SPYING ON THE BOMB

JEFFREY T. RICHELSON

SPYING ON THE BOMB

AMERICAN NUCLEAR INTELLIGENCE

from **NAZI GERMANY** *to*

IRAN *and* **NORTH KOREA**

W. W. NORTON & COMPANY | NEW YORK

Copyright © 2007, 2006 by Jeffrey T. Richelson

All rights reserved
Printed in the United States of America
First published as a Norton paperback 2007

For information about permission to reproduce selections from this book, write to
Permissions, W. W. Norton & Company, Inc., 500 Fifth Avenue, New York, NY 10110

Manufacturing by The Maple-Vail Book Manufacturing Group
Book design by Judith Abbate/Abbate Design
Production Manager: Devon Zahn

Library of Congress Cataloging-in-Publication Data

Richelson , Jeffrey
  Spying on the bomb : American nuclear intelligence, from Nazi Germany to Iran and
North Korea / Jeffrey T. Richelson — 1st ed.
        p. cm.
  Includes bibliographical references and index.
  ISBN-13: 978-0-393-05383-8 (hardcover)
  ISBN-10: 0-393-05383-0 (hardcover)
 1. Espionage, American.   2. Nuclear weapons information.   3. Nuclear weapons—
research.   4. Nuclear arms control—United States.   I. Title.
        UB271.U5R53 2006
        327.1'747—dc22

                                                                        2005014415

ISBN 978-0-393-32982-7 pbk.

W. W. Norton & Company, Inc., 500 Fifth Avenue, New York, N.Y. 10110
www.wwnorton.com

W. W. Norton & Company, Ltd., Castle House, 75/76 Wells Street, London W1T 3QT

1 2 3 4 5 6 7 8 9 0

In memory of **EDNA RICHELSON**

FOR AS LONG AS WAR IS A THREAT, the spy is a ticking seismograph on top of the Jungfrau measuring distant atomic explosions on the other side of the world, or instruments carried in an aircraft that measure uranium or plutonium contents of the atmosphere.

— IAN FLEMING

CONTENTS

PHOTOGRAPHS APPEAR ON PAGES 171–186 AND 381–396.

LIST OF MAPS

PREFACE

FOLLOWING THE DISCOVERY of nuclear fission in 1939, several nations began programs to develop the ultimate weapon. Scientists in the United States, including many who had studied in Germany or had recently escaped from the German campaign of conquest, were concerned that the eminent scientists who remained, including Werner Heisenberg, might be able to produce a nuclear weapon for Adolf Hitler's use. The United States tried to find out whether those fears had a sound basis. In addition to relying on traditional intelligence methods, the Americans explored ways in which the signatures of nuclear activity could be detected.

In 1944, scientists deployed with the invading Allied armies discovered that the Germans had made little progress toward an atomic bomb. But the relief felt from that discovery would be replaced in a few years by fear of what the Soviet Union might accomplish in the nuclear field. America's work on monitoring German progress toward the ultimate weapon provided a foundation for the far more extensive and long-lasting intelligence effort to uncover Soviet nuclear secrets.

The Soviet Union was not the only nation whose nuclear activities were of concern to the United States in the next decades. Other hostile nations seeking to become nuclear powers—most prominently the People's Republic of China, particularly given the loose talk about nuclear war that came from Chinese leaders—also worried American presidents. At least one president seriously considered a preemptive strike to prevent China from developing the bomb.

That friendly nations might try to join the nuclear club was another mounting concern. In the 1960s and 1970s, U.S. presidents tried their best to discourage Israel, Taiwan, South Africa, and India from building a nuclear arsenal—fearful that every time a new nation joined the nuclear club, more nonnuclear nations would see it as a means to improve their status in the world. The United States feared that nuclear acquisition would prompt regional arms races and ultimately increase the risk of nuclear war, especially in the Middle East and on the South Asian continent. More recently, the nations seeking to join the nuclear club—Saddam's Iraq, Islamic Iran, and North Korea—would be at the very top of any list of nations that the United States would want to deny membership in the nuclear club.

For over five decades the United States has devoted considerable resources to monitoring the quests by friends and foes to acquire nuclear weapons and improve their nuclear capabilities. The efforts to collect and analyze intelligence on foreign nuclear weapons programs have continued to involve both traditional methods such as human intelligence, aerial reconnaissance, and communications intelligence, and newer ones such as the detection of the signatures of nuclear detonations and of the production of fissile material.

The collected data has had many uses: keeping policymakers informed of foreign nuclear activities, determining and estimating the nuclear warfare capabilities of other nations, planning military operations to disrupt nuclear activities, supporting diplomatic initiatives to forestall nuclear weapons development, assisting inspectors from the International Atomic Energy Agency, and monitoring compliance with a number of arms control treaties. The latter include the 1963 Treaty Banning Nuclear Weapons Tests in the Atmosphere, in Outer Space, and Under Water; the 1968 Treaty on the Non-Proliferation of Nuclear Weapons; the 1974 Treaty on the Limitation of Underground Nuclear Weapon Tests (limiting tests to yields of no more than 150 kilotons); and the Comprehensive Nuclear Test Ban Treaty that prohibits all nuclear testing.

Spying on the Bomb traces the evolution of the U.S. nuclear intelligence effort, its successes and failures, from its origins in the early days of World War II to the first years of the twenty-first century. There is no simple explanation for success or failure in these endeavors. Given the different periods, different individuals, varying targets, and different technologies available for collecting intelligence, that should not be surprising.

The book's focus is largely on the early nuclear programs of about fifteen nations, and the U.S. effort to determine if they were trying to acquire nuclear weapons, how far they had gotten, and their attempts to improve those capabilities. Thus, the core of the book examines the work of the CIA and other intelligence agencies in identifying and providing the details about those nuclear programs, as well as the agencies' efforts to monitor and evaluate nuclear testing—rather than their efforts to gather information on nuclear arsenals or during nuclear crises.

Each chapter focuses on the nuclear activities of one or a small number of nations during different periods starting in the 1940s and progressing to the new century. In addition, the chapters intermingle accounts of what was actually happening in foreign nuclear weapons programs, based on memoirs and other non-U.S. intelligence–derived material, with the U.S. intelligence community's understanding of what was taking place.

As a result, Spying on the Bomb focuses on the institutions, technologies, and people that have been part of the U.S. intelligence community—including Robert Furman, Moe Berg, Henry Lowenhaupt, the CIA, the Air Force

Technical Applications Center, Joe T., and bhangmeters—as well as on the institutions, technologies, and people that have been part of foreign nuclear weapons efforts—including Andrei Sakharov, Jaffar Dhia Jaffar, Homi Bhabha, the Soviet "Layer Cake" bomb, the Lanzhou Gaseous Diffusion Plant, and the Pokhran test site.

—JEFFREY T. RICHELSON

SPYING
ON THE
BOMB

chapter one

A TERRIFYING PROSPECT

ALAMOGORDO, NEW MEXICO, was established in 1898, with the expectation that it would be one of many communities supporting the western expansion of the railroad. For the next thirty-five years, the city and railroad grew in tandem. But by December 1941, when the United States entered World War II, Alamogordo was a "small town of 4,000 people existing on its economic past and a small tourist industry." One element of the wartime expansion of the U.S. armed forces was the establishment of the Alamogordo Bombing and Gunnery Range, subsequently renamed the Alamogordo Army Air Field.[1]

In May 1944, Dr. Kenneth T. Bainbridge, a Harvard University experimental physicist employed at another, far more secret, military installation in New Mexico, led an expedition through parts of the state. He was looking for a remote place where he and his colleagues at Los Alamos could determine whether their efforts to transform the theories of nuclear physics into a dramatic new weapon—an atomic bomb—had been successful. The Manhattan Project's scientific director, J. Robert Oppenheimer, had come along for the ride. The two physicists were searching for a piece of territory measuring approximately 17 by 24 miles that was just far enough from Los Alamos to make the town safe from the effects of a bomb test.[2]

They found what they were looking for in the northwest sector of the Alamogordo airfield, located about 60 miles northwest of the city and 210 miles south of Los Alamos. The flat scrub region was known from Spanish colonial times as the Jornada del Muerto, the "Journey of Death," for thirst had claimed the lives of many who attempted to travel through the region in the years before the railroad arrived. With the approval of the commander of the Second Air Force, which controlled the airfield, they staked a claim to the site. Oppenheimer would give it the code name Trinity, in reference to a sonnet by John Donne and in tribute to a dead lover.[3]

Under the guidance of the Army Corps of Engineers, contractors proceeded to convert the desolate territory into a test area. Three earth-sheltered bunkers with concrete slab roofs were built ten thousand yards from the designated ground zero. On July 16, 1945, the bunker to the north contained recording instruments and searchlights, while the one to the west held searchlights and high-speed cameras. The southern bunker was the control center. Five miles south of the control center was a base camp, with tents and barracks. Twenty miles northwest of ground zero, at Compañia Hill, was a viewing site for VIPs.[4]

For several early morning hours on July 16, Oppenheimer and Maj. Gen. Leslie Groves, head of the Manhattan Project, were together at the control shelter hoping that assorted weather problems would not interfere with the test. At 5:10 a.m. Groves returned to the base camp, which provided a better observation point. Meanwhile, the visitors at Compañia Hill, including Los Alamos physicists Hans Bethe and Edward Teller, ignored instructions to turn their faces away at the time of the blast, "determined," Teller recalled, "to look the beast in the eye."[5]

The device to be tested relied on implosion—the rapid compression of a plutonium sphere by a symmetrical detonation of conventional explosives. If the device worked as planned, the imploded sphere would be sufficiently dense to set off a chain reaction, producing an atomic explosion. Another type of atomic bomb, and the one that would destroy Hiroshima, relied on a "gun" that fired one mass of U-235, a uranium isotope, at another, with an expectation that a chain reaction of "fast neutrons" (moving at tens of thousands of kilometers a second) would result. The exponential increase in the splitting of nuclei would result in an atomic detonation due to the energy released when nuclei break apart. While designers were so confident that the uranium "gun" device would work that they did not feel the need to test it, there was less confidence in the plutonium implosion bomb.[6]

The uranium and plutonium that would fuel the bombs had been produced at two very distant locations. A massive complex at Oak Ridge, Tennessee, contained three means of producing U-235 for use in the bomb: an electromagnetic isotope separation plant, a gaseous diffusion plant, and a thermal diffusion plant.* The plutonium for the test device at Trinity had come from another enormous site, the project's Hanford Engineer Works, in Washington State, where three plutonium production reactors and three separation facilities had been built.[7]

At exactly 05:29:45 the test device, located on a platform on top of a hundred-foot-high steel tower, was detonated, and a brilliant burst of light, equivalent to several suns at noon, filled the sky for 20 miles in every direction. A huge fireball formed and lasted for several seconds. It then mushroomed

---

* Electromagnetic separation of U-235 from U-238 relies on exploiting the different curvatures of the paths of ions of different masses when they travel through magnetic fields. Gaseous diffusion involves passing uranium hexafluoride (UF6), derived from uranium ore, through a porous barrier that preferentially passes the lighter molecules containing U-235, which travel a little faster on average. In the thermal diffusion method, UF6 is subjected to strong temperature differences to separate the uranium isotopes.

and rose to over ten thousand feet before it dimmed. A massive cloud rose to about forty-one thousand feet. Light from the explosion was seen clearly in cities up to 180 miles away, including Albuquerque, Santa Fe, and El Paso.[8]

While it would take some time before Groves and Oppenheimer discovered just how successful they had been, that the plutonium device had detonated with the force of twenty thousand tons of TNT, it was clear to all observers that the test had been a success—even before surveying the resulting devastation. One of those present, Isidor Rabi, would recall that "suddenly there was an enormous flash of light, the brightest light I have ever seen or that I think anyone has ever seen. It blasted; it pounced; it bored its way into you."[9]

By the time of the test, Adolf Hitler's Nazi Germany, the catalyst for developing an atomic bomb, had already been defeated. Germany had been unable to develop its own atomic bomb before the Allies defeated its troops on the battlefield and took control of German territory. Several years earlier it had not been at all clear to Oppenheimer and his colleagues at Los Alamos that they would beat Hitler's scientists in the race to exploit atomic energy for military purposes. Germany, after all, was the home of many of the world's greatest physicists, the country where Oppenheimer and others had gone to do graduate work, and the place where fission itself had first been discovered.

IN DECEMBER 1938, fifty-nine-year-old Otto Hahn, Germany's leading radiation chemist, and his student, Fritz Strassmann, were following up on the experimental work of Irène and Frédéric Joliot-Curie and Enrico Fermi when they discovered that the bombardment of uranium nuclei by neutrons appeared to give rise to barium nuclei—an unprecedented occurrence in the history of nuclear reactions. It appeared to represent the splitting of an atom into lighter elements rather than a transformation of one element into another just a few steps down the periodic table. Their article, cautiously reporting those results, appeared in the January 6, 1939, issue of the Berlin scientific journal *Die Naturwissenschaften* (The Natural Sciences). In March and April, the British journal *Nature* published two papers by Frédéric Joliot-Curie and his research assistants, Hans von Halban and Lew Kowarski, at the Collège de France in Paris, which confirmed the results of Hahn and Strassmann.[10]

Lise Meitner, Hahn's former colleague and longtime collaborator at the Kaiser-Wilhelm Institute for Chemistry in Berlin, and her nephew, Otto Frisch, pondered the results, which Hahn had written them about in December. They did their pondering in Sweden, since Meitner, an Austrian of Jewish heritage, had been driven out of Germany when the Third Reich swallowed her country, making her a German citizen and subject to Hitler's racial laws. The pair soon concluded that Hahn's results demonstrated a splitting or "fission" of the uranium nucleus, and communicated their results in a two-page paper that appeared in *Nature* on February 11, 1939.[11]

That explanation had enormous significance. The splitting of the uranium atom into two radioactive substances meant that a number of neutrons could then be emitted simultaneously, ultimately leading to a chain reaction—an exponential increase in the splitting of nuclei—and the release of enormous quantities of energy. The papers appearing in *Die Naturwissenschaften* and *Nature* led to the publication of over fifty articles on uranium fission in Europe and the United States between January and June of 1939. Among them was "Can the Energy Contained in the Atomic Nucleus Be Exploited on a Technical Scale?" by Siegfried Flugge, one of Hahn's colleagues, which also appeared in *Die Naturwissenschaften*.[12]

The possibility that atomic fission might serve as the basis for a super-weapon did not go unnoticed by physicists on both sides of the Atlantic, nor on both sides of the ideological divide between democracies and dictatorships. In early August 1939, writing from Peconic, Long Island, Albert Einstein alerted President Franklin Roosevelt to the promise and threat of the new discovery. In his two-page letter, Einstein informed FDR that "recent work . . . leads me to expect that the element uranium may be turned into a new and important source of energy in the immediate future." The father of relativity theory went on to tell Roosevelt that "it may become possible to set up a nuclear chain reaction" and that "this new phenomenon would also lead to the construction of bombs," possibly "extremely powerful bombs of a new type."[13]

The following year Otto Frisch, who had made it to England, and another refugee scientist, Rudolf Peierls, demonstrated, in a memorandum delivered to two members of the British Air-Warfare and Defence Committee, that the prevailing skepticism about the feasibility of an atomic bomb was unfounded. Because of the small proportion (0.7 percent) of the fissionable uranium isotope (U-235) found in natural uranium, almost all of which is made up of the unfissionable U-238, an explosive chain reaction had appeared to be unlikely. When Soviet physicists learned, in February 1939, of the discovery of fission, they recognized the military significance and began their own investigations. In late 1941, after the German invasion had put a stop to the activities of the Soviet "Uranium Commission," physicist Georgi Flerov would write Igor Kurchatov, head of the fission effort, on the short-term feasibility of a bomb effort. He would follow up with a letter to Joseph Stalin in April 1942.[14]

IN GERMANY, Paul Harteck, a professor of physical chemistry at the University of Hamburg and an army consultant, and his assistant, Wilhelm Groth, wrote Erich Schumann, the physicist who headed the Heereswaffenamt (the Army Weapons Office of the Army Ordnance department), in April 1939:

"We take the liberty of calling to your attention the newest developments in nuclear physics, which, in our opinion, will probably make it possible to produce an explosive many orders of magnitude more powerful than the conventional ones." They observed that the "country which first makes use of it has an unsurpassable advantage over the others."[15]

At about the same time Schumann received the letter from Harteck and Groth, the Reich Ministry of Education was contacted by Göttingen University physicist George Joos, after attending a physics colloquium presentation by Wilhelm Hanle on a "uranium burner." Joos also wished to alert the German government to the potential of atomic fission as a source of energy. To look into such matters, the ministry's Reich Research Council chartered a group of physicists, designated the Uranverein (Uranium Club).[16]

Meanwhile, although Harteck did not receive a response until August, which prompted a second letter, Schumann had turned the first letter over to one of his principal staff members, Kurt Deibner, a member of the Nazi Party with a Ph.D. in physics and, according to one historian, "a reasonably competent expert on both explosives and nuclear physics." In September, after the outbreak of war, Army Ordnance moved to take over the Uranium Club.[17]

On September 25, Germany's most renowned nuclear physicist, Werner Heisenberg, was summoned to Berlin, as part of the mobilization for war, to join the Uranverein. One of a small group of young men who led the quantum revolution in physics, he had received his doctorate at the age of twenty-two and became a full professor of theoretical physics at the University of Leipzig in October 1927, just a few months short of his twenty-sixth birthday. Earlier that year, in a twenty-seven-page paper, *On the Perceptual Content of Quantum Theoretical Kinematics and Mechanics*, he formulated the uncertainty principle, which stated that it was impossible to precisely measure *both* the location and the velocity of an electron. That principle became a key component of quantum mechanics, along with Niels Bohr's complementarity principle and the Max Born–Wolfgang Pauli statistical interpretation of Erwin Schrödinger's wave function. Five years after his revolutionary paper, Heisenberg was awarded the Nobel Prize in Physics.[18]

When Heisenberg arrived the next day at the Uranverein, he found a number of his colleagues waiting for him. Harteck was there, along with fission codiscoverer Otto Hahn. Hans Geiger, who had given his name to the device capable of detecting radioactivity, was also in attendance, along with Carl Friedrich von Weizsäcker and Walter Bothe. The research interests of the twenty-seven-year-old von Weizsäcker, son of the secretary of state for foreign affairs, spanned both nuclear theory and astrophysics. He had explored the nature of the nucleus as well as the origins of the universe. Bothe, whose work had included investigating the makeup of cosmic rays, was the leading nuclear experimental physicist remaining in Germany and head of the Institute of

Physics at the Kaiser-Wilhelm Institute for Medical Research in Heidelberg, where he found refuge after being booted out of the University of Heidelberg for his lack of Nazi ardor. But that did not stop the army from "requesting" his appearance at the Uranium Club meeting, or Bothe from complying.[19]

A debate ensued as to whether the club should help build a fission bomb. One attendee at the meeting, Deibner's assistant Erich Bagge, recalled that Bothe ended the discussion with the pronouncement, "Gentlemen, it must be done." Geiger chimed in, arguing that "if there is the slightest chance that it is possible it must be done."[20] Neither appears to have considered an atomic bomb in the hands of Adolf Hitler to be a terrifying prospect.

After the Berlin session concluded, the attendees headed back to their institutes. Research agendas were assigned by Diebner and Bagge, under the authority of the Army Weapons Office. The office proceeded to take control of the government-sponsored Kaiser-Wilhelm Institute for Physics in the Berlin suburb of Dahlem, with Diebner assuming command, while Dutch-born director Peter Debye headed to the United States on a forced leave of absence that would last a lifetime. The Uranium Club became the War Office Nuclear Physics Research Group.[21]

Heisenberg returned to Leipzig and produced a secret two-part technical report for the weapons office. *The Possibility of the Technical Acquisition of Energy from Uranium Fission* explored the prospects and means for exploiting physics theory to develop military hardware. In part one, dated December 6, 1939, he concluded that a reactor (or "pile"), in which fission could be controlled to produce energy rather than an explosion, was technically feasible. He investigated the use of different moderators, which were needed to slow down the neutrons so that they would not be absorbed by U-238 but would fission the U-235 instead, and concluded that graphite and heavy water were best. (In heavy water 99 percent or more of the two hydrogen atoms in each molecule of water has been replaced by deuterium, an isotope of hydrogen with an extra neutron in its nucleus.) He also explored different configurations of uranium and moderator. Additionally, uranium could be used as the basis for a bomb of tremendous power if it could be highly enriched so as to significantly increase the proportion of the rare U-235 isotope while reducing the proportion of U-238.[22]

In the second part of his report, delivered on February 29, 1940, Heisenberg was more skeptical of the promise of nuclear fission. He omitted any mention of fission as the basis for a bomb, noting the engineering difficulties involved. One problem was Germany's lack of technical capability to enrich uranium by separating U-235. In addition, while Germany did possess a large supply of uranium ore owing to its seizure of Czechoslovakia's Joachimsthal mine, it lacked the means required to process it on an industrial scale into uranium oxide and then into the necessary metal plates, cubes, and powder.

Adding to Heisenberg's caution was his conclusion that graphite would not make an appropriate moderator, leaving only heavy water, which Germany did not possess.[23]

But such skepticism did not prevent Heisenberg and other German scientists and institutions from exploring the path to the development of reactors and bombs. Between 1939 and the end of 1941, staff members of sixteen universities and institutes produced secret technical reports on various aspects of atomic energy. Included were the Berlin-based Kaiser-Wilhelm institutes for physics and chemistry and the Heidelberg institute for medical research. Faculty attached to the physics institutes from universities in Göttingen, Cologne, Hamburg, Giessen, and Vienna also made contributions. And one company, the Linde Ice Machine Company, contributed a solitary technical paper (a patent) concerning the process for producing heavy water. Among the more prolific authors were army consultant Harteck, whose group worked on the separation of isotopes, von Weizsäcker, and Bothe.[24]

Of particular importance were papers by von Weizsäcker, Bothe and Peter Jensen, and Fritz Houtermans. Calculations by von Weizsäcker's assistants had supported Heisenberg's conclusion about the futility of using graphite as a moderator, and a January 1941 paper by Bothe and Jensen, *The Absorption of Thermal Neutrons in Electrographite*, seemed to provide further confirmation of that judgment, leading the Germans to focus exclusively on heavy water as a moderator.[25]

In a July 1940 paper, *The Possibility of Obtaining Energy from U^{238}*, von Weizsäcker built on the discovery that after a U-238 atom captures a neutron, it decays in an average of twenty-three minutes to element 93, now known as neptunium. He argued that neptunium could be substituted for the hard-to-obtain U-235 as the key ingredient of an atomic bomb. While von Weizsäcker was wrong, in that neptunium decayed within less than three days into the longer-lived plutonium, such work opened up the alternative plutonium path to the atomic bomb—thanks to Fritz Houtermans.[26]

Houtermans was an unlikely member of the uranium project. He grew up in Vienna, the son of a half-Jewish mother, with communist politics. He had been a classmate of Oppenheimer's during the American's time in Germany. His reputation as a theoretical physicist, partly the result of his coauthorship of a paper on energy production in stars, meant that he had no trouble finding employment in the Soviet Union when he fled Germany in the mid-1930s. In 1937 he was arrested by the Soviet secret police when the Stalinist purges reached the University of Kiev, his employer. After a thirty-month stay in the Soviet prison system, he was returned to Germany, where the Gestapo promptly locked him up, suspecting that he was a Soviet spy. Houtermans was able to get in touch with physicists such as Max von Laue, the deputy head of the Kaiser-Wilhelm physics institute, and was quickly released.[27]

Von Laue also found him a job with Manfred von Ardenne's laboratory, Institut A. Von Ardenne was a "gifted inventor" whose income came from obtaining contracts to do scientific work for a variety of clients, including the post office. His laboratory's staff included several members trying to develop techniques for separating isotopes. In August 1941, Houtermans completed *The Question of Starting a Nuclear Chain Reaction*, reporting that a reactor using natural uranium as a fuel could produce plutonium, which could then be removed by chemical means and used as an explosive.[28]

Despite the attention devoted to reactor and bomb development, the papers by the German scientists revealed a number of critical misunderstandings, omissions, or errors. The papers did not contain any calculation of the critical mass of a U-235 bomb, the recognition that a U-235 bomb would depend on fast neutrons (although Heisenberg understood this to be the case), or an equation for the internal multiplication of neutrons with respect to time—the latter being critical to attaining a chain reaction. In addition, the paper by Bothe and Jensen mistakenly confirmed Heisenberg's conclusions about graphite's inappropriateness as a moderator because they failed to understand that while industrial graphite would not work, highly purified graphite would.[29]

Along with such theoretical investigations, the group undertook experimental work. In July 1940, construction began on a small laboratory near the Kaiser-Wilhelm Institute for Biology and Virus Research in Berlin-Dahlem. Ultimately, it would consist of a six-foot-deep circular pit lined with brick and a wooden laboratory barracks about twenty feet long. Named the "Virus House" to keep the curious away, it became, in October 1940, a facility for exploring the workings of a uranium reactor.[30]

In the fall of 1941 the Nazi blitzkrieg had appeared on the verge of producing a quick victory, but the winter brought serious setbacks to Hitler's armies. With all available resources being diverted to bring about a successful end to the war, long-term projects were considered a luxury. Schumann, the Army Weapons Office research director, sent a letter to the directors of the various institutes involved in the uranium project, notifying them of a meeting scheduled for December 16. He noted that "given the present personnel and raw materials shortage, the nuclear power project requires resources that can only be justified if there is certainty that an application will be found in the near future."[31]

After the meeting, during which Heisenberg, Bothe, Hahn, Harteck, and others delivered papers, Schumann reported to the head of the weapons office, Gen. Emil Leeb, and requested a decision on the army's future role in the project. By late January 1942, the office decided to cede control of the effort, and the Kaiser-Wilhelm Institute for Physics returned to its traditional place in the Kaiser-Wilhelm Society, where it would stay until April.[32]

Ceding control did not mean that the office had completely lost interest. In February, it issued a long report titled *The Production of Energy from Uranium*, a detailed description and analysis of the uranium project's work through the end of January. Its first chapter briefly reviewed the potential employment of atomic energy for reactors and bombs. The report maintained that using plutonium rather than uranium would make it easier to build a bomb, and suggested that the critical mass for a plutonium bomb was in the range of 22 to 220 kilograms. However, either route would involve a long-term effort requiring "a very large isotope separation plant or the successful extraction of [plutonium] in large quantity from a reactor." It was an effort, the report concluded, that should be undertaken, given its importance for both the economy and the German military.[33]

The continued interest of the weapons office in the subject was also in evidence when a three-day conference sponsored by the office opened on February 26. Its first day overlapped the one-day meeting the weapons office cosponsored with the Reich Research Council and held at the House of German Research in Berlin-Steglitz. After the opening address by Erich Schumann, titled "Atomic Physics as a Weapon," the attendees at the council meeting heard another seven, relatively nontechnical lectures by the key scientists involved in the atomic energy program. Hahn, as might be expected, talked about fission of the uranium nucleus, while Bothe addressed the results of research on energy production. Klaus Clusius lectured on the enrichment of uranium isotopes, and Harteck addressed the issue of heavy water. According to the manuscript version of Heisenberg's lecture, "The Theoretical Basis for Energy Production from Nuclear Fission," he reported that fission could produce "an explosive of unimaginable force." He also stressed the importance of pure U-235 in producing a chain reaction, and of employing alternative means to obtain it, including uranium enrichment and the development of a reactor. In addition, he endorsed the use of plutonium as a nuclear explosive, citing von Weizsäcker's work.[34]

Very few of the high-level dignitaries invited to attend the meeting— including armaments chief Albert Speer, interior minister Heinrich Himmler, air force chief Hermann Goering, Hitler aide Martin Bormann, field marshal Wilhelm Keitel, and navy commander-in-chief Erich Raeder—actually did so. It certainly did not help that mistakenly enclosed with the invitation was the agenda for the army's three-day conference, consisting of twenty-five highly technical topics, rather than the simpler agenda for the council's meeting. That the actual council meeting featured a lunch of "experimental" food such as assorted deep-frozen and enriched dishes, baked or fried in synthetic fats, probably also deterred attendance. Himmler did sent a short note, thanking education minister Bernhard Rust for "your kind invitation" while informing him that "unfortunately" his duties prevented him from attending.[35]

Not long after Heisenberg completed his lecture at the research council's conference, the army-sponsored meeting at the Kaiser-Wilhelm physics institute opened. Over the following three days virtually all of the project's scientists presented papers. Technical papers included Bothe's report on the measurement of nuclear constants, Weizsäcker's description of a new theory of resonance absorption in a reactor, and reports on the behavior of fast neutrons in uranium. Hahn and Strassmann focused on the creation of an isotope of neptunium. But the greatest attention was devoted to the development of a reactor.[36]

In April, Abraham Esau, head of the physics section at the research council, had, in the wake of the army's action, persuaded education minister Rust to restore his control of the uranium project, including the Kaiser-Wilhelm Institute of Physics. But in May, faced with complaints about the education ministry's inadequate support for fundamental research, Speer obtained Hitler's approval for a reorganization of the research council, and the appointment of Goering to head it, a change that took place in June. Esau continued as head of the physics section and eventually became Goering's deputy for "all questions of atomic physics."[37]

Just a few days earlier, on June 4, Heisenberg and several of his colleagues, including Hahn and Harteck, assembled in the Kaiser Wilhelm Society's Harnack House to brief Speer and the three military heads of weapons production. When, after the lecture, Speer asked Heisenberg about the feasibility of atomic bombs, Germany's top physicist told him that while the scientific problem had been solved, the "technical prerequisites for production" were such that it would take years to achieve the goal. Speer, willing to think big, asked for requests for funds and materials. The scientists asked for only several hundred thousand marks and some small amounts of steel, nickel, and other priority metals, and resisted the armaments chief's suggestions that they take a couple of million marks and correspondingly more material. The scientists' reaction, and their explanation that such resources could not be utilized at the time, led Speer to assign the project a lower priority than a number of other projects, including Wernher von Braun's missile program.[38]

The project did receive approval for construction at the Kaiser-Wilhelm Institute for Physics, which Heisenberg assumed command of on July 1. With the construction funds, the institute built a bunker to house Germany's first major large nuclear reactor, allowing an expansion of Virus House reactor experiments. At the same time, the theoretical efforts of the scientists and their institutes continued. From the beginning of 1942 through August 1943, over seventy-five additional technical papers dealing with reactor operations, the production of heavy water, isotope separation, and a variety of additional topics were prepared.[39]

But all the work and all the experiments did not result in any renewed optimism. In a July 8, 1943, letter, Rudolph Mentzel of the Reich Research Council informed a member of Goering's staff that while "the work has progressed considerably in a few months [it] will not lead in a short time towards the production of practically useful engines or explosives." However, he added a silver lining: "enemy powers cannot have any surprise in store for us."[40]

AT THE TIME Mentzel wrote his letter, the U.S. atomic bomb effort had been underway for nineteen months, a fact that not one of Germany's many intelligence services had discovered. On December 6, 1941, two years to the day after Heisenberg turned in the first part of his technical report, and after German scientists had completed over a hundred further reports, the United States established what would become known as the Manhattan Project, a concerted scientific and industrial effort to develop an atomic bomb. Beyond concerns about their chances of success, Allied scientists worried about German progress. Through the scientific underground they had heard of the Uranverein and of Heisenberg's and von Weizsäcker's involvement. In an August 1943 memo to Oppenheimer, Hans Bethe and Edward Teller noted that "recent reports, both through the newspapers and through secret service, have given indications that the Germans may be in possession of a powerful new weapon which is expected to be ready between November and January," a weapon they identified as an atomic bomb. As Isidor Rabi recalled, the questions were, "Where was the enemy in this field of work? What did the Nazi's have? . . . Where were the [Nazi scientists]? What means did they have at their command?"[41]

The United States would not begin to make a serious and systematic attempt to answer such questions until the fall of 1943. In March 1942, Vannevar Bush, head of the Office of Scientific Research and Development (OSRD), informed President Franklin D. Roosevelt that "I have no indication of the status of the enemy program, and have taken no definite steps toward finding out." But, in September 1943, Army chief of staff Gen. George C. Marshall did take steps. Marshall asked Leslie Groves whether he would be willing to assume responsibility for determining what the Germans were doing in the field of atomic weaponry and how well they were doing it.[42]

According to Groves, Marshall apparently felt that "the existing agencies were not well co-ordinated; and that, as result, there were many gaps not being covered." In addition, the army's chief of staff thought that agencies such as the Office of Strategic Services (OSS), the Office of Naval Intelligence (ONI), and the army's G-2 would not always understand the significance of some of the information they might collect. At the same time, concern for the security of the atomic bomb project suggested limiting those agencies' exposure to information that might reveal America's progress toward an atomic capability—information, for example, that might indicate an atomic bomb could be constructed relying on plutonium rather than uranium.[43]

Groves also discovered, to his surprise, "that there was considerably more friction between the various intelligence agencies than I had previously suspected." Therefore, there "seemed to be no alternative" to his taking on this added mission. Given the secrecy involved, nothing was put in writing. It was agreed that Marshall would notify the head of G-2, Maj. Gen. George Strong, while Groves would alert the OSS and ONI of his new responsibility.[44]

Not long before Marshall's request, Groves had established an intelligence section to investigate German progress, and selected twenty-eight-year-old Maj. Robert Furman to run it. His new intelligence chief, a Quaker, had grown up in Trenton, New Jersey, as the son of a bank teller and with two early ambitions—to be a builder and have his own business. He would achieve those goals later in life, remaining active in his construction company into his eighties. But the Depression made those dreams impossible to realize in the 1930s. Furman did receive a degree in civil engineering from Princeton in 1937. Graduation was followed by a job with the Pennsylvania Railroad, which fired him. He also did not last long as a construction inspector for the Federal Housing Authority. His next employer was the Turner Construction Company in New York, which hired him as a timekeeper. Then in December 1940, Furman was called up for active duty with the corps of engineers.[45]

Service in the Reserve Officer Training Corps (ROTC) during his time at Princeton resulted in his being commissioned as a field artillery officer after training with horse-drawn, 75 mm field guns. By 1940 the army had newer field guns and no longer relied on horses to move them. Instead, 2nd Lt. Robert Furman became a junior officer in the project that Groves supervised—the building of the Pentagon—and had an office near his chief's. The same was true for his new assignment as head of the Manhattan Engineer District's (MED) intelligence operation (which subsequently became known as the Foreign Intelligence Section). Groves gave him an office next to his at MED headquarters on Twenty-first Street and Virginia Avenue, in the Foggy Bottom section of Washington. Selected on a Thursday in August, he began work the following Monday. A physical contrast to his corpulent boss, Furman would match him in terms of a penchant for secrecy, and would be referred to as the "Mysterious Major" by one scientist who worked with him in trying to ferret out Nazi nuclear secrets.[46]

While briefing Furman on his new assignment, Groves told him of the atomic bomb project and explained the concern of Los Alamos scientists about possible German progress in developing an atomic bomb. Many of the scientists working for the Manhattan Project, such as Oppenheimer, had studied in Germany and considered Heisenberg and Hahn, among others, as experts in the field. Teller had earned his doctorate under Heisenberg's tutelage. Without any solid information on the subject, "Groves had difficulty keeping the scientists' minds on [their] work," Furman recalls. Groves repeated his conclusions about the fragmented U.S. intelligence effort and gave Furman the job of finding all that could be discovered on the status of the German effort.[47]

There had been previous opportunities to gather information about Germany's atomic activities and some thought given to its progress before Furman's appointment. In March 1941, Houtermans sent a message along with an emigrating German physicist, Fritz Reiche. The message, which eventually found its way to Groves, warned that "a large number of German physicists are working intensively on the uranium bomb under the direction of Heisenberg." Houtermans also maintained that Heisenberg was attempting to obstruct the effort, a claim not likely to provide much reassurance as it was unverifiable and no guarantee of future behavior. An item in a Berlin newspaper the day following the February 26, 1942, Reich Research Council meeting noted that "many members of the Party, the State, and Industry were present under the chairmanship of the president, Reich Minister Rust." The conference, the paper noted, "dealt with problems of modern physics that are of decisive importance for national defense and the German economy." The exact details were a state secret.[48]

Samuel Edison Woods, while serving as America's commercial attaché in Berlin prior to Germany's declaration of war on the United States, had a number of sources of information. One was former economics professor and financial consultant Dr. Erwin Respondek, whom Woods referred to by the code name Ralph. Respondek had contacts in the German general staff, industry, and the Nazi Party, and at the Kaiser-Wilhelm physics institute, including a number of sources who knew something about the German atomic effort— Max Planck, Herman Muckermann, a retired scientist who had worked at the Berlin physics institute before 1933 and had scientific contacts across the country, and Herbert Müller, who worked at a center for legal research affiliated with the Kaiser-Wilhelm Society. When Woods was forced to leave Germany, he told Respondek that he could stay in touch through August Ochsenbein, a Swiss diplomat stationed in Berlin.[49]

In the fall and winter of 1942, Respondek organized all the facts he had available, including the names of the principal scientists. Through Ochsenbein, he delivered his report, including the claim that five million Reichmarks had been set aside for "leading professors of scientific institutions" to test the principles involved in the development of an atomic bomb, while another thirty million marks was available for technical tests. "The military authorities are anxiously awaiting [the] results of [these] tests," Respondek claimed.[50]

Scientists who had fled Germany knew that research had started. At first they represented the primary source of information about the German program and its personnel. In some cases they continued to receive information from colleagues back home. In October 1942, Victor Weisskopf, who had fled Germany in 1937, received news from his former mentor, Wolfgang Pauli, that Heisenberg had become director of the Kaiser-Wilhelm physics institute in Berlin and had agreed to give a lecture in Zurich in December.[51]

One of those who provided some analysis of the status of the German program and its personnel was Arthur H. Compton, a pioneer in the study of cosmic rays, cowinner of the 1927 Nobel Prize in Physics, and head of the University of Chicago's deceptively named Metallurgical Laboratory, which conducted research into the requirements for plutonium production capability. In early June 1943, Compton wrote a memo to the Manhattan Project's Maj. Arthur V. Peterson titled "Situation in Germany," a report based on his discussions with several refugee scientists and a review of German physics journals.[52]

Part of Compton's memo discussed the activities of Bothe, Hahn, and former physics institute director Peter Debye, who had landed a teaching job at Cornell. Compton wrote that Bothe was involved in studies of neutron diffusion and, over the previous two years, had published articles on subjects related to chain reactions in the form of a reactor or bomb. That the results of his research were published indicated "no close censorship over such material in Germany at the present time." Similarly, publication of a paper by Hahn on the radioactivity of cesium and Hahn's invitation to a Finnish scientist to come check his data suggested "no great secrecy there with regard to general problems of nuclear physics." Compton also concluded that Debye's successful means of partially separating uranium isotopes, the thermal diffusion of liquids, was probably "being applied at Berlin."[53]

The memo went on to state that it was a "reasonable guess" that "Heisenberg and his colleagues, especially Weizsäcker . . . are concerned with studies of the chain reaction as a source of power using, perhaps a combination of heavy water and uranium enriched in 235 content." In addition, he noted that "there is no indication that we find of German concern with [plutonium], though [neptunium] is reported in their discussions." If the Germans were working on an atomic bomb, rather than development of a reactor, "it would seem most probable that it is from the point of view of separated 235 following the method of thermal diffusion of the liquid." Compton continued, "The openness of the discussions of neutron diffusion, however, makes it appear possible that this aspect of the chain reaction is not being developed."[54]

The United States would also have access, starting in late 1943, to the intelligence produced by Great Britain. The British intelligence effort went back to late 1941, when the Directorate of Tube Alloys was established to direct British work on an atomic bomb. In May 1942, a member of the Secret Intelligence Service (SIS) was assigned to Tube Alloys to organize the collection of relevant information and help with its analysis.[55]

Britain's intelligence chiefs considered it impossible and unwise to infiltrate agents into Germany. It was unlikely that any agent would obtain accurate information on such a complex issue. Further, the detailed briefing an agent would receive would, if he was captured, threaten the security of the Allied bomb program. It was better, British officials believed, to rely on information delivered through neutral or occupied countries on the whereabouts and activities of Heisenberg and other scientists likely to be associated with any attempt to develop a bomb.[56]

By this means, British intelligence did manage to obtain information on German atomic energy activities. By 1942, a young scientist at the University of Stockholm was reporting to the SIS on the whereabouts of German scientists and on contacts between his Swedish colleagues with Germany. That spring a Norwegian scientist began providing information on German scientists. There was also a source within Germany: Paul Rosbaud. An Austrian with a background in chemistry, Rosbaud had become the science adviser to the Springer-Verlag publishing house, whose collection of scientific journals included the very one that published Hahn and Strassman's paper reporting their discovery of fission. (Indeed, Rosbaud had speeded up its publication to provide a warning to the West.) Through his work he met individuals likely to be key figures in any German program and managed to transmit some information on their atomic activities to the British, via Switzerland and the Norwegian resistance.[57]

It was through these and other individuals, open sources, and some foreign governments (communications intelligence made no contribution) that the British, between late 1941 and September 1943, received a number of reports and indications of what the Germans had or had not accomplished. In the summer of 1942, a report alleged that Heisenberg was responsible for producing a U-235 bomb and developing fission as an energy source. In June, Rosbaud traveled to Oslo, where he apparently passed on to the Norwegian resistance the news about Speer's curtailment of support for bomb development. Also in 1942, a German scientific journal carried a detailed report on the thermal diffusion method of isotope separation. That same year another report indicated that Klaus Clusius was employing ore from the Joachimsthal mine in his research on isotope separation. During a visit to Rome in the summer of 1943, Max Planck said that Heisenberg claimed, "in his usual optimistic way," that in three or four years uranium could be employed to produce energy.[58]

Beyond tracking the movements and activities of key German scientists, the British also had information about German attempts to procure material for a bomb. They had discovered that after the occupation of Belgium in 1940, the Germans had access to the largest stock of uranium oxide in Europe, held at the refinery of the Union Miniére at Olen. SIS reported, prior to the fall of 1943, that the enemy was trying to increase the production of heavy water at a facility at Vemork in occupied Norway. University of Trondheim physics professor Leif Tronstad, who had been involved in setting up the facility, provided details about the expansion of heavy-water production. In March 1942, the SIS contacted a knowledgeable employee at the plant, who helped obtain photographs and drawings of the facility along with details of the German plan to increase production. That intelligence ultimately resulted in a combination of commando and aerial assaults, starting in February 1943 and concluding in November, that shut off the Norwegian source of the water.[59]

When taken in its totality, the information in the hands of British intelligence assessors in the fall of 1943 led them to conclude that Germany probably did not represent a serious threat in the area of atomic weapons. Reasons for their confidence included Britain's ability to monitor Heisenberg's movements along with their inability to find any link between him and the type of large-scale industrial enterprise required of any serious atomic bomb project. There were no mysterious disappearances or travels. In addition, the articles published in German scientific journals, beginning in early 1943, and related to the development of a plutonium production reactor appeared at much later dates after completion than what was normal for scientific papers, and the British concluded that originally they had been classified owing to their potential military relevance but that their content was no longer considered useful to ongoing potential weapons projects.[60]

While the British had become sanguine about the threat from any German bomb program, there was greater concern on the other side of the Atlantic. Furman passed the British view on to the scientists, but it was agreed, he recalls, that "we couldn't take the chance." Unlike the British, who were using all their resources to fight the war, the United States could afford to devote greater attention to the issue.[61]

Two of Furman's first tasks were contacting other U.S. organizations that might be able to assist him in monitoring the German program and determining what information his group and others should be collecting. Furman recalls going "from one agency to another, explaining in broad terms what [information I] wanted." Information on earthquakes "or anything that looked like earthquakes," in terms of their size or intensity, would be of interest. He also wanted to be informed about large industrial facilities with "a lot going on," including the movement of scientists, but with only a little going out. The little going out might be a bomb. He carried with him a letter from army intelligence chief Strong, which helped open doors.[62]

One of Furman's first meetings was with J. Robert Oppenheimer, probably in Washington, D.C. Locating Germany's leading scientists was the first step in any intelligence effort, Oppenheimer emphasized. Finding the scientists would lead to the center of German nuclear research, if there was one. To get Furman started, he provided some of the names that would naturally be on a watch list.[63]

Furman also received a warning from Oppenheimer that a German program might not be a mirror image of the U.S. effort. The huge isotope separation plants being built at Oak Ridge in Tennessee might not have any counterparts in Germany, even if the Germans had an active program. Since isotope separation was, like much of the bomb effort, a new endeavor, plans could change frequently. While the Americans had concluded that the separation process was extraordinarily difficult and required huge plants, the Germans might have discovered a far more elegant approach that required only a fraction of the resources the scientists at Los Alamos believed necessary. With respect to the separation of U-235, "someone might," Oppenheimer noted, "come up with a way to do it in his kitchen sink." It was a warning Furman did not forget.[64]

Oppenheimer also provided advice in a September 22 letter. He began by reiterating the importance of investigating "the whereabouts and activities of the men who are regarded as specialists in this field and without whom it would certainly be difficult to carry out a program effectively," and added Klaus Clusius to the names he had previously provided. But most of his letter focused on detecting any German atomic activities by monitoring the Germans' interest in certain raw materials and the construction of, and activities at, the type of plants required to produce material for a bomb.[65]

One absolute requirement for any bomb program would be uranium, stocks of which, the letter noted, had been captured by the Germans in Belgium. "It would be extremely important," Oppenheimer wrote, "to know with what urgency and on what scale these sources are being worked." German attempts to obtain or produce certain related substances, including graphite, heavy water, and beryllium—all of which might be used in the operation of a reactor—would also be of interest. With respect to heavy water, the letter stated that any production "beyond a liter or so a month seems to us indicative" and that the production at the Vemork plant seemed to be inadequate for success of a bomb program, but "it would be interesting to find out what the output of the [Vemork] plant is and where the material is being shipped."[66]

In attempting to locate plants that might be used to produce bomb material, Oppenheimer advised that they were unlikely to be "smaller than one city block" and would require large amounts of power. In addition, it was likely that any plants would be heavily guarded, out of bombing range from Britain, and not too near the Russian border—making Bohemia a likely location. If the Germans were to operate a reactor for the production of plutonium, "they will be operating it where water is plentiful and where the flow from the plant passes either through open country or through country inhabited by an 'inferior race' whom they do not mind killing off."[67]

Oppenheimer also noted that a large chemical company, such as I. G.

Farben, could carry out a bomb program. In that case "it would be quite possible to conceal the plant among other war projects on the grounds of the company." While the need to keep unwitting employees in the dark about such activities seemed to mitigate against such an approach, "it may not be ruled out." Further complicating the intelligence task was the fact that "the physical nature of the plant is sufficiently flexible so that external inspection can probably not identify it."[68]

The Los Alamos scientific director also suggested that if agents could be dropped with the right equipment or could transmit material back to the United States, one method of detecting an operating reactor would be "to investigate the radioactivity of rivers some miles below any suspicious and secret plant." A few cubic centimeters of water from any of the rivers would allow scientists back home to determine if a reactor was in operation.[69]

The day after Oppenheimer completed his letter to Furman, Philip Morrison, a young physicist with the Metallurgical Laboratory at the University of Chicago, submitted a memo to lab official Samuel K. Allison, who passed it on to Leslie Groves a few weeks later and suggested that it be followed up. Morrison, a twenty-eight-year-old New Jersey native, had received his doctorate in physics from Berkeley in 1940, where Oppenheimer served as supervisor for his thesis, *Three papers in quantum electrodynamics*. After brief teaching stints at San Francisco State University and the University of Illinois, Morrison joined the Met Lab in December 1942, where he would stay until moving to Los Alamos in August 1944. His memo laid out a variety of ways in which the extent of a German bomb program might be investigated. Morrison listed them in the order he considered feasible, which he noted "is probably the inverse order of effectiveness."[70]

First on Morrison's list was a literature survey of journals in not only physics, but also electronics, chemical engineering, economic geology, clinical and industrial medicine, and physical chemistry. Analysts would look for increased activity in research on alpha-particle counters, diffusion membranes, therapy for fluorine burns, and possibly radiological problems. The survey's objectives would be to determine the scale of research in particular fields as well as to extend U.S. knowledge of key personnel, particularly nonacademics.[71]*

More complex was the "economic survey," which could be combined

---

* As Morrison noted in a subsequent memo, the "fundamental special material in the whole process, besides the metal, is probably fluorine. Even metal production depends on fluorine at one step, and almost all separation methods known require the use of uranium hexafluoride." P. Morrison to R. R. Furman, Reports from the FEA, March 16, 1944, RG 77, Entry 22, Box 170, Folder 32.60-1, NARA.

with other information possessed by British or U.S. intelligence agencies. Morrison suggested that a group conducting the survey could prepare a list of raw materials (including uranium, fluorine, boron, and deuterium) with probable locations of origin, transport routes, and key personnel. Reports from enemy territory could be used to try to determine if there was any new or increased activity. The survey group would also examine plant construction, looking for isolated construction, special health precautions, location near a river, heavy concrete walls, along with a number of other possible warning signs. In addition, Morrison recommended that "a careful study should be made of fluorine, its use in German industry before 1940, and any change in its use thereafter."[72]

The final item on the list was the one Morrison characterized as "probably the one which would offer the most information," and "the most difficult." The easy part would be the preparation of a list of experts in physics, engineering, and chemistry. More difficult would be looking for contacts between scientific and engineering and industrial personnel, a sign that an attempt was being made to transform theory into an atomic capability. Some information, the memo suggested, might be found in the scientific and engineering circles of Zurich and Stockholm, which "should be full of gossip."[73]

PART OF THE INTELLIGENCE agenda laid out by Oppenheimer and Morrison could be addressed simply by the collection of German scientific literature. But if there was a serious German program to build an atomic bomb, uncovering its details would require more information than librarians could provide. It would require human intelligence (or HUMINT, in today's jargon), aerial reconnaissance, and possibly a variety of technical schemes for detecting the "signatures" of an atomic program.

Between the time when Furman began his job as intelligence chief and D-Day, a variety of human sources provided information. In January 1944, in Britain, a London intelligence and liaison office was established under the supervision of Horace K. (Tony) Calvert, a young Oklahoma City lawyer who had been working in the project's counterintelligence and security section. In addition to serving as liaison with British intelligence and reviewing German physics journals for information of interest, Calvert and his group also interviewed an assortment of German refugees, sometimes successfully, to extract information about the location of laboratories and industrial facilities in their homeland, the mining of fissionable materials, and the all-important whereabouts of Heisenberg, Hahn, and other key scientists.[74]

Human sources were also available in the United States. One was Charles W. Wright, a foreign materials specialist of the Bureau of Mines who had traveled extensively in Europe and visited a variety of mines. In an early

December interview with Lt. Col. Howard W. Dix of the OSS, Wright provided some information on the metals, including uranium, extracted from
Joachimsthal. A week later, Dix also interviewed Dr. Alois Langer of the West-
inghouse Research Laboratory in Pittsburgh. Langer, who had come to the
United States in 1936 as an exchange student from Germany, provided
sketches of the locations of various mines and the inside of an unspecified facility designated the "factory." Later that month, a prisoner of war, detained in
the Midwest, provided some data on the location of German scientists, but
had little information about any experiments.[75]

There were also key refugee scientists to consult. One was former Kaiser-
Wilhelm physics institute director Peter Debye. Others included Hans Bethe
and Victor Weisskopf, now working on building a bomb for the Allies. Part of
Robert Furman's job was to interview them and to find out what they knew
about German atomic activities. Then in December 1943, Furman had a new
and very important scientist to consult: Danish physicist Niels Bohr, who had
escaped from Denmark to Sweden and on to Scotland late in September,
after learning earlier that month that the Gestapo was planning to arrest
him.[76]

Some of Bohr's work, particularly his collaboration with Princeton University's John Wheeler, which resulted in a 1939 paper in *Physical Review*, was vital
to the understanding of nuclear fission and the importance of U-235. But Furman wanted to talk to Bohr because he had recent knowledge about the Germans. He had already spoken to the Danish physicist during a trip to London
before the physicist's mid-December appearance at MED headquarters. Subsequently, Furman would repeatedly bring Bohr back to those offices and question
him about a variety of topics, including Bohr's September 1941 meeting with
Heisenberg in Copenhagen, which left him with the impression that Heisenberg
was working on an atomic bomb, as well as his 1942 and 1943 meetings with
Hans Jensen (coauthor with Bothe of the report that ruled out graphite as a feasible moderator for a reactor). Furman also went through his list of German scientists of interest, and Bohr told him "what they did, where they had worked before
the war, whom they knew, how they felt about the Nazis." Bohr had already
talked to the British about such things, who had conveyed the information to
Furman during his visit, but, according to one account, "it is very likely that Bohr
was never questioned at greater length, or in more detail, about his knowledge of
the German bomb program . . . than he was in December 1943."[77]

Outside of the United States and Britain, collecting intelligence on the
German program was a more difficult task. Interviewing scientists and others
on friendly territory is one component of human intelligence operations. The
use of intelligence officers to collect information covertly on hostile or neutral
territory is another. In July 1942, the Office of the Coordinator of Information,
established a year earlier, had become the OSS, America's first central intelli-

gence agency. Throughout the war, the OSS, headed by William "Wild Bill" Donovan, would perform a variety of tasks, including analysis, special operations, counterintelligence, and clandestine human intelligence collection.[78]

Furman was not about to run a clandestine collection operation on his own, so he and Groves went to visit Donovan in October 1943. They hoped that Donovan would be willing to employ some OSS resources to look for signs of a German bomb program, including unusual scientific activities, large factories with no significant output, and the movements of key German scientists, as well as obtain a few cubic centimeters of water from rivers near suspect locations for analysis. Groves was pleased with the outcome of the meeting for two reasons—Donovan's promise of full cooperation and his aide's "artful description of targets while giving little away."[79]

Donovan did more than pledge cooperation. He created a technical section of his agency's Secret Intelligence branch, and on November 10, 1943, sent a cable to future director of central intelligence Allen Dulles, who had been the service's man in Bern for about a year. The cable requested that Dulles provide information on the whereabouts of three individuals, code-named Henno, Poli, and Bono. Later that day another cable matched real names to the code-names, identifying the quarry as three Italian physicists—Gilberto Bernardini of the University of Bologna, and Gian Carlo Wick and Fermi-protégé Edoardo Amaldi, both of the University of Rome. By the end of December, cables requesting similar information on another thirty individuals followed.[80]

One individual Dulles could turn to for help was fifty-three-year-old Paul Scherrer, designated Flute in OSS cables. A Swiss physicist that Dulles had met through his social network, Scherrer had early interests in business and botany but they gave way to a long-term involvement with physics and mathematics. Since 1920 he had been a professor at Zurich's Federal Technical College (ETH) and went to the same professional conferences attended by Germany's top nuclear physicists. Further, Scherrer had been friends with many of them, including Heisenberg, for a long time.[81]

Although he was never formally an agent, paid or otherwise, for the OSS, Scherrer was a valuable and frequent contributor to its intelligence effort. His frequent contact was Frederick Read Loofbourow, an executive with Standard Oil of New Jersey who had been sent to Switzerland in 1942 by the Board of Economic Warfare to collect intelligence on German oil production. When the Swiss border was closed, Loofbourow found himself stuck, and Allen Dulles had a new intelligence officer.[82]

Some of the intelligence Loofbourow relayed from Flute was transmitted in cables from Dulles to OSS headquarters in March and May 1944, cables that bore the designation Azusa, indicating that they involved atomic intelligence. The earlier cable consisted solely of information provided by Scherrer. It reported that Allied bombing had destroyed the left side of the Kaiser-

Wilhelm Institute for Chemistry in Berlin-Dahlem, disorganizing it, and that Tag (the OSS code name for Otto Hahn), "a fine person and not a Nazi," was heading the reorganization effort. At Heidelberg's Kaiser-Wilhelm Institute for Medicine, Ernst (Wolfgang Gentner, Bothe's assistant and an anti-Nazi) was constructing a cyclotron. Lender (von Weizsäcker) was reported to be in Strassburg, and was described as having "extremely pro-Nazi sympathies" and characterized as being a "pure theorist." With regard to Heisenberg (Christopher), Scherrer reported that "the greatest living German physicist" was working on cosmic rays and long-range projectile trajectories as well as disseminating Nazi propaganda.[83]

The May cable reported that Scherrer had discovered a number of facts of interest, as a result of talking to Gentner during a visit to Switzerland. Allied air raids had bombed out the institutes at Munich, Leipzig, and Cologne along with the chemistry institute in Berlin-Dahlem. In contrast, the Kaiser-Wilhelm physics institute in Berlin-Dahlem, where Heisenberg was in residence, had gone untouched. Flute also revealed that alternative installations were being prepared in the country region of Gau Württemberg to allow the institutes, including Heisenberg's, to operate safely. The cable further described the whereabouts and activities of a number of physicists. Gentner seemed "more Nazi" than previously and told Scherrer that the Reich chancellery was paying for the production of a two-hundred-million-volt cyclotron at Bisingen, although Flute believed it was actually a proton accelerator.[84]

While Paul Scherrer was not paid by the OSS, Morris "Moe" Berg, code-named Remus, did receive a paycheck from General Donovan's organization. He had joined on August 2, 1943, at age forty-one, at an annual salary of $3,800, after a year of working for the coordinator of inter-American affairs, Nelson Rockefeller. A 1923 graduate of Princeton, Berg had grown up in Newark, where his father, a Jewish immigrant from the Ukraine, operated a drugstore fifteen hours each day. At the Ivy League school, Berg had been a baseball star and had studied seven languages, including ones of practical importance (French, German, and Italian) and others that were largely of historical interest (Latin and Sanskrit).[85]

The six-foot one-inch, 195-pound Berg followed his undergraduate baseball career with a fifteen-year stint as a Major League Baseball player, mostly as a catcher. His professional career began in 1923 with the Brooklyn Dodgers and ended in 1939 with the Boston Red Sox. In between he wore the uniforms of the Chicago White Sox, Cleveland Indians, and Washington Senators. Beyond longevity, his baseball career did not amount to much. Over fifteen years he played in only 663 games, playing in more than 76 in a season only once. His career totals in hits (441) and runs-batted-in (206) constituted two good seasons for a star player. His lifetime batting average of .243 earned him the same tag given to many other players—"Good field, no hit."[86]

What made Berg useful as a spy—his intelligence and knowledge of for-eign languages—also made him, during his baseball career, the subject of "countless sports columns and Sunday-supplement stories" despite his mediocre accomplishments. He was repeatedly described "as the brainiest player in the major leagues." Along with showing up for a couple of thousand games over fifteen years, he spent part of an off-season semester studying at the University of Paris, read a large number of books and newspapers, passed the New York State Bar Exam in 1929, took a position as an associate with a Wall Street law firm, and appeared on the NBC radio game show *Information Please* in 1938, where he demonstrated that he knew that *poi* was Hawaiian bread and *loy* was French for "law."[87]

As an intelligence officer he was not easy to control, and his whereabouts would at times be a mystery to those paying his salary. Allen Dulles would write to OSS chief William Donovan that Berg "is as easy to handle as an opera singer. . . . His work is at times brilliant, but also temperamental."[88]

In late 1943, Berg was assigned to a new project, code-named Larson. Ostensibly, the objective was the exfiltration of Italian rocket and missile experts by boat and their subsequent transportation to the United States. Only a few in the OSS, along with Groves and Furman, knew that the actual pur-pose was to interview a number of Italian physicists, including Amaldi and Wick, most of whom were at the University of Rome, about the whereabouts and activities of Heisenberg, von Weizsäcker, and others. Berg received his assignment in an early-evening meeting with the balding, bespectacled head of the service's technical section, Howard Dix. Also attending, but not speak-ing, was Furman, whose name but not affiliation was provided to Berg. Nobody used the words *atomic bomb*, and as Berg would write, "most of the talk was cryptic." But he was able to figure out what Furman wanted and why. However, he would not have the opportunity to carry out his assignments until the spring of 1944 because of the reluctance of Gen. Mark Clark, the com-mander of the U.S. Fifth Army, which controlled the Italian frontier, to per-mit any of General Denovan's representative to enter.[89]

While Berg was cooling his heels, OSS was still receiving intelligence from its outpost in Bern, not all of it from Flute. An April 3, 1944, Azusa cable reported that a scientist code-named Henry was working in the field of crys-talogy at the Kaiser-Wilhelm physics institute, while another source, code-named Minister, was engaged in work on the electron microscope, and that Frédéric Joliot-Curie "has just been given 300,000 French francs by the Nazis toward his research in the reduction of heat formation during the atom-splitting reaction."[90]

Occasionally, the U.S. naval attaché in Stockholm, Cap. Werner Heiberg, received information from Paul Rosbaud during his travels to Scan-dinavia. In the spring of 1944, Rosbaud provided Furman's intelligence section, through Heiberg, with short reports, each no more than a dozen words, which confirmed that Heisenberg and his institute had been driven from Berlin by Allied air raids. Although the information may have been no different from reports on the subject received from the British, Furman was informed of the identity of Heiberg's source, whereas the British kept the identity of their sources confidential.[91]

GROVES AND FURMAN did not rely solely on traditional means of intelligence gathering. Allied acquisition of an atomic bomb would mean an unprecedented advance in weapons capability, delivered by science and technology. Furman hoped to employ atomic science and industrial technology in determining where the Germans stood in the race for an atomic bomb.

A key individual in that effort was physicist Luis W. Alvarez, the grandson of Irish-born missionaries. Tall and blond, he looked neither Latino nor Irish, but Scandinavian. "Brilliant, arrogant, and ambitious" is one characterization of the future Nobel laureate—who, along with several colleagues, would first propose the now widely accepted theory that the extinction of the dinosaurs sixty-five-million years ago was the result of a comet or large meteor hitting Earth. After undergraduate and graduate careers at the University of Chicago and work with the University of California and MIT radiation laboratories, he joined the University of Chicago's Met Lab in late 1943, before moving to Los Alamos in the spring of 1944.[92]

In his memoirs, Alvarez wrote that he "was so far down the Met Lab structure [that he] didn't appear on any organizational chart." Nevertheless, one day he discovered that Leslie Groves was aware of his existence when he was summoned to meet the project head in a Met Lab office. Groves wanted to know if there was some technological means to determine if the Germans were operating plutonium-producing reactors. If it was possible to locate such reactors, aerial attacks could halt or at least interrupt their operations. Alvarez was given a week to come up with an answer and cautioned not to tell anyone else in the Met Lab of his new assignment.[93]

Alvarez devised a scheme for the remote detection of a radioactive gas emitted by operating reactors. Xenon-133, a noble gas, has a five-day half-life, during which it produces distinctive gamma and beta radiation. Alvarez concluded it would be possible to build a filtering device that could process thousands of cubic meters of air and trap any radioactive xenon atoms that appeared in the mixture. The filtering device could be built into the front of an airplane and sample the air as it flew across Germany. When the plane returned, any xenon it picked up could be identified by its unique radioactive traits.[94]

Alvarez moved his office to the University of Chicago campus so he could have access to the physics library. His task had been given the highest priority-rating within the Manhattan Project, allowing him to go anywhere he wanted to, to arrange to have anything he needed built. To learn more about the handling of noble gases, he traveled to a General Electric plant in Cleveland, which used argon, another noble gas, in its lightbulbs. With the help of GE experts, he designed equipment that could be carried in the bombardier's compartment of a Douglas A-26 and arranged with GE for its construction.[95]

The device passed an air sample through activated charcoal, which trapped xenon and radon (another noble gas) but not oxygen or nitrogen. Since radon has a much higher boiling point than xenon, it is possible to separate one from the other. After the flight, the activated charcoal would be heated to boil off the radon and xenon into a stream of helium gas. The gas stream would then be passed through activated charcoal again, but at a temperature that would freeze the radon and allow the xenon to get through. Additional activated charcoal, at dry-ice temperature, would absorb the xenon. With the helium pumped out, the final filter would be heated to extract the pure xenon. The highly concentrated sample that would remain could then be analyzed for radioactive xenon, the presence of which would confirm an operating reactor. When the specially equipped plane was tested in the vicinity of Cleveland, flying at four hundred feet, nothing was detected—although, Furman recalls, it "scared a lot of cows."[96]

Furman also consulted Alvarez, in May 1944, by which time he had moved to Los Alamos. Writing him at "P.O. Box 1539, Santa Fe, New Mexico," Furman asked for advice on a project that followed up on Oppenheimer's September 1943 suggestion "to obtain samples of water from Lake Constance and the upper reaches of the Rhine River which are accessible from Switzerland without flying in either special testing apparatus or personnel." Alvarez was asked to draft a cable providing instructions to "the people in Switzerland" who would be doing the work.[97]

Alvarez suggested issuing instructions that samples of water from the lake and river "should be in . . . containers, with a label to indicate the geographical position and the date (including the time of day) at which the sample was collected." He also advised that the cable specify that the river water should be collected from the fastest-flowing part, and "lake water should be taken as near shore and as close to small rivers which empty into the lake on the German side." Men in fishing boats, equipped with water bottles as part of a lunch basket, could most easily collect the water without arousing suspicion.[98]

OF COURSE, the penultimate rationale of the effort to collect information about the German program—whether through open sources, human intelligence, or technical methods—was to determine exactly who was involved in the program and what they had accomplished. Such information could be used to provide reassurance or to justify and aid in action designed to destroy or inhibit German atomic activities. Action might involve bombing missions; it might involve the assassination of one or more of the Reich's key atomic scientists.

A systematic effort to convert raw data into informed judgment had begun by late 1943, when Philip Morrison started implementing the ideas in his September proposal. At the end of November, he finished his *Report on the Enemy Materials Situation*, which he revised shortly before Christmas. Relying solely on public sources, his two-and-a-half-page analysis estimated the amount of uranium ore accessible to the Germans, and examined the availability of possible moderators for a reactor—beryllium, heavy water, and graphite. With respect to graphite, which the Germans had already rejected as a suitable moderator, Morrison concluded that "the Germans, under pressure, could manufacture adequate amounts."[99]

Just a few days before he completed the December version of his enemy materials report, Morrison had finished another, lengthier study. The main body of *Report on Enemy Physics Literature: Survey Report P* ran seven and a half single-spaced pages and was largely based on Morrison's examination of the articles that appeared in the 1942 and 1943 issues of *Die Naturwissenschaften*, two physics journals, and an inorganic chemistry journal. A three-page appendix listed the location of enemy physics laboratories, their specialities, and some of their personnel.[100]

Morrison concluded that the Germans were well aware of the key facts concerning chain reactions, including their "technical promise and difficulty," and inferred that the enemy was also well aware of the properties of plutonium. He also noted that from 1940 to the middle of 1942, the German research program was capable of producing the scientific background for, and even allowing the initial design of, a plutonium production plant. The only piece of data that was not consistent with an ongoing effort was the "apparent release from full-time secret work of two leading physicists"—a reference to Heisenberg and von Weizsäcker. In any case, there was a need for initiating a search for a plutonium plant, relying on both espionage and "physical means," presumably the type of means that Luis Alvarez was and would be working on. Finally, Morrison noted that, given the advanced stage of fluorine chemistry and the large scale of their chemical industry, the Germans might be more likely to pursue uranium enrichment via gaseous diffusion than plutonium production. Thus, the existence of a plant involved in the production of hexafluoride or a related material, such as the I. G. Farben site at Leverkusen, was perhaps more likely than that of a "high-powered" plutonium plant.[101]

In addition to analyzing raw data about the status of any German program, Morrison spent some time analyzing the British interpretation of the data. A December 22, 1943, summary of the more sanguine British view was apparently prepared by Furman during his visit to London in late 1943. In it, he noted the varied reasons for British skepticism. Those reasons included, but were not limited to, the immense size of any such project (which would preclude total secrecy); the absence of any indication of any scientist "doing anything but quite normal research, the results of which are published in scientific publications"; a lack of sufficient ore for a full-scale production program; the operation of the heavy-water plant in Norway at less than full capacity; the timing of the discovery of uranium fission (too late to be incorporated into Nazi war planning); and the combination of the Nazis' initial confidence that the war would be won easily and later concerns (severely limiting the use of resources for experimental projects). Furman noted that the British placed great importance on meetings between Lise Meitner and Otto Hahn and Meitner and Max von Laue. During a 1943 visit to Sweden, Hahn, when asked by Meitner how the fission project was going, replied, "It isn't going."[102]

Furman pointed to some limitations to the British analysis, including lack of solid information on the activities of fifty-one of the sixty scientists in the field. Based on the information they did have, the British had concluded the Germans planned only experimentation and pure research during the war. In that conclusion, he wrote, "It is felt the British are skating rather thin."[103] What neither the British nor Furman had available were the German Army Ordnance weapons office report of February 1942 or any of the technical reports prepared by scientists at the assorted institutes and universities doing research in the field of fission. Indeed, no one in either the British or the U.S. intelligence establishment was even aware that such reports existed.

In any case, a more detailed critique, signed by Met Lab official Samuel Allison, although probably drafted by Morrison, was provided to Groves in early January. The memo disputed the "notion that nothing unusual is happening in Germany," and pointed to the analysis in *Survey Report P* of the long delays before articles related to fission are published in contrast to other areas of physics, which—contrary to the British view—was not considered reassuring. Allison added that there was no reference in the German literature to plutonium. While noting that Heisenberg, since late 1942, had dropped intensive efforts on "work similar to ours," the author also pointed to the visits of Harteck and Jensen to the Norwegian heavy-water plant, indicating the interest of top-rank German scientists in heavy-water production. The critique argued that the British ability to explain known industrial activity without reference to a bomb project was greatly inferior approach to "an active search by technical experts for positive data." Finally, Allison argued, the two tons of heavy water that the Germans probably had from the Norwegian plant represented a minimum, and it appeared that the moderator was "being made elsewhere in enemy territory."[104]

Another element of the analytic effort was the Foreign Intelligence Section's periodic *Report on Enemy Activities*. The March 7, 1944, report, authored by Furman, was provided to Groves along with a letter from its author. Furman noted that "it has been determined that the enemy has the necessary material and is accomplishing important research work." The report covered the activities of German scientists, uranium, moderators, enemy research centers, German industrial activity, and Italian activity. It mentioned Heisenberg's current position as head of the Kaiser-Wilhelm physics institute and his reduced work in the area of fission. Other scientists whose activities were noted included Clusius, Walther Gerlach, Jensen, Harteck, and von Weizsäcker. After noting the delay between the time of completion and the time of publication of articles related to fission, the continued participation of key scientists in university instruction, the absence of any articles on plutonium, and the comments of von Laue and Hahn that German development of a bomb was not progressing, the report concluded that "the pretense of study and research as usual has been an enemy security policy but that a great deal of work other than the normal research is evidently taking place," a conclusion consistent with the variety of German technical reports being produced but of which the United States had no specific knowledge.[105]

The report stated that "sufficient uranium is available to the enemy," a finding based on a combination of German stocks at the beginning of the war, what was seized from Belgium, and possible extraction of additional ore from Joachimsthal. It also revealed the existence of a new institute with a huge technical staff that worked on problems of armament production. In addition, the report revealed the failure to find any industrial plant that could be used for the separation of isotopes, and observed that "other groups have not found to date enemy plants for the manufacture of rockets and pilotless aircraft which leaves every doubt that a factory could be uncovered which is engaged in the project work."[106]

Later that month Furman received a report by Karl Cohen, another contributor to the analytical effort. Cohen, a chemist, worked under Harold Urey at Columbia University on isotope separation via liquid thermal diffusion. Like Morrison, he had wondered what the Germans were up to with regard to atomic weapons. He also reached a similar solution to begin the process of finding out: a review of the literature, while keeping in mind possible German attempts at deception.[107]

In his March 27 *Report on German Literature on Isotope Separation*, Cohen drew on articles in a variety of physics, chemistry, and engineering journals published between 1939 and 1942, and surveyed alternative separation methods, including the centrifuge, electromagnetic separation, and thermal diffusion techniques, with particular emphasis on the latter. "The enemy," Cohen wrote, "has given the most serious consideration to the liquid thermal diffusion method. . . . His publishing program on L.T.D. is deliberately designed to mislead us." Further, Cohen argued, the publications that he and Morrison were seeing were the result of a *planned partial publication* program. He pointed to the absence of articles on reactors, chain reactions, and experiments on separating uranium hexafluoride. The German motive was "to deceive us about the extent and progress of his program, and so cause us to relax the pressure on our own." "The German publication program," Cohen concluded, "is thus a blind for diligent work."[108]

Cohen went on to sketch his assessment of the history and current status of the German program. Research was started in 1940, and by the beginning of 1941, "certainly by Spring 1941," there was sufficient data for the Germans to begin construction. While it was possible that they began "to build immediately at top speed," it was more probable that they were delayed by preparations for the attack on the Soviet Union. "We may safely assume," Cohen continued, "that the program received all-out attention as soon as it was evident that the war would last several years more—say by the Spring of 1942." Based on his estimate of the time required to build a full-scale thermal diffusion plant, Cohen concluded that the Germans had "a completed plant by the Fall of 1943, and possibly much sooner." It would then take, he believed, eighteen months to produce uranium enriched to 90 percent (that is, 90 percent U-235), giving the Germans an atomic weapon in the spring of 1945.[109]

A cover letter from Urey that accompanied Cohen's report expressed his skepticism that the Germans had made much progress in the area, a much more optimistic conclusion than Cohen's. "On the other hand," he noted, "[a] 10% chance is too much to neglect," and seconded Cohen's proposals for certain measures to determine the actual status of the program. Those steps included contact with Werner Kuhn, a German physicist living in Switzerland who had worked on isotope separation before leaving Germany, and close scrutiny of German engineering journals for signs of unusual activity, including advertisements for specialized personnel and reports of meetings.[110]

THE GERMANS HAD, of course, been engaged in covert work on atomic energy, as Cohen feared. There were the classified technical papers and reactor experiments, of which the United States and Britain had little or no knowledge. But that covert program was far less substantial and successful than Cohen estimated. By the time he prepared his report in March 1944, the German program was even more scattered than it had been when Robert Furman began investigating its status six months earlier.

By the beginning of 1944, there had been at least three significant developments. One involved program management. Albert Speer forced Abraham Esau, who supervised the program for the Reich Research Council, to resign, in part because of the hostility from project scientists, who opposed his attempts to centralize their work. Replacing Esau was Walther Gerlach, a physics professor at the University of Munich. Both Heisenberg and Hahn gave their blessing, and on January 1, 1944, Gerlach became the deputy to the Reichmarshall (Goering) on the questions of atomic physics.[111]

The second development concerned hardware. The bunker laboratory at the Berlin-Dahlem institute had been completed by the end of 1943. The main laboratory consisted of a water-filled pit, rapid air and water pumps in case of an accident, remote-control apparatus for handling radioactive materials, a ventilation and heating system, and heavy-water tanks with a purification system. Other rooms included a workshop and several smaller laboratories, where further research on uranium and heavy water was conducted. As protection from aerial assault and radiation from the uranium furnace, the facility was surrounded by two meters of iron-reinforced concrete.[112]

While the bunker laboratory was safe from aerial attack, the bunker did not have living quarters for all the project members. Berlin was becoming more dangerous as the intensity of U.S. and British bombing increased, and in August 1943 was the target of large-scale raids, whose objectives included disruption of scientific efforts that might lead to a German bomb. But earlier that year, even before the bombing intensified, German authorities began to consider moving the work of the uranium project to safer locations in the countryside.[113]

Gerlach appears to have told Heisenberg of a cluster of small, peaceful villages in the Swabian Alps region of the Black Forest, just south of Stuttgart and Tübingen. With the bombing intensifying in the summer and fall of 1943, Heisenberg decided to relocate all personnel who would not be needed for the latest series of reactor experiments in Berlin. By the end of the year, about one-third of the fifty-five-member staff of Heisenberg's institute, including assistant director Max von Laue, were gone from the capital. Their new workplace was a large and nearly vacant textile factory in Hechingen, which provided sufficient space to allow them to set up offices as well as rooms for measurement of materials and construction of equipment.[114]

Heisenberg and his institute were not alone in seeking to avoid Allied bombs and continue their work. British raids on Hamburg in August 1943 burned out the city's center, and convinced Paul Harteck to transfer his experiments in isotope separation from the University of Hamburg to Freiburg. Hahn and his Berlin-based chemistry institute, which had been involved in fission studies, also sought a safer environment, which was why, on the night of February 15, Hahn was in the south of Germany, preparing to move his institute to Tailfingen, a village not far from Hechingen. That night British bombers scored a direct hit on his institute, and it burned to the ground.[115]

Also outside of the main target areas was a new Nazi university, located in

Alsace, at Strassburg (as the Germans spelled Strasbourg, which they had seized in 1940). It had been established in late 1942 and early 1943. Its faculty included a key member of the Uranverein, von Weizsäcker. Another faculty member was Rudolf Fleischmann, a colleague of Bothe's whose experience included radiochemistry and rare-element chemistry.[116]

Despite the air raids and the dispersal of personnel, research continued at the bunker laboratory in Berlin and an army weapons station in Gottow under Kurt Diebner. During the winter of 1943–1944, the Kaiser-Wilhelm physics institutes in Berlin and Heidelberg had collaborated to construct a model reactor at the bunker laboratory, employing one and a half tons of heavy water and uranium plates of equal weight. However, experiments using horizontal layers of uranium plates and varying the width of the layers failed to provide hope of a future chain reaction. In contrast, Kurt Diebner and his group in Gottow obtained better results with a uranium metal cube design, with cube lattices being lowered into a cylindrical aluminum container filled with heavy water.[117]

MOE BERG'S LONG WAIT for approval from the Fifth Army ended in the spring of 1944. During the winter months, in preparation for his mission, he had read Max Born's *Experiment and Theory in Physics* and studied quantum theory and matrix mechanics, which introduced him to Heisenberg and the uncertainty principle. At a meeting shortly before his departure, Furman told Berg that he wanted to know which German and Italian scientists were still alive, their locations, and their travel plans. Furman apparently provided him with a list of scientists to contact, which contained data on their age, political affiliation, and address. And, without using the words *radioactive* or *atomic bomb*, Furman instructed Berg to find what he could about German secret weapons.[118]

On May 4, carrying a .45 pistol in one pocket, and two thousand dollars in OSS money in the other, and dressed in black, white, and gray, Berg boarded a military airplane at a field outside Washington, D.C., for the flight that would take him to Newfoundland, Scotland, and finally London. Not long after takeoff, Berg was embarrassed when his pistol slipped out of his pocket and fell into the lap of George Shine, the army major occupying the next seat—something that certainly never happened to James Bond. Berg explained to Shine, "I'm inept at carrying a gun."[119]

Exactly one month later Rome was liberated. That same day Berg left for Bari, on the Adriatic Sea, where he was to have dinner with Army Air Forces Gen. Nathan Twining on June 5. Twining provided a plane so that Berg could return to OSS headquarters in Caserta, outside of Naples, where a driver picked him up and delivered him to Rome four hours later. The next day, as Allied forces were landing on Normandy, Berg checked into the Hotel Excelsior. In the afternoon, an OSS operative who was familiar with the city led Berg to the home, at 50 via Parioli, of Edoardo Amaldi, next to whose name on his list of Italian physicists Berg had marked a "1."[120]

A leading experimental physicist, Amaldi had worked closely with Fermi in studying the consequences of bombarding the nucleus with neutrons. Berg knocked on his door and arranged to talk with him the following day, which he did during a lunch at the Arturo restaurant, whose patrons used golden forks to consume their meat and pasta. Berg also managed to get in touch with Gian Carlo Wick, a theoretical physicist who had gone to Germany to study in 1931, where he became acquainted with Heisenberg. Berg also took Wick out for lunch, where they spoke privately.[121]

In addition to talking to the two Italian physicists individually, Berg met with them jointly. The results of those conversations were relayed to OSS headquarters in a June 12 cable. Berg reported that Amaldi had not worked on fission since 1941 because the University of Rome was not equipped for experimentation, and had been working largely on the scattering of neutrons. Amaldi also told the catcher-turned-spy that his only contact with Germany since the beginning of the war was when Otto Hahn visited Rome in 1941 to deliver three popular lectures under the auspices of the German Cultural Institute. Neither in his lectures nor in his three meetings with Amaldi did Hahn discuss the use of fission for military purposes, a subject about which he was "extremely secretive," according to Berg's cable. Hahn and Strassmann, Amaldi thought, would be the most important scientists involved in a German atomic bomb project, which he believed must be underway (although he thought it would not be possible to complete for a decade). A secondary group consisted of Bothe and his pupils. Amaldi did not place Heisenberg in either group; while Amaldi considered him a first-class theoretical physicist, he was not an experimental physicist.[122]

Wick complemented Amaldi's information nicely, since he was able to tell Berg about Heisenberg. Some of what he told him constituted his assessment of his former teacher, whom he had a "great love for" and "sentimental interest in." According to Wick, Heisenberg was probably an anti-Nazi, but with "too deep a sense of patriotism not to work for his country." Like Amaldi, Wick found Germans he spoke to very secretive and "non-talkative" when it came to atom bombs and reactors. He also told Berg of the most recent letter he had received from Heisenberg, postmarked Berlin and dated January 15, 1944. The portion that Berg quoted in his cable had informed Wick that his former teacher was living in the "Nernack House" in Berlin, while his family was living in the Bavarian Alps. Heisenberg's institute, as of his writing, was still standing, although the Leipzig physics institute had been largely destroyed, along with the first edition of his book on cosmic rays. Wick had provided a not-too-precise update of Heisenberg's whereabouts. He was in a woody region in the southern part of Germany, but Wick either would not or could not give Berg more details. In terms of their importance to an atomic bomb project, Wick rated Clusius most important, followed by Heisenberg, Bothe, Hahn, and Strassmann.[123]

About the same time Berg was preparing his cable for Washington, he made, what was to him, another important discovery. He acquired a copy of *Zeitschrift fur Physiks*, whose contents included an article on neutron diffusion, an article he apparently believed Philip Morrison, back at the Met Lab, needed to review as soon as possible. So, instead of sending it back via pouch, Berg decided to deliver it himself. According to Morrison, one day in mid-June Berg showed up at his office in Chicago, sweaty and tired, journal in hand. One look at the journal and Morrison knew Berg's long journey had been a waste of time. Every month, the Met Lab received the journal's latest issue through a Swiss distributor. Morrison didn't tell Berg that he could have stayed in Rome. He just thanked him for his efforts and sent him back.[124]

On June 19, not long after Berg returned to Rome, Robert Furman arrived. Berg gave him a tour of the Vatican, while Furman gave Berg another assignment. As soon as possible, he was to go to Florence and investigate an optical laboratory, the Galileo Company. Furman was concerned because of the similarity between lens assembly and the design of a system to compress fissionable material in a plutonium bomb, and the fear that the Galileo Company and Germany were in close contact. "As soon as possible" turned out to be two months later, after the Allied armies entered Florence. Berg arrived and contacted the company's owner, Dr. Paolo Martinez, who reassured him that his firm only produced an array of products appropriate for its name, including range finders, periscopes, searchlights, and telescopes.[125]

WHILE BERG was trying to ferret out information on German scientists from the ground, the United States and Britain were looking for signs of a German atomic bomb program from the air. Early that summer the Royal Air Force had brought back some photographs taken over the Joachimsthal uranium mine. Tony Calvert, in London, sent a set of the photos to Furman, who passed them on to the OSS. The spy service took them to a German mining engineer living in the United States, and asked his opinion without telling him why they were of interest.[126]

The engineer noted that while it was not a gold mine, "it's definitely a mine for heavy metal." He offered a number of possibilities, including tungsten and bismuth, while ruling out lead. By examining the mine tailings, the piles of crushed rock that remained after the uranium had been removed, he estimated that the mine was producing only a few tons of crude ore each day. That would convince Furman that the Germans had not accelerated production at Joachimsthal, although he continued to worry that other mines might have been established.[127]

In the fall of 1944, three A-26 Invader aircraft, lightweight attack bombers that could descend to treetop level and quickly climb high enough to elude antiaircraft fire, carried Luis Alvarez's xenon detection equipment over three areas of concern in Germany. The sites had been selected by Furman's staff, who combined the data they could find in German books, newspapers, and technical reports with aerial reconnaissance and other intelligence data. No xenon-133 was found.[128]

In November another set of photos produced what Leslie Groves would describe in his memoirs as "our biggest scare to date." In July Tony Calvert had requested coverage of the Hechingen-Bisingen area. The photos from a November mission over the area showed new construction of a series of small factory buildings of identical design. The extent and speed of the construction effort caused alarm, for it included new railway lines being built toward the plant sites, the establishment of nearby slave labor camps, and new power lines being strung in the vicinity. Given the information on the relocation of Heisenberg and other key scientists to the area, Groves wondered if the images showed Germany's equivalent of Oak Ridge.[129]

His fears were soon followed by relief. Douglas Kendall, Britain's chief of aerial reconnaissance, noticed that all the plants photographed were in the same twenty-mile-long valley, and all were located on the same geological contour. A trip to the Geological Museum in London allowed Kendall to determine that prior to the war, German geologists had uncovered a seam of oil-bearing shale in the valley. Photo interpreters, given that bit of data, were able to show that the factories represented nothing more threatening than a desperate German attempt to find petroleum, which was in short supply. The issue was not closed, however, since a report from Sweden claimed that traces of uranium could be found in oil shale. Furman went to Pittsburgh to talk to an expert on the subject, who was able to confirm that the pipes next to each plant were intended to cook the oil out of the shale.[130]

IN DECEMBER, Berg was still on the ground, but now in Switzerland. If delivery of a physics journal represented one end of the spectrum of secret service work, what Berg was possibly going to do in Switzerland represented the other end.

By the fall of 1944, based on Heisenberg's letter to Wick and other intelligence, Furman could be reasonably confident that Heisenberg was in Hechingen. On December 8, there was word from Bern that Heisenberg was going to give a lecture in Zurich, one in a series arranged by Paul Scherrer. As a result, Morris Berg arrived at the ETH lecture hall on December 18, carrying a gun. His assignment was to listen very carefully to Heisenberg's remarks, and if he became convinced that the Germans were close to an atomic bomb, Berg was to shoot him while he was still in the auditorium.[131]

The idea of depriving Heisenberg of his life or liberty was not new. In 1942 refugee scientists Hans Bethe and Victor Weisskopf had proposed kidnapping him, but Groves and Furman did not begin looking for the right man for the job until 1944. OSS chief Donovan sent Carl Eifler, a 280-pound graduate of the Los Angeles Police Academy and former undercover customs inspector, to Furman. When Furman asked Eifler if he could "deny Germany [Heisenberg's] brain," he said he could, and planning began. But Donovan called it off in late June, perhaps unconvinced that Eifler's plan was feasible, for it involved leading Heisenberg out of Germany on foot, putting him on a plane in Switzerland, and parachuting him into the Mediterranean, where he would be picked up by a submarine.[132]

Bringing a gun into a lecture hall and shooting someone was considerably easier. And so Berg sat behind Otto Hahn and Carl F. von Weizsäcker, other logical targets if one were to begin knocking off key German scientists, and listened as Heisenberg lectured on the nonpolitical and nonmilitary topic of S-matrix theory to an audience of about twenty professors and graduate students. The S stood for *scattering*, and the theory was one approach to explaining strong interactions between particles. It is doubtful, even with his exploration into the world of physics the previous winter, that Berg could really make sense of what Heisenberg was talking about. But nobody gave any signs of being alarmed, and Berg's gun stayed in his pocket. Soon Berg had a second chance, attending Scherrer's dinner for Heisenberg. Leaving at the same time as his potential victim, he chatted with him as they walked on dimly lit Zurich streets. But Heisenberg's comments at dinner that the war was lost gave Berg even less of a motive to kill him, even if he had the means and a golden opportunity.[133]

EARLIER THAT MONTH a group of American soldiers and scientists arrived at the University of Strassburg, where von Weizsäcker had been a prominent faculty member. Designated Alsos, the unit's primary mission was to uncover as much as possible about the status of the German bomb program. Its methods would include reviewing seized documents, interviewing enemy scientists after their capture, and examining any construction projects that might have been undertaken.

The inspiration for Alsos came to counterintelligence officer John Lansdale early in 1943. By the time his idea became a reality, Lansdale was working for Groves. But in early 1943, Landsale was a member of the army's G-2. He convinced his boss, army intelligence chief Gen. George V. Strong, who then presented chief of staff George Marshall with Lansdale's idea of a unit that would trail Allied troops through Italy and investigate German scientific developments, although the primary purpose would be to find out what progress the Germans had made with respect to atomic weaponry. Strong noted that such operations might be used in other enemy and enemy-occupied territory in the future. General Groves also approved of the idea, although he was less than thrilled at the designation for the project, which seemed like a breach of operational security. *Alsos* was Greek for "a sacred grove." But Groves feared that changing the designation would be noticed and cause speculation.[134]

On November 26, 1943, Groves, along with the two most senior officials of the OSRD, which had been established to oversee the exploitation of science in the cause of the war effort and whose director reported directly to President Roosevelt, met to decide who would lead Alsos. Their choice for military commander was Lt. Col. Boris T. Pash, who had been serving as head of the counterintelligence branch of the Western Defense Command of the Fourth Army. Groves and Pash had already met, Pash having directed an espionage investigation of the University of California at Berkeley's Radiation Laboratory, and Groves would later write that his "thorough competence and great drive had made a lasting impression on me." The son of a Russian émigré, Pash spoke Russian fluently and was energetic in trying to unmask communists. One of his major targets had been the Los Alamos scientific director, J. Robert Oppenheimer, who, he concluded, was a secret Communist Party member and possibly a spy.[135]

Less than a month later, Pash was in Naples, where the Alsos unit—consisting of Pash, an executive officer, four agents of the Army's Counterintelligence Corps, four interpreters, and four scientists (one army, one navy, and two from the OSRD)—had established its headquarters on December 17. In February 1944, Alsos members were able to locate and interrogate a few Italian scientists in Sicily and southern Italy. What they discovered seemed to indicate that Germany was not employing Italian scientists or resources in a bomb program. But key targets such as Amaldi and Wick were in Rome, and the Allied advance toward the Italian capital had stalled, so Pash and his team returned to Washington.[136]

Alsos operations in Italy convinced OSRD chief Vannevar Bush that a similar operation, with the unit trailing Allied forces as they made their way through Western Europe and into Germany, could help uncover important intelligence on the German program. On February 29, 1944, in a letter to Groves, he recommended that Alsos be continued. Groves followed up, and during the first half of March he sent a memo to Maj. Gen. Clayton L. Bissell, the new army intelligence chief, which recommended that "a similar scientific mission with the same objectives be made ready for use in other European territory as soon as progress of the war permits." General Staff indecision delayed approval, leading Groves to insist that Bissell bring the matter to General Marshall's attention. On April 4, the army's deputy chief of staff gave Alsos the go-ahead for post–D-Day operations. Its mission was to secure "all available intelligence on enemy scientific research and development, particularly with regard to military application," although the primacy of its atomic mission was understood.[137]

While the basic mission had not changed, the nature of the target had, and the likelihood of finding key information was greater. For its second venture into Europe, Alsos would have an advisory committee for nonatomic matters, a scientific director, and a larger military and civilian staff, largely selected by Groves and Bush. By the end of August, Alsos would include more than thirty scientists as part of the combined military and civilian personnel that would, at its height, number about one hundred. They agreed that Pash should again head the unit and then made another key appointment on May 15, when they chose Samuel A. Goudsmit to serve as scientific director.[138]

Goudsmit, an atomic physicist, was on leave from the University of Michigan to work on radar at the MIT Radiation Laboratory, and had just spent six months in Britain. A native of the Netherlands, he had been educated in Europe and was fluent in a number of European languages. He had been recruited to join Michigan by Walter Colby, who in 1944 was a senior official of OSRD.[139]

In the 1920s, in collaboration with George Uhlenbeck, Goudsmit had introduced the concept of the spinning electron into physics, which offered an explanation for previously puzzling data on the properties of light emitted and absorbed by atoms. The discovery put Goudsmit into close contact with German physicists who would become involved in the uranium project. After taking the job at the University of Michigan, he became involved in organizing a renowned summer school. In late July 1939, Heisenberg lectured there for a week and stayed with him. Goudsmit had the perfect combination of knowledge and ignorance for the job: he knew physics and key German physicists, but was largely unaware of what Oppenheimer and others were doing at Los Alamos. Should he be captured by the Germans, even their most skilled torturers would have been able to extract very little information from him about the Manhattan Project. Ten days after his appointment, Goudsmit was in Washington. On D-Day he left for London. Goudsmit also had a very personal motivation for returning to Europe: his last communication from his parents was a letter with the address of a Nazi concentration camp.[140]

Goudsmit was not part of the first Alsos mission after his appointment. On June 4, 1944, with the American Fifth Army taking control of Rome, Pash headed back to Italy to try to make contacts with the Rome physicists who were out of reach during Alsos's 1943 Italian mission. He was able to stay for only a short time, but did make contact with Amaldi—Moe Berg had been the *second* American to show up on June 6. After Pash returned to England, an Alsos unit arrived in Rome on June 19 and began six days of investigations. Joining them was Robert Furman (who also received his Vatican tour from Moe Berg). Wick and Amaldi were questioned about their activities but had no direct information on German fission research since they had never been asked to participate. Wick was able to tell Alsos of his trip to Germany in the summer of 1942, describe the correspondence between German scientists that he had reviewed, and provide brief accounts of the locations and activities of some of the German physicists.[141]

Goudsmit would see action in France, after Allied troops secured the beachhead at Normandy and moved into the country. He was preceded by Pash, who arrived in Rennes on August 9 and examined the laboratories of the university there, along with catalogues and papers that suggested additional targets. The primary target was the nation's leading nuclear scientist, Frédéric Joliot-Curie. When Pash arrived at L'Arcouest, the coastal village where Joliot-Curie had a summer home, he found neither his target nor his wife. On August 24, Pash was also disappointed to find Joliot-Curie away from his home in the suburbs of Paris, although his servants told him that he was in Paris, probably working at his laboratory. On August 25, Pash, along with Tony Calvert and two members of the Army's Counterintelligence Corps, became the first Americans to enter liberated Paris, riding in jeeps and accompanied by the Second French Armored Division. That same afternoon they found Joliot-Curie in his laboratory at the Collège de France.[142]

Two days later, Goudsmit and other Alsos team members arrived, set up offices at 2 place de l'Opéra, and interviewed Joliot-Curie. On August 29, the French scientist and Calvert flew back to London, where he was questioned by Goudsmit and several British officials. Joliot-Curie told them that German scientists had used his laboratory and cyclotron during the occupation, identifying Kurt Diebner, Walter Bothe, and Abraham Esau as his visitors. He told Goudsmit and the others that he believed they had made very little progress toward developing an atomic bomb, which reinforced the view that the Germans were not as far along as had been feared. But, as Goudsmit would write, it was plain that Joliot-Curie "knew nothing of what was going on in Germany."[143]

In September and October, the Alsos team's operations in Belgium and southern France produced some valuable intelligence, much of it due to the work of team member Capt. Reginald Augustine. In early September, the existence of Union Minière uranium refinery at Olen, in Belgium, came to Pash's attention, and he was ordered to locate and confiscate any uranium ore at the site. When the team arrived at Union Minière offices in Antwerp, twenty-eight miles west of the target, Augustine learned that over a thousand tons of refined ore had been shipped to Germany, and another seventy tons were still in a warehouse in Olen. Records turned up by Augustine also showed that France had received more than eighty tons of refined ore on June 4, 1940, shortly before the Nazi invasion. After being alerted by Pash, Groves sent Robert Furman to join forces with Pash, to locate the missing ore and place it under Allied control.[144]

On September 19, they traveled to Olen, where Pash, Furman, and two of his agents began their hunt, which was not without a considerable degree of personal risk. On some occasions they took German fire. On another Furman was nearly thrown from a jeep as they dashed across a railroad crossing. After six days they found what they were looking for. They obtained samples to bring back to Brussels for analysis. The next day they returned to Olen, where the Germans shot at them once more but were unable to stop them from arranging for numerous small barrels of uranium to be transferred to Britain, which took place within a matter of days.[145]

Not long afterward, new information was obtained concerning the uranium ore that had been sent to France: the serial numbers of the seven railway cars that had hauled it away. That clue led to an arsenal in Toulouse, in southern France. Equipped with Geiger counters, Alsos members were able to discover thirty-one tons of the material, about three railcars' worth, in a warehouse. Pash arranged for it to be hauled away to Marseilles by a special truck convoy with combat support. They would never find the remaining four cars' worth.[146]

In September, Alsos was also able to satisfy the request Groves and Furman had made for water from the Rhine River. Maj. Robert W. Blake carried a bucket and a coiled rope to the Nijmegen bridge in Holland. The water he retrieved was placed in bottles, each "carefully wrapped and marked for identification," Pash recalled. A liberated bottle of French wine was included in the shipment, as a joke, with a note asking that it be given "special attention." It would not be long before Washington radioed Pash's unit, informing them, "Water negative. Wine positive." It wasn't a joke or a wine review. Some radioactivity had been detected in the wine, and it was thought this might mean something sinister. Goudsmit explained to Pash that a certain amount of radioactivity in wine or mineral water was to be expected. Washington was not appeased however, and demanded more wine.[147]

November would bring more fruitful data. Information that had been acquired by Alsos in Rennes, Paris, and Holland indicated that some Nazi atomic research was being conducted in Strassburg. In Paris, a 1944 catalogue for the university in Strassburg was of particular interest—so much so that Alsos scientists, Pash would write, "studied [it] as if it were a spicy French novel with photographs." Investigators also concluded that special equipment used in atomic research had been ordered for the university. Thus, Strassburg was a target Goudsmit thought to be of major significance. With the Sixth Army Group moving eastward and Strassburg expected to be an early November target, Pash headed to Paris to prepare. Intelligence from Washington (Groves and Furman) and London (Calvert), along with information he acquired on his own, meant that Alsos would enter the city with a good idea of who to talk to and where to go.[148]

The Sixth Army Group's entry into Strassburg was delayed a few weeks, but on November 25 Pash led a small task force into the city. It proceeded to take over the homes and workplaces of the targeted scientists. A primary target was Professor Rudolph Fleischmann, whose whereabouts had been discovered during an Alsos visit to a French optical company. While Fleischmann had cleared out the day before, he had left papers behind, including revealing letters. The next day, he and six other German scientists on Pash's list were apprehended. Von Weizsäcker was not among them, having fled before the Allied forces had arrived, and apparently taking from his home "everything . . . but the pot-bellied stove that remained in the living room."[149]

Both Furman and Goudsmit (who had stayed behind in Paris to meet with Vannevar Bush) arrived within days. Goudsmit reached a key conclusion, after only forty-eight hours of interviewing scientists, including Fleischmann; reviewing the correspondence, manuscripts, and documents found in their offices, as well as some unburned papers recovered from von Weizsäcker's stove; and inspecting their labs: "the evidence at hand proved definitely that Germany had no atom bomb and was not likely to have one in a reasonable time." The review showed that the Germans had been unsuccessful in their attempts to separate U-235, and appeared to have only recently succeeded in manufacturing uranium metal. After Philip Morrison examined the results of the Strassburg mission, he too was convinced that there was "no German bomb threat."[150]

Specific items, many of which led to the conclusions of Goudsmit and his colleagues, were contained in a December 8 preliminary report, written by Goudsmit and DuPont corporation chemist Fred Wardenburg. It began with a description of the organization and location of the Reich Research Council, noting that the council's department for nuclear physics was headed by the "Reichmarshall's deputy for Nuclear Physics." More importantly, it revealed that the Kaiser-Wilhelm Institute for Physics had been moved in part to Hechingen, and provided the street address and phone number. Heisenberg, von Weizsäcker, and Karl Wirtz (an expert on heavy water and isotope separation) were among those who could be found there, at least part of the time. The review of the Strassburg data also seemed to indicate that the Hechingen group was solely concerned with theoretical physics, with no evidence of experimental work being uncovered.[151]

The report also noted that "uranium figures prominently in the work being done at Hechingen," and that a June 12, 1944, letter established the connection of two prominent German industrial concerns—Degussa and Auer—with the uranium project. Examination of von Weizsäcker's personnel correspondence revealed, the report stated, that only a portion of his time was being spent on the project. Intelligence that Goudsmit and Wardenburg also culled from other documents included a lack of evidence of any "uranium work on a production scale"; a proposal to separate uranium isotopes using liquids instead of gas; references to experiments, including those of Diebner at Gottow; and "disappointments with UF 6," due to "its nasty properties." In addition, Goudsmit and Wardenburg wrote that "the lack of secrecy in Germany with regard to nuclear physics matters is striking." Examples included envelopes and letterheads with the title "Reichmarshall's Deputy for Nuclear Physics," and stationery for the Hechingen institute bearing its complete address.[152]

While the Strassburg material tended to support the conclusion that British intelligence analysts had reached in 1943, that a German bomb was not a serious threat, it did not lead Groves or Furman to want to suspend the Alsos mission. Goudsmit would recall that initially his military and civilian colleagues were not as convinced as Alsos that fears of a German atomic bomb were without substance (although Morrison recalls that he was). They worried that the papers could have been planted, in an attempt at deception, and considered an aerial attack on the Hechingen area. Instead, it was decided to continue on, to locate and interrogate Heisenberg, von Weizsäcker, and other key scientists. Documents, laboratories, the tons of missing ore from Olen, and heavy water remained important targets.[153]

Targets suggested by the Strassburg documents were investigated in March, when Alsos arrived in Heidelberg, and then in April in Stadtilm. Key scientists, including Walter Bothe and Richard Kuhn, were captured and interrogated, although Bothe refused to talk about military-related work until Germany's surrender. Germany's only operational cyclotron was seized. Walther Gerlach's office in Stadtilm/Thüringen was located. Although Gerlach was gone, he had left behind papers and documents of interest. Kurt Deibner, who had also been in Stadtilm conducting experiments at Germany's first uranium reactor laboratory, located in the cellar of an old schoolhouse, was gone too. The Gestapo had collected him along with key papers so he could continue his research elsewhere. What Alsos found supplemented and confirmed the Strassburg discoveries. The pile and associated laboratories, Goudsmit wrote, exhibited a "pitiful smallness." Bothe told his interrogators that he believed the separation of uranium isotopes by thermal diffusion was impossible and all work on separation in Germany had relied on the centrifuge method. After initially claiming not to know of any theoretical or experimental work in Germany on the military applications of atomic fission, Bothe admitted that the cyclotron had been considered as means of obtaining material for a bomb. The importance of Hechingen (where Heisenberg could be found, along with the experimental reactor that had been moved from Berlin-Dahlem to nearby Haigerloch), Bisingen, and Tailfingen to the south (where Hahn could be found) was also confirmed. Unfortunately, responsibility for that zone had been assigned to the French army, which was arriving to take control.[154]

When the State Department was reluctant to negotiate a change in zones without a reason, which Groves would not give, he took action—wanting to ensure that nothing of interest to the Soviets would fall into French hands. Actually, the troops in question were from the French colony of Morocco and noted for their destructiveness. On April 5, Groves met with Marshall and secretary of war Henry Stimson, a meeting that produced agreement that Alsos teams, accompanied by U.S. combat forces, should not wait. They were to move into the area, capture and interrogate any German scientists they found, gather up documents, and destroy any installations that merited destruction before the French arrived. That plan would become known as Operation Harborage.[155]

Before launching Harborage, Alsos was able to clear up one further mystery—what had happened to the several thousand tons of uranium ore that the Germans had acquired from Belgium. It was discovered, on April 16 and 17, in several Stassfurt caves. It was then transported to Hanover in U.S. Army trucks. British aircraft flew away with some of it, while most was sent on to Antwerp so it could be shipped to Britain by sea.[156]

Less than a week later, Harborage began. On April 22, Pash and his men crossed the bridgehead at Horb on the Neckar River and headed for Haigerloch, which was captured the following day, just before the French arrived. The next day, Lansdale and Furman, who were once again in the field, went into the town, accompanied by the British contingent. They discovered a cave in the side of a cliff, inside of which was a large chamber with a concrete pit about ten feet in diameter. Inside the pit Germany's top physicists had attempted to build a reactor, which included graphite blocks under a metal cover in a center cylinder. Lansdale took measurements, while others searched for uranium fuel and heavy water for the reactor. They took photographs and then combat engineers assisted in dismemberment of the facility.[157]

Pash left a member of the British contingent in charge of the cave, while he and one company of the 1279th Engineer Combat Battalion continued on, occupying Bisingen and Hechingen without opposition. Among the twenty-five scientists and technicians Alsos quickly apprehended were von Weizsäcker, Karl Wirtz, and Erich Bagge. Interrogations produced more information, and on April 24 Alsos arrived in the nearby village of Tailfingen.

There, they added Otto Hahn and Max von Laue to their collection, seizing their research facilities. When the other German scientists claimed they had destroyed secret reports and documents, Hahn provided the Alsos group with his collection. Heisenberg was not in the area, they learned. Two weeks earlier he had headed, by bicycle, to visit his family in the mountain village of Urfeld in the Bavarian Alps, which was still in German hands.[158]

On April 26 and 27, Alsos investigators would continue to discover more about key aspects of the German program. On the April 26 Lansdale, along with British intelligence officers Eric Welsh and Michael Perrin, learned from the captured scientists the location of the heavy water and uranium ore for the Hechingen reactor. The heavy water could be found about three miles from Haigerloch, in three steel barrels in the cellar of an old gristmill. They would be sent by truck to Paris and then on to the United States. The uranium had been hidden in a hill, where it had been buried and then plowed over. It was dug up and also sent to Paris, and then on to the United States.[159]

On April 27, just before he and the other recently captured scientists were to be transported to Heidelberg, von Weizsäcker revealed that, contrary to his earlier claim, he had not burned all his papers. He had hidden some in a metal drum in a cesspool behind a house. When the drum was retrieved, Goudsmit and the rest of the team discovered a complete set of reports about German efforts to build a bomb. A cable from Brig. Gen. Eugene Harrison, the Sixth Army Group's Intelligence chief, eventually passed on to Marshall and Stimson, was effusive: "The Alsos mission . . . hit the jackpot in the Hechingen area." Alsos had conclusive proof that the feared German program was actually, in Goudsmit words, "small-time stuff." The program clearly had not moved beyond preliminary research, had not produced a chain reaction, and had not discovered an effective means of enriching uranium.[160]

The only loose ends were Heisenberg, whom Pash wanted to capture before he was picked up by Soviet forces or killed by the SS, and a few other top scientists. On May 2, two days after Hitler's suicide, Pash and his team reached Urfeld. Locals provided the directions and Pash and his men climbed a steep cliff to Heisenberg's cabin, where they found the Nobel Prize winner waiting for them on his veranda. The threat from German troops forced a retreat, but they were able to return the following day, collect both Heisenberg and his documents, and head for Heidelberg. About the same time, Walther Gerlach was picked up in his lab at the University of Munich, Kurt Diebner was apprehended about twenty miles from Munich, while Paul Harteck was run to ground in Hamburg.[161]

After Heisenberg's capture, almost all his colleagues began talking. Diebner was an exception. Goudsmit recalled that "we could get nothing out of Diebner. He was as sullen as a real prisoner"—although probably not nearly as sullen as he would have been in a Nazi-style concentration camp. On July

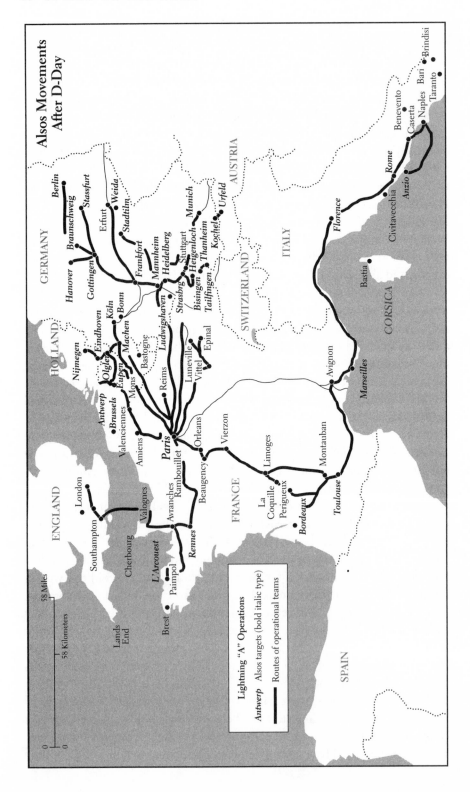

Alsos Movements
After D-Day

Lightning "A" Operations

Antwerp   Alsos targets (bold italic type)

━━━   Routes of operational teams

3, ten captured scientists were moved to an estate in the English countryside, Farm Hall, which had previously been used for training officers of the Special Operations Executive. The ten included Heisenberg, Hahn, Bagge, Diebner, Gerlach, Harteck, von Weizsäcker, von Laue, Horst Korsching, and Karl Wirtz. Von Laue was interned with an eye to the future, because of his anti-Nazi stance and refusal to do war work. Korsching and Wirtz had both worked on isotope separation. In addition to talking with interrogators, they talked among themselves, conversations that were recorded by eavesdropping devices planted at the suggestion of R. V. Jones, the head of scientific intelligence for the British SIS. Those microphones would record the astonishment, even disbelief, of Heisenberg and others when they first learned in early August that the United States and Britain had succeeded in doing what they had failed to do—build an atomic bomb.[162]

chapter two

LIGHTNING STRIKES

THE GERMAN ATOMIC BOMB program turned out to be far less successful than U.S. scientists and intelligence officials feared in 1943. By the time of the Nazi defeat in the spring of 1945, German scientists had not even completed a functioning reactor, and were in no position to *attempt* to build a bomb. There were no German counterparts to Los Alamos, Oak Ridge, or Hanford. Yet the effort to collect and analyze information about what the Germans were doing and what they had accomplished had not been conducted in vain.

During the the latter stages of the war, the Allied intelligence effort provided reassurance that Adolf Hitler would not be able to avert defeat by using a superweapon—that the war would not turn against the Allies at "one minute to midnight," in the words of OSS officer Howard Dix.[1] The effort also had significant benefits for the Cold War. The Allies' capture of records and personnel, including Heisenberg and other key scientists, kept them out of Soviet hands. In addition, the search for any German attempt to build a bomb constituted a practice run for the far lengthier, more extensive, and more sophisticated program about to unfold to uncover Soviet nuclear secrets.

BEFORE THE END of 1945, the Soviet effort to build an atomic bomb was underway. Operation Borodino, named after the locale where Russian soldiers had halted Napoleon's advance in 1812, had been propelled forward first by word of U.S. and British activities in the field and then by the destruction of Hiroshima and Nagasaki. Soviet physicists, including Yuli Khariton and Yakov Zeldovich, had learned about fission from the scientific grapevine as well as the journals that told physicists around the world of the discovery. In 1921, at the age of seventeen, Khariton had made such a favorable impression on Nikolai Semenov, the deputy director of the prestigious Physicotechnical Institute in Petrograd (later Leningrad), that Semenov invited him to join the institute. In 1926, Khariton headed for Cambridge University. He returned two years later with a doctorate and established an explosives laboratory at the Institute of Physical Chemistry. Zeldovich, ten years younger than Khariton, also found himself, at seventeen, being invited to work at the physics institute in Leningrad.[2]

In October 1939 they transmitted two papers to the Soviet *Journal of Experimental and Theoretical Physics*. The first concluded that a fast-neutron chain reaction in U-238 was not possible, while the second examined the possibility of a slow-neutron chain reaction in natural uranium and concluded that U-235 and heavy water were means of attaining such a reaction. A third paper, on the kinetics of a chain reaction, followed in March. Other papers, by Georgi Flerov and Lev Rusinov and Flerov and Konstantin Petrzhak, explored other important elements of fission.[3]

Such research spurred Vladimir Vernadskii and Vitali Khlopin to write Nikolai Bulganin, the country's deputy premier and chairman of the government's council on the chemical and metallurgical industries. Vernadskii, a Russian mineralogist who had been elected to the Academy of Sciences in 1906, was a pioneer in the study of radioactive materials. Khlopin, a chemist, headed the Leningrad-based Radium Institute. Their July 12, 1940, letter drew Bulganin's attention to the discovery of fission and its potential. Four days later, the presidium of the Academy of Sciences met to consider the matter and requested a further report from Vernadskii and two academy colleagues.[4]

On July 30 the academy established the Special Committee on the Uranium Problem to oversee atomic energy research, with Khlopin as chairman. The committee of about a dozen scientists also included Khariton, Vernadskii, Physicotechnical Institute head Abram Ioffe, and Igor Kurchatov. Kurchatov, a contemporary of Khariton, was the son of a surveyor and teacher who had been born in the Chelyabinsk region of the southern Urals in 1903. He had received his undergraduate physics degree in 1923, then enrolled at the Polytechnic Institute in Petrograd. A possible career in shipbuilding was derailed in 1925 when Ioffe invited him to join his institute. In 1932 Kurchatov's focus shifted to nuclear physics, and between July 1934 and February 1936, he and his coauthors published seventeen papers on artificial radioactivity.[5]

But the initial, official Soviet investigation of fission would be a short one. On June 22, 1941, less than a year after the commission was established, the German army breached the Soviet frontier and headed for Moscow. Its rapid advance did not allow Soviet scientists the luxury of investigating the mid- or long-term benefits of atomic energy. Instead, they turned their attention to the immediate problem of defeating the invading Nazi army.[6]

The halt was only temporary. The atomic activities of the Soviet Union's major allies eventually helped convince Soviet dictator Joseph Stalin to order a resumption of research. In early November 1941, Lavrenti Beria, the head of the People's Commissariat of Internal Affairs (NKVD), whose responsibilities included foreign espionage, received word from the Soviet embassy in London that scientists in Britain were conducting theoretical work on an atomic bomb employing uranium. Among the London embassy's sources were British Foreign Office official Donald Maclean and the Treasury's John

Cairncross, both of whom had access to information on the British atomic program. Stalin, not for the first time, was reluctant to believe the NKVD's foreign spies. But Beria, who himself was suspicious of foreign deception, continued to compile reports until he was able to offer more conclusive proof. Some of that additional information was provided by the Soviet General Staff's Chief Intelligence Directorate (GRU), whose roster of agents included Klaus Fuchs, a German émigré physicist working in the British program. The information from Fuchs and others justified the Soviet code name for atomic intelligence—Enormoz (Enormous).[7]

In March 1942, Beria presented Stalin with the additional evidence he had accumulated. Later that year Stalin met with Ioffe, Khlopin, Vernadskii, and Peter Kapitza, who would win a Nobel Prize for his experimental work in low-temperature physics, to discuss the issue. On February 11, 1943, the State Defense Committee approved an atomic energy research and development program. The next month, Stalin selected Kurchatov as the project's scientific director and head of the vaguely named Laboratory No. 2, which was established in April in the northwest sector of Moscow.[8]

Kurchatov was still sporting the pharaoh-like beard he had grown while recovering from pneumonia in early 1942, which he promised "no scissors would touch till after victory." According to a former student and biographer, it hid his "strong, resolute chin." Bearded or not, Laboratory 2's director was a "natural leader, vigorous and self-confident," according to author Richard Rhodes. One of Kurchatov's contemporaries described him as an individual with a "great sense of responsibility for whatever problem he was working on, whatever its dimensions might have been," and recalled that he "would sink his teeth into us and drink our blood until we'd fulfilled [our obligations]."

His laboratory had a dual mission: designing a nuclear reactor to determine the feasibility of a nuclear chain reaction and developing methods (including gaseous diffusion) for separating U-235 from natural uranium. The mission expanded in the spring of 1943 to include the production of plutonium and the investigation of its properties, after Kurchatov examined intelligence from the Allied bomb program revealing that plutonium rather than U-235 was the most promising path to development of a bomb.[9]

The August 1945 attacks on Hiroshima and Nagasaki demonstrated the success of the Allied bomb program and led Stalin to implore his scientists to give the Soviet state a similar capability. He told Kurchatov and other senior officials, "Comrades—a single demand of you. Get us atomic weapons in the shortest possible time. As you know Hiroshima has shaken the whole world. The balance has been broken. Build the bomb—it will remove the great danger from us!" Later in the month, the State Defense Committee voted to establish the Special Committee on the Atomic Problem, and the Council of People's Commissars created a First Chief Directorate to organize and manage the bomb program. Beria was named chairman of the committee and chief of the directorate. Stalin gave him two years to produce a bomb.[10]

The decision meant that more people, money, and equipment would be devoted to the program. In addition, the indigenous Soviet effort would be augmented by the continued flow of espionage material. By 1945, the NKVD and GRU had spies at Los Alamos and several other Allied atomic sites in the United States, Canada, and Britain. David Greenglass, Theodore Hall, and Klaus Fuchs were at Los Alamos, and Allan Nunn May was in the project's Montreal laboratory. They could tell their Soviet masters about topics, such as implosion, that the official U.S. history of the Manhattan Project, Henry Smyth's *General Account of the Development of Methods of Using Atomic Energy for Military Purposes*, released in August 1945, did not. Aside from information, the NKVD provided the human and technical resources required, including labor camp prisoners to expedite uranium-mining operations in Central Asia.[11]

Still, the Soviet secret police chief faced the same type of tasks and challenges that Leslie Groves had faced: design a bomb, obtain the necessary nuclear material (uranium and/or plutonium), construct the device, and test it. To do so required scientists, laboratories and institutes where they could work, uranium ore, facilities for the conversion of ore into sufficiently enriched uranium or plutonium, installations where bomb components could be constructed and assembled, and a test site. New atomic-related facilities would start to spring up across the Soviet Union.

Kurchatov continued as scientific director from his post at Laboratory No. 2 and assumed responsibility for the construction of an experimental reactor, designated F-1 (for First Physics Uranium Pile), at the site. The number of personnel in his reactor group grew from eleven at the beginning of 1946 to seventy-six by the end of the year. That June, a special building was erected at the laboratory to house the reactor, and on Christmas Day it produced the first controlled nuclear chain reaction in the Soviet Union.[12]

Uranium enrichment required expeditions into Soviet Central Asia and mining activities that would employ a hundred thousand miners and other workers by the end of the decade. But it was the defeated enemy that provided the largest and most immediate source of ore, the result of the Germans' tapping of uranium deposits in central Europe, particularly in Czechoslovakia. By the end of 1945, the Soviets had collected a hundred tons of uranium oxide stored in Germany, the first substantial amount acquired by the Soviet project.[13]

Enrichment of the uranium was entrusted to two secret sites. One, the home for an electromagnetic separation facility, was located in the Urals, about 100 miles north of Sverdlovsk and 825 miles southeast of Moscow. Consistent with Soviet practice of giving classified facilities the name of a nearby city and a post office box number, it was designated Sverdlovsk-45. Construction of the second site, consisting of a gaseous diffusion plant and satellite town, began in January 1946, near Neviansk, about 30 miles northwest of Sverdlovsk. It was assigned the code name Sverdlovsk-44.[14]

Chelyabinsk-40, about ten miles east of Kyshtym, fifty miles north of Chelyabinsk (itself about 115 miles south of Sverdlovsk), was the home of a plutonium production reactor (Plant A), a separation facility (Plant B), and a metallurgical plant (Plant V) to purify the plutonium and convert it into metal for use in a bomb. Construction began in 1947, using about seventy thousand labor camp prisoners. Kurchatov arrived there in the fall of 1947, along with the frigid weather, to supervise the effort, living in a railroad car next to the construction site. The reactor was built underground, in a concrete shaft, to protect it from aerial attack. After eighteen months of effort it became fully operational on June 22, 1948. The site's location placed it close to railways and roads, two lakes that could supply huge quantities of water needed for the reactor, and the Chelyabinsk Electrode Plant, the main supplier of purified graphite. Plant B started operations on December 22, 1948, and began to produce plutonium in February 1949.[15]

Most secret of all was the installation established at Sarov, the site of a defunct monastery, which the Soviet government had used to house war orphans in the 1920s and prisoners in the 1930s. Located about 250 miles southeast of Moscow and about 40 miles south of Arzamas, the new secret city, isolated and surrounded by wooded lands, was designated Arzamas-16 (and was also known, at various times, as the Volga Office, Installation No. 558, Kremlev, Moscow Center 300, and Arzamas-75). During the war it had been home to a plant that turned out artillery shells. In the atomic age Sarov housed a far more lethal enterprise, Design Bureau-11 (KB-11), responsible for designing Soviet atomic bombs. KB-11's first scientific director was Yuli Khariton, who had helped select the site. Construction of the bureau began in 1946, and physicists and other scientists began arriving the following year. Secrecy was so great that the city of Sarov soon disappeared from Soviet maps, being cut off from the rest of the world by a barbed-wire fence and guards that patrolled a one-hundred-square-mile zone. The scientists were "prisoners themselves, even if their cage was gilded," observed author Richard Rhodes.[16]

German scientists who had been persuaded or coerced to join the Soviet bomb program augmented the work of Soviet physicists and institutes. Manfred von Ardenne, under whose auspices Fritz Houtermans had produced his groundbreaking work on plutonium, arrived in the Soviet Union on May 22, 1945, to lead an institute staffed by German scientists. Located at Sinop, near Sukhumi in Georgia, the organization was designated "Institut A," just as von Ardenne's German institute had been named. His Soviet-sponsored group investigated techniques (including electromagnetic separation) for enriching uranium. Starting with a staff of about twenty in 1945, the number of Germans working at Institut A would grow to about three hundred by the late

1940s. Among von Ardenne's key scientists was Peter Adolf Thiessen, former director of the Kaiser-Wilhelm Institute for Physical Chemistry.[17]

A second institute, also near Sukhumi, at Agudzheri, was designated "Institut G," and headed by Gustav Ludwig Hertz, the winner of the Nobel Prize for Physics in 1925 for work that played an important part in the development of quantum theory. As chief of the Siemens-Halske Laboratories during the war, he had developed a gaseous diffusion process for isotope separation, one of several areas Hertz's institute was assigned to investigate.[18]

Other German scientists were assigned to other Soviet institutes. In 1946 chemist Max Vollmer was sent to work at Scientific Research Institute 9 (NII-9) in Moscow, where he headed a design bureau responsible for developing a method for producing heavy water, a project that failed to produce any benefits. In 1948, Vollmer and his associates were transferred and given a new focus, the extraction of plutonium from fission products. Nikolaus Riehl, who had been the head of scientific research at the Auer Company, wound up working on uranium purification at Elektrostal, about forty-five miles east of Moscow. After a stint at Institut A, Max Steenbeck, who had been a Siemens research scientist, worked on uranium enrichment at Laboratory 2 during 1947 and 1948.[19]

Construction of a test site began in 1947, in the vicinity Semipalatinsk, in the Kazakhstan desert—"an arid, partly hilly steppe with a few derelict dried-up wells and salt lakes." Headquarters for the military unit responsible for test preparations was established on the shore of the Irtysh River, about forty miles northeast of the testing ground and approximately seventy-five miles from Semipalatinsk. Originally given the designations Mountain Seismic Station and Object 905, it received new cover names in 1948—Training Proving Ground No. 2 of the Defense Ministry, and the Semipalatinsk Experimental Proving Ground.[20]

In May 1949, Kurchatov and his colleagues began final preparations for the test, but were temporarily delayed when the test tower started to tilt dramatically owing to a shift in its concrete foundation. They considered detonating the bomb at ground level, but decided to erect another tower, delaying the test by two months. Finally, on August 29, 1949, Kurchatov was ready to test the first Soviet atomic bomb, a plutonium bomb designated RDS (Reaktivniyi dvigatel Stalina—Stalin's Rocket Engine)-1. RDS-1 was based on the U.S. design for a plutonium implosion weapon, from information provided by Klaus Fuchs. The test had a code name: Pervaya Molniya (First Lightning).[21] But the United States had no idea that lightning was about to strike.

WHILE U.S. INTELLIGENCE AGENCIES would provide no advance warning of the test, it was not for a lack of trying. Even during World War II, despite the rosy perception of the Soviet Union shared by many in Franklin

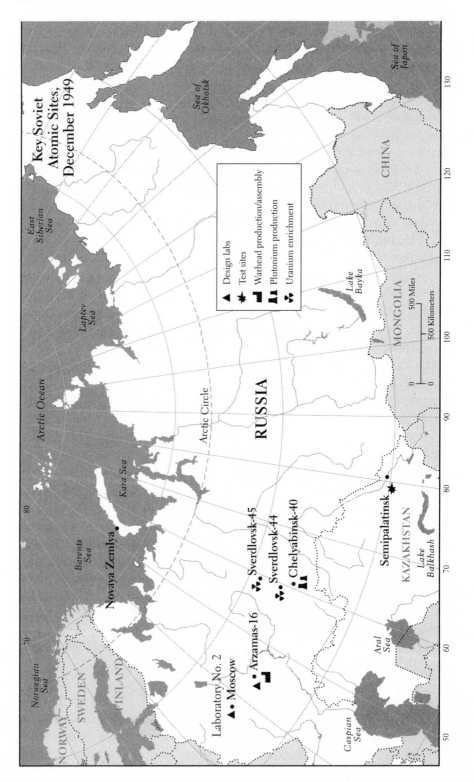

Roosevelt's administration, America's ostensible ally was also an intelligence target. The Venona project—the interception of Soviet diplomatic traffic and the sometimes successful effort to read that traffic—started during the war years, and would provide critical information about Soviet espionage, including atomic espionage, during the 1940s.[22]

Not surprisingly, with the defeat of the Axis enemies, and as relations between the United States and the USSR deteriorated, the Soviet state became the primary focus of the American intelligence effort. In addition, one of the war's lessons, freely available to all nations, was that an atomic bomb was not just a possibility, but a capability that could be attained by countries with sufficient expertise and resources. The United States would be concerned in the decades that followed with what other nations were doing, if anything, to acquire an atomic capability. In 1946, the primary concern was the Soviet Union.[23]

In 1946, the resources that the U.S. government had at its disposal to investigate Soviet progress in the atomic energy field were, in comparison to those that would become available in succeeding decades, limited. It had two primary means of collection: human intelligence and communications intelligence. After President Harry Truman's dissolution of the OSS in October 1945, the Strategic Services Unit (SSU) was established within the War Department. It absorbed the OSS secret intelligence and counterintelligence branches, along with some of their personnel—including Moe Berg. Communications intelligence remained the responsibility of the army and navy (and also became a responsibility, after its creation in 1947, of the air force).[24]

Throughout 1946 the SSU sent Leslie Groves reports about foreign developments in the atomic energy field. On the next to last day in January, Lt. Col. Selby M. Skinner, the SSU's liaison officer, reported that "a very good source" had recently told the SSU of "a secret Czech-Russian Treaty by the terms of which . . . the uranium production in Jachymov [Joachimsthal] goes to Russia." While the SSU held the source in high regard, it still credited the reliability of the information as no more than moderate.[25]

That same day the SSU also passed on some information that had been received from Berg. The former baseball player reported that Peter Kapitza had invited Neils Bohr to visit Russia, but Bohr "will not himself go to Russia." Based on his conversation with Lise Meitner, Berg concluded that she would not accept any offer from the Russians, and passed on her belief that her friend Gustav Hertz "most likely went to Moscow against his desires." She also asserted her certainty that there would be no collaboration between the Russians and the Danes, information Berg believed she obtained from Bohr.[26]

By February, an SSU agent in the eastern zone of Germany provided information on where Hertz and other German scientists could be found. Von Ardenne's group was residing in one of the small communities between

Anaklia and Poti on the east shore of the Black Sea. Another agent reported that Hertz, Thiessen, and Vollmer were living on another stretch of the Black Sea coast, between Sukhumi and Poti. The agent also informed his SSU contacts that since their housing and laboratories were still under construction, Hertz and his colleagues had not done any work as of early November 1945.[27]

On March 5 the SSU conveyed information from a "reliable" source that there were contradictory reports about whether there was any mining activity going on at Joachimsthal, and Czech officials were refusing to discuss the mines. The source doubted that machinery at the mine could have been quickly restored to operational status or that the "great number of rail cars" needed to ship enough ore to get even meager returns were available. In addition, the source had observed no activity pointing toward an investment of much-needed capital for the mine. A March 15 report conveyed claims that a mining engineer had made to the same source—that the mining area was not occupied by the Russians, that the mines were idle, and that the laboratories were "absolutely idle."[28]

Lt. Col. Edgar P. Dean, a member of Groves's staff based at the American embassy in London, was not uncritical of SSU reports. In commenting on an earlier one, he characterized an SSU comment as "pure imagination," while dismissing another paragraph in the same report as revealing "ignorance of facts and only conjecture." But Dean was impressed by the March 5 report, describing it as "the best single report to emerge from the welter of contradictions [in] the last five months." However, an apparently knowledgeable official, whose exact identity is unknown owing to the illegibility of his signature and absence of a letterhead (although the "Top Secret" marking survived), wrote to senior British atomic intelligence official Eric Welsh that while he agreed with the first two paragraphs of the report, the claims concerning the machinery, the lack of a suitable number of railcars, and the need for new capital "appear to me to be complete nonsense to anybody who knows the facts."[29]

Sometime in May, Lt. Col. Peer de Silva of the SSU counterintelligence (X-2) branch sent the unit's headquarters a Ramona report—Ramona having replaced Azusa as the code word indicating atomic intelligence—on Peter Kapitza. The information obtained, de Silva noted, was of "doubtful authenticity." It claimed that the Soviet government had established laboratories for Kapitza and "allows him unlimited credit at the Soviet State Bank." The SSU source also claimed that Kapitza was head of the "atomic bomb research committee," a position actually held by Beria. De Silva's characterization of the information in the report did not prevent the intelligence community from believing, at first, that Kapitza was the head of the atomic bomb effort.[30]

June brought two more SSU reports on possible Soviet exploitation of scientists and resources. One concerned the physics and chemistry institutes in

Vienna, whose activities had been investigated by Moe Berg. It noted that the top two officials of the Radium Institute had been flown to Moscow for questioning and returned to Vienna, after turning down jobs in the Soviet Union. The director of the Radium Institute was, however, providing instruction in nuclear physics to Soviets in Vienna. A second letter informed its readers that a Soviet general had interviewed a Manchuria-based geologist, inquired about the presence of uranium mines in Manchuria, and was told of ones that had been discovered. He proceeded to quiz the geologist on the quality of the minerals, the tonnage capacity of the mine, and how much had been mined and where the product was taken.[31]

That the Manhattan Engineer District was still very interested in Soviet attempts to mine uranium ore was evident by a report completed in early December 1946. "Russian Mining Operations in the German-Czech Border Region" was written by intelligence analyst Henry S. Lowenhaupt, who had obtained a doctorate in chemistry from Yale in 1943. During his time at Yale he had worked part-time on uranium enrichment by chemical methods. After basic training at Oak Ridge, he was assigned to work for Groves in Washington, and in 1945 began to focus on foreign nuclear-related activities. In late 1946, now a civilian, Lowenhaupt was still at the beginning of a long and distinguished career in intelligence.[32]

His nine-page, single-spaced report covered nine different sites and, as he acknowledged in the opening paragraph, was a compilation of "probably reliable" to "possibly reliable" intelligence because "not one single absolutely reliable informant has submitted a report on any area mentioned." The report provided no overall assessment of Russian mining activity, although it did note that, with the exception of Joachimsthal, which been turned over to the Czechs under a secret agreement, all of the uranium mines were under direct Soviet operational and security control.[33]

A FEW MONTHS after Lowenhaupt completed his report, he became an employee of the Central Intelligence Group (CIG), although his job remained the same. Established by President Truman on January 22, 1946, the CIG was given the mission of coordinating the intelligence reports and estimates of the government's other civilian and military intelligence units, employing personnel from those other organizations. In July, the CIG established the Office of Special Operations to conduct espionage and counterintelligence operations, and in October that office assumed the mission of the SSU, with a limited number of SSU personnel joining the new office.[34]

A little over six months after the birth of the CIG, on August 1, legislation established the Atomic Energy Commission (AEC) in place of the MED. Lt. Gen. Hoyt Vandenberg, the CIG's director, sought to preempt any AEC takeover of the atomic intelligence mission, suggesting that the personnel and records of Groves's foreign intelligence section be transferred to his central intelligence organization. Such a transfer would have to be approved by the National Intelligence Authority (NIA)—the four-person committee, whose members included the secretaries of war, navy, and state and Truman's military adviser, that had been established by the president to supervise the CIG.[35]

By mid-August, Vandenberg had transformed his proposal into a draft NIA directive on the coordination of atomic intelligence activities, which was discussed at an NIA meeting on August 22, after acting secretary of state Dean Acheson blocked its approval, unsure of whether the AEC would continue to have access to the information needed in its search for uranium ore. While there was strong support for the proposal, Truman, who was away from the capital, wanted to consider the issue further when he returned. Additional delay followed owing to opposition to Truman's choice to head the AEC, David Lilienthal, and the president's desire to wait until all members of the AEC had been appointed before considering the intelligence issue.[36]

Groves's doubts that Lilienthal and his staff could be trusted to handle his organization's intelligence files responsibly was one reason why he supported the idea of turning his intelligence section's personnel and files over to the CIG. In a November 21, 1946, memo to the AEC, Groves argued that it was "vital to the security of the United States that foreign intelligence in the field of atomic energy be maintained and strengthened." Since the CIG was responsible for the coordination and direction of all foreign intelligence activities, and the best nucleus "upon which to build" its atomic energy intelligence component was the MED Foreign Intelligence Section, it followed that the CIG should absorb the section. The AEC, as Groves envisioned the arrangement, would be the recipient of the CIG's collection and analysis of information on ore deposits and discoveries, mining activities, and foreign scientific developments that the AEC needed to know about to perform its mission.[37]

By the time the NIA convened for its ninth meeting, on February 12, 1947, the issue was ready to be resolved. The meeting was attended by George C. Marshall, the recently approved secretary of state, Robert Patterson and James Forrestal, the secretaries of war and navy, Fleet Admiral William D. Leahy, Truman's representative, Vandenberg, and a number of observers. It was agreed that the AEC would be able to examine the files to be transferred to the CIG and retain those on uranium deposits. With that matter settled, the NIA approved the transfer of the MED's intelligence files to the CIG. By February 18, Henry Lowenhaupt was officially an employee of the CIG, and before the end of March the Foreign Intelligence Section had become the

Nuclear Energy Group, Scientific Branch, Office of Reports and Estimates, Central Intelligence Group. Its primary responsibility was to prepare "estimates of the nuclear energy capabilities and intentions of foreign nations."[38]

The transfer to the CIG would only be the beginning of several years of organizational turmoil for Lowenhaupt and his colleagues. On July 26, 1947, Truman signed legislation transforming the CIG into the Central Intelligence Agency (CIA), which was no longer dependent on other agencies for its personnel or funding. By December, the AEC had established its own Intelligence Division, an action that had been urged earlier that year in a report on atomic energy intelligence by Sidney Souers, Vandenberg's predecessor as director of central intelligence. Then, on March 5, 1948, less than a year after the nuclear energy group had been established in the Office of Reports and Estimates (ORE), the group was transferred, without any change of mission, to the Office of Special Operations and became its Nuclear Energy Branch. Finally, on the last day of 1948, in response to an outside review prepared by Allen Dulles and two colleagues that criticized the agency's scientific intelligence effort, director of central intelligence Roscoe Hillenkoetter reattached the nuclear energy unit to the scientific branch of the reports and estimates office and transformed the branch into the Office of Scientific Intelligence (OSI), which would be home to the agency's nuclear intelligence analysts for decades to come.[39]

The creation of a nuclear energy group within CIG/CIA was one of three major developments in the nuclear intelligence area in the late 1940s. In December 1947, Maj. Gen. Albert F. Hegenberger returned to the United States from his assignment in Japan, where he had served as commanding general of the First Air Division. On December 5 he was assigned to the Special Weapons Group, an organization that reported to the air force's deputy chief of staff for materiel and interacted with the Armed Forces Special Weapons Project (established in light of the AEC's supplanting of the MED, and headed by Groves) and the AEC on matters concerning atomic bombs. Nine days later, Maj. Gen. William Kepner, the Special Weapons Group commander, established a new section within his group, designated Section One, and named Hegenberger commander. By the end of July 1948, Hegenberger's unit, AFMSW-1, was transferred to the office of the deputy chief of staff for operations, and thus became AFOAT-1: Air Force Deputy Chief of Staff for Operations, ATomic Energy Office, Section 1.[40] AFOAT-1 was to play a key role in tracking the nuclear activities of foreign nations, employing different methods than the CIA and other intelligence agencies.

Late 1947 also witnessed the creation of an interagency committee that would assume a significant role in the analysis of nuclear intelligence. Despite his initial reservations, Rear Adm. Thomas Inglis, the chief of naval intelligence, along with Hillenkoetter and the army and air force intelligence chiefs, signed a memorandum on December 31, establishing the Joint Nuclear Energy Intelligence Committee (JNEIC). The committee would eventually meet on an almost weekly basis and collaborate with the CIA's Nuclear Energy Branch in preparing studies of foreign nuclear programs.[41]

THROUGH JULY 1949, the analysts at the CIG/CIA, JNEIC, the AEC's

Intelligence Division, the Joint Chiefs of Staff (JCS) Joint Intelligence Committee, and the military intelligence services had been the beneficiaries of whatever intelligence could be obtained by the United States and Britain concerning the Soviet nuclear effort.

A March 1947 letter, written by Nikolaus Riehl's secretary, was intercepted and confirmed that Riehl was at Elektrostal near Moscow, along with others who had worked with him at the Auer Company. Early 1947 also saw the defections of four German atomic scientists who had traveled to the Soviet Union for job interviews and had been returned to East Germany. One, Dr. Adolf Krebs, reported that the Hertz group was working on isotope separation problems at Sukhumi while von Ardenne's institute was located nearby. He also told his debriefers that Max Vollmer was working on heavy-water production (which came as a surprise), with Riehl and his group producing uranium metal. In addition, he revealed that the former director of the Joachimsthal mine was heading a group near Tashkent, in Central Asia, searching for uranium.[42]

U.S. knowledge of uranium mining in Czechoslovakia benefitted from both British and CIA collection activities. In 1946, Britain had discovered that one ten-ton freight car of uranium ore was being shipped from Joachimsthal to Elektrostal every ten days. In addition, the Soviets required the former Bitterfeld plant of I. G. Farben to turn out thirty tons of highly pure metallic calcium each month, enough for the manufacture of sixty tons of uranium metal. Sources within the Soviet program furnished specifications on the amount of impurities permitted in the calcium; that information established beyond a doubt that it was for atomic use. CIA clandestine collection efforts produced a bill of lading for three freight-car loads of calcium from Bitterfeld to Post Box 3, Elektrostal, which proved that there was a uranium factory at Elektrostal producing the metal in quantity and employing methods at least partially developed by Riehl. It also led to the conclusion that the Soviet program included a functioning or planned reactor to make plutonium for nuclear weapons, since the metal being produced was not needed to enrich uranium but was required for the production of plutonium in a reactor.[43]

In 1948, British interrogation of a former German prisoner of war revealed the existence of the plutonium facility (Chelyabinsk-40) near Kyshtym, one of a number of POW reports on Kyshtym. A copy of the report was passed to the U.S. naval attaché in London and to a representative of U.S.

naval intelligence in Germany. Reports from U.S. sources in Europe noted that some leading Soviet physicists and chemists had been assigned to the facility. That same year, a POW told his American interrogators of the Soviet gaseous diffusion effort, and that it was in a primitive stage.[44]

During 1948–1949, U.S. intelligence efforts also yielded new information on mining in Czechoslovakia. The new data, provided by a single source who was considered reliable, indicated that the Soviets were extracting between five and eight times as much uranium as Britain had thought likely, and between four and six times as much as British experts believed possible. Further intelligence, from intercepted letters and refugee reports, confirmed the source's claims.[45]

Beyond reports from spies, refugees, and former POWs, communications intelligence was obtained by the military communications intelligence (COMINT) agencies. By August 1949, those agencies consisted of the Army Security Agency, the Naval Security Group Command, and the Air Force Security Service. There was also the Armed Forces Security Agency, established that May to coordinate and supervise the military-service efforts.[46]

In the latter half of April, central intelligence chief Hillenkoetter, in a memo to the executive secretary of the National Security Council, urged that the communications intelligence effort against the Soviet atomic energy target be stepped up (along with an increased use of other collection methods). Secretary of defense Louis Johnson directed the JCS to review the issue. In June, he was informed by the JCS and the U.S. Communications Intelligence Board (the interagency committee that supervised the communications intelligence effort) that "for many months the production of information regarding the atomic energy program of the USSR has been accorded the highest priority in the COMINT field." He was also advised that "no more effort can be diverted from other highly important problems without serious detriment to those problems." According to one account, communications intelligence had produced "some useful intelligence about Soviet work in the field of atomic energy."[47]

Former air force intelligence officer Spurgeon Keeny recalls that there was "a lot" of communications intelligence on Soviet atomic energy activities. Keeny had been drafted in 1948, and received a commission in the air force. He finished college during the war, received his master's degree in physics from Columbia in 1946, and was a member of the first class of the Russian institute at Columbia. His background made him a logical candidate for the service's Directorate of Intelligence, located in the Pentagon. He recalls that a number of factors contributed to the availability of communications intelligence—the geographical breadth of the Soviet Union, which resulted in an absence of landlines and the widespread use of radiotelephones, as well as "lots of plaintext" transmissions. The intercepted communications, along with the assorted varieties of human intelligence, and the examination of Soviet scientific literature, meant that early on in the Soviet program, the United States "knew [the] location of most main activities." Kyshtym, Keeny recalls, was identified even before the British provided the United States with that information.[48]

Intelligence from human and technical sources provided valuable information on where Soviet and German scientists were working on an atomic bomb, and what they were doing at various sites. But it did not answer what was, at the time, the burning question: when would the Soviets have an atomic bomb? Even Lavrenti Beria did not know for sure, although he had far more information available to him than U.S. intelligence analysts. That extra information would surely have helped American analysts in their effort to provide a reasonable estimate of an initial Soviet nuclear capability. The lack of complete information was reflected in American estimates in two ways: the differences between intelligence agencies as to when the Soviets were *most likely* to have the bomb, and the range of years given in individual estimates as to when the Soviets *might* end the U.S. nuclear monopoly.

In 1946, the CIG, noting that "our real information . . . is relatively meager," judged that the Soviets would first test a bomb sometime between 1950 and 1953. That same year, the air intelligence element of the Air Staff (at the time, still part of the U.S. Army) suggested that the Soviets might detonate a bomb toward the end of 1949. In July 1947, an analysis by the three major service intelligence organizations produced some agreement—including the observations that some details of the Hanford plutonium production plant may have been provided to the Soviet Union via espionage, that the Soviets did not yet have a working reactor, that the Soviet Union lacked skilled engineering and experienced technical personnel, and that uranium ores available from many areas within the Soviet Union or Soviet-controlled territory were of low uranium content. There was disagreement, however, in a key area. The intelligence chiefs of the army and navy believed that the Soviet Union "could not have atomic weapons now," could possibly have them in 1950, and would "most probably" have them during 1952. The assistant chief of the Air Staff for intelligence concluded that the Soviet Union might already have an atomic weapon and would most probably have one between 1949 and 1952.[49]

In 1948, the JCS's Joint Intelligence Committee estimated mid-1950 as "the earliest date by which the Soviets [might explode] their first bomb," and mid-1953 as "the probable date." That July, the *Estimate of the Status of the Russian Atomic Energy Project*, provided to President Truman by Hillenkoetter, echoed the committee's finding. It confessed that "it continues to be impossible to determine the exact status of or to determine the date scheduled by the Soviets for the completion of their first atomic bomb," but agreed that "on the basis of the information in our possession, it is estimated that the earliest date by which it is remotely possible that the USSR may have completed its first atomic bomb is mid-1950, but the most probable date is believed to be mid-1953."[50]

By early 1949 the air force had concluded that 1950 was the earliest date. In March, Willard Machle, the CIA's director of scientific intelligence, informed Hillenkoetter that the JNEIC "has sufficient data to make the following estimate": "mid-1950 is the earliest possible date for Soviets to complete their first atomic bomb, and mid-1953 is the most probable date for completion." Machle noted that the estimate was based on three conclusions: that the Soviets did not begin development of an atomic bomb until late 1945, that they were attempting to build a plutonium bomb, and that they had sufficient uranium for the operation of one plutonium reactor.[51]

He went on to explain that the mid-1950 date was based on the U.S. British, and Canadian experience with atomic energy, while the mid-1953 date was the result of comparing Soviet and Western industrial performance in other fields of similar size and complexity. He also noted that "during the past years information has been received which furnishes a picture of the organization of the Soviet atomic energy program and certain localities involved." He cautioned, however, that the "available information as well as uncertainties inherent in industrial development make it impossible to state with greater accuracy the dates cited above."[52]

MUCH, MAYBE ALL, of the uncertainty surrounding the timing of the first Soviet bomb test would have been eliminated if the United States (or Britain) had a high-level spy in the Kremlin or KB-11, or if it had been possible to eavesdrop on conversations between Khariton and Kurchatov or Kurchatov and Beria. Instead, the Americans had to settle for the hope that any Soviet atomic detonation would be detected shortly after the fact, and that it would be possible to acquire intelligence on the nature of the explosion, including the type of bomb (uranium or plutonium) and its power.

That hope centered on an interim system for the long-range detection of atomic explosions that had been established after World War II. Rather than depending on the word of a spy, an intercepted communication, or the photograph of a mushroom cloud, the system relied on the inevitable by-products of an atomic detonation to announce its occurrence, by-products that could be detected by having the right equipment in the right place at the right time.

In 1945 and 1946, believing it unlikely that the Soviet Union would develop a bomb but not test it, Leslie Groves, then still head of the Manhattan Project, and Gen. Curtis LeMay, the Army Air Force's research chief, initiated separate projects to determine if an atomic detonation could be detected from outside of Soviet territory. They were not the only early advocates of investigating the feasibility of long-range detection. Officers from each of the services, including Edwin Siebert, the head of the army's G-2, also suggested the need for a detection system.[53]

The possibility of detection emerged from the data produced by the July 1945 Trinity test. Two Met Lab scientists, Anthony Turkevitch and John Magee, suggested, with the Krakatoa volcanic explosion of 1883 in mind, that debris from an atomic explosion might be blown around the world, debris that would carry the radioactive fission products of the detonation. To test their hypothesis, a B-29 was modified to carry an air scoop on top of the plane's fuselage. Connected to the scoop was a tube that led to a perforated metal cylinder lined with soft tissue paper, similar to the paper used in air filters at the Trinity test site.[54]

In the aftermath of the Hiroshima blast, five flights were flown, at altitudes between 15,000 and 30,000 feet. Two flights originated from Wendover Field in western Utah, a site designated W-47. The first, on August 10, was completed when it landed in Bakersfield, California, while the other went on to Seattle after landing in Bakersfield. Another two flights departed from Seattle to Alaska and returned, and the fifth, on August 15, arrived at W-47 from Seattle. After each flight the paper was removed and checked for radioactivity.[55]

An analysis of the data completed that fall led to the conclusion that radioactive dust had been detected and that it "seems reasonable that the activity observed is due to the fission products from Hiroshima". This conclusion may have been drawn without proper consideration of the greater volume of dust that resulted from the Trinity test as well as the flight paths of the B-29s, which took them over the Hanford reactor site. In any case, the analysis concluded that the type of air filter employed "would seem to be a practical means of detecting an atomic bomb explosion almost anywhere with proper meteorological conditions."[56]

At about the same time, the Army Air Force began exploring another potential means of long-distance detection of atomic bomb tests, an effort designated Project Mogul. It was inspired by geophysicist W. Maurice Ewing's wartime discovery that at a depth of four thousand feet in the ocean there was a layer of water through which sound waves could travel unlimited distances without contact with the surface or ocean bottom. In October 1945, Ewing suggested to Gen. Carl Spaatz, the Army Air Force's commander, that a similar channel might exist in the atmosphere.[57]

That observation led Col. Roscoe C. Wilson, Spaatz's deputy chief of staff for research and development, to initiate a program to explore the feasibility of monitoring such a sound channel for signs of a nuclear detonation thousands of miles away. Since it was believed that the channel was located at approximately 45,000 feet, and B-29s were only capable of flying at little more than 30,000 feet, it would be necessary to place the sonic detectors on balloons that could float at a constant altitude. Such balloons did not exist at the time, and one early part of Mogul included research on how to make them a reality.[58]

Key factors in developing long-range detection methods were the atmospheric tests the United States was conducting to improve its own nuclear arsenal and to evaluate the vulnerability of its forces to atomic attack. Operation Crossroads, conducted on Bikini atoll in the Pacific, was one instance. On July 1, 1946, a flotilla of thirty-eight obsolete U.S. and Japanese ships, ranging from battleships to submarines, was the target of a 23-kiloton bomb detonated 520 feet above them in an attempt to determine just how vulnerable such ships were. A second bomb would be detonated underwater on July 25. Another element of Crossroads, consistent with Groves's interest in developing monitoring techniques, was to evaluate possible ground- and air-based detection methods.[59]

Microbarographs located on Pacific islands recorded sonic data, while Geiger counters on those islands measured radioactivity at ground level. Air operations included drones flown into the atomic cloud to gather dust and air samples, and aircraft capable of measuring airborne radioactivity tracking the cloud out to about 500 miles. B-29s, carrying filters capable of collecting the minute dust particles that a detonation would produce, were deployed to sites in the Pacific (Guam, Okinawa, and Hawaii), on the West Coast (Spokane), and elsewhere (Tucson, Tampa, and Panama), ranging 1,600 to 8,000 miles from ground zero. Each day, the aircraft patrolled at 30,000 feet and the filters were examined for signs of the blast.[60]

The results of the Crossroads experiments indicated that much work needed to be done. While seismographs in California detected the underwater July 25 explosion, they failed to record the airburst of July 1. In addition, seismographs were not capable of distinguishing between a low-yield atomic explosion and a large-scale conventional one. In a September 18 memo to Groves, Maj. Philip G. Krueger concluded that "it is possible by monitoring the air currents at various points around the world to determine if an atomic bomb has been detonated in the air." Detailed analysis of wind conditions might make it possible to determine the direction to the blast, and, "by additional judicious reasoning," approximately when and where it occurred. However, Krueger noted two limitations: very high counts of radioactivity were required to conclusively establish that a bomb had been detonated, and positive results could be most reasonably expected when the blast occurred at a distance of 2,000 miles or less. Thus, at the time, none of the methods tried could promise an unambiguous means of detecting a Soviet test that took place deep within Soviet territory. Col. Lyle E. Seeman, the associate director at Los Alamos, noted that "no instruments exist at present to insure success."[61]

Long-range detection was also of interest to General Vandenberg, director of the CIG. About the time Krueger completed his memo, Vandenberg sent one of his own to Groves, requesting information about the performance of experimental long-range detection techniques and seeking recommendations on what could be done to develop a reliable detection system. When Groves replied several months later, he told Vandenberg that the instruments and procedures for long-range detection required further development.[62]

The following spring, as research on long-range detection continued in secret, another prominent official suggested that such programs should be pursued. This time it was a member of the AEC, Commissioner Lewis L. Strauss — a lifelong Republican who owed his position, in part, to Truman's need to appear nonpartisan in his appointments to the new body. Strauss had joined the naval reserve in 1926 as a lieutenant commander, and spent fifteen years as a reserve officer attached to the Office of Naval Intelligence (ONI). When war came, he was called to active duty, but with the Bureau of Ordnance. He left the navy, at the end of the war, as a rear admiral. When he joined the AEC in 1947, he gave up a position that was far more lucrative than any government job, a partnership in the Wall Street firm of Kuhn, Loeb, and Company.[63]

In an April 11, 1947, one-paragraph memo to his fellow commissioners, who also were unaware of what was being done elsewhere in the government to develop a long-range detection program, Strauss wrote that "it would be interesting to know whether the intelligence arrangements of the Manhattan District made any provision in the past for the continuous monitoring of radioactivity in the upper atmosphere. This would be perhaps the only means that we would have for discovering that a test of an atomic weapon has been made by any other nation." He went on to suggest that if the CIG had no such system in place, the commissioners might want to recommend that it develop one and, in the event of the CIG's refusal to do so, that the AEC might consider taking action on its own.[64]

Strauss followed up his memo in meetings with Vandenberg and Colonel Seeman, but was kept in the dark about the status of the effort. He came away dissatisfied and approached army secretary Kenneth C. Royall, army chief of staff Dwight Eisenhower, and secretary of the navy James Forrestal — in Forrestal's case to determine if his service could fly monitoring missions in the Arctic and off the Asian mainland. While the navy had a very limited number of planes that could perform such a mission, the Army Air Force's Air Weather Service was already flying WB-29s in the areas suggested by Strauss.[65]

A big step toward establishing a full-scale detection program came on May 21, when representatives from the army, navy, AEC, CIG, and the Joint Research and Development Board met as the Long-Range Detection Committee, organized in response to a March memo from Vandenberg. By the time of the meeting, Vandenberg had become the air force's chief of staff, but the initiative continued under his successor, Roscoe Hillenkoetter. The committee identified three basic objectives for a detection system: determining the time and place of all large explosions on earth, obtaining samples of the explosive products from water or air or both, and establishing the nature of the explosions by chemical and radiological analysis of the samples collected. Techniques that were considered worthy of exploration included monitoring sonic and seismic activity at terrestrial stations, detecting sounds via an underwater system, and collecting samples using ships and aircraft equipped with containers and filters. The committee also concluded that air-sampling operations to provide data on the existing levels of radioactivity could be started without delay. In addition, the group suggested that direction of the project should be the responsibility of the Army Air Force.[66]

The next year was filled with the usual bureaucratic maneuvers involved in establishing new activities—exchanges of memos, committee meetings, and disputes over the division of responsibilities. Groves claimed that his Special Weapons Project was most capable of analyzing any data obtained by a monitoring network. AEC Chairman Lilienthal responded to a June 30 memo by Hillenkoetter, which estimated that it would take two years to have a complete monitoring network in place, with a memo of his own. He told Hillenkoetter that the AEC regarded it as essential that "a working arrangement, even though less than 'complete,' for the detection of atomic explosions in other parts of the world be established without much delay." In contrast, in January 1948, James Conant, chairman of the Research and Development Board's Committee on Atomic Energy, informed board chairman Vannevar Bush that his committee had "grave doubts as to whether [Hillenkoetter's] optimistic view [in his June 30 letter] is justified."[67]

Some of the difference in viewpoints as to when the United States could and should have a viable long-range detection program was due to varying degrees of access to information, and different assumptions. The belief that detection capabilities were more advanced than they actually were and a fear that a Soviet bomb might be imminent led some, such as Lilienthal, Strauss, and Le May, to press for quick action. Groves and others knew that more work had to be done before any form of detection could be reliable, and they mistakenly believed, *because* of their knowledge of another highly secret program, that a Soviet bomb was not imminent.[68]

Some of the anxiety of those pushing for a detection capability was diminished when the issue of assigning responsibility for the monitoring effort was settled. After meetings between senior officials, it was agreed that the Army Air Force was best equipped to handle the mission. On September 16, following the instructions of the secretary of war, Eisenhower sent a memo to Spaatz, instructing him to assume "over-all responsibility for detecting atomic explosions anywhere in the world."[69] That order would result in the formation of AFMSW-1 and its successor, AFOAT-1. What remained was to develop adequate technical detection capabilities and create a network based on those capabilities.

Work had continued on some potential detection capabilities while the issue of an institutional home for the long-range monitoring program was being debated. In November 1946, New York University was awarded a contract for the development of balloons that could loiter for as long as forty-eight hours at a predetermined altitude between 33,000 and 66,000 feet while carrying sonic detection equipment. The university's director of research, Capt. Athelstan Spilhaus, a geophysicist, had served during the war under Col. Marcellus Duffy, now the officer in charge of Project Mogul.[70]

Spilhaus assembled the Constant Level Balloon Group, which included his wartime assistant, Charles Moore. Between June 4 and July 7, 1947, the group launched eight trains or clusters of polyethylene balloons from the Army Air Force base in Alamogordo. Each balloon carried a low-frequency microphone, of which the capability to pick up distant, preset explosions was tested. Some balloon groups operated at maximum altitudes of over 48,000 feet; others, in the range of 15,000 to 19,000 feet. Further development followed, and by the end of the year balloons meeting Mogul requirements were available.[71]

Another opportunity to test assorted potential long-range detection techniques came in April and May 1948, when three bombs (X-Ray, Yoke, and Zebra) were detonated on Eniwetok. The tests were designated Operation Sandstone, while the Special Weapons Group's monitoring effort was code-named Operation Fitzwilliam.[72]

The arrangements for Fitzwilliam were in large part the work of Dr. Ellis A. Johnson, the scientific director for AFMSW-1. A graduate of MIT, he had spent a few years there as an instructor before moving on to the Carnegie Institution's department of terrestrial magnetism in 1935. On loan to the Naval Ordnance Laboratory to work on magnetic mines, he was at Pearl Harbor on December 7, 1941. While there he solved the problem of American submarine torpedoes that failed to explode when they hit their Japanese targets. After the war he returned to Carnegie, but took a leave of absence when invited to join the new monitoring organization.[73]

The scientific program that Johnson and his colleagues developed involved testing the three primary candidates for employment in long-range detection—radiological, seismic, and sonic—while exploring the potential of other, exotic techniques.* Attempting to observe a light flash reflected off the dark side of the moon after an explosion was one of those techniques. Measur-

---

* Seismic techniques involved detecting the waves that would pass through the earth's surface in the event of nuclear detonation. Such techniques were already in use for detecting earthquakes. Sonic techniques detected the sound waves created in the atmosphere from a detonation.

ing the magnetic effects of the dynamo action in the ionosphere caused by the pressure waves from a detonation, and detecting a blast-induced "dimple" in the ionosphere were the others. The complete test program consisted of nineteen projects, carried out by eight different agencies, dispersed halfway around the world.[74]

The primary element of the radiological experiments were the air-sampling missions conducted by the Air Weather Service. Along with the regular flights of filter-equipped aircraft that took off from bases in Guam and elsewhere, the weather service employed eight WB-29s on special sampling missions. The aircraft, based at Kwajalein, were fitted with radiation intensity recorders as well as with a device to collect atmospheric gas samples and filters to collect airborne particles. WB-29s also flew from bases on both coasts of the United States as well as in Bermuda, the Azores, and North Africa.[75]

One participant in the far-eastern segment of the aerial sampling program, designated Operation Blueboy, was Arnold Ross, the chief radio operator for Flight C of the 373rd Reconnaissance Squadron, Very Long Range Weather. In a 1985 letter, Ross recalled, on the basis of the personal logbook he had kept, that

> we left Lagens [in the Azores] on the 14th of May and proceeded to Wheelus Field, Tripoli, Libya. Using Wheelus as home base . . . we flew high altitude (35,000 feet) missions through Egyptian airspace, up to the Turkish border, through the Mediterranean area, and on one occassion, on 30 May we flew a 15 hour mission from Wheelus to the Cape Verde Islands. On all of these missions, the filter box was used, with filters being changed every hour on the hour. When removed from the filter box they were placed in a lead lined container, and upon completion of Operation Blueboy on 6 June 1948, the containers were returned to Washington.[76]

All together the Fitzwilliam air-sampling missions involved 466 sorties and 4,944 hours of time in the air. The area of coverage stretched from the polar regions in the north to the equator in the south, and from Manila in the Pacific to Tripoli in Africa.[77]

To test the feasibility of seismic detection, a team from the Coast and Geodetic Survey operated short-range diagnostic seismographs on the Runit, Parry, and Aniyaaii atolls in the vicinity of Eniwetok. Naval Ordnance Laboratory seismographs were installed at eight different sites in the Pacific, including on Kwajalein and Eniwetok. Both the ordnance lab and the Army Signal Corps established networks of sonic sensors. The navy detectors were located at six of the eight seismograph sites, while the signal corps network included five sites that extended from Japan to Germany (with sites in Hawaii, California, and New Jersey in between). Each army station was equipped with an array of twenty or more acoustical sensors.[78]

The air force's sonic detection equipment was carried on the Project Mogul balloons. For each of the three detonations, balloons were launched from progressively more distant sites to test the feasibility of sonic detection. The launch from Kwajalein (450 miles away) was followed by launches from Guam (1,200 miles) and Hawaii (2,750 miles). Mogul balloons were also launched from bases in New Mexico and Alabama.[79]

Naturally, the exploratory efforts for more exotic detection methods were less extensive. Two Army Signal Corps teams, hoping to detect the optical signatures of the detonations after they bounced off the moon, set up on Guam and Eniwetok, with telescopes coupled to photoelectric detectors and cameras. The search for electromagnetic effects took place on Eniwetok and Kwajalein, where naval ordnance personnel deployed high-sensitivity magnetometers. The search for an ionospheric dimple was confined to Kwajalein, where an ionospherograph—a pulsed radiotransmitter that periodically swept the frequency band between 1 and 25 megahertz—had been installed. Back in New Mexico, some Los Alamos scientists set up photoelectric recording equipment to determine if there was a notable change in the sky's illumination due to a nuclear test over 5,000 miles away.[80]

For most of the techniques tested in Fitzwilliam, the results were poor or worse, particularly with regard to distant atmospheric tests. The 49-kiloton blast of April 30, designated Yoke and the largest of the three, could not be detected by seismometers more than 500 miles from the site of the blast. Sonic detectors worked better, but their range was still too limited to detect tests in the Soviet heartland. The Yoke test was detected at 1,700 miles while the 18-kiloton blast of May 14 was detected at 1,000 miles. The data produced by the Mogul balloons was no better than that from the sonic detection devices on the ground, equipment whose operation did not involve the operational and security problems associated with balloons. As a result, the effort was abandoned.[81]

None of the exploratory techniques appeared to be useful. If any light ricocheted off the moon as the result of the tests, it was not detected. The magnetic experiment also came up empty, "with no indication of magnetic phenomena recorded," according to the team leader. The search for an ionospheric dimple never got a chance after it was discovered that the ionospherograph interfered with the radio control of the drone aircraft as well as the telemetry of other experiments. And the photoelectric equipment in New Mexico gave no indication of increased illumination in the sky on the one occasion when the devices were operational—at the time of the third test.[82]

The good news was that airborne radiological detection showed promise.

Ground-based equipment for detecting the radioactivity proved to be relatively insensitive if located more than approximately 600 miles from the blast. The problem, according to an analysis of the results, was "the small concentrations of debris" that fell back to earth more than 600 miles from the test site. The results using aircraft were quite different. A variety of radiation detectors, when carried by aircraft flying at altitudes of 25,000 to 35,000 feet, proved capable of detecting and tracking radioactive clouds of atomic debris to distances of about 2,000 miles from Eniwetok.[83]

While the results indicated that airborne detection devices could be used to track a radioactive cloud, they could not unequivocally establish its cause, which might be from a reactor accident or a nuclear explosion. Another approach, collecting the airborne dust created by a detonation, was also tested because it allowed the fission products to be subjected to chemical and physical analyses to establish that an atomic bomb had been tested. Here the results were particularly valuable and impressive. Samples collected over Tripoli, about 12,000 miles from the test site, were successfully subjected to radiochemical analysis. It was also discovered that debris brought back to earth by rainfall as far as 9,000 miles from the detonation site, gathered at radiological ground stations equipped with precipitation collectors, could also be analyzed to confirm an explosion and details of the device.[84]

While rainfall collection was far cheaper and less dangerous than airborne monitoring, it also depended on a certain amount of luck. The radioactive cloud not only had to pass over a rainwater collection station, but also had to do so at a time when nature contributed some rainfall. In contrast, launching aircraft was a matter of choice, not chance. Based on analysis of the fission products of the Sandstone tests, Ellis Johnson was able, on July 8, to tell members of the AEC that "the Air Force was confident of being able to detect by radiological means an atomic airburst."[85]

Johnson and his staff envisaged creation of an interim radiological detection system based on airborne monitoring, with experimental sonic and seismic detection networks being added in the future. But failure to obtain approval from higher authority outside of the monitoring organization for research projects he considered vital, including the initial airborne network, led him to resign as technical director. It would not be until the spring of 1949 that the Joint Chiefs would formally give their blessing to the creation of an interim long-range detection system, by which time Johnson's successor had also resigned over the multiple reviews by multiple committees that forced multiple revisions of the AFOAT-1 program.[86]

The process of establishing an interim network had begun well before final JCS approval. Shortly after the Sandstone tests and the detection effort concluded, Johnson had transformed the set of radiological ground stations into the network that would be part of the interim detection system, closing two Pacific stations (at Wake Island and at Henderson Field, Guadalcanal) and moving their equipment to a new station at Lagens Air Force Base in the Azores. Each of the twenty-four ground stations, located in a huge arc extending from Guam northward to Alaska and then southward to the Canal Zone, was equipped not only to detect radioactivity but also to gather airborne debris. One very simple piece of equipment was a shallow tank that collected rainfall. The interim network also included six sonic stations operated by the Army Signal Corps. Originally there were stations in Alaska, Hawaii, California, New Jersey, Germany, and the Philippines, although the network may have undergone some revision before August 1949.[87]

In July 1948, AFOAT-1 assigned the code name Workbag to Air Weather Service participation in the monitoring program (the entire monitoring effort was first code-named Whitesmith, and subsequently Bequeath). Four Air Weather Service reconnaissance squadrons, with about fifty-five filter-equipped WB-29s, formed the backbone of the interim detection network. The WB-29s flew from Guam, Alaska, California, and Bermuda. Collectively their efforts covered the Northern Hemisphere from the pole to the equator and from Korea to as far west as Libya, excluding only the North Atlantic region.[88]

Two other contributors to the atomic detonation detection capability at the beginning of August 1949 were the U.S. Navy and the United Kingdom. The navy's effort, Project Rainbarrel, was initiated by Herbert Friedman, a Naval Research Laboratory (NRL) physicist. As a result of his work with the radiation detectors established at naval monitoring stations as part of the navy's own detection efforts, he discovered that rainfall could carry with it the debris from an atomic detonation. Based on his suggestion, Peter King, head of the laboratory's chemistry division, and Luther Lockhart, another NRL chemist, developed a method of separating some of the rainfall-carried debris for chemical analysis. The navy was already operating naval stations at Manilla; Honolulu; Kodiak, Alaska; and Washington, D.C.—all equipped with two devices, one that constantly recorded the level of gamma radiation while the other collected airborne radioactive material. In April 1949, the Kodiak and Washington stations were equipped with a rainfall collector—a rooflike aluminum structure 2,500 square feet in area that rested on ten-foot-high posts. Along the perimeter were runoffs that permitted water to flow into storage tanks. If there was no rain to carry the debris into the tanks, "roof scrubbing" would be conducted to collect the dry fallout.[89]

When informed of the Sandstone tests, the British rushed to establish an interim network of their own. After a subsequent meeting between military representatives of the United States, Canada, and the United Kingdom, during which the subject of monitoring was discussed, the British followed up by establishing radiological ground stations at airfields in Scotland,

Northern Ireland, and Gibraltar, while Royal Air Force bombers at those bases were fitted with filters similar to those carried by WB-29s. By the summer of 1949, British monitoring aircraft were conducting routine missions covering the North Atlantic, flying from Gibraltar (code-named Nocturnal) and Britain (Bismuth).[90]

The final piece of the network were two laboratories, located in Berkeley and Boston and operated by Tracerlab, a private contractor that had been established in March 1946 to manufacture equipment for measuring radioactivity. The company would first become involved with the long-range detection program in February 1948, and would take part in the Fitzwilliam operation. Its laboratories provided the crucial radiochemical analysis of the debris collected by aircraft and ground stations.[91]

JUST AS LESLIE GROVES, Robert Oppenheimer, and assorted Los Alamos scientists were present at the Trinity test site in July 1945, Beria, Kurchatov, and other key figures in the Soviet program could be found at Semipalatinsk in late August 1949. One key difference though was that neither Oppenheimer nor his scientific colleagues had any reason to believe that they would be shot or wind up in a prison camp if the test failed. The same could not be said for Kurchatov, Khariton, and their associates.[92]

Beria, their potential executioner, had arrived at the test site during the second half of August to review preparations. On the night of August 28 and into the next morning, he, Kurchatov, Khariton, and others watched the bomb be put together. By about two o'clock in the morning, it was almost fully assembled and was wheeled out of the assembly area toward the platform where it was to be detonated. Kurchatov made his way to the command post, while Beria headed off to a cabin near the command post and slept for a few hours. The device was raised to the top of the platform, where the final assembly was completed.[93]

Very early that morning, Kurchatov gave the order to detonate "Stalin's Rocket Engine-1." One witness recalled that "on top of the tower an unbearably bright light blazed up. For a moment or so it dimmed and then with new force began to grow quickly. The white fireball engulfed the tower and the shop and, expanding rapidly, changing color, it rushed upwards. The blast wave at the base, sweeping in its path structures, stone houses, machines, rolled like a billow from the center." Another of those present recalled that "the steel tower on which the bomb had been hoisted had disappeared together with the concrete foundation . . . in place of the tower there yawned a huge crater." Beria responded to the successful test by embracing Kurchatov and Khariton and then kissing each on the forehead.[94]

After returning to his hotel, Kurchatov prepared his handwritten assessment of the test. He was able to report that the goal of a 20-kiloton blast had been achieved. For the next two weeks, analysis of the test results continued at the site of the blast. The levels of radioactivity in the air and in the soil were measured, the path of the radioactive cloud was tracked by aircraft, and cars journeyed into areas where debris had fallen to the ground to determine the extent to which the soil had been contaminated.[95]

WHILE THE UNITED STATES would have no opportunity to examine the results at the test site, or read Kurchatov's report, the radioactive cloud could not be contained inside Soviet borders. By late August the airborne segment of America's interim detection network had been operating on a routine basis for several months. The filter-equipped WB-29s of the 375th Weather Reconnaissance Squadron (WRS) normally flew every other day, along two tracks. One, designated Ptarmigan, involved a 3,500-mile journey, from Eielson Air Force Base at Fairbanks, Alaska, to the North Pole and back. Loon Charlie, the second track, was longer by 100 miles and took the plane and its crew from Eielson to Yokota, where a new crew took over and flew the plane back to Alaska. Together, the tracks flown by the WB-29s put them in position to collect airborne dust traveling eastward from any point in the Soviet Union.[96]

By September 3 there had been 111 instances in which the radiation count on filter paper carried by a WB-29 had exceeded 50 per minute, a number that resulted in an Atomic Detection System Alert. Each of the first 111 alerts had been explained by natural occurrences—volcanic explosions, earthquakes, or normal fluctuations in background radioactivity. But Alert No. 112 was the real thing.[97]

On September 3, a WB-29 piloted by 1st Lt. Robert C. Johnson flew for thirteen and a half hours from Japan to Alaska, at eighteen thousand feet, on the return segment of a Loon Charlie flight that had taken off from Misawa owing to special circumstances. While the flight was uneventful, its aftermath was not. Postflight analysis showed that a filter paper exposed for three hours had a radioactivity measurement of 85 counts per minute. The second filter paper was checked and yielded 153 counts per minute. When word of these developments arrived at AFOAT-1's well-guarded Data Analysis Center at 1712 G Street, N.W., in Washington, D.C., sometime after dinner on the third, it produced an increase in activity at AFOAT-1 and in the air. Technical director Doyle Northrup and members of his staff were summoned to the center to examine the data. Flights from Alaska to Hawaii and from California to Alaska were scheduled for Sunday and Monday, September 4 and 5, respectively. Subsequently, a special mission covered portions of the Beaufort Sea, to the north and east of Alaska. On Monday evening a report arrived from Japan stating that at ten thousand feet and just to the east of Japan, a filter paper on a WB-29 that had taken off from Guam on a routine weather reconnaissance mission registered over 1,000 counts per minute.[98]

By the time the aerial monitoring of First Lightning ceased, the Air Weather Service had flown ninety-two special air-sampling flights. In addition, British Royal Air Force planes had also contributed. On September 10, with President Truman's approval, Britain was informed that a mass of debris-laden air would be passing north of Scotland. A special flight was launched that day from Scotland and journeyed to the Arctic Circle before returning with more debris. Two days later, a routine flight from Gibraltar collected fresh evidence and other special British flights followed. All together, the aerial sampling effort produced over 167 radioactive samples with counts of 1,000 per minute or more.[99]

Other components of the interim network were checked to see if they yielded any information on what the Soviets had done. The air force's ground-based filter units produced positive results from Fort Randall in South Dakota, Shemya Island in the Aleutians, and a station in northern Japan. Naval research stations also contributed to the pool of data and debris that analysts would examine. Starting on September 9, gamma ray detectors on a station on Kodiak Island, Alaska, indicated a rise in background radioactivity. The following day air monitors at the NRL in Washington also detected increased radioactivity. Two collections of rainfall from Kodiak, covering the periods September 9–12 and September 13–17, were found to contain large amounts of debris.[100]

Two elements of the interim network, at first appearance, provided no confirmation that a detonation had occurred. The Army Signal Corps's network of sensors showed no acoustic waves associated with an explosion, just as the Coast Survey's seismic network yielded no evidence of seismic waves indicating an atomic blast in the Soviet Union. Such data would have allowed a more precise determination of the location, time, and yield of the Soviet test.[101]

The initial readings of the filters left much to be done. Beyond verifying that a detonation did occur, there were the questions of when and where, and whether the device was a uranium or a plutonium bomb. The analytical effort spanned the country and the Atlantic, and included some of America's most renowned scientists.

Beginning on September 6, air force couriers began delivering filters to Tracerlab's Berkeley laboratory. Lab director Lloyd Zumwalt recalled that "we worked on them through the night." It was not long before their analyses revealed the presence of fresh fission products on the filters. That the products appeared to have been created simultaneously indicated that they were more likely the result of a bomb than a reactor accident. On September 7, Zumwalt was also able to tell William Urry at the data analysis center in Washington that it was likely a plutonium bomb. By September 10 Tracerlab had concluded that the bomb had been detonated between August 26 and August 29 and that it was a plutonium bomb containing a large amount of uranium, indicating a uranium tamper was employed to help create a chain reaction by reflecting neutrons back into the plutonium.[102]

The NRL also quickly began to analyze samples produced by the aerial collection effort, and on September 14 its scientists provided an oral briefing to Maj. Gen. Morris Nelson, who had been Hegenberger's deputy and became his successor at AFOAT-1. The NRL scientists identified the fission products of five elements, but suggested that they should cease work on the air force samples and begin investigating the larger samples that had been produced by the navy's rainfall collection effort.[103]

Doyle Northrup also decided to ask scientists at Los Alamos to conduct their own radiochemical analysis of the samples, and on September 10 a filter sample was sent to their radiochemistry group. Weeks before the Los Alamos report arrived in early October, it had become apparent to almost all the experts examining the data that the United States had detected the Soviet Union's first atomic bomb test, which would be designated both Joe-1 and Vermont.[104]

There were some high-level doubters who did not believe, or did not want to believe, that America's atomic monopoly had come to an end. One of the skeptics was secretary of defense Johnson. Another was Truman's national security adviser Sidney Souers, who hoped there had been a reactor accident. As a result of such doubts, General Nelson asked a panel of scientists, with no air force affiliation, to examine the data. The prestigious group included Vannevar Bush, who had left government service to return to the Carnegie Institution in Washington; former AEC commissioner Robert Bacher; J. Robert Oppenheimer; and Adm. William Parsons, a member of the Military Liaison Committee to the AEC. They were chartered by Gen. Hoyt S. Vandenberg, former intelligence chief and now air force chief of staff, to meet on September 19 to review AFOAT-1's data and conclusions.[105]

When the group assembled at 10:00 a.m. on September 20, Bush, who served as chairman, along with Oppenheimer and his colleagues, heard largely oral presentations about the analyses and conclusions of the British, Los Alamos, and NRL scientists. Additional presentations were made by members of the AFOAT-1 staff, and Northrup submitted a three-page memo. The essence of the memo consisted of eleven "facts bearing on the problem" and six conclusions. The facts included the key Tracerlab findings concerning the likely dates that the material was fissioned, the composition of the material, and the presence of uranium, as well as the first results from the Los Alamos and NRL analyses. The memo also reported on the British flights and their results. The main conclusions were those reached earlier in the month: the Soviet Union had detonated a plutonium bomb with a uranium tamper, sometime between August 26 and August 29.[106]

Estimates of the location of the test site were produced by the six-member Special Projects Section of the U.S. Weather Bureau, one of many small units located in nonsensitive agencies that did very sensitive work during parts of the Cold War. The section was headed by Lester Machta, who held a doctorate in meteorology from MIT. Established in late 1946 or early 1947, it studied the movement of air currents, to assess potential exposure to fallout from U.S. nuclear tests. It included several recruits from the University of Chicago, including Kenneth Nagler and Lester Hubert. Hubert recalls that he was finishing graduate school, where he had studied wind patterns at high altitudes in the Pacific and South Pacific, when he was recruited.[107]

Based on three possible test dates (August 27–29), the meteorologists produced a series of probability contours, such that for a given date all points within the contour had an equal probability of having been the point of detonation. Their work led to the conclusion, based on AFOAT-1's estimate that August 27 was the most likely date for the test, that the test site could be found between longitude 35° and 170° east, an enormous expanse of territory that included points west of Moscow and as far east as places in Siberia. The most likely site was somewhere near the northern part of the Caspian Sea.[108] That conclusion had two implications: the blast could have occurred almost anywhere in the Soviet Union, but not outside it.

The panelists were convinced by what they heard. The next day they sent a copy of Northrup's report, along with a cover letter, to Vandenberg. In their letter they told him that it was their unanimous belief that the phenomena detected were "consistent with the view that the origin of the fission products was the explosion of an atomic bomb whose nuclear composition was similar to the Alamogordo bomb," and echoed Northrup's memo with regard to the dates and location of the blast.[109]

Vandenberg passed the letter and attached memo on to Johnson, along with his own memorandum, before the day was out. He told the defense secretary, "I believe an atomic bomb has been detonated over the Asiatic land mass during the period 26 August 1949 to 29 August 1949. . . . Conclusions by our scientists based on physical and radiochemical analyses of collected data have been confirmed by scientists of the AEC, United Kingdom and Office of Naval Research."[110]

The following day, Truman, who had received a number of reports on the event over the preceding two weeks, read the Vandenberg memorandum. On September 22 the NRL report was completed and, based on the analysis of collected rainwater, provided further confirmation of the detonation. Then, at eleven o'clock on Friday morning, September 23, after consultations, a review of the evidence with the JCS, receipt of recommendations from Johnson and the AEC, and notification that the United Press would have the story on the street in an hour, Truman told the American public, "We have evidence that within recent weeks an atomic explosion occurred in the U.S.S.R." He went on to note that such a development had been expected and cited a statement he made in 1945 to that effect. He closed with the observation that "this recent development emphasizes once again . . . the necessity for truly effective enforceable international control of atomic energy."[111]

The next day the headlines and substantial portions of the news sections of the *New York Times* and *Washington Post* were devoted to the president's announcement and related stories. "Truman Reveals Red A-Blast" was the *Post*'s headline. Both papers noted that there was no claim that the Soviet Union had a bomb, although high-level officials warned against assuming that the explosion was the result of a reactor accident. There was also discussion of the various means by which the United States might have detected the blast. The *Post* noted that some scientists believed the omission of an exact time of the explosion might have been due to its detection by radiological, rather than seismic or sonic, means, although it is unlikely that such information would been revealed even if the United States had it. William L. Laurence, the scientific correspondent for the *Times*, contributed an article on the Soviet bomb having arrived several years ahead of the schedule predicted by U.S. intelligence and national security officials.[112]

Identifying the reasons why the Soviet Union shattered the American nuclear monopoly ahead of when the Americans estimated the Soviets "could" have a bomb, much less when it was "most likely" to have one, is not difficult. Some, like Leslie Groves, were privy to the secrets of the Murray Hill Area and Combined Development Trust—projects to locate and purchase as much high-grade uranium ore as possible before the Soviet Union could obtain any—knowledge that had influenced their estimate of when the Soviet Union would break the U.S. nuclear monopoly. They believed that the combination of the trust's acquisition of the ore and Soviet inability to extract sufficient bomb material from low-quality ore ensured a prolonged U.S. atomic monopoly.

But the analysts at the CIA and the Joint Staff were off in their estimates for other reasons: uncertainty as to when the Soviets began their program, the inability to penetrate the highly secret world of the Soviet bomb program, the lack of complete knowledge about the success of Soviet atomic espionage efforts, and perhaps a failure to appreciate, despite the example of Los Alamos, what a group of highly qualified nuclear physicists could accomplish if given the resources they required. The conditions that the Germans had lacked—scientists who understood how to build a bomb, a country that was not under assault, and the availability of the required resources—were present in the case of the Soviet Union.

The CIA's failure to provide advance warning of the Soviet test predictably resulted in some tough questioning by some of the legislators who served on the Congressional Joint Committee on Atomic Energy (JCAE). During an executive session on October 17, Hillenkoetter told his audience some of what the JNEIC and CIA had concluded about the Soviet program, including the existence of three water-cooled reactors that used graphite as a moderator. Hillenkoetter could not provide a definite answer as to whether there were other reactors, but he told the congressmen, "We think that that is all they have." He also estimated that more than 150,000 individuals were involved in the program. Both Hillenkoetter and Dr. Walter F. Colby, the chief of the AEC Intelligence Division, reported that the United States had not picked up any traces of large-scale efforts to separate U-235. Hillenkoetter also acknowledged, in response to a question, that the CIA had not been able to acquire very many, if any, Soviet documents.[113]

One committee member was particularly concerned with the lack of warning. Senator Eugene Millikin was "very much interested in why we were taken by surprise on the Russian explosion" and observed that "it seems that we muffed it at least a year and maybe longer." In defense, Hillenkoetter responded, "I don't think we were taken by surprise," and then proceeded to explain the reasons for the surprise, including the lack of solid information on when the Soviet program started. Millikin was not satisfied by the admiral's comments, observing, "We apparently don't have the remotest idea of what they are doing until after they have done it. . . . I just get no comfort out of anything that the Admiral has said to us. We have not had an organization adequate to know what is going on in the past and he gives me no assurance that we are going to have one in the future." His judgment was shared by AEC chairman David Lilienthal, who noted at the time, "In my opinion our sources of information about Russian progress are so poor as to be merely arbitrary assumptions."[114]

The implications of a Soviet bomb were profound. By mid-1950, the CIA had revised upward its estimate of the Soviet atomic bomb stockpile. It was now projected that the Soviets would possess 10 to 20 bombs by mid-1950, 25 to 45 by mid-1951, 45 to 90 by mid-1952, and 70 to 135 by mid-1953. And U.S. defense spending would have to be adjusted upward as well. Omar Bradley, who was chairman of the JCS at the time, recalled that "the news came as a terrible shock to Louis Johnson. It caught him with his economy ax poised and in mid-air for yet another blow. He swung and continued to swing for some months, but . . . it was clearly a time to build our military forces, not pare them." Part of that buildup, Lewis Strauss argued, should be a vigorous program to build an H-bomb.[115]

The lull between Soviet tests would last two years and one day after President Truman's announcement of Joe-1. Although there may have been a lull in Soviet testing, there was no lull in U.S. attempts to gain further insight into the status of the Soviet atomic energy program. Sometime after the first Soviet test, the CIA contacted a retired mining engineer who had worked in Kyshtym before the 1917 revolution. While there he had overseen many mining operations and had accumulated papers and photos of Kyshtym as well as detailed maps of the entire area. He no longer had the papers in his possession, but was able to tell the agency's representatives where to find them—in the collection of his papers at Stanford University. The former engineer was also former president Herbert Hoover.[116]

Additional help in understanding the Soviet program came sometime in 1950 when a colonel in the the Ministry of Internal Affairs (MVD) defected. Icarus, as he was code-named, had worked in the Moscow office of the First Chief Directorate and later at a Soviet-run uranium-mining operation in East Germany. He was able to tell his CIA debriefers the names and addresses of the Soviet Union's "atomic representatives" in Berlin—information that allowed the agency to begin an extensive investigation of their activities, an investigation that would bear fruit in later years. By mid-1951 the CIA had acquired a sample, manufactured in East Germany, of material used in U-235 production.[117]

The agency was also able to report that a fifth large Hanford-type plutonium production reactor might be under construction and that between 340,000 and 480,000 persons were working full-time on the Soviet atomic bomb effort. There was considerable uncertainty, however, in a number of areas, according to the JCAE staff. While the CIA "appears to have established the location of many Soviet project sites with some certainty (largely through the aid of refugees from Russia) . . . relatively little is known about the kind of plants actually established at these sites." In addition, estimates of the number of graphite and heavy-water reactors and the size of U-235 plants "are based in large measure (the Committee staff understands) upon the amount of raw materials assumed to be on hand." While the CIA's information on raw materials in Eastern Europe and European Russia was quite good, "there is no proof that the Soviets have not discovered rich uranium sources in Siberia."[118]

The two technical components of the detection system that had moved beyond the formative stage remained the key elements of the monitoring effort in the early 1950s. The Army Signal Corps continued operating the acoustic stations and providing reports to AFOAT-1. By May 1951 the United States was sampling the air masses moving out of the USSR and over the Middle East. Flights were conducted once every seventy-two hours over a limited flight path from Dhahran, Saudi Arabia, to Lahore, Pakistan—a frequency that was not sufficient to intercept all the clouds moving out of the area. The lack of backup ground filter units in the Near East made the deficiency more serious. At the time, Britain was in the process of equipping with filters the Royal Air Force Transport Command aircraft that flew daily round-trips between London and Singapore, with stops in Libya, Iraq, Pakistan, and India.[119]

A SECOND ELEMENT of aerial atomic intelligence operations was even more sensitive than test detection. Its genesis can be found in Luis Alvarez's idea to monitor Germany for signs of xenon-133, to determine if a plutonium production reactor was in operation. That gas was not the only noble gas emitted as a by-product of plutonium production. Krypton-85 was another. It also does not occur naturally in the atmosphere and is only found there if some nation put it there. If the United States could determine the amount of krypton-85 emitted from Soviet reactors, it would be possible to estimate the amount of plutonium produced, since the number of grams of plutonium produced is directly proportional to the number of grams of krypton-85 produced by the fission of U-235 in a reactor. In the process of dissolving uranium to recover plutonium, krypton-85 gas is released into the atmosphere along with the dissolving gases in an amount proportional to the number of grams of plutonium recovered.[120] An estimate of the amount of plutonium produced could help determine the number of plutonium bombs that might be carried on Soviet bombers.

In June 1950, the Ad Hoc Committee on Atomic Energy, reporting to the Intelligence Advisory Committee (which consisted of the chiefs of America's major intelligence organizations), recommended maintenance and active support for such an effort. Since U.S. spyplanes could not overfly Soviet reactors to obtain direct readouts of the level of krypton-85, the effort required a more complex approach. It required that U.S. and British analysts, based on the results of aerial sampling, determine the worldwide level of krypton-85, which had stood at zero in 1944, and subtract from it the contribution due to non-Soviet reactors. What was left was the Soviet contribution. By late March 1951, scientists determined that it would be possible to calculate the post-1945 releases of krypton-85 from the Hanford facility as well as from the reactor at Chalk River, Canada. If, as expected, the British began plutonium production later in the year, it would be necessary to add that amount to the U.S. and Canadian totals. In addition, AFOAT-1 and the AEC had worked out a method of measuring the worldwide level of krypton-85, and it was expected that before the end of the year it would possible to estimate that level to within 5 percent of the true value. On July 1, the Research and Development Board's committee on atomic energy estimated that by mid-1952 it would be possible to produce a quantitative assessment of Soviet krypton-85 production "with a precision equal to ten percent of U.S. generation."[121]

BY 1951, there had also been some progress in expanding the network of ground stations used to gather atomic intelligence. In July 1950, the first ground filter units, designed to trap radioactive debris, were produced and installed at McClellan Air Force Base in California, at Eielson in Alaska, and on Guam. Beginning in 1950, the Special Weather Unit, under the control of the air force, began operations at Puerto Montt in Chile, and was probably involved in similar operations. Near the end of 1950, or early the next year, the first seismic station dedicated specifically to the Atomic Energy Detection System, as the AFOAT-1 monitoring network was called, was installed near College, Alaska. In April 1951, Team 301, which operated both seismic and acoustic equipment, began operating in Ankara, Turkey.[122]

That was only the beginning of several attempts, some immediately successful, to establish such facilities on allied territory. In September 1951, Frederik Møller, the director of the Norwegian Defense Research Establishment (NDRE), received a request from Colonel McDuffy of the U.S. Air Force, requesting permission for an American team to search Norway for suitable sites for seismic and acoustic detection stations. The stations would be operated for two years by an American staff and then turned over to Norway. In Washington that month, the Danish ambassador was told during a meeting at the State Department that the United States was interested in installing a ground filter unit at Thule, Greenland.[123]

MEANWHILE, AS THE U.S. and allied intelligence services tried to uncover their secrets, Soviet bomb designers worked to improve the plutonium bomb design that their spies had stolen from the United States—something they believed, even before the August 1949 test, could be done. Sometime in 1949, Yakov Zeldovich, at the time head of the theoretical department at Arzamas-16, and three of his colleagues—E. I. Zababakhin, Lev Altshuler, and K. K. Krupnikov—drafted a proposal for a bomb that would halve the weight of the plutonium bomb while doubling its yield. V. M. Nekrutkin suggested a different means of producing implosion, which made it possible to significantly reduce the bomb's diameter.[124]

The result of their work, RDS-2, exploded at 9:19 on the morning of September 24, 1951, at the Semipalatinsk test site, with a yield of just over 38 kilotons. Joe-2 was followed by Joe-3 less than a month later. On October 18, RDS-3, dropped from a Tu-4 Bull bomber rather than placed on a tower, detonated with a yield of 42 kilotons. The successful tests resulted in Kurchatov and Khariton each being named a Hero of Socialist Labor for the second time.[125]

The data collected on the September 24 blast by U.S. detection systems was reviewed by a panel reporting to the Defense Department's Research and Development Board. The panel, which included Oppenheimer and Bacher as its members, concluded that "there was a fission explosion on 24 September 1951 . . . in the vicinity of Lake Balkhash." The conclusions as to the time and place of the detonation were based on its detection by the experimental acoustic network, which had exhibited improved performance since 1949. While the time was correct, the center of Lake Balkhash is about 350 miles from Semipalatinsk—but still far closer to the actual test site than "somewhere near the Caspian Sea" as estimated in 1949.[126]

The panel also reported on the preliminary analysis, which indicated that "an implosion weapon using plutonium was fired." Further, the scientists concluded that at the time of their review there were no indications of U-235 having been employed and the results were "inconsistent with the presence of any large amounts of this material."[127]

The October test would be followed by another lull, one that would last for almost two years. But while there was no testing activity, the Soviet program continued to develop during that time, just as it did during the period between the first and second tests. In 1949 the gaseous diffusion plant at Sverdlovsk-44 had been unable to produce uranium enriched to more than 75 percent, requiring the electromagnetic separation facilities at Sverdlovsk-45 to be employed to raise the enrichment level to 90 percent. In 1950 the technical difficulties at Sverdlovsk-44 were overcome and the plant was able to produce tens of kilograms of uranium each year, enriched to the 90 percent level. In July 1950 the second of the Chelyabinsk-40 production reactors became operational, an event that would be repeated by four additional reactors by the end of 1952. To further augment the plutonium production capabilities of Sverdlovsk-44 and Chelyabinsk-40, yet another facility was established in 1950. This one, Krasnoyarsk-26, was located on the Yenisei River, about thirty-one miles to the northeast of Krasnoyarsk.[128]

In December 1951 the Soviet Union moved toward mass production of atomic bombs when the Avangard Electromechanical Plant (Plant 551), established in 1949 to produce twenty RDS-1–type bombs a year, and located near Arzamas-16, produced its first bomb. The year 1951 also witnessed the completion of the second gaseous diffusion plant at Sverdlovsk-44.[129]

THE SOVIET TESTS of 1951 would be followed by another hiatus, which also lasted about two years before being shattered by a dramatic Soviet advance. During that interval the United States experienced both success and setbacks in building its network to monitor future tests.

In January 1952 Norway's Møller replied to McDuffy and informed him that due to political considerations, his country's minister of defense demanded that the stations be partly staffed by Norwegians. The original plans then underwent substantial revision, with five stations becoming two "micro-meteorological research stations," and received the defense minister's approval. However, for reasons that are not clear, the plan would lay dormant for several years.[130]

The request to the Danish ambassador proved more successful. In October 1952, Team 220 was established at Thule Air Base. A few months earlier, in May, a mobile seismic station, Project Rockpile, was set up in Korea. A number of seismic-monitoring devices were also located in Iran. The operation, known as B/65, involved at its peak three officers and thirteen enlisted personnel above and beyond those assigned to the air attaché's office, which was employed as a cover by the AFOAT-1 personnel.[131]

However, by the end of 1952 the shah's continuation of power in Iran seemed problematic. The air force's Directorate of Intelligence expressed concern to the air attaché in Iran about the security of the AFOAT-1 operation. As a result the seismic and acoustic instruments covertly located at four sites on a hunting preserve were removed. However, to avoid the "impression of lack of confidence in the shah," the instruments were replaced by dummy boxes and the removal was made to appear as a routine overhaul.[132]

Despite such setbacks, the detection organization commanded at the end of 1952 by Brig. Gen. Donald Keirn, a former liaison officer for the Manhattan Engineer District, had grown to eight hundred employees. It also utilized the services of hundreds of other personnel and dozens of additional agencies both in the air force and outside of it.[133]

Late 1952 also saw an organizational change that would prove important to the atomic intelligence effort. On October 24, 1952, in a top-secret, eight-page memorandum on communications intelligence activities, President Truman abolished the ineffective Armed Forces Security Agency (AFSA) and transferred its personnel to the National Security Agency (NSA), created earlier that day by a draft of National Security Council Intelligence Directive No. 9 (which would be formally issued in December).[134] Whereas AFSA was unable to exercise significant supervision over the military COMINT agencies, NSA, as befitted its name, would serve as a national manager—and atomic intelligence was one of the most national of intelligence requirements.

FOR MUCH of his time at Los Alamos and after, while others were consumed with developing an atomic bomb and then improving it, Edward Teller focused on the possibility of an even more destructive weapon—a hydrogen bomb or "Super." The explosive force of such a bomb would come, not from fission, but fusion. Two isotopes of hydrogen, deuterium (extracted from water) and tritium, would be fused to form a nucleus of helium and a neutron. The energy released in the process would be far greater than that released from fission, with bomb yields in the megatons rather than kilotons. On January 31, 1950, President Truman publicly authorized the development of such a bomb, and in March issued a secret directive that labeled the project "a matter of the highest urgency" and authorized the production of up to ten H-bombs a year.[135]

Between his initial proposal and Truman's authorization of the project, Teller had produced a number of alternative designs for the bomb. Ultimately, he would have to share credit with mathematician Stanislaw Ulam. A 1951 suggestion by Ulam, and its modification by Teller, resulted in the concept of radiation compression—using the radiation (X-rays) rather than the shock wave from an atomic bomb to compress the thermonuclear fuel. Compression would make the fuel burn faster, ensuring that heat production outstripped heat loss in the fuel. Their design also involved separating the fission bomb (the primary) from the thermonuclear fuel (the secondary) and using the bomb casing to channel the radiation produced by detonating the primary toward the thermonuclear fuel of the secondary.[136]

On November 1, 1952, Mike, as the test of the device produced according to the Teller-Ulam theory was designated, resulted in the incineration of the Pacific island of Elugelab, substituting a crater about two hundred feet deep and a mile and a half wide. The yield of the explosion was more than 10 megatons, exceeding expectations by 50 percent—an "outstanding success," as Lewis Strauss would write several months afterward. For the test, the deuterium was maintained in a liquid state by a massive refrigeration system, which turned the device into a 50-ton, two-story "bomb"—not something one could load onto a bomber.[137]

Just as Edward Teller began thinking about a hydrogen bomb before design work for the first atomic bomb had been completed, Soviet physicists considered the possibility of employing fission as the first step in producing a fusion reaction. The first was Yakov Frenkel, who headed the theoretical department at Ioffe's institute. He raised the issue of a fusion bomb in a September 1945 memo to Kurchatov, who was already aware of the possibility because of his access to the intelligence on the American efforts provided by the NKVD and GRU. That month Soviet intelligence obtained reports on aspects of the "classical Super" that Teller had proposed. Another intelligence report from 1945 provided information on means of boosting the yield of a fission bomb through the fuel used in a hydrogen bomb.[138]

Kurchatov instructed Khariton to investigate, in collaboration with Zeldovich and two other physicists. On December 17, Zeldovich read their report, *Utilization of the Nuclear Energy of the Light Elements*, to the Technical Council of the Special Committee. Khariton and his colleagues recommended setting off a nuclear explosion in a deuterium cylinder through "nonequilibrium combustion."[139]

In the succeeding years, while Kurchatov and Khariton continued working on the primary task of developing an atomic bomb—first by copying the

U.S. design and then developing their own—Soviet physicists at home and intelligence officers abroad continued their investigations concerning fusion. In London, on September 28, 1947, Soviet intelligence officer Aleksandr S. Feklisov met with spy Klaus Fuchs and posed ten questions, the first of which concerned the Super. Fuchs told Feklisov of the studies being conducted by Teller and Enrico Fermi. A little over a month later, in early November, Zeldovich reported to the First Chief Directorate the latest research results of the group that he headed (which had been established in June 1946). Their report mirrored American thinking of the time, in that it envisioned the shock wave from a fission bomb igniting the thermonuclear fuel.[140]

The program escalated in 1948, with Zeldovich being placed in charge of operations at KB-11 in February, Fuchs delivering materials containing new theoretical information on the Super in March, and the Council of Ministers approving a resolution in June that ordered the Sarov design bureau to investigate, both theoretically and experimentally, all possible advanced atomic and hydrogen bombs. The resolution also mandated a role for the Physics Institute of the Academy of Sciences of the USSR. The hydrogen project was given the code name RDS-6. Another resolution directed that a special theoretical unit be established at the physics institute under fifty-three-year-old Igor Tamm, who had organized the institute's theoretical department in 1934—and would share the 1958 Nobel Prize with two other Soviet physicists for his work on the "Cerenkov effect."[141]

Among those working in Tamm's group was Andrei Sakharov, who at age twenty-seven was Tamm's junior by well over two decades and had joined the Academy of Sciences physics institute in 1945, three years after graduating from Moscow State University. In September and October 1948 Sakharov came up with an idea, analogous to the "Alarm Clock" concept conceived by Edward Teller—a bomb consisting of layers of fusion material (lithium-6 deuteride) placed into concentric shells of an enlarged implosion device—apparently without any access to intelligence about Teller's notion. The Sloika, translated as "Layer Cake," also would rely on alternate layers of deuterium and U-238. In January, Sakharov issued his report on the new concept, which drew strong support from Khariton. Sakharov then found himself being ordered by Beria to attend an almost weeklong series of conferences held in Sarov in early June to review the status of the atomic and hydrogen bomb projects. It was Sakharov's first visit to the secret city, where he would spend eighteen years of his life. The key result of the conference was a scientific research plan that called for work on both Sakharov's Layer Cake design and on the Truba (Tube)—the name for the Soviet version of the classical Super. Sakharov himself would devote himself solely to finding ways to transform his idea into reality.[142]

His idea took another step toward being transformed into an actual weapon the following February, when the Special Committee passed a resolution, "On Measures to Develop the RDS-6." The First Chief Directorate, Laboratory 2, and the design bureau at Sarov were instructed to organize further theoretical, experimental, and design work to construct both the Layer Cake (RDS-6s) and the Tube (RDS-6t). Khariton was appointed as director of operations for their construction, and Tamm and Zeldovich were named his deputies. The RDS-6s was to have a yield of 1 megaton and weigh up to 5 tons.[143]

A variety of measures were investigated to produce the thermonuclear fuel needed for the bomb. The fuel was not deuterium and the expensive, hard-to-produce tritium that had originally been thought necessary. In November 1948 Vitali Ginzburg, a member of Tamm's group, suggested that lithium deuteride, a compound of lithium-6 and deuterium, was a preferred alternative. Not only would lithium deuteride, a chalklike solid, be easier to handle than tritium and deuterium, but lithium-6 would produce the required tritium during the explosion when it was bombarded by neutrons. At Ioffe's institute in Leningrad, Boris Konstantinov developed an effective and cheap method of obtaining lithium-6, but one that required a new plant. A member of Lev Artsimovich's group at Laboratory 2 eventually developed a method for separating lithium isotopes and produced enough lithium-6 to fuel the Layer Cake device. The process for producing the required deuterium was developed at the Institute of Physical Problems in Moscow, which had been established in 1934 as consolation prize for Peter Kapitza when he was forbidden to return to the English laboratory where he had spent the previous thirteen years.[144]

On June 15, 1953, Tamm, Sakharov, and Zeldovich signed the final report on the development of RDS-6s, which estimated that the device would explode with a force of between 200,000 and 400,000 tons of TNT. This time the Soviet scientists did not have to fear Stalin's reaction if the test did not live up to expectations, since the Soviet dictator had died two months earlier. And by the end of the month they no longer had to worry about Beria, who was arrested on June 26 by Stalin's successors and charged with assorted offenses, including being a "bourgeois renegade" and "agent of international imperialism." His arrest was followed first by his replacement by Viacheslav Malyshev, deputy chairman of the Council of Ministers, and then by his execution. The First Chief Directorate became the Ministry of Medium Machine Building.[145]

Even if Stalin and Beria had been around, they would not have been able to complain about the results of the first test of Sakharov's bomb. When it was tested at Semipalatinsk on August 12, 1953, it produced an explosion measured at 400 kilotons, at the very top of the estimated range. Sakharov recalled that he had taken a sleeping pill the night before and turned in early. He rose, along with the others who were there to witness the test, when alarm bells at the hotel went off at four in the morning. Two and a half hours later he reached his station, about twenty miles from his bomb, where he was to watch the test with other young scientists from Sarov.[146]

In his memoirs Sakharov recalled the moment of detonation and the aftermath:

> We saw a flash, and then a swiftly expanding white ball lit up the whole horizon. . . . I could see a stupendous cloud trailing steamers of purple dust. The cloud turned gray, quickly separated from the ground and swirled upward, shimmering with gleams of orange. The customary mushroom cloud gradually formed, but the stem connecting it to the ground was much thicker than those shown in the photographs of fission explosions. More and more dust was sucked up at the base of the stem, spreading out swiftly. The shock wave blasted my ears and struck a sharp blow to my entire body; then there was a prolonged, ominous rumble that slowly died away after thirty seconds or so. Within minutes, the cloud, which now filled half the sky, turned a sinister blue-black color.[147]

THE LAYER CAKE was certainly different from the standard fission bomb, American or Russian. Whether it was truly a thermonuclear bomb was another question. At the time it was the position of the Joint Atomic Energy Intelligence Committee (JAEIC), as the JNEIC had been rechristened in late November 1949, that "a field test of a device involving a thermonuclear reaction is within Soviet capability at any time." But that judgment was not based on hard evidence. In March 1952 air force secretary Thomas Finletter had characterized U.S. intelligence on the subject as "meager." At the beginning of 1953 the JAEIC and CIA issued an estimate which stated that "there is no evidence of thermonuclear development activities at the present time." Among the factors considered were the individuals involved in the Soviet bomb program. The only concrete warning came courtesy of Soviet premier Georgi Malenkov, during an August 8 speech to the Supreme Soviet, when he claimed that the United States no longer "had a monopoly" on the hydrogen bomb.[148]

Then, on August 12 the United States detected seismic signals and subsequently collected airborne, and possibly rainfall, debris that indicated a possible Soviet test. When AEC chairman Lewis Strauss returned to Washington on August 19, after a trip to New York, and conferred with other members of the commission, acting director of central intelligence Gen. Charles Cabell, and acting secretary of state Walter Bedell Smith, he discovered that two possibilities needed to be eliminated before the United States could be sure that the Soviets had tested an atomic or thermonuclear weapon: that the signals were not the result of a concurrent earthquake in the Greek islands and that the debris did not originate with a previous U.S. test. Strauss was assured by AFOAT-1 representatives that they would have definitive information that afternoon.[149]

At six o'clock that evening Strauss received a call from Cabell, who told him that a report on the scientific findings would be ready at about 8:30 that night and that he would bring it to his office. The meeting that began at 8:30 included Strauss, several other commissioners, Cabell and three other members of the CIA, State Department representative Gordon Arneson, and AFOAT-1 technical director Northrup. Northrup told them that while his organization's conclusions were incomplete, there was no doubt that a fission and thermonuclear reaction had taken place within Soviet territory. At 10:30 Strauss received a call from a member of the AEC staff who informed him that Moscow radio had announced that the Soviet Union had tested an H-bomb in the last several days.[150]

The following day, Strauss told the world, "The Soviet Union conducted an atomic test on the morning of August 12. Certain information came into our hands that night. Subsequent information on the subject indicates that this test involved both fission and thermonuclear reactions."[151]

A panel of scientists whose charter was to review information from Soviet atomic and nuclear weapons tests took another look at the data. The Foreign Weapons Evaluation Panel was better known as the Bethe Panel, taking its name from chairman Hans Bethe, who had left Los Alamos to return to teaching and research at Cornell, his first position in the United States after arriving from Germany in 1935. While no longer a government employee, he still played a major role in advising the national security bureaucracy on weapons and intelligence issues, and was instrumental in developing techniques to distinguish between a fission explosion and a thermonuclear blast. The panel also included Enrico Fermi, Richard Garwin, who for over forty years would play a key role as an outside adviser to U.S. intelligence organizations on technical issues, and Lothar W. Nordheim.[152]

Bethe and his colleagues examined the seismic and acoustic data that had been obtained as well as the data that had been produced by subjecting the debris to mass spectrographic and radiochemical analyses. Seismic data was considered the best means of estimating yield. Even so, analysis of that data indicated a yield of between 500 kilotons and 2 megatons, with the most likely value being 700 kilotons. Acoustic data indicated a somewhat lower yield.[153]

The first of the general conclusions about "Joe-4," and undoubtedly the key conclusion, based on analysis of the debris, was that "there must have been a substantial thermonuclear reaction." But the presence of a substantial thermonuclear reaction did not make the device a true thermonuclear bomb, in the view of Bethe and others. The JCS Joint Intelligence Committee concluded in October that the test represented the Soviet counterpart to Teller's

Alarm Clock bomb rather a true hydrogen bomb. In his report Bethe noted that its conclusions were "subject to considerable doubt" and that "it is a bold undertaking . . . to determine both the composition and the geometry of a bomb which you have never seen," while also writing that "certain conclusions are much more firm than others." One of the conclusions he considered firm concerned the proper classification of RDS-6s. Almost thirty years later, he would write that "this was not a true H-bomb . . . it was not the real thing." Richard Garwin agrees, noting that the test was "the first large scale burning of thermonuclear material, [but] not radiation implosion by any means."[154]

chapter three

THE VIEW FROM ABOVE

THE SOVIET TEST of Sakharov's Layer Cake bomb would be followed, within thirty days, by four fission bomb tests: an airdrop on August 23 of the RDS-4 Tatyana, which would eventually be issued to bomber regiments, and three tower tests between September 3 and September 10. The airdrop produced a yield of 28 kilotons, while its successors produced smaller blasts, each below 6 kilotons.[1]

During one of the 1953 Soviet tests, the Air Weather Service unveiled a new aerial sampling capability. Maj. James T. Corn and Lt. William H. Wright flew a modified B-57A to an altitude of fifty-four thousand feet into the debris cloud—a flight that marked the start of the special B-57s being used for intelligence missions. Under a classified program designated Black Knight, the air force directed the Air Material Command to procure six Martin Model-294 aircraft, which became the RB-57D Intruder.[2]

SOMETIME AFTER those four tests, the CIA's nuclear intelligence analysts began preparing another assessment of the Soviet nuclear program. The information available to those analysts included the data gathered during and after Soviet tests, the results of krypton-85 monitoring, communications intelligence, and human intelligence. A national intelligence estimate provided a brief review of Soviet atomic weapons activities since 1945, and noted that while there was no doubt that espionage, German assistance, and Western scientific and technical literature made significant contributions to the Soviet program, the independent research required to adapt the information obtained to Soviet needs "was apparently carried out with a high degree of competence." It also revealed that the Soviets had departed from U.S., British, and Canadian atomic energy practices on a number of occasions.[3]

Beyond history, the report offered some admissions of uncertainty and information gaps, some estimates and facts, and some speculation about alternative stockpiles. The exact extent of the Soviet capability to produce nuclear weapons remained uncertain, and the reason why U-235 production lagged behind plutonium production was unknown. In the latter case, there was "only meager evidence . . . available . . . relevant to the isotope separation program." The lack of intelligence on that program was, the analysts wrote, "one of the most serious gaps in intelligence information on the Soviet atomic energy program." That gap was one reason why there was "no clear evidence" to guide analysts trying to estimate the specific types and numbers of weapons that would make up the Soviet stockpile.[4]

The report did estimate that the total East German production of uranium metal available to the Soviet Union up to the end of 1953 was between ten and fifteen thousand tons, and noted that an equal amount could have been produced from domestic and other Soviet satellite sources. The CIA's analysts also noted that the Soviets were depending on very low-grade uranium ore, the type of ore that Leslie Groves and others had believed could not be effectively exploited to produce bomb-grade material. The analysts did try, despite their limited knowledge, to calculate the number of warheads the Soviets might have available between the end of 1953 and mid-1957, under different combinations of weapons type and yield. But the numbers produced—somewhere between 12 and 550 at the end of 1953 and from 80 to 2,400 in mid-1957—primarily demonstrated how much the United States did not know about the Soviet nuclear program.[5]

During the remaining months of 1954, the Soviet atomic energy program continued to be a moving target for U.S. intelligence agencies and to provide more data through ongoing testing. On March 10, 1954, construction began on a gaseous diffusion plant, Combine 820, in Angarsk—about thirty miles north of the western tip of Lake Baikal. Then, on July 10, a government decree established the Naval Scientific Research Test Range, code-named Installation 700. Novaya Zemlya, a convex-shaped island over five hundred miles in length located between the Soviet mainland and the Arctic Ocean, whose southern tip is at the same latitude as Alaska, was chosen as the home for the new test site. In addition to substantial snowfall, the island also experiences winds of up to one hundred miles per hour, winter months of total darkness, and life-threatening cold weather. While the site's stated purpose was to test the effects of nuclear weapons, primarily torpedoes, on naval equipment, its remote location made it a viable alternative site for high-yield tests that could cause significant environmental problems for the small towns and villages near Semipalatinsk.[6]

The initial test of 1954 was also the first Soviet one outside of Semipalatinsk. On September 14, as part of a field exercise, a modified version of the 40-kiloton RDS-3 bomb was detonated over the Totsk range, about one thousand miles to the northwest of the usual test site. Four further tests, in late September and early October, validated designs for tactical weapons, with yields ranging between 0.03 and 4 kilotons. Before the testing activity for October, and the year, was over, there would be another four tests. The first, of a device developed for the T-5 torpedo, failed. The most notable of the remaining three was the October 23 test of the RDS-3I bomb—an RDS-3 equipped with a neutron initiator. The modification was intended to allow about a 50 percent increase in yield. The bomb designers' expectations were fulfilled when the device produced a blast equivalent to 62,000 tons of TNT.[7]

THE FIRST PART of 1955 was marked by the publication, within the intelligence community, of two studies that provided some indication of what American nuclear intelligence analysts knew or believed about the Soviet atomic energy program. One is the still classified national intelligence estimate on the Soviet program, prepared by the Joint Atomic Energy Intelligence Committee and released in April. That estimate, as the ones before it, was primarily a scientific and technical analysis of the Soviet ability to produce fissionable material, as well as the types of warhead sizes and yields the Soviets could turn out in the near future, and informed speculation on alternative stockpiles they could possess.[8]

The previous month, the Nuclear Energy Division in the Office of Scientific Intelligence had completed a revision of the atomic energy section of the National Intelligence Survey (NIS) on the Soviet Union. The NIS was a lengthy top-secret compendium of what the CIA knew about countries of interest. The seventy-seven-page treatment of Soviet nuclear activities included a discussion of the program's history and growth, its current management structure, the personalities involved, research facilities, uranium mining, and the production of fissionable materials.[9]

The report reflected a combination of knowledge and ignorance, at least at the top-secret level. It provided a detailed account of the roles of the First and Second Chief Directorates in supervising the Soviet program—information that appeared to have come from knowledgeable sources. At the same time, the authors of the survey admitted that they had no current knowledge of the activities of the two directorates, or even if they still existed. There was also a description of the assorted laboratories and institutes, mostly in the Moscow area, as well as those created for German scientists.[10]

The list and commentary on ninety-six scientists filled up nineteen pages. Kurchatov, Khariton, Artsimovich, Flerov, Sakharov, and others who had played major roles in the Soviet development of atomic weapons were all included. Kurchatov was noted to be the head of Laboratory No. 2, and described as "probably the key scientist directing research on reactors and weapons for the atomic energy program." That "probably" was one possible example of the limits of U.S. knowledge at the time. So was the lack of information on Sakharov's role in designing the Layer Cake bomb. There were references to sites in the Urals and Siberia involved in uranium enrichment and plutonium production, but no specific locations were given. As the authors noted about the sites, "Important details remain undetermined."[11]

One explanation for some missing data was not a lack of knowledge but the level of classification of the survey. While the uninitiated might assume that there is nothing more sensitive than "top secret," in World War II the United States began creating classifications that were, in effect, above top secret. Several of those, each designated by a code word, which was itself classified, covered intelligence obtained by communications intercepts. The authors of the survey relied on a number of different sources: returned German and Japanese prisoners of war, defectors, intercepted letters from German scientists, open literature, and espionage directed principally against uranium-mining activities. Communications intelligence was not one of them. But, by 1955, the United States had apparently discovered the existence of Sarov by detecting unusually heavy telephone traffic between the secret city and Moscow. Thus, the CIA knew more than it was telling the readers of the survey.[12]

But it is clear that some of the omissions were not due to restricted communications intelligence knowledge, but rather no knowledge at all. In April German scientists began returning from Sukhumi to East Germany. In 1951 the CIA, in anticipation of their return, initiated Operation Dragon. Largely relying on the analysis of mail intercepted by the Army Security Agency, the CIA began to prepare defection pitches targeted at the returnees. CIA attempts to induce Hertz, von Ardennes, Vollmer, and Max Steenbeck to defect failed, but some of their subordinates were more receptive. In addition, Nikholaus Riehl, upon learning that he could no more keep the money from his Stalin Prize than a runner-up on *Jeopardy* could keep his winnings, decided to take the CIA up on its offer.[13]

The agency knew from reading their mail that the defector returnees would not be able to offer fresh information, as they had not been allowed to work in the Soviet nuclear program for three years. While their Soviet masters had intended the cooling-off period to reduce any damage from defections or loose talk, "skillful and exhaustive interrogation . . . revealed technical details, individual names . . . in a richness unbelievable to one who has never witnessed this procedure," according to Henry Lowenhaupt.[14]

The returnees were able to confirm the CIA's supposition that the Germans working in the vicinity of Sukhumi had focused on isotope separation. Naturally, they were able to provide more detail on the von Ardenne group's research into isotope separation, and the Hertz group's investigation of a modified form of gaseous diffusion. Beyond that, the interrogations helped the CIA pin down the precise location of one of the secret cities in the Urals. The agency had concluded that there was a gaseous diffusion plant in the northern Urals, as indicated in the national intelligence survey. And it knew the existence of some sort of atomic facilities at Nizhnyaya Tura and Verkh Nevyinsk, but not which one was the diffusion plant. Several returning POWs had actually been to the plant but knew it only as "Kefirstadt," a nickname derived from the name of the area's favorite nonalcoholic beverage — *kefir*. The best guess was Nizhnaya Tura. But that guess turned out to be wrong. The new batch of defectors told the CIA that Kefirstadt was actually Verkh Neyvinsk. The agency had found Sverdlovsk-44.[15]

WHILE THE CIA was debriefing the Germans who had been sent home, Soviet scientists and technicians continued their work. In an eight-day span, beginning on July 29 and ending on August 5, the Semipalatinsk area experienced three more atomic tests. All were low-yield tests of the RDS-9 developed for the T-5 torpedo. Then, on September 21, another RDS-9 device was detonated. But this time, the test occurred about one hundred feet underwater, in Chernaya Bay, located near the southern end of Novaya Zemlya. In contrast to the July and August tests, the purpose of this one was not weapons development, but to determine the damage that could be done by a T-5 when its nuclear warhead exploded.[16]

Testing was not the only way in which the Soviet nuclear program had expanded by the end of September 1955. In April, concerned that a too heavy workload would result in a decline in the quality of the research and development being done at Arzamas-16, Soviet leaders established a second weapons design bureau. The Scientific Research Institute was built about fifty miles south of Sverdlovsk and twelve miles north of Chelyabinsk-40, in the city of Snezhinsk. Its first scientific director was K. I. Shechelkin, whose name and specialty (the combustion and detonation of gases), but not his role as Khariton's first deputy, had been noted in the national intelligence survey. The secret city's new designation was Chelyabinsk-70. Before the year was out, there would be further developments. In November the first plutonium production reactor at Tomsk came online, while a second heavy-water reactor would began operating at Chelyabinsk-40 in late December.[17]

The most important development of the year occurred sometime after Andrei Sakharov boarded a train at Moscow's Yaroslavl station. He was accompanied by bodyguards from a special KGB detachment who had been assigned to him since the summer of 1954. They served as both guardians and watchers. No counterpart of Moe Berg was going to assassinate one of the Soviet Union's key weapons designers, and that designer was not going to associate with "undersirables." Sakharov apparently reached the test site in time to view a test on November 6. Although the blast equaled the force of 250,000 tons of TNT, it "made no special impression on me," he recalled years later. Two weeks later, Sakharov was anticipating something special when a plane carrying a nuclear device in its bomb bay took off from an airfield near Semipalatinsk. The device was the product of what Sakharov would refer to as the "Third Idea," and promised to give the Soviet Union a full-fledged thermonuclear capability, one that would pass scrutiny even before the Bethe Panel.[18]

The first proposal for a two-stage thermonuclear device had been made in 1953. Then, on January 14, 1954, Zeldovich and Sakharov sent Khariton a memo titled "Concerning Utilization of the Gadget for Implosion of the RDS-6s Supergadget" that included a schematic of a different two-stage device and an estimate of its performance. The device would contain both an atomic bomb and a thermonuclear core, and the gases from the detonation of the atomic bomb would compress the thermonuclear core. There was no suggestion of creating a thermonuclear detonation through radiation compression, the Teller-Ulam idea being pursued in the United States.[19]

That concept of radiation compression came to Sakharov and others a few months later, in March and April. It followed the U.S. Bravo test on March 1, whose yield of 14 megatons made it very clear that U.S. weapons designers had developed a high-yield thermonuclear device. "Intensive analytical dissection and interpretation of all the available evidence," presumably including Soviet analysis of the American debris, followed. The subsequent Soviet-accelerated research and design effort resulted in the technical specifications for an experimental two-stage, radiation compression, thermonuclear device being completed on February 3, 1955, with the device being designated RDS-37. By the time the theoretical and engineering work had been done, about thirty physicists, including Sakharov and Zeldovich, had made contributions, along with a team of mathematicians.[20]

But Sakharov and the others at Semipalatinsk were to be disappointed that November day, not because the bomb did not live up to expectations, but because it was not dropped at all. The weather had changed after the plane lifted off. Low clouds made it impossible to use visual sighting to deliver the bomb or optical systems to monitor the detonation, so the test was aborted and rescheduled for a few days later. On November 22, Sakharov recalls an hour of tedious waiting, and then the announcement that the plane was over its target. That was followed by notification that "the bomb has dropped!" and "the parachute has opened!" The countdown finally reached the "five, four, three, two, one, zero stage."[21]

Sakharov saw "a blinding yellow-white sphere expand, turn orange in a fraction of a second, then turn bright red and touch the horizon, flattening out at its base. Soon everything was obscured by rising dust which formed an enormous, swirling, gray-blue cloud." It was not long before he "felt heat like that from an open furnace on my face . . . in freezing weather, tens of miles from ground zero." Several minutes later he was jumping from the platform, as "the sudden shock wave was coming at us, approaching swiftly, flattening the grass." The test, he would write, "crowned years of effort. It opened the way for a whole range of devices with remarkable capabilities."[22]

WHILE THE SOVIETS were busy upgrading their nuclear infrastructure and conducting further weapons tests, the United States was enhancing its detection capabilities on land and in the air. In March 1954, Col. Jack Gibbs, the deputy chief of AFOAT-1, was seeking guidance from the State Department's Gordon Arneson concerning the possible establishment of a seismic station in Australia. Arneson suggested relying on the U.S. ambassador in Australia to raise the issue, notifying the United Kingdom of U.S. plans, and stressing that "the seismic installation in question is directed solely toward the Soviet Union *and that the equipment involved would not be suitable for monitoring of any future British tests that might take place on or near the continent of Australia* (emphasis added)."[23]

In December, Colonel Gibbs again consulted the State Department, inquiring about the feasibility of conducting seismic surveys in southern Germany, Spain, Norway, and Sweden. The seismic stations that the United States was operating at Camp King, Germany (Team 313A), and Thule Air Base, Greenland, were not producing the expected results, and AFOAT-1 was seeking two replacement stations—one in Norway or Sweden to replace Thule, and one in Spain or Germany to replace Camp King. The following June, a letter from a State Department official to L. Corrin Strong, the American ambassador in Oslo, requested his views about how the Norwegian government would react to a request to permit a U.S. team to survey Norwegian territory in search of a suitable site. The letter explained that such a station would consist of four small huts to house the instruments and a central recording station, with the huts being spaced along a four-mile line. Two officers and twelve airmen, "who could be in civilian clothes," would be needed to man the central recording station around the clock.[24]

A more important issue for the ambassador was undoubtedly the U.S. desire to tell the Norwegians as little as possible about what the Americans would be doing, at least in part because of legal restrictions on the sharing of nuclear intelligence. Norwegians would not be involved in the operation of the station, nor would the government receive finished intelligence derived from the signals detected. The raw data obtained could be shared, but those signals would be "relatively meaningless until correlated with similar data from several stations." The issue would come before the Norwegian Cabinet Defense and Security Committee that summer. After discussion, particularly of whether they should demand that Norway play a greater role in operating the station and have greater access to the data it produced, it was agreed to leave negotiations in the hands of the National Defense Research Establishment and the Intelligence Staff. As a result, on September 5, an American site survey team began its trek across southern and northern Norway, conducting a "granite reconnaissance" in search of a suitable site.[25]

The approach to Australia was also successful. Sometime in 1955, early enough for the station to be operational before the year was out, the United States and Australia entered into a secret agreement to permit AFOAT-1 to establish a seismic station in the vicinity of Alice Springs, a small remote city in the Australian outback. The unit was designated Team 421 and the station code-named Oak Tree. By the end of 1955, with the Thule site having been closed in June, the seismic network consisted of nine fixed stations, a mobile team, one research station, and one standby station. Foreign sites included those in Australia (Alice Springs), South Korea (mobile), the Philippines (Clark Air Force Base), Germany (Camp King), and Turkey (Ankara). Within U.S. borders there were ground stations in Wyoming (at Pole Mountain, Douglas, and Encampment) and Washington (Larson Air Force Base).[26]

AFOAT-1, also at the end of 1955, continued to have the benefit of reporting from its three electromagnetic pulse stations, eight acoustic stations operated by the Army Signal Corps as well as five stations operated by the Coast and Geodetic Survey. America's nuclear test monitors were also getting a little help from British and Canadian friends. One British acoustic station, Tag Day, had operated throughout the year, while a seismic station, Beaver, had been activated during the year at American request. Another acoustic station had also been operating during 1955. Both Tag Day and Beaver, one of which was located in Pakistan, "lay in close proximity to . . . Semipalatinsk." Canada furnished data from its own ground and aerial filter operations and conducted radiochemical analyses of debris and air samples collected by both Canadians and Americans.[27]

Airborne debris collection remained a key element of the monitoring activity, and was performed by the 56th Weather Reconnaissance Squadron (WRS) at Yokota Air Base in Japan, and the 58th WRS at Eielson Air Force Base in Alaska—along trajectories now labeled Buzzard Delta and Loon Charlie. Special flights were also flown by the 53rd WRS at Burtonwood, England, and the 55th WRS at McClellan Air Force Base in California. To improve their collection capabilities, that August the Air Weather Service began replacing WB-29 aircraft with the more modern WB-50, which could collect debris samples at thirty thousand feet, five thousand feet higher than the WB-29. Concern that debris from some atomic bombs might be carried in fast-moving airstreams at very high altitudes, with little fallout to the altitudes patrolled by the WB-50, led to the use of T-33 jet trainers for sampling operations, starting with a July 12 mission out of Yokota Air Base in Japan. The T-33 would not be the only aerial supplement to the WB-29s and WB-50s.[28]

GIVEN THE NUMBER and diversity of Soviet tests in 1955, the ground and aerial collection systems operated by the United States and Britain received a good workout, confirming the utility of the multiple means of detection. On July 29, the date of the first Soviet test of 1955 (Joe-15), the Ankara station as well as two additional acoustic sites detected signs of a possible low-yield explosion, in the area of 5 kilotons. Analysis of aerial samples confirmed that despite initial British skepticism due to the failure of its Pakistan station to detect any sign of a test, an atomic blast had been detected. There was no disagreement between the United States and Britain over the reality of Joe-16, the 12-kiloton test of August 2. That morning two British and two American stations detected what appeared to be an explosion of some sort, first picked up by acoustic sensors and seismic signals. That the event was an atomic test was subsequently confirmed by aerial debris, although the debris was apparently not suitable for extensive analysis. In both cases the initial estimates of yield overstated the power of the blasts. The yield of the second test was estimated at between 15 and 60 kilotons, with 30 kilotons being most likely, a figure 250 percent greater than the actual yield.[29]

The shift in test sites from Semipalatinsk to Novaya Zemlya did not prevent either U.S. or British acoustic and seismic stations from detecting Joe-17, an underwater test on September 21. Conclusions as to the time and day of the test were based on seismic data, while the judgment that the explosion probably occurred underwater was the result of examining both seismic and acoustic data. U.S. analysts concluded that since there was a large discrepancy between the strength of the seismic signal and that of the acoustic signal, the explosion was probably "well tamped" as the result of having taken place underwater. They noted that at the apparent location of the test the depth of the water was between one hundred and two hundred feet. Once again, they significantly overestimated the yield of the 3.5-kiloton blast, concluding that the "true yield [is] on the order of 20 kilotons."[30]

The detection system missed one test entirely, a low-yield detonation that occurred on August 5, though it did not miss the final two Soviet tests of 1955. The first of those tests did not come as a surprise to Britain, nor presumably the United States. There had been evidence for two months, minister of defense Selwyn Lloyd informed British prime minister Anthony Eden on November 7, that "the Russians were preparing to carry out a large scale nuclear explosion." At dawn of the previous day British stations in the United Kingdom and Pakistan detected the large explosion. Varied types of U.S. stations also detected the blast and contributed in different ways to characterizing it. Electromagnetic data provided the time; seismic data, the location (near Semipalatinsk); and acoustic data, the best estimate of yield—200 kilotons, an estimate that was reasonably close to the actual 250-kiloton yield.[31]

Analysis of the acoustic data obtained from the thermonuclear test of November 22, Joe-19, also helped produce an estimate—1.7 megatons—that was very close to the actual yield of 1.6 megatons. Other detection techniques allowed the U.S. analysts to go beyond simply announcing that a test had taken place. Radiochemical analysis of the debris confirmed the thermonuclear nature of the test. Electromagnetic data established the time, while seismic data pinpointed the location. The height at which the bomb detonated was estimated through analysis of seismic signals and the debris.[32]

Debris from one or both of the November tests, most probably the November 22 blast, was also collected by modified B-36 aircraft, which sampled some of the gases released during a nuclear explosion, at altitudes up to forty thousand feet. Missions using the B-36 were dubbed Sea Fish. The first was flown from Guam by the 6th Bomb Wing, while the second took off from Fairchild Air Force Base in Spokane. Both missions succeeded in bringing back debris for analysis.[33]

THE PROGRAM to determine the amount of krypton-85 being emitted by Soviet plutonium production reactors into the atmosphere, designated Music, continued in 1955, but was also a source of contention with America's closest nuclear intelligence ally, Great Britain, for the United States was more content with the utility of the program than the British were. In a 1953 estimate on Soviet capabilities for attacking the United States, the CIA had claimed that while estimates of Soviet U-235 production were subject to large uncertainties, the estimates for plutonium production were "reasonably firm." Even so, the authors suggested that the numbers they provided for the Soviet stockpile for the three years beginning in mid-1953 (120, 200, 300) could be as much as one-third less than the actual numbers, or twice as high, giving the "uncertainty in the evidence concerning the production of fissionable material" as their prime reason.[34]

But the British were also skeptical of the reliability of the Music effort, and annoyed at American postponements of meetings to discuss the issue. A conference had originally been scheduled for October 1954, and then put off until January 1955. When that meeting was also postponed, and the Americans suggested rescheduling for June, a senior British official wrote in a confidential memo that "there are many difficulties in making the assessment, for example how much gas is produced, and what happens to it, from U.S. and U.K. production, how much is produced, and what happens to it, from U.S. trials, and how the gas is distributed in the atmosphere."[35]

He continued that "this is a sorry tale. We ourselves need to take decisions urgently to continue or close a number of our overseas stations engaged in this programme. We have considerable doubts whether the programme continues to be worthwhile in view of the possible margins of error in the assessments resulting from it, but the assessment of the Russian plutonium stock is fundamental to intelligence on their total weapons supply."[36] Eventually, the differences between the allies with regard to estimating plutonium production would be resolved, but it would take several more years.[37]

OVER THE COURSE of 1956, there were eight tests at the Semipalatinsk test site, including two thermonuclear ones with yields of 900 kilotons. Meanwhile, the United States would seek to extend its network of ground stations that could provide data on the occurrence, location, and yield of such tests. The first overseas electromagnetic pulse station, apparently located in Pakistan, began operations in August 1956. Reestablishing a nuclear detection capability in Iran, involving either seismic or electromagnetic detection, was also discussed. While the 1955 site survey in Norway led to the conclusion that none of the sites were suitable for a seismic station, in 1956 the possibility of establishing an electromagnetic pulse facility in the vicinity of the Rygge Air Base southeast of Oslo became a subject of discussion between the two governments.[38]

But the most important development that year in the U.S. quest to monitor Soviet nuclear activities involved an aircraft whose nuclear intelligence mission was not its most important. On July 4, Hervey Stockman took off from Wiesbaden, Germany, in a plane designated the U-2, which he guided over Poznań, Poland, before heading for Belorussia. The next leg of his mission included a turn north to take him over Leningrad, where Soviet submarines were being built in the city's shipyards. He also overflew several major military airfields before heading back to Germany.[39]

The concept for the aircraft Stockman was flying originated with Kelly Johnson of Lockheed Aircraft, and was strongly supported by key presidential advisers Edwin Land and James Killian. Their support led to a program code-named Aquatone and managed by the CIA's Richard Bissell, a special assistant to agency director Allen Dulles. The plane produced by Johnson and his staff at the secretive Lockheed "Skunk Works" in Burbank could fly at 70,000 feet, at a speed of 500 knots, to a range of 3,000 nautical miles, with a pilot as the lone crew member. The special focal-length camera it carried could photograph objects as small as a man within a strip 200 miles wide by 2,500 miles long.[40]

Stockman's mission, the first for a U-2 over Soviet territory, was followed by another four overflights within a week. Among the targets were Moscow, a bomber test facility at Ramenskoye airfield outside of the capital, bomber bases, the Kaliningrad missile plant, the Fili airframe plant, and the Khimki rocket-engine plant. Those flights were followed by a hiatus, decreed by President Dwight Eisenhower in response to unexpected Soviet protests of the overflights, which the CIA had not expected to be detected. It would be November before the next U-2 lifted off on a mission that would take it over Soviet territory, and even then it was under presidential orders to stay as close to the border as possible, a flight path that precluded photographing possible atomic installations located in the center of the country or in Siberia.[41]

U-2 activity in the summer of 1957 would be much more extensive, with targets well within the interior of the Soviet Union and China. Flying from Incirlik Air Base in Turkey, Lahore Air Base in Pakistan, and Atsugi Air Base in Japan during a twenty-three-day period in August, the spy planes conducted Operation Soft Touch—seven overflights of the Soviet Union and two of the People's Republic of China. Those overflights would substantially add to the U.S. intelligence community's knowledge of not only Soviet military forces and industrial capability but also its nuclear facilities.[42]

Soft Touch targets included the Soviet space launch facility (later known as Tyuratam), the antiballistic missile radar test site at Sary Shagan, and the aircraft construction facilities in Omsk and Novosibirsk, as well as nuclear installations selected by the Ad Hoc Requirements Committee, responsible for selecting targets for U-2 missions, in late May. The most important central Asian and Siberian atomic targets were near Krasnoyarsk, Semipalatinsk, and Tomsk. In July, Henry Lowenhaupt was instructed "to work up target briefs for all atomic targets in the enormous geographical area of central Asia and Siberia." Because of the secrecy surrounding the U-2 program, Lowenhaupt did his work in the "Blue Room," a small centrally located secure area that was actually painted light green.[43]

Lowenhaupt's work involved selecting a flight path that would allow photography of the highest-priority targets as well as coverage of as many of the lower-priority targets as possible. Those lower-priority targets included the uranium concentration plants in the Fergana Valley, including one near Taboshar, and another near Andizhan—facilities that had been located thanks to a 1947 refugee who had driven a bread truck to each of them. The job required familiarity with the defector, refugee, espionage, and technical intelligence reports.[44]

In putting together the target brief for Krasnoyarsk, Lowenhaupt had, in addition to the the reports from Icarus, the testimony of a German prisoner of war who had spent several years there as a construction worker. Imagery was also recovered, earlier in the year, from the short-lived Genetrix balloon program, which commenced and ended in 1956 and had involved camera-carrying balloons sailing over Soviet territory. The few pieces of hard intelligence actually produced by the program included photographs of the Krasnoyarsk area, which showed an enormous construction effort—new apartment houses, laboratories, warehouses, machine shops, and a vast mining enterprise. Higher-resolution U-2 images, it was hoped, would reveal more information about what was actually going on at the site.[45]

Although the Semipalatinsk test site was also on the target list, there was considerable uncertainty about its precise location. To come up with specific coordinates for the U-2 pilot to overfly, Lowenhaupt asked Donald Rock, Northrup's deputy at AFOAT-1, to compute the average of the seismic epicenters of the five highest-yield detonations in the target area. The result was "a spot in the featureless desert some seventy miles due west of Semipalatinsk," Lowenhaupt recalled.[46]

But the primary nuclear target was the Siberian Chemical Combine, Tomsk-7, located nine miles northwest of Tomsk. While Kurchatov knew exactly where it was and what went on there, Lowenhaupt did not. He had only a minimal amount of information about its location and purpose, owing to the city's closure in 1952 and the inability of attachés to photograph it from the Trans-Siberian Railroad. While there had been a number of comments in intelligence reports suggesting the presence of something related to atomic energy in the vicinity of Tomsk, in 1957 "the resulting evidence . . . was all contained in just three reports, two of which did not inspire much confidence, and the analysis of a fur hat," Lowenhaupt would recall a decade later.[47]

The latest report conveyed the comments of a German claiming to have been employed as a blacksmith in Tomsk in 1955. He had told his army interrogator that the local residents had suggested, tongue in cheek, that "Atomsk" would be a more appropriate name for the city, and that there was an underground secret plant to the northeast of the Tomsk railroad station.[48]

Earlier, another returned German informed a British interrogator that he had heard of an industrial unit that "manufactured fillings for atomic weapons locally known as the Post Box," and had seen a large building in Tomsk with all its windows barred and a large sign identifying it as "Information Office, Personnel Department, Post Box." Subsequently, he mentioned that while riding a bus, he had seen railway trains carrying coal, wood, and building materials entering the the closed area. He also reported that from a distance of about four to five miles north of Tomsk, he could see three large chimneys emitting smoke. His interrogator observed that the source was plagued by a very poor memory, appeared to be suffering from some kind of mental problem, and was preoccupied with emigrating to Canada.[49]

A more persuasive report came from another German, a returned prisoner of war. In 1949, he had been employed as a tailor in a small factory northwest of Beloborodova, about seven miles north of Tomsk. During his interrogation by air force intelligence officers, he claimed that in April or May 1949, about twelve thousand penal laborers were put to work in a fenced-off area between his factory and the village of Iglakovo, along the Tom River. Among his customers were military officers of the construction staff that managed the project who came to get their uniforms properly fitted. The tailor's Soviet supervisor told him that the officers would be supervising the construction of an atomic energy plant.[50]

A CIA officer, John R. Craig, also obtained physical evidence in the form of a fur hat that had been worn by one of the Germans who had recently lived in Tomsk. The hat was turned over to AFOAT-1 and the Atomic Energy Commission. Analysts concluded that its exterior contained fifty parts per billion of uranium that was, without a doubt, slightly enriched in U-235. They were able to eliminate the possibility that the uranium came from fallout or from a reactor. Tests for plutonium, radio-iodine, and separated lithium all came back with negative results. The hat was consistent with the hypothesis that somewhere in the Tomsk area, there was a uranium enrichment plant. While the U-235 may also be residue from fabrication of nuclear warhead components, the size of the atomic facility seemed, to Lowenhaupt, too large for that to be the case. It was also unlikely to be a reactor with an associated chemical plant or a lithium isotope separator. Lowenhaupt thus classified the target as a uranium separation plant and centered it on the spot where the German tailor had seen twelve thousand prisoners go to work.[51]

The Soft Touch missions began on August 4, and the missions of August 21 and 22 brought back key imagery of the Soviet nuclear targets. On August 21, pilot Sammy Snyder lifted off from Lahore Air Base and piloted his spyplane over part of the Semipalatinsk test facility and eventually on to Tomsk. On August 22, James Cherbonneaux also left Lahore and flew directly over the testing ground, and discovered why he had been given those coordinates. On several occasions he had overflown the U.S. test site in Nevada and was able to recognize a test site when he saw one beneath him—large circular areas that had been cleared and graded, with paved support roads connecting to distant block houses. A slight adjustment in his course took Cherbonneaux over the center of a cleared area, where he noticed a large isolated shot tower, with a nuclear weapon "cab" in the center. At one of the block houses, close enough to witness a blast but not suffer from it, he detected a number of parked vehicles. It occurred to Cherbonneaux that the tower might be holding a nuclear bomb about to detonate.[52]

Upon returning to Lahore, the relieved pilot told his debriefers what he had seen, but found his tale greeted with skepticism. While they were reluctant to credit Cherbonneaux's observation skills, they did believe the images he brought back, as well as the report they received within twenty-four hours that less than four hours after his overflight the eighth Soviet test of 1957, Joe-36, had occurred. The photographs showed the bomb and the aircraft that was used to drop it. They also showed evidence of a recent low-yield test.[53]

Two of the Soft Touch nuclear targets—Kyshtym and Krasnoyarsk—hid under cloud cover while U-2s were overhead. But Sammy Snyder brought back images of sufficient value to impress Allen Dulles and be shown to Eisenhower. The tailor's information about location was as accurate for Tomsk as Donald Rock's had been for Semipalatinsk. Allen Dulles is reported to have said, "You mean you really did know that something atomic was going on 'way out there in the wilds of Siberia!" Of course, knowing that *something* is going on is quite different from knowing *exactly* what is going on. The clear, vertical photographs of Tomsk provided plenty of surprises to the photointer-preters and nuclear intelligence analysts at CIA. The photographs revealed, in addition to the expected U-235 separation plant, a plutonium-producing reac-tor area and a plutonium chemical separation facility in midconstruction.[54]

The extent of the atomic enterprise at Tomsk-7 was clear from the mis-sion report, which noted that the installation "covers an irregular shaped area of about 40 square miles on the right bank of the Tom River. No single energy complex in the western world includes the range of processes taking place here." It went on to specify that "on the west edge of the area, a large thermal power plant with an estimated capacity of 400 megawatts is undergoing fur-ther expansion. . . . East of this plant is . . . the feed and production section and gaseous diffusion plants. One gaseous diffusion building is uncompleted. On the east edge is . . . the reactor area. One of the two reactors appears to be in the final stages of construction. . . . On the northeast edge a plutonium chem-ical separation area is uncompleted."[55]

Full "exploitation" of the Tomsk imagery was not an overnight process and involved far more than simply identifying the key facilities of the com-plex. While obtaining the imagery was the dangerous part, turning it into fin-ished intelligence was the hard part. It took Richard Kroeck, from the agency's Photographic Intelligence Center, a full five months to complete his interpre-tation of the photographs that were snapped in a matter of minutes. Working along with Kroeck was the OSI's William F. Howard, who directed the com-plementary engineering analysis. The combined efforts provided the agency with an evaluation of not only what facilities could be found in those forty square miles, but also what was inside them, their interrelationships, and how it all worked.[56]

THE NUCLEAR WEAPON CAB that Cherbonneaux had seen during his overflight was for a low-yield device that was tested on September 13, the third test since his mission. The Soviet test program for 1957 concluded in late December after sixteen tests, the most powerful being one of the four con-ducted on Novaya Zemlya—a 2.9-megaton blast on October 6. That Arctic island was the site of five more tests during the first three months of the new year, with yields ranging from 40 kilotons to 1.5 megatons. Although Semi-palatinsk could not compete with its northern neighbor in terms of the size of its blasts, it doubled the frequency of testing, with ten between the first of January and March 22.[57]

The fifteen tests in early 1958 provided the usual variety of signals and debris associated with such events. A significant contribution to U.S. understanding of the Arctic tests was made by a detachment from the Strategic Air Command (SAC). SAC had tried to usurp the CIA's control of the U-2 program and came away with the responsibility for noncovert overflights. The detachment flew specially modified U-2s, designated U-2A-1s, from Eielson Air Force Base in Alaska as part of Operation Toy Soldier. The modifications included a new hatch for the equipment bay, which contained a device to gather gaseous samples and store them in six spherical, shatterproof bottles. The hatch also carried an air scoop connected to a filter paper system, which allowed four filter papers to be rotated, placing a fresh one in front of the airduct at appropriate times. The U-2 itself had an advantage over other planes in that it could operate at substantially higher altitudes, where the debris from thermonuclear, megaton explosions rose and where the winds were minimal and the airflow more stable.[58]

The deployment to Eielson began on January 30, with the first three of the ten modified U-2s assigned to SAC. Almost everyday over the next two months its pilots flew "long and boring" missions that frequently lasted eight hours or more, taking their planes far to the north, over Point Barrow, where the fallout from the Arctic tests usually appeared within a day. The SAC U-2 flights from Eielson were supplemented by CIA flights, also involving modified U-2s, along a track north from Atsugi.* Initially, the samples brought back to Eielson were sent to the AFOAT-1 laboratory at McClellan Air Force Base, but eventually Eielson had a lab of its own, since the very short half-lives of some of the radioactive samples demanded quick analysis.[59]

Within a month after the March 22 test, another station joined the growing network of U.S. and allied ground stations dedicated to monitoring Soviet testing. Near the end of 1957, the United States had made another approach to Norway, this time proposing establishment of an electromagnetic station, in the form of a ten-ton trailer requiring between six and ten operators, to help monitor the Arctic tests. Within a few months the allies were able to agree on establishing a Norwegian-manned, American-financed station at Hoybukt-moen. The two nations agreed to pretend that the station, code-named Crock

---

* The CIA received the first five modified U-2s, and Detachment C began flying missions from Eielson in June 1957, before it began flying them from its home base at Atsugi. During a flight headed northeast along the Kurile Islands, CIA pilot John Shinn made the first interception of nuclear debris in a U-2. See Chris Pocock, *The U-2 Spyplane: Toward the Unknown* (Atglen, Pa.: Schiffer, 2000), p. 120.

Pot, was a "weather research station." On April 18, it became an around-the-clock operation.[60] But it would be a while before that monitoring station or any other detected a Soviet test.

On the last day of March, Soviet foreign minister Andrei Gromyko appeared before the Supreme Soviet and proposed that in order "to contribute in every way to the great goal of mankind's deliverance from the threat of atomic war . . . the Soviet Union should unilaterally cease the testing of all kinds of atomic and hydrogen weapons." In addition, he challenged the United States and Britain to do the same. Igor Kurchatov also addressed the legislative body, complaining that during World War II, America and Britain had conducted their work on the atomic bomb "under conditions of most strict secrecy and did not help us," resisting any temptation he might have had to add "at least not intentionally." He asserted that the casualties at Hiroshima and Nagasaki were needed by "American military politicians . . . to begin a campaign of unparalleled atomic blackmail and cold war against the USSR." He also offered reassurance that the Soviet Union possessed the means to detect "distant explosions of atomic and hydrogen bombs." Not surprisingly, the rubber-stamp legislative body approved a resolution declaring a moratorium.[61]

Soviet tests would not resume until September, but through the summer several U.S. analysts continued trying to unravel the Soviet atomic energy infrastructure, relying, rather significantly, on photographs provided by the secretive Soviets themselves. One of those analysts was OSI's Charlie Reeves, an MIT graduate who had worked his way through school as a heavyweight boxer and had been recommended to the CIA by the president of the New England Electric Power Company because of his professional experience and linguistic talent. In August 1958 Reeves was faced with the task of assembling data on suspected Soviet atomic energy facilities in the Urals, as a means of estimating the consumption of electric power at those sites. Such estimates could be used to gauge the production of fissionable materials, since a plant's production of such materials was directly proportional to the amount of power consumed.[62]

Reeves started with a single picture of the Sverdlovsk Central Dispatching Station of the Urals Electric Power System that appeared in the July issue of *Ogonek*, the Soviet equivalent of *Look*. The picture of the inside of the dispatching station showed what looked to Reeves like a schematic diagram of major power plants, with their transmission lines and user substations—all the information required for control of the entire Urals electric system. The CIA analyst then examined at least 103 articles in Soviet newspapers and technical journals, four reports of visits by delegations, eleven POW returnee reports, approximately twenty-five local photographs, as well as some of the photographs that had been obtained by the Genetrix program. Among the items consulted were the December 1948 issue of *Elektricheskiye Stantsii*, which contained a short report of a Moscow conference on a planned expansion of power in the Urals, and a 1958 book celebrating the fortieth anniversary of electric power in the Urals.[63]

As a result, by April 1959 Reeves was able to map out the power distribution network in the Urals and determine the approximate power supplied to three of the Soviet Union's most important facilities for producing fissile material. The U-235 production plant at Verkh Neyvinsk (Sverdlovsk-44) received 850 to 1,000 megawatts; the plutonium reactor at Kyshtym (Chelyabinsk-40), 105 to 195 megawatts; and the unidentified complex near Nizhnyaya Tura (Sverdlovsk-45), up to 100 megawatts.[64]

Another Soviet photo proved vital in enhancing U.S. understanding of the Tomsk-7 reactor, although this one was somewhat more difficult to obtain than the one that appeared in *Ogonek*. The same month that the Soviets resumed testing, they also participated in the two-week-long Second Conference on the Peaceful Uses of Atomic Energy in Geneva, Switzerland. Among the featured topics was controlled fusion research; among its themes was collaboration, with U.S. and Soviet scientists calling for world cooperation "to unravel the mysteries of fusion power for peace."[65]

Hoping to derive some useful intelligence about Soviet atomic energy developments, Charles Reichardt, the AEC's director of intelligence, went to the conference. From his temporary office at American delegation headquarters, he was prepared to serve as a liaison between intelligence officers and scientists attending the conference and to support intelligence collection activities, whether overt or clandestine. Henry Lowenhaupt was also there to assist, with files on the Soviet personalities attending, a list of what the Soviets had published on nuclear energy, and his memories of what U-2 imagery had shown about the nuclear facilities in Siberia.[66]

Opportunity arrived about halfway through the conference when the Soviets announced that an atomic power station "somewhere in Siberia" had just begun operations. The chief Soviet delegate, V. S. Emelyanov, told his audience that one of the six natural-uranium reactors planned for the station was already operating, but declined to pinpoint the location. When a reporter asked where to send a letter to plant workers, he offered to mail the letter himself. The announcement was followed by visual evidence, in the form of a seventeen-minute color film and related exhibit in the conference exhibition hall. The description of the facility as shown in the movie led Lowenhaupt to believe it could well be the one north of Tomsk that had shown up on U-2 photographs from August 1957.[67]

But the intelligence that could be derived from having a copy of the film was far greater than what could be obtained simply by viewing it. The Soviet delegation, however, would not let a copy out of its possession, particularly since I. I. Rabi, the head of the American delegation, had already promised the Soviets copies of all the U.S. movies shown at the conference. To get the most out of viewing the film, OSI's John R. Craig recruited a group of reactor design engineers, whose firm employed them to evaluate Soviet reactor engineering practices for the OSI, to watch the film, with each engineer looking and listening for specific items. They also proposed taking still photographs of the movie, using two Leica cameras and the very high-speed film Lowenhaupt and Craig had brought along.[68]

The results included detailed notes on the content of the film, along with photographs that turned out to be vital to subsequent analysis. Information was also gathered by non-AEC American delegates, some of whom had been asked by the CIA's Domestic Contact Service to inquire about specific subjects. Others were assigned specific "situational gambits" devised by an air force intelligence officer who was in contact with the CIA representatives at Geneva.[69]

Back in Washington, OSI's Frank McKeon began the analysis by comparing the photographs from Geneva with U-2 images of the Tomsk reactor. The objective was to understand the internal workings of the reactor in order to estimate how much plutonium it could produce—the plutonium that would go into Soviet nuclear warheads. Attaining that understanding required obtaining data on a multitude of items, including the number of fuel rods, reactor dimensions, turbine performance, and the flow of cooling water through the reactors.[70]

Producing such data demanded the application of an array of interpretation and research skills. In late October the agency's Photographic Intelligence Center contributed a one-page brief interpreting the content of the motion picture photography showing the outside of the reactor building. The center, working with photographs of the building's interior, was also able to provide measurements of the size of the reactor as well as the size of the blocks containing the fuel rods. The latter information, when combined with McKeon's conclusion that there were 2,100 fuel rods, led to the assessment that the reactor was graphite-moderated (since the average space between the 2,100 rods when placed in the twenty-six blocks that contained them averaged 8.5 inches—close enough, given measurement limitations, to the 8 inches expected for a graphite-moderated natural-uranium reactor).[71]

Charlie Reeves relied on his ability to read technical Russian fluently, as well as his research skills and his five-shelf library, to provide answers needed about the facility's turbines. Days were spent looking at engineering drawings of Russian turbines for a match to the ones shown in the Geneva photography. Neither the Leningrad VK-100-2 nor the Leningrad SVK-150 MW, a picture of which he found in his personal copy of *Energetecheskoe Stroitel'stvo SSSR Za 40 Let*, were it. But *Elektricheskiye Stantssi*, again, had the answer. This time it was the November 1957 issue. On page 46, he found the matching turbine and its specifications, which permitted an estimate of the power level of the reactor.[72]

All the intermediary findings led to the conclusion that the reactor would produce a small amount of electric power and a large quantity of plutonium. The analysis of the Geneva photography not only allowed a more detailed assessment of Tomsk, but also became, Lowenhaupt recalled, "the key to understanding Russian facilities for the production of plutonium for nuclear weapons."[73]

DURING THE SUMMER of 1959 the CIA continued its attempts, on the ground and in the air, to acquire more information on the Soviet nuclear program. No information was available from collection of debris, since the Soviets had followed President Dwight D. Eisenhower's declaration of a testing moratorium, which commenced after a U.S. test on October 31, 1958, with another of their own. Eisenhower hoped that the United States, the Soviet Union, and Britain, which also ceased testing, could negotiate a test ban treaty. The moratorium would continue until early September 1961, when the Soviets resumed testing, followed later that month by the United States.[74]

But there were other means of uncovering Soviet nuclear activities. On July 8, Allen Dulles and Richard Bissell met with President Eisenhower. When they left the White House that day, they had his approval for Operation Touchdown. The U-2 mission would depart from Pakistan and, after completing its mission, land in Iran. Its targets included the test ranges at Tyuratam and Sary Shagan, the Semipalatinsk proving ground, Dolon airfield and its Bear bombers, and the never-before-photographed Kyshtym.[75]

At six o'clock the following morning, pilot Marty Knutson took off from Peshawar Air Base, and while his U-2 was periodically detected by Soviet air defense radars, he was able to complete his mission and land in Iran. The imagery from the mission provided analysts of Soviet missile programs with valuable information, as it revealed the existence of a second launch complex under construction at Tyuratam. But the agency's nuclear intelligence analysts in OSI were disappointed. The key areas of interest at Kyshtym were almost entirely obscured by clouds.[76]

That summer Raymond Garthoff was working in the agency's Directorate of Intelligence. He had joined the agency in late 1957 and was assigned to the Office of National Estimates. His graduation from Princeton in 1948, shortly after his nineteenth birthday, was followed by graduate studies at Yale, where he learned to speak and read Russian. While at Yale he also served with the 469th Strategic Intelligence Research and Analysis Team, a military reserve unit that engaged in library research on aspects of Soviet war potential. Before the end of 1949, with his master's degree in hand, and his doctorate just a couple of years away, he was looking for a job. His search yielded three alternatives: teaching at Yale, working for the CIA, or joining the RAND Corporation. RAND was the winner, but by 1957 he was ready to join the CIA.[77]

On July 23, 1959, Garthoff arrived in the Soviet Union, part of the contingent touring the country with Vice President Richard Nixon. Garthoff's job was to serve as an interpreter for Vice Admiral Hyman Rickover, the head of the navy's nuclear propulsion program. But Garthoff came equipped with more than language skills. He spotted and photographed a large, and previously unidentified, munitions storage center near Novosibirsk. Near Sverdlovsk he noticed and covertly photographed from his airplane seat two new SA-2 antiaircraft missile sites. He also scooped up samples of soil and water from Novosibirsk, Beloyarsk, Sverdlovsk, and Pervouralsk, samples that he recalls as "contributing to our understanding of the pattern of Soviet nuclear activities in those key and inaccessible regions."[78]

Shortly after returning, he was asked by Sherman Kent, the head of the Office of National Estimates, if he would do it again. This time he would be interpreting for John McCone, the chairman of the AEC, who would shortly be leading a high-level delegation to visit a number of Soviet nuclear facilities. Garthoff agreed, unaware at the time that Soviet intelligence had discovered his position with the CIA, thanks to a Swedish officer working for the GRU.[79]

Part of his trip with McCone, which began on October 9, involved personal encounters with some of the key members of the Soviet atomic weapons program, including Igor Kurchatov at the Institute of Atomic Energy and A. I. Alikhanov at the Institute of Theoretical and Experimental Physics. The delegation also visited a uranium mine and uranium concentration and processing plant in the Ukraine. McCone, Garthoff, and other members of the delegation were first flown to Dnepropetrovsk, which was followed by a 120-mile drive to a uranium mine near Pervomaisk, and then to the processing plant at Zheltye Vody. To prevent the Americans from tracing their trip and determining exactly where they had been taken, the drive had been a long and circuitous one. It succeeded in confusing the visitors but failed in its objective. After arriving in the village near the uranium mill, they encountered some of the village's inhabitants, including some boys, about twelve years old, whom the KGB had apparently failed to brief. When Garthoff asked where they were, the boys promptly told him "Zheltye Vody." Their official hosts did provide detailed information on ore concentration, the separation process, and the purity of the product. But they had nothing to say about the current or cumulative quantity of production or about the mine's production as a percentage of total Soviet production.[80]

Despite the extra attention from the delegation's Soviet security escorts, Garthoff still managed to bring back some photographs. He came equipped with several cameras, including a CIA camera with fast black-and-white film as well as his personal camera with color film, both of which he used "liberally." He later recalled that his photographs of the mine tailings taken from ground level "complemented very well overhead [that is, U-2] photography." The two sets of images permitted a more accurate determination of the height of the tailings, and were valuable in allowing analysts to estimate the mine's cumulative production. Appreciation for his work would extend not only to the head of the Office of Central Reference, who wrote a glowing memorandum to Garthoff's boss at the national estimates office, but also to agency director Allen Dulles, who invited him to a luncheon at his Georgetown home.[81]

THE SUMMER OF 1959 also marked a change in name for the Washington headquarters and field units of the air force's nuclear monitoring organization. On July 7, AFOAT-1 became the Air Force Technical Applications Center (AFTAC) and the 1009th Special Weapons Squadron became the 1035th Field Activities Group (1035th FAG). AFTAC also had an unclassified nickname — Project Clear Sky. However, its mission, as was AFOAT-1's, was officially classified.[82]

The name change was prompted by a presidential award Doyle Northrup received in January 1959 for his work at AFOAT-1. Northrup would recall in an oral history interview years later that the "citation was so *directly exactly* what I had been doing — and it had always been classified secret — that the Air Force practically went into a tizzy." Among those most upset was Maj. Gen. Jermain Rodenhauser, who had assumed command of the detection organization the previous August. According to Northrup, Rodenhauser went to the air force's chief of staff and said, "This is a terrible security breach, and what we had better do is change the name." So AFOAT-1 became AFTAC, a change Northrup described as "really comical," explaining that he had "a list of all the [unclassified and easily available] Department of Defense telephone directory listings for all those years and it shows D.L. Northrup, Technical Director, Don Rock, Assistant Technical Director . . . and all of a sudden those people changed from AFSMW-1 to AFOAT-1 to AFTAC and that's supposed to fool somebody."[83]

At the time of the name change, AFTAC was concerned, even more than usual, with increasing its ability to detect nuclear detonations through means other than air sampling — because of the prospect of a prolonged atmospheric testing halt. Late the previous August, in 1958, President Eisenhower had proposed negotiations among the United States, Britain, and Soviet Union to permanently end nuclear testing. He also announced that the United States would halt testing for a year from the time negotiations began. The Soviets soon agreed to negotiations beginning on October 31. With that date looming, all parties began a round of tests. The Soviet test series, which started on

September 30 and ended on November 3, included twenty-one tests. Of the nineteen at Novaya Zemlya, six had yields of over 1 megaton.[84]

During, and shortly after those tests, AFTAC had improved its ability to detect and gather intelligence on them. By the end of 1958, the B-36s that had been used to conduct the Sea Fish high-altitude gas-sampling missions had been replaced by jet-powered B-52s. In addition, the T-33 sampling aircraft operated by the Alaskan Air Command and Pacific Air Forces was replaced with a RB-57, providing an additional sampling capability above fifty thousand feet. December also marked the commencement of seismic detection operations at Pinedale, Wyoming, and May 1959 saw the opening of a seismic station at Flin Flon, Canada—although the Crock Pot station in Norway had been closed the previous month due to its failure to produce the information expected.[85]

Throughout 1959, AFOAT-1/AFTAC was laying the groundwork for increasing its capabilities, both by expanding the number of stations using already developed techniques and by forging ahead with experimental work to validate new techniques. AFTAC would inform the State Department's special assistant for atomic energy of its interest in conducting a site survey in a particular country, which might be followed by a letter from the special assistant to the American ambassador asking his opinion on the wisdom of making such a request to his hosts.

In March 1959 the special assistant was Philip J. Farley, who notified John J. Muccio, the ambassador to Iceland, of "Air Force" interest in possibly establishing an electromagnetic station in the Langanes area of Northwest Iceland to improve coverage of "atomic events in the northwest quadrant of the USSR." Later in the month, an AFOAT-1 inquiry into the feasibility of establishing a detection station in East Pakistan, complementing the one in Lahore, brought back the response that there were no U.S. forces in the area to provide cover. Also rejected in the region were Cambodia, Laos, Malaya, Burma, and Singapore. South Vietnam was considered unlikely owing to the existing ceiling on military personnel. That left Thailand. At the end of the year the special assistant's office reviewed the possibility of seismic, acoustic, or electromagnetic stations in Thailand, Ceylon, and Ecuador and noted potential problems: the ambassador wanted to limit the number of American military personnel in Thailand, the government of Ceylon was "hanging by a thread," and the Ecuadorians might demand "an excessive *quid pro quo*."[86]

Despite such objections, Ceylon, Ecuador, Thailand, and a large number of other nations had been listed as part of AFTAC's expansion program, which had been approved by the Air Staff in the early fall. The expansion was expected to improve the ability to detect tests in the Southern Hemisphere or at high altitudes. The five-year program called for new electromagnetic, seismic, and acoustic stations. Stations employing a new technique—backscatter radar, which would detect the ionospheric disturbances caused by nuclear detonations at high altitudes—were also part of the plan. All together, it envisioned sixty-five stations being added to the existing network of thirty-five stations—stations located on every continent, in major countries, and on the most obscure islands.[87]

WHILE AFTAC endeavored to expand and improve its ground and aerial nuclear intelligence capabilities, the CIA tried to develop a revolutionary new intelligence capability—one that would significantly improve the spy agency's ability to monitor a large slice of Soviet military activities, including missile and bomb deployments, military exercises and troop movements, and nuclear activities ranging from uranium mining to reactor construction to test preparations.

The man who was responsible for implementing President Eisenhower's February 1958 decision to assign the CIA responsibility for developing a photographic reconnaissance satellite was Richard Bissell. As with the U-2, Bissell headed a CIA–air force–contractor program, code-named Corona, to develop the reconnaissance system. On February 28, 1959, a little over a year after the president's go-ahead, test launches began from Vandenberg Air Force Base in California. But it would not be until August 18 and 19, 1960, that a camera-equipped Corona satellite would be successfully placed in orbit, photograph targets in the Soviet Union and other denied areas, and return its images back to earth the next day via a film capsule that was ejected from the satellite and recovered in the air in the vicinity of Hawaii.[88]

The satellite's orbit allowed it to overfly the entire Soviet Union, at times passing only 116 miles above its target. The camera carried on that August flight was designated Keyhole-1 (KH-1), its forty-foot resolution being far inferior to that of the U-2. But the spyplane would not be flying over Soviet territory any more, because Soviet air defenses had shot down a U-2 piloted by Francis Gary Powers on May 1 in the vicinity of Sverdlovsk, preventing Kyshtym and a number of other important targets from being photographed that day. Fortunately, successful satellite missions were conducted on December 7–10, 1960, and June 16–19, 1961, using the KH-2 camera, with a resolution of about twenty-five feet. In August the first mission using the KH-3 camera, with a resolution that varied between twelve and twenty-five feet, flew, and of the final four successful missions of 1961, three would be KH-3 missions.[89]

Top priority for the early Corona missions were areas where intercontinental ballistic missiles might be deployed, for the U-2 missions had not been able to cover enough Soviet territory to determine whether there was a "missile gap," as Democrats had charged during the 1960 election year. Finding airfields with heavy bombers, which could reach the United States carrying atomic bombs, was the second priority. Nuclear energy targets were third. For the August 18 mission they included Kyshtym and Nizhnyaya Tura, the name by which Sverdlovsk-45 was known in the U.S. intelligence community.[90]

The Corona missions gave the army, navy, and CIA interpreters at the CIA-managed National Photographic Interpretation Center (NPIC)—which had been established in January 1961 as one of President Eisenhower's last acts—a reason for updating reports on assorted Soviet atomic energy complexes. A February report focused on the uranium metal plant and related facilities at Novosibirsk, comparing the more recent satellite images to those obtained by the U-2 photos from Soft Touch, a comparison that revealed a number of additions and changes.[91]

It sometimes took a while before a target showed itself to the Corona cameras. A forty-four-page report issued in June, concerning the uranium-mining and -milling complex at Mayli-Say in the Fergana Valley, apparently relied more on the older U-2 imagery and a study by the U.S. Geological Survey (of the area's geology) than on Corona images, possibly because the target was obscured by cloud cover. Throughout 1960 and a substantial part of 1961, clouds interfered with attempts to photograph Kyshtym. But during a September 1961 KH-3 mission, the clouds finally parted. The photographs showed that canals had been constructed to route the Techa River around Lake Kyzyl-tash and that two large cascaded basins with a combined area of approximately thirty miles had been created for retention and evaporation of drainage from the lake.[92]

Much earlier that year, in February, the CIA's espionage branch, the Directorate of Plans or Clandestine Service, had received a report of a possible accident at Kyshtym. The source had both relevant firsthand knowledge and hearsay evidence. The latter included reports from "several people that large areas north of Chelyabinsk were contaminated by radioactive waste from a nuclear plant operating at an unknown site near Kyshtym." The source also revealed that "it was general knowledge that the Chelyabinsk area had an abnormally high incident of cancers." Twenty years later a 1981 CIA report noted that the creation of the retention basins and construction of the bypass canals may have become necessary owing to the repeated release of "significant fission and activation products" from reactor operations and from site runoffs.[93]

THE IMAGES OBTAINED by U-2 overflights prior to May 1960 and acquired by Corona satellites since then, the data and debris gathered by the Atomic Energy Detection System, the analysis of open-source material (including official Soviet statements as well as newspapers and magazines), communications intelligence, and human intelligence, both overt and clandestine, all went into producing a 1961 national intelligence estimate that was approved by the U.S. Intelligence Board on October 5, 1961: NIE 11-2-61,

The Soviet Atomic Energy Program. Estimates with identical titles had been published since at least 1956, with each year's edition providing additional certain knowledge of the Soviet program as well as revised estimates of key parameters such as the quantity of fissile material produced.[94]

The 1961 report, which consisted of forty-five pages of text and twenty-five pages of photographs and maps, covered all aspects of the Soviet program: organization, nuclear reactors, nuclear materials production, nuclear weapons, possible allocations of fissionable material to weapons stockpiles, and research laboratories. Neither human nor communications intelligence provided information on the Soviet designations for the country's secret cities—for example, there is no reference to "Arzamas-16" or "Chelyabinsk-40." But more importantly, the estimate reported on the existence of atomic activities at such sites and specified the type of activity.[95]

The report noted the presence of the gaseous diffusion plants at Tomsk and Verkh Neyvinsk, and suggested there was probably a third one at Angarsk, about which "considerable information" had become available in the preceding year. Angarsk had begun operations in 1954, but the authors reported that "we have been unable to confirm U-235 production in this area." It estimated that the Soviets had produced about 167,000 pounds of U-235 by mid-1961, although the navy's intelligence chief dissented, arguing that it was based on assumptions not supported by the available evidence.[96]

The two sites that the estimate unequivocally identified as being associated with plutonium production, and provided a bit of detail about, were Kyshtym and Tomsk. The authors also noted that the site near Krasnoyarsk (Krasnoyarsk-26, where production had begun in August 1958) and "perhaps that at Angarsk" (where it had never taken place) might also include some plutonium production facilities. Outside of those locations it was doubtful there were any other large plutonium production facilities, since it "was unlikely that any sites large enough to have significant plutonium production capacity would have remained wholly unassociated by intelligence with the Soviet atomic energy program." Indeed, there were no other plutonium production sites.[97]

The secret city of Sarov was, as noted, apparently first detected by communications intelligence, and then identified as the principal site for nuclear weapon research, design, and development. The estimate reported that the U-2 images taken in February 1960 of the area revealed "a large and elaborate nuclear weapon research and development complex comparable in size to the combined facilities of the Los Alamos Scientific Laboratory and the Sandia Corporation in Albuquerque." It was also noted that recent analysis of July 1959 U-2 photography indicated the existence of a facility near Kasli that was "probably concerned with nuclear weapon research and development." What the analysts had found was Chelyabinsk-70, the Soviet Union's second weapons design bureau.[98]

Those with access to the national intelligence estimate could also read about Semipalatinsk, view a photograph, and examine drawings of the site — one of which showed the main shot area and the associated facilities, and another which showed the layout of the apparent ground zero. The text reported that three facilities had been constructed outside the fenced shot area since 1957. They consisted of a new research facility (most probably associated with laboratory experiments related to nuclear weapons development and located to the northwest of the main shot area), a rectangular grid pattern about three miles by five miles in size, and an apparent ground zero also located to the north-northwest of the main shot area.[99]

PRODUCING A NATIONAL ESTIMATE is usually a long and involved effort. And during the last part of that process, the test ban moratorium came to an end, with a Soviet weapons test at Semipalatinsk on September 1. During the halt in testing, while the United States, Britain, and the Soviet Union had been negotiating a possible test ban, some had been concerned that the Soviet Union was using the negotiations as means of halting U.S. and British testing while secretly conducting its own tests. During a December 1960 interview with *U.S. News & World Report*, AEC chairman John McCone stated that he believed the Soviets were probably conducting clandestine tests, possibly underground, in order to gain on the United States.[100]

The possibility of cheating and the need to detect it had, of course, occurred to the U.S. intelligence community, even before the moratorium had been declared. In December 1957, the community had produced a special national estimate on the topic: *Feasibility and Likelihood of Soviet Evasion of a Nuclear Test Moratorium*. The analysis focused on the ability of the Atomic Energy Detection System to sense an explosion and confirm that it was a nuclear blast. The estimators concluded that the existing system had an excellent capability (90 to 100 percent) for detecting airbursts of 10 kilotons or greater, a good capability (60 to 90 percent) with respect to 5- to 10-kiloton airbursts, and a fair one (30 to 60 percent) for 3- to 5-kiloton bursts. There was a poor capability (0 to 30 percent) for airbursts less than 3 kilotons.[101]

The report also observed that while it was conceivable that tests could be staged in remote areas such as Antarctica or southern waters, "such possibilities would probably be excluded by the Soviets, since various intelligence collection efforts could be almost certain to spot the activities which would be associated with test preparations, if not the test itself." With respect to establishing a detonation's nuclear origin, the estimate noted that it would be necessary to obtain radioactive debris, which was "generally possible" for tests involving fission conducted between the surface and thirty-five to forty-five thousand feet.[102]

Herbert Scoville, the head of the CIA's OSI, reported McCone's remarks to CIA chief Allen Dulles and noted that the intelligence community had "reached the conclusion that balancing the potential gains versus the risk of detection, it appears unlikely that the Soviets have been conducting clandestine nuclear tests." He also mentioned that he had recently heard an air force briefing purporting to provide evidence of such clandestine tests, and that while the agency was making a detailed analysis of the material presented, he believed that "the Air Force has provided no significantly new information and has primarily twisted the raw data to prove a prejudgment."[103]

In late April, Dulles, and then the U.S. Intelligence Board, approved a national intelligence estimate titled *The Possibility of Soviet Nuclear Testing During the Moratorium*. The three-page analysis examined the technical motivations and political considerations affecting Soviet actions, the techniques that could be employed to minimize the risk of detection, and the evidence of possible testing. With regard to the latter, it noted that the United States had collected no nuclear debris or other conclusive evidence of Soviet nuclear tests since November 3, 1958. Other than nuclear debris, conclusive evidence might be hard to come by since "other indicators of testing activity are susceptible to alternative explanations." There had been seismic events in the Soviet Union that could have been the result of tests, and there had been indications from other intelligence sources that raised the possibility of Soviet evasion by underground testing, but those indications "are also susceptible to alternative explanations."[104]

The most suspicious evidence concerned the area around Osh, and Semipalatinsk. The data concerning Osh, undoubtedly measurements gathered by AFTAC seismic stations, was considered most consistent with the Soviets' having conducted one or more detonations using high explosives in the winter of 1959–1960, as part of their seismic improvement program or to study methods of clandestine testing. U-2 photography during April 1960 showed evidence of testing after the U-2 mission in August 1957. But those who prepared the estimate considered the most likely explanation to be that the tests had occurred between August 1957 and November 1958. The assessment that the Soviets had conducted tests during the moratorium "cannot be drawn from the available evidence," they concluded—a judgment disputed by the intelligence chiefs of the armed services and Joint Staff.[105]

On August 30, 1961, a U.S. listening post on Cyprus, probably one of the stations that monitored radio and television broadcasts for the Foreign Broadcast Information Service, picked up a Tass transmission of items for the provincial papers that included a statement scheduled for release at seven that evening. The statement announced that the Soviet Union was going to resume nuclear testing. An alert monitor had "fished this item out of the reams of copy being teletyped from Moscow to the Caucasus in Cyrillic characters," Glenn Seaborg recalled. About two hours later, the information had reached the State Department, and not long after that the president knew.[106]

U.S. detection stations were probably notified within twenty-four hours. In any event, as Herbert Scoville, in his capacity as chairman of the JAEIC, reported on September 1, an explosion had been detected earlier that day by three acoustic stations. The estimated location was in the vicinity of Semipalatinsk while the estimated yield was in the 50- to 500-kiloton range, with a best estimate of 150 kilotons. The Soviets had indeed tested in the vicinity of Semipalatinsk, but the yield of 16 kilotons was far lower than the initial estimates relying solely on acoustic measurements.[107]

BEFORE THE YEAR was out, another fifty-eight tests would follow, almost all conducted at either Novaya Zemlya or Semipalatinsk—the exceptions were a small number of missile-related tests at Kapustin Yar. Herbert Scoville was busy issuing statements like those he issued on September 1 and November 4, the latter reporting the detection of two explosions. The November 3 detonation, apparently with a yield of less than 10 kilotons, was an atmospheric blast in the vicinity of Semipalatinsk, first reported by two acoustic and ten electromagnetic stations. The second explosion, on November 4, took place on the east coast of Novaya Zemlya, the JAEIC chairman reported. The estimated yield was between 1 and 6 megatons, most probably 3 megatons. Its power was certainly sufficient to light up much of the U.S. detection network, with signals being reported from eight acoustic, nine seismic, and ten electromagnetic stations.[108]

But that test was little more than a stick of dynamite compared to the Soviet test of October 30, also at Novaya Zemlya. Andrei Sakharov had appealed to Nikita Khrushchev and the rest of the Soviet leadership to cancel the test of the bomb he had helped design. The device, designated RDS-220, was about 6.5 feet in diameter and 26 feet long, and weighed about twenty-five tons. To ensure that the bomber dropping it did not become one of its victims, the bomb relied on an enormous set of four parachutes. In its most powerful form it could explode with the force of 100,000,000 tons of TNT—100 megatons. Concerns over the possible effects of such a blast led Khrushchev and his colleagues to order its yield reduced to a still impressive 50 megatons.[109]

Decades later, Sakharov recalled being in Moscow at the beginning of October 1961 to discuss calculations concerning the "Big Bomb," and that it was assembled in a special workshop on top of a platform car. "A few days later, when everything was ready, the superstructure would be dismantled and, under the cover of darkness, the platform would be coupled to a special train that would transport the device along an open track all the way to the air-field where it would be loaded into the bomb bay of a waiting plane."[110]

On October 30, a specially modified Tu-95N bomber, flown by Maj. Andrei Durnovstev, took off with its payload, headed for a drop point over Novaya Zemlya. Sakharov sat by a telephone, waiting for news. A call that morning informed him that the plane had taken off. He recalled that he and his fellow scientists at Sarov "just couldn't keep our minds on our work. My colleagues were hanging around in the corridor, continually dropping in and out of my office." At noon he received another call and was told "there's been no communication with the test site or the plane for over an hour. Congratulations on your victory!"* Ninety minutes later, Sakharov received another call, learning that the mushroom cloud had reached a height of over forty miles.[111]

Due to the advance planning, the Soviet Tu-95 escaped without damage. The same could not be said for the specially equipped American plane monitoring the test. There appears to have been significant prior warning of the planned test date from intelligence sources—human intelligence, communications intelligence, or both—and from Khrushchev himself, who had bragged openly that the Soviets could detonate a 100-megaton bomb. After discussions between Scoville, acting in his capacity as JAEIC chairman, and Gerald Johnson, the assistant to the secretary of defense for atomic energy, a crash program had been initiated to modify a KC-135 to carry broadband electromagnetic and special optical equipment to monitor the test. The modification effort, code-named Speedlight, was carried out under the supervision of Doyle Northrup by an air force unit known as Big Safari, with headquarters at Wright-Patterson Air Force Base in Ohio, and detachments at the headquarters of key aircraft manufacturers. By October 27 the plane was ready to depart for its overseas staging base.[112]

Given Novaya Zemlya's location in the Arctic, it was possible for the Speedlight aircraft to fly relatively close to the test area. Given the force of the explosion, it proved almost too close. The plane returned not only with the data it had been sent to gather but also with a scorched fuselage. Had the Soviets decided on a 100-megaton blast, the plane and its pilots would not have made it back.[113]

The Bethe Panel scrutinized the data and concluded, correctly, that the blast exceeded the 50-megaton objective by 7 megatons, large enough to ensure that "the whole earth's atmosphere just vibrated for days after," Northrup recalled. The panel also determined that the yield had been constrained by encasing the weapon in lead rather than uranium.[114]

---

* The lack of communication was a sign of success because ionized particles released by a powerful explosion interfere with radio transmissions. The more powerful the explosion, the longer the communications gap. Andrei Sakharov, *Memoirs* (New York: Knopf, 1990), p. 219.

In the aftermath of the huge blast there were repercussions in the Soviet Union and the United States. Khrushchev asked his scientists about the targets against which such a bomb could be used. West Germany could not be on the target list, they told him, because the westerly winds would blow the fallout over East Germany, inflicting damage not only on the East Germans but, more importantly, on the Soviet forces stationed there. On the other hand, Britain, Spain, France, and the United States were viable targets.[115]

In the United States, in addition to leading to the production of similarly modified planes, the success of the initial Speedlight mission produced a letter of appreciation from President Kennedy to Robert McNamara, asking his defense chief to "extend his sincere appreciation to the personnel" who participated in the operation. "The expeditious preparation of the complex technical equipment and the bold execution of this operation are excellent examples of the effective use of our resources. I am proud of those who took part in this operation," Kennedy continued.[116]

CIA and other intelligence analysts evaluated the data collected from the Soviet tests of September and October and used it in a national estimate on Soviet strategic military posture that was completed in November. The estimate broke down the tests by their differing purposes, which included evaluating complete weapon systems, researching and developing future offensive systems, as well as obtaining weapons effects information needed to develop an antiballistic missile system. The new national estimate concluded that the new tests had given the Soviets increased confidence in weapons design, and had augmented their understanding of thermonuclear weapon technology and weapons effects. In addition, the "1961 test series will permit the Soviets to fabricate and stockpile, during the next year or so, new weapons of higher yields in the weight classes presently available," which had significant implications for the Soviet ability to deliver their warheads to U.S. targets via missile rather than via slower and more vulnerable aircraft.* The analysts correctly concluded that the October 31 detonation was a test of a 100-megaton device at reduced yield so as to limit fallout.[117]

WHEN PRESIDENT John F. Kennedy wrote to Robert McNamara, praising those involved in Speedlight, the Soviet Union was no longer the only

---

* By November 1961 those with access to the latest national intelligence estimate on Soviet strategic forces knew that the feared missile gap did not exist, knowledge that was the direct result of the Corona missions. But, of course, Soviet intercontinental ballistic missiles (ICBMs) were inevitable, and Soviet tests that revealed the relationship between warhead size and yield also revealed Soviet ICBM options with regard to missile range, yield, and size.

Communist state whose nuclear aspirations were of concern. There was no doubt that the People's Republic of China was seeking to join the nuclear club, despite the substantial entrance fee—in terms of men, money, and resources. By late 1961 the club included not only its charter members, the United States and the Soviet Union, but also Great Britain and France. Britain had joined in October 1952, with a test off the northwest coast of Australia, and France in February 1960, when it detonated an atomic bomb in the Sahara Desert.[118]

But while French acquisition of the bomb was certainly not viewed with pleasure by Eisenhower or his successor, China's pursuit of atomic weapons was far more distressing. Walt Rostow, who served as head of the State Department's policy-planning council during part of Kennedy's brief presidency, and then as national security adviser under Lyndon Johnson, recalled that Kennedy considered a possible Chinese nuclear test as "likely to be historically the most significant and worst event of the 1960s."[119] That event had its origins midway through the previous decade.

chapter four

MAO'S EXPLOSIVE THOUGHTS

BY JANUARY 1955, Mao Tse-tung and the Chinese Communist Party had been in power for over five years, after having driven the Nationalist regime of Chiang Kai-shek off the mainland and onto the island of Taiwan. It was during the second week of January that Premier Zhou Enlai met with nuclear scientist Qian Sanqiang, economic affairs official Bo Yibo, and two representatives of the Ministry of Geology, Li Siguang and Liu Jie. Qian, the head of the Institute of Physics, had graduated from the physics department of Qinghua University in 1936, and spent the war years in German-occupied France, doing theoretical work with Irène Joliot-Curie and earning his doctorate from the University of Paris. He had returned to China in 1948, becoming a professor of physics at Qinghua University. Qian provided Zhou with a tutorial on atomic weaponry, as well as an overview of the nation's nuclear-related manpower and facilities. Zhou interrogated Liu about the geology of uranium, and reviewed the basics of atomic reactors and weapons with Qian. At the end of the meeting, Zhou told his guests to prepare for a repeat performance, this time for Mao and other senior officials.[1]

On January 15, Mao, senior members of the party's Politburo, and others met in a conference room in Zhongnanhai, a massive walled compound in Beijing, where China's Communist rulers resided. There was only one topic on the agenda: the possibility of initiating a nuclear weapons program. Li, Liu, and Qian were there, and it was not long after the meeting began that they were lecturing China's senior leaders on nuclear physics and uranium geology. In addition to information, the scientists brought along some uranium and a Geiger counter for Politburo members to try out.[2]

At the end of the meeting there were toasts from Mao and Zhou, with the premier calling on the scientists "to exert themselves to develop China's nuclear program," which was given the code designation 02. But it was not the clicks of the Geiger counter that had led Mao to decide, before the meeting ended, that China should acquire nuclear weapons. There had been a war in Korea, whose endgame included a U.S. threat to employ nuclear weapons if an armistice could not be worked out, the confrontation over the Nationalist-held islands of Quemoy (Jinmen) and Matsu (Mazu) that began the previous fall, the U.S.-Taiwan defense treaty signed in December, and a desire for international prestige and influence.[3]

Mao's decision was followed on July 4 by the Politburo's appointment of the unimaginatively named Three-Member Group, consisting of Nie Rongzhen, Chen Yun, and Bo Yibo, to serve as a policy board for the nuclear program. Nie, a senior battlefield commander during the revolution, had served as acting chief of the General Staff from 1950 to 1953. Chen, a senior member of the Politburo as well as vice premier, played a significant role in industrial development. Bo was apparently chosen for his managerial acumen. Two other organizations were established that month to implement Mao's decision. The Third Bureau, which remained under the Ministry of Geology until November 1956, was to lead the search for uranium. The deceptively named Bureau of Architectural Technology was to supervise construction of the experimental nuclear reactor and cyclotron, which was to be provided by the Soviet Union.[4]

On November 16, 1956, the Third Ministry of Machine Building, headed by Song Renqiong, was established to direct China's nuclear industry. Song, who served as a senior commander and political commissar during the civil war, became responsible for the policy direction that had been provided by the Three-Member Group. Before the end of 1959, a reorganization would result in the Third Ministry becoming the Second Ministry of Machine Building, with eleven bureaus to oversee the various stages of atomic bomb production, from uranium mining to bomb design to testing.[5]

In 1958 a second crisis over the Taiwan Straits, as well as U.S. nuclear weapons deployments on Taiwan, reinforced Mao's belief that China needed an atomic arsenal. That July also marked the creation of the Beijing Nuclear Weapons Research Institute, China's temporary counterpart to Sarov and Los Alamos. Heading the institute was Li Jue, an administrator rather than a scientist, who would also be placed in charge of the nuclear weapons bureau (Ninth Bureau) of the Second Ministry.[6]

For the designs produced by the Beijing institute to progress beyond the blueprint stage, China needed uranium and facilities to turn the uranium into fissionable material and then into bombs. The first phase of that process began shortly after Mao's decision, when two prospecting teams, Team 309 and Team 519, were sent out to find uranium. By early 1958, their efforts had produced a list of eleven candidate sites, from which eight would be chosen for further investigation. In May, one thousand miners began construction, in Hunan province, of the Chenxian Uranium Mine.[7]

Institutions dedicated to research on the means of getting the most out of the mining effort were also established in 1958. At Hengyang, about 150 miles north of Chenxian, the Uranium Mining and Metallurgy Design and

Research Academy was created, to design hydrometallurgical plants and explore the mass production of uranium oxides. That August, construction began on the Hengyang Uranium Hydrometallurgy Plant (Plant 414, later 272), located on the banks of the Xiang River, at the site of a defunct political prison camp, which would process all the ores from Chenxian and other mines using magnetic separators.[8]

The Second Ministry also created the Uranium Mining and Metallurgical Processing Institute in Tongxian, a few miles east of Beijing, to engage in research on uranium ores and their processing. In August 1960 a subsidiary element of the institute, the Uranium Oxide Production Plant (Plant 2), was established to rapidly produce several tons of the oxide. A few months later the institute was also instructed to build a plant, Plant 4, for the production of uranium tetrafluoride.[9]

Construction also began in 1958 of two facilities earmarked to provide crucial material for China's uranium bombs. Baotou, in Inner Mongolia, about 445 miles from Beijing, became the site for the Baotou Nuclear Fuel Component Plant, also known as Plant 202, which would provide uranium tetrafluoride to be converted into uranium hexafluoride and used to produce enriched uranium. In October construction began on Plant 202's Uranium Tetrafluoride Workshop, and, in 1959, on the Lithium-6 Deuteride Workshop—indicating that China was already looking past the atomic bomb to a hydrogen bomb.[10]

The site for the Lanzhou Gaseous Diffusion Plant—in a U-shaped valley on the banks of the Huang He (Yellow River) about 15 miles northeast of Lanzhou—had been selected in February 1957. Lanzhou appeared to satisfy several requirements. Its interior location made it difficult for U.S. spyplanes to overfly, while the Huang He provided water that could be used for cooling and power generation (although not without a special filtration system to separate the considerable sediment). In addition, it was necessary to build substantial numbers of converters for the diffusion cascade, pumps, valves, coolers, and instruments, as well as several million feet of corrosion-resistant piping. Lanzhou, with a population of over seven hundred thousand, contained a thermal power plant, nearby coal fields, and assorted machine-building, metallurgy, and chemical factories.[11]

The year 1958 also saw the beginning of planning for China's first plutonium production reactor, also in north-central China. Its location at the foot of the Qilian peaks in the isolated Gobi Desert, in the western sector of Gansu province, was selected by Nie Rongzhen. He surveyed the desert area over 185 miles to the west of the ancient town of Suzhou, which had a population of less than fifty thousand. Nie also approved the Soviet designs for the facilities to be constructed and arranged for a workforce of thousands to build them. In August 1959 construction began for the Jiuquan Atomic Energy Joint Enterprise, initially known as Plant 404.[12]

When completed, the complex included a plutonium production reactor, a chemical separation plant, and more. Its Plutonium Processing Plant would refine the plutonium metal for bombs and warheads. Jiuquan would also be the home of the Nuclear Fuel Processing Plant, for converting enriched uranium hexafluoride to uranium metal, as well as the Nuclear Component Manufacturing Plant. A satellite city was also built, consisting of a large residential area with its own shopping and recreation facilities.[13]

And in August 1958 a select group of officers and men from the People's Liberation Army garrison at Shangqiu, in Henan province, boarded a train that took them west in search of a test site. Unlike Kenneth Bainbridge or their Soviet counterparts, they did not know that they were looking for a nuclear test site. All that their secretive superiors had told them was that they would be roaming the western part of China in search of appropriate locations for a secret facility. They were given no information about how long their assignment would take or exactly where it would take them.[14]

Their first stop, ten days into their journey, was at Dunhuang in northwestern Gansu province. They examined parts of the Gobi Desert, to learn what it would be like when they began their search in earnest. After a week they returned to Dunhuang, sat in a movie theater, and discovered that their real mission had two parts: to choose a location for the test site and then to build it. For the next three months they searched for a suitable location for the site, housing, and command posts.[15]

By October, while the issue had not been settled, several potential locations had been identified. To bring the selection process to a close, Zhang Yunyu, who had been named commander of the test site, arrived in Dunhuang to personally inspect the alternatives. One potential site, about 85 miles to the northwest, had been recommended by the survey team's Soviet advisers, with the expectation that explosions at the site would not exceed 20 kilotons, which they considered sufficient for China's nuclear weapons program.[16]

However, examination of high-altitude wind direction data at the proposed site eliminated it. Downwind from the test site were the residents of the Dunhuang region, who would suffer the consequences of tests conducted at the Soviet-proposed site. Zhang recommended that the search move to the west, a recommendation accepted by China's rulers back in Beijing. Zhang stayed in Dunhuang, but ordered the survey team west. They were soon in the county of Turpan, in the Xinjiang Uygur autonomous region, about 340 miles northwest of Dunhuang and north of the Taklimakan Desert. Without adequate maps, survey aircraft conducted initial reconnaissance missions.[17]

By the middle of December, the aerial surveys had spotted some good candidate sites, and on December 22, survey teams set off to conduct ground reconnaissance. Units of twenty soldiers "covered this ancient kingdom of Loulan by jeep, basically following the routes of the ancient Silk Road between Yanqi and Turpan and Yanqi and Lop Nur," according to two historians of the Chinese program.[18]

In the winter of 1958–1959, one of the teams arrived at the oasis Huangyanggou and liked what they found. The surrounding area was a large desert valley, more than 60 miles wide and 37 miles long, with the Tian Shan mountain range to the north. Water was readily available for both drinking and construction. There were no residents within 280 miles in the downwind direction and no significant settlements within a 140-mile radius. It would be possible, further examination revealed, to satisfy the requirements for a ground zero and a command post close enough to each other to permit observation without risking the lives of the observers. On October 16, 1959, the Lop Nur Nuclear Weapons Test Base was established.[19]

Originally Mao and his cohorts expected that the first device tested at Lop Nur would be built with considerable Soviet assistance, and for several years it looked as if he would get it. In mid-January 1955, the Soviets had announced that they would provide assistance to China and several East European nations in the field of peaceful uses of atomic energy. Their help to China would include a cyclotron, a nuclear reactor, and fissionable material for research. Altogether, between 1955 and 1958 the Soviet Union and China reached six agreements on nuclear issues, including the October 15, 1957, New Defense Technical Accord, which contained a Soviet promise to provide a prototype atomic bomb and missiles, along with related technical data.[20]

But by 1959 the Sino-Soviet alliance was in the process of falling apart. Since 1956 Mao's regime had been issuing grand pronouncements on both domestic and foreign policy issues that were more radical and truculent than Soviet policies. One casualty was the atomic assistance pacts. In June 1959 the Soviets notified the Chinese Communist Party that they would not provide promised mathematical models and technical information to assist the Chinese effort. It was a refusal that signified the deterioration of relations between the Communist states as well as accelerated the decline. By the time Soviet assistance ceased, in 1960, the Soviets had not delivered a single key component for the plutonium production reactor to be built at Jiuquan, much less the "sample" bomb.[21] The Chinese were now on their own, and that would have a substantial impact on the road they took to get to the front door of the nuclear club.

The Soviet reversal also meant that China would have to place greater reliance on its own nuclear physicists, including Deng Jiaxian, Yu Min, Peng Huanwu, Guo Yonghuai, Hu Side, and Wang Ganchang. Deng had earned his doctorate in the United States, from Purdue University in 1950, and returned to China that same year, helping to establish the Chinese Academy of Sciences's Institute of Modern Physics ("Modern" subsequently being deleted from its name). He was also among the founders of the Beijing Nuclear Weapons Research Institute, where he headed the Theoretical Forum, which examined the theory of bomb design. Yu Min, unlike Deng, gained his doctorate from a Chinese university, enrolling in the graduate program in the physics department at Pekin University in 1949, at the age of twenty-three. In 1960 he began theoretical research on nuclear weapons, eventually becoming Deng's deputy. By the time Yu began his graduate work, Peng, born in 1915, had obtained two doctorates, one from Edinburgh University, where he had studied under Max Born and became well known for his work on quantum field theories and cosmic rays.[22]

In 1935, at the age of twenty-six, Guo Yonghuai left China with an undergraduate degree in physics from Beijing University and headed for Canada and the applied mathematics department at the University of Toronto, which awarded him a master's degree in 1940. His next stop was the California Institute of Technology, where his studies on compressible fluid mechanics culminated in his receiving a doctorate in 1945. The next year he began a seven-year stay at Cornell, leaving in 1953 when the United States lifted its prohibition on Chinese students leaving the country. Five years later he became the first head of the chemical physics department of the China Science and Technology University. In 1960 he was appointed a deputy director of the Beijing Nuclear Weapons Research Institute.[23]

Wang Ganchang, an expert in radioactivity and bubble chambers, graduated from Qinghua University in 1929, did his graduate work in Germany, studied under Lise Meitner at Berlin University, received his doctorate in 1934, and returned to China that same year. In 1956 he was a researcher at the Dubna Integrated Atomic Nuclear Institute in the Soviet Union. After his return, he became deputy director of the Institute of Atomic Energy.[24]

WHEN JOHN F. KENNEDY sat behind his desk in the Oval Office for the first time, he knew little about how China's quest for an atomic bomb had progressed over the previous six years. But it was not because he had not yet been briefed. The CIA and America's other intelligence agencies, despite the imagery provided by Corona and U-2 missions and the efforts from 1957 of modified Navy P-2V Neptune aircraft to detect the signatures of atomic activity (in addition to their main electronic intelligence mission), knew little of what the Chinese were doing or had done in the atomic field. China was, former OSI chief Karl Weber recalled, "a real mystery . . . big, really foreign, hard to get a handle on."[25]

That mystery was reflected in the intelligence reports that had been prepared on the Chinese program. In June 1955 Sherman Kent, the head of the

CIA's Office of National Estimates, prepared a short memorandum on possible Chinese development of atomic weapons and delivery systems. The fifty-two-year-old Kent, the son of a three-term California congressman, had received a doctorate in history from Yale in 1933, and during World War II had served in the OSS research and analysis branch as a division chief. After a brief postwar tour in the State Department's intelligence office he returned to academic life. Then, in late 1950 he joined the CIA as deputy chief of the national estimates office, becoming its head in 1952. In a volume of essays in his honor, he was described as "perhaps the foremost practitioner of the craft of analysis in American intelligence history."[26]

Kent concluded that "China almost certainly would not develop significant capabilities for the production of nuclear weapons within the next 10 years unless it were given substantial external assistance." Without such assistance, development of an effective nuclear weapons program "would probably take well over 10, and possibly 20 years." Kent based his assessment on what he knew or believed about China's scientific and industrial capabilities—including its lack of an ability to process uranium ore as well its having "almost no scientific tradition in theoretical and experimental physics"—and his assessment of China's willingness to divert significant resources from conventional economic and military needs.[27]

But Mao and his associates had decided to divert the resources necessary, and by 1960 China was actively engaged, without Soviet assistance, in constructing its first generation of atomic facilities. To the extent that the CIA and other agencies could photograph such activities, intercept signals about them, and recruit spies who could explain their significance, U.S. analysts might be able to accurately assess the status of the Chinese program. To help the intelligence collectors in their task, in October 1960, the OSI requested the geography division of the agency's Office of Research and Reports to analyze the geography of China in order to identify the most likely locations for reactors, gaseous diffusion plants, and test sites.[28]

That very request demonstrated how little the United States knew about Chinese atomic activities, an ignorance that was reflected in key intelligence estimates published at the end of the year. A national intelligence estimate issued on December 6 noted that "our evidence with respect to Communist China's nuclear program is fragmentary as is our information about the nature and extent of Soviet aid." Seven days later, another estimate, *The Chinese Communist Atomic Energy Program*, spelled out what little America's intelligence agencies knew or believed.[29]

The December 13 estimate, which one State Department official described as "one of the most significant recent intelligence products," was considerably different in tone from Kent's analysis half a decade earlier. It noted that China was "energetically developing her native capabilities in the field of atomic energy," a conclusion based in part on the images brought back from a September 1959 U-2 mission, which revealed a two-thousand-foot-long building at Lanzhou that had some of the characteristics of a Soviet gaseous diffusion plant. In addition, China had "acquired a small but highly competent cadre of Western-trained Chinese nuclear specialists." The authors also mentioned a number of concrete manifestations of the Chinese program, including indications that its control was vested in the Second Ministry of Machine Building. Further, China was probably constructing ore concentration and uranium metal plants, and over ten uranium ore deposits were being mined.[30]

The big question, just as it had been with the Soviet Union in the late 1940s, was *when*. CIA analysts assumed China would conclude—as had the Soviets, British, and French—that the plutonium route to the bomb was the easiest. They estimated that China's first plutonium production reactor could go critical in late 1961, with the first plutonium possibly becoming available in 1962. The most probable date for a test was sometime in 1963, but possibly as late as 1964 or as early as 1962. Much would depend on the extent of Soviet assistance, which the analysts noted might decline as a result of the tensions between the two Communist powers.[31]

During 1961, while analysts at the CIA and the other intelligence agencies tried to determine exactly what progress China had made toward an atomic capability, other elements of the government began to explore the implications of such a capability, and what the United States might do to lessen or eliminate its impact.

A June 1961 report produced for the Joint Chiefs of Staff concluded that Chinese "attainment of a nuclear capability will have a marked impact on the security posture of the United States and the Free World, particularly in Asia." A few months later, George McGhee, the State Department's director of policy planning, suggested that China's acquisition of nuclear weapons would pose more political and psychological problems than military ones. According to that study, a nuclear China could reap politically significant "psychological dividends" by helping to create the impression that "communism is the wave of the future." For many Asians, a nuclear test would raise the credibility of the Communist model for organizing a backward nation's resources as well as their estimates of Chinese "military power relative to that of their own countries and the [United States'] capabilities in the area." A heightened sense of China's power could create a bandwagon effect, with greater political pressures on states in the region to accommodate Beijing and loosen ties with Washington.[32]

McGhee suggested to secretary of state Dean Rusk that one way to reduce the psychological impact of a Chinese bomb was to encourage, and perhaps even assist, India to develop a bomb. India's atomic energy program,

McGhee informed his boss, was sufficiently advanced so that within a few months it could produce enough fissionable material for an atomic device. McGhee wanted a noncommunist Asian state to "beat Communist China to the punch." While it would be difficult, he wrote, to get Indian prime minister Jawaharlal Nehru, an opponent of nuclear testing, to approve, he might be "brought to see the proposal as being in India's interests," since an Indian bomb could neutralize any Chinese attempts to employ nuclear blackmail against India and its neighbors.[33]

McGhee's scheme found uneven support at the State Department, and it was diluted to a quiet, exploratory effort by White House science adviser Jerome Weisner during his upcoming trip to South Asia. Weisner would meet with Homi Bhabha, the chairman of India's Atomic Energy Commission, and inquire about the effect a Chinese nuclear weapons capability might have on India's nuclear program, a question that might lead to an Indian request for assistance. The proposal was approved by undersecretary of state Chester Bowles but vetoed by Rusk, who was not convinced that "we should depart from our stated policy that we are opposed to the further extension of nuclear weapons capability." If the United States abetted nuclear proliferation, Rusk argued, it "would start us down a jungle path from which I see no exit."[34]

THROUGHOUT 1961 and into 1962, the State and Defense Departments as well as the National Security Council (NSC), the latter at Kennedy's urging in January 1962, pondered what might be done about the embryonic Chinese nuclear program. Meanwhile, the intelligence community sought to accumulate more information about it. In October 1961, the CIA's *Central Intelligence Bulletin* noted that Lo Jui-ching, the People Liberation Army's chief of staff, had "reaffirmed China's determination to become a nuclear power."[35] But, as expected, he provided no details about China's quest.

Providing those details was partially the responsibility of the Corona satellites. While there had been only one successful Corona mission prior to the December 1960 national estimates, eight additional successful Corona missions had been conducted through the end of February 1962. Whatever intelligence on Chinese atomic facilities had been derived would have been available to to the CIA analysts when they began preparing the April 1962 national intelligence estimate titled *Chinese Communist Advanced Weapons Capabilities*. Not only were there more photographs that could be exploited, but they were of higher quality. Instead of the KH-1 camera, with its forty-foot resolution, which produced the imagery employed in the 1960 estimates, the eight missions employed the KH-2, KH-3, and KH-4 cameras, each with progressively higher resolution. A December 1961 KH-3 mission provided the first imagery of Lop Nur since the Chinese had selected it as a site, although CIA photointerpreters only recognized it as a "suspect site" at the time.[36*]

In addition to the imagery from Corona missions, there were even higher-resolution images, albeit far fewer of them, from U-2 missions. Beginning in 1961, under a program designated Tackle, U.S.-trained Chinese Nationalist pilots, known as the "Black Cat" squadron, began flying over China from a base at Taoyuan on Taiwan. Despite the substantial risk involved, they were able to cover a number of mainland targets, flying as many as three missions a month, some of the pilots penetrating Chinese airspace for eighteen hundred miles before turning back. While Lop Nur was beyond their reach, possible atomic sites in north-central China were not.[37] The increased imagery, however, still left much in doubt.

The September 1959 images of of the Lanzhou building that had some of the characteristics of a gaseous diffusion plant revealed "no . . . provision for an electric power supply." Imagery from a Corona mission in late February and early March 1962 showed "no further indication of provision for an electric power supply or of preparation for construction of a second building," a building that would be needed to obtain weapons-grade U-235. The analysts went on to note that the Corona photographs showed "arrested development" at a nearby hydroelectric power station. Thus, if "the [Lanzhou] site were to be a gaseous diffusion plant, the Chinese probably could not produce weapon-grade uranium-235 there before 1965, even if construction of another building were started now."[38]

The photography turned up no evidence that China was building a plutonium production facility: "recent photographic coverage of certain suspect areas produced negative results." It was possible, according to the authors of the estimate, that a production reactor was located outside the area covered. Despite the lack of supporting evidence, the estimators continued to assume that China was taking the plutonium path to the bomb. "Assuming," they wrote, "an accelerated and highly successful program for the production of plutonium since 1960, the Chinese Communists could detonate an all-plutonium device in early 1963." They considered it unlikely, however, that the Chinese would meet such a schedule, and predicted that the "first Chinese test would probably be delayed beyond 1963, perhaps as much as several years."[39]

The conclusions of the April and subsequent intelligence reports helped reinforce the need to examine the implications of, and policy options to deal with, a Chinese nuclear capability. In August, a group of RAND Corporation

---

* The KH-2 was employed on five missions; the KH-3, on two; and the KH-4, on one. See Dwayne A. Day, John M. Logsdon, and Brian Latell, *Eye in the Sky: The Story of the Corona Spy Satellites* (Washington, D.C.: Smithsonian, 1998), p. 232.

analysts concluded that a nuclear-armed China would pose a significantly broader challenge to America's position in Asia than it had previously, and was most likely to exploit its new status in the political arena and through low-level military operations. They also noted that while the pronouncements of Chinese leaders created an impression of recklessness and irresponsibility, their statements appeared to be "motivated by the internal and international value they derive from creating and maintaining the image." In contrast, actual Chinese behavior and doctrine "place a great emphasis on a cautious and rational approach to the use of military force."[40]

The following month Dean Rusk approved a new proposal from policy-planning chief George McGhee, this one for a coordinated overt-covert propaganda campaign that would involve the State and Defense Departments and CIA. The campaign would combat the "vast ignorance and strong emotionalism" in most of Asia with regard to nuclear matters, heighten Asian awareness of "U.S. and Free World strength," and neutralize "awe and unreasoned fear" of China. Besides emphasizing the United States' strategic nuclear superiority, the campaign would suggest that China's nuclear program was behind schedule, in hopes of producing a "what took you so long" reaction to any Chinese detonation.[41]

Along with the efforts to shape world opinion, Robert Johnson, an East Asian specialist, began a series of major studies on the implications and consequences of a Chinese nuclear test and a "regionally significant" nuclear capability. Johnson had arrived in Washington in 1951 to work at the NSC, after obtaining his doctorate from Harvard and spending a couple of years teaching there. His graduate work had been in political economy and government, not Asia, but during his first decade at the NSC a Rockefeller Public Service Award allowed him to spend ten months traveling through Asia, working on a project on Chinese and Indian influences in the region. He "went around and talked to all sorts of people," he recalls, "got a good education on Asia," and found out that "neither [India nor China] had much influence."[42]

When the Kennedy administration took office, most of the NSC staff were sent elsewhere, but Johnson remained and was assigned responsibility for East Asia. By the fall of 1962 he had been transferred to the State Department's policy-planning unit to be its East Asia expert. His mandate was not only to determine the impact of a Chinese nuclear capability but also to consider the policy changes that might be needed to counter its political and diplomatic effects.[43]

EARLIER THAT YEAR, the Uranium Mining and Hydrometallurgy Institute at Tongxian (Plant 4) had begun producing uranium tetrafluoride in quantity. In September the nation's senior defense and nuclear officials, after reviewing the progress of the nuclear program, proposed that China try to test an atomic bomb within two years. The following month Li Jue and other leaders of the Beijing institute provided senior officials with their plan to bring China into the nuclear club during the winter of 1964. It was probably that plan that led officials from the Second Ministry to order the Lanzhou gaseous diffusion plant to produce the necessary highly enriched uranium six months ahead of schedule—by early 1964. Then, in November the Chinese Communist Party Central Committee established the fifteen-member Central Special Commission, lead by Zhou Enlai, to oversee the nuclear weapons program.[44]

Not long after its establishment, the commission speeded up the planned move of Li Jue's institute from Beijing to Qinghai province, where it would become the Northwest Nuclear Weapons Research and Design Academy, more discretely known as the Ninth Academy. The commission accelerated work on key buildings, including those for neutron physics and radiochemistry. Finally, in March 1963 some sections of the Beijing institute began to move to their new home.[45]

The institute's scientists found themselves in a very different environment than Beijing—much the same as Oppenheimer and scientists from Berkeley, Chicago, and New York did when they moved to an isolated part of New Mexico, or as Andrei Sakharov did when he left Moscow for Sarov. Qinghai, in China's remote northwest, was isolated and largely inaccessible, which satisfied the key criteria of the Chinese officials responsible for selecting the site for the nation's weapons design bureau.[46]

Beyond movement of personnel, there was also movement toward the day when China would test an atomic bomb. The Institute of Atomic Energy (initially code-named 601 and later 401) had grown out of the Institute of Physics, and its scientific activities were conducted in Touli, a town about twenty miles south of Beijing. Sometime before July 1960 it had been assigned the task of beginning research and development on the production of uranium hexafluoride. By October 1963 it had produced enough to send to Lanzhou for test runs of the plant's diffusion cascade. In November the plant in the Jiuquan complex also produced satisfactory uranium hexafluoride, while Plant 414 at Hengyang produced uranium oxide that was sufficiently pure to justify the plant beginning mass production.[47]

IF THE CIA and other interested intelligence agencies had known of the developments in 1962 and 1963, they would have revised at least one key assumption about the Chinese program: that it revolved around the production of plutonium. But their knowledge of China's efforts was still limited. On January 10, 1963, former Atomic Energy Commission chairman John McCone—who replaced Allen Dulles as director of central intelligence in

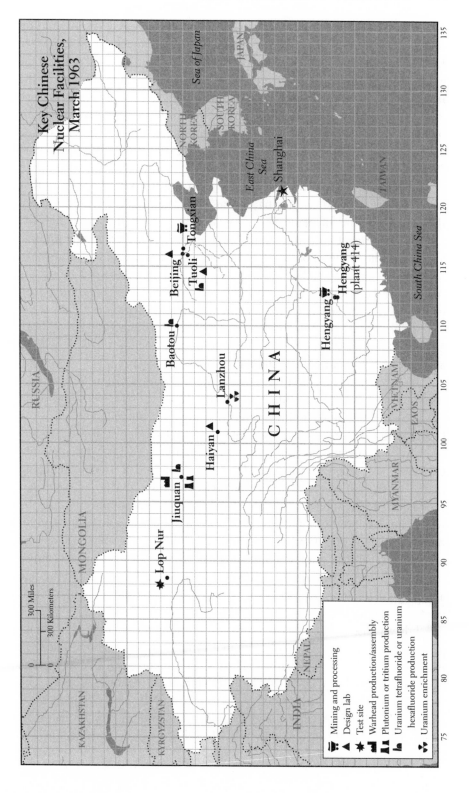

November 1961 after Dulles was forced to depart because of the Bay of Pigs fiasco—met with McGeorge Bundy, Kennedy's national security adviser. Bundy described the president's fear that a nuclear China "would so upset the world political scene [that] it would be intolerable." Further, Bundy told the intelligence chief that Cuba and the Chinese nuclear program were the "two issues foremost in the minds of the highest authority and therefore should be treated accordingly by CIA." McCone had to acknowledge, however, that the agency knew little for certain about China's progress—hence the need for an expanded effort.[48]

In the months that followed, pilots from the Black Cat squadron flew their U-2s over China, as they had throughout 1962—although not without the occasional loss of plane and pilot. A March 1963 flight detected the nuclear complex at Baotou. Satellite coverage was also increasingly routine, allowing photography of parts of China, including the suspect site at Lop Nur, that were out of range of the Taiwan-based U-2s. Launch crews at Vandenberg Air Force Base in California successfully orbited five Corona satellites, each equipped with the advanced KH-4 camera system, during the first half of the year. Intelligence from those missions would be added to whatever had been acquired from the thirteen 1962 Keyhole missions whose imagery became available after the April 1962 national estimate was prepared.[49]

In July a new type of imaging satellite was added to the U.S. arsenal when the first Gambit satellite, carrying the KH-7 camera, went into orbit. Whereas the Corona satellites performed an "area surveillance" mission, Gambit was designed for a "close look" mission. Its lower orbit was one reason why a photograph taken by a KH-4 camera included 1,075 square nautical miles, but one taken by a KH-7 camera covered a mere 120 square nautical miles. However, whereas the KH-7 saw less, what it did see it saw much more clearly. In contrast to the ten- to twenty-five-foot resolution of the KH-4, the initial resolution of the KH-7 was, at its best, four feet. The combination of higher resolution and the camera's ability to take oblique shots was of particular value in photographing nuclear installations. Interpreters examining KH-7 images of the sides of nuclear facilities could determine the size and shape of the transformers, allowing an accurate assessment of how much power was being used.[50]

July was also marked by two estimates summing up what the U.S. intelligence community knew or believed about the Chinese program. The first, issued on July 10, two days before the first KH-7 camera was placed into space, was the work of the Arms Control and Disarmament Agency (ACDA). The second, a special national intelligence estimate—SNIE 13-2-63, titled *Communist China's Advanced Weapons Program*—was in draft form at that time, although it was formally approved by the U.S. Intelligence Board on July 24.

Both estimates devoted considerable attention to Lanzhou and Baotou. The national estimate reported that photography of Lanzhou, obtained that March and June, showed progress being made on a nearby hydroelectric installation, which intelligence experts believed was designed to supply the plant. Although much work remained to be done, some power was available. In addition, the analysts reported two transmission lines, one of which appeared to be completed, connecting the diffusion plant with a thermal electric plant at Lanzhou. There was also a substation at the diffusion plant, and, it was noted, the installation of transformers alongside the main building had begun, although only two of a probable thirty-eight were shown to be in place.[51]

The national estimate also informed its readers that the main building at Lanzhou was big enough to allow for the production of lightly enriched uranium, which could be used in reactors. It would take at least twice as much floor space than provided by that building to produce weapons-grade U-235, according to the analysts, who also noted the existence of an adjacent area within the facility's security perimeter that was apparently intended to allow the required expansion. However, even if "work was underway and all of the highly specialized separation equipment was promptly available, the earliest date at which weapon-grade U-235 could be produced would be in 1966." A more likely time was 1968–1969, "considering the great technical difficulties involved and the large amount of additional construction needed." Had the analysts known that the Second Ministry of Machine Building had directed Lanzhou to produce enough uranium for a bomb by the beginning of 1964, they might have had second thoughts about their projection.[52]

The ACDA study, not surprisingly, echoed the national estimate's findings with regard to Lanzhou, although it added some details that helped explain the estimate's conclusions. The size of the existing diffusion building, approximately 1,900 feet by 150 feet, was large enough to contain about eighteen hundred compressor stages. However, at least double the floor space, enough for about four thousand stages, would be required to produce uranium enriched to 93 percent U-235.[53]

With respect to work at Baotou, the national estimate noted that recent photographs of the area revealed a facility with "elaborate security arrangements." Its authors believed that a small air-cooled plutonium production reactor, with a capacity of about 30 megawatts, was part of the installation, along with related chemical separation and metal fabrication facilities. The reactor was judged to be sufficient for a token weapons program, but not for "a sizable . . . program based on plutonium alone." Whether the reactor was in operation, they reported, could not be determined from the photographs.[54]

In the absence of hard data, the analysts considered alternative scenarios.

If the reactor was in operation, they did not believe it could have reached criticality before early 1962. An additional twenty-one to twenty-four months would be needed for the completion of the process—one year for fuel element irradiation within the reactor and an additional nine to twelve months for cooling of the irradiated fuel, chemical separation, and fabrication of a device. Therefore, the earliest a device could be ready would be early 1964. However, running into even normal difficulties would postpone the date to late 1964 or early 1965. If the reactor reached criticality later than early 1962, the date of the first detonation would be delayed even further.[55]

The analysts also suggested that China must have planned to construct other plutonium production facilities, based on the belief that the Chinese program called for composite weapons containing both U-235 and plutonium. In that case, the quantity of plutonium that could be produced at the reactor believed to exist at Baotou was far too small to be compatible with the amount of U-235 that could be produced at Lanzhou. However, there had been photographic coverage "of many of the likely areas for reactor sites without identifying another production reactor, and there is no significant collateral evidence indicating the existence of such a reactor." But the estimators could not exclude the possibility that there were other, undetected plutonium production facilities under construction. If that were the case, "the Chinese could have a first detonation at any time."[56]

As with Lanzhou, the conclusions of the ACDA report on Baotou were derived from the the national estimate. It also, once again, provided some additional information, including the facts that the entire area was enclosed by multiple fencing and a wall with guard towers at the corners and, more importantly, that the Baotou "reactor" was too small to produce enough plutonium in a year for more than one or two weapons. The ACDA study also devoted a paragraph to two locations in the vicinity of Beijing where nuclear research was underway, both elements of the Institute of Atomic Energy. It noted that the research at the location twenty miles southwest of Beijing, at Touli, involved a Soviet-supplied heavy-water reactor as well as a Soviet-supplied cyclotron.[57]

The authors of the national estimate acknowledged that despite the influx "of a considerable amount of information, mainly from photography . . . the gaps in our information remain substantial and we are therefore not able to judge the present state or to project the future of the Chinese program as a whole with any very high degree of confidence." What they did not, and of course could not, tell their readers was what they did not know: the role of the Institute of Atomic Energy at Touli in producing ten tons of hexafluoride for Lanzhou, or the mission of the Jiuquan complex. Nor could they report the extent of their errors. Lanzhou was months, not years, away from producing enough highly enriched uranium for a weapon, while Baotou had been established to produce uranium tetrafluoride not plutonium. Chiang Kai-shek's intelligence services believed that the Lanzhou reactor was active during 1963, but no one in Washington appears to have given any credence to that report.[58]

THE ESTIMATE, looking beyond questions of how and when China might first achieve an atomic capability, also explored the ultimate concern of U.S. policymakers—how China's behavior might change once it had a nuclear arsenal. The estimators "did not believe that the explosion of a first device, or even the acquisition of a limited nuclear weapons capability," would result in China adopting "a general policy of military aggression or even be willing to take significantly greater military risks." Chinese leaders, it was expected, would realize just how limited their capabilities were. Yet the estimate also suggested that "the Chinese would feel very much stronger and this mood would doubtless be reflected in their approach to conflicts on their periphery. They would probably feel that the U.S. would be more reluctant to intervene on the Asian mainland and thus the tone of Chinese policy would probably become more assertive." In a footnote, the acting director of the State Department's group of intelligence analysts—the Bureau of Intelligence and Research (INR)—noted that the two conclusions appeared contradictory.[59]

About the same time, a State Department colleague, Walt Rostow, George McGhee's successor as policy-planning director, gave a less ambiguous assessment. Rostow was undoubtedly influenced by Robert Johnson's two-hundred-page study, *A Chinese Communist Nuclear Detonation and Nuclear Capability*, whose conclusions about the consequence of a Chinese bomb were "generally quite sanguine," Johnson recalls. Rostow wrote that the minimal nuclear capability Beijing could develop was unlikely to "convince . . . anyone" that it could be "used as an umbrella for aggression." Not only would "U.S. overwhelming nuclear superiority" deter Beijing, but also its "desire to preserve its nuclear forces as a credible deterrent might tend to make China even more cautious than it is today in its encounters with American power."[60]

But the argument that China might behave itself when it became a nuclear power did not prevent President Kennedy from exploring how to rein in, or even "take out," China's nuclear program. In his January meeting with McCone, McGeorge Bundy said that Kennedy believed "we should be prepared to take some form of action unless they [the Chinese] agreed to desist from further efforts in this field."[61]

By the time the ACDA study and special national intelligence estimate were issued, the State Department, the office of the assistant secretary of defense for international security affairs, and the JCS had explored a variety of options. More importantly, on July 14 the undersecretary of state for political affairs, Averell Harriman, arrived in Moscow to try to finalize an agreement on a treaty banning nuclear tests in the atmosphere, in outer space, or under water. Harriman had a second mission. He was to emphasize to Khrushchev that a nuclear China, even as a small-scale nuclear power, "could be very dangerous to us all." The president wanted Harriman to explore Khrushchev's views on "limiting or preventing Chinese nuclear development and his willingness either to take Soviet action or to accept U.S. action aimed in this direction."[62]

Harriman succeeded in finalizing the agreement on the test ban treaty. But any cables he sent back to Kennedy reporting on his second mission would have been disappointing to the president. Khrushchev proved uninterested in taking any action, even political, against China. As long as France was unwilling to sign the test ban treaty, he would not agree to isolate Beijing. The Soviet ruler also played down the Sino-Soviet split and rejected the idea that a nuclear China would threaten the Soviet Union. Nor did he agree that a nuclear-armed China would be a threat to others, claiming that Beijing would become "more restrained"—"whenever someone lacked [nuclear] means he was the one who shouted the loudest."[63]

But Khrushchev's reassurances and lack of interest did not soothe Kennedy or end U.S. interest in finding a way to stop China's nuclear quest. In an August 1 press conference, Kennedy spoke of a "menacing situation." He noted that it would take some years before China became "a full-fledged nuclear power," but "we would like to take some steps now which would lessen that prospect." The day before, William Bundy, McGeorge's brother and assistant secretary of defense for international security affairs, tasked the JCS to develop a contingency plan for a conventional attack designed to cause "the severest impact and delay to the Chinese nuclear program."[64]

And while the Soviet Union may not have been interested in taking action against China and its nuclear program, another country was not only willing but eager. In September, Gen. Chiang Ching-kuo—Chiang Kai-shek's son, minister of defense, and much-feared "security czar"—visited Washington. There he met with central intelligence director McCone to discuss long-standing differences between the United States and Taiwan over military operations against the People's Republic. A day after meeting McCone, he met with President Kennedy.[65]

Undoubtedly fearing that a China with nuclear weapons would eliminate any possibility of a return to the mainland, Chiang Ching-kuo raised on several occasions the issue of attacking China's nuclear facilities. At CIA headquarters, he participated in discussions on the possibility of an air strike. Later, in the company of Ray Cline, the deputy director of intelligence and the agency's former station chief in Taiwan, and William Nelson, Cline's successor as chief of station, Chiang met McGeorge Bundy. He suggested that the United States provide "transportation and technical assistance" for a commando attack on the Chinese nuclear installations. Bundy told Chiang that the "United States is very interested in whether something could be planned" that would have a "delaying and preventive effect on the nuclear growth of China." Such measures, he cautioned, needed "most careful study."[66]

On September 11 an extended discussion between Kennedy and Chiang prompted the president to question the feasibility of sending commandos against Chinese nuclear installations. He asked "whether it would be possible to send 300 to 500 men by air to such distant . . . atomic installations as that at Baotou, and whether it was not likely that the planes involved would be shot down." Chiang reassured Kennedy that the commando raid proposal "had been discussed by CIA officials yesterday and they had indicated that such an operation was feasible." Kennedy's query suggested some doubts about the proposal's feasibility, and other comments emphasized the importance of "realistic" plans to "weaken the Chinese Communist regime." To avoid another Bay of Pigs operation "based more on hope than on realistic appraisals," Washington and Taipei needed better intelligence about conditions on the mainland. In that way, Kennedy observed, "whatever action is undertaken would fit the actual situation."[67]

A few days later, Chiang met with McCone to formalize the understandings he had reached with Kennedy and his advisers. With respect to possible action, McCone and Chiang agreed to establish a planning group to study the feasibility of attacks by Nationalist teams against China's nuclear sites. Any operations would require joint approval by their nations' highest authorities.[68]

In the weeks after Chiang Ching-kuo's visit, the Kennedy administration continued to review ways of preventing China from acquiring an atomic bomb. The CIA as well as the Pentagon studied the possibility of air dropping Taiwanese sabotage teams and other covert options. On November 18 Maxwell Taylor, chairman of the JCS, informed his colleagues that their next meeting would include a discussion of "how we can prevent or delay the Chinese from succeeding in their nuclear development program." Kennedy's favorite general noted that developing an atomic bomb was "fraught with troubles—technological, scientific, economic, and industrial." A coordinated program of covert activities designed to intensify those troubles could significantly delay the Chinese program. The title of the agenda item—"Unconventional Warfare Program BRAVO"—indicates that a paramilitary action was to be considered. That such an action had been examined seriously is indicated by the unsuccessful attempt in the fall of 1963 to fly a U-2 equipped with an infrared camera over the suspected plutonium reactor at Baotou. The objective was to determine whether the reactor was in operation, and thus off limits to military attack.[69]*

In addition, the JCS responded to William Bundy's request for a contingency plan for a conventional attack to retard Chinese nuclear development. In mid-December, they completed a plan for a multiple-sortie attack designed to inflict severe damage and delays. Nevertheless, the large number of sorties required probably led the JCS to propose looking into a possible nuclear attack on the same facilities, an idea that was obviously rejected.[70]

Kennedy was willing to consider more than military options. He and his advisers sought to obtain Soviet cooperation on a nonproliferation agreement that would be aimed, in part, at China. Rusk discussed the issue with Soviet foreign minister Andrei Gromyko at the United Nations in the fall of 1963. Gromyko then discussed the issue with Kennedy on October 10. Showing some willingness to exert indirect pressure on China, Gromyko acknowledged that an agreement would make China's "political situation more difficult and delicate," presumably by increasing its isolation and raising pressures on it to follow nonproliferation standards.[71]

THE UNITED STATES began 1964 with a new president, Lyndon Baines Johnson, after John Kennedy was assassinated in Dallas on November 22. In China, Mao and Zhou were still in charge, and China continued its pursuit of an atomic bomb. On January 14, 1964, Wang Jiefu, the director of the Lanzhou plant, and his colleagues arrived at the central control department, where Wang ordered the enriched uranium to be siphoned off into special containers. That was done at 11:05 that morning, with the goal of producing 90 percent enriched uranium achieved. The following day the Second Ministry sent a message of congratulations to the plant and a report to Mao, who scribbled "very good" on his copy.[72]

A few months later the Nuclear Component Manufacturing Plant at the

---

* The issue of China's acquisition of an atomic capability was discussed not only behind closed doors, but also by leading journalists, including the well-connected and influential Stewart Alsop. In *Saturday Evening Post* columns published in September and October 1963, Alsop wrote about "the madness of Mao Tse-tung" and the necessity and feasibility of military action against Beijing's nuclear program. He asserted that the "president and his inner circle . . . have agreed in principle that China must be prevented, by whatever means, from becoming a nuclear power." "Nuclear sterilization," Alsop wrote, was a "technically easy problem" that could be accomplished with a "few rather small bangs." See Stewart Alsop, "The Real Meaning of the Test Ban," and "The Madness of Mao Tse-tung," *Saturday Evening Post*, September 28 and October 26, 1963, respectively.

Jiuquan complex produced the first nuclear components for the bomb, although it had been a struggle. Producing a uranium core had run into a variety of problems, including the development of air bubbles in the casting. Alternative plans and techniques were tried, and data collected, in a series of experiments. One promising approach, when tested, proved successful. On April 30, technicians at Jiuquan began machining a uranium core. By the early morning of May 1, the first core was ready, but not until after there had been a slight mishap due to a technician's stage fright.[73]

Then, on June 6 the Northwest Nuclear Weapons Research and Development Academy (the Ninth Academy) conducted a full-scale simulated detonation test, lacking only the nuclear components. The test was successful, indicating that the device would detonate as designed. In July and August the technical staff at the Northwest academy assembled three bombs, putting together the explosive assembly, tamper, uranium core, and initiator plus electrical assembly.[74]

On August 19, with pairs of white and velvet curtains draped over the windows to keep the sunlight out, what was apparently the assembly of the third bomb began. Electrostatic copper wires had been installed at the doors to ground the static electricity of anyone entering the assembly area. The first stop for those who would handle the assembly was a room where they changed into white coveralls and cloth slippers. The workers also received a message of encouragement and warning from Mao and Zhou, who told them to "be bold but cautious."[75]

Their boldness and caution would have to be exercised in view of two high-ranking dignitaries who were there to watch the assembly process. One was Zhang Aiping, head of the First Atomic Bomb Test Commission and the First Atomic Bomb Test On-Site Headquarters. The fifty-six-year-old Zhang had served as deputy chief of the People's Liberation Army general staff, as chief of staff for the Advance Command of the Taiwan Liberation Forces in Fujian, and as deputy director for the National Defense Science and Technology Commission, an appointment he had had since 1961. The other was Liu Xiyao, the vice minister of the Second Ministry. The assembly was a prolonged process, even without glitches. It would take two days from the time it began until the assembly team reached the last item on its checklist. At that point Zhang and Liu were invited to approach the security line and supervise the insertion of the uranium core into the shell case. When that was completed, the two senior officials applauded.[76]

In mid and late August the devices, minus the enriched uranium components, were shipped on a special train to Lop Nur, under conditions of extreme secrecy. The train was escorted by armed police, while the route was protected by police from the Ministry of Public Security. All the coal used for the train was sifted to make sure there were no hidden explosives, waiting to derail China's first nuclear test. In addition, the regions that the train passed through had their high-voltage power cut off. When the devices arrived at the station, they were then taken by truck to the test base.[77]

Getting Lop Nur ready for the detonation was the responsibility of Zhang Aiping and two key subordinates, test base commander Zhang Yunyu and scientist Cheng Kaijia. During the summer before the bomb had been assembled, their crews had put up an iron tower with an elevator that would carry "596," as the bomb was designated, approximately four hundred feet above ground.[78]

TO GET A FIX on China's nuclear progress, the U.S. intelligence establishment worked overtime to penetrate the ring of secrecy surrounding the effort. Early in 1964, Robert Johnson and other officials at the State Department read CIA reports stating that Chinese officials had said that the first test would "definitely" occur in 1964. China expert Allen Whiting, an INR analyst at the time, recalled reading agent reports on Premier Zhou Enlai's visit to Mali. According to one of those reports, Zhou told Premier Mobido Keita that China would test a bomb in October. In mid-March the CIA reported that Soviet delegates to the International Atomic Energy Agency (IAEA) believed that China already had a nuclear device and would be capable of detonating it in no more than a year. Nevertheless, no one yet regarded such reports as decisive; thus, Robert Johnson wrote, "We really don't know when the first detonation would occur."[79]

Overhead reconnaissance efforts were particularly important. U-2 missions flown by the Black Cat squadron helped monitor developments at Lanzhou and elsewhere. A September 1963 mission had returned photographs of the gaseous diffusion and thermal power plants at Lanzhou. The images allowed photo-interpreters to conclude that a new wing, approximately 134 feet wide, was under construction at the diffusion plant, and a building that had been under construction during a previous overflight had been completed.[80]

That spring Lop Nur was added to the list of U-2 targets, one of several secret operations directed against Chinese missile and nuclear activities conducted in concert with the Indian government. In 1962, to aid India in its conflict with China, the CIA had provided India U-2 photographs of the Chinese border. The next year the agency suggested establishing a temporary U-2 detachment in India, which would permit missions to be conducted against Lop Nur and other targets in Xinjiang. In the spring of 1964, India agreed to the secret deployment of a U-2 detachment at Charbatia, an old wartime base on the country's east coast. Two or three missions followed, with the United States obtaining images of Lop Nur and India receiving current intelligence on Chinese deployments along its border. Of course, it was an arrangement that India, which prized its "nonaligned" status, sought to conceal. In May, after a mission over Xinjiang, the brakes on the returning U-2 failed and it rolled off the end of the runway. Out of fear of public disclosure, members of the Indian Aviation Research Centre, responsible for India's aerial reconnaissance programs, "manhandled" the aircraft into a hangar until U.S. technicians could repair it.[81]

There had also been seven successful Corona missions between the publication of the July 1963 estimate and mid-July 1964. One mission carried a KH-4 camera, while the other six carried the improved KH-4A. The 4A camera was a stereo system with a resolution of between nine and twenty-five feet, and its images encompassed 1,440 nautical miles of territory. China was not, however, always adequately covered. James Q. Reber was the chairman of the Committee on Overhead Reconnaissance (COMOR), the interagency body responsible for deciding which targets would be photographed, when, and by what satellites or aircraft. In April he was informed by McCone's deputy that McCone and deputy secretary of defense Cyrus Vance were interested in increasing the amount of Chinese territory covered in KH-4 missions, given delays in U-2 missions and the fact that the one successful KH-4 mission of 1964 had covered only one-fifth of China's territory. Reber recommended to the National Reconnaissance Office (NRO) that more emphasis be given to China on the next satellite mission.[82]

In late July 1963 a satellite code-named Lanyard carrying a KH-6 camera with a resolution varying between four and six feet was successfully launched. While most of its targets were in the Soviet Union, at least one "spot in central China" was photographed. Imagery was also provided by the KH-7 Gambit satellites, ten of which were successfully orbited between July 1963 and the end of July 1964. A KH-7 mission in late April 1964 photographed Jiuquan and Baotou. The images from that mission were probably sharper than from the first missions, as the camera's resolution continued to improve (to two feet by mid-1967).[83]

Overhead imagery played the key role in producing reports on what were first identified as a possible atomic energy complex in Jiuquan and a possible plutonium production facility at Baotou. The same could be said for Lop Nur, which was a target not only for U-2s, but also for Corona and Gambit satellites. Lop Nur was photographed during a February 1964 KH-4A mission, as well as during the late April 1964 KH-7 mission. While the February mission showed no apparent change from previous coverage, the April imagery revealed that a tower had been constructed at the site, the tower that would eventually host China's first atomic bomb.[84]

The overhead photography allowed McCone to tell President Johnson on July 24 that the U-2s and satellites had observed five installations associated with the Chinese program "in various stages of assembly and operation." That led the intelligence chief to conclude that the Chinese had overcome some, if not all, of the problems associated with the Soviet cutoff of aid. However, despite the intelligence effort devoted to monitoring the Chinese effort, McCone also informed Johnson that he could not "foretell when the Chinese would explode a device." A three-page summary, apparently prepared for McCone's presentation, stated that "evidence on Communist China's nuclear weapons program is still insufficient to permit confident conclusions as to the likelihood of Chinese Communist detonation in the next few months. . . . We believe that Communist China's leaders are determined to set off a nuclear device at the earliest possible moment in order to secure military, psychological, and political advantages."[85]

Before the end of August the intelligence community would address the issue of "when" in a new estimate. That month, the photointerpreters at NPIC also completed a study, largely based on overhead imagery, of the suspect Jiuquan complex. The seven-page report consisted of text, images, and drawings based on the imagery. It described the complex as including a production area, thermal power plant, a workshop area, a main housing, as well as other facilities. It also noted that successive photographs showed expansion of the complex, and resulted in its December 1963 characterization as a "suspect" atomic energy complex being changed to "probable."[86]

Beyond identifying the components of the complex, the interpreters provided details, including measurements of the components at Jiuquan and how they had expanded over the years. The interpreters also noted the apparent similarity between some of the reactor buildings at Kyshtym and a "probable" reactor building at the complex. Such caveats were often used in the report. One sentence referred to "one possible reactor building completed, a large probable reactor building under construction, and a possible chemical separation plant."[87]

Such uncertainty about Jiuquan and the other components of the Chinese atomic weapons program, McCone and Johnson certainly hoped, would be reduced as the United States continued its intelligence campaign against those targets. Part of that effort included the August 5 launch of a Corona satellite carrying a KH-4A camera. On August 9, the satellite ejected one of its two recovery capsules, containing four days' worth of imagery. While the plane that was supposed to snatch the capsule out of the air near Hawaii missed, frogmen were able to fish the valuable photographs out of the Pacific.[88]

The images contained in the capsule included photographs of the chemical and plutonium facilities at Jiuquan as well as of Lop Nur. The interpretation of those photographs led the CIA experts on China's nuclear program in the OSI to conclude that "the previously suspect facility" at Lop Nur "is a nuclear test site which could be ready for use in about two months." That judgment was part of a August 26 special national intelligence estimate, *The Chances of an Imminent Communist Chinese Nuclear Explosion*, which directly confronted the issue of "when."[89]

While the analysts were now convinced that Lop Nur was "almost certainly" a test site that *could* be in used in two months, they believed that detonation "will not occur until sometime after the end of 1964." That conclusion was driven by what would prove to be another faulty assumption: that China "will not have sufficient fissionable material for a test of a nuclear device in the next few months." Their conviction resulted from the continued belief that China's first bomb would be fueled by plutonium, not uranium (the Lanzhou plant, which had already produced the required U-235, was described as "behind schedule"), and that only one plutonium reactor—believed to be at Baotou—could not produce enough plutonium for a bomb until at least 1965.[90]

The intelligence analysts also believed that even if there were no major obstacles, it would take at least eighteen months, and more likely twenty-four, after the startup of the Baotou reactor before a nuclear device would be ready for testing. The earliest date that the Chinese could test, given these assumptions, would be mid-1965.[91]

The estimators raised the possibility that China might have another source of fissionable material. One option would be a facility started with Soviet help, prior to its withdrawal of assistance, at about the same time as work on the Lanzhou gaseous diffusion facility began. If it existed, overhead imagery had not yet identified it.[92]

Intelligence analysts also mentioned the possibility that China might have acquired fissionable material from a "non-Soviet foreign source": France. A year earlier, on August 15, 1963, a State Department cable referred to indications of "French-Soviet and French-Chinese cooperation in the atomic energy field prior to the withdrawal of Soviet technicians from Communist China." It also noted a continuing personal relationship between the high commissioner of the French Atomic Energy Agency and several members of China's Institute of Atomic Energy.[93]

The analysts were also unsure what the activity at the test site signified. They noted the incongruity of bringing the site to a state of readiness without having a device nearly ready for testing, since it was technically unwise to install much of the instrumentation more than a few weeks before an actual test. However, they also observed that uneven progress in various phases of the Chinese program would not be surprising. In addition, given Lop Nur's remote location and the poor transportation available, China might need a long lead time to prepare the installation. On balance then, the estimators believed that the detonation would not occur until at least early 1965.[94]

Such conclusions were disputed within and outside the intelligence community. Two prominent nuclear advisers and brothers, Albert and Richard Latter, told the CIA's deputy director for science and technology, Bud Wheelon, that the CIA's Office of Scientific Intelligence, which had responsibility for studying foreign nuclear programs, was "screwing up" in assuming that a first bomb would rely on plutonium. OSI chief Donald Chamberlain, a chemical engineer who had left his professor's position at Washington University in St. Louis to join the agency, had misjudged the Chinese program and "got stubborn about it," Wheelon recalls. He took the Latters to see McCone, who listened to their complaints.[95]

Allen Whiting argued that a test was imminent, doubting that the Chinese would put up the tower at Lop Nur, discovered in Corona imagery, unless they were planning a test. The agent reports of Zhou's statements about a nuclear test in October further convinced Whiting that the CIA estimates were too cautious. That evidence, along with the public and private statements of Chinese leaders, led him to recommend to INR director Thomas Hughes that the United States invoke a contingency plan by announcing the upcoming test before the Chinese did, in an effort to lessen the impact and "reassure neighboring countries that the United States was watching and aware."[96]

WITH THEIR ESTIMATE under scrutiny, CIA analysts began to restudy the data. At the same time, some U.S. officials were still thinking about military options or at least threatening to use force. On September 4, 1964, assistant secretary of state William Bundy suggested to his staff the possibility that a speech by Rusk could include a suggestion that Washington might take preventive action against Chinese nuclear facilities. Bundy's proposal quickly produced opposition from Robert Johnson, who reasoned that any advance warning could help the Chinese blunt an attack, and would have a negative political impact internationally—by stirring fears of war while providing Beijing with a justification for its nuclear weapons program.[97]

How Bundy responded to Johnson's advice is not known, but the seemingly imminent Chinese test made the question of preventive action ripe for a presidential decision. The Chinese nuclear danger had been discussed that summer at several of President Johnson's Tuesday lunchtime meetings of his top national security officials. On September 15 critically important decisions were made. McCone, McNamara, Rusk, and McGeorge Bundy met in Rusk's dining room at the State Department. Three days earlier McCone, again ahead of his analysts, had told Rusk that activity at Lop Nur and certain clandestine reports indicated that a test was imminent. Rusk then informed McCone that Soviet ambassador Anatoli Dobrynin had told former U.S. ambassador to the Soviet Union Llewellyn Thompson the same thing.[98]

On September 15 they decided that it would be better to let the Chinese test occur than to take "unprovoked unilateral U.S. military action." Attacks on Chinese nuclear facilities would be possible only in the event of "military hostilities." Although cautious on unilateral action, the advisers were sufficiently worried about Beijing's nuclear progress to consider the possibility of joint steps with the Soviets, such as a warning to the Chinese not to test, or "even a possible agreement to cooperate in preventive military action." Whether anyone at the table expected the Soviets to be any more receptive than they had been in 1963 is unknown. In any event, Rusk was to make early contact with Ambassador Dobrynin.[99]

McCone suggested the need for further information on developments at Lop Nur, and recommended that the president be asked to approve a U-2 overflight of the test site. The CIA director met initial resistance from Johnson's senior advisers. For his part, Rusk noted that he knew a Chinese test was inevitable and he could not think of any action he would take if he was informed of the precise timing. McCone suggested that advance notice could be the basis for contacts with the Soviets as well as U.S. allies in Europe and Asia. But the general view was that the embarrassment and consequences of a failed mission outweighed any potential benefits. Neither Rusk nor Bundy would recommend the flight.. Before the day was out, however, McCone promised a mission with a greater chance of success, one that flew from Ban Takhli in Thailand to Lop Nur and back, and it gained the approval of the president's advisers and Johnson himself.[100]

THE TAKHLI–LOP NUR U-2 mission was canceled sometime in late

September or early October, because, as Thomas Hughes, the INR director at the time, observed, "nobody wants a U-2 shot down in the middle of a political campaign"—a consideration that, Hughes remembers, resulted in "a bewildered reaction of [the] collectors [at the United States Intelligence Board] at what politicians might do next." Also influencing the decision to cancel was data obtained from a September satellite mission.[101]

Only the Soviet archives can confirm if Rusk met Dobrynin to discuss a joint approach; if they did, no U.S. records of the talks survived. But on September 25 McGeorge Bundy attempted to sound out the ambassador. A statement that Khrushchev had made on September 15, the same day that Johnson and his advisers discussed the Chinese nuclear problem, may have encouraged Bundy to believe that Moscow might be in the mood to consider joint action. Responding to Mao's hostile comments about Soviet border rights in the Far East, Khrushchev warned that the Soviets would use all "means at their disposal" to protect their borders, including "up-to-date weapons of annihilation."[102]

Despite Khrushchev's tough talk, Dobrynin was not interested in discussing any anti-Chinese initiatives with Bundy. Just as in May 1963, Bundy proposed a "private and serious talk about what to do about this problem." In response, Dobrynin admitted the "depth and strength" of the Sino-Soviet split, which he blamed on Mao's "personal megalomania," but he took a Chinese nuclear capability for "granted." Chinese nuclear weapons, he argued, had "no importance against the Soviet Union or against the U.S." A Chinese test would have a "psychological impact" in Asia, but that was of "no importance for his government."[103]

The Soviet government's negative response effectively settled the argument over direct action. The presidential election, only weeks away, undoubtedly had some impact on Johnson's thinking. In the heat of the campaign, with Johnson running on a "peace platform" against the hawkish Barry Goldwater, the last thing he wanted to contemplate was any military action against China, with all of the risks involved. Whether election concerns were a bottom-line consideration, however, is an imponderable.

Johnson's determination to avoid confrontation with China was made evident in his Vietnam policy, and very likely shaped his stance on preemption. Although he worried that inaction on Vietnam would benefit China, Johnson wanted to avoid military measures that might lead to a wider war. Even if Johnson had been less concerned with China's reaction and leaned toward preemption, he would have had to face significant doubts about the feasibility of stopping the Chinese bomb by overt or covert action. Airstrikes would have required hitting facilities deep in the Chinese interior, requiring U.S. aircraft to "run the gauntlet of China's air defense network" with less than complete information about that network's disposition and capabilities.[104] Even more important, "less than complete information" also described U.S. knowledge about China's nuclear program. Neither John McCone nor anyone else in the U.S. intelligence community could have even come close to giving Johnson assurances that they could tell pilots or commandos exactly what targets had to be destroyed to prevent a Chinese nuclear test.

AROUND THE TIME of the Bundy-Dobrynin meeting on September 25, the U.S. intelligence establishment, probably relying on KH-7 images of Lop Nur taken in mid-August and KH-4A images from mid-September, decided that the preparations at the Lop Nur site were basically complete. Also suggestive was an agent report from a member of the Malian government delegation that had recently visited China; it stated that the Chinese had scheduled a test for October 1, China's national day.[105]

By late September the White House and the State Department were ready to make an announcement. After Whiting indirectly leaked word of a Chinese test to CBS News, on September 29, reporters queried State Department spokesman Robert McCloskey about the accuracy of television reports of an impending test. With President Johnson's consent, Secretary of State Rusk had already approved a statement for the press, which McCloskey read. He stated—for background only and not for attribution—that "from a variety of sources, we know that it is quite possible that [an] explosion could occur at any time." Downplaying the event's immediate significance, he observed that the Chinese were a "long way" from having nuclear delivery systems.[106]

The importance of intense satellite coverage was emphasized in a "Top Secret" October 2 COMOR memo, which noted that "the most pressing Chi Com intelligence problem . . . will concern the Chinese nuclear program," and that "most of our knowledge of Chinese progress in the nuclear field has been derived from satellite photography." Searching for additional facilities and monitoring known ones would require continued use of Corona and Gambit satellites. The high priority assigned to covering the Chinese nuclear program and the new Soviet missile silos had led the U.S. Intelligence Board to request that the NRO be prepared to double the number of Corona and Gambit launches over the following three months, so that possibly up to six KH-4A and four KH-7 cameras would be orbiting the earth during the year.[107]

Imagery from the first of the Corona launches in the final quarter of 1964, along with imagery obtained from Corona and Gambit satellites in September (an October 8 Gambit launch failed to reach orbit), undoubtedly had much to do with what Donald Chamberlain told deputy director of central intelligence Marshall Carter on October 15. The OSI chief wrote that the most recent information, which also included reports of a stand-down of all aviation in the area and unusual sampling of weather, had confirmed that Lop Nur was probably ready to host an atomic test. Beyond describing specific items that turned up in overhead photography—including a 340-foot tower surrounded by a double fence, arrays for instrument emplacement, two small towers, and a variety of bunkers and platforms—Chamberlain observed that the "high priority given to the completion of site construction suggests that a test is scheduled in the fairly near future." He also noted that the high level of flight activity to and from the area halted in September 1963, when the site was essentially complete, but had resumed in late September 1964, possibly reflecting final preparations.[108]

While Chamberlain and OSI were getting closer to the truth about "when," they were still off base about "how." Nuclear fuel, in the form of U-235, could not come from Lanzhou, Chamberlain wrote, because "the plant . . . is only partially complete and thus could not contribute fissionable material for a nuclear test in the near future." But CIA scientists had restudied the Baotou "reactor" site and concluded that adequate primary and backup electric power circuits for reactor operation had been installed by March 1963, resulting in a reduction in the confidence about the August 1964 judgment that the reactor had not begun operation until early 1964. In addition, the scientists wrote, "We no longer believe that evidence on plutonium availability justifies the on-balance judgment reached in August 1964. We believe the Lop Nur evidence indicates that a test could occur at any time." But they hedged their bets by concluding that "we believe a test will occur sometime within the next six to eight months."[109]

THE "NEXT SIX to eight months" included the very next day—the second day of a five-day window that Mao and other senior leaders had selected for the first test. On the same day that Chamberlain sent his memo to Carter, those responsible for assembly of the bomb at the test site received instructions to "shoot the basket," a phrase suggested by the basketball players at Lop Nur. The uranium core had arrived by air and the other components by train. Those trips, had the United States known they were taking place, would have represented an opportunity, at least in the world of fiction and film, for a daring commando raid that could have delayed the first Chinese test. But the components arrived safely at the test site and were housed in an assembly workshop to which only five people had access. The command gave the go-ahead to insert the uranium component and initiator into the high-explosive assembly.[110]

Before 6:30 in the evening of October 14, the entire bomb was assembled and moved by cart to the bomb tower's elevator, where custody was transferred in writing and with ceremony to the tower crew. The crew's chief was Chen Nengkuan, a forty-one-year-old with a Ph.D. from Yale University who had returned to China in 1958 after eleven years abroad. Chen had supervised the development of the explosive assembly and headed a team that conducted over a thousand experiments to explore the principles for detonating an atomic bomb. Chen issued the order, "Hoist up!," that would start the bomb's journey to the top of the tower. When it arrived, technicians began the process of installing it, taking readings from all the tower's onboard instruments, and inserting the detonating caps in the implosion assembly. The next morning, on the basis of weather reports, the test was scheduled for the next day at three in the afternoon. In the early morning hours of October 16, Zhang Aiping and Liu Xiyao conducted a final inspection of the preparation beneath the tower and approved connecting the detonator at 6:30 a.m. Northwest Nuclear Weapons Research and Design Academy director Li Jue and test site commander Zhang Yunyu rode the elevator to the tower's summit, where technicians affixed the electrical connections and conducted the final checks.[111]

After Li and Zhang finished their last-minute work, they, along with the tower team, moved to the far-safer test-site control room, fourteen miles away.

Zhang turned over to the control room chief the key to the tower electrical controls. With that act, all that was left was the countdown, which began seconds before the designated zero hour of 3:00 p.m. on October 16. Ten seconds after it began, the order "*Qibao!*" (Fire!) was issued, the People's Republic of China detonated an atomic bomb with a yield of 20 kilotons.[112]

One minute after the explosion, an artillery unit fired shells with parachutes to collect air samples from the cloud. An hour after the explosion, a modified Ilyushin aircraft with sampling devices flew directly into the mushroom cloud, while a second began a thirty-six-hour flight to gather air samples for later evaluations of the fallout. Chinese workers, wearing protective gear, drove into the test site to collect data on radiation and shock wave effects. Special armored units headed straight for ground zero to test the combat capability of their vehicles after an atomic blast.[113]

Zhang Aiping and Liu Xiyao reported the results to Mao, Zhou, Nie Rongzhen, and other senior leaders. A few hours later Radio Beijing began broadcasting the news to the entire world. The Chinese government issued a statement hailing the test as "a major achievement of the Chinese people," denouncing "the U.S. imperialist policy of nuclear blackmail," and characterizing the atom bomb as "a paper tiger." The following day the test was reported on the front pages of the *New York Times*, *Washington Post*, and newspapers around the world.[114]

THE U.S. INTELLIGENCE establishment did not have to wait for Radio Beijing to give it the bad news. Eleven of the thirteen electromagnetic pulse detection stations in the Atomic Energy Detection System picked up indications of a test, and their data also produced the estimated time of the detonation and contributed to the yield estimate of 19 kilotons (in contrast to China's own estimate of 22 kilotons). In addition, seven acoustic stations detected signals indicating a test, signals that, along with those from the electromagnetic stations, were used to estimate the yield and location of the detonation.[115]

In an attempt to neutralize any political repercussions, President Johnson, who only hours earlier learned that Nikita Khrushchev had "retired," issued a reassuring statement based on a draft prepared long in advance. Johnson reaffirmed U.S. defense commitments to Asia, even if China were to develop an effective nuclear arsenal; characterized the test as "a tragedy for the Chinese people, who have suffered so much under the Communist regime"; and downplayed the test's significance, stating that "there is no reason to fear that it will lead to imminent war." In his memoirs Johnson wrote, "I was not concerned for the immediate future. A long and expensive road separated setting off a nuclear blast and developing the powerful and accurate missile to carry nuclear weapons across seas and continents. Some future President would have to face the question of how to deal with this situation."[116]*

Meanwhile, the CIA, AFTAC, and other agencies continued to collect and analyze data about the test. Of particular importance were the aerial debris collection flights. On the day of the test, but before it occurred, the State and Defense Departments notified a number of military attachés that, in anticipation of a Chinese test, the air force had a "high priority requirement to obtain air samples" in Taiwan, Turkey, Iran, Pakistan, India, and Thailand, using Air Weather Service C-130 or WB-50 aircraft that would fly from airfields in those countries.[117] Those messages were overtaken by the events, but that did not prevent special aerial missions from collecting valuable debris from the test.

Missions designated Toe Dancer included Air Weather Service C-130, WB-50, and WB-57 aircraft that flew from airbases in Japan (Yokota), Libya (Wheelus), Alaska (Eielson), and California (McClellan). The Strategic Air Command also supplied B-52s from Castle Air Force Base in California, as well as WU-2s from Davis Monthan Air Force Base in Arizona and from Eielson. Collectively the planes flew eighty-five sorties, racking up 721 hours in the air, from October 16 to December 5.[118]

Nuclear debris from the test was gathered during more than thirty individual sorties by planes flying from Yokota, with the best collection occurring on October 17 at 29,000 and 30,000 feet in the vicinity of Japan. The cloud then moved eastward, crossing over, on successive days, the Aleutians and the northern Pacific, reaching Canada and the western United States on October 20. During that period aerial missions flying at between 10,000 and 20,000 feet also gathered valuable debris, which was collected on the U.S. East Coast on October 23 and 24 at 14,000 feet.[119]

When John McCone met with President Johnson and other officials on October 17, there was no longer any question as to when China would first detonate an atomic bomb. But the question of how it accomplished the feat was still a mystery. McCone opened the meeting with a briefing on the Chinese program, mentioning the presence of a small heavy-water reactor at the nuclear energy institute in Beijing, as well as the "existence of [a] suspected U-235 plant at [Lanzhou] which was not completed and we did not expect

---

* Johnson's view was shared by Barry Goldwater. The Republican presidential candidate, speaking in Mansfield, Ohio, told his audience that Communist China had not yet become a "nuclear threat" and that a warhead had no military value "unless you can get it from here to there." Without outside assistance, it would take China at least twenty-five years to develop a suitable missile, he stated. Charles Mohr, "Goldwater Doubts Chinese A-Threat," *New York Times*, October 18, 1964, pp. 1, 57.

[to] be in operation for 2 to 3 years." The CIA chief also referred to the imaginary air-cooled reactor at Baotou, which the CIA had believed went operational in late 1963 or early 1964, as well as the real one at Jiuquan, which he noted was first photographed in 1962 and then again in February 1964 and might have been operational as early as 1962. Photography of Lop Nur, he noted, had shown considerable activity at the site.[120]

As to where the fissile material for the bomb came from, McCone stated that the output of the two reactors could have provided sufficient plutonium. He also noted that "while we had extensive U-2 and satellite photography over [China], there was an important area in and about Chungking and east on the Yangtze River on which the photography was unsatisfactory and hence there might exist there or elsewhere in China, a reactor or a production complex which we did not know about."[121]

After McCone's presentation, it must have come as quite a shock to Johnson and the others when AEC chairman Glenn Seaborg addressed the president and his cabinet during the afternoon of October 20, the same day a Corona satellite snapped a picture of ground zero at Lop Nur. Seaborg and his fellow commissioners had been surprised to learn what he told LBJ: that radiological analysis had shown that the Chinese bomb was a "uranium-235 device—an implosion design using uranium rather than plutonium." U.S. officials quickly saw this as "quite an accomplishment" that, as William Bundy put it, "probably advanced the date that Chicoms would be [a] full nuclear power."[122]

At eleven o'clock the next morning, Seaborg called John McCone and told him it seemed clear that the Chinese bomb had relied on U-235. McCone told the AEC chairman that he would explore further the source of the U-235, commenting that it might have come from the Soviet Union before the schism between the Communist giants or it might have come from Lanzhou. Two months later Seaborg reported to the Committee of Principals, a group of senior officials, including Rusk and McNamara, that reviewed arms control policy, that further analysis of the debris led to the conclusion that the U-235 did not come from the Soviet Union. Nor did it come from U-235 supplied by the United States to European allies. Rather, it appeared that China had produced the material itself.[123]

THOUGH CHINA was now a member of the nuclear club, some still considered attacking its nuclear facilities a viable option. In a December 1964 paper, ACDA official George W. Rathjens challenged the analysis and conclusions of Robert Johnson. He argued that Johnson had underestimated the effects of Chinese nuclear capabilities, asserting that the United States would be far more devastated than China by the destruction of two or three of its major cities. Rathjens also claimed that Johnson had given "inadequate weight to the near term anti-proliferation effects of destroying Chinese nuclear capabilities." He concluded with the observation that if Johnson's analysis was judged to be deficient, "further consideration of direct action against Chinese nuclear facilities, or at least consideration of . . . that possibility with the Soviet Union may be warranted."[124]

While there was no chance that senior officials, including President Johnson, would approve of a postdetonation strike at China's nuclear facilities, those facilities still remained of great interest to those officials, the U.S. intelligence community, and war planners. Monitoring the facilities would provide hard intelligence on future nuclear developments as well as assist war planners in deciding which ones should be attacked in the event of war and with what degree of force. U-2s and satellites would continue to play a major role in keeping watch on China's nuclear research centers, production facilities, and test site. And there was still the tantalizing question of where the Chinese had obtained the uranium for their first atomic test.

On January 8, 1965, a Black Cat pilot, Johnny Wang Shi Chuen, took off from Taoyuan on a flight that lasted a little over seven hours, almost six hours of which was spent over the mainland. He made it to Lanzhou without equipment failures or surface-to-air missiles being fired at him. The infrared camera demonstrated that the facility was indeed operational and could have been the source of U-235 for the October blast. Unfortunately, two days later Maj. Jack Chang left on a mission from which he never returned. His target was Baotou, but Chinese air defense forces shot him down about two hundred miles south of Beijing. The next morning, Beijing radio announced that it had shot down yet another U-2.[125]

The imagery from Johnny Wang's mission, as well as other aerial and satellite imagery, helped analysts prepare the 1965 national intelligence estimate on China's advanced weapons program, which was published in late January. The estimate reported that while the first Chinese test used U-235 and had a yield of about 19 kilotons, U.S. analysts were unable to estimate the device's weight or dimensions with any confidence. In addition, it noted that Lanzhou was the most likely source of U-235 for China's bomb, and that non-Chinese sources were "highly unlikely." The estimate was wrong, however, in suggesting that the Lanzhou facility could only produce low-enriched uranium, which would require further enrichment to weapons grade, probably by an as-yet-unidentified electromagnetic separation facility. It also continued to erroneously characterize Baotou as a plutonium production site. The estimators further wrote that they had "no good basis for estimating the current level of production of fissionable material." Nevertheless, they believed that China would have enough material over the next two years to stockpile a few bombs as well as conduct a test program.[126]

A little over three and a half months after the estimate was issued, the CIA

Werner Heisenberg
(on left), Max von
Laue, and Otto Hahn.
AIP EMILIO SEGRE
VISUAL ARCHIVES,
GOUDSMIT COLLECTION

Robert Fuman (on left) and
Samuel Goudsmit.
COURTESY OF ROBERT S. NORRIS

above | **A**-26 Invader aircraft, used to carry xenon-133 detection equipment over Germany. PHOTOVAULT/WERNHER KRUTEIN PRODUCTIONS, INC.

above | **A**merican troops discover Heisenberg's reactor. AIP EMILIO SEGRE VISUAL ARCHIVES, GOUDSMIT COLLECTION

top left | **M**oe Berg (on right) and Paul Scherrer. MOE BERG PAPERS, MANUSCRIPTS AND ARCHIVES DIVISION, THE NEW YORK PUBLIC LIBRARY, ASTOR, LENOX AND TILDEN FOUNDATIONS

Tomsk-7 nuclear facility, photographed by a U-2 on August 21, 1957.
NATIONAL ARCHIVES VIA TIM BROWN

Arzamas-16, the Soviet counterpart of Los Alamos,
as photographed by a U-2 on February 5, 1960.
NATIONAL ARCHIVES VIA TIM BROWN

The cylinder with China's first bomb being moved
to the tower at Lop Nur on October 15, 1964.
ROBERT S. NORRIS

Deng Jiaxian (center) and Yu Min (right),
early Chinese nuclear weapons designers.

Jiuquan Atomic Energy Complex, as photographed
on September 22, 1966, by a KH-7/Gambit satellite.

Lanzhou Gaseous Diffusion Plant, as photographed on May 10, 1966, by a KH-7/Gambit satellite.

Lop Nur shot tower, photographed
on December 8, 1966, during a
KH-7/Gambit mission.

The Mururoa French nuclear test in the Pacific, as photographed by a KH-7/Gambit satellite on May 26, 1966. NATIONAL ARCHIVES VIA TIM BROWN

A close-up of the entrance to the test shafts at Mururoa, as photographed by a KH-7/Gambit satellite on May 26, 1967.

NATIONAL ARCHIVES VIA TIM BROWN

Marcoule Plutonium Production Plant,
France, photographed on June 11,
1967, by a KH-7/Gambit satellite.

Pierrelatte Uranium Enrichment Plant, France,
photographed on June 11, 1967, by a
KH-7/Gambit satellite.

The Negev Nuclear Research Center (Dimona)
in Israel, photographed by a KH-4B/Corona
satellite on September 29, 1971.

Vaults in which
South African
nuclear weapons
were stored.
ROBERT WINDREM

Henry Gomberg, the University of Michigan Professor who
was instrumental in convincing the United States that Israel
was operating a plutonium production reactor in the Negev.
MOSES GOMBERG PAPERS, BOX 2, BENTLEY
HISTORICAL LIBRARY, UNIVERSITY OF MICHIGAN

was reporting on the second Chinese test, conducted on May 14. Based on the data collected, particularly by Atomic Energy Detection System sensors, and analyses by OSI, AFTAC, and other elements of the nuclear intelligence establishment, the CIA reported the time of the blast as 10:00 a.m. local time, and the estimated yield at about 40 kilotons. The evidence also suggested to American analysts that the test was an airburst, "possibly an air drop from one of China's dozen or so obsolescent B-29 type bombers," based on the absence of seismic signals as well as a Chinese announcement claiming that China had exploded the device "in the air over China's western areas."[127]

Exactly what postdetonation imagery was obtained by U.S. satellites is not clear, although coverage of Lop Nur throughout 1965 was significant. By early October the site had been photographed nine times by KH-4 cameras—five times completely and four times partially. Lanzhou and Baotou were also targeted by both Corona and Gambit satellites: Lanzhou was photographed by a KH-7 camera on March 16 whereas images of Baotou were obtained in January, March, and April.[128]

The extent of coverage of Jiuquan was discussed in a September 1965 photographic interpretation report, which noted that usable photographs of the complex had been taken at least once by a U-2, three times by Gambit satellites, and eighteen times by Corona spacecraft since the first Chinese test. Of particular interest to the interpreters was what they could see in the most recent pictures: cell-like structures on the outside of the reactor building which they believed to be reactor shielding forms and shielding. Analysis of those structures would permit determination of reactor characteristics, information that could then be used to estimate Communist China's ability to produce fissionable material.[129]

IMPROVEMENTS IN the Corona, Gambit, and U-2 systems had helped increase the ability of the United States to collect photographic intelligence about developments at Chinese nuclear facilities as well as the aftermath of test shots. In 1965, the Atomic Energy Detection System was also upgraded in several important areas. That system still included key contributions from electromagnetic, airborne, acoustic, and seismic systems, although budget constraints had reduced the number of electromagnetic stations from over twenty to twelve. By the end of 1964 the remaining sites received advanced equipment and plans were being made to expand the network.[130]

In the summer of 1963, the fleet of planes used for aerial sampling consisted of sixty-seven aircraft operated by the Air Weather Service (forty-three RB-50s, twenty-three RB-57s, one RB-47) and seventeen operated by SAC (eight B-52s and nine U-2s). That fleet was expected to change significantly over the succeeding years as RB-47 and W-130 aircraft replaced the RB-50 and

RB-57 planes. RB-47E aircraft were phased into the Air Weather Service inventory from June through December 1963. Routine operations with the C-130 aircraft, which began in December 1962, also resulted in the retirement of five of the seventeen RB-50 aircraft from the Air Weather Service inventory by December 31, 1963. The modification of twelve B-57 aircraft, involving the installation of gamma ray spectrometers for detection of debris at high altitudes and gas-sampling equipment, began in 1963. By December 1965 the Air Weather Service received eleven of twelve RB-57 aircraft. In December 1965, Air Weather Service WC-135 aircraft, which carried equipment for debris sampling, whole air sampling, and tracking of radioactive clouds, replaced the RB-50 aircraft and began flying sampling missions.[131]

Responsibility for two army acoustic intelligence networks had been transferred from the Army Signal Corps to the Army Security Agency, whose primary goal was signals intelligence, in July 1962. One network, designated Red Wind, consisted of a processing and reporting center at Fort Monmouth, New Jersey, and six overseas collection facilities. Its mission was to detect the acoustic signals from Soviet space and missile launches. The second acoustic network, Dawn Star, had a different target: Soviet and, from 1964 on, Chinese nuclear weapons tests.[132]

By the fall of 1965, the Dawn Star network consisted of a processing center at Vint Hill Farms Station, Virginia, where it had been relocated from Fort Monmouth after being merged with the Red Wind processing center, and overseas sites. Collection sites, each designated as an Army Security Agency Signal Research Unit, were located in Germany (Zweibrücken), Iran (Teheran and Meshed), Turkey (Belbasi), Hawaii (Helemano), Thailand (Bangkok), Japan (Misawa Air Base, Itazuke Air Base), and Greenland (Thule Air Base). A site at Yong Do, Korea, was shut down in September.[133]

The most important 1965 development involving AFTAC and the Atomic Energy Detection System occurred in the summer, when AFTAC began receiving data from six satellites, the first two of which had been launched in 1963 and the fifth and six in July 1965. Those six satellites had been lifted into 67,000-mile circular orbits by Atlas-Agena D boosters from the Eastern Test Range at Cape Kennedy. Designated Vela, they were part of a research program begun by the Advanced Research Projects Agency in August 1959 to investigate means of detecting nuclear explosions. One component was Vela Uniform, the seismic detection of detonations; another was Vela Sierra, the surface-based detection of high-altitude explosions; the third was Vela Hotel, satellite-based detection of nuclear detonations at high altitude or in outer space. Eventually the term *Vela*, Spanish for "watchman," became synonymous with the satellite component of the program.[134]

The lack of a satellite detection capability had been identified in a December 1964 JCS report to secretary of defense Robert McNamara as one of two acute deficiencies in the U.S. ability to monitor compliance with the 1963 limited test ban treaty, which prohibited the United States, Soviet Union, and the United Kingdom, its signatories, from conducting nuclear tests in outer space, in the atmosphere, or underwater. The other was the absence of a means of detecting underwater tests. Turning over the Vela research satellites would help address those deficiencies. While small, measuring less than five feet in diameter, they were equipped with sensors to detect the X-rays, gamma rays, and neutrons emitted from a nuclear explosion.[135] Besides providing more confidence in the U.S. ability to monitor the test ban treaty, the satellites improved the ability to monitor the nuclear tests of two countries that had not signed the treaty: China and France.

The U.S. nuclear intelligence analytical capability was also augmented in 1965. That August, William F. Raborn, the director of central intelligence, and Glenn Seaborg, who had succeeded John McCone as chairman of the AEC, signed a memorandum of understanding. The memo established a Special Projects Group, also known as Z Division, as part of the Lawrence Livermore National Laboratory. The division would focus its analytical talent, made up of individuals with physical and social sciences background, initially on the Soviet and then the Chinese nuclear programs. Dale Nielsen, the division's first chief, recalled, "We looked at the weapons fired by Russia, and later by China, to see what they were shooting."[136]

Raborn also agreed to an October recommendation from CIA deputy director of science and technology Albert Wheelon to establish the Nuclear Intelligence Panel. The group, whose members were drawn from the national labs, academia, and industry, would serve as an advisory panel on estimates of fissionable material and weapons production. With Louis H. Roddis Jr. of the Pennsylvania Electric Company as its chairman and Hans Bethe among its eleven members, the new unit was an enhanced version of a panel that had been established by Allen Dulles during his tenure as director of central intelligence.[137]

VELA AND OTHER nuclear intelligence assets would prove useful in 1966, as China conducted its third, fourth, and fifth nuclear tests, as well as improved its capability to produce nuclear fuel. On May 9 a Hong-6 bomber, a modified version of the Soviet Tu-16, released an atomic bomb that was far more potent than any of China's previous bombs. The weapon, which was detonated in the air, produced a yield of over 200 kilotons. Two weeks later, after American nuclear intelligence analysts had a chance to analyze the debris resulting from the test and other data, the OSI correctly reported that China had used thermonuclear material, which would have been identified as lithium-6 deuteride, to achieve the boost in yield.[138]

The second test of 1966 occurred in October—the same month that the plutonium production reactor at Jiuquan was completed and started up—with another nuclear first. On October 27 members of the People Liberation Army's Second Artillery Corps fired a DF-2 missile, armed with a 20- to 30-kiloton warhead, from Shuanghcengzi, the Chinese missile test center, toward Lop Nur. After traveling about five hundred miles, it detonated as planned and on target. Beijing did not try to keep the test or its method of delivery secret. The following week, a CIA publication, the Office of Current Intelligence's *Weekly Summary*, reported that the limited, indirect evidence available suggested that Beijing was telling the truth when it claimed its missile had carried the warhead to Lop Nur. It added that the detonation occurred about a hundred miles east of the Lop Nur test site and had a yield between 20 and 200 kilotons. Beyond noting technical details, the CIA authors commented that "the test came at a time when the regime was badly in need of a showy achievement," and "served as a psychological boost to the Vietnamese Communists."[139]

A two-page special national intelligence estimate on China's advanced weapons programs, updating the longer national estimate that appeared in July, which was approved by the U.S. Intelligence Board the day before the *Weekly Summary* appeared, also reported on the detonation and its location, along with the apparent accuracy of China's claim that the bomb arrived at the test site via a ballistic missile. Looking toward the future, it noted that China would be aiming to develop a high-yield thermonuclear weapon. At the same time the estimators did not expect near-term success. They observed that while the third Chinese test device contained some thermonuclear material, it "performed quite inefficiently and apparently was heavy and bulky, indicating that the Chinese have much to learn about thermonuclear technology." They would not rule out "the possibility that the Chinese will be able to develop a thermonuclear warhead by the early 1970s."[140]

BUT THE NUCLEAR WEAPONS designers at the Northwest Nuclear Weapons Research and Design Academy were farther along than the U.S. intelligence community believed. The initial intent to develop a hydrogen bomb went back to 1959 when China's leaders first drew up a plan that included the development of fission and fusion weapons. The next year, with weapons designers at the Beijing Nuclear Weapons Research Institute focusing their attention on the atomic bomb, the Second Ministry instructed the Institute of Atomic Energy to form a "leading group" to conduct research on thermonuclear materials and reactions. Key members of the group included Huang Zuqia, a student of Peng Huanwu, as well as Yu Min and Qian Sanqiang. Then in September 1963, as soon they had finished their work on 596, the bomb designers in Qinghai were ordered to shift their attention to a thermonuclear device. The Northwest institute's theoretical department, headed by Deng Jiaxian, assumed primary responsibility for designing China's first fusion weapons.[141]

In May 1964 Mao urged that work on the hydrogen bomb be speeded up, and Zhou Enlai followed in July with a directive to build a bomb that could be carried on a missile—a two-stage thermonuclear device, not simply a boosted fission weapon. By the winter of 1964–1965, aided by their reading of foreign literature, the Chinese were completing the production line for lithium-6 deuteride, the first quantities of lithium-6 having been separated at the workshop at Baotou on September 17 and the first lithium-6 deuteride produced the following week. But Chinese scientists still had much to learn about how it performed or the exact conditions necessary to achieve a thermonuclear reaction. They had yet to discover how to use a uranium bomb to induce the desired reaction. Physicists from both the Northwest academy and the Touli institute searched for answers throughout the winter. In February 1965 Qian Sanqiang ordered fifty of his top scientist and engineers at Touli to measure the lithium deuteride molecule and analyze its reactions.[142]

Design of the proper initiator required a trip by Yu Min, deputy director of the Northwest academy's theoretical department, to Shanghai to make extensive calculations. Yu departed for Qinghai in late September 1965 and in about two months was able to inform his bosses that he had "found a shortcut." A test on May 9, 1966, was one sign of progress. A Hong-6 bomber dropped a 200- to 300-kiloton uranium bomb that contained lithium-6. Another occurred at the end of the year—on December 28. A device containing U-235 and lithium-6 deuteride and mounted on a tower detonated with a force of between 300 and 500 kilotons. It was reported about ten days later to readers of the CIA Weekly Summary as "probably a tower shot which yielded several hundred kilotons." Both tests allowed for the evaluation of the scientists' ideas about burning thermonuclear fuels, and resulted in approval to test a two-stage, 3-megaton device.[143]

Early May 1967, assembly of a fusion device was completed at the Nuclear Component Manufacturing Plant at Jiuquan, and on May 9 the Fifteen-Member Special Commission informed the commander of the Lop Nur test base that he should complete preparations for a test no later than June 20. That order was fulfilled with time to spare, and on June 17, a few hours before the test, the thermonuclear device was lifted onto a Hong-6 bomber. Once in the air there were problems. The pilot had trouble flying the plane, while the navigator failed to release the bomb on schedule, at 8:00 a.m. When the bad news arrived in Beijing, Zhou radioed the crew with encouragement, telling them "to remain calm and act resolutely."[144]

At 8:20 a.m. the bomb was released, followed by an enormous, 3-megaton explosion—"steel plates 400 meters from ground zero melted, as did concrete blocks whose surfaces turned to glass. The shock wave struck a 54-ton locomotive 3 kilometers from ground zero and shoved it 18 meters. Semi-buried fortifications were sliced apart, and brick houses 14 kilometers away collapsed. The spectacular fireball rapidly became a massive mushroom cloud." Less than a week later, an article in the CIA *Weekly Summary* noted that "Communist China's successful detonation of a high-yield thermonuclear weapon . . . shows its continuing progress in nuclear weapons design." It also observed that the "test was China's biggest so far, with a yield in the range of several megatons." In August a new national estimate on China's advanced weapons program noted that "China probably now has a few fission weapons in its stockpile deliverable by bomber, and has demonstrated the capability to produce thermonuclear weapons with megaton (mt) yields."[145]

The analysts who prepared the estimate did not have all the information they might have wished or expected, which was the catalyst for a U-2 mission to Lop Nur. On the night of May 7, 1967, Jenliang "Spike" Chaung took off from Takhli and flew his spyplane across Burma, northeastern India, and the Himalayan mountains, headed to Lop Nur. Along with a camera, the pilot carried an "emplaced sensor," a device that would be covertly deployed to a location where it could monitor a targeted activity. Designated Tabasco, it had been developed for OSI by Sandia Labs under the supervision of the CIA's Office of Research and Development. After being ejected from the U-2, the fifteen-foot-long capsule would descend to three thousand feet, at which point its parachute was to open and carry it down to a spot near, but not too near, the Chinese test site. When the nose of the device pierced the surface of the desert and embedded itself in the ground, the petals on the tail were to open, deploying solar cells and an antenna. After the device's airwave and ground motion sensors collected data from a Chinese test, it would transmit them to the U.S. signals intelligence site on Taiwan at Shu Linkou.[146]

When Spike reached the test site early the following morning, he dropped the Tabasco device. After completing the photographic reconnaissance portion of his mission, he headed back to Takhli, landing after almost nine hours in the air. But the Tabasco sensor that he had gone to such trouble to deliver did not perform satisfactorily on June 17. So another Black Cat pilot, Bill Chang, lifted off in the early morning hours of August 31, also from Takhli, and flew an almost identical path to Lop Nur. His U-2 was equipped with a high-frequency transmitter and trailing antenna. Chang loitered over the area where Spike had dropped the Tabasco capsule, to tune up the communication link between the sensor and the station on Taiwan. After ten minutes he resumed his course. After nine hours and twenty minutes in the air he was able to land back at Takhli, although not until he had evaded SA-2 missiles that sought to bring him down.[147]

THE TABASCO SENSOR'S next opportunity to provide data on a Chinese test, if Chang's mission was successful, was in December. On December 24 a device was dropped from a Hong-6 and exploded with a force of 15 to 25 kilotons. There was no signal from Tabasco. In the months before the test Lop Nur was monitored by two types of Gambit satellites: the original model, which carried the KH-7 camera, and an advanced version equipped with the KH-8 camera. On the very last KH-7 mission, which began on June 4, 1967, and ended on June 12, Lop Nur was photographed three times, twice with good results. By that point the resolution of the KH-7 images could reach two feet. Higher-resolution KH-8/Gambit spacecraft had been orbited in July 1966 and on eight subsequent occasions through the early part of December.[148]

The United States also had a new version of Corona available, starting in the fall of 1967. On September 15 the first Corona carrying a KH-4B camera, with six-foot resolution, went into orbit. In addition to a higher resolution, KH-4B cameras carried more film and could stay in orbit longer — up to eighteen days, compared to the four- to fifteen-day lifetimes for the KH-4A. Over the remainder of the year, there would be another five KH-4B and another six KH-4A launches, all of which concluded with both film capsules from the satellites being recovered.[149]

In late April the first pair of advanced Vela satellites were launched from what was then Cape Kennedy. An addition to each satellite was a pair of optical flash detectors, known as bhangmeters, that could measure the intensity of light, as a function of time, from a nuclear explosion. The satellites also came equipped with eight X-ray detectors, four gamma ray detectors, two Geiger counters, an extreme ultraviolet radiation detector, and electromagnetic pulse detectors.[150]

The improved Velas and Dawn Star, along with aerial debris collection, undoubtedly played a role in providing the raw data to those responsible, in the CIA, JAEIC, AFTAC, Z Division, and other organizations, for assessing the December 24 test. That data would have allowed an estimate of the yield, as well as the judgment that the fallout from the blast contained lithium-6.[151]

In a secret memo to Dean Rusk, written two days after the test, INR's George Denney Jr. reported that "preliminary technical analysis of Communist China's seventh nuclear test, together with [Beijing's] continuing silence about the event, suggests that the test could have been a failure." Denney went on to explain that the estimated yield was 10 kilotons, the preliminary debris sampling showed presence of lithium deuteride in the device, and the previous Chinese thermonuclear tests had produced yields of 250, 300, and 3,000 kilotons. He continued, "Given the thermonuclear content and other technical evidence, the low yield of the seventh device suggests that something may have gone wrong during the detonation."[152]

IN 1969, President Richard Nixon suspended the Tackle program of U-2 flights over the Chinese mainland. In 1971 he canceled it as part of his quest to improve relations with China. But a constellation of intelligence collection systems would continue to provide data on various aspects of the Chinese program.[153]

Those systems would repeatedly cover the key facilities that had been established in the late 1950s and early 1960s—the assorted mines, Lanzhou, Baotou, Jiuquan, Lop Nur, and the Northwest Nuclear Weapons Research and Design Academy. Some of those facilities did not play a role in China's initial nuclear test: Mass mining produced the uranium ore from which the U-235 for the first bomb was made. And the Institute of Atomic Energy, not Baotou, provided the uranium tetrafluoride used in building the first bomb. But the mines and Baotou would play key roles in creating the successors to "596."[154]

America's spies would also have new nuclear facilities to investigate, those established as part of the "Third Line" program—the creation of a duplicate, and more advanced, set of nuclear facilities, steel and machine building factories, mines, and railroads that would also serve as a strategic reserve in the event of war. To reduce their vulnerability the facilities would be built in remote areas of China, in narrow valleys, or near mountains. Work on the facilities began in 1964, was disrupted by the Cultural Revolution, and continued on until the 1970s. Among the key nuclear facilities of the Third Line was a complex in Guanyuan which contained a plutonium production reactor and chemical separation plant, and apparently replaced Jiuquan. There was also a nuclear fuel component plant in Yibin, and a gaseous diffusion plant at Heping, which probably became operational around 1975.[155] Eventually, the Third Line facilities would replace many of the ones that were of such concern—including Lanzhou, Jiuquan, and Baotou—in the 1960s. Lop Nur, however, would remain an active nuclear site and a target for the U.S. intelligence community for decades to come.

chapter five

AN ELATED GENERAL, A SMILING BUDDHA

IN THE LATE 1960s, Lop Nur, Semipalatinsk, and Novaya Zemlya were not the only nuclear testing sites that commanded the attention of the men and women who selected the targets for the Corona and Gambit reconnaissance satellites.* In contrast to the sites in the Soviet Union and China, others were not located within a vast expanse of territory. Instead, they could be found on two tiny atolls in the South Pacific. And rather than belonging to a sworn adversary, they belonged to an ally, albeit a troublesome one.

FRANCE'S FIRST STEPS toward an atomic bomb can be traced back to a meeting held in the spring of 1939. One participant, Edgar Sengier, was the managing director of Union Minière, which controlled access to the uranium ore in the Belgian Congo. Another participant, along with several professional colleagues, was Frédéric Joliot-Curie, whose work had ultimately led Otto Hahn and Fritz Strassman to discover fission. Joliot-Curie and his fellow scientists proposed developing and then exploding a uranium bomb in the Sahara Desert. Sengier agreed in principle, promising to provide the ore and assist in the bomb's development. He would soon provide eight tons of uranium oxide.[1]

In addition to uranium oxide from the Congo, Joliot-Curie and his col-

---

* Until 1967 selecting targets was the responsibility of the Committee on Overhead Reconnaissance. In July 1967, the Committee for Imagery Requirements and Exploitation (COMIREX) was established by director of central intelligence Richard Helms, and assigned two missions: making the targeting decisions for imagery overflights and deciding how the task of exploiting the imagery obtained would be divided among the National Photographic Interpretation Center, Defense Intelligence Agency, and military service interpreters at organizations such as the Air Force Foreign Technology Division and the Naval Scientific and Technical Intelligence Center. See Jeffrey T. Richelson, *America's Secret Eyes in Space: The U.S. Keyhole Spy Satellite Program* (New York: Harper & Row, 1990), pp. 252–256.

leagues wanted heavy water. They believed they had identified two means of producing an unrestrained chain reaction—with U-235, and with natural uranium mixed with heavy water to slow down neutrons and increase the rate of fission—and that the second way was the easiest. In November 1939, Joliot-Curie, who had been recalled to military service and appointed head of the army's Group 1 of Scientific Research, recommended to minister of armaments Raoul Dautry that France acquire 880 pounds of uranium metal from the United States and Norway's entire stock of heavy water.[2]

The second task was entrusted to Lt. Jacques Allier, an officer in the Deuxième Bureau, at that time still the elite French intelligence service. Allier, whose civilian career was in banking, had been dealing with Norwegian affairs since 1923. On February 28, 1940, he boarded a train from Paris to Amsterdam to begin his journey. Upon arrival in Norway he discovered that the Germans had tried to purchase the existing heavy-water supply and order more. But while France could not best the Germans on the battlefield, they did win this battle in the secret war. On March 9, Allier completed negotiations for Norway's entire heavy-water supply, about 407 pounds, which would be turned over to France as a wartime loan, in exchange for 15 percent of the profits from any technical developments obtained from its use. Exactly a week later the entire supply was in Paris.[3]

With uranium oxide and heavy water in hand, the French physicists prepared to begin reactor-related experiments. But just as the German invasion of the Soviet Union in 1941 delayed that nation's effort to develop atomic weapons, so the German invasion of France in June 1940 stopped the "clock of French research" on atomic weapons. After the German invasion the primary concern was keeping the raw materials that France had acquired out of Hitler's hands. The heavy water went to Britain along with Joliot-Curie and his colleagues Hans Halban and Lew Kowarski. Some of the uranium oxide went to Morocco, where it would remain hidden in a mine for six years—keeping it out of the hands of first the Germans and then the Americans and British. Joliot-Curie went back to Paris, where he would later tell Kurt Diebner that he had no idea what happened to the uranium oxide or heavy water.[4]

In the fall of 1945, with the war over, another trip by Allier to Norway produced another commitment. The Norwegian foreign minister and Norsk Hydro-Electric agreed to provide France with the first five tons of heavy water produced after the war. The purchase arrangements would be completed in May 1946. That same year, Gen. Bloch Dassault, the brother of airplane builder Marcel Dassault, oversaw the quiet repatriation of the uranium oxide.[5]

France had not only acted to obtain the raw materials for atomic weapons, but also tried to determine what the Germans knew. At the end of the war, the First Army's Operational Intelligence Service managed to snatch two or three scientists from the Russians. They also received the help of a

"Captain Durand" in assessing recovered documents concerning nuclear physics. One day, an assistant to Col. Leon Simoneau, head of the intelligence service, told his boss that it was "astonishing" how closely Durand resembled Joliot-Curie. Considering that Durand and Joliot-Curie were one and the same, it was not astonishing at all.[6]

On one of the occasions in the spring of 1945 when Joliot-Curie was not pretending to be anyone other than himself, he met with Gen. Charles de Gaulle, leader of the Free French Forces who would become president of the provisional French government. Also in attendance was Pierre Auger, who, along with Halban, Kowarski, Jules Gueron, and Bertrand Goldschmidt, worked in the Manhattan Project's Montreal laboratory. The duo insisted that it was time to set up a French atomic energy organization. De Gaulle, who during a trip to Canada had learned from the French physicists there of the atomic bomb effort, accepted their recommendation and told them to "take Dautry with you" — in reference to Raoul Dautry, who had become the minister for reconstruction.[7]

Their efforts culminated in a October 18, 1945, decree establishing the Commissariat à l'Énergie Atomique (CEA), the French Atomic Energy Commission, reporting directly to the president of the provisional government. No program to build nuclear weapons was established along with the commission. The CEA was independent of the military establishment, and its first objective, the construction of a small reactor, was to be accomplished in the light of day. Joliot-Curie became the high commissioner, and at the beginning of January 1946 his six-member executive committee — Kowarski, Goldschmidt, Gueron, Irène Joliot-Curie, Pierre Auger, and Francis Perrin, who had published the first approximate formula for determining the critical mass of uranium — was appointed. Dautry was appointed administrator-general.[8]

The CEA's initial workplan involved five components. In the vicinity of Paris, a nuclear physics research center would be created, and the first two reactors established. An intense uranium-prospecting effort would be required. Offices and laboratories needed to be built. Private corporations and a gunpowder factory at Le Bouchet, twenty-five miles south of Paris, would process minerals and prepare extremely pure materials. The last step would involve the construction of a 100,000-kilowatt reactor, which could produce 5 percent of the electricity that France had consumed in 1938.[9]

That spring Dautry and Joliot-Curie agreed that "the wide-open and windy plateau" of Christ-de-Saclay would be the future site of CEA's Saclay Nuclear Research Center. To serve as temporary quarters, they used an old fortress at Fort de Chatillon, on the Paris outskirts. By the end of 1947, the plant at Le Bouchet was completed and began refining the uranium oxide that had been returned from Morocco, which proved to be of much higher quality than the oxide retrieved from Le Havre after the war. The purified material it produced was used to feed France's first reactor, at Chatillon, EL-1 or ZOE (Zero power, uranium Oxide, Eau lourde [heavy water]), which went critical in December 1948. ZOE would be employed for research and training and produce minute amounts of plutonium and radioisotopes.[10]

Before the end of 1948 the prospecting effort was underway and producing results. There was an exploratory mission to Madagascar, but more important and more promising were prospecting discoveries within France. Uranium was discovered at La Crouzille, in the Limousin, as well as in the Autun region. As a result, France would not have to rely on foreign sources of uranium.[11]

A second plant was built at Le Bouchet during the spring and summer of 1949, this one a laboratory-scale extraction facility. The uranium oxide fuel rods of the ZOE reactor were processed there to extract small quantities of plutonium. The first milligram, in the form of a purified salt, was produced in November 1949. By the end of 1951 one hundred milligrams had been extracted, which was sufficient for research purposes.[12]

That year had proved significant in France's progress toward an atomic weapons capability. Early in the year Robert Spence, a British colleague of Bertrand Goldschmidt, told him that Glenn Seaborg's proposition—there was no "best solvent for [extracting] plutonium, the best is the one that one knows how to use best"—had been invalidated. Spence, however, would not reveal what solvent the Americans had discovered was unequivocally superior. But he had said enough. There was a secret waiting to be uncovered; all that was necessary was to know it existed. Goldschmidt assigned two of his assistants to compile a complete bibliography of all recent U.S. publications concerning solvent extraction in mineral chemistry. A few weeks later they informed him that tributyl phosphate (TBP) had been successfully employed for the difficult separation of adjoining elements. Shortly afterward, one of Spence's colleagues happened to visit. During their drive to Le Bouchet, Goldschmidt casually asked him if the British were working on TBP as well. Goldschmidt recalled that "he could not keep from replying: 'Oh. You know!' We thus 'discovered' the exceptional properties of this solvent."[13]

In April 1951 Francis Perrin replaced Joliot-Curie as high commissioner of the CEA. Joliot-Curie, a Communist, had become increasingly hostile to the notion of France developing atomic weapons, fearful that they might be employed some day against the Soviet Union. In August, Félix Gaillard became the secretary of state for atomic energy. Over the next few months he appointed Pierre Guillaumat to become administrator-general of the CEA, and requested preparation of a five-year plan. Completed by the end of 1951, and approved by the National Assembly the following July, it called for the construction of two plutonium production reactors and a plutonium extraction facility at Marcoule on the Rhone River. The plan was silent about the real purpose of the facility, the production of atomic weapons, but an infra-structure would be required when the time arrived.[14]

Also during 1951 the army's chief of staff created the Committee on Spe-cial Armaments (Commandement des Armes Spéciales). Among the first studies were those exploring the use of atomic weapons in combat. But while such theoretical studies increased military interest, it was a real-world military defeat that helped foster the notion that France should possess the bomb. In May 1954 French troops were defeated by the Viet Minh at Dien Bien Phu, signaling the end of French colonialism in Indochina and dealing a severe blow to French prestige. Development of an atomic bomb was seen as a means of restoring France's status, and ensuring a greater voice among the Western allies. That the United States considered using atomic weapons in support of the French effort, but decided against such a dramatic action may have further spurred on the French.[15]

Before the end of the year, on December 26, Prime Minister Pierre Mendès-France, who had presided over the Dien Bien Phu debacle, met with his cabinet and other officials to discuss the possibility of joining the nuclear club. They decided that the idea should be studied, and Gen. Albert Buchalet was appointed to head the Bureau of General Studies, subsequently renamed the Department of New Techniques (in 1956) and then the Military Applica-tions Directorate (in 1958), within the CEA.[16]

In May 1955 the first funds for bomb studies were covertly transferred from the Ministry of the Armed Forces to the CEA, and Buchalet's bureau began work. The CEA's nuclear development plan called for an extension of the basic nuclear infrastructure, including a graphite-moderated reactor and a chemical-processing plant to produce plutonium. And just as, two years later, the Taiwan Straits crisis of 1958 would reinforce Mao's desire for nuclear weapons, so the Suez Crisis of 1956 did for France. The United States pres-sured its allies to withdraw their forces, while the Soviet Union threatened nuclear attack if they failed to do so. The event, according to one observer, "demonstrated to the French military . . . that strategic dependence on the United States might prove worse than futile."[17]

ON JANUARY 7, 1956, G-1, the plutonium production reactor at Mar-coule, went critical and in September reached full power. By that time, Col. Charles Ailleret, the most outspoken advocate of nuclear weapons in the armed forces, had been elevated to the rank of general and placed in charge of the Committee on Special Armaments. A November 30 memorandum instructed the CEA to conduct preliminary studies for a test explosion, pre-pare the scientific aspects of the test, provide the required plutonium, and build a facility for enriching uranium. Ailleret's group was assigned responsibility for preparing for the test, including selection of the site. The next month, the Committee on Military Applications of Atomic Energy, which included military personnel as well as the most senior officials from the CEA, was established.[18]

The search for a suitable site began in 1957. There would be only two serious candidates—the Sahara Desert in the French colony of Algeria, and the Tuamotu islands in Polynesia—although a number of additional islands, including the Kerguelen Islands, Réunion, and New Caledonia, were the subject of preliminary studies. In July the Sahara was selected. Polynesia was rejected, at least in the short term, because of the distance from France and lack of an airport. Ailleret wrote at the time that the rejection should last "as long as we are not setting off megaton-size thermonuclear devices." He also noted that "from a technical point of view, and without any evaluation or prediction regarding future political developments, it appears that only the [Sahara] is suited for the construction of an atomic testing complex." The Sahara was still a provisional choice, apparently because the problem of establishing a water supply had not yet been solved.[19]

On April 11, 1958, Prime Minister Félix Gaillard signed a directive ordering the construction of a device, to be tested in the first quarter of 1960. By July the supreme authority over France's nuclear program passed to Charles de Gaulle. The Fourth Republic had been a casualty of the Algerian war, as the French military tried to maintain control of the colonial outpost and the Algerian National Liberation Front (FLN) sought to drive them out. De Gaulle was invited to step in and assume leadership of a Fifth Republic. On July 22 de Gaulle confirmed Gaillard's April 11 decision.[20]

Throughout 1958 and 1959, in France and in Africa, the French effort progressed. The CEA's industrial directorate, which had built the Marcoule reactor, supervised the production of plutonium at the site, the separation plant having become operational in 1958. The Military Applications Division was responsible for weapons design and building the experimental device.[21]

Concerns about the water supply notwithstanding, the moratorium on atmospheric testing that began in late 1958, and the potential internationalization of the Algerian war, did not prevent the construction of the test center in the Sahara. Several potential underground sites in France were investigated, as were possible sites in the Pacific because of fears that international agreements or events in Algeria would preclude testing there. Ground zero was established about forty-five miles south of the oasis at Reggane, with a base camp and a landing strip about seven miles to the east, at the edge of the Tidikelt plateau.[22]

At 7:00 a.m. Paris time on February 13, 1960, the plutonium device, resting on a 344-foot tower, was detonated on Aillert's orders in the remote Saharan site, marking France's entrance into the nuclear club. Code-named Gerboise Bleue, the test produced a blast of between 60 and 70 kilotons, making it the most auspicious entry into the nuclear club. The blast "lighted the desert and paled the full moon still visible in the morning sky." President de Gaulle expressed his elation with a "Hurrah for France!" reaction to the news. He went on to note that "since this morning [France] is stronger and prouder." Other nations were less thrilled. Not surprisingly, the Soviet Union was not pleased. The U.S. reaction was one of resignation and regret. Several African nations strenuously objected to being exposed to the fallout from the French test. Ghana froze the assets of all French concerns "until such time as the effects on the population of Ghana . . . become known."[23]*

Before the year was over, France conducted three more tower tests in the Sahara, although of much lower yields, with only the Gerboise Blanche test of April 1 producing a blast close to 20 kilotons. The last of the three tests, Gerboise Verte, occurred on April 25, 1961, and produced a yield of less than 1 kiloton. The device was detonated "hastily and prematurely" because three days earlier, Gen. Maurice Challe, the former commander-in-chief of French forces in Algeria, initiated the "The Revolt of the Generals," in opposition to de Gaulle's plan to disengage from Algeria. Detonating the device ahead of schedule ensured that it would not fall into the hands of Challe and his associates.[24]

U.S. CONCERN over French involvement with atomic energy had begun long before France had a nuclear weapons program. Operation Harborage had been intended to keep Werner Heisenberg, his colleagues, and their documents out of French as well as Soviet hands. Joliot-Curie inspired suspicion because of his Communist politics. Leslie Groves believed he first collaborated with the Germans, only joining the resistance when it became clear that the Third Reich was doomed.[25]

Suspicion extended beyond Joliot-Curie. A February 1946 memo from Selby Skinner of the Strategic Services Unit to Groves's representative, W. R. Shuler, noted that "a reliable source" conveyed a rumor that "French scientists have the formula and techniques concerning atomic explosives, and that they are now willing to sell this information." They were not targeting Allies or their own government, the memo reported, but were supposed to be interested in "selling the discovery to one of the smaller nations." The six scientists

---

* The story merited front-page coverage in the *New York Times* as well as the *Washington Post and Times-Herald*. But while the story received column-one treatment in the *Times*, the biggest headline in the *Post* concerned the snowstorm that had blown into the Washington area and threatened to deposit eight inches before it departed.

named included Joliot-Curie, Madame Curie, and four professors identified as Bertrand, Pascal, Coupard, and Cappard.[26]

Several additional, more conventional reports or studies about French atomic activities were produced before the year was out. In their February 28 overview of foreign nuclear capabilities, W. R. Shuler and David Gattiker devoted one section to France, focusing on Joliot-Curie and mineral resources. The professor was attempting to form a European scientific bloc to "counteract the Anglo-American bloc." One of those approached was an unsympathetic Paul Scherrer. The second section noted Joliot-Curie's claim that France had two hundred tons of uranium which had not been discovered by the Germans.[27]

In August one of Groves's representatives in London transmitted a study titled "Atomic Energy Research in France," which ran a bit over six single-spaced pages and was classified Top Secret. The author addressed the CEA and its functions, other research organizations, personalities, raw materials, political considerations, and capabilities. It noted the plan to locate the CEA headquarters in Fort de Chatillon, and identified the facilities being employed at the time. The section on other organizations covered nineteen institutions, from the National Center for Scientific Research to the Cancer Institute. Fifteen different individuals, mostly scientists, were briefly discussed, including the usual suspects: the Joliot-Curies, Kowarski, Goldschmidt, and Gueron. The report also identified the principal bottleneck for the CEA as being "the lack of large stocks of fissionable material with which to carry on large-scale experimentation." France, it continued, did not have access to uranium supplies, a comment perhaps made in the absence of knowledge about the uranium ore hidden in Morocco.[28]

Henry Lowenhaupt made a contribution to the analysis of the French program in November when he reported on the significant elements in a speech Joliot-Curie gave to the CEA. The Top Secret designation of his report may indicate that the speech was obtained from clandestine sources or the reports about atomic energy developments were politically sensitive, or both. One item of undoubted interest was Joliot-Curie's statement that France had available a uranium supply that had been built up before June, and enough uranium "throughout the empire" to conduct the first stage of their work. He also suggested that through close French cooperation with Britain, "England could be aided in getting 'out of the grasp of the United States.'"[29]

Various branches of the U.S. intelligence establishment continued to keep tabs on who was who in the French program during the early 1950s (and certainly beyond). In April 1951 the Division of Biographic Information, in what was then the State Department's Office of Intelligence and Research, sent the department's intelligence chief a short, secret report on new CEA chairman Francis Perrin. The report focused on his background (professor of atomic and molecular physics at the Collège de France since 1946), his politics (leftist), and his "reputation for honesty, reliability, and sound judgment among U.S. representatives in Berlin."[30]

In December 1952 Garrison B. Coverdale of Army Intelligence sent a memo to the CIA and to the State Department's special assistant for atomic energy, apparently based on reporting from the army attaché in Paris and focusing on CEA personnel developments. Jacques de Courlon, who had been invited to join the CEA, was described by one of the attaché's sources as "an excellent geophysicist, but politically leftist." There was also discussion of what role a particular individual would play in the commission's work, and on the unannounced replacement of the commission's secretary-general.[31]

What other intelligence was collected about French atomic activities and personnel during the first part of the 1950s, and what conclusions were drawn from it, is not evident. However, in the late 1950s and early 1960s, as France advanced toward membership in the nuclear fraternity, a variety of reports and studies were completed. An article in the May 29, 1957, issue of the *Central Intelligence Bulletin* noted that the French government that replaced defeated Prime Minister Guy Mollet's might be unable to renew his assurances that France would forgo such a program if an early disarmament agreement was reached. "Pressures," it stated, "seem to be mounting in France in favor of a national nuclear weapons program."[32]

The following month, the intelligence community estimate titled *Nuclear Weapons Production in Fourth Countries: Likelihood and Consequences* reported the belief of community analysts that France could produce its first nuclear weapons in 1958. The authors explained that plutonium "in weapons quantities is now beginning to become available" and planned production facilities would be developed to the point that weapons with yields in the range of 20 to 40 kilotons could be produced at an annual rate of 3 in 1958, 50 in 1962, and 110 in 1967. The estimate also reported that France was "on the verge of deciding a nuclear weapons production program" but that there were two impediments—opposition from much of the public and the concern of some French officials that French production of atomic bombs could lead other nations, including West Germany, to build their own bombs.[33]

A little over a year later, another intelligence community assessment of the likelihood and impact of new nations joining the nuclear club informed its readers, "We believe (although we have no reliable evidence to demonstrate) that France has probably conducted a fairly significant amount of theoretical weapons research during the past few years." In addition, the estimators concluded that it would take France another five years to develop an independent capacity to produce significant quantities of U-235, so that until then any independent French capability would be based on plutonium. The American analysts also believed that France could produce and test its first fission weapon of 20 to 40 kilotons by late 1958 or early 1959, noting that the French were establishing a test site in the Sahara.[34]

Then, in September 1958, the CIA's *Current Intelligence Weekly Summary* reported that France "may have the capability of exploding a nuclear device . . . at any time, and intensive preparations for a test have been reported recently"—although such preparations would not begin in earnest until 1959. It surmised that de Gaulle's government might want to conduct a test prior to the beginning of the testing moratorium that was scheduled to begin on the last day of October, overestimating the general's concern for world public opinion. The weekly summary explained that a French nuclear test had not previously been expected to occur before 1959, although France had enough plutonium. What was not expected to be available before 1959 were the instruments used to obtain scientific data from a test. However, the CIA reported, it appeared that a German scientist who headed the joint French-German Research Institute in Alsace was "working feverishly" in midsummer on instrumentation for an impending test and had made several trips to the Reggane test site.[35]

But whatever the German scientist was doing, he was not preparing for a test in 1958. When Dwight Eisenhower visited France in September 1959, the nuclear club still only had three members, but the American president told de Gaulle of his concern that France had decided to develop an atomic arsenal. About two months later, the November 13, 1959, report by the CIA's Office of Scientific Intelligence, *The French Nuclear Weapons Program*, told readers that France would soon be a member and that a U.S-Soviet testing moratorium would not stop it. The study indicated that the CIA had learned a great deal about French progress, some of that knowledge having been acquired from a U-2 overflight of France as well as from commercial airliners with covertly placed cameras. Among the targets were the facilities at Marcoule.[36]

In addition to examining the politics and history of the program, the paper provided an assessment of key facilities, the production of fissile material, weapons research and development, the test center, and the expected timing and nature of the test. France, it noted, was able to obtain most of its uranium from domestic sources, although small quantities were imported from Madagascar. The study also credited France with a reserve of ten thousand tons and an active exploration program in Africa.[37]

The paper reviewed French plutonium production and extraction. It summarized the history, capabilities, and performance of the three reactors at Marcoule. It provided details on the beginning of construction of the chemical separation plant, as well as the chemicals used, including tributyl phosphate, in the extraction process. According to OSI, there had been a considerable delay in getting the separation plant into operation, but U.S.

intelligence agencies had been unable to determine the nature of the trouble. There were also delays in the production of weapons-grade plutonium, largely due to problems with the separation process and "dirty plutonium" (plutonium unsuitable for weapons purposes due to its having too high a concentration of plutonium-240 or having been contaminated by the separation process). Nevertheless, OSI was able to conclude that kilogram quantities of plutonium did not become available for weapons development purposes until the summer of 1959. However, when the Marcoule center was in full operation, probably in late 1960, it would be able to produce approximately 220 pounds of plutonium per year. By 1965, with completion of a planned nuclear reactor program, that total could rise to 1,210 pounds.[38]

The scientific intelligence report also reviewed developments in French uranium enrichment capabilities, noting that research had started at Saclay in 1955, and construction on two pilot plants had begun two years later—the first being used to test gaseous diffusion barriers. Ground was broken for a full-scale plant at Pierrelatte, fifteen miles south of Montélimar, in the fall of 1958. According to the study, plans called for the plant to be in partial operation within three years and in full production in four. The initial capability would enrich uranium to only about 3 percent U-235, enough to improve the efficiency of French reactors but not nearly enough to be used for weapons. Plans were being considered, although no decision had been made, to build additional stages, to produce weapons-grade material.[39]

The discussion of uranium enrichment also provided some evidence of where the CIA was getting its information, and what intelligence about the French program it had been unable to acquire. Information on French research on gaseous diffusion had come from at least two sources: papers presented by the French at the same September 1958 Geneva conference that had been a source of intelligence on Tomsk in Siberia and the debriefing of U.S. scientists who had visited the Saclay pilot plant. But when it came to the gaseous diffusion barriers to be used in the operational plant, the CIA was in the dark.[40]

The report's examination of weapons research and development largely focused on the organizations involved. While the Department of New Techniques was officially subordinate to the CEA, it appeared, according to the report, to be a joint CEA–Ministry of National Defense organization. Three organizations were identified as "probably" doing research and development on nuclear weapons under the new techniques department: the Centre d'études de Bruyere-le-Chatel, which reportedly conducted theoretical and applied studies of the critical mass required for nuclear explosions and prepared weapons models; the Army's Armament Research and Manufacturing Directorate, which was reported to have been involved in the research and development of detonators; and the Centre d'études de Vaujours (Research Center at Vaujours), located east of Paris. It also reported that the head of the army directorate's atomic section, Prof. Paul Chanson, was reputed to be "one of the guiding lights" for atomic bomb construction.[41]

The study's final presentation of facts concerned the Reggane test center, which it noted was scheduled for completion in the fall of 1958. It correctly identified Charles Ailleret as the chief of Special Arms as well as the commander of the test center. The actual test area was believed to be almost sixty miles due south of the test center headquarters, "in a remote part of the Sahara."[42]

The test itself was predicted to be a 300-foot tower shot with a yield of about 20 kilotons, a significant underestimate of the actual yield of 60 to 70 kilotons. But the analysts were correct in their prediction that the device would probably be a plutonium implosion bomb, an estimate based on their conclusion that the French would not be able to produce sufficient amounts of highly enriched uranium for a bomb until 1965, unless they received it from the United States or the United Kingdom or enlarged the Pierrelatte facility.[43]

About two weeks before the test, the CIA *Current Intelligence Weekly Summary* noted that there had been a number of postponements, primarily due to technical difficulties, which included producing the proper plutonium isotope, problems of weapons research and development, and a shortage of trained personnel. It was speculated that the most recent delay might have been the result of France's wanting to install test measuring equipment, much of it purchased from American firms, to obtain maximum diagnostic data.[44]

Another issue of the weekly summary, published about two weeks after the test, correctly informed its readers to expect another three tests, involving lighter, smaller devices than the one detonated on February 13. It noted that the second test was scheduled before May and might occur sooner, with the third and fourth shots planned for the fall, and possibly including an underground test. France's interest in underground testing may have been the result, the summary suggested, of "widespread international condemnation of its first test."[45]

THE REACTION, both in Africa and around the world, to the first four French tests made it clear to de Gaulle that atmospheric testing in the Sahara was not a viable long-term option. The premature detonation of April 1961 would be France's last atmospheric test in Africa, but not its last test. Geological conditions forced subsequent underground tests to be conducted in horizontal galleries rather than deep vertical shafts, and thirteen were conducted between November 7, 1961, and February 16, 1966, at In Ecker, in southern Algeria, as France sought to develop operational weapons for its Mirage IV bombers. Most of the tests were less than 20 kilotons, but the Rubis test of October 20, 1963, exceeded 50 kilotons and the Saphir/Monique test of February 27, 1965, produced a blast equivalent to 110,000 tons of TNT.[46]

Long before the last test in Algeria, on March 18, 1962, France and Algeria had signed the Evian Agreement. France recognized its former colony's independence and agreed to turn over control of the Sahara in five years. It had been clear in 1961 to all but the hard-core supporters of a French Algeria that the colony would become independent and would prohibit any French testing, even underground. France would need a new test site, a site that would have to accommodate high-yield thermonuclear tests. In July 1961 Gen. Jean Thiry, who had assumed responsibility for test site selection, listed four possibilities. Three were located in the South Pacific— New Caledonia, the Marquesas, and Réunion—and one in the South Atlantic, the Kerguelen Islands.[47]

Other sites were considered over the next year, and when the selection commission made its choice on March 22, 1962, it chose to locate the Centre d'Expérimentations du Pacific (Pacific Test Center) at Gambier–South Tuamotu in French Polynesia, which had been the favorite of French leaders from the start. Actual detonation points could be set up on nearby Mururoa, and perhaps at Temoe, Fangataufa, Maria, and Marutea. The choice was made official by the Defense Council on July 4, and the orders were confirmed before the end of the month. Work was to start in early 1964 so that the center would be operational at the end of 1966. The desire to reduce the amount of time to complete a test site meant the sites would be designed for atmospheric testing, since a surface site could be completed a year earlier than one for underground testing.[48]

Mururoa is a coral atoll, a ring-shaped coral reef enclosing a lagoon that is the visible rim of an extinct underwater volcano. The atoll is about 6 by 18 miles, and the average depth of its lagoon is between approximately 100 and 130 feet—deep enough for large ships. Its coral ring is between 650 and 985 feet wide, except for a gap about 2 $1/2$ miles wide that connects the lagoon to the Pacific Ocean. Mururoa is located about halfway between Australia and South America, about 720 miles from Tahiti, in the extreme southeast corner of the Tuamotu Archipelago. One of five archipelagos making up French Polynesia, Tuamotu consists of about eighty atolls. In May 1963 the first detachment of engineers assumed control of the planned test site, followed in September by the first group of Polynesian workers. By January 1964 five hundred men were working on the atoll.[49]

Fangataufa, about 25 miles southeast of Mururoa, became the secondary Pacific Ocean test site. Measuring about 3 by 5 miles, it was originally a closed atoll, requiring the French army to blast a 250-foot gap through the coral ring to permit access from the ocean. A third atoll, Hao, located about 280 miles northwest of Mururoa, initially served as a base where the test devices were assembled. Device components arrived on planes, which were able to land on one of the longest runways in the South Pacific, built by the

French military. Eventually, the nuclear assembly facility would be transferred to Mururoa.[50]

By early July 1966 France began atmospheric testing in the Pacific. On
July 2, a specially equipped cruiser, the De Grasse, kept a safe distance from
Mururoa. On board were Gen. Jean Thiry, then director of the French test
program, Adm. Jean Lorrain, commander of the task force for the Pacific tests,
and Jean Viard, technical director for the tests. Presumably it was Thiry who
ordered the detonation of the pure-plutonium AN 52 warhead on a barge at
the test site. The test, code-named Aldébaran, produced a blast of 30 kilotons.
Seventeen days later Fangataufa was initiated into the nuclear era. Test
Tamouré was an airdrop, with a Mirage IVA aircraft ejecting an AN 11 bomb
that exploded with a force equivalent to about 60,000 tons of TNT.[51]

Another three tests, in September and October, followed before the year
concluded. The September 11 test had the supreme French VIP in attendance: President Charles de Gaulle. The device, a prototype of a planned
intermediate-range ballistic missile warhead, was carried into the air by a balloon, where it detonated with a yield of 120 kilotons. The next-to-last test of
the year, on September 24, was code-named Rigel and represented a step
toward a French thermonuclear capability. A boosted fission device containing plutonium and small quantities of thermonuclear material was detonated
on a barge at Fangataufa and produced a yield of 150 kilotons.[52]

De Gaulle might have been most interested, not in the test he attended,
but the one on September 24. In 1966 the temperamental general reversed
his previously relaxed attitude toward French attainment of a thermonuclear
capability. While in 1962 he was willing to wait until 1970 for France to
advance beyond fission weapons, in 1966, with China on its way to developing a fusion device, de Gaulle wanted results and he wanted them quickly.
The French president told Alain Peyrefritte, who had recently been named
minister for research and atomic and space affairs, "I want the first experiment
to take place before I leave! Do you hear me? It's of capital importance. Of the
five nuclear powers are we going to be the only one which hasn't made it to
the thermonuclear level? Are we going to let the Chinese get ahead of us?" De
Gaulle gave Peyrefritte a new deadline—1968.[53]

One step toward beating that deadline was taken in April 1967, when the
uranium enrichment plant at Pierrelatte became operational. The uranium
produced was used in the three tests conducted on Mururoa during June and
July, all of which involved research on the use of U-235 as a fissile material,
apparently in the fission primary of a thermonuclear weapon.[54]

But the most significant developments occurred back in France. Work by
physicists Pierre Billaud, Luc Dagens, and Michel Carayol, and possibly help
from a friend, made 1968 a realistic goal. In January, Billaud, following up on
work by Dagens, completed a paper that advanced French weapons designers'

thinking toward the same concept that U.S. and Soviet weapons designers had: a two-stage weapon using the principle of radiation implosion first worked out by Ulam and Teller. His work, "while not solving the entire problem," unleashed a new round of reflections. In early April, Carayol produced a brief paper that presented, and justified mathematically, his architectural idea for such a two-stage fusion device.[55]

Then, in late September, according to Billaud, André Thoulouze, the French military attaché in London, arrived in Paris, bringing along information from Sir William Cook, who had been appointed director of the thermonuclear research, development, and testing program at the British Atomic Weapons Research Establishment at Aldermaston in 1954. Cook allegedly advised Thoulouze that in developing a hydrogen bomb, French scientists should not "look for complications" but should "try a simple design." More specifically, the British scientist reportedly suggested that using X-rays to compress the thermonuclear fuel, rather than more complicated techniques, was their best bet. Cook's information provided reassurance that Carayol's design was correct. Billaud notes that "had this outline not already been in existence we would have had a difficult time understanding this information, and may have suspected an attempt at misleading us. In fact, there was a kind of reciprocal validation: Carayol's sketch authenticated the seriousness of the source, while the latter confirmed the value of Carayol's ideas."[56]*

Those ideas bore fruit well before de Gaulle's deadline expired, but not before China tested its first hydrogen bomb. Billaud traveled to the South Pacific to watch France's first thermonuclear test, code-named Canopus, on August 24, 1968, at Fangataufa. The U-235 fission primary was used to ignite the lithium-6 deuteride secondary. The three-ton device was carried into the air by balloon and was detonated at approximately 1,970 feet, producing a blast of 2.6 megatons. De Gaulle proclaimed it a "magnificent scientific, technical and industrial success, achieved for the independence and security of France by an elite of her children." The contamination was apparently so extensive that the atoll was declared off-limits for the next six years. Two weeks later, on September 8, the second test, Procyon, took place on Mururoa and produced a yield of 1.2 megatons.[57]

The French testing program took a holiday in 1969, which French offi-

---

* Billaud believes that the British government approved Cook's disclosure. However, it was treated as a very sensitive piece of information, so much so that some of the young engineers involved in the French program were not told why they were being instructed to work on one particular design, and not another that they believed superior. Some in Britain and France reacted with skepticism to the claim that Cook provided technical advice. See "Did UK Scientist Give France Vital Clues About H-bomb?" *Nature*, December 5, 1996, p. 392.

cials claimed was due to budgetary limitations, while others suspected that contamination of Mururoa from the September 8 test was the real reason. Between 1970 and September 15, 1974, France conducted twenty-nine tests, all atmospheric, with twenty-eight on Mururoa and one on Fangataufa. The most notable of the eight 1970 tests was Licorne, a 1-megaton test on Mururoa on July 3. Six hours after its conclusion, French officials returned to the island, and minister of defense Michel Debré, who would die in 1996 at the age of eighty-four, swam in the lagoon in an attempt to neutralize criticism of the environmental impact of the tests.[58]

The thirteen tests conducted in 1971 and the two succeeding years primarily focused on the development of two warheads: the 500-kiloton MR41 boosted-fission warhead that was to be deployed on the M1 and M2 submarine-launched ballistic missiles, and the 1-megaton TN 60 warhead destined to be carried by the M20 submarine-launched ballistic missile. There was a single test apparently designed to test the warhead for a tactical missile. The French finally bowed to international pressure and ended their atmospheric testing program with the eighth test of 1974, on September 15. Those tests involved a small tactical atomic bomb and an airdrop from a Jaguar A aircraft.[59]

THE FRENCH NUCLEAR TESTS in Algeria and the South Pacific from

1961 to 1974 were of sufficient interest to U.S. officials that the U.S. nuclear intelligence establishment went to significant lengths to monitor them. On August 4, 1961, a group of midlevel officials from the State Department and air force met in the office of Philip J. Farley. Farley, Dean Rusk's special assistant for atomic energy and outer space matters, was not there and Col. L. B. Williams presided over the meeting. The catalyst for the meeting was a July 26 letter from Air Force Technical Applications Center commander Jermain P. Rodenhauser, who had inquired about the possibility of establishing Atomic Energy Detection System stations in countries close to Algeria, to monitor the underground tests that "a reliable intelligence source" claimed would take place there from October 1961 through 1962.[60]

The idea of establishing stations in Mali or Niger was soon dismissed. Two State Department officials observed that neither government was likely to give its consent, and even if one did it would be "almost impossible to conceal such activities from the French." The third nation whose proximity to Algeria made it a subject of discussion was Libya, where the United States had a military presence at Wheelus Air Base. State Department official Richard St. F. Post noted that "certain factors" might make it possible to place detection equipment in Libya.[61]

There were two possible cover stories for a collection effort. Post pointed out that the 64th Engineer Battalion was engaged in a mapping survey project in the Ghat-Sebha-Ghadames triangle, the precise location to establish a station. In addition, the detection equipment could be brought into Libya without difficulty under the guise of being for the survey team. At the same time, the similarity of the detection equipment to that used in oil exploration created another option, since most of the territory of interest was covered by oil concession land, and most of that land had been rented to American oil companies. Post continued that it might be possible to conduct the operation without informing either the Libyan government or the nation's chief of state, King Idris.[62]

In a letter dated August 15, Howard Furnas, the acting special assistant for atomic energy and outer space, informed Rodenhauser of the conclusions reached at the August 4 meeting. Furnas also suggested that Rodenhauser determine whether the possible covers for a detection site were truly feasible. In addition, he noted that the State Department was weighing the foreign policy implications of the proposal and that the U.S. ambassador to Libya had been asked for his views. Furnas also mentioned the damage to the U.S. position in Africa if the existence of such a covert collection operation were revealed.[63]

It is not clear from the declassified record whether a station was established in Libya during 1961, or after.* It *is* clear that U.S. leaders and their intelligence support apparatus remained interested in French nuclear progress. In the summers of 1962 and 1963, special national estimates titled *French Nuclear Weapons and Delivery Capabilities* were completed. In April 1963 the CIA reported indications of technical difficulties at the Pierrelatte gaseous diffusion plant. Later that month or early the next, President Kennedy was made aware of reports from Bonn, Rome, and Brussels alleging that France had requested financial and technical assistance from West Germany to complete the Pierrelatte facility. In a May 7 national security action memorandum, national security adviser McGeorge Bundy informed key officials that Kennedy wanted CIA chief John McCone and Atomic Energy Commission chairman Glenn T. Seaborg to prepare an appraisal of the gaseous diffusion project.[64]

In addition to responding to the president's request, CIA analysts also spent part of May completing a study, *The French Nuclear Strike Force Program*, which concluded that France's initial operational nuclear arsenal would consist of Mirage IV bombers equipped with 50- to 60-kiloton fission warheads, which would be followed by a fleet of submarines carrying intermediate-range

---

* The U.S. ability to detect French tests in Algeria in 1965 is illustrated by a Joint Atomic Energy Intelligence Committee statement of March 3, 1965, noting the detection of a French test on February 27 and giving a yield estimate of 125 kilotons. See ACDA to U.S. Mission Geneva, Amembassy Moscow, Amembassy Paris, "Soviet and French Underground Nuclear Tests," March 4, 1965.

missiles armed with thermonuclear warheads. At the very end of the month, Glenn Seaborg personally followed up on John McCone's assertion that France was sharing its nuclear weapons know-how with West Germany. On his return from a visit to unclassified Soviet nuclear facilities and laboratories, he stopped in Paris to have lunch with Bertrand Goldschmidt. "His vehement denial of any such activity," Seaborg recalled, "was completely convincing to me and I had no trouble convincing President Kennedy and the CIA director that such collaboration in nuclear weapons was not occurring."[65]

In late July, the U.S. Intelligence Board approved a completed special national intelligence estimate, *The French Nuclear Weapons Program*. Most of the estimate focused on delivery systems, the cost of the nuclear program to the French economy, and political considerations. Only a few pages of the estimate focused on the size of France's stockpile or its ability to produce U-235. The intelligence community's analysts had concluded that France would not be able to produce weapons-grade U-235 until 1967, when they expected the gaseous diffusion plant under construction at Pierrelatte to be completed.[66]

A CIA study on the French nuclear energy program that was completed in early 1964 examined the availability of uranium, research facilities and their functions, nuclear weapons research institutions, production of plutonium and U-235, and the nine nuclear weapons tests that had taken place through October 20, 1963. It concluded with a brief examination of French plans to establish a new testing area in the South Pacific.[67]

The desire to closely monitor French progress in producing fissile material and in completing the new test center led the intelligence community to conduct space and aerial overflights of key targets over the following years. Overflights by satellites carrying KH-7 cameras between January 22, 1966, and June 12, 1967, produced ten images of Pierrelatte, four of which were obtained during conditions of good visibility. On eight occasions between December 8, 1966, and June 12, 1967, Marcoule was photographed, with five of those occasions producing good-quality images. In the mid-1960s, at least, the CIA also had a couple of human sources inside the French government who provided intelligence on France's nuclear program—sources that the agency's operations directorate was "pretty proud" of, according to a former senior intelligence official.[68]

Interest in developments at the test center spurred what would become the only operational U-2 missions launched from an aircraft carrier. On several occasions between 1957 and 1967, the navy tried, but failed, to obtain a joint agreement between the CIA and air force to develop such a capability. In mid-1963, Kelly Johnson, the Lockheed airplane designer who had conceived of the U-2, deputy CIA director Marshall Carter, and Brig. Gen. Jack Ledford, head of U-2 operations for the CIA, met at the officers' quarters at Edwards Air Force Base in California, where the CIA U-2 detachment was located. Their discussion of the advantages of being able to launch a U-2 without securing suitable foreign bases led to Project Whale Tale, the modification of some U-2s to permit carrier operations.[69]

As a result, in May 1964 a U-2G, a U-2C with the necessary modifications, was aboard the USS *Ranger* when it set sail for the mid-Pacific, and its ultimate target was Mururoa. The images the U-2 produced, from the only two operational missions the spy plane ever flew off a carrier on May 19 and May 22, were available to the authors of a 1965 CIA study that focused solely on the test center. After providing a brief history of French nuclear testing and the selection of the test center, the *The French Pacific Nuclear Test Center* reviewed the different installations in the region, including the Mururoa testing area, the Hao support base, and the Tahiti headquarters. The report noted that while Fangataufa had been designated an observation post by General Thiry, the atoll would probably be used as a test site at some point in the program. The CIA analysts also summarized the history of the construction effort, noting that "construction of a test site . . . halfway around the world has placed a tremendous logistics burden on France." Nevertheless, they concluded that testing would begin on Mururoa in 1966 as scheduled. They also correctly predicted that the testing program would include barge and balloon tests, and pinpointed 1968–1970 as a period during which France would probably conduct tests of a thermonuclear warhead with a megaton yield.[70]

The Mururoa test center, and the atmospheric tests conducted there through September 1974, were the target of a wide variety of U.S. intelligence collection efforts. Monitoring the test center was done through open sources, including French newspapers and government publications, and more secret sources, including Corona and Gambit satellites. On sixteen occasions between June 30, 1966, and August 20, 1968, Corona satellites (carrying KH-4A or KH-4B cameras) targeted the French South Pacific test site. And on at least two occasions during the KH-7 portion of the Gambit program—on March 13, 1966, during Mission 4016 and on May 26, 1967, during Mission 4037—the United States obtained high-resolution images of the area, images of the site before the first test of each year. Undoubtedly, the KH-8 component of the Gambit program also contributed to the monitoring of the test center from its beginnings in July 1966 through September 1974, a period during which forty KH-8 cameras were shot into orbit.[71]

Dino Brugioni, a former official at the National Photographic Interpretation Center (NPIC), recalls that the French were "sneaking down there" and not eager to acknowledge their use of U.S. construction practices, but the imagery from the KH-7 missions, as well as other sources of intelligence, allowed the United States to monitor their activities. In addition, he concluded that despite the image of "beautiful Tahiti" associated with French Polynesia, the places where the French were working were "not paradise."[72]

Beginning in June 1971 Brugioni and other photointerpreters at NPIC had an additional asset at their disposal: the first of eighteen Hexagon satellites carrying the KH-9 camera was placed in a 114- by 186-mile orbit at an inclination that took it over the entire planet. After the final Corona mission of May 1972, the KH-9 cameras in orbit would provide the intelligence community with the wide-area imagery that had been Corona's responsibility. The images covered four times more territory (80 by 360 miles in a single frame), were far sharper (with a ground resolution of one to two feet), and were far more numerous, since Hexagon satellites carried four film return capsules in contrast to the two carried by later Corona models.[73]

While imagery satellites could monitor test site construction, test site preparation, and the destructive impact of a detonation, the United States needed a whole variety of systems to detect and evaluate the French testing program in the South Pacific. To increase the capability of the Dawn Star acoustic network to monitor those tests, U.S. Army Signal Research Unit No. 15, reporting to the Army Security Agency, was established at Brisbane, Australia, in the fall of 1967. That unit, along with a temporary station at Fiji, detected the French tests during the summer of 1968. The Fiji station was deactivated that September.[74]

Monitoring the 1968 tests was also a responsibility of the Strategic Air Command's 55th Strategic Reconnaissance Wing. The wing's effort, designated Burning Light, employed two KC-135R aircraft—modified tankers whose primary sensor measured and recorded the electromagnetic pulse from nuclear detonations while secondary sensors photographed the density and opacity of the resulting nuclear cloud. The data gathered would help the United States predict the effects of low-altitude nuclear detonations—information of particular interest to the Pentagon's Defense Nuclear Agency, which was the primary customer for Burning Light data. While the plane was flown by crews from the reconnaissance wing, the sensors were installed and operated by personnel from AFTAC.[75]

The 1968 tests resulted in fifteen Burning Light missions, which began and concluded at Hickam Air Force Base in Hawaii. While the French government did not provide SAC and AFTAC with advance warning of the tests, the eavesdroppers at the National Security Agency did. Communications intercepts allowed NSA to notify SAC of the approximate time of a test. Before that time a KC-135 would begin orbiting in the vicinity of Mururoa or Fangataufa until there was a detonation. (At some point, possibly as early as 1968, the advance notice that NSA was providing SAC may have originated with a far smaller eavesdropping operation—that of New Zealand. In the late 1960s or early 1970s the New Zealand Government Communications Security Bureau, through its NR [Navy Receiver] 1 station at Waiouru, began monitoring communications, including telexes, between France and the Pacific test center. The Joint Intelligence Bureau also used the intercepts to prepare reports on the French program that were provided to the United States and other allies.)[76]

The French did not test in 1969, so the Burning Light aircraft had a year off, but between May 15 and August 6, 1970, thirteen Burning Light missions collected data on the eight atmospheric tests France conducted in the South Pacific, six at Mururoa and two at Fangataufa. Those missions were only one part of Nice Dog operations, Nice Dog being the overall designation for long-range collection against French nuclear testing (each year's effort also had its own code name). Another component of the 1970 effort was ship-based monitoring of the tests, conducted by the 455-foot-long USNS *Wheeling*, a missile-range instrumentation ship, also known by the code name Pock Mark.[77]

The small French test program for the summer of 1972, three tests, was reflected in the smaller Burning Light effort of nine sorties as part of the Nice Dog/Dial Flower collection effort. The following year's test series was slightly larger, with five tests between July 21 and August 27, 1973, tests which led to an antibomb rally in Papeete that attracted five thousand people and protests from several Latin American countries. The United States continued monitoring the French tests, an activity designated Hula Hoop that year—which included both Pock Mark and Burning Light missions, the latter performed by two NC-135A aircraft provided by the Air Force Systems Command. On board were personnel from the Defense Nuclear Agency, U.S. Air Force Security Service, AEC, and AFTAC. Also employed to monitor the tests was the USNS *Corpus Christi*, an aircraft repair ship operated by the Military Sealift Command and code-named Pot Luck. Both ships carried SH-3A helicopters that were used in data collection. A third ship, the USNS *Huntsville*, also participated in the effort, with drones equipped for nuclear sampling being launched from its deck.[78]

The briefing given to the crew of the Pock Mark vessel stressed the classified nature of the mission, even though U.S. and French spokesmen had noted the presence of U.S. ships in the vicinity of the testing site from the very first South Pacific test. The crew was also assured that the ship's positioning was based on both the data to be collected as well as safety factors. At the time of detonation there would be a slight jolt, followed by a wind of up to eighteen knots per hour. "Thermal output will be detected as a slight warming of the skin by topside personnel," they were told, but "no nuclear radiation will be experienced because of the ship's upwind position."[79]*

---

* It is not clear whether any aerial sampling aircraft were employed to gather the debris from the French tests in 1973, or during other testing campaigns. The WB-57 aircraft stationed at Yokota Air Base, Japan, could have been used for that purpose. There were also U-2Rs that conducted Olympic Race aerial sampling missions, including those that followed Chinese tests in July 1973 and June 1974. None of the SAC or Pacific Command histories

Successful monitoring of the tests using ships and aircraft equipped with specialized nuclear intelligence gear depended on more traditional intelligence disciplines—human intelligence, imagery, and communications intelligence to provide warning of the upcoming tests. Burning Light aircraft, based in Hawaii, were not dispatched until notice of an upcoming detonation was received. After flying 2,600 miles and arriving in the vicinity of the test range, they orbited the area before, during, and after the detonation. The planes refueled before entering their orbit, so they had just enough to circle for about two and a half hours and then return to Hawaii. In some cases, accurate intelligence was negated by unforeseen delays. During the 1973 tests, both Burning Light aircraft were launched to cover each test, but the detonation of July 28 was delayed due to technical difficulties. By the time it went off, the two NC-135As were more than 1,500 miles north of the test area, on their way back to Hawaii.[80]

Burning Light missions also experienced problems in 1974, the final year of French atmospheric testing. The first test, on June 16, went uncovered by the single NC-135A that had been assigned to the mission because intelligence sources failed to warn that a test was imminent. There were also repeated postponements and cancellations of tests in June and July. The problem was further complicated in August by fifteen days of continuously bad weather, not the sort of problem expected of a tropical paradise, which complicated traditional testing arrangements. Rather than being launched on the basis of solid data, NC-135A missions largely depended on "guess work." As a result of the 1974 experience, the Defense Nuclear Agency and the AEC jointly decided to terminate the Burning Light mission on August 16, about a month before the last French atmospheric test.[81]

Of course, the United States had assets that did not require advance notice of a planned test but were constantly on watch. In 1965 the first of four hydroacoustic stations was established, and another five were in operation by the end of 1966. The stations were adjuncts to the navy's Sound Surveillance System (SOSUS) network of hydrophones, ocean-bottom listening devices that could detect the sound emanating from underwater events. Development of the SOSUS network began in 1954, based on Maurice Ewing's discovery of an underwater sound channel, with the primary objective of detecting and characterizing Soviet submarines. By the late 1960s,

---

that discuss the monitoring of French nuclear tests refer to such aerial sampling efforts, although they do with regard to China. See Strategic Air Command (SAC), *History of SAC Reconnaissance Operations, FY 73* (Offutt Air Force Base, Neb.: SAC, 1974), p. 84; Strategic Air Command, *History of SAC Reconnaissance Operations, FY 74* (Offutt Air Force Base, Neb.: SAC, 1975), pp. 65, 67.

networks of hydrophones and associated ground stations received the SOSUS data (via cable) off the coasts of the United States as well as in the Atlantic and Pacific oceans.[82]

In addition, the Vela satellites circled 67,000 miles above the earth. The two final pairs of advanced Velas had been launched in 1969 and 1970. While their design life had been short, the satellites would exceed expectations and one, 6911, was operational well into the 1980s. The Defense Support Program (DSP) satellites also contributed to intelligence. Whereas the first DSP satellite, launched in November 1970, went into an elliptical orbit, subsequent launches in May 1971, March 1972, and June 1973 successfully delivered the spacecraft into their intended geostationary orbits 22,300 miles above points on the equator. In that orbit the speed of their rotation allowed them to to keep the same, substantial portion of the earth under constant surveillance as the earth turned on its axis.[83]

The primary mission of the satellites was the detection of Soviet missile launches, whether fired for test purposes or with more sinister intent. Their data was transmitted back, in the early years of the program, to the appropriate ground station—either the one at Nurrungar, Australia, or Buckley Air Force Base in Colorado. To gather the data, each of the twenty-three-foot-long, ten-foot-wide, two-thousand-pound DSP spacecraft was equipped with a twelve-foot-long Schmidt infrared telescope containing an array of detectors. In addition to monitoring missile launches, the telescope could sense a number of other infrared events, including the heat from an atomic explosion as well as from the resulting fireball.[84]

The satellites also carried a variety of additional sensors—bhangmeters, an atmospheric fluorescence detector, an X-ray locator system—to help in its secondary mission of detecting nuclear explosions in the atmosphere or space. The fluorescence detector could register nuclear detonations that took place between 31 and 1,240 miles, recording the optical time history of the nitrogen fluorescence signals produced when X-rays from a nuclear detonation outside the atmosphere (an exoatmospheric detonation) excited air molecules at the top of the atmosphere. The X-ray locator measured the direction and arrival of X-rays from near-earth exoatmospheric detonations. In addition to estimating the location and time of a blast, the locator sensors made it possible to estimate a blast's yield and yield-to-mass ratio, as well as establish additional characteristics of the explosion.[85]

During the summer of 1973 there was only one DSP satellite, sent into orbit in March 1972, that could detect a test at Mururoa. Although it was located over the equator at 70° west longitude, over Latin America, its footprint extended well into the South Pacific. And it successfully detected all five French tests conducted that summer. By the following summer another DSP satellite had joined the operational constellation. Stationed above the Pacific, at 134° west longitude, it ensured that two DSP satellites could provide data on the tests of that summer and the tests during the summer of 1974.[86]

The last test in the summer of 1974, on September 15, would be not only the final French atmospheric test of 1974 but also the final French atmospheric test. Mururoa would be the site of repeated tests in the coming decades, but those tests would take place underground. Although the DSP's sensors would be of little use in monitoring those tests, the U.S. intelligence community would continue to gather intelligence through other means, in response to its mandate to monitor nuclear testing across the globe and to permit analysts to estimate the future capabilities of France's nuclear arsenal.

FRANCE'S CESSATION of atmospheric testing after the detonation of September 1974 represented a victory for governments and activist groups seeking a halt to such tests. But just a few months earlier, another test, although conducted underground, meant defeat for those, including the U.S. government, who had hoped that no new nations would join the nuclear club — ever.

In mid-May 1974, two-dozen scientists and engineers, including Dr. Rajagopala Chidambaram, were encamped near the Indian village of Pokhran. Pokhran is in the northwestern Indian state of Rajasthan, bordered on the north and northwest by Pakistan, in a desert area where winter temperatures can reach 82 degrees while summer can see the thermometer hit 115, a far less pleasant environment than Mururoa.[87]

Chidambaram and his colleagues were hoping that their preparations to make India the sixth nation to test a nuclear device would not be detected by a U.S. spy satellite. While it is doubtful that the names Hexagon and Gambit would have meant anything to the Indian scientists, they certainly knew that the United States had such capabilities. They looked up at the night sky, hoping not to see the light of an American reconnaissance satellite passing overhead.[88] The idea of assisting India in obtaining nuclear weapons had been proposed a dozen years earlier, but rejected, and the U.S. policy was to discourage nations — whether allies, neutrals, or enemies — from joining the nuclear club. Life would be easier for Indian leaders if they could present the world with a fait accompli, rather than testing in the face of diplomatic pressure.

Like France, India's path to an atomic weapons capability was an incremental and prolonged one. Homi Bhabha, the father of the Indian bomb effort, moved in the same circles as Joliot-Curie and other atomic physicists of the pre–World War II era. In 1927 he left India to study engineering at Cambridge University. Eight years later Cambridge awarded him a doctorate, in physics rather than engineering. The focus of his work had been in the area of cosmic rays, a subject that, as two historians of twentieth-century physics explained, became an Indian specialty because "India's high mountains and deep mines enabled the physicists to do important research with inexpensive instruments." Bhabha went on to become an important contributor to the meson theory of nuclear forces, which centered on a particle (called the meson, as Bhabha had suggested) first discovered during research on cosmic rays.[89]

Before returning to India in 1939, Bhabha visited the institutes and laboratories of the top physicists working on the Continent, including Neils Bohr, James Franck, and Enrico Fermi. While in India the Second World War erupted, stranding him in his homeland. With nowhere else to go, he accepted the position of "reader" in theoretical physics at the Indian Institute of Science in Bangalore. In 1941, at the age of thirty-one, he received two honors. He was promoted to professor of cosmic ray research and elected a Fellow of the Royal Society. Three years later he wrote to the Sir Dorabji Tata Trust, requesting that the philanthropy provide funds for a nuclear research institute to help develop indigenous expertise, so that when nuclear energy for power production became feasible "in . . . a couple of decades," India would not need to rely on foreign assistance.[90]

Before the end of 1945 the Tata Institute of Fundamental Research opened, with Bhabha as its director. The following year Bhabha took on the additional job of chairman of the newly formed Atomic Energy Research Committee, created to promote nuclear physics education in Indian colleges and universities. Then, in 1948, Prime Minister Jawaharlal Nehru, who had written that "the future belongs to those who produce atomic energy," submitted legislation to create India's Atomic Energy Commission (AEC). The Atomic Energy Act established the legal framework under which the Commission would operate. Surpassing the restrictions in British and U.S. legislation, the act imposed a veil of secrecy over atomic energy research and development and established government ownership of uranium, thorium, and all other relevant raw materials. The secrecy, Nehru argued, was necessary to protect the nation's raw materials and knowledge from colonial exploitation as well as to ensure countries with which India might cooperate that their nuclear secrets would be safe in Indian hands.[91] The legislation would be the first portent of the extreme secrecy that would envelop the Indian nuclear weapons effort in the years that followed.

When the dust cleared from the legislative debate, India had its Atomic Energy Commission, which, along with the Atomic Energy Research Committee, reported to the Department of Scientific Research. The three-member commission was established on August 10. Bhabha became its first chairman, while S. S. Bhatnagar, a chemist with a sideline in Urdu poetry, and K. S. Krishnan, the director of the National Physical Laboratory, were named his fellow commissioners.[92]

The 1950s saw further bureaucratic developments, creation of plans, and attempts to acquire the resources needed for an atomic energy program. A 1951 nuclear cooperation agreement with France was followed the next year with Nehru's unveiling of a four-year plan to move India toward a nuclear capability; the plan included surveys for atomic materials and extracting thorium from monazite. Bhabha began gathering technical information on reactor theory, design, and related technologies. In 1954 another bureaucratic entity was created, the Department of Atomic Energy, and Bhabha became its secretary. The next year, ground was broken for the first Indian reactor, a research reactor named Aspara, at Trombay, on the Indian west coat, just north of Bombay. In January 1957 Trombay became the headquarters of the Atomic Energy Establishment, which was assigned the mission of directing Indian nuclear research and development. Not surprisingly, Bhabha was named director.[93]

In 1958, Nehru's government adopted Bhabha's plan to employ atomic energy to stimulate economic development, which he had outlined in a November 1954 address to the Conference on the Development of Atomic Energy for Peaceful Purposes. The first stage involved the construction, with Canadian assistance, of natural uranium–fueled reactors to produce power and plutonium. A second set of reactors, fueled by the recycled plutonium and thorium, would then be built. The plutonium-thorium fuel, when fissioned in the second-generation reactors, would produce U-233 as a by-product. The U-233, along with thorium, would then be used in yet another set of reactors, to produce more U-233 than consumed by fission. Owing to India's extensive supply of thorium, an unlimited supply of thorium—U-235 fuel would be created. At least that was Bhabha's expectation.[94]

Turning the multistage plan into reality required India to master nuclear technology, a process started with the construction of the Aspara reactor. Of greater significance was the offer Canada made that year to build the 40-megawatt, heavy water–moderated CIRUS (Canadian-Indian, U.S.) research reactor, which burned natural-uranium fuel. Also of importance for the future Indian atomic weapons program was Canada's failure to attach significant restrictions on the use of the plutonium produced by CIRUS beyond a promise, contained in a secret annex to the agreement, that the reactor and its product would only be used for peaceful purposes. Then, in 1958, while CIRUS was under construction, Bhabha decided to build a plutonium extraction plant at Trombay. Ground was broken for the plant, which was given the name Phoenix, in April 1961. It would become part of the establishment complex at Trombay, which by 1961 included over one thousand scientists and engineers and their offices, and eventually Phoenix, nuclear reactors, and a uranium enrichment plant.[95]

Ostensibly, India's effort was devoted to the peaceful purpose of creating energy. Nehru repeatedly pledged that the Indian nuclear activities were for "peaceful purposes only," although he was also willing to use Indian nuclear know-how for deterrent purposes, noting in January 1958 that India had the capability to build a bomb "in three or four years if we divert sufficient resources in that direction." In contrast, in 1958 Bhabha privately told an English friend that he wanted India to develop nuclear weapons. A French colleague, Bertrand Goldschmidt, recalled, "Bhabha always wanted the bomb."[96]

That desire was enhanced by China's march toward the bomb. In 1959, in reaction to concern over China's atomic weapons program, Bhabha told a parliamentary committee that India could build its own bomb without foreign assistance. But while India would continue to advance toward building a nuclear weapon in the first part of the 1960s, it did so without an explicit decision. In August 1960 Nehru told his parliament's lower house, the Lok Sabha, that the first Indian nuclear power station would be built at Tarapur, north of Trombay, and that the nation would also move forward with the proposed plutonium extraction facility at Trombay. Then, in 1963 Canada reached agreement in principle to build a natural-uranium power reactor in Rajasthan, the Rajasthan Atomic Power Station Unit 1 or RAPS-I, while the U.S. government approved American construction of two light-water power reactors at Tarapur, to the north of Trombay. India agreed to accept IAEA safeguards on the U.S.-supplied fuel for the Tarapur reactor.[97]

Early in 1964 Bhabha presented a paper to a conference on "Current Problems of Disarmament and World Security" in India, in which he argued that nuclear weapons represented one means of a smaller country deterring a larger, more powerful country, such as China. Then, in May 1964 Nehru died. His death was followed by Lal Bahadur Shastri's accession to the position of prime minister and, coincidentally in June, by the first spent fuel from the CIRUS reactor entering the Trombay plutonium-reprocessing facility.[98]

During the summer and fall, as the Chinese test grew closer, there was increasing pressure for Indian development of a bomb. Less than a week after Dean Rusk's warning of the upcoming Chinese test, Bhabha began public and private efforts to push Shastri and his government to approve additional work on bomb development. During a visit to London he claimed that India's scientists could develop and test an atomic bomb within eighteen months if permitted, but said, in an attempt to generate domestic support in favor of a bomb, that he did not expect "such a decision will be taken." Eight days after the test Bhabha, on All-India Radio, told his audience that "atomic weapons give a State possessing them in adequate numbers a deterrent power against attack from a much stronger State."[99]

On November 27 the issue was taken up in parliament when the opposition party, the right-wing Jana Sangh, introduced a resolution calling for India to develop and deploy atomic weapons. The resolution was defeated by a voice vote, as Shastri wished. The prime minister believed that India should press for nuclear disarmament rather than become part of a nuclear arms race, and feared the impact on the economy of diverting resources to build a bomb. But that was not the end of the story. In his speech Shastri reminded the legislators that India was still able to produce a bomb within "two or three years" if necessary. Most importantly, while he reaffirmed India's commitment to peaceful nuclear activities, he extended the concept beyond the production of nuclear energy to include peaceful nuclear explosives that could be used for tunneling through mountains, canal construction, and deepening and widening ports, a concept that formed the basis for the U.S. Plowshare program.[100]

Shastri's revised formulation of peaceful nuclear activities left the door open for Bhabha's pursuit of nuclear weapons, since the physics of peaceful and military nuclear detonations were identical. In addition, as Bhabha was aware, India's claim of peaceful intent allowed nuclear cooperation with the United States and Canada to continue, whereas an acknowledged atomic bomb program would have led those countries to terminate their assistance to the Indian nuclear program.[101]

There is some evidence that in 1965 Bhabha sought to obtain a U.S. Plowshare device or blueprints that would, he believed, reduce the time required for India to build one from eighteen to six months. If he did try, he failed. Had he been successful, he might have lived to see India detonate an atomic device. But on January 24, 1966, Bhabha's Air India flight slammed into the highest mountain in western Europe, the 15,800-foot-tall Mont Blanc in the French Alps. The plane crashed in almost the same spot where another Indian plane, the "Malabar Princess," did in November 1950. The 1966 crash killed the fifty-six-year-old Bhabha and all 116 of his fellow passengers.[102]

His death required Indira Gandhi, who succeeded Shastri as prime minister after a heart attack killed him two weeks before Bhabha's death, to fill the numerous positions that Bhabha had occupied. Others had to assume the role of advocating Indian development of atomic weapons. Dharma Vira, cabinet secretary and AEC member, became interim commission chairman, and was replaced several months later by another commission member, Vikram Sarabhai, an opponent of nuclear explosions of any kind. Like Bhabha, the new chairman had received his physics training at Cambridge University. Homi Sethna, a chemical engineer who had supervised the construction of the plutonium separation plant at Trombay, replaced Bhabha as director of the Atomic Energy Establishment. Sethna and Raja Ramanna, another leading scientist at Trombay, would lead the effort to develop an atomic device.[103]

Sarabhai's opposition to the development of nuclear explosives led him to order a halt to work on the topic. That limited authorized development of an atomic bomb, but did not stop it. The separation facility at Trombay continued to extract plutonium from the fuel rods used in the CIRUS reactor, although at a much slower rate than expected, while the nuclear establishment developed the expertise to transform the plutonium metal into bomb cores.[104]

During 1968, at a time when the government's leadership, including

Indira Gandhi, was focused on the proposed nonproliferation treaty* rather than development of an Indian nuclear capability, a small group of scientists at the Bhabha Atomic Research Centre (BARC), as the Atomic Energy Establishment had been renamed in January 1967 in homage to their late leader, began a concerted effort to move India into the nuclear club. In late 1967 or early 1968 Ramanna, then the chief of the physics group at BARC, instructed Chidambaram to develop the equation of state for plutonium, which required both theoretical analysis and experiments with shock waves. The thirty-two-year-old scientist, who had received his doctorate in physics from Madras University, had been assigned a task that was fundamental to determining how much high explosive was needed to compress plutonium to a specified density, as well as the explosive yield of a device.[105]

Chidambaram then began recruiting and supervising physicists and engineers, from BARC and the laboratories of the Defence Research and Development Organization (DRDO), who were asked to design the components of the chemical high-explosive device that would be needed to implode the plutonium core of a bomb. Ramanna and Chidambaram, along with senior experimental physicist and Ramanna deputy P. K. Iyengar, selected contributors to the effort and coordinated their activities, in cooperation with DRDO director B. D. Nag Chaudhuri.[106]

While Sarabhai eventually became aware of the efforts taken in defiance of his instructions, he did not seek to halt them. As a result, Ramanna, Chidambaram, and their associates could proceed until they were able to build and ready to test a device—provided they received approval from the prime minister, whomever he or she might be when the time arrived.[107]

The new decade would bring India increasingly close to that time. Construction of a new research reactor began in 1970 at Trombay. While the size and costs associated with the Plutonium Reactor for Neutron Investigation in Multiple Assemblies (given the approximate acronym *Purnima*, the Indian word for "festival") were small, it would provide crucial data for the design of India's first atomic device. The reactor allowed Indian scientists to evaluate the behavior of plutonium-based chain reactions as well as study the system

---

* The treaty, formally the Treaty on the Non-Proliferation of Nuclear Weapons, and also known as the Nuclear Non-Proliferation Treaty, was signed before the end of 1968. It obligated the five acknowledged nuclear-weapon states of the time—the United States, the Soviet Union, France, the United Kingdom, and the People's Republic of China—to refrain from transferring nuclear weapons, other nuclear explosive devices, or their technology to nonnuclear weapon states. Nonnuclear weapon states who signed the treaty agreed not to acquire or produce nuclear weapons or other nuclear explosive devices.

when it just exceeded critical. The data could then be employed to identify critical parameters and determine how to achieve optimum yield. While much of the information obtained from the reactor was already published by the United States and other nations, Indian scientists wanted to be sure they would not become the victims of deception. At the same time, the reactor facilitated Indian deception, for India's plans for atomic power stations employing fast-breeder reactors using plutonium cores provided cover for the reactor's utility in bomb development.[108]

Throughout 1972 India moved toward the day when it would detonate a device. The Purnima reactor began operations in May, allowing Indian physicists to refine their understanding of fast neutrons and fast fission. That same month, Homi Sethna, who had succeeded Sarabhai as AEC chairman in February after Sarabhai's death in late December 1971, gave Ramanna and his colleagues the green light to begin work on a device. In early September Indira Gandhi visited Trombay for a tour. Afterward, Sethna invited her to his office, where he showed her a model of the device he had designed. Sethna soon asked her, "Should we do it or not?" According to Sethna, the prime minister told him, "Get it ready. I will tell you whether to do it or not." Toward the end of the year a search for a possible test site began.[109]

Once the decision was made to proceed with construction of a device, commonly referred to as the Smiling Buddha, work accelerated on each phase of the project: the electrical system in the device, the neutron initiator (code-named Flower), the charges that would implode the plutonium, and the diagnostic equipment and instruments. Ramanna, now the director of BARC, supervised the effort in conjunction with the head of the DRDO, B. D. Nag Chaudauri. Chidambaram and Satinder Kumar Sikka, who would go on to play a leading role in India's pursuit of a hydrogen bomb, worked together on bomb design while the Terminal Ballistics Research Laboratory in Chandigarh produced the conventional high-explosive system to implode the plutonium.[110]

In January 1973 Ramanna, after being informed that the plutonium extraction plant at Trombay, which had been shut down in 1970 due to its erratic performance, would not become operational again until late 1973 at the earliest, ordered the Purnima reactor shut down so that its plutonium oxide fuel rods could be melted down to obtain enough plutonium for the test device. In March the DRDO reportedly tested the high-explosive system to determine if it would produce the necessary symmetrical detonation. By the middle of the year Chidambaram had concluded that the shaft for the explosion would have to be 350 feet deep to prevent poisonous fumes from being vented.[111]

The 61 Engineer Regiment, stationed in Jodhpur in Rajasthan, was assigned responsibility for digging the shaft for the device. The regiment's commander, under instructions from Ramanna to tell only those with a need to know what the shaft was for, informed his engineers that they would be digging a deep well to supply water to the range. Digging began in October 1973 but ran into a series of problems, including hitting water in January. Despite the cover story, the project had been given the code name Operation Dry Enterprise, which reflected the need for a dry shaft, since water or humidity could seriously damage the device. Digging would resume in February, when the test had been envisioned to take place, and continue into May.[112]

On May 13 Iyengar, Ramanna's deputy, and four others began assembling the device, whose components had been transported to the test site by a number of means. A regular Indian Airlines flight flew the trigger, concealed in a thermos to prevent the leak of radioactivity and accompanied by Iyengar and T. S. Murthy, a key member of the team that developed the bomb's neutron initiator. An army convoy transported the plutonium sphere, placed in a specially designed box, along with measurement equipment, from Trombay to Pokharan, a 560-mile journey through hills, plains, and desert. During the entire three-day journey Chidambaram and P. R. Roy, head of the core fabrication team, ate and slept next to the box and took it with them whenever they left their truck.[113]

On May 15, with assembly completed, the device was lowered into the shaft, which was then sealed with sand and cement.[114] For the next three nights Chidambaram and his colleagues would wonder if their plans would be or had already been uncovered by a U.S. spy satellite, and then be obstructed by American pressure.

CHIDAMBARAM NEED NOT have worried, despite the CIA, NSA, and other intelligence organizations having monitored Indian nuclear activities for decades. Those agencies had relied on a combination of open sources, diplomatic reporting, communications intelligence, and satellite photography to track Indian nuclear developments. The AEC also monitored India's nuclear progress, given the U.S. role as a nuclear supplier. The intelligence gathered helped inform policymakers throughout the 1950s, 1960s, and early 1970s about India's nuclear status. A 1958 assessment by the CIA's Office of Scientific Intelligence provided reassurance that India's nuclear intentions were peaceful. The section on possible military applications was a single paragraph in length, which noted Nehru's pledge that his government and future Indian governments would use atomic energy for peaceful purposes. The section closed with the observation that "there is no indication in government or scientific circles of a change from the traditional Indian pattern of passivity and mediation."[115] In later years, U.S. decisionmakers would worry that India's leaders would decide that neutralizing the threats from China and Pakistan, as well as an Indian desire for international prestige, required a nuclear program that produced bombs as well as energy.

In late June 1961 a State Department message conveyed the JAEIC's interest in Indian nuclear developments. Sent to American embassies and consulates in North America, Europe, and Asia—including Bonn, Paris, Karachi, New Delhi, and Bombay—the secret cable passed on a series of technical questions about the Indian nuclear program. Its recipients were told that beyond technical matters, they should also report on political and economic considerations that might influence a decision to embark on an expanded program, and the relationship of any expanded program to India's capability and intentions to develop nuclear weapons.[116]

Any useful information that had been provided in response to a similar message, sent out early in the previous month, would have been employed in writing the September 1961 national intelligence estimate titled *Nuclear Weapons and Delivery Capabilities of Free World Countries Other Than the US and UK*. The analysts noted that India "is deliberately improving its overall capabilities in the nuclear field, possibly in anticipation that a future decision to develop an operational capability may be required." In addition, India had three nuclear reactors in operation, including one (CIRUS) that could produce enough plutonium for about one or two weapons a year; preliminary construction had started on a plutonium separation plant, which was unlikely to begin operations before 1964–1965; and India was seeking to develop its own sources of uranium. In the event of decision within the "next year or two" to develop nuclear weapons, India would probably have a "modest capability, using aircraft and fission weapons, by 1968–1969," the estimate concluded. It also judged, however, that India's leaders would not make such a decision unless they were convinced that no disarmament agreements were possible and China's foreign policy "was clearly growing more truculent."[117]

Those conclusions were affirmed about two years later by a national estimate on the likelihood and consequences of nuclear proliferation, which addressed the likely impact of a Chinese nuclear detonation on India. Such an event would probably not lead India to respond in kind, the CIA analysts believed. However, India was likely to continue its current nuclear efforts to the point where a crash weapons program could be instituted to produce a bomb in a relatively short time.[118]

As predicted in the September 1961 national estimate, despite plans that the Phoenix separation facility at Trombay would be completed in 1963, it did not begin operations until 1964. At 5:00 p.m. on March 31, in an informal ceremony attended by Homi Sethna and other scientists and engineers involved in building the facility, an inactive uranium fuel rod was pushed into the plant by Homi Bhabha. It did not require secret intelligence efforts to discover those and other facts about the new plant. They were reported in a Department of Atomic Energy press release, and forwarded to the Department of State by the American consul in Bombay.[119]

Beyond monitoring the growth of the Indian nuclear infrastructure, U.S.

intelligence continued to address the issue of whether China's entrance into the nuclear club would cause India to pursue a nuclear weapons capability. During the time between the 1961 estimates and Phoenix commencing operations, India had fought and lost, in 1962, a limited war with China. Then in October 1964 China joined the nuclear club. A national intelligence estimate on the prospects for nuclear proliferation, completed shortly after the Chinese test, noted a number of factors that would affect India's decision, including the scope and pace of the Chinese program, Sino-Soviet relations, and guarantees from other nations. However, the analysts concluded that the chances were "better than even" that within a few years India would seek to join the nuclear club. They also noted that India had the basic facilities needed for a modest program, including the Phoenix facility, and estimated that by 1970 the country could have an arsenal of about a dozen 20-kiloton weapons.[120]

While the estimators were predicting "within a few years," the CIA's spies, or at least one of them, was telling the agency that Prime Minister Shastri and other Indian leaders were not yet ready to commit to a nuclear weapons program. On October 22, 1964, the day after the new estimate on proliferation was approved by the U.S. Intelligence Board, a CIA Intelligence Information Cable, based on reporting from the field, was disseminated. Titled "Indian Government Policy on Development of Nuclear Weapons," it claimed that although India had the ability to produce an atomic bomb quickly, it did not plan to do so "as yet." The author explained that India's government was convinced that "the Chicoms [Chinese Communists] will not have an offensive nuclear capability for at least five years." In the interim, if the situation changed, the Indians were relying on the assurance from President Johnson that the United States would come to the aid of any nation threatened by China.[121]

A week later the American embassy in New Delhi transmitted its assessment of the situation to secretary of state Rusk, which echoed that of the CIA's source in India. "Our current estimate," the diplomats wrote in cableese, "is that in foreseeable future India's leaders will continue stand on position of responsibility and adherence to no-bomb policy." It also reported on a conversation between an embassy official and a member of the Indian Ministry of External Affairs, who stated that pressure to build a bomb was growing and that Bhabha was the "leading advocate . . . and . . . was actively campaigning for India to go down the nuclear road." While the External Affairs official felt that India would not reverse course, he did reveal that the matter was under "active consideration" and that Shastri had authorized Bhabha to produce an estimate of what would be required for India to conduct an underground detonation.[122]

Not surprisingly, assessment of the Indian nuclear program continued within the CIA and other agencies. In early November, OSI completed a secret study of the Indian nuclear energy program which focused on infrastructure rather than the "will they or won't they" question. It addressed the functions of the Atomic Energy Establishment, the existence and capabilities of the three reactors in operation (including Aspara and CIRUS), the state of India's uranium reserves, and the capacity of the heavy-water plant at Nangal. In addition, it reported on plans to build three nuclear power stations in India—at Tarapur, in Rajasthan, and in Madras. The study also noted that a plant for the production of plutonium metal, necessary for weapons manufacture, was underway and could be in operation in the fall of 1965.[123]

The following month, Harry Rowen, of the Defense Department's International Security Affairs office, completed a draft titled "The Indian Nuclear Problem," which focused not on India's nuclear resources, but what the country was likely to do with them and the consequences. He concluded that India might soon begin a weapons program since "the pressures for a weapon are likely to be irresistible after the Chinese test their next device in the absence of some better alternative." The consequences of such a program would include there being "one more national state [that] could some day attack the United States." It would also add to the states that could start nuclear actions "with a fair chance of spreading and involving the United States."[124]

Whether India would, sometime in the future, decide to join the nuclear club was a mystery to analysts for years—a question that no one, not even the Indian government itself, could answer. Collection systems such as Corona and Gambit were of no use in trying to unravel such mysteries. They could, however, provide significant intelligence on nuclear developments in the world's second most populous country.

On April 29, 1965, a Corona satellite carrying a KH-4A camera blasted off from Vandenberg Air Force Base. Whereas the second film capsule ejected went into a higher orbit rather than down to earth, the first capsule, ejected on May 4, was snatched out of midair over the Pacific. In addition to the photographs it contained of targets in the Soviet Union and China, it included a direct overhead image of the Trombay complex. Later that year more detail may have been accumulated when a KH-7–carrying Gambit satellite orbited the earth for five days, beginning on September 30.[125]

Whatever information NPIC photointerpreters extracted from any KH-7 photos of Trombay, along with the intelligence derived from the Corona images, would have been accessible to analysts in OSI and other portions of the intelligence community who prepared the October 21, 1965, special national intelligence estimate titled *India's Nuclear Weapons Policy*. The report reviewed the same basic facts and repeated some of the judgments that had appeared in the October 1964 estimate on proliferation: that India had all the facilities necessary to produce plutonium, could quickly transition from a peaceful to a military nuclear program, and could build an arsenal of a dozen bombs by 1970.[126]

The estimate also warned its readers that India's joining the nuclear club within months was not out of the question. The American intelligence analysts believed India probably had enough plutonium on hand to produce a nuclear device, and if its leaders had decided in late 1964 or early 1965 to develop nuclear weapons, a test might occur within months. However, they noted, such an event would require weapons design to be well advanced and establishment of a test site in the immediate future. The CIA, NSA, and other intelligence collection efforts had provided "no evidence that such activities are well advanced."[127]

Work on weapons technology and design, which in its early stages is "easy to conceal and difficult to identify," was probably underway. And intelligence, either secret or open source, did indicate that India had expanded significantly the electronic facilities at its nuclear establishment and may have begun to set up a high-explosive test site—both of which could be, but were not necessarily, related to an imminent test. It was possible, then, that even if India didn't join the nuclear club in a few months, it could before the end of 1966.[128]

Looking ahead, the estimators noted that if India did decide to construct an atomic device and test it underground, it might claim that it was exploring the potential of nuclear explosions for peaceful purposes. A decision to build a bomb is one the analysts thought "unlikely that we would immediately learn of," although they expected the intelligence community would be able to detect "advance indications of the first detonation."[129]

The search for advance indications relied in part on what the foreign service officers at the American embassy in New Delhi could uncover. In late March 1966 the embassy received an airgram from the State Department providing what had become a boilerplate description of the Indian program, noting the lack of information on a decision by the Indian government to develop nuclear weapons as well as the capability of the CIRUS reactor to produce the necessary plutonium if it did so. The same message also tasked the embassy to report information in five areas: signs of activity in remote areas that might indicate test site construction, indications of the covert establishment of nuclear research facilities or tightened security at known installations, evidence of continued use of the CIRUS reactor to produce "clean uranium," Indian procurement or development of small electronic neutron generators and high-quality explosive detonators, and the testing of highly instrumented high-explosive shapes or sections.[130]

Whatever information the embassy's political, scientific, and economic officers could come up with was of interest at the highest levels of the U.S. government. On June 9, 1966, a little over five weeks after the State Department's tasking to the embassy, President Johnson met with his National Security Council. Noting that in the aftermath of the third Chinese test there was an increased urgency in dealing with the Indian nuclear weapons issue, he directed the Defense and State Departments, along with the Arms Control and Disarmament Agency and other agencies, to examine a variety of issues concerning the Indian program. Johnson asked that the study address the extent to which the United States might use its economic leverage to discourage Indian development of a bomb, how far the United States should go in meeting Indian security concerns, how various arms control agreements might have an impact on Indian intentions, and "what price the U.S. should be prepared to pay for such agreements."[131]

The report delivered to the president on July 25 identified two key issues. One was the political and prestige factors that might propel India toward a nuclear capability. The other was the more tangible problem of India's need to be able to deter or neutralize Chinese nuclear blackmail. The report's authors did not believe a decision was "imminent," indicating that the New Delhi embassy's collection efforts produced no smoking gun. Nor did they expect a "go nuclear" decision to be made within the year.[132]

One means of curbing India's desire for nuclear weapons, the report suggested, was sharing U.S. intelligence analysis of China's programs, which might "without falsely discounting ChiCom progress, make clear difficulties and limitations still confronting the ChiCom nuclear weapons program and aid in keeping the potential ChiCom nuclear threat in strategic perspective as far as India's interests are concerned." At the same time, in order to obtain as much warning as possible about a shift in "India's present no-bomb policy," an "increased priority should be assigned to the collection and analysis of relevant intelligence data." Johnson approved the recommendations on August 1.[133]

The gathering of information about Indian nuclear activities through the remainder of the decade illustrated the varied sources employed. Corona missions in November 1966, May 1967, and November 1967 produced imagery of the Trombay complex. There was also KH-7 imagery, of unknown quality, from a February 1966 mission. The assorted papers presented by senior Indian scientists were also undoubtedly gathered up by the CIA and other agencies, such as the paper Homi Sethna coauthored on the fuel reprocessing plant at Trombay, prepared for the November 1967 New York conference titled *Recent Advances in Reprocessing Irradiated Fuels*.[134]

The American embassy continued to dig out data on topics such as uranium exploration in India. While some information was available in annual reports and other authorized publications from the Department of Atomic Energy, detailed technical data was withheld for reasons of security. As the embassy noted in a May 1968 cable to Washington, current estimates of Indian uranium reserves were not available, and "the overall scope of field exploration and development programs may only be assessed through interpretation from a variety of disconnected chemical analysis reported to be indicative of ores contained in certain areas under exploration, and from personal observation and verbal inquiries by Embassy staff personnel."[135]

U.S. foreign service personnel in India also kept an eye on the new power plants that were under construction in the late 1960s and early 1970s, including the ones forty miles south of Madras and in Rajasthan. In 1971 the consulate in Madras provided a five-page report, including a map courtesy of the Indian atomic energy department, which focused on progress of the Madras Atomic Power Project, slated for completion in 1973—a facility not subject to safeguards that could be used to produce plutonium. The 1971 report updated earlier State Department findings from 1968 and 1969. It was followed by an embassy report in August 1972, which stated that the Rajasthan station had become operational earlier in the month.[136]

Monitoring developments concerning the Madras and Rajasthan projects was not restricted to America's diplomats. NSA's eavesdroppers also made a contribution, in August 1972. An NSA report, classified "Top Secret Umbra," indicating it was based on sensitive communications intelligence, reported on French financing for the Madras project, specifically that "the Banque National de Paris, on 22 June reported that it had been asked to set up a credit agreement . . . to finance an Indian atomic energy project." The same report also informed its readers that Sweden was supplying material for the project, and that a French company, in Orsay, had informed Indian nuclear officials that the Swedish material "would be shipped within a short time."[137]

It did not take such secret intelligence to keep the Indian nuclear weapons problem in front of key decisionmakers such as President Richard Nixon, or his national security adviser, Henry Kissinger. Kissinger had been cautioning Gandhi against a test since 1970, when press reports suggested, prematurely, that India was considering conducting a nuclear test. The State Department, then under the command of William Rogers, informed India that employment of the plutonium from the CIRUS reactor for a test would be considered a violation of India's pledge of peaceful uses of the heavy water that had been provided by the United States.[138]

On May 18, 1972, Kissinger, in Nixon's name, commissioned another study of Indian nuclear developments. The resulting study, by an NSC interdepartmental group, again noted that India's nuclear energy program afforded the country the ability to conduct a test on short notice and "of mounting a rudimentary weapons program on short notice." The group also wrote, six days before Indira Gandhi's visit to Trombay, that "there is no firm intelligence that Mrs. Gandhi has given a political go-ahead for detonating an underground nuclear device (which the Indians would undoubtedly label a peaceful nuclear device)." It further reported that "our intelligence assessment is that over the next several years the chances are about even that India will detonate a nuclear device."[139]

EVEN HAD CHIDAMBARAM not been concerned about America's spy satellites, he probably would not have gotten much sleep on the night of May 17. None of the other scientists there were able to get more than an hour's worth, undoubtedly due to a combination of anxiety and oppressive heat. By 8:00 a.m., when the detonation was scheduled, Ramanna, Sethna, Nag Chaudhuri, and Iyengar were in place to observe the test, about three miles from the shaft.[140]

A slight delay was caused when a jeep carrying a member of the ballistics research laboratory broke down near the shaft, forcing him to walk over a mile rather than wait for the vehicle to repaired. At five minutes past eight, Pranab Revati Dastidar, BARC's electronics expert, pushed the red button. The lack of an immediate reaction led Ramanna and Sethna to fear the device was not going to detonate, but then they saw a small mountain of sand rise from the ground before collapsing. Iyengar recalls thinking, "Now I believe all those mythological stories about Lord Krishna lifting a hill."* Legend has it that Sethna called the prime minister's office, spoke to P. N. Dhar, her principal secretary and one of the few individuals other than those working on the project who knew of its existence, and told him that "the Buddha is smiling."[141]

Less than an hour later, everyone listening to All-India Radio was in on the secret. India's version of the BBC interrupted its programming at 9:00 a.m. for a special announcement: "At 8:05 a.m. this morning, India successfully conducted an underground nuclear explosion for peaceful purposes at a carefully chosen site in western India." Dhar had informed the U.S. ambassador to India, Daniel Patrick Moynihan, a half hour after the test.[142]

Later in the day, Gandhi publicly congratulated the scientists at a news conference with Sethna. "It is a significant achievement for them and the whole country. . . . We are proud of them. They have worked hard and done a good, clean job." At the same time, she told newsmen, "There's nothing to get excited about . . . we are firmly committed to only peaceful uses of atomic energy." Ramanna reported that the blast created a 650-foot crater and an artificial hill, and called the test "a spectacular sight." A Western diplomat characterized the prime minister's pronouncement as "gobbledygook," explaining that "it is gobbledygook for them to claim that now that they have the ability they won't use it to make weapons."[143]

THAT MOYNIHAN—and apparently, every other U.S. official—was surprised by the test meant that despite the prolonged concern about India "going nuclear" and the efforts of the CIA, National Reconnaissance Office, NSA, State Department, and other intelligence collection and analysis

---

* Lord Krishna is a mythical Hindu deity who reportedly appeared in human form in 3328 BC and disappeared 125 years later.

agencies, the intelligence community had failed to provide advance warning. In a Top Secret report, the CIA characterized the test as "a well kept secret" that "took the world by surprise." The Indian drilling activities in Pokhran were apparently interpreted as involving the search for water, the Indian cover story, or oil.[144]

The failure was not an epic one though, and may have had more to do with the extraordinary secrecy surrounding the Indian program and the dual-use nature of the facilities, than with the inadequacy of America's intelligence establishment. While thousands were involved in India's nuclear program, only fifty to seventy-five scientists were actually part of the effort to design and build an explosive device. Work on the plutonium core was done by the scientists alone. One of them, C. Ganguly, recalled, "We had to do it ourselves, there were no technicians or helpers." Knowledge outside the group of scientists was so tightly restricted that only three additional individuals, including Gandhi and her principal secretary, knew what was being planned. The minister of defense was informed only eight days before the test; the minister of external affairs, only two days ahead of time. The rest of the cabinet was kept in the dark until after the detonation. In the years after the test, Raja Ramanna was asked by several people about India's ability to restrict prior knowledge of the test to so few individuals and the strict silence of those in the know prior to the detonation. In his autobiography he suggested that "it was the magnitude of the operation and the enormity of its implications that led us all to honour the oath of secrecy so diligently."[145]

While the CIA and other agencies may have failed to provide advance warning, they were able to assess the test based on intelligence gathered from open sources, imagery, human sources, and various components of the Atomic Energy Detection System. A Top Secret Codeword article on the test that appeared in the May 20 issue of the *Central Intelligence Bulletin* reported the claim of Indian AEC chairman Sethna that the detonation occurred at a depth of slightly more than 325 feet and was completely contained—with no venting of radioactive substances. It also relayed Sethna's claims that the device was entirely developed by India and relied on implosion. He was noncommittal, the article noted, as to whether India would conduct further tests.[146]

Beyond reporting Indian claims concerning aspects of the blast, analysts tried to evaluate some of those assertions concerning yield, the absence of venting, the geological conditions of the test site, and other aspects of the test. One of those analysts was Milo D. Nordyke of Lawrence Livermore National Laboratory, who produced two papers on the Indian test. In a May 29 paper he started by accepting the Indian claims concerning the depth of the test as well as a yield of 10 to 15 kilotons. If such numbers were accurate, then the apparent size of the crater created and the absence of venting indicated the device had been detonated in hard, dry rock—the type of rock that a peaceful nuclear explosion might be used to excavate. He concluded that "all the known facts appear to support the Indian statements that their nuclear test was carried out to further their PNE (peaceful nuclear explosions) program." In September, Nordyke received information indicating that rather than harder rock, the explosion took place in shale and at a depth of 357 feet. Given the size of the crater, he concluded that the yield of the Indian test was probably around 10 kilotons.[147]

In June the State Department's Bureau of Intelligence and Research focused on nontechnical issues related to the Indian detonation. It reported that the "euphoria that characterized the response of the Indian public" to the test "has been overtaken by uncertainty about the relationship between nuclear explosions and development needs and about the durability of India's proclaimed status as a non-weapons nuclear state." Much of the analysis focused on press and political reaction to the test and the question of whether India should develop nuclear weapons, the costs of future testing, the impact on the nonproliferation treaty, and the impact of the public on future decisions.[148] The post-test political analysis in many ways echoed the pretest analyses noting the differing views and competing pressures over India's future use of atomic energy—illustrating that the test, unlike the first tests in other nations, had far from settled the issue of whether India would become a nuclear weapons state.

SIX DAYS AFTER the Indian test, Lt. Gen. Daniel O. Graham, deputy to the director of central intelligence, William Colby, sent a memo to the directors of several intelligence agencies (NSA, Defense Intelligence Agency, and INR); the heads of the CIA directorates for intelligence, operations, and science and technology; and the chairman of the JAEIC. He informed them that he had requested the Intelligence Community Staff to assess the community's performance with respect to the Indian nuclear test.[149]

The postmortem that Graham ordered for Colby was completed in July and ran fifteen pages in length. The executive summary, the only portion of the postmortem that has been declassified, begins by stating the obvious: "In the months prior to India's 18 May nuclear test, the intelligence community failed to warn US decision makers that such a test was being planned. This failure denied the US Government the option of considering diplomatic or other initiatives to try to prevent this significant step in nuclear proliferation."[150]

The summary then noted that the intelligence community had "estimated as far back as 1965 that India would 'in the next few years' detonate a nuclear device" and that "its inability to predict the actual event was due essentially to two factors," one of which was the "inadequate priority against an admittedly difficult target"—not the first or last time that an intelligence failure would be attributed, at least partially, to a lack of attention. Fixing the problem would require "a more focused and dedicated effort by existing collection assets, chiefly in the HUMINT [human intelligence] area," Graham informed Colby. There was also, according to the authors of the postmortem, a lack of adequate communications among those elements of the community, both collectors and producers, whose combined talents were essential to resolving the problem."[151]

By the next January, there had been a number of intelligence community responses to the postmortem's recommendations, which included a COMIREX review of why intelligence analysts had failed to ask the National Photographic Interpretation Center at the CIA to analyze images they had specifically requested be obtained by America's spy satellites and the assignment of technical specialists abroad to support the CIA case officers involved in collecting proliferation intelligence. Intelligence reporting on proliferation subjects had increased tenfold and the AEC had established a "proliferation watch" effort to develop better indicators of proliferation activity. In addition, the Human Sources Committee of the U.S. Intelligence Board had established an ad hoc group to work with the JAEIC.[152]

chapter six

"PARIAHS"

BY 1975 INDIA WAS not the only nation whose ambiguous or opaque nuclear intentions were of concern to the United States. Israel, widely believed to be a member of the nuclear club, neither confirmed nor denied possessing such special weapons. South Africa and Taiwan were considered candidates to join the nuclear club before the end of the decade.

The three nations were also united in that some circles considered them international pariahs. Israel was repeatedly condemned by Arab states, the Communist world, and assorted Third World regimes—and often rebuked in the United Nations—for measures it took in self-defense. South Africa was ostracized, sanctioned, and embargoed because of the white government's racial policy of apartheid, which resulted in the separation and subjugation of the millions of blacks who constituted the vast majority of the nation's population. Taiwan had been expelled from the UN in 1972, owing to Richard Nixon and Henry Kissinger's desire to open a new relationship with the People's Republic of China—even if it had to be at the expense of a longtime ally whose citizens were far freer than those of the People's Republic.[1]

That each nation considered itself under siege by neighboring states that could command more resources and larger armies made the nuclear option worth considering. The three nations' isolation from much of the world, particularly when it came to the acquisition of advanced weaponry, made them, to some extent, natural allies for a time. And their willingness and ability, in at least two cases, to build a nuclear arsenal without openly testing it made monitoring their pursuit of a nuclear capability an even greater challenge for America's nuclear intelligence establishment.

ISRAEL WAS THE FIRST of the three to decide to develop a nuclear arsenal. Like India and France, it began work on nuclear energy without an explicit commitment to nuclear weapons. Israel's first prime minister, David Ben-Gurion, was well aware of the potential role that science and technology could play in national defense. He also believed, and stated so repeatedly, that Israel could rely only on its own strength—not on international guarantees, the promises of other nations, or UN resolutions—to ensure survival. In the spring of 1952 he started his nation on the path to nuclear weapons with the creation of the Israeli Atomic Energy Commission (IAEC).[2]

Ben-Gurion was acting on the recommendation of Ernst David Bergmann, the head of the Division of Research and Infrastructure in the Ministry of Defense. Bergmann, an organic chemist, had been expelled from the University of Berlin in 1933 by the newly installed Nazi government. From Germany he emigrated to Palestine, where he became the scientific director of the newly created Daniel Sieff Research Institute in Rehovot. In August 1948, he was appointed head of the scientific department of the new Israeli Defense Forces (IDF). Appointments as scientific adviser to minister of defense Ben-Gurion (who held that position as well as prime minister) and as head of the new research and infrastructure division followed in July 1951 and early 1952, respectively. With creation of the IAEC, he received a second government job: chairman of the commission.[3]

Among the six others who made up the commission was Hebrew University's Israel Dostrovsky, who would play a key role in Israel's development of atomic weapons. Born in Russia in 1918, his family emigrated to Palestine the next year. His studies in physical chemistry took him to London, where University College awarded him a doctorate in 1943. After spending the next five years in England, he returned to Palestine in 1948, where he founded the Department of Isotope Research at the Weizmann Institute. At the same time, in his capacity as a major in the IDF Science Corps, he established Hemed Gemel, a special branch of the corps that would play a key role in Israel's bomb project. Among its first projects was sending geologists into the Negev desert in search of uranium.[4]

In the years immediately following the creation of the IAEC, Israel's internal nuclear research progressed and external nuclear contacts expanded. In 1952–1953, a research team under Dostrovsky developed a new process relying on distillation to produce water enriched with heavy oxygen. A similar process to produce heavy water was the next step. A chemical method for separating uranium from phosphate deposits was also under development. Optimism about the commercial potential led Bergmann to use these methods to cultivate contacts with France and Norway, nations that might be able to satisfy Israeli requirements for nuclear engineering and reactor technology, which neither the United States, Canada, nor Britain were willing to provide.[5]

Bergmann's initiative led to cooperation with both Norway and France. Of particular importance to Israel was the relationship established with the French atomic energy commission. Israeli scientists were granted access to the Saclay Nuclear Research Center as well as Chatillon. Toward the end of 1953, Zvi Lipkin and Israel Pelah were sent to study reactor physics at the centers. They were followed by Amos de Shalit, who, instead of returning to Israel after his stay at MIT, spent four months at Saclay studying reactor physics.[6]

Ben-Gurion resigned as Israeli prime minister and defense minister in 1953. But in early 1955 his party's leadership, in the wake of the Lavon affair, requested that he take charge of the Defense Ministry again.* Before the end of the year he had become prime minister for the second time. In between he apparently decided that not only should Israel begin a nuclear energy program, but its ultimate goal should be the production of nuclear weapons.[7]

Ben-Gurion's decision was followed by a recruiting drive by the Defense Ministry's Research and Planning Division (EMET). The targets were advanced students in mathematics, engineering, and the sciences. The initial recruits were chosen by division chief Bergmann and Jenka Ratner, a key deputy and the future chief of the bomb project. A few went to Saclay's Institute of Nuclear Science and Techniques and Chatillon for graduate work. Only after obtaining their security clearances and being sworn to secrecy were the recruits told that they had been selected to help develop an Israeli nuclear device.[8]

In July 1956 Bergmann prepared a detailed memorandum, which he submitted to Shimon Peres, the director general of the Ministry of Defense since 1953, with whom he would strike an "intimate partnership," according to Peres. The science adviser offered two basic options: purchasing a small reactor from the United States, Canada, or France or attempting to obtain a much larger, more capable reactor. The cabinet considered the alternatives and chose to start small, with a reactor purchased from the United States and located at Nebi Rubin, south of Tel Aviv.[9]

But an opportunity to advance Israel's quest for nuclear weapons, with French assistance, arose out of a foreign policy fiasco. France had already become an important military supplier to Israel, largely owing to Peres. It provided Mystere fighters, AMX tanks, and plenty of ammunition. The director general of the Defense Ministry, and future prime minister, also played a significant role in obtaining additional assistance that went far beyond training scientists at Saclay and Chatillon.[10]

Shortly after Egyptian president Gamal Abdel Nasser announced the nationalization of the Suez Canal in late July 1956, French defense minister

---

* The Lavon affair, named for Minister of Defense Pinhas Lavon, involved an attempt to damage U.S.-Egyptian and British-Egyptian relations through attacks on U.S. and British facilities in Egypt, carried out by Israeli military intelligence assets with the expectation that the attacks would be attributed to Egyptians. See Ian Black and Benny Morris, *Israel's Secret Wars: A History of Israel's Intelligence Services* (New York: Grove Weidenfeld, 1993), pp. 107–117.

Maurice Bourges-Maunoury asked Peres to meet with him. The question he put to Peres was whether Israel was willing to participate in a military operation, along with France and Britain, to seize the canal. Peres, seeing an opportunity to obtain an atomic reactor from a grateful France, one with fewer strings attached than Israel could get from the United States, agreed.[11]

In mid-September, before the military campaign began, the Commissariat l'Énergie Atomique and IAEC agreed, in principle, on the sale to Israel of a small research reactor similar to the EL-3 at Saclay. But the military campaign turned into a debacle when Soviet leaders threatened missile attacks on the homelands of the invaders and Eisenhower responded with condemnation rather than support. On November 8, Ben Gurion sent Peres and foreign minister Golda Meir on a covert mission to France to determine what kind of support the French would provide in case the Soviets made good on their threats against Israel. The French foreign minister, Christian Pineau, noted France's inability to shoot down Soviet missiles and urged Israel to comply with the ultimatum. Peres apparently suggested that Israeli withdrawal would require another means of protecting its security and asked Pineau and the other French participants in their meeting, Bourges-Maunoury and aide Abel Thomas, "What would you think if we prepared our own retaliation force?" Bourges-Maunoury and Thomas responded favorably, leaving them with the task of convincing CEA chairman Frances Perrin and the current prime minister, Guy Mollet, to take French support to a much higher level.[12]

What Israel wanted was an upgraded version of the reactor that the CEA had planned to provide Israel, one similar to the large G-1 (40-megawatt thermal power) reactor at Marcoule, which was capable of producing between twenty-two and thirty-three pounds of plutonium a year. In addition, Israel wanted France to provide the technology required to extract plutonium from the spent reactor fuel, and requested that Saint Gobain Nucléaire, the same company responsible for building the Marcoule extraction facility, build an underground plant attached to the reactor. The underground facility would have four components: a preparation workshop for spent fuel, laboratories for the analysis of irradiated spent fuel, a facility to store wastes from the reactor, and a reprocessing plant to extract plutonium.[13]

It would take a year before the two nations were ready to sign an agreement. The political part involved the pledge, from Shimon Peres to Pineau, that the reactor complex would be used for peaceful purposes. The technical portion covered the reactor and some other elements of the facilities to be constructed. Other technical issues were covered by oral understandings. There was no reference at all in the official documents to the reprocessing plant. Rather, the plant was the subject of a contract between SGN and another French firm, serving as an intermediary for Israel.[14]

In addition to the reactor and processing plant, Israel needed to obtain uranium and heavy water. But France could not supply the heavy water needed for the reactor, since it had been relying on the Israeli process, which, in the end, could not be developed for commercial production. Israel found another source—the same nation that had supplied France with heavy water before and after World War II. In February 1959 the Israeli representative in Oslo and the Norwegian foreign affairs chief exchanged documents that laid the groundwork for the sale of twenty-two tons of heavy water, with Israel promising, once again, to use it only for peaceful purposes and pledging that Norway would have the opportunity to verify that Israel was living up to its commitment.[15]

By that time, construction of the nuclear facility was well underway. It had begun, in secret, sometime in late 1957 or early 1958. Overall responsibility for the construction of the reactor, separation plant, and related facilities was placed in the hands of Col. Manes Pratt, head of the Ordnance Corps during the war of independence. Like Leslie Groves, he was an engineer, not a scientist, a quick study, and a perfectionist. Shimon Peres, who selected Pratt for the job, recalled that he was looking for "a man who would not compromise over detail, whether vital or ostensibly marginal." Peres also wrote of Pratt that "within a few months he became Israel's foremost expert in nuclear engineering."[16]

Pratt's project was located in the Negev desert, which comprises about half of Israeli territory and which Mark Twain, after an 1867 visit, described as "a desolation that not even imagination can grace with the pomp of life and action." Annual rainfall in the Negev actually varies from twelve inches in the northern part to barely two in the Arava Valley, along the Jordanian border. While some thought had been given to building the facility at a seashore location where water needed for cooling would be plentiful, safety considerations dictated a location far from major population centers. The secret construction site, where the Negev Nuclear Research Center would come into existence, was in the central part of the desert, about eight and a half miles from the town of Dimona and approximately twenty-five miles from the Jordanian border.[17] Over time "Dimona" would become synonymous with the nuclear facility built nearby.

By the latter half of 1959 excavation work for the reprocessing plant, under the supervision of SGN, was underway. The digging took place next to and below the reactor construction site. In France, dozens of Israeli scientists and technicians conducted research and trained at a number of CEA facilities, including Saclay and Marcoule.[18] But political changes in France threatened to bring the joint effort to a halt well before the research center could be completed.

The potential stumbling block was French president Charles de Gaulle, who was determined to end his nation's close military collaboration with Israel, in part because of fear of Arab reaction if the extent of cooperation became known. In 1959 he had been talked out of his plan to simply abrogate the nuclear agreement. In 1960, after the departure of pro-Israeli atomic energy minister Jacques Soustelle, French foreign minister Maurice Couve de Murville made three demands, conveyed via the Israeli ambassador. Israel was to publicly acknowledge the existence of the Negev project, declare that the reactor was to be used for peaceful purposes, and permit international inspections. Unless Israel complied, France would refuse to supply the natural uranium needed to fuel the reactor.[19]

Accepting the French demands, particularly for international inspections, would threaten the plan to produce fissile material for atomic bombs. At the same time, the natural uranium France was providing was needed for the project. High-level discussions between de Gaulle and Ben-Gurion followed in June 1960. During a meeting in the Elysée Palace, the French president asked why Israel needed a nuclear reactor at all. Before the talks concluded, the Israeli leader pledged that he would not approve construction of a nuclear device or a separation plant. But it took three months of negotiations between Couve de Murville and Peres to produce a final agreement. France, while terminating official involvement through the CEA, would allow French firms to fulfill their contracts to build the reactor and drop its demand for international inspections. Israel would acknowledge the existence of the project and affirm its peaceful intent—both of which Ben-Gurion did before the Knesset that December, telling his audience that the atomic energy produced would be used to develop industry and agriculture.[20]

As a result of the agreement, the reactor was completed and handed over to Israel sometime in 1963 or 1964, after the start-up stage. Israel faced the problem of completing the reprocessing plant without Saint Gobain's assistance. However, with the plans and specifications that the company had provided in hand, Israel was able to take over most of the effort. Three areas of lesser sensitivity were completed by a French company, the Société Industrielle d'études et de Construction Chimiques, between its return in 1963 and its departure in June 1965.[21]

By 1965 the Dimona facility was the most controversial component of the Israeli program. But there were other facilities whose personnel would play significant roles in the research and development and construction of Israel's first atomic bombs. The Soreq Nuclear Research Center, also located in the Negev, fifteen miles south of Tel Aviv, was formally established in 1958. Two years later the reactor purchased from the United States became operational. It was with unintended irony that, in 1961, *Architectural Forum* wrote of Soreq that the "secret nature of the work within is suggested by the steeply battered, fortress-like walls which clearly and powerfully resist the visitor."[22]

From 1961 to 1963 the scientific director for Soreq (and the IAEC) was Yuval Ne'eman, a Tel Aviv native who obtained his bachelor's degree in mechanical engineering from the Israeli Institute of Technology in Haifa (the Technion, also known as Israel's MIT) and his doctorate in physics from London University in 1962, where he had studied while serving as defense attaché. By the time he started work at Soreq he was already a world-renowned physicist, having contributed papers such as *Derivation of Strong Interactions from a Gauge Invariance*, and having developed, along with Murray Gell-Mann, the classification scheme for elementary particles known as the Eightfold Way. During his time at Soreq and the IAEC, he would help shape Israel's atomic bomb project.[23]

In addition to, or ahead of, Soreq was RAFAEL, the Armament Development Authority, which replaced EMET in 1958. The authority was the professional home of Jenka Ratner and his technical director, Avraham Hermoni, who had been assigned the responsibility for the design and fabrication of Israel's first atomic device. Other scientists contributing to the program were affiliated with the Weizmann Institute (as the Sieff Institute had been renamed in 1949), the Technion, and Hebrew University.[24]

Their joint efforts, the assistance from France, and the heavy water from Norway allowed the first plutonium for a bomb to be extracted in 1965. Then, one day in late 1966, Israel's weapons designers convinced themselves that their country had joined the nuclear club, although they did not offer the world proof by blowing anything up. Whether they became convinced because they tested an implosion device minus fissile material or conducted a near-zero-yield test is not clear. But the memoirs of Munya Mardor, the head of RAFAEL at the time, suggest that whatever tests they conducted turned out well. Mardor, in a manner consistent with Israel's policy of nuclear ambiguity, wrote,

> On November 2, 1966, a test with special significance was conducted. It meant an era of development, and a step that brought one of our primary weapons-systems to its final phases of development and production in RAFAEL. The test was completely successful, for we received an unequivocal experimental proof of the adequacy of the system that was developed at RAFAEL. We have waited for that result for many years.[25]

The November success meant that seven months later, at the beginning of the Six-Day War, Israel's arsenal included—along with its fighters, tanks, and soldiers—two or three nuclear weapons, although the speed of Israel's victory meant that Israeli leaders never had to contemplate their use as they would in the later Yom Kippur War.[26]

Producing further warheads required the reactor in the Negev, which could turn out enough plutonium each year for one or two weapons, to be fed with uranium. In 1968 Israel resorted to an unconventional method to acquire the fuel. In a joint operation the Institute for Intelligence and Special Tasks (better known as the Mossad) and the Science Liaison Bureau (LAKAM) stole two hundred tons of natural uranium. A Mossad-controlled ship, the *Scheersberg A*, picked up the uranium at Antwerp, ostensibly to carry it to Italy. Instead it rendezvoused with an Israeli cargo ship somewhere between Cyprus and Turkey and transferred the nuclear fuel. The ship showed up in Turkey without the uranium and missing two pages of its log, but with a new crew.[27]

SOUTH AFRICA'S FIRST VENTURE

SOUTH AFRICA'S FIRST VENTURE into uranium exploration and mining dates back to 1944, when Britain asked Prime Minister Jan Smuts to assist in the search for material needed for the Allied atomic bomb project. The South African Chamber of Mines soon discovered that uranium coexisted with gold in virtually every goldmine and borehole in the portion of the country known as the Rand. For the next four years, until the Atomic Energy Board (AEB) was established, in 1948, the prime minister's office managed the uranium production.[28]

While uranium production increased substantially over the next decade, South Africa did not have an actual atomic energy program. Then, in September 1959 the cabinet approved the atomic energy board's proposed research and development program. Dr. A. J. A. "Ampie" Roux was appointed research director and began trying to develop a core of nuclear scientists and engineers, sending them to overseas nuclear research organizations for training. In 1961 general nuclear research and development work began at the Pelindaba Nuclear Research Center, about twelve miles west of Pretoria. Four years later, ground was broken at Pelindaba for Safari, South Africa's first research reactor. Over thirteen hundred pounds of 2 percent enriched uranium and over five metric tons of heavy water, supplied by the United States, allowed the reactor to go critical in 1967.[29]

By that time some prominent South African officials had already raised the prospect of acquiring nuclear weapons. In 1965 Andres Visser, a member of the AEB, advocated building a nuclear arsenal for "prestige purposes" and reportedly said, "We should have the bomb to prevent aggression from loudmouth Afro-Asiatic states." Later that year, during the inauguration ceremony of the Safari reactor, Prime Minister H. F. Verwoerd proclaimed that it was "the duty of South Africa to consider not only the military uses of the material but also to do all in its power to direct its uses to peaceful purposes," implying that South Africa was already pondering the military uses of atomic energy.[30]

With Safari in operation, South Africa had a training ground for a program designed to produce plutonium. While the Safari operation was visible, a parallel uranium enrichment program was not. It had begun in a small warehouse in central Pretoria, and moved in the mid-1960s to Pelindaba, to allow more sophisticated experiments to be conducted under stricter security. By the end of 1967 the uranium had been enriched on a laboratory scale. In early

1969, after reviewing the program's progress, the government authorized construction of a pilot plant. That year it also authorized a committee to explore economic and technical questions concerning the use of peaceful nuclear explosives for mining.[31]

In July 1970 Prime Minister John Vorster told Parliament that South African scientists had developed a unique method for enriching uranium, and announced his government's intent to build a pilot facility to test the new method, along with the creation of the Uranium Enrichment Corporation. (While there were suspicions that the process was similar to the jet nozzle system, developed by Professor Erwin Becker of the Institute for Nuclear Processing Techniques in West Germany, its resemblance was only superficial. The South African method was closer to an ordinary centrifuge, "except that the centrifuge wall was stationary and a vortex mechanism rapidly spun the uranium hexafluoride (UF_6) and hydrogen gas inside a stationary tube." Centrifugal force separated the U-235 from the U-238, which exited through different concentric holes in at the ends of the tube.) The Y-Plant would be located at Valindaba, adjacent to the Palindaba center, Vorster said. He also emphasized that the the work at Valindaba was intended only for peaceful uses. Of course, the facility's name, which in Zulu means "we don't talk about this at all," probably did not help allay suspicion.[32]

That guarantee did not rule out developing nuclear explosives, no more than it would for India. In March 1971 the AEB received permission from the minister of mines, Carel de Wet, to conduct a preliminary investigation into the feasibility of producing a nuclear explosive device. The initial investigation was limited in scope, restricted to an examination of the literature, theoretical calculations, and studies of the ballistics of gun-type devices. Manpower devoted to the effort was also minimal, with only three engineers working on the ballistic and theoretical implosion studies.[33]

But with the defense minister and chief of the South African Defence Force proclaiming in 1971 and 1972 that a Soviet-orchestrated assault was inevitable, the restriction to theoretical work did not last long. In 1972 and 1973 a small group from the atomic energy board worked, in conditions of secrecy, at a propulsion laboratory at Somchem in Cape Province. They studied mechanical and pyrotechnic subsystems for a gun-type device and then designed and tested a scale model with a projectile containing nonnuclear material. The test took place at Somchem in May 1974, the same month India was testing its completed device in the Pokhran.[34]

Before the year was out, South Africa took two additional steps toward joining the nuclear club. The first stages of the lower end of the Y-Plant's cascade became operational. And, after receiving a report from the AEB saying that it could do so, Vorster and his government, possibly motivated by the overthrow of the dictator in Portugal by left-wing military officers, who could not be counted on to maintain the Portugese colonial presence in Mozambique and Angola, decided to authorize the construction of at least one fission device—a single device as a "peaceful nuclear explosive." The program was treated as a top-secret effort, one South African official claimed, because of the "expected sensitivity surrounding the enrichment project and because the world was fast turning against PNE [Peaceful Nuclear Explosions]."[35]

Vorster also authorized funding for a testing site. The site would have to be large enough and sufficiently far from any international borders to contain any physical and radiological effects within the country. Locating that site began with the use of a variety of maps—geological, hydrological, and geographical—and ended with the selection of an area north of Cape Province, in the Kalahari Desert. Because the presence of representatives from the AEB at such a location might create suspicion, the Defence Force bought the site, guarded it, and established the "Vastrap" test site.[36]

TAIWAN'S INTEREST in developing an atomic bomb, if not created by China's October 1964 test, was certainly heightened by that traumatic event. The concern of Taiwan's rulers was evident in the cables from the U.S. embassy to Washington that conveyed their views. One reported that "top GRC [Government of the Republic of China] leaders have expressed private view [that the detonation] can cause 'crisis of confidence' eroding people's will [to] resist Peiping on both Taiwan and elsewhere." Another passed on Chiang Kai-shek's characterization of the "free people of Asia . . . as 'uncertain and scared.'"[37]

In 1967, with China having conducted several additional tests and increased concern about Chinese intentions, the Ministry of Defense's Chungshan Institute of Science and Technology produced a proposal for developing nuclear weapons at a price of $140 million. The projected cost was based on an estimate from the German company Siemens, which offered to supply a heavy-water reactor, a heavy-water production plant, and facility for the production of ballistic missiles for $120 million.[38]

The proposal was given to Ta-You Wu, head of the government's National Science Council and director of the Science Development Advisory Committee of the National Security Council, for review. Wu had received his doctorate in 1933 from the University of Michigan, where he had studied under future Alsos scientific director Samuel Goudsmit, and spent considerable time overseas, heading the theoretical physics division of the Canadian National Research Council from 1949 to 1963. He was also the author of several highly technical books, including *Vibrational Spectra and Structure of Polyatomic Molecules* and *Kinetic Equations of Gases and Plasmas*.[39]

Wu's reaction to the proposed "Hsin Chu" program was less than favorable.

He believed that the plan was severely flawed on economic, technical, and political grounds—that it underestimated the actual cost, which he believed would exceed $140 or $150 million, while overestimating the chance of success. Development of a plutonium production plant would "rouse the suspicion of the international community," he wrote. Producing ballistic missiles as part of the plan would, he judged, cost more than Taiwan, with its limited cash reserve of a few-dozens-million American dollars, could afford.[40]

As an alternative, Wu suggested focusing first on acquisition of a reactor, which could be purchased from the United States if Taiwan could accept IAEA safeguards. Once that was accomplished, "we can . . . then find ways to develop the other two projects," he wrote in reference to the heavy-water and plutonium separation plants. He also suggested the nuclear program be controlled by a civilian body in conformity with international practice, and because military control would be considered suspicious, which led to the Atomic Energy Council's assumption of responsibility. The military did retain some involvement in that Lt. Gen. Tang Jun-Po, a Cambridge-trained mathematician and the chief of Chungshan's Preparatory Committee, was reappointed as a "standing committee member" of the council.[41]

Wu also recommended purchase of a safeguarded nuclear reactor, which would permit Taiwan to legally obtain heavy water from the United States. While the Ministry of Defense's science institute wanted such a reactor, the Taiwan Electricity Company did not, favoring the purchase of light-water reactors. A compromise solution allowed the electric company to buy light-water reactors, and in 1969 the Institute of Nuclear Energy Research (INER), located at the same site as the Chungshan institute, about twenty-seven miles southwest of Taipei, obtained a small heavy-water research reactor from Canada.[42]

All of Wu's recommendations were accepted. In September 1969 work on the Canadian-supplied Taiwan Research Reactor began. The reactor was only one of several INER nuclear projects initiated in 1969 and 1970. Also in the works were a plant to produce natural uranium fuel, a reprocessing facility, and a plutonium chemistry laboratory. All three were built by Taiwan, with equipment obtained from an assortment of countries, including the United States, France, and Germany.[43]

During the first half of the 1970s the INER facilities gradually began coming online. In 1972 or 1973 the fuel fabrication facility started operations, employing natural uranium provided by South Africa. The twenty to thirty metric tons of fuel it was expected to produce each year was about twice as much as the research reactor required. In 1973 the 40-megawatt-thermal, natural-uranium, heavy-water Taiwan Research Reactor, the same type of reactor that India used to generate the plutonium for its 1974 detonation, began operations. The United States supplied the heavy water via Canada, which also supplied twenty-five metric tons of natural-uranium fuel rods.

Reportedly, the reactor did not perform well initially, producing only about twenty-two pounds of plutonium by the end of 1975, in contrast to the thirty-three pounds per year it could have produced in that period if it had operated at full power for 80 percent or more of the time.[44]

THE EARLIEST available example of the U.S. intelligence community's interest in the atomic energy activities of the pariah states is a volume of a 1956 Office of Scientific Intelligence study on the nuclear activities of the nations of Asia and Africa. The six pages devoted to South Africa note the existence and responsibilities of the AEB, the absence of nuclear reactors and creation of a Nuclear Physics Institute, and South Africa's role as "one of the world's principal producers of uranium."[45]

Israel's known nuclear activities were probably summarized in a companion volume covering the Middle East. In any case, there was no suspicion that Israel envisioned a future arsenal that contained nuclear weapons. In 1957, a national intelligence estimate observed that Israel "would require major foreign assistance to produce even the first nuclear weapon within the next 10 years." Its expression of interest in 1956 in purchasing a 10-megawatt, natural uranium–fueled, heavy water–moderated reactor did not cause concern.[46]

Knowledge of the Soreq project led U.S. intelligence analysts to view any statements made by Bergmann between 1958 and 1960 as references to that effort, even when his statements seemed to refer to a facility considerably larger than the small reactor the United States had agreed to help build. And when Bergmann was asked directly about Israeli nuclear plans or the extent of cooperation with France, he provided answers that revealed nothing about what was going on in the Negev. In June 1958 he did respond to a series of questions from the U.S. embassy in Tel Aviv. While "somewhat perturbed" by the questions, he answered them "in some detail," claiming that while Israel had decided to build a heavy-water plant, its capacity had not been determined. He did not mention construction of a reactor.[47]

But between 1958 and 1960 intelligence from a variety of sources started raising the possibility that Israel was secretly engaged in building a reactor to produce fissile material, and then made it a near certainty. In May 1959 the U.S. naval attaché in Tel Aviv heard, through a British source, that the April resignation of Dan Tolkovsky, the head of RAFAEL, might be the result of his opposition to Peres's plan for a nuclear-armed Israel. In the absence of confirmation, no further inquiries were made. Then, in June, the Norwegian foreign ministry told an Atomic Energy Commission representative about the agreement to sell heavy water to Israel. The representative did not inquire further at the time and the information was not circulated to other intelligence agencies for over eighteen months.[48]

The CIA's human intelligence efforts also yielded some information in early 1960. In April the Clandestine Service discovered that the Norwegian-Israeli agreement called for the sale of twenty tons of heavy water. Earlier that year the agency also "obtained information that specific Israeli observers would be present at the first French nuclear weapons tests," but that information, too, was never passed on "because it could not be confirmed that any observers actually attended."[49]

Two of the intelligence community's most sensitive collection methods of the time—communications intelligence and the U-2—also provided data. In mid-1959 a communications intercept provided some information about the Negev site, but was discounted because the other information it provided was "demonstrably untrue," according to an intelligence community assessment.[50]

Harder to ignore was the imagery obtained from U-2 overflights of Israel. Those overflights began in late August 1956. Israel, Egypt, Jordan, Lebanon, and Syria had all been U-2 targets, with the imagery revealing, to the surprise of CIA photointerpreters, the presence of French-supplied fighter planes and fighter-bombers at Israeli airfields. President Dwight Eisenhower ordered that U-2 coverage be increased, and the spy planes flew from Adana, Turkey, to fulfill his orders.[51]

Among the sites that U-2s regularly snapped pictures of was a bombing range in the Negev, where the Israeli defense forces staged exercises. Starting in early 1958, the images from the missions slowly revealed something more significant. That the Dimona project would be discovered by such overhead surveillance was a major concern to Israeli officials. Peres has recalled that "the first stage of construction was a vast excavation. A bird's eye view would have revealed great gashes dug into the desert. A spy plane or satellite would have had the same view, which was enough to send twinges of trepidation through the minds of my cabinet opponents."[52]*

Early on there was more to see than gashes in the desert. An initial clue was the fencing off of a large, barren area about a dozen miles from Dimona. Also a new road connected the site to Beersheba, twenty-five miles to the north. Dino Brugioni, second in command at the CIA's Photographic Intelli-

---

* In his memoirs, Shimon Peres reported that Isser Harel, head of the Mossad, feared, that a trip to Washington by Soviet foreign minister Andrei Gromyko during the last months of the Eisenhower administration was the result of the Soviet Union's discovery of what was going on a Dimona. Harel's anxiety was based on a report that a Soviet satellite had recently overflown and photographed Dimona and the Soviets were planning to make a "dramatic protest." Harel's fears were baseless—it would be several years before the Soviet Union acquired the capability to take pictures from space. See Shimon Peres, *Battling for Peace: A Memoir* (New York: Random House, 1995), pp. 120–121.

gence Center, and other interpreters at first assumed that Israel was establishing an ammunition testing facility.[53]

Subsequent photos from the spy planes showed construction workers and heavy machinery and then the great gashes in the desert. It was also clear that two underground sites were being dug—Brugioni had watched the Germans dig underground facilities during World War II and recognized the piles of dirt as a sign. An attempt was made to estimate their size by measuring the "spoil," the amount of dirt in cubic feet being removed from the ground every day.[54]

The digging was followed by pouring of cement into heavy foundations. Soon Brugioni and his colleagues began to suspect what was going on, for they had visited nuclear weapons facilities in the United States so that they would understand the meaning of such images. Years later he recalled, "We spotted it right away. What the hell was that big of a plant, with reinforced concrete doing there in the middle of the desert? . . . Whenever you build something nuclear you build it thick and deep. They were pouring a hell of a lot of concrete. We knew they were going deep."[55]

Then there was imagery of workers pouring what appeared to be the concrete footings for a reactor's circular dome. Arthur Lundahl, chief of the Photographic Intelligence Center, assumed that Eisenhower would be very interested to hear, and see, that Israel was probably in the midst of building a nuclear reactor. Lundahl prepared a briefing for the chief executive, which included slides showing both the French Marcoule plutonium-producing reactor and the very similar-looking Israeli site. When he returned, he reported to Brugioni that Eisenhower listened to his briefing but had nothing to say. However, Eisenhower didn't tell the CIA to stop overflying the site, which Brugioni, as was his responsibility, named Beersheba for the nearby city.[56]

The accumulation of data did not lead the CIA and other intelligence organizations to conclude that Israel was, without doubt, building a plutonium-producing reactor and reprocessing facility in the Negev. But it did lead to further inquiries. In late March 1958, OSI had communicated its interest in any information that could be obtained concerning Israeli nuclear activities, particularly its production of heavy water and uranium. Then, in September Israel was designated a Second Category Priority under the director of central intelligence's National Scientific and Technical Intelligence Objectives listing.[57]

Fourteen months after OSI's expression of interest, and an accumulation of U-2 imagery that allowed monitoring of the "probable" nuclear site, new information focused additional attention on developments in the Negev. In June 1960 the U.S. embassy in Tel Aviv began hearing rumors that the "French were collaborating with the Israelis in an atomic energy project near Beer Sheeba." When the embassy informally asked Israeli officials about what was going on in the Negev, they were told the facility was, of all things, a textile plant. In early August the embassy forwarded reporting that Israel was constructing "a major reactor with French assistance." Later that month the CIA learned that a secretary with the embassy in Tel Aviv had visited Beersheba with her boyfriend months earlier, who told her that the French were building a reactor at Beersheba.[58]

The embassy report was one topic of discussion when the Joint Atomic Energy Intelligence Committee met on August 25, and committee members were asked to report whatever information they had for the next meeting, to be held on September 8. Throughout September Israeli nuclear activities continued to be a subject of discussion between the United States and Israel and within the U.S. national security establishment. In response to additional inquiries, Israel changed its story—Dimona was no longer a textile factory, but a "metallurgical research installation." In the middle of the month the CIA responded to a query from the State Department about the embassy's early August report, informing the denizens of Foggy Bottom that it had "no confirming information" concerning the Negev construction site but had instructed its officers in the field to obtain answers to specific questions about the facility. The State Department also instructed the embassy in Tel Aviv to gather more data.[59]

In October and November U.S. intelligence received help from its British cousins. In late October and early November they passed along to the CIA station in London their assessment that a reactor was under construction in the vicinity of Beersheba. Then, on November 8, they delivered ground photography of the site. The following day, after a quick analysis of the imagery, the CIA concluded that "the site was probably a reactor complex."[60]

The CIA station encouraged military attachés to find reasons to travel to the desert in the vicinity of Dimona. The station was willing to equip them with wine for picnics and special automatic cameras with preset lenses for some clandestine photography. On November 8, the air attaché in Tel Aviv was ordered to obtain additional photographs of the "Beer Sheba site." He first laid eyes on Dimona during a personal trip in July, and was told by his Israeli liaison officer that the installation was a "a metallurgical research laboratory." He was able to take a long-range photo on November 16 to fulfill his order, and found that the Israelis were sticking to their story—he was photographing a metallurgical research laboratory.* Additional information came from the

---

* His photographs were not made available to the JAEIC until early December. About the same time, the JAEIC also received ground photographs obtained by the army attaché—photographs taken in early August, but the significance of which were not appreciated due to the attaché's ignorance of the nature of his target. See Director of Central Intelligence, *Post-Mortem on SNIE 100-8-60: Implications of the Acquisition by Israel of a Nuclear Weapons Capability*, January 31, 1961, pp. 13–14. The Israelis also made photog-

U.S. embassy in Paris later that month, when it reported, in response to a CIA request, that an AEC representative had questioned an "appropriate member" of the CEA about French participation in "the alleged construction of a nuclear power plant in Beer Sheeba." The CEA official "stated flatly" that neither the CEA nor any French company was assisting Israel in construction of such a facility, and claimed that the French-Israeli connection was limited to uranium and heavy-water production. The cable also reported that an American representative of a U.S. firm that built nuclear reactors had returned from Israel less than three months ago and agreed that the Israeli government was "not now constructing a power reactor."[61]

But further evidence cast serious doubt on those claims. It came not from a spy satellite, U-2, communications intercept, or a highly placed spy, but from University of Michigan nuclear scientist Henry Gomberg, head of the institution's Phoenix Project, which focused on the peaceful uses of nuclear energy. On November 26 Gomberg, in Paris on his way back from Israel, informed the U.S. embassy that he had an "urgent and secret" item regarding the Israeli nuclear program to discuss. On December 1 he returned to Washington and was debriefed at the State Department by representatives of the AEC, CIA, and State Department, including Philip Farley, still the special assistant to the secretary of state for atomic energy. Gomberg told his audience that he believed the facility in the Negev, which he had been told was a large experimental agricultural station, was a "Marcoule-type reactor being constructed with French technical assistance."[62]

Gomberg's reasons included both positive and negative evidence. He reported that he had been shown a photograph of the Dimona installation, which "apparently included a steel containment sphere which would be usable only for a nuclear power reactor," and that the facility's characteristics "were those of the Marcoule reactor." In addition, when he visited the Technion, he found that the specific skills being taught by the institute's personnel-training program were unsuited for any acknowledged activity. Also, some of those who had completed training could not be located at any known facility. His suspicions were further raised during a visit to a facility designated Plant or Laboratory No. 4 (Machon 4). It was clear to Gomberg that his hosts had been instructed to be careful with what they told him, and that something was being hidden from him. One worker did slip, to the distress of Gomberg's

---

raphy more difficult by planting large trees to block the line of vision, and increasing patrols of the Dimona perimeter. One American attaché was nearly shot after exceeding the limitations established by the embassy for monitoring Dimona. See Seymour Hersh, *The Samson Option: Israel's Nuclear Arsenal and American Foreign Policy* (New York: Random House, 1991), p. 57.

guide, by mentioning that the laboratory expected to be handling gram quantities of plutonium and curie quantities of polonium in the near future. Neither material would come from any acknowledged Israeli facility, but, presumably, from either another Israeli reactor or France.[63]

In a meeting Gomberg had with Ernst Bergmann, the science adviser revealed that in three weeks Ben-Gurion would be issuing a statement concerning Israel's atomic energy program. After meeting with Gomberg, Bergmann gave a preview of the prime minister's statement to the American ambassador, Ogden Reid. He told the diplomat that Ben-Gurion would note the existence of a new 10- to 20-megawatt natural-uranium and heavy-water reactor that would go critical in about eighteen months. Bergmann also stated that while the reactor employed some French equipment, it was exclusively of Israeli design and would be used "for research in desert plants, drought resistant seeds, short-life isotopes and radio biological research not now possible at [Soreq]."[64]

Bergmann was using the simplest deception technique: lying. His words were not taken seriously but were considered one element of an Israeli effort to deceive the United States. On December 2 the JAEIC concluded that "a 200 megawatt reactor appeared [to be] under construction near Beer Sheba." On December 8 the CIA's Office of National Estimates issued a special national intelligence estimate based on the latest information available—SNIE 100-8-60, *Implications of the Acquisition by Israel of a Nuclear Weapons Capability*, which focused on the serious implications of such an occurrence.[65]

The National Security Council met that same day, and Dimona was a prominent topic of discussion. Central intelligence chief Allen Dulles told the council that Israel, with French assistance, was building a nuclear facility in the Negev, a facility that probably included a reactor capable of producing weapons-grade plutonium. He also noted Ben-Gurion's expected announcement, while reporting that experts from the CIA and the AEC believed "that the Israeli nuclear complex cannot be solely for peaceful purposes." Dulles also stated that the Soviet Union and Arab countries would undoubtedly interpret the facility as intended for weapons production and that the Arab reaction would be "particularly severe."[66]

By this time the Eisenhower administration had about six weeks left in office, before a Democratic administration led by John F. Kennedy would take over. Nevertheless, the administration acted on the information rather than just leaving the problem for its successor to handle. On December 9 Christian Herter, who had replaced John Foster Dulles as secretary of state, summoned Israeli ambassador Avraham Harman and presented him with the intelligence community's conclusions, ground photographs, and the observation that the site appeared to be more appropriate for a reactor ten times as large as the declared size. Herter also noted the discrepancies between Israeli statements to the U.S. ambassador and the reports from U.S. scientists and industrial representatives.

Herter spoke of the U.S. suspicion that Israel had initiated a secret program to develop nuclear weapons, warned Harman of the consequences, and requested an accurate report on Israel's nuclear program. Harman claimed ignorance, telling Herter that he would request "urgent advice."[67]

On December 20, the same day the *New York Times* reported on Israel's original claim that Dimona was a textile factory and that the facility had been the subject of a presidential briefing the previous day, Harman provided a formal response. The ambassador told Herter that a 24-megawatt research reactor, rather than the 100- to 300-megawatt reactor the United States suspected, had been under construction for a year and would be completed in another three or four years. He also claimed that it had purely peaceful purposes—developing knowledge for industrial, agricultural, medical, and other scientific uses of atomic energy—and would not be used to make an atomic bomb.[68]

Neither Harman's statement nor Ben-Gurion's reassurances, offered the following day in the Knesset, ended the administration's quest to dissuade Israel from joining the nuclear club or finding out more about the Negev facility. On December 21 the State Department instructed Ambassador Reid to remind the Israeli prime minister that the United States "is firmly opposed to proliferation of nuclear weapons capabilities and therefore deeply interested in having [a] full and frank account [of] Israeli atomic activities." Three days later Reid met with Ben-Gurion to pass on the message and sent Washington an account of the meeting. Then, on the last day of the year, Reid received new instructions because neither the State Department nor other interested agencies were reassured by Ben-Gurion's responses to Reid—despite the State Department's public statement on December 21 that Dimona "does not represent a cause for special concern." The United States wanted Israel to answer five questions. The questions sought information on Israeli plans for disposing of the plutonium produced by Dimona, Israeli willingness to accept safeguards with regard to the plutonium produced as well as visits from the IAEA or other "friendly quarters," the possible existence of a third reactor in the construction or planning stages, and whether Israel could unequivocally state that it had no plans to develop nuclear weapons.[69]

On January 4 Reid got his answers: plutonium would revert to the uranium supplier, nationals of friendly powers would be permitted to visit, IAEA safeguards would not be accepted until others agreed to the same safeguards, no third reactor was contemplated, and nuclear weapons were not being planned. Ben-Gurion's answers did not prevent Harman from having to spend four hours on January 11 discussing the Israeli atomic energy program with Herter, who on January 17 instructed Reid to continue pressing the Israeli prime minister to allow a visit from foreign scientists in the near future.[70]

TWO DAYS LATER, Herter journeyed to the White House for a meeting whose participants included Eisenhower, the incoming and outgoing secretaries of state, defense, and treasury, and Senator John F. Kennedy. The president-elect, on the eve of his inauguration, asked Herter which nations were candidates to join the nuclear club. "Israel and India," Herter replied, adding that Israel had a reactor capable of producing about two hundred pounds of weapons-grade plutonium by 1963. He recommended that Kennedy demand inspection and control to keep atomic weapons out of the Middle East.[71]

Kennedy acted on Herter's advice. Shortly after taking office, he asked secretary of state Dean Rusk for a report on Israel's atomic energy program, which he received on January 30. The two-page memo, with an attached chronology, summarized the facts, as they were known, about the Israeli program as well as noting the diplomatic exchanges between Israel and the Eisenhower administration about the existence and purpose of Dimona. Rusk also stressed the two reasons for continued U.S. interest: a general opposition to proliferation and the "grave repercussions" that Israeli acquisition of nuclear weapons would have in the Middle East, including the possible deployment of Soviet nuclear weapons to the region.[72]

Rusk also told the new president that while Ben-Gurion's assurances appeared to be satisfactory and his explanation for the secrecy surrounding Dimona—the fear of an Arab boycott of the foreign firms involved in its construction—plausible, "it [is] the intention of our intelligence agencies to maintain a continuing watch on Israel as on other countries to assure that nuclear weapons capabilities are not being proliferated." In addition, the secretary's memo reported that his department was encouraging Israel to permit a qualified scientist from the United States or another friendly nation to visit Dimona.[73] For the thirty-four months Kennedy occupied the Oval Office, the CIA and other agencies sought to improve their understanding of the Israeli program, while the president and State Department sought to ensure regular visits to verify Israeli claims that Dimona was not intended to support a nuclear weapons program.

One element of the intelligence community's attempts, in early 1961, to do a better job of monitoring Israel's nuclear program was the preparation of a postmortem on the December 8, 1960, special national intelligence estimate and the collection and analysis activities that preceded it. A major focus of the review, which was completed at the end of January, was why the CIA and its sister agencies had taken so long to understand what was going on at Dimona. The postmortem distributed blame among a number of factors. In several cases, information that was obtained prior to 1960, such as the CIA's June 1959 intelligence on Israel's acquisition of heavy water, had not been adequately disseminated to the entire atomic energy intelligence establishment.

There was also a failure to properly interpret intelligence on Israeli reactor plans and "promptly and persistently" seek additional information. In addition, Israel's status as a second-priority intelligence target reduced "the effort and urgency attributed to this problem."[74]

The postmortem also produced several recommendations. Most dealt with the general problem of collecting and interpreting data on possible "nth" country nuclear programs, such as the suggestion that the CIA's clandestine service should "expeditiously disseminate all information [on nth country nuclear developments] that it collects on this subject." With specific regard to Israel the review recommended that "a concerted effort should be made to obtain information on the characteristics of Israeli reactors, how and where the plutonium produced will be processed and used, plans for weapons development, and the extent of foreign assistance and collaboration." It was not long after the postmortem was turned over to the U.S. Intelligence Board that the CIA disseminated its report on Gomberg's views of Israeli nuclear activities, based on his discussion with the U.S. ambassador in Tel Aviv in November 1960.[75]

Beyond assessing its past shortcomings, the intelligence establishment continued to collect new information. Thus, the CIA was able to report, in the April 27, 1961, issue of its Top Secret Codeword *Central Intelligence Bulletin*, "that photographs of the site show that the top of the reactor containment vessel was not closed until some time between November 1960 and February 1961." The article also noted that under normal construction techniques, reactor operations would begin a year to eighteen months after closure of the containment vessel. Of particular importance was the observation that "the statement . . . that Israel has started construction of an underground plutonium factory indicates that chemical separation of the irradiated fuel is to take place in Israel."[76]

But direct access to Dimona might allow more informed conclusions than the intelligence effort permitted. The Kennedy administration, including the president himself, continued to press Israel to fulfill its pledge to permit outside scientists to visit. On April 10, after numerous reminders and repeated Israeli excuses, Israel, through its ambassador in Washington, informed the State Department that the week of May 15 would be acceptable for a visit.[77]

On the evening of Wednesday, May 17, Jesse William Croach Jr. and Ulysses Merriam Staebler, both of whom had been selected by the AEC for the mission, arrived at Tel Aviv airport. The forty-three-year-old Croach had received his bachelor's degree in physics from Harvard in 1940 and joined DuPont that year. In 1961 he was working at the AEC's Savannah River Laboratory, which DuPont operated. Staebler was the senior assistant director of the AEC's Division of Reactor Development and had been a member of the

U.S. delegation to the 1955 and 1958 Geneva conferences on the peaceful use of atomic energy.[78]

Thursday's visits began with a trip to the reactor at Soreq, which was followed with a visit to the Weizmann Institute at Rehovot. On Friday morning the two American scientists traveled to Haifa and the Technion. The next day they were taken, by car, from Tel Aviv to the site of real concern, Dimona, arriving at about 11:00 a.m. Only two groups of Israelis were at the site that Saturday: security personnel and the eight who took part in the discussion. Leading the Israeli delegation was Manes Pratt.[79]

Staebler and Croach were told that all their questions would be answered, no written material would be given to them, and no pictures would be allowed. Manes also informed them that all information on the site was still considered classified. He then provided a background and history of the project, one consistent with previous Israeli statements to the United States, and described Dimona as a prelude to the creation of nuclear power plants. Beyond summarizing Pratt's presentation, Staebler and Croach provided a brief description of what they had seen, including a plutonium-processing pilot plant, the waste disposal facility, a hot cell for the small-scale separation of plutonium, a pilot plant for converting uranium ore to uranium metal, and the state of construction. They also drew a diagram of the facility, with the location and shapes of twenty-six numbered items, from the reactor to the temporary canteen. They reported that the Israelis wanted enough plutonium to experiment with as a power source and that they considered shipping it long distances for processing to be impractical.[80]

At least as important as the details of what they were told and what they saw was their overall judgment. That was conveyed in a memorandum to Kennedy's national security adviser, McGeorge Bundy, based on their discussions with State Department officials on May 25, three days after their return. Staebler and Croach were "satisfied that nothing was concealed from them and that the reactor is of the scope and peaceful character previously described to United States officials by representatives of the Government of Israel."[81] They had given Israel a clean bill of health.

Only four days after Bundy received the memo, Kennedy, just before leaving for his first encounter with Nikita Khrushchev, met with Ben-Gurion at the Waldorf-Astoria in New York. By that time he had received word from Bundy about the results of the Dimona visit, as well as briefing papers indicating that the CIA and other intelligence agencies still believed Israel was intent on developing nuclear weapons. However, the nuclear issue was largely brushed aside at their meeting, with Kennedy requesting, but not insisting, that scientists from a neutral country be allowed to visit Dimona.[82]

The issue did not, however, disappear from Kennedy's mind after the meeting—or stop being a concern to the U.S. intelligence community. That

September, a national intelligence estimate, *Nuclear Weapons and Delivery Capabilities of Free World Countries Other Than the US and UK*, suggested that Israel "possibly" had "already made the decision to develop operational nuclear capabilities." It went on to explain that Israel had "strong incentives to develop a nuclear capability against its Arab neighbors," and had received considerable assistance from France. It noted that with the addition of plutonium separation facilities, the Israelis could probably produce, by 1965–1966, enough weapons-grade plutonium for one or two weapons each year. The estimate also observed that there "is considerable evidence that Israel is engaged in nuclear weapons and related fields," and while the Israeli program "may not be directed specifically toward an operational nuclear capability we believe that the Israelis intend at least to put themselves in the position of being able to produce nuclear weapons fairly soon after a decision to do so." Dimona would provide the necessary experience to develop a plutonium production capability, the estimate reported.[83]

Such reporting undoubtedly helped spur Kennedy and Rusk to continue to push for inspections. On September 26, 1962, after failing to persuade Sweden earlier in the year to take on the inspection task, and after continuing to press Israel on the need for another visit, the second U.S. trip to Dimona took place. Since CIA attempts to infiltrate agents into the facility had failed, the visit represented the only chance to collect on-site intelligence, although, as it turned out, not a very good one. The two U.S. scientists who arrived to conduct a routine inspection at Soreq were escorted to Dimona by Soreq scientific director Yuval Ne'eman. Their visit fell far short of an in-depth examination of the facility. The U.S. ambassador described it as "unduly restricted to no more than forty five minutes." They were also prohibited from entering one large building, probably the building that contained the entrance to the underground reprocessing plant. Not surprisingly, the visitors found no evidence that Dimona had any military connection. On that basis, the United States told Arab governments that "the latest observations again confirm Israeli statements that [the] reactor [is] intended for peaceful purposes only."[84]

But just as the reassurances from the 1961 meeting were followed by an intelligence community product that painted a different picture, so the 1962 meeting was preceded and followed by a Pentagon study on nuclear *diffusion*, the term used prior to *proliferation*, in which Israel was depicted as likely to be more interested in nuclear weapons than nuclear power. In both the July 1962 and February 1963 versions of the study, Israel was placed ahead of Sweden and India as the next nation to likely acquire nuclear weapons after China.[85]

In March 1963 Sherman Kent, still the head of the Office of National Estimates, who had written of the prospect of Chinese nuclear weapons in 1955, turned his attention to the implications of an Israeli nuclear arsenal, a capability he assumed Israel would announce to the world. Kent's brief paper, despite its "Secret" classification, made no references to any intelligence collected about Israeli nuclear activities, or any previous analytic work. In eight pages Kent examined the implications for Israeli policy, the reaction of the Arab states, and Soviet reactions. He expected that a nuclear capability would make Israel tougher in dealing with its neighbors and give it an additional sense of security. Arab reaction "would be one of dismay and frustration," with a "period of highly emotional outbursts." The United States would be a principal target of Arab resentment. Meanwhile, the Soviets would be presented with both opportunities and problems: they would have the opportunity to increase Arab dependence on them but would probably be unwilling to accept requests from Arab countries for help in developing their own nuclear capability.[86]

Whether Kennedy was inspired by Kent's speculative analysis or some solid piece of intelligence, toward the end of March he directed increased attention to the Israeli nuclear issue. McGeorge Bundy, in a national security action memorandum—NSAM 231, *Middle Eastern Nuclear Capabilities*—informed Rusk, AEC chairman Glenn Seaborg, and director of central intelligence John McCone that "the President desires, as a matter of urgency, that we undertake every feasible measure to improve our intelligence on the Israeli nuclear program as well as other Israeli and UAR [United Arab Republic] advanced weapon programs, and to arrive at a firmer evaluation of their import." The memo also passed along the chief executive's desire that the next informal inspection of Dimona "be undertaken promptly and . . . be as thorough as possible."[87]

One consequence of the memo may have been the increase in Corona coverage of Dimona that occurred in the succeeding months. In 1962 only two Corona missions—in July and December—had photographed the reactor complex. In 1963, on five occasions from April to August, Corona satellites passed overhead and snapped photographs of the facility. Dimona was covered by clouds during the April mission, but the subsequent four attempts produced good imagery.[88]

Efforts to gather information using human sources also continued. Col. Carmelo V. Alba, the U.S. military attaché in the mid-1960s, spent weekends patrolling the Negev, equipped with a long-range telescopic camera. At least once a month he shipped photographs to Washington, one of which showed "smoke coming out of the dome," Alba recalled. On one occasion, John Hadden, who arrived in Tel Aviv in 1963 to assume command of the CIA station there, sent Alba to Beersheba to examine the mailboxes at the city's apartment complexes in search of French names.[89]

A clear consequence of the memorandum was further pressure on Israel for additional visits to Dimona. On April 2 the U.S. ambassador to Israel, Walworth Barbour, informed Ben-Gurion that Kennedy wanted U.S. scientists to be permitted to visit Dimona twice a year, in May and September. That began a new round of meetings and messages between U.S. and Israeli representatives, including letters between their chief executives, over access to Dimona. The United States pressed while Israel stalled, unwilling to agree to a regular schedule of two visits each year.[90]

In May, Kennedy wrote Ben-Gurion directly, warning the Israeli leader that U.S. support for Israel "would be seriously jeopardized in the public opinion of this country and in the West, if it should be thought that this Government was unable to obtain reliable information on a subject as vital to peace as the question of Israel's efforts in the nuclear field." That same month, Ben-Gurion responded, agreeing to further annual visits, but no more, and suggesting late 1963 or early 1964, when the reactor reached its "start-up" time, as most appropriate.[91]

But on June 12 the State Department informed McGeorge Bundy that the CIA, AEC, and Arms Control and Disarmament Agency all agreed that "the Prime Minister's terms fail to meet our minimum requirements." A key problem, the State Department explained, was that "a reactor of this size would be at the optimum discharged every two years if devoted to research, but at approximately six month intervals if the object was to produce a maximum of irradiated fuel for separation into weapons grade plutonium." In order to verify that Dimona was not being used to produce material for bombs, a visit in July 1963 and then twice-yearly visits starting no later than June 1964 would be necessary. Further, U.S. scientists would have to have access to the entire site and any related facilities such as fuel fabrication facilities or a plutonium separation plant. In addition, the scientists would need adequate time for a thorough examination of the site.[92]

Those requirements shaped Kennedy's tough reply to Ben-Gurion, dated June 15, which again threatened Israel with a loss of American support if it did not comply. But Ben-Gurion never read the letter, instead announcing his resignation that very day in the midst of domestic political turmoil. On July 5 Kennedy tried again, with a letter to Ben-Gurion's successor, Levi Eshkol. Kennedy again raised the prospect of a "seriously jeopardized" commitment to Israel if U.S. scientists were not able to conduct proper inspections of Dimona. In August, after further discussions between and within the two governments, Eshkol responded with a letter that agreed to a U.S. visit before Dimona reached the start-up stage. He also informed Kennedy, "I believe that we shall be able to reach agreement on the future schedule of visits," although he did not explicitly accept the twice-a-year requirement.[93]

Kennedy did not live to see another U.S. visit. Thirteen days after he died in Dallas, Eshkol invited U.S. representatives to visit Dimona between January 10 and 15, 1964. The two-day visit actually began on January 17, with Ulysses Staebler, Richard Cook, vice president of the company that built Soreq, and Clyde L. McClelland, a nuclear physicist with the Arms Control and Disarmament Agency, starting with the Weizmann Institute and Soreq. The next day was devoted to their inspection of Dimona, which lasted eleven hours.[94]

Among their conclusions was that the reactor "was clearly designed as an experimental reactor, capable of operation at 15 to 20 percent above [the] design power of 26 megawatts." The Israelis had told them that construction of a plutonium-reprocessing facility had apparently been delayed for an indefinite time. Until Israel built such a facility and fabricated a device, which would take two to three years, it could not, without foreign assistance, become a nuclear weapons state. Staebler and his colleagues concluded that "the plant has no weapons-making capability at present, but continuing periodic inspections are recommended."[95]

A CIA analysis in late January, undoubtedly prepared with access to the scientists' report, stated that "there appears to be little doubt that the center is now designed and intended for nuclear research" but that the reactor's capacity and fuel supply and preparation facilities "would permit the Israelis to redirect the program in the future toward achievement of a small nuclear weapons capability should they so decide." It also noted that "construction of complex and expensive plutonium recovery facilities would be needed for such a capability."[96]

Despite the U.S. desire for biannual inspections, the next one would not occur until late January of 1965. In the interval between visits, the United States continued to use its other means of gathering information about Dimona. A July 1964 Corona mission included coverage of the reactor site, and three possible Gambit missions might have produced high-resolution images.[97]*

The 1965 inspection team began its work on Thursday, January 28, with visits to the Weizmann Institute and Soreq. Ulysses Staebler was back for his third visit and McClelland for his second. They were joined by Floyd L. Culler, assistant director of reactor technology at Oak Ridge National Laboratory. Based on their ten-hour Saturday visit to Dimona, they concluded that "there is no evidence of further activity on [plutonium] extraction from irradiated fuel" and "while there appears to be no near term possibility of a weapons development program at the Dimona site, the site has excellent development and production capability that warrants continued surveillance at maximum intervals of one year."[98]

The State Department passed along their conclusions to national security adviser McGeorge Bundy in a memo. It stated that Israel "may have suc-

---

* Soreq was photographed by a Corona satellite, for the first time, in 1964. It would also be photographed at least once a year by a Corona satellite between 1967 and 1971. See "Soreq," www.globalsecurity.org, accessed March 9, 2004.

ceeded in concealing a decision to develop nuclear weapons," and noted a number of Israeli actions that would be consistent with covert weapons activity, including the secrecy surrounding Dimona, the limited time visitors were allowed to inspect the facility, the missiles Israel was acquiring from France that could carry nuclear warheads, and the statements of Israeli officials that indicated their military planning allowed for use of nuclear weapons.[99]

In addition to the State Department's caution over the conclusions of the Dimona visitors, there was also skepticism coming from the embassy in Tel Aviv. While the officers there were not formally part of the intelligence community, and they may not have had access to all the data that had been collected on the Israeli effort, they were still able to produce useful analysis that suggested Israel might well be on a path to develop nuclear weapons.

In March the director the Near Eastern affairs office of the State Department sent a memo to his boss, the assistant secretary for Near Eastern and South Asian affairs, reporting on what officers in the Tel Aviv embassy told a member of his staff during a recent trip to Israel. The author began the section on nuclear developments with the statement, "All indications are toward Israeli acquisition of a nuclear capability." He went on to observe that Israeli officials appeared to believe that the United Arab Republic would have a nuclear capability within five to seven years. In addition, he reported that science attaché Robert T. Webber, who held a doctorate in physics from Yale, "has calculated that the target date for acquisition of a nuclear weapons capability by Israel is 1968–9," and that the attaché "has discovered information indicating that Israel has already acquired the know-how for Plutonium metal production." The attaché also believed that he had convincing evidence "that parts of the Dimona facility had been purposely mothballed to mislead the visiting team." The attaché, as well as other embassy officers, believed Israeli scientists were preparing "all necessary elements for production of a nuclear device, leaving undone only last-minute assembly."[100]

In April, William N. Dale of the American embassy in Tel Aviv provided the State Department with his own evaluation of the Dimona project. He began examining the value of Dimona as a research establishment devoted to Israel's scientific needs. Examining its financial costs and scientific benefits, he concluded, "It is *not* a sensible research project fitting into the total picture of the accomplishments, activities, and needs of Israel's science." Purely on a scientific basis it appeared to be "a colossal blunder" which dissipated more than half of Israel's funds for the construction of research and development facilities for the past six years.[101]

Dale went on to observe that "nearly all of the considerable facilities at Dimona seem to be devoted to the various stages of fueling and operating the reactor and handling the Plutonium which is to be produced." He concluded that it was likely "the Israelis have been deliberately developing their nuclear potential with national security in mind." Although the Israelis may not have definitely decided to develop nuclear weapons, "they are constructing a high plateau of scientific techniques and facilities so that they can move to the making of weapons in a relatively short time." He continued his analysis with a nine-point step-by-step description of the path to a nuclear weapon, starting with provision of an adequate supply of uranium and concluding with preparation of a test site, and evaluated Israel's progress in each area. In addition, Dale provided a possible time line that included beginning construction of a chemical separation plant in 1965, operation of the plant beginning in 1967, and assembly and detonation of a test device the next year.[102]

Analysts with OSI, JAEIC, and AEC probably had considerably more access to the data collected about Dimona than the officers at the embassy in Tel Aviv. But they were still unable to convert persistent suspicion into conclusive evidence that Israel was committed to developing nuclear weapons and was less than eighteen months from reaching that objective. Even by May 1, 1967, almost six months to the day after the "test of special significance," the jury was still out. Undersecretary of state Nicholas Katzenbach, in a memo to President Johnson, wrote, "We have no evidence that Israel is actually making a bomb . . . our periodic inspections of [Dimona] . . . have uncovered no evidence of weapons activity."[103] If Katzenbach's memo accurately reflected the intelligence community's understanding of Dimona, Israel had developed a nuclear weapon under the noses and feet of U.S. inspectors and spies—both literally and figuratively.

BY 1967 Taiwan's nuclear program had also attracted the attention of America's intelligence establishment as well as that of U.S. diplomats in Europe and the Middle East. On September 27, 1965, a Corona satellite equipped with a KH-4A camera snapped a photograph of the Taiwan Nuclear Research Facility. The following March the embassy in Tel Aviv transmitted an excerpt of a story that appeared in the Israeli newspaper *Ha'aretz* concerning the visit of senior Taiwanese atomic scientists to Soreq. The embassy's science attaché pursued the matter with the administrative director of Soreq, who told him the visit had actually occurred the previous December, that one of the visitors was the head of a nuclear research center on Taiwan, and that they had been escorted by Ernst Bergmann, the latter fact leading the embassy to conclude that the visitors had received "VIP treatement."[104]

Also in March 1966 the Bonn embassy reported that an official from the German science ministry had informally requested an embassy officer's view on a Taiwanese request to purchase a multipurpose research reactor from the Siemens company. The next month it was the embassy in Taipei that had information to offer. It reported what a Taiwanese official had disclosed about the visit of John D. McCullen and three other scientists from the IAEA. The team was in Taiwan to do a siting survey for the possible location of two atomic power plants to be located on the north and south ends of the island. One potential location would place a reactor in the vicinity of the military's Chungshan Institute of Science.[105]

In June the embassy in Taipei directly confronted the issue of Taiwanese intentions to develop nuclear weapons. In a Secret dispatch it reported the claim of Dr. Hsu Cho-yun—chairman of the history department of National Taiwan University, protégé of a reported member of the Chungshan Institute's council, and often privately critical of his government's policies—that the institute was "continuing to push ahead with its program of developing an atomic weapon." Hsu also told an embassy representative that Lt. Gen. Tang Jun-po, as vice minister of defense for scientific development, actually believed that developing an atomic weapon was impractical and beyond the country's resources, but that Chiang Kai-shek insisted the effort be made. Hsu further revealed that Taiwan was having trouble buying the necessary items to conduct nuclear research. For one reason or another, contacts with Israel, West Germany, and Japan failed to produce positive results.[106]

Through the rest of the decade, the Taiwanese effort was monitored both from space and on the ground. Corona missions in September 1966 and February 1969 produced photographs of the same nuclear research facility that had been photographed in 1965, with the 1969 images being obtained by the KH-4B with its six-foot resolution. In the interval, the embassies in Bonn and Taipei continued to monitor Taiwanese atomic energy activities, including 1967 plans to purchase a 50-megawatt heavy-water nuclear power plant from West Germany.[107]

BY 1969 South Africa's Pelindaba Nuclear Research Center had joined Dimona and Taiwan's nuclear facility as Corona targets. On December 22, 1968, a KH-4A camera snapped an image of the partially cloud-covered facility. The capsule returned to earth the next day, carrying other images taken during the last phase of the Corona mission, including one of Dimona. Dimona, a far more urgent concern despite the periodic inspections, had been targeted on each of the eight Corona missions that took place in 1968— in one case being photographed during the first and second parts of the mission so that each of the film capsules contained an image. The result was eight usable photographs, three taken by higher-resolution KH-4B cameras. In 1969 Dimona was a target on only half of the six Corona missions, the three that produced KH-4B images. Undoubtedly, Dimona was also a target for at least several of the fourteen KH-8–equipped Gambit satellites that orbited in 1968 and 1969.[108]

While monitoring Dimona from the reaches of space would continue for decades after 1969, the periodic "visits" by U.S. scientists would not. Visits in 1966 and 1967 produced no evidence of weapons-related activity at Dimona and did not reveal any plutonium-processing capability. The July 1969 inspection by the AEC's three-man team—George B. Pleat, the commission's assistant director for reactor products, Edwin Kintner, and Edward L. Nicholson, of Oak Ridge—would be the last. It took place under a series of restrictions—no more than three scientists, measurement instruments were prohibited, collection of samples was prohibited—that suggested Israel had something to hide. The three visitors left Dimona after an eighteen-hour Saturday inspection, angry and frustrated at having been quizzed about their own research, possibly as a diversionary tactic, as well as the ground rules they operated under. But they left without finding a reprocessing plant or evidence of its existence.[109]

After the 1969 visit, the United States gave up on sending scientists to visit Dimona. Of course, the CIA and other intelligence agencies continued trying to discover the truth about Israel's nuclear activities. Dimona remained a regular target of U.S. imagery satellites. It was photographed six times by Corona satellites in 1970 and 1971, which yielded five good KH-4B photographs. Undoubtedly a number of high-resolution KH-8 images were also obtained.[110]

The intelligence analysts at OSI, the JAEIC, and other nuclear intelligence organizations continued to sift through the evidence produced by those satellites, NSA's eavesdropping efforts, and diplomatic and CIA reports, including the report that in 1968 some fissionable material from Dimona was diverted from normal peaceful uses and disappeared. Some analysts estimated that Israel had obtained more than thirty pounds of weapons-grade plutonium by early 1968. There was also circumstantial evidence, which included Israel's contract with Dassault Aviation for twenty-five missiles that could carry warheads weighing one thousand to twelve hundred pounds and reports of Israel purchasing uranium oxide from Argentina and possibly Africa. As a result, by 1970 the United States was conducting its Middle Eastern policy on the assumption that Israel either possessed or could quickly assemble an atomic bomb.[111]

In July of that year the *New York Times*, in addition to reporting the role of that assumption in U.S. Middle East policy, revealed some continuing dispute over whether the evidence was conclusive and whether Israel could be considered to have an atomic bomb before the mechanism was completely assembled. Presidents Johnson and Nixon reportedly received intelligence assessments that Israel had the capacity to assemble an atomic device on short notice and that some senior officials believed it had already done so. The most recent CIA judgment, that Israel had the technical capacity to produce atomic weapons, was conveyed by director of central intelligence Richard

Helms to the Senate Foreign Relations Committee a couple of weeks before the *Times* story. One senior official told the *Times* that if the Israelis did not actually possess a weapon, "they're seven and a half-months pregnant." No national intelligence estimate on the subject was produced, however, due to the sensitivity of the issue.[112]

IN 1970 South Africa was one of the world's largest uranium producers. Its nuclear activities had yet to become a sensitive topic but began to attract increasing attention from America's intelligence collectors and analysts. In May the *Weekly Surveyor*, a publication of the CIA's Directorate of Science Technology, which the OSI reported to at the time, contained an item on a visit by an executive of the South African Nuclear Fuels Corporation to the United States. The article noted that the executive was investigating the possibility of licensing uranium hexafluoride technology, apparently with the objective of allowing South Africa to supply uranium, of which it is one of the world's largest producers, in "a more saleable form that would enable the purchaser to send the product directly to an isotope enrichment plant without arranging for additional processing." In October the *Weekly Surveyor* reported the claim by South African AEB chairman A. J. A. Roux that his nation's new isotope separation process was low in capital cost but required substantial power, and noted that "the isotope separation process . . . is still unknown."[113]

The following year, South Africa's atomic progress received full-scale treatment in an OSI study, *Atomic Energy Activities in the Republic of South Africa*. It began with the reassuring statement that "the Republic of South Africa has no capability for the production of fissionable material and there is no evidence of activity related to the development of nuclear weapons." The report went on to note the announcement of the new technology for uranium enrichment, the exact nature of which remained a mystery to the CIA's scientific intelligence analysts, as well as South Africa's role as a major supplier of uranium oxide. The overview section of the study concluded with identification of the National Nuclear Research Center at Pelindaba as the principal research facility, and a description of the center's Safari-1 reactor, which it noted was upgraded in February 1969 from 6.6 to 20 megawatts.[114]

The remainder of the report discussed the organization of the South Africa atomic energy effort and the production of uranium, provided additional detail about the Safari-1 reactor, and noted that a pilot plant to test the new uranium isotope separation method was under construction near Pelindaba. It also observed that "no details of this plan were revealed and a tight security system was established for the plant's protection."[115]

While the South African program does not seem to have been the subject of any CIA analysis in 1972, it was the subject of four articles in the *Weekly*

Surveyor during 1973 and 1974, often combining South African press accounts, such as a June 1974 *Rand Daily Mail* article on the nation's uranium enrichment program, with commentary. The first three articles reported on the South Africans' plans to build the uranium enrichment plant "based on their [still] secret process," to stockpile large quantities of uranium, and the judgment that the secret uranium isotope process was probably aerodynamic.[116]

The final article, from July 1974, reported the recent comments of AEB vice president Louw Alberts, that South Africa possessed the ability to build an atomic bomb, while claiming that it was South African policy to use nuclear knowledge for peaceful purposes. The article's authors, members of the OSI and Office of Weapons Intelligence, commented that "South Africa is not currently in position to produce nuclear weapons." They noted that the only South African reactor was a research reactor under IAEA safeguards, and that the pilot uranium enrichment plant was expected to become operational sometime that year and to produce only low-enriched uranium. However, changes in the process could permit production of weapons-grade uranium, in which case a "crude fission device could be produced within this decade." At the time, South Africa, they observed, lacked all the other facilities necessary to produce nuclear weapons, and it would take several years to build them after a decision to go forward with a nuclear weapons program.[117]

TAIWAN'S NUCLEAR ASPIRATIONS were also the subject of various reports and assessments during the early 1970s, which resulted in U.S. approaches to various foreign governments. In December 1972 the assistant secretary of state for East Asian and Pacific affairs, Marshall Green, was informed that the State Department had recently discovered that Taiwan was considering purchasing essential material for a reprocessing plant from commercial sources in West Germany. The German embassy had approached the State Department to inquire whether the United States would be willing to assume responsibility for safeguards at the plant since most of the reprocessed reactor cores would be of U.S. origin. It was also reported that at a meeting earlier that month, interested offices and agencies concluded that Germany should be informed that construction of a reprocessing plant would create problems for the United States—that U.S. safeguards would apply only when its materials were being reprocessed. Thus, full-safeguard, around-the-clock coverage of the plant would require a separate agreement.[118]

At the beginning of 1973 the State Department acted on the information it had acquired in its attempt to block Taiwan's acquisition of a reprocessing plant. On January 4 departmental headquarters sent out a message addressed to the embassies in Taipei, Bonn, and Brussels. The Taipei embassy was instructed to inform the Taiwanese government of the "serious problems involved in ROC [Republic of China] acquisition of nuclear fuel reprocessing plant" and that acquisition of such a plant without IAEA safeguards "would evade [the] intent" of the nonproliferation treaty. The diplomats in Bonn were to tell the West Germans that the United States believed the sale of major components to Taiwan for a reprocessing plant, in the absence of adequate safeguards, would be highly undesirable. The department's representatives in Brussels were asked to urge the Belgian government not to authorize any Antwerp-based firms to provide architectural and engineering services, and possibly equipment, for the Taiwanese plant.[119]

That the United States was keeping a close watch and converting intelligence into action was illustrated by another cable, sent sixteen days later, to the same embassies. The message told its recipients that the State Department was particularly troubled by a report from Bonn that Taiwan had already signed a contract with the Uhde-Lurgi Group for reprocessing plant parts. State was also concerned about discrepancies between the Taiwanese claim that the objective was to build a small-scale laboratory facility and information from Bonn that the plant would be able to reprocess fifty tons of irradiated fuel each year. Walter McConaughy, the ambassador in Taipei, was requested to reemphasize U.S. concerns to Chiang Kai-shek's government, while it was suggested that the ambassador in Bonn speak to higher levels in the West German government to counter any pressure coming from the Uhde-Lurgi firm.[120]

Before the end of the month McConaughy met with the Taiwanese foreign minister to stress U.S. concerns and warn of the consequences of pursuing a reprocessing capability. Doing so risked "jeopardizing the ROC's projected four great nuclear power plants, which are of overriding consequence to the future of the entire ROC economy." The ambassador's warnings appeared to have the desired results, as Taiwan's foreign minister informed him on February 8 that "in compliance with US wishes ROC had decided against [the] recommendation of some of its scientists to purchase [a] nuclear reprocessing plant."[121]

Whatever reassurance was provided by the ambassador's February 8 cable to Washington was probably dissipated to a certain extent the next day, when two members of the British embassy—counselor John Wilberforce and first secretary Christopher Makins—called on three State Department representatives to discuss nuclear developments in Taiwan. One purpose of their visit was to inquire as to whether the Americans saw anything unusual in Taiwan's request for proposals to supply 66,000 pounds of natural-uranium metal for the heavy-water research reactor nearing completion in Taiwan. In addition, the Americans were told that British intelligence, undoubtedly either the spies of the Secret Intelligence Service or the eavesdroppers of the Government Communications Headquarters, had reported "activity at a facility in northwest Taiwan which they suspect is related to the development of a nuclear weapons capability."[122]

The embassy in Taiwan was able to contribute to U.S. understanding of Taiwan's nuclear program with a February 24 telegram titled "Chung Shan Nuclear Research Institute," which "helped answer some but by no means all of the questions on the Institute's activities." The message reported that the nuclear facilities in the institute were formally turned over to the Chinese Atomic Energy Council in February 1968 but there existed a strong military element in that the director and deputy of the institute, Chien Chi-Peng and Li Yu-Hao, came from the military where they worked under Gen. Tang Chun-po. Also noted was the Canadian-built research reactor at the INER, which went critical the previous month and had been managed from the beginning by Adm. Hsia Hsin, Tang's deputy, "ostensibly because Hsia is a civil engineer."[123]

The telegram also reported that a pilot reprocessing laboratory, which could handle no more than gram-size quantities, was under construction using imported parts. The plan to buy a German reprocessing plant with a fifty-ton capacity was instigated by Chungshan director Chien, a purchase that members of the Chinese Atomic Energy Council claimed he did not have the authority to consummate. The authors suggested that Chien may have had the authority to use military, but not council, funds. The cable concluded with brief discussions of the Institute of Nuclear Research's waste disposal facility and "extremely elaborate and complex decontamination facility, containing a room large enough for a contaminated vehicle to be driven into it for decontamination." In addition, it contained a decontamination cell "into which a man in a 'space suit' can be admitted."[124]

Such reports helped the analysts at the Bureau of Intelligence and Research, back in Washington, produce their assessments of Taiwan's nuclear intentions. In late March they completed a report, in response to the British counselor John Wilberforce's inquiry about Taiwan's plans. It opened with the observation that "the Republic of China's intentions regarding the development of nuclear weapons have been far from clear." It also noted that the United States had occasionally received information indicating that senior Taiwanese officials were interested in initiating measures which could at least provide an option for developing nuclear weapons.[125]

Other Taiwanese officials, it was reported, opposed such steps. Existing and planned civil nuclear facilities reflected both viewpoints, according to the INR's analysts. They pointed to Taiwan's early interest in acquiring a natural uranium–fueled, heavy water–moderated research reactor at the Chungshan Institute as the product of a desire to provide a modest plutonium production capability. On the other hand, more recent decisions, including the two boiling-water power reactors under construction, were examples, the authors concluded, of decisions that "have gone against . . . pro-weapons advocates." In light of the most recent developments, the State Department intelligence analysts "were inclined to believe that no organized program for the production of nuclear weapons has been authorized or initiated by the ROC." They also noted that the U.S. science attaché in Taipei, a frequent visitor to Chungshan, "has observed no indication of any covert program to develop nuclear weapons."[126]

Shortly after that analysis was completed, INR analysts met with members of the State Department's scientific affairs bureau to discuss Taiwan's nuclear activities. One topic of conversation involved two reports, one of which alleged the existence of a Japanese nuclear weapons factory on Taiwan, which the science representatives considered "sensational." One of the representatives, Daniel Brewster, considered the reports as the work of a "kook." Thus, they were doubtful about the urgency or even the need to send a team to visit Taiwan. They argued that with only one reactor in operation, Taiwan would have to run it constantly at full capacity to generate enough plutonium for a nuclear weapon—and that it was unlikely that secrecy about such a program could be maintained.[127]

INR representative Lawrence Finch agreed that Taiwan was several years away from being able to build a nuclear weapon. But INR did think a visit would be useful. As a result, the bureau had already obtained a list of installations that should be visited, and would request from the CIA a list of personalities that a team should meet. The bureau also planned to ask the CIA's opinion on the reliability of the sources of the "sensational reports." Within ten days, the idea of a visit was presented to Victor Cheng, the secretary general of Taiwan's Atomic Energy Council, who "welcomed [the] suggestion" that a U.S. study group visit Taiwan to consider the course of U.S.-Taiwan nuclear cooperation. On April 17 the State Department informed the Taipei embassy that in addition to the "ostensible purpose," the team "would have the further objective of acquiring information about identity and progress of ROC coterie which advocates development of nuclear weapons capability." The team would seek to talk to selected individuals who might have knowledge of Taiwan's activities in the area and visit all sites of interest. The team, the State Department cable noted, "would be composed of two or three nuclear experts able to ask penetrating questions."[128]

The team that arrived in mid-November consisted of four individuals—two from the AEC, director of international programs Abraham Friedman and Tokyo scientific representative Gerald Helfrich; one from the ACDA, Frank S. Houck; and the deputy director of the State Department's scientific bureau, Nelson Sievering. They apparently visited six or seven institutes and organizations—including the Atomic Energy Council, the Chungshan Institute, and the INER—and spoke with Atomic Energy Council chief Cheng and foreign minister Shen. In a November 23 assessment of the mission, the deputy chief of mission in Taipei, William H. Gleysteen Jr., noted that "all of us who were involved believe the exercise was worthwhile and successful," and while "we cannot guarantee that certain people will not continue to nudge the ROC into activities associated with a nuclear weapons program but short of a flat statement to Premier Chiang I think we have done everything possible to underscore the firmness of our position."[129]

IN THE FALL of 1974 the intelligence community's efforts to collect and analyze data concerning the nuclear activities of Israel, Taiwan, and South Africa contributed to a September 1974 special national intelligence estimate, *Prospects for Further Proliferation of Nuclear Weapons*. The judgment on Israel was clear. "We believe," a memorandum summarizing the estimate stated, "that Israel already has produced nuclear weapons." The authors explained that their conclusion was "based on Israeli acquisition of large quantities of uranium, partly by clandestine means; the ambiguous nature of Israeli efforts in the field of uranium enrichment; and Israel's investment in a costly missile system designed to accommodate nuclear warheads." They also wrote, "We do not expect the Israelis to provide confirmation of widespread suspicions of their capability, either by nuclear testing or by threats of use, short of a grave threat to the nation's existence."[130]

Taiwan and South Africa, the estimate observed, "will be much influenced in their decisions not only by the general course of proliferation but by such factors as growing feelings of isolation and helplessness, perceptions of major military threat and desires for regional prestige." Any weapons capability they might develop "probably would be small and delivery probably would depend on aircraft, though there is some possibility that one or another might be able to purchase a nuclear-capable missile system from a foreign supplier."[131]

The judgment on Taiwan was not only a statement of fact but also a warning to U.S. policymakers. "Taipei," the analysts reported, "conducts its small nuclear program with a weapon option clearly in mind, and it will be in a position to fabricate a nuclear device after five years or so." The estimate noted that the international role of Taiwan, which had been booted out of not only the UN Security Council but also the UN in favor of mainland China, was "changing radically, and concern over the possibility of complete isolation is mounting." Taiwan's decisions would be influenced by U.S. policies in two key areas, the analysts predicted—American support for the island's security and American attitudes about the possibility of a nuclear-armed Taiwan. In conclusion, they noted that "Taipei's present course probably is leading it toward development of nuclear weapons."[132]

South Africa, the estimators believed, was a somewhat less serious threat to develop a weapon during the decade. It "apparently has developed a technology for enriching uranium that could be used for producing weapons-grade material," and "probably would go forward with a nuclear weapons program if it saw a serious threat from African neighbors beginning to emerge." However, the estimate claimed that "so serious a threat is highly unlikely in the 1970s."[133]

BY 1975, as the estimate concluded, Israel had acquired nuclear weapons. The underground plutonium-processing plant at Dimona was producing the fissile material needed for those weapons. In Taiwan, there was plenty of nuclear activity. Five nuclear research reactors were in operation, and four nuclear power plants—each with two reactors—were either being built or planned. The first plant was scheduled to become operational in 1977.[134]

While in 1975 some South Africans were operating and constructing facilities that would permit the nation's rulers to build a bomb if they chose to do so, others were evaluating the strategic situation to determine if they should develop a nuclear arsenal. In March 1975 the chief of staff informed the chief of the South African Defence Force of a recent study by the force's director of strategic studies. It concluded that a "direct and/or indirect nuclear threat against South Africa has developed to the point of being a real danger," requiring a reappraisal of the nation's strategic policy. In addition, "there is a danger that an enemy assuming an African identity such as terrorist organizations, or a OAU [Organization of African Unity] 'liberation army' could acquire and launch against us a tactical nuclear weapon." China, the study's authors believed, was the most likely nation to "associate itself with such a venture."[135]

The memo apprised the South African defense chief of a number of other judgments reached by the director of strategic studies. The joint thrust of several conclusions was that regional limited and localized use of nuclear weapons had again become conceivable, and need not escalate to a large-scale war involving the United States and the Soviet Union. Further, South Africa's defense strategy needed to take into account the potential nuclear threat. The memo concluded by providing a rationale for a South African nuclear weapon, observing that "should it become generally known that the RSA [Republic of South Africa] possesses a nuclear weapon [and] that it would use it if we were subjected to nuclear attack, such a deterrent strategy could be used as a positive weapon in our defence."[136]

LITTLE IS KNOWN on the details of the U.S. assessment of the Israeli nuclear weapons program in 1975, beyond a report published in the *New York Times* that January. The article claimed that senior American intelligence analysts believed that Israel had produced more than ten nuclear weapons, each with a yield similar to the bombs that devastated Hiroshima and Nagasaki. The report also noted the analysts' belief that Israel had planes and missiles—the Phantom F-4 and Jericho—that could deliver the weapons to targets hundreds of miles away.[137]

With regard to South Africa, one continuing topic of intelligence analysis in 1975 was the nature of the uranium enrichment process. A March analysis in the CIA's *Weekly Surveyor* scoffed at the South African claim to have produced an original enrichment process. The author(s) reasoned that the "South Africans have stated that after study, they would adopt either the Becker nozzle or their own process, whichever turns out to be more commercial. If the South Africans can make this choice at the late stage of their construction program, their so called 'unique' process must indeed be quite similar to the Becker nozzle."[138]

The next month the same CIA publication reported that South Africa's pilot uranium enrichment plant at Valindaba was active, noting the government's statement that it had gone into operation during the weekend of April 5–6. The commentary section of the article noted that the pilot facility consisted of three processing buildings and it was unlikely that all three had gone into operation. It was possible that only one building was in operation, and that only certain elements of the process—"believed to be based on aerodynamic principles like the Becker nozzle process"—were being tested.[139]

An article in the May 5 issue of *Weekly Surveyor* noted that "details about [the] South African aerodynamic enrichment process remain closely guarded." The item also observed that South Africa could adapt the process to produce weapons-grade material, and reported the government's claim that it had the capability to build nuclear weapons but its policy was to employ the enriched uranium for peaceful purposes. It added that "Pretoria, however, has not signed the Non-Proliferation Treaty."[140]

ON MARCH 11, 1976, a senior CIA official indiscreetly disclosed one of the agency's conclusions about Israel's nuclear weapons program. Carl Duckett, the agency's deputy director for science and technology, participated in an informal seminar in front of local members of the American Institute of Aeronautics and Astronautics. The briefing was part of a campaign of increased CIA openness to offset the unfavorable publicity from press and congressional disclosures. One hundred and fifty individuals paid $6.50 for cocktails, a light buffet, and close to two hours of discussion with high-ranking CIA officials. Although the briefing was unclassified, attendees were asked not to take notes or quote the officials to the press. When questioned about Israel's nuclear capability, Duckett did not hesitate, responding that the CIA estimated Israel had ten to twenty nuclear warheads available for use. Four days later his comments were reported in the *Washington Post*. The day after the *Post* story, the *New York Times* reported that the current estimate was based not simply on circumstantial evidence such as the purchase of aircraft or missiles, but on "empirical evidence."[141]

Several months after Duckett's comments, the *Weekly Surveyor* carried one of at least five articles published that year concerning the South African nuclear program. The first of those articles, in the June 28 issue, reported that a member of the South African AEB had told an agency source that the Valindaba pilot plant was complete but not yet in operation because of unresolved questions about its safety. An article in a July issue focused on discussions between "a U.S. nuclear industrialist" and officials of the South African Electricity Supply Commission. The industrialist reported that the South Africans had made a flat statement that their country was developing a capability to reprocess spent fuel. The analyst(s) observed that while such a statement "is in contrast to earlier statements by South African officials [it] may be true."[142]

In September a *Weekly Surveyor* article focused on policy plans rather than hardware. It reported that the director of the life sciences division of South Africa's AEB, C. R. Jansen, had stated in May, "We're going to have an atom bomb. We can't afford it but we're going to have it anyway." Then, it went on to note that this "is one of several recent indications from knowledgeable South Africans that the government intends to develop nuclear weapons." Yet, the author(s) of the article also wrote, "In spite of this evidence . . . and the likelihood that it is conducting theoretical studies applicable to nuclear weapons development, there is no convincing evidence that nuclear weapons are being developed at this time." The possibility was then raised that "considering South Africa's usual extreme concern for secrecy, such direct references to nuclear weapons development may be intended specifically for U.S. or other foreign audiences."[143]

The final two *Weekly Surveyor* items of 1976 illustrate the CIA's extraction of intelligence about the South African nuclear program from published photographs. Examination of photographs of the processing equipment in the Valindaba plant, which had originally appeared in the March 1976 issue of the magazine *Panorama*, revealed the "inefficient reciprocating compressors." In late November an article reported that published photographs of the Valindaba processing equipment indicated the plant consisted of several hundred stages which could be used to produce uranium enriched to more than 20 percent U-235—"although no significant requirements for such high-enrichment levels are foreseen from South African descriptions of its nuclear program." A more complex arrangement of stages would have been more efficient for a plant devoted solely to energy production, the article noted.[144]

ALTHOUGH THE VARIOUS statements by South African officials, and the workings of its nuclear facilities, merited attention in 1976, the activities of Taiwan were of more concern. In March 1974 secretary of state and national security adviser Henry Kissinger had signed a national security decision memorandum which directed the withdrawal of U.S. nuclear weapons from Taiwan before the end of the year. In 1975 Chiang Kai-shek died, and Chiang Ching-kuo, his son, assumed the presidency.[145] The first event could create a further incentive for Taiwan to acquire nuclear weapons; the second could make the decision the responsibility of one man.

There had been IAEA inspections of the Taiwanese facilities in the early 1970s, but they had been conducted with fewer inspectors than truly needed and with inadequate equipment. But by 1975–1976 the IAEA concluded that the nuclear activities being conducted by INER, where a small-scale, "hot-cell" reprocessing laboratory had been established, merited greater attention.[146]

In early 1976 ten fuel rods containing about five hundred grams of plutonium turned up missing, creating concern that Taiwan might have secretly extracted fissile material. An examination of INER's records indicated that fuel elements had been moved, probably to the fuel fabrication plant. Such a transfer should have been detected by the IAEA surveillance cameras, but they turned out to be faulty. The international agency could not determine whether the rods had gone to the fuel fabrication plant or somewhere else.[147]

Additionally, inspectors discovered that the Plutonium Fuel Chemistry Laboratory at INER could produce plutonium metal, and was doing so using U.S.-supplied plutonium, leading them to insist that the facility be subject to regular inspections. Such discoveries led the IAEA's inspector general Rudolf Rometsch to visit INER in May 1976. After first rebuffing his request for a tour of the chemistry laboratory, INER officials agreed. At a dinner that same night with Taiwan's nuclear officials, Rometsch told them he could support all civilian-related nuclear activities but was concerned about some of things he had seen that day.[148]

Two months later, in July, the IAEA returned to INER to determine if unsafeguarded fuel had been placed in the reactor, to establish a nuclear material baseline at both the reactor and the fuel fabrication plant, and to upgrade the surveillance system. The inspectors took detailed measurements of about half of the spent fuel on site to determine if the readings were consistent with Taiwan's claims as to where the fuel rods had been located in the core, in contrast to just testing the rods for radioactivity. When the inspectors found discrepancies in Taiwan's declaration, Taiwanese officials claimed their declaration had contained errors—a response the IAEA found hard to accept.[149]

One reprocessing facility, probably the hot cell, was also inspected. Its being open for construction activities allowed inspectors to enter the cell, which did not seem to have handled any irradiated material. The inspectors also verified that the small size of the cell precluded it from being employed to separate kilograms of plutonium.[150]

But U.S. officials were still concerned about Taiwan's intentions, as was an ACDA official, who said, "I don't like Taiwan reprocessing secretly or openly, large or small." Their concern stemmed not only from the results of the IAEA inspections but also from secret intelligence reports, which stated that Taiwan had recently started reprocessing nuclear reactor fuel to build up a stockpile of plutonium. Administration officials were reportedly unable to determine whether the reprocessing violated an agreement between the United States, IAEA, and Taiwan.[151]

The intelligence reports flowed out of an operation run by a CIA officer working undercover in Taiwan, Robert Simmons. After his years in the agency, Simmons went on to become staff director for the Senate Select Committee on Intelligence and a U.S. congressman from Connecticut. But from 1975 to 1978 he ran an operation that purloined Taiwanese government plans and files concerning its nuclear weapons aspirations.[152]

Some of that intelligence may have been employed by the intelligence community analysts who produced the May 1976 study titled *Prospects for Arms Production and Development in the Republic of China*. Much of the sections on the nuclear program, nuclear weapons, and nuclear scientists focused on what technology and skills Taiwan possessed, what it would need to do to produce nuclear weapons, and the calculus involved in such a choice. The secret study did state that "during 1974 and 1975 a group of [Taiwanese] nuclear scientists reportedly used computer facilities at the Chungshan Institute of Science and Technology to conduct extensive theoretical design calculations for a first generation nuclear device." In addition, "experiments were carried out, presumably in the area of high explosives, shockwaves, and detonation systems. Problems were encountered in the experiments but these were solved and the program was considered a success in September 1975."[153]

In late August, the *Washington Post* reported that "U.S. intelligence reports over the past six months indicate that Taiwan has been secretly reprocessing spent uranium fuel," and that ACDA officials "said they have been stalling on an application to export two additional nuclear power plants to Taiwan as a signal to stop secret reprocessing." The disclosure was apparently engineered by U.S. officials to send a warning to Taiwan, following a number of private warnings from the Ford administration over the previous year. Taiwanese officials and diplomats, of course, denied that any covert nuclear activity was underway. Rather, they suggested that there had been confusion over the small, hot-cell reprocessing facility at INER that Taiwan was seeking U.S. permission to open, permission that was required because the spent uranium fuel to be used was originally supplied by the United States.[154]

On September 14, under American pressure, Chiang Ching-kuo promised the U.S. ambassador that Taiwan would not acquire its own reprocessing facilities or engage in activities related to reprocessing, and that his government's policy was "not to manufacture nuclear weapons." Three days later a diplomatic note containing the same pledge followed. Soon afterward, U.S. officials stated that any breach of Taiwan's promise would "fundamentally jeopardize" nuclear cooperation, including American supply of the low-enriched uranium used in Taiwan's power plants.[155]

Neither the warning nor the promise completely resolved the matter. In November the U.S. ambassador to Taiwan, Leonard Unger, met with James C. H. Shen, Taiwan's ambassador to the United States, a meeting that Unger described in a top-secret "memorandum of conversation." Unger wrote that he had told Chen that he "had been disturbed at some indications received here that [Taiwan] was perhaps not living up completely to the assurances that we had received about nuclear reprocessing." Unger acknowledged that the information "was not all that firm," but was still concerned even at the possibility that Taiwan was continuing with plans for reprocessing. Shen expressed surprise as well as interest in knowing more about Unger's information, and said, given Taiwan's pledge, that it would be stupid to try to set up reprocessing facilities.[156]

But it was not long before the United States received "intelligence" from IAEA inspections that suggested Taiwan might be emulating Israel's nuclear deception, although with less skill. Late in 1976 or early in 1977 the agency's inspectors discovered a "canal gate," or port, at the bottom of the spent fuel pond near the Hot Laboratory. The gate, which had been concealed by scrap and other debris, exited to a vertical shaft. While INER officials claimed that the gate had been part of the original Canadian design for the transfer of spent fuel to the hot cell, it was not included in the facility's design information.[157]

The inspectors also discovered five fuel assemblies, three in the core and two in storage, that looked to be identical to other research reactor fuel but contained only 70 percent as much uranium. Institute officials explained that the fuel rods contained 10-centimeter pieces of uranium rods separated by solid pieces of aluminum. Such rods would appear to be standard fuel rods, and no discrepancy would have been detected prior to July 1976, since at the time the rods were simply tested for radioactivity. Such fuel rods could have been cut into small pieces in the spent fuel pond without releasing radioactivity, making them far easier to transport. While full-size spent fuel elements could not be fitted into the small reprocessing laboratory, some U.S. officials speculated that the look-alikes were intended to solve that problem.[158]

Such discoveries led to further U.S. expressions of concern, which were not alleviated by Chiang Ching-kuo's statement that while "we have the ability and the facilities to manufacture nuclear weapons . . . we will never manufacture them." To help ensure that weapons would not be manufactured, the United States insisted that Taiwan shut down the reactor, and in 1977 Los Alamos scientists radioactively scanned every element in the core. The process verified the irradiation history of the fuel rods in the core, as declared by Taiwan, making it probable that any future diversions would be detected—although it could not settle questions about diversions that might have taken place earlier.[159]

To further satisfy U.S. proliferation concerns, Taiwan dismantled its reprocessing facilities and the hot cells in the Hot Laboratory were employed to study spent fuel without separating plutonium or uranium. In 1978, in response to a U.S. demand, Taiwan returned 863 grams of plutonium.[160]

THE CONCERN over Taiwan's nuclear program during 1977 was not only matched but exceeded by the anxiety about South Africa's hidden nuclear activities, and with good cause. That concern would reach a climax when the United States received information from a source less likely than the IAEA about the white regime's intentions.

By mid-1977 work was completed on two large nuclear devices, based on a gun-type design, at the AEB's site. However, the Valindaba Y-Plant was not able to keep up with the weapons designers, and had not produced enough highly enriched uranium to allow the devices to include a highly enriched uranium core. The devices were to be used instead in fully instrumented "cold tests," with the test device containing a depleted uranium core.[161]

About the same time the first devices were completed, so was the drilling of two sufficiently deep boreholes, 590 to 655 feet down, to accommodate the first oversized devices for an actual test. A third shaft was abandoned because of unsuitable geological conditions. In the hopes of deceiving foreign intelligence services that might be monitoring the activity in the Kalahari involving the conspicuous drilling and heavy equipment, the process was disguised as construction of an underground military ammunition depot.[162]

The cold test, with a simulation of all the activities associated with a full-scale test, was to be conducted on site in August 1977. Since installing the necessary instrumentation trailers, cables, and other equipment used in a test would mean a significant increase in activity at the site, another covering activity was needed. The National Institute for Defence Research agreed to simultaneously test its version of what was known as the "Stalin Organ," a truck-mounted multiple rocket launcher.[163]

But the cover story would not hold. On June 30 a Soviet reconnaissance satellite, Cosmos 922, was launched from Plesetsk and passed over the Kalahari site on July 3 and 4. Possibly it was instructed to take photographs on the basis of a tip from a Soviet spy in the South African defense establishment,

Commander Dieter Gerhardt. After the return of the film from that mission, and its analysis by the Space Intelligence Directorate of the GRU Cosmos 932 was sent into orbit on July 20. In contrast to the area surveillance mission of Cosmos 922, Cosmos 932 had a close-look mission. It returned to earth on August 2 and the film was turned over to the GRU for analysis.[164]

On August 6 the South African prime minister, John Vorster, delivered a message to President Jimmy Carter when he spoke at a Foreign Affairs Association dinner in Pretoria. Vorster warned that U.S. policy of pressuring South Africa to abandon apartheid would lead to "chaos and anarchy in South Africa," and "the end result for South Africa" would "be exactly the same as if it were subverted by Marxists." He also claimed that Carter's policy did not reflect the sentiments of the American people.[165]

That afternoon another message concerning South Africa had been delivered to Carter, which made Vorster's broadside particularly ill-timed. During the afternoon, Vladillen M. Vasev, the acting chief of the Soviet embassy in Washington, arrived at the White House carrying a personal message from Soviet general secretary Leonid Brezhnev for Carter. The message Vasev delivered to William Hyland, the senior National Security Council officer on duty that afternoon, was that Soviet intelligence had detected secret preparations by South Africa to test an atomic device in the Kalahari Desert. Brezhnev was asking for Carter's assistance to stop the test. Vasev also informed Hyland that Brezhnev was planning to send similar appeals to the leaders of Britain, France, and West Germany. Failure to prevent a South African explosion "would have the most serious and far-reaching aftermaths for international peace and security."[166]

Two days later, TASS, the Soviet press agency, told the world what Brezhnev had already told Carter. It carried an article claiming that South Africa was preparing for a nuclear test, and charged that "the possession of nuclear weapons by the racist regime of Pretoria would constitute a most direct threat to the security of the African states; it would lead to a sharp escalation of instability and tension in southern Africa and would increase the nuclear threat to all of mankind."[167]

The United States had been aware of activities at the site when it received Brezhnev's message, and took steps to update its knowledge following the the Soviet claim. As soon as Vasev left, Hyland telephoned Zbigniew Brzezinski, who was vacationing in Maine, and then Carter's office in Plains, Georgia, and relayed the Brezhnev message to presidential press secretary Jody Powell. Hyland then called, in quick succession, deputy secretary of state Warren Christopher, since secretary of state Cyrus Vance was in Jordan, and then director of central intelligence Stansfield Turner. An initial assessment was ordered for that Monday, August 8.[168]

To provide the basis for an independent assessment, the U.S. intelligence community took a number of steps. On the day after Vasev's visit, an unmarked light aircraft flew over the borehole sites, the instrumentation and cable trenches, the area that would house the instrumentation trailers, the office, and the accommodation block. The South Africans failed to identify the plane, and no flight plan that took a plane over the site had been filed. The plane belonged to the U.S. military attaché's office in Pretoria and was equipped with suitable cameras.[169]

At least one U.S. reconnaissance satellite was reprogrammed to examine the test site on its next pass. At the time, the United States had two imagery spacecraft circling the earth. A Hexagon carrying a KH-9 camera had been launched on June 27 and would remain in orbit until the end of the year. In December 1976 a new class of imagery satellite had been launched. Code-named Kennan, the satellite employed the KH-11 optical system to obtain imagery. Rather than record images on film that had to be returned to earth, the KH-11 converted imagery of a scene into numbers, from 1 to 256, representing the lightness or darkness of each pixel in the scene. The numbers were then electronically transmitted back to the Mission Ground Site at Fort Belvoir, Virginia, just south of Washington, D.C., via a Satellite Data System relay satellite in highly elliptical orbit. The KH-11 was designed to quickly obtain imagery and would have been perfectly suited for use in such a situation.[170]

The combined result of the aerial and satellite missions were images showing construction that experts said was typical of a nuclear test site. The images revealed a cluster of sheds and other buildings around a prominent tower, along with a solidly built structure a bit removed from the rest, in a remote stretch of sand. Cables were in place. Experts believed they were viewing a pattern of preparations around an instrumentation tower. One official told the *Washington Post*, "I'd say we were 90 percent certain" that the construction was preparation for an atomic test. Another official commented, "People were pretty confident that this was what it might be." Yet another remarked, "We were not 100 percent sure but the technicians were less iffy than they had been about some incidents in the past."[171]

One official noted, "It was very likely [a nuclear test site] but with some ambiguity about the purpose." Indeed, some U.S. intelligence analysts believed that the construction effort was not part of preparation for a test. Rather, they viewed it as an elaborate con job, conducted for the impact its discovery would have on the major powers. The dissenters argued that the South African regime intended to dramatize, at a low cost, its claim to be a nation with major military capabilities and one that would not let outsiders dictate a change in its social system.[172]

In addition to directing that the National Reconnaissance Office employ its satellites to monitor the test site, the National Intelligence Officer for Africa,

William Parmenter, was asked to coordinate an interagency study on South Africa's nuclear intentions. On Friday, August 12, he requested, via a memo, oral contributions from agencies represented on the National Foreign Intelligence Board at a meeting to be held the following Monday at 10:00 a.m. in Room 5G00 at CIA headquarters. The meeting, chaired by Parmenter, would include representatives, in some cases multiple representatives, from the CIA, army, navy, air force, Defense Intelligence Agency, and NSA.[173]

On August 18 Parmenter sent the findings to the National Foreign Intelligence Board for its consideration. The nine-page, Top Secret Codeword study examined the domestic, military, and foreign policy considerations involved in a decision to test, the question of sanctions, South Africa's peaceful nuclear power activities, and the timing of a test. While based partly on technical analysis of the South African program, it also reflected, in the view of the authors, "the Community's knowledge of the Afrikaner people and their leaders; their perceptions of themselves and the outside world; and the policy imperatives to which they seem most likely to respond."[174]

The intelligence community analysts held out the promise that U.S. and other pressures might forestall a South African test for the short term. The assessment began with the judgment that "the South African government plans to proceed through the various stages of a nuclear weapons program, including the eventual testing of a weapon." Domestic political concerns argued in favor of testing, and those concerns outweighed fear of adverse foreign reactions. In addition, Vorster's inclination toward actions which "project power and toughmindedness," as well as "his personal contempt for world opinion" directed at influencing his decisions, would lead him to favor testing. And "on balance," military considerations, including the fear "of being invaded by Communist-backed black regimes and even by Soviet and Cuban forces," also argued in favor of testing.[175]

The second of the key judgments offered some near-term hope, though. "We can discern no over-riding pressure on South Africa's leaders to rush to test a weapon in the immediate future; indeed we think foreign policy considerations could lead them to adopt a flexible attitude toward its timing." The analysts went on to explain that while there might be "considerable pressure" on Vorster within his cabinet to go ahead with a scheduled test, the prime minister might be persuaded to delay a test for a short time if he perceived that a major change in U.S. policy toward South Africa was possible or believed that sensitive ongoing negotiations would be undermined by a test.[176]

By the time the assessment arrived at the National Foreign Intelligence Board, the diplomatic offensives of the two superpowers as well as France, Britain, and German were well underway. South African denials continued, such as the one of August 10, which included a deputy secretary of the

Department of Foreign Affairs wondering where the Soviet Union had gotten the "romantic notion about a Kalahari Test Site." South Africa was also busy cleaning up the site in case of an actual inspection. Two days after the attaché's plane photographed the Vastrap site, a senior nuclear program official received a phone call at nine in the evening on a secure line. He was told, "You must pack and leave immediately for Pretoria since inspection of the site is imminent. The rest of the AEB team must leave as soon as possible by road!" To ensure that an inspection did not yield signs of a planned test, the National Institute for Defence Research and the AEB staff began a crash program to dismount and remove critical equipment that could not be explained as being for conventional military use. On August 11 Carter returned to Washington, where the basic intelligence assessment of South African activity in the desert was ready. Three days later Carter directed that a full reply be sent to Brezhnev the next day, which stated that the U.S. assessment agreed with that of the Soviet Union, that there was enough evidence to suspect that South Africa was preparing for a nuclear test.[177]

The United States urged French, British, and West German action to help avert the expected test. U.S. ambassador-at-large Gerard Smith, former head of ACDA, was recalled from vacation and sent to Paris, armed with intelligence information, possibly satellite photographs, to persuade the French of the need to act. The United States and other governments exercised concerted pressure, which reportedly included France's threat to break diplomatic relations and terminate its assistance in constructing the nuclear power plants that it had sold South Africa—a sale for which the French had taken some flak. The United States followed by sending to Pretoria a precise statement of the assurances it wanted. "We were pretty severe in private," one U.S. official noted. On Sunday, August 21, Carter received the news that South Africa had agreed to give the assurances demanded.[178]

On that basis, at an August 23 news conference, President Carter announced, "South Africa has informed us that they do not have and do not intend to develop nuclear explosive devices for any purpose, either peaceful or as a weapon," and "that the Kalahari test site which has been in question is not designed for the test of nuclear explosives, and that no nuclear explosive test will be taken in South Africa now or in the future." Carter also told his audience that while "we appreciate this commitment from South Africa and its information," the United States would "continue to monitor the situation very closely" and would renew its efforts to convince South Africa to place all its nuclear facilities under international safeguards and to sign the 1968 nonproliferation treaty.[179]

The requirement for continued monitoring was certainly made clear by the third, and final, key judgment of the August 18 interagency assessment.

The analysts wrote that "while we . . . ascribe some flexibility . . . to the South African position regarding the timing of a test, we do not see any circumstances arising which would lead to a termination of their long-standing program to develop a nuclear weapon." They could see "no credible threat from the West which would be sufficient to deter the South African government from carrying out a test." Rather, "threats would, in our judgment, be more likely to harden South African determination."[180]

chapter seven

THE DOUBLE FLASH

JOHN VORSTER HAD TAKEN the simple expedient of lying when confronted with allegations that South Africa was on the verge of a nuclear test. He followed that nuclear lie with another, claiming during an October 1977 interview that "I am not aware of any promise that I gave to President Carter"—and that he had only repeated his oft-made statement that South Africa was "only interested in peaceful development of nuclear facilities." In response, the State Department released portions of an October 13 letter from Vorster to Carter, which included the pledge that South Africa did not have, and would not develop, nuclear explosives for any purpose.[1] That letter also turned out to be a lie, for throughout 1977 and for the rest of the decade and beyond, South Africa would secretly continue along a path leading to its possession of a small nuclear arsenal.

In 1977 South Africa and Israel began carrying through on an agreement that had been reached in April 1976 when Vorster—who the British had jailed during World War II for his Nazi sympathies and refusal to serve in the military—visited Israel to meet with Israeli prime minister Yitzhak Rabin and other Israeli leaders. The two pariahs had agreed to trade thirty grams of yield-boosting tritium from Israel, code-named *teeblare*—Afrikaans for "tea leaves"—for fifty tons of uranium from South Africa, code-named mutton. The tritium would be flown to South Africa in 2.5-gram installments over eighteen months.[2]

During the same year that South Africa and Israel began implementing their secret nuclear trade agreement, South Africa's minister of defense issued a white paper asserting that "we are today involved in a war, whether we wish to accept it or not." That belief led to acceleration of the program and a Vorster meeting with his senior aides. He directed them to draft a memorandum describing the nation's nuclear path, which he approved in April 1978. What Vorster sanctioned was a strategy that called for South Africa's clandestine development of nuclear weapons, revealing that capability to the United States and other countries if South African territory was threatened, and then, if the secret disclosure had no effect, a public announcement and possibly a test. The program did not envision actual military use, for fear of retaliation.[3]

That September Vorster left office to become the nation's president, and was replaced by defense minister Pieter Willem Botha, commonly known as

"P.W." and "the big crocodile." Shortly after becoming prime minister, Botha established a cabinet committee to deal with the military uses of atomic devices. It would deliver its first recommendations the following summer, including construction of seven weapons. In the interim, cabinet members, at a meeting held on October 31, 1978, decided that the state-owned Armaments Corporation (Armscor), the Defence Force, and the Atomic Energy Board should begin work on a nuclear weapons program, a program that was immediately classified as top secret. Armscor would be responsible for designing and building the devices.[4]

The year was notable not only for the formation of policies and committees but also for the production of fissile material and construction of another nuclear device. In January the Valindaba Y-Plant produced its first batch of highly enriched uranium, although it was 80 percent U-235 rather than the 90 percent preferred by weapons designers. Production would continue for the rest of 1978 and well into the next year at the 80 percent level, until operations came to an abrupt halt in August 1979, when a major chemical reaction contaminated the plant and put it out of commission for over seven months. The year 1978 also saw the AEB complete construction of a second, smaller device, intended for an instrumented test, before bomb construction was assigned to Armscor.[5]

DURING 1978 and the first eight months of 1979, the U.S. intelligence community was, as Jimmy Carter had promised, monitoring South Africa's nuclear activities and evaluating any data collected. Monitoring included use of the imagery and signals intelligence satellites operated by the National Reconnaissance Office, National Security Agency and CIA communications intercept operations, as well as attempts to recruit human sources with knowledge of South African nuclear activities. It also included the continued use of aircraft belonging to the defense attaché's office. As a result, in April 1978 South Africa expelled three American diplomats who were alleged to have used the defense attaché's plane to take aerial photographs of "strategic installations," which apparently included the nuclear enrichment plant at Valindaba.[6]

Two months before the expulsions, the CIA's Office of Economic Research prepared a paper for an interagency assessment of South Africa's nuclear options, noting "there is no doubt that South Africa can afford to develop and test nuclear explosive if it chooses." Articles that appeared in the agency's *Scientific Intelligence Weekly Review* between December 1978 and the end of April 1979 discussed the capacity of the Valindaba plant, problems at the plant, and the presence of military personnel at the Pelindaba nuclear research center.[7] Then, in late September 1979 the focus suddenly shifted from assessing South Africa's progress toward developing an atomic bomb, to whether it had already built and tested one.

ABOUT 10:15 P.M. on September 21, at Patrick Air Force Base in Florida, technicians from the Air Force Technical Applications Center were conducting a routine readout of Vela 6911, which had been launched on May 23, 1969. That Vela satellite, along with the final pair launched in 1970, orbited the earth at a distance of seventy thousand miles—leaving the U.S. one short of the four needed to keep all of the earth under surveillance on a continuous basis. By 1979, Vela 6911 had substantially exceeded its projected lifetime, and if not for the controversy that followed the September 21 readout, might have been best known for its contribution to space science. For years it had provided data on Cygnus X-1, first believed to be an X-ray double star and then the subject of a bet between physicists Stephen Hawking and Kip Thorne as to whether it was really a black hole. (It is and Thorne won the bet.)[8]

Vela satellite bhangmeters had, over the years, detected a variety of light flashes, including lightning. Many were of no concern because their line of sight did not lead back to earth. Others did not have the optical signature of a nuclear detonation. In some of those cases, their origin was apparent. In others, the cause was a mystery, and the detected signal became part of the collection of Vela "zoo events."[9]

During the readout of Vela 6911, AFTAC personnel watched as a stylus drew a figure representing the variations in light intensity, as monitored by the two satellite bhangmeters. There was no data from a third optical sensor, whose mission was to provide the geographic origin of any noticeable flash of light, because it was out of commission. Nor would there be any reading from the satellite's electromagnetic pulse sensors, which were no longer functioning. But what the technicians saw was sufficient cause for concern. The stylus drew a figure with a double hump, indicating a brief intense flash of light, a dramatic decline in intensity, and then a second, longer-lasting flash. Such double flashes had always been associated with nuclear detonations, where the fireball's surface is rapidly overtaken by the expanding hydrodynamic shock wave, which acts as an optical shutter and hides the small but extremely hot and bright early fireball behind an opaque ionized shock front which is comparatively quite dim. The initial flash normally lasts only a millisecond and emits about only 1 percent of the total thermal energy, although it is the point of maximum intensity. It appeared that some nation or nations, in some part of the world covered by Vela 6911, had detonated a nuclear device in the atmosphere.[10]

The area in view of the Vela bhangmeters was 3,000 miles in diameter, encompassing the southern tip of Africa, the Indian Ocean, the South

Atlantic, and a bit of Antarctica. Examining the satellite readout indicated that the double flash was recorded at about 3:00 a.m. local time. Less than a hour after its technicians noted the signs of a double flash, AFTAC, based on a preliminary analysis, initiated a "pre-alert." After further analyses, Alert 747 was declared at 3:30 a.m.[11]

Sometime that evening President Carter and other top government officials—including national security adviser Zbigniew Brzezinski, secretary of state Cyrus Vance, and secretary of defense Harold Brown—were informed of the possibility that a nuclear detonation had occurred. The next morning a committee of ten to twelve officials gathered to deal with the potential crisis. Gerald Funk, at the time the senior Africa specialist on the National Security Council staff, remembers Brzezinski calling to tell him to "get my toucus into work, that we had a little bit of a problem." Funk also recalled that "we first convened a meeting in the Situation Room of the White House," with Frank Press, the presidential science adviser "there and in charge." During that and other meetings early in the crisis, Funk's assumption was "that there had been in fact a legitimate sighting . . . that satellite had never failed to react positively, and had never given a false signal."[12]

Others called to the meeting included Spurgeon Keeny, then the number-two man in the Arms Control and Disarmament Agency, who received a call from Harold Brown, an old friend from college, and Gerald G. Oplinger, Brzezinski's aide for global issues. Oplinger recalled that "we went around and asked 'Was it a test?'" The CIA and Defense Intelligence Agency representatives "said the odds were at least ninety percent that it had been a nuclear explosion," according to Oplinger. Keeny was skeptical that a truly informed judgment could be reached so quickly.[13] Everybody realized that they were just at the beginning of an investigation.

PRESIDENT CARTER and his chief policy advisers needed two questions answered: Were the indications of a nuclear test, which the specifics of the Vela signal suggested was in the 2- to 4-kiloton range, correct? And if there had been a test, who was responsible? The first question could be addressed in two ways: by looking for corroborating data and by exploring the possibility that the Vela had malfunctioned or detected an event whose optical signature cleverly duplicated that of a nuclear blast.

Verification that a test had taken place, as well as the identity of the culprit, *could* come from conventional intelligence methods—a spy at the heart of the guilty government, an intercept of communications between high-level officials or between the test site and officials in the culpable nation, or even overhead photographs that revealed test preparations. In addition, the CIA, AFTAC, and other intelligence agencies could search data gathered by other components of the Atomic Energy Detection System for signals confirming a detonation had taken place. Much of that search would have taken place anyway, as it had for acknowledged tests in order to determine their characteristics, but the uncertainty and the high stakes added to the urgency.

Part of that search would involve examining the data gathered by the other military satellite systems that carried sensors capable of detecting nuclear explosions. On September 22, 1979, the air force was operating three Defense Support Program satellites, equipped with both bhangmeters and infrared sensors, the latter capable of detecting the heat from a detonation. F-6, which hovered over the equator, 22,300 miles above Brazil, could "see" portions of the South Atlantic. The best view of the area of the suspect flash was from F-7, the Eastern Hemisphere satellite stationed over the Horn of Africa, whose sensors could view part of the South Atlantic, the northern portion of Antarctica, and all of the Indian Ocean.[14]

In addition, sensors were carried aboard two NRO Jumpseat spacecraft, which operated in highly elliptical orbit, and whose antennas intercepted a variety of communications, particularly from the northern reaches of the Soviet Union. Those spacecraft also carried an infrared sensor designated Heritage, which had the potential to detect the heat from a nuclear test.[15]

One Satellite Data System (SDS) spacecraft, which also operated in highly elliptical orbit, was equipped with nuclear detonation detectors. The first two SDS craft had been launched in 1976; their primary mission was to relay the electronic signals from the low-earth-orbiting Kennan (KH-11) imagery satellites back to the ground station at Fort Belvoir, Virginia, where they would be converted into images. Other missions that had been assigned to the spacecraft included serving as a communications relay between the remote tracking stations employed by the air force to exercise command and control of its satellites, as well as relaying communications to U.S. strategic bombers flying over the northern polar region. In 1974 the air force had decided to assign yet another mission to the SDS craft: carrying bhangmeters to augment polar coverage of nuclear detonations. The third SDS satellite, and the first to be equipped with the detonation detectors, was orbited in August 1978.[16]

Further, Defense Meteorological Satellite Program (DMSP) satellites might have detected a blast. In normal circumstances two of the satellites circled the planet in five-hundred-mile orbits. Their primary mission was to provide weather information—crucial to programming reconnaissance satellites as well as conducting military operations. Going along for the ride on the satellites launched in February 1976 and April 1978 was a gamma X-ray detector provided by AFTAC.[17]

The records of the other passive nuclear detonation systems operated by AFTAC could also be searched to see what they might have picked up on September 22. Those no longer included the acoustic sensors of the Dawn Star network, which had been shut down in 1975. But they did include the seismic sensors spread across the planet, as well as the seabed sensors employed for the Sound Surveillance System.[18]

Active measures could also be taken by AFTAC, the CIA, and other intelligence organizations. The Vela detection "set off one of the most extensive air sampling operations in recent years," according to AFTAC historian Gerald Wright. The first planes arrived in the area on September 25, and began over a month of air-sampling operations. By the time they ended on October 29, five different WC-135B aircraft flew a total of twenty-two missions, which involved almost 222 hours of flying time. Other aircraft flew another three missions, spending eight hours aloft in search of debris. The aerial missions were flown to gather any debris emanating from four possible test locations. The Kalahari Desert, where two years earlier South Africa had been preparing for a test, was one location. Another was Prince Edward Island, which along with nearby Marion Island was a South African possession located between South Africa and Antarctica, far from shipping and commercial routes. In addition, two ocean locations could have been the source of acoustic and underwater signals that had been detected. Airflow from other parts of the general area of interest was also targeted. The CIA took a lower-tech approach, sending personnel into western Africa to gather tree leaves, which might be coated with radioactive residue from a blast.[19]

CORROBORATIVE DATA might also be found in the records of government agencies outside the intelligence and military communities, for the effects of nuclear detonation could have been detected by scientific instruments operated by other elements of the government and private scientific institutions, with missions far removed from nuclear detonation detection. Such instruments included earth resources satellites such as Landsat, civilian weather satellites like Nimbus and Tiros, and even the Arecibo Ionospheric Observatory in Puerto Rico. In addition, scientific institutions in the United States and abroad might have inadvertently collected data of significance. Over the next year, some of this data would be searched for and acquired by the United States, while other data would be volunteered once word of the possible blast became public.

In November corroborating data appeared to come from the Institute of Nuclear Science in Gracefield, New Zealand, located just north of Wellington, the nation's capital. The institute had discovered an increase in radioactive fallout in rainwater samples collected between August 1 and October 28. The rainwater contained short-lived radioisotopes such as barium-140, praseodymium-143, and ytrrium-91, all fission products of a nuclear explosion. The institute's director, B. J. O'Brien, noted that "we didn't see much of an increase, just enough to suggest they came from a small nuclear test."[20]

The increase in fallout was measured for radioisotopes with half-lives no longer than fifty-nine days, so that if they came from a nuclear detonation, it would have had to have been a recent one. The half-life of barium-140 is twelve days, while the half-lives of praseodymium-143 and yttrium-91 are thirteen and fifty-nine days, respectively. O'Brien observed, "What we see in our fallout here would be consistent with a nuclear explosion having a force equivalent to two to four kilotons" and "what we've seen couldn't have come from an old test. . . . Whatever it is, it is a recent event." A White House source was also impressed, telling the *Washington Post* that "radioactive fallout was the key missing element in what we thought originally was a clandestine nuclear test" and that "the fallout in New Zealand could well be that missing element."[21]

But before the end of the month, the institute was backtracking, issuing a statement saying "there is no evidence of fresh radioactive fallout during the past three months." After the initial announcement, New Zealand's National Radiation Laboratory conducted its own analysis of the rainwater and found no evidence of fallout. The discrepancy was officially explained as resulting from the laboratory's being equipped to detect only levels of radiation that would endanger health, so that slight fluctuations of radiation would escape notice. However, when scientists at the Gracefield institute tried, they were unable to replicate their initial findings. Subsequently, a U.S. government laboratory also tested the water and found no signs of radioactivity.[22]

Another possible confirmation came from scientists working at the ionospheric observatory at Arecibo, Puerto Rico, site of the world's largest single radio telescope, one thousand feet in diameter. Established in 1963 as a result of Cornell University professor William Gordon's quest to study the ionosphere, it was also used to collect the signals from Soviet radars after they bounced off the moon, but became best known for its role in searching for signals from any extraterresttial civilizations that might be trying to alert others of their existence.[23]

The scientists, Lewis Duncan and Richard Behnke, were using the observatory's radio telescope to watch the upper atmosphere to gather baseline data in support of an experiment in which they planned to watch an Atlas Centaur rocket tear a hole in the ionosphere during its launch. Several hours after the apparent Vela detection, the telescope sensed a ripple moving through the ionosphere. The scientist who saw the ripple, which he called a pattern of "ducted ionospheric disturbances," would later note that the time and direction of the ripple's appearance was consistent with the Vela flash. A nuclear explosion can send a shower of electrons outward through the ionosphere in such a manner as to cause it to "bob up and down a little," according to the scientist.[24]

GIVEN THE INITIAL IMPRESSION that Vela had witnessed a nuclear detonation and the importance of such an event, senior U.S. officials could not wait until all the evidence was in and analyzed before considering the possible implications. A discussion paper, prepared by the State Department for an October 23 meeting involving the secretaries of state, defense, and energy, the director of the ACDA, the chairman of the Joint Chiefs of Staff, director of central intelligence Stansfield Turner, and presidential science adviser Frank Press, laid out the issues.[25]

The paper noted that the intelligence community had "high confidence, after intense technical scrutiny of satellite data, that a low yield atmospheric nuclear explosion occurred in the early morning hours of September 22 somewhere in an area comprising the southern portions of the Indian and Atlantic Oceans, the southern portion of Africa, and a portion of the Antarctic land mass." However, efforts to acquire radioactive debris "have been fruitless," although debris "could have escaped our collection effort." It reported that there was no corroborating seismic or hydroacoustic data, but "those systems' existing capabilities to detect low yield nuclear events in the region of interest is poor."[26]

The paper also noted that the Vela detection was not yet public knowledge, but that information "could leak at any time" and observers would assume that South Africa had tested a nuclear bomb. In that case, there were three concerns: One was that "the efficacy of U.S. intelligence systems generally and test ban monitoring capabilities specifically" would be questioned. In addition, public knowledge would impinge on U.S. global nonproliferation as well as African policy interests. The "nonproliferation stakes could be high," the paper observed, if the Vela detection "caused a rupture in our nuclear negotiations with South Africa," which included trying to persuade the Botha administration to sign the Nuclear Non-proliferation Treaty. On the other hand, failing to take action in response to the event could make it more difficult to deter proliferation elsewhere, including in Pakistan and India.[27]

It was also feared that public disclosure of the event would have a negative impact on efforts to achieve settlements in Rhodesia and Namibia. In Rhodesia, the paper noted, "disclosure of a possible South African nuclear capability might have some cautionary effect on the negotiating positions of the parties . . . but most likely would sharpen the lines already drawn."[28]

One choice facing the administration was whether to confront South Africa, "the most likely responsible party." There was a case for not taking the issue up with the Botha government. The evidence was not strong enough to permit an accusation, and South Africa was "likely to treat our raising of the subject as an accusation." If guilty, the South Africans would deny involvement, and if not guilty they would "react violently and probably conclude that there is no further point in discussing broader nuclear issues" with the United States.[29]

On the other hand, not to go to the South African government would leave the United States "vulnerable," particularly if the intelligence on the September 22 event became public, to charges that the Americans were unwilling to confront the likeliest perpetrator. On balance, it was concluded "there seems more to be gained than lost" by raising the issue with the South Africans.[30]

Only days after the paper was written, the feared leak occurred, making a meeting between the U.S. ambassador and South African officials inevitable. ABC News reporter John Scali, who had attained fame by serving as an intermediary between a Soviet intelligence officer and the U.S. government during the Cuban missile crisis, reported the detection on the evening of October 25. In response to Scali's report, the State Department released a statement that evening, acknowledging that the "United States Government has an indication suggesting the possibility that a low-yield nuclear explosion occurred on September 22 in an area of the Indian Ocean and South Atlantic including portions of the Antarctic continent, and the southern part of Africa." The statement also noted that "no corroborating evidence has been received to date." In a press conference in Gainesville, Florida, the following day, secretary of state Cyrus Vance observed that "it is not clear that there has been a nuclear detonation" and "we don't know that anything has happened in South Africa."[31]

Over the next days, South African officials, acting as if they had been accused, and with stories on the incident appearing in the international and South African press, proclaimed ignorance, denied that their nation had anything to do with the explosion, and suggested alternatives. In response to the State Department announcement, foreign minister Roelof F. Botha proclaimed, "I know absolutely nothing about the matter." J. Wynand de Villiers, the AEB's chairman, labeled suggestions that South Africa might have detonated a nuclear device as "complete nonsense," and went on to say, "If there was anything of the sort, my first reaction would be that some other power might have undertaken a test, but it was definitely not South Africa."[32]

Vice Admiral J. C. Walters, the chief of South Africa's navy, suggested that the cause might have been an accident aboard a Soviet nuclear submarine, adding that the presence of Soviet Echo II class submarines, each equipped with eight nuclear-armed cruise missiles, in the vicinity was common knowledge. He called the theory of a submarine accident a "real possibility." It was not an assessment shared by the White House. "It was considered," one official told the New York Times, "but we gave up on the idea very quickly."[33]

WHILE SOUTH AFRICAN involvement in a covert nuclear test attracted the most attention, it was not the only possibility. The October 22 State Department discussion paper, while focusing on South Africa, observed that "we must consider the possibility that Israel could have detonated a device in this remote geographical area," an action that, if verified, could have significant consequences for U.S. policy toward Israel, the Middle East peace process, and the incentives of Arab states to acquire nuclear weapons.[34] And while the collectors in the U.S. intelligence community sought to obtain evidence of a test and identify a perpetrator, some analysts as well as knowledgeable observers tried to identify the risks and benefits of a covert test to a number of nations. One result was a December 1979 interagency intelligence assessment, *The 22 September 1979 Event.*

In the aftermath of the event the NSC had asked for an estimate, based on the assumption that a test had taken place, of which country or countries might have been responsible. Producing the estimate was the responsibility of the national intelligence officer for nuclear proliferation, who coordinated his effort with the intelligence community representatives of the Interagency Intelligence Working Group on Nuclear Proliferation.[35]

The report, completed in December, began by stating that the technical analyses suggested an atmospheric nuclear detonation had taken place near the earth's surface, within a broad area that consisted primarily of oceans and was generally cloudy and with a yield equivalent to less than 3 kilotons.[36]

It then mentioned and dismissed a variety of possibilities. Pakistan and Taiwan "probably lacked sufficient fissile material for even a single nuclear explosive device." Brazil, Argentina, and Iraq "almost certainly lacked the fissile material and non-fissile components required to fabricate and test nuclear explosive devices." China and France had not signed the partial test ban treaty and were free to test in the atmosphere. They also lacked any "technical or political motivation" to conduct a clandestine test in the southern Indian or Atlantic Ocean.[37]

The Soviet Union was also mentioned and dismissed, although not without dissent, on the grounds that it would have to assume "inordinate political risks" in its relations with the United States to conduct a covert atmospheric test in violation of the partial test ban treaty. The DIA felt differently, arguing that if an atmospheric test were in the Soviet Union's technical interest, "an anonymous test near an unwitting proxy state such as South Africa could have provided an attractive evasion method." The Energy Department suggested that while the Soviets had no technical reason to conduct such a test, it could serve a political purpose—creating suspicion that South Africa was the guilty party, disrupting peace efforts, and polarizing moderate elements in southern Africa.[38]

The possibility of an accident—the "unintended firing and near-surface detonation of a nuclear weapon during military exercises"—was considered and judged unlikely. While an unintended explosion would have produced the double-flash signature, it would have been of lower yield than what was indicated by the Vela signals. In addition, an accident would have required multiple safety measures to have been neutralized. The memorandum also noted the absence of any known weapons carriers in the area on September 22, as well as the absence of any other signs that would be consistent with such an incident, including the disappearance of any nuclear weapons carriers or the presence of ongoing search-and-rescue operations.[39]

The report then, not dissuaded by official denials, turned to the two prime suspects: South Africa and Israel, either individually or jointly. The authors reviewed the history of South Africa's nuclear activities, including the aborted test of 1977, and the role of Prime Minister P. W. Botha during his tenure as defense minister in expanding his government's military capabilities. They commented that if Botha decided in favor of a test, an atmospheric test "over unfrequented international waters," while entailing some risk of being discovered violating the partial test ban treaty, "would have offered a relatively quick, safe, and easy way" for South Africa's weapons designers to test a device without leaving behind clear evidence. In contrast, an attempt to test underground would have been more likely to be discovered ahead of time, as in 1977, and would have left tangible indications of a detonation.[40]

In addition to examining South Africa's motivation to test, the analysts looked at some circumstantial evidence. The Simonstown harbor and naval base had been declared off limits from September 17 to 23, while the Saldanha naval facility, whose tenants included a naval search-and-rescue unit, suddenly was placed on alert for September 21 to 23. Neither event, however, could be taken as a dramatic clue. The memorandum reported that while the Simonstown closure could have helped screen sensitive loading or unloading operations as well as ship movements, the U.S. defense attaché had been told by "several reliable sources" that harbor defense exercises had been conducted during the seven days beginning September 17. The defense attaché noted that the closure was "a regular practice linked to internal defense." And while the alert at Saldanha appeared "unusual," in that no explanation was given and no activity was observed around or in the port, the analysts were unable to state with any assurance that the alert was unique. In addition, Gen. Magnus Malan, chief of South Africa's Defence Force, was reported to be in South America when the Vela detection occurred.[41]

Also noted were statements by Botha that hinted at South Africa's possession of nuclear weapons. On September 25, three days after the double flash, he told a provincial congress of his ruling National Party that "South Africa's enemies might find out we have military weapons they do not know about."

A month later, on October 24, during a dinner attended by past and present members of the AEB, he was reported to have paid tribute to South African nuclear scientists who had been engaged in "secret work of a strategic nature." Their names, he said, could not be mentioned and they would never receive the recognition they deserved. Also of interest were the words and silence of foreign minister Roelof Botha, the day after the prime minister's dinner remarks. He ridiculed speculation that the Vela had detected a South African test, but declined to say, when asked, that South Africa had not been responsible.[42]

Most skeptical of South Africa having conducted a test was the State Department's Bureau of Intelligence and Research, which considered the evidence against South Africa "inconclusive." While the INR believed that South Africa had an ongoing nuclear program, had probably acquired enough fissile material for a device, and might eventually take the risk of testing, the bureau also believed that the same factors that deterred South Africa in August 1977 were still effective in September 1979. The State Department's intelligence organization did agree that if a test had taken place, South Africa was the most likely perpetrator.[43]

The possibility of a secret Israeli test also received significant attention. Several different circumstances could have pushed Israel to test in secret, and in the atmosphere, in violation of its commitment to the partial test ban agreement. The "Israelis might have conceivably foreseen [the need] . . . for . . . low yield nuclear weapons that could be used on the battlefield, or might have considered desirable a small tactical nuclear warhead for short range Lance surface-to-surface missiles," the memorandum observed. In addition, Israeli strategists "might even have been interested in developing a fission trigger for thermonuclear weapons." In absence of access to designs that had been tested, Israeli nuclear weapons designers would probably, it was asserted, want to test prototypes — and "a low yield nuclear test conducted at sea could have enabled them to make basic measurements of the device's performance."[44]

Political calculations, however, would mitigate against such a test. Israel's leaders could not ignore a number of risks, including the adverse reaction from the United States, possible increased Soviet assistance to the Arab states, the likelihood of serious damage to the two-year-old peace treaty with Egypt, and the likely erosion of support among traditionally friendly West European states. In addition, the Department of Energy suggested that for Israel to explode a nuclear device in the vicinity of South Africa, and leave that country to take the blame, was not consistent with Israel's policy or attitude toward its fellow pariah.[45]

THE POSSIBILITY of a joint Israeli–South African test, with South Africa testing Israeli designs in exchange for technical information, was also evaluated in the memorandum. According to its authors, both nations would have considered the trade-off between the benefits of cooperation and the security risks involved in a joint effort. Israel would have expected responsibility for a test to attributed to South Africa, and "would have calculated that South Africa, as a pariah state in need of reliable friends would have had every reason to preserve security and remain silent in the face of speculation about the Israeli role." For such a test to be worth the risk for South Africa, Israel would have had to offer advanced weapons technology. South Africa would probably have had enough confidence in Israeli security, the DIA suggested, to consider a joint test.[46]

While the interagency memo had noted that as of September 1979 India probably had enough fissile material for a bomb, it did not really explore the possibility of Indian responsibility. Former Atomic Energy Commission intelligence officer Arnold Kramish did, in an article published in the summer of 1980. Kramish argued that the signals detected by Vela 6911 were most likely those from a nuclear blast and asked the same question the U.S. intelligence community had asked: who was most likely to be responsible?[47]

Kramish dismissed Israel, South Africa, and Pakistan as likely culprits. Israel would not want to risk disruption of the implementation of its peace treaty with Egypt and the wrath of the United States, while South Africa was concerned with the stability of the transition from white rule in Rhodesia-Zimbabwe. Pakistan's possession of a bomb was, Kramish believed, questionable. While he had no direct or circumstantial evidence to offer, Kramish suggested that the momentum of Indian nuclear weapons development as well as concern over the threat from Pakistan may have pushed India in the direction of a test. Employing the Pokhran test site would have been "politically dangerous and unlikely to escape detection." The presence of Indian navy ships or scientific vessels in the southern Indian Ocean would not be unusual, he wrote. The locale would also divert suspicion to South Africa.[48]

Sam Cohen, best known for his key role in development of the neutron bomb, had another candidate. Cohen, writing in early 1981, dismissed Israel and India as candidates, in part because they had signed the partial test ban treaty. They would not risk, he argued, the consequences of violating it. Cohen also suggested that the lack of radiation in the area after the Vela detection could be explained by a test of a neutron warhead. South Africa, never known to have tested any bombs at all, was unlikely, he argued, to start with a test of a sophisticated device.[49]

"But now take France," he wrote. "The French would have a much different risk equation, never having signed the partial test ban treaty. They had halted atmospheric tests in French Polynesia only because of political pressure. Since an atmospheric test would be the best way to measure the effects of a neutron bomb, which, Cohen noted, many observers believed France was developing, a covert test in an area where the risk of detection was low might be an attractive option.[50]

Cohen had two pieces of circumstantial evidence to offer. If Vela 6911 did register a test, it occurred within the three-thousand-mile-wide circle covering the Indian Ocean, South Atlantic, southern tip of Africa, and a small part of Antarctica. In that area lie the Kerguelen Islands, one of the areas once considered as a possible French nuclear test site, where the French had maintained a small scientific center with a staff of about one hundred since 1950. Cohen also noted that in June 1980, France had announced that it had tested a neutron bomb, "but not when and where."[51]*

BY THE TIME the intelligence community's analysis of who was likely to be responsible for a test was completed in December 1979, and as collection efforts continued, a number of panels or organizations tried to analyze the available data and to evaluate the possibility that the Vela signal was the result of a malfunction or natural phenomenon—efforts that would produce a series of reports over the next several years.

On September 25, just as the AFTAC aircraft had begun their air-sampling operations on the other side of the world, Richard Garwin, a University of Chicago–trained physicist and longtime adviser to the CIA and NRO on satellite reconnaissance issues, was asked to come to CIA headquarters for half a day. Harold Agnew, director of the Los Alamos National Laboratory, and Steve Lukasik, the former director of the Advanced Research Projects Agency, joined him to serve as three-man panel "to render some judgment as to whether this actually had been a nuclear test," Garwin recalled.[52]

Garwin reported that "all we had were Vela reports" and "there were no other data . . . and there were little negative data because there had not been enough time to determine whether other detection systems had received similar signals or not." He suggested waiting for more information to be gathered from debris collection and underwater sensors. But when pressed to give a best estimate because the "CIA had to tell the president something" before an

---

* Both pieces of evidence were weak. By 1979 there was a joint French-Soviet meteorological facility on Kerguelen, making it somewhat unlikely that the French would involve it in a covert nuclear test. In addition, a number of underground tests in French Polynesia during 1970s have been associated with the French neutron bomb program.

item appeared in the newspapers, he came up with a 60 percent probability that there had been a nuclear test.[53]

The next month Garwin received another summons, this time asking him to serve on a panel established by presidential science adviser Frank Press to evaluate the incoming data on the September 22 event. Eight other scientists, with a variety of backgrounds, would join Garwin as members of the committee. They included William Donn of the Lamont-Doherty Geological Observatory, Ricardo Giacconni of the Harvard Smithsonian Center for Astrophysics, Richard Muller of the University of California at Berkeley, Wolfgang K. Panofsky of the Stanford Linear Accelerator Center, Allen Peterson of the Stanford Research Institute, and F. William Sarles of MIT's Lincoln Laboratory. Also serving was a scientist with a long history of involvement in nuclear detection issues—Manhattan Project veteran Luis Alvarez, then at the University of California at Berkeley. Jack Ruina, an old friend of Press's, a professor of electrical engineering and computer science at MIT, and former head of the Pentagon's Advanced Research Projects Agency, was appointed chairman. Ruina described the group as a panel of people from across the political spectrum.[54]

Ruina and his colleagues were given a three-part mission: to review both classified and unclassified data that could help determine whether the Vela signal had been the result of a nuclear detonation, to consider the possibility that the signal was a "false alarm" resulting from a satellite malfunction, and to investigate whether the signal might have been of natural origin, possibly the result of two or more natural phenomena. The group would begin work on November 1, supported by the Office of Science and Technology Policy (OSTP), which Press headed.[55]

BEFORE THE END of that month several technical analyses were completed. Los Alamos scientist Guy Barasch examined the possibility that the flashes detected by Vela 6911 were the result of a natural phenomenon. Vela bhangmeters had been triggered hundreds of thousands of times by lightning, cosmic particles, and direct sunlight. He concluded that naturally occurring signals would not be confused with signals from a nuclear detonation, whose light signature is "unmistakable." While pulsed light sources that matched *either* the intensity or the duration of a nuclear detonation occur in nature, or could be built, no known source matched *both* characteristics. In particular, Barasch dismissed the possibility that the Vela signal came from a lightning "superbolt," lightning that is over a hundred times more intense than typical lightning and usually occurs over water when cold polar air moves in over warm, moist oceanic air. Barasch noted that "to achieve the pulse shape and peak-radiated power simulating a one-kiloton nuclear explosion, lightning would have to be both 400 times more energetic and 100 times longer in duration than ever observed for the superbolts."[56]

Another two technical studies would follow in December and January. *Possible Origins of Event 747 Optical Data*, written by three employees of the Santa Barbara–based Mission Research Corporation—Dale Sappenfield, David Sowle, and Trella McCartor—appeared in December. The three authors examined the same possibility that the Press panel was asked to consider—that the Vela signal was of nonnuclear origin. They would find a possible explanation in the reflection of sunlight off some small irregularly shaped object, provided it passed in front of the Vela sensors with the proper trajectory. However, all such objects would be "highly contrived" and would have to be matched to a "restricted trajectory." In addition, they were unaware of other occurrences where such objects created double flashes that were clearly not caused by nuclear detonations. As a result, it was hard, Sappenfield and his colleagues wrote, to believe that the first time such an object produced a double flash, it made one so similar to the signal created by a nuclear detonation.[57]

The trio also considered two factors that could raise doubts about whether Vela 6911 had actually detected a nuclear detonation. One discrepancy was "late first maximum"—that the maximum intensity associated with the first flash occurred later than expected relative to the maximum of the second flash. The second factor, which would play a significant role in the Press panel's conclusions, was that the two bhangmeters did not yield equivalent or "parallel" readings for the maximum intensity of the second flash, as would be expected when the event they were sensing was many thousands of miles away.[58]

The authors did not find the first anomaly particularly troubling, believing that it was the result of "experimental conditions surrounding the nuclear explosion." The different readings produced by the bhangmeters for the second flash were of far greater concern. The authors considered and rejected several potential explanations, including "smog, X-ray veil, surface effects, and bomb mass effects." The malfunctioning of one of the bhangmeters was the only explanation they could find, the probability of which they considered "much higher than the probability of any non-nuclear explanation of either or both sensor signals." A nuclear detonation was thus the only possible source of the Vela signal that did not seem "very improbable" to the trio.[59]

In January, two scientists from the Stanford Research Institute reported on their rush evaluation of the possibility that the double-flash signal resulted from a meteoroid. The only conclusions they were able to offer after their three-week study was that the scenario suggested by the Mission Research Corporation (MRC) authors and the one suggested by Gary H. Mauth of Sandia, which involved two meteoroids, were extraordinarily unlikely. Two meteoroids were likely to be responsible for a double flash like the one received by

Vela only once in one billion years. However, meteoroid data from the Pioneer space probe indicated that the MRC and Sandia models did not exhaust "the possible means for producing optical signals from meteoroids." However, given the limited time for the study, the authors were unable to reach any firm conclusion concerning the probability that the Vela signal was produced by a meteoroid encounter.[60]

THE REPORTS PRODUCED in late 1979 and early 1980 resulted from quick assessments, using whatever data was available, of the likelihood that the September 22 double flash represented a nuclear detonation. Authors and panels whose reports were published in the spring and early summer of 1980 had the advantage of more, although far from complete, data, as well as more time to analyze data on issues ranging from possible corroborative evidence to the feasibility of a sensor malfunction to a nonnuclear origin for the Vela signal.

Reports issued in May by Los Alamos and Sandia would not, specifically, attract public attention, although they reflected the opinion of those in the labs who worked on the issue, an opinion that would often be presented in the months ahead. The Los Alamos report was authored by Henry G. Horak, who had joined Los Alamos in the fall of 1967 after obtaining a doctorate in astronomy from the University of Chicago, developing an expertise in astrophysics, and teaching at the University of Kansas. In his paper, he noted that the bhangmeters on DSP Flights 6 and 7 did not trigger, and offered two explanations consistent with a nuclear test having occurred: the event did not take place within the satellites' field of view, or the signal was weakened during transmission through clouds and, as a result, wasn't strong enough to reach the necessary threshold of brightness for detection. It was also possible, he noted, that Vela 6911 had detected the blast through a break in the clouds, or through thin clouds.[61]

Horak confronted the issue of discrepant bhangmeter readings and suggested that the substantial difference in bhangmeter results for the second flash could have been caused by "optical background changes during the much longer second pulse." The bottom line for Horak was that when one looked at all the data associated with the Vela signal—the double flash, the intensity of the flashes, and the time difference between the various portions of the signal—it was "strong evidence that a nuclear explosion actually produced Vela Alert 747."[62]

The May 1980 Sandia report, authored by Gary Mauth, noted that none of the other satellites equipped with bhangmeters, including DSP and SDS satellites, had detected the double flash that the Vela did. He also disputed the notion of Sappenfield and his colleagues that the different bhangmeter readings could be explained by a malfunction, noting that laser calibration tests on Vela 6911, conducted on two occasions in November 1979, revealed no problems.[63]

Most importantly though, taking into account such factors as Vela 6911's performance history and the very remote probability that the signal could be explained by encounters with meteoroids, Mauth came to the same conclusion as the Santa Barbara trio and Horak as to the likely cause of the Vela signal. It was reasonable to conclude, he argued, that the discrepancy in bhangmeter readings was the result of satellite motion enhancing the apparent strength of the signal recorded by the more sensitive bhangmeter during the second flash. As a result, the Vela signals were "fully consistent with those expected from a low-yield atmospheric [nuclear detonation]."[64]

BY THE TIME the Los Alamos and Sandia reports had been completed, Ruina and his colleagues on the Press panel finished their investigation, meeting for the third and final time in early April 1980. During meetings, the panel received briefings by AFTAC, the DIA, and other agencies. Not all those briefings were unanimously well received—Luis Alvarez recalled the DIA briefing as being one in which the group was shown "and quickly discarded confirming evidence from a wild assemblage of sensors." Keeny recalls that Alvarez was "outraged by [the] DIA people," believing they flagged possible "blips" in various sensor readings without considering whether such blips were part of the normal environment. One briefing was given to a select subgroup of the panel, and involved relevant human intelligence gathered by the CIA on topics such as the movements of South African and Israeli ships.[65]

In any case, the information received from those briefings, along with additional documentation, allowed Ruina and his associates to examine Vela performance, review the data that might corroborate a nuclear origin of the signal, and review the studies produced by Los Alamos, Sandia, and other agencies. They also commissioned and reviewed statistical studies of the light signals that had previously been detected by Vela satellites as well as computer models of natural phenomena that might have generated the double-flash signal.[66]

The Press panel's written report, issued in late May, contained an assessment of the effort to obtain potential corroborating data, an analysis of the Vela signal and possible nonnuclear explanations, and the group's conclusions.

The search for confirming data from other satellites carrying bhangmeters was unsuccessful, because "these other satellites were looking at different parts of the earth and due to weather conditions had very little coverage overlap with the . . . satellite that observed the light flash." Nor were there any electromagnetic pulse or magnetic disturbance data that could be correlated with the September 22 signal. The debris collection effort, involving both aircraft and ground sampling, and hampered by the weather, also failed to produce positive results—a failure, the group observed, that did not provide conclusive evidence that no nuclear explosion had occurred.[67]

The group also did not put much weight in an acoustic signal received at a "distant recording site in the northern hemisphere at an appropriate time." A second site in the Northern Hemisphere failed to detect an acoustic signal, as did sensors in Australia, which sound propagation models suggested would be the more likely recipient of such a signal—although AFTAC's data indicated that no signal was likely to be received at any of those sites from a low-yield explosion. There was also, the panel concluded, a significant probability of a signal arriving "within the large time window allowed," owing to the uncertainty about the location of the Vela signal.[68]

Ruina and his colleagues had also been briefed by the Naval Research Laboratory during their last meeting in April, on signals that were picked up at SOSUS sites. Signals a few decibels above background noise were detected at the several sites at times consistent with their direct arrival from a source near Prince Edward Island, far from shipping or commercial routes, and for rays reflected from the Antarctic ice shelf. The report noted that the data was "analyzed by a filtering procedure that was not normally employed with SOSUS data." In any event, the presidential panel considered the NRL study too incomplete to serve as corroborating data because the data on the frequency and strength of background signals was insufficient to resolve "the ambiguity in signal identification and source locations."[69]

The traveling ionospheric disturbance detected at Arecibo was not considered "useful evidence" at the time the panel concluded its deliberations. The Arecibo scientists who detected that ripple, Richard Behnke and Lewis Duncan, met with the panel in Washington, a meeting they said was "mass confusion . . . an exercise in distraction." Members of the panel disputed their major findings—that the ripple came from a source at least 310 miles away, moving from south to east at a speed, between 600 and 750 meters per second, typical of ionospheric ripples. The group claimed that Behnke and Duncan had made major errors in their calculations, which resulted in fallacious findings concerning the direction and speed of the disturbance. Duncan would say that it surprised him that "people have tried as much as they have to discredit [their findings] and that critics had failed to appreciate the sophistication of the incoherent-scatter radar (the radio telescope) at Arecibo and the methods used." Duncan, himself, was not fully convinced that Arecibo had detected a nuclear test.[70]

Panel member Richard Garwin agreed that the ionospheric ripple was the most plausible corroborating signal considered, and that its movement from south to north was "striking and unusual" since most disturbances moved in the opposite direction. However, Garwin added, the record of observations using the advanced radar at Arecibo was too small to allow many generalizations. In addition, he doubted that such a large disturbance could have been created by a low-yield detonation like the one Vela 6911 appeared to detect.[71]

In the absence of data confirming the detection, the panel placed great importance on its analysis of the Vela signal. The group's report noted that it "has the right duration and the characteristic double-humped shape was recorded by both bhangmeters." Three separate means of producing an estimate of yield, normally derived from the time of the maximum intensities of the first and second flashes, were also in rough agreement, which further supported the hypothesis that a nuclear blast had been detected.[72]

However, the panel argued, before accepting the proposition that the double flash represented a nuclear detonation, it was necessary to demonstrate that the signal had no additional characteristics that ruled out a nuclear origin. It was also important that no alternative explanation was more likely to be true—that is, another class of signals of which the September 22 signal was more likely to be a member.[73]

One potential problem for the scientists was that the total intensity of light detected by Vela 6911 was "considerably larger than expected for a hypothesized explosion with this measured yield." The anomaly could be explained if the signal had been transmitted through clear skies—if the region where the light source originated had been essentially free of clouds. At the same time, the absence of nuclear debris could only be explained, they wrote, if there was heavy cloud cover and "local rainout." Those seemingly contradictory requirements could be reconciled if the light were transmitted through a small local gap in the clouds, a possibility that Horak had noted in his paper.[74]

But, as with others who had examined the Vela detection, the most troubling issue for the nine members of the Press panel was the discrepancy in bhangmeter readings at the peak intensity for the second flash, which, they stated, had not happened with the twelve previous nuclear detonations detected by Vela 6911. As the panel explained, the readings for the bhangmeters would not be expected to be identical, since one was more sensitive than the other, but if on one occasion one bhangmeter recorded a 20 and the other a 10, then on other occasions when that first bhangmeter recorded a 20, the other should also record 10 or a nearby value, with some variation possible due to changes in the background during the recording of data. But in the case of the September 22 signal, the size of the discrepancy, the panel wrote, "assumes major significance," and "throws doubt on its interpretation as a nuclear event."[75]

The report went on to explain that "during the second hump, the ratio of bhangmeter signals is significantly different from what would be expected from a nuclear explosion near the surface of the earth. Such anomalous behavior was never observed in bhangmeter recordings of previous nuclear explosions. Thus, although the September 22 event displays many of the characteristics of nuclear signals, it departs in an essential feature."[76] That observation, was followed by another:

> It is very difficult to account for such a departure if the source of the September 22 signal was at a great distance from the bhangmeters, i.e. on the surface of the earth. On the other hand, if the source of the September 22 signal were close to the satellite sensors, the relative intensity of the light incident on the two bhangmeters could be quite different from cases where the source is far away. That is, an object passing near the satellite might be more in the field of view of one sensor than the other, whereas at a distance the field of view of both sensors is essentially the same.[77]

The panel noted its consideration of a number of alternative explanations, including unusual astronomical events, ordinary lightning, superbolts of lightning, sunlight reflecting off other satellites, sunlight reflecting off meteoroids passing near the satellite, and sunlight reflecting off particles ejected from the collision of meteoroids upon impact with the spacecraft. The group dismissed the first five alternatives—meteoroids of sufficient size were considered too rare and traveled too rapidly through the field of view to generate the double-flash signal with the required time difference between the first and second flash, while other satellites were too far away to reflect enough light to trigger the Vela bhangmeters, for example.[78]

The sixth alternative was another matter: "a meteor impact with the Vela satellite appears to be the best candidate for a nonnuclear origin of the signal." Such an impact, the scientists argued, could generate a large number of particles with greater mass than the meteoroid, particles that would move with a low speed relative to the satellites. They could well generate "the complicated time histories seen in the unexplained zoo events as well as in the September 22 event."[79]

Panel member Luis Alvarez recalled that "some on the committee proposed that a micrometeorite might have struck the satellite and dislodged a piece of its skin. Reflecting sunlight into the optical system on one sensor but not into that of its neighbor, the debris might have caused the questionable event. We constructed a believable scenario based on the known frequency of such micrometeorite impacts that reproduced the observed light intensity and pattern."[80]

The meteor impact theory became the panel's best explanation of what happened on September 22, although it could not rule out the possibility that the signal had a nuclear origin. Ruina said that his group had begun its work assuming it would conclude that the Vela 6911 signal was the result of a nuclear detonation, but by their last meeting the consensus was that the difference between known blast signals and the double flash detected on September

22 was too great to accept the flash as proof of an explosion in the absence of corroborating data. One panel member summarized the shift in opinion in terms of odds, saying that "on the first day we were betting four-to-one that it was an explosion, and at the end we were betting four-to-one that it was not."[81]*

THE PANEL'S CONCLUSION had been expected, and challenged by some, as far back as January. An article in the *Washington Post* reported that "scientists at [Los Alamos], in the Department of Energy and even a few technical people at the State Department question why there should be such equivocating" since "every sign they've seen identifies the event of September 22 as a nuclear explosion." An anonymous State Department official told the *Post* that "the Vela satellite picked up a signature like this 41 times before. . . . In every one of those 41 instances, there was never any question about the fact that a nuclear test had taken place. Each of those 41 was undeniably a nuclear explosion. This one was too." A Los Alamos scientist, noting that the second pulse of a nuclear detonation produces exactly ninety-nine times more light than the first pulse, stated, "This is what the Vela saw the night of September 22." Subsequent to the report's release, one expert at Sandia asserted that the White House's reflected sunlight theory "strains credibility."[82]

Not surprisingly, just as reports prior to the Press panel's study concluded that the September 22 detection had resulted from a nuclear blast, so did subsequent reports. The DIA report, *The South Atlantic Mystery Flash: Nuclear or Not?*, was released to a select audience in late June 1980. It was written by Dr. John E. Mansfield, who held a doctorate from Harvard in physics and worked for 1965 Nobel Prize winner Julian Schwinger, and Lt. Col. Houston

---

* Another panel, the CIA's Nuclear Intelligence Panel (NIP), whose members included Harold Agnew, Louis Roddis Jr., and Edward Teller, reached a different conclusion. According to Donald Kerr, who chaired the panel's study, and who had served in the Carter administration as acting director of defense programs at the Energy Department, and became the CIA's deputy director for science and technology in 2001, "We had no doubt it was a bomb." See Seymour Hersh, *The Samson Option: Israel's Nuclear Arsenal and American Foreign Policy* (New York: Random House, 1991), pp. 280–281. The panel reviewed data from the event during a February 11–13, 1980, NIP meeting, according to a memorandum: Chairman, JAEIC, Memorandum for: Director of Central Intelligence, Deputy Director of Central Intelligence, Subject: Judgments of the DCI's Nuclear Intelligence Panel on the 22 September 1979 Event, February 14, 1980. The panel's report (*Judgments of the DCI's Nuclear Intelligence Panel on the 22 September 1979 Event*, n.d..), attached to the memo, was released in 2004 in response to a Freedom of Information Act request—with all discussion of facts as well as the panel's conclusions redacted.

T. Hawkins, who had recently joined DIA, as head of the Nuclear Energy Division's Nuclear Weapons Branch, at the time of the incident. The authors noted that much of the search for corroborating evidence failed–that while data "possibly related [to the double-flash] were . . . found in the records of a number of instruments . . . in each [case], the signal was very weak, embedded in noise, or of a phenomenon not well understood." As a result, intelligence analysts and review panels tended to discount those signals as possible corroboration of a nuclear blast.[83]

Among the topics discussed by Mansfield and Hawkins were the absence of detected radioactivity, the traveling ionospheric disturbance detected at Arecibo, and the possibility that one or more micrometeoroids caused the signal. They noted that explosions near or at the ocean's surface result in a large volume of sea water being vaporized or physically lofted into the radioactive cloud. The water then immediately begins to fall back to the ocean, so that a large portion of the debris from the explosion falls into the ocean just a few thousand yards from the point of detonation.[84]

Their treatment of the ionospheric disturbance that Behnke and Duncan detected included both a detailed description of the detector and a calculation of the probability of one or more northward-traveling ionospheric disturbances from random events passing the Vela circle at the Vela time as being not more than 0.02–making it very unlikely, although not impossible. In their discussion of micrometeoroids, they argued, based on the calculations performed by Stanford Research Institute scientists, that the odds of a single meteor observation with a peak intensity and duration, with no additional requirements such as rise time and double pulse, was one in one hundred billion.[85]

Although much of their reasoning, the data they employed, and even their conclusions remain officially classified to this day, within weeks after their report was completed, its conclusions were reported in the press. On July 15, 1980, both the *New York Times* and *Washington Post* carried stories asserting that the DIA report, although "hedged with uncertainties," concluded that the signal detected by Vela 6911 came from a nuclear detonation in the South Atlantic. The stories also carried comments from anonymous White House and Defense Department officials disputing the conclusion reached by Mansfield and Hawkins. (Years later, Ruina would dismiss the study as being on "college freshman level . . . maybe college senior" from a technical standpoint," while Richard Garwin recalled that it involved a statistical analysis that would have justified any hypothesis over time.)[86]

But the news coverage prompted the White House to do more than issue anonymous criticism. On the same day the stories ran in the *Post* and *Times*, the White House released an only-mildly redacted version of the Press panel's report. The White House official said that it was purely a coincidence that the two papers came to light in the same week.[87]

Four days after Mansfield and Hawkins submitted their report, the NRL turned in a three-hundred-page study, *Report of NRL Investigations Concerning the 22 September 1979 VELA Alert*. The NRL's involvement in the effort to determine the significance of the Vela detection began with a letter from John Marcum, OSTP's senior adviser for technology and arms control, to Alan Berman, the director of research at the laboratory—an institution that began operations in 1923, and whose campus-like headquarters are located in an isolated corner of Washington, D.C. Berman had received his doctorate in physics in 1952 from a far older institution, Columbia University, where he was a contemporary of Frank Press's. He had been named NRL's director of research in 1967 and become accustomed to receiving requests from Press to look into some "strange problem."[88]

Marcum asked that the laboratory undertake "an immediate study" of ionospheric data that might have a bearing on whether the bhangmeters on Vela 6911 had actually witnessed the light from a nuclear explosion. In addition, the NRL was to study any other signals that might be available through its own experiments or experiments undertaken by other observatories. The laboratory's effort was dubbed Project Search.[89] The major result of NRL's work, its report, has never been released. However, the paper trail of memos and letters gives a partial view of the laboratory's extensive research effort as well as some of the conclusions it reached.

On February 14, 1980, Berman, according to a sanitized memo, contacted a "foreign national" and asked him to contact several seismic observatories and find out if they had detected any unusual signals at the time of the Vela detection. The same individual was asked to determine whether an experiment in equatorial scintillations, which had a propagation path between Adelaide, Australia, and Papua New Guinea's Manus island, or a particular high-frequency over-the-horizon radar had detected any unexpected signals. It would appear that the foreign national was Australian, and the radar was the Jindalee radar that began experimental operations in October 1976.[90]

The following day, a member of Berman's staff, Frank Kelly, telephoned Dr. Robert A. Helliwell of Stanford University in search of data, information, and suggestions. Helliwell reported that he was supervising a project, which had stations in Antarctica and Canada, to make wideband synoptic recordings of ELF (extremely-low-frequency) and VLF (very-low-frequency) noise. The recorders were on for only a portion of each hour, but he promised to have his workers check to see if they were on at the time of the Vela sighting. He also provided leads about other American and foreign researchers who were monitoring ELF and VLF noise in the Antarctic, and suggested that information might be available from a French research station at Kerguelen Island. On February 25 Kelly called Dr. Nelson Spenser of the Goddard Space Flight Center because he had been told that Spenser's Atmospheric Explorer Satellite might have detected ionospheric disturbances associated with the September 22 double flash. Spenser agreed to check to see if the satellite's sensors had been turned on, and if so, if they had recorded any signal of interest. The same day Kelly was in touch with an individual connected with ship-based VLF studies, who also promised to find out if any relevant data had been gathered.[91]

John Goodman, whom Berman had released from all other duties the day after Marcum's letter arrived so he could work on the Vela investigation, spent part of February 27 inquiring about the availability of infrared and other data from the Landsat earth resources satellite and the Tiros and Nimbus weather satellites. Goodman also penned a brief memo that day, recording that he had requested and was expecting copies of images taken by an air force DMSP spacecraft on September 22. Meanwhile, Berman spoke to an official from another organization, possibly AFTAC, who was responding to the research director's question about signals that might have been detected by a particular seismic station. The results were negative, as they were with respect to another station that might have detected a signal.[92]

Goodman also informed Berman that day of a series of findings: examination of data from the navy's Omega land-based VLF communications system as well as the service's Transit navigation satellite system, which used very high and ultra-high frequencies, proved negative. In addition, Goodman's memo raised questions about the Arecibo data. While it was apparent that Behnke and Duncan had detected an ionospheric disturbance, a "back of the envelope calculation" did not support the idea that it originated from an explosion in the South Atlantic, off South Africa. However, it was possible, Goodman reported, that the mathematical analysis being employed was not the proper one for a surface explosion.[93]

During the first days of March, John Goodman explored the possibility of obtaining data from a number of satellite systems. He had discovered the First GARP (Global Atmospheric Research Program) Global Experiment, a joint program of the World Meteorological Organization and the International Council of Scientific Unions. The program involved five geosynchronous and three polar orbiting weather satellites, as well as a number of ocean buoys that measured surface atmospheric pressure and sea surface temperature—sixteen of which were located at longitudes and latitudes monitored by Vela 6911. It was hoped that the weather satellite data would reveal the presence of any storms near South Africa and Arecibo.[94]

On March 5 Goodman received a call concerning some of the data obtained by the DMSP. One of the military weather satellites did "see an enhancement" of high-frequency noise at the approximate time of the double flash, near the conjectured location of the possible test. The noise, however, could have resulted from environmental conditions. At the same time, a more active cause, including lightning or a nuclear detonation, was possible. In a memo written that day, Goodman observed that the DMSP data "would appear, at present, to be quite interesting." The NRL was also processing data concerning the electron content of the ionosphere at the time of the Vela signal in its search for corroborative data. In addition, there was hope that a military research satellite, launched in January 1979 and known as SCATHA (an acronym for Spacecraft Charging at High Altitudes), might have relevant data from a high-frequency experiment.[95]

NRL representatives continued to reach out to a number of American and foreign institutions that might have inadvertently gathered data relevant to the investigation. Frank Kelly was trying to obtain high- and low-frequency magnetic field data from a Japanese research station in Showa, Antarctica, and the Japanese Radio Research Laboratory was expected to provide data. VLF data from Kerguelen was also due to arrive at the NRL. The Smithsonian Astrophysical Observatory in Massachusetts had been asked to provide VLF records from sites in Latin America, the Middle East, Australia, and the United States. Even Air Traffic Control tapes were being searched for data. The remote possibility that neutrinos associated with the conjectured nuclear explosion had been detected by a massive neutrino detection system at the University of Pennsylvania led the NRL to ask the professor who ran the system to determine if any unusual background counts were observed. Consideration was also given to obtaining samples from American ichthyologists who were due to be aboard a French supply ship traveling to the Crozet Islands in the South Atlantic. The Americans would be collecting samples of the islands' fish fauna for their studies, fauna that might contain radioactivity transported by the air or water from the Prince Edward Island area, about six hundred miles away.[96]

Three weeks before the NRL turned in its final report, Lothar H. Ruhnke, the head of the research department's atmospheric physics branch, summarized some of the preliminary results and made some recommendations. He noted that an analysis was conducted to determine the probability of detecting radioactivity in the air and rainwater from a 2-kiloton explosion on September 22, 1979, at Marion Island. An important factor in the analysis was the major cyclone that approached the island on the day of the double flash and moved eastward. Based on satellite data and conventional weather maps, a trajectory analysis showed that a possible radioactive cloud was caught by the storm and stayed with it until at least September 28.[97]

Comparing the trajectories of the radioactive cloud, its horizontal expansion, and the paths of the AFTAC aerial sampling missions led to the conclusion that only one mission, flown on September 28 to 58° south latitude and 150° east longitude, could have intercepted the radioactive cloud. By that time, "fission products had decayed by rainout below the level of detectability with the exception of the gamma count." Later, Ruhnke noted that it was necessary to conclude that if, under the prevailing meteorological conditions, there had been a 2-kiloton explosion on September 22, it could not be detected by airborne sampling methods more than five days later (that is, after September 26).[98]

Nor could such a blast be detected by the existing ground-based sampling network under average meteorological conditions. Ruhnke suggested that it might be possible to find evidence in snow samples from the glaciers of the Kerguelen Islands. Even one year after a detonation, the snow should still show considerable signs of radioactivity. He recommended an expedition to obtain radioactivity profiles of the snow on a glacier, down to a depth of one meter. His suggestion was passed on to Frank Press by Berman. But the French, according to Berman, "told us to go pound sand."[99]

Such NRL collection and analysis efforts were undoubtedly described in its lengthy report. The most significant element of the report, which, in conjunction with the Vela signal, led Berman and his associates to believe a nuclear device had been detonated on September 22, was the analysis of the hydroacoustic signals detected—the same signals the White House panel had dismissed as inconclusive, but which Berman describes as being comparable to those received from French tests in the Pacific.[100]

The September 22 signals had been obtained from two sets of sensors: the SOSUS hydrophones, used by the navy to monitor Soviet submarine movements and by AFTAC to detect nuclear detonations, and the sensors of the Missile Impact Location System (MILS), which had been deployed throughout the South Atlantic to measure when and where test missiles fired from Cape Canaveral splashed down—information vital to evaluating missile accuracy. To determine if the signal was possibly the result of natural phenomena, the NRL searched the logs for "every minute of every day" for thirty days before the event and thirty days afterward and found none.[101]

The NRL scientists used the SOSUS/MILS data in conjunction with a working assumption: if the Vela 6911 signal had been from a nuclear test, then the most likely site was in the Prince Edward Island–Marion Island area. If one wanted to conduct a clandestine test, that area was a "splendid place to go," Berman notes. The islands' high mountains would be a good place to locate observation sensors. A barge carrying a nuclear device could be placed in the shallow water near the islands.[102]

That hypothesis was reinforced by calculations done by the Naval Observatory, which Berman had asked to determine the time of sunrise in the Prince Edward Island area—knowing that weapons designers preferred tests to take place shortly before then. Such timing allowed the blast to be seen and measured against a dark background, as well as permitting aircraft monitoring the blast effects to launch shortly after detonation. The answer that came back from the observatory placed sunrise ten minutes after the Vela detection.[103]

Analysts under Berman's direction then developed a model of the hydro-acoustic signature that might be expected from a blast at Prince Edward Island. A massive acoustic signal would be expected to travel south, bounce off Antarctica, and travel north. Using the laboratory's sophisticated computer capability, the analysts calculated the time when the original signal should have reached Antarctica, and then the speed at which it would have traveled north. It was then possible to compare the theoretical times with records of the SOSUS and MILS network. Berman recalls that a signal arrived "within a few seconds" of the time such a signal would have been expected to arrive at the SOSUS and MILS sensors in its path. It was "not positive proof," Berman notes, but it was "interesting evidence."[104]

After its report was completed, the NRL continued to receive new information and to analyze it. In late July, Berman wrote Press adviser John Marcum to report that Marion Island ionosonde records from late on the night of September 21, 1979, extending to October 1, 1979, had been received and subjected to a "very preliminary analysis." That analysis showed an "effect of currently unexplained origin" between 2:45 and 3:00 a.m. on September 22. The "rather striking anomaly" was a "a major biteout or depletion of the ionospheric electron density" in the vicinity of Marion Island, while no similar effect appeared in the records for Johannesburg, Kerguelen, and Grahamstown.[105]

On September 25, 1980, Berman received a letter from Dr. L. Van Middlesworth, a professor in the physiology and biophysics department at the University of Tennessee's college of medicine who for the previous twenty-five years had been examining samples of sheep thyroids from around the world. Van Middlesworth wrote that he had detected iodine-131 in the thyroids of sheep slaughtered in Melbourne, Australia, in November 1979. He also reported that subsequent to that time, no evidence of iodine-131 was ever detected in Australian sheep thyroids. In early November, Berman informed Marcum that based on their analysis of the data, the head of the radiation survivability and detection branch of the NRL and his staff "believe that Dr. Van Middlesworth's data constitutes a positive case for the proposition that Australian sheep ingested the fission product [iodine-131] during the month of October 1979." Further, Berman wrote that it was not "inconsistent with the observed evidence" that iodine isotope detected in the thyroids "could have been associated with a postulated nuclear detonation in the vicinity of Prince Edward and Marion Islands."[106]

AT THE TIME of the release of the Press report, the NRL's conclusion was not known outside of government circles, but at the end of August 1980 it was revealed in the pages of *Science* magazine. The disclosure came not from an anonymous source at the NRL, but from research director Alan Berman.

Berman, who was irritated by the Press panel's dismissal of his organization's work as "incomplete" and "ambiguous," pointed out that when the panel's report was drafted in April, the NRL had not yet completed its work. He also noted that the NRL had assigned seventy-five people to work on the project for several months, whereas the White House panel "undertook no study of its own [but] listened to presentations. . . . They heard various opinions and came to their own." The preponderance of evidence indicated that a nuclear blast had taken place, according to Berman. And, in response to a question from the *Washington Star*'s John Fialka, the NRL research director remarked that "a hydro-acoustic signal was detected which had characteristics similar to those received from known nuclear detonations."[107]

Science also reported the criticism by a White House staff member of the navy lab's analysis. The anonymous staffer called the issue of the hydro-acoustic signal a "dead horse." He asserted that the NRL study was fraught with ambiguity because two signals had been detected: a weak one followed by a strong one.* If they came from the same source, he continued, the initial signal had to have arrived directly, while the second was a reflected signal. Most of the mathematical analysis was based on the second signal, and no amount of sophisticated mathematics, according to the staffer, could determine with confidence the origin of the reflected signal. In addition, the aide claimed that if the event had originated at Prince Edward Island, as the NRL study assumed, it should have been detected by another satellite, but was not.[108]

IN THE IMMEDIATE YEARS after the completion of the Press panel, DIA, and NRL reports, the national labs as well as private contractors would complete additional studies. None would provide conclusive proof that a test did, or did not, take place.

In August 1980, Sappenfield and his two colleagues at Mission Research Corporation completed an expanded version of their December 1979 study. They reached the same basic conclusion as they had nine months earlier—that the likelihood of a nuclear explosion was much higher than the likelihood of any nonnuclear explanation for the triggering of the bhangmeters. They concluded for the first time that the reading of the less sensitive bhangmeter was more likely to be correct, and that the data from that sensor indicated a surface burst. They also argued that there were some serious flaws

---

* The aide was apparently referring to a weak signal that arrived before the signal that the NRL concluded had been reflected off Antarctica. Berman has noted the arrival of a very weak signal following the Vela detection. Interview with Alan Berman, Alexandria, Va., March 27, 2003.

with the Press panel's meteoroid theory—that the natural speed of objects spun off the satellite by a meteoroid would be one-tenth the speed required to generate the double-flash signature, and that the objects would be going in the wrong direction.[109]

In April 1981 a trio of Los Alamos scientists noted that about two minutes after the Vela detection, a Tiros-N weather satellite detected an "electron precipitation event." While the event was "unusually large," they did not find it to be unique, and suggested it was probably due to natural causes. They also noted that a patch of auroral light suddenly appeared in the sky above Syowa Base in Antarctica a few seconds after the Vela event, which was consistent with, but not proof of, an electromagnetic pulse resulting from a surface nuclear burst.[110]

In addition, the authors noted that it was possible to study natural and weapons-related perturbations of the ionosphere by monitoring long-path VLF transmissions, and that the U.S. Navy operated eight Omega VLF transmitters for navigational purposes. Since a nuclear explosion might have affected transmissions in the region, they examined transmissions along two different paths that cross that region. Neither yielded evidence of any abnormal variations at the time of the double flash.[111]

A January 1982 report by Carl J. Rice of the Aerospace Corporation, whose mission was to provide technical support to NRO and air force space programs, focused on the infrared data obtained by the two DSP satellites (Flights 6 and 7) whose footprints overlapped that of Vela 6911. A pair of signals, with the appropriate differences in time and intensity corresponding to a double flash, would suggest that a nuclear test had occurred, as would a single, but sufficiently bright, pulse. One problem facing the author was the lack of precise information about where the "detonation" took place. The initial signal from a low-yield detonation would not necessarily stand out from the variety of other infrared signals that the DSP spacecraft would pick up during their scans of the South Atlantic region. An initial signal of sufficient intensity would be noticed, as would a lower-yield signal at a precise suspect location. In the end, no confirmation of a test could be found—while at least one signal merited special attention, it was insufficiently intense and "very unlikely to represent the nuclear event in question."[112]

In May, four Los Alamos scientists completed their study of the Vela signal. They discounted a number of explanations for the discrepancies in the bhangmeter readings, including atmospheric absorption of the signal or cloud cover. They went on to present their own model for the September 22 event, a model that remains largely classified but may have relied on the effect of surface bursts on bhangmeter readings. However, it does seem likely that the authors shared the belief of many of their colleagues at Los Alamos and Sandia that the September 22 event was a nuclear test, as they wrote that "our model is consistent with the apparent absence of nuclear debris, the collection of which is required by some analysts for absolute confirmation of an atmospheric detonation."[113]

WHILE THE OFFICIAL STUDIES of the Vela incident would decline over the years, there would be continued speculation and reporting in the media. One of the first allegations came on February 21, 1980, when CBS aired a story by correspondent Dan Raviv, who quoted from a book—*None Will Survive Us: The Story of the Israeli Atom Bomb*—written by Israeli journalists Eli Teicher and Ami Dor-on. Although a novel, it recounted Israel's path toward nuclear weapons—apparently accurately enough that the Israeli censor refused to permit its publication. Raviv also interviewed the authors, who claimed the September 22 event was a nuclear test conducted by Israel with South African assistance. In response, a spokesman for Israeli defense minister Ezer Weizman quoted him as stating that "nothing like that took place."[114]

A similar charge was made on December 21, 1980, when Israeli state television broadcast a British-made program on Israeli–South African nuclear cooperation, which alleged that the 1979 flash came from a test of a new naval nuclear warhead, developed jointly by South Africa and Israel.[115]

In his 1991 book, investigative journalist Seymour Hersh reported that Vela 6911 had detected, according to former Israeli government officials "whose information has been corroborated," the test of a low-yield nuclear artillery shell and that the test was not the first, but the third Indian Ocean test. At least two ships from the Israeli navy had sailed to the site ahead of time, and a group of Israeli military officials and nuclear experts, as well as the South African navy, observed the test, according to Hersh. A similar accusation was made by Dieter Gerhardt, who was subsequently convicted of spying for the Soviet Union, but at the time was commander of the Simonstown naval base near Cape Town. He said that shortly before the Vela detection, a fleet of Israeli ships had made a port call at the naval base and that the flash was the result of a joint Israeli–South African test, Operation Phoenix. The test was supposed to have gone unobserved, according to Hersh's source: "There was a storm and we figured it would block Vela, but there was a gap in the weather—a window." It has also been suggested that Israel may have received information that the Vela bhangmeters were no longer working.[116]

In April 1997 an article in the Israeli *Ha'aretz* daily newspaper stated that South African deputy foreign minister Aziz Pahad confirmed that the double flash had resulted from a test, although he did not suggest that Israel was involved. In July the Los Alamos *Laboratory News Bulletin* ran an article based on the supposed revelation, with the headline "Blast from the Past: Lab Scientists Received Vindication." The *Albuquerque Journal* also followed up on the apparent disclosure, reporting comments from David Simons, a Los Alamos physicist, who had joined the lab's verification program in 1979, that similar discrepancies had been observed in Vela bhangmeter signals from earlier atmospheric tests.* It also reported the belief of one expert who helped design the satellite that the panel's explanation of how a near-perfect image of a nuclear explosion could be caused by a meteoroid strained credulity. He added that when an explanation was needed, "the zoo animals come marching out of the woodwork."[117]

Later that month *Aviation Week & Space Technology* ran a similar story, stating that "a South African government official has confirmed that his nation detonated a nuclear weapon in the atmosphere in September 1979." But Pahad's press secretary disputed the reports, stating that Pahad had merely noted the "strong rumor" that a test had occurred, and suggested the allegation should be investigated.[118]

MANY WHO directly confronted the issue at the time—whether as intelligence producers or consumers—believe that a test did take place and that Israel was probably responsible. Adm. Stansfield Turner, Carter's director of central intelligence, believes the Vela detection of September 22 was of "a man-made phenomenon." Several natural phenomena would have had to take place at the same time to simulate a nuclear blast, requiring a degree of coincidence Turner finds implausible. Leonard Spector, an expert on nuclear proliferation, who was at the time an aide to Senator John Glenn and received a number of intelligence briefings on the incident, recalls that he was "uncomfortable with the Ruina report." His impression is that the accretion of evidence points to Israel.[119]

Another former Glenn aide who attended some of the same Vela incident briefings with Spector, as well as others that Spector did not have the clearances to attend, was his boss, Leonard Weiss. Weiss gave up his position as a professor of applied mathematics at the University of Maryland to join the senator's staff, where he worked on nonproliferation issues for over two decades. When he first heard of the incident, he "jumped on it" and asked for a briefing. He recalls that his briefers were "too zealous in trying to tell us that nothing happened." His initial conclusion was that a test had taken place, and he

---

* According to one individual involved in the Vela incident debate, the same bhangmeter discrepancy occurred on a previous Chinese test, possibly the atmospheric test of September 13, 1979. Richard Garwin recalls that the only significant discrepancy was between the September 22 event and all nuclear detonations detected by Vela 6911. Private information; e-mail from Richard Garwin, November 4, 2004.

was prepared to say so in an interview with the *CBS Evening News*. Before he could, the White House warned Glenn that if such a claim was made, "all hell would break loose." Glenn told his aide, as the television crew was setting up in Weiss's office, that while he could go on the air, he could not make such an unequivocal claim.[120]

A few weeks after that interview Weiss finally received access to AFTAC's data base of zoo events—access that he had sought, and originally been denied, given claims that the Vela signal might have been the result of a zoo event. Weiss recalls that when he examined the Vela zoo, he was "astounded"—it was clear to him that "this was no zoo animal." Rather, it was the "classic wave produced by a nuclear explosion," with its double hump. It was "unmistakable." The inability to detect radiation associated with a test was not surprising, he remembers, because for some French tests, of which the United States had advanced knowledge, monitoring aircraft were not able to find the plume or found it late. He also recalls that there was "hardly anybody in the intelligence community who didn't think it was a test."[121]

That view was not shared by Press panel member Luis Alvarez. In his 1987 memoirs, he wrote, "I doubt that any responsible person now believes that a nuclear explosion occurred because no one has broken security, among South Africans or elsewhere."* During the summer of 1994 many of Alvarez's colleagues on the presidential panel met in San Diego at a meeting of the JASON group, which consists of scientists from outside the government who provide their expert advice to the Department of Defense. They received CIA briefings, largely on the lack of new evidence concerning the incident that had appeared in recent years, and, according to Jack Ruina, "found no reason to change their mind."[122]

New information in the early 1990s suggested that South Africa was not responsible, at least not by itself, for any test that occurred on September 22, 1979.† As of 1995 the U.S. intelligence community had not reached an *official* consensus about the cause of the double flash. But according to one account, based on interviews with U.S. officials, "unofficially, the widespread view in

---

* Given the decades-long veil of secrecy concerning many highly classified projects in the United States, including satellite reconnaissance projects, Alvarez was far from being on solid ground. Daniel Ellsberg has noted that "secrets that would be of the greatest importance to [the public, Congress, and the press] can be kept from them reliably for decades by the executive branch, even though they are known to thousands of insiders." The veil of secrecy is far tighter in Israel, where military censors are able to review and withhold news considered damaging to national security. See Daniel Ellsberg, *Secrets: A Memoir of the Pentagon Papers* (New York: Viking, 2002), p. 43.

† See chapter 9.

the U.S. government was that the Vela satellite had detected the test of a low-yield nuclear bomb and that Israel alone was responsible."[123]

Spurgeon Keeny, in early 2003, described himself as "uncertain" as to whether Vela 6911 detected a nuclear explosion on September 22, 1979. He noted that an Israeli technician studying at MIT, and "clearly an Israeli agent," as well as a few Israeli officials hinted that Israel did conduct a test that day. However, he argued, if Israel had conducted a test, it would have involved a major expedition. The resulting spread of knowledge about the activity, along with the conflicts of personalities that make up Israeli politics, would have resulted in disclosure of the test, he believed. Ruina, in 2004, argued that if it was a nuclear explosion, it was clearly in the 2- to 3-kiloton range—in contrast to the standard yield of first tests, between 15 and 20 kilotons. That Israel might have detonated a low-yield neutron bomb is a hypothesis he considered "far fetched, then and now."[124]

There remains a lack of hard evidence, and if Israel did indeed test a nuclear weapon that day, it is unlikely that former Israeli officials will come forth or that Israeli documents confirming Israeli involvement will emerge—at least any time soon.

chapter eight

ROGUES

WHATEVER ANXIETY the Vela incident produced in America's top national security officials represented only a fraction of the concern they would experience in response to the efforts of a trio of rogue states to acquire nuclear weapons. By 1980 North Korea, Libya, and Iraq were virtually personal possessions of Kim Il Sung, Muammar Qadhafi, and Saddam Hussein, respectively.[1] Each was supported by a military and security apparatus that controlled, and often terrorized, his nation's population. Gen. Mohammad Zia ul-Haq, the leader of Pakistan, was not in the same class as Hussein, Qadhafi, and Kim, but his nuclear policies would still cause considerable anxiety.

KIM, NORTH KOREA'S "Great Leader," was the ruler with the longest tenure. Born in 1912, by early 1934 he had become a member of the Northeast Anti-Japanese United Army, a Communist guerilla force. In 1940, with Japanese forces in the midst of a crackdown on partisan activities, Kim fled across the border into the Soviet Union, where he was arrested by Soviet border guards. Along with other survivors of his group, he became a charter member of the 88th Special Independent Sniper Brigade in August 1942, a unit that reported to the Soviet Far East Command's Reconnaissance Bureau. In September 1945, after Japan's defeat in World War II, Kim returned to Korea as a captain in the Soviet army but gradually became the Soviets' first choice to assume leadership of the new Communist Korean state. In the thirty-one-plus years from September 1948, when the Democratic People's Republic of Korea (DPRK) was established, to 1980, Kim's regime had managed to invade South Korea, seize a U.S. intelligence ship in international waters, shoot down a U.S. electronic reconnaissance aircraft, killing all aboard, and engage in assorted acts of terrorism and abduction. More bad behavior would follow in the 1980s.[2]

About two decades after Kim became head of the DPRK, a group of Libyan military officers, known as the Free Officers, ousted the pro-American King Idris, who was vacationing abroad. They then terminated U.S. use of Wheelus Air Base and set Libya on a new, revolutionary course, which included supporting and conducting acts of terrorism. It was not long after the September 1, 1969, coup that Capt. (and later Col.) Muammar Qadhafi, who claimed to be only twenty-seven years old, emerged as the key figure in the council. Like Kim, he would become the focus of a personality cult. Several volumes of his *Green Book*, an exposition of his "Third Universal Theory," which not surprisingly denounced the concept of representative government, would be published in Libya so that his "wisdom" could be disseminated among the nation's citizens. This wisdom saw Libya pursue a nuclear bomb, a major confrontation with the United States, and an act of terrorism that killed hundreds of air travelers in a single morning.[3]

In contrast to Qadhafi, Saddam Hussein's path to power ran through a political organization rather than the military. In 1957, at the age of twenty, the future Iraqi dictator joined the socialist Baath Party. The next year, a military coup swept away Iraq's monarchy. Ten years later Saddam played a major role in the coup that installed a Baathist regime, becoming deputy chairman of the Revolutionary Command Council and the second most powerful man in Iraq, behind President Ahmed Hassan al-Bakr. Long before July 1979, when he became Iraq's president after al-Bakr resigned, ostensibly for health reasons, Saddam had become the most powerful. His formal ascent to the top position was followed by a bloody purge of the party and then, in 1980, war with Iran.[4]

General Zia ul-Haq was also not above using violence to eliminate political opponents, but he was far more selective. In July 1977 he ousted Pakistan's civilian leader, the flamboyant Zulfikar Ali Bhutto. In April 1979, despite the pleas of foreign leaders, including Jimmy Carter, Bhutto met death at the end of a rope in a Rawalpindi prison, having been convicted of assorted crimes, including murder. Zia would become an increasingly devout adherent of Islam until his death in a 1988 plane crash, which also took the life of U.S. ambassador Arnold Raphael. He was replaced by an elected prime minister, Benazir Bhutto, a product of Radcliffe and Oxford, and the daughter of the man whose execution he had engineered.[5]

SADDAM WAS the driving force behind Iraq's attempt to acquire nuclear weapons. Iraq's nuclear program had modest origins, beginning with the creation of the Iraqi Atomic Energy Commission in January 1959. In the mid-1960s the Soviet Union agreed to provide nuclear research facilities, including a small 2-megawatt research reactor. Reactor operations began in late 1967 or early 1968 at the new Nuclear Research Center at Tuwaitha, located about thirteen miles southeast of Baghdad.[6]

In December 1974 French prime minister Jacques Chirac arrived in Iraq, where he was hosted by Saddam. India's detonation of its first atomic device earlier that year may have sparked an Iraqi desire to develop similar capabilities. The late 1974 meeting represented a first step toward the contract signed in Paris in late August 1976, a contract worth over one billion francs to France's nuclear industry. In exchange, Iraq received two small reactors, including a 70-megawatt thermal "experimental" reactor, similar to the Osiris reactor at France's nuclear research center at Saclay. The similarity led the French to call the reactor-to-be Osiraq, although Saddam renamed it Tammuz I—the smaller reactor became Tammuz II—to commemorate the Baathist revolution, which occurred in July (*Tammuz* in Arabic). Tammuz I would look like a large, open swimming pool with a reactor core at the center.[7]

A reprocessing capability would also be needed to extract the plutonium from the spent reactor fuel, a requirement satisfied by another contract, this one with an Italian firm. Iraq would be provided with five new laboratories. Four were "cold labs" that lacked the shielding needed to permit work with irradiated plutonium or other radioactive substances. However, the fifth lab was a radiochemistry lab, with three hot cells, that was expected to be operational before the end of 1981.[8]

While foreign firms could provide the hardware for Iraq's nuclear program, Iraq itself had to provide the key personnel. In some cases their participation was the result of coercion, not choice. It was made clear to Khidir Hamza, who was teaching in a small Georgia college, after obtaining a master's degree at MIT and a doctorate in theoretical nuclear physics at Florida State University, that he had to return to Iraq for his father's sake. Hamza, who would eventually be appointed to head the weapons design segment of the Iraqi nuclear weapons effort, returned to Iraq in 1970. In 1975, along with another prominent Iraqi physicist, Mahdi Obeidi, he visited the Los Alamos laboratory to learn about new technologies for enriching uranium.[9]

In the latter half of 1981, thirty-eight-year-old Jaffar Dhia Jaffar, who had been appointed vice chairman of the Iraqi Atomic Energy Commission by 1979, became the head of his nation's effort to join the nuclear club. Jaffar had returned to Iraq in April 1975, one of four thousand scientists recruited between 1974 and 1977 to work on Iraq's nuclear program. British-trained, he had obtained his bachelor's and master's degrees at the University of Birmingham and then moved on to the University of Manchester for his doctorate. In the early 1970s he had left his job at the commission to visit the European nuclear research center CERN, where he became familiar with cyclotron technology, and the British nuclear center at Harwell. In early 1975, shortly before his return to Iraq, he had applied for a professorship at Britain's Imperial College, where he had previously worked as an assistant researcher, but was turned down.[10]

By that time he had become "an urbane Shiite bon vivant who loved 'starred' restaurants, excellent whiskey, bridge, squash, and tailor-made suits from Milan, his favorite city." His return to Iraq may have been the result of his application being rejected or of as-yet-unknown coercion. But in 1980 coercion was one means of persuasion. In 1979 Hussein al-Sharistani, the commission's chief of research and a friend, was arrested. A combination of the intensely religious Sharistini's close ties with Shiite clergy, which included his uncle, the war with Shiite-ruled Iran, unfounded rumors of his complicity in attempts to sabotage Tammuz I, and Saddam's paranoia resulted in his being tortured for twenty-two days at the Abu Ghraib military barracks.[11]

In February 1980, after attempts to get his friend released, Jaffar found himself under house arrest, a sentence that lasted twenty months. Both men were offered a choice: remain prisoners or resume work on Iraq's nuclear program and receive extravagant benefits. Upon being told that the main objective was a nuclear weapon, Sharistani, according to his account, refused and continued to refuse. Jaffar took some convincing, which included a brief stay in prison, where he was forced to watch guards break the back of an elderly man, but eventually capitulated. He became the head of Iraq's nuclear weapons program in September 1981.[12]

In other cases, such as that of Imad Khadduri, no coercion was needed. His six-year stay in the United States during the 1960s "heightened his appreciation of the richness and warmth of Arab culture" and led him to decide that he would only marry an Iraqi and that their children would be raised in the "warm and generous atmosphere of the deeply rich Iraqi culture." He first joined the Tuwaitha center in 1968. After obtaining his doctorate from the University of Birmingham, he rejoined the Nuclear Research Center in January 1974, going to work in the reactor department. Later that year he proposed an expedition to locate uranium, which "struck it rich" near Al Qaim, in the vicinity of the Syrian border. In 1978 he would collaborate with Jaffar to produce *The Possible Production of Pu^{239} from the IRT-5000 Reactor*, a study of the possible use of the Soviet-provided reactor at Tuwaitha to produce weapons-grade plutonium. Eventually Khadduri would play a key role in Iraq's overt and covert acquisition of science and technical information.[13]

Another willing participant was Egyptian physicist Yehya al-Meshad, who had studied nuclear engineering in the United States and the Soviet Union. After working for the Egyptian Atomic Energy Commission from 1961 to 1968, he became a professor of nuclear engineering at the University of Alexandria. He spent two years in the mid-1970s teaching at Baghdad's University of Technology. During that time al-Meshad also assisted the Iraqi atomic energy effort, producing, in collaboration with Khadduri, a computer code that permitted the calculation of critical mass. Rather than seek employment in the United States or Europe, al-Meshad offered to stay in Iraq, telling Khadduri that he wanted to raise his children in a Moslem country, and was hired by the atomic energy commission in 1977.[14]

WHILE IRAQ'S nuclear efforts in the 1970s did not particularly concern U.S. or West European leaders, the same could not be said about Israeli prime minister Menachem Begin and several of his key advisors. Saddam himself had provided the warning, when, in September 1975, he described the search for a reactor as part of "the first Arab attempt at nuclear arming." That message was repeated in 1978 by Naim Hadad, a senior member of the Revolutionary Command Council, who declared, "If Israel owns the atom bomb, then the Arabs must get an atom bomb." Iraq's refusal to accept low-enriched uranium to fuel the Tammuz I reactor, rather than the originally promised highly enriched uranium, also concerned Israel, since the latter could be diverted for use in a weapon.[15]

Israel tried, in a variety of ways, to halt the project. Attempts were made to influence international opinion by providing information about the reactor to media outlets, including the *London Daily Mail*. Between 1975 and 1981, Israeli officials held discussions with French officials to convey their concern. In July 1977 the Israeli ambassador in Paris had requested that France substitute the low-enriched "caramel" that Iraq would refuse the following year. Covert action included the sending of multiple threatening letters to scientists and technicians involved in the project—letters signed by the fictitious "Committee to Safeguard the Islamic Revolution."[16]

Israel also employed covert measures. On April 6, 1979, the storerooms of a French nuclear plant at La Seyne-sur-Mer, where the Tammuz I reactor core was under construction, received some uninvited visitors, who blew the core up just days before it was to be shipped to Iraq. The previously unknown, and never heard from again, "French Ecological Group" called to take responsibility—although the French security service, the DST, suspected the attack had been engineered by Israel's Institute for Intelligence and Special Tasks, better known as Mossad.[17]

While no one was killed in the April 1979 attack, the same could not be said of the suspected Mossad action in June 1980. On June 14 a chambermaid discovered Yehya al-Meshad's body in his hotel room in Paris, where he had traveled to complete arrangements with the French for the supply of nuclear fuel to Iraq. The Egyptian physicist had been bludgeoned and left to die. While there was no proof of Israeli involvement, the Mossad—which had also used violence in the 1960s to "discourage" German scientists from working on the Egyptian missile program—was a logical candidate. At the same time, the nature of the attack and his being left alive did not appear to be consistent with a Mossad operation.[18]

The final strike against the Tammuz project came about a year later, from the air. This time there would be no doubt about who was responsible, nor any Israeli reticence in acknowledging its involvement, which brought the expected UN condemnation. Israel's action might not have taken place had Iran's aerial attack on the Tuwaitha site, in the early days of the Iran-Iraq war, been more successful. After it became apparent that the Iranian attack had inflicted only minor damage, Israeli officials began considering letting the Israeli air force finish the job. While a number of senior Israeli officials, including Mossad chief Yitzhak Hofi, deputy prime minister Yigal Yadin, and chief of military intelligence Gen. Yehoshua Saguy, opposed such an attack, a majority, most importantly Begin, favored a strike.[19]

Primary responsibility for developing plans that would allow Israeli pilots to evade Iraqi air defenses and destroy their target belonged to the Israeli air force's operations chief, Aviem Sella, who would become better known in the 1980s for his role in the Jonathan Pollard spy case. The operation, developed under the code name Scorch Sword by Sella and his staff, was carried out on June 7, 1981, as Operation Babylon. Eight Israeli pilots, including Ilan Ramon—who later died in the explosion of the space shuttle *Columbia* in February 2003—flew their F-16s over Saudi Arabia and Jordan, evaded Iraqi antiaircraft defenses, and destroyed the reactor core and the buildings nearby.[20]

Imad Khadduri recalls that "the bombing occurred in late afternoon and after most of the staff had returned home. We heard the blasts and ran to the rooftops. We could see the cloud plumes even tens of kilometers away. We sadly watched the unchallenged Israeli warplanes streaking west in the setting sun." Hamza remembers the Israeli jets sweeping over the rooftops "with a ground-shaking roar" and "an explosion, then another, then another." The F-16s were "buzzing like hornets over the aluminum dome of the French reactor."[21]

The next day, the Israeli government released a statement acknowledging the role of its air force in the attack. The release also explained that "for a long time we have been watching with growing concern the construction of the [Tammuz I] atomic reactor. . . . From sources whose reliability is beyond any doubt, we learn that this reactor, despite its camouflage, is designed to produce atomic bombs." The timing of the attack, according to the Israeli statement, was determined by the plan to complete the reactor in July 1981 and begin operations in September. Since bombing the reactor after it had become operational would result in "radioactive lethal fallout over the city of Baghdad," it was necessary to "act without further delay to ensure our people's existence."[22]

THE ISRAELI RAID led Iraq to review the future of its nuclear program, a review which concluded that while Baghdad should continue its project to acquire nuclear weapons, it should take a different path to reach its objective.

Rather than developing a plutonium bomb, which required reactors such as Tammuz I, Iraq should covertly develop a uranium enrichment capability while appearing to remain in compliance with the Nuclear Non-Proliferation Treaty. A key factor was the desire of the military and security services to avoid attention being drawn to the program, attention that could complicate procurement and development activities. The argument, according to Jaffar, was "let Israel believe it destroyed our nuclear capacity, accept the sympathy being offered for this aggression and proceed in secret with the program."[23]

On September 3, 1981, the reeducated Jaffar Dhia Jaffar arrived at the Nuclear Research Center at Tuwaitha, with the covert mission of providing Saddam and his regime with atomic weapons. The center itself, under Khalid Said, was designated Department 6000 of the Iraqi Atomic Energy Commission, while Jaffar's unit, Research and Development, was known as Department 3000.[24]

Between 1982 and 1987, Jaffar and his associates established at least six secret weapons laboratories at Tuwaitha. The Nuclear Physics Building contained labs for the research and testing of calutrons (also referred to as "baghdatrons") for electromagnetic separation. Centrifuges were the object of study in the Chemical Research Building, while a solvent extraction method developed by the French was the focus of the activities in the Polymer Chemistry Research Laboratory. Reprocessing was the responsibility of the Chemical and Radiochemical Analysis Laboratory.[25]

In the summer of 1987, Department 3000 was renamed, and purposely misnamed, Petrochemical-3—two 1980s refinery projects had been designated PC-1 and PC-2. The project was also reorganized into four key groups. Group 1, headed by Mahdi Obeidi, was assigned responsibility for developing a gas centrifuge process. Jaffar, in addition to his other duties, headed Group 2, which soon came to focus on electromagnetic isotope separation, a technology considered obsolete in the West. Administrative support, which included document acquisition and covert procurement as well as some manufacturing and engineering tasks, was the mission of Group 3, headed by Dhafir Selbi, who had joined the British-run Iraqi Petroleum Corporation after receiving an engineering degree from Baghdad University and moved on to the atomic energy commission in the late 1970s. Selbi played a key role in switching the focus of Group 2 to electromagnetic separation. Khidir Hamza was appointed as the head of Group 4, responsible for bomb design, but was soon replaced by Khalid Said after misappropriating several air conditioners for personal use.[26]

Reorganization was not the only key development in 1987 and 1988. In 1987 Iraq recruited a Yugoslav firm to build its first electromagnetic isotope separation production facility, in Tarmiya, north of Baghdad. The facility was expected to produce thirty-three pounds of weapons-grade uranium per year, according to a September 1987 document titled "New Procedures for Setting Up and Operating the Third Phase of a Separation System." Late that year Iraq decided to build a replica of Tarmiya at Ash Sharqat, about 130 miles northwest of Baghdad, in anticipation that it would become operational at about the same time as Tarmiya and be the second production facility.[27]

There were also significant developments in the gaseous diffusion program in the late 1980s. Possibly due to a conflict between Jaffar and Obeidi, who at that time headed the gaseous diffusion effort, the group charged with developing gaseous diffusion technologies was transferred from Tuwaitha to a new site near Rashdiya, on the northern edge of Baghdad, which was subsequently named Engineering Design Center. In 1987 or 1988 the Iraqi leadership concluded that the gaseous diffusion effort was not living up to expectations, and decided to deemphasize it in favor of centrifuges as a means of providing low-enriched uranium for the electromagnetic separation program.[28]

In late 1988 almost all of the nuclear weapons effort was placed under the direction of Hussein Kamel, Saddam's powerful son-in-law, who had become the head of the Ministry of Industry and Military Industrialization when the ministry was established that May. Jaffar became deputy minister while the directors of the major programs were made ministry director-generals. Appointed to supervise the entire weapons of mass destruction effort—to be Iraq's Leslie Groves for chemical, biological, and nuclear weapons—was the senior deputy minister of the ministry, Gen. Amir Hammoudi al-Saadi, who had received a doctorate in chemistry from the University of Munich, and had overseen the development of the Al-Abbas missile, a variant of the Soviet Scud.[29]

By the end of 1988 the groundwork had been laid for a dramatic expansion of the Iraqi nuclear effort. But Iraq already had a number of facilities of its nuclear complex up and running. The Tuwaitha Nuclear Research Center had been deprived of the Tammuz I reactor by the Israeli raid, but was still operating the Soviet IRT-5000 and the French Tammuz II reactors, although they could not provide the plutonium needed for a bomb. Also operational were a variety of administration and research facilities, including the radiochemical building, an isotope production laboratory, Building 86 for the mechanical design teams, a building that housed the labs for the electronic department, and the power substation. There also was the Akashat phosphate mine and the Al Qaim facility for the production of uranium oxide, the direct result of Imad Khadduri's search for uranium in 1974.[30]

IN JUNE 1981, the same month that Israel handed Iraq's nuclear weapons program a major setback, Qadhafi told *Time* magazine that he and his nation were not interested in such weapons. "We put the production of nuclear weapons," he proclaimed, "at the top of the list of terrorist activities. As long as the big powers continue to manufacture atomic weapons, it means that they are continuing to terrorize the world. . . . I have nothing but scorn for the notion of an Islamic bomb. . . . Any such weapon is a means of terrorizing humanity, and we are against the manufacture and acquisition of nuclear weapons."[31]

Of course, he was lying. About a week after his *Time* interview and a few days after the Israeli raid on Tammuz I, the Libyan leader apparently held a secret meeting with five key advisers. He told them that he would employ "all Libya's financial resources" to obtain a nuclear weapon from Pakistan or the technology to produce weapons-grade enriched uranium. But the meeting did not represent a sudden change of heart caused by the Israeli raid, for Libya's quest for atomic weapons had started over a decade earlier.[32]

In 1970 Qadhafi had sent Abdul Jalloud, vice chairman of the Revolutionary Command Council, to Cairo to ask for Egyptian president Gamal Abdel Nasser's help in obtaining nuclear weapons from China. Although Nasser told his visitor that such weapons were not for sale, Jalloud traveled to China incognito and on an Egyptian passport, by way of Pakistan and India. As Nasser predicted, China was not willing to sell Libya a weapon. Zhou Enlai exhibited "perfect Chinese courtesy," but stressed the virtues of self-reliance and offered some general assistance in the area of nuclear research.[33]

In the face of China's refusal to provide a ready-made bomb, Libya began a two-track program to enhance its nuclear capabilities. Covert operations were conducted to quickly acquire nuclear weapons or at least the crucial ingredients and equipment needed to build them. They reportedly included a standing offer of one million dollars in gold to anyone who would provide Libya with an atomic bomb.[34] Overt activities were geared toward developing a nuclear research and energy program similar to the programs in other developing nations, as well as acquiring bomb-related material.

In 1973 Libyan representatives offered to purchase twenty large electromagnets from a French firm, Thompson-CSF, apparently for electromagnetic separation, but the French government vetoed the sale. That same year, Libya reportedly reached a secret agreement with Pakistani president Zulkifar Ali Bhutto. Libya would finance the Pakistani nuclear weapons program in exchange for "full access" to "the entire capability" to be developed. In addition, Libya requested that Pakistan provide training in hot-cell operations. It was also reported that Libya was willing to finance a large reprocessing plant that Pakistan was interested in buying from France, if Pakistan provided some of the plutonium produced.[35]

The following year, as part of its effort to develop an open, apparently benign nuclear program, Libya asked a U.S. manufacturer of research reactors used in developing nations if it would like to sell Libya a full reactor, along with some fuel. The firm was quite willing to say yes, but the White House, State Department, and Congress said no. That same year Argentina, which possessed one of the most advanced nuclear programs of developing countries, agreed to provide Qadhafi's regime with general assistance as well as equipment and training related to uranium prospecting, extraction, and purification.[36]

In 1975 Qadhafi demanded that Palestine Liberation Organization chief Yasser Arafat undertake a clandestine project—he was to assemble a group of Arab scientists to build a bomb—a command, Arafat was afraid to tell Qadhafi, that was impossible to carry out due to a lack of qualified personnel. More overtly, that June the Soviet Union announced that it had agreed to build a small, 10-megawatt research reactor in Libya, along with an atomic research center. A year later another Libyan-Soviet nuclear agreement was reached in principle, this time for construction of a 440-megawatt nuclear power reactor. Both sales were made possible by Libya's ratification of the Nuclear Non-Proliferation Treaty, although the country would not reach a safeguards agreement with the inspection authority—the International Atomic Energy Agency—until 1980.[37]

Libya's quest to obtain assistance in developing nuclear weapons continued in 1978, with approaches to both India and Pakistan. During a July visit to New Delhi for the signing of an agreement on peaceful nuclear cooperation, Jalloud, then the Libyan prime minister, reportedly pressed Indian officials to pledge that their government would help Libya to obtain "an independent nuclear capability." India's refusal over the next year to provide weapons-related assistance resulted in Libya's termination of oil shipments to India, but no change in New Delhi's refusal to help Libya gain entrance to the nuclear club.[38]

While Libya's cutting off of oil exports was designed to coerce India to do something it had not promised to do, Libya's purchase of several hundred tons of uranium concentrate from Niger between 1978 and 1980 was designed to induce Pakistan to fulfill a promise. The yellowcake was to be supplied to Pakistan's clandestine uranium enrichment program to "remind" its recipient to provide the nuclear weapons technology promised in 1973.[39]

In late 1981 the small research reactor that the Soviets agreed to build for Libya in 1975 began operations. Its home was the Tajoura Research Center, outside Tripoli and near the Okbah ibn Nafi Air Base (formerly Wheelus Air Base). Primary responsibility for reactor operations had been entrusted to Dr. Fathi Noor and Dr. Fathi Skinji, who were also in charge of the nuclear engineering faculty at Tripoli's Al Fatah University. Noor was trained at the University of California at Berkeley, while Skinji had studied in India and Britain.[40]

The following years involved a number of failed Libyan attempts to enhance its ability to develop nuclear weapons. In 1982 negotiations began with a Belgian firm that was willing to provide a plant for the production of uranium tetrafluoride. Two years later Belgian nuclear officials announced the imminent signing of a nuclear cooperation agreement with Libya, which would incorporate the sale of the tetrafluoride plant as well as provision of architectural-engineering services for the Soviet nuclear power plants that were still the subject of negotiations. The whole deal fell apart, however, when the United States objected and the Belgian government canceled the pending agreement. A year earlier Libya's attempt to buy a research reactor from Argentina also met with failure.[41]

In late 1984 Brazilian-Libyan discussions began on the supply of uranium prospecting and development services. Then, early in 1986, negotiations with the Soviet Union over the 440-megawatt reactor collapsed, and then started again in May, although by the end of 1988 no agreement had been concluded.[42] As the end of the decade approached, Libya's path to an atomic bomb faced significant roadblocks.

PAKISTAN'S QUEST for nuclear weapons began a couple of years after Libya's, but would be far more successful. Pakistan had first entered the nuclear arena in March 1956, with creation of the Atomic Energy Council, which consisted of a governing board and the Pakistan Atomic Energy Commission (PAEC). In 1960–1961 the Pakistan Institute of Nuclear Science and Technology (PINSTECH) was completed in Rawalpindi and in 1963 a 5-megawatt light-water research reactor was installed there. In May 1965 Canada agreed to provide a nuclear power plant to be located at Karachi, which would be designated the the Karachi Nuclear Power Project (KANUPP).[43]

But it was the country's devastating defeat in the 1971 Indo-Pakistani war—which resulted in the large, physically detached eastern portion of Pakistan becoming the independent nation of Bangladesh—that became "the turning point in the history of Pakistan's nuclear program," according to Indian defense analyst Matin Zuberi. Defeat led President Yahya Khan, in the face of military unrest, to turn power over to the eloquent, flamboyant, and arrogant Zulfikar Ali Bhutto. Bhutto had headed the natural resources and foreign affairs ministries (from 1958 to 1962 and 1963 to 1966, respectively), established the Pakistani People's Party in 1967, and joined Khan's government in 1971. Bhutto became president and chief martial law administrator, and after the elections that followed, he became prime minister. From the mid-1960s on, in his speeches and his writings, Bhutto had suggested that Pakistan might need to join the nuclear club, and pledged that the Pakistani people would make the necessary sacrifices for a bomb, even if it meant that they had "to eat grass."[44]

After assuming control of the government in December 1971, Bhutto placed the nuclear program under his direct control. Then, on January 20, 1972, he secretly met with a collection of the nation's top scientists and nuclear aides in Multan, a city in the center of Pakistan that was the home to commerce and industry as well as mosques, shrines, and beggars. He told his audience that what he wanted from them was an atomic bomb. It was an announcement that left the scientists "absolutely dumfounded," according to one participant who attended the meeting. After Bhutto's announcement, discussion followed on how long it would take to make Pakistan a nuclear weapons state. Bhutto wanted a bomb in his hands in three years, but one scientist pointed out, "It isn't like firecrackers you know. We don't know how long it will take." But Bhutto was told it was a mission that could be accomplished given sufficient resources and facilities, which he promised to provide.[45]

Former PAEC chairman Munir Ahmed Khan claims that India's nuclear test spurred Pakistan to become more determined to obtain its own weapons. But it was in March 1973, more than a year before the first Indian test, that Pakistan and France's Saint Gobain Nucléaire signed a contract for the basic design for a large reprocessing plant. A second contract would be signed in October 1974. The facility was to be located at Chashma (Hot Spring), about 120 miles southwest of Islamabad, in the north-central part of the country. Pakistan had several reactors that might eventually provide the material to be reprocessed into fissile material, despite their being under IAEA safeguards. One was the heavy-water, natural-uranium KANUPP reactor, completed in 1972. Another was a 500-megawatt reactor to be built near the planned Chashma reprocessing facility. There were also heavy-water reactors at Multan and Karachi, the later of the two becoming operational in 1976.[46]

That same year a team from the PAEC conducted a survey of the Chagai Hills region, a remote section of the Baluchistan desert near the Iranian border, and selected the mountain at Ras Koh for a test site. A geological survey of the area followed to verify that there was no ground water as well as to ensure that the 2,295-foot mountain could withstand a 20-kiloton test. Brig. Mohammad Sarfaraz was assigned to prepare an underground test site and created the Special Development Works, which would complete its first tunnel—3,325 feet long and 8 to 9 feet in diameter—in 1980.[47]

Also in 1976, U.S. anxiety over Pakistan's possible use of the planned reprocessing facility to produce fissile material for bombs reached the point where President Gerald Ford sent his secretary of state, Henry Kissinger, to Paris in what proved to be a failed attempt to halt sale of the SGN reprocessing plant. But in August 1977, the month after Bhutto was ousted by his military, the French did suspend deliveries for the plant. The suspension was not a reaction to Bhutto's fall from grace, but followed U.S. disclosure to French officials of intelligence concerning Pakistan's actual nuclear plans. In June 1978, a few months after Pakistan refused to accept a form of reprocessing for the plant that would have prevented the production of weapons-grade pluto-nium, the French government's Council on Foreign Nuclear Policy formally decided to terminate the SGN contract, although up to 95 percent of the blueprints for the facility may have already been provided to Pakistan.[48]

Whatever construction continued on the Chashma reprocessing plant throughout the 1980s did not bring it close to completion. During that decade Pakistan did establish two facilities with a reprocessing mission—an experi-mental unit at PINSTECH in Rawalpindi, and the nearby "New Labs" pluto-nium extraction plant, possibly capable of extracting twenty-two to forty-four pounds of plutonium each year, although it is not clear that it produced any weapons-grade material during the decade.[49]

In any case, by the time France backed out of the Chashma contract, Pakistan was also pursuing the uranium enrichment path to the bomb. In 1975 Pakistan began to acquire the hardware and technology needed for a facility containing high-speed centrifuges to separate U-235 from U-238. The key figure in that effort was Dr. Abdul Qadeer Khan, characterized by a British newspaper as "the most successful nuclear spy since Klaus Fuchs and Allan Nunn May took their secrets to the Kremlin." Born in 1936 in Bhopal, part of British India at the time, Khan arrived in Europe in the early 1960s for graduate studies. His first stop was Germany, where he became fluent in Ger-man while studying at the Technische Universität in West Berlin. He then went to the Netherlands to study at the prestigious Technical University of Delft from 1963 to 1967, a stay that concluded when he received a degree in metallurgical engineering. He completed his studies in Belgium, whose Catholic University of Leuven awarded him a doctorate in 1972.[50]

Graduate work in Europe was followed by employment there, when Khan was hired by the Physical Dynamics Research Laboratory (FDO) in Amster-dam, a subsidiary of the Dutch firm Verenigde Machine-Fabrieken. The firm worked closely with the Uranium Enrichment Corporation (URENCO), a company established in 1970 to guarantee Britain, West Germany, and the Netherlands their own supply of enriched uranium to fuel their reactors.[51]

URENCO's enrichment plant, located in Almelo, the Netherlands, relied on highly classified ultracentrifuge technology to separate U-235 from U-238, by spinning the two isotopes up to 100,000 revolutions per minute. Khans's work at FDO and Almelo, where on occasion he would be assigned to translate technical documents, required a standard background investiga-tion by the Dutch security service, the BVD, which did not turn up any rea-son to terminate his employment. As a result of his work at FDO and Almelo,

Khan became familiar with the design plans for the enrichment facility as well as the companies that provided parts for the ultracentrifuges. In the fall of 1974, a few months after India detonated a nuclear device, he spent sixteen days in the Almelo facility's most sensitive area, translating from German into Dutch a highly classified technical report on a dramatic advance in centrifuge technology.[52]

During his time at FDO, Khan made regular trips to Pakistan. At the end of 1974, during one those of visits, he contacted some influential Pakistanis, suggested that the nation should attempt to develop a uranium enrichment capability, and explained what type of facilities would be needed. In February 1975 Munir Khan submitted a proposal to Bhutto for an enrichment project whose components included a centrifuge plant, a uranium mine at Baghalchor in Dera Ghazi Khan, a plant to manufacture uranium hexafluoride, and a weapons design program. Research and development work on enrichment technology began under the cover of a fictitious Directorate of Industrial Liaison, located in the barracks at Chaklala airport.[53]

In October 1975 the Dutch Ministry of Economic Affairs requested that FDO assign Khan to work that would deprive him of access to information about the sensitive centrifuge technology. Two months later Khan left for Pakistan, with his wife and daughter, on what appeared to be just another of his regular trips home. But rather than return to FDO, Khan sent a letter of resignation in his place, effective March 1, 1976.[54]

Beyond the impending transfer, Khan may been motivated to resign by the request of Pakistani officials. After arriving in Pakistan that December, he reportedly was asked to evaluate how much progress had been made toward building a bomb since his last visit. His assessment that little had been accomplished, due to attempts at empire building, led to his being asked to quit his job at Almelo, return home, and play a key role in the nuclear program.[55]

Khan brought back more than accumulated expertise and the knowledge that was in his head. Through his translation work, he obtained key plans, technical documents, and listings of component suppliers for the Dutch centrifuge — all of significant value to a nation working to develop its own capability. Upon his return, and seeing no progress being made, Khan wrote to Bhutto, who responded by inviting him to a meeting. Khan suggested that the project be made autonomous, and in July 1976 it was detached from the PAEC and Khan was transformed from being a critic of the uranium enrichment effort, which was designated Project 706, to its director.[56]

He assumed command of the newly created Engineering Research Laboratory (which would be renamed the Dr. A.Q. Khan Research Laboratories on May 1, 1981), whose mission was to design centrifuges and determine what items needed to be acquired. Among his most important tasks was overseeing the ongoing search for a site for a full-scale uranium enrichment facility. Ultimately, Kahuta, just to the east of Islamabad, in the rugged Himalayan foothills, was selected because it was close enough to the capital to permit close contact with key officials while also being, in Khan's words, "out of normal traffic," which was an important security consideration.[57]

In July 1977, one year after Khan assumed responsibility for the program, the design of the Kahuta facility was finalized. Land was purchased and construction began under the direction of Brig. Gen. Anees Ali Sayeed, head of the military's Special Works Organization. The following year a test of the uranium enrichment process was successful, which led to the search for a site for a pilot plant that could be in operation while construction of the much larger Kahuta plant was underway. Sihala, just to the southwest of Kahuta, was selected, and within a year the pilot plant was in operation. Kahuta would become operational in 1984. In December 1987 construction began on a second uranium enrichment plant, at a site in Golra, about six miles west of Islamabad.[58]

By the early 1980s a plant for transforming uranium powder into the uranium hexafluoride feedstock for the enrichment facilities had been established at Dera Ghazi Khan, about 225 miles southwest of Kahuta, near the Indus River. With help from the information Khan had brought back with him, Pakistan acquired and smuggled the plant, piece by piece, from West Germany between 1977 and 1980. Through the 1980s Khan oversaw an extensive procurement effort that yielded over six thousand tubes of maraging steel for centrifuges (from the Netherlands), precision equipment for a reprocessing plant (from Switzerland), electronic equipment for centrifuges (from a company in the United States, via Canada and Turkey), and a metal finishing plant (from the United Kingdom).[59]

By early 1984 Kahuta had produced enriched uranium, according to Khan. Subsequently, President Zia claimed that only low-enriched non-weapons-grade uranium had been produced. In March 1986 it was reported that Pakistan's enrichment efforts had progressed to the point where Kahuta was producing uranium enriched to 30 percent U-235, still far from weapons grade but a significant step in that direction. That same year, cold tests of an implosion device were conducted at Chaghai Hills. In 1987 Pakistan purchased a West German purification and production facility, capable of producing between five and ten grams of tritium a day. Also in 1987, in an interview with *Time* magazine, Zia claimed that Pakistan had not yet enriched uranium to weapons-grade level and did not intend to manufacture nuclear weapons, but also asserted that "Pakistan is capable of building the Bomb whenever it wishes."[60]

By the time of Zia's interview, Pakistani scientists responsible for designing the bomb had been at work for about seven years somewhere within the Wah Cantonment Ordnance Complex. About thirty miles northwest of Islamabad, the complex was first established in 1947 as the home for the Pakistan Ordnance Factories, whose first weapons production effort involved rifles and ammunition.[61]

IN THE LATE 1980s A. Q. Khan and Pakistan had yet to provide aid to North Korea's nuclear program, which had its origins in July 1955 when representatives of the North Korean Academy of Sciences attended a nuclear energy conference in Moscow. The next year, Kim Il Sung's regime signed an agreement on nuclear research with its Soviet ally, and North Korean scientists began arriving at the Dubna Nuclear Research Institute for training. In 1959 a second agreement on nuclear cooperation was signed with the Soviet Union, while a first agreement was reached with the People's Republic of China.[62]

In late 1964, after China's successful detonation of an atomic bomb, Kim sent a delegation to China to make the same sort of request Qadhafi's representative made over a decade later. Kim wanted China's assistance in developing nuclear weapons, but Mao sent the Koreans away empty-handed. The next year, Moscow did sell North Korea a small 2- to 4-megawatt research reactor. The reactor was built near the Kuryung River, in the vicinity of Yongbyon, about sixty miles northeast of the capital city of Pyongyang, and placed under IAEA safeguards at Soviet insistence. Soviet and North Korean scientists also established a nuclear research center at the site.[63]

Reportedly, Kim made another effort to get China to provide aid to a North Korean nuclear weapons program in 1974, when South Korea was exploring development of similar weapons. Then in the late 1970s, according to one Russian intelligence official, Kim instructed the Ministry of Public Security to initiate a nuclear weapons program, which was to include a rapid expansion of the Yongbyon facilities.[64]

Heading the program was Lee Sung Ki, who had obtained a doctorate in engineering from Kyoto Imperial University in prewar Japan. He had served as dean of Seoul's National University's college of engineering, and achieved worldwide recognition for developing vinalon, a synthetic fiber made from coal. Although born in the South, during the Korean War he defected to the North, where he became a close friend of Kim's as well as his primary scientific adviser. Other key members of the early North Korean nuclear weapons effort included Do Sang Rok and Han In Suk. Do was a quantum field theorist who first published papers on quantum mechanics in Japan and the United States as early as 1930. He built his own particle accelerator and conducted the North's first experiment on nuclear reactions. Han, born in South Korea, studied physics in Japan and Germany, and taught physics briefly at the National University after World War II before defecting to North Korea. After the Korean War he studied physics at

Moscow University, returning to Pyongyang in 1960 and publishing assorted papers on nuclear physics.[65]

In the early 1980s, in a major step toward developing nuclear weapons, North Korea began work on a 20- to 30-megawatt research reactor in the Yongbyon area, near the Soviet-supplied reactor. The graphite-moderated, gas-cooled reactor was similar to some older European models, and was well suited to the production of plutonium, requiring neither enriched uranium nor heavy water, which North Korea could not easily or cheaply acquire. By September 1982 construction had apparently begun on the new reactor's nuclear core and the nuclear control building. By the end of 1984 the reactor's cylindrical smokestack could be identified, and other buildings were near completion. In 1986 reactor operations began.[66]

NOT SURPRISINGLY, in the 1980s the nuclear activities of all four countries were of more than passing interest to U.S. intelligence analysts. One early task was to assess the impact of Israel's air strike on the Tammuz I reactor. A technical assessment would have been conducted by the imagery interpreters at the CIA's National Photographic Interpretation Center, who would have had a variety of satellite images available. A KH-8 Gambit satellite had been launched on the last day of February 1981 and remained in orbit until June 20. In addition, there were two KH-11s in orbit, able to return their imagery of the damaged facility within moments of passing overhead.[67] The interpreters would have tried to determine the extent of the damage to different segments of the facility, and passed that information on to reactor experts at the CIA and national laboratories, who could then estimate the time it would take to make repairs.

There was also a need for political analysis. A July 1, 1981, interagency assessment was prepared by the CIA's Office of Political Analysis and informally coordinated with analysts in the Defense Intelligence Agency, National Security Agency, Energy Department, Bureau of Intelligence and Research, and the military services. The authors reviewed Arab reactions, the immediate repercussions of the strike, and longer-term problems. With regard to the consequences for Iraq's nuclear program, the authors wrote, "It will take Iraq several years to rebuild its nuclear facilities, even if Baghdad finds cooperative suppliers of nuclear technology."[68]

That judgment was repeated about two years later in a Top Secret CIA study, *The Iraqi Nuclear Program: Progress Despite Setbacks*, apparently based on a combination of diplomatic reporting, human intelligence, and communications intelligence. The strike represented a "significant setback to the Iraqi nuclear program." In addition to destroying the reactor containment vessel and control, Iraq's short-term options for acquiring weapons-grade material, using Tammuz I to produce plutonium or diverting the reactor's highly enriched uranium fuel, had also been set back. The strike did not, however, "change Iraq's long-range nuclear ambitions," which included a "significant . . . domestic nuclear capability" and "probably an eventual nuclear weapon capability."[69]

The CIA's analysts could not be more definitive because, as they reported, "we still see no identifiable nuclear weapon program in Iraq . . . nor of the existence of any Iraqi nuclear weapons design group." They noted that Iraq had taken some steps in that direction. Should the country be able to obtain foreign assistance in key areas such as the manufacturing and testing of high explosives and the design, fabrication, and testing of a weapon, Iraq "possibly could have a viable design completed on paper within a few years." However, in the absence of significant foreign assistance "the Iraqis will not be able to produce the material for a nuclear weapon before the 1990s." Further, that necessary foreign assistance included "the foreign supply of a nuclear reactor—preferably a power reactor—of substantial size fairly soon." To the analysts, construction of a reactor from which plutonium could be extracted—whether a production or power reactor—appeared to be the only feasible means of producing the fissile material needed for an Iraqi bomb in the late 1980s or early 1990s.[70]

The analysts were not willing to totally dismiss Iraq's ability to acquire the necessary foreign assistance, given Iraq's past success with foreign suppliers and its "potential oil leverage." They noted that, according to State Department reporting, shortly before Israel's attack on the Tammuz I reactor Iraqi officials had met with representatives of the Italian firm SNIA-Techint. The meeting was dedicated to working out the final details of a feasibility study for supply of a power reactor that would have given Iraq "access to significant quantities of plutonium . . . in nine or ten years." Overall, Italy "probably will continue helping Iraq in numerous areas of nuclear technology, possibly even including reprocessing and plutonium chemistry."[71]

Iraq also had nuclear relationships with Pakistan and Brazil. Contacts with Pakistan had taken place from time to time over the preceding few years, and possibly included some cooperation after the Israeli attack on Tammuz I. CIA knowledge about what transpired between Iraq and Pakistan was limited, requiring the analysts to admit, "We do not know the exact nature of the recent contacts, but they appear to have been related to purchases of uranium and nuclear equipment." It was also noted that Iraqi-Brazilian contacts had increased since the two countries had signed a cooperation agreement, and Brazil might provide assistance if Iraq wanted to construct a 2- to 5-megawatt research reactor. In addition, Spain might be willing to provide assistance, and could build a reactor with a far higher power level than Brazil could provide, although it would be close to impossible to secretly divert plutonium from such a reactor. An overt diversion would require Iraq to withdraw from the Nuclear Non-Proliferation Treaty.[72]

Of course, France might be willing to rebuild Tammuz I, a project the CIA estimated would require three years. This time the French would probably insist on providing the lower-enriched fuel, such as the previously rejected caramel, which would eliminate the danger of Iraq diverting fresh highly enriched uranium for use in a bomb. Even with the lower-enriched fuel there were methods to produce plutonium—twenty two pounds per year if a blanket was built around the core. Such a technique would, the analysts believed, "be very difficult for Iraq to do without being detected by the IAEA or the French."[73]

Iraq might attempt, the study noted, to avoid safeguards by secretly constructing a reactor. Such a project would be difficult to carry out because, the analysts believed, the reactor would have to be built with the help of Spain or Brazil, whose involvement would have to be concealed. A secret project of that size, with the number of personnel involved and the large amount of material required, was not likely to remain secret for long, the CIA concluded.[74]

Beyond reactors, the report noted a number of other Iraqi acquisition activities related to the development of nuclear weapons. Iraq had been "working hard" to obtain, largely from Italy, the fuel cycle needed to support a reactor and extract plutonium: uranium supply, fuel fabrication, reprocessing, and waste treatment. Not long before the CIA study was written, Iraq's National Computer Center had expressed interest in acquiring advanced Japanese computers for Baghdad University, which the authors suspected were earmarked for the Iraqi Atomic Energy Commission.[75]

Iraq had also shown, according to the top-secret analysis, an interest in capabilities related to a uranium bomb, including the acquisition of lasers and related equipment. Because the Iraqis had previously requested Italian assistance with laser isotope separation, the authors suspected that they were interested in developing an enrichment capability using that technique. Saddam's regime had also expressed interest in acquiring a facility to convert uranium into metallic form.[76]

The CIA further noted that Iraq might make greater efforts to acquire fissile material in secret, and without approval of the seller's government. It had already acquired some uranium through a clandestine purchase, and continued "to show a great interest in obtaining fissile material clandestinely—on the black market or elsewhere." In 1979, according to the report, swindlers offered to sell high-grade uranium to Iraq. The CIA did not discover whether the uranium was natural, depleted, or highly enriched—although the proposed price suggested that it was of the highly enriched variety—but did not believe that any uranium acquired was usable in a weapon. However, Iraq was expected to keep trying: "dissatisfaction with what have probably been hoaxes so far will not be likely to deter Iraq from further attempts." In addition, such attempts were expected to fail: "no other country, we believe, has been successful in acquiring nuclear materials covertly."[77]

Despite the CIA's skepticism in 1983 that Iraq would seek to construct a reactor in secret, and the belief that Spain or Brazil would have to build it, information obtained in 1986 by another U.S. government intelligence organization—the U.S. Army Operational Group (a component of the U.S. Army Intelligence and Security Command)—indicated that China had completed a study in 1986 which evaluated the feasibility of building a reactor at one of four different sites in Iraq by 1990. The study team had been asked to take into account a variety of factors, including the availability of water and electricity, the ability to defend the facility from attacks, and the ability to camouflage the site so that it would not be detected by satellite reconnaissance. Site selection was to take place in 1987, construction to be completed in 1989 or 1990, and the facility was to be camouflaged.[78]

In 1988, in the aftermath of the war with Iran and after Iraq had committed itself to developing a nuclear weapon, a CIA study on Iraq's national security goals expressed the view that "Iraq regards the development of nuclear weapons as essential to offset Iran's geographic and demographic superiority." In addition, Iraq probably believed that Iran would develop a chemical weapons capability within a year or two to neutralize Iraq's advantage. Further, there was concern that Iran would develop or obtain nuclear weapons.[79]

EXAMPLES OF the U.S. intelligence community's collection and analysis efforts directed at Colonel Qadhafi's nuclear dreams in the 1980s are less numerous than those concerning Saddam Hussein's aspirations. In 1975, the CIA had produced an intelligence memorandum titled *Qadhafi's Nuclear Weapons Aims*. It noted that "the acquisition of nuclear weapons was a stated objective" of the Libyan dictator in 1974, and "so far he has chosen the path of developing an indigenous program to achieve his aim." His negotiations with assorted Western firms for nearly simultaneous construction of the required nuclear facilities was interpreted as indicating that "Libya has opted for a crash nuclear program." But, the memorandum continued, "it will probably take at least a decade for Libya to produce a nuclear weapon."[80]

A decade later Libya did not have a nuclear weapon, but the CIA was still interested in its quest to obtain one, as demonstrated by the February 1985 top-secret study by the agency's Office of Scientific and Weapons Research. *The Libyan Nuclear Program: A Technical Perspective* relied on intelligence obtained by satellite photography of Tajoura and other facilities, communications intercepts, human intelligence, and careful monitoring of foreign government announcements and the world's media.

The twenty-one-page study provides an overview of key organizations and facilities. Two of those pages explore the origins of the Libyan Secretariat of Atomic Energy, its components and their missions, as well as key personnel. It identified Dr. Fathi Noor (spelled "Nuh" in the CIA study) as head of the secretariat's Committee for Scientific Affairs, which included divisions for power, exploration and mining, fuel, and technical training and cooperation. Dr. Fathi Skinji (aka Abd al-Fatah Eskanji) is identified as the former director of the Atomic Energy Establishment, the secretariat's predecessor, and the current head of a committee responsible for the technical review of the nuclear power plant contract with the Soviet Union. The structure and activities of the Tajoura Nuclear Research Center, which included basic research as well as research in three other areas—radiochemistry, fusion, and nuclear and material science—were also examined.[81]

A significant portion of the study evaluated Libyan efforts to acquire key technologies and material—including uranium, uranium conversion, uranium enrichment, and fuel fabrication—while another section focused on problems plaguing the Libyan program.* One was the lack of trained personnel, partly the result of restrictions imposed by some foreign nations on what subjects Libyan students were allowed to study in their countries, and partly because of the low educational standards at Al Fatah University, Libya's main center for nuclear science. Other issues involved the stalled deal with the Soviet Union for the 440-megawatt reactor and assorted financial problems.[82]

The overall assessment of the program by the CIA analysts was a bleak one, which simultaneously made it good news to key U.S. national security officials, from President Ronald Reagan on down, who were worried about Libya's quest to join the nuclear club. The Libyan program was "so rudimentary that it is not clear whether plutonium or uranium will be chosen as the basis for a weapon." What was clear was that "the program has major problems, including poor leadership and lack of coherent planning, as well as political and financial obstacles to acquiring nuclear facilities." As a result, the weapons analysts believed it "highly unlikely the Libyans will achieve a nuclear weapon capability within at least the next 10 years."[83]

That assessment was echoed later that year when the National Intelligence Council, consisting of the nation's top intelligence analysts and reporting to the director of central intelligence, produced a secret review on the dynamics of nuclear proliferation. Libya required attention, the review noted, not because the Libyan nuclear program had any prospect of producing a weapon within the next decade, but "because Qadhafi may once again attempt to buy or steal a weapon or its components."[84]

---

* The study also reports (p. 1) two attempts to purchase a bomb from China: one in 1973 and one 1976.

PAKISTAN'S NUCLEAR PROGRAM had also been of interest to the CIA and other elements of the U.S. intelligence community as far back as the 1970s. In September 1974 the intelligence community judged that Pakistan as well as Iran, Egypt, Brazil, and Spain would require at least a decade to develop nuclear weapons—unless they received significant foreign assistance or were able to purchase fissile material. Countries might be driven to acquire nuclear arms for reasons of prestige or in reaction to the nuclear efforts of antagonists, according to the community's analysts, and Pakistan and Iran were the countries likely to feel the strongest impulse to do so.[85]

That judgment ensured that Pakistan's nuclear efforts would continue to be watched with particular interest. More than two years later the CIA's *Weekly Surveyor* carried an article on Pakistan's desire to purchase uranium from Niger, which the agency's analysts believed was "undoubtedly intended" to provide fuel for the Canadian-supplied KANUPP reactor. The interest in buying nuclear material from the African country was reportedly the result of a new Canadian policy that would have limited such sales to nations that had ratified the nonproliferation treaty or agreed to IAEA safeguards on their nuclear program—neither of which Pakistan had done.[86]

The uranium would first have to be fabricated into fuel rods to power the reactor—a task beyond the capabilities of Pakistan, but not China. The possibility that China would take the uranium Pakistan had purchased from Niger and turn it into nuclear fuel as well as provide the heavy water for the KANUPP reactor was discussed in a June 1977 *Weekly Surveyor* item, which noted the upcoming extended visit of a Chinese delegation.[87]

The following spring one or more CIA analysts completed a thirty-eight-page Top Secret Codeword report on the Pakistani nuclear program. The author(s) observed that Pakistan "is strongly motivated to develop at least a potential nuclear capability, in part for prestige purposes but more strongly because it genuinely believes its national security could ultimately be threatened by India." A decision to develop a nuclear capability would be strongly supported by the military, according to the analysis. At the same time, there was "no visible sense of urgency about the matter and a decision to proceed may be postponed for many years." One indication of that lack of urgency was that the Pakistani nuclear weapons design group "appears to be operating at a relatively low priority."[88]

The bulk of the paper, at least in its declassified form, concerned the technical base of Pakistan's nuclear program, the French reprocessing plant and alternative sources of plutonium, along with the bottom line—Pakistan's potential to produce nuclear weapons. A section on the program's technical base noted that PINSTECH was the center of Pakistani atomic energy research activities, and that the central element of the research center was a research reactor capable of producing a maximum of one hundred grams of plutonium per year. But the KANUPP reactor—its characteristics, history, problems, fuel requirements, and plutonium production capability—constituted the major focus of the section. According to the CIA analysis, if the reactor was operated in a manner optimized to produce weapons-grade plutonium, it could make between 132 and 264 pounds of reactor-grade plutonium, which could then be reprocessed into plutonium suitable for use in weapons.[89]

Almost six pages of the CIA analysis was devoted to possible sources of weapons-grade plutonium, either the reprocessing plant the French had agreed to provide in 1976 or alternative sources. The paper noted that "the odds appear to be sharply increasing that the plant will not be completed, at least according to original specifications, in the foreseeable future." If the plant were to be built, it would be under international safeguards intended to prevent it from being used to provide weapons-grade material. The same analysis noted, however, that "short of round-the-clock physical inspection of a reprocessing plant it is questionable whether safeguarding such a facility is really effective," given that the time between diversion of fuel and production of weapons could be very short.[90]

Even without the planned Chashma facility, Pakistan had other potential sources of plutonium, the CIA analysts reported. PINSTECH "probably had a laboratory-scale fuel reprocessing facility," and modifications might allow it to produce enough plutonium for a single weapon sometime in the first half of the 1980s. Such a course, however, would leave Pakistan years away from developing the reprocessing capability that would permit it to stockpile weapons. Another option was for Islamabad to build a small, crude reprocessing plant on its own. Under the best of circumstances, such a facility could be built in a few months and produce several kilograms of plutonium each day— enough for several weapons—within an extremely brief period. According to the analysis, it would be at least five years before Pakistan would be capable of building such a plant.[91]

In assessing Pakistan's potential to produce nuclear weapons, the CIA noted that a host of variables, including delivery systems, would influence production capability. Production of a low-yield bomb designed to be carried inside an aircraft would probably require two years from the time that a device was tested, but the bomb would be so large that the only means for getting it to its target would be Pakistan's "relatively slow and vulnerable B-57s." The number of weapons that could be produced by employing the KANUPP reactor would depend on whether the reactor was operated primarily to produce power or weapons-grade plutonium. In any case, the study estimated that Pakistan had already accumulated about two hundred or so kilograms of reactor-grade plutonium, enough for thirty to forty weapons.[92]

Such intelligence on the Pakistani program resulted in a direct expression of concern. In 1979 Robert Gallucci, a thirty-three-year-old member of the State Department's policy-planning staff, spoke with the department's undersecretary, David Newsom, about Pakistan's nuclear activities. In addition to information, he also had a proposal: rather than try to get Zia to call a halt to the program, the United States should obtain Zia's pledge that Pakistan would not enrich uranium beyond a low level and would agree to a monitoring system. Part of that strategy was to confront Zia with U.S. knowledge, including satellite images, of the Pakistani effort.[93]

Newsom was convinced, and obtained whatever approval was necessary from his superiors. He also told Gallucci that he wanted him to travel to Pakistan to help the U.S. ambassador deliver the message to Zia. When Gallucci noted that as a member of the policy-planning staff he didn't normally take such trips, Newsom told him "you'll take this one." So he left Washington, he recalls, "with dirty pictures under my arm." On the day he and Ambassador Arthur Hummel were to see Zia, illness kept him from the meeting.[94]

HUMMEL DID SEE ZIA, but with no great impact. Zia had his story and he was sticking to it. After Hummel briefed him on what the United States knew about Pakistan's uranium enrichment program, Zia responded, "That's absolutely ridiculous. Your information is incorrect. We have to clear this up. Tell me any place in Pakistan you want to send your experts and I will let them come and see." But Zia was simply stalling, and no visits would ever take place.[95]

Gallucci's trip was not wasted, as he was able to accomplish more than serving as a delivery boy for highly classified satellite photographs. A bit of subterfuge allowed him to bring back some ground-level photographs of Kahuta. He managed to persuade Hummel to let him take a drive near the facility. He had first raised the idea with the embassy's political officer, who said he would go only if ordered by the ambassador. Gallucci then told Hummel that the political officer wanted to go, and Hummel gave the order. They took along an INR representative, who came equipped with a camera which was put to good use.[96]*

That September, Pakistan's program was a subject of discussion at a September meeting of the General Advisory Committee of the Arms Control and

---

* The Gallucci trip to Kahuta stimulated the French ambassador and the embassy first secretary to visit the area in June 1979. They were on a public road in an unrestricted area when the road was blocked by two vehicles. Six Pakistanis pulled the diplomats from their car and gave them a severe beating. One victim told the U.S. embassy that he assumed the Pakistanis organized the attack to scare people away from the facility. See Dennis Kux, *The United States and Pakistan, 1947–2000: Disenchanted Allies* (Baltimore: Johns Hopkins University Press, 2001), p. 240.

Disarmament Agency. Charles Van Doren, acting director of ACDA's non-proliferation bureau, expressed concern about Pakistan's "building a conversion plant to convert the materials to [uranium hexafluoride] which is the feed for the enrichment plant," which led the United States to tighten up "on the export control side." He also reported that "there is increasing evidence of their preparing a test site, and we have some reliable, or fairly reliable seeming reports that this test may be ready in one of two locations that have been specified, by November or December of this year." Van Doren described the situation as "a railroad train that is going down the track very fast, and I am not sure anything will turn it off."[97]

That year, foreign sources had told the Carter administration that Pakistan had started construction of a nuclear test site and that it might detonate its first bomb by the end of the year. U.S. intelligence had detected unusual construction in the southern region of Pakistan but could not determine if the activity was actually connected to the country's nuclear program. As a result, the intelligence community still believed that Pakistan was at least two years away from building and testing a bomb.[98]

By the fall of 1980 the U.S. intelligence community had gathered data that Pakistan was indeed constructing a reprocessing plant and possibly had begun work on a test site. Either the CIA's spies, the NSA's eavesdroppers, or the NRO's imagery satellites, or some combination of the three, had provided evidence that a building just outside the PINSTECH fence was to be a small reprocessing facility, about one-tenth the size of the planned Chashma facility. Despite its size, it appeared, based on intelligence concerning the equipment it would contain, that it would be able to produce between twenty-two and forty-four pounds of plutonium each year beginning in 1981, which would be enough for between one and three weapons.[99]

Discovery of the possible test site was undoubtedly due to the U.S. reconnaissance satellites that had been in orbit. During most of the first eight months of 1980 there had been two Kennan (KH-11) spacecraft in orbit, which were joined in mid-June by a Hexagon (KH-9). They apparently detected the sporadic construction of a tunnel for which there appeared to be no other explanation, as well as photographing surrounding towers. "Work at the site appears to have stopped again for the moment," a government official told the *Washington Post* in September 1980. But there was still reason for concern, for "if they do plan to stage a test there, it would not take them long to get it ready."[100]

Over the next four years, Pakistan did not test a weapon and the U.S. intelligence community continued to gather information on its nuclear program. Not surprisingly, when Howard Hart arrived in May 1981 to take over as CIA chief of station in Islamabad, he came with instructions to emphasize intelligence collection to support the secret war in Afghanistan and to discover Pakistan's nuclear secrets. When he left a little over three years later, the U.S. ambassador, Dean Hinton, wrote a classified evaluation letter in which he reported that Hart's "collection efforts on the Pakistani effort to develop nuclear weapons is amazingly successful and disturbing." He continued, "I would sleep better if he and his people did not find out so much about what is really going on in secret and contrary to President Zia's assurances to us"—a statement he presumably meant as a compliment and not as a complaint.[101]

CIA intelligence gathering allowed various elements of the intelligence community to produce more informed assessments that spurred U.S. action. In 1981 INR, partly based on information that Kahuta had begun operations as well as the discovery of certain illegal export activities, observed that "we have strong reason to believe that Pakistan is seeking to develop a nuclear explosives capability" and "Pakistan is conducting a program for the development of a triggering package for nuclear explosive devices." In 1983 U.S. intelligence reported that China had provided Pakistan with a complete design of a 20-kiloton nuclear weapon, which it had tested at Lop Nur. That same year, the Pentagon noted the "unambiguous evidence that Pakistan is actively pursuing a nuclear weapons development program." The assessment also identified the Kahuta facility as key to the Pakistani weapons program, declaring that its "ultimate application . . . is clearly nuclear weapons." Such intelligence led President Reagan, in August 1984, to draft a letter to President Zia, warning of "grave consequences" if Pakistan enriched uranium beyond 5 percent. Zia pledged not to do so, a pledge that high-level officials frequently repeated.[102]

Reagan also sent former deputy CIA director Gen. Vernon Walters to Pakistan several times during the mid-1980s to express U.S. concerns. During one visit, Walters showed Zia a blueprint of Pakistan's bomb that had been passed to the CIA by a foreign intelligence service, which had stolen it from A. Q. Khan's hotel room. The U.S. ambassador, Ronald Spiers, recalled the drawing as looking like something out of a science fiction magazine. When Walters showed Pakistan's president a satellite photograph of Kahuta, he got much the same reaction as Hummel did several years earlier. Zia claimed that "this can't be a nuclear installation. Maybe it is a goat shed." According to atomic energy commission chairman Munir Ahmed Khan, the "show and tell" briefings had no impact on the nuclear program other than to give Pakistani officials an idea of what the United States knew.[103]

Despite those assessments and U.S. warnings, there was still uncertainty about details of the Pakistani program. The National Intelligence Council's September 1985 review of the dynamics of nuclear proliferation used the adjective *probably* on three occasions in its discussion of Pakistan: Pakistan probably had a workable design for a nuclear weapon, while separated weapons-grade plutonium probably would not be available for several years after a pilot-scale reprocessing plant began operations. In addition, although the Pakistanis were theoretically capable of producing very small quantities of highly enriched uranium, they were probably at least a year or two from being able to produce enough for an atomic device.[104]

In late October of 1986 President Reagan certified that Pakistan "does not possess a nuclear explosive device," which was consistent with the projections of the NIC from a year before. Legislation requiring such certification or a presidential waiver, which was necessary if Pakistan was to continue receiving hundreds of millions of dollars in U.S. aid, had been passed in 1985, and was a consequence of arrests in 1984 of three Pakistanis who were trying to illegally obtain fifty electronic triggering switches, krytrons, used for atomic bombs. Providing such aid to Pakistan was of particular importance to the Reagan administration, because Pakistan played a key role in supporting the U.S. effort to aid the Afghan guerrillas fighting the Soviet troops who had invaded their country six years earlier. But the president's certification concealed some disconcerting intelligence.[105]

The DIA reported that sometime between September 18 and September 21, Pakistan detonated a high-explosive device as part of its effort to develop an implosion device—its second test of the year, and one of many that had been conducted over several years. In addition, intelligence reports stated that Pakistan had far surpassed the 5 percent enrichment level that Zia had promised Reagan would be Pakistan's limit. According to the reports, Pakistani scientists had succeeded in producing, at Kahuta, uranium composed of 93.5 percent U-235.[106]

Other activities belying Pakistan's claims that it was not developing nuclear weapons were described in a special national intelligence estimate completed earlier in 1986. The estimate probably included relevant information from a high-level spy in the Chinese nuclear program who had access to information on Chinese nuclear contacts with Pakistan. That asset reported, by the end of 1985, that Chinese technicians were providing assistance at a suspected Pakistani bomb development site (probably Wah), and that Chinese scientific delegations were also spending a substantial amount of time at Kahuta. The spy also revealed that Pakistani scientists from Wah had shown a nuclear weapon design to some Chinese physicists in late 1982 or early 1983 and sought their opinion as to whether the design would produce the desired nuclear blast. In addition, the CIA's agent reported on the triggering mechanism for Pakistan's bomb design, which appeared to be very similar to the one used by China in its fourth nuclear test. The estimate concluded that Pakistan would possess a small nuclear weapon at a future, but unspecified, date. According to U.S. officials who spoke to the *Washington Post* at the time, the unspecified date could come within two weeks or even less. Pakistan, according to one official, was only "two screwdriver turns" from having a fully assembled atomic bomb.[107]

Further evidence of Pakistan's pursuit came the following year, as a result of escalating tensions between India and Pakistan. Pakistan feared that large-scale Indian military maneuvers, designated Operation Brasstacks, might be a prelude for an invasion. Very late in January, when the maneuvers were at their peak, A. Q. Khan was reported to have told a visiting foreign journalist that Pakistan had already achieved nuclear weapons capability. The following month Zia told *Time* magazine, "You can write today that Pakistan can build a bomb whenever it wishes."[108]

Then in July the FBI arrested Arshad Z. Pervez, a Pakistani-born Canadian, for trying to purchase twenty-five tons of specially strengthened maraging steel from a Reading, Pennsylvania, company, steel that would have been shaped into extra-strong, ultrafast gas centrifuges for Kahuta. But the company tipped off U.S. law enforcement authorities, who were watching and listening when Pervez made his pitch to an undercover agent in a Toronto hotel room. Pervez also revealed to the agent his interest in beryllium, which is used as casing for the fissile material in an atomic bomb to increase the device's yield. Two days later two Americans were arrested in Sacramento for illegally exporting to Pakistan advanced instruments and computer items used in developing nuclear weapons.[109]

Over the succeeding two years the United States built up a detailed dossier on the Pakistani program, through satellite images of PINSTECH, Kahuta, and continuing construction at Chashma and other facilities; communications intercepts of talkative Pakistani scientists and military officials; and probably a few well-placed human sources in Pakistan and China. Once again, the intelligence was used in an attempt to get Pakistan to halt its march toward becoming a nuclear weapons state—this time during an early 1989 visit to Washington by army chief of staff Gen. Mirza Aslam Beg, who along with Zia's successor, President Ghulam Ishaq Khan, directed their country's nuclear weapons program.[110]

Beg met with outgoing national security adviser Gen. Colin Powell and Brent Scowcroft, Powell's designated successor. They conveyed the message that the United States considered Pakistan to be very close to crossing the line, which would prevent the president from issuing the certification required for aid. The meetings apparently had the desired effect, at least in the short term, because the U.S. intelligence community soon reported that Pakistan had halted the production of highly enriched uranium, the activity that produced the greatest anxiety in Washington.[111]

In May, George H. W. Bush's director of central intelligence, William Webster, told the Senate Committee on Governmental Affairs that "clearly, Pakistan is engaged in developing a nuclear capability." Then in June Pakistani prime minister Benazir Bhutto arrived in Washington for the first state visit during Bush's administration. Her first stop was Blair House, where she was met by Webster, who gave Bhutto an unprecedented and rather unusual briefing. Never before had a DCI briefed a foreign leader on his or her country's nuclear weapons program. The briefing took place despite concerns that the disclosure, even though sanitized to protect sources and methods, would lead Pakistan to tighten the security cloak around its program. And it sent the message that the United States was aware of exactly how close Pakistan was to joining the nuclear club. It also provided Bhutto with information on Pakistan's nuclear efforts, including a mock-up of the bomb designed by her scientists, that had been kept from her by the military and program scientists.[112]

Further, Webster let Bhutto know that if Pakistan were to convert the highly enriched uranium gas produced at Kahuta into uranium metal, the United States would consider Pakistan to have acquired a bomb. Such a conclusion, Bhutto knew, would likely result in President Bush refusing to certify Pakistan's nonnuclear status. Continuing aid to Pakistan would then require a presidential waiver, the probability of which dropped dramatically after the last Soviet soldier departed Afghanistan the year before. The next day, Bhutto addressed Congress and assured the attending senators and representatives that Pakistan neither possessed a nuclear device nor intended to obtain one. While her assurances may have been sincere, in the end they would mean little. In the meantime, they helped justify President Bush's certification in October that "Pakistan does not now possess a nuclear explosive device."[113]

That same month, an analysis appearing in *Science and Weapons Review*, a top-secret journal published by the CIA's Office of Scientific and Weapons Research, asserted that "Islamabad is pressing forward with efforts to acquire and deploy advanced weapons in reaction to India's growing military capability" and that "a relative decline in the deterrent value of Pakistan's conventional forces is leading [it] to seek ballistic missiles and a rapidly deployable nuclear weapons capability."[114]

By May 1990 the information available to U.S. nuclear intelligence analysts, probably largely from human intelligence and communications intercepts, led them to believe that Pakistan had started machining uranium metal into bomb cores. During a visit to Pakistan, deputy national security adviser Robert Gates discussed the matter with President Ghulam Ishaq Khan and General Beg, who claimed there was no change in Pakistan's nuclear status. But Gates wasn't convinced and told them that unless Pakistan melted down the bomb cores that had been produced, his president would be unable to certify Pakistan's nonnuclear status in the fall.[115]

A few months later President Khan did take dramatic action, but not the action that Gates had in mind. He dismissed Benazir Bhutto, charging her with corruption and nepotism, dismissed the national assembly, and called for new elections. Meanwhile, America's nuclear intelligence analysts—from the Joint Atomic Energy Intelligence Committee, CIA, DIA, Z Division, and elsewhere—all informed President Bush that Pakistan "possessed" a nuclear device. Reluctantly, in the fall of 1990 Bush accepted the interagency recommendation that he refuse to certify Pakistan's nonnuclear status. His decision certainly was made easier by the withdrawal of Soviet forces from Afghanistan in 1988, eliminating the need to placate Pakistan in order to ensure her support of the U.S. effort to arm the resistance.[116]

UNCOVERING DETAILS of what was going on inside North Korea's nuclear program would be one of the U.S. intelligence community's greatest challenges. Obstacles included the lack of an embassy, which could provide a home for a CIA station; the secrecy surrounding the North Korean program; and the oppressive secret police apparatus. But in the mid-1960s, when the CIA and other agencies began first taking notice of North Korean nuclear efforts, they did have one means of gathering intelligence that the North Koreans could not interfere with—the Corona spy satellite. Satellite overflights of Yongbyon, which began in 1961, had first spotted nothing more than a few small buildings at the site, but by 1965 the photographs showed construction activity. From 1966 to the end of the Corona program in May 1972, Yongbyon was photographed on thirty-six occasions by various versions of the KH-4 camera, which produced eighteen good-quality images.[117]

The analyses of North Korean nuclear activities in the 1980s also owed much to the NRO's spy satellites—Corona's successor, Hexagon, the high-resolution Gambit, and the real-time Kennan (which would be redesignated Crystal sometime in 1982)—although there was clearly some input from other sources. In 1980 one of those satellites obtained images of the Yongbyon area, which showed components of a nuclear reactor near a large hole, apparently dug for the reactor's foundation. A July 1982 CIA report noted that a new nuclear research reactor was "being built at the southern edge of North Korea's Yongbyon Nuclear Research Center" and that the facility was similar to the reactor the Soviet Union had supplied, and Corona had photographed under construction, in 1965.[118]

The report also mentioned the training provided to North Korea's nuclear physicists by the Soviet Union, and that they possessed the theoretical and technical skill to build a small reactor. Whether their Soviet ally was providing assistance in building the new reactor, the CIA could not say—although it offered some reassurance, observing that even if the North Koreans were relying solely on their own resources, perhaps because they did not want to place the reactor under IAEA safeguards, it would not be completed for several years and, in any case, was not designed to produce the quantities of plutonium needed for a nuclear weapons program.[119]

In the spring of 1984 another CIA item, clearly relying to a significant extent on satellite photography, provided an update on the reactor's status. The April 20 *East Asia Brief* noted that a cooling tower had been constructed, and speculated that the reactor would probably be graphite moderated and use natural uranium for fuel. Completion of the project was estimated to take another three years, during which time the North Koreans would need to develop advanced engineering skills to master the remote-control operations needed to handle highly radioactive materials.[120]

By January 1985 the reassurance that the new reactor could not provide fuel for nuclear weapons was missing from a State Department briefing paper, which apparently had been prepared for secretary of state George Shultz's meeting with Soviet foreign minister Andrei Gromyko in Geneva. The paper noted that "overhead photography" had revealed the construction in North Korea of a nuclear reactor that could be used for the production of weapons-grade plutonium. The paper also reported that the intelligence collected on North Korean nuclear activities had led the the United States to request its allies as well as China and the Soviet Union to deny Kim Il Sung's regime sensitive nuclear materials—an appeal that produced positive reactions among the allies but less cooperation from the two major Communist powers.[121]

In 1986, a top-secret CIA assessment, *North Korea: Potential for Nuclear Weapons Development*, commented that until 1984 the North Korean nuclear program had not been viewed as a serious proliferation threat. Up to that time the "available evidence had painted a picture of a rudimentary program incapable of very advanced research." The 1986 study was thus not only an assessment, but a reassessment based on information developed since 1984 as well as a reinterpretation of earlier intelligence.[122]

The specifics of that new information are absent from the declassified version of the study, although it may well have involved further satellite images showing a reactor larger than expected. In any case, the assessment also speculated on possible North Korean motives for developing nuclear weapons, including forcing political concessions from South Korea, hedging against South Korean development of a bomb, obtaining leverage for a free hand to conduct paramilitary operations without provoking a response, deterring a U.S. nuclear response to a North Korean attack, and a means for carrying out an all-out attack.[123]

In the next two years, on at least two occasions, the CIA addressed North Korea's nuclear efforts. A secret April 1987 report, in addition to retracing the history of the Hermit Kingdom's nuclear activities, repeated the judgment that the new 30-megawatt reactor, which had been completed in 1986 but had not yet been acknowledged by North Korea, could be used to produce weapons-grade plutonium. The CIA analysts also believed that Pyongyang had developed portions of the front end of the fuel cycle—uranium mining, milling, conversion, and fuel fabrication—to provide fuel for the reactor. North Korea's accession to the nonproliferation treaty (NPT) in December 1985 was explained as a result of its need to obtain additional nuclear assistance, particularly from the Soviet Union.[124]

About a year later another CIA report characterized North Korea's nuclear efforts as "expanding." Readers of the "Secret Noforn" study were informed that the new 30-megawatt reactor had been completed the previous October, and that at least part of the rationale for the country's nuclear program was the production of nuclear energy—pointing to the initiation of a major hydroelectric power project in the southwest and the construction of thermal power plants across the country. "Nonetheless," the analysis stated, "the possibility that Pyongyang is developing a reprocessing capability and its footdragging on implementing NPT provisions, suggest close scrutiny of the North's nuclear effort is in order."[125]

BY OCTOBER 1, 1990, the deadline for President Bush to certify that Pakistan had not crossed the line to become a nuclear weapons state, Saddam Hussein's Iraq had crossed another type of line—the border with Kuwait. Just two months earlier, on August 2, Iraqi troops poured into Kuwait to claim the country as Iraq's nineteenth province. The following January the U.S.-led effort to oust the Iraqi forces began with an aerial attack, and concluded successfully in February, just days after the ground campaign began. Fortunately, Iraq had not yet joined the nuclear club, but it had made significant progress toward it in the previous two years.

The Tuwaitha Nuclear Research Center remained the intellectual center of the project, and the home to nuclear physics labs, five working baghdatrons, and facilities for centrifuge testing as well as uranium research and development. Building 80 appears to have been the site of a pilot electromagnetic isotope separation plant.[126]

The Tarmiya complex, about a half hour north of Baghdad by car, now consisted of almost four hundred buildings distributed over more than two square miles. Inside one massive building, 250 feet by 370 feet, designated Building 33, were the first operational baghdatrons, where the initial step of enriching uranium to weapons grade was to take place. By January 15, 1991, nine magnets had been installed in one section, and three of a planned seventeen in another. There was room for at least seventy more. A nearby building contained the equipment that could finish the job, raising the U-235 content to 93 percent. Close to Building 33 were two satellite facilities, whose 132 one-megawatt transformers provided the vast quantities of electricity needed to operate the baghdatrons. Meanwhile, Ash Sharqat, Tarmiya's twin, still under construction, was 85 percent complete.[127]

Several facilities supported the EMIS effort. The Al Rabiyah Manufacturing Plant contained large mechanical workshops designed and constructed for the manufacture of large metal components for the electromagnetic effort. The Al Qaim facility produced uranium oxide as well as uranium tetrachloride. The Jesira plant, also known as the Mosul Production Facility, also produced uranium tetrachloride.[128]

South of Baghdad, in the vicinity of An Walid, was Al Furat, which was still under construction in early 1991. With assistance from Interatom, a subsidiary of the German company Siemens, Iraqi scientists and technicians had constructed a workshop for the design and fabrication of centrifuges. Mass production was to follow. While the baghdatrons alone could provide only enough fissile material each year for three bombs, cascades consisting of thousands of centrifuges could provide the nuclear fuel for twenty additional devices each year. To decrease the number of centrifuges required, uranium enriched to the 20 percent level at Tarmiya would be used as feed material. The centrifuges would finish the job.[129]

By 1991 the partially completed Al Atheer complex, located south of Baghdad and deceptively designated the "Al Atheer Materials Center," consisted of almost one hundred buildings. Its actual function was weapons design and bomb assembly. Its buildings contained "computer-controlled drills and lathes and the presses, induction furnaces, and plasma coating machines that were necessary to shape and mold the uranium bomb cores." The weapons design facility was equipped with IBM PS/2 personal computers, as well as a larger NEC-750, to test different bomb configurations. Also present was a firing bunker that permitted tests of the conventional explosives required to implode the bomb's core. A subfacility, Al Hateen, included a variety of diagnostic tools, such as flash X-ray to study the blast waves produced by high explosives. There was also the Al Musayyib complex, which included a test range for shaped charged detonations, a nuclear weapons lab, production facilities, and a power plant.[130]

Led by Jaffar Dhia Jaffar, the Iraqi program had made significant progress beyond filling buildings with equipment. The Iraqi calutrons, the baghdatrons, may have been the most sophisticated electromagnetic isotope separators ever produced. According to one analysis of the program, "the Iraqis seemed to have mastered the technique and were well on the way to producing weapons quantities of highly enriched uranium." The maximum level of enrichment was to 9.5 percent, almost halfway to the 20 percent target, at which point the baghdatrons would take over. The centrifuge enrichment program had also proved successful, with uranium hexafluoride being introduced into centrifuges at Al Furat during the first half of 1990 and the separation of uranium isotopes being achieved. In addition, large quantities of uranium hexafluoride and uranium tetrachloride had been produced in Buildings 15 and 85, respectively, at Tuwaitha. Weapon design had also been advancing. According to David Dorn, a weapons inspector with the UN Special Commission, Iraqi bomb designers "calculated at least five different designs for a nuclear weapon. While they were all primitive, each one was an improvement over its predecessors."[131]

Iraqi progress had been achieved with more than a little help from friends—and during the 1980s Iraq had a wide variety of friends motivated by security interests, money, or both. Fear of the consequences of an Iranian victory in the war with Iraq that had started in 1980 led U.S. policymakers in the Reagan administration to tilt toward Iraq—with money, intelligence, and license approvals. Between 1984 and 1990 the administration approved high-speed computer exports to Iraq worth 96 million. During that same period the Commerce Department issued licenses authorizing the sale of nearly $1.5 billion of sensitive technology to Saddam's regime, with much of the technology destined for the Iraqi Atomic Energy Commission.[132]

Asian and European companies and governments also provided a helping hand. A Japanese firm sold Iraq a high-speed video system for observing implosion tests, while China provided lithium hydride, which could be used to produce tritium. The Yugoslav Federal Directorate of Supply and Procurement handled construction of the entire Tarmiya complex, while another Yugoslav company provided the equipment. Other European suppliers included France, Italy, Sweden, Switzerland, the United Kingdom, the Soviet Union, and West Germany. At least thirteen companies in the Federal Republic of Germany provided hardware, training, or materials to the Iraqi program, particularly to its centrifuge component.[133]

While individual governments knew about the specific Iraqi purchases they authorized, determining the actual progress Iraq had made toward becoming a member of the nuclear club would have required a substantial intelligence effort—and Iraq sought to increase the chances that any intelligence effort would produce misleading results.

With Israel's attack on the Tammuz I reactor in mind, Jaffar, along with Iraq's intelligence experts, developed a plan to minimize the chances of U.S. and other foreign intelligence services discovering Iraq's nuclear secrets. They were aware how imagery interpreters worked—their search for "signatures" associated with particular activities. U.S. provision of satellite photographs, or information derived from satellite images, to Iraq during its war with Iran certainly did not hurt the Iraqis' understanding. To undermine the effectiveness of such searches, the Iraqis designed buildings that were not suggestive of what was going on inside. Facilities were constructed to prevent emissions, radioactive or other kinds, from leaking out. The civilian capability of dual-use plants provided cover. In one case, a facility that produced baghdatrons also produced window frames. Buildings built to house similar activities often had very different designs.[134]

Hiding the mission of the Tarmiya facility involved several gambits. To convey the impression that what was going on inside was of limited importance, the entire complex was surrounded by a light fence rather than the normal security barriers used for a nuclear weapons facility. Knowing that U.S. and other imagery interpreters might well suspect a uranium enrichment facility if they saw large quantities of electricity being produced for, and transmitted to, a facility, the Iraqis engaged in some deception and some denial. They built the 100-megawatt plant that provided power for the facility's transformers ten miles away, and then buried the cables carrying the power to Tarmiya underground.[135]

BY 1991 North Korea also had nuclear activities spread out across its territory. Uranium was being mined at two locations: Hungnam, in the southern half of the country and along the Sea of Japan, and Pyongsan in the far south. Pyongsan may also have been the home to a uranium enrichment facility. Apparently the sole site for uranium refining was Kusong, in the west, which reportedly had a daily capacity of 660 pounds of uranium ore. Nuclear research activities were conducted in three locations: Kimch'aek, also located on North Korea's east coast, the capital of Pyongyang, and Yongbyon.[136]

Yongbyon, actually the Yong-dong territory to its west, about fifty-five miles north of Pyongyang, remained the center of North Korea's nuclear research activities, with the 0.1-megawatt critical assembly, the Soviet-supplied research reactor that had been upgraded to 8 megawatts, and a 30-megawatt reactor. Construction was also underway on a 50- to 100-megawatt reactor, about a mile and a half south of Yong-dong and about 1.2 miles north of the 30-megawatt reactor. Its purpose appeared to be plutonium production, and a reprocessing facility also seemed to be under construction.[137]

THE LATE 1980s brought heightened concern about the Iraqi as well as the North Korean nuclear programs. One manifestation was the October 1988 special conference of intelligence analysts from Z Division, the Pacific Northwest Laboratory, and Savannah River Laboratory on Iraq and North Korea.[138]

Just two months before, the eight-year Iran-Iraq war had ended, but not before it cost Baghdad 375,000 casualties and half a trillion dollars. Saddam also piled up debts of $80 billion. To aid Iraq's military effort, early in 1985 the United States started sending to Iraq, on a regular basis, satellite data, either photos or the information derived from the photos, particularly after Iraqi bombing raids. In August 1986 the CIA established a direct, top-secret link between Washington and Baghdad to provide Saddam's military with better and more timely satellite intelligence. Data from satellite imagery would arrive "several hours" after a bombing raid to allow assessment of damage and aid in planning the next attack. By December 1986 the Iraqis were receiving selected portions of images obtained by KH-11 spacecraft and SR-71 spy planes.[139]

The attention devoted to developments on the battlefield meant that coverage of areas in the Persian Gulf, including the parts of Iraq that were home to nuclear facilities, was not as extensive as some might have liked. John A. Gentry served as senior analyst on the staff of the national intelligence officer for warning during 1987–1989. He recalled attending a joint CIA–National Intelligence Council meeting in 1988, as the representative of Charlie Allen and David Einsel, the national intelligence officers for warning and proliferation, respectively. The topic under discussion involved the priorities for employing "one technical collection asset" against nuclear, biological, and chemical (NBC) weapons programs in the Persian Gulf region.[140]

The national intelligence officers and some components of the CIA, particularly the Office of Scientific and Weapons Research, wanted to devote more attention to the "NBC" targets. According to Gentry, they argued that they "were not receiving enough data to adequately monitor the programs, that there were windows of opportunity to best learn of the development of the programs that would close, and the issue would become more important to consumers in the future." The CIA's Office of Near East and South Asian Analysis (NESA) objected, arguing that its customers were primarily interested in developments on the Iran-Iraq battlefield. The NESA eventually lost, and collection priorities were shifted in favor of collection against weapons of mass destruction targets, but, according Gentry, "collection opportunities were lost during the period the collection resources were devoted to other targets."[141]

Additional developments during the last half of 1988 augmented the general concern about the need to monitor regional nuclear, biological, and chemical weapons programs with a specific concern about nuclear developments in Iraq. William A. Emel, who headed the Proliferation Intelligence Program in the Energy Department's Office of Foreign Intelligence at the time, recalled that during "the last half of 1988 information was being received that heightened concern about a possible Iraqi nuclear weapons program"—apparently information about covert Iraqi procurement activities. In February 1989 he attended what he has described as "a special intelligence conference overseas"—probably a reference to a conference involving British and possibly additional foreign intelligence representatives—"during which Iraq was identified as of significant concern." And early in 1989 the Director of Central Intelligence's Nuclear Proliferation Working Group identified Iraq as a key country on which to focus community resources.[142]

By early 1989 collection resources included three KH-11s (launched in December 1984, October 1987, and November 1988), one Onyx radar imagery satellite (capable of producing images at night or through cloud cover), at least two signals intelligence satellites (one member of the three-satellite Mercury constellation and one member of the two-satellite Orion constellation) whose footprints would cover Iraq, the SR-71 aircraft, NSA's eavesdropping operations, including the joint CIA-NSA Special Collection Service unit at the U.S. embassy in Baghdad, and the CIA's intelligence officers and their agents.

Analytical resources were spread across the National Intelligence Council, the CIA and DIA, the Department of Energy headquarters and the department's laboratories, including Livermore, Los Alamos, and Oak Ridge, and the State Department's intelligence and research bureau. One small manifestation of the increased focus on Iraq was the creation by the Energy Department's intelligence office of an Iraq Task Force in April and May 1989, to be headed by experts at Oak Ridge. The new group was charged with producing weekly technical assessments of intelligence information concerning Iraq, particularly Iraqi procurement efforts, and maintaining close coordination with the CIA and NSA.[143]

But there was also resistance to the idea that Saddam was anywhere close to developing nuclear weapons. In 1991 Roger K. Heusser, the former deputy director of the Energy Department's office of classification and technology policy, told a congressional committee that national experts he spoke to in early 1989 claimed it would take Iraq ten years to get an atomic bomb, and told him not to be concerned. But his review of data concerning Iraqi procurement efforts led him to believe the threat was more immediate. Those not considering the issue to be an urgent one included Robert Walsh, head of the Energy Department's intelligence office, who vetoed suggestions that the secretary of energy, Adm. James Watkins, be briefed on the concerns of his subordinate intelligence experts. Such attitudes led A. Bryan Siebert, Heusser's boss, to send a memo to John Rooney, responsible for export control matters. Siebert wrote, "I am very concerned that Intelligence seems unable to review the intelligence data through anything other than a 'if you don't see it, it ain't there' lens. I would bet my job that Iraq is moving toward a nuclear weapons program and the time to try and stop it is now."[144]

In the months following Iraq's invasion of Kuwait in August, the U.S. intelligence community intensified its efforts to determine the extent of Iraqi nuclear progress. Satellite reconnaissance activity—which included a stealth imagery satellite, code-named Misty and launched in February 1990—increased. Monitoring of Iraqi communications was also stepped up. In addition, the flight of foreign workers that resulted from the crisis provided another source of intelligence, as did international businessmen with ties to Iraq. European governments began a crackdown on nuclear-related smuggling.[145]

Satellite reconnaissance offered the promise of detecting new construction activities and older facilities that might not have been noticed during the Iran-Iraq war. Imagery interpreters at NPIC might find evidence of the large plants required to produce highly enriched uranium. Since it would take about one thousand centrifuges to produce enough fissile material for between one and one and a half 15-kiloton bombs each year, and they needed to operate in concert as part of a cascade, any plant would be large and thus highly conspicuous. The probability of detection would be further enhanced because the facility would have to be near a railroad siding, access roads, and other accessories, including a major source of electrical power.[146]

The interpreters already knew of the installations at Erbil, Mosul, and Tuwaitha. By November 1990 the NRO's spies in space had not detected any signs of construction at those sites, or elsewhere, indicative of a full-scale gas centrifuge plant. Reports, possibly based on satellite imagery, showed that Iraq had begun building an underground uranium-processing facility in a remote, mountainous section of the country.[147]

Intelligence assets were undoubtedly targeted against both internal Iraqi communication links—between Tuwaitha and Baghdad, for example—and communications with known and possible suppliers of nuclear-related material in Europe and Asia. Iraqi officials overheard in communications intercepts might reveal a number of details about the nuclear program. While foreign workers would not have information on Saddam's decisions with regard to nuclear weapons, or on whatever progress his scientists had made in the production of fissile material or bomb design, they could report on construction activities—where facilities had been constructed and key characteristics of those facilities. Interviews with international businessmen revealed that Iraq had been receiving more weapons of mass destruction–related materials than previously believed. The crackdowns on nuclear-related smuggling provided new information on the type of equipment Iraq was seeking to acquire and, by implication, what it lacked.[148]

But the intensified collection and analysis effort still left the CIA and other interested agencies with significant intelligence gaps. According to a late November 1990 report in the *New York Times*, "credible information on Saddam Hussein's tightly guarded bomb program is scarce, and American intelligence analysts have only recently begun to train attention on the subject. The Central Intelligence Agency began to devote substantial numbers of analysts and computer research to Middle East technical and scientific developments only in the last 18 months, when the collapse of communism in Eastern Europe freed qualified employees to tackle the subject."[149]

And one government official noted that while "we have a good handle on how long it would take them [to build a bomb] with what we know they have . . . the question is what they have that we don't know about." Intelligence officials observed that Iraq's weapons programs were among the most tightly held secrets in one of the world's most regimented police states. "This is the hardest kind of collection problem," one intelligence official remarked.[150]

Intelligence gaps meant that assumptions as well as facts played a key role in estimates on the status of the Iraqi quest for nuclear weapons. And alternative assumptions led to different, sometimes substantially different, estimates. As one government official remarked in November 1990, "If you put a dozen intelligence experts around a conference table and ask them to tell you when Iraq will have a bomb, you'll get a dozen answers, from six months to 10 years."[151]

One official who had examined the most recent CIA assessment noted that "while the hypothesis is possible—in other words that they could design a bomb—there are still questions about whether it would be sufficiently powerful to constitute a military capability." Some of those who questioned Iraq's near-term capability believed that Iraq's nuclear scientists lacked the design and fabrication capability to make use of the small amount of highly enriched uranium that Iraq had received from France as fuel for the Tammuz I reactor, and that the complex production techniques required to produce a usable nuclear explosive were beyond Iraq's capabilities."[152]

Others took a more pessimistic view. One Department of Defense official found the CIA's most recent assessment more alarming than others. "Within a year they could come up with a crude bomb. . . . It is a real threat," he said, "certainly within the realm of possibility." One intelligence official noted, "This man has a history of looking for the magic weapon in the Iran-Iraq war, the silver bullet that can solve all his problems. . . . We certainly expect him to accelerate any program, such as his nuclear program, that would give him that 'silver bullet' capability against U.S. forces." That assessment was consistent with information obtained by an allied Arab government's intelligence service, and apparently provided to the United States, that Saddam had pushed his nuclear scientists to obtain an atomic bomb within a year.[153]

That Iraq might be able to obtain a bomb far sooner than the optimists believed was a key element of President George Bush's 1990 Thanksgiving Day address to U.S. troops stationed in the Persian Gulf. He told his audience that "those who would measure the timetable for Saddam's atomic program in years may be seriously underestimating the reality of that situation and the gravity of the threat. Everyday that passes brings Saddam one step closer to realizing his goal of a nuclear weapons arsenal. And that's why more and more, your mission is marked by a sense of urgency."[154]

The president's remarks were based on portions of the report that had been recently completed by the Joint Atomic Energy Intelligence Committee, and which also appeared in a special national intelligence estimate. One scenario assumed that Iraq would undertake a crash program to build a bomb, that it would use only its known supply of uranium, and that Iraq possessed advanced bomb-making technology. The central conclusion as to when Iraq might have a bomb was not precise—within "six months to a year, and probably longer." Further, the bomb would be of low yield and would be too bulky to deliver by missile or aircraft, and there would be a significant chance that it would not detonate.[155]

On November 29, a week after the president's Thanksgiving Day address, the UN passed another resolution in response to Iraq's failure to withdraw its troops from Kuwait. If the Iraqi dictator did not remove his troops by January 15, a U.S.-led coalition was authorized to remove him by force. On January 15, George Bush signed a national security directive authorizing the commencement of military operations, and the air campaign began in the predawn hours of January 17. After five weeks of aerial attack, the ground campaign began on February 24. Four days later, with coalition forces having driven Iraqi forces from Kuwait and having made significant inroads into Iraqi territory, the United States declared a cease-fire. On March 3, Gen. H. Norman Schwarzkopf met with his Iraqi counterpart at a remote air base in Iraq to spell out the terms of the cease-fire.[156]

On April 2, a new UN Security Council resolution demanded that Iraq disclose all of its weapons of mass destruction activities—from research and development to weapons stockpiles—and submit to inspections of the sites it declared as well as additional sites chosen by the UN-authorized inspection agencies—the UN Special Commission on Iraq (UNSCOM) and the IAEA.[157] The resolution opened the way for the UN and the U.S. intelligence community to determine the ground truth about suspected Iraqi nuclear, chemical, and biological weapons facilities, in some cases guided by intelligence obtained by the CIA and other U.S. and allied intelligence agencies.

THE YEAR 1991 ended with the hope that the nuclear weapons programs in two rogue states had been stopped. The upcoming inspections of sites associated with the Iraqi nuclear program, and the destruction or rendering harmless of the equipment at those sites, held out the promise that Saddam's nuclear dreams would never be realized. Then on December 31, North and South Korea initialed a joint declaration banning nuclear weapons from the Korean peninsula, as a step toward "peaceful unification of the homeland."[158]

That agreement appeared to offer relief from the fears that had been generated by monitoring of North Korea's nuclear behavior since 1989. In March of that year CIA analysts completed a special analysis, *NORTH KOREA: Nuclear Program of Proliferation Concern*. The study noted that "North Korea is rapidly expanding its nuclear-related activities" and that the new plants detected at Yongbyon might be part of a civilian power-generation program to alleviate the "chronic energy shortages" plaguing the Hermit Kingdom.[159]

But it was also reported that while North Korea had promised Soviet and IAEA officials that it would open formal safeguard negotiations that month, the "North has repeatedly missed target dates for such talks, and the IAEA is concerned that Pyongyang may find new pretexts to postpone any talks." In addition, the analysts observed loopholes in the safeguards agreement. It would be up to North Korea to notify the IAEA as to when the agreement would go into force as well as to identify the facilities to be inspected, permitting the North Koreans to delay implementation indefinitely or to limit inspections to select facilities. North Korea, the CIA concluded, might "be willing to risk the international censure that a nuclear weapons program would bring in order to maintain a decided military advantage over the South."[160]

The concern that was present in 1989 and beyond in the White House, Foggy Bottom, Langley, and other segments of the U.S. national security establishment responsible for worrying about Korea and proliferation was often fueled by the images from the various satellites operated by the NRO. That concern, in turn, stimulated consultation with allies and adversaries as well as negotiations with North Korea.

In Seoul, on June 30, a U.S. team briefed working-level officials from several South Korean agencies on new intelligence, derived from satellite imagery, that North Korea was stepping up its efforts to develop a nuclear weapons capability. The indications of North Korean nuclear activity had also been discussed with the Soviet Union and China, in hopes of gaining their cooperation in halting any North Korean movement toward nuclear weapons. What the imagery showed was a second facility, a long narrow factory-like building near the Yongbyon reactor that appeared to be a reprocessing plant. A reprocessing plant, once in full operation, would be able turn the spent fuel from the research reactor into enough fissile material each year for one or two bombs.[161]

Beyond briefing the South Korean government, U.S. officials initiated a diplomatic offensive to get North Korea to deliver on its promises to subject its nuclear facilities to international safeguards. The Americans also repeatedly sought Soviet help, with secretary of state James A. Baker raising the issue with Soviet foreign minister Eduard A. Shevardnadze when they met in Wyoming that September. Baker then went public with the issue in San Francisco in October, when he observed that "nuclear proliferation, notably North Korea's reactor program, remains dangerous," during a speech on arms control.[162]

Eighteen months later the issue had still not been resolved. Satellite photos showed the 30-megawatt reactor unattached to any electric power lines. Kim Il Sung refused to permit international inspection of his nation's nuclear facilities until the United States removed all its nuclear weapons from South

Korean territory. Kim's refusal produced various threats. The Soviet Union warned that it would stop providing supplies for the nuclear program. South Korea's defense minister threatened substantially more, stating that his country might decide to launch a commando attack against the suspected reprocessing facility. The remark, which North Korea characterized as "virtually a declaration of war," was then disavowed by his government.[163]

The United States meanwhile continued to pursue diplomacy. There was disagreement as to exactly how much farther North Korea had to travel to arrive at the nuclear club's front door—the DIA estimated three to five years, Z Division and other Energy Department experts believed it would take somewhat longer, while the State Department's INR was somewhere in between. But there was no disagreement on the importance to act while there was still time. Thus, in late May undersecretary of state Reginald Bartholomew headed for Beijing to stress the need for a "broadly based, concerted international consensus" to get North Korea to comply with its obligations under the nonproliferation treaty.[164]

By November, a "steady trickle" of new intelligence had suggested that several new installations at Yongbyon were nearly complete, including the suspected reprocessing plant. Some intelligence also indicated that other nuclear installations, possibly some underground facilities, were being built elsewhere in North Korea. The intelligence was, however, as in the past, far from complete: satellite photos, some sketchy information from defectors, along with information and assumptions about the depth of North Korean technical skills and access to key technologies. James Lilley, who served as ambassador to South Korea in the late 1980s, told the *New York Times,* "As far as I know, you don't have the wealth of defectors in Korea . . . to lay it all open."[165]

But he also noted, "No one can afford to assume a country like North Korea is bluffing. . . . You end up with a lot of people dead in the sea that way." As a result, the additional intelligence, however incomplete, along with Kim's continued refusal to open the nuclear facilities for international inspection, further heightened fears in the United States, Japan, and South Korea. The South Korean Defense Ministry issued a white paper, not subsequently disavowed, stating that the project "must be stopped at any cost."[166]

But it appeared that an agreement signed by North and South Korea on the final day of 1991, which followed a nonaggression agreement signed earlier that month, stopped North Korea's pursuit of nuclear weapons, possibly just in the nick of time. Recent U.S. intelligence indicated that the reprocessing plant could be producing plutonium by mid-1992. In the "Joint Declaration for a Non-Nuclear Korean Peninsula," both Koreas promised not to test, produce, receive, possess, or deploy or use nuclear weapons. They also promised not to maintain facilities for reprocessing or enriching uranium. In addition, the declaration called for inspections of each other's facilities, but left the details to be determined by the South-North Joint Nuclear Control Committee. Further, the declaration would become effective on February 19, 1992.[167]

The agreement offered the possibility, with Iraq's nuclear program already set back, if not ended, by the Gulf War, that two of the four nations whose quest to join the nuclear club had troubled U.S. policymakers throughout the 1980s would remain outside the club for the foreseeable future.

chapter nine

"PARIAHS" REVISITED

THE INCREASING ATTENTION the United States devoted to the quest for nuclear weapons by rogue states Iraq, Libya, and North Korea did not mean that earlier concerns, including the nuclear activities of the "pariah" states, were forgotten. In the mid-1980s a major new source of information about the Israeli nuclear program became available to the U.S. intelligence community. A CIA asset in Taiwan received assistance in escaping to the United States in 1987, but not before providing information crucial to stopping renewed Taiwanese nuclear weapons activity. In the early 1990s South Africa's claim to have developed and then destroyed a nuclear arsenal required the attention of America's intelligence collectors and analysts.

IN THE MID-1980S the Negev Nuclear Research Center near Dimona continued to turn out the plutonium needed to provide additional bombs for Israel's "secret" nuclear arsenal. The center consisted of ten different "machons" or institutes. The sixty-foot, silver-domed, heavy-water reactor constituted Machon 1. Machon 2 was the most sensitive building in one of Israel's most sensitive facilities. Two activities took place in Machon 3: processing of natural uranium for the reactor and conversion of lithium-6 into a solid that would be placed in a nuclear warhead. A waste treatment plant for the radioactive remains from Dimona's chemical reprocessing plant could be found in Machon 4. Machon 5 would coat the uranium rods, prepared in Machon 3 for use in the reactor, with aluminum. Machon 6 provided basic services, such as chemicals, and power to the other machons. Machon 8 (apparently, there was no Machon 7 at the time) contained a laboratory for testing the purity of samples from Machon 2 and experimenting on new manufacturing processes. It was also the home of Special Unit 840, whose scientists developed a gas centrifuge means of enriching uranium. A laser isotope reprocessing facility could be found in Machon 9. In Machon 10 depleted uranium, with little or no U-235, would be chemically separated for eventual use in bullets, armor plating, and artillery and bomb shells.[1]

IN 1980 the U.S. intelligence community completed a new special national intelligence estimate on Israel's nuclear capability, which concluded that it had an arsenal of between twenty and thirty warheads. The study also reported that the Dimona reactor had been upgraded to increase its cooling capacity, indicating that a greater quantity of plutonium was being produced. And there was also no longer any doubt of the existence of a completed chemical reprocessing plant, although its location was uncertain.[2]

While the estimate was more comprehensive than past estimates, there were still clear information gaps about the Israeli program. One way to fill those gaps would be to recruit an insider. Despite the close alliance between Israel and the United States, both had, from time to time, conducted human intelligence operations that attempted to uncover the other's secrets. In the 1980s the United States acquired intelligence from a major in Israel's army, while Israel's Scientific Liaison Bureau received a vast quantity of highly classified U.S. intelligence information provided by Jonathan Pollard.[3] But the individual who provided the United States with significant new information on Israel's covert nuclear weapons program was not an asset of the CIA, or any other intelligence organization—American or foreign.

Mordechai Vanunu was about five months short of his thirty-second birthday in May 1986. He had been born in Marrakesh, Morocco, in October 1954, the second of seven children, and had emigrated to Israel with the rest of his family in 1963. While it was his father's preference to resettle near Haifa, immigration officials ignored Solomon Vanunu's wishes and sent the family to Beersheba—an act that would have dramatic, and unanticipated, repercussions for both Israel and Mordechai in the future.[4]

High school was followed by compulsory military service, which Vanunu hoped to spend with the air force. But his failure to pass the entrance exam resulted in a tour of army duty instead. After serving as a corporal in the engineering corps during the 1973 Yom Kippur War, and spending 1974 blowing up army installations in the Golan Heights before Israel returned part of the territory to Syria, he enrolled at Tel Aviv University to study physics. By the end of his first year he had dropped out, after discovering that the full-time work he needed to pay for college prevented him from keeping up with his studies. In 1976 he returned to Beersheba, looking for employment.[5]

During the first few months after his return, Vanunu held assorted odd jobs. One day he ran into a friend of his brother's who worked at Dimona and suggested that he might look there for employment. After passing an initial exam and surviving the security interviews, he became one of about forty recruits who received an additional two months of instruction in the basics of nuclear physics and chemical engineering, technical English, first aid, and fire prevention. He passed the final exam and began a full-time job as a shift manager in August 1977, working from 11:30 at night to 8:00 in the morning, at Dimona's Machon 2.[6]

Only 150 of Dimona's 2,700 employees were permitted access to the top-secret, below-ground, six-level facility. Parts of Levels 2 to 4 were occupied by the production hall, which contained the main chemical laboratory, where plutonium was separated from uranium. Vanunu was assigned to the main control room, on Level 2, "a 100-foot long maze of polished instrument panels, switches, illuminated dials, gauges and flow charts" used to monitor production hall operations. Level 3 received the fuel rods, lowered from the ground floor. The rods were then stripped of their aluminum casing and dissolved in nitric acid, with the resulting solution moving through pipes to automated units that extracted the plutonium. Scientists working in Level 3 laboratories evaluated the purity of the chemicals used for plutonium extraction. On Level 4 another control room, smaller than the one two levels above, monitored the transformation of plutonium into pure metal, in addition to the production of tritium.[7]

Level 5 was the most sensitive level of all. It was where Vanunu worked briefly, in Unit 95, as part of a team producing the hydrogen bomb ingredient lithium-6. It also was where the process for manufacturing Israel's bombs began, with plutonium discs being machined into spheres. At the very bottom, Level 6 contained storage tanks to hold the radioactive solutions in the event of an emergency.[8]

A little over eight years later, in October 1985, Vanunu would be formally laid off, not because of the quality of his work or elimination of his job, but due to his having become, in the eyes of Israeli officials, a security risk. By 1984 his political views and activism had become clear, including his election to the Council of Students, which represented left-wing and Arab organizations. He was heavily involved in the defense of four Arab students arrested on suspicion of carrying literature from the Palestine Liberation Organization. His face could also be found in newspaper photographs snapped at demonstrations supporting the idea of a Palestinian state. Not surprisingly, security officials at Dimona received a flood of reports about Vanunu's activities.[9]

Security at the site was the responsibility of Israel's version of the British MI-5, the Sherut Bitachon Klali or General Security Service, also known as the Shin Bet (for the first two letters of its Hebrew name) or Shabak (the acronym formed from its Hebrew title). The organization had somehow not noticed Vanunu's first few years of activism, and it was not until June 1984 that plant officials confronted him. While Vanunu would be watched by the security service, he was initially neither fired from Dimona nor transferred from the sensitive Machon 2.[10]

What his Shabak watchers discovered was that Vanunu did not halt his political activities, which were becoming even more worrisome to Israeli authorities. In March 1985 he was one of a very small group of Jews who showed up at a huge Arab demonstration near Beersheba, also attended by camera-carrying security agents. Informants reported that he had also attended a Communist Party membership meeting in Beersheba. The result was another summons to the Dimona security office and a contentious encounter with the head of the office and a senior Shabak official. It ended with Vanunu's refusal to sign a statement acknowledging his activities, after a warning that he could be sent to prison for disclosing information about what went on at Dimona.[11]

That he had not lost his job was due to the favorable evaluation of his performance by his supervisors, as well as his having gone to great lengths to avoid discussing his work in public. In addition, plant officials believed that the high degree of compartmentalization at the facility prevented any worker, especially a control room monitor, from learning exactly what was going on in the most sensitive sections of Machon 2. But the breaking point came when Vanunu called for the creation of a Palestinian state in the midst of a rally during which the PLO flag was unfurled, which was illegal in Israel. Under pressure from plant officials, Vanunu, who had been planning to leave before the end of the year, accepted $7,500 in severance pay and a letter stating that he was a good employee who had only been laid off owing to budget cuts.[12]

On January 19, 1986, no longer tied to a job, Vanunu boarded an Athens-bound ferry in Haifam, a first step in travels that would take him to Bangkok, Burma, Nepal, and then, in May 1986, to Australia. Among those he met down under was Oscar Guerrero, a freelance Colombian journalist with a shady reputation who "oozed insincerity" and was "nothing more than a buccaneering conman," according to one account. His new friend, on learning Vanunu's story, persuaded him that it could be sold for a substantial sum of money. After failing to interest *Newsweek* and assorted local Australian papers, the pair attracted the curiosity of the *London Sunday Times*. The prestigious British paper sent Peter Hounam, who served as the chief investigative reporter for the paper's Insight column from 1986 to 1994, and who had a physics degree, to meet with Vanunu.[13]

Hounam was sufficiently impressed to bring Vanunu back to London, where he was interrogated by nuclear physicists selected by the *Times*. One of those physicists was Frank Barnaby, who had worked for the British atomic weapons establishment at Aldermaston prior to serving as head of the Stockholm International Peace Research Institute (SIPRI) for ten years. He spent three days with Vanunu, first in secret locations near London and then at the *Sunday Times* offices, and found his story credible. He recalled, "I vigorously cross-examined Vanunu, relentlessly asking the same question in a number of different ways and at different times." His cross-examination of Vanunu convinced Barnaby that Vanunu had, as he claimed, worked as a technician on several processes in Dimona.[14]

Vanunu's credibility was enhanced by having more than his memories to offer. Before leaving Dimona, he had pulled off what would have been, had he been working for a foreign intelligence service, a dramatic espionage coup—one for which he would have been handsomely rewarded. In September 1985 he had smuggled a camera into the top-secret facility. The first day, while he was on the 3:30 to midnight shift, he ascended to the roof of Machon 2 and snapped fifteen minutes' worth of pictures, including one or more of the reactor dome.[15]

The next night, while working the overnight shift, he was able to exploit the presence of a skeleton crew. For forty minutes, starting at the 2:00 a.m. meal break, he roamed the building and photographed Dimona's most secret areas. By the time he finished, he had pictures of the laboratories and control room on Level 3 as well as the production hall and plutonium separation equipment on Level 4. Vanunu and his camera even penetrated Level 5, the only area officially off-limits to him, with the help of a negligent supervisor who habitually left the key that allowed access in an open locker. Once inside, Vanunu was able to photograph the glove boxes where the plutonium discs were machined into spheres, along with the instrument panels that controlled the activity. Also in Level 5 was a full-scale model of a hydrogen bomb that Vanunu did not neglect. Altogether, the two-day effort yielded fifty-seven images, including one of "Golda's Balcony," where the Israeli prime minister had stood in admiration of the three-story production hall.[16]

The *London Sunday Times* article appeared on October 5, 1986, and reflected the detailed debriefing of Vanunu as well as the result of his extraordinary adventure in covert photography. In addition to describing his past life, the history of the Israeli nuclear program, and how the *Times* acquired the story, it provided details about Dimona that were probably previously unknown to all but a few Israelis. If so, foreign intelligence services from the CIA to the KGB were able to acquire a gold mine of intelligence for the purchase price of that day's edition.

Vanunu disclosed, and the *Times* reported, the security precautions at Dimona, which included the raking of the perimeter by a tractor so that an intruder would be betrayed by his footprints, infantry and helicopter patrols, observation posts on nearby hilltops, and missile batteries with orders to shoot down any aircraft that strayed into the airspace above the facility. The paper also told its readers of the false walls on the top floor that hid the service elevators carrying men and materials to the six levels below ground.[17]

More importantly, the article detailed Machon 2. It described the facilities and activities on each level, from the canteen and office on the first floor to the storage tanks on the sixth level and everything in between. It also provided, in addition to the type of drawing of the Dimona facility that could have been made using satellite photography, drawings of the individual levels that could not have been obtained from space—photos showing where control rooms, labs, and other facilities were located.[18]

Also described were the activities of individual production units, such as Units 12 to 22, which received the dissolved uranium after the aluminum had been stripped, as well as Units 31 and 37, which, respectively, further concentrated the plutonium that had been extracted from the uranium and then baked it after it had cooled and been mixed with other chemicals. Units 93, 95, and 98 produced tritium, lithium-6, and deuterium, respectively.[19]

The article also revealed, based on Vanunu's disclosures and the analysis by the physicists consulted by the *Times*, Dimona's output. Israel appeared to have a far more substantial arsenal than believed, in terms of both numbers and types of weapons. Discussions with Vanunu led the *Times* physicists to conclude that if Dimona was producing eighty-eight pounds (forty kilograms) of plutonium a year, then enough of the fissile material had been produced for an arsenal, depending on the sophistication of the bomb design, of between one hundred 20-kiloton weapons and two hundred weapons of varying yield—about seven to ten times the previous estimates of Israel's atomic strength. It was also clear that Israel possessed the ability to produce lithium-6. Among the pictures Vanunu showed the *Times* were two that appeared to show a lithium deuteride hemisphere, which could be employed in constructing a thermonuclear weapon.[20]

The pictures and information in that early October report gave the U.S. intelligence community the first detailed evidence that Israel was able to produce thermonuclear weapons. One intelligence official familiar with the previous U.S. intelligence studies of Israel's nuclear capabilities commented that Vanunu's information was stunning and that "the scope of this is much more extensive than we thought. This is an enormous operation."[21]

The revelations left the CIA and other intelligence agencies hungry for more details that could add to the revelations as well as help the agencies attempt to verify Vanunu's claims. Had it been possible to contact him either directly or through an intermediary, undoubtedly attempts would have been made. But Israel had been warned of what Vanunu was doing by the Australian Security Intelligence Organization, which also informed the British Security Service of Vanunu's trip to Britain. And five days before the *Times* story appeared, Vanunu vanished after falling victim to a "honey-trap" operation. Since the Israeli government promised British prime minister Margaret Thatcher that he would not be abducted in Britain, he was lured to Rome by a female member of the Mossad. Instead of the sex he believed was waiting for him, he received a dose of drugs to incapacitate him. A trip back to Israel on a rusty cargo ship used by the Israeli navy for intelligence collection, followed. On November 9 the government of Israel acknowledged that the former Dimona employee was in custody. Trial and seventeen years in prison would follow.[22]*

While Vanunu's kidnapping ruled out the possibility of additional questioning, U.S. intelligence was still able to acquire more information than what appeared in the *Times* article, including *Times* reporters' notes of their interviews with him, which contained a description of each machon's functions. Among the organizations that carefully scrutinized the *Times* report, the photographs, and the reporters' notes was Z Division. The Livermore specialists were skeptical of the conclusion that the Israeli nuclear stockpile was as high as reported, aware of the current CIA and Defense Intelligence Agency estimates that Israel possessed twenty-four to thirty weapons. "On the basis of what Z Division knew," a White House aide remarked, "it could not relate those kinds of numbers to what they could see in the Vanunu photographs."[23]

What puzzled Z Division was the lack of evidence in the Vanunu material of additional cooling capacity for the Dimona reactor. An increased capacity would have been required if the reactor's capability had been expanded to about 150 megawatts, which would have been necessary for it to produce enough plutonium for as many warheads as the story claimed Israel possessed. But Vanunu, in a segment of the interview that was not published, and which Z Division did not have access to, explained that a new cooling unit had been installed during the time he was working at Dimona, an account confirmed by American nonproliferation experts.[24]

Copies of Vanunu's photos of full-sized models of Israeli weapons were provided to weapons designers at Los Alamos and Livermore so that additional intelligence could be extracted. It was assumed that, as was commonly the case, the mock-ups were accurate replicas of the weapons in terms of external design and size. On that basis, the experts at the New Mexico and California laboratories concluded that Israel was capable of producing a neutron bomb, the type of bomb that might have produced the Vela double flash in September 1979.[25]

Vanunu's data also assisted U.S. intelligence experts in charting the progress of the Israeli nuclear program. He revealed that Unit 92 had been

---

* Under the terms of his release in 2004, Vanunu is prohibited not only from leaving Israel but also from speaking to foreigners, entering Internet chat rooms, or approaching foreign embassies. Following Vanunu's release, Peter Hounam arrived in Israel to make a documentary about him and was arrested. See Paul Martin, "Israeli Nuclear Foe Still Fighting," *Washington Times*, July 7, 2004, pp. A1, A18; Sharmila Devi, "Israeli Arrest of UK Reporter Branded a 'Farce,'" *Financial Times*, May 27, 2004.

extracting tritium from heavy water since the 1960s, leading U.S. experts to conclude that the program's physicists had been trying since the early days of Dimona's production to make boosted-fission weapons.[26]

MORDECHAI VANUNU and Col. Chang Hsien-Yi of Taiwan had a few things in common. During the 1980s both were connected to the nuclear programs of "pariah" states, and as a result had accumulated significant knowledge about their nations' pursuit of nuclear weapons. Among the undoubtedly many differences were two of particular interest to the U.S. intelligence community. One was that Chang, rather than being a technician, was the deputy director of Taiwan's Institute of Nuclear Energy Research. And rather than having to first read about his disclosures in a newspaper, the CIA was able to get them directly from Chang. He had been recruited as a CIA asset in the 1960s while he was still a military cadet. Since then he had been providing information about Taiwan's intermittent quest to join the nuclear club.[27]

In 1967 Chang graduated from the military's Chung-Cheng Institute of Technology, which had been established the previous year from the merger of the Army Engineering Institute, Naval Engineering Institute, and Survey College of the Combined Services Force. During the 1970s, while he was ascending the ranks of Taiwan's nuclear weapons establishment, Chang was also being nurtured and cultivated by the CIA, which used both ideology and money. James Lilley, the former CIA China hand and ambassador to South Korea and then China, commented, "You pick a comer, put the right case officer on him and recruit him carefully . . . and keep in touch. Then in the early 80's, it began to pay off."[28]

What information Chang passed on in the 1970s is not clear, but in 1987 he was perfectly positioned to alert the United States when Taiwan began to build a small-scale plutonium extraction facility in violation of its 1976 promises as well as its commitments under the nonproliferation treaty. In the intervening years, the United States had taken a number of steps to reduce the chances that Taiwan's research reactor would be used as source of weapons-grade plutonium. They included persuading Taiwan to employ a reactor core that used both low-enriched uranium oxide and natural uranium, as well as taking control of the reactor's spent fuel. By 1987 about 172 pounds of plutonium in spent fuel had been shipped to the United States, but large quantities of the spent reactor fuel was still in containers at the reactor site. And President Chiang Ching-kuo, possibly out of concern for his nation's security as a result of the United States establishing closer ties with the People's Republic, authorized construction of the multiple hot-cell facility. Bomb development work took place at the Chungshan Institute as well as at Chang's institute nearby.[29]

In December 1987, as the program was accelerating, Chang, with the CIA's aid, never returned from his vacation, defecting to the United States along with his family. As did Vanunu, he brought along more than memories, including a large quantity of documents detailing the progress Taiwan was making toward becoming a nuclear weapons state. Referring to the material Chang brought with him, Lilley commented, "You couldn't get this stuff from intercepts and you couldn't get it from overhead" and "you had to get it from a human source."[30]

With Chang safely in the United States, the Reagan administration, which had been concerned about Taiwan's nuclear activities for several years and considered confronting its leaders a year earlier, decided to act. President Chiang had died in January 1988 but the program was continuing under successor Lee Teng-hui, possibly without his knowledge. Confidential discussions followed, during which the administration stressed the "great importance we attach to nuclear nonproliferation." In February a State Department delegation traveled to Taipei and was informed that Taiwan agreed to both U.S. demands. Taiwan would not only cease work on the plutonium extraction facility but also close down its largest civilian research reactor, the 40-megawatt reactor in Lung Tan, a reactor similar to the one India had used to produce the plutonium for its first test.[31]

"This was a case where they actually did something right," Lilley concluded. "They got the guy out. They got the documentation. And they confronted the Taiwanese."[32]

LIKE MORDECHAI VANUNU, Frederik Willem de Klerk provided the world at large with significant new details about his nation's nuclear weapons program. But unlike Vanunu, de Klerk was not a political outsider who disclosed nuclear secrets to a foreign newspaper. When he addressed a special joint session of parliament as well as a national radio audience on March 24, 1993, he had been South Africa's state president since August 15, 1989.[33]

A month earlier, in February 1993, two Los Alamos scientists visited friends in South Africa's nuclear establishment and had a separate meeting with Atomic Energy Corporation officials J. Wynard de Villiers and Waldo Stumpf. One of the Los Alamos representatives was James McNally, who had spent about two decades in the field of nuclear weapons design and testing and had served as deputy assistant director of the Arms Control and Disarmament Agency's verification and intelligence bureau in the late 1980s. The other was former DIA official Houston T. Hawkins. Since his time with DIA, Terry Hawkins had served in the office of the secretary of defense, with the Defense Nuclear Agency, and from 1988, in the International Technology Division of Los Alamos, the lab's intelligence unit. He had also been a member of several of the multitude of interagency groups, including the Interagency Hard Target Kill Working Group and the President's Verification Review Panel.[34]

In 1991 South Africa had agreed to become a signatory to the nonproliferation treaty and to open its nuclear facilities to inspection by the International Atomic Energy Agency. But there was still skepticism that South Africa had been completely forthcoming about its nuclear history. The two visitors "kept pressing hard" their scientist friends, urging them to do more to persuade skeptics in South Africa and abroad that Pretoria "had come clean," including acknowledging its past nuclear program. AEC chairman de Villiers was unfriendly and unhappy at the prospect of meeting the U.S. scientists, though he asked, "What's another two US spies?" Stumpf, the AEC's chief executive officer, was more friendly than de Villiers, who was described as being "markedly colder than in past discussions." But even Stumpf was less friendly than in past discussions with McNally. One participant in the meeting described Stumpf as "not very accommodating" and the two South Africans as "very testy" and "not very happy campers."[35]*

In his State Department debriefing McNally credited the pressure he exerted while in South Africa as contributing to de Klerk's address, a view shared by the Bureau of Intelligence and Research staffer who conveyed McNally's account of his South Africa trip. De Klerk's speech would be only one of several notable developments during his tenure as president. The presidency followed his becoming the leader of the *verligte* (enlighted) forces of the ruling National Party and then of the party itself, and a successful rebellion against the sitting president, P. W. Botha, after he suffered a stroke but refused to resign the presidency. By 1993 de Klerk had lifted the ban on the African National Congress, freed Nelson Mandela, ended apartheid, and laid the groundwork for the 1994 elections that would terminate white rule in South Africa.[36]

Shortly after the middle of March, de Klerk announced that he would be taking the uncommon step of addressing a joint session of parliament on March 24. His announcement, he recalled, "caused wild speculation among the local and foreign media," for there was no obvious reason for such a session at that time. While there was much speculation as to what de Klerk

---

* McNally also spoke with a scientist friend concerning the Vela incident, who told him that he knew all the weapon scientists in the South African program and there "just weren't enough around to do the job." McNally told his State Department debriefer that the small group of South African weapon scientists were largely Western educated and he did not believe they could have pulled off a September 1979 test without word leaking out. See INR/SPA –[deleted], To: [assorted State Department officials], Subject: February 1993 Visit to South Africa by US Nuclear Weapon Scientists, May 28, 1993.

would be talking about, "none of [the] guesses came close to the mark," de Klerk would write in his memoirs.[37]

In his speech, copies of which would be carefully studied by the CIA and other intelligence agencies, the South African president admitted that "at one stage South Africa did indeed develop a limited nuclear capability." He explained that the plan was to build an arsenal of seven fission bombs, "which was considered the minimum for testing purposes and for the maintenance, thereafter, of a credible deterrent." By the time he became president, six devices had been completed.[38]

When de Klerk assumed the presidency, he was already aware of the weapons program because he had served as minister of mines and energy, which made him responsible for the Atomic Energy Corporation (AEC), established in 1982 through the merger of the Uranium Enrichment Corporation and the Atomic Energy Board. In his memoirs he recalled that while he "had no enthusiasm for [that] massive spending program . . . it had already reached a point of no return when I became involved."[39]

When he replaced Botha, it appeared evident to him as well as to other senior officials, he told parliament, that it was in "our national interest that a total reverse . . . of our nuclear policy . . . was called for." He went on to cite a number of factors—the conclusion of military operations in Angola, the end of the Cold War, and the breakup of the Soviet bloc. There was "the prospect of moving away from a confrontational relationship with the international community in general and with our neighbors in Africa . . . to one of cooperation." In addition, South Africa could reap benefits, including access to new technology, if it would join other countries as a signatory to the nonproliferation treaty. What de Klerk did not mention was the additional consideration of ensuring that a black-dominated government would not possess nuclear weapons.[40]

THE ARSENAL that South Africa possessed when de Klerk assumed power had been assembled during the 1980s. In addition to the uranium-mining and -processing sites, the nuclear infrastructure included the Y-Plant at Pelindaba East (Valindaba) for uranium enrichment and three facilities or complexes involved in various aspects of nuclear weapons research and development and assembly: the Pelindaba Nuclear Research Center, the Building 5000 complex near Pelindaba (which consisted of four buildings), and a large windowless building belonging to Armscor subsidiary Kentron (renamed Advena in 1988), located about ten miles west of Pretoria. Signs at the Kentron/Advena site announced that photography was prohibited, and advised the unauthorized that they were approaching "at your own risk." Overseeing the effort was the AEC.[41]

The primary mission was the production of highly enriched uranium and the manufacture of fission devices. The program also involved research on implosion and thermonuclear weapons, and research and development related to the production of plutonium for use in implosion devices as well as lithium-6 and tritium for use in boosted devices—the latter at a facility in the Gouriqua area on the Cape Coast.[42]

Due to problems at the Y-Plant, it was not until November 1979 that enough highly enriched uranium had been produced for a gun-type device. The first bomb, including its enriched uranium core, was assembled by the Atomic Energy Board to verify that everything fitted properly. After the device was disassembled, it was turned over to Armscor and the two halves of the device were placed in separate, high-security vaults—a precaution taken for future devices. Assembling the weapon required four codes, one held by the president. To prevent premature detonation, the device would only be armed once the aircraft transporting it reached a specified altitude.[43]

A second device was produced in December 1982, with one being added to the arsenal approximately every eighteen months, matching the schedule of the enrichment plant. In addition to adding new bombs to the stockpile, the older ones were upgraded as South Africa improved their reliability. A review of the program in September 1985 reaffirmed that it would be limited to the production of seven gun-type devices, although some limited theoretical work on advance concepts such as implosion devices and lithium-6 production was authorized. The seventh bomb was under construction in 1989 when the program was canceled.[44]

Each of the bombs weighed about one ton and was six feet long and a little over twenty-five inches in diameter. Altogether four primitive gun-type designs were employed, all similar to the "Little Boy" atomic bomb that had been detonated over Hirsohima. Because South Africa's nuclear weapons designers had no means to test the bombs without detection, and no tests were planned, they were packed with about twice as much highly enriched uranium than normally used for a gun-type device to provide extra insurance that they would detonate. Theoretical calculations indicated they would probably explode with a force between ten and eighteen thousand tons of TNT, but some estimates were as low as 5 kilotons. Former AEC chairman de Villiers noted that without a test the AEC "just didn't know the yield."[45]

Although South Africa's atomic bombs were built under the assumption that they would not be tested, there was renewed activity at the Kalahari test site in 1988. President P. W. Botha asked for an estimate of how much time would be required to prepare the site for a nuclear test. Obtaining the answer required Armscor to examine the condition of one of the test shafts. It first cast a concrete floor around the site and then erected a 66-foot-high and 328-foot-long hangar over it. The cover story, if needed, was that the new facility was being used to store and repair vehicles. Technicians proceeded to pump the water out of the shaft, then lowered a specially designed probe which allowed them to determine that the shaft was intact and could be used. Preparations for a test would take between one and two weeks.[46]

Botha's inquiry was the result of the ongoing military and political conflict over independence for Namibia, located to the northwest of South Africa and south of Angola. U.S., Soviet, and Angolan representatives tried to forge a diplomatic solution that would result in independence for the longtime South African colony as well as the withdrawal of Cuban forces from Angola. Cuban forces battled soldiers from South Africa and the Angolan opposition group Unita. In late 1987 and early 1988 they had fought near the southern Angolan town of Cuito Cuanavale. In June, Cuban dictator Fidel Castro warned that South Africa risked "serious defeat" and hinted that his troops might cross into northern Namibia. In August a cease-fire was negotiated and on December 22, South Africa, Cuba, and Angola agreed to Namibia's independence as well as a schedule for the withdrawal of Cuban forces.[47]

Botha's actions have been explained as his trying to raise the stakes so that the two superpowers would conclude that a failure to settle the issue might lead to catastrophic consequences, or his hedging against a breakdown in the negotiations that started after the cease-fire. The first explanation is based on the belief that the construction activity at the test site began prior to the cease-fire. But according to Frank Pabian, who for many years was Z Division's South Africa expert, the shed was first built one or two months after the cease-fire, suggesting that the construction was an "insurance policy" in case the peace process failed.[48]

Whatever the explanation, it was the last hurrah for the South African nuclear weapons program. In October 1989, following the government's conclusion that South Africa should reverse its nuclear course, an experts committee was appointed to provide specific recommendations, which it did the next month. Based on its recommendations, de Klerk directed a committee, consisting of senior officials of the AEC, Armscor, and South African Defence Force under the the chairmanship of the AEC's chief executive officer Waldo Stumpf, to oversee the denuclearization process. The process was to include dismantling the six completed devices, melting and recasting the partially finished seventh device and returning it to the AEC, destroying all the hardware components of the devices along with technical and manufacturing information, and terminating the operation of the Y-Plant as soon as possible.[49]

Y-Plant operations ceased on February 1, 1990, and decommissioning began. Two options were considered for dismantling the arsenal. The first called for destroying one-half of each of the six completed devices before destroying the second parts. The alternative involved destroying one device at a time, which would leave South Africa with some nuclear weapons capability until the very last device was destroyed. Wynand Mouton, a former professor of nuclear physics at Stellenbach University and principal of the University of the Orange Free State, whom de Klerk had first met while he was minister of education in the 1980s and who had been appointed to audit the dismantlement process, recommended the second approach and de Klerk accepted his recommendation.[50]

Mouton's appointment was an attempt to prevent any diversion of weapons materials by South African conservatives who might want to use them to preserve apartheid. He was given access to a massive amount of classified documents, shown slides of the bomb's inner workings, and given a look at the six-foot-long devices during a tour of the Advena facility. Mouton witnessed some of the bombs being dismantled and accompanied several shipments of the highly enriched uranium from Advena to Pelindaba. Approximately twenty trips, spread over four nights, were needed to move the remaining nuclear materials and components, in the trunks of Toyota sedans, to the AEC for storage. The South African military was instructed to monitor the route, although no explanation was provided for the order. In his final report, Mouton certified that the weight of the nuclear cores approximated the weight of the enriched uranium at the conclusion of the dismantlement process, but not that he could account for all of South Africa's nuclear weapons-grade uranium.[51]

The next step on South Africa's denuclearization "to do" list was accession to the nonproliferation treaty. On July 10, 1991, South Africa agreed that its nuclear activities would be governed by the treaty, with all of its nuclear materials and facilities subject to international safeguards. In September it signed a safeguards agreement with the IAEA and in late October submitted an inventory of nuclear material and facilities under its jurisdiction.[52]

WHILE THE U.S. intelligence community attempted to follow South Africa's nuclear activities, those managing the South African program were also determined to limit the information that could be collected from space, in the air, and on the ground—with the 1977 Kalahari incident no doubt firmly in mind. As in other nations, compartmentalization, through the use of code words, restricted knowledge of the nuclear program or parts of the program to those with a "need to know." The names Kraal (an Afrikaaner word for the stone wall that farmers once built to protect livestock, roughly translated as "Circle") and Kierktoring ("Church Tower") designated the program at different times, while Melba was the code name for the first device. No more than ten people knew all the details of the program. It was never discussed in the cabinet or State Security Council. Even foreign minister Roelof F. Botha was not briefed until four years after he became a cabinet member. To further limit the chance of disclosure of program activities to the CIA, KGB, or press, severe limitations were placed on who could be hired. Physicists, chemists, and engineers had to either be South African citizens or have resided in the country for at least fifteen years.[53]

As the August 1977 incident demonstrated, there was always the threat of U.S. or Soviet satellites detecting nuclear weapons activities. To reduce the chances that imagery interpreters in Washington or Moscow would take an interest in the Kentron/Advena nuclear weapons facility, the building's green roof was installed before construction of its internal walls or any significant equipment was sent to the site. Proposals to place sophisticated communications equipment on the roof were vetoed to avoid attracting attention. The precautions would prove successful, with its nuclear role remaining a secret until the South African government disclosed its function in March 1993. Another building, one closer to Valindaba, had become the focus of suspicion, a building that South African officials swore was never the scene of nuclear weapons work.[54]

The CIA, National Security Agency, and other U.S. intelligence agencies continued, of course, to gather whatever information they could on the South African program and make sense of the data collected. The interagency committee assigned to select targets for the National Reconnaissance Office's imagery satellites continued to designate targets in South Africa. On May 11, 1982, a Keyhole satellite photographed the Simonstown Naval Base. The Kalahari test site, the Y-Plant, and other suspected nuclear facilities were likely photographed during that and other Keyhole missions during the decade.[55]

Communications intelligence coverage may have been conducted partially by geosynchronous satellites such as Rhyolite and Vortex along with the eavesdroppers of the CIA–NSA Special Collection Service working out of the U.S. embassy in Pretoria. The embassy was also home to a CIA station, whose officers were undoubtedly attempting to penetrate various components of the South African government.

Analysts also examined trade journals for evidence. Thus, Z Division analyst Frank Pabian became aware, probably shortly after it was published, of an item in *Engineering Week*, published in Johannesburg. The article, "From Bomb-filing to Advanced R&D," which appeared in the journal's annual Arsmcor survey, described the test and evaluation range at Boskop, operated by an Armscor subsidiary. It noted that the range included an "advanced detonics laboratory featuring flash x-ray analysis and ultra-high-speed photography . . . for recording detonation phenomena." That indicated to Pabian that by 1989 South Africa "had acquired the imaging equipment necessary to fulfill the requirements of an implosion-type nuclear weapons research and development program."[56]

Information obtained in the early 1980s through a still classified source, probably a human one, was the basis for a March 1983 top-secret report by the CIA's intelligence directorate, *New Information on South Africa's Nuclear Program and South African-Israeli Nuclear and Military Cooperation.* That source "expands and confirms our knowledge of South Africa's nuclear weapons program," although it is clear from the report that the knowledge being added and confirmed is largely historical.

"Its scientists," the report stated, "were tasked to develop gun-assembly, implosion, and thermonuclear designs." After noting the 1977 detection of the Kalahari test site (which the report incorrectly stated occurred in 1979) and subsequent "international uproar," it went on to tell its readers that *we have had no direct indication of any subsequent activities in the weapons program"* (emphasis added) and "we believe, however, that South Africa already either possesses nuclear devices or has all the components necessary to assemble such devices on very short notice."[57]

The information already known by the CIA and confirmed by the source included the intended use of the Kalahari site for testing, that South African scientists anticipated a yield of 20 kilotons had they tested, and that research on both a gun-assembled device using two modified naval guns and on the firing system for an implosion device was conducted at the Somerset West explosives facility over the period at least from 1973 to 1977. In addition, the source confirmed that favorable nuclear weapons modeling results convinced South African scientists that nuclear testing was not required, and that a plutonium separation plant was contemplated in 1977 to give South Africa a complete nuclear fuel cycle. The report also contained the judgment that the Valindaba plant, which had been producing highly enriched uranium since 1978, had produced enough fissile material for several nuclear weapons.[58]

South African–Israeli nuclear cooperation was another subject, according to the report, where little information had been gathered. It noted that South Africa had supplied Israel with depleted uranium for antitank shells as well as natural-uranium rods between 1972 and 1978. But other than South Africa's sale of ten tons of nominally safeguarded uranium to Israel in 1963, the analysts wrote, "we have little confirmed information about South African-Israeli nuclear cooperation, despite numerous reports and/or rumors linking the two states."[59]

A national intelligence estimate published in October 1984, *Trends in South Africa's Nuclear Security Policies and Programs,* was classified Top Secret Codeword and apparently based in part on communications intelligence. Despite its high classification level it did not reveal that the CIA and other intelligence agencies had gained access to current South African nuclear secrets, but rather that they had failed to.

The analysis did state the agency's belief that South Africa had already stockpiled the components for several test devices or first-generation nuclear weapons and the conclusion, given the size of the nuclear program, that she could stockpile each year sufficient highly enriched uranium for two to four nuclear devices, depending on their design. With regard to any recent research and development of atomic weapons the study could only observe that it was "reasonable to assume that research and development has continued."[60]

The report noted continued disagreement within the intelligence community as to the cause of the September 1979 double flash. It also stated that a South African bomb was still considered a possible source of the Vela detection, which indicated that the intelligence community was not aware of when South Africa first acquired sufficient fissile material for a bomb (November 1979) or that the characteristics of South Africa's atomic devices were incompatible with the estimated yield of the September 1979 signal.[61]

The signature of South Africa's president on the nonproliferation treaty in July 1991 meant that the United States would soon have an additional source of information about his country's nuclear activities: the reports of the IAEA inspectors who would be arriving in South Africa to verify the accuracy of the inventory of nuclear materials and facilities submitted that October.

While such inspections promised to advance U.S. understanding of the nuclear programs of de Klerk and his predecessors, American officials still feared that South Africa might not tell the whole truth. In September 1991 Randall M. Fort, the chief of the State Department's intelligence bureau, addressed the issue of Pretoria's intention to declare its full stock of highly enriched uranium. Fort wrote that while the INR's information was not complete, the organization "currently believes the government of South Africa is inclined to declare all of its enriched-uranium stockpile to the IAEA."[62]

He went on to enumerate three reasons for the South Africans to comply with its IAEA safeguards obligations: fear of exposing or transferring covert stockpiles to a future black-majority government, a desire to improve ties with the international community and to have trade sanctions lifted (including those related to peaceful nuclear trade and technology), and the reduced conventional threat in the region.[63]

That same month, South Africa signed its safeguards agreement with the IAEA. South Africa's record of all nuclear material production dating back more than fifteen years was turned over to the IAEA for verification on October 30, 1991. Pretoria's most important claim was that it produced about 880 pounds of highly enriched uranium. Work on verifying the accuracy of that and other claims would begin with inspections in mid-November.[64]

LONGTIME IAEA DIRECTOR GENERAL Hans Blix was requested to report back to his board of governors on the "completeness of South Africa's declaration of nuclear material and facilities." Blix, who had served as a mem-

ber of Sweden's delegation to the UN until 1981, when he became IAEA chief, appointed a special IAEA safeguards team. Five meetings held in South Africa and Vienna followed. South Africa also declared its imports and exports of nuclear materials and technology and gave the IAEA the authority to inspect any relevant location, including the nuclear test site and the Advena weapons fabrication plant.[65]

The most important site the IAEA inspectors visited was the pilot enrichment plant (Y-Plant), as part of the effort to determine just how much enriched uranium had been produced, as well as to look into reports that it might contain equipment for manufacturing weapons components. Determining how much U-235 had been produced and accounting for it would give the IAEA confidence that there had never been, or no longer were, any nuclear devices in South Africa and that no U-235 (or U-235 bombs) had been shipped abroad. Blix's special team carried out an extensive audit of historical operating and accounting records at the selected facilities. Inspectors discovered some sophisticated equipment at the Y-Plant that could be used in the bomb program but no hidden nuclear material.[66]

Early in August 1992 a helicopter carried a team of inspectors to the Vastrap test range in the Kalahari Desert to inspect the test site that South Africa had constructed in 1988. Inspectors dug soil samples around the concrete-capped shaft so that laboratory analysis could search for the residue of an atomic bomb test. The tests would show the presence of natural uranium but no evidence of a nuclear detonation. The inspectors also did not find any evidence that the South Africans might not have declared all the highly enriched uranium produced at Valindaba, but hidden some of it.[67]

In late September Blix told the IAEA General Conference that "there is inherent difficulty in verifying the completeness of an original inventory in a country in which a substantial nuclear program has been going on for a long time. . . . Even so . . . no evidence has been found suggesting that the original inventory is not complete."[68]

But the inherent difficulty Blix wrote about contributed to lingering doubts in various elements of the U.S. intelligence community. Undoubtedly, discovery after the Gulf War of the extent to which the IAEA failed to uncover the scope of the Iraqi nuclear program contributed to U.S. concern that the agency might be fooled again. That concern would lead to parallel efforts by the United States and other countries to determine if South Africa's declarations to the IAEA were full and complete. Stumpf would find those efforts "quite frustrating," "irritating," and "even irresponsible" and wondered why those countries did not trust the IAEA.[69]

Earlier in the year, a secret March 1992 INR memo noted a recent CIA assessment that apparently questioned the completeness of South Africa's disclosure. INR was less inclined to be suspicious and more willing to postpone judgment. It noted that "the South Africans reportedly kept poor operating records of enriched-uranium output" and that "we continue to receive information which, over time, may permit us to reach conclusions as to whether South Africa is meeting its NPT obligations—but we cannot reach any conclusions yet."[70]

In late August 1992 the intelligence community was still debating the issue of South African compliance. The proliferation assessments working group of the Nonproliferation Center drafted a paper on South Africa's nuclear inventory that was apparently skeptical of its veracity.[71]

The Nonproliferation Center had been first established on September 17, 1991, within the CIA's Directorate of Intelligence and subordinated to the Office of Scientific and Weapons Research. Its mission was to track worldwide development and acquisition of production technology, designs, components, or complete military systems in the areas of weapons of mass destruction and advanced conventional weaponry. In April 1992 director of central intelligence Robert Gates raised the unit's status by making it a DCI center and removing it from control of the scientific and weapons research office. The center's director, Gordon Oehler, a twenty-year agency veteran who had headed the scientific and weapons research office and held a doctorate in physics from Rensselaer Polytechnic Institute, became the senior intelligence community spokesperson on proliferation-related issues.[72]

An INR response, at the end of the month, to the center's assessment conveyed the bureau's strong belief that the "body of information is ambiguous" and that contradictions needed to be resolved before any firm judgments could be offered with confidence. It went on to state that while some information supported the notion of an "honest declaration," other data supported the "cheating" scenario. Considerable information was susceptible to either interpretation. The memo argued that, at the time, there was no basis for assigning a greater likelihood to the "cheating scenario" and that it was premature to offer any general verdict on South Africa's conduct.[73]

The INR response also noted a considerable difference in the estimates as to how much highly enriched uranium the Y-Plant had produced over the past fourteen years, from as much as 2,420 pounds (1,100 kilograms) to as little as 1,100 pounds (500 kilograms). While the INR and other agencies considered the higher end of the scale more likely, a range with 1,320 pounds (600 kilograms) as its minimum was also plausible, according to the memo. The author further noted that the working group meeting was not attended by the Department of Energy, "whose technical contributions have been essential toward framing [U.S. Government] estimates of South Africa's HEU [highly enriched uranium] production."[74]

Two days after the INR response, the bureau followed up with another, similarly worded dissent, which it submitted as a footnote to the working group paper, stressing the ambiguity of much of the evidence. It argued that the key remaining uncertainties, particularly the output of the pilot enrichment plant, might be resolved over time. Thus, "while the amount of HEU reportedly declared raises doubts and serious questions, it also falls within the range . . . of plausible HEU production levels."[75]*

Then in mid-September the INR addressed another memo to the Nonproliferation Center, protesting the elimination of some portions of the footnote. The shorter version failed to spell out in full the argument that the evidence was subject to differing interpretations. It also contained less exposition than the INR would have liked about the range of plausible highly enriched uranium production levels.[76]

In December, Gary D. Dietrich, the chief of INR's Office of Strategic and Proliferation Affairs, wrote INR director Douglas P. Mulholland, commenting that the intelligence the United States possessed about the South African program was still far from definitive. The memo, which may have been written in response to a recent CIA report concerning the Vela incident, noted that the INR believed that South Africa's only well-developed nuclear weapon design "at the time" was a gun-assembly weapon that would not require nuclear testing. Implosion weapon development, according to the memo, "almost certainly had not reached the test phase." In addition, the memo noted that "there is evidence that South Africa may not have produced enough weapons-grade uranium by late 1979 for a test device."[77]

Another December report mentioned that the primary nuclear proliferation concern for South Africa "is to establish whether Pretoria has declared to the IAEA its entire inventory of in-country nuclear material and operational nuclear facilities." Many, if not most, U.S. analysts, the report stated, believed that if South Africa had not declared all the highly enriched uranium it produced, the missing material probably had been transferred abroad. The possibility that South Africa was concealing the fissile material, possibly in an underground facility, within South Africa was considered remote.[78]

The concerns of analysts and officials in the CIA and elsewhere in the intelligence community that South Africa might have hidden significant quantities of highly enriched uranium and other components of nuclear warheads were partially based on what was described as "highly sensitive intelligence . . . from human sources and photoreconnaissance satellites." That intelligence included claims or indications that "a lot of stuff [in the operating records] was altered or filled in" during several months when South Africa claimed it was conducting a search to locate them, according to a U.S. official.[79]

---

* The minimum plausible amount of HEU specified in the INR memo was still significantly greater than the 880 pounds declared by South Africa, but see pp. 397–398.

In addition, there was concern that hidden material may have been transferred to another nation. The concern reached a level such that an unclassified version of an intelligence community report transmitted to Congress in
January 1993, and signed by President George H. W. Bush, noted that "the
United States has serious questions about South Africa's compliance with its
Article II and Article III obligations." Article II of the nonproliferation treaty
prohibits the manufacture or transfer to another country of nuclear weapons
while Article III requires international safeguards on all "special fissionable
material" and forbids its undeclared export.[80]

An anonymous official, speaking to the *Washington Post*, explained that
"the biggest concern is how much [fissile] material they have produced." Analysts, he reported, believe "they declared only a portion" of the material in the
documents provided to the IAEA, fueling fears that the remainder was hidden
or possibly exported to Israel.[81]

IAEA investigators proved unable to resolve some of the discrepancies in
South Africa's nuclear accounting. Despite their extensive efforts—which
included more than eighty inspections (by March 1993), short-notice visits to
undeclared military facilities, including the Vastrap test range in the Kalahari,
and reviews of fifteen years of records—discrepancies remained between the
amount of uranium material going into the two South African enrichment
plants and the quantity of bomb-grade material that the plants reportedly produced. Complicating the problem were the idiosyncratic accounting systems
used to monitor the program during the prolonged period when its existence
was a secret. Those systems made it impossible to conclusively demonstrate
that every last ounce of fissile material could be accounted for.[82]

The IAEA was inclined to believe that the discrepancies were a product
of inevitable limits of nuclear accounting, and doubted that South Africa
would have any motive to hold on to nuclear weapons material. In addition,
the inspectors were impressed by South Africa's willingness to agree to short-
notice inspections of the Y-Plant and the Vastrap range. There were dissenters, particularly within the U.S. intelligence community. One U.S.
official commented, "I think there is more to it than simply a physics problem" and "if you put yourself in the position of the U.S. government, you
have the IAEA's effort to reconstruct the [nuclear] material, and you have
your own intelligence archive about what has been going on [in South
Africa] for 15 years. That intelligence is not consistent, but even after win-
nowing, there are questions."[83]

At the time, one U.S. official questioned whether the intelligence community would ever be satisfied that South Africa's nuclear capability had been
eliminated, observing that "you can never prove a negative." He also noted,
"You are left at bottom with taking someone's word for it. . . . The conse-

Jaffar Dhia Jaffar, appointed senior administrator of
the Iraqui nuclear weapons program in 1981.

Mahdi Obeidi, head of the centrifuge effort at Rashdiya, turned over booklets and centrifuge parts hidden in his garden to U.S. troops after the fall of Baghdad.
CENTRAL INTELLIGENCE AGENCY VIA ROBERT WINDREM

A.Q. Khan, a central figure in Pakistan's development of nuclear weapons and the proliferation of nuclear weapons technology.
UNITED STATES INFORMATION AGENCY VIA ROBERT WINDREM

India's Pokhran test site after the
May 11, 1998, detonation.
AFP/GETTY IMAGES

The Defense Communications Electronics
Evaluation and Testing Activity (DCEETA), at Fort
Belvoir, Virginia, the main ground station for the
receipt of KH-11 and advanced KH-11 imagery.

ROBERT WINDREM

Tuwaitha centrifuges, discovered
by IAEA inspectors after the
1990–1991 Persian Gulf War.
ACTION TEAM 1991–1998/IAEA

WC-135, the remaining U.S. aircraft used to gather the airborne particles produced by nuclear testing.

Tarmiya, site of Iraqi electromagnetic isotope separation efforts before the 1990–1991 war.

David Kay was head of an IAEA inspection team in Iraq after the 1990–1991 war and served as the director of central intelligence's adviser to the Iraq Survey Group after the 2003 war.

AL FURAT MANUFACT

DECEMBER 1998

George J. Tenet, director of central intelligence from July 1997 to July 2004.
CENTRAL INTELLIGENCE AGENCY

...G FACILITY, IRAQ

SEPTEMBER 2002

CONSTRUCTION NEARLY COMPLETE

Al Furat, a centrifuge production site before the 1990–1991 Gulf War, as photographed by advanced KH-11 satellites in December 1998 and September 2002.
U.S. GOVERNMENT

Arak, Iran, site of a planned heavy-water
production plant and 40-megawatt reactor,
photographed by an Ikonos satellite in
August 2001.

SPACE IMAGING/INTA-SPACE TURK

A September 2002 Ikonos photograph of
Natanz, Iran, site of a pilot fuel enrichment
plant employing centrifuges and planned
future site of a full-scale enrichment plant.
SPACE IMAGING/INTA-SPACE TURK

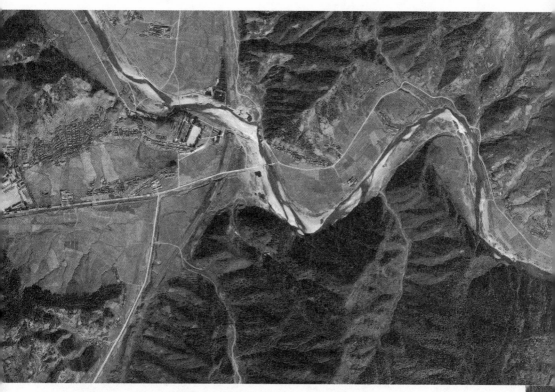

Hagap, North Korea, a candidate for the location
of an underground uranium enrichment
facility, photographed by an Ikonos satellite
in October 2000.

SPACE IMAGING

Yongbyon Nuclear Research Center, North Korea, the focus of
U.S. concerns about North Korean nuclear weapons efforts,
photographed by an Ikonos satellite in August 2002.

SPACE IMAGING

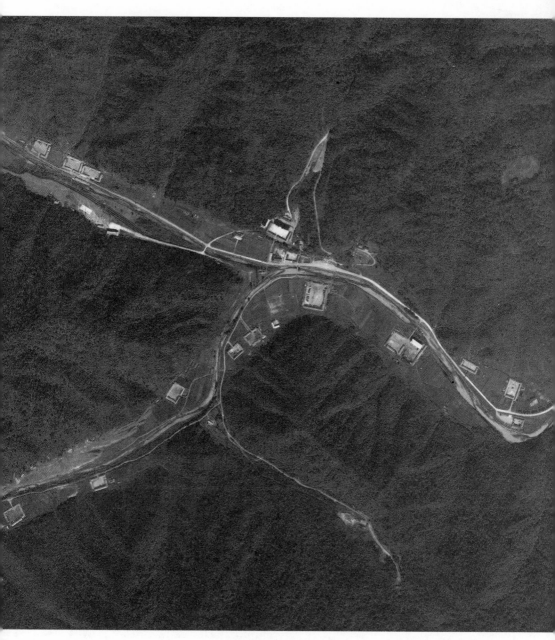

A September 2002 Ikonos photograph of Kumchang-ri, North Korea, home to an underground facility that the United States believed might be related to nuclear weapons efforts but was empty when inspected.

quence is that maybe the South Africans have a bunch of bombs and maybe they will wind up in the hands of terrorists. That is the best we will ever be able to do."[84]

NEAR THE END of de Klerk's speech in March 1993, he assured his listeners that "South Africa's hands are clean and we are concealing nothing. Permission has now been granted by the government with a view to international inspection for full access to the facilities and records of facilities which in the past were used for the preparation of a nuclear deterrent capability."[85]

In the aftermath of de Klerk's speech, international inspectors did more than take the South African president's word that his country had disarmed and had come clean, although they would certainly be handicapped by the government's destruction of an estimated twelve thousand documents relating to the weapons program. They would spend five months carrying out inspections at facilities and locations that South Africa declared to have been involved in the nuclear program.[86]

An IAEA team visited in April and was presented with records on the dismantling of the enriched uranium components of the weapons and shown destroyed or partially destroyed weapons components. The team also audited the records on the shipment of enriched uranium between the AEC and the Kentron Circle facility, which allowed the team to conclude that the enriched uranium originally applied to Armscor had been returned to the AEC.[87]

In May they were planning to analyze the ink and paper records of a key South African nuclear plant in the hope of alleviating continued U.S. concerns. The planned tests were intended to determine the age of the records, which would answer the question of how much highly enriched uranium the South Africans had produced.[88]

Based on the intelligence received, some U.S. intelligence officials suspected that the South Africans had forged some of the records in 1992, to understate the amount of bomb-grade material they had produced between 1976 and 1990. That would allow some of the enriched uranium to be stockpiled, hidden by renegade white officials, or transferred to other nations, such as Israel—although U.S. intelligence agencies had not collected any concrete evidence to support such fears. The South Africans claimed that the records were not falsified and provided accurate information on the quantity of fissile material produced.[89]

The suspicions were fueled by information obtained in 1992 that suggested alterations of the records, combined with the claim that only 880 pounds of enriched uranium had been produced, in contrast to the more than 2,400 pounds that might have been produced if the Valindaba plant was operating at full capacity. "It's the minimum possible, reflecting what might have happened if everything went wrong," one official said. Other factors that undoubtedly undermined South African credibility were the claims of no foreign involvement in its nuclear weapons program as well as differing accounts by South African officials concerning when Valindaba began producing fissile material.[90]

IN SEPTEMBER the IAEA transmitted a letter from the director general Hans Blix, *The Denuclearization of Africa*, with an attachment, *The Agency's Verification Activities in South Africa*. The attachment listed and described the facilities visited by the IAEA's inspectors, including the Armscor/Circle establishment near Pelindaba, the Armscor/Advena Central Laboratories, the Vastrap site in the Kalahari, the site at Gouriqua, and an explosives test facility, among others.[91]

It also reported that "consultations with officials of the Atomic Energy Corporation (AEC) and detailed examination of the historical records of specific periods of operation and intervening shutdown periods, since the start-up of the pilot enrichment plant have resulted in substantial reduction of the magnitude of the apparent discrepancy in the uranium-235 balance associated with this plant." It went on to state that "it is reasonable to conclude that the amounts of HEU which could have been produced by the pilot enrichment plant are consistent with the amounts declared in the initial report."[92]

Two months later DCI James Woolsey transmitted a national intelligence estimate to a much more select audience. The study reportedly assigned a low probability to South Africa's having retained a "bomb in the basement" but also concluded that there would never be 100 percent certainty. The estimate also could not provide a definitive conclusion concerning whether South Africa had declared all its enriched uranium to international inspectors.[93]

The last declassified word from the U.S. intelligence community on the subject is an INR report of December 19, 1993, *South Africa: Nuclear Case Closed?* It noted that de Klerk's March claims—that South Africa had manufactured six gun-assembled nuclear weapons and had planned to complete a seventh weapon using highly enriched uranium as well as having done preliminary work on implosion and advanced-weapons designs—were consistent with information available to the United States.[94]

The study also noted that reporting indicated the dismantlement or decommissioning of all dedicated nuclear weapon facilities, including the Armscor weaponization complex. In addition, there had been drastic cutbacks at virtually all dual-use nuclear installations. One Armscor facility, apparently intended for second-generation nuclear weapons, had been converted to produce conventional technologies. The Kalahari test site, whose boreholes were filled in a public ceremony, was inactive, according to the report.[95]

It also noted that before de Klerk's revelations, South Africa had gone to considerable lengths to avoid admitting the military orientation and advanced stage of the nuclear program—though it was under no legal obligation to do so. "The March disclosures," the report commented, "apparently set the record straight concerning previous obfuscation, and Pretoria has invited the IAEA to visit virtually any suspect site and interview any individual in the former program."[96]

The study characterized South Africa's inventory declaration as "credible but problematic." It noted that "South Africa's nuclear-material inventory— declared to the IAEA . . .—is [redacted] to verify given the incompleteness of our own information." The amount of enriched uranium produced at the Valindaba plant, according to the analysis, "[deleted] corresponds to the mid range of previous US estimates of actual plant production but is well below plant capacity." South African officials described, "in impressive detail," plant operating problems that were technically plausible but were previously unknown to the United States nonetheless, according to the INR report.[97]

With regard to the possibility of fissile material having been transferred abroad, it noted that, "moreover, the evidence for a transfer abroad is not strong, and prospects for an in-country cache are very remote." As for other aspects of cooperation, the report observed that de Klerk's claim that South Africa never conducted a nuclear test could not be refuted. As for his claims that South Africa never engaged in nuclear weapons cooperation with another country, it commented that "we have no firm evidence that would contradict a claim of direct weapons cooperation, though what evidence we have suggests earlier cooperation in a looser sense."[98]

The IAEA, the INR noted, was satisfied, with the agency reporting to its board of governors in September that it felt that "Pretoria's inventory declarations were consistent with the amount of highly enriched uranium that could have been produced at the Valindaba plant." The State Department intelligence bureau also noted that the IAEA had "conducted over 20 inspection missions, examined many thousands of records [deleted] and received US briefings on most aspects of the weapons program [deleted]."[99]

IN OCTOBER 1984, when the national intelligence estimate titled *Trends in South Africa's Nuclear Security Policies and Programs* was written, the United States had little recent knowledge of the South African weapons program. Although U.S. officials claimed to have been aware of details of the

South African program revealed by President de Klerk in 1993, no specifics were provided on exactly what information was acquired and when.

Despite those claims, it appears that the IAEA inspections, with South African cooperation, added substantially to U.S. knowledge of the South African nuclear weapons effort, including its production of highly enriched uranium, as well as its being unable in September 1979 to detonate an atomic weapon, particularly one with the characteristics needed to generate the Vela signal.

chapter ten

BIG BANGS

In his March 1993 address in Pretoria, F. W. de Klerk told the world that his nation was no longer interested in being a member of the nuclear club. But during the first half of the decade, at test sites in different parts of the world, other nations would demonstrate their continued desire to maintain and improve their nuclear arsenals. Those activities would be followed closely by U.S. nuclear intelligence analysts, who sought to determine exactly what those nations were doing and why.

FRANCE WAS AMONG those countries. During the 1980s the French had used their Mururoa and Fangataufa testing grounds on ninety-two separate occasions. Included were eight tests in 1984 used to validate an improved warhead for the multiple-warhead M4 submarine-launched ballistic missile that would enter service in 1985 on the *L'Inflexible*, to test an improved warhead for the ASMP air-to-surface missile that would be first deployed on Mirage IVP aircraft in 1986, and to conduct research for a warhead intended for the never-to-be-deployed Hades short-range tactical missile.[1]

The French testing campaign in the 1980s was also notable for the two nonnuclear explosive devices that tore through the *Rainbow Warrior*, a ship operated by the Greenpeace environmental group, on July 10, 1985. The environmental group was planning to use it to lead a flotilla of vessels to the vicinity of Mururoa to protest the French testing activities. It would soon be discovered that the bombing, which destroyed the ship and killed Greenpeace photographer Fernando Pereira, was the work of the General Directorate for External Security (DGSE), the French secret service.[2]

During 1990 and 1991, while South Africa was dismantling its arsenal and signing the nonproliferation treaty, France conducted another twelve tests, nine at Mururoa and three at Fangataufa. While the yields of the tests varied widely, from 10 to 130 kilotons, they did have a common purpose. Each was for evaluating the performance of the miniaturized, hardened TN 75 warhead that was to rest atop the M45 submarine-launched missile, which was to be carried aboard the Triomphant-class submarines beginning in the mid-1990s. The Commissariat l'Energie Atomique had promised that the warhead would be "virtually invisible to radar."[3]

A three-year moratorium followed, imposed by French president François Mitterand. But that hiatus ended in 1995, when his successor, Jacques Chirac, assumed power. The CEA as well as nuclear specialists in the Ministry of Defense convinced the new chief of state that a new testing campaign would serve two purposes. It would allow French weapons designers to perfect a new warhead for the M5 missile, scheduled to enter service with the third Triomphant-class submarine around the turn of the century, and to ensure the reliability of the French arsenal once the country signed the comprehensive test ban treaty. The treaty, whose origins went back to the 1950s, would go beyond the prohibition of the 1974 threshold test ban treaty and prohibit all nuclear tests of any yield.[4]

The moratorium ended with an underground test on September 5, 1995, which Chirac had postponed from August in response to President Bill Clinton's plea that France not conduct a test while he was in the region celebrating the fiftieth anniversary of the end of World War II in Hawaii. The test took place at 12:30 p.m. at Mururoa, when the nuclear device inside the sixty-five-foot-long canister at the bottom of a shaft about a half mile deep detonated with a force of 8 kilotons, an explosion that was detected in Australia within minutes. French television pictures of the event showed the turquoise lagoon rise several feet, turn a milky white for several seconds, and then settle back into its original state. French nuclear scientists watched the test from deck chairs on the atoll and politely applauded the explosion. French defense chief Charles Millon issued a statement declaring that the testing program was "indispensable to enable us to guarantee the reliability and safety of our nuclear arsenal in the long term."[5]

The new series of tests was met with strong protests from governments and activists. While Russia, Great Britain, and the United States had ceased testing between 1990 and 1992, France and China had continued. Japan, Australia, and New Zealand were among the nations that lodged complaints. New Zealand, whose prime minister in 1984 had suggested the French do their testing "somewhere near Strasbourg," recalled its ambassador from Paris. Australian foreign minister Gareth Evans objected that the test "is not the action of a good international citizen; it is not the action of a good neighbor." Throughout the region there were consumer boycotts of French wine, cheese, and fashion products. In Papeete the protests were violent. A flotilla of twenty-five protest ships, including the *Rainbow Warrior II* and *Greenpeace*, ringed Mururoa. Once again the French interfered, seizing both vessels as they moved toward the exclusion zone, although without killing anyone.[6]

A second test, at Fangataufa, followed on October 1. The fifth, and last, test of 1995 took place in late December. The protesters would have what they wanted—an end to French testing—on January 27, 1996 when France conducted its final nuclear test, number 210. Approximately eight months later, on September 24, it signed the comprehensive test ban treaty along with the other acknowledged nuclear powers.[7]

THE FRENCH TESTS in the 1990s did draw the attention of both real and fictional spies. To protest the 1995 round of tests, actor Pierce Brosnan refused to attend the French premiere of the film *Goldeneye*, his debut appearance as James Bond, leading to the premiere's cancellation. Meanwhile, on the other side of the world, very real spies were monitoring those nuclear tests.[8]

When Mitterand announced his moratorium in April 1992, analysts with the New Zealand External Assessments Bureau who followed French testing were shifted to other duties. Once testing resumed in 1995, New Zealand's Government Communications Security Bureau (GCSB) resumed intercepting French military communications to and from Mururoa. Analysts at the assessments bureau also went back to monitoring French testing activity. They used the signals intercepted by GCSB concerning French military aircraft movements to and from Mururoa, along with other information, to evaluate and predict the times and yields of French tests. Their reports were of interest not only to New Zealand officials, but also to those in the U.S. intelligence community who monitored French testing activity—and the Americans received the product of the New Zealand analysts' work, as they had in the past.[9]

The reports from New Zealand about French nuclear activities helped the United States target its more substantial intelligence capabilities on nuclear developments in the South Pacific. In the mid-1990s the National Reconnaissance Office was operating both later versions (launched in late 1987 and 1988) of the original KH-11 satellites, as well as one advanced electro-optical satellite—the Improved Crystal, launched in November 1992, which was equipped with infrared sensors for nighttime imaging. Another Improved Crystal would be in orbit at the time of the final two French tests. All would pass over the French test grounds and could return their high-resolution imagery in real time.[10]

Were any of the Vela satellites still operational, they would, of course, have been useless in detecting French tests. Other satellite systems—including the Defense Support Program, Defense Meteorological Satellite Program, Global Positioning System, and Satellite Data System satellites—able to detect atmospheric tests were also of no use against underground tests.* Aer-

---

* The Global Positioning System (GPS) is a constellation of twenty-one primary satellites, and three spares, in near-circular orbits 11,000 miles above the earth at an inclination of 55 degrees to its equator. While the satellites are best known for their role in allowing the precise location of individuals and objects, by 1995 they had been performing an important secondary mission for over decade. Every GPS satellite since GPS-8, launched in 1983, had carried

ial monitoring would be of no value unless nuclear material escaped from the underground test shaft, and it does not appear any attempt was made to collect such debris. But the Air Force Technical Applications Center was still operating seismic stations and underwater arrays that could detect the earth-shaking signals produced by a nuclear weapons test.

By 1995 AFTAC's seismic network included stations on four continents, although the number had declined with the end of the Cold War. There were stations in North America (Cambridge Bay, Canada; Flin Flon, Canada; Eielson Air Force Base, Alaska; Lajitas, Texas), Asia (Chiang Mai, Thailand; Wonju, Korea), Australia (Alice Springs), and Europe (Belbasi, Turkey). In addition, as part of AFTAC's response to the September 1979 Vela incident, it engaged the U.S. Geological Survey to establish a set of nine stations distributed across Latin America, Antarctica, and Africa. The first of those stations to become operational was located in South Africa (in February 1993) while the final station to come online was the Argentina station (in November 1994), so all were in operation when the French began their new round of tests.[11]

The end of the Cold War had also taken its toll on the Navy's Sound Surveillance System and AFTAC's collocated stations. But at least some of the arrays that resided in portions of the Pacific Ocean and their associated ground stations remained in operation, and the hydroacoustic signals generated by the French tests at Mururoa and Fangataufa would have been detected by the arrays and been transmitted to the naval facility that recorded their data.[12]

WHILE THE U.S. intelligence community continued to take an interest in French nuclear testing activities in the 1990s, it did not take nearly as great an interest as it did in earlier years. In the 1960s it had produced a number of national intelligence estimates, the community's most prestigious product. But in the 1990s, it would not publish a single national, or special national, intelligence estimate on French nuclear weapons programs.[13]*

------

a Nuclear Detonation (NUDET) Detection System (NDS) package on board. The NDS includes X-ray and optical sensors, bhangmeters, electromagnetic pulse sensors, and a data-processing capability that can locate a nuclear explosion to within one hundred meters. Data is reported on a real-time basis directly to either AFTAC or ground stations at Diego Garcia, Kwajelein Atoll, Ascension Island, or Kaena Point, Hawaii. See Jeffrey T. Richelson, *The U.S. Intelligence Community*, 4th ed. (Boulder, Colo.: Westview, 1999), pp. 218–219.

* There was even less need after 1996 to gather information about the French program. The U.S.-French nuclear cooperation that had begun in the early 1970s expanded further, and included an exchange of each country's data base of nuclear weapons tests. The United

In contrast, there was still great interest in China's continuing efforts to upgrade its nuclear capabilities. China, like France, would sign the comprehensive test ban treaty on September 24, 1996, and cease testing. But, like France, China had conducted nuclear tests throughout the first half of the decade and into 1996, stopping with its forty-fifth test on July 29, 1996, by which time, according to CIA estimates, the Chinese had an arsenal of between two hundred and three hundred warheads.[14]

From the late 1960s and up to the final Chinese test, the Americans had continued to gather intelligence on China's nuclear activities. Each new generation of imagery satellite photographed Lop Nur, Baotou, Jiuquan, and the other elements of China's nuclear weapons establishment, while the National Security Agency continued to monitor Chinese communications for relevant data, and the CIA's operations directorate tried, and occasionally succeeded in, recruiting human sources—as illustrated by the information obtained in the 1980s on the links between the Pakistani and Chinese programs.[15]

Through China's twenty-seventh test, on October 16, 1980—the sixteenth anniversary of its first test—significant intelligence was also obtained from the satellites equipped with nuclear detonation detection sensors as well as aerial collection of the nuclear debris that resulted from the explosions. In 1976, for example, Strategic Air Command U-2Rs conducted Olympic Race debris collection operations following China's tests of January 23, 1976, and November 17, 1976.[16]

Thanks to advance warning from AFTAC that a test was imminent—which the organization had probably received as a result of the combined work of the Gambit (KH-8) and Hexagon (KH-9) satellites orbiting the earth during the final months of 1975 and into 1976, and America's eavesdropping operations—SAC had a U-2R ready at Osan Air Base in Korea for China's first test of 1976. The plane flew its first sampling mission on January 24, over the Sea of Japan, and gathered debris from the test. Four more missions followed but failed to collect additional debris.[17]

While the test of January 23 was relatively small, characterized by the CIA as being of low yield, the November 17 test was estimated at 4 megatons, the largest Chinese test since joining the world's nuclear fraternity. In order to sample the resulting debris from the large nuclear cloud as it slowly moved eastward through the stratosphere, U-2Rs flew from four locations—from

---

States also provided the results of computer simulations on the workings of the "primary" (fission bomb) component of thermonuclear bombs. See R. Jeffrey Smith, "France, U.S. Secretly Enter Pact to Share Nuclear Weapons Data," *Washington Post*, June 17, 1996, p. A9; Kenneth Timmerman, *The French Betrayal of America* (New York: Crown, 2004), p. 267.

Osan as well as air force bases in Alaska (Eielson), California (Beale), and New Hampshire (Pease). The planes logged 143 hours of flying time conducting seventeen sampling missions, six of which yielded debris.[18]

But China's October 1980 test would be its last atmospheric test, as the nation joined the other declared nuclear powers in observing the terms of the 1963 partial test ban treaty. During the remainder of the decade China would conduct another seven tests.[19] Thus, by the time the 1990s began, the U.S. nuclear intelligence community would have had a decade of experience in monitoring Chinese nuclear testing activity without the benefit of satellites equipped with nuclear detonation gear or the guarantee that there would be atmospheric debris.

While over the years France and Russia had moved the locations of their main test sites, Lop Nur had remained China's one and only site for nuclear weapons tests. It was also the world's largest test area, occupying over 62,000 square miles, with over 1,200 miles of highways. About one-fifth of the site was used for testing purposes. The entire facility consisted of three districts. The northwest district included the scientific city of Malan, where test site headquarters and the residences for scientists, engineers, and technicians were, and still are, located. The southeast district was where China had set off atmospheric tests, while the central district was where underground tests were conducted. The Qinggir region, in the eastern part of the district, was used for vertical shaft tests. Tests were conducted in horizontal tunnels in the Beishan region, to the southwest of Qinggir, and the Nansahn region, to Qinggir's northwest.[20]

Gathering the details about the test site—where the shafts were, whether they were horizontal or vertical, and how deep they were—was part of the nuclear test intelligence effort. Information was also needed on the geology of the test site. That some of the vertical shafts had been dug in Carboniferous granite and Upper Paleozoic metasandstone and conglomerate was important. The magnitude of the seismic signals from an underground test is a product not only of the true yield of the device but also the type of rock that the resulting seismic signals pass through on their way to a monitoring station. Therefore, turning the magnitude into an estimated yield required consideration of the site's geology. Some of the needed information could be found in, or teased out of, the open Chinese literature, such as articles that appeared in 1980 and 1983 in the journal *Shuiwendizhi Gongchengdizhi* with the titles "Physical Geological Reactions to Underground Nuclear Explosions" and "A Preliminary Study of Abnormal Movement of Groundwater Influenced by an Underground Nuclear Explosion." But there was also a need to produce classified studies such as the Joint Atomic Energy Intelligence Committee's 1992 *Geology of the Qinggir Underground Nuclear Test Site, China*, based partly on secret sources.[21]

Of course, those in the U.S. intelligence community—whether at the CIA in northern Virginia or at Z Division in northern California—who monitored Chinese nuclear testing activities in the 1990s wanted to know about more than the rocks at Lop Nur. They also wanted information about the people involved in the test program—about their responsibilities, skills, and backgrounds, information that helped in understanding China's testing activities.

One means of gathering such information involved Chinese nuclear scientists visiting facilities such as Livermore and Los Alamos, an activity that began in the late 1970s. Those scientists, according to a Livermore counterintelligence briefing, "sought close personal relationships with individual Lab employees." The Chinese delegation that visited Livermore in February 1994 included Hu Renyu, director of the Chinese Academy of Engineering Physics, which ran the nuclear weapons program, along with academy deputy director Hu Side. Also along for the visit was Ye Lirun, the chief engineer at Lop Nur.[22]

Even more valuable were the U.S. scientists who were permitted to travel in China and visit China's nuclear weapons facilities, including the test site. The first was Harold Agnew, the veteran of Los Alamos, who had become the institution's director in 1970. In January 1979, a few months before he was due to retire, Agnew received an invitation to a reception for Deng Xiaoping at Washington's Ritz-Carlton Hotel. Also attending the gathering was Chen Ning Yang, a prominent Chinese physicist who had studied, along with Agnew, under Enrico Fermi. Yang introduced Agnew to the deputy director of the Second Ministry of Machine Building, K. C. Wang, and suggested that Agnew eat dinner with the official in a back room. During dinner, Wang asked some questions about Agnew's scientific interests. Two weeks later Agnew received another invitation, which he also accepted—to visit China.[23]

Shortly after his arrival at Shanghai airport a group of six individuals, who Agnew concluded were weapons scientists, showed up to take charge of him. Their first stop was Beijing, where the scientists wanted Agnew to give an address in the Great Hall of the People. As a result, Agnew found himself behind a podium, with thirty or more Chinese weapons scientists in front of him. Over the following weeks, Agnew's tour continued, with visits to Beijing's Forbidden City and a massive bomb shelter underneath the city, with the weapons scientists as his companions.[24]

Once he returned to New Mexico, Agnew drafted a report that intrigued U.S. intelligence officials, who were hungry for more information about the Chinese bombmakers. In addition to memories, Agnew brought back photographs and a tiny spiral notebook in which his Chinese colleagues had written their names in Mandarin as well as English. The chief of Los Alamos's International Technology Division (ITD), the lab's intelligence unit, had Agnew's report typed up, stamped "Secret," and sent back to Washington, where it left analysts at the CIA and Defense Intelligence Agency hungry for more.[25]

Daniel B. Stillman, the head of ITD, hoped to provide more. He encouraged George A. "Jay" Keyworth II, head of the lab's physics division, to follow in Agnew's footsteps. Although reluctant, his respect for Agnew, who also urged him to go, led him to agree. With intelligence collection a clear objective, Keyworth was given some pointers by the new CIA liaison to Los Alamos, Robert S. Vrooman. He also received a visit from CIA representatives stationed in Denver, probably from the agency's Domestic Collection Division, which collected intelligence from U.S. residents who traveled abroad. Keyworth recalled that "they gave me tips, taught me methods—'Here are some ways you can do things.' It was just like the spy books, writing things that can't be seen."[26]

In 1980 Keyworth's plane deposited him in Shanghai, and he soon discovered that his host was Gen. Zhang Aiping, first commander of the Lop Nur test site who had become chairman of the National Defense Science and Technology Commission in 1975. In 1977 he had also become a deputy chief of the General Staff, as well as member of the Chinese Communist Party Central Committee. He was also believed to be a close associate of Deng Xiaoping.[27]

Keyworth's quarters were in a presidential guest house in Beijing. To neutralize the bugs he assumed were liberally distributed throughout his rooms, he would turn on the shower to maximum intensity and record each day's events on microcassettes as he stood in a cloud of steam, using the lone CIA technical device he had taken along. His reports covered what he learned, what his hosts seemed to know, and what they wanted to know. When he slept, the cassettes were in his pillowcase, and when he was awake, he carried them with him. Return trips followed in 1980 and 1981, trips that lasted for weeks and brought back more secretly recorded reports.[28]

In May 1981 Keyworth's role as "scientist-spy" ended just before he was about to leave for a visit to Lop Nur—he was informed that he was about to be nominated as President Ronald Reagan's science adviser. The next year, Agnew volunteered to take Keyworth's place if the CIA would provide him with a map of China and airfare for his wife. A flight to western China was followed by a drive to test site headquarters at Malan. At night Agnew ate in the home of Gen. Zhang Zhishang, the test site's commander, and they traded stories of life at the Nevada site and Lop Nur. Agnew's days as the first American visitor to the test site included watching a movie and examining color photographs of China's atmospheric tests that no American had seen, as well as a look at the tunnels that had been dug for testing.[29]

Eight years later, the man who sent Agnew's first report to Washington, and asked Keyworth to go to China, made his first trip. By 1990 Daniel Stillman had worked at Los Alamos for twenty-five years. He had come to the lab as a specialist in devices used to simulate and measure nuclear detonations. In

1978 he became head of ITD, Los Alamos's version of Livermore's Z Division. In June 1988 lunch with five Chinese weapons scientists, including Professor Yang Fujia, the director of the Shanghai Institute of Nuclear Research, at a conference in Albuquerque led to an invitation to visit a number of Chinese facilities. China's suppression of the Tiananmen Square uprising in June 1989 would delay the trip until spring 1990, when Stillman and his deputy, Terry Hawkins, arrived for their tour. One stop was the Southwest Institute of the Chinese Academy of Engineering Physics at Mianyang, which was scattered in several valleys, often under cloud cover, making satellite photography difficult. But photographs of the facilities could be found in a brochure Hawkins brought back and which he felt lucky to get his hands on—"When I was in DIA doing real intelligence work, I would have given ten million dollars for this book," he observed.[30]

Stillman would make nine visits through the summer of 1999, continuing to tour Chinese nuclear facilities and equipped with video recorders and cameras—first as representative of Los Alamos and then, after his October 1993 retirement, as a private citizen, sometimes escorting Los Alamos officials. In a talk at MIT in 2001, he recalled, "I visited virtually all of China's nuclear weapons laboratories." In Shanghai, he visited Fudan University and the Shanghai Institute of Nuclear Research, where scientists worked on neutron initiators and sources. In Mianyang, near Chengdu, he toured the headquarters of the Chinese Academy of Engineering Physics, "China's equivalent to our Los Alamos, Sandia, and Lawrence Livermore nuclear laboratories."[31]

Stillman also visited the Northwest Institute of Nuclear Technology, which designed and produced diagnostic equipment to monitor nuclear weapons tests. It also assembled the instrumentation trailers used for each test as well as conducted radiochemical analysis after the test to determine the yield of the detonation. Lop Nur was also on his itinerary. There he toured several vertical-shaft test sites and was able to walk in a tunnel that had been used for a horizontal test. He was also told that China's first seven tests had employed uranium consisting of 93.5 percent U-235.[32]

The visits were followed by reports detailing where he went, who he saw, and what they said. The written record produced by Stillman's visits included the names of more than two thousand Chinese scientists working at the nuclear weapons facilities, detailed histories of the Chinese program from senior scientists, descriptions of his inspections of nuclear weapons labs and Lop Nur, and reports of interviews with Chinese weapons designers. There were also photographs of the nuclear facilities. All that was passed on to debriefers from the U.S. intelligence community who came to visit him after each trip.[33]

Vrooman observed that "Danny's approach was disarmingly simple: You just go to China, find the guys who designed the bombs and ask them questions." According to Robert Daniel, a former CIA officer and congressman who headed the Energy Department's intelligence office in 1991 and traveled to China with Stillman in October 1990 and in 1991, "We saw things no outsider had ever seen before . . . we went to the test site . . . and saw them getting ready to place a device down a 600-meter hole." George Keyworth concluded that "the whole activity that he was involved in was extraordinarily successful for the United States." Stillman's assessment was that "the information the Chinese scientists willingly gave to me and my fellow travelers would have cost the government several millions of dollars to collect by traditional methods." As for his trip to Lop Nur, he observed that "more Americans have walked on the Moon than on China's nuclear weapons test site."[34]

NOT SURPRISINGLY there were critics of the entire exchange and contact effort, which included not only the high profile visits of Agnew, Keyworth, and Stillman, but groups of Chinese and American scientists visiting each others' facilities and attending conferences—after which many of the U.S. scientists would be debriefed by CIA representatives. The skeptics believed that whatever increased understanding the United States obtained about the state of the Chinese nuclear weapons program was outweighed by what Chinese scientists would learn about ways to improve China's nuclear capabilities.[35]

Whether the benefits outweighed the costs may have been a matter of debate, but it was certainly clear that the CIA and other U.S. intelligence organizations watching China's nuclear activities benefited from the information obtained. That information, however, did not eliminate the need to spy on China's nuclear program using imagery, signals intelligence, seismic detection, and spies as China proceeded with its nuclear test program.

Testing activity at the site in the 1990s would begin on July 26, 1990, and August 16, 1990, with yields of at least 15 and 50 kilotons, respectively. The CIA's Office of Scientific and Weapons Research located the July test at the Qinggir Underground Test Site East and noted that "the current test may be related to development of a warhead for a Chinese short-range ballistic missile." The same analysis also speculated that the upcoming August test was being conducted for the same reason.[36]

It would be almost two years before China would test again. In early January 1992 an article in the CIA's *Science and Weapons Review* estimated that China would conduct two nuclear tests that year, with at least one taking place in May. One possible source for the information in the report, as well as other information on the Chinese nuclear program, was Hua Tianqiang, a senior engineer and director of the intelligence unit at the nuclear research institute of the Shanghai Academy of Sciences who had access to a variety of secrets about that program. Hua disappeared in mid-October while touring Emei Mountain in Sichuan Province, an area full of crags, caves, and forests. In the following weeks groups searched the region and came up empty. After three months Chinese authorities began to suspect that either he had been killed in an accident or by a wild animal, or he had been smuggled out of the country by a foreign intelligence service.[37]

In any case, U.S. imagery satellites detected preparations for a test weeks ahead of time, and on May 21 China detonated a nuclear device, with a yield estimated to be between 700 kilotons and 1.8 megatons. The second and last test of the year followed on September 25, with a far smaller yield of 15 kilotons. The approximately two hundred recipients of the elite, top-secret *National Intelligence Daily* read about the test in the May 22 edition. The following day the unclassified *Washington Times* revealed some of what U.S. officials told reporter Bill Gertz. The "huge underground blast," the paper reported, was a test of a warhead for a new intercontinental ballistic missile under development. U.S. intelligence agencies were also expecting that radioactive gases from the explosion would be vented into the atmosphere and spread to areas outside of Chinese territory, despite the test having taken place at a depth of more than three thousand feet.[38]

Intelligence coverage of the event and its aftermath included detection at AFTAC seismic stations and satellite images obtained by KH-11 and advanced KH-11 satellites as they passed overhead, images that showed a cave-in around the center of the blast. And, as expected, despite the blast having occurred far underground, a radioactive cloud passed over the Sea of Japan. A WC-135 from a base in Japan flew through the cloud to monitor the level of radioactivity and gather whatever debris it could.[39]

In August 1992 the May 21 test would be the subject of an article in the CIA's *Science and Weapons Review*, which examined the reported claim of Chinese deputy premier Deng Xiaoping, carried in a Hong Kong newspaper, that the test was actually a multiple-device test. The CIA article noted that if it was a multiple-event test, it would have been the first known one of that type in the Chinese program, that obtaining high-quality diagnostic data from multiple devices is the major problem in conducting multiple tests in a single test shaft, and it was unclear why the Chinese would wish to test two devices with identical yield given the cost and complexity of testing more than one device in a single shaft.[40]

As had been predicted, a second test followed that year, on September 25. Another seven would follow that one. The sole test of 1993, on October 5, would be followed by two tests in 1994 (on June 10 and October 7), two in 1995 (on May 15 and August 17), and the final two in 1996 (on June 8 and

July 29). Yields of the tests were estimated, in open sources, as ranging from 1 to 5 kilotons for the July 29, 1996, test to 40 to 150 kilotons for the October 1994 and May 1995 tests.[41]

Intelligence gathering directed at the Chinese program would continue to provide notice of impending tests. By mid-September 1993, if not earlier, the U.S. intelligence community had concluded that another Chinese test would occur in the near future, based on satellite imagery of the Lop Nur site, which indicated that Chinese engineers had recently lowered a device down a deep shaft, among the final preparations for a test. And in May 1996 under-secretary of defense Walter Slocombe told reporters that preparations for a test were underway at the Lop Nur test site, and that "what we see them preparing to do is to conduct a nuclear test." Slocombe's remarks were based on the same intelligence that allowed the authors of an article in the May 31 issue of the CIA's *Proliferation Digest* to note that two of the four test sites at Lop Nur were in late-stage preparations, one was in early-stage preparations, and one was in the site-preparation stage.[42]

U.S. intelligence gathering and analysis allowed not only short-term alerts based on observed activities, but also longer-term projections of Chinese testing and explanations of the objectives associated with the tests. The February 19, 1993, issue of the *National Intelligence Daily* noted that "China has accelerated its nuclear test schedule and plans to conduct seven tests by 1996" devoted to strategic and, possibly, tactical systems development, and speculated that the speedup in its schedule might be the result of "growing international pressure for a comprehensive test ban in 1996." The October 1994 edition of *Proliferation Digest* explained that the planned tests were part of China's nuclear weapons modernization program, which included the development of warheads for new intercontinental and submarine-launched ballistic missiles as well as technologies to enhance confidence in the reliability of warheads that would be part of China's stockpile after it signed the comprehensive test ban.[43]

The same classified publications that contained long-term projections of Chinese activity also provided updates on China's test plans. The August 29, 1994, edition of the *National Intelligence Daily* reported that China had planned a test early in the month but postponed it for six weeks. That September, readers of the *NID* learned that the director of Chinese nuclear weapons research had indicated that China would continue testing through 1996, with a minimum number of tests, unless some failed. The next month, *Proliferation Digest* reported that the Chinese testing program was facing delays that could set back China's adherence to the comprehensive test ban treaty. In March 1995 the *Digest* and *NID* contained items noting that China appeared to have taken steps to put its nuclear testing program back on schedule. In

April 1996, an *NID* informed its readers that "China is accelerating its nuclear testing preparations at Lop Nur."[44]*

Of course, the Chinese program was far from transparent and the information available to CIA analysts was not sufficient to leave them confident that they always understood what the Chinese were doing in the remote western part of China. A September 1994 joint CIA-DIA memorandum observed that although their analysis indicated that China had several modernization goals, "the specific purpose of each Chinese test is unknown." A November 1995 article in *Proliferation Digest* illustrated that point. It noted that "an underground event—probably a nuclear test—occurred between 4 and 6 September at China's nuclear test site." While three probable nuclear testing scenarios had been evaluated—test of a nuclear artillery shell, a safety test, or a hydronuclear experiment—none was considered "completely consistent with all of the evidence."[45]

WHILE THE CHINESE ceased testing in July 1996, a controversy over the significance of one test emerged in 1995 and would continue until the end of the decade and beyond. The controversy was not contained within the highly classified world of the nuclear intelligence establishment, but would result in a very public trial for a Los Alamos scientist, Department of Justice and intelligence community investigations, congressional inquiries, and, of course, books and articles.[46]

It began with China's nuclear test of September 25, 1992. Like the test that May, the United States collected a variety of data on preparations for the test and the test itself, using imagery satellites, the seismic stations spread across the planet, and a WC-135 to intercept the radioactive gases that were vented into the atmosphere and passed over the Sea of Japan. The test, which took place in a tunnel at the Qinggir site, was estimated to have generated the equivalent of about 10,000 tons of TNT, a small fraction of the energy released by the test in May.[47]

---

* An April issue of *National Intelligence Daily* demonstrated that the U.S. intelligence sources were able to provide information on the worries of military personnel at the Lop Nur site. An article reported that "some military personnel at . . . Lop Nur . . . are concerned because the three nuclear tests planned for this year may require them to remain at the test site for long periods of time. *The site has been contaminated by fallout from 17 years of atmospheric nuclear tests and improper venting from most of the underground tests.*" See Director of Central Intelligence, "China: Nuclear Test Plans Prompt Health Concerns," *National Intelligence Daily*, April 19, 1994, p. 10.

But it was not until almost three years later that the intelligence gathered concerning the test began to have a dramatic impact. During the summer of 1995 Dan Bruno, the Energy Department's chief counterintelligence investigator, was called into the office of Notra Trulock III, the head of the department's Office of Energy Intelligence, established in 1990 as the Office of Intelligence by merging the department's foreign intelligence, threat assessment, and counterintelligence offices.[48]

Trulock had started his intelligence career as an eavesdropper. Graduation from Indiana University, with a degree in political science, was followed by a stint with the Army Security Agency beginning in 1971. After attending the Defense Language Institute in Monterey, California, to learn Russian, he headed for West Germany to listen to the radio traffic transmitted by Soviet troops across the border. When he returned to the United States, he put in several years at NSA, starting in 1975, where he became a specialist in the analysis of command and control systems. That job was followed by positions in the contract research world and at the National Defense University and, starting in 1990, at the Los Alamos Center for National Security Studies. In October 1993 he returned to Washington to join that what was then the Energy Department's Office of Intelligence. In May 1994 he became director of the renamed office.[49]

Trulock's message to Bruno was a simple one: "The Chinese have stolen the design of the W88," the country's most "highly optimized" warhead. Each W88 warhead, eight of which reside on top of each of the twenty-four Trident II (D5) submarine-launched ballistic missiles carried by Ohio-class submarines, would detonate with a force of 455 kilotons.[50] Chinese acquisition of W88 technology would certainly increase their ability to produce smaller, but more deadly missiles.

The basis for Trulock's statement came from work done at Los Alamos. It began with Bobby Henson, a former hydrogen bomb designer assigned to the laboratory's intelligence division who had considerable experience in analyzing the results of Chinese atomic tests. He had begun in 1967 when he was asked to study China's initial test of October 1964. From there he went on to examine the data on each of China's nuclear tests. The data from September 25, 1992, and later tests would lead him to a disturbing conclusion.[51]

The seismic signals from those tests indicated smaller yields, which Henson believed meant China was learning to build smaller primaries—the atomic bombs used to set off the thermonuclear fuel. Smaller and therefore lighter primaries opened up a number of possibilities for China's strategic force—more warheads per missile, missiles with more mobility, missiles with longer ranges—none of which were good for the United States. That could mean a Chinese missile force that was harder to monitor, more likely to survive a U.S. attack, and capable of delivering greater death and destruction to the United States.[52]

The intelligence about the September 25, 1992, test included the fact that Chinese weapons scientists, for the first time since 1980, used a horizontal tunnel and ran a far larger set of fiber-optic cables out of the entrance. The implication was that the test device's performance had been monitored by an exceptionally large number of sensors, an indication that something unusual was taking place. To Henson that meant the Chinese were capable of producing smaller H-bombs, that, as he would remark, "they quit driving a Model T and started driving a Cadillac."[53]

Henson then began to wonder how the Chinese had made such a dramatic advance, whether they had developed the Cadillac themselves or simply stolen it from someone's driveway. Given that he was less than enamored with the contacts between U.S. and Chinese weapons scientists, believing them to be a security risk, and doubted the Chinese scientists' ability to make such a rapid advance, he was open to the possibility that espionage was involved. Then, in the summer of 1994 he attended a lecture given by Chinese theoretical physicist Sun Chen Wei, an explosives expert who worked on nuclear primaries. During his lecture Sun mentioned how Chinese scientists had relied on ball-shaped primaries for decades, but that in the last few years "we've just been working with these watermelons," using his hands to illustrate his point.[54]

Sun's remarks startled Henson because he had just disclosed what was officially highly classified nuclear weapons design data in the United States—the watermelon configuration reduced the size and number (to two) of explosives used to trigger nuclear blasts. Although outside experts understood that some primaries of U.S. nuclear weapons were spherically shaped, the fact that China's primaries were similarly shaped alarmed Henson and suggested that his conclusions from studying the Chinese test data had some substance. Then, in January 1995 he was informed that a classified cable was awaiting his attention. When he read it, he discovered that a Chinese nuclear expert, recruited by U.S. intelligence years earlier, had revealed that the device tested in September 1992 was miniaturized and used a hollow plutonium, watermelon-shaped core. The cable also explained that the primary was an oblong plutonium shell wrapped in high explosives and about as wide as a soccer ball. A follow-up test, which used a similar core surrounded by insensitive high explosives, also detonated as expected.[55]

It had taken America's weapons scientists over a dozen tests to make really small primaries behave as desired. To also succeed with the insensitive high explosives on the first try, without help from a source in the United States, was not possible, in Henson's view. He went to see another Los Alamos intelligence analyst, Larry Booth. The result was an April 25 coauthored Top Secret Codeword memo and an appointment to see Trulock, who listened to what they had to say and decided to ask for a second opinion.[56]

The person Trulock consulted was John Richter, a Los Alamos physicist, an expert on primaries, and the chief designer for forty nuclear test devices. In May 1995 he traveled to Washington and read the same cable that had excited Henson and also examined the data from the September 25, 1992, test. He concluded that a primary had been tested and its width (nine inches, similar to that of a soccer ball) was pretty close to that of the W88. Before the end of the month, Richter joined Henson and Booth in producing a new memo for Trulock. It told the Energy Department's intelligence chief that the Chinese had probably tested the primary for the W88, and that they had likely acquired the necessary design information from a spy.[57]

That China might have tried to obtain data that would help improve its nuclear capabilities by any means possible—from assiduous collection of unclassified (open-source) material through espionage—was hardly a shock. In 1984 a DIA "estimative brief" noted that "qualitative improvements that the Chinese are developing for their nuclear warheads will depend on the benefits that [the] Chinese are now deriving from both overt contact with U.S. scientists and technology, and the covert acquisition of U.S. technology."[58]

The Henson-Booth-Richter memo led Trulock to call in Bruno and inform officials in his department as well as the FBI of "potential espionage involving nuclear weapons data." Bruno's suggestion that a scientific working group be established to "assist in the development of a logical investigative effort" led to the creation of the Kindred Spirit Analysis Group, "Kindred Spirit" being the designation for the investigation of possible espionage. Appointed to head the group was Michael Henderson, a longtime primary designer at Los Alamos. The panel also included, in addition to Richter, Booth, and Henson, additional Los Alamos scientists, and representatives from Sandia, Livermore, the CIA (a nuclear physicist), and DIA (a senior nuclear intelligence analyst).[59]

By late July some of the weapons designers and CIA analysts were unconvinced that espionage was the only reasonable explanation, suggesting that indigenous development, possibly combined with some Russian help, might explain the advance. A majority, including some representatives of Los Alamos, were leaning toward dismissing the notion that espionage was the cause for China's new capabilities. But before the issue could be settled, new data became available.[60]

That information had first arrived earlier in the year in the arms of a middle-aged Chinese man claiming to be a missile expert. He was what was known as a "walk-in," someone who brought documents or volunteered to spy (or both) rather than being targeted and recruited by an intelligence service. Indeed, almost all the success that either the CIA or KGB had during the Cold War in penetrating the other's national security organizations (other than through technical means) was due to walk-ins, including Oleg

Penkovskiy and Aldrich Ames. The initial beneficiary of this walk-in was Taiwan's internal security service.[61]

Among the documents he delivered was a twenty-page memo, dated 1988, prepared for the China's First Ministry of Machine Building, which employed missile designers and builders. A five-year strategic plan for China's future missile forces, it described in text, diagrams, and graphs the characteristics of both Chinese and American weapons. There were descriptions and hand-drawn sketches of a variety of U.S. strategic warheads for the Trident, the MX and Minuteman intercontinental ballistic missiles, and the cruise missile. The document noted five key attributes of the warhead and accurately described the shape of the primary as well as the width of the casing surrounding it to within a millimeter (four hundredths of an inch), a description Trulock characterized as "pretty damn accurate." Taiwan passed both the defector and the documents to the CIA station in the American Institute in Taiwan, which had served as the unofficial U.S. embassy since President Jimmy Carter had recognized the People's Republic of China (PRC) as China's "legitimate" government.[62]

The walk-in made frequent trips back to China and returned with more documents—over seven hundred, totaling thirteen thousand pages, before he was through. A CIA translation team was flown to Taiwan to begin working on them. A CIA polygrapher worked on the walk-in, and found his answer to whether he was operating on behalf of a foreign intelligence agency deceptive. He was then flown back to the United States so the CIA and FBI could try to determine whether the entire operation had been managed by China's intelligence services.[63]

Theories as to why Beijing might have sent the documents varied. The goal might have been to intimidate Taiwan, or discourage the United States from defending Taiwan should China attack, to misinform the CIA, or divert attention from a more valuable agent. It was also possible that somebody had just made a mistake. Richter suggested that China might have wanted to know if the information it had gathered on U.S. weapons was correct, and was hoping to judge so by the American reaction to the walk-in's documents. What was certain was that the documents contained a great deal of classified information, including the description of the W88.[64]

By this time Henson's conclusions were no longer driving the Kindred Spirit investigation. While seismic signals and satellite images generated initial suspicion, the words and gestures of a Chinese weapons designer and classified Chinese documents revealing secret details of the most advanced U.S. warheads provided the basis for continuing investigations. The alleged espionage became part of a broader congressional investigation into Chinese acquisition of U.S. technology led by California congressman Christopher Cox. The investigation concluded that "the PRC stole classified information on every currently developed U.S. intercontinental ballistic missile (ICBM) and submarine-launched ballistic missile (SLBM)," a conclusion that did not go unchallenged. A Los Alamos scientist, Wen Ho Lee, would come to be suspected of providing China with classified data on U.S. nuclear weapons systems. In the end he would experience a lengthy pretrial detention and lose his job, but regain his liberty. While it was established that he created a private collection of the computer programs used to design U.S. nuclear weapons and left them vulnerable to outside hackers, including those who might be in the pay of foreign intelligence services, and had put the codes on portable cassette tapes, which he claimed to have destroyed, there was no definitive proof of espionage. The case would end with almost everyone involved tarnished, whether justly or not, in one way or another.[65]

In March 1999 director of central intelligence George J. Tenet selected Robert Walpole, the national intelligence officer for strategic and nuclear programs, to lead an interagency group that would assess possible damage to U.S. national security from any disclosure of classified nuclear weapons information to China. Walpole, who joined the CIA in 1978 as an imagery analyst and spent five years as the deputy director of the Nonproliferation Center, would lead a team of intelligence analysts from across the intelligence community and the national labs. Tenet also appointed an outside review group, headed by Adm. David Jeremiah, former vice chairman of the Joint Chiefs of Staff, to head an outside panel that would review the Walpole group's report and write one of its own.[66]

The next month Jeremiah's panel—whose members also included Richard Kerr, a former deputy director of central intelligence, Gen. Brent Scowcroft, national security adviser in two administrations, and John Foster, the head of defense research and engineering in the Nixon administration—issued their report, which according to a statement from Tenet agreed with those produced by Walpole's group. The outside panel concluded that China had obtained via espionage classified U.S. nuclear weapons information that probably accelerated its nuclear modernization program, had obtained at least basic design information on the W88, and had acquired information on a variety of U.S. weapons design concepts, including those of the neutron bomb. The group also concluded that "China's technical advances have been made on the basis of classified and unclassified information derived from espionage, contact with US and other countries' scientists, conferences and publications, unauthorized media disclosures, declassified US weapons information, and Chinese indigenous development. The relative contribution of each cannot be determined."[67]

WHILE CHINA had been the last of the acknowledged nuclear powers to halt testing, the Soviet Union had been the first. But in 1997 some in the U.S. nuclear intelligence community suspected that Russia might be conducting low-yield nuclear tests. Although the comprehensive test ban treaty had not come into force, Russia had pledged to refrain from further testing. If it were conducting secret tests, in violation of that pledge, that was something the United States and its political leadership needed to know.

Not surprisingly, during the Cold War there had been suspicions that the Soviets might be cheating on one or both of the nuclear testing treaties as well as other arms control agreements. In late 1979 the DIA had raised the possibility that the Vela detection that September might have been due to a Soviet test, in violation of the 1963 partial test ban treaty. During Ronald Reagan's presidency there were concerns about Soviet compliance with the antiballistic missile treaty, the strategic arms limitation treaty, and the agreement concerning biological weapons. And during the middle of the Reagan years the Soviet Union's possible failure to comply with the other nuclear testing treaty—the 1974 threshold test ban treaty, which restricted weapons tests to those with a yield no greater than 150 kilotons—was a serious matter.[68]

Between 1976, when the Soviets pledged to abide by the still unratified treaty, to the end of 1984, the Soviets had conducted 128 underground weapons tests. The tests in the Semipalatinsk region took place in three distinct areas: The eastern and central testing areas were commonly known as the Shagan River and Degelen Mountain test sites. A third site, to the west, was referred to in the U.S. intelligence community as the Konystan testing area, due to its proximity to the nearby town. There had been no tests at Konystan site since 1980.[69]

By 1985 analysis of the seismic signals detected by AFTAC's nineteen detachments—which included manned sites at Alice Springs, Australia; Lakenheath, United Kingdom; Torrejon, Spain; Clark Air Force Base, Philippines; Crete, Greece; Okinawa and Misawa, Japan—seemed to indicate that a number of tests had exceeded the 150-kiloton limit, in some cases significantly. Concern that the Soviets were not living up to their pledge of treaty compliance was noted in a secret national security decision directive signed by President Ronald Reagan on January 14, 1984. *Soviet Noncompliance with Arms Control Agreements* reported that while "the available evidence is ambiguous and we have been unable to reach a definite conclusion, this evidence indicates that Soviet nuclear testing activities for a number of tests constitutes a likely violation of legal obligations under the Threshold Test Ban Treaty of 1974 . . . which banned underground nuclear tests with yield exceeding 150 kilotons."[70]

The same judgment conveyed in the 1984 directive was repeated in a publicly released February 1, 1985, report on arms control compliance, as well as two identically titled directives, signed by Reagan in February and December 1985. The December directive, NSDD 202, also elaborated on the reason for concern: "If the yields of Soviet nuclear tests have been substantially above 150 kilotons, then Soviet testing would allow proportionately greater gains in nuclear weapons development than the U.S. could achieve." The directive also observed that violations, even if of little apparent military significance, could become "precedents for future, more threatening violations."[71]

That the nuclear intelligence analysts at the CIA and other intelligence organizations were forced to rely on ambiguous evidence indicated that the agency was not operating a human source who could provide a definitive answer, although the United States had received some human intelligence from a source with knowledge of activities at the Degelen Mountain test area in recent years. Nor, clearly, had NSA's eavesdropping efforts settled the issue. And while the National Reconnaissance Office's imagery satellites could monitor pretest activities on the surface and some of the surface effects of an underground test, the images could not, in the absence of other information, reveal the force with which Soviet bombs exploded beneath the earth. And while AFTAC had no problems collecting the seismic signals generated by the Soviet tests, estimating the yield of the tests from those signals was not a simple matter—and became a topic of contention within the intelligence community.[72]

The fundamental problem was the same one that had led the United States to gather information about the geological structure of Lop Nur. While the magnitude of the "body waves" generated by an underground nuclear explosion, which pass through the earth's mantle and core, can be transformed into an estimate of the explosion's yield through a simple mathematical formula, the result needs to be adjusted. The adjustment, a "discount factor," takes account of the specific geological structure at the test site, because it influences the magnitude of the waves generated by an explosion. In contrast to some of the rocks beneath the Nevada site, which were believed to be partly molten, the Soviet test site at Semipalatinsk was geologically older and more stable. As a result, the magnitude of the body waves generated by a blast of any given yield would be stronger when the blast took place at Semipalatinsk.[73]

Because the treaty had not been ratified, neither the Soviet Union nor the United States had exchanged information on the geological coordinates of the boundaries of each test site, the geology of the testing areas, the geographic coordinates of underground tests, and the yield, date, time, depth, and coordinates for two tests from each geophysically distinct testing area where tests had or were going to be conducted—as called for in the treaty protocol. By the early 1980s some unclassified Soviet publications that concerned the geology of the Shagan River test area were available, but they did not provide the definitive information required by U.S. nuclear intelligence analysts.[74]

In 1985, in the absence of definitive data, CIA and Energy Department experts argued that the discount factor then being used, 30 percent, was too low, and contended that too much emphasis had been placed on the body waves and that more weight should be given to the "surface waves" that travel through the earth's upper crust—an argument also made by outside seismic experts who followed the controversy such as Columbia University's Lynn Sykes and the U.S. Geological Survey's Jack Evernden.[75]

In October 1985 the Defense Advanced Research Projects Agency (DARPA) Seismic Review Panel completed an analysis which concluded that the method being used to estimate the yield of the Soviet tests was, as had been charged, based on erroneous assumptions. That information was then forwarded to the JAEIC. It was also supported by another report, one commissioned by AFTAC itself. In mid-December the committee echoed the reports' recommendation, that the intelligence community adopt the defense research agency panel's suggestion that the discount factor be increased to a level that would reduce the estimated yield of Soviet tests by 20 percent.[76]

The recommendation was not without opposition, including the Defense Intelligence Agency as well as assistant secretary of defense Richard Perle, who feared that a recalculation would become public and would be used by the Soviet Union to build and test more powerful weapons. The recommendation was pending before DCI William J. Casey when NSDD 202 was issued. On January 21, 1986, a little over a month after the directive was signed, Casey, despite the opposition, approved the recommendation.[77]

Casey's approval did not automatically end the controversy. Some believed that a number of tests would still be evaluated as being over 150 kilotons. In February 1987 Reagan signed another directive on Soviet noncompliance, which noted an ongoing review of methodologies for estimating Soviet nuclear test yields. The new directive stated that until the review was completed, the conclusion of the December 1985 directive, that a number of Soviet tests constituted likely violations of the threshold treaty, "stands."[78]

The issue of Soviet compliance with the threshold test ban treaty would fade away, as the U.S.-Soviet relations took a dramatic turn—first with the assumption of power by Mikhail Gorbachev and then, after the failed coup of August 1991, with the collapse of the Soviet Union and Boris Yeltsin's rise to power as president of Russia. But in 1996 there was concern within the U.S. national security establishment about Russian compliance with another testing treaty that the Soviet successor state had pledged to abide by—the comprehensive test ban treaty.

This time the troubling seismic signals were not coming from Semipalatinsk. In early 1990 Col. Gen. Vladimir Gerasimov informed the Supreme Soviet that nuclear testing would end at Semipalatinsk by 1993, and any further testing would be conducted at Novaya Zemlya, where 130 nuclear tests had been conducted between 1954 and 1989.[79] Even without such a plan, the collapse of the Soviet Union would have necessitated a change in the main test site. On Christmas Day 1991, when the Soviet Union's existence ended,

Semipalatinsk became part of, not the Russian-successor state, but the new nation of Kazakhstan.

Far to the north, and within the Russian successor state, the Central Test Site, as Novaya Zemlya was designated, had been closed down following the collapse of the Soviet Union. Then, in 1992 it was reopened to allow Russian leaders to order a resumption in testing. In March 1996 it was reported that, according to Clinton administration officials, "U.S. intelligence agencies suspect Russia secretly set off an underground nuclear test this year." The information that led to such suspicions included both seismic data and satellite imagery. According to one U.S. official, "There was some activity you would expect to see that is associated with a nuclear test," possibly a reference to drilling of a large hole or laying of cables. The same official also noted, however, that the data was "inconclusive."[80]

Another anonymous official reported that a number of Pentagon officials had few doubts and believed Russia had tested a small nuclear weapon. "There's no question it was a nuclear test," the official told the *Washington Times*, "the only question is the yield." The official went on to tell the paper that "it was a low-yield test in mid-January," and that intelligence reports located the test on the northern island of the test site.[81]

But despite the certainty of some officials, the case was less clear to others. Seismologists in Europe looking for evidence of a Russian test had not detected any underground blasts. Back in the United States, one senior official who was willing to be named, secretary of defense William J. Perry, told a congressional committee that "there is some evidence on the subject, there's also some ambiguity in the evidence." Sometime after Perry's statement, it was concluded that the seismic disturbance had been caused by an earthquake rather than an explosion.[82]

But in the summer of 1997 there would be new concern and controversy over whether the Russians had been fully complying with the terms of the now signed, but still unratified comprehensive test ban treaty. The catalyst was a seismic signal coming from the vicinity of Novaya Zemlya on August 16, which registered at 3.2 on the Richter scale—consistent with a very small nuclear blast of between 0.1 and 1.0 kiloton, which might indicate scaled-down tests of a warhead primary. The signal was first detected, not by one of AFTAC's sites, but by a station in Russia, at Norilsk, operated by the Russian Defense Ministry. That station had been designated as one of the 320 monitoring sites that would gather the data used to monitor compliance with the comprehensive test ban treaty.[83]

The signals from Norilsk were automatically relayed to the International Data Center in Arlington, Virginia, where signals from each of the monitoring network's stations were analyzed. Within minutes of the Norilsk signal's arrival, additional data was received from two monitoring sites in Norway, one in Finland, and another in Sweden. Together they indicated that the event that generated the signal occurred at 5:00 a.m. Novaya Zemlya time, a time consistent with past Russian nuclear tests.[84]

After the data center informed AFTAC of the event, on August 18 the U.S. nuclear detection organization passed on the information to the CIA. Some of the CIA's analysts were alarmed, in part because some of the signals recorded by seismometers looked like those from previous nuclear tests at the site. Satellite images also appeared consistent with a test. The constellation of advanced KH-11 satellites passing overhead had returned imagery over the previous months showing Russian scientists unusually active at the test site. Helicopters were flying technicians around the site. On the ground, those technicians were lowering equipment, plugging test holes, and stringing cables for diagnostic equipment. Activities photographed on August 14 and 16 were, according to one intelligence analyst, "a dead ringer for [those in] test shots" conducted during the previous ten years and prompted AFTAC to order a WC-135 to fly downwind of the test site on the first of those dates. Several weeks earlier there had also been a visit from Viktor Mikhailov, Russia's atomic energy minister.[85]

To further study the data, the CIA called a meeting of the Nuclear Test Intelligence Subcommittee, a component of the JAEIC, which included representatives from the key agencies involved in analyzing test-related intelligence. Signals from the stations in Russia and Finland were thrown away because their sensors were not properly calibrated. The subcommittee then concluded that while the seismic event might have originated at the test site, its origin was probably at sea.[86]

On August 16 the International Data Center reached a more definitive conclusion based on computer analysis of the signals from the sensors or arrays in Norway, Sweden, Finland, and Russia, pinpointing the location of the event as being more than 60 miles from the test site. Further analysis completed by August 18 confirmed that conclusion.[87]

The nuclear test intelligence group may have been more open to the explanation that a test had occurred for a number of reasons: their access to the highly classified images showing activity at the test site, concern about the validity of the data obtained by the sensors in Finland and Russia, as well as their responsibilities. But the message that the JAEIC subcommittee conveyed to policymakers was even more categorical than the conclusions of the subcommittee. An initial alert message, dated August 18, erroneously described a probable nuclear test as having taken place at the test site, without any qualification, and the coordinates from a previous test on Novaya Zemlya were given as those for the event instead of the most probable coordinates, which corresponded to a location at sea about forty miles from the test facility. "We were trying to be very, very careful," one official told the *Washington Post*.

A policymaker who read the alert message said it conveyed "very high confidence that it was explosive . . . and right at Novaya Zemlya."[88]

Based on the alert, officials at the National Security Council called an interagency meeting on August 20 and ordered that an extensive effort be made to get an explanation from Moscow. The Russian ambassador was called to the State Department to hear of U.S. concerns, while the senior American diplomat in Russia issued a similar statement at the Foreign Ministry in Moscow. In response, Moscow would claim that the seismic signals had been caused by an underwater earthquake, and that activity at the test site was related to preparations for treaty-sanctioned "sub-critical" nuclear tests involving chemical explosions that blast apart fissile material without producing a chain reaction.[89]

The CIA, in Notra Trulock's judgment, "jumped the gun" and acted as if it wanted the event to be a test. In particular, according to Trulock, CIA seismologist Larry Turnbull, one in a long line of intelligence and defense officials who had worried about "evasive" nuclear testing by foreign countries, and Nonproliferation Center chief John Lauder "drove the intelligence process harder than it should have been pushed." There was a lot of talk of tunnels, branching off under the ocean bed, to permit covert testing. An underwater tunnel would have to have been well under the ocean, according to former Arms Control and Disarmament Agency deputy director Spurgeon Keeny, and would have required an "impossible engineering feat." Keeny considered that the whole episode was a "shocking example of the rigidity of the intelligence community, particularly CIA."[90]

Near the end of the month, U.S. officials confirmed their concern about a possible Russian test. On August 27 the NSC released a statement which read, "We do have information that a seismic event with explosive characteristics occurred in the vicinity of Novaya Zemlya." Ralph Alewine, director of the Pentagon's nuclear treaty office, added that "the information is still under review, and we are discussing this with other countries including Russia." An anonymous Pentagon official noted that the seismic signal created "very sharp" waves on the detection equipment, waves not usually associated with an earthquake. From Martha's Vineyard, where he was with a vacationing President Bill Clinton, White House spokesman Joe Lockhart reported, "We are currently in conversation and dialogue with [the Russian government]."[91]

Not long afterward, the test intelligence subcommittee formally began to retreat, with one official describing it as "the last to join the crowd." The group issued a new classified report in early September, which included additional data and stated that there was no connection between the test site activities and the seismic event and that the event occurred at sea. Before the middle of the month British government scientists seconded the opinion, telling the

Defense Department that the event had "a similar location and mechanism" as an earthquake that occurred in the Kara Sea eleven years earlier.[92]

But that was not the end of story. While the CIA had no evidence that the August 16 signal had been caused by a detonation, it was reluctant to conclude that it was the result of an earthquake. One intelligence official explained that "we like our judgment to be based on positive evidence." An alternative explanation that some officials were interested in investigating in late August involved the possibility of a sudden compression of the hull of one of the obsolete nuclear submarines that Russia had dumped into the Kara Sea and the signal being the result of the shock waves generated by that compression.[93]

In an attempt to put the issue to rest, because questions remained both within and outside the government, DCI George J. Tenet appointed a four-member panel to examine the evidence. The members included Sidney Drell, a Stanford University physicist, member of the President's Foreign Intelligence Advisory Board, and longtime adviser to the U.S. intelligence community; Richard Kerr, who had spent three decades with the CIA and served as deputy director of central intelligence (1989–1992); Eugene Herrin, a professor of geological sciences at Southern Methodist University who had also chaired the DARPA Seismic Review Panel for fifteen years; and Roger Hagengruber, who held a doctorate in experimental nuclear physics from the University of Wisconsin and was vice president of the Sandia National Laboratories.[94]

The panel evaluated the imagery, communications intelligence, seismic signals, and the results of the AFTAC-directed WC-135 flight. The data included not only that gathered in the immediate aftermath. There was also the negative evidence that accumulated during two months of intelligence community efforts to find potentially corroborating evidence. There were no signals indicating telltale underwater blast sounds, no signs of unusual radioactivity, and no evidence of underwater drilling or other special activities in the Kara Sea prior to, during, or after the event.[95]

In late October the members of the panel delivered a two-page secret report to Tenet. They reported that two seismic events had been detected on August 16, about four hours apart. The second one was smaller but had the same signature as the initial event, "indicating it to be of the same source." The centroid of the region, according to the report, "was located in the Kara Sea some 130 km southeast of the test area." Most importantly, they noted that "available data leads to a firm conclusion that the site of the seismic activity is offshore, and, therefore, almost certainly not associated with the activities at [Novaya Zemlya]."[96]

The panel also concluded that "the seismic event on 16 August triggered a process that worked in many respects as it should within the monitoring community," adding that "given the brief reporting times and limited data, the association of the seismic event with a nuclear test at NZ was sound." Furthermore, the panel reported that until the seismic event "became unambiguously centered in the Kara Sea," the intelligence community "needed to act with the emphasis and dispatch associated with a subkiloton nuclear test at the NZ site."[97]

As a result of the report, both the CIA and the White House formally dropped any claim that the August 16 event had resulted from a clandestine nuclear test. On October 28 Tenet transmitted the report to higher authority, with a covering memo summarizing the panel's key findings. A White House spokesman told one newspaper, "We agree with the judgment of the DCI based on the findings of the outside panel that this event was not nuclear."[98]

Many also believed that the event in the Kara Sea was an earthquake, rather than an underwater volcano. In October, Harold P. Smith, assistant to the secretary of defense for nuclear, chemical, and biological programs, told the *Washington Post*, "I personally think it was an earthquake," and added that other scientists at the Pentagon agreed. It was a view also shared by at least one member of the DCI's panel, Eugene Herrin, who remarked that "it was not an ambiguous event. . . . It's an earthquake."[99]

U.S. spy satellites would continue to keep watch on Novaya Zemlya for the rest of the decade. In September 1998 images returned by those satellites revealed, to the interpreters at the National Imagery and Mapping Agency, activity at the test site that was normally associated with an underground test, including vehicle activity near a deep hole at the site and trucks unloading filter material at the mouth of the shaft. A Pentagon spokesman acknowledged, "We have observed some activity at this Russian test range suggesting that some nuclear-related experiments are underway."[100]

What the imagery interpreters had seen and warned of in September was the beginning of a series of five subcritical tests that would take place between September 14 and December 13.[101] But earlier in the year, the interpreters had not warned about another nation beginning a series of full-scale nuclear tests.

chapter eleven

POKHRAN SURPRISE

IT WAS 8:00 A.M. on May 11, 1998, when an aide handed John Lauder, who had become head of the DCI's Nonproliferation Center in November 1997, what appeared to be a wire-service report. It stated that India had detonated one or more nuclear devices at its Pokhran test site. Lauder's immediate response was to ask his aide, "Is this some sort of joke?"[1] But his aide was not joking. Almost twenty-four years after its initial nuclear detonation, India had conducted another. This time there was no pretense that a peaceful nuclear explosion was involved.

DURING THOSE TWENTY-FOUR years, India had continued to develop its civilian and military nuclear capabilities, and on three occasions had come close to conducting further nuclear tests. Soon after Morarji Desai was sworn in as prime minister in March 1977, he convened a meeting of his cabinet's political affairs committee to discuss Indian nuclear strategy. Although no test was approved, Desai, according to Homi Sethna, gave him the "green signal to refine the design [of the explosive device]," which involved reducing the weight and diameter of the device through miniaturization.[2]

Intelligence about Desai's instructions to Sethna apparently reached U.S. officials, since in May 1977 President Carter hurriedly appointed Robert Goheen as U.S. ambassador and requested he meet with Desai immediately and ask him to restrain India's nuclear weapons program. When the two met, Desai pledged, "I will never develop a bomb."[3]

By January 1981 Desai had been displaced as prime minister by Indira Gandhi. That month she met with Raja Ramanna, director of the Bhabha Atomic Research Center, who reported that Indian scientists had asked permission to test two devices: a streamlined version of the 1974 device that could be delivered by aircraft, and a more advanced boosted-fission device that would produce four times the force with the same amount of plutonium. He also noted intelligence reports indicating that Pakistan's bomb program was moving ahead. Gandhi gave her approval.[4]

Specifically, she approved the digging of two shafts for the devices and instructed that the bomb team get the devices ready. In February 1981 the 113

Engineer Regiment began work at Pokhran, where it had to battle both oppressive heat and an assortment of vipers, cobras, and scorpions. Team members were not told the purpose of the shafts, and to prevent U.S. and Soviet spy satellites from detecting their work, digging was done under camouflage netting. Trespassers were subject to being shot on sight. In May 1982 Gandhi would give approval for the tests, but then called it off only hours later.[5]

Gandhi's reversal was the direct consequence of the images obtained by the National Reconnaissance Office's spy satellites of the era—the KH-8, KH-9, and KH-11—and whatever other intelligence the CIA and National Security Agency had managed to collect about activities at Pokhran. That May, India's foreign secretary, Maharaja Krishna Rasgotra, traveled to the United States. During a private meeting, U.S. undersecretary of state for political affairs Lawrence Eagleburger asked him, "What are you doing in Pokhran?" After Rasgotra denied that anything was taking place, Eagleburger took out maps and satellite pictures of the area. He pointed to them and told his guest that "there is a lot of activity going on there and it looks like you are sinking shafts. Are you going to conduct a test again?"[6]

Ragostra, who had been kept in the dark about India's nuclear plans, told Eagleburger that to his knowledge there was no such plan but he would investigate when he returned. It was hours after Gandhi approved the test that he briefed her on his meeting with the undersecretary and told her that there would be major unfavorable consequences should India test. The prime minister listened but had no comment. Hours later she canceled the planned tests.[7]

The CIA and other intelligence agencies continued, of course, to monitor Indian nuclear weapons developments. In July 1982 a CIA study of the Indian program reported that scientists at the Bhabha Atomic Research Center had been conducting research on laser isotope separation. In October NSA produced a report on India's shortage of heavy water, classified Top Secret Umbra, indicating that at least some of the information in the report came from high-level communications intercepts. NSA's analysts noted that India's inability to produce sufficient quantities of heavy water, along with its aversion to international safeguards, was a major factor constraining its nuclear power program. The report also inventoried the country's heavy-water plants, from its first at Nangal in Uttar Pradesh to its fifth and largest at Kota in Rajasthan, and facilities to upgrade the quality of heavy water, including the operational ones at the Madras Atomic Power Station and the Rajasthan Atomic Power Station along with the one under construction at the Narora Atomic Power Station.[8]

Both the CIA and NSA probably also reported, later in the 1980s, on India's covert acquisition of heavy water from foreign sources, including Norway. The CIA detected an illegal shipment of beryllium from West Germany to India late in the decade. In May 1989 director of central intelligence William Webster told the Senate Committee on Governmental Affairs that one of the indicators to the CIA of a country's interest in developing thermonuclear weapons was the acquisition of beryllium, which he explained was "usually used in enhancing fission reaction." In addition, the CIA had noted a number of other indicators of Indian interest in developing a hydrogen bomb, including purification of lithium, which is needed to produce the tritium used in thermonuclear explosions, and the separation of lithium isotopes.[9]

THE WORK on nuclear weapons by India and Pakistan was far from the only source of tension between them in the 1980s and beyond. In addition to the other nation's nuclear progress, several incidents undoubtedly encouraged continued work on advanced weapons. In 1986–1987 India conducted Operation Brasstacks, a triservice military exercise of unprecedented size involving nine divisions and three brigades, held in training areas near the border with Pakistan. In response, Pakistan's army extended and expanded its normal field training. Before the resulting crisis was over, the two countries had massed more than a quarter of a million troops on their border, threatening to turn normal winter exercises into a major confrontation.[10]

Then in 1990 the two adversaries squared off over Kashmir, the territory on India's northern border that the two had claimed for over forty years, ever since the 1947 collapse of the British Empire in India. Over the course of several months India assembled two hundred thousand troops, including paramilitary forces and five brigades of the Indian Army Strike Corps, its most sophisticated attack force. Pakistan deployed its primary armored tank units along the Indian border and, according to one account, placed its nuclear weapons arsenal on alert. The United States, either through NSA eavesdroppers or the CIA-NSA Special Collection Service unit in Islamabad, intercepted a message to the Pakistani Atomic Energy Commission directing it to assemble at least one nuclear bomb. How close the two nations actually came to war, particularly nuclear war, is a matter of dispute. But the situation was serious enough for President Bush to send deputy national security adviser Robert Gates to the subcontinent to caution Pakistani and Indian leaders against the use of force and urge them to adopt assorted confidence-building measures.[11]

During the first half of the 1990s India and Pakistan continued their work on nuclear weapons as well as the means to deliver them, including ballistic missiles. In January 1992 Robert Gates, who had become director of central intelligence in 1991, told a congressional committee that while there was no evidence that India maintained, assembled, or deployed nuclear devices, "such weapons could be assembled quickly." The next month, Shahryar Khan, Pakistan's foreign minister, told the *Washington Post* that his nation possessed the components to assemble at least one nuclear bomb. By

the end of that year India's inventory of weapons-grade plutonium was estimated to have reached seven hundred pounds, and the expectation was that
the inventory would reach over nine hundred pounds by the end of 1995. By
1995 Pakistan was still in the early stages of work on a ballistic missile that
could cover northwestern India, including New Delhi. But it had acquired
M-11 missiles from China, which had a range of 186 miles. India was more
advanced, having successfully tested the two-stage Agni in 1994, whose
expected range was 1,240 miles.[12]

In April 1995 prime minister Narasihma Rao simultaneously approved
development of the Agni II and instructed the army to prepare the shafts at
Pokhran needed to conduct nuclear tests. Rao was responding to the requests
of two of India's most important military scientists. One was A. P. J. Abdul
Kalam, head of the Defence Research and Development Organization since
1992, who had achieved fame as the mastermind of India's missile and space
launch vehicle programs, including the Agni. The other was Rajagopala Chidambaram, who had become chairman of the Indian Atomic Energy Commission in 1993. Their scientists had been advocating testing for three
reasons, including the need to perfect and demonstrate the technological
innovations they had made. They also felt that their work could be validated
only by full-scale tests and that recruiting top-flight scientists and engineers for
the program required testing.[13]

Appointed as mission director that August was K. Santhanam, the defense
research organization's chief technical adviser. Santhanam had joined the
organization in 1986 after a career that included heading the health physics
division of the atomic research center as well as stints in the Research and
Analysis Wing, India's CIA, where he read intelligence reports on the Pakistani and Chinese nuclear programs and briefed the government, and with
the foreign ministry.[14]

Following Rao's instructions, the 8 Engineer Regiment at Pokhran began
to refurbish the two shafts that had been built in 1982, and began digging a
third. The deeper of the three shafts, code-named White House, was discovered to be filled three-quarters of the way to the top with water, the result of its
having been capped after the previous regiment at Pokhran got tired of maintaining it. It took until November to complete the process of pumping out the
accumulated water and finish refurbishing the shaft.[15]

While the engineer regiment was busy on the ground in Pokhran, U.S.
imagery interpreters in the United States were taking an interest in its activities. Located at Fort Belvoir, Virginia, just south of the nation's capital, was the
main ground station for the KH-11 and advanced KH-11 satellites—with the
cover name Defense Communications Electronics Evaluation and Testing
Activity (Defense CEETA) and the designation Area 58. Also located there
was the Priority Exploitation Group, a contingent from the CIA's National

Photographic Interpretation Center, whose job was to examine incoming satellite imagery to determine if any of it merited immediate attention. Further analysis of imagery of strategic importance was done at NPIC headquarters, a windowless building in the Washington Navy Yard, located in a rundown section of Washington.[16]

At the time, the interpreters could have had access to images from as many as six satellites: the two KH-11s launched in 1987 and 1988; the first advanced KH-11, orbited in 1992; the Misty stealth satellite, which had been operating since the spring of 1990; and the two Onyx radar imagery satellites launched in December 1988 and March 1991. In addition to obtaining images during daylight hours, it was also possible to acquire images at night, using the advanced KH-11's infrared sensor or the radar-imaging capability of the Onyx satellites.[17]

Starting in November 1995 images from at least some of those satellites showed increased scientific and technical activity at the Pokhran test site. When the U.S. ambassador to India, Frank Wisner Jr., was in Washington at the beginning of the month, he paid a courtesy call on secretary of state Warren Christopher. Minutes after that meeting he learned that imagery from a satellite passing over Pokhran had caught sight of suspicious activity, including cables running through L-shaped tunnels, apparently to transmit diagnostic data from an underground test.[18]

It was not completely clear whether that activity was related to preparations for a nuclear test or some nonnuclear experiment intended to increase India's expertise in making nuclear weapons. One U.S. official told the *New York Times* in December, "We're not sure what they're up to." The official added, "If their motive is to get scientific knowledge, it might be months or years before they do the test. If it's purely for political reasons, it could be this weekend. We don't know the answer to those questions." Intelligence officials also told the *Washington Post* that the images, which showed the clearing out of a deep underground shaft and possible preparations for instrumentation, depicted "activities [at the test site] going beyond what we've seen in the past" and that Indian scientists were trying to develop boosted atomic bombs as well as a hydrogen bomb. The Indian government first denied plans for a nuclear test and then characterized the *Times* report as "highly-speculative."[19]

That politics might be a motivating force, and a test could come sooner than later, was a serious possibility. With an election coming up, Rao's party was facing a serious challenge from the right-wing Hindu nationalist Bharatiya Janata Party (BJP), which called for India to come out of the nuclear closet. A secret cable drafted by State's intelligence and research bureau noted that "Rao's effort to recover his political reputation and to refute BJP charges that he has compromised the defense of India could soon result in the testing of a nuclear device in the Rajasthan desert." A State Department official observed that if India exploded a nuclear bomb, it "would be a matter of great concern and a serious setback to nonproliferation efforts."[20]

In an attempt to prevent a test, Wisner met with A. N. Varma, Rao's private secretary, on December 15, only hours after returning from Washington. He was equipped, as other American representatives before him had been when challenging foreign nations about military activities, with satellite imagery—in this case a single image, which he showed Varma and then "put in his back pocket," according to Strobe Talbott who was undersecretary of state at the time. Wisner warned that a test would backfire and bring sanctions. President Bill Clinton followed with a call to Rao, urging him not to proceed with any tests. The effort proved successful, or at least not unsuccessful, when foreign minister Pranab Mukherjee denied that India was preparing to conduct a nuclear test.[21]

Of course, Indian officials had denied that there was any substance in the first place to the public reports of India preparing to test nuclear weapons. The press minister for the Indian embassy in Washington claimed that the movements seen by U.S. satellites "have been absurdly misinterpreted." Close surveillance of the test site continued, with U.S. satellites producing four images a day in January 1996—an activity certainly not discouraged by accounts early that month in the Indian press, monitored by the CIA's Foreign Broadcast Information Service, of more army troops and increased activity at Pokhran, including fencing off the old test site and laying down cables.[22]

Then in mid-May, the results of India's parliamentary elections made Mukherjee's pledge irrelevant. While the BJP finished with less than a majority of seats, it did have the largest plurality and received the first opportunity to put together a government. On May 16 its leader, Atal Behari Vajpayee, took the oath as prime minister and received fifteen days to win a parliamentary vote of confidence for his government—which would require it to add 75 votes to the 186 it could count on from the party's representatives.[23]

During the campaign the BJP had promised to reevaluate India's nuclear policy. Vajpayee himself had asked, in December 1964 after China's first test, "What is the answer to the atom bomb?" He also provided his answer: "the answer to an atom bomb is an atom bomb, nothing else." When the party's general secretary claimed, in early April, that if the BJP came to power it would test a nuclear weapon, another party spokesman claimed that while it was the party's position that India should possess a nuclear deterrent, "the issue of testing has not been discussed." Maybe no discussion was needed, or it was discussed in the six weeks between early April and Vajpayee's appointment, but almost immediately after he assumed the prime ministership Vajpayee told Kalam and Chidambaram to proceed with the tests, which were to involve an improved version of the 1974 device as well as a boosted-fission bomb.[24]

Once again NRO's constellation of imagery satellites provided indications that a test might be upcoming, picking up signs of renewed activity that spring, although they failed to detect that the team at Pokhran had placed at least one nuclear device in a test shaft. While senior U.S. officials did not expect an imminent test, the Clinton administration did follow up on the new intelligence and urged Indian officials to refrain from testing.[25]

But it was not Bill Clinton, spurred on by the information gathered from space, that prevented an Indian test. Instead, it was Vajpayee and developments on the ground. With a vote of confidence pending, the prime minister decided to wait for the outcome before giving the final go-ahead. On May 28, 1996, failing to attract the additional 75 supporters, the BJP lost the vote of confidence and was replaced by a United Front government consisting of thirteen parties. But in March 1998 the BJP would return to power when it won 250 seats in the parliamentary elections, 22 short of a majority but sufficient to give Vajpayee the opportunity to form a government. And this time the coalition he assembled prevailed, albeit by a slim margin, in the confidence vote that followed before the month was over.[26]

DURING THE CAMPAIGN the BJP issued an election manifesto with the title "Our Vision, Our Will, Our Way," which covered topics ranging from cow protection (a total ban on the slaughter of cows was called for) to policy on weapons of mass destruction. It echoed 1996 campaign rhetoric with respect to nuclear weapons, noting that "the BJP rejects the notion of nuclear apartheid" and would "re-evaluate the country's nuclear policy and exercise the option to induct nuclear weapons." The BJP saw a nuclear-armed India as a way not only of deterring Pakistan, but of deterring another nation that presented an even greater threat—China.[27]

On March 20, the day after Vajpayee and the BJP assumed control of the Indian government for the second time, the new prime minister was visited by Chidambaram. "It was not," one of the Indian leader's aides recalled, "a pure courtesy call." The atomic energy chief was there to make the case for conducting nuclear tests. Early the next month, on April 6, Pakistan tested its Ghauri missile, which could hit targets 930 miles away and carry a payload of 1,540 pounds. Two days later, Chidambaram and Kalam received the answer they were hoping for when they were summoned to see the prime minister and told to go ahead with the tests, with Vajpayee telling them that the Ghauri test was the last straw. A contingent of one hundred scientists and engineers soon packed up and headed for the test site.[28]

Sometime during the night of May 1 an Indian air force Antonov-32 plane took off from Santa Cruz airport in Mumbai, carrying the plutonium cores to be used in the tests. The cores weighed between eleven and twenty-two pounds and had been produced at the BARC in Trombay and stored in underground vaults in Mumbai. Two hours later a convoy of trucks lined up at the Jodhpur airport and the crates were loaded onto one of them. To make the whole activity appear routine, no extra security was provided, and the convoy set out for the test site under the cover of darkness. Once it arrived at Pokhran, the crates were moved to temporary labs, code-named Prayer Hall, where the bomb team began mating the cores with the conventional explosives, detonators, and triggers, which had been flown in separately.[29]

On the morning of May 7 a team of scientists from the Kalam's defense research organization and Chidambaram's Department of Atomic Energy arrived in Jodhpur. That night they left for Pokhran, arriving early the next morning. On May 10 preparations for lowering the devices into the shafts began. The device with an expected subkiloton yield was the first lowered down its shaft, which was sealed by 8:30 in the evening. A hydrogen bomb was lowered into the shaft code-named White House, about 655 feet deep. It was sealed with concrete and sand by 4:00 a.m. on May 11, while a fission bomb was lowered into a third shaft, designated Taj Mahal, which was sealed by 7:30 a.m. Back in New Delhi senior officials had only just learned of the impending tests. Defense minister Georges Fernandes was told on May 9, while the military service chiefs and foreign minister were let in on the secret the following day.[30]

The tests were scheduled for 9:00 a.m. on May 11. Chidambaram and Kalam waited in a tiny bunker, code-named Deer Park, containing computers and control panels with an assortment of colored switches. They wore battle fatigues in accord with their cover identities as Major-General Natraj and Major-General Prithviraj, identities adopted to prevent knowledge of their repeated visits to the test site from leaking. But at eight that morning the test was put on hold, because of a west wind that would have blown any radioactive debris accidentally released not only toward nearby villages but also into Pakistan.[31]

While the wind was still a problem at noon, it would eventually subside, and at 3:45 p.m. the Pokhran test site would be rocked by India's first nuclear test since 1974. Ten minutes later a phone rang in a room in the prime minister's residence, where Vajpayee and five other senior Indian officials, including Fernandes and the defense, home, and finance ministers, were gathered. When the prime minister's principal secretary picked up the phone, he heard a voice cry, "Done!," telling him that the tests, which would subsequently be designated Operation Shatki, had been a success.[32]

At 5:00 p.m. Indian time, 7:30 a.m. in Washington, Vajpayee walked over to reporters and cameras waiting outside his office and announced that India had tested three nuclear weapons. Later, his government issued an official statement providing specifics: the weapons included a fission device, a low-yield device, and a thermonuclear device and the measured yields were "in line with expected values." No radioactivity was released into the atmosphere, according to the statement. Two days later, on May 13, the government issued another statement, announcing that two subkiloton tests were carried out at Pokhran earlier that day.[33]

The Indian claims came as a surprise to the United States once again. The CIA and other intelligence agencies had provided no warning of a second round of tests. At a classified briefing on Capitol Hill on May 12, Nonproliferation Center chief John Lauder gave no indication that further tests were anticipated. And on May 13 deputy assistant secretary of state for nonproliferation Robert J. Einhorn told a Senate committee, "I personally woke up this morning and I did not know about it."[34]

THE SURPRISE INDIAN TESTS left the U.S. intelligence community

with three clear tasks. The most pressing was gathering intelligence on how Pakistan planned to respond and when. Then there was the need to gather and evaluate intelligence on the Indian tests—to verify, if possible, Indian claims about what had taken place and to obtain information about the tests that India did not wish to volunteer. It would also be necessary to consider why the almost $30 billion that the United States spent each year on its large array of intelligence agencies, analysts, and collection systems had failed to buy advanced warning of India's tests.

That India's nuclear tests would make a Pakistani test a certainty—and sooner rather than later—seemed clear to U.S. intelligence analysts. The State Department's intelligence and research bureau commented on May 13 that "though some Pakistani officials will counsel patience to allow the weight of the international opprobrium to fall exclusively on India, mounting domestic political pressure makes a Pakistani nuclear test virtually inevitable." The following day State informed national security adviser Sandy Berger that various sources, including the Pakistani press and (apparently) communications intercepts, indicated that Pakistani president Nawaz Sharif had given the "green light" for tests.[35]

Also on May 14 director of central intelligence George Tenet told the House and Senate intelligence committees that U.S. satellites had detected Pakistani preparations for an underground test. In closed session, the CIA chief presented satellite imagery showing an increase in equipment, technicians, and security activities at the Ras Koh test site in the Chagai Hills. The satellite images also indicated heavy traffic on the roads, with some being used for the first time, and heavier traffic on others.[36]

What the satellites were seeing were preparations for a nuclear test, but a nuclear test that Pakistan was well prepared for. Six months earlier, a multidisciplinary team of Energy Department nuclear experts—from Z Division, Oak Ridge Laboratory, and Savannah River Laboratory—noted that Pakistan was making significant progress in developing nuclear weaponry. The key intelligence that led to this conclusion concerned Pakistan's progress in producing yield-enhancing tritium. While the information had been acquired by the CIA and initially kept away from the Energy Department's intelligence personnel, a CIA detailee to Energy was able to get his agency to share the crucial intelligence.[37]

By May 27 most of the U.S. intelligence community believed that Pakistan was close to conducting its first test—although an INR analysis, consistent with other analyses it had produced since mid-May, suggested that Sharif "probably still hopes to avoid having to order a test." But "it could happen any time," a U.S. intelligence official told the *Washington Times*. The test site activities continued to be the target of both U.S. imagery satellites as well as those capable of intercepting communications from 22,300 miles above the earth. The sum of U.S. intelligence indicated that a nuclear device had been placed in an underground shaft and that the sensors, cables, and other equipment needed to monitor a detonation were in place.[38]

Sometime on May 27 President Clinton himself collected a definitive bit of human intelligence from Pakistan's president, intelligence indicating that his efforts to prevent a Pakistani test were going to fail. According to Strobe Talbott, during a phone conversation "a timorous sounding Sharif apologized to Clinton for 'disappointing' him, but [he] simply had no choice but to go ahead with the test."[39]

At 3:30 p.m. on May 28 seismic stations recorded the signals commonly associated with nuclear testing, and Sharif issued a statement claiming that "Pakistan today successfully conducted five nuclear tests" and congratulating "all Pakistani scientists, engineers and technicians for their dedicated team work." In a somber early-evening television address, Sharif announced, "Today, we have evened the score with India." Two days later Pakistan one-upped its adversary by announcing a single test, at a site about sixty-two miles from the May 28 tests, bringing the number of claimed Pakistani tests to six.[40]

THE PAKISTANI CLAIMS meant that now two nations' assertions about their nuclear accomplishments needed attention from U.S. nuclear intelligence experts. The nuclear intelligence community and its customers would want to know if the claims about the number of tests conducted, their yields, and the nature of the devices—for example, whether the claimed hydrogen bombs were indeed thermonuclear—were accurate.

Among the sources of data were the written statements released by the Indian and Pakistani governments, and the oral remarks. There was also the question-and-answer session held on May 17 by AEC chairman, Chidambaram, Kalam, BARC director Anil Kakodkar, and DRDO chief adviser for technology Santhanam. Kalam repeated the claim that the tests on May 11 included a hydrogen bomb, a fission device, and a subkiloton device, while Chidambaram stated that the hydrogen and fission devices were six-tenths of a mile (one kilometer) apart and the yield of the hydrogen device was 45 kilotons. Chidambaram also reported, as he had previously, that the fission device was significantly lighter and more compact than the 1974 bomb and produced a yield of 12 kilotons, while the yield of the third device was 0.2 kiloton. Kalam also told his audience that the test had been approved thirty days prior to May 11.[41]

The scientists at the press conference released a videotape of the blasts that allowed viewers to see the countdown at the test site, hear a deep boom, witness the ground shake violently, and see a huge cloud of dust rise into the sky above the test site. Cheers could also be heard. Views from a helicopter showed a crater that appeared to be seventy feet deep and several hundred feet wide. One could also see what appeared to be a concrete walkway leading into the shaft. Its sides had been shattered and covered with netting, twisted steel, and broken sandbags.[42]

Analysts would pay close attention to the BARC Newsletter, whose May 1998 issue contained a note written by Kakodkar and S. K. Sikka, a longtime research associate of Chidambaram. They reported the yield of the hydrogen device as 45 kilotons and of the fission device as 15 kilotons. The three smaller devices were described as "experimental" and their yields given as 0.2, 0.5, and 0.3 kiloton.[43]

There were additional things U.S. intelligence analysts would have liked to know that the Indian scientists weren't telling. During the press conference, AEC chairman Chidambaram would not reveal the ingredients used in the hydrogen bomb or the depth of the shafts. Kalam had no comment when asked about how many warheads India needed, when production would begin, and whether the "U.S. surveillance system was deliberately fooled by you or was it accidental?"[44]

To gather whatever information it could on the Indian and Pakistan tests, the U.S. intelligence community employed a variety of assets. Imagery satellites photographed the test sites in the aftermath of the detonations, while communications intelligence systems on the ground and in space continued to intercept and analyze whatever relevant communications they could. The imagery from advanced KH-11 satellites could show where radiation from the tests had hit the surface, rapidly deoxidizing the rock and turning the mountainside white.[45]

Satellite imagery can also be employed to identify "throw-out" craters and their ejecta blanket, created by explosions at shallow depths, as well as any domelike structure (referred to as a retarc — for "crater" backwards) created by detonations at greater depths. The surface signatures of an underground blast, along with knowledge of the geology of the site (which influences the surface features) and the depth at which a device was buried, could be used to produce estimates of its yield.[46]

In addition, a WC-135, stationed at Offutt Air Force Base in Nebraska, was deployed to South Asia in search of any debris that had been injected into the atmosphere. It was an opportunity that was almost missed. By May 1998 the nation's aerial nuclear sampling fleet, whose mission was designated Constant Phoenix, was down to a single plane, the result of the decline in worldwide nuclear testing and budget constraints. Later, Terry Hawkins, the director of the nonproliferation and national security division at Los Alamos, would observe that "sampling capability is really important. If a nuclear explosion occurs somewhere, and if you want to attribute it to a country that conducted the test, the only credible way to do that is to get a piece of the debris and analyze it." But by May 1998 there had not been a nuclear test for almost two years, and the plane used for debris collection was scheduled for six months of maintenance, with its 1,200-pound collection system headed for storage. The Indian tests resulted in a crash effort to reconstitute the aircraft in time to fly the sampling missions, manned by the last remaining personnel trained to use the equipment for detecting and gathering debris.[47]

In addition to imagery, communications intelligence, and debris collection, seismic signals were available to American nuclear intelligence analysts from both unclassified seismic detection systems as well as the stations operated by the Air Force Technical Applications Center or allies. In the immediate aftermath of the Indian tests, the AFTAC-collected seismic signals seemed to indicate a combined yield for the May 11 Indian tests of only 15 to 20 kilotons, about a third of that claimed by Indian scientists. Such a relatively low yield, even for a single test, raised questions as to whether the tests really included a full-fledged, first-generation hydrogen bomb, which could be expected to produce yields up to a half million tons of TNT or more. Nor was there proof in the seismic signals that more than one test had been conducted, since only one signature had been detected.[48]

There was even more skepticism concerning the Indian claims about the May 13 tests. No seismic signal could be detected that would serve as confirmation that India had conducted even one, much less two, tests that day—not by the International Data Center network, or the U.S. Geological Survey, or the seismic station at Nilore in Pakistan, which detected the May 11 explosions, and apparently not by any of the AFTAC stations.[49]

At their press conference Indian scientists tried to answer some of the skepticism that had emerged within days after the tests, largely owing to the seismic data obtained by unclassified stations. Chidambaram emphasized that India had detonated a true hydrogen bomb—a plausible claim since BARC reportedly began, in the mid-1980s, separating lithium-6, which could then be placed in reactor cores and transformed into tritium or mixed with deuterium to produce lithium-6 deuteride. "We used a fission trigger and a secondary fusion," he said. Kalam and his colleagues explained the thermonuclear yield of 43 kilotons as the result of a decision to limit yield in order to minimize damage to nearby villages. It was also suggested that the simultaneous detonations caused "interference" in the seismic signals being used to evaluate yield. Failure to detect the May 13 tests were, the scientists explained, due to their having been conducted in a sand dune.[50] Their explanations, of course, were available not only to the world at large but to the U.S. nuclear intelligence establishment.

Such explanations still left some outside experts unpersuaded, in part because India's 1974 claim that its bomb had exploded with the force of fifteen thousand tons of TNT, when subsequent analysis produced estimates in the 6 to 8 kiloton range, indicated a willingness to exaggerate its accomplishments. "They definitely hyped it the first time around," noted George Perkovich, an expert on the Indian nuclear weapons program.[51]

"The whole thing sounds odd," Herbert A. York, a former nuclear bomb designer and Pentagon chief of research and engineering observed. "It's not odd enough to make me say it's not true, but it's still a very strange story." Experts also noted India's claim that it had conducted a full thermonuclear test without having gone through the intermediate step of testing a boosted-fission device using thermonuclear material, as did other nations. In addition, experts speculated that the two tests of May 13, which had the equivalent of two hundred and six hundred tons of TNT according to India, might have been failed boosting tests. "Maybe they tried and failed," observed former Livermore bomb designer Ray E. Kidder. Peter Zimmerman, a physicist and former arms control official, wrote that sand dunes were porous and carried the risk of letting radioactive gases escape, making them a strange choice for a medium within which to conduct a nuclear test.[52]

The public controversy over the yields of the May 11 and May 13 tests would continue for several years. Numerous foreign experts argued that the total yield was significantly lower than the claimed yield, and the yield of the alleged hydrogen bomb test was closer to 30 than 43 kilotons, while others, particularly Indian scientists, defended the Indian government's estimates.[53] But settling that issue would not settle the more important concern about India's tests—did they demonstrate that India possessed a hydrogen bomb?

In late November the trade journal *Nucleonics Week* reported that analysts at Z Division had completed several months of analysis of seismic, human, and signals intelligence, which apparently included intelligence on contacts between the Department of Atomic Energy and senior Indian decisionmakers. They concluded that India had attempted to detonate a hydrogen bomb on May 11, not just a boosted-fission device. However, "the secondary didn't work," according to one of the journal's sources. While the fission primary detonated as planned, the heat failed to ignite the second stage, which contained the thermonuclear material. As a result, "if India really wants a thermonuclear capability, they will have to test again and hope they get it right," one U.S. official said.[54]

PAKISTAN'S CLAIMS were also subject to similar scrutiny and skepticism. While no one doubted that India's adversary had detonated at least one nuclear device, there was no initial evidence of more than one. The unclassified global seismic monitoring network detected a signal from deep beneath Pakistani territory on May 28, a confirmation that Pakistan had conducted a nuclear test. The preliminary measurements of the signal's magnitude indicated a yield of between 8 and 17 kilotons. As with India's May 11 tests, there was only one signal, which could have been caused by a single detonation or the five simultaneous explosions claimed by Pakistan.[55]

U.S. intelligence analysts believed that it was likely that at least two bombs had been tested but were skeptical of the claim that five had exploded. They thought that while it was not implausible to detonate two bombs at identical moments, it would be technically challenging as well as highly unusual to fire off five detonations simultaneously. Analysts also speculated that the device or devices had not performed up to specifications. U.S. data indicated that the magnitude of the blast(s) was between 9 and 12 kilotons, with 6 kilotons being the most likely value, which was less than the estimated yield of even one of the principal bombs in the Pakistani arsenal. One obvious possibility was that Pakistan had exaggerated its achievements in order to match India's claims. "We don't believe either nation is really telling the truth about what they did," one U.S. official commented.[56]

Unlike India's claim of follow-on tests, Pakistan's assertion that it tested again, shortly after its initial tests, was backed up by seismological data. But the faintness of the signal picked up indicated to many specialists that the test was either a failure or successful but small. One of those specialists, University of Arizona seismologist Terry C. Wallace, remarked at the time, "It's a small event."[57]

There was also skepticism, within at least some segments of the U.S. nuclear intelligence community, concerning A. Q. Khan's claim that the Pakistani bombs used highly enriched uranium—a conclusion reached after analysis of debris collected by the WC-135 dispatched to South Asia in May 1998, specifically debris collected from the May 30 test. That December the CIA informed President Clinton, in a highly classified report based on a preliminary analysis done at Los Alamos, that the debris contained low levels of weapons-grade plutonium. The finding implied that Pakistan had been manufacturing or importing plutonium, which would allow the development of smaller warheads and thus either longer-range missiles or missiles with more deadly payloads, without detection by American intelligence agencies.[58]

The conclusion reached by the Los Alamos scientists came as a surprise to other elements of the U.S. nuclear intelligence community. The United States had been routinely monitoring work on a reactor at Khushab in the Punjab, where construction had begun in the late 1980s, but which Islamabad had first announced as going critical in the spring of 1998. There was also an awareness of increased Pakistani research and development activities with respect to plutonium production. But prior to the Pakistani tests, the U.S. officials claimed that Pakistan had no significant reprocessing capability other than the small pilot facility at the Pakistan Institute of Nuclear Science in Rawalpindi.[59]

The conclusion by the Los Alamos scientists was not shared by their counterparts at Lawrence Livermore, those who worked or consulted for Z Division. It was not the first disagreement. Former Energy Department intelligence chief Notra Trulock has noted that Los Alamos's International Technology Division was fiercely competitive with Livermore's Z Division and "IT's harshest invective was reserved not for a foreign espionage operation, but for a Z-division report or Z-division personnel." David Kay, the former UN weapons inspector and chief of the Iraq Survey Group, recalled that it was "interesting to watch them denigrate each other's assessment."[60]

In this case the Livermore scientists claimed that Los Alamos first contaminated the May 30 sample. Any opportunity to reevaluate disappeared when the sample was lost. A second sample was available at another laboratory, but whether it was an identical sample was another matter of dispute. One U.S. intelligence official acknowledged that "there is some disagreement here, and experts at the labs need to sort it out."[61]

BUT THE MOST PRESSING question facing the U.S. intelligence community was why it had failed to provide advance warning of India's intentions, possibly allowing the United States to exert diplomatic pressure as it did in 1995 and preventing India's tests and Pakistan's reaction.

The United States was not the only nation that had been surprised by the tests. Russian president Boris Yeltsin and his foreign minister, Yvgeny Primakov, characterized the tests as a "big surprise." An official of the Russian Foreign Intelligence Service, the SVR, told one newspaper that the service "had no information" about India's plans to carry out the tests, despite the reputation of India being "transparent" to Russian intelligence and the presence of a large number of India specialists in the SVR, including director Vyacheslav Trubnikov.[62]

But the Russians did little to mitigate the concern that the U.S. intelligence community, with significantly greater resources, particularly in space, had failed to provide notice of such a significant event. And it was a failure that stretched across the entire nuclear intelligence establishment, from the CIA and INR in the Washington area to Z Division in California. When Phyllis Oakley, the director of INR, was grilled at a closed Senate hearing on May 14, 1998, she conceded, "We were wrong. We were all wrong." One former intelligence official recalled that the "guys at Livermore thought they owned the Indian program" and "blew off BJP claims that they would test." The State Department, he said, accepted their view. Senator Richard Shelby, chairman of the Senate Select Committee on Intelligence, labeled the episode "a colossal failure of our intelligence-gathering system, perhaps the greatest failure in a decade." He also bemoaned the lost opportunity for the president or secretary of state to attempt to intervene diplomatically. A senior administration official characterized the failure "as a very big deal, especially because nonproliferation is supposed to be the No. 1 priority of the intelligence community."[63]

On May 13 former director of central intelligence James Woolsey suggested that the failure to detect blast preparations could be traced back to a decision earlier in the decade to cut the projected size of the reconnaissance satellite constellation.[64] However, it would soon become clear that the problem was not in space but on the ground. The United States had the intelligence that would have provided last-minute warning of a test, but it went unanalyzed until after India's first round of tests had been completed. That intelligence was in the form of imagery from an advanced KH-11 satellite that was in the hands of interpreters in the Priority Exploitation Group.

Beginning on October 1, 1996, the interpreters at Fort Belvoir reported to a new organization, the National Imagery and Mapping Agency (NIMA) within the Department of Defense. NIMA had been established on the initiative of director of central intelligence John Deutch to combine the national imagery interpretation and mapping efforts. The new entity absorbed the NPIC, the Defense Mapping Agency, the Central Imagery Office, the imagery interpretation elements of the CIA's Directorate of Intelligence and Defense Intelligence Agency, along with other offices and programs. The imagery interpreters at Fort Belvoir would be given a new designation but their mission remained the same.[65]

On May 8 a satellite transmitted imagery showing signs of renewed activity at the test site, including the presence of bulldozers nearby. That imagery may also have shown activity at the wellheads on top of deep holes where the nuclear devices would be detonated—if not, other imagery taken about the same time did. But not until sometime in the early hours of May 11 did an Area 58 interpreter notice something of interest in newly received images of the Indian test site—fences being removed and some panels, possibly motion detectors, being laid on the ground. The analyst marked the imagery for further analysis by the more experienced day-shift analysts, who were not expecting a test, and were presumably asleep rather than on alert. By the beginning of their workday, the opportunity for warning had passed.[66]

The BJP's platforms and the statements of Indian officials might also have been a source of warning. Days after the first Indian tests, Senator Daniel Patrick Moynahan, a former U.S. ambassador to India, posed the question, "Why don't we learn to read? . . . The political leadership in India as much as said they were going to begin testing." In early March AEC chairman Chidambaram stated publicly, "We are technologically prepared to go nuclear, but it is for the policy-makers to decide whether to go nuclear." At about the same time, Lal Krishna Advani, president of the BJP, and soon to become home minister, described a nuclear-free world as "a distant dream." But in classified reports analysts from the CIA, DIA, and State Department discounted the promise to go nuclear as mere campaign rhetoric, possibly believing it would not stand up to the threat of sanctions. It was a view communicated to higher levels and accepted. During his mid-April meeting with Pakistani leader Nawaz Sharif, U.S. ambassador to the UN Bill Richardson dismissed the BJP's vow to develop nuclear weapons as "election rhetoric."[67]

There might also have been an opportunity to uncover Indian plans to test if the CIA had had a human source in one of the villages in the Pokhran area, since the imminence of a test had been an open secret in those villages. Alternatively, attention to a Sikh community newsletter in Ontario, Canada, which speculated on an upcoming test four days before it happened, could have provided advance warning.[68]

THE U.S. INTELLIGENCE community's lack of attention was augmented by India's deception campaign. It employed the same technique that foreign officials had used for years in the face of a U.S. challenge concerning the nuclear intentions: they lied. State Department spokesman Jamie Rubin labeled it a "campaign of duplicity." In late March 1998, senior foreign policy adviser N. N. Jha reassured officials at the American embassy that over the next three to six months his government would be reviewing Indian national security policy and had no plans for weapons tests. Possibly Jha offered his assurances in good faith, with no knowledge of what was being planned. But his message, and one that was repeated to American officials in March and April, was false.[69]

On April 14 UN ambassador Bill Richardson met with Vajpayee and others in New Delhi, stressed U.S. opposition to nuclear testing, and was persuaded that there was no plan for tests. Sandy Berger, the president's national security adviser, did not raise the issue directly during a May 1 meeting in Washington with India's foreign minister, but praised India's restraint in not responding to Pakistan's missile test and came away reassured. That the Indian officials were telling their Clinton administration contacts exactly what they wanted to hear—that restraint would prevail—made it easier to believe.[70]

Some of the Indian officials were not aware they were providing misinformation because they did not know that the prime minister had already given Kalam and Chidambaram the go-ahead for the tests. The small number of Indian officials let in on the planned tests made it easy for others, including the foreign minister, to tell plausible lies since they did not believe they were being deceptive. Of course, no matter how plausible or sincere the lies, hard intelligence would convince those in the CIA and other agencies who monitored Indian nuclear activities that a test was in the works.

Indian officials and scientists, who certainly had not forgotten Frank Wisner's use of satellite imagery to make his point in 1995, tried to limit what U.S. spy satellites photographed in 1998. "They knew from the 1995 experience we were watching them closely," one U.S. official observed. Indian countermeasures included burying the cables and wires running into the shaft where they conducted the tests, placing camouflage netting over the test area, and conducting as many operations as possible at night or when satellites were not overhead. Working largely during the night the 58 Engineers dug two new shafts during the first half of April. On the night of May 5 the regiment laid the cables at the various shafts and then tried to cover their tracks, replacing the vegetation in the hopes that satellite images would show no sign that the area had been disturbed. The Indians also took advantage of the sandstorms that occur during May and block the view of KH-11–type satellites.[71]

The 58 Engineers also believed that its activity could be detected by U.S. imagery interpreters by tracking the movements of sand mounds required to seal the shafts. Mounds that occurred through the forces of nature would form in the direction of the blowing winds. Mounds created by bulldozers could stand out from those created naturally. To prevent discovery, the winds were monitored to ensure that any artificially created mounds were aligned with the wind.[72]

The Indians also tried, successfully, to prevent imagery from revealing vehicle movements that signaled increased and test-related activity. Each vehicle had an assigned parking space for the day. No matter how extensively they were used at night, they would be back in their designated spaces by morning, hoping to give the impression that nothing of consequence was happening at the test site.[73]

Also contributing to the failure to detect the tests well in advance was the limited targeting of the satellites on the test site. By mid-April, having heard the reassurances of Indian officials, the Imagery Requirements Subcommittee of NIMA's Central Imagery Tasking Office—which decided which targets would be photographed by U.S. spy satellites, from what angle and height, and when—decided to concentrate on India's missile sites, with the reasonable expectation that a response to Pakistan's Ghauri test would be forthcoming. Coverage of the nuclear test site was scheduled at three-day intervals, in stark contrast to the four images a day being obtained in January 1996. And the less the satellites saw, the more administration fears decreased.[74]

India's success in preventing U.S. spy satellites from seeing signs of the planned tests days to weeks in advance was matched by its success in preventing acquisition of other types of intelligence. India's Intelligence Bureau ran an aggressive counterintelligence program, and the CIA, despite a large station in New Delhi, was unable to recruit a single Indian with information about the Vajpayee government's nuclear plans. Instead, the deputy chief of the CIA station in New Delhi was expelled after a botched try at recruiting the chief of Indian counterintelligence operations. Former ambassador Frank Wisner recalled that "we didn't have . . . the humans who would have given us an insight into their intentions."[75]

Nor had NSA's eavesdropping activities detected test preparations. "It's a tough problem," one nuclear intelligence expert told investigative journalist Seymour Hersh, because India's nuclear weapons establishment would communicate via encrypted digital messages relayed via small dishes through satellites, using a system known as VSAT (very small-aperture terminal), a two-way version of the system used by satellite television companies.[76]

IT WAS SHORTLY AFTER the first Indian tests that director of central intelligence George Tenet appointed a panel, headed by former Joint Chiefs of Staff vice chairman Adm. David Jeremiah, to review intelligence community performance. While the full report remains highly classified, Jeremiah did hold a press conference when the report was finished, in early June 1998. The CIA also released a set of unclassified recommendations.

In his press conference Jeremiah noted that the identification of Indian nuclear test preparations represented a difficult collection problem as well as a difficult analytical problem. Since the program was not derived from a foreign one but was indigenous, some characteristics were difficult to observe. He mentioned the attention to limiting the number of Indian officials aware of the program as well as efforts to limit observable actions related to test preparations.[77]

He also noted the assumption, both in the intelligence and policy communities, that the BJP would behave as a Western political party, making promises in a political platform but not necessarily keeping those promises once they reached office and were confronted with the problems or costs of keeping their pledge. It was also assumed that the BJP would not be willing to suffer the economic sanctions that would follow a test.[78]

Unclassified recommendations discussed at the press conference ranged across all aspects of intelligence community activity. It would be necessary to add rigor to analysts' thinking, bringing in outside experts in a more systematic fashion; to reexamine the formal warning process in anticipation of altering it significantly; and to find means to better integrate regional and technical analyses. There was also a need to devote more resources to the processing and interpretation of imagery, relative to the resources expended on collecting imagery. For years the collection of imagery far outpaced the ability of the machines and people on the ground to turn it into finished intelligence.[79]

It was also recommended that collection priorities be realigned so that high-priority issues within individual nations, such as Indo-Pakistani weapons of mass destruction programs, would be treated with similar urgency as rogue states. Another recommendation was to create a management structure to integrate collection systems so that collection is tasked as a "system of systems" rather than as individual activities.[80]

Asked to what degree the failure to predict the tests was an intelligence failure and to what degree it represented an Indian success in keeping its plans secret, the admiral responded that the two factors had equal weight. As to whether advance warning could have been used to avert tests, his personal opinion was, "No, I don't think you were going to turn them around."[81]

In a statement issued the day of Jeremiah's press conference, Tenet accepted all of Jeremiah's recommendations and stated that he was "making it my highest priority to implement them as quickly as possible."[82]

chapter twelve

INSPECTORS AND SPIES

SHORTLY AFTER 11:00 A.M. on March 3, 1991, Lt. Gen. Sultan Hashim Ahmad and Lt. Gen. Salah Abud Mahmud arrived in Safwan, just north of the border with Kuwait, to meet with Gen. Norman Schwarzkopf, commander in chief of the U.S. Central Command. Ahmad was the deputy chief of staff of the Iraqi Ministry of Defense, while Mahmud had been commander of Iraq's recently decimated III Corps. Both of them "to Western eyes bore extraordinary resemblances to Saddam Hussein, with their black berets, dark olive uniforms, and heavy black mustaches," recalled Gen. Sir Peter de la Billiere, the British deputy commander of the coalition forces.[1]

Three days earlier, President George H. W. Bush declared a cease-fire in the Persian Gulf War after the allied forces led by Schwarzkopf had routed Iraqi forces, first driving them out of Kuwait and then back toward Baghdad. When NBC anchorman Tom Brokaw asked Schwarzkopf what he planned to negotiate with the Iraqis, the general snapped, "This isn't a negotiation. I don't plan to give them anything. I'm here to tell them exactly what we expect them to do."[2]

A day earlier the UN Security Council passed the first of ten 1991 postwar resolutions telling Saddam Hussein's regime what it expected now that his army had been defeated. The second of those resolutions, passed by a twelve-to-one vote on April 2, with only Cuba voting no, consisted of thirty-four points, including the demand that Iraq "unconditionally accept the destruction, removal, or rendering harmless, under international supervision of all chemical and biological weapons and all stocks of agents; and all related subsystems and components of all research, development, support and manufacturing facilities." Ballistic missiles with a range greater than 150 kilometers (93 miles), along with related major parts and repair and production facilities were also to be destroyed.[3]

Intending to make a clean sweep of Iraq's ability to produce and deploy weapons of mass destruction, the Security Council ordered Saddam's regime not to obtain or develop nuclear weapons or nuclear weapons–usable material or "any subsystems or components or any research, development, support or manufacturing facilities" involved in producing such weapons or weapons-usable material. Iraq was also ordered to provide the UN secretary general and the director general of the International Atomic Energy Agency, within fifteen days, with a declaration that fully disclosed Iraq's nuclear weapons facilities and material.[4]

Further, Iraq was also to place any weapons-usable material under the control of the IAEA. In addition, it "requested" that the IAEA director general, Hans Blix, carry out "immediate on-site inspections of Iraq's nuclear capabilities based on Iraq's declarations and the designation of any additional locations by the [U.N. Special Commission on Iraq—UNSCOM]." The atomic energy agency was also requested to develop a plan, within forty-five days, for the "destruction, removal, or rendering harmless" of all the nuclear weapons–related material prohibited by the resolution.[5]

Assigning the IAEA to investigate Iraq's progress toward an atomic bomb and destruction of weapons-related material came only after a diplomatic dispute between the United States and Britain on one side and France on the other. The first Anglo-American draft of the April 2 resolution gave the unit that would become known as UNSCOM the responsibility for disarming Iraq of all weapons of mass destruction. The IAEA had been created primarily to advance the peaceful uses of atomic energy. Nuclear weapons states provided nuclear technology to be used for peaceful purposes and the IAEA, through consensual "safeguards inspections," accounted for weapons-grade uranium and plutonium. The agency's legacy did not lie in overcoming denial and deception. Its failure prior to the Gulf War to notice Iraq's huge nuclear weapons effort—despite direct and repeated access to Tuwaitha because Iraq was a signatory to the nonproliferation treaty—left certain members of the Bush administration deeply skeptical of the agency's ability to carry out the nuclear disarmament mission.[6]

One problem, according to former IAEA inspector David Kay, was that the agency's technical personnel had no weapons background. In the case of Tuwaitha, they had been easily misled, being shown portions of only three of the hundred buildings at the site. The facility was cleverly laid out, including the distribution of buildings and the use of trees to provide visual screening. The clever routing of the site's internal road system made it very difficult for any outsider, Kay recalled, "without access to overhead intelligence to accurately understand the size of the center and the relationship of the buildings to each other." The agency's deputy director general for technical assistance, who had never seen any overhead images of the site, had no idea how much his inspectors were not being shown. Not surprisingly, the inspectors never asked about the rest of the site or for permission to see it. But the IAEA supporters in the Bush administration argued that to refuse to assign the agency the inspection mission would fatally cripple it at a particularly inopportune time—right before the conference reviewing the nonproliferation treaty, a treaty that the IAEA played a crucial role in enforcing. The IAEA supporters won out and the IAEA was assigned the nuclear disarmament role in the April 2 resolution, while UNSCOM was given the mission of verifying Iraqi compliance with regard to all other varieties of weapons of mass destruction.[7]

IN EARLY MAY a letter from the UN secretary general, Javier Perez de Cuellar, was delivered to the Iraqi foreign minister, spelling out the rights of the UNSCOM teams that would be arriving in Iraq to inventory and destroy Iraqi chemical, biological, and missile facilities and weapons. Those rights would soon be extended to the IAEA teams investigating Iraqi nuclear programs. There were to be no restrictions on their movements in and out of Iraq, no interference with their access to any site or facility designated for inspection, no attempt to prevent interviews with relevant personnel, and no restrictions on communications, whether by radio, satellite, or mail. In addition, Iraq was obligated to provide requested documents relevant to disarmament, which the teams could examine and copy. The teams also would have the right to use aircraft to photograph facilities and activities and to take and analyze samples of any kind.[8]

There were obvious parallels between the UNSCOM and IAEA teams and the Alsos effort at the end of World War II—the mandate to investigate efforts of a defeated enemy to develop weapons of mass destruction and virtually free reign to accomplish that mission. And the United States would have access to the product of their efforts. There were also important differences. Alsos had been strictly a U.S.-conceived and -directed effort, with some British participation. The UN teams in Iraq included scientists from nations such as France and Russia, while the Alsos teams had tried to prevent French and Russian scientists from acquiring information about the German effort or getting their hands on German scientists.

More importantly, the Allies had occupied all of Germany in 1945. There was no surviving German government that sought to interfere with their activities. In 1991 the United States and its allies occupied only the southern portion of Iraq, while Saddam remained in power. In 1993 he established the National Monitoring Directorate, ostensibly to handle Iraqi government dealings with the inspection teams, but as part of the Iraqi objective to make the teams work as unproductive as possible. From 1991 each of the regime's numerous intelligence services was involved in the concealment effort, with the Special Security Organization, headed by Saddam's son Qusay Hussein, coordinating their efforts. Qusay also headed the Concealment Operations Committee, established in May 1991. The Special Republican Guard and the Military Industrialization Commission were part of the concealment effort too.[9]

The first of the IAEA inspections began in May 1991. The Iraqi declaration of April 19 was of no help. Signed by Saddam himself, it claimed that Iraq possessed no nuclear materials covered by the resolution. It was amended on April 27 to acknowledge Iraq's possession of additional nuclear material and facilities, including a "peaceful" research program, with headquarters at the Tuwaitha Nuclear Research Center—still far from the truth. When the inspectors did find documents, they would be faced with the "multiple, constantly shifting, and overlapping codes for individual components" that Iraq had employed for all its weapons programs.[10]

The inspectors, in preparation for their first inspection, would also have very limited help from the U.S. intelligence community, which professed to have little specific knowledge of the Iraqi nuclear weapons effort and nothing like a comprehensive overview. There had been no systematic overhead imagery of central Iraq. Among the items missed by the United States and other nations was Iraq's acquisition of soft iron magnets for its calutrons, which were purchased from an Austrian firm, shipped through Hamburg, and trucked across Turkey. It was the type of activity easily detected in Hollywood films—where the United States has an ever-present eavesdropping capability and operates spy satellites that can constantly track trains, cars, and other vehicles—but not in the real world.[11]

On May 14 a Romanian BAC-111 aircraft landed at Saddam International Airport carrying thirty-four specialists in physics, chemistry, and nuclear engineering. Inspections began the next day and lasted until May 21. The team arrived equipped with a variety of detection gear, prepared to measure the gamma rays given off by uranium samples, to identify uranium enrichment efforts, as well as to detect the Cerenkov glow emitted by high-speed electrons, which when viewed through night-vision devices can reveal whether the plutonium in spent fuel rods is still there or has been removed to make bombs. The team was also prepared to sample vegetation, take smear samples from building walls, and analyze the soil—all for signs of illicit nuclear activity.[12]

The IAEA1 team, headed by veteran IAEA inspector Dimitri Perricos, spent most of its time exploring the huge nuclear research facility at Tuwaitha, which had some buildings destroyed by coalition bombing. Before the inspectors arrived, Iraq added to the destruction, leveling the large calutron test facility and covering it with dirt, as well as destroying the laser and centrifuge test facilities at the site. The inspectors were, however, able to accomplish their key objective and locate the enriched uranium believed to be at the site. What they were not expecting to find were the 2.26 grams of plutonium that turned up during their search.[13]

The inspectors also sorted through the rubble at Tarmiya. Iraqi army officers stationed there claimed that one facility, which appeared to be a factory, had produced electrical transformers—although the plant was too large and complex to be a simple manufacturing site. "We were perplexed by the building setup," Perricos recalled. "If this was for the manufacture of transformers there were too many buildings, too much chemistry." A Western intelligence service had suggested that it might have housed centrifuges, but the team found no evidence of their presence. The pictures of the facility's layout did remind some of a more primitive form of uranium enrichment—World War II–era calutrons.[14]

There were early indications that Iraq was going to be less than fully cooperative. It was apparent to the team that Iraq had conducted, as former UNSCOM inspector Tim Trevan recalled, "extensive clearing operations before the inspection to remove much of the equipment that had been at al-Tuwaitha." The Iraqis neither declared the equipment nor would reveal its current location. While some of the relocated equipment was shown to the inspectors, other items remained hidden.[15]

It did not take long before Iraqi interference with the nuclear inspectors became more blatant. The second IAEA inspection team was led by David Kay, a fifty-one-year-old Texan with a doctorate in international affairs from Columbia University who had worked in the Pentagon before joining the IAEA in 1983. Like Perricos, he was a veteran of many IAEA safeguards inspections. But in contrast to Perricos's good cop, Kay would often play the bad cop in dealing with the Iraqis. Mahdi Obeidi recalls that Kay "had a brash confrontational style. He rode around Iraq, acting like a cowboy on big horse, and over time all the scientists became afraid he would expose their former work." Also in contrast to the first inspection team, Kay's would be armed with some significant intelligence from the United States, including a fact revealed by satellite images—that immediately after the inspection at Tuwaitha, the Iraqis had uncovered and removed disc-shaped objects that had been buried outside of Tuwaitha.[16]

Initial analysis of the photographs by IAEA as well as U.S. analysts left both groups puzzled about the intended use of the large cylindrical objects on the trucks. A suggestion that the equipment in the images were calutrons was initially dismissed, in the belief that the Iraqis would not attempt to enrich uranium using antiquated World War II technology that required huge expenditures of money and energy. Earlier suggestions from one or more analysts at either Los Alamos or Sandia (or both) that Iraq might be employing calutrons had been rejected at higher levels of the Energy Department. IAEA head Blix, and his deputy, Mohamed ElBaradei, were among the doubters. But John Googin, a retired nuclear weapons engineer and veteran of Oak Ridge and the Manhattan Project, when shown the images had no trouble in confirming that the inspectors and the satellites had indeed photographed calutrons.[17]

Kay's team arrived in Baghdad on Saturday, June 22, armed with intelligence provided, via the United States, from two Iraqi engineers who had fled west and were familiar with Iraq's nuclear weapons program. In addition, the team knew that U.S. intelligence had been able to track suspicious objects (the calutrons) from Tarmiya to the Abu Ghraib military barracks near Baghdad, a site not mentioned in Iraq's declarations concerning its weapons of mass destruction activities. On June 23 the IAEA2 team showed up at the barracks, ready to conduct a surprise inspection and demanding full access.[18]

Despite Iraq's claim that it had nothing to hide, Iraqi soldiers blocked the entrance to the site that Sunday. The attempt was not a total loss, however. From their positions outside the barracks, inspectors could see, and used telephoto lenses to photograph, trucks, cranes, and a forklift moving out heavy, draped objects—the calutrons that the U.S. intelligence community had tracked from Tarmiya to Abu Ghraib. Kay's team tried again on Tuesday and was again denied admittance. It was only on the third try, the following day, that the team was let in—but by then all the incriminating evidence was gone. IAEA chief Blix noted that there was "no longer any trace of the activities and objects" his inspectors had seen a few days earlier.[19]

The day after the team's futile return visit to Abu Ghraib, the fifteen permanent representatives of the UN Security Council, Secretary General de Cuellar, and two senior UN officials were shown photos obtained by one or more KH-11 satellites. The United States wanted it to be clear that the failure to find anything there was due to Iraqi duplicity not Iraqi compliance. The secret images showed uncrated calutrons being moved onto trucks just before inspectors arrived at Tuwaitha, Tarmiya, and Abu Ghraib.[20]

The inspectors faced interference again on June 28, when Kay and his team arrived in Fallujah, intent on exploring the Military Transportation Facility, based on a tip from the CIA. The agency's information indicated that the regime had collected various items from its nuclear program at the site. Satellite photographs had shown the facility's buildings, a fenced perimeter, a water tower outside the fence, and a single front gate. Other intelligence, probably another set of photos, indicated the calutrons had been moved, from Abu Ghraib to Fallujah.[21]

The convoy of vehicles arrived at the transportation facility carrying the inspectors, their equipment, and their "minders"—Iraqi officials whose ostensible mission was to serve as guides and liaisons between the inspectors and their targets but were not supposed to know in advance what site was to be inspected. Kay then told the chief minder that he wanted to inspect the site, and reminded him that while his team was waiting to enter, only UN vehicles should enter or leave the site, and no equipment was to be moved. Kay also sent some of the inspectors to watch the exits, and one of "Kay's cowboys"—as Robert Gallucci characterized them—climbed a nearby water tower, which allowed him to monitor the entire site.[22]

It came as no surprise that the Iraqis tried to deny the team access. In the midst of his telling the Iraqis what was required of them, Kay received a call over portable radio from the inspector perched in the water tower. The bomb-making equipment that the U.S. intelligence reports claimed was at the site, and Iraq denied possessing, was being loaded onto trucks that were getting ready to leave.[23]

Kay and his team could do nothing to gain entrance, because heavily armed soldiers blocked their way. But the inspectors stationed at the exits would be able to photograph the trucks when they departed. One, Rick Lally, had brought his own new and expensive camera. When the trucks left, he started snapping pictures, then jumped into a UN vehicle along with other inspectors and continued taking photos as the UN vehicle chased the trucks. The chase ended when an Iraqi vehicle drove the inspectors' car off the road. The Iraqis then tried to force Lally, at gunpoint, to turn over the camera and film—a demand he successfully deflected, having hidden the film and claiming that the device was actually a new type of binoculars.[24]

The inspectors' photographs were not the only images demonstrating that the Iraqis were willing to make a great effort to hide the equipment stored at the military transportation facility. Another set came, not from ground level or from the perspective of a water tower, but from outer space, as one or more of the National Reconnaissance Office's constellation of imagery satellites recorded the Iraqi convoy driving away from Kay and his inspectors. Not surprisingly, the convoy was out of view of the satellites before it reached its destination, but the images obtained by the inspectors and satellites revealed new information about Iraq's nuclear weapons program.[25]

The consolidated report on the first two IAEA inspections provided the U.S. intelligence community with data, unobtainable prior to the war, on the inner workings of Tuwaitha. It also assessed how effective the coalition aerial attacks had been in destroying or disrupting the facilities at the nuclear center. It described the status of the research reactors, the hot cells, a variety of laboratories, and the chemistry and chemical engineering building—while the laboratory and workshop building was totally destroyed, all three compartments of the hot cells in the radiochemistry laboratories were intact. The report also evaluated the overall development of the Iraqi program, with a description of the findings during the first team's inspection of the Tarmiya complex, which it labeled as a "possible nuclear facility," as well as its examination of several other sites suspected of fabricating calutron components.[26]

The Iraqi actions of late June, which included firing over the heads of one group of inspectors on June 28 as they followed the convoy out of Fallujah, produced sharp reactions from the United States and UN. The international body sent a high-level delegation, which included UNSCOM chief Rolf Ekeus as delegation head, the IAEA's Blix, and Yasushi Akashi, the UN's undersecretary general for disarmament affairs. They met with Iraqi foreign minister Ahmed Hussein on June 30 and with deputy prime minister Tariq Aziz the following day. The message they conveyed, backed up by serious U.S. preparations for military action, led to a July 5 letter from Saddam to the UN secretary general, promising compliance and a new list of nuclear-related items that would be of interest to the inspectors.[27]

After Kay's team left Iraq on July 3, a new IAEA team arrived, with Dimitri Perricos at the head of the thirty-seven inspectors. Early in their visit they were escorted into a large conference room at the Al Monsour Hotel, where they met with a collection of Iraqi nuclear experts. The experts appeared uncertain about what they could say when suddenly, according to Cal Wood, a Livermore physicist, a "well-dressed man in the back, in impeccable English with a British accent, said 'I will answer all your questions.'" The man was Jaffar Dhia Jaffar, who inspectors and U.S. intelligence knew held a senior position in the Iraqi nuclear program, but who had not yet realized he was Iraq's J. Robert Oppenheimer.[28]

Jaffar acknowledged that the Iraqis had made some progress in the field of uranium enrichment, and even arranged for visits to sites where Iraqis had destroyed or concealed calutrons. Inspectors visited seven desert sites and found thirty magnets. They also heard explanations of how the Iraqis had tried to blow up some of the calutrons, but accomplished nothing more than lifting them up off the ground, only to have them land undamaged.[29]

Jaffar claimed, however, that the enrichment effort did not have a military objective, that there was no plan to use the highly enriched uranium for nuclear weapons. The objective, he said, was to provide fuel for research reactors and a future nuclear power program—an assertion the inspectors considered implausible given the existence of two types of equipment used for separation, one with low capacity and high-separation ability and another with high capacity and low-separation capability.[30]

As part of Iraq's limited disclosure, the Perricos team was shown a video of the February 1990 inauguration of the Tarmiya plant. The video, along with blueprints of the plant, allowed the inspection team to calculate that the facility could produce up to thirty-three pounds of 93 percent enriched uranium each year. They also concluded that Ash Sharqat, which was 85 percent complete at the beginning of the war, was a duplicate of Tarmiya, and not a factory for the plastic coating of equipment as Iraq claimed. Together the facilities would produce enough highly enriched uranium for two nuclear bombs a year.[31]

By the time they had completed their inspection on July 18, Perricos's team was convinced that they had seen only part of a full-scale nuclear program, and that the enrichment programs, particularly the gas centrifuge technique, had been more advanced than Iraq was willing to admit. They also believed that a substantial effort would be required to track down all the items that had been transferred from Tuwaitha, Tarmiya, and Ash Sharqat.[32]

The Iraqis had made a significant effort to hide the true nature of Tarmiya and Ash Sharqat from the inspectors. In addition to removing key equipment from the facilities, they had also tried to cover up telltale signs of the original layout, including rails and return irons for the separators, by laying down a new cement floor at each site.[33]

At the time the third IAEA inspection was winding down, David Kay and his team were preparing to build on their work. IAEA4 would seek to uncover more about the centrifuge enrichment program, to produce a detailed evaluation of the calutron effort, and to search for evidence of weaponization facilities. The team's arrival in Baghdad, on July 27, had been delayed a day because President Bush was threatening military action against Iraq unless the country revealed the full extent of its nuclear weapons program. The team arrived with orders to report its location to UNSCOM in New York at three-hour intervals to ensure that if the United States did undertake military operations, team members would not become unintended casualties.[34]

On the first morning, the Iraqis revealed more about their nuclear activities, which made it clear that they had conducted a covert program to produce natural-uranium fuel elements from nuclear materials the Iraqi government had not, as it was obligated to, disclosed to the IAEA under the Safeguards Agreement. In addition, two experiments conducted at Tuwaitha's Experimental Reactor Fuel Fabrication Laboratory were intended to produce fuel elements containing plutonium. The center of the experiments was the IRT-5000 reactor core. Despite two IAEA inspections each year, the experiments had not been detected, apparently because Iraq had removed the experimental fuel elements before each inspection.[35]

Kay's group conducted a no-notice inspection of the Mosul Production Facility at Al Jazirah, which uncovered its true mission, the production of uranium hexafluoride to be used in gas centrifuges—although the building for uranium hexafluoride production had been leveled. They also visited the Al Furat complex, which Iraq admitted had been built to produce gas centrifuges. The plans for Al Furat, according to Iraqi authorities, spanned another five years. The construction and operation of the centrifuge production plant was to be completed by the end of 1991, while the first 100-machine cascade was to be in operation by mid-1993. By early 1996 a 500-machine cascade was to be in operation. As much as fifty-five pounds of uranium, enriched to at least 90 percent U-235, would be produced each year.[36]

Al Atheer, suspected of having a connection with nuclear weaponization, was also on the team's list. Jaffar had claimed that no official decision had been taken to develop nuclear weapons, and that any design activities "had been only individual exercises by interested scientists." After visiting the site, Kay and his team came to a different assessment. The unit's report noted that "one of the most visible weaponisation activities is high explosive testing," and the existence of a firing bunker belonging to the Hatheen Establishment of Al Musayyib and "now heavily damaged" near the Al Atheer materials research center. It also mentioned that the bunker had been used a few times for crude testing of conventional explosives and was "capable of supporting significant physics experiments critical to nuclear weapons development." In addition, it reported that "some construction work is under way at this site despite the damage, and this suggests that such a facility has a very high priority."[37]

After completing its work on August 10, Kay's team prepared a report for the UN Security Council, which stated that "Al Atheer and its companion facilities at al-Hateen and al-Musayyib constitute a complete and sufficient potential nuclear weapons laboratory and production facility within one common fence line. This combined facility is so big and well equipped that it can clearly do much more than the limited non-weapons activities that the Iraqis claim as its purpose. It is certainly a top candidate for future monitoring."[38]

A direct consequence of the new evidence of Iraq's nuclear weapons ambitions was a new UN resolution, 707, adopted on August 15. It was, according to former UNSCOM inspector Tim Trevan, the "strongest outpouring of vitriol and bile in the history of the U.N." The resolution, which even Cuba supported, condemned "Iraq's serious violation of a number of its obligations under . . . resolution 687 (1991) and of its undertakings to cooperate with the Special Commission and the IAEA." Those failures represented, the Security Council declared, "a material breach of the . . . resolution . . . which established a cease-fire." The resolution also demanded that Iraq immediately halt any attempts to conceal movement or destruction of equipment relating to its weapons of mass destruction programs without consent from the UN, make available any previously denied equipment, and permit overflights throughout Iraq for a variety of purposes, including inspection and surveillance.[39]

Passage of the resolution was followed by a U.S. offer to fly U-2 missions over Iraq, an offer accepted by Ekeus, with the understanding that the missions, which would be designated Olive Branch, would be under his control. But the first two post-overflight briefings were not well received. The United States provided a limited number of photographs that had been degraded to conceal the U-2 camera's capability, and were delivered weeks after the mission was completed. The photos provided no information about the time they were taken or the longitude and latitude of the target, information normally imprinted on U-2 images. The second briefing, held in Ekeus's office on the thirty-first floor of UN headquarters in New York and attended by intelligence analysts, some senior U.S. Air Force officers, and U.S. ambassador to the UN Thomas Pickering, provoked an outburst from Ekeus. Reminding his guests that the U-2 missions were to be a UN operation, he asked what they had produced. It was a rhetorical question, and after providing his answer—a few lousy fuzzy photographs of no use to anyone—he tossed them in his garbage can.[40]

Ekeus's complaints produced the desired results. At the third briefing, held soon after the next U-2 flight, the photographs were remarkably sharp and useful, and had the time stamped on them along with the name of the facility photographed. The United States also turned over negatives of the images shown at the briefing, which could be analyzed by the imagery interpreters that UNSCOM had recruited. The interpreters, along with the Information Assessment Unit established by Ekeus, provided the inspectors with their own independent interpretation and analysis capability.[41]

BY JUNE 1991, as result of defector debriefings, U.S. analysts believed they could pin down the exact location of key documents describing Iraq's weaponization program. A proposal to blockade the building where the documents were believed to be while a search was conducted ran into initial opposition from Blix as well as Perricos, who were accustomed to consensual safeguards inspections. But the United States insisted that an IAEA inspection go forward, headed by Kay, or that the effort be conducted by UNSCOM. Blix reluctantly agreed.[42]

Kay's team arrived on September 22 for what was to be the sixth inspection. Serving as his deputy was Robert Gallucci, who joined the UN effort in April, after having spent three years teaching at the National War College and then briefly rejoining the State Department to advise on the disarmament of Iraq. At 5:30 on the morning of September 23, Kay and his team of forty-four gathered in the lobby of the Rasheed Hotel, accompanied by their Iraqi minders, and headed for the multistory L-shaped Nuclear Design Center across the road—"arriving unannounced and in force, like cops on a drug bust," according to *Newsweek*. Hoping to avoid alerting the Iraqis if they made a significant discovery, they had selected a set of code words to be used in their radio communications.[43]

After Kay's team secured the building, the inspectors spread out to check each floor. The intelligence provided by the CIA indicated that the key documents could be found in a basement room in a building annex, leaving a significant area to be searched. At 10:00 a.m. Kay was on the eighth floor when a message containing the magic word came across his radio, indicating that the team had hit paydirt. The documents had been found in the basement, as the CIA had predicted. Since the elevators were out of commission, Kay trotted down the stairs. When he arrived in the basement, he found several trunks filled with documents, including a report from Al Atheer concerning the progress made on developing an implosion-type weapon up to May 1990.[44]

Kay's first priority was to get the evidence out before the Iraqis discovered what his team had found. He took advantage of one American inspector's stomach infection, which caused severe dehydration. Kay requested one of his medics to evacuate him, taking him directly to Habbaniyah air base, where a UNSCOM aircraft would take him to Bahrain. The plane also carried some of the documents, which Kay had hidden in the inspector's jacket. The plane took off at two in the afternoon and reached Bahrain less than three hours later. By the end of the day copies of the documents had been faxed to the IAEA in Vienna and UNSCOM in New York.[45]

Finally, around 3:30 in the afternoon, the Iraqis tumbled to what was going on, and demanded that they be given a full inventory of the confiscated documents. Throughout, the inspectors had been making their own inventory and marking the relevant documents. Kay gave the order for the UNSCOM vehicles to be loaded with the trunks and transfer them back to the field office, but the Iraqi minders blocked the team's departure. At 4:30 Iraqi officials arrived and began an inventory of the documents on the inspectors' trucks. Jaffar, who the Al Atheer report identified as the leader of the weaponization program and deputy chairman of the Iraqi Atomic Energy Commission, also showed up and demanded a complete inventory. Kay had his own demand— that the team be allowed to leave at 6:30. Instead, at seven, the Iraqis confiscated the materials at gunpoint, an act photographed by the team. At two in the morning the Iraqi minders turned up to return the documents to Kay's team, minus, a quick check of their inventory showed, all of the ones the inspectors considered relevant.[46]

Four hours later, Kay's team gathered at the hotel again, prepared to pursue a lead from the Al Atheer report, and found themselves outnumbered by their minders by a three-to-one ratio. They loaded up the vehicles as if they were preparing for a major expedition, although they were planning on going only one hundred yards, to the headquarters of Petrochemical-3. By 6:20 they had arrived. They immediately discovered large quantities of relevant documents, which guaranteed that their Iraqi minders were unhappy from the start of the day. Kay instructed the team to load the documents onto their vehicles as soon as they were discovered, but at 10:50, the chief minder ordered all activity to stop. When the inspectors tried to ignore his orders, they were forcibly removed from the building. Kay, told to unload the documents from the vehicles and leave, responded that they were not leaving without the documents. At 12:30 Jaffar arrived and also demanded that the team return all the documents and films they had confiscated.[47]

Team members proceeded to circle their wagons in the parking lot—a Land Rover, a Toyota, and an old bus. That was the beginning of a four-day standoff in which the days were hot and the nights cold, as there was no cloud cover to prevent the temperature from rapidly falling after the sun went down. The inspectors' diet consisted of watermelon and military Meals-Ready-to-Eat (MREs). In addition to eating and waiting, they also secretly transmitted some of the data they acquired to a satellite, which relayed it to a secret National Security Agency site in Bahrain.[48]

The Iraqi government organized demonstrations and made assorted accusations. Finally, on the afternoon of September 27, at UN headquarters in New York, an agreement was reached allowing the team to leave with the documents. Both sides would review and inventory the seized documents and films at the UNSCOM office in Baghdad, and Iraq would retain the inventory. Irrelevant documents would be returned to Iraq, but the final decision as to relevance would be Kay's.[49]

On September 28, at 5:46 a.m. Baghdad time, the team was finally released. The inspectors then spent the entire day reviewing the sixty thousand or so documents they had brought back, which included a copy of the Al Atheer progress report. The next day UNSCOM's support staff shipped documents out to Bahrain, while the team searched three further sites. Not surprisingly, whatever documents that had been there had already been cleaned out or destroyed—on the third day of the standoff, the team had seen smoke from a fire on the top floor of one of the two targeted buildings.[50]

The team's report (which included the entire Al Atheer report as an annex) noted that it had "obtained conclusive evidence that the Government of Iraq had a program for developing an implosion-type nuclear weapon and it found documents linking this program to Iraq's Ministry of Industry and Military Industrialisation, the Iraqi Atomic Energy Commission (IAEC) and the Iraqi Ministry of Defense." It also informed the Security Council that "contrary to Iraq's claims of having only a peaceful nuclear program, the team found documents showing that Iraq had been working on the revision of a nuclear weapon design and one linking the IAEC to work on a surface-to-surface missile project—presumably the intended delivery system for their nuclear weapon."[51]

The documents revealed that Al Atheer was the center for nuclear weapons design work, despite Iraq's declaration that it housed no nuclear activity of any sort, and that extensive weaponization work had also been conducted at Tuwaitha. Other documents revealed the existence of a project to produce a sizable amount of lithium-6, a key component for thermonuclear weapons (although ultimately it would be determined that only small quantities had been produced and little, if any, theoretical work had been done on hydrogen bomb development). They also established a link between Iraq's work on gaseous diffusion and uranium enrichment techniques to the weapons effort. Further, the documents showed that Jaffar Dhia Jaffar, despite his claims that Iraq had not been trying to develop nuclear weapons, was one of the program's senior officials. Indeed, the team finally concluded that Jaffar was the program's director.[52]

THE INSPECTION of late September was David Kay's (and Robert Gallucci's) last for the IAEA. But over the next year, eight agency teams visited Iraq. The October and November 1991 teams supervised the destruction of uranium enrichment and processing equipment and removed stocks of irradiated nuclear fuel from the country. From April through July 1992 inspectors directed the destruction of equipment and facilities at Al Atheer, Tarmiya, and Ash Sharqat.[53]

On January 23, 1991, little over a week into the aerial campaign, and about a month before the ground war began, President Bush had reassured the nation that "our pinpoint attacks have put Saddam out of the nuclear bomb building business for a long time." And on several occasions in late January, General Schwarzkopf said the coalition's attacks "had destroyed all their nuclear manufacturing capability."[54]

Those assertions were based on the assumption that the CIA and other key intelligence agencies had a good understanding of the Iraqi nuclear program—its size, scope, and progress—prior to the initiation of the air war. Over the course of 1991 the U.S. intelligence community would learn far more about the Iraqi nuclear program, in part from independent intelligence collection—overhead imagery, eavesdropping, and human intelligence (including the debriefing of defectors). But the UN inspections played a major role in transforming the intelligence collected into firm conclusions about the status of the Iraqi program before the war.

In late May 1991 four Iraqis drove up to a U.S. Marine checkpoint near Dohuk, a hamlet in northern Iraq that had been established to protect the Kurds. One occupant, who was accompanied by his wife, brother, and a friend, told one Marine, "I am Saddam Hussein's top nuclear scientist." He was whisked away for debriefing, along with his family and friend—taken first to Turkey and then to Munich.[55]

As was not unusual with defectors, he was exaggerating. He was not Jaffar Dhia Jaffar, but a physicist who had worked at the Ash Sharqat calutron facility. He disclosed the progress that Iraq had made in advancing the World War II–era technology, and claimed to know of several sites where such facilities existed. He also reported that the coalition bombing campaign had missed a number of key facilities, including a large underground uranium enrichment facility inside a mountain north of Mosul. In addition, he passed on some inaccurate hearsay—the assurances of a colleague that the Petrochemical-3 facility already had eighty-eight pounds of highly enriched uranium. He claimed that Saddam expected to have a bomb by the end of the year. The defector also reported that nuclear weapons material and equipment had been transferred to the substitute site before the beginning of the Gulf War, and provided information concerning Iraqi use of gas centrifuges and research on chemical high explosives to trigger nuclear detonations. One U.S. analyst characterized the defector as "the one guy, out of thousands, who came forward and who actually had useful information about Saddam's nuclear program."[56]

The defector's report spurred even more extensive satellite imagery of Iraq, including Tuwaitha. Some of the images showed that after the inspectors left the facility on May 21, 1991, the Iraqis disinterred the disc-shaped objects that they had buried there—the objects Oak Ridge veteran John Googin was able to identify as calutrons.[57]

That defector was not the only Iraqi official to come forward with tales about the nuclear program. By September, according to one account, at least three Iraqi officials with extensive knowledge of the program had defected to allied intelligence agencies since the end of the war in February.[58]

By late September the accumulation of data from defectors, spy satellites, and UN inspections gave the U.S. intelligence community a far better grasp of the Iraqi nuclear weapons program, as well as its other weapons of mass destruction programs, than it had possessed at the beginning of the year. It was also the view of the IAEA that by that time despite the Iraqi government's strategy of "obstruction and delay . . . to conceal the real nature of its nuclear projects . . . the essential components of the clandestine program have been identified." A significant factor in the agency's ability to accomplish that task, the IAEA noted, was "the provision of intelligence information" by its member states.[59]

Among the new insights was Iraq's attempt to employ three different technologies to produce highly enriched uranium: electromagnetic isotope separation (calutrons), thermal diffusion, and gas centrifuges. In addition, a minute quantity of plutonium had been produced at Tuwaitha, by cheating on international safeguards. The extent to which Iraq had acquired a wide range of sophisticated and restricted nuclear weapons technologies, including carbon-fiber rotors used in gas centrifuges and super-hard maraging steel that could be used in centrifuges or a bomb itself, was understood for the first time.[60]

Related to the appreciation of the different technologies employed was the identification of all but one of the key facilities that made up the Iraqi program, along with their purpose. By the end of September 1991 the U.S. intelligence community understood that the prewar Iraqi program included facilities at Tuwaitha (Nuclear Research Center), Al Qaim (uranium concentration plant), Al Jazirah (manufacturing of uranium oxide and uranium tetrachloride for the EMIS program), Tarmiya (EMIS Plant), Ash Sharqat (EMIS plant), Al Atheer (Materials Center for nuclear weapons production and development), and Al Rabiyah (Manufacturing Plant with workshops designed and built for the manufacture of large metal components for the Iraqi EMIS program). Inspectors did show up at the Rashdiya centrifuge development center during the fourth IAEA inspection, based on a tip from a defector in the summer of 1991, and again in January 1992, but its true function would not be appreciated until much later.[61]*

Understanding virtually the full range of facilities and technologies that constituted the prewar Iraqi program brought with it an understanding of what the intelligence community had failed to discover about the Iraqi program: Al Atheer's role in weapons design, Al Furat's secret mission of building centrifuges, and the pursuit of electromagnetic separation to produce enriched uranium. Al Atheer was not linked to the nuclear program until a week before the war ended. Even then, the three buildings essential to any effort to assemble and test bomb components were not detected. The extent that the United States and its allies underestimated and misunderstood the Iraqi program constituted a "colossal international intelligence failure," according to one Israeli expert. IAEA Hans Blix acknowledged that "there was suspicion certainly," but "to see the enormity of it is a shock."[62]

The additional information about not only the scope of the Iraqi program but also its actual progress led to revised estimates of when Iraq could have had its first atomic bomb, and when it would have been able to produce bombs in quantity. The Joint Atomic Energy Intelligence Committee estimate of 1990, which suggested that a crash program could have produced a bomb within a year, gave way to new judgments based on discovery of problems that the Iraqis had experienced with respect to enriching uranium and

---

* The report of the ninth IAEA inspection team explains the Iraqi cover story for the site—that it was first built in the 1980s by the Ministry of Agriculture for research and development in water irrigation technology but was turned over to the Ministry of Industry and Minerals in 1988, which established an Engineering Design Center in the northern part of the site while attempting to establish a paper mill/vocational training center under the forestry ministry in the southern part. After exploring the complex, the team reported that "there was no physical evidence or other signs of recent modifications which might suggest that this facility served some other purpose than what was declared." The report did note that the director of the center "was unable to produce a single piece of paper related to its projects," claiming that all records and reports were maintained at the locations where the staff was working or at the ministry. See S/23505, Note by the Secretary General, January 30, 1992 w/enclosure: *Report on the Ninth IAEA On-Site Inspection in Iraq Under Security Council Resolution 687 (1991), 11–14 January 1992*, pp. 14–15.

In late 1992, after repeated questioning, the Iraqis admitted that Rashdiya was home to one of the country's senior centrifuge experts but claimed his presence simply resulted from his desire to work at that location. They continued to claim that the principal centrifuge sites were at Tuwaitha and Al Furat. In the absence of solid evidence inspectors disagreed as to the nature of Rashdiya's activities throughout 1993 and 1994. See David Albright, "Masters of Deception," *Bulletin of the Atomic Scientists*, May/June 1998, pp. 45–50 at p. 48.

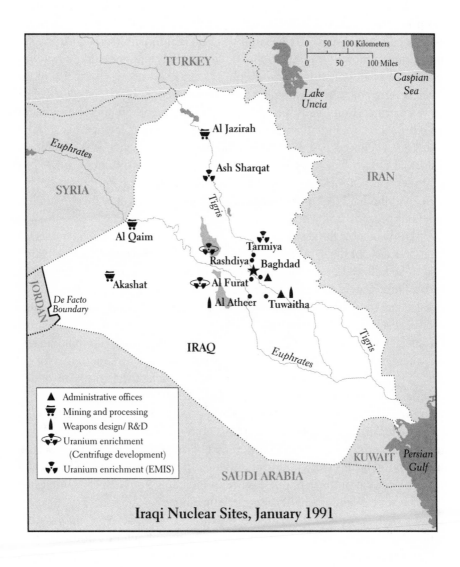

Iraqi Nuclear Sites, January 1991

perfecting implosion. By mid-1992 it was estimated that it would have taken Jaffar and his colleagues another two to three years after the beginning of the Gulf War, or more, to have a working bomb.[63]

In the immediate aftermath of the war, there was still uncertainty within the U.S. intelligence community and the IAEA as to who actually headed the Iraqi program. Both U.S. and IAEA officials believed there was a yet-to-be-identified "mastermind." The existence of such an unknown official, possibly a foreigner, followed from the belief of UN officials that none of the Iraqi scientists they had encountered, including Jaffar, knew about all aspects of the nuclear program, from enrichment efforts to weapons design. UNSCOM executive chairman Rolf Ekeus was "rather convinced that there must be someone who links the enrichment and design sides." But by early October, David Kay's IAEA team believed, based on its examination of the Petrochemical-3 employee lists, that Jaffar Dhia Jaffar not only was a "senior administrator" in the program who was "intimately linked to the uranium enrichment program," but also "had the lead technical and administrative responsibility for the nuclear weapons program as a whole."[64]

The belief that the key elements of the Iraqi program had been identified by late 1991 did not mean an end to further inquiries, as several defectors' claims had to be followed up and there was every expectation that Iraq would seek to reconstitute its weapons of mass destruction capability. At least one defector had insisted that Iraq's nuclear program involved one or more underground facilities, including a uranium enrichment plant in a mountain in the vicinity of Mosul. No such facility was discovered there. And no evidence turned up that Iraq had anywhere near eighty-eight pounds of weapons-grade enriched uranium. Nor did the efforts of the tenth IAEA inspection team, which searched for an underground plutonium production reactor at the Saad-13 State Establishment in Salah Al-Din province, bear fruit—a search possibly inspired by the 1986 Chinese reactor study. The team would ultimately report that "information and documents gathered during the inspection do not support the reports that such an underground facility exists at this site." Earlier searches, by the ninth inspection team, of specific sites where intelligence, presumably from defectors, indicated such a reactor might be hidden also came up empty.[65]

By that time the CIA had also discounted other defector information indicating that Iraq had secretly enriched a sufficient quantity of uranium to produce one to three nuclear devices. As more data was gathered, intelligence analysts reached a consensus that Iraq had probably produced only a few grams of plutonium and only a few pounds of uranium.[66]

In mid-April 1992, following the destruction of Al Atheer, Iraqi trucks were photographed, probably by one or more KH-11 satellites, hauling equipment back into known manufacturing facilities, having apparently concluded they would not be receiving further visits from IAEA inspectors.[67]

Such intelligence was undoubtedly one factor in the assessment presented in 1993 to the House Foreign Affairs Committee by Robert Gallucci, back at the State Department as an assistant secretary of state. "Over the long term," he told the representatives, "Iraq still presents a nuclear threat. We believed that Saddam Hussein is committed to rebuilding a nuclear weapon capability, using indigenous and imported resources," a judgment that had been reached by the National Intelligence Council at least as early as June 1991.[68]

Between Gulf War aerial attacks and IAEA-supervised demolition, key Iraqi nuclear facilities lay in ruins. Tuwaitha, according to the IAEA, had been "devastated," with much of its equipment destroyed during the war. Al Qaim, Al Jazirah, Tarmiya, and Al Atheer were also severely damaged. But Gallucci noted that Iraq had retained "its most critical resource for any nuclear weapons program": skilled personnel and expertise. Iraq had also retained "a basic industrial capability to support a nuclear weapons program, including a large amount of dual-use equipment and facilities." He also observed that if sanctions were to be lifted, Iraq would have access to additional financial resources for overseas procurement activities. Finally, Gallucci reported, "Iraq has still refused to provide the UN with details of its clandestine procurement network, a network which could therefore be reactivated in the future."[69]

Gallucci's statement, along with the written statements the IAEA submitted to the same committee before which the assistant secretary appeared, implied the need for continued monitoring of personnel, rebuilding efforts, and nuclear commerce. The IAEA noted that "Iraq could constitute a weapons program faster than another state that had never tried. The capable scientists remain. How they are currently employed is difficult to ascertain because they had been dispersed." The agency also told the committee that it was "highly probable" that some documents about the nuclear weapons program "remain safely hidden away." The physical facilities would of course "have to be rebuilt at great cost."[70]

THE IAEA was correct. Just as Carl Friedrich von Weizsäcker had tried to hide some of his nuclear documents at the end of World War II, Mahdi Obeidi, following orders from Qusay Hussein in 1992 to keep the documents for the centrifuge project safe, hid his set in a fifty-gallon drum, which he then buried beneath a lotus tree in his rose garden. Inside were the detailed plans and design drawings required to manufacture centrifuges. Altogether there were more than two hundred booklets, instruction manuals for constructing each piece of the centrifuge and then assembling them.[71]

Along with the documents were the prototypes for four of the most advanced centrifuge components, which were small enough to fit in a suitcase. One of the parts was the ball bearing on which the centrifuge rotor sits. About the shape of a toy top, it balances the centrifuge rotor tube as it rotates at speeds in excess of sixty thousand revolutions a minute. Another was the centrifuge motor, about the size of a round loaf of bread, which contains magnets and coils that drive the centrifuge. By creating an extraordinarily powerful electromagnetic field, the magnets spin the centrifuge without actually touching it. There were also two segmented aluminum-nickel-cobalt magnetic discs connected by slight thread steel, which made up the magnetic upper bearing. From their place at the top of the centrifuge, the discs hold the rotor in place in a vacuum as it spins at supersonic speeds. Also stored in the drum was the bellows, a thin, gun metal–colored disc about six inches in diameter and two inches tall, which connected centrifuge tubes end-to-end — increasing the length of the centrifuge, resulting in a version that can enrich uranium substantially faster.[72]

CONCERN THAT IRAQ would seek to reconstitute its nuclear, chemical, biological, and ballistic missile programs, based on both its obsessive prewar quest and the continuing attempts to obstruct and deceive UN inspectors, guaranteed continued inspections by the UN and close monitoring by the United States and other nations. In an August 1993 letter William Studeman, the acting director of central intelligence, informed a Senate committee that "efforts undertaken by the IAEA to collect samples from Iraqi waterways offer us the greatest assurance that Iraq does not have a secret supply of bomb-usable material."[73]

Other components of the Iraqi program — equipment, technology, and materials — still needed to be kept under scrutiny by the IAEA and United States. The international agency's plan for a long-term monitoring effort, which led Iraq to establish the National Monitoring Directorate to interact with and obstruct the inspectors, would be complemented by the efforts of the U.S. and other national intelligence communities. The following year, the Arms Control and Disarmament Agency noted that "the United States believes Baghdad is continuing its effort to circumvent inspections and preserve as much nuclear-related technology as possible for a renewed weapons effort."[74]

In April 1995 Hans Blix's report to the Security Council provided some reassurance. He informed the council that "the essential components of Iraq's past clandestine nuclear program have been identified and have been destroyed, removed, or rendered harmless . . . [and] the scope of the past program is well understood." He also reported that "areas of residual uncertainty have been progressively reduced to a level of detail, the full knowledge of which is not likely to affect the overall picture."[75]

But there was more to learn than just some details. In August 1995 the UN inspectors, the CIA, and other interested intelligence agencies would reap a significant intelligence bonanza when Lt. Gen. Hussein Kamel, a cousin and son-in-law of Saddam's, would flee Iraq. Kamel, along with his brother Saddam Kamel, also a son-in-law of Saddam's, arrived in Jordan on the night of August 7 in a convoy of black Mercedes automobiles that carried him out of Iraq and away from the immediate threat posed by increasing family infighting, which was constantly exacerbated by Saddam's out-of-control son Uday.[76]

If the brothers knew nothing more than the details of that infighting, they would have been of interest to the CIA and other intelligence organizations. But they knew much more. Saddam Kamel was a lieutenant colonel in the Amn al-Khass presidential security service. Hussein Kamel had even more intelligence value, having served as undersecretary at the Ministry of Industrialization and Military Industry and subsequently as minister of defense. Of particular importance to the CIA and IAEA, he had been responsible for oversight of Iraq's weapons of mass destruction programs, and knew the details of their current status and the attempts to conceal past activities and current capabilities.[77]

Six months after his defection Hussein Kamel would return to Iraq, having failed to establish himself as a future leader of Iraq while in exile. Not surprisingly, despite Saddam's pledge of amnesty, he would die in a shootout engineered by Saddam, while Uday and Qusay watched. But in the months shortly after his defection he was debriefed by a variety of international and national organizations. On the evening of August 22 in Jordan, he met with UNSCOM chief Rolf Ekeus, the IAEA's Maurizio Zifferero, and UNSCOM's Nikita Smidovich, who were interested in what Kamel had to say about Iraq's chemical and biological weapons programs. An interpreter from the court of the King of Jordan attended. The meeting began at ten minutes before eight and concluded approximately three hours later.[78]

Kamel began by noting that Iraq initially had one reactor and four different projects to produce fissile material. He also reported that "a few months ago they had a new project, designated 'Sodash,'" that involved burying equipment, some of which had been recently recovered, while other parts were "made to disappear." In response to Zifferero's questioning, Kamel indicated the equipment was related to the electromagnetic separation project at Tarmiya.[79]

Zifferero and Kamel also discussed Mahdi Obeidi's centrifuge project at Rashdiya, whose existence, and Obeidi's role as director, Kamel disclosed. The defector also told his audience that the Iraqis at the site were manufacturing centrifuges using maraging steel as well as carbon fibers, and they preferred the carbon-fiber centrifuges. When asked why Iraq had been willing to acknowledge the centrifuge effort but had not disclosed the Rashdiya site, instead claiming that the work took place at Tuwaitha, Kamel responded that "it was the strategy to hide, not to reveal the sites" and "they said that to divert attention."[80]

Later in the debriefing, Zifferero turned to a reference to a "final experiment" in one of the documents recovered by the IAEA teams. What Zifferero wanted to know was whether the final experiment was a test or combat use. Kamel did not specifically answer that question, but characterized all the work related to testing as "only studies" and stated that Iraq "had never reached a point close to testing."[81]

A key focus of the studies, Kamel told Zifferero, was finding a way to employ less enriched uranium in an effective bomb. He also disputed the notion that the crash project would have relied on Soviet-supplied uranium, explaining that while the French uranium was sufficiently enriched for use in bombs, the Soviet-supplied material was only 80 percent enriched and without an operational centrifuge program there was no means to boost it to bomb grade.[82]

Earlier Zifferero had asked a key question: "Were [sic] there any continuation of, or present nuclear activities, for example, EMIS, centrifuge?" Kamel provided some reassurance for the immediate future but confirmed fears that Saddam Hussein had not abandoned his longtime quest for nuclear power status. "No," he answered, "but blueprints are still there on microfiches."[83]

Kamel's defection spurred the Iraqi government into action. Knowing that his disclosures could be highly embarrassing and provide hard details about Iraq's recent weapons of mass destruction programs as well as the continued denial and deception campaign, Saddam tried to undercut the impact. Five days before Kamel's meeting in Jordan with Ekeus, Zifferero, and Smidovich, Iraq issued a new declaration acknowledging that it had filled warheads with biological agents (anthrax and botulinum) and that it had started a crash program to develop a nuclear weapon. New information on the chemical and ballistic missile programs was also provided. In addition, Saddam's threat, made in mid-July, to toss out the UN inspectors was rescinded. Iraq would further admit that Obeidi was the leader of the centrifuge program (which led to a meeting with IAEA inspectors, who also received a tour of the Engineering Design Center at Rashdiya), and that Iraqis were conducting a survey of less populated areas in the desert to dig a vertical shaft and horizontal chamber for a test.[84]

Iraq also "identified" the culprit responsible for concealing the truth about Iraq's weapons efforts: none other than Lt. Gen. Hussein Kamel. After the declaration, Iraq turned over 680,000 pages of new material, much of which it claimed had been hidden on Kamel's chicken farm in Haidar, a suburb of Baghdad. The episode did not, of course, represent the beginning of a new Iraqi attitude toward the UN inspectors or an end to attempts at concealment. The following years would be filled with continued Iraqi obstruction and harassment of the inspectors, refusal to turn over documents or actively assist the inspectors, and complaints by the UN Security Council about Iraqi actions. Saddam's announcement on October 31, 1998, that Iraq would cease all cooperation with UNSCOM led to a withdrawal of all the inspectors, IAEA and UNSCOM, from Iraq by mid-December. Operation Desert Fox, a four-day bombing campaign, began on December 16.[85]

When the inspectors departed Iraq, they had, according to IAEA chief Blix, compiled a "technically coherent picture of Iraq's clandestine nuclear programme. These verification activities have revealed no indication that Iraq possesses nuclear weapons or any meaningful amount of weapons-usable nuclear material, or that Iraq has retained any practical capability (facilities or hardware) for the production of such material." But, the IAEA noted, a statement "that it has found 'no indication' of prohibited equipment, materials, or activities in Iraq is not the same as a statement of their 'non-existence.'"[86]

The departure of the inspectors would have a significant impact on the ability of the CIA and other interested U.S. intelligence agencies to monitor any Iraqi attempts to rebuild its weapons of mass destruction programs. One constellation of NRO satellites could still send back detailed images of suspect facilities, while another could intercept Iraqi communications. Both the NSA and CIA also had capabilities for monitoring Iraqi communications at home and abroad, possibly detecting attempts to purchase materials related to nuclear or other weapons programs. In addition, the CIA could still attempt to recruit Iraqi assets and debrief defectors. But there would no longer be inspectors on the ground who could enter a suspect facility to determine if the deductions of imagery interpreters about what was going on inside were correct, or confirm the inferences drawn from a suspicious telephone conversation, or investigate the claims of a defector. Iraq was again a denied territory.

chapter thirteen

FLAWED INTELLIGENCE

AMONG THE IRAQI defectors whose claims would be harder to check out was one who by early 2001 had claimed that a Gen. Ra'ad Ismail was involved in the Iraqi nuclear program and headed Iraq's "Committee on the Use of Nuclear Weapons." Another defector, who appeared later in 2001 and whom the Defense Intelligence Agency put great stock in, was Adnan Ihsan Saeed al-Haideri. Saeed described himself as a civil engineer who had worked, as recently as the previous year, on renovations for the nuclear, biological, and chemical weapons programs in underground wells, private villas, and beneath the Saddam Hussein Hospital in Baghdad. He also claimed that some production and storage facilities were hidden in the rear of government company buildings and private villas in residential areas. Others had been concealed underground in what appeared to be water wells but which had been lined with lead-filled concrete and contained no water. It was all part of a program that, according to Saeed, was referred to as "Substitute Sites." Saeed would be interviewed at least twice by U.S. intelligence officials.[1]

Another defector, according to one account, left Iraq before the end of 2000 and was subsequently debriefed at length on at least four occasions by DIA representatives. The defector was brought to the attention of Western intelligence organizations by the Iraqi National Congress, the opposition group headed by Ahmed Chalabi. In his late thirties, the defector claimed to have worked for the Iraqi Intelligence Service and told of Saddam's renewed efforts to develop weapons of mass destruction as well as of Iraq's support and training for foreign terrorists. If what he told his DIA debriefers matched what he told a reporter from the magazine *Vanity Fair*, he revealed that a project code-named al-Bashir, located at Faham, a populated residential section of Baghdad, was at the heart of Iraq's efforts to acquire nuclear weapons. Scientists at the site, he reported, had examined the possibility of reestablishing the small Isis reactor destroyed in the 1991 war. His next assignment, had he not defected, would have been to procure material for the project. Subsequently, the CIA would determine that a defector "whose story appeared in *Vanity Fair* magazine . . . had embellished and exaggerated his access." As former director of central intelligence James Woolsey observed, "If defectors are all you've got, that's a problem."[2]

Preferable to defectors would have been intercepts of Iraqi communications or sources within the Iraqi government who could provide hard data on Saddam's nuclear, biological, and chemical weapons efforts. Unfortunately, according to the Senate intelligence oversight committee, "the Intelligence Community did not have a single HUMINT source collecting against Iraq's weapons of mass destruction programs in Iraq after 1998," apparently having decided that "the difficulty and risks inherent in developing sources or inserting operations officers into Iraq outweighed the potential benefits."[3] But the United States did receive intelligence from foreign intelligence services, including those of Italy and Britain, as well as information about events outside of Iraq that appeared to have a significant bearing on Saddam's nuclear plans.

ON OCTOBER 15, 2001, the CIA's Directorate of Operations issued an intelligence report based on information provided by Italy's Service for Information and Military Security (SISMI), a report that had been in the service's files for a couple of years but in the wake of the events of September 11 was considered worth transmitting to the United States. The SISMI report focused on Niger, a landlocked African nation with a population of around eleven million, whose exports included uranium, livestock, cowpeas, and onions, and which the CIA characterized as "one of the poorest countries on earth."[4]

The Italian report charged that Niger was planning to ship several tons of uranium to Iraq, which had purchased over three hundred tons of the material in the early 1980s. According to the report, the uranium sales agreement had been under negotiation since at least early February 1999, when a delegation including the Iraqi ambassador to the Vatican arrived. SISMI claimed that the agreement had been approved by the State Court of Niger in 2000, and then by Nigerien president Mamadou Tandja, who proceeded to inform Saddam of the good news. Niger's minister of foreign affairs was also alleged to have informed one of his ambassadors in Europe that Niger had concluded an accord to provide several tons of uranium to Iraq.[5]

The CIA report was followed by a discussion between Barbro Owens-Kirkpatrick, the U.S. ambassador in Niamey, Niger's capital, and the director general of the French-led consortium that was responsible for operating the uranium mines. The director general said "there was no possibility" that the government of Niger had diverted any of the three thousand tons of yellowcake produced in its two mines. But a second report from the CIA's operations directorate followed on February 5, 2002, also based on information from SISMI. Included in the new report were additional details about the agreement as well the verbatim text of the alleged accord — text derived, it would be discovered, from a forged document.[6]

Seven days later, the DIA produced an item titled *Niamey Signed an Agreement to Sell 500 Tons of Uranium a Year to Baghdad*, repeating information in the CIA report. It concluded that "Iraq probably is searching abroad for natural uranium to assist in its nuclear weapons program." The DIA item caught the eye of Vice President Dick Cheney, who asked his morning briefer for the CIA's analysis. The agency's Weapons Intelligence, Nonproliferation, and Arms Control Center (WINPAC)—which had been established in March 2001 by merging the Nonproliferation Center, Arms Control Intelligence Staff, and the Weapons Intelligence Staff from the Office of Transnational Issues—noted some reasons to be cautious about the DIA claim. Its assessment stated that "information on the alleged uranium contract . . . comes exclusively from a foreign government service report that lacks crucial details," which the CIA was trying to clarify and corroborate.[7]

In response to Cheney's interest, the Directorate of Operations Counterproliferation Division (CPD), established in the 1990s to facilitate counterproliferation operations that cut across regions handled by different divisions of the operations directorate, decided to contact Joseph Wilson. The retired diplomat, whose first posting as a foreign service officer, in the 1970s, was to Niger, subsequently served in Togo, Burundi, South Africa, the Congo, and Baghdad, where he secured the release of Americans held hostage in 1990, before becoming ambassador to Gabon in 1992. In doing so, the division was following up on a suggestion from the ambassador's wife, Valerie Plame, a member of the CPD who one colleague recalled as having been the best shot with an AK-47 during her training with the agency. Plame had written the division's deputy chief on February 12, nominating her husband for the assignment—informing him that "my husband has good relations with the PM and the former Minister of Mines (not to mention lots of French contacts), both of whom could possibly shed light on this activity." It would not be Wilson's first mission to Niger for the agency. He had traveled to Niger on the CIA's behalf in 1999, but was unable to uncover any information of interest to the agency.[8]

On February 19 Wilson attended a meeting along with analysts from the CIA and the State Department's Bureau of Intelligence and Research, as well as representatives of the Africa and counterproliferation divisions, the latter serving as hosts. The gathering revealed that there was little support for the whole idea. The State Department intelligence analyst saw no need for the effort, arguing that the embassy already had good contacts. The others thought little could be accomplished, since the Nigeriens would be unlikely to admit that they had concluded a uranium sales agreement with Iraq, even if such an agreement existed. After the meeting, an analyst from WINPAC e-mailed a colleague at the proliferation division: "it appears that the results from this source will be suspect at best, and not believable under most scenarios." But the Counterproliferation Division concluded that it had no other options and sending Wilson was worth a try.[9]

The following day the division provided "talking points" to guide the former ambassador. He was to inquire if Niger had been approached, been involved in discussions, or entered into any agreements concerning uranium transfers with any "countries of concern"—the Clinton administration's politically correct euphemism for what had previously been called "rogue states." The former ambassador was also to ask if any uranium might be missing from Niger or might have been transferred.[10]

Wilson arrived in Niger six days later, already skeptical because of his belief that the French, Spanish, German, and Japanese firms that ran the uranium consortium made it unlikely there would have been any deal. The city was very much as he remembered—"seasonal winds had clogged the air with dust and sand. Through the haze I could see camel caravans crossing the Niger River (over the John F. Kennedy Bridge), the setting sun behind them." His first significant meeting was with the U.S. ambassador, who asked him to restrict his inquiries to former government officials, on the grounds that meetings with present officials would complicate her efforts. Wilson agreed and "spent the next eight days drinking sweet mint tea and meeting with dozens of people," including people associated with Niger's uranium business as well as former officials.[11]

Among those Wilson talked to were a former Nigerien prime minister and a former minister of mines and energy. In early March, a day after his return, he met with two CIA operations directorate officers, who would turn his oral report into a routine memo of less than two pages. Wilson told them that Ibrahim Mayaki, foreign minister from 1996 to 1997 and prime minister from 1997 to 1999, claimed to be unaware of any contracts between Niger and any rogue state for the sale of yellowcake, and told his visitor that he would have known of such contracts. Similar reassurances were provided by Mai Manga, the former minister for energy and mines, who told Wilson there had been no sales outside of IAEA channels since the mid-1980s and he knew of no contracts between Niger and any rogue state for the sale of uranium.[12]

No sales did not mean no contact. Mayaki also told Wilson that in June 1999 he was approached by a businessman and asked to meet with an Iraqi delegation which he discovered was headed by information minister Mohammed Saeed Sahhaf, who about four years later would become better known as "Baghdad Bob" or "Comical Ali" for his televised counterfactual claims of Iraqi combat successes in the second Gulf War. The minister wanted to discuss "expanding commercial relations" between Niger and Iraq. Since Niger had nothing else to export that Mayaki believed to be of interest to Iraq, the former prime minister assumed that the delegation was trying to obtain yellowcake. The meeting did take place but, Mayaki reported, he let the matter drop because of UN sanctions on Iraq.[13]

The story that the State Department and CIA were receiving from current and former Nigerien officials continued to differ from the accounts given by SISMI to U.S. intelligence. On March 25, 2002, the operations directorate issued its third and final report from SISMI, a report which stated that the 2000 agreement by Niger to provide uranium specified that five hundred tons of uranium would be delivered each year and when the deliveries would begin.[14]

By the fall the CIA was also the recipient of reports produced by Britain's Secret Intelligence Service. Those reports, based on British contacts, rather than just the SISMI documents, claimed that Iraq had sought uranium from several sources in Africa, including Niger, Somalia, and possibly the Democratic Republic of the Congo.[15]

IN EARLY 2001 America's spies and intelligence analysts received information about another commodity Iraq was attempting to purchase. If the Iraqis did obtain uranium from Niger or elsewhere, they would need to enrich it to weapons grade, and one means to do so involved a gas centrifuge. What the intelligence community discovered was that Iraq was trying to purchase sixty thousand high-strength 7075-T6 aluminum tubes with an outer diameter of eighty-one millimeters. Their potential use in centrifuge rotors made them a controlled item under the Nuclear Suppliers Group guidelines, and any Iraqi purchase was prohibited under two UN Security Council resolutions. Upon first receiving the report about Iraq's desire to acquire the tubes, the CIA concluded that they were intended for use in an uranium enrichment program.[16]

In contrast to the claims concerning the purchase of uranium from Niger, the CIA had solid evidence that Iraq had concluded an agreement with a foreign source to obtain the tubes and that they were on their way. That evidence came in the form of a shipment of two thousand tubes, which left a factory in southern China in mid to late May 2001 and traveled by slow barge to Hong Kong, en route to Jordan and then Iraq. The order had come ostensibly from a Jordanian firm to an Australian company, which was owned by the Kam Kiu Aluminum Extrusion Company in Tai Shan, near Hong Kong. But an Australian intelligence agency, probably the Defence Signals Directorate, which might have intercepted some or all of the assorted faxes, e-mails, or telephone conversations relevant to the order, knew about the shipment and its intended ultimate destination.[17]

Adding to the concern was another CIA human intelligence report, passing on information from a foreign intelligence service, that informed its readers that Saddam "was closely following the purchase and analysis of 114,000 7075-T6 aluminum tubes." Rather than stop the initial shipment of two thousand tubes, the entire supply the manufacturer had ready when they were shipped, the United States let the transaction proceed. But shortly after the crates holding the tubes arrived, just inside the gates of the port of Aqaba, CIA officers and members of the Jordanian security service showed up and chased off the two Iraqi men waiting for the shipment to clear customs. The CIA then took possession of the tubes.[18]

THE CIA also had gathered, or been given, information that Iraq had completed, in April 2002, construction of a new building for the Iraqi Atomic Energy Commission (IAEC). The report asserted that the building was an alternative to the existing offices and was built for the "operations room" of the commission. It also noted that the commission was planning to open at another location a new high-level polytechnic school that would offer doctorates in all branches of nuclear energy. There were also reports that the CIA interpreted other information as indicating that scientists had been reassigned to the IAEC apparently as part of an effort to reconstitute the nuclear weapons program.[19]

Reports from foreign intelligence services indicated that "as of late 1999, several groups from Iraq's nuclear establishment remained intact, although the majority of key nuclear scientists, but no engineers or technicians, either had retired, died, or left Iraq." The CIA report based on that information also commented that "as of late 1999, it was unlikely that any nuclear weapons work was taking place." There was, according to the report, a loose professional alliance of employees of Iraq's pre–Gulf War program, as a result of their work in the engineering and design center of the Military Industrialization Commission.[20]

Other intelligence findings appeared to be consistent with a renewed Iraqi nuclear effort. Several open-source and classified reports showed Saddam meeting with IAEC officials and praising their work. Others mentioned increased security at the Commission's offices, and one, from 1998, noted the practice of having intelligence officers accompanying commission officials on foreign travel. There were also reports that scientists had been consolidated into facilities associated with the nuclear program and retained equipment that could be used in renewal efforts. Intelligence work further revealed that several scientists who had worked on the Iraqi calutron program were now at a research and engineering facility at Al Tahadi, a facility engaged in a variety of high-voltage and magnetics work.[21]

THE INTELLIGENCE OBTAINED from U.S. technical and human sources in the years after the departure of the inspectors, along with that received from foreign services, provided the basis for intelligence assessments on Iraq's nuclear weapons program, including the Joint Atomic Energy Intelligence Committee's June 1999 report, *Reconstitution of Iraq's Nuclear Weapons Program: Post Desert Fox*. That report, along with others, concluded that while the UN inspectors had destroyed portions of Iraq's nuclear infrastucture, and neutralized the remainder, Iraq retained the basis for reconstituting its program—although it did not appear to have done so. The JAEIC also believed that Iraq was continuing low-level clandestine theoretical research and personnel training, while attempting to acquire dual-use technologies and materials. And while it would take Iraq five to seven years, even with foreign assistance, to produce enough weapons-grade material for a bomb, Iraq could have a crude nuclear weapon within a year if it obtained the fissile material from a foreign source.[22]

Starting in 2001 and continuing into 2002, analysts devoted considerable attention to the implications of the information obtained about Iraq's alleged quest to purchase uranium from Niger and its attempt to procure tens of thousands of aluminum tubes. Behind the scenes, analysts from different agencies were drawing significantly differing conclusions about either the credibility of the information or its implications.

Such debates were part of the history of the U.S. intelligence community from the beginning of the Cold War, and potentially one of its greatest strengths. Good intelligence, like good science, requires the conventional wisdom to be challenged and, when a better explanation is available, replaced. Over the years, intelligence analysts from the CIA, the State, Energy, and Defense Departments, and the military services had argued over a multitude of issues, including the existence of a missile gap, the capabilities of the Soviet SS-9 intercontinental ballistic missile, Soviet compliance with the test ban and antiballistic missile treaties, and whether China had shipped M-11 ballistic missiles to Pakistan.

The aluminum tubes controversy involved analysts from four different agencies: CIA, DIA, INR, and the Energy Department's Office of Intelligence, supported by expertise in labs such as Oak Ridge. The CIA was the first to publish an assessment of the significance of Iraq's quest for aluminum tubes in an issue of the *President's Daily Brief*, the most exclusive document published by the intelligence community. Containing information from the most sensitive sources, the brief is normally delivered to fewer than ten individuals in the entire government. A broader audience, the readers of the *Senior Executive Intelligence Brief* (formerly the *National Intelligence Daily*), was informed on April 10, 2001, about the tubes and that they "have little use other than for a uranium enrichment program." The CIA analysis, which was the responsibility of a single WINPAC analyst, stated that "using aluminum tubes in a centrifuge effort would be inefficient and a step backward from the specialty steel machines that Iraq was poised to mass-produce at the outset of the Gulf War" and that "Iraq successfully used outdated enrichment technologies, such as electromagnetic isotope separation . . . before the war."[23]

That WINPAC analyst, who has become known as "Joe" or "Joe T." because of the CIA's request to media outlets that his last name be withheld to preserve his ability to work overseas, was the only analyst in the center with hands-on experience with centrifuges. After graduating in the late 1970s from the University of Kentucky, with a bachelor's degree in mechanical engineering, he joined the Goodyear Atomic Corporation and was assigned to work at Oak Ridge. In 1985 his project to learn how to test and operate European centrifuges, which were one-quarter the height of American ones, was canceled and he moved on to performing hazard analyses. Then in 1997 he was shifted to working at Oak Ridge's National Security Program Office, tracking the sales of material that could be used in nuclear arms. Two years later he retired and joined the CIA's Nonproliferation Center.[24]

Whatever his expertise, Joe T.'s analysis did not convince experts in the Department of Energy's Office of Intelligence. On April 11 the office published its own analysis, *Iraq: High-Strength Aluminum Tube Procurement*, which questioned the CIA's judgment. The Energy Department acknowledged that based on the reported specifications, "the tubes could be used to manufacture gas centrifuge rotor cylinders for uranium enrichment." However, the department's analysis noted that the specified tube diameter was half that of tubes for the centrifuge machine Iraq had successfully tested in 1990, and only marginally large enough for practical centrifuge applications, while other specifications were not consistent with use in a gas centrifuge. In addition, while the quantity of tubes being sought indicated large-scale production, "we have not seen related procurement efforts." Further, the department's analysis noted that the tubes' specifications suggested a centrifuge design very different "from any Iraq is known to have."[25]

The Energy Department's intelligence assessment concluded that while the gas centrifuge application could not be ruled out, the procurement effort was more likely directed toward a different objective, such as the production of conventional ordnance. At the time, however, the analysts at Energy had not "identified an Iraq-specific, military, or other noncentrifuge application that precisely matches the tube specifications."[26]

Within a month they did find a nonnuclear explanation. On May 9, 2001, a Technical Intelligence Note reported that further investigation revealed that Iraq had purchased tens of thousands of tubes in the 1980s and 1990s with identical dimensions—900 millimeters long, 81 millimeters in diameter, with walls 3.3 millimeters thick—to build the Nasser 81 rocket. UN inspectors had counted 66,237 tubes on the ground in 1996.[27]

Over the next sixteen months, through the end of August 2002, the CIA and Energy positions would remain unchanged—although there would be further research and additional reports. Each would attract support from other intelligence organizations. The DIA sided with the CIA, while the State Department's INR aligned itself with the Energy Department in questioning whether the aluminum tubes were a sign of an Iraqi attempt to reconstitute its nuclear weapons program.

Greg Thielmann, who was near the end of a twenty-five-year career in the State Department, including a previous tour of duty in the INR during the early 1990s, was, at the time, head of the bureau's Strategic Issues Division — a component of its Office of Analysis for Strategic, Proliferation, and Military Issues. He recalls having been "agnostic" on the aluminum tubes issue when it first arose in 2001, and listening to Joe T. but being unpersuaded. The WIN-PAC analyst was no "wunderkind," "did not seem to have all the answers," and was "not particularly persuasive in fending off alternative explanations." In addition, when Thielmann's analysts spoke to experts at Oak Ridge, they found that they didn't accept the CIA analysis.[28]

Still, from July 2001 to July 2002, the CIA produced at least ten intelligence assessments or reports on Iraq's efforts to acquire aluminum tubes, all of which echoed the CIA analysis of July 2, 2001, that followed the inspection of the tubes seized that spring. The July 2 assessment stated that "the tubes are constructed from high-strength aluminum (7075-T6) and are manufactured to the tight tolerances necessary for gas centrifuges." The CIA also claimed that the tubes matched those of a publicly available gas centrifuge design from the 1950s, known as the "Zippe centrifuge" — for its designer, Gernot Zippe — the plans for which Mahdi Obeidi had made such an effort to get in the 1980s. The agency concluded that "the specifications for the tubes far exceed any known conventional weapons application, including rocket motor casings for 81-mm multiple rocket launchers."[29]

In August and September 2002 the CIA published two further papers on the tubes. Its August 1, *Iraq: Expanding WMD Capabilities Pose Growing Threat* provided a one-page outline of the CIA view—that the tubes' materials, exceedingly stringent tolerances, high cost, and secrecy surrounding procurement attempts indicated they were intended for use in a centrifuge. A more detailed analysis titled *Iraq's Hunt for Aluminum Tubes: Evidence of a Renewed Uranium Enrichment Program* followed in September. In addition to the factors noted in the August analysis, the new assessment noted the anodized coating of the tubes and stated the agency's conclusion that the tubes matched known centrifuge rotor dimensions.[30] Also included was an analysis of the National Ground Intelligence Center (NGIC), a component of the U.S. Army Intelligence and Security Command, based in Charlottesville, Virginia. Its mission is to analyze the weaponry and tactics of foreign ground forces. In an August 13, 2001, e-mail, center analysts wrote that while they could "not totally rule out the possibility" that the tubes could be used for rockets, they believed that the tubes were poor choices for rocket bodies. Thus, NGIC believed there was a low probability that the tubes were intended for use in conventional rockets. In September 2002, the center's conclusion remained unchanged. The material and tolerances of the tubes were "highly unlikely" to be intended for rocket motor cases.[31]

To provide additional data for the September analysis, Joe T. hired two engineers with ties to Oak Ridge to conduct "spin tests" that might demonstrate that the tubes could withstand the extreme rotational speeds required to enrich uranium in its gaseous form. The engineers, who were instructed not to reveal their testing activity to Oak Ridge's intelligence office, succeeded in spinning a tube to sixty thousand revolutions per minute and concluded that the tubes could be used in a centrifuge program, as did Joe T. — even though most of the tests ended in failure.[32]

The DIA evaluation mirrored that of the CIA, starting with an August 2, 2001, internal background paper which compared the alternative views of the CIA and the Energy Department and noted that "DIA analysts found the CIA . . . presentation to be very compelling." The paper repeated the CIA's reporting of the tubes' characteristics with regard to material, outer diameter, inner diameter, wall thickness, length, and tolerance, as well as the agency's observation linking the tubes to the gas centrifuge rotor described by Zippe. The claim that the tubes were consistent with earlier Iraqi gas centrifuge rotor designs was repeated in a November 2001 supplement to the *Military Intelligence Digest*. Over a year later, in September 2002, DIA produced *Iraq's Reemerging Nuclear Weapons Program*, which acknowledged alternative uses for the tubes but again asserted that use in a gas centrifuge program was more likely because the specifications for the tubes were consistent with earlier Iraqi centrifuge designs.[33]

Among the Energy Department intelligence products questioning the CIA-DIA position was the Technical Intelligence Note of August 17, 2001 — *Iraq's Gas Centrifuge Program: Is Reconstitution Underway?* — which included an extensive eight-page analysis of whether the tubes were destined for use in a rocket or a centrifuge program. The paper was produced by Dr. Jon A. Kreykes, head of Oak Ridge's national security advanced technology group; Dr. Duane E. Starr, an expert on nuclear proliferation threats; Dr. Edward Von Halle, a retired Oak Ridge nuclear expert; and Dr. Houston G. Wood III, a professor of engineering at the University of Virginia who assisted in the design of the forty-foot American centrifuge and had consulted with Zippe. The authors noted that Iraq had informed the IAEA that the Nasser State Establishment had, since at least 1989, obtained and used a large quantity of high-strength aluminum tubes to manufacture 81-millimeter rockets. The specifications of those tubes, including the type of aluminum (7075-T6), outer diameter (81 millimeters), inner diameter (74.4 millimeters), and length (900 millimeters), matched the specifications of the tubes they had been trying to covertly acquire in 2001. The report also mentioned that the IAEA had found large numbers of tubes stored in various locations around the Nasser facility.[34]

The Energy Department's intelligence analysis also argued that while the tubes could be used to produce centrifuge rotors, they were not well suited for that purpose. The intelligence note stated that the the variety of aluminum used for the tubes "provides performance roughly half that of the materials Iraq previously pursued"—which would require many thousands of centrifuges to produce weapons-grade uranium, something that no proliferator had ever done. Before the 1991 war, Iraq had sought rotors made from maraging steel and carbon-fiber composites, which are more efficient in separating uranium. Using the 7075-T6 aluminum would require Iraq to produce twice as many rotors and other key centrifuge components, including end caps, bearings, and outer casings.[35]

The Energy Department analysis raised other objections. The tube diameter was smaller than that for any known operating centrifuge and about half the diameter of the tubes used in Iraq's pre–Gulf War prototype machine. Further, "the tubes are too thick for favorable use as rotor tubes, exceeding the nominal 1-mm thickness of known aluminum rotor tubes by more than a factor of three." The anodized surface requested by Iraq was also a problem, for "it is not consistent with a gas centrifuge application." The report also pointed out that use of eighty-one-millimeter aluminum rotors for a centrifuge would require Iraq to undertake program development all over again. Thus, "a gas centrifuge application is credible but unlikely and a rocket production application is the more likely end-use of these tubes."[36]

The controversy continued unresolved through August 2002. An attempt was made to have the JAEIC settle the debate, which Thielmann characterizes as "an issue made for the JAEIC," although accounts differ concerning whether the CIA opposed such an effort at a time when the JAEIC was headed by an Energy Department official. Some Energy officials have claimed that the CIA sought to prevent the committee from considering the issue, while a CIA official claimed that the agency was the first organization to seek JAEIC's intervention. The committee did hold a formal session in early August, with more than a dozen experts on each side attending. But a second meeting scheduled for later in August was postponed, and a planned September meeting also never took place.[37]

ABOUT SIX MONTHS after its first analysis of the aluminum tubes issue, the CIA produced the first finished intelligence product concerning the reports of alleged Iraqi attempts to buy uranium from Niger. The article,

"Iraq: Nuclear-Related Procurement Efforts," appeared in the October 18, 2001, issue of the *Senior Executive Intelligence Brief*. It reported that a foreign government service had obtained information that Niger as of early that year planned to sell Iraq several hundred tons of uranium. The brief also noted the lack of corroboration that an agreement was actually reached or that uranium was transferred. The amount mentioned, according to the analysis, would be sufficient for at least one nuclear weapon.[38]

This time the skeptic's role was played by the INR, which issued an assessment on March 1, 2002, whose title—*Niger: Sale of Uranium to Iraq Is Unlikely*—clearly conveyed its judgment. The INR reiterated the views expressed in the meeting with Joseph Wilson in February. France controlled the uranium industry, the State Department's analysts wrote, and "would take action to block a sale of the kind alleged in a CIA report of questionable credibility from a foreign government service." It did allow that "some officials may have conspired for individual gain to arrange a uranium sale," but believed that President Tandja's government was unlikely to risk damaging relations with the United States or other key aid donors.[39]

An Energy Department report, *Nuclear Reconstitution Efforts Underway?*, cited the intelligence on the alleged transaction as one of three indications that Iraq might be reconstituting its nuclear program but also observed that the quantity of uranium specified "far exceeds what Iraq would need even for a robust nuclear weapons program." As with the aluminum tubes issue, the DIA's conclusions duplicated those of the CIA. In its September 22 assessment, *Iraq's Reemerging Nuclear Program*, it stated that "Iraq has been vigorously trying to procure uranium ore and yellowcake." It also described the intelligence on the alleged Iraq-Niger deal as well as the intelligence on Iraqi efforts to acquire uranium from Somalia and the Democratic Republic of the Congo.[40]

BY SEPTEMBER 2002 George W. Bush had been president for less than two years. But in that time, U.S. national security policy had changed dramatically from the days of Bill Clinton—partly as a result of the administration's senior decisionmakers and partly because of events. The attacks of September 11, 2001, on the World Trade Center and the Pentagon had led Bush to declare war on terrorism and, most immediately, the Taliban regime in Afghanistan.

In his January 29, 2002, State of the Union Address, the president singled out three other regimes for particularly pointed criticism: Iraq, Iran, and North Korea. "States like these and their terrorist allies," the president said, "constitute an axis of evil, arming to threaten the peace of the world." By the fall of 2002 it had become clear that the administration was willing to go to war to deal with the first of those three regimes—one that remained in violation of its commitments under the 1991 cease-fire agreement. In a speech at the Veterans of Foreign Wars convention in Nashville, Vice President Cheney told his audience that "we know that Saddam has resumed his efforts to acquire nuclear weapons." A week later secretary of defense Donald Rumsfeld followed up with the claim that "we know they've kept their nuclear scientists together and working on these efforts," adding that "one has to assume they've not been playing tiddlywinks, that they've been focusing on nuclear weapons."[41]

Then on September 12 Bush traveled to New York to address the UN, and challenged the body to confront Iraq's failure to live up to the commitments it had made over a decade earlier, after its defeat in the Gulf War. That same day the White House issued a paper titled A *Decade of Deception and Defiance: Saddam Hussein's Defiance of the United Nations*, which charged that "Iraq has stepped up its quest for nuclear weapons and has embarked on a worldwide hunt for materials to make an atomic bomb. In the last 14 months, Iraq has sought to buy thousands of specially designed aluminum tubes which officials believe were intended as components of centrifuges to enrich uranium."[42]

It was possible that a resumption of UN inspections could provide an alternative to war, but that was by no means a certainty. Facing the possibility of being asked to vote on a resolution approving military action, two members of the Senate Select Committee on Intelligence—Richard Durbin and Bob Graham—each wrote to director of central intelligence George J. Tenet requesting a national intelligence estimate on the status of Iraq's weapons of mass destruction programs that would update the last estimate, produced about two years earlier. While the CIA had been working on an unclassified white paper dealing with Iraq's nuclear, biological, chemical, and missile programs for several months, no classified estimate had been planned, despite an earlier congressional request for a new study.[43]

By the morning of September 12, two days after Tenet received Graham's request and three days after receiving Durbin's letter, Robert Walpole, still serving as the National Intelligence Officer for Strategic and Nuclear Programs, had been instructed by Tenet to begin work on the national intelligence estimate. Walpole was responsible both for overall management and for producing the nuclear and ballistic missile portions of the estimate, while three other national intelligence officers were to handle the other parts. Biological warfare was the responsibility of Lawrence Gershwin, who held the science and technology portfolio, while the chemical and unmanned-aerial-vehicle portions of the estimate were to be produced under the supervision of retired Army major general John Landry, who handled conventional military issues. Finally, Paul Pillar, the national intelligence officer for the Near East and South Asia, was assigned to assess regional reactions and some terrorism issues.[44]

Under normal circumstances the production of a national intelligence estimate could take months, starting with the assignment of initial tasks and the bringing together of relevant information, followed by production of drafts of its various sections, discussion of disagreements among the representatives of the agencies involved in the drafting, revision of the drafts, final agreement as to the wording, and incorporation of any still dissenting views. In this case, the process was severely compressed, leaving the four intelligence officers and the National Intelligence Council staff a mere two weeks to complete their work.[45]

As a result, already existing assessments would be used as the basis for each section. The first section of the estimate, "Saddam's Pursuit of Nuclear Weapons," would be derived from the recently completed studies by the CIA and DIA. The CIA's *Iraq's Hunt for Aluminum Tubes* served as the foundation for the section's discussion of the aluminum tubes issue, while DIA's *Iraq's Emerging Nuclear Weapons Program* became the primary source for the estimate's treatment of nuclear reconstitution. A coordination meeting on September 25 demonstrated that the issues that divided the agencies over the previous year continued to divide them. The CIA and DIA had no reservations about relying on the CIA's aluminum tube analysis as the basis for the exploration of the issue in the estimate—with the CIA arguing that the tubes were similar to those used in Iraq's prewar design and nearly matched the tube size used in another type of gas centrifuge. Further, the CIA argued that Iraq would build what it *could* rather than what would be optimal, and that Iraq no longer had access to the foreign assistance that would allow construction of a more advanced model. The Energy Department and INR still believed the tubes were intended for use in a conventional rocket program. Both the National Imagery and Mapping Agency and the National Security Agency supported the CIA-DIA position, making it four to two in favor of the nuclear explanation of the aluminum tube acquisition.[46]

Despite its vote against the CIA and DIA on the aluminum tubes issue, the Energy Department did agree with those two agencies that Iraq was reconstituting its nuclear weapons effort. That vote was cast by acting department intelligence chief Thomas S. Ryder, whose background was in human resources rather than intelligence and who had been in his new position for only five months. One senior nuclear official described him to the *New York Times* as "a heck of a nice guy but not savvy on technical issues." In supporting the position that Iraq was reconstituting its nuclear program, Ryder rejected the advice of experts from the department's nuclear weapons research laboratories and senior members of his own staff, who were in favor of joining INR in a dissenting footnote that would have begun "Energy and INR."[47]

On October 1 the National Intelligence Council published *Iraq's Continuing Program for Weapons of Mass Destruction*, a ninety-two-page document containing the majority views of the agencies represented in the production of the estimate, as well as minority views—including an eleven-page annex with the INR's dissenting views, particularly with regard to the nuclear weapons issue. A "key judgments" section at the beginning of the document provided an executive summary for busy officials who did not have time to read the entire assessment. In that section, they were told that "Baghdad . . . if left unchecked . . . probably will have a nuclear weapon during this decade."[48]

The section contained several other assessments concerning the status of Saddam's quest for nuclear weapons. It reported the intelligence community's judgment that "Baghdad started reconstituting its nuclear program about the time the UNSCOM inspectors departed—December 1998"—the first time that judgment had been made in a post–Gulf War national estimate. The community also believed that while "Saddam does not *yet* have nuclear weapons or sufficient material to make any, he remains intent on acquiring them." And if Iraq "acquires sufficient fissile material from abroad it could make a nuclear weapon within several months to a year." Without material from abroad, Iraq would probably not be able to produce a weapon until between 2007 and 2009, the community concluded, due to its inexperience in building and operating centrifuge facilities and challenges in obtaining the required equipment and expertise. A weapon might be manufactured between 2005 and 2007, in the "much less likely scenario" in which Iraq "obtains suitable centrifuge tubes this year and has all the other materials and technological expertise necessary to build production-scale uranium enrichment facilities."[49]

The section also elaborated on the reasons why "most agencies" believed that nuclear reconstitution was underway. At the top of the list was "Saddam's personal interest in and Iraq's aggressive attempts to obtain high-strength aluminum tubes for centrifuge rotors—as well as Iraq's attempts to acquire magnets, high-speed balancing machines, and machine tools"—all of which constituted "compelling evidence." A further indication of reconstitution was "Iraq's efforts to re-establish and enhance its cadre of weapons personnel as well as activities at several suspect nuclear sites"—an assessment undoubtedly based in part on NRO satellite images of sites such as Tuwaitha and Al Qaim, which were also photographed by commercial satellites late that summer and showed new construction or operational activities. High-resolution commercial imagery publicized by one Washington research group showed "an apparently operational facility at the site of Iraq's al-Qaim phosphate plant and uranium extraction facility." The section also reported that all agencies involved in the estimate agreed that "about 25,000 centrifuges based on tubes of the size Iraq is trying to acquire would be capable of producing approximately two weapons' worth of highly enriched uranium per year."[50]

At the end of the paragraph listing the "compelling evidence" of reconstitution was a parenthetical remark that the Energy Department's intelligence office "agrees that reconstitution is underway but assesses that the tubes probably are not part of the program." In a box at the very end of the key judgments section, INR elaborated on its skepticism about any ongoing reconstitution effort as well as the argument that the aluminum tubes Iraq was seeking to obtain were signs of such an effort. The bureau did believe that Saddam continued to desire nuclear weapons and that the available intelligence indicated that Iraq was making at least a limited effort to acquire nuclear weapons capabilities. But INR also believed that "the activities we have detected do not . . . add up to a compelling case that Iraq is currently pursuing . . . an integrated and comprehensive approach to acquire nuclear weapons."[51]

The State Department intelligence office elaborated: "Lacking persuasive evidence" that Iraq was rebuilding its nuclear weapons program, "INR is unwilling to speculate that such an effort began after the departure of UN inspectors or to project a timeline for the completion of activities it does not now see happening." As a result, the organization could not predict when Iraq might acquire a nuclear weapon.[52]

INR then went on to argue that evidence of "Iraq's efforts to acquire aluminum tubes is central to the argument that Baghdad is reconstituting its nuclear weapons," but the bureau "was not persuaded that the tubes in question are intended for use as centrifuge rotors." The dissent was based on the technical analysis of the Energy Department's experts, "who have concluded that the tubes Iraq seeks to acquire are poorly suited for use in gas centrifuges to be used for uranium enrichment." At the same time, INR found "unpersuasive the arguments advanced by others to make the case that they are intended for that purpose." It was "far more likely," the intelligence bureau wrote, that the tubes were intended for a different purpose, probably the production of artillery rockets. In addition to the Energy Department's conclusion, INR noted other factors suggesting that the tubes had a nonnuclear use—the method of testing and the "atypical lack of attention to operational security" in the procurement effort.[53]

The majority view, that the aluminum tubes were a significant indicator of Iraqi reconstitution as spelled out in the national estimate, was derived from the CIA's September analysis. The intelligence community's conclusion that the tubes were for use in a centrifuge centered on several factors outlined in the estimate and previously in the CIA analysis of the tubes: Saddam had a personal interest in the procurement of aluminum tubes, which suggested a high national priority; the composition, dimensions, and extremely tight manufacturing tolerances of the tubes far exceed, by a substantial margin, the requirements for nonnuclear applications but made them suitable for use as rotors in gas centrifuges; the amount the Iraqis were willing to pay for each 7075-T65 aluminum tube suggested that the tubes were intended for a special project of national interest; Iraq insisted that the tubes be shipped through intermediary countries in an attempt to conceal the ultimate user; procurement agents were unusually persistent in seeking numerous foreign sources for tubes, often departing from Iraq's traditionally cautious approach to potential vendors; the aluminum tube built to Iraqi specifications was successfully spun in a lab setting to sixty thousand revolutions per minute, indicating it was suitable as a centrifuge rotor; the dimensions of the tubes seized were similar to those used in the Zippe and Beams-type gas centrifuges; and Iraq was conducting internal-pressure tests to induce a hoop-stress level similar to that obtained by an operating rotor.[54]

The key judgments section contained no mention of the intelligence concerning alleged Iraqi attempts to acquire uranium from any African country, including Niger, owing to a consensus that such efforts were not a key part of the argument that Iraq was trying reconstitute its nuclear weapons program, as well as the belief that the reports of Iraqi attempts to acquire uranium were inconclusive. However, "in the interest of completeness," according to DCI Tenet, the main body of the assessment noted that Iraq possessed about 550 metric tons of yellowcake and enriched uranium, stored at Tuwaitha and inspected annually by the IAEA, and "Iraq also began vigorously trying to procure uranium ore and yellowcake." Acquiring either "would shorten the time Baghdad needs to produce nuclear weapons."[55]

The estimate went on to note that a foreign intelligence service, not specifying, even in the top-secret national estimate, that it was the Italian SISMI, had reported that as of early 2001, Niger planned to send several tons of "pure uranium" to Iraq. As of early 2001, it continued, Niger and Iraq were reportedly still working out arrangements, which could be for up to five hundred tons of yellowcake, according to the foreign service. In addition, the readers were informed of the reports stating that Iraq had also sought to obtain uranium from Somalia and possibly the Democratic Republic of the Congo.[56]

Whether Iraq had actually acquired uranium from any African country, the intelligence community could not say, and the estimate reported that lack of knowledge. It also noted the existence of reports suggesting that Iraq was shifting from domestic mining and milling of uranium to foreign acquisition. Iraq did possess significant phosphate deposits, from which uranium had been extracted prior to Operation Desert Storm, but intelligence information on whether nuclear-related phosphate mining and/or processing had resumed was "inconclusive," the estimate stated.[57]

In the annex, INR challenged the nuclear reconstitution interpretation of much of the data. The bureau argued,

> Some of the specialized but dual-use items being sought are, by all indications, bound for Iraq's missile program. Other cases are ambiguous, such as that of a planned magnet-production line whose suitability for centrifuge

operations remains unknown. Some efforts involve non-controlled industrial material and equipment—including a variety of heavy machine
tools—and are troubling because they would help establish the infrastructure for a renewed nuclear program. But such efforts (which began well
before the inspectors departed) are not clearly linked to a nuclear end-use.
Finally, the claims of Iraqi pursuit of natural uranium in Africa are, in
INR's assessment, highly dubious.[58]

THE ESTIMATE'S MAJORITY conclusions were not dramatically different, or in some instances different at all, from those produced by several allied
agencies. In March 2002 the British Joint Intelligence Committee observed
that "although there is very little intelligence we continue to judge that Iraq is
pursuing a nuclear weapons programme." The committee also concluded that
the program was based on uranium enrichment by gas centrifuge, and noted
that "recent intelligence indicates that nuclear scientists were recalled to work
on a nuclear programme in the autumn of 1998" although it could not say
whether large-scale development work had recommenced. The March assessment also estimated that it would take five years for Iraq to produce a nuclear
weapon if sanctions were removed or became ineffective, but if Iraq acquired
fissile material from abroad that "timescale would shorten."[59]

In September the British government issued a white paper, *Iraq's
Weapons of Mass Destruction: The Assessment of the British Government.* The
product of the Joint Intelligence Committee, it asserted that Iraq was continuing to work on nuclear weapons, in violation of its commitments under the
nonproliferation treaty as well as UN Security Council Resolution 687. The
assessment went on to inform its readers that after the departure of the UN
inspectors in 1998, there "has been an accumulation of evidence indicating
that Iraq is making concerted efforts to acquire dual-use technology and materials with nuclear applications." In addition, it noted the existence of "intelligence that Iraq has sought the supply of significant quantities of uranium from
Africa" despite the absence of any civilian nuclear program or nuclear power
plants that would provide a legitimate reason for seeking the material.[60]

The white paper identified a number of attempts to obtain equipment or
other material that could be used in the production of nuclear weapons. Vacuum pumps, which could be used to create and maintain pressures in a gas
centrifuge, as well as complete magnet production line of the proper specifi-
cation for use in the motors and top bearings of such a centrifuge, were two
examples. Also noted were Iraq's attempts to obtain anhydrous hydrogen fluoride and fluoride gas. The paper observed that while the former is used in the
petrochemical industry, and Iraq commonly imported significant quantities, it
is also used in converting uranium into uranium hexafluoride for use in a gas

centrifuge. There were other attempts to buy other equipment—a large fila-
ment winding machine and large balancing machine—relevant to centrifuges. Finally, there were the "repeated attempts to acquire a very large
quantity (60,000 or more) of specialized aluminum tubes."[61]

The white paper also tackled the issue of when Iraq might obtain a
nuclear weapon and came up with conclusions similar to those of most U.S.
agencies. Without effective sanctions or with no sanctions at all, it would take
Iraq at least five years to produce sufficient fissile material and design a
weapon. However, if Iraq were able to obtain the required weapons-grade
material and other essential components from foreign sources, it would be
possible for Saddam to have a bomb within one to two years.[62]

The two key Australian assessment agencies weighed in on the issue of
Iraqi nuclear reconstitution. In September the civilian Office of National
Assessments, which reports to the prime minister, stated that "Iraq is highly
unlikely to have nuclear weapons, though intelligence on the programme is
scarce. It has the expertise to make nuclear weapons, but almost certainly
lacks the necessary plutonium or highly-enriched uranium." However, the
office also observed that "procurement patterns are consistent with an effort to
develop an enrichment capability." The timeline estimated for Iraq to build a
nuclear weapon was similar to that estimated by Britain's Joint Intelligence
Committee—four to six years, but shorter "in the unlikely event that Iraq was
able to acquire fissile material from elsewhere."[63]

The Defence Intelligence Organization, Australia's version of the DIA,
stated, at about the same time the National Intelligence Council's national
estimate was published, that Iraq did not possess nuclear weapons—which was
in agreement with all other agencies. The organization also noted that Iraq's
nuclear "expertise has been in decline through natural attrition and loss of
skills." It characterized the intelligence "on recent attempts to buy dual-use
items for the production of weapons grade uranium" as "patchy and inconclusive." There was agreement with the Office of National Assessments that Iraq
could produce a weapon in four to six years if it had to produce the fissile material, but that time could be shortened in the unlikely event that sufficient fissile
material was obtained from a foreign source. The defense intelligence unit also
specified how much the timeline could be reduced—to within a year.[64]

OVER THE SIX MONTHS after publication of *Iraq's Continuing Program
for Weapons of Mass Destruction*, some of the intelligence contained in the
estimate was presented to the American public as well as the UN. At the same
time, further intelligence was gathered, analyzed, and debated—sometimes
behind the scenes, and sometimes in public forums and the press.

Only days after the classified national estimate was published, the CIA released its white paper, *Iraq's Weapons of Mass Destruction*. The twenty-five-page document's key judgments section reported that Iraq's "aggressive attempts to obtain proscribed high-strength aluminum tubes are of significant concern," and that "all intelligence experts agree that Iraq is seeking nuclear weapons and that these tubes could be used in a centrifuge program." It did acknowledge that while most intelligence specialists agreed on their intended use, "some believe that these tubes are probably intended for conventional weapons programs"—an internal dispute that had become public knowledge owing to leaks to the media, first of the administration's position and then of the dissenting view.[65]

The white paper also noted Iraq's retention of nuclear scientists and technicians, program documentation, and "sufficient dual-use manufacturing capabilities to support a reconstituted nuclear weapons program." It also repeated the conclusions of the classified estimate that Iraq was unlikely to be able to produce enough fissile material for a deliverable bomb until the later half of the decade, but could have a weapon within a year if it is able to procure the material from a foreign source.[66]

The following week started with a speech by President Bush, on October 7, at the Cincinnati Museum Center, which provided a view of what the United States knew, thought it knew, and didn't know. He told his audience that "many people have asked how close Saddam Hussein is to developing a nuclear weapon. Well, we don't know exactly." He did report that in 1998, a high-ranking nuclear engineer who had defected revealed that "despite his public promises, Saddam . . . had ordered his nuclear program to continue."[67]

The president continued, again reflecting the content of the recent intelligence estimate, that "Iraq is reconstituting its nuclear weapons program. Saddam . . . has held numerous meetings with Iraqi nuclear scientists, a group he calls his 'nuclear mujahideen'—his nuclear holy warriors." In addition, satellite photographs revealed "that Iraq is rebuilding facilities at sites that have been part of its nuclear program in the past." Also noted was Iraq's quest for aluminum tubes as well as "other equipment needed for gas centrifuges."[68]

Finally, the president repeated the conclusion of the intelligence community that "if the Iraqi regime is able to produce, buy, or steal an amount of highly enriched uranium a little larger than a single football, it could have a nuclear weapon in less than a year." If that happened, the president warned, then Saddam "would be in a position to dominate the Middle East. He would be in a position to threaten America. And Saddam Hussein would be in a position to pass nuclear technology to terrorists."[69]

One of the satellite photographs released immediately after the president's speech, probably obtained by an advanced KH-11, showed that at least one Iraqi nuclear facility had been rebuilt in recent years. The facility, Al Furat, was originally intended to house a centrifuge enrichment cascade operation. Construction was suspended in 1991, and it was bombed in 1998. The December 1998 and September 2002 satellite images showed that it had been rebuilt in the interval—according to the White House, beginning in 2001.[70]

ON OCTOBER 9, 2002, two days after Bush's speech, Elisabetta Burba, a foreign correspondent for the Italian journalist magazine *Panorama*, gave the U.S. embassy in Rome copies of documents relevant to the alleged Iraq-Niger uranium transaction, documents she received from a former member of Italy's Defense Information Service (SID), a predecessor of SISMI. One, ostensibly a July 27, 2000, letter from the president of Niger to Saddam Hussein, mentioned an agreement signed in Niamey on July 6, 2000, that called for Niger to provide five hundred tons of uranium each year to Iraq and conveyed presidential approval. Another, purportedly from the foreign affairs ministry to the Nigerien ambassador in Rome, included the protocol of the agreement along with a covering letter. Burba wanted to know if the embassy could authenticate the documents, because her source had requested 15,000 Euros in return for their publication, and she suspected they were fakes.[71]

The documents, which were the basis of the report SISMI had provided to the CIA in February 2002, would be passed not only to the CIA, but also to other concerned parties in the intelligence community and the IAEA. INR's Iraq nuclear analyst was immediately skeptical. He e-mailed intelligence community colleagues, requesting that the documents be provided to the Nuclear Interdiction Action Group, which was scheduled to meet the following day. In the message he commented, "You'll note that it bears a funky. Emb. of Niger stamp (to make it look official, I guess)."[72]

In January 2003 he again e-mailed intelligence community colleagues with another observation concerning the documents. One of them purported to be an agreement for a joint military campaign, including both Iraq and Iran, that he considered so ridiculous it was "clearly a forgery." He noted that that document had the same alleged stamps for the Niger embassy in Rome, leading him to conclude that "the uranium purchase agreement is probably a forgery."[73]

Early the next month the United States provided electronic copies of the alleged documents to the IAEA, along with U.S. government talking points which mentioned the reports of Iraqi attempts to acquire uranium from Niger but noted that the Americans could not confirm the reports and had questions with respect to some specific claims. In any case, the memo conveyed U.S. concern that "these reports may indicate Baghdad has attempted to secure an unreported source of uranium yellowcake for a nuclear weapons program."[74]

In early March the IAEA provided the U.S. mission in Vienna with its assessment of the Niger documents. Based on analysis of the documents and interviews with Iraqi officials, the IAEA's Iraq Nuclear Verification Office concluded that the documents were forgeries and provided no confirmation that Iraq had tried to obtain uranium from Niger. Glaring problems included the October 10, 2000, letter from the minister of foreign affairs, which was allegedly signed by Abele Habibou, who had not served in that job since 1989, a fact quickly determined by an Internet search. It was also clear that the signature of the president of Niger, Mamadou Tandja, had been faked. One senior IAEA official commented, "These documents are so bad that I cannot imagine that they came from a serious intelligence agency."[75]*

In the interval, the United States had received other information that went beyond the signing of an agreement. Rather, information reached a navy organization that a large quantity of uranium from Niger was being stored in a warehouse in Cotonou, Benin. Allegedly, the uranium had been sold to Iraq by Niger's president. The report issued by the navy unit, on November 25, 2002, also provided the name and telephone numbers of a West African businessman who was reported to know about the transaction. On December 17 the reports officer for the Defense Attaché Office in Abidjan, Ivory Coast, a member of the DIA-run Defense HUMINT Service (DHS)—created in the mid-1990s through the merger of the military service human intelligence activities—examined the warehouse but saw only what appeared to be bales of cotton.[76]

No attempt was made to contact the businessman named in the navy report. Nor was it possible to determine whether the cotton bales concealed a shipment of uranium, since the DHS officer was not equipped with any radiation detection equipment—even though such equipment, which could be concealed in an attaché case, had been available for decades and was used by navy intelligence personnel in the 1970s to investigate whether Soviet ships carried nuclear weapons on board.[77]

---

* According to one theory, the former Italian intelligence agent, who also had contacts with the French DGSE, was given the documents by that organization, in the hope of trapping the United States and the United Kingdom into making unsupportable statements about the documents, which would then be exposed as forgeries. See "Italian Ex-Spy Discusses Own Role in Iraq-Niger Uranium Traffic Hoax," *Il Giornale*, September 21, 2004, p. 4; Bruce Johnston, "Italy Eyes French Ruse to Dupe U.S. over Iraq," *Washington Times*, September 6, 2004, p. A11.

It has also been reported that the DGSE is believed to be the foreign intelligence service that provided the British SIS with intelligence that Iraq was trying to acquire uranium from Africa, but prohibited the British from passing on that information to the United States. See Beth Gardiner, "Britain Defends Uranium Data on Iraq," *Washington Times*, July 13, 2003, p. A7; Michael Smith, "Withheld Iraq Report Blamed on French," *Washington Times*, July 14, 2003, pp. A1, A10.

The conclusion that the Niger documents were forgeries as well as the failure to find any uranium in the Benin warehouse did not convince DIA that the other reports of a Niger-Iraq deal were wrong. In a top-secret memo to defense secretary Donald Rumsfeld on March 8, DIA stated that "we believe the IAEA is dismissing attempted Iraqi yellowcake purchases, largely based upon a single set of unverified documents concerning a contract between Niger and Iraq for the supply of 'pure uranium.'" The memo also added that the United States had not shared some information with the IAEA suggesting a Nigerien-Iraqi uranium deal—possibly the late 2001 fax found in the possession of a Somali businessman which described arrangements for shipping unidentified commodities in amounts that appeared similar to the amount of the alleged Iraq-Niger uranium deal, although the fax did not mention uranium, Iraq, or Niger.[78]

In March 2003 several CIA assessments accepted the IAEA's conclusions about the documents. On the broader issue of the possible sale of uranium to Niger, the National Intelligence Council reported in an April 5 memorandum, *Niger: No Recent Uranium Sales to Iraq*, that "we judge it highly unlikely that Niamey has sold uranium yellowcake to Baghdad in recent years." The memo also noted that the intelligence community had come to agree with the IAEA assessment that the Niger documents were forgeries and that the reports of the warehouse in Benin holding yellowcake to be shipped to Iraq and of a 1999 visit by an Iraqi delegation to Niamey did not "constitute credible evidence of a recent or impending sale." The memo added that "the current government of Niger . . . probably would report such an approach by the Iraqis." It did not discuss whether there had been any change to the assessment, made in the October 1, 2002, national estimate, that Iraq had been "vigorously trying to procure uranium ore and yellowcake" from Africa.[79]

BY APRIL 5, 2003, U.S. and allied troops were only days from capturing Baghdad. On September 12, 2002, in his speech to the UN General Assembly, President Bush had challenged the international body to force Iraq to disarm, implying that if it failed to do so the United States would handle the job along with any willing allies. Four days later, Iraq announced that it would admit inspectors from the UN Monitoring, Verfication, and Inspection Commission (UNMOVIC), which had replaced UNSCOM and was now headed by Hans Blix, and the IAEA, now headed by Mohamed ElBaradei. On November 8 the Security Council unanimously adopted Resolution 1441, which declared Iraq in material breach of existing resolutions and gave the country seven days to accept the resolution, and thirty days to provide a full declaration of all of its weapons of mass destruction programs. The resolution also specified that new inspections were to begin within forty-five days, and inspectors were to have access to all sites, including presidential sites. In addition, the inspectors were to be free to interview Iraqis in private and take them outside Iraq.[80]

Iraq accepted the resolution four days later, not surprisingly with a defiant letter, and inspections began on November 27. The nuclear inspectors did what previous inspection teams did—they sampled the air, soil, and water over large portions of Iraq. They also revisited sites that had been connected with the Iraqi nuclear program, including Al Furat on November 30—a visit that annoyed Brig. Gen. Samir Ibrahim Abhar, the director of the facility, which had been renamed the al-Milad Company. But the inspectors also had some new tools, including a device designated Alex, which could identify hardened metals used to make nuclear weapons.[81]

The inspectors had a more difficult time gaining access to the scientists who might know the status of various weapons programs and what material, if any, had been hidden across and under parts of Iraq. Some were apparently sent abroad. Not until late December did Iraq provide a list of five hundred scientists involved in the programs of interest to the inspectors. Even then, interviews would take place either with Iraqi officials present or with tape recorders—in the open or concealed—in operation.[82]

On December 7 Iraq submitted its declaration, which Blix criticized for containing "little new information." Ten days later WINPAC analysts completed a paper, U.S. Analysis of Iraq's Declaration, 7 December 2002. They made only two points concerning Iraq's nuclear claims: Iraq failed to explain procurement of the aluminum tubes the intelligence community had "assessed" could be used in a nuclear program; and the declaration "does not acknowledge efforts to procure uranium from Niger, one of the points addressed in the [British government white paper]." The Bush administration characterized the declaration as an additional material breach of Iraq's obligations.[83]*

---

* An e-mail from INR's Iraq nuclear analyst to an Energy Department analyst on December 23 indicated surprise that INR's well-known alternative views on both the aluminum tubes and the uranium information were not included in the points before they were transmitted to the National Security Council. The Energy analyst responded that it was "most disturbing that WINPAC is essentially directing foreign policy in this matter. There are some very strong points to be made in respect to Iraq's arrogant non-compliance with UN sanctions. However, when individuals attempt to convert those 'strong statements' into the 'knock out punch,' the Administration will ultimately look foolish—i.e., the tubes and Niger!" See U.S. Congress, Senate Select Committee on Intelligence (SSCI), Report on the U.S. Intelligence Community's Prewar Intelligence Assessments in Iraq (Washington, D.C.: SSCI, 2004), p. 60.

In the weeks that followed, the inspections continued, as did U.S. intelligence analysis and collection operations focused on possible Iraqi nuclear activity. Some, but by no means all, of the information obtained by the U.S. intelligence community about suspect chemical, biological, and missile sites was passed to the inspectors to aid their efforts. No information about suspect nuclear sites was given to the IAEA.[84] The end results were further U.S. reports on the aluminum tubes and uranium issues, as well as reports from Blix and ElBaradei to the UN Security Council.

In January 2003, WINPAC produced a paper at the request of the chairman of the Joint Chiefs of Staff for information, in addition to that concerning the aluminum tubes, indicating that Iraq was reconstituting its nuclear program. With regard to uranium acquisition, the center paper stated that "fragmentary reporting on Iraqi attempts to procure uranium from various countries in Africa in the past several years is another sign of reconstitution. Iraq has no legitimate use for uranium."[85]

Blix and ElBaradei briefed the Security Council concerning the results of their inspections on January 27, in accord with Resolution 1441's call for an interim progress report within sixty days after inspections began. Just over a week earlier, the inspectors had found documents related to uranium enrichment in the home of Faleh Hassan, a fifty-five-year-old scientist with an expertise in laser enrichment who was once associated with the Iraqi nuclear program. While in his cover letter ElBaradei observed that "we have to date found no evidence that Iraq has revived its nuclear weapons program," the updated report notes that "little progress has been made in resolving the questions and concerns that remained as of 1998" and that "further verification activities will be necessary before the IAEA will be able to provide credible assurance that Iraq has no nuclear weapons programme."[86]

Eight days later, secretary of state Colin Powell addressed the council and the world, in an attempt to demonstrate that Iraq was, as it had in the past, still trying to deceive the inspectors and the world about the status of its nuclear, biological, chemical, and ballistic missile programs. He told his audience, "The material I will present to you comes from a variety of sources. Some are U.S. sources and some are those of other countries. Some of the sources are technical . . . other sources are people who have risked their lives to let the world know what Saddam is up to." He showed satellite photos and played communications intercepts which he said provided strong evidence that Baghdad still was not complying with its international obligations. His argument that "Saddam Hussein is determined to get his hands on a nuclear bomb" rested heavily, albeit not exclusively, on the intended use of the seized aluminum tubes.[87]

Powell told the members of the Security Council and a large television audience that Saddam was so determined to obtain a nuclear bomb that Iraq "has made repeated covert attempts to acquire high-specification aluminum tubes from 11 different countries" and that "these tubes are controlled by the Nuclear Suppliers Group precisely because they can be used as centrifuges for enriching uranium." He also commented, "By now, just about everyone has heard of these tubes"—a reference to the numerous media reports about the debate that followed the first media reporting on the issue in September 2002—and acknowledged, "There are differences of opinion." Powell, as a representative of the U.S. government and not just the State Department, went on to argue the view, held by the majority of intelligence community agencies, that the tubes were intended for centrifuges, rather than express the skepticism of his own intelligence bureau, INR.[88]

Starting in February, the United States, Britain, and Spain called on the Security Council to vote on a new resolution, giving Iraq an ultimatum to quickly come into complete compliance with UN requirements or face military action. During that time Blix and ElBaradei continued their reports to the Security Council on the status of their inspections. On February 14 the two inspections chiefs again addressed the council to update its members on the status of their work. The IAEA chief reported that since resuming work, his teams had conducted 177 inspections at 125 locations. He also provided a survey of the means used to investigate possible Iraqi nuclear activities—the collection of water, sediment, vegetation, and air samples for analysis, as well as use of handheld and car-borne gamma ray detection systems.[89]

On the key issue of the aluminum tubes, ElBaradei was skeptical of the case that Colin Powell had presented to the same group nine days earlier. Late in January Joe T. had arrived in Vienna and met with members of the IAEA staff to discuss the issue. In the conference room that overlooked the Danube River from thirty-two floors up, Joe told the inspectors that they were making a serious mistake, and that Iraq's claim that the tubes were purchased for a rocket program was a transparent lie. The tubes were, he claimed, "overspecified," "inappropriate," and "excessively strong." Despite his assertiveness, his audience was not convinced and it was their view ElBaradei conveyed to the UN. He noted Iraq's claim that it was seeking to acquire the tubes as part of a program to reverse-engineer a rocket, and that the IAEA had verified such a program existed, and that the IAEA was still investigating the issue and had asked for an explanation concerning the tolerance specifications Iraq had placed on the tubes.[90]

His last report before the war would be on March 7. He surveyed the variety of methods his teams used to monitor Iraq for signs of nuclear activity, ranging from a multitude of sampling activities to interviews with Saddam's nuclear scientists. The IAEA chief reported that there was no indication nuclear activities had resumed in the buildings that had been identified through satellite imagery as being rebuilt or erected since 1998. Nor were there any signs that Iraq attempted to import uranium since 1990, a judgment based on an investigation of the February 1999 visit to Niger by the Iraqi ambassador to the Vatican and the conclusion that the documents provided to the IAEA were forgeries. The IAEA chief informed the Security Council that his agency had found no indication that Iraq had attempted to import aluminum tubes for use in centrifuge enrichment, for some of the same reasons that led Energy Department analysts to reach the same conclusion.[91]

After several weeks of unsuccessful diplomacy, and with the opposition of France, Germany, and Russia remaining undiminished, Bush and British prime minister Blair concluded that the council would not approve the new resolution. On March 17 Bush followed the withdrawal of the resolution with a new offer to Saddam: he and his sons could leave Iraq in forty-eight hours or face military action. Saddam refused his last chance, and on March 19 U.S. military operations began—after receiving human intelligence, incorrect as it turned out, claiming to pinpoint Saddam's current location, thus creating hope that he might be killed in an air strike. Less than a month after the initial air attacks, U.S. forces captured Baghdad, bringing Saddam's reign to an end as well as any fantasies he may have harbored about ruling a nuclear-armed Iraq.[92]

WITH THE FALL of the regime, there would be a chance to search the entire country, without obstruction from minders, concealment operations committees, or Iraqi intelligence experts on denial and deception. Initially, the search for stockpiles and illicit weapons activities was the responsibility of the Army's 75th Exploitation Task Force, as part of its job of informing combat troops about things to avoid, precautions to be taken, or events for which they might have to prepare. As the task force moved through Iraq, reports that chemical or biological weapons might have been uncovered were followed by the news that further investigations produced negative results.[93]

In May a larger, more capable group was established to hunt for the missing weapons and related material. It was a move that the administration's undersecretary of defense for intelligence, Stephen Cambone, told reporters had been planned shortly after the beginning of hostilities. The Iraq Survey Group, consisting of about 1,300 to 1,400 individuals, was created with members from the United States, Britain, and Australia. Appointed to head the group, whose motto was "find, exploit, and eliminate," was Maj. Gen. Keith Dayton, a former defense attaché in Moscow and, in May 2003, the director of the DIA's directorate of operations and the Defense HUMINT Service.[94]

The headquarters for the survey group was established in Baghdad, in one of a series of villas, lodges, and buildings ringing an artificial lake at one of Saddam's former palace compounds, which also served as a Baath Party playground. One member recalled working in "the best office I've ever had"—an office with twenty-foot ceilings and chandeliers But, accommodations for the group members were at first, according to another, "barely tolerable." During one of his first nights there, "a great dust storm covered everything and nearly everyone with a fine layer of dust and sand." Until air-conditioning was installed, many slept on cots outside to seek relief from the heat, which exceeded one hundred degrees during the day. Eventually a diet of hamburgers and hot dogs gave way to food served in an air-conditioned dining facility.[95]

At headquarters a detachment of about 190 survey group members identified documents of immediate importance and shipped them off to Qatar, where several hundred others at the group's processing center translated and summarized the contents. The group's analytic center was also established in Qatar with a staff of over a hundred, including experts from the CIA, the DIA, and the Energy and State Departments, as well as from British and Australian intelligence agencies. Back in Baghdad, along with the document exploitation group, were interrogation and debriefing experts, technical analysts to evaluate material suspected of being related to weapons of mass destruction, human intelligence collection teams, and a support staff. About two hundred people would be involved in actual search operations. It had been decided before the search group began that it would pay less attention to fixed sites and put more emphasis on places where intelligence community analysts concluded there was a likelihood of finding material or individuals of interest.[96]

Not long after Stephen Cambone announced the creation of the Iraq Survey Group, director of central intelligence George Tenet announced that he was appointing a "Special Advisor for Strategy regarding Iraqi Weapons of Mass Destruction (WMD) Programs," and calling him "the ideal person for this new role," citing "his understanding of the history of the Iraqi programs and knowledge of past Iraqi efforts to hide WMD." The adviser was none other than David Kay, now sixty-three, who had spent the years since leaving the IAEA as secretary general of the Uranium Institute; then as a vice president of Scientific Applications International Corporation, a mammoth defense and intelligence consulting firm; and finally as a senior fellow at the Potomac Institute, a small Virginia-based think tank. According to Kay, the creation of his position and the survey group was the result of "frustration" with the pace of the search for banned weapons.[97]

Kay's appointment served to give the CIA a higher profile in the hunt for Iraqi weapons of mass destruction, and was explained by one senior official as an effort to coordinate the work in Iraq of all U.S. agencies with expertise in the area of unconventional weapons. While Kay was formally an adviser, he would be spending his time in Baghdad and other locations in Iraq, with the survey group, which was to provide him with "direct support." Reportedly the CIA gave him the code name Ramrod—an apt reference to his new job.[98]

Among the materials that had already been acquired by the group were the booklets and centrifuge parts that Mahdi Obeidi had hidden under the lotus tree in his garden. When IAEA officials interviewed him earlier, after the resumption of inspections, Obeidi did not tell them of his hidden stash, knowing how Saddam would respond. But shortly after the dictator was driven from power in April, Obeidi, concerned that he could suffer the fate of some German scientists after World War II and be whisked away by a foreign country or terrorist group to help develop an atomic bomb, tried to turn himself and his hidden material over to U.S. officials. Rebuffed at first, eventually he was able to make contact with the CIA—although the first meeting did not go well, in part because his interviewers appeared to know little about either him or the centrifuge program. But on June 2 he led investigators to his rose garden and his secret stash. One administration official emphasized that the discovery "validates our long-standing view that Iraq had hidden nuclear technology." The IAEA argued that the fact that the documents and parts remained underneath Obeidi's lotus tree was evidence that Iraq had not attempted to reconstitute its nuclear program.[99]

Obeidi's gift, along with his comments and revelations, made up some of the data Kay had available when he prepared an interim report on the group's progress. Also available were the debriefings of Jaffar Dhia Jaffar, who was interviewed by American and British experts in the United Arab Emirates, where he had fled. Both denied the nuclear program had been restarted, and Obeidi also disputed the notion that the purchase of aluminum tubes was related to centrifuge production. Another nuclear scientist questioned by the survey group should have fled. Majid Hussein Ali was found dead after the group interviewed him—he had been shot twice in the back.[100]

Kay delivered his interim report on October 2, before the House and Senate intelligence committees as well as the defense subcommittee of the House appropriations committee. He reported that the "environment in Iraq remains far from permissive for our activities, with many Iraqis that we talk to reporting threats and overt acts of intimidation," and threats and attacks being directed at Iraq Survey Group personnel. Three attacks on group facilities or teams had taken place the previous month alone—the survey group's base in Irbil was bombed and two staff members seriously injured, a team person had his vehicle blocked by gunmen and only escaped by firing back through the windshield, and Baghdad headquarters had been subject to a mortar attack.[101]

Kay was not able to report that any stockpiles of chemical or biological weapons had been discovered, or that previously identified weapons of mass destruction facilities had been in operation in recent years. But he could report that "we have discovered dozens of WMD-related program activities and significant amounts of equipment that Iraq concealed from the United Nations during the inspections that began in late 2002." Kay revealed that the survey group had found a clandestine network of laboratories within the Iraqi

Intelligence Service suitable for chemical and biological warfare research, new work on biological warfare agents, a continuing covert capability to produce fuel propellant useful only for Scud missiles, and clandestine attempts to obtain from North Korea technology related to eight-hundred-mile-range ballistic missiles.[102]

There were also violations in the nuclear area, Kay reported. The survey group had obtained "documents and equipment, hidden in scientists' homes that would have been useful in resuming uranium enrichment by centrifuge and electromagnetic isotope separation (EMIS)"—some but not all of which came from Mahdi Obeidi. Kay also reported, based on testimony from Iraqi scientists and senior government officials, "Saddam . . . remained firmly committed to acquiring nuclear weapons." Those officials also told the group that "Saddam would have resumed nuclear weapons development at some future point." Some believed that any end of sanctions would have been followed by nuclear reconstitution, while one believed that by 2000 Saddam had run out of patience with waiting for sanctions to end and wanted to restart the program.[103]

Kay also reported that beginning around 2000, Dr. Khalid Ibrahim Said, senior official with the Iraqi Atomic Energy Commission and the Baath Party started several small and relatively unsophisticated research projects relevant to nuclear weapons development. While those initiatives did not, the DCI's special adviser noted, constitute a renewal of the nuclear effort, they could have been useful in developing "a weapons-relevant science base for the long-term." Kay also informed the members of Congress that his group did not yet know if Said's projects had been initiated by a higher authority, and that Said was in no position to provide further information, having been killed on April 8 when the car he was riding in tried to run a Coalition roadblock. According to one account, "his loss grieved Kay's nuclear investigators, who had many questions for him."[104]

Kay also reported that "we have not uncovered evidence that Iraq undertook significant post-1998 steps to actually build nuclear weapons or produce fissile material." However, based on examinations of documents and interviews with Iraqi scientists, it was clear that some of the key technical groups from the pre–Gulf War program remained largely intact, working on nuclear-relevant dual-use technologies. Some of those scientists believed the groups were preserved to allow reconstitution of the program, although none could produce official directives or plans to that effect.[105]

In some cases, Kay noted, groups worked on projects that could preserve essential skills needed for the production of fissile material or nuclear weapons development. And then there were scientists, such as Obeidi, who "at the direction of senior Iraqi government officials," preserved documents and equipment from their pre-1991 nuclear weapons–related research— which they did not disclose to the IAEA. One Iraqi scientist told his interrogators that it was a "common understanding" among the scientists that material was being preserved for reconstitution of nuclear weapons–related work. And the survey group's nuclear team, Kay stated, had "found indications that there was interest, beginning in 2002, in reconstituting a centrifuge enrichment program. Most of this activity centered on the activities of Dr. Sa'id."[106]

In his report, Kay observed that the work of the survey group was far from over. But in a few months he would be finished with the group. In mid-December he returned from Baghdad, where he had been living for six months, and visited CIA headquarters. Several newspapers reported that while at Langley he told CIA officials that he was thinking of leaving, in part because the search was taking far longer than he had first expected, and was putting a strain on his family. Subsequently, Kay would say that he resigned largely because he objected to the administration's decision in November to transfer intelligence resources from the hunt for weapons to counterinsurgency efforts within Iraq.[107]

Toward the end of January 2004, the CIA released a statement announcing that Kay would be stepping down from his job as special adviser. Tenet praised him as "a model private citizen who willingly lent his unique expertise to his government in a time of need." Simultaneously, the CIA chief announced the appointment of Charles A. Duelfer, at the time a public policy analyst at the Woodrow Wilson International Center for Scholars, to replace Kay. The new special adviser had received a master's of science degree from MIT and served as deputy assistant secretary of state for arms control and multilateral defense matters before joining the UN Special Commission in 1993 as its deputy executive chairman—a position he held until it folded in 2000.[108]

Duelfer's appointment may have come as surprise to some, given his public skepticism that any chemical or biological weapons would be discovered by the survey group or anybody else. Only two weeks before, in a television interview, he remarked, "The prospect of finding chemical weapons, biological weapons is close to nil at this point." When asked about his skepticism during a conference call with reporters on the day of his appointment, he told one reporter, "My goal is to find out what happened on the ground. What was the status of the Iraqi weapons program, what was their game plan. . . . I have the responsibility to do that now as an investigator. Other comments I've made as an academic or as a scholar were the judgments or prognostications of an outsider."[109]

As Duelfer promised to put his skepticism aside, his predecessor joined the ranks of the skeptics—at least with respect to the prospect of finding stockpiles of weapons. In an interview with Reuters on the day his resignation was announced, David Kay expressed his belief that Iraq had illicit weapons at the conclusion of the Persian Gulf War, but the UN inspections and Iraq's own decisions "got rid of them." Interviews with Iraqi scientists convinced him that sometime around 1997 and 1998, Iraq descended into a "vortex of corruption" which resulted in governmental activities spinning out of control as an isolated and fantasy-prone Saddam Hussein authorized major projects without consulting others. As a result, proposals for weapons programs became money-making scams that overwhelmed whatever was left of actual programs.[110]

After about two months on the job, Duelfer provided his first impressions to Congress. He reported that "in the nuclear arena, the ISG has developed information that suggests Iraqi interest in preserving and expanding the knowledge needed to design and develop nuclear weapons." One effort Duelfer deemed significant involved a high-speed rail gun program, which was directed by two scientists associated with Iraq's pre-1991 nuclear weapons program. Documents examined by the survey group showed that the gun project was intended to achieve speeds of 1.24 to 6.2 miles per second. While the ostensible purpose for the effort was the development of an air defense gun, such speeds, Duelfer noted, "are what are necessary to conduct experiments of metals compressing together at high speed as they do in a nuclear detonation."[111]

Additionally, the scientists' laboratory contained documents describing diagnostic techniques that are important for nuclear weapons experiments, including flash X-ray radiography, laser velocimetry, and high-speed photography. Documents discovered outside the laboratory described a high-voltage switch that can be used for nuclear weapon detonation, laser detonation, nuclear fusion, radiation measurement, and radiation safety. Such topics, Duelfer commented, "are certainly not related to air defense." "It is this combination of topics," he reported, "that make us suspect this lab was intentionally focused on research applicable for nuclear weapons development."[112]

The survey group also had continued trying to determine whether Iraq was seeking to develop uranium enrichment technologies, and revisited the issue of the high-tolerance aluminum tubes, a controversy that would appear to have been settled. Duelfer noted the same point that had been raised by the CIA and DIA—that while the tubes were ostensibly for small rockets, the manufacturing tolerances specified were much higher than what would normally be required for rockets. "Technical reasons for the high tolerances were explained by a number of Iraqis," he informed the committee, "but there are still a number of discrepancies to examine with regard to these tubes."[113]

Six months later Duelfer took the witness chair in the Hart Senate Office Building at around 2:30 in the afternoon, to deliver his final, massive, three-volume report. As a summation of what the Iraq Survey Group had discovered and what it concluded over its eighteen-month existence, the report repeated much of what appeared in the earlier statements by Kay and Duelfer, including the receipt of documents and equipment from scientists' homes related to uranium enrichment, the rail gun project, and the concealment of documents concerning the nuclear weapons effort.[114]

The report also noted the regime's efforts to sustain the talent base for a nuclear program. Starting around 1992, Baghdad, according to the report, "in a bid to retain the intellectual core of the former weapons program . . . transferred many nuclear scientists to related jobs in the Military Industrialization Commission (MIC)," jobs that would help the scientists "maintain their weapons knowledge base." In addition, the regime prevented scientists in the former weapons program from leaving their jobs or Iraq, while, in the late 1990s, personnel from the MIC and Iraqi Atomic Energy Commission received significant pay raises in an attempt to retain them.[115]

Despite those efforts, Duelfer told the Senate Armed Services Committee, "there was decay in the team." "Unlike other WMD areas," he explained, "nuclear weapons development requires thousands of knowledgeable scientists as well as a large physical plant. Even with the intention of keeping these talented people employed, a natural decay took place and the time it would take for Iraq to build a nuclear weapon tended to increase for the duration of the sanctions." The special adviser also told the senators that "despite this decay, Saddam did not abandon his nuclear ambitions."[116]

JUST AS the survey group found that the reality in Iraq with respect to chemical and biological weapons and ballistic missiles differed from what the U.S. intelligence community predicted, so too did they find a discrepancy between the state of Iraq's nuclear program and its portrayal in the October 2002 national intelligence estimate, *Iraq's Continuing Weapons of Mass Destruction Program*. There was no sign of uranium from Africa, or of the use of aluminum tubes to build centrifuges, and no real reconstitution. The gap between the expectations created by the estimate and the administration's statements and what the survey group found led some, including David Kay, to call for an investigation as well as an overhaul of the intelligence community's structure. With two other members of the "axis of evil" threatening to become significant nuclear powers, the United States could not afford to delay taking actions that would seemingly enhance its intelligence community's capability to correctly assess nuclear developments in those nations.[117]

chapter fourteen

TROUBLE WAITING TO HAPPEN

CONCLUSIVE EVIDENCE THAT Saddam Hussein had not reconstituted his nuclear weapons program was obtained by the Iraq Survey Group after U.S. forces deposed the Iraqi dictator from power, an action which also ensured that he never would reconstitute the program. But while Saddam began 2004 in custody, awaiting trial for his myriad crimes, the other two charter members of the axis of evil were still very much in business.

BY LATE 2004, an Islamic regime had ruled Iran for a quarter of a century, since it dethroned the shah in November 1979. While many in the country, including some in the government, yearned for a freer society than the mullahs desired, the regime remained in power—supported by the Revolutionary Guards, the Ministry of Intelligence and Security, and other instruments of oppression. In addition to terrorizing its own citizens, the regime had become the world's primary state sponsor of terrorism. The Iranian-supported and -directed Hezbollah carried out the 1983 attacks on the U.S. embassy and Marine barracks in Beirut and the subsequent bombings of the Israeli embassy and a Jewish community center in Argentina. Another Iranian-sponsored terrorist act occurred in June 1996, when a fuel truck packed with explosives blew up outside the Khobar Towers in Dharan, Saudia Arabia, where U.S. military personnel were living.[1]

The regime has made substantial progress in establishing a nuclear infrastructure that would allow it to achieve what Saddam had dreamed of—a nuclear weapons capability. Overall administrative responsibility for the civilian nuclear program probably lies with the Atomic Energy Organization of Iran, first established by the shah in 1974, while the Islamic Revolutionary Guards Corps is believed to be in charge of Iran's weapons of mass destruction programs. The apparent intellectual center of the nuclear weapons effort is the Nuclear Technology Center located in Esfahan, about 260 miles south of Tehran and one of the major tourist stops in Iran, with its historical buildings, bridges, and other attractions. The center is the home of Chinese-supplied minireactors, subcritical assemblies, and a fuel fabrication laboratory. It employs as many as three thousand scientists and is suspected of being Iran's Los Alamos or Sarov, home to nuclear weapons designers.[2]

Esfahan is also the site of several nuclear-related construction projects. Chinese firms are working on the Zirconium Production Facility, which will produce cladding for reactor fuel. Also under construction in the area is the Uranium Conversion Facility, which will produce uranium hexafluoride, metallic uranium, and uranium oxide. Construction started in 2003 on the Fuel Manufacturing Plant, which, Iran has stated, would fabricate fuel assemblies for the IR-40 reactor being built at Arak and the Bushehr Nuclear Power Plant.[3]

The Bushehr plant, located in southwestern Iran, on the Persian Gulf, is probably the best known of the Iranian nuclear sites, as a result of U.S. efforts to induce Russia to cease its assistance to the project. During the Iran-Iraq war of 1980–1988 the two light-water, low-enriched uranium reactors at Bushehr, which Germany had begun work on during the shah's regime, were damaged by Iraqi attacks. Russia then accepted an $800 million contract to finish construction of the first reactor, a mission it announced as completed in October 2004—after spurning U.S. requests to halt the project. The facility will have the capability of generating 1,000 megawatts of electric power, but a year's worth of spent fuel will contain about 550 pounds of plutonium. In an attempt to alleviate concerns that Iran would be able to use that plutonium to develop a nuclear arsenal, Russia took the unusual step of paying Iran to take the spent fuel, which operators of nuclear power plants usually are glad to get rid of.[4]

What appear to be two key components of any Iranian nuclear weapons program are located in the vicinity of Arak, about 150 miles south of Tehran, and Natanz, a small mountain town about 10 miles farther south that had been better known for its fruit orchards. Two heavy-water facilities—a heavy-water production plant and the 40-megawatt Iran Nuclear Research Reactor (IR-40)—are planned for the vicinity of the Qareh Chay River, about 35 miles from Arak, under the supervision of Mohammad Qannadi, the deputy for production of fuel of the Iranian atomic energy organization. According to the head of the organization, Gholamreza Aghazadeh, basic reactor design was completed by the end of 2003, and Iranian officials announced in April 2004 that construction would begin in June. Some have estimated that the reactor, which Iran claims is intended for medical research and development, will allow Iran to produce about eighteen to twenty-two pounds of weapons-grade plutonium annually each year, enough for one or two nuclear weapons.[5]

Work on the Natanz project, which was originally described as an effort aimed at the eradication of deserts, is reported to have started in 2000. According to an Iranian resistance group (which the State Department classifies as a terrorist organization), about twenty-five acres of territory has been set aside for the effort and is surrounded by barbed wire. One component of the project is the Pilot Fuel Enrichment Plant, which will eventually contain approximately one thousand gas centrifuges to enrich uranium. By February 2003 over one hundred of the centrifuges were already operational. The second element is the yet-to-be-completed Fuel Enrichment Plant, a very large facility with foot-thick walls and sections twenty-five feet underground. It is estimated that, when completed, the project will employ more than fifty thousand centrifuges and be able to produce enough highly enriched uranium for several nuclear weapons a year.[6]

A variety of other installations spread across Iran make up the rest of the country's nuclear infrastructure. In the capital is the Tehran Nuclear Research Center, with an operating research reactor, a radioisotope production facility, laboratories, and a waste-handling facility. At the University of Tehran is a 5-megawatt research reactor, provided to the shah's regime by the United States and subject to IAEA inspections, with fuel provided by Argentina. In another part of the city, at the Physics Research Center of the Sharif University of Technology, more covert nuclear activities may have taken place, including an experimental centrifuge uranium enrichment program as well as research on plutonium separation. In Anarak and Karaj are waste storage sites, while uranium deposits and mines are located in Yazd province, where Iran discovered over five thousand metric tons of the substance in 1985.[7]

Also part of the Iranian nuclear effort are the front companies that procure material for the program. Kala Electric in Tehran has obtained material and equipment for the Natanz facility from India and China. Mesbah Engineering Corporation, also in Tehran, has performed similar services for the Arak plants. The Center for Atomic Research, an arm of the Iranian atomic energy organization, employs a front company, Kaavosh Yaar, to procure material that the center might not be able to obtain if requested directly.[8]

According to the not-always-reliable Iranian resistance, several other secret Iranian nuclear facilities may be at various stages of construction, including a uranium enrichment facility at Kolahdouz, about nine miles west of Tehran and concealed in a large military facility; the Ardekan Nuclear Fuel Site for uranium enrichment in central Iran, scheduled for completion in 2005; and an underground nuclear facility with an unknown purpose at Darkhovin, on the Karun River south of Ahvaz that is under the control of the Revolutionary Guards. Such facilities may be part of what several Western intelligence agencies, including the CIA, suspect may be a nuclear weapon program parallel to one connected to the Natanz and Arak facilities.[9]

WHILE IRAN'S DEPUTY PRESIDENT proclaimed in 1991 that Iran should collaborate with other Islamic states to produce an Islamic bomb, almost all statements concerning Iran's nuclear program have stressed that it was intended only for peaceful purposes. In February 2003 President Moham-

mad Khatami assured "all peace-loving individuals in the world that Iran's efforts in the field of nuclear technology are focused on civilian applications and nothing else." But such statements, similar to the deceptive ones of earlier foreign leaders claiming no interest in nuclear weapons, did nothing to alleviate U.S. concerns that the oil- and natural gas–rich country was not interested in atomic energy simply to provide electricity—that ultimately the mullahs wanted atomic weapons.[10]

To monitor nuclear developments in the Islamic republic, the United States has employed high-tech intelligence systems and human intelligence. In addition, it has obtained reports from allies such as Britain and Israel, and carefully scrutinized the reports of IAEA inspectors who, as a result of Iran's being a party to the nonproliferation treaty, were able to examine the country's declared nuclear facilities.

Among the intelligence gathered by those means was the sale to Iran, by China, of a calutron to the Center for Agricultural Research and Nuclear Medicine at Karaj. While the calutron was one normally used for peaceful purposes, and not easily adaptable for use to turn out weapons-grade uranium, the news worried U.S. officials, who feared that Iran might eventually be able to produce a version that could be used for military purposes. A draft version of a national intelligence estimate on Iran, written in the fall of 1991, shortly after the discovery of the calutron sale, and with knowledge of other Chinese assistance, including providing the small research reactor at Esfahan and training Iranian engineers and scientists, concluded that Iran's leadership was committed to developing nuclear weapons. Other intelligence available to the analysts included Iran's attempts to purchase nuclear technology abroad, including nuclear fuel, equipment for handling and processing fissile material, and nuclear reactors. The estimate also concluded that Iran's nuclear program was disorganized and only in the first stages of development, an overly optimistic assessment in the view of some administration officials and outside experts.[11]

The concern about Iran's nuclear intentions was conveyed to Congress in early 1992 by director of central intelligence Robert Gates, who testified that Iran was seeking to acquire an atomic bomb and could well have one by 2000 if the West did not act to stop it. The "suspicious procurement pattern" with respect to nuclear technology that led to such a conclusion also led to stepped-up intelligence collection, including increased satellite coverage of Iranian nuclear sites. The United States passed intelligence to the IAEA's inspectors in Vienna.[12]

Further, the conclusion that Iran was seeking to become a nuclear weapons state spurred attempts to forestall future sales, while the attempted purchases served to reinforce the intelligence community's conclusions about the mullahs' intentions. Twice in 1992, sometime after Gates testified, the United States was able to block the sale of nuclear goods to Iran. Richard T. Kennedy, the U.S. ambassador to the IAEA, managed to persuade Argentina not to sell Iran nuclear fuel fabrication equipment, which was packed and ready to be shipped and would have allowed Iran to convert natural uranium into precursors to weapons-grade uranium. Another U.S. diplomat, ambassador to China J. Stapleton Roy, visited a nuclear facility outside Beijing to examine a model of the reactor that Iran wanted to purchase. After lobbying by U.S. diplomats, an official of the China National Nuclear Corporation told a trade journal that China "could not supply" the reactor to Iran for technical reasons.[13]

Such successes did not lead the U.S. intelligence community to believe that Iran would not keep trying to acquire advanced weapons technology. The title of a secret February 1, 1993, report by the Joint Atomic Energy Intelligence Committee—*Iran's Nuclear Program: Building a Weapons Capability*—conveyed that judgment.[14]

At about the same time there were reports that Iran had recruited several nuclear engineers from the former Soviet Union. Even more potentially disturbing were the persistent reports that Iran "somehow acquired three nuclear warheads from a former Soviet test range."[15] Undoubtedly, U.S. intelligence agencies sought more information on such claims while continuing to monitor Iranian attempts to acquire material that could be employed to produce its own bombs.

In 1994 U.S. and other Western intelligence agencies received information that some Iranians had visited the Ublinsky Metallurgical Works in the former Soviet republic of Kazakhstan, a plant from which they had purchased large quantities of low-enriched uranium and beryllium in August 1992. This time their target was highly enriched uranium stored at the facility. Armed with the knowledge of Iranian interest as well as the assessment that the material was stored, according to a senior U.S. intelligence official, "in a highly unsecure way," the United States arranged to purchase all 1,320 pounds of the highly enriched uranium. The operation, approved by President Bill Clinton on October 7, 1994, and designated Sapphire, involved thirty-one U.S. specialists and concluded with three C-5 military transports flying nonstop from Kazakhstan to Dover Air Force Base in Delaware, with the uranium then being transported by convoy to a storage site in Oak Ridge, Tennessee.[16]

That success, not surprisingly, did not end Iran's quest for nuclear weapons–related technology nor alleviate U.S. apprehension—much like a television show in which the heroes defuse a serious threat one week, only to be faced by another just as serious the following week. Early in 1995 several U.S. officials, presumably based on raw or finished intelligence, told the *New York Times* that Iran might be much closer to producing nuclear weapons than previously believed—although the concern was based less on what Iran had actually done than what it was planning to do. One official asserted that "if the Iranians maintain this intensive effort to get everything they need they could have all their components in two years. Then it will be just a matter of technology and research. If Iran is not interrupted in this program by some foreign power, it will have the device in more or less five years."[17]

Beyond providing U.S. officials with intelligence about Iranian nuclear efforts, the intelligence community also presented information on the same subject to Russian foreign minister Andrei V. Kozyrev, with the approval of the Clinton administration, in an attempt to get his government to cut or reduce its nuclear ties to the Islamic regime. The written report provided to the Russians claimed Iran had a crash program to build nuclear weapons, which would be accelerated by construction of the Russian reactors. It cited specifics, including Iran's importing other equipment needed to build nuclear weapons, particularly from Germany; its attempt to buy enriched uranium from Kazakhstan; and the similarity of Iranian smuggling efforts and those used by the Pakistani and Iraqi nuclear weapons programs.[18]

Giving such sensitive intelligence to Russia, one official remarked, was unusual, noting that "we used to only share information when we wanted to accuse them of some type of violation. Now we're sharing information so we can cooperate." More precisely, intelligence was being shared to assist those in the Russian government who opposed nuclear ties with Iran, and give them ammunition to counter officials from the Defense Ministry, Atomic Energy Ministry, and intelligence agencies who wished to proceed with the deal. In case sharing intelligence was not enough, the United States also offered to share money, nuclear aid that might exceed $100 million as well as some of the $2 billion in contracts earmarked to build light-water reactors for North Korea.[19]

That April the United States tried a similar strategy with Beijing when the State Department provided Chinese officials with an intelligence report, similar to the one given to Russia, detailing Iran's attempts to import equipment for building an atomic bomb. This time the objective was to get China to back away from its deal with Iran to build two 300-megawatt pressurized water reactors at Darkhovin. The report was provided in advance of the April 17 two-hour meeting and lunch shared by secretary of state Warren Christopher and Chinese foreign minister Qian Qichen, at New York's Waldorf Astoria. However, neither the contents of the report nor Christopher's remarks convinced Qian, at the time, to reverse China's position.[20]

While the administration could not ban China or Russia from dealing with Iran, it could prevent U.S. firms from doing business with Iran, and at the end of April it announced a ban on all trade with that country—20 percent of whose crude oil exports had been sold to U.S. firms and branches the previous year. Christopher told reporters that "we know that Iran is seeking a capability to produce both plutonium and highly enriched uranium, the critical materials for a nuclear bomb." He charged that Iran had been frustrated in its efforts to produce weapons-grade materials at home so it "has aggressively sought to buy them abroad." Christopher added, "A regime with this kind of a record simply cannot be permitted to get its hands on nuclear weapons." Not surprisingly, some European nations, including France and Germany, believed the embargo was an overreaction. French foreign minister Alain Juppé asserted that "the right thing to do is to conduct a political dialogue with Iran."[21]

But U.S. pressure seemed to produce results. A few days after the embargo was announced, it became known that Russia, while planning to continue the Bushehr reactor project, intended to refrain from selling Tehran a gas centrifuge plant—a copy of the protocol signed in Iran the previous January by Russian atomic energy minister Viktor Mikhailov was obtained by the United States, leading to American pressure to kill the deal. In addition, China eventually suspended plans to supply the two power reactors that Warren Christopher had objected to in his meeting with Qian. U.S. complaints also led the Czech government to block plans by one of its nation's companies to sell reactor equipment to Iran. By 1997 it seemed that the U.S. attempts to curb Iran's pursuit of atomic weapons had an impact. While the CIA had estimated in 1992 that Iran could have a bomb by 2000, in 1997 John Holum, director of the Arms Control and Disarmament Agency, was estimating that Iran would not be able to produce a nuclear weapon until at least 2005.[22]

Continued intelligence collection against Iranian nuclear activities resulted in another diplomatic approach to Russia in 1997. New information, probably obtained from human intelligence or electronic intercepts or both, revealed ongoing high-level technical exchanges between Russian and Iranian engineers and technicians. Intelligence also indicated that Russian experts might still be advising Iran on uranium-mining and -processing efforts, despite a previous Russian promise to halt such activity.[23]

The next year, it was the Chinese who received a reminder about U.S. concerns over nuclear deals with Iran. U.S. intelligence discovered that just weeks after China had pledged it would halt nuclear assistance to Iran, other than completing two small projects, a new deal was in the works. China would, as promised, break a contract to build a uranium conversion facility, which was still of concern even though it would have been under IAEA safeguards. But one of China's state-run corporations had started or was still involved in secret negotiations with Tehran over the possible sale of hundreds of tons of material for uranium enrichment. In January 1998, the National Security Agency intercepted at least two communications between a senior Iranian official in Esfahan, undoubtedly from the Nuclear Technology Center, and mid-level Chinese counterparts in Beijing. The negotiations, opened by Iran, concerned millions of dollars' worth of anhydrous hydrogen fluoride, also known as hydrofluoric acid. While it has several commercial applications, including production of aviation fuel, the acid can be used to produce fissile material.[24]

Smaller quantities can be used to separate plutonium oxide from the spent fuel of a nuclear reactor and purify it into metallic plutonium. Larger quantities can be used as a feeder material for turning yellowcake into uranium hexafluoride. The amount Iran wished to purchase would be sufficient to provide a lifetime supply for a uranium enrichment facility. In addition to any discussions of amount and price, the communications also referred to a cover story and to falsified end-user documents to conceal the fact that the ultimate destination for the chemical was one of Iran's top nuclear institutes.[25]

NSA's intercepts caused Robert Einhorn and Gary Samore, the top State Department and National Security Council counterproliferation officials, to summon acting Chinese ambassador Zhou Wenzhong to a meeting to lodge a complaint about what his government's Chinese Nuclear Energy Industry Corporation was willing to sell to Iran. Within two weeks, after a series of high-level contacts, Chinese officials in Beijing told Washington that the sale would not take place. The *Washington Post* reported that the United States claimed to have "additional intelligence, so sensitive that it cannot be fully described," which provided reassurance that China was indeed cutting off its assistance to Iran.[26]

Once again, such a counterproliferation victory only delayed the day when a new assessment would cause concern. In late 1999 director of central intelligence George Tenet informed senior Clinton administration officials, based on a newly completed estimate, that Iran might have acquired the capability to make a nuclear weapon. But the "might" was not based on hard evidence of developments in Iran—which might show up in satellite photographs—but rather the judgment that the CIA, NSA, and other agencies did not have high confidence in their ability to monitor Iran's attempts to procure nuclear materials and technology—including weapons themselves—from abroad.[27]

The CIA could not be certain that Iran had acquired nuclear weapons, but announced that Iranian acquisition could not, as it had been in the past, be ruled out. Despite the cautious nature of the report, it stimulated a strong debate within the Clinton administration, with some analysts believing that Iran's nuclear efforts were still moving slowly. Those analysts pointed to the lack of evidence that Iran had succeeded in building its own weapon, stealing one, or acquiring enough fissile material. Meanwhile, some officials viewed the estimate as a CIA attempt to avoid the criticism it suffered after its underestimation of Iraq's nuclear program before the 1991 Gulf War and failure to provide warning of the 1998 Indian tests.[28]

Despite the CIA's concern about its ability to track Iranian nuclear procurement attempts, the year provided another success, in both intelligence collection and use of the information gathered. During the spring of 2000 American intelligence agencies uncovered plans for the D. V. Efremov Institute in St. Petersburg to provide Iran with a laser facility that could be used for uranium enrichment. Once U.S. officials became aware of the proposed transaction, they began urging Russian officials to cancel it because, in the words of one official, "there is no question that the turn-key facility was intended for" Iran's nuclear weapons program. During a session in New York to prepare for the September 6, 2000, meeting between Clinton and Russian president Vladimir Putin, the subject was raised again and Russian officials told White House aides that the contract had been suspended and was under review by the Russian government to determine if the facility could be used for uranium enrichment.[29]

A month later, John A. Lauder, still in charge of the DCI Nonproliferation Center, told the Senate Foreign Relations Committee that there was continued concern over Moscow's nuclear ties to Tehran. Lauder informed the senators that "Iran is seeking nuclear-related equipment, material, and technical expertise from a variety of foreign sources, most notably in Russia. Tehran claims that it seeks foreign assistance to master nuclear technology for civilian research and nuclear energy programs. However, the expertise and technology gained— along with contacts established—could be used to advance Iran's nuclear weapons effort." In addition, Lauder noted that work continued on the Bushehr reactor, and that while the project "will not directly support a weapons effort . . . it affords Iran broad access to Russia's nuclear industry." An additional concern was that "Russia's entities are interacting with Iranian nuclear research centers on a wide variety of activities beyond the Bushehr project." Many of the projects, Lauder pointed out, while ostensibly for civilian nuclear uses, had a direct application to the production of weapons-grade fissile material.[30]

ALMOST THREE YEARS LATER, in the summer of 2003, director of central intelligence George Tenet filed a "721" report with Congress—an unclassified report on foreign nations' acquisition of technology related to weapons of mass destruction and advanced conventional weapons—which Congress, in Section 721 of the 1997 fiscal year intelligence appropriations, required be filed every six months. Drafted by the CIA's Weapons Intelligence, Nonproliferation, and Arms Control Center (WINPAC) and coordinated with the intelligence community, the eleven-page single-spaced report dealt first with Iran.

Owing to its being unclassified, the report did not directly discuss the data collected by U.S. intelligence activities directed at Iran's nuclear program— whether by spy satellites, eavesdropping operations, or human intelligence. But it did convey the fundamental conclusions that would be found in the classified estimates that did include such sensitive details. "The United States remains convinced," the section on Iranian nuclear activities began, "that Tehran has been pursuing a clandestine nuclear weapons program, in violation of its obligations as a party to the Nuclear Nonproliferation Treaty (NPT)."[31]

The report also expressed the continuing concern that Iran's efforts to develop a complete fuel cycle for its civilian program provided an excuse and cover for activities designed to produce weapons-grade material. In particular, the intelligence community was concerned about the true purpose of Natanz—whose existence, along with that of the heavy-water plant at Arak, had been revealed to the world in the summer of 2002 by the National Council of Resistance of Iran, the political arm of the People's Mujaheddin. Satellites operated by the National Reconnaissance Office had detected the digging at Natanz earlier, and possibly Natanz is what an anonymous official referred to when he told reporter Seymour Hersh in 2001 that "we know that they are going deep and clandestine." Arak, on the other hand, was not flagged as being nuclear related because from above it looked like a common factory.[32]

The WINPAC-drafted report noted that commercial imagery showed what the higher-resolution advanced KH-11s revealed, that Iran was burying the Natanz facility "presumably to hide and harden it against military attack." That imagery, and certainly the NRO's imagery, also showed two large underground structures, each about 340,000 square feet in size, that could be cascade halls designed to house centrifuges, as well as several white-roofed above-ground structures whose function could not be determined.[33]

The analysts also had the benefit of information produced by IAEA inspectors from their first inspection of Natanz, in February 2003, during which they discovered uranium centrifuges. It was one of several visits the Iranians would tolerate because of a desire to avoid the economic and political consequences of unequivocally walking away from the nonproliferation treaty. The information available about the Arak and Natanz facilities indicated to the U.S. analysts who produced the 721 report that "Iran appears to be embarking on acquiring nuclear weapons material via both acquisition paths—highly enriched uranium and low burn-up plutonium."[34]*

---

* Even France was concerned. In the summer of 2003, at a Nuclear Suppliers Group (NSG) information exchange meeting in Pusan, the French presented a paper titled "Latest Developments in the Nuclear Program of Iran, in Particular on the Plutonium Way." It began with the observation that "recent disclosures, arising mainly from regime opponents, satellite imagery, purchasing attempts and intelligence reports tend to confirm suspicions about the existence of an Iranian hidden nuclear program." It concluded with the advice that "NSG participating governments . . . exercise the most serious vigilance on their exports to Iran and Iranian front-companies."

The IAEA inspection of February 2003 was only the first of several that would, in effect, provide the U.S. intelligence community with not only the benefits of on-site access to key Iranian nuclear facilities but also the advantage of trained inspectors with, if not a "license to spy," then a "license to investigate." Inspections would follow every few months in 2003 and 2004. In February 2004 the inspectors would turn up sophisticated uranium enrichment equipment as well as blueprints for a previously unknown Iranian enrichment project that involved testing a faster and more efficient centrifuge, the P(akistan)-2. They also discovered that Iran had produced and then experimented with polonium, an ingredient in initiating the chain reaction that produces a nuclear detonation.[35]

Over the remainder of the year the effort to get Iran to fully reveal its nuclear program to the IAEA and to cease activities that could lead to nuclear weapons alternated between temporary success and failure. In March 2004 Iranian defense minister Ali Shamkhani acknowledged his country's military had built centrifuges, but claimed they were for civilian use. Meanwhile, foreign minister Kamal Kharrazai promised that when Iran's "relations with the IAEA return to normal, we will definitely resume enrichment." Days later, Iran barred further nuclear inspections after an IAEA resolution, milder than the one preferred by the United States, criticized Iran's leadership for failing to fully disclose the nation's past nuclear activities. Iran's top nuclear official, Hassan Rouhani, denounced the rebuke as "unfair and deceitful." In the view of the United States it was Iran that was deceitful. In early May John Wolf, the assistant secretary of state for nonproliferation, told some fellow diplomats that "despite professions of transparency and peaceful intent, Iran is going down the same path of denial and deception that handicapped international inspectors in North Korea and Iraq."[36]

In April Iran would agree to a new round of inspections, with the inspectors arriving days after the Islamic republic claimed that it had stopped building centrifuges. In June, when the IAEA prepared its assessment, based on the April inspections, it would sharply criticize Iran's leaders for repeatedly misstating details about its nuclear program and its pursuit of uranium enrichment technology. The agency noted that Iranian officials had finally admitted that an Iranian company had contacted a European intermediary about buying four thousand P-2 gas centrifuges, far more than needed for simple research, as well as importing magnets for the P-2s. The IAEA also questioned Iran's claims that the 36 percent enriched uranium found in Iran had come from centrifuge parts imported from Pakistan, on the grounds that the amounts found on the parts were larger than traces that would result from prior use.[37]

While the IAEA inspections continued to provide the United States and others with high-level information on past Iranian activities and present capabilities, the CIA, NSA, and other U.S. intelligence agencies continued their own quest to gather data on what Iran was doing and planning in the nuclear field. One stream of information apparently came from defecting Iranian nuclear scientists and possibly from some who remained inside the program, at least until their arrest. By April the Revolutionary Guards were "overseeing" about four hundred nuclear officials to prevent further leaks of information, such as the revelations of nuclear facilities at Arak and Natanz. In June an Iranian newspaper reported that two employees of the Atomic Energy Organization of Iran had been arrested for providing secret information to foreigners.[38]

Another potential source of human intelligence on the Iranian nuclear program—the large Iranian community in Southern California—is the target of a CIA station in Los Angeles. The station has, for years, cultivated contacts with members of that community. The agency's representatives seek information from Iranians who have traveled to Iran or communicate with relatives in the country.[39]

In early November 2004 the CIA was also the recipient of a "walk-in." Similar to the individual who provided Taiwan's intelligence service with documentary material from China's nuclear program, the new walk-in brought more than one thousand pages of material, which he claimed were actual Iranian drawings and technical documents. The subjects covered in the documentation included nuclear warhead design and modifications to Iranian ballistic missiles that would allow them to carry a nuclear warhead. In late 2004 the CIA was trying to assess whether the documents were real or simply fabrications.[40]

Beginning in April 2004, the CIA employed two types of unmanned aerial vehicles—the I-Gnat and the Predator—as part of the collection effort aimed at Iran's nuclear activities. The Predator, the more capable of the two, has a five-hundred-nautical-mile range and can carry a four-hundred-pound payload. Use of the drones allows the CIA to fly radar, electro-optical, and infrared imagery systems closer to Iranian targets to get a better view than could be obtained by satellites. At least some of the drones also carried air filters to pick up particles indicative of nuclear activity that cannot be detected from space.[41]

NRO imagery satellites at various times in 2003 and 2004 undoubtedly transmitted images of sites in Lavizan-Shian, a northeastern neighborhood of Tehran. One site had been of interest to the United States, IAEA, and other governments since at least May 2003, when the National Council of Resistance of Iran claimed that the Lavizan-Shian Technical Research Center was associated with biological weapons research. It was subsequently discovered that a radiation detection device was delivered to the site from overseas, as well as spare parts for the machine, raising the possibility that the center might be connected to the Iranian nuclear program. Then, between January and March 2004, the buildings were dismantled by the Ministry of Defense and the rubble hauled away.[42]

In November 2004 the National Council claimed that nuclear-related equipment from the demolished site had been moved to a new location in the Lavizan District—ensuring that the new location would become a target of U.S. satellites, if it wasn't already. The group charged that the Ordnance Factory Support Center at the new location had been supplanted by the Modern Defensive Readiness and Technology Center, which it described as "a major nuclear site strictly kept secret" that performs "11 kinds of activities in nuclear and biological warface."[43]

Another target for the advanced KH-11, Misty, and the Onyx radar imagery satellites to focus on in 2004 was located about twenty miles southeast of Tehran—the Parchin military complex, an enormous site owned by Iran's military industry, made up of hundreds of buildings and test sites. Its announced function is the research, development, and production of ammunition, rockets, and high explosives. Within the complex is an isolated, separately secured area that U.S. analysts believe may be involved in the research, testing, and, possibly, production of nuclear weapons.[44]

Imagery interpreters with the National Geospatial Intelligence Agency (NGA), as the National Imagery and Mapping Agency was renamed in 2003, would have even better-quality imagery to work with than the commercial imagery available to experts outside government. In the isolated area, interpreters would see some facilities more useful for armaments research or testing of rocket motors. They would also see high-explosive testing facilities that could be part of a nuclear weapons program, as well as buildings that might contain flash X-ray and fast cameras for recording the explosion.[45]

The interpreters might also conclude that nearby is a high-explosive testing bunker, which bears some resemblance to the bunker at Al Atheer in Iraq, where explosives are detonated outside and evaluated from within the bunker. Such a bunker, which is partly buried, allows the study of large explosions for assorted purposes, including nuclear weapons development, and would increase analysts' suspicion that its ultimate purpose is for a test of a full-scale mock-up of a nuclear device, with natural or depleted uranium in place of a highly enriched uranium core.[46]

Despite the resources available to the U.S. intelligence community, its understanding of the Iranian nuclear program, as of early 2005, was far from complete. At the time, the community was conducting a broad review of its Iran assessments—a review ordered by the acting chairman of the National Intelligence Council. Meanwhile, a presidential-congressional review group, the Commission on the Intelligence Capabilities of the United States Regarding Weapons of Mass Destruction, had concluded that American intelligence on Iran was inadequate to permit solid conclusions about that country's weapons programs.[47]

Some additional information was available in 2005 thanks to the Iranians and the IAEA. Starting in the last quarter of 2004, Iran's FARS news agency posted photos of several of the nation's nuclear facilities. Included were exterior, interior, and panoramic views of the Qatran Heavy Water Facility near Arak, as well as interior and exterior photos of Esfahan. In late March 2005, Tehran television reported on President Khatami's visit to the Natanz facility. The video showed the inside of buildings, corridors, maps of the site, the mouth of a tunnel, and the outside of some buildings.[48] Whether U.S. intelligence analysts were able to extract any significant new intelligence from such photos—as analysts in the 1950s were able to from Soviet photos—is not known.

Under pressure from the IAEA, the United States, and European nations, Iran's leaders agreed to a January 2005 inspection of the Parchin base, although they permitted the inspectors to visit only one of four areas that the IAEA had identified as being of interest. While there the inspectors took environmental samples, which were still being analyzed several months later. If any new information had been gleaned from those samples, it would have been a pleasant surprise to some American officials who expected the inspectors to be allowed only in areas where there was no ongoing nuclear work and where evidence of past work had been removed. Nor was much expected from the soil samples, since the Iranians "are great at removing soil," according to one American nuclear expert, who also added that "they have mastered the art of cat-and-mouse when it comes to inspections." In February, Iran rejected a request from the IAEA for a follow-up visit.[49]

As part of its interaction with the IAEA, Iran did make some admissions that either confirmed the conclusions of U.S. intelligence analysts or added to their knowledge. It admitted that as long ago as 1987 the country had discussed acquiring technologies necessary for building nuclear weapons. Of more current relevance were the admissions that Iran had converted thirty-seven tons of uranium into gas, indicating that it was in a position to rapidly begin enriching uranium, and that it had conducted small-scale experiments to create plutonium.[50]

Some seemingly reassuring news appeared during the summer of 2005, when a new national intelligence estimate—based largely on satellite imagery, communications intercepts, and the discoveries of IAEA inspectors—was issued. It did report that Iran was determined to build nuclear weapons. But it also concluded that Iran would be unlikely to produce enough highly enriched uranium for a nuclear weapon before "early to mid–next decade," with 2015 being the most likely time that Iran would have enough fissile material for a bomb. The estimate's conclusion was reported to be consistent with the revised estimates of British and Israeli intelligence analysts and more optimistic than previous estimates that Iran could accomplish the task within five years. Whether that estimate proves to be accurate, or is simply the consequence of a lack of good information about the Iranian program and an overreaction to the recent overestimate of Iraq's nuclear efforts in 2003, remains to be seen.[51]

NORTH KOREA'S AGREEMENT in December 1991 that the Korean peninsula should be free of nuclear weapons was followed, in January 1992, by its signing in Vienna a safeguards agreement with the IAEA. The agreement required North Korea to report all nuclear programs to the agency as well as gave the IAEA the authority to conduct a variety of inspections of North Korean nuclear installations and programs. There was, however, a catch. Chang Mun Son of the nation's foreign affairs ministry explained that "we need time to have this ratified" in the national legislature and the process could take as much as six months.[52]

Not surprisingly, within a month "Great Leader" Kim Il Sung was making statements that questioned whether the United States had truly removed all nuclear weapons from the Korean peninsula, and demanding the withdrawal of "foreign forces" from South Korea. He also asserted that "it is unimaginable for us to develop nuclear weapons that can wipe out the Korean people. No one can possibly question this." That month Kim's subordinates rejected the South's pleas to move ahead with the implementation of the denuclearization agreement through the joint inspection of each other's nuclear facilities.[53]

Kim did allow the IAEA to conduct six inspections between June 1992 and February 1993. In April the atomic energy ministry announced that the IAEA would be permitted to visit three reactors in various stages of construction or operation. Two of the reactors were at Yongbyon: a 30-megawatt plant under construction and a 5-megawatt facility that opened in 1986. The third was the 200-megawatt reactor under construction at Taechon, sixty miles north of Pyongyang. In May 1992, North Korea handed over to the IAEA a document, about a hundred pages long and over an inch thick, on its nuclear facilities and activities, a document that included the surprise disclosure that North Korea had produced a small amount of plutonium.[54]

Later that month IAEA director Hans Blix arrived in the Hermit Kingdom for a preinspection visit. Two weeks before his visit the nation's deputy prime minister, Kim Dal Hyon, claimed, "We have no plutonium reprocessing facility." Yet Blix was taken to a partially completed six-story-tall, 600-foot-long industrial facility that was to be used for just that purpose. The North Koreans described it as "Radiochemical Laboratory," but at a Beijing press conference, shortly after the visit, Blix said, "If it were in operation and complete, then it would certainly in our terminology be called a reprocessing plant."[55]

The IAEA chief also told the press that construction of the reprocessing facility was 8 percent complete, that 40 percent of the equipment had been installed, and that there "were several pieces [of equipment] missing," which raised the possibility that some equipment had been removed to prevent discovery that the facility was actually in operation. He was also taken to two underground shelters near the Yongbyon research reactor, which he described as "large cavities under the hill" and appeared to be empty. His team also found electric power distribution grids outside two large nuclear power plants, indicating that the plants would be used to generate power. Such power lines were not evident on previous satellite photos.[56]

But then, during the initial inspections in the summer of 1992, the IAEA gathered samples of material caught during various stages of reprocessing as well as different varieties of nuclear waste produced during the reprocessing stages. After analysis of the samples in laboratories in Vienna as well as at the Air Force Technical Applications Center's McClellan Laboratory in California, the inspectors concluded that North Korea not only had separated plutonium in March 1990 from damaged fuel rods, as it claimed, but had done so on several different occasions and from different sources. As a result most inspectors concluded that the North had reprocessed more plutonium than the eighty grams it had admitted to the agency.[57]

In February 1993 the IAEA invoked a provision in the safeguards agreement that allowed it to call a "special inspection" of two concealed but apparent waste sites at Yongbyon, whose wastes were believed to contain telltale evidence of undeclared plutonium production. North Korea turned down requests from the IAEA to visit the sites, on the grounds that they were exempt nonmilitary facilities. The IAEA board of governors gave North Korea until March 25 to agree to the special inspections. Rather than open the door to more embarrassing discoveries, North Korea first turned down the IAEA request and then turned its back on the nonproliferation treaty, announcing its intention to withdraw on March 12, 1993, effective on June 12. Kim suspended the threat when the Clinton administration agreed to a high-level meeting in June.[58]

Kim's suspension of the threat did not mean a suspension of problems in dealing with his regime. On April 8 the North Koreans shut down the small, 5-megawatt reactor, in preparation for unloading the core in early May. Blix and his inspectors wanted to view that unloading to guarantee that none of the spent fuel was diverted to produce weapons-grade plutonium. They wanted to set aside a few hundred of the thousands of fuel rods, from a variety of locations in the core, for inspection, which would allow them to verify North Korea's claim that the original core fuel had remained in the reactor, rather than having been removed for reprocessing. But despite their plea, the North started unloading the reactor without the requested safeguard measures.[59]

While the North did allow the inspectors to view the unloading, it refused to permit them to select and store any fuel rods for subsequent testing. In

Pyongyang, in May, the North offered to let the inspectors sample the rods after they were placed in the nearby spent fuel ponds. Since the inspectors would be unable to to determine what part of the core the rods had come from, they refused. "Without such identification," according to the agency, "future measurements would be meaningless and the agency's ability to verify non-diversion would be lost." In a May 27 letter to UN Security Council members, Blix reported that the "fuel discharge rate at the reactor was proceeding at a very fast rate." By June 2 the IAEA chief concluded it was too late for a systematic sampling of the fuel rods, which "seriously eroded" the agency's ability to verify that diversion had not taken place.[60]

THROUGHOUT THE TWO YEARS since Blix's May visit to North Korea until his exasperated letter of June 1994, the U.S. intelligence community was trying to learn as much as possible about the North's nuclear program. Some of what it discovered was a result of the inspectors' visits, which were, on occasion, assisted by intelligence provided by the United States. A key asset in tracking North Korean nuclear activities was America's fleet of reconnaissance satellites. At the time that Blix arrived in May 1992, the NRO's imagery constellation consisted of two Crystal (KH-11) birds, one advanced Crystal, two Onyx radar imagery satellites, and one Misty stealth satellite.

Satellite images obtained in early February 1992 showed construction of deep tunnels in the vicinity of the Yongbyon center, which appeared to be part of an effort to harden the facility against any attack by U.S. or South Korean forces and possibly part of a program to hide nuclear weapons components from IAEA inspectors. At about the same time, the United States detected, apparently via satellites, North Korea moving equipment away "from a highly restricted facility associated with the clandestine production of nuclear weapons," the plutonium-reprocessing facility at Yongbyon.[61]

Sometime not long before Blix's visit, one or more of those satellites detected activity at the site of the North's newest reactor: Workmen began demolishing freshly built walls and rerouting newly laid pipes so they were able to quickly install electric turbines in a new room. When they were through, they had grafted onto the completed reactor some power-generating equipment in what U.S. officials considered a clumsy attempt to create the impression that the reactor was intended to produce electricity—a ruse that initially worked during Blix's May 1992 visit.[62]

At the time, the CIA, although it had provided satellite imagery of the North Korean site to IAEA experts since 1976, also held much back, probably including imagery from newer systems. But after the IAEA discovered discrepancies in the North Korean claims of having conducted minimal reprocessing, the CIA became more forthcoming. In late 1992 the agency informed the

IAEA that satellite reconnaissance had shown North Korean workers hurriedly constructing a new storage site for nuclear wastes directly across from the storage site completed in 1976. Days before the inspectors arrived in the fall, an NRO satellite transmitted an image showing the old site being concealed under dirt and dozens of newly planted trees and shrubs, in an apparent attempt to fool the inspectors into taking their samples from the new facility while hiding the existence of the old waste site. A later image revealed that most of the trees died after the inspectors departed.[63]

The agency also told the nuclear inspectors that U.S. satellites had obtained images of North Korean workers digging trenches in the frozen ground through the winter of 1991 near one of the two suspected waste storage facilities. The apparent objective was to bury pipes between the two facilities and hide their connection from the IAEA's inspectors.[64]

Imagery of the two waste sites, obtained in 1992, became the focus of the IAEA's governing board in February 1993, as they seemed to indicate yet another attempt at deception by the North. The images revealed two sites near the reprocessing facility large enough to hold substantial quantities of liquid and solid nuclear waste. One set of images showed an outdoor waste site believed to be associated with the Soviet-supplied IRT reactor that had been under IAEA safeguards since 1977. In the first images, the facility's layout resembles waste sites near other research reactors supplied by the Soviet Union, including one near a Soviet-supplied reactor in Iraq. Adding to U.S. suspicion, subsequent images showed a site that had been covered and landscaped in an effort to hide it from inspectors on the ground and satellites in space.[65]

The second covert waste site, known to the CIA as "Building 500," was about 490 feet east of the reprocessing facility, and separated from it by a small hill was a building about 165 feet long that could be connected to the reprocessing facility by underground pipes. The first images showed a two-story building with two trenches connecting it to the reprocessing facility. Later images show only the top floor because a slab of concrete had been placed to conceal the lower floor, while the trenches do not appear in the later images because they were filled in. The photos also showed that dirt had been pushed around the facility's lower level in an additional attempt at concealment. When the inspectors arrived in September 1992, North Korean officials told them that there was nothing underneath the warehouse.[66]

After the secret images were shown to Blix and his inspectors, the IAEA chief followed up with an informal request to the North Koreans to allow an IAEA team to drill and take samples at one of the suspected waste sites. When the North refused, Blix asked Washington to allow the images to be displayed at the special IAEA meeting in February. His proposal was supported by the State Department, with undersecretary of state Arnold L. Kanter arguing that "it behooved us to share the photographs" because the United States had been "leading the charge" concerning suspected nuclear waste sites. Not surprisingly, it ran into initial opposition from mid-level CIA analysts. But they were overruled by director of central intelligence Robert Gates.[67]

When Gates and Kantner left office, at the end of the Bush administration, CIA analysts mounted another effort to kill the plan by providing what were, according to one official, "wholly inadequate" images of the sites, deliberately degraded to hide the satellite capabilities. In the end, the Clinton administration concluded that the failure to provide adequate imagery might impede the IAEA's ability to press the North to be more open about its nuclear activities; however, it did allow the imagery to be slightly fuzzed by computer technology.[68]

On February 22, 1993, representatives from the thirty-five member states of the IAEA Board of Governors met in closed session in Vienna. Included were delegates from Libya, Algeria, and Syria—all of whose weapons of mass destruction programs were targets of the same satellites that produced the images of North Korea. The board members examined a series of grainy black-and-white images that showed a storage facility under construction as well as what appeared to be an older facility at Yongbyon being covered with dirt and later with trees and shrubs planted on top. The message sent by the images was that North Korea had buried nuclear waste under a camouflaged mound and constructed a newer facility to serve as a decoy.[69]

After the presentation Ho Jin Yun, the North's senior representative at the IAEA meeting, denounced the images as fakes and accused Blix of illegal actions and using intelligence information provided by a "third power." The board was not influenced by the outburst and immediately approved a tough resolution demanding that North Korea permit inspections, "without delay," of the waste storage sites.[70]

North Korea refused, making the images that the NRO's satellites continued to send back even more important. In the fall of 1993 one or more of those satellites detected the delivery of chemical reagents to the Yongbyon complex, indicating continued reprocessing activity.[71]

THE INTELLIGENCE GATHERED by satellites and other means became, along with basic nuclear science and conclusions about the North Korean regime's priorities, the basis for the intelligence community's estimates, during 1992, 1993, and the first half of 1994, about Pyongyang's nuclear capabilities and intentions.

In late February 1992 central intelligence chief Robert Gates told the House Foreign Affairs Committee, in open session, that his analysts believed North Korea was hiding parts of its nuclear weapons program despite its pledge of denuclearization and openness to inspections. "We have some information that I can't go into here in this setting," he said, "that suggests that they have a deception plan for hiding their nuclear capabilities." Later, he told his audience that there were "grounds for questioning the North's sincerity, given that it has not even admitted the existence of, much less declared the pluto-nium production reactors and a reprocessing center at the Yongbyon nuclear research center." When asked how long it would take for Kim's scientists to build an actual nuclear bomb, he replied, "We think a few months to as much as a couple of years"—an estimate based on the possibility that North Korea had produced enough fissionable material to make at least one bomb.[72]

There was at least one dissenting view in the intelligence community to Gates's harsh assessment: the State Department's Bureau of Intelligence and Research. Its director, Toby Gati, characterized Gates's statement as an "absolutely worst case analysis." The INR and others in the State Depart-ment believed that there was insufficient hard evidence to make that predic-tion and that North Korea, owing to its limited industrial capability, would require two years or more to build a bomb. An administration official sug-gested the two conclusions were, at least in part, a matter not of differing interpretations of evidence but different perspectives. "The C.I.A. has to be absolutely certain that if anything bad happens they predicted it first, so that it cannot be accused of a repeat of what happened in Iraq," the official said. On the other hand, the "State Department is responsible for solving the problem diplomatically, and the natural inclination is to say that there is still sufficient time to solve this problem."[73]

Throughout 1993 the intelligence community as a whole continued to take a more pessimistic view than the State Department. Early in 1993, dur-ing his last days as DCI, Gates said that despite eight months of IAEA inspec-tions the limited access of the inspectors as well as "disturbing evidence of continuing efforts to deceive"—apparently a reference to efforts to hide radioactive waste products from the Yongbyon reactors—had left important unresolved questions. Gates also said that "we don't know" whether North Korea had made a decision to end its nuclear weapons program "and we will just have to keep monitoring it very, very closely."[74]

Gates's replacement as the nation's intelligence chief was James Woolsey. Shortly after taking office, he too told Congress that North Korea might have enough plutonium for a nuclear weapon. He would repeat that judgment in late November, reporting that U.S. intelligence agencies had believed "for some time" that North Korea "could have enough nuclear material for a weapon and perhaps two." He went on to explain that the assessment was based on the nature of the Yongbyon facility and the plant's schedule for plu-tonium reprocessing, adding that "we're not saying that they do have a weapon designed and assembled, but it is a possibility."[75]

That month the U.S. intelligence community produced two new estimates concerning North Korea and its nuclear program. The first, a special national intelligence estimate, warned that without inspections of key North Korean nuclear facilities, it might be impossible to discover how much plutonium had been produced, but that administration efforts to obtain Pyongyang's approval for inspections were likely to fail.[76]

The majority view of the agencies preparing the estimate, which was also the view of the CIA, was that while the North Koreans might be convinced to accept new inspections of the civilian reactor containing spent fuel laden with plutonium and the reprocessing facility at Yongbyon, they would not permit inspections of the two nuclear waste sites believed to contain evidence of how much plutonium had been produced. A strong dissent came from the INR, which continued to believe that North Korea might eventually permit inspections. Another dissent, but in the opposite direction, came from the Defense Intelligence Agency, whose analysts had concluded that Kim's regime was using the ongoing negotiations over inspections to buy time while continuing weapons development.[77]

The second estimate, a national intelligence estimate, restated what Gates and Woolsey had said earlier in the year. It informed President Clinton, who had pledged that "North Korea cannot be allowed to develop a bomb," that there was more than a 50 percent chance that the country might already possess a very small nuclear arsenal, consisting of one or two bombs—which would be consistent with the study's estimate that North Korea could have extracted as much as twenty-six pounds of plutonium, enough for two bombs under optimum conditions, when it shut down its reactor for seventy days in 1989. "What the intelligence community is saying is that the horse is already out of the barn," one official observed. "It's too late."[78]

Not only did the report describe as "better than even" the chance that North Korea already had a nuclear bomb, but it also suggested there was little prospect that diplomatic or economic sanctions would get Pyongyang to give up its arsenal. The North, according to the estimate, had invested significant amounts of its scarce cash to produce plutonium, develop the high-explosive trigger required for a nuclear explosion, and build a medium-range missile that could hit Japan. Further, it said that sanctions might only result in a North Korean attack on the South.[79]

Given the difficulty in monitoring the North Korean program, there was, not surprisingly, no conclusive proof that North Korea had even one nuclear weapon. While the United States had detected craters near Yongbyon consistent with experiments with the conventional explosives required to detonate a nuclear bomb, no specific satellite image, communications intercept, or agent report provided confirmation of the community's majority view. It was therefore possible to challenge the majority view, and the State Department's INR did just that. It argued that the quantity of plutonium North Korea could have obtained from reprocessing was likely to be less than the amount required for a single bomb, owing to North Korea's poor equipment for extracting fuel rods.[80]

Critics of the INR's view claimed that the bureau had consistently underestimated North Korea's nuclear abilities, including disputing the existence of a North Korean plutonium-reprocessing plant. Further, the critics maintained, the INR had accepted North Korea's assertion that the giant building at Yongbyon was, as Israel had claimed about Dimona, a textile factory—specifically, that it was the home to a production line for vinalon, the synthetic fiber that former nuclear program chief Lee Sung Ki developed. At the same time, some State Department officials believed the other intelligence agencies were producing a worst-case analysis to protect themselves from subsequent accusations of failing to provide proper warning.[81]

ON JUNE 16, 1994, North Korea, in defiance of U.S. warnings, unloaded the fuel rods from its 5-megawatt reactor. The prospect that the North might plan on extracting the plutonium in those rods and turning it into fissile material for one or more bombs meant that Washington faced a crisis. The Clinton administration responded by moving toward the imposition of sanctions and reviewing its decision to send significant military reinforcements to South Korea.[82]

That month Kim Il Sung reissued a long-standing invitation to former President Jimmy Carter to visit North Korea. When Carter arrived, Kim told him that he was willing to free his regime of its nuclear activities and operations. Kim's action apparently followed word from China that the Chinese would not veto a first round of economic sanctions, which the Clinton administration had proposed to UN Security Council members. In response, the U.S. dropped its sanctions proposal and began a new round of high-level negotiations with Pyongyang.[83]

At the time of Carter's visit, there was talk in Washington of not only sanctions but also drastic military action. Attacking the Yongbyon complex to halt reprocessing activity was a matter of public discussion. It was also a matter of discussion at the highest levels of the Clinton administration, and contingency plans were developed to strike Yongbyon if North Korea tried to turn the reactor fuel into bombs.* Just as John Kennedy and his advisers had considered eliminating China's nascent nuclear capability in the early 1960s, Bill

---

* The Defense Department had been studying the requirements for an attack on the Yongbyon facility for a considerable period of time. It examined options ranging from attacks with cruise missiles to commando raids. See Joel S. Wit, Daniel B. Poneman, and Robert L. Gallucci, *Going Critical: The First North Korean Nuclear Crisis* (Washington, D.C.: Brookings, 2004), p. 103.

Clinton and his advisers pondered whether their only option was an air strike on the North Korean nuclear center—even though a bloody war might well follow. According to the North's foreign minister, Kim Yong Nam, economic sanctions alone would "bring devastating consequences."[84]

But the high-level negotiations, led by Robert Gallucci, resulted in the agreed framework of October 21, 1994, a deal in which the United States would provide North Korea with a combination of nuclear, energy, economic, and diplomatic benefits in exchange for a halt in its threatening nuclear activities. North Korea agreed to "freeze its graphite-moderated reactors and related facilities," with the freeze being monitored by the IAEA. The framework also obliged the North to store eight thousand fuel rods removed from the 5-megawatt reactor in May 1994, "in a safe manner that does not involve reprocessing in the [North]" and called for talks on their ultimate disposition. In addition, the North Koreans were to implement the 1991 denuclearization agreement with the South. Clinton administration officials reportedly said that a confidential minute to the agreed framework forbade Pyongyang from building new nuclear facilities elsewhere in the country.[85]

The payoff to the North for freezing its nuclear program was to include two light-water reactors, with the United States organizing an international consortium for financing them. The Clinton administration, South Korea, and Japan would establish a Korean Peninsula Energy Development Corporation (KEDO) to coordinate provision of the reactors. Prior to completion of the light-water reactors, the framework required the United States to facilitate the provision, at no cost, of alternative energy—heavy oil—as compensation for freezing the nuclear program. When new reactors were completed, the North was to dismantle the ones that had been frozen under the framework. North Korea, in addition, reaffirmed its commitment to the 1991 denuclearization declaration as well as the nonproliferation treaty. The United States and North Korea were also, under the agreement's terms, to open liaison offices in Pyongyang and Washington and establish full diplomatic relations if the two governments made progress on "issues of concern to each side." In addition, the framework required that three months after its signing both sides would reduce barriers to trade and investment.[86]

What would happen subsequent to the agreement had been a matter of dispute in the U.S. intelligence community that summer. Many analysts believed that North Korea had no real intention of negotiating away its nuclear program. DIA experts thought that Pyongyang would operate a covert nuclear program regardless of what agreements it signed. On the other hand, INR was somewhat optimistic, arguing that the North wanted a deal that would lead to better relations with the United States.[87]

BY THE TIME the accord was signed, North Korea had a new ruler. On July 7 Kim Il Sung was in his villa in the Myohyang Mountains, about a hundred miles north of Pyongyang, when he collapsed with a massive heart attack and died at two o'clock the following morning. Well before his death Kim had designated a successor, his son Kim Jong Il—the "plump, bespectacled, moon-faced man" who had been designated as the country's "Dear Leader."[88]

Born in February 1942 in the Russian Far East and, until high school, known by his Russian name, Yuri, Kim graduated from Kim Il Sung University in 1964 and then went to work with the Workers Party central committee, where films, theater, and the arts were his special responsibility. At the October 1980 party congress, he was simultaneously awarded senior positions in the Politburo, the Military Commission, and the Party Secretariat as well as being designated his father's successor. In December 1991 he was named supreme commander of the People's Army.[89]

One author characterized Kim Il Sung and his son as being, in many respects, a "study in contrasts." While Kim Il Sung was a guerrilla fighter, the founder of the North Korean state, and an outgoing and outspoken individual, his son never served as a soldier for even a day, was excessively reclusive, and appeared uncomfortable in the midst of a roaring crowd.[90] At the same time, given Kim Jong Il's position of absolute authority, with his father as a role model, and past North Korean behavior as a guide, the chances were good that the signing of the agreed framework would be no more than a temporary respite from concern over North Korean nuclear activities.

The agreed framework had included a U.S. pledge to make the "best efforts" to produce a contract supplying the new reactors within six months after the accord's signing—by April 21, 1995. As that date approached, negotiations were stalled on the origin and name of the reactors, because North Korea wanted no open acknowledgment that South Korea would be furnishing them. The North threatened to abandon the agreement by reloading the 5-megawatt reactor at Yongbyon while the South insisted that Pyongyang acknowledge the origin of the reactors. Ultimately, Washington was able to find a description that satisfied both Pyongyang and Seoul, one that applied only to the South Korean reactors without explicitly naming their country of origin.[91]

A new crisis having been avoided, the U.S. intelligence community continued to gather whatever information it could, from whatever sources it could, about North Korean nuclear activities. While the intelligence community was used to receiving help from its friends, particularly Britain and Australia, aid from the Russian Foreign Intelligence Service, the SVR, the successor to the Soviet KGB's foreign intelligence directorate, was relatively new. In the early 1990s and extending to sometime after the agreed framework was signed, the SVR operated nuclear monitoring equipment, provided by the CIA, in its Pyongyang embassy, and possibly other locations in the country. "We have tried to get information every which way we can," remarked one individual familiar with U.S. intelligence operations.[92]

The CIA-supplied equipment was intended to detect emissions of krypton-85, to help analysts determine if reprocessing was underway at Yongbyon. "Krypton is a very good technical indicator that is hard to hide," one person familiar with the program noted, adding that "if you are able to situate the sniffers in the right places, then you could have confidence that you can find out whether plutonium reprocessing is going on or not."[93]

In early 1997 the U.S. intelligence community received information from another source it wasn't counting on. Hwang Jang Yop, one of the North's most senior officials and the architect of its self-reliance (*juche*) philosophy, defected while in Beijing by walking into the South Korean consulate and asking for safe transit to Seoul. The seventy-four-year-old former philosophy student at Moscow University and confidant of Kim Il Sung had become an advocate of reform, including Chinese-style market reforms, and as a result, a subject of surveillance and criticism.[94]

None of his past positions—speaker of the Supreme People's Assembly, secretary of international affairs for the Workers Party, and chairman of the Foreign Affairs Committee of the rubber-stamp parliament—were likely to have given him access to North Korea's closely held nuclear secrets. And when he was debriefed after his arrival in Seoul, undoubtedly by both CIA and South Korean representatives, it became apparent that his knowledge of military matters was less extensive than that of propaganda activities. But he did tell his debriefers that not only did North Korea possess nuclear weapons but she had planned an underground test, which was only canceled after a warning from the foreign ministry.[95]

Hwang's claims gave the U.S. intelligence community yet another task: to find an underground test site in North Korea, a country well trained in tunneling and hiding those activities from the NRO's spy satellites. The effort apparently failed, possibly because such a site never existed and Hwang was yet another defector with a tale of an imaginary underground facility. But U.S. satellites did find something suspicious, and perhaps nuclear, in 1997 or 1998.[96]

Possibly by the end of 1997, and certainly by the summer of 1998, U.S. imagery satellites detected activity at a site known as Kumchang-ri, twenty-five miles northeast of Yongbyon. The imagery showed a massive tunneling and digging operation for a huge underground complex, involving about fifteen thousand workers "swarming around the new site, burrowing into the mountainside." The immediate fear among U.S. officials was that the North was building either a nuclear reactor or reprocessing plant under the mountain, an effort intelligence analysts estimated would take between two and six years, depending on the extent of foreign assistance. "There is a volume of activity that certainly suggests that kind of activity," an administration official told the *Washington Post*, adding that "we have deep concerns about this."[97]

The fear created by the images was reinforced by other intelligence, probably either communications intelligence or human intelligence. One American official characterized it as "a very, very serious development to say nothing of incredibly stupid, because it endangers the nuclear accord and humanitarian aid." Some U.S. officials speculated that with Kim Jong Il about to receive all the titles that had been held by his father, he was trying to placate his "right wing." Others raised another possibility, that Kim was creating another bargaining chip.[98]

By early 1999, despite what were undoubtedly substantial efforts, the U.S. intelligence community had not been able to determine exactly what the North Koreans were doing. White House national security adviser Sandy Berger told reporters at a breakfast meeting that "under paragraph four of the agreed framework the North Koreans agreed not to build other graphite reactors and we need to satisfy ourselves that that is not happening." The activity at Kumchang-ri "gives us concerns and raises suspicions," he told his audience.[99]

It was one more issue among a host of issues—including North Korea's ballistic missile program, its involvement in a number of criminal enterprises, its failure to permit full inspections of its nuclear facilities as promised under the agreed framework—which, when added to the nation's desperate economic situation, threatened to produce a second Korean war. Pyongyang repeatedly denied that the site had a nuclear purpose, although it acknowledged that it was intended for "a sensitive military purpose."[100]

Finally, after prolonged negotiations, which began in August 1998 and included a North Korean demand for a $300 million one-time inspection fee, a U.S. threat to terminate the agreed framework, and a U.S. promise of additional food aid, an American inspection team was given permission to take a look under the mountain. The fourteen-person team began its visit to the site on May 20, 1999, and concluded on the evening of May 22. Repeated satellite monitoring of the facility between May 6 and May 12 revealed continued construction along with increased vehicle traffic and personnel activity, although not the removal of any large equipment. When the team showed up, there was only an extensive underground tunnel complex for the members to see—no workers, no construction activity, no equipment.[101]

At the end of June State Department spokesman Jamie Rubin issued a statement based on the analysis of the observations and data collected at the underground facility. The statement reported that "there was no indication that equipment was ever installed at this location." In addition, Rubin stated the obvious—that the Kumchang-ri site did not contain a plutonium production reactor or reprocessing plant—and more: The size and configuration of the underground area was unsuitable for a plutonium production reactor, especially a graphite-moderated reactor similar to the one at Yongbyon. Nor was the site well designed for a reprocessing plant, although the site, with substantial modifications, could support such a facility. Finally, the United States could not rule out the possibility that the underground facility was intended for another nuclear-related purpose, "although it does not appear to be currently configured to support any large industrial nuclear functions." A follow-up visit in 2000 found conditions remained the same.[102]

THE FOLLOWING YEAR brought the end of the Clinton administration and the start of George W. Bush's presidency. There was also a subtle change in the intelligence community's description of North Korea's nuclear weapons capability. In a speech in August 2001 to a conference at Texas A&M University, deputy director of central intelligence John McLaughlin went beyond stating that the community's analysts believed North Korea had reprocessed sufficient plutonium for one or two bombs. Instead he told his audience that "the North probably has one or two nuclear bombs." By the summer of 2003 the intelligence community would also conclude that the North "has validated the designs without conducting yield-producing nuclear tests."[103] Concern over the North Korean nuclear effort increased in 2001 for yet another reason.

One large industrial nuclear function not mentioned in Rubin's statement is uranium enrichment. Whether Kumchang-ri was intended for such a purpose is not clear, but by 1999 there were concerns in the U.S. intelligence community and Clinton administration that the North would seek to expand whatever nuclear arsenal it already had by pursuing the harder-to-detect uranium enrichment path to the bomb. Early that year, director of central intelligence George Tenet told a Senate committee that the intelligence community was "deeply concerned" about a "covert" nuclear weapons program in violation of the 1994 agreement.[104]

In March 1999 a report from the Department of Energy's intelligence office stated that the North Korean Daesong Yushin Trading Company had recently ordered two frequency converters, which can provide a special electrical current to gas centrifuges, from a Japanese firm. The attempt to acquire that was a clear sign, according to the Energy Department analysis, that the North "is in the early stages of a uranium enrichment capability"—with a small-scale program as a precursor to a large one. "On the basis Pakistan's progress with a similar technique, we estimate that the DPRK [Democratic People's Republic of Korea] is at least six years from the production of [highly enriched uranium], even if it has a viable centrifuge design," the report continued. "On the other hand, with significant technical support from other countries, such as Pakistan, the time frame would be decreased by several years." The report suggested that given their close ties in missile development, support from Pakistan was likely.[105]

The "shards of evidence" of a North Korean–Pakistani nuclear relationship going back to 1997 turned into "pretty clear suspicions by 1998," according to a senior Bush administration official. It was during those years that Kim Jong Il and his generals decided to pursue uranium enrichment. By the summer of 2002 the United States had acquired "clear evidence" that pointed to a North Korean uranium enrichment program, which the intelligence community believed had started about two years earlier. In 2001 the North began seeking centrifuge-related materials in large quantities, including high-strength aluminum used in uranium enrichment. It also obtained equipment that could be used for uranium feed and withdrawal systems. In addition, recent satellite imagery showed major construction activity that appeared to be for an enrichment facility, apparently at another suspected underground installation, possibly one at Hagap in Changang province. The intelligence community concluded that the facility could produce enough weapons-grade uranium for two or more nuclear weapons a year when it became fully operational, possibly as soon as the middle of the decade.[106]

In November 2001 Z Division completed a highly classified report which concluded that North Korea had begun building a uranium enrichment plant. It also claimed that Pakistani scientists were the source of instructions on how uranium is enriched. By May 2002 more intelligence led Vice President Cheney, among others, to push the National Intelligence Council to produce a national intelligence estimate on whether a uranium enrichment facility was actually under construction. When it was completed in June, the estimate was adamant that the North had moved on from research and development to actual purchases of materials to construct a gas centrifuge facility. The estimate also, a U.S. intelligence official told author Seymour Hersh, "points a clear finger at the Pakistanis. The technical stuff is crystal clear—not hedged and not ambivalent."[107]

As a result, assistant secretary of state James Kelly arrived in Pyongyang in early October and confronted the North Koreans with U.S. knowledge of their secret program. The North Koreans did what had become traditional: they lied, calling the allegations "fabrications." But overnight they had a change of heart, and the next day vice foreign minister Kang Sok-ju, a senior official in the regime, acknowledged the existence of the program. However, there was no apology, and Kang was "assertive, aggressive about it," according to a U.S. official. He did offer a proposal for yet another round of negotiations—this time a bilateral nonaggression pact and an agreement by the United States to cease "stifling" North Korea's economy. Some experts believed that the proposal for a nonaggression pact was a stalking horse for the North's long-standing proposal of a bilateral peace treaty between the United States and the North.[108]

In response to North Korea's refusal to halt the enrichment program, the Bush administration decided to void the agreed framework, and persuaded the Korean Peninsula Development Organization to suspend heavy-oil shipments. The North's counter response to the halt in oil shipments, as well as the "pre-emptive nuclear attack" it claimed Washington was preparing, was to announce in December 2002 that it would restart the 5-megawatt reactor, resume construction of two larger reactors that had been frozen under the agreement, and resume operations at the plutonium-reprocessing plant. Toward the end of the month North Korean officials disabled IAEA cameras and began breaking agency seals around the reprocessing plant. The North also began moving fresh fuel rods into the reactor in preparation for restoring it to operational status. On December 28 Pyongyang announced it would expel all of the IAEA's inspectors who had remained on site since 1994, leading one Korea expert to state, "If they kick out the inspectors the world has absolutely no eyes—no cameras, no inspections."[109]

By the middle of that month the U.S. intelligence community had determined that North Korea had purchased and received twenty tons of tributyl phosphate from China. While the substance can be used in making plastics, ink, and paint, it can be employed in plutonium reprocessing too. U.S. intelligence agencies had also detected, undoubtedly through satellite reconnaissance, activity at Yongbyon.[110]

Then in January 2003 the North withdrew from the nonproliferation treaty, and the United States issued a communiqué, also signed by Japan and South Korea, which stated that "the United States is willing to talk to North Korea about how it will meet its obligations to the international community," but that "the United States will not provide quid pro quos to North Korea to live up to its obligations."[111]

While North Koreans on the ground were making pronouncements about what they were doing at Yongbyon, U.S. eyes in space continued watching developments there and elsewhere in the Hermit Kingdom, to try to determine what was actually happening. In January the NRO's mechanical spies had detected signs that North Korea might be removing spent fuel rods from storage, the first step in a process that would take only months and result in an expansion of North Korea's nuclear arsenal. The images sent back during January showed extensive activity at the nuclear research center, including trucks pulling up to the building housing the storage pond where the rods had been kept since 1994. What the satellites could not see was exactly what the North Koreans were putting in the trucks.[112]

Analysts believed that it was probable, but not certain, the trucks were there to move the fuel rods into the "Radiochemistry Laboratory" to extract weapons-grade plutonium. "There's still a debate about what exactly we are seeing and how provocative it is," one senior U.S. official noted, adding that "the North Koreans made no real effort to hide this from us." One possibility was that the North was moving the fuel rods so that they wouldn't be a target for a bombing raid. If the satellites were seeing the first steps in reprocessing and the production of new bombs, it would be a "fateful step," former Clinton administration counterproliferation official Robert Einhorn observed.[113]

In late February spy satellites were showing a constant level of activity around the reprocessing plant. On February 26 they transmitted images of a plume of steam coming from the 5-megawatt reactor at Yongbyon, allowing CIA chief George Tenet to alert the White House that the North Koreans had restarted the reactor. But the North appeared to have trouble with the reprocessing facility, despite the extensive activity detected around the site. There was no detection of the brownish plume that would indicate reprocessing. "They are working 24/7," a senior administration official said, "but it is not going as fast as they wanted to." According to the official, steam had been seen intermittently coming out of the power plant next to the six-story reprocessing plant. "They are definitely trying hard," he added.[114]

The next month, during talks in Beijing with the United States and other nations, representatives of Kim's government claimed that the North possessed nuclear weapons and that it had nearly finished reprocessing the spent nuclear fuel into weapons-grade plutonium. Pyongyang threatened to conduct a nuclear test and, far worse, to "export" nuclear materials—leaving it to the imagination of U.S. representatives who the "importers" might be. The North then asked to be bought off, with a combination of oil shipments, food aid, security guarantees, energy assistance, economic benefits, and construction of light-water reactors.[115]

The United States was unable to determine if the North Korean claims had any validity—aerial missions were flown to try to detect krypton-85, but failed to do so. "We have seen lights on and people [at the reprocessing facility] but we don't know what is going on inside," one official remarked. Secretary of state Colin Powell would tell a Senate committee on April 30 that "we can't establish as matter of fact with our intelligence community, but they say they did."[116]

In the light of North Korea's claims that it had completed reprocessing of eight thousand fuel rods, which would provide enough plutonium for five or six weapons, White House officials ordered the intelligence community to conduct a thorough review of whether North Korea could produce weapons-grade plutonium without detection. "We think they are bluffing," a senior administration official said, but "we felt the need to go back and review every possibility, in the off chance that we missed something."[117]

In early May satellite reconnaissance showed signs of renewed activity around the Yongbyon reactor and reprocessing facility, including smoke emanating from it, but that didn't allow the conclusion that it was in opera-tion. "It's fair to say that the experts have come to no hard conclusions," White House spokesman Ari Fleischer told reporters. And one senior intelli-gence official told the New York Times, "We don't have confirmation that they are reprocessing on a large scale." Small-scale production was a real pos-sibility, however.[118]

With efforts to detect krypton-85 coming up empty, the lack of confirma-tion continued into July. "We don't believe that the main reprocessing facility has been very active," a senior administration official said at the time. NRO imagery satellites had detected an advanced nuclear testing site in Youngdok-tong, where equipment had been set up to test conventional explosives that, when detonated, could implode a plutonium core and set off a nuclear explo-sion. The implication of the images to some intelligence officials was that North Korea was planning on manufacturing more sophisticated weapons that could be carried atop its medium- and long-range missiles.[119]

At the beginning of July one administration official asked, "Could there be a second reprocessor?" and acknowledged that "no one knows for sure." Then, new evidence that North Korea might, indeed, have a second secret reprocessing plant arrived—just eleven days after Pyongyang claimed that it had completed reprocessing the eight thousand fuel rods—in the form of ele-vated levels of krypton-85 being detected by airborne sensors flown near North Korea's borders. One senior administration official characterized the intelli-gence as "very worrisome, but still not conclusive." Reportedly, computer analyses that tracked the gases as they were blown across the Korean peninsula appeared to rule out the possibility that they originated from Yongbyon. Rather, the analyses suggested the existence of a second plant, perhaps buried in a mountain—which was consistent with information from an agent of the South Korean National Intelligence Service, who also reported the existence of a second plant. But a subsequent report showed that the gas had come from Yongbyon, indicating reprocessing activity at that site.[120]

More confusion about the North's nuclear activities followed in Septem-ber, when U.S. monitoring suggested that operations at Yongbyon had been halted—whether due to a technical problem or a "goodwill gesture" by Kim was a question satellite intelligence could not answer. Then early the next month, the North claimed to be producing plutonium bombs, which led Sec-retary of State Powell to note, "This is the third time they have told us they'd just finished reprocessing the rods. We have no evidence to confirm that."[121]

TO ADD TO the confusion, late in 2003, the North Koreans retracted their confession to James Kelly, claiming that they had no uranium enrichment program. It was a plea of innocence they would repeat into 2004. At the same time, the United States had a golden opportunity to gather some on-the-ground intelligence at Yongbyon when the North Koreans invited an unoffi-cial U.S. delegation to visit the nuclear site—the first time the North permitted foreigners to enter its key nuclear facilities since it expelled the IAEA monitors in December 2002.[122]

The group consisted of Keith Luse and Frank Jannuzi of the Senate Committee on Foreign Relations staff; Stanford University professor John Lewis, coauthor of books on the Chinese nuclear program; Siegfried Hecker, former director of Los Alamos; and Charles L. "Jack" Pritchard, former U.S. special envoy for negotiations with the North and at the time a scholar at the Brookings Institution. The five received a tour of the Experimental Nuclear Power Plant, the North Korean name for the 5-megawatt reactor, escorted by the facility's chief engineer, Li Song Hwan, who also led the group on a tour of the spent fuel storage pool building. In addition, the visitors were driven by the 50-megawatt reactor, whose construction had been suspended in 1994, and were able to view hot-cell operations at the Radiochemical Laboratory, escorted by chief engineer Li Yong Song.[123]

Some of what Hecker was able to report was known to the United States through satellite reconnaissance: that the 5-megawatt reactor was in opera-tion, and there had been no construction activity at the site of the not-completed 50-megawatt reactor. The North Koreans also made claims that could not be verified by Hecker or his colleagues: that they had reprocessed all eight thousand fuel rods to extract plutonium, that the radioactive material shown the group was actually plutonium, and that the North actually pos-sessed nuclear weapons.[124]

But the visitors were able to provide current intelligence on the repro-cessing effort. According to Hecker, "We noted that the North Koreans had the requisite facilities, equipment, and technical expertise for large scale plu-tonium reprocessing." The visitors also reported that the North Koreans used the standard PUREX (plutonium uranium extraction) processing to separate plutonium from the fission products and uranium fuel. They could further testify to the fact that their hosts were able to answer "all of the technical ques-tions about reprocessing chemistry very competently." In addition, they were undoubtedly able to add to the U.S. store of knowledge about the officials they met.[125] And lastly, they brought back some valuable nuclear material that they did not have to smuggle past their North Korean hosts.

In April the intelligence community raised its estimate of the North Korean arsenal to eight bombs, based on the conclusion that all eight thou-sand fuel rods had been reprocessed. Among the evidence used in making that judgment were traces of plutonium by-products found on clothing worn by members of the delegation. Just as an examination of a hat that had been worn in the vicinity of Tomsk had provided information on Soviet nuclear activities in the late 1950s, so the analysis of the delegation's clothing in 2004 provided data on North Korean nuclear activities. Traces of the by-products, such as americium, collected from the clothing were evaluated to indicate how recently the plutonium had been processed. The same study estimated that the uranium enrichment program would be operational by 2007 and produce enough material for at least six additional weapons each year.[126]

Since the estimates were based partially on circumstantial evidence, as well as different judgments on the power and efficiency of the North Korean reactors, there was less than unanimous agreement, and disagreement in different directions from the consensus view. The Energy Department's intelligence office suggested the estimated number of weapons should be higher, while the DIA believed that the uranium enrichment program would be operational by the end of 2004. Not surprisingly, the State Department's INR was the most skeptical of such claims.[127]

The only certainty that existed as 2005 arrived was that North Korea's nuclear program was one of the most critical issues facing U.S. national security decisionmakers in the years ahead. For over two years, the United States had attempted to do what it thought it had done in 1994—halt the program. But continued negotiations and discussions, and the involvement of not only the United States but also China, South Korea, Russia, and Japan in talks with Kim's regime had not resolved the crisis. Nor had the North heeded the pleas of the IAEA.[128]

Meanwhile, the U.S. nuclear intelligence establishment continued to try to ferret out as many of the North's nuclear secrets as it could. Its collection and analysis operations were conducted in the face of a series of North Korean actions and claims that threatened to further escalate the confrontation over the North's nuclear program. On February 10, North Korea claimed, for the first time, that it possessed nuclear weapons. By mid-April there was concern that North Korea would soon be able to add to its nuclear inventory. Selig Harrison, a North Korean specialist, was told, during meetings with North North Korean officials in Pyongyang between April 5 and 9, that there were plans to "unload the reactor [at Yongbyon] to create a situation."[129]

That led to new attention being given to the images obtained by American spy satellites during the period of Harrison's visit. Those photographs undoubtedly showed as much, and more, than the images produced by commercial satellites—photographs of a reactor that had apparently been shut down or shifted to a very low power level. Such images were consistent with, but not proof of, the beginning of preparations to reprocess the rods into weapons-grade plutonium. Such an action would allow the North Koreans to add up to three weapons to whatever nuclear arsenal they already possessed. But as one Bush administration official noted, the imagery was not conclusive, "it is still too murky to tell exactly what the North Koreans are doing."[130]

That murkiness made it possible for U.S. intelligence analysts to debate exactly what the North Koreans had planned. By the end of April some analysts were suggesting that the shutdown was inspired by the need to perform maintenance, while others argued the action was the prelude to the removal of fuel rods. During the first week of May, satellite images showed a platform and large crates near the reactor. Then on May 11, North Korea announced that it had removed eight thousand spent fuel rods from its 5-megawatt reactor at the Yongbyon center as one of several "necessary means" to add to its nuclear arsenal.[131]

Toward the end of the April, an additional worry was added to the list—also the result of examining images produced by the NRO's advanced KH-11 satellites. What the imagery interpreters at the National Geospatial Intelligence Agency saw were signs of heightened activity at North Korean missile sites and other locations that could be used for an underground nuclear test. Once again the imagery did not allow a definitive conclusion. One official commented that "much of what we see is open to interpretation."[132]

Even more troubling was imagery of activities in North Korea's northeastern region of Kilju. Starting in October 2004, imagery of the region led intelligence analysts to suspect that it might be the site of a nuclear test. Then in April 2005, worrisome activity in the region accelerated. For the first time, imagery showed the digging of a tunnel—similar to the one used in Pakistan for its 1998 nuclear tests, and located under a mountain suitable to contain a nuclear device with the yield of the one that shattered Hiroshima. And not only did the imagery show the excavation of a tunnel, but it showed that rock and other sealing material had been put back into the hole—standard practice when a hole has been dug for an underground nuclear test, to create a barrier that prevents blast effects and radioactivity from escaping.[133]

One senior intelligence official remarked that "you see them stemming the tunnel, taking material back into the mine to plug it up." He also stated that "there's grout and concrete that goes into the hole, and normally you don't see that in a mine. A mine you want as open as possible." "There's a lot of activity," he noted, "taking stuff in as opposed to taking it out." There were also photographs which revealed construction of a reviewing stand, presumably for dignitaries—just as they had built a reviewing stand for the 1998 launch of their Taepo Dong 1 missile with its satellite payload. A senior U.S. intelligence official told the New York Times that "what we're seeing is everything you need to test" and "we've never seen this level of activity."[134]

There was sufficient concern to prompt a warning from Stephen J. Hadley, the president's national security adviser. During an appearance on the May 15 edition of CNN's Late Edition, Hadley remarked that if the North were to conduct a nuclear test, "action would have to be taken." Although he did not provide specifics, Shinzo Abe, the secretary general of Japan's governing Liberal Democratic Party, appeared on Japanese television the same day and promised that if North Korea conducted a nuclear test, Japan would "bring the issue to the U.N. and call for sanctions against North Korea."[135]

Of course, there was the possibility that the activities shown in the satellite images were not related to a nuclear test—that the grandstands had been built for another purpose, or that the digging and filling of a hole might be in pursuit of another objective. Intelligence analysts and policymakers also understood that what was turning up in satellite images, whether with regard to developments at Yongbyon or potential test sites, might represent some combination of deception and signaling, for it occurred in the midst of the ongoing back and forth between the United States, the Koreas, China, Japan, and Russia about the status and future of the North Korean nuclear program that continued well into 2005.[136]

In mid-September 2005 North Korea agreed to give up "all nuclear weapons and existing nuclear programs" and submit to international inspections in exchange for a variety of benefits—including economic aid, security commitments, electricity from South Korea, discussion at the "appropriate time" of provision of a light-water reactor, and, possibly, a normalization of relations with the United States. But much of the detail remained to be worked out, and within days North Korea was asserting it would have to receive the reactor before it dismantled its nuclear weapons program.[137]

NOT ALL THAT LONG after the United States began trying to build nuclear weapons, it began to worry about another nation trying and succeeding. The Nazi effort never approached success, as the Alsos mission would discover in the fall of 1944. But the understandable fear that Germany's world-famous physicists and scientists, including Werner Heisenberg and Otto Hahn, might hand Hitler a bomb had spurred intelligence collection, using human and technical means, to find out what progress, if any, they had made toward the ultimate weapon. And available intelligence, in that case, served as a basis for action—in the form of bombing raids—and as the basis for near action, when Moe Berg arrived to hear Heisenberg lecture, carrying a gun and a license to kill.

Little could be done to prevent the Soviet Union from acquiring nuclear weapons, but determining when the Soviet Union acquired the bomb, and then how many bombs it had in its arsenal and their capabilities, became a key mission for U.S. intelligence agencies for forty-five years. During that time, the United States developed sophisticated techniques—imagery and signals intelligence satellites such as Corona, Kennan, and Rhyolite; spy planes such as the U-2 and RC-135—and managed to recruit human assets in assorted countries. These techniques could be, and were, applied to a variety of intelligence targets, including the nuclear weapons programs of adversaries and allies.

The intelligence effort also focused specifically on gathering information about foreign atomic energy activities, largely managed by what is today the Air Force Technical Applications Center. That enterprise developed and operated satellites, aircraft, ground stations, and underwater arrays that could detect the special signatures of nuclear explosions, including light flashes, X-rays and gamma rays, nuclear debris, acoustic signals in the air and under the seas, and seismic signals. Those techniques proved vital both in identifying when a nuclear weapon had been detonated in the atmosphere or underground and in providing intelligence on whether it was an atomic bomb or hydrogen bomb, whether it relied on plutonium or uranium for fissile material, and its yield—all key items of information in assessing the Soviet Union's nuclear capabilities as well as its compliance with the partial test ban treaty of 1963, the threshold test ban treaty of 1974, and the as-yet-unratified comprehensive test ban treaty.

The techniques would also prove useful when other nations progressed from developing nuclear bombs to detonating them—France in 1960, China in 1964, India and Pakistan in 1998. There appears to be only one instance when a nuclear test *might* have occurred and the U.S. Atomic Energy Detection System failed to provide unambiguous data: the September 1979 double flash.

Systems that detect the signatures of nuclear detonations are far less useful in providing advance notice that a nation is seeking to develop nuclear weapons. In such cases, imagery satellites, eavesdropping systems, and human sources may be much more likely to provide sufficient warning for U.S. policymakers to act on, whether that action be a military strike to eliminate or set back the weapons program, or diplomatic intervention to persuade a nation to think twice before officially joining the nuclear club. The U.S. intelligence community has a mixed record, which is not surprising given the difficulty of collecting conclusive information on certain aspects of nuclear weapons development, such as uranium enrichment and weapons design, and the lengths to which nations have gone to hide their programs so that they would be able to confront the world with a fait accompli.

Thus, the CIA misread the images and other data it received in the early 1960s concerning the nature of the Chinese program—its focus on uranium enrichment rather than plutonium—in part because of a preconceived expectation about what route China would take to join the nuclear club. National intelligence estimates from the early 1960s, using data from U-2 and Corona missions, often were simultaneously correct in identifying secret installations deep inside China as being part of the nuclear program and wrong as to their specific mission.

Uncertainty about the completeness of the intelligence on the Chinese program was one factor in discouraging U.S. leaders from authorizing a pre-emptive military strike to prevent Mao's regime from acquiring nuclear weapons. But the satellite images that convinced INR analyst Allen Whiting in the late summer and early fall of 1964 that a test was imminent did allow a preemptive strike of another kind: the State Department's notification to the public and the world in late September that China would soon test, permitting the United States to downplay the significance of the event.

Had the CIA been able to recruit a knowledgeable source within the Chinese program in the early 1960s—one who could tell the agency what satellites and intercepts did not—the CIA would, of course, have had a far better understanding of the Chinese effort. But the Chinese program at that time proved impossible to penetrate with human sources. In subsequent years, the Israeli, South African, and Indian programs apparently have proved immune from whatever human penetration attempts were made by the CIA. The failure left the agency guessing or in ignorance of, among other things, the extent of Israel's nuclear capability, the uranium enrichment process developed by South Africa, and India's plans to conduct nuclear tests in 1974 and 1998, although the latter failure was also the result of satellite imagery not being interpreted in a timely fashion. Whether that latter failure truly cost U.S. leaders an opportunity to dissuade India from testing is doubtful given the commitment of the BJP to a nuclear-armed India.

The intelligence community can also point to several instances when technical or human sources provided significant advance knowledge of foreign nuclear intentions or activities, which permitted timely U.S. intervention. Monitoring of Taiwan's nuclear efforts, in the 1970s and 1980s, assisted by a key spy in the program, allowed the United States to dissuade that nation from proceeding with nuclear weapons development. Satellite reconnaissance images proved vital in helping the United States halt South Africa's activities at the Kalahari test range in 1977 and in preventing India from going ahead with a planned test in 1995.

As rogue states have sought to develop, and in one case may have succeeded in developing, atomic weapons, the stakes involved in the nuclear intelligence effort have become higher than ever. From the 1980s on, the U.S. intelligence community needed to be very concerned about Iraq's and North Korea's quest for atomic weapons. Yet the intelligence community failed twice with respect to Iraq. First, it grossly underestimated the program in the late 1980s. The extent of that underestimation only became clear after the 1991 Persian Gulf War, when IAEA inspectors were able to seize documents and visit Iraq's nuclear facilities. Only then did they learn of Iraq's multiple programs for producing highly enriched uranium as well as its efforts in weapons design. The failure to appreciate the extent of the Iraqi program before the Gulf War can be explained, in part, by the concentration of intelligence resources, including satellites, on developments on the battlefields where Iran and Iraq fought from 1980 to 1988.

In 2003 the intelligence community failed again, erroneously concluding that Iraq was reconstituting its nuclear program, as indicated by its attempts to acquire aluminum tubes for use in centrifuges, its rebuilding of facilities that had been associated with the nuclear program, and Saddam's meeting with his "nuclear mujaheddin."

Certainly past Iraqi behavior had given intelligence analysts a good reason to believe intelligence which seemed to establish that Iraq had stockpiles of biological and chemical agents, was continuing to produce more, and was reconstituting its nuclear program. The Iraqis had relentlessly pursued weapons of mass destruction, including nuclear weapons; defied the UN inspection regime; failed to account for significant quantities of biological and chemical agents; and conducted an elaborate and sophisticated denial and deception campaign. Indeed, by October 2003 the Iraqi Survey Group had turned up a variety of instances in which Iraq had violated its disarmament commitments with regard to nuclear, biological, and ballistic missile prohibitions—just not the ones described in the October 2002 national intelligence estimate.

But there were important dissenting voices on the key piece of evidence for reconstitution, the aluminum tubes—the State Department's INR and, more importantly, the Energy Department's Office of Intelligence, supported by the national laboratories. Unfortunately, a single CIA analyst was allowed to determine the CIA's position on the significance of the aluminum tubes, which then became the intelligence community's position based on a vote among six agencies. That officials, such as the director of WINPAC, did not inform George Tenet of the differing views contributed to the failure. Tenet's failure, once he learned of the dispute in September 2002, to ensure that the issue was brought before the JAEIC or to at least seek outside opinions was, unfortunately, all too typical of his tenure as director of central intelligence. He was more interested in boosting the morale of the CIA than serving as a true director of central intelligence. Thus, the hypothesis that the aluminum tubes Iraq was seeking to illegally purchase were intended for use in centrifuges was not unreasonable. There was no dispute that they could be used in such a manner, and Iraq's past willingness to use inefficient means, such as electromagnetic isotope separation, increased the plausibility of that hypothesis. It deserved, however, to be the minority view at best, not the majority view of the intelligence community.

What does not seem to be a valid explanation is that political leaders, including the president, dictated the content of the estimates to provide a "pretext for war" or to "hoodwink" the American public. It was George Bush who questioned the persuasiveness of the information presented to him concerning Iraq's weapons of mass destruction program and George Tenet who reassured him that it was a "slam dunk"—and it was Bush who told Tenet that he did not want analysts to stretch to make the case. Neither the Senate Select Committee on Intelligence nor the Commission on the Intelligence Capabilities of the United States Regarding Weapons of Mass Destruction found evidence that analysts were subject to pressure to produce intelligence to support policy, and were told by analysts that they were not.[138]*

But even in the absence of complicity from political leaders, the overestimation of Iraq's weapons of mass destruction programs certainly could undermine the credibility, both at home and abroad, of the U.S. intelligence community and national leaders who justified action on the basis of its findings. As one former CIA analyst has observed, "When the United States confronts future challenges, the exaggerated estimates of Iraq's WMD will loom like an ugly shadow over the diplomatic discussions."[139]

One can easily imagine that those exaggerated estimates might make it difficult for the United States to allege that Syria, for example, was engaged in extensive covert nuclear or biological weapons programs, and then request international support to halt those activities. The concern that estimates are exaggerated is an immediate problem in dealing with Iran and North Korea. For some nations, the shortcomings of the U.S. intelligence community with regard to weapons of mass destruction in Iraq may provide an excuse, rather than an actual reason, for foreign leaders to oppose acting decisively. Not surprisingly, in March 2005, Chinese foreign minister Li Zhaoxing questioned the accuracy of U.S. intelligence on the North Korean nuclear program, allowing China to refrain from adopting a tougher position toward the North.[140]

With respect to both Iran and North Korea, the United States can point to valuable, albeit not flawless, intelligence about their nuclear activities obtained by American agencies, and to examples of how that intelligence has

---

* While disparity between what the Bush administration claimed with regards to Iraqi weapons of mass destruction programs and what was found, and not found, by the Iraq Survey Group (ISG), reflects poorly on the case it made for the invasion of Iraq, it does not follow that there was no good case for war. As the report of the ISG made clear, Saddam Hussein had not given up his desire for weapons of mass destruction and was violating his disarmament commitments in a variety of ways not detected by UN inspectors. In the near future, the sanctions regime would have been terminated, with a considerable push from some of the major recipients of oil-for-food funds—Russia and France—and Saddam would have been free to resume his pursuit of weapons of mass destruction, including nuclear weapons. For expositions of this view, see William Safire, "Roth Plot II," *New York Times*, December 20, 2004, p. A29; Robert Kagan, "Whether This War Was Worth It," *Washington Post*, June 19, 2005, p. B7.

aided counterproliferation and diplomatic efforts. Numerous Iranian attempts to acquire nuclear-related materials have been blocked by U.S. efforts that were guided by intelligence—from the preemptive purchase of uranium from Kazakhstan to persuading China not to sell the mullahs tons of a chemical used in uranium enrichment. In conjunction with the inspections conducted by the IAEA, U.S. satellite imagery has undoubtedly been important in monitoring developments at the Natanz and Arak sites when the inspectors are not present, and in monitoring activities at the Parchin military complex.

The responsible U.S. intelligence agencies—the CIA, NSA, and NRO—did track and monitor the activities of a network run by Pakistan's A. Q. Khan that transferred nuclear weapons–related plans and technology to several nations, including Iran, Libya, and North Korea—although it was not able to neutralize its activities in the 1980s and 1990s. Former DCI George Tenet told an audience that "we were inside his residence, inside his facilities, inside his room." Penetration of Khan's network, specifically of the Scomi Precision Engineering company, which produced specialized centrifuge parts, resulted in advance knowledge that a freighter, the German-owned *BBC China*, was headed for Libya with thousands of the parts as cargo. American spy satellites—probably advanced KH-11s that photographed it in ports and at sea, and advanced Parcae electronic intelligence satellites that could have monitored its electronic emissions—tracked the *BBC China*'s voyage. After it passed through the Suez Canal on its way to Libya, Washington ordered the ship seized. Its diversion to Italy in October 2003 may have led to the successful conclusion of the ongoing diplomatic contacts that resulted in Libya giving up its weapons of mass destruction and allowing IAEA inspectors to investigate its nuclear capabilities.[141]

However, it appears that U.S. intelligence agencies failed to detect the connection between Khan's nuclear supply operation, which provided Iran's program with key blueprints, technical guidance, and uranium enrichment equipment, and Iran. According to Gary Samore, who directed NSC nonproliferation efforts in the Clinton administration, "We have some intelligence successes with Iran, we knew some of their enrichment efforts. . . . What we didn't know was the Pakistan connection—that was a surprise. And the extent of Pakistan's ties was, in retrospect, the surprise of 1990s."[142]

While the United States has been monitoring North Korean nuclear activities since the 1960s, in the last two decades its program has become particularly worrisome—and probably has resulted in North Korea having a small number of warheads. U.S. intelligence, through satellites and other means, has uncovered much that the North Koreans undoubtedly wish had remained hidden. That has allowed the IAEA or the United States to confront North Korea when, predictably, it has failed to live up to its promises to

refrain from taking steps toward producing fissile material, whether plutonium or uranium.

At the same time, much remains unknown about the North Korean program. Satellite intelligence goes only so far. North Korean defectors have
proved, according to one account, to be "notoriously unreliable." The
regime's installation of underground fiber-optic communication links has dramatically reduced the intelligence obtained from communications intercepts.
Those limitations are exacerbated by North Korea's skill at building underground facilities.[143]

ALTHOUGH THERE IS undoubtedly room for improvement in its performance, the failure to find a satisfactory solution to the problem of the Iranian and North Korean nuclear programs is not a failure that can be laid at the
door of the U.S. intelligence community. The primary responsibility, of
course, lies with the leaders of the two regimes, who are incapable of compre-
hending that their nuclear weapons efforts have no legitimacy because their
regimes are illegitimate, given their human rights violations, which include
the suppression of free speech; their enforcement of state-sanctioned religion
(whether fundamentalist Islam or North Korean communism); and their
severe restrictions on private property and trade. Nor has it helped that the
United States, key nations in Europe, Russia, and China have not been united
in making it clear to the two regimes that they will not be permitted to maintain nuclear arsenals.[144]

In November 2004 Britain, France, and Germany struck an agreement
with Iran, with the Islamic regime promising to suspend, but not terminate,
uranium enrichment in exchange for political and economic benefits. Then in
late May 2005, after Iranian threats to resume uranium enrichment and U.S.
and European warnings, Iran agreed to pledge that it would continue its freeze
on uranium enrichment. The following day, the World Trade Organization
announced that it would begin talks to welcome Iran as a member. The
announcement came after the United States dropped its long-standing opposition to Iranian membership in the organization—as it had promised Britain,
France, and Germany if Iran agreed to continue the freeze. They hoped that
such an agreement would postpone the day when Iran would be capable of
producing a nuclear weapon and then allow time for Iran's regime to either
change from within or change its mind about joining the nuclear club.[145]

But the summer and fall of 2005 brought more conflict over Iran's program. Iranian threats to resume uranium enrichment were followed by actual
resumption. There were also U. S. and European threats to punish the Islamic
regime for such action, as well as Iran's rejection of a U.S.-supported Euro-

pean proposal to provide Iran with nuclear reactors and fuel. In addition, an American briefing titled "A History of Concealment and Deception" was presented to the U.N. representatives of more than a dozen countries, with the intent of convincing them that Iran is avidly pursuing nuclear weapons. In late September, the IAEA's governing board voted (twenty-two to one, with twelve absentions) to report Iran to the U.N. Security Council for having violated its obligations under the nuclear nonproliferation treaty, noting its "absence of confidence that Iran's nuclear program is exclusively for peaceful purposes." But rather than immediately report its finding, it delayed transmitting its report until after a second board vote in November. In November, the United States and its allies decided to put off referring the problem to the Security Council in favor of relying on Russia, China, and India to persuade Iran to halt nuclear activities—undoubtedly for a price.[146]

Some clearly believe that political and economic settlements with Iran and North Korea are within the realm of possibility—that the right packages of benefits can convince the two regimes to abandon any quest for nuclear weapons. Possibly, Iran will be willing to give up that goal, and the cycle of threats, negotiations, and dashed hopes will cease. Likewise, the fall 2005 agreement with North Korea might lead to a lasting solution to the threat of a North Korean nuclear arsenal.

But it may well be that European-style pragmatism, when dealing with rogue regimes, is nothing more than a doomed attempt at appeasement. There is certainly reason to be skeptical that the two regimes will live up to the commitments they make—given the nature of both, their ability to act in secret, and their track record in reneging on agreements they have made. Alternatively, they may only comply with agreements that provide a loophole allowing them to pursue their nuclear dreams. Thus, the November 2004 agreement allowed Iran to continue to produce plutonium. In either case, there may be no solutions short of severe sanctions, military action, or regime change.[147]

Either way, continued aggressive and inventive intelligence collection and analysis on their nuclear programs, and those of other rogues, will be necessary to permit a clear understanding of the threat, and to guide decisionmakers in choosing what courses of action to take or avoid.

EPILOGUE THE U.S. INTELLIGENCE ORGANIZATIONS responsible for collecting and analyzing intelligence on foreign nuclear weapons programs at the beginning of 2006 were largely the same ones that had performed those functions for decades. The CIA was still running spies and technical collection programs, while the Air Force Technical Applications Center remained responsible for managing the Atomic Energy Detection System. The NSA monitored communications, and NRO satellites produced imagery and intercepts. Analysts at the CIA, the DIA, the National Geospatial Intelligence Agency, Z Division, and other agencies pored over the collected data to try to understand foreign nuclear capabilities and intentions.

But there was at least one important difference. On December 8, 2004, President Bush had signed into law the Intelligence Reform and Terrorism Prevention Act of 2004. The act, many of whose provisions came from recommendations contained in the report of the National Commission on Terrorist Attacks Upon the United States, established the post of Director of National Intelligence (DNI). It also eliminated the job of Director of Central Intelligence (DCI), leaving the CIA director responsible only for the operations of the agency.[1]

The DNI's job came with more power over budgets and non-CIA personnel than the DCI had ever had, although not nearly as much as those favoring an intelligence czar would have liked. In February 2005, President Bush announced that his nominee for national intelligence director was John D. Negroponte, a longtime diplomat who was serving as ambassador to Iraq and whose previous jobs included ambassador to the UN and ambassador to Honduras.[2]

A key responsibility of the nation's new intelligence chief, along with directing the intelligence effort against Al-Qaida and other terrorist groups, would be overseeing the intelligence community's work against Iranian and North Korean targets. In January 2006, to assist him with the later job, Negroponte appointed two mission managers. He tapped Joseph De Trani as mission manager for North Korea—thus, making him responsible for integrating the collection and analysis of information on the Hermit Kingdom. De Trani had served as director of the European and East Asian operations divisions for the CIA, as well as head of the agency's Office of Technical Service and Crime and Narcotics Center. At the same time, S. Leslie Ireland was announced as mission manager for Iran. A Middle East specialist, Ireland had served in both the CIA (as special advisor for Iran collection issues, among other posts) and the Department of Defense (as country director for Iran and Kuwait in the office of the secretary).[3]

At the time, work was already well under way on the annual threat assessment Negroponte would present to assorted congressional committees. In his early February 2006 appearance before the Senate Select Committee on Intelligence, Negroponte, in open session, told his audience that North Korea's claim to have nuclear weapons "is probably true." Those weapons appeared to Pyongyang "as the best way to deter superior US and South Korean forces, to ensure regime security, as a lever for economic gain, and as a source of prestige."[4]

In closed session Negroponte probably discussed the national intelligence estimate that either had recently been completed or was on its way to completion. That estimate concluded that North Korea had probably fabricated the fuel for more than a half-dozen nuclear weapons since the beginning of 2001 and was continuing to produce roughly a bomb's worth of new plutonium each year. The assessment left unclear how much of the plutonium had been fabricated into bombs.[5]

In the two pages devoted to Iran in his threat assessment, Negroponte covered Iranian support to terrorism and the insurgency in Iraq, regime stability, the threat to the Persian Gulf states, Iranian conventional military power, as well as the Iranian nuclear program. He told the congressional committee that "Iran conducted a clandestine uranium enrichment program for nearly two decades in violation of its IAEA safeguards agreement, and despite its claims to the contrary, we assess that Iran seeks nuclear weapons." In addition, the community believed "that Tehran probably does not yet have a nuclear weapon and probably has not yet produced or acquired the necessary fissile material." "Nevertheless," his assessment continued, "the danger that it will acquire a nuclear weapon and the ability to integrate it with ballistic missiles Iran already possesses is a reason for immediate concern."[6]

THE ANALYSIS AND conclusions in the estimate on which Negroponte briefed Congress were based in part on a stolen Iranian laptop computer, one example of the continuing intelligence efforts dedicated to gathering and analyzing data on the country's nuclear ambitions. The laptop, which had been obtained in mid-2004 from a longtime Iranian contact, contained studies on the essential features of a nuclear warhead, including a sphere of detonators to trigger a nuclear explosion. The documents also examined the question of how to position a heavy ball—presumably consisting of fissile material— inside the warhead so as to guarantee the stability and accuracy needed as it descended toward its target. In addition, they specified an explosion about two thousand feet above the target—a preferred altitude for a nuclear blast.[7]

Nuclear experts at Sandia National Laboratories in Albuquerque, after conducting computer simulations based on the drawings in the laptop concerning Iran's Shahab-3 missile, concluded that they represented an effort to expand the missile's nose cone so that it could carry a nuclear warhead. Indeed, the drawings showed eighteen different approaches to producing a satisfactory combination of size, weight, and diameter to accommodate a nuclear warhead. The Sandia experts concluded that none of them would work—possibly explaining the DNI's comments that implied Iran still needed to find a way to integrate a nuclear warhead with its ballistic missiles.[8]

The documents on the pilfered computer also included sophisticated drawings of a 130-foot-deep underground shaft, with remote-controlled sensors to measure pressure and heat—the type of shaft used for an underground nuclear test. A test control team was to be located six miles away. There were also designs, with the most recent ones dated February 2003, for a small-scale facility to produce UF4, uranium tetrafluoride, or "green salt," an intermediate product in the transformation of uranium into a gaseous form. Absent from the documents was evidence—in the form of construction orders or payment invoices—that the projects had gotten beyond the drawing-board stage.[9]

Aside from past experience with their source, U.S. intelligence officials found the documents on the laptop, which were written in Persian, convincing because of their consistency and technical accuracy, as well as their portrayal of a progression of developmental work from 2001 to early 2004. Gary Samore, a former Z Division analyst and head of nonproliferation at the National Security Council in the Clinton administration, told reporters that "the most convincing evidence that the material is genuine is that the technical work is so detailed that it would be difficult to fabricate."[10]*

---

* Some experts were more skeptical about the contents of the laptop. Joseph Cirincione of the Carnegie Endowment for International Peace raised the question of whether the work was an uncoordinated effort by an ambitious sector of the rocket program or part of a step-by-step effort to develop a nuclear weapon within a decade. A European diplomat claimed, "I can fabricate that data," and stated, "It looks beautiful but is open to doubt." David Albright, president of the Institute for Science and International Security, stated that the information concerned a reentry vehicle for a missile rather than a warhead—although given the other information reported, it would seem that the reentry vehicle in mind was a nuclear warhead. See William J. Broad and David E. Sanger, "Relying on Computer, U.S. Seeks to Prove Iran's Nuclear Aims," *New York Times*, November 13, 2005, pp. 1, 2; David Albright, "To Whom It May Concern," n.d., www.isis-online.org, accessed December 2, 2005.

The content of the stolen laptop was the subject of a briefing senior U.S. intelligence officials presented to the top echelon of the IAEA in Vienna in July 2005. At the same time, the United States hoped to benefit from the agency's inspections in Iran throughout 2005 and 2006. In late 2005 Iran was less forthcoming than the IAEA, and the United States, would have wished in response to the atomic energy agency's requests for information. "Full transparency is indispensable and overdue," wrote IAEA director general Mohamed ElBaradei. And there was a chance things could get worse, with Iran threatening to bar the agency's inspectors from its declared nuclear sites altogether if the agency referred Iran to the UN Security Council for possible sanctions.[11]

But the agency, during visits to Iran that October and November, received access to buildings of interest at Parchin and took environmental samples, and "did not observe any unusual activities in the buildings visited." It also reported that the UF6 being produced at the Uranium Conversion Facility at Esfahan "has remained under Agency containment and surveillance measures." In contrast to those items of information, another that it reported—that civil engineering and construction of the reactor at Arak was continuing—was intelligence that U.S. satellite reconnaissance could provide on its own.[12]

At the end of January 2006 the IAEA had more to contribute, providing data that U.S. intelligence officials would have been more than a little pleased to have acquired through a spy or communications intercept. Iran showed the international agency more than sixty documents concerning uranium metal. Included was a fifteen-page document describing the procedures for the reduction of UF6 to metal in small quantities, and the casting of enriched and depleted uranium metal into hemispheres, common in the production of nuclear weapon components. Iran claimed the document had been provided, along with other material, by A. Q. Khan's network at Khan's initiative. However, Iran did not permit the agency to make a copy. Iran also provided some documentation on some of its efforts to acquire dual-use material, including laser equipment and electric drive equipment.[13]

The threatened end of "cooperation" with the IAEA followed in early February, after the agency's board of governors voted to report Iran to the UN Security Council for failure to be sufficiently forthcoming. Iran, which had reopened its uranium enrichment facility at Natanz during the first part of January, requested the agency remove, by the middle of the month, its remaining seals and surveillance systems from Iranian facilities. Still, in a report at the end of the month the agency was able to report that on February 11, Iran began enrichment tests by feeding a single P-1 centrifuge with UF6 gas and that a ten-centrifuge cascade was undergoing vacuum tests and began receiving UF6 on February 15.[14]

WHILE THE DATA from the laptop computer and IAEA helped America's spies in understanding Iran's nuclear activities, there were still gaps—thanks in part to Iran's less than complete cooperation with the IAEA. In its early 2006 reports, the international agency stated that it had not been provided a copy of the document on the fabrication of uranium metal hemispheres, and noted that Iranian officials had refused to discuss the "green salt" project, claiming that such a project did not exist.[15]

Satellite imagery helped in monitoring further developments in construction during the late winter and early spring of 2006. High-resolution commercial imagery of the Uranium Conversion Facility at Esfahan, obtained in late March, provided evidence of construction of a third tunnel entrance to the facility. Commercial imagery of Natanz in late February provided an up-to-date overhead view of the location of the underground cascade halls for the fuel enrichment plant, and of further construction next to the Pilot Fuel Enrichment Plant.[16] Imagery interpreters at the National Geospatial Intelligence Agency may have seen those photos, but certainly were able to examine the more detailed images that would have been produced by advanced versions of the government's KH-11 satellite.

Of course, the satellite photos were far from perfect guides to what progress Iran was making in uranium enrichment and weapons design. Tehran itself offered some information. In mid-April, Muhammad Saeedi, deputy chief of Iran's atomic energy organization, announced that his nation had 164 operating centrifuges, was capable of enriching uranium, and would seek to quickly put 54,000 centrifuges on line. Before Saeedi's statement, U.S. intelligence analysts believed Iran was still years away—five to ten at least—from becoming a nuclear weapons state. And his statement did not change their mind. "Our timeline hasn't changed," Thomas Fingar, chairman of the National Intelligence Council, said. Kenneth Brill, who as head of the National Counterproliferation Center (established to coordinate proliferation intelligence across the intelligence community) reported to Negroponte, observed that "an announcement is one thing" and "it will take several years to build that many centrifuges."[17]

More information on Iran's uranium effort became available later that month, when ElBaradei reported on the results of a trip to Iran by five IAEA inspectors during the first part of April—the first inspection trip since Iran had suspended cooperation in February. In addition to discussions with atomic energy officials in Iran, the inspectors visited both Esfahan and Natanz.

In a report described as having "an unusually bleak tone," the agency confirmed that Muhammad Saeedi's claim of Iran having begun small-scale uranium enrichment was accurate. The agency's director general also reported that all the nuclear material declared by Iran to the IAEA could be accounted for, and that environmental samples taken from the Lavisan-Shian Physics Research Center were still being analyzed. They were first analyzed at an agency laboratory in Seibersdorf, Austria, and then sent to a network of laboratories around the world to confirm the results. Once the samples were fully evaluated, before the middle of May, the agency could state that they contained traces of highly enriched uranium, implying that unless there had been contamination of equipment from abroad, Iran had enriched uranium to far beyond the level needed for civilian reactors.[18]

A significant reason for the report's bleak tone was Iran's continuing refusal to provide information or documents with regard to many aspects of its nuclear program. In his late-April report, ElBaradei wrote that his agency was still waiting for Iran's "clarifications" with respect to its effort to purchase assorted dual-use equipment for the physics research center, and needed further access to the procured equipment. Other problems included Iran's refusal to discuss the green salt project, or address questions relating to high-explosive testing and the design of a missile reentry vehicle. The title of a *New York Times* article that May aptly summarized the situation: "Iran's Secrecy Widens Gap in Nuclear Intelligence."[19]

OF COURSE, it was the job of U.S. intelligence, in the absence of Iranian transparency, to close that gap by clandestine means, including human intelligence. In March 2005 the commission investigating America's ability to spy on weapons of mass destruction programs had listed Iran among the nations for which "human intelligence is still not delivering the goods."

The commission had also reported that with regard to Iran's pursuit of nuclear weapons, "the Intelligence Community frequently admitted to us that it lacks answers." Just a little over a year later, in mid-April 2006, secretary of defense Donald Rumsfeld described Iran's nuclear program as "a very difficult target for our intelligence community" and that he was "not confident" in the Intelligence Community's estimate that it would take Iran five to ten years to join the nuclear weapons club, citing the possibility of the Islamic republic receiving foreign help.[20]

A report by the staff of the House Permanent Select Committee on Intelligence, *Recognizing Iran as a Strategic Threat: An Intelligence Challenge for the United States*, released in August, stressed the need for America's spies to do a better job collecting and analyzing intelligence on Iran, including its nuclear weapons program. The report asserted that "the United States lacks critical information needed for analysts to make many of their judgments with confidence about Iran" and that a special concern was the major gaps in America's knowledge of Iranian nuclear, biological, and chemical programs. The staffers who prepared the report also argued that while "Iran, being a denied area with active denial and deception efforts, is a difficult target for intelligence analysis and collection, it is imperative that the U.S. Intelligence Community devote significant resources against this vital threat."[21]

The committee staff suggested a number of steps that the Intelligence Community needed to take to upgrade its understanding of Iranian nuclear developments: improving analysis, using more open-source intelligence, "the availability of which is augmented by Iran's prolific (if persecuted) press"; improving coordination on Iran-specific issues; augmenting linguistic capabilities; and, of course, enhancing human intelligence capabilities. With respect to the latter, the report's authors noted that "the nature of the Iranian target poses unique HUMINT challenges; since American officials have so little physical access to Iran, it is difficult to collect information there."[22]*

A few days after the House committee released its report bemoaning the state of U.S. intelligence on Iran, the nation's president, Mahmoud Ahmadinejad, showed up at Arak for its official launch and provided some public remarks and video for analysts to ponder, including the statement that the plant was operational. That latter bit of information would be significant to U.S. intelligence analysts if they were not already aware of the plant's status, for "if . . . it's operational, if it's producing heavy water, that would be a big breakthrough," according to former weapons inspector David Albright.[23]

U.S. intelligence also received some new information at the end of the month from the IAEA, despite the limits Iran had put on the agency's access. In addition to confirming that Iran continued to produce low-level enriched uranium at Natanz, it also reported that it had discovered new traces of highly enriched uranium in a year-old sample taken from equipment at a technical university, equipment that the IAEA had inspected in conjunction with its investigation of the activities at the physics research center.[24]

On October 3, about a month after the IAEA report was released, and after having seen whatever data U.S. imagery satellites, communications intelligence, human sources, and other collection methods had produced on Iran's nuclear activity since his congressional testimony of early February, DNI John Negroponte told a Voice of America audience that "we don't have any fast facts that could demonstrate to you a particular date by which we're

---

* Some of the specific claims about the status of the Iranian program made in the report were challenged by the IAEA. See Vilmos Cserveny, Director, Office of External Relations and Policy Coordination, Letter to Hon. Peter Hoekstra, September 12, 2006; David E. Sanger, "Nuclear Agency for U.N. Faults Report on Iran by U.S. House," *New York Times*, September 15, 2006, p. A3; Jacqueline Shire and David Albright, Institute for Science and International Security, "Iran's Nuclear Program: Flawed House Intelligence Report Should Be Amended or Withdrawn," November 9, 2006.

certain Iran will have a nuclear weapon. But yes, it is our judgment, based on all the information available to us, that Iran is determined to acquire nuclear weapons and, secondly, they are on a path to achieve that within the next several years. The estimate that we have made it that somewhere between 2010 and 2015 . . . Iran is likely to have a nuclear weapon if it continues on its current course."[25]

OF COURSE, while the United States and IAEA were trying, throughout 2005 and 2006, to acquire more information about exactly what the Iranians were doing, diplomatic efforts continued in an effort to prevent Iran from becoming a nuclear weapons state. In November 2005, the Bush administration and the three European nations known as the EU-3 (Britain, France, and Germany) approved offering Iran the opportunity of conducting limited nuclear activities within Iran, but having all of its uranium enriched in Russia. The United States and Europe also agreed to put off attempts to refer Iran's case to the UN Security Council in order to give Russia, China, and India the opportunity to persuade Iran to halt its suspicious nuclear activities.[26]

During the first several months of 2006 there were developments, but few that were positive. The Iranians cancelled a high-level meeting with the IAEA scheduled for early January. A few days later Iran broke the IAEA seals on the uranium enrichment facility at Natanz. President Ahmadinejad insisted that Iran had the right to its peaceful nuclear program and that "no excuse could deprive the country from this right." On February 4 the IAEA's governing board voted to refer Iran's nuclear activities to the UN, by a vote of 27 to 3, with Syria, Venezuela, and Cuba voting no. But in mid-March Iran announced that it was rejecting the proposal that uranium enrichment for Iranian reactors take place in Russia.[27]

Throughout the remainder of March and the two following months the UN pleaded for Iran to halt its nuclear activities, while Iran remained defiant and Russia and China dissented over possible sanctions. The United States and the EU-3 came up with a revised offer to Iran, which included assisting the Islamic republic with building a light-water nuclear reactor for civilian use in return for halting its objectionable nuclear operations. The offer also included the United States lifting its sanctions on the sale of commercial jets, agricultural equipment, and telecommunications technology to Iran.[28]

Ahmadinejad was immediately dismissive, addressing the United States and EU-3 in front of a cheering crowd in Arak, "Do you think you are dealing with a 4-year old child to whom you can give some walnuts and chocolates and get gold in return?" A few weeks later, at the beginning of June, the United States, EU-3, China, and Russia reached agreement on a new offer. Along with the promise of U.S. assistance for an Iranian civilian nuclear energy program, it left open the possibility that Tehran could continue to enrich uranium once the IAEA certified that Iran's nuclear program was a peaceful one.[29]

Iran's initial, nineteen-page response included a presentation of the Islamic republic's beliefs concerning the unfortunate impact of massive weapons spending, Iran's legal position, engagement as a means of conflict resolution, and the conditions that would make negotiations constructive, rather than specifics concerning what was being offered and what Iran would want. An actual response would, Iran's president said, take over a month, which seemed like "an awful long time" to President George Bush.[30]

At the end of June, calls from the United States, Russia, and the other industrialized nations that make up the G8, for Iran to give a "clear and substantive response" the following week would fall on deaf ears. Three weeks after the G8 demand, Iran promised that it would respond on August 22, unless its case was referred to the UN Security Council. Running out of patience, the Security Council passed a resolution on July 31 demanding that Iran suspend its uranium enrichment and reprocessing activities by the end of August or face sanctions. Iran promised to ignore the deadline, and on August 21 refused to allow inspectors access to Natanz.[31]

The August 31 deadline came and went and Iran did not blink. On the other hand, several of the nations that had demanded Iranian compliance did. Within days after the deadline, Russia was hinting that it would not support sanctions. Russian foreign minister Sergey V. Lavrov told students at Moscow State Institute of International Relations that "we cannot support ultimatums that lead everyone to a dead end and cause escalation." It took France a few weeks to join Russia and China, with President Jacques Chirac proclaiming that "I am never in favor of sanctions."[32]

In late September, the United States along with the EU-3, China, and Russia set a new deadline—early October—although the events of early September gave Iran no reason to expect there would be consequences if it failed to comply. On October 1, Ahmadinejad told students that Iran would not halt its uranium enrichment activities and that "nobody has the right to make Iran back down over its rights." By the end of October, with another deadline having been ignored, the United States and its European allies were squabbling among themselves over terms of a resolution that would punish Iran, with the United States believing the proposed resolution was too weak to be effective.[33]

In November, negotiations within the United States, EU-3, and Russia would continue, with Iran threatening more noncooperation with UN inspectors if the body's Security Council approved sanctions. At virtually the same time that it was issuing its threat, President Ahmadinejad claimed that Iran would soon complete its nuclear fuel program: "I'm very hopeful that we will be able to hold the big celebration of Iran's full nuclearization in the current year," he said in Tehran. Iran also promised to build a heavy-water reactor at Arak without IAEA help, if necessary. Meanwhile, the IAEA reported that it found unexplained plutonium traces in a nuclear waste facility in Iran.[34]

On December 23, almost four months after the UN deadline, the UN Security Council voted to approve sanctions that banned the import and export of materials employed in uranium enrichment, reprocessing, and ballistic missiles. The sanctions reflected the demands of Russia and China. As a result, the freeze on the assets of twelve Iranians and ten companies said to be involved in nuclear and ballistic missile programs was qualified to give countries more leeway to unfreeze assets than had been envisioned in earlier drafts of the resolution. In addition, while the United States and European nations would have preferred a mandatory travel ban on Iranians believed to be involved in prohibited nuclear activities, the resolution only called on nations to "exercise vigilance" over their borders. Russia's objections also meant that there were no sanctions against the nuclear power plant that the Russians were building at Bushehr. The resolution did demand that Iran immediately suspend uranium enrichment and reprocessing within sixty days or face further sanctions.[35]

Iran responded with further defiance. Iran's ISNA news agency quoted President Mahmoud Ahmadinejad as saying that "nuclear technology is our right, and no one can take it away from us" and asking, "What kind of Security Council is this that is completely in the hands of the Zionists, the United States and Britain?" The Iranian Parliament approved a resolution that the government should "revise its cooperation with the International Atomic Energy Agency based on the interests of Iran and its people."[36]

But during 2006, it was North Korea's nuclear weapons program that took center stage.

WHILE THE NUCLEAR confrontation with Iran held the spotlight for most of the year, it was North Korea's actions in October of 2006 that had the most dramatic impact. For most of the year there had been no progress in the multilateral efforts by the United States and its four partners—Russia, China, Japan, and South Korea—to halt or reverse North Korea's nuclear weapons program.

Kim Jong Il's September 2005 pledge to abandon his nuclear weapons program and rejoin the Nuclear Non-Proliferation Treaty "at an early date" proved to be another instance of false hope—at least for those who were optimistic enough to believe such promises. North Korea insisted that it receive a power reactor before it disclosed the details of its nuclear program while the United States insisted that disclosure come first.[37]

In determining what the North Koreans were doing while the diplomats talked, the United States used a report from former Los Alamos chief Siegfried

Hecker and colleagues who had returned to North Korea in August 2005 to talk with government representatives. While Hecker's group did not return to Yongbyon, they did sit down with Ri Hong Sop, the facility's director. They were told at their meetings that the fuel rods for the country's 5-megawatt reactor had been unloaded in April and that North Korea was going to complete a 50-megawatt reactor within the next two years—which would represent a tenfold growth in the regime's ability to produce fissile material. In November, Hecker told an audience at a conference in Washington what he had presumably already told U.S. government representatives, that the North was "moving full speed ahead with its nuclear weapons programs."[38]

America's spies also had their secret sources of information, one of which was satellite imagery. Included in that imagery was certainly a higher-resolution version of the photograph obtained by a commercial satellite that showed preparation for construction at the 50-megawatt reactor site, including restoration of a building near the reactor.[39]

At about the time Hecker was speaking in Washington, representatives from the United States, China, Russia, Japan, South Korea, and North Korea met in Beijing for three days to continue discussions. The top American negotiator at the talks, assistant secretary of state Christopher Hill, told the press that "I think we're going to talk about concepts of how to go forward." During those three days, the Chinese representative would appeal for flexibility, while the United States and North Korea would stick to their positions as to whether disarmament or reward should come first. North Korea would also complain about financial difficulties it was suffering as a result of financial sanctions the United States had imposed on a Macao bank that it had concluded was laundering $100 bills produced by North Korea's counterfeiting operation—the sanctions resulting in the bank's assets, including those belonging to North Korea, being frozen. At the conclusion of the meeting Beijing characterized the talks as "pragmatic and constructive."[40]

While there had been talk of more talks in January, the North Koreans weren't interested.

In April, the negotiators were all in the same place—Tokyo—but they were there to attend the Northeast Asian Cooperation Dialogue, an academic conference on international security sponsored by the University of California at San Diego. There was no dialogue between the negotiators concerning Pyongyang's nuclear activities. The North was offering to resume talks only if the United States would lift the financial sanctions on the Macao bank.[41]

Over the next six months President Bush's top advisors reportedly recommended a new approach, including commencing negotiations for a peace treaty in the midst of efforts to get North Korea to abandon its nuclear weapons program, and of Bush and South Korean president Roh Moo Hyun agreeing to work together to restart the stalled talks. After a September meeting with Roh, Bush stressed the benefits to Kim Jong Il of returning to the negotiating table and giving up nuclear weapons. "First and foremost," he said, "the incentive is for Kim Jong Il to understand there is a better way to improve the lives of his people than being isolated."[42]

But, as Bush was well aware, improving the lives of his people has never been very high on the North Korean dictator's "to do" list. Bush had told journalist Bob Woodward a few years earlier, "I loathe Kim Jong Il!" because he was starving his people. Inducements are "not valued according to whether they are good for the North Korean economy or people, but whether they help keep Kim Jong Il in power," according to two observers of the regime. And Kim's behavior in 2006 would only serve to increase the North's isolation. In July the regime test-fired six missiles over the Sea of Japan, including an intercontinental missile that failed or was aborted, in defiance of warnings from Japan, South Korea, the United States, and China. But worse was yet to come.[43]

On October 3 North Korea's foreign ministry announced that it would conduct a nuclear test, claiming it was doing so in the midst of increasing U.S. hostility toward the regime—specifically Washington's "financial squeeze," which it described as a "de facto declaration of war." That squeeze included increasing pressure from the United States on foreign banks not to handle transactions involving the North's military and political elite. North Korea never specified a date or location for the test.[44]

Objections from other nations and the United Nations followed. The Bush administration transmitted a secret message to North Korea through its mission to the UN, warning it not to go ahead with a test. Assistant Secretary of State Hill warned publicly that the North "can have a future or it can have these weapons. It cannot have both." He added that "we are not going to live with a nuclear North Korea, we are not going to accept it." In Russia, in a meeting with his South Korean counterpart, Foreign Minister Lavrov "stressed the unacceptability" of a North Korean test. China suggested North Korean restraint rather than "taking actions that may intensify the situation." The UN Security Council urged Kim not to test, stating that it would endanger regional stability and produce worldwide denunciation.[45]

OF COURSE, even without North Korea's announcement, America's spies had been monitoring North Korea for activity at its nuclear sites and signs of a possible test. There were seven potential test sites to be monitored, the primary one being at P'unggye, a few-dozen miles from the city of Kilju—although it was possible that P'unggye was only a high-explosive site associated with the nuclear weapons program. Commercial satellite photography showed two suspected tunnel openings in a mountain several miles from P'unggye, as well as barracks for support personnel and a multitude of cables running into the tunnel. Three layers of security and a number of warehouses in a valley below the test site were also visible in commercial images, as was a rail station in the area. Imagery showed that it had recently been upgraded with "VIP" features.[46]

American spy satellites had returned images of activity at the site in August and September. The images showed movements of people, vehicles, and fencing. But it was not clear whether the images showed actual test preparations or activity staged to make it appear that a test was imminent—possibly timed to the September 2006 visit to Washington of South Korean President Roh.[47]

Part of the problem in determining what the North Koreans were actually planning was the lack of a historical record with regard to North Korean testing. One intelligence official commented that "the Chinese used to white-wash the curbs before a test to look good for [VIPs]. That was always a good indication something was imminent. [Today], we see everything necessary for a test. . . . They should be ready to go. But it's hard to tell what North Korea's intent is." Another noted that "we don't have a wonderful timetable that says they have to do 14 things to prepare for a test and they have done seven of them. There is no precedent for assessing how North Korea does its test preparations."[48] But soon there would be.

In South Korea, the Korea Earthquake Research Center had been put on twenty-four-hour alert in August, probably as a result of the satellite images showing activity at P'unggye, and the Defense Ministry had sent soldiers to examine the center's video displays for any indications of a test. It was Sunday night on October 8 in Washington when North Korea announced that it had detonated a nuclear device. According to the North Korean Central News Agency the test was "a historical event that has brought our military and people huge joy." South Korean officials announced that they had detected a seismic event measuring about 3.6 on the Richter scale as having occurred at 10:36 a.m. local time, Monday, October 9, in Korea.[49]

The announcement produced the expected condemnations. President Bush characterized the very claim of a test as a "provocative act." Even the People's Republic of China, North Korea's best friend and benefactor, was annoyed. The Chinese foreign ministry in Beijing stated that North Korea "has ignored the widespread opposition of the international community and conducted a nuclear test brazenly on October 9." Russian president Vladimir Putin told Bush of Russia's strong concern about North Korea's activities, and the French foreign minister called the test "a very grave act" that required "a firm response" from the international community. Japanese prime minister Shinzo Abe told a news conference in Seoul that North Korea's possession of nuclear weapons constituted a "major threat" extending "beyond northeast Asia."[50]

WHILE LEADERS and foreign ministries were busy making public statements condemning the claimed test, American nuclear intelligence analysts were busy evaluating the data they had from the event while intelligence collectors attempted to gather more. A U.S. intelligence source told the *Washington Post* that satellite imagery, intercepts, and seismic signals would all be used to put together a picture of the test and improve understanding of the North's actual nuclear capabilities.[51]

The seismic data available to the United States included those obtained from South Korea as well as the signals obtained by the U.S. Geological Survey (USGS) and AFTAC. The USGS detected a seismic event with a 4.2 magnitude at the same time that the South Korean earthquake center detected the claimed North Korean detonation. Exactly which AFTAC arrays also picked up seismic signals is not public knowledge, but they probably included the ones in South Korea, Thailand, and Australia.[52]

The data left no doubt that an explosion, rather than an earthquake, had taken place in North Korea, but it was not a very impressive one for a nuclear explosion. Other nations' first tests had produced yields of at least 10 kilotons; France's first detonation had produced a yield of over 60 kilotons. But according to one intelligence official the United States "assessed that the explosion in North Korea was a sub-kiloton explosion." At that yield, "we don't know, in fact, whether it was a nuclear explosion," he added, raising the possibility that the North had set off a large chemical explosion in an attempt to mimic a nuclear detonation.[53]

There were also other possibilities, all of which involved a nuclear explosion having occurred. One was that only a fraction of the device's plutonium core exploded, due to asymmetrical implosion or poisoned plutonium (a core that contained too much plutonium 240). Another possibility was that the North had used less plutonium than anticipated because it had less available than had been believed. Less likely explanations were that Pyongyang had manufactured a smaller, more sophisticated device, and that engineers had intended to test the device's design instead of its yield.[54]

One indication that the explosion had not been a North Korean deception effort came from what U.S. spy satellites had not seen: any signs of chemical explosives having been unloaded at the site. Information indicating that the device had not performed as expected came to a senior Bush official from "Asian contacts," most probably a Chinese official. What the U.S. official was told was that the North Koreans had expected the device to produce a 4-kiloton yield.[55]

U.S. spy satellites continued to photograph the test site, looking for a crater that might provide additional data about the test as well as signs that, in the face of the test's partial failure, the North might be preparing for a second

A July 31, 2006, Orbview-3 image of the area north
of Kilju, North Korea, where North Korea's first
nuclear test would take place on October 9, 2006.
GEOEYE

round. Undoubtedly, the NSA tried to glean whatever it could from North Korean communications. There was also an expectation that nuclear debris from the test could be captured because the strength of the detonation was not sufficient to melt and pulverize nearby rock into impregnable barriers, increasing the chances that radioactivity would leak into the atmosphere. One intelligence official noted that "over time, whenever the prevailing winds blow out over the Gulf of Japan, it will be more likely that we get some detection."[56]

Detection of the xenon, krypton, cesium, and other radioactive isotopes associated with a plutonium detonation would provide the best confirmation of a test and the composition of the bomb, particularly since "it would be more difficult to mimic the radioactive isotopes you get from a nuclear blast" than to conduct an actual nuclear test, according to a nuclear expert at the Council on Foreign Relations. In the hopes of detecting those isotopes, AFTAC ordered the remaining WC-135 Constant Phoenix aircraft to launch from Kadena Air Base and fly over the Sea of Japan.[57]

The first results from the air-sampling missions did not provide conclusive proof. The WC-135 did not appear to bring back any evidence of radioactive debris that would have been expected to be circulating in the atmosphere. A Chinese official confirmed that China had also failed to find radioactive evidence: "We have conducted air monitoring and found no radiation in the air over Chinese air territory so far." According to Daryl Kimball, the executive director of the Arms Control Association, "Sampling devices may simply have been in the wrong place at the wrong time, or the amount of radioactive material may have been too small to detect because this may have been a failed test of a small nuclear device."[58]

But by Friday, October 13, press reports stated that U.S. aerial sampling operations, guided by computer models that identified when the planes would have the best chance of gathering conclusive evidence, had produced evidence of radioactivity associated with a nuclear explosion. Analysts had also produced an estimate of the yield of the test—a mere 200 tons of TNT or 0.2 kiloton. But the U.S. government was not yet ready to officially confirm that North Korea had become the eighth nation to test a nuclear device. Frederick Jones, a spokesman for the National Security Council, told reporters that "when the intelligence community has a determination to present, we will make that public."[59]

While the United States was not willing to make an official statement that day or the next, it did vote for UN Security Council Resolution 1718, as did all other fourteen members of the council. Its primary provision prohibited the sale or transfer to North Korea of material that could be used to produce weapons of mass destruction. It also banned international travel and froze the overseas assets of individuals associated with Pyongyang's weapons programs. The most debated component of the resolution permitted inspection of cargo to and from North Korea to detect prohibited material, a provision that was less than enthusiastically supported by China and Russia but was not as tough as the United States desired in that it didn't include the authority to stop ships in international waters. Predictably, North Korean ambassador Pak Gil-yon informed the council that his government "totally rejected" the resolution, and accused the group's members of "gangster-like" action and of "double standards" that ignored the nuclear threat posed by the United States.[60]

Two days later, the United States was willing to state officially that North Korea had conducted a nuclear test and to provide some information on when it had accumulated definitive evidence. The Office of the Director of National Intelligence issued a one-paragraph statement: "Analysis of air samples collected on October 11, 2006 detected radioactive debris which confirms that North Korea conducted an underground nuclear explosion in the vicinity of P'ungyye on October 9, 2006. The explosion yield was less than a kiloton."[61]

The statement did not mean that U.S. nuclear intelligence analysts were through exploring all the data on the North Korean test. Nor were the collectors at the National Clandestine Service, NRO, or NSA done gathering data. One question that remained for which a definitive answer was lacking was the cause of the test's low yield. The analysts had reached three firm conclusions: the bomb's fissile material was plutonium rather than uranium, it was extracted from its 5-megawatt nuclear reactor, and it was produced either during the administration of the first President Bush (1989–1993) or after 2003.[62]

According to some nuclear experts the findings represented "good news" because they suggested that North Korea's plutonium program was probably the only one currently capable of producing material for a bomb. In addition, according to Siegfried Hecker, they indicated that "we have a reasonably good idea of how much plutonium they have made."[63]

Collectors and analysts were also devoting attention to the possibility of a second North Korean nuclear test, perhaps fueled by the world's perception that the first test had been a partial failure. Concern that Kim might be planning a second test was partly the result of new satellite images showing increased activity around two additional North Korean test sites. That activity had begun a few days earlier, and included ground preparation at one site as well as the construction of some buildings and other structures, according to a U.S. defense official. However, the imagery did not, a senior South Korean official noted at the time, indicate that a second test was imminent.[64]

By the end of the month there had been no second test, and North Korea had agreed to rejoin the six-party disarmament talks, probably motivated to a great degree by the money crunch created by U.S. financial sanctions and China's post-test order to some of its major banks to halt monetary transactions with the North. Assistant Secretary of State Hill said he expected "substantial progress" at the talks and they would take place without preconditions. Others were less optimistic, with one unidentified administration official asking, "Where's the stick?" and adding, "We're celebrating the six-party talks, but we're back to endless chatter."[65]

IN THE FIRST half of 2007, developments with regard to the Iranian nuclear program unfolded in much the same manner as they had in the later part of 2006. The United States tried to persuade its European allies, Russia, and China to turn up the pressure on Tehran. China did urge Iran to give a "serious response" to the UN sanctions. But European governments initially resisted demands from the Bush administration that they move quickly to enforce the sanctions approved in December, citing technical and political problems related to Europe's extensive economic relations with Iran and its oil companies.[66]

President Ahmadinejad, meanwhile, pressed on, despite criticism from the nation's most senior dissident cleric, Grand Ayatollah Hossein-Ali Montazeri. In January, Iran barred thirty-eight inspectors from entering the country in retaliation for the sanctions imposed in December. IAEA chief Mohamed ElBaradei reported that Iranian officials had told him that they planned to begin installing uranium enrichment equipment in their Natanz facility in February. And in early February, European diplomats reported that Iran had set up two cascades of 164 centrifuges at the facility. Later in February, Ahmadinejad characterized his nation's nuclear program as a train "without brakes."[67]

During the first half of April Iran's mercurial president claimed that his country had started enriching uranium on an industrial scale. In a nationally televised speech from Natanz, Ahmadinejad told his audience, "With great pride I announce as of today, our dear country is among the countries of the world that produces nuclear fuel on an industrial scale." Ali Larijani, Iran's top nuclear negotiator, appeared to confirm to reporters that Iran had begun enriching uranium through a 3,000-centrifuge cascade.[68]

Iran's intransigence did result in additional penalties. In early February the IAEA board of governors suspended twenty-two of its fifty-five aid programs to Iran, including those designed to assist Iran's development of nuclear power, to assist its radiation processing of metals and plastic, as well as to improve its nuclear management and strategic planning. In addition, European governments agreed to extend economic sanctions, resulting in a new UN Security Council resolution in late March that targeted Iranian arms exports, the state-owned Bank Sepah (already under Treasury Department sanctions), and the Revolutionary Guard Corps. The resolution prohibited the sale or transfer of Iranian weapons to any nation or organization, and asked nations to "exercise vigilance and restraint" in providing weapons to Iran.[69]

Russia also told Iran that it would not provide fuel for the nearly complete Bushehr Nuclear Power Plant unless it suspended its uranium enrichment program. But that came a month after Russia had threatened to slow work on the plant after a dispute with Iran erupted over Iran's desire to pay its bills in euros rather than dollars, creating the suspicion that Russia was using the UN sanctions as a convenient excuse to pressure Iran.[70]

Throughout the dispute there was, of course, a desire by both the IAEA and the U.S. Intelligence Community to find out exactly what Iran was doing—to determine the extent to which their boasts were backed up by actual deeds, and what they might be doing that they were not talking about. Certainly, both were interested in what might be gleaned from the tour of the Esfahan uranium conversion facility that Iranian officials gave to diplomats and journalists in early February, which included the claim from the officials that the facility had manufactured 250 tons of uranium hexafluoride. America's spies also benefited from the IAEA disclosure in late February that Iran was operating or about to switch on approximately one thousand centrifuges.[71]

In addition, in February the IAEA reported that satellite imagery indicated that the heavy-water production plant at Arak was still in operation, imagery that might have been obtained from commercial sources or provided by the United States. Certainly, U.S. imagery satellites would have photographed that site and every other nuclear site in Iraq, and the IAEA would (or did) gladly accept such images. The international agency was apparently, however, less enthralled with other information provided by the United States. According to one report, "U.S. intelligence shared with the U.N. nuclear watchdog agency has proved inaccurate and none has led to significant discoveries inside Iran." It quoted an anonymous senior diplomat at the IAEA: "Since 2002, pretty much all the intelligence that's come to us has proved to be wrong"—a statement that might have been more a testament to the unreliability of human intelligence than to failures unique to the U.S. Intelligence Community since it also applied to the intelligence provided by other Western intelligence services.[72*]

But in April the IAEA had an opportunity to gather data on Iran's uranium enrichment activities firsthand—which would help inform not only the IAEA but a variety of national intelligence agencies, including the CIA. During a visit to Riyadh, during the first half of April, IAEA chief ElBaradei

---

* The report also again raised the question of the validity of the documents found on the laptop computer, quoting a UN official as stating, "We don't know. Are they genuine? Are they real?" See Bob Drogin and Kim Murphy, "U.N. Calls U.S. Data on Iran's Nuclear Aims Unreliable," *Los Angeles Times*, February 25, 2007, pp. A1, A9.

questioned Iranian claims to be operating 3,000 centrifuges, suggesting that only several hundred were in operation.[73]

However, that assessment did not survive the inspection carried out a few days later, on April 15 and 16—inspections that required only a couple of hours notice and had recently been agreed to by the Iranians. The inspectors verified that Iran was indeed operating 3,000 centrifuges at the newly opened underground facility at Natanz, although they were not in position to determine how efficiently they were running.[74]

In another short-notice inspection of Natanz, on May 13, the IAEA inspectors found that Iranian engineers had apparently overcome their difficulty in keeping the 1,300 centrifuges spinning at the enormous speeds needed to enrich uranium suitable for nuclear reactors. The inspectors also reported another 300 centrifuges were being tested and could become operational within a week. In contrast to his statements of a month earlier, ElBaradei viewed the Iranian claims of progress less skeptically, observing that "we believe they pretty much have the knowledge about now to enrich. From now on, it is simply a question of perfecting that knowledge." Matthew Bunn, assistant director of Harvard University's Belfer Center for Science and International Affairs commented that the new information meant that "whether they're six months or a year away, one can debate. But it's not ten years."[75]

IN LATE DECEMBER, while the UN was approving sanctions against Iran for its nuclear activities, the talks that would hopefully reverse or halt the North Korean nuclear program were going nowhere, concluding with no "tangible progress" and Pyongyang threatening to "improve its nuclear deterrent." But private talks in Berlin between Christopher Hill and North Korean envoy Kim Kye-gwan led to an action plan in February that was endorsed by China, South Korea, Japan, and Russia.[76]

Under the terms of the agreement, North Korea promised to shut down and seal the Yongbyon facility, including its reprocessing component, within sixty days, and invite IAEA inspectors to return "to conduct all necessary monitoring and verifications as agreed." Eventually the facility was to be abandoned entirely. Pyongyang pledged to discuss with the other participants in the six-party talks all of its nuclear programs, including the extraction of plutonium from fuel rods, that would be abandoned in accord with the agreement. A list of those activities was to be provided by the time Yongbyon was shut down. The United States and North Korea would also begin bilateral talks aimed at "resolving pending bilateral issues" and moving toward full diplomatic relations. The United States also agreed to begin the process of removing from Kim Jong Il's regime the designation of state sponsor of terrorism. The agreement also specified that North Korea would receive an initial shipment of 50,000 tons of heavy fuel, beginning within sixty days, with another 950,000 tons to follow.[77]

The agreement was criticized by former Bush administration ambassador to the UN (and before that State Department nonproliferation chief) John Bolton, for "rewarding [the] bad behavior of the North Koreans by promising fuel oil" and giving up financial leverage by agreeing to lift banking sanctions. Bolton's successor in the State Department, Robert Joseph, resigned, in part because of his discomfort with the agreement. It was not long before it appeared there might be no agreement after all, as delays in transferring $25 million in frozen North Korean funds led Pyongyang's delegates to refuse to take part in the joint meetings in Beijing concerning implementation of the action plan. But during the first week of April, the United States announced that it had found a way around the legal and technical problems that had prevented return of the money—one week before the target date for shutting down Yongbyon.[78] But when the deadline arrived in April, North Korea claimed it could not access the money and refused to shut down the reactor. NRO spy satellites continued to monitor the facility. Near the end of April one U.S. official noted, "There is no evidence to indicate, nor is there reason to believe, that it has shut down." By mid-May the North Koreans had still not halted operations at Yongbyon.[79]

But should Yongbyon actually be shut down and talks eventually progress beyond the shutting down of that facility and on to issues such as the declaration of all the North's nuclear programs, and delivery of all the fissile material produced by Kim's regime, the U.S. Intelligence Community will be asked to provide its estimate of whether the regime can be counted on to keep its word.

One issue will be whether the North's declaration of its stockpile of nuclear weapons and the quantity of fissile material produced is accurate or even close to accurate. Given the debate that took place within the U.S. Intelligence Community in the early 1990s concerning the veracity of South Africa's declarations to the IAEA, it is not hard to imagine that it might be difficult, if not impossible, for the CIA and other intelligence agencies to establish with high probability that North Korea's claims are not duplicitous.[80]

The second issue will be the status of North Korea's uranium enrichment program, which the United States first accused North Korea of operating in 2002. Whereas a North Korean representative apparently acknowledged the program, Pyongyang representatives have since denied the existence of such an effort. The United States reached the conclusion that North Korea was pursuing such a program, a violation at the very least of the 1991 denuclearization agreement, based on the North's purchase of twenty centrifuges from Pakistan (in exchange for No Dong missiles) as well as its massive purchase of aluminum tubes. Even agencies such as the State Department

Bureau of Intelligence and Research that had challenged the assertion that Iraq's purchase of such tubes was linked to nuclear ambitions were in agreement that the North's acquisition of the tubes was related to uranium enrichment. According to John Bolton, "There was no dissent at the time, because in the face of the evidence the disputes evaporated."There was also some tentative intelligence that the North was building a factory to produce centrifuges.[81]*

In March 2007, some news reports suggested that the Intelligence Community's confidence in the overall existence of the program had dropped from high to moderate—while there was high confidence that North Korea had pursued uranium enrichment in the past, there was only moderate confidence that it was still doing so. In response to suggestions that the Bush administration had not been on solid ground in challenging North Korea on the uranium enrichment issue in 2002, North Korea mission manager Joseph De Trani issued a press release noting that "the intelligence in 2002 was high quality information that made possible a high confidence judgment about North Korea's effort to acquire a uranium enrichment capability. The Intelligence Community had then, and continues to have, confidence in its assessment that North Korea has pursued that capability." He went on to state that "we have continued to assess efforts by North Korea since 2002. All Intelligence Community agencies have at least moderate confidence that North Korea's past efforts to acquire a uranium enrichment capability continue today."[82]

That the Intelligence Community has moderate rather than high confidence in this judgment apparently stems from a dearth of information on the North's current activities, which may be a product of North Korea's lack of progress in the area, its complete cancellation of the program, or the type of successful operational security measures that have kept other nuclear weapons programs hidden from U.S. intelligence.[83] That also raises the question of how well the Intelligence Community will be able to assure U.S. national security officials that North Korea's claims concerning its uranium enrichment program, or lack thereof, are actually true.

THROUGHOUT 2006 and early 2007, America's spies continued to monitor the Iranian and North Korean nuclear programs, including collecting and analyzing data on the North Korean test of October 9. As with the tests of

---

* For a challenge to the argument that the 2002 data provided persuasive evidence that North Korea was pursuing uranium enrichment, see David Albright, "North Korea's Alleged Large-Scale Enrichment Plant: Yet Another Questionable Interpretation Based on Aluminum Tubes," February 23, 2007, www.isis-online.org.

other nations—from the Soviet Union in 1949 to India and Pakistan in 1998—the intelligence on the North Korean nuclear test collected and analyzed by U.S. intelligence organizations was intended to produce a better understanding of the North's nuclear weapons capabilities.

The results of the intelligence effort directed against all aspects of the Iranian and North Korean programs (supplemented by the data provided by the IAEA with respect to Iran) might give the president and other senior officials the information they need to intelligently guide their actions among policy options—whether verifying or challenging North Korean compliance with nuclear disarmament agreements or using military force against Iranian nuclear facilities—and to persuade the public, legislators in the United States, and foreign governments of the wisdom of their actions.[84]

But the events of 2006 and early 2007 also illustrated that America's nuclear intelligence efforts concerning Iran and North Korea might well have a limited impact in terms of shaping international responses, no matter how successful the efforts. A blind-faith belief in negotiations often cannot be undermined by intelligence reporting, since it can always be argued that if only the United States and other nations offer the right package of inducements (possibly including overlooking such matters as a nation's counterfeiting of U.S. currency), the offending party's behavior can be changed. Thus, one writer for a major newspaper wrote, in the aftermath of North Korea's nuclear test, that "moral suasion and sustained bargaining" were "the proven mechanisms of nuclear restraint," while a former U.S. CIA official and ambassador to South Korea wrote that "the only path to success with North Korea is negotiation."[85]

Such a worldview may be ill equipped to accept the idea that certain regimes and leaders are incorrigible and negotiate only as a stalling tactic until they have attained a deterrent capability against the United States and other nations that might act against their nuclear programs. Iranian nuclear negotiator Hassan Rouhani told his nation's Supreme Cultural Revolution Council in September 2005 that Iran, in dealing with the IAEA, had agreed to suspend activities only in areas where it was not experiencing technical problems and that the Esfahan uranium conversion facility was completed while negotiating with the EU-3. Rouhani informed the council that "while we were talking with the Europeans in Tehran, we were installing equipment in parts of the facility . . . by creating a calm environment, we were able to complete the work."[86]

Intelligence data may also fail to persuade nations who claim they are opposed to sanctions, or seek to weaken them, because they would not accomplish the stated objective, when the actual reason for their opposition is based on their calculation of their national interest—in terms of their trade relations with the offending nation or their desire to undermine American power and influence—or simple cowardice. It is hard, after all, to take seriously Russian and Chinese claims that they are opposed to the use of coercive measures and threats in international diplomacy, given their policies toward some of the former Soviet states and Taiwan, respectively. And even if one understands a South Korean reluctance to intercept North Korean ships because of a fear that such action by the *South* could escalate to war, it is hard to be charitable about the South's reluctance to invoke any significant economic penalties for the North's test.[87]

Nevertheless, the more accurate U.S. nuclear intelligence analysts can be about the status of the nuclear programs of nations like Iran and North Korea, the better the chance of minimizing the threat from such nations—by keeping decisionmakers apprised of those nations' nuclear progress, monitoring compliance with agreements and treaties, and watching for transfers of nuclear technology, particularly to terrorist groups.

ABBREVIATIONS AND ACRONYMS

ABBREVIATIONS AND ACRONYMS

ACDA	Arms Control and Disarmament Agency
AEB	Atomic Energy Board (South Africa)
AEC	Atomic Energy Commission
AEC	Atomic Energy Corporation (South Africa)
AFOAT-1	Air Force Deputy Chief of Staff for Operations, Atomic Energy Office, Section 1
AFSA	Armed Forces Security Agency
AFTAC	Air Force Technical Applications Center
BARC	Bhabha Atomic Research Centre (India)
CEA	Commissariat l'Énergie Atomique (France)
CIA	Central Intelligence Agency
CIG	Central Intelligence Group
CIRUS	Canadian, Indian, U.S.
COMINT	Communications Intelligence
COMIREX	Committee on Imagery Requirements and Exploitation
COMOR	Committee on Overhead Reconnaissance
CREST	CIA Records Search Tool
DARPA	Defense Advanced Research Projects Agency
DCI	Director of Central Intelligence
DGSE	General Directorate for External Security (France)
DHS	Defense HUMINT Service
DIA	Defense Intelligence Agency
DMSP	Defense Meteorological Satellite Program
DNI	Director of National Intelligence
DPRK	Democratic People's Republic of Korea
DRDO	Defence Research and Development Organization (India)
DSP	Defense Support Program
ELF	Extremely Low Frequency
EMET	Research and Planning Division (Israel)
EMIS	Electromagnetic Isotope Separation

ETH	Federal Technical College (Switzerland)
FAG	Field Activities Group
GARP	Global Atmospheric Research Program
GRU	Chief Intelligence Directorate (Soviet General Staff)
HEU	Highly Enriched Uranium
HHPL	Herbert Hoover Presidential Library
HTPL	Harry Truman Presidential Library
HUMINT	Human Intelligence
IAEA	International Atomic Energy Agency
IAEC	Israeli Atomic Energy Commission
ICBM	Intercontinental Ballistic Missile
INER	Institute of Nuclear Energy Research (Taiwan)
INR	Bureau of Intelligence and Research
ITD	International Technology Division
JAEIC	Joint Atomic Energy Intelligence Committee
JCAE	Joint Committee on Atomic Energy
JCS	Joint Chiefs of Staff
JFKL	John F. Kennedy Library
JNEIC	Joint Nuclear Energy Intelligence Committee
KANUPP	Karachi Nuclear Power Project
KGB	Committee on State Security (Soviet Union)
KH	Keyhole
LAKAM	Scientific Liaison Bureau (Israel)
LANL	Los Alamos National Laboratory
MED	Manhattan Engineer District
MILS	Missile Impact Location System
MIT	Massachusetts Institute of Technology
MVD	Ministry of Internal Affairs (Soviet Union)
NARA	National Archives and Records Administration
NDRE	Norwegian Defense Research Establishment
NGA	National Geospatial Intelligence Agency
NIA	National Intelligence Authority
NIE	National Intelligence Estimate
NII	Scientific Research Institute (Soviet Union)
NIMA	National Imagery and Mapping Agency
NIS	National Intelligence Survey
NKVD	People's Commissariat of Internal Affairs (Soviet Union)
NPIC	National Photographic Interpretation Center
NPT	Nonproliferation Treaty
NRL	Naval Research Laboratory
NRO	National Reconnaissance Office
NSA	National Security Agency
NSAM	National Security Action Memorandum

NSC	National Security Council
NSCID	National Security Council Intelligence Directive
NSDD	National Security Decision Directive
ONI	Office of Naval Intelligence
OSI	Office of Scientific Intelligence
OSRD	Office of Scientific Research and Development
OSS	Office of Strategic Services
OSTP	Office of Science and Technology Policy
PEG	Priority Exploitation Group
PINSTECH	Pakistan Institute of Science and Technology
PNE	Peaceful Nuclear Explosion
POW	Prisoner of War
PSF	President's Security Files
RAFAEL	Armament Development Authority (Israel)
RAPS	Rajasthan Atomic Power Station
RDS	Stalin's Rocket Engine
ROC	Republic of China
SAC	Strategic Air Command
SCATHA	Spacecraft Charging at High Altitudes
SCS	Special Collection Service
SDS	Satellite Data System
SGN	Saint Gobain Nucléaire
SID	Defense Information Service (Italy)
SIPRI	Stockholm International Peace Research Institute
SIS	British Secret Intelligence Service
SISMI	Service for Information and Military Security (Italy)
SNIE	Special National Intelligence Estimate
SOSUS	Sound Surveillance System
SSCI	Senate Select Committee on Intelligence
SSU	Strategic Services Unit
SVR	Foreign Intelligence Service (Russia)
TBP	Tributyl Phosphate
UKNA	United Kingdom National Archives
UN	United Nations
UNSCOM	U.N. Special Commission on Iraq
URENCO	Uranium Enrichment Corporation
USASA	United States Army Security Agency
USGS	United States Geological Survey
USIB	United States Intelligence Board
VLF	Very Low Frequency
WINPAC	Weapons Intelligence, Nonproliferation, and Arms Control Center (CIA)
WMD	Weapons of Mass Destruction
WRS	Weather Reconnaissance Squadron

ACKNOWLEDGMENTS

A VARIETY OF INDIVIDUALS and institutions played a significant role in the production of this book. There are those who have researched and written about foreign nuclear weapons programs and U.S. nuclear intelligence efforts—in books, magazines and journals, newspapers, and on the Web sites of a variety of organizations. Although they did not undertake their work for my benefit, nonetheless it would have been impossible for one person to reproduce even a fraction of their work and I am grateful for their contributions.

A number of institutions have allowed me to examine their holdings or have provided documents in response to my requests. These include the California Institute of Technology, the American Institute of Physics, the Herbert Hoover Presidential Library, the Harry S. Truman Presidential Library, and the National Archives and Records Administration (NARA). Other organizations responded to some of my many Freedom of Information Act requests by releasing relevant documents, in whole or in part, including the Central Intelligence Agency, Defense Intelligence Agency, National Reconnaissance Office, State Department, Air Combat Command, and Los Alamos National Laboratory. I appreciate the work of the people who processed my requests and reviewed the documents.

A number of individuals are also due thanks. Both Robert S. Norris of the Natural Resources Defense Council and William Burr of the National Security Archive provided relevant documents as well as read each chapter and provided valuable suggestions and comments. Thomas Powers and Matin Zuberi provided helpful comments and suggestions with respect to selected chapters. Chris Pocock alerted me to relevant files in the U.K. National Archives and kindly copied a number of interesting documents that the archives contained. Others who provided information and suggestions include Matthew Aid, Desmond Ball, Hans Kristensen, Robert Windrem, and Dwayne Day. At the National Security Archive Magda Klotzenbach repeatedly printed out significant documents that were essential to this book.

Tim Brown's work was crucial to my being able to identify the dates and frequency of aerial and satellite coverage of a number of nuclear targets, as well as to my presenting some of the imagery obtained. He searched the data sets at NARA to determine when certain targets were photographed by the U-2, KH-4, and KH-7 reconnaissance systems and the quality of the imagery produced. He also located examples of the imagery in NARA's holdings, a particularly difficult task for U-2 imagery, and reproduced a selection for this book. As a result, a number of the images included in this book are appearing for the first time in an unclassified work.

Mark Brender and Valerie Webb of Space Imaging were instrumental in my being able to obtain their company's images of nuclear installations in Iran and North Korea.

I owe an enormous debt to those individuals who were willing to be interviewed for this book, either in person or via telephone. They include Alan Berman (Alexandria, Va., March 27, 2003), Dino Brugioni (January 23, 2003, February 21, 2003), Robert Furman (Rockville, Md., February 13, 2003), Robert L. Gallucci (Washington, D.C., June 22, 2004), Richard Garwin (July 24, 2004), Houston T. Hawkins (October 28, 2004), Lester Hubert (September 15, 2004), Thomas L. Hughes (Washington, D.C., September 8, 2004), Robert Johnson (Washington, D.C., May 9, 2003), David Kay (Arlington, Va., April 28, 2003), Spurgeon Keeny (Washington, D.C., February 6, 2003), Myron Kratzer (September 2, 2003), Philip Morrison (January 29, 2003), Jack Ruina (July 19, 2004), Leonard Spector (Washington, D.C., March 5, 2003), Waldo Stumpf (September 13, 2004), Greg Thielmann (Arlington, Va., October 20, 2004), Notra Trulock (Washington, D.C., March 28, 2003), Stansfield Turner (April 17, 2003), and Leonard Weiss (Silver Spring, Md., March 19, 2003).

In addition, others interviewed for past projects—the late Richard Bissell (Farmington, Conn., March 16, 1994), Jack Ledford (Arlington, Va., October 7, 1999), the late Karl Weber (Oakton, Va., May 5, 1999), and Albert Wheelon (Washington, D.C., April 9, 1997, and Montecito, Calif., November 11–12, 1998)—provided information that proved helpful for this book.

I would also like to thank the National Security Archive for its support, in a variety of ways. Of course, special thanks go to my editor, Leo Wiegman, Sarah Mann, and the others at W. W. Norton involved in the production of this book.

NOTES

CHAPTER 1: A TERRIFYING PROSPECT

1   "The History of Alamogordo," www.alamogordo.com, accessed August 8, 2003.

2   Richard Rhodes, *The Making of the Atomic Bomb* (New York: Simon and Schuster, 1986), p. 652; Leslie R. Groves, *Now It Can Be Told: The Story of the Manhattan Project* (New York: Da Capo Press, 1983), p. 289; Kal Bird and Martin Sherwin, *American Prometheus: The Triumph and Tragedy of J. Robert Oppenheimer* (New York: Knopf, 2005), p. 304.

3   Rhodes, *The Making of the Atomic Bomb*, p. 652; Peter Wyden, *Day One: Before Hiroshima and After* (New York: Simon & Schuster, 1984), p. 203; Gregg Herken, *Brotherhood of the Bomb: The Tangled Lives and Loyalties of Robert Oppenheimer, Ernest Lawrence, and Edward Teller* (New York: Henry Holt, 2002), pp. 128–129.

4   Rhodes, *The Making of the Atomic Bomb*, p. 653.

5   Ibid., p. 668; Maj. Gen. L. R. Groves, Memorandum for the Secretary of War, Subject: The Test, July 18, 1945, pp. 9–10.

6   www.atomicarchive.com/Fission," accessed September 5, 2003.

7   Robert S. Norris, *Racing for the Bomb: General Leslie R. Groves, the Manhattan Project's Indispensable Man* (South Royalton, Vt.: Steerforth Press, 2002), pp. 200–201, 205, 224, 365–366.

8   Groves, Memorandum for the Secretary of War, Subject: The Test, pp. 1–2.

9   Rhodes, *The Making of the Atomic Bomb*, p. 672; Wyden, *Day One*, 213n; I. I. Rabi, *Science: The Center of Culture* (New York: World Publishing, 1970), p. 139.

10 Maurice Goldsmith, *Frédéric Joliot-Curie: A Biography* (London: Lawrence and Wishart, 1976), p. 65; Rhodes, *The Making of the Atomic Bomb*, p. 262; Leo Mahoney, *A History of the War Department Scientific Intelligence Mission (ALSOS), 1943–1945* (Ann Arbor, Mich.: University Microfilms International, 1993), p. 59; Kristie Macrakis, *Surviving the Swastika: Scientific Research in Nazi Germany* (New York: Oxford University Press, 1993), p. 163.

11 R. V. Jones, "Introduction," in Samuel A. Goudsmit, *ALSOS* (Los Angeles, Calif.: Tomash, 1983), p. ix; Goldsmith, *Frédéric Joliot-Curie*, pp. 67–68; David Bodanis, *E=mc²: A Biography of the World's Most Famous Equation* (New York: Berkley, 2000), pp. 100–113; Jeremy Bernstein, *Hitler's Uranium Club: The Secret Recordings at Farm Hall* (New York: Springer-Verlag, 2001), p. 11 n. 18. Also see Ruth Lewin

Sime, "The Search for Transuranium Elements and the Discovery of Nuclear Fission," *Physics in Perspective*, 2, 1 (March 2000), pp. 48–62. The Meitner-Frisch article was titled "Disintegration of Uranium by Neutrons: A New Type of Nuclear Reaction" (Rhodes, *The Making of the Atomic Bomb*, p. 856).

12   Goldsmith, *Frédéric Joliot-Curie*, pp. 71–72.

13   "Albert Einstein to Franklin D. Roosevelt, August 2, 1939," in Michael B. Stoff and Jonathan F. Fanton, *The Manhattan Project: A Documentary Introduction to the Atomic Age* (Philadelphia: Temple University Press, 1991), pp. 18–19.

14   "The Frisch-Peierls Memorandum, 1940," in Philip L. Cantelon, Richard G. Hewlett, and Robert C. Williams (eds.), *The American Atom: A Documentary History of Nuclear Policies from the Discovery of Fission to the Present* (Philadelphia: University of Pennsylvania Press, 1984), pp. 11–15; Paul Lawrence Rose, *Heisenberg and the Nazi Atomic Bomb Project: A Study in German Culture* (Berkeley: University of California Press, 1998), pp. 101–102; David Holloway, *Stalin and the Bomb: The Soviet Union and Atomic Energy* (New Haven: Yale University Press, 1994), pp. 75–79.

15   Bernstein, *Hitler's Uranium Club*, pp. 1, 364; Mark Walker, *German National Socialism and the Quest for Nuclear Power, 1939–1949* (New York: Cambridge University Press, 1989), pp. 17–18; Rose, *Heisenberg and the Nazi Atomic Bomb Project*, p. 95.

16   Walker, *German National Socialism and the Quest for Nuclear Power*, p. 17; Bernstein, *Hitler's Uranium Club*, p. 3; Thomas Powers, *Heisenberg's War: The Secret History of the German Bomb* (New York: Knopf, 1993), p. 94; David Cassidy, *Uncertainty: The Life and Science of Werner Heisenberg* (New York: W. H. Freeman, 1992), pp. 419–420.

17   Bernstein, *Hitler's Uranium Club*, pp. 2, 363.

18   Cassidy, *Uncertainty*, pp. ix, 91–92, 215, 226, 228, 231, 242, 247; Bernstein, *Hitler's Uranium Club*, p. 364. On the complementarity principle and the statistical interpretation of Schrödinger's wave function, see Helge Kragh, *Quantum Generations: A History of Physics in the Twentieth Century* (Princeton: Princeton University Press, 1999), pp. 209–210, and Robert P. Crease and Charles C. Mann, *The Second Creation: Makers of the Revolution in Twentieth-Century Physics* (New Brunswick, N.J.: Rutgers University Press, 1996), p. 61.

19   Bernstein, *Hitler's Uranium Club*, pp. 3, 24; "Albert Einstein to Franklin D. Roosevelt, August 2, 1939," pp. 10–11; Kragh, *Quantum Generations*, pp. 169, 183–185, 235, 260, 265, 271, 350–351; Macrakis, *Surviving the Swastika*, p. 168.

20   Bernstein, *Hitler's Uranium Club*, p. 3.

21   David Cassidy, "Introduction," in Bernstein, *Hitler's Uranium Club*, p. xxiii; Macrakis, *Surviving the Swastika*, p. 168; Powers, *Heisenberg's War*, p. 16.

22   Cassidy, "Introduction," p. xxiii; Cassidy, *Uncertainty*, p. 421.

23   Cassidy, *Uncertainty*, pp. 420–423; Cassidy, "Introduction," pp. xxiv–xxv.

24   Lore R. David and I. A. Warheit, *German Reports on Atomic Energy: A Bibliography of Unclassified Literature* (Washington, D.C.: U.S. Atomic Energy Commission, 1952), passim; Macrakis, *Surviving the Swastika*, p. 167.

25   David and Warheit, *German Reports on Atomic Energy*, p. 10; Cassidy, "Introduction," pp. xxiv–xxv; Bernstein, *Hitler's Uranium Club*, p. 58.

26   David and Warheit, *German Reports on Atomic Energy*, p. 9; Bernstein, *Hitler's Uranium Club*, p. 30.

27   Bernstein, *Hitler's Uranium Club*, pp. 33–34; Rose, *Heisenberg and the Nazi Atomic Bomb Project*, p. 136; Powers, *Heisenberg's War*, p. 84; Bird and Sherwin, *American Prometheus*, p. 63.

28   Cassidy, "Introduction," p. xxvi; David and Warheit, *German Reports on Atomic Energy*, p. 13; Bernstein, *Hitler's Uranium Club*, p. 13.

29   Rose, *Heisenberg and the Nazi Atomic Bomb Project*, pp. 9–10; Cassidy, "Introduction," p. xxv.

30   Macrakis, *Surviving the Swastika*, p. 169.

31   Ibid.; William L. Shirer, *The Rise and Fall of the Third Reich: A History of Nazi Germany* (New York: Simon & Schuster, 1960), p. 903.

32   Macrakis, *Surviving the Swastika*, p. 169; Rose, *Heisenberg and the Nazi Atomic Bomb Project*, p. 173.

33   Macrakis, *Surviving the Swastika*, p. 169; Rose, *Heisenberg and the Nazi Atomic Bomb Project*, pp. 167–171.

34   Macrakis, *Surviving the Swastika*, p. 170; "Vortragsfolge," Samuel A. Goudsmit Papers, Box 25, Folder 13, American Institute of Physics, College Park, Md.; Cassidy, *Uncertainty*, pp. 444–445; Rose, *Heisenberg and the Nazi Atomic Bomb Project*, pp. 174–175, 177–178; Werner Heisenberg, "A Lecture on Bomb Physics: February 1942," *Physics Today*, August 1995, pp. 27–30.

35   Cassidy, *Uncertainty*, p. 444; Goudsmit, *ALSOS*, pp. 170–171; Heisenberg, "A Lecture on Bomb Physics."

36   Macrakis, *Surviving the Swastika*, p. 171.

37   Ibid., p. 174; Rose, *Heisenberg and the Nazi Atomic Bomb Project*, p. 173; Cassidy, *Uncertainty*, pp. 451–452; Albert Speer, *Inside the Third Reich* (New York: Macmillan, 1970), p. 225.

38   Cassidy, *Uncertainty*, pp. 455–458; Macrakis, *Surviving the Swastika*, p. 173; Bernstein, *Hitler's Uranium Club*, p. 40; Speer, *Inside the Third Reich*, p. 226; Rose, *Heisenberg and the Nazi Atomic Bomb*, pp. 179–184. Whether Heisenberg, through his comments to Speer and other actions, sought to sabotage, for moral reasons, any German attempt to build an atomic bomb has been a subject of major controversy for decades, as are his motives in meeting with Niels Bohr in Copenhagen in September 1941. The two primary books on the issue, which reach diametrically opposite conclusions, are Powers, *Heisenberg's War*, and Rose, *Heisenberg and the Nazi Atomic Bomb Project*. The issue is also discussed in *Hitler's Uranium Club* (which includes transcripts of conversations among the key German atomic scientists during their immediate postwar captivity in England), Cassidy's *Uncertainty*, and John Cornwell's *Hitler's Scientists: Science, War, and the Devil's Pact* (New York: Viking, 2003), and has been the subject of articles, letters, and exchanges in the *New York Review of Books*, *Bulletin of the Atomic Scientists*, *Nature*, and *Physics Today*.

I do not examine the issue in this book because I do not believe it is of great relevance from the point of view of those involved in collecting and analyzing intelligence on a possible German atomic bomb effort, or of those who approved the U.S.-British effort out of concern about the Germans might be doing. Analysis and policy decisions would have to be made on the basis of hard facts, or lack thereof, of what the Germans were doing, not trust in the benevolence of physicists who were under Hitler's thumb. For what it's worth, I do not believe that Heisenberg understood that an atomic bomb could be built but sought to sabotage, along with others, the German effort. See Bernstein, *Hitler's Uranium Club*, pp. 113–140, especially p. 117, for Heisenberg's reaction to Hiroshima, which does not seem to be the reaction of a scientist who *knows* an atomic bomb is feasible.

39   Macrakis, *Surviving the Swastika*, pp. 174–175; David and Warheit, *German Reports on Atomic Energy*, pp. 17–33. Since *German Reports* does not specify the month of publication, the January–August 1943 number is an estimate.

40   Bernstein, *Hitler's Uranium Club*, p. 45.

41   Powers, *Heisenberg's War*, p. 187; H. A. Bethe and E. Teller to J. R. Oppenheimer, August 21, 1943, J. Robert Oppenheimer Papers, Box 20, H. A. Bethe Folder, Manuscript Division, Library of Congress; Rabi, *Science*, p. 141. The concern about a German atomic bomb was not restricted to those inside the Manhattan Project or even the U.S. government. In December 1943, articles in *Newsweek* and the *Rochester Democrat and Chronicle* raised the specter of a Nazi A-bomb. See James S. Murray, Memorandum for Officer in Charge, Subject: D.S.M. Project, December 16, 1943, RG 77, Entry 22, Box 165, NARA; "Uranium Seen as Key to New Secret Bombs," *Rochester Democrat and Chronicle*, December 26, 1943.

42   Rhodes, *The Making of the Atomic Bomb*, p. 405; Groves, *Now It Can Be Told*, p. 185.

43   Groves, *Now It Can Be Told*, p. 185.

44   Ibid., pp. 185–186.

45   Powers, *Heisenberg's War*, pp. 217, 286.

46   Ibid., p. 218; Interview with Robert Furman, Rockville, Md., February 13, 2003; Goudsmit, *ALSOS*, p. 16.

47   Powers, *Heisenberg's War*, pp. 218–219; Goudsmit, *ALSOS*, p. 16; Furman interview.

48   Macrakis, *Surviving the Swastika*, pp. 171, 244 n. 36; Bernstein, *Hitler's Uranium Club*, p. 35; Rose, *Heisenberg and the Nazi Atomic Bomb Project*, p. 143. On pp. 143–145 Rose discusses the apparent paradox of a German scientist both making a key discovery that increases the prospects of a German bomb *and* warning the Allies of Germany's bomb project.

49   John V. H. Dippel, *Two Against Hitler: Stealing the Nazi's Best-Kept Secrets* (New York: Praeger, 1991), pp. x, 21, 29, 80–81.

50   Ibid., p. 93.

51   John Lansdale Jr., "Military Service" (unpublished manuscript, 1987), pp. 37, 40; Norris, *Racing for the Bomb*, pp. 288–289.

52   Groves, *Now It Can Be Told*, pp. 9, 54; Arthur H. Compton to Major A. V. Peterson, "Situation in Germany," June 2, 1943, RG 77, Entry 22, Box 170, Folder 32.60-1,

NARA. On Compton's work, and Nobel Prize, see Kragh, *Quantum Generations*, pp. 161, 194, 435.

53   Compton to Peterson, "Situation in Germany."

54   Ibid.

55   F. H. Hinsley, E. E. Thomas, C. A. G. Simkins, and C. F. G. Ransom, *British Intelligence in the Second World War, Volume 3, Part 2* (New York: Cambridge University Press, 1988), p. 932; F. H. Hinsley, E. E. Thomas, C. F. G. Ransom, and R. C. Knight, *British Intelligence in the Second World War, Volume 2* (New York: Cambridge University Press, 1981), p. 124.

56   Hinsley, Thomas, Simkins, and Ransom, *British Intelligence in the Second World War, Volume 3, Part 2*, p. 932.

57   Hinsley, Thomas, Ransom, and Knight, *British Intelligence in the Second World War, Volume 2*, pp. 125–126; Bernstein, *Hitler's Uranium Club*, p. 44; R. V. Jones, *Reflections on Intelligence* (London: Mandarin, 1990), p. 284.

58   Hinsley, Thomas, Simkins, and Ransom, *British Intelligence in the Second World War, Volume 3, Part 2*, pp. 933–935, 938; Hinsley, Thomas, Ransom, and Knight, *British Intelligence in the Second World War, Volume 2*, p. 124; Arnold Kramish, *The Griffin* (Boston: Houghton Mifflin, 1986), pp. 129–130.

59   Hinsley, Thomas, Ransom, and Knight, *British Intelligence in the Second World War, Volume 2*, pp. 123–124, 127; R. V. Jones, *The Wizard War: British Scientific Intelligence, 1939–1945* (New York: Coward, McCann & Geohegan, 1978), p. 206; Charles Cruickshank, *Special Operations Executive in Scandinavia: The Official History* (New York: Oxford University Press, 1986), pp. 198–202; Jeffrey T. Richelson, *A Century of Spies: Intelligence in the Twentieth Century* (New York: Oxford University Press, 1995), pp. 149–151.

60   Jones, "Introduction," p. xi; Jones, *Reflections on Intelligence*, p. 284.

61   Furman interview.

62   Ibid.

63   Powers, *Heisenberg's War*, p. 223.

64   Ibid.

65   J. R. Oppenheimer to Major Robert Furman, September 22, 1943, J. Robert Oppenheimer Papers, Box 34, Robert Furman Folder, Manuscript Division, Library of Congress.

66   Ibid.

67   Ibid.

68   Ibid.

69   Ibid.

70   E-mail, Philip Morrison to author, January 21, 2003; "Philip Morrison," web.mit.edu, accessed May 9, 2002; P. Morrison to S. K. Allison, September 23, 1943, and Samuel K. Allison to Brig. Gen. L. R. Groves, October 11, 1943, both in RG 77, Entry 22, Box 170, Folder 32.60-1, NARA.

71   Morrison to Allison, September 23, 1943.

72   Ibid.

73   Ibid. On the other side of the Atlantic, Rudolf Peierls had done work similar to Morrison's for the British. See Powers, *Heisenberg's War*, p. 74.

74   Vincent C. Jones, *Manhattan: The Army and the Bomb* (Washington, D.C.: Center of Military History, 1985), p. 282; Powers, *Heisenberg's War*, p. 214.

75   H. W. Dix to Colonel O'Conor, Subject: Joachimsthal, December 2, 1943; Lt. Col. H. W. Dix to Brig. Gen. Leslie R. Groves, January 11, 1944; and SI, Special Projects Section to W. H. Shepardson, Chief, SI, Subject: Azusa, Report of Present Status, January 24, 1944—all in RG 226, Entry 210, Box 431, Folder 2, NARA.

76   Powers, *Heisenberg's War*, p. 242; Jeremy Bernstein, "What Did Heisenberg Tell Bohr About the Bomb?" *Scientific American*, May 1995, pp. 92–97.

77   Bernstein, *Hitler's Uranium Club*, p. 13; Powers, *Heisenberg's War*, pp. 242–243; Rhodes, *The Making of the Atomic Bomb*, p. 849.

78   Bradley F. Smith, *The Shadow Warriors: O.S.S. and the Origins of the C.I.A.* (New York: Basic Books, 1983), passim.

79   Powers, *Heisenberg's War*, pp. 227–228; Norris, *Racing for the Bomb*, p. 290.

80   Powers, *Heisenberg's War*, p. 228; Richard Harris Smith, *OSS: The Secret History of America's First Central Intelligence Agency* (Berkeley: University of California Press, 1981), p. 204; Kragh, *Quantum Generations*, p. 239.

81   Peter Grose, *Gentleman Spy: The Life of Allen Dulles* (Boston: Houghton Mifflin, 1994), p. 214; Powers, *Heisenberg's War*, pp. 167, 272–273.

82   Grose, *Gentleman Spy*, p. 214; Powers, *Heisenberg's War*, p. 271.

83   Office of Strategic Services Official Dispatch (from Bern, Switzerland to Office of Strategic Services), March 24, 1944, RG 226, Entry 134, Box 219, Folder 1370, NARA; Office of Strategic Services, Official Dispatch (from Office of Strategic Services to Bern), November 30, 1943, RG 226, Entry 134, Box 219, Folder 1371, NARA; Bernstein, *Hitler's Uranium Club*, p. 48.

84   Office of Strategic Services Official Dispatch (from Bern, Switzerland, to Office of Strategic Services), May 11, 1944, RG 226, Entry 134, Box 219, Folder 1370, NARA.

85   Powers, *Heisenberg's War*, pp. 294–295; Nicholas Dawidoff, *The Catcher Was a Spy: The Mysterious Life of Moe Berg* (New York: Pantheon Books, 1994), pp. 17, 53.

86   Powers, *Heisenberg's War*, p. 295; "Moe Berg," www.baseball-reference.com, accessed June 30, 2005; Dawidoff, *The Catcher Was a Spy*, p. 50.

87   Dawidoff, *The Catcher Was a Spy*, pp. 4, 21, 31–33, 36–37, 54–56, 61, 70, 82; Powers, *Heisenberg's War*, pp. 294–295; Norris, *Racing for the Bomb*, p. 290.

88   Dawidoff *The Catcher Was a Spy*, p. 214.

89   Ibid., pp. 161–162.

90   Office of Strategic Services Official Dispatch (from Bern, Switzerland, to Office of Strategic Services), April 3, 1944, RG 226, Entry 134, Box 219, Folder 1370, NARA.

91   Powers, *Heisenberg's War*, pp. 287–288.

92   Luis W. Alvarez, *Alvarez: Adventures of a Physicist* (New York: Basic Books, 1987), pp. 22–24, 38, 86; Rhodes, *The Making of the Atomic Bomb*, pp. 143, 273, 349; Herken, *Brotherhood of the Bomb*, p. 20; Peter D. Ward and Donald Brownlee, *Rare Earth:*

Why Complex Life Is Uncommon in the Universe (New York: Copernicus, 2000), p. 164; Powers, *Heisenberg's War*, p. 222.

93   Alvarez, *Alvarez*, p. 120.

94   Ibid. Xenon is one of six noble gases (along with helium, neon, argon, krypton, and radon), all but one of which was discovered by Sir William Ramsey in the 1890s. These gases do not form compounds readily, and all have the maximum number of electrons in their outer shell, making them stable. See www.chemicalelements.com/groups/noblegases.html.

95   Alvarez, *Alvarez*, p. 120.

96   Ibid.; Furman interview; Powers, *Heisenberg's War*, p. 223.

97   Maj. R. R. Furman to Mr. Luis Alvarez, May 12, 1944, LANL Archives.

98   Luis W. Alvarez to Maj. R. R. Furman, May 17, 1944, LANL Archives.

99   P. Morrison to S. K. Allison, "Report on the Enemy Materials Situation," November 30, 1943/December 23, 1943, RG 77, Entry 22, Box 170, Folder 32.60-1, NARA.

100   P. Morrison to S. K. Allison, "Report on Enemy Physics Literature: Survey Report P," December 20, 1943, RG 77, Entry 22, Box 170, Folder 32.60-1, NARA.

101   Ibid., p. 7.

102   "Summary," December 22, 1943, RG 77, Entry 22, Box 170, Folder 32.60-1, NARA.

103   Ibid.

104   Samuel K. Allison to Brig. Gen. L. R. Groves, January 7, 1944, RG 77, Entry 22, Box 170, Folder 32.60-1, NARA.

105   Maj. R. R. Furman, Memorandum to Brig. Gen. L. R. Groves, Subject: Report on Enemy Activities, March 7, 1944, RG 77, Entry 22, Box 170, Folder 32.60-1, NARA.

106   Ibid.

107   Powers, *Heisenberg's War*, pp. 219–221.

108   Karl Cohen, "Report on German Literature on Isotope Separation," March 27, 1944, RG 77, Entry 22, Box 170, Folder 32.60-1, NARA. Oppenheimer was also concerned about German scientific articles that were a little too reassuring, and wrote to Furman earlier in the month to express his concerns. See Powers, *Heisenberg's War*, p. 285.

109   Cohen, "Report on German Literature on Isotope Separation," p. 9.

110   Harold C. Urey to Maj. Gen. L. R. Groves, April 4, 1944, RG 77, Entry 22, Box 170, Folder 32.60-1, NARA; Powers, *Heisenberg's War*, p. 380.

111   Macrakis, *Surviving the Swastika*, p. 177.

112   Ibid.; Cassidy, *Uncertainty*, p. 487.

113   Macrakis, *Surviving the Swastika*, p. 176; Powers, *Heisenberg's War*, p. 335.

114   Cassidy, *Uncertainty*, p. 488.

115   Ibid., p. 489; Powers, *Heisenberg's War*, pp. 336–337.

116   Morrison to Allison, "Report on Enemy Physics Literature."

117   Macrakis, *Surviving the Swastika*, pp. 177–178.

118   Dawidoff, *The Catcher Was a Spy*, pp. 167–168.

119   Ibid., p. 169.

120   Ibid., pp. 172–173.

121 Ibid., pp. 173–175, 177–179.
122 Berg to Buxton, Shepardson, and Dix, June 12, 1944, RG 226, Entry 210, Box 431, Folder 2, NARA.
123 Ibid.
124 Dawidoff, *The Catcher Was a Spy*, pp. 181–182.
125 Ibid., pp. 184, 187–188.
126 Powers, *Heisenberg's War*, p. 375.
127 Ibid.
128 Charles A. Ziegler and David Jacobson, *Spying Without Spies: Origins of America's Secret Nuclear Surveillance System* (Westport, Conn.: Praeger, 1995), p. 7.
129 Powers, *Heisenberg's War*, pp. 376–377.
130 Ibid., p. 377.
131 Dawidoff, *The Catcher Was a Spy*, pp. 194, 199–202. A letter from Howard Dix to William F. Quinn, the head of the Strategic Services Unit in 1946 (the successor to the OSS secret intelligence and counterintelligence branches), gives the date of the lecture as December 23. It does not mention that Berg had the option of killing Heisenberg. Letter, Howard Dix to Col. Wm. F. Quinn, September 30, 1946.
132 Dawidoff, *The Catcher Was a Spy*, pp. 191–194.
133 Ibid., pp. 202–207; Helmut Rechenberg, "Werner Heisenberg: The Columbus of Quantum Mechanics," www.cerncourier.com/main/article/41/10/16, accessed October 8, 2003.
134 Lansdale, "Military Service," pp. 37–38; Groves, *Now It Can Be Told*, pp. 190–191; Norris, *Racing for the Bomb*, p. 285; Maj. Gen. G. V. Strong, Memorandum to Chief of Staff, [no title], Washington, D.C., September 25, 1943.
135 Rhodes, *The Making of the Atomic Bomb*, pp. 605–606; Groves, *Now It Can Be Told*, pp. 192–193; Norris, *Racing for the Bomb*, p. 286; Lansdale, "Military Service," p. 38; Jones, *Manhattan*, p. 281.
136 Groves, *Now It Can Be Told*, pp. 192–193; Jones, *Manhattan*, pp. 281–282.
137 Groves, *Now It Can Be Told*, p. 207; Jones, *Manhattan*, pp. 285–286; Norris, *Racing for the Bomb*, pp. 286–287.
138 Groves, *Now It Can Be Told*, p. 208; Jones, *Manhattan*, p. 285; Norris, *Racing for the Bomb*, p. 296.
139 Norris, *Racing for the Bomb*, p. 296; Powers, *Heisenberg's War*, p. 314.
140 Bernstein, *Hitler's Uranium Club*, pp. 46–47; Kragh, *Quantum Generations*, p. 163; Goudsmit, *ALSOS*, pp. 15, 47; Powers, *Heisenberg's War*, p. 352; Brian Greene, *The Elegant Universe: Superstrings, Hidden Dimensions, and the Quest for the Ultimate Theory* (New York: W. W. Norton, 1999), p. 171.
141 Groves, *Now It Can Be Told*, pp. 209–210.
142 Ibid., pp. 211–212.
143 Ibid., pp. 213–215; Goudsmit, *ALSOS*, p. 34; Norris, *Racing for the Bomb*, p. 299.
144 Boris T. Pash, *The ALSOS Mission* (New York: Charter, 1969), pp. 83, 85–86; Norris, *Racing for the Bomb*, p. 299.

145   Pash, *The ALSOS Mission*, pp. 91–92; Norris, *Racing for the Bomb*, pp. 299–300; Groves, *Now It Can Be Told*, p. 219.

146   Norris, *Racing for the Bomb*, p. 300; Jones, *Manhattan*, p. 287.

147   Pash, *The ALSOS Mission*, pp. 133–134. Perhaps Washington saw through the joke and realized they had an opportunity to acquire some French wine, quickly and cheaply.

148   Ibid., pp. 87, 130; Norris, *Racing for the Bomb*, p. 300.

149   Groves, *Now It Can Be Told*, pp. 221–222; Goudsmit, *ALSOS*, p. 66; Pash, *The ALSOS Mission*, p. 156; Norris, *Racing for the Bomb*, pp. 300–301.

150   Norris, *Racing for the Bomb*, p. 301; Goudsmit, *ALSOS*, pp. 67, 70–71; Pash, *The ALSOS Mission*, p. 156; Morrison e-mail.

151   S. A. Goudsmit and F. A. C. Wardenburg, Subject: TA-Strassburg Mission, December 8, 1944, RG 77, Entry 22, Box 166, NARA; Powers, *Heisenberg's War*, p. 367. Information on Heisenberg and Weizsäcker being in Hechingen had been obtained by the OSS during the November 15–24 period from a Swiss source, Professor Edgar Meyer. The information was transmitted in full to Furman on December 20. OSS Bern, Report B-710, "Location of Forschungsstelle E.," November 24, 1944; Colonel H. W. Dix to Major Robert R. Furman, December 20, 1944.

152   Goudsmit and Wardenburg, Subject: TA- Strassburg Mission.

153   Goudsmit, *ALSOS*, p. 75.

154   Ibid., pp. 88–90; Pash, *The ALSOS Mission*, pp. 156–157, 187, 197; Groves, *Now It Can Be Told*, pp. 231–233; Norris, *Racing for the Bomb*, p. 303.

155   Groves, *Now It Can Be Told*, p. 234; Lansdale, "Military Service," p. 55; Jones, *Manhattan*, p. 290; Norris, *Racing for the Bomb*, p. 303.

156   Norris, *Racing for the Bomb*, p. 304.

157   Ibid.; Groves, *Now It Can Be Told*, p. 241; Goudsmit, *ALSOS*, p. 98.

158   Goudsmit, *ALSOS*, p. 108; Groves, *Now It Can Be Told*, pp. 241–242; Pash, *The ALSOS Mission*, pp. 216–217; Norris, *Racing for the Bomb*, pp. 304–305.

159   Norris, *Racing for the Bomb*, p. 305.

160   Ibid., p. 305.

161   Groves, *Now It Can Be Told*, p. 242; Norris, *Racing for the Bomb*, p. 306.

162   Groves, *Now It Can Be Told*, p. 244; Goudsmit, *ALSOS*, p. 121; Bernstein, *Hitler's Uranium Club*, pp. 363–365; Powers, *Heisenberg's War*, pp. 428–429.

CHAPTER 2: LIGHTNING STRIKES

1   Thomas Powers, *Heisenberg's War: The Secret History of the German Bomb* (New York: Knopf, 1993), p. 292.

2   David Holloway, *Stalin and the Bomb: The Soviet Union and Atomic Energy, 1939–1956* (New Haven: Yale University Press, 1994), pp. 9, 51–52; I. N. Golovin, *I.V. Kurchatov: A Socialist-Realist Biography of the Soviet Nuclear Scientist* (Bloomington, Ind.: Selbstverlag Press, 1968), p. 31; Richard Rhodes, *Dark Sun: The Mak-*

ing of the Hydrogen Bomb (New York: Simon & Schuster, 1995), p. 32; Steven J. Zaloga, *Target America: The Soviet Union and the Strategic Arms Race, 1945–1964* (Novato, Calif.: Presidio, 1993), p. 29.

3   Holloway, *Stalin and the Bomb*, pp. 52–53, 55; Yuli Khariton and Yuri Smirnov, "The Khariton Version," *Bulletin of the Atomic Scientists*, May 1993, pp. 20–31 at p. 23.

4   Holloway, *Stalin and the Bomb*, pp. 29–33, 61.

5   Ibid., pp. 31, 36–38, 62; Arnold Kramish, *Atomic Energy in the Soviet Union* (Stanford: Stanford University Press, 1959), p. 24; Golovin, *I.V. Kurchatov*, pp. 10–13; Rhodes, *Dark Sun*, p. 29.

6   Holloway, *Stalin and the Bomb*, p. 75.

7   Ibid., pp. 82–84; Jerrold Schecter and Leona Schecter, *Sacred Secrets: How Soviet Intelligence Operations Changed American History* (Washington, D.C.: Brassey's, 2002), p. 48; Rhodes, *Dark Sun*, pp. 163–164; Christopher Andrew and Vasili Mitrokhin, *The Sword and the Shield: The Mitrokhin Archive and the Secret History of the KGB* (New York: Basic Books, 1999), p. 118.

8   Holloway, *Stalin and the Bomb*, pp. 86, 96; Thomas B. Cochran, Robert S. Norris, and Oleg A. Bukharin, *Making the Russian Bomb: From Stalin to Yeltsin* (Boulder, Colo.: Westview, 1995), p. 7; Yury A. Yudin, *Manuscript on the History of the Soviet Nuclear Weapons and Nuclear Infrastructure* (Moscow: Ministry of Atomic Energy, n.d.), pp. 10, 49; Paul Podvig (ed.), *Russian Strategic Nuclear Forces* (Cambridge: MIT Press, 2001), pp. 68–69; Steven Zaloga, "The Soviet Nuclear Bomb Programme—The First Decade," *Jane's Soviet Intelligence Review*, April 1991, pp. 174–181 at 174–175; Helge Kragh, *Quantum Generations: A History of Physics in the Twentieth Century* (Princeton: Princeton University Press, 1999), p. 437.

9   Podvig (ed.), *Russian Strategic Nuclear Forces*, p. 69; Holloway, *Stalin and the Bomb*, p. 93; Rhodes, *Dark Sun*, pp. 29–30, 48.

10 Steven Zaloga, *The Kremlin's Nuclear Sword: The Rise and Fall of Russia's Strategic Nuclear Forces, 1945–2000* (Washington, D.C.: Smithsonian Institution Press, 2002), p. 7; Podvig (ed.), *Russian Strategic Nuclear Forces*, p. 69; Holloway, *Stalin and the Bomb*, pp. 116, 134.

11 Holloway, *Stalin and the Bomb*, pp. 105–106; Yudin, *Manuscript on the History of the Soviet Nuclear Weapons and Nuclear Infrastructure*, pp. 42–49; Henry De Wolf Smyth, *Atomic Energy for Military Purposes: The Official Report on the Development of the Atomic Bomb Under the Auspices of the United States Government, 1940–1945* (Princeton: Princeton University Press, 1945).

The importance of foreign espionage in support of the Soviet atomic bomb program has been a source of considerable controversy for two reasons: the debate between former Soviet intelligence officers and Soviet weapons scientists over the role that espionage material played in the development of the initial Soviet bombs, and the controversy over which American and British citizens served as Soviet spies at Los Alamos or elsewhere during World War II. On the first subject, see the May 1993 issue of the *Bulletin of the Atomic Scientists*, specifically the articles by David Holloway ("Soviet Scientists Speak Out," pp. 18–19), Yuli Khariton and Yuri

Smirnov ("The Khariton Version," pp. 20–31), and Sergei Leskov ("Dividing the Glory of the Fathers," pp. 37–37).

While it is generally accepted that the Venona decrypts establish that more Americans and Britains provided classified information to Soviet intelligence than have been identified publicly, the controversy concerns whether some very prominent scientists, including J. Robert Oppenheimer, did so. The books making such charges include Schecter and Schecter, *Sacred Secrets*, and Pavel Sudoplatov and Anatoli Sudoplatov with Jerrold L. and Leona Schecter, *Special Tasks: The Memoirs of an Unwanted Witness—A Soviet Spymaster* (Boston: Little, Brown, 1994). Among the works challenging such allegations are Thomas Powers, *Intelligence Wars: American Secret History from Hitler to Al-Qaeda* (New York: New York Review Books, 2002), pp. 59–79; David C. Cassidy, *J. Robert Oppenheimer and the American Century* (New York: Pi Press, 2004), pp. 198–200; Priscilla Johnson, "Flimsy Memories," *Bulletin of the Atomic Scientists*, July/August 1994, pp. 30–36; and Hans A. Bethe, Kurt Gottfried, and Roald Z. Sagdeev, "Did Bohr Share Nuclear Secrets?" *Scientific American*, May 1995, pp. 84–90. In 1995 the FBI stated that there was no evidence to confirm the allegations that Oppenheimer, Enrico Fermi, Niels Bohr, and Leo Szilard were witting sources of Soviet intelligence. In addition, the FBI stated that it had classified evidence indicating that such allegations were false. See The White House, Opening Statement by Chairman Les Aspin, President's Foreign Intelligence Advisory Board, "FBI Inquiry into Allegations of Atomic Scientist Espionage Made in Sudoplatov Book," May 1, 1995.

Works that deal, in whole or part, with Soviet World War II atomic espionage operations include Christopher Andrew and Oleg Gordievsky, *KGB: The Inside Story* (New York: HarperCollins, 1990); Andrew with Mitrokhin, *The Sword and the Shield*; John Earl Haynes and Harvey Klehr, *Venona: Decoding Soviet Espionage in America* (New Haven: Yale University Press, 1999); Joseph Albright and Marcia Kunstel, *Bombshell: The Secret Story of America's Unknown Atomic Spy Conspiracy* (New York: Times Books, 1997); Allen Weinstein and Alexander Vassiliev, *The Haunted Wood: Soviet Espionage in America—The Stalin Era* (New York: Random House, 1998); Robert Chadwell Williams, *Klaus Fuchs—Atom Spy* (Cambridge: Harvard University Press, 1992); H. Montgomery Hyde, *The Atom Bomb Spies* (New York: Ballantine, 1980); Rhodes, *Dark Sun*; and Michael Dobbs, "Code Name 'Mlad,' Atomic Bomb Spy," *Washington Post*, September 25, 1996, pp. A1, A20–A21.

12   Holloway, *Stalin and the Bomb*, pp. 180–182; Zaloga, *The Kremlin's Nuclear Sword*, p. 9; Golovin, *I.V. Kurchatov*, p. 56.

13   Pavel V. Oleynikov, "German Scientists in the Soviet Atomic Project," *Nonproliferation Review*, 7, 2 (Summer 2000), pp. 1–30 at pp. 8–10; Zaloga, *The Kremlin's Nuclear Sword*, pp. 7–8;

14   Holloway, *Stalin and the Atomic Bomb*, p. 190; Oleg Bukharin, Thomas B. Cochran, and Robert S. Norris, *New Perspectives on Russia's Ten Secret Cities* (Washington, D.C.: Natural Resources Defense Council, 1999), pp. 18–19, 28–29; Zaloga, *The Kremlin's Nuclear Sword*, p. 8. For a history and status report on Soviet/Russian

closed cities, see Richard H. Rowland, "Russia's Secret Cities," *Post-Soviet Geography and Economics*, 37, 7 (July 1996), pp. 426–462.

15   Zaloga, "The Soviet Nuclear Bomb Programme," p. 178; Zaloga, *The Kremlin's Nuclear Sword*, p. 9; Podvig (ed.), *Russia's Strategic Nuclear Forces*, p. 70; Holloway, *Stalin and the Atomic Bomb*, pp. 184, 186, 188; Yudin, *Manuscript on the History of the Soviet Nuclear Weapons and Nuclear Infrastructure*, p. 17; Golovin, *I.V. Kurchatov*, p. 59.

16   Bukharin, Cochran, and Norris, *New Perspectives on Russia's Ten Secret Cities*, p. 10; www.sandia.gov/ASCI/russia/sarov.html, accessed October 28, 2003 Holloway, *Stalin and the Atomic Bomb*, pp. 196–197, 202; Rhodes, *Dark Sun*, pp. 242–243, 285.

17   Oleynikov, "German Scientists in the Soviet Atomic Project," pp. 10–12; Holloway, *Stalin and the Bomb*, p. 190; Henry S. Lowenhaupt, "On the Soviet Nuclear Scent," *Studies in Intelligence*, 11, 4 (Fall 1967), pp. 13–29 at p. 14.

18   Oleynikov, "German Scientists in the Soviet Atomic Project," pp. 12–13; Holloway, *Stalin and the Bomb*, pp. 110, 190–191; Lowenhaupt, "On the Soviet Nuclear Scent," p. 14; Kragh, *Quantum Generations*, pp. 56–57, 132.

19   Oleynikov, "German Scientists in the Soviet Atomic Project," p. 13; Holloway, *Stalin and the Bomb*, pp. 57, 178, 191. For Riehl's account, see Nikolaus Riehl and Frederick Seitz, *Stalin's Captive: Nikolaus Riehl and the Soviet Race for the Bomb* (Washington, D.C.: American Chemical Society and Chemical Heritage Society, 1996).

20   Zaloga, *The Kremlin's Nuclear Sword*, p. 10; Yudin, *Manuscript on the History of the Soviet Nuclear Weapons and Nuclear Infrastructure*, pp. 15, 81.

21   Zaloga, "The Soviet Nuclear Bomb Programme," p. 179; Zaloga, *The Kremlin's Nuclear Sword*, p. 10; Holloway, *Stalin and the Atomic Bomb*, p. 138; Khariton and Smirnov, "The Khariton Version," p. 20.

22   On Venona, see Haynes and Klehr, *Venona*; Herbert Romerstein and Eric Breindel, *The Venona Secrets: Exposing Soviet Espionage and America's Traitors* (Washington, D.C.: Regnery, 2000), pp. 3–28.

23   The worldwide interest of the Manhattan Engineer District's Foreign Intelligence Section is demonstrated by a late 1945 memo outlining ten different areas of information that would provide leads about foreign nuclear activities, including the names, locations, positions, and activities of personnel; the names and locations of institutions involved in nuclear physics; the names, locations, and activities of large industrial firms that could be involved in atomic activities; the existence of large plants, particularly those that produced little output; and the location of plants producing heavy water, graphite, or carbon. See "Atomic Energy (Nuclear Physics)," December 11, 1945, RG 77, Entry 22, Box 170, Folder 32.60-A-1, NARA. Also see Lt. Col. P. de Silva, X-2, to Lt. Col. S. M. Skinner, SI, Subject: RAMONA (Spain), May 1, 1946, w/att: "Establishment of a German Laboratory in Spain," RG 226, Entry 210, Box 431, Folder 2, NARA.

24   David F. Rudgers, *Creating the Secret State: The Origins of the Central Intelligence Agency, 1943–1947* (Lawrence: University Press of Kansas, 2000), pp. 43, 45.

25   Lt. Col. S. M. Skinner to Col. W. R. Shuler, January 30, 1946, and Brig. Gen. John

B. Magruder, Director, SSU, to Maj. Gen. Leslie Groves, Subject: Liaison, January 7, 1946, both in RG 226, Entry 210, Box 431, Folder 2, NARA.

26   Lt. Col. S. M. Skinner to Col. W. R. Shuler, Subject: Activities of Scientists, January 30, 1946, RG 226, Entry 210, Box 431, Folder 2, NARA.

27   Lowenhaupt, "On the Soviet Nuclear Scent," p. 15.

28   Strategic Services Unit/Germany, Report LC-545, "Reactions to the Question of the Jachymov Mines in Czechoslovak Government Circles," March 5, 1946, and Strategic Services Unit/Germany, Report LC-555, "Visit to Jachymov Mines Early in March," March 15, 1946, both in RG 77, Entry 22, Box 163, NARA.

29   Lt. Col. Edgar P. Dean, "New Reports on the Situation at Joachimsthal," April 17, 1946, and [author unknown] to Eric Welsh, April 25, 1946, both in RG 77, Entry 22, Box 163, NARA. The unknown author challenged the claim that a large number of boxcars would be needed to remove the ore. He maintained that only two trucks per year would be needed. He also argued that rehabilitating the mine would not require any unusual activity noticeable to an outside observer. In addition, he stated that he had visited the mines in May 1945 and the machinery was going "full blast" and was "in good working order." It was "inconceivable to believe that the machinery would have been left in a state in which it could deteriorate during a few months."

30   Lt. Col. P. de Silva to Lt. Col. S. M. Skinner, Subject: Ramona (USSR-4), n.d., and Lt. Col. P. de Silva to Lt. Col. S. M. Skinner, Subject: Follow-up on RAMONA disseminations, May 20, 1946, both in RG 226, Entry 210, Box 431, Folder 2, NARA; Letter, Dino Brugioni to author, January 18, 2004.

31   Lt. Col. S. M. Skinner to Lt. Col. Richard H. Free, June 13, 1946, and Lt. Col. S. M. Skinner to Lt. Col. Richard H. Free, Subject: Manchuria, June 13, 1946, both in RG 226, Entry 210, Box 431, Folder 2, NARA.

32   H. S. Lowenhaupt, "Russian Mining Operations in the German-Czech Border Region," December 5, 1946, RG 77, Entry 22, Box 163, NARA; Interview with Henry S. Lowenhaupt, Springfield, Va., April 15, 1999.

33   Lowenhaupt, "Russian Mining Operations in the German-Czech Border Region."

34   Rudgers, Creating the Secret State, pp. 40, 118.

35   Arthur B. Darling, The Central Intelligence Agency: An Instrument of Government, to 1950 (University Park: Pennsylvania State University Press, 1990), pp. 161–162; Thomas Troy, Donovan and the CIA: A History of the Establishment of the Central Intelligence Agency (Frederick, Md.: University Publications of America, 1981), pp. 406–407, 471–472.

36   Darling, The Central Intelligence Agency, p. 162; Hoyt S. Vandenberg, NIA 6, "Coordination of Intelligence Activities Related to Foreign Atomic Energy Developments and Potentialities," August 13, 1946; "Minutes of the Sixth Meeting of the National Intelligence Authority," August 21, 1946; Telegram from the President's Chief of Staff (Leahy) to President Truman, August 21, 1946; and "Minutes of the Seventh Meeting of the National Intelligence Authority"—all in C. Thomas Thorne Jr. and David S. Patterson (eds.), Emergence of the Intelligence Establishment (Washington, D.C.: U.S. Government Printing Office, 1996), pp. 394–402, 412–416 at p. 415, respectively.

37   Robert S. Norris, *Racing for the Bomb: General Leslie R. Groves, the Manhattan Project's Indispensable Man* (South Royalton, Vt.: Steerforth Press, 2002), p. 467; Leslie Groves, Memorandum to the Atomic Energy Commission, Subject: Foreign Intelligence Set-up, November 21, 1946, in Thorne and Patterson (eds.), *Emergence of the Intelligence Establishment*, pp. 458–460.

38   Darling, *The Central Intelligence Agency*, p. 165; "Minutes of the 9th Meeting of the National Intelligence Authority," February 12, 1947, and Brig. Gen. E. K. Wright, DDCI, "Establishment and Functions of the Nuclear Energy Group, Scientific Branch, Office of Reports and Estimates," March 28, 1947, both in Thorne and Patterson (eds.), *Emergence of the Intelligence Establishment*, pp. 487–493 at p. 488 and pp. 503–505, respectively. The NIA directive specifying the director of central intelligence's authority in the area of atomic intelligence was not issued until several weeks after Wright's memo. See National Intelligence Authority Directive No. 9, "Coordination of Intelligence Activities Related to Foreign Atomic Energy Developments and Potentialities," April 18, 1947, in Thorne and Patterson (eds.), *Emergence of the Intelligence Establishment*, pp. 510–511.

39   Brig. Gen. E. K. Wright, DDCI, Memorandum, Subject: Additional Functions of the Office of Special Operations, March 5, 1948, CREST, NARA; George S. Jackson and Martin P. Clausen, *Organizational History of the Central Intelligence Agency, 1950–1953* (Washington, D.C.: Central Intelligence Agency, 1957), pp. VI-3, VI-16, VI-16 n. 2; Ludwell Lee Montague, *General Walter Bedell Smith as Director of Central Intelligence, October 1950–February 1953* (University Park: Pennsylvania State University Press, 1992), p. 174; Sidney W. Souers, "Atomic Energy Intelligence," July 1, 1947; John Ranelagh, *The Agency: The Rise and Decline of the CIA* (New York: Simon and Schuster, 1986), p. 728.

40   Charles A. Ziegler and David Jacobson, *Spying Without Spies: Origins of America's Secret Nuclear Surveillance System* (New York: Praeger, 1995), pp. 65, 92, 95, 150; Biography: Major General Albert F. Hegenberger, www.af.mil/news/biographies, accessed July 1, 2002. The military, field element of AFOAT-1 was known as the 1009th Special Weapons Squadron, of which Hegenberger was the commanding general. See Science Applications International Corporation, *Fifty Year Commemorative History of Long Range Detection: The Creation, Development, and Operation of the United States Atomic Energy Detection System* (Satellite Beach, Fla.: SAIC, 1997), pp. 4–5.

41   Col. Laurin L. Williams, War Department General Staff, Memorandum for Director, Central Intelligence Agency, Subject: Establishment of Proposed Joint Nuclear Energy Intelligence Committee, November 7, 1947; Darling, *The Central Intelligence Agency*, p. 230; Memorandum, W. Machle, Assistant Director, OSI to DCI, "Briefs on Nuclear Energy Intelligence Situation," March 18, 1949; C. P. Cabell, Director of Intelligence, USAF, Memorandum for: Director of Central Intelligence, Subject: Reports of the Joint Nuclear Energy Intelligence Committee, July 28, 1949, CREST, NARA.

42   Lowenhaupt, "On the Soviet Nuclear Scent," p. 17.

43   Ibid., p. 18; Paul Maddrell, "British-American Scientific Intelligence Collaboration During the Occupation of Germany," *Intelligence and National Security*, 15, 2 (Summer 2000), pp. 74–94 at p. 77; Henry S. Lowenhaupt, "Chasing Bitterfield Calcium," *Studies in Intelligence* 17, (Spring 1973), pp. 21–30.

44   Peter Grose, *Gentleman Spy: The Life of Allen Dulles* (Boston: Houghton Mifflin, 1994), p. 391; Maddrell, "British-American Scientific Intelligence Collaboration," p. 77; Brugioni letter.

45   Maddrell, "British-American Scientific Intelligence Collaboration," p. 78.

46   James Bamford, *The Puzzle Palace: A Report on NSA, America's Most Secret Agency* (Boston: Houghton Mifflin, 1982), p. 47.

47   Rear Adm. R. H. Hillenkoetter, Director of Central Intelligence, Memorandum for: The Executive Secretary, NSC, Subject: Atomic Energy Program of the USSR, April 20, 1949; Louis Johnson, Memorandum for the U.S. Communications Intelligence Board, June 2, 1949; Adm. Louis Denfeld, Memorandum for the Secretary of Defense, Subject: Atomic Energy Program of the USSR, June 30, 1949; Maj. Gen. C. P. Cabell, Chairman, USCIB, Memorandum for the Secretary of Defense, Subject: Atomic Energy Program of the U.S.S.R., June 23, 1949—all in RG 330, Entry 199, Box 61, Folder CD 11-1-2, NARA; Matthew Aid, "The Russian Target: The U.K.-U.S. Cryptologic Effort Against the Soviet Union: 1945–1960," paper prepared for the Annual Conference for the Society of Historians of American Foreign Relations, Washington, D.C., June 6–8, 2003, pp. 27–28.

48   Interview with Spurgeon Keeny, Washington, D.C., February 6, 2003. A somewhat different view of the vulnerability of Soviet communications concerning their nuclear program can be found in Oleg Bukharin, "US Atomic Energy Intelligence Against the Soviet Target," *Intelligence and National Security*, 19, 4 (Winter 2004), pp. 655–679. According to Bukharin (p. 665), most communications between nuclear facilities and Moscow were by Teletype or telephone and involved the use of landlines or microwave systems rather than easier-to-intercept short-wave radio communications.

49   Central Intelligence Group, ORE 3/1, *Soviet Capabilities for the Development and Production of Certain Types of Weapons and Equipment*, October 31, 1946; Lawrence Aronsen, "Seeing Red: US Air Force Assessments of the Soviet Union, 1945–1949," *Intelligence and National Security*, 16, 2 (Summer 2001), pp. 103–132; Service Members of the Joint Intelligence Committee, J.I.C. 395/1, "The Capabilities of the USSR in Regard to Atomic Weapons," July 8, 1947.

50   Charles A. Ziegler, "Intelligence Assessments of Soviet Atomic Capability, 1945–1949: Myths, Monopolies, and *Maskirovka*," *Intelligence and National Security*, 12, 4 (October 1997), pp. 1–24 at p. 13; Letter, R. H. Hillenkoetter to B. B. Hickenlooper, July 1, 1948, w/att: "Estimate of the Status of the Russian Atomic Energy Project," July 1, 1948, RG 330, Entry 199, Box 61, Folder CD 11-1-2, NARA; R. N. Hillenkoetter, Director of Central Intelligence, Memorandum for the President, Subject: Estimate of the Status of the Russian Atomic Energy Project, July 6, 1948, PSF, HTPL.

51   Keeny interview; Machle, "Briefs on Nuclear Energy Intelligence Situation."

52   Machle, "Briefs on Nuclear Energy Intelligence Situation."

53   Ziegler and Jacobson, *Spying Without Spies*, p. 13; "Beginnings of AFOAT-1," document declassified for Advisory Committee on Human Radiation Experiments, CIA Accession Number CIA-030695-A.

54   Ziegler and Jacbson, *Spying Without Spies*, p. 38; J. M. Blair, D. H. Frisch, and S. Katcoff, LA-418, "Detection of Nuclear-Explosion Dust in the Atmosphere," October 2, 1945, pp. 1–2 LANL Archives.

55   Blair, Frisch, and Katcoff, "Detection of Nuclear-Explosion Dust in the Atmosphere," pp. 2–3; Norris, *Racing for the Bomb*, p. 11.

56   Ziegler and Jacobson, *Spying Without Spies*, p. 39; Blair, Frisch, and Katcoff, "Detection of Nuclear-Explosion Dust in the Atmosphere."

57   Ziegler and Jacobson, *Spying Without Spies*, pp. 41–44.

58   Ibid., p. 44.

59   Ibid., pp. 46–47.

60   Ibid., p. 48.

61   Ibid., pp. 49–50, 102; Maj. Philip J. Krueger, Memorandum for General Groves, Subject: Remote Air Sampling, September 18, 1946, LANL Archives. Ziegler and Jacobson (*Spying Without Spies*, p. 53) argue that Krueger's conclusion about the ability to detect a blast was naïve since it didn't take into account other potential causes of high radiation, such as a reactor accident. Further, they claim the measurements did not demonstrate that detection of an airburst at high altitudes, in contrast to the low-altitude Bikini detonation, was feasible. It is possible that a high-altitude detonation might not produce a large enough quantity of radioactive dust for collection at long range to permit "the identification of specific radioisotopes through chemical analysis."

62   Doyle L. Northrup and Donald H. Rock, "The Detection of Joe-1," *Studies in Intelligence*, 10, 4 (Fall 1966), pp. 23–33 at p. 24.

63   Ziegler and Jacobson, *Spying Without Spies*, p. 70; Greg Herken, *Brotherhood of the Bomb: The Tangled Lives and Loyalties of Robert Oppenheimer, Ernest Lawrence, and Edward Teller* (New York: Henry Holt, 2002), p. 169; Omar N. Bradley and Clay Blair, *A General's Life* (New York: Simon & Schuster, 1983), p. 514.

64   Lewis L. Strauss to Commissioners, Memorandum, April 11, 1947, Papers of Lewis L. Strauss, Box 68, Folder: Monitoring of Soviet Tests, HHPL; Strauss would continue to depict himself as the central figure in the creation of a long-range detection system, both in contemporaneous classified memos and in his memoirs. See Lewis L. Strauss, Memorandum for the Files, Subject: History of the Long-Range Detection Program, July 21, 1948, Papers of Lewis L. Strauss, Box 113, Folder: Tests and Testing, HHPL; Lewis L. Strauss, *Men and Decisions* (Garden City, N.Y.: Doubleday, 1962), pp. 201–207.

65   Ziegler and Jacobson, *Spying Without Spies*, p. 73; Strauss, *Men and Decisions*, p. 202.

66   R. H. Hillenkoetter, Director CIG, Memorandum for the Secretary of War, Subject: Long Range Detection of Atomic Explosions, June 30, 1947.

67   Lauris Norstad, Director of Plans and Operations, Memorandum for the Secretary of War, Subject: Long-Range Detection of Atomic Explosions, September 3, 1947; Hillenkoetter, Memorandum for the Secretary of War, Subject: Long Range Detection of Atomic Explosions, June 30, 1947; David E. Lilienthal, Memorandum for Director, Central Intelligence Group, Subject: Long Range Detection of Atomic Explosions, July 10, 1947, Papers of Lewis L. Strauss, Box 68, HHPL; J. B. Conant, Chairman, Committee on Atomic Energy, to Dr. V. Bush, Chairman, Research and Development Board, Subject: The Long Range Detection of Atomic Bomb Explosions, January 2, 1948.

68   Ziegler and Jacobson, *Spying Without Spies*, pp. 84–86.

69   Walter Todd, Deputy Director of Intelligence, "Long Range Detection of Atomic Explosions," September 15, 1947; Dwight D. Eisenhower, Memorandum for the Commanding General, Army Air Forces, Subject: Long Range Detection of Atomic Explosions, September 16, 1947.

70   Benson Saler, Charles A. Ziegler, and Charles B. Moore, *UFO Crash at Roswell: The Genesis of a Modern Myth* (Washington, D.C.: Smithsonian Institution Press, 1997), pp. 74–75. The book explains how Mogul and other tests in the Roswell area helped create the myth of a UFO crash. Also see James McAndrew, *The Roswell Report: Fact vs. Fiction in the New Mexico Desert* (Washington, D.C.: U.S. Government Printing Office, 1995); James McAndrew, *The Roswell Report: Case Closed* (Washington, D.C.: U.S. Government Printing Office, 1997); Philip J. Klass, *The Real Roswell Crashed-Saucer Coverup* (Amherst, N.Y.: Prometheus, 1997); B. D. Gildenburg, "The Cold War's Classified Skyhook Program: A Participant's Revelations," *Skeptical Inquirer*, May/June 2004, pp. 38–42.

71   Saler, Ziegler, and Moore, *UFO Crash at Roswell*, pp. 75, 78–79.

72   Rhodes, *Dark Sun*, p. 320; Ziegler and Jacobson, *Spying Without Spies*, p. 117.

73   Ziegler and Jacobson, *Spying Without Spies*, pp. 118–119; Strauss, *Men and Decisions*, p. 206.

74   Ziegler and Jacobson, *Spying Without Spies*, pp. 125–126; Department of the Air Force, *Operation Fitzwilliam, Annex "A": Design of Experiment for Fitzwilliam*, May 11, 1948, pp. A-1, A-2.

75   Ziegler and Jacobson, *Spying Without Spies*, pp. 128–129.

76   Letter, Arnold Ross to author, April 1, 1985.

77   Ziegler and Jacobson, *Spying Without Spies*, p. 129.

78   Ibid., p. 130.

79   Ibid.

80   Ibid., p. 131; J. F. Kalbach, LAMS-732, *Attempt at Remote Detection of a Nuclear Explosion*, Los Alamos Scientific Laboratory, June 7, 1948, p. 2.

81   Ziegler and Jacobson, *Spying Without Spies*, p. 133.

82   Ibid; Kalbach, *Attempt at Remote Detection of a Nuclear Explosion*, p. 2.

83   Ziegler and Jacobson, *Spying Without Spies*, p. 134.

84   Ibid.

85   Ibid., p. 138; Strauss, "History of the Long-Range Detection Program," p. 5. The

statement that airborne methods could be used to detect an airburst depended on an unexpected discovery during the analysis of the debris collected during Fitzwilliam. Also, although airborne detection would not be useful if the Soviets engaged in underground testing, it was believed that they would opt for atmospheric testing. See Ziegler and Jacobson, *Spying Without Spies*, pp. 135–138.

86   Ziegler and Jacobson, *Spying Without Spies*, pp. 144, 147–150, 153–158.

87   Ibid., pp. 176, 186.

88   Ibid., p. 186–187, 199; Northrup and Rock, "The Detection of Joe-1," p. 28.

89   Herbert Friedman, Luther B. Lockhart, and Irving H. Blifford, "Detecting the Soviet Bomb: Joe-1 in a Rainbarrel," *Physics Today*, 49, 11 (November 1996), pp. 38–41; Northup and Rock, "The Detection of Joe-1," p. 28; Ziegler and Jacobsen, *Spying Without Spies*, pp. 191–193.

90   Ziegler and Jacobsen, *Spying Without Spies*, pp. 195–196; Richard Aldrich, *The Hidden Hand: Britain, America, and Cold War Secret Intelligence* (New York: Overlook Press, 2001), pp. 228–229.

91   Ziegler and Jacobsen, *Spying Without Spies*, pp. 121–125, 187.

92   Holloway, *Stalin and the Bomb*, pp. 214–215; C. J. Chivers, "It Was Once Ground Zero, Now Little but Danger Is Left," *New York Times*, March 3, 2005, p. A4.

93   Holloway, *Stalin and the Bomb*, pp. 214–215.

94   Ibid., pp. 216–217. There is some disagreement as to whether the bomb was detonated at six in the morning, according to Kurchatov's original plan, or a few hours earlier. See Lester Machta, "Finding the Site of the First Soviet Nuclear Test in 1949," *Bulletin of the American Meteorological Society*, 73, 11 (November 1992), pp. 1797–1806 at p. 1802n.

95   Holloway, *Stalin and the Bomb*, p. 218.

96   Ziegler and Jacobson, *Spying Without Spies*, p. 201; Charles C. Bates and John F. Fuller, *America's Weather Warriors* (College Station: Texas A&M University, 1986), p. 137.

97   Northrup and Rock, "The Detection of Joe-1," p. 23.

98   Ibid., pp. 23, 29–30; Ziegler and Jacobson, *Spying Without Spies*, pp. 204–205; Mary Welch, "AFTAC Celebrates 50 Years of Long Range Detection," *Monitor*, October 1997, pp. 8–32 at p. 9.

99   Northrup and Rock, "The Detection of Joe-1," pp. 23, 30–31; Ziegler and Jacobson, *Spying Without Spies*, p. 206; W. C. Penney, "An Interim Report of British Work on Joe," September 22, 1949, PSF, HTPL.

100   Northrup and Rock, The Detection of Joe-1," pp. 30–31; Friedman, Lockhart, and Blifford, "Detecting the Soviet Bomb," p. 41.

101   Northrup and Rock, "The Detection of Joe-1," p. 31.

102   Ibid.; Ziegler and Jacobson, *Spying Without Spies*, pp. 205–208.

103   Ziegler and Jacobson, *Spying Without Spies*, p. 207.

104   Ibid., pp. 207–208; David E. Lilienthal, *The Journals of David E. Lilienthal*, Vol. 2, *The Atomic Energy Years, 1945–1950* (New York: Harper & Row, 1964), p. 570n.

105   Ziegler and Jacobson, *Spying Without Spies*, pp. 208–209; Herken, *Brotherhood of the Bomb*, p. 200.

106   Ziegler and Jacobson, *Spying Without Spies*, p. 211; Doyle L. Northrup, Technical Director, AFOAT-1, Memorandum for Major General Nelson, Technical Memorandum No. 37, Subject: Atomic Detection System Alert No. 112, September 19, 1949, PSF, HTPL; Letter, V. Bush, J. Robert Oppenheimer, Robert Bacher, and W. S. Parsons to General Hoyt S. Vandenberg, September 20, 1949. The final Los Alamos analysis was not completed until early October. See R. W. Spence, "Identification of Radioactivity in Special Samples," Los Alamos Scientific Laboratory, October 4, 1949.

107   Machta, "Finding the Site of the First Soviet Nuclear Test in 1949," p. 1797; Interview with Lester Hubert, September 15, 2004; "Dr. Lester Machta, Founding Director of ARL (1919–2001)," www.arlnoaa.gov, accessed January 2, 2004.

108   Machta, "Finding the Site of the First Soviet Nuclear Test in 1949," p. 1803; U.S. Weather Bureau, *U.S. Weather Bureau Report on Alert Number 112 of the Atomic Detection System*, September 29, 1949, pp. 2–3, 6–8, PSF, HTPL; "Dr. Lester Machta, Founding Director of ARL (1919–2001)."

109   Ziegler and Jacobson, *Spying Without Spies*, p. 211; Robert J. Donovan, *The Tumultuous Years: The Presidency of Harry S. Truman* (New York: W. W. Norton, 1982), p. 99; Kenneth W. Condit, *The History of the Joint Chiefs of Staff: The Joint Chiefs of Staff and National Policy, Volume II, 1947–1949* (Washington, D.C.: Joint Chiefs of Staff, 1964), p. 253; Letter, Bush, Oppenheimer, Bacher, and Parsons to Vandenberg, September 20, 1949.

110   Memorandum by the Chief of Staff, U.S. Air Force, Hoyt S. Vandenberg to the Secretary of Defense on Long Range Detection of Atomic Explosions, September 20, 1949, PSF, HTPL; Ziegler and Jacobson, *Spying Without Spies*, pp. 210–211; Northrup and Rock, "The Detection of Joe-1," p. 32. That same day, a CIA memorandum reported that the "current estimate of the Joint Nuclear Energy Intelligence Committee is that the earliest possible date by which the USSR might be expected to produce an atomic bomb is mid-1950 and the most probable date is mid-1953." The authors were still using the JNEIC July estimate. See CIA Intelligence Memorandum No. 225, Subject: Estimate of Status of Atomic Warfare in the USSR, September 20, 1949, in Michael Warner (ed.), *The CIA Under Harry Truman* (Washington, D.C.: CIA, 1994), pp. 319–320.

111   Ziegler and Jacobson, *Spying Without Spies*, p. 211; Condit, *The History of the Joint Chiefs of Staff*, pp. 523–524; Peter W. King and Herbert W. Friedman, *NRL Report CN-3536, Part I: Collection and Identification of Fission Products of Foreign Origin*, September 22, 1949; Northrup and Rock, "The Detection of Joe-1," p. 33; "Statement by the President on Announcing the First Atomic Explosion in the USSR, September 23, 1949," in Philip L. Cantelon, Richard G. Hewlett, and Robert C. Williams (eds.), *The American Atom: A Documentary History of Nuclear Policies from the Discovery of Fission to the Present* (Philadelphia: University of Pennsylvania Press, 1991), p. 112.

112   Edward T. Folliard, "Truman Reveals Red A-Blast; No Widespread Alarm Felt; Stockpiling May Be Speeded," *Washington Post*, September 24, 1949, pp. 1, 3; N. S. Haseltine, "U.S. Learned of Blast Through 'Mechanical Means,'" *Washington Post*, September 24, 1949, pp. 1, 2; Anthony Leviero, "Atom Blast in Russia Disclosed; Truman Again Asks U.N. Control; Vishinsky Proposes Peace Pact," *New York Times*, September 24, 1949, pp. 1-2; William L. Laurence, "Soviet Achievement Ahead of Predictions by 3 Years," *New York Times*, September 24, 1949, pp. 1-2.

113   Joint Committee on Atomic Energy, *Report of the Central Intelligence Agency: Construction Rider on Appropriations Measures*, October 17, 1947, pp. 7-8.

114   Ibid., pp. 46, 54, 61; Lilienthal, *The Journals of David E. Lilienthal, Volume II*, p. 486.

115   Central Intelligence Agency, ORE 32-50, *The Effect of the Soviet Possession of Atomic Bombs on the Security of the United States*, June 9, 1950, p. 2; Bradley and Blair, *A General's Life*, pp. 514-515.

116   Dino A. Brugioni, "The Kyshtym Connection," *Bulletin of the Atomic Scientists*, March 1990, p. 12.

117   Lowenhaupt, "On the Soviet Nuclear Scent," p. 20; Joint Committee on Atomic Energy, *The CIA Semi-Annual Report*, August 16, 1951; Herken *Brotherhood of the Bomb* (hereafter *BoB*) Documents, Box 10, National Security Archive.

118   Joint Committee on Atomic Energy, *The CIA Semi-Annual Report*, n.p.

119   Science Applications International Corporation, *Fifty Year Commemorative History of Long Range Detection*, p. 97; Memorandum for General Maude, Subject: Proposed U.S./U.K. Cooperation within Area 5 of the Technical Cooperation Program, May 4, 1951, RG 341, Entry 214, NARA.

120   Brig. Gen. R. C. Maude, Chief, AFOAT-1, Doyle Northrup, Technical Director, AFOAT-1, Memorandum for: Mr. Robert Lebaron, Deputy to the Secretary of Defense for Atomic Energy, Subject: Notes on Technical Cooperation with British and Canadians in the Field of Atomic Energy Intelligence, March 27, 1951.

121   Rear Adm. R. H. Hillenkoetter, DCI, Memorandum for: Executive Secretary, National Security Council, Subject: Atomic Energy Intelligence, June 28, 1950; R. C. Maude, Northrup, Memorandum for: Mr. Robert Lebaron, Subject: Notes on Technical Cooperation with British and Canadians in the Field of Atomic Energy Intelligence; "AE 207/1.1," p. 1, attachment to Joint Panel on Technical Objective IO-7, Memorandum to the Chairman, RDB [Research and Development Board] Committee on Atomic Energy, Subject: Review of DOD Program for Long Range Detection of Atomic Operations, July 1, 1951.

122   Science Applications International Corporation, *Fifty Year Commemorative History of Long Range Detection*, pp. 72, 84; Mary Welch, "AFTAC Celebrates 50 Years of Long Range Detection," *The Monitor*, October 1997, pp. 8-32 at p. 12; Letter to Hon. Walter Howe, American Ambassador, Santiago, October 22, 1958.

123   Olav Riste, *The Norwegian Intelligence Service, 1945-1970* (London: Frank Cass, 1999), p. 193; Max Van Rossum Daum, Lt. Col. USAF, Acting Chief, Intelligence Branch, to Deputy Chief, AFOAT-1, Proposed Site for GFU at Thule, Greenland,

September 10, 1951. Just a few months earlier, in July, William P. Snow, the counselor of the U.S. embassy in Oslo, received a Top Secret cable concerning "a rather delicate problem." R. Gordon Arneson, a special assistant to the secretary of state, wanted to know if Snow could arrange to see Norwegian foreign minister Lange to inform him of the U.S. desire to establish a series of acoustic and seismic detection stations on Norwegian soil. Apparently, this strategy for raising the question was abandoned. Arneson's memo also informed Snow that the detection stations could be operated by personnel from the U.S. Weather Bureau, if that would make the stations more acceptable to Norway. The special assistant further noted that the United States wanted to get an agreement in principle within a month to four weeks, and for "the real purpose of the equipment to be known only to a minimum number of Norwegians." See R. Gordon Arneson, Special Assistant to the Secretary to William P. Snow, Counselor of Embassy, American Embassy, July 11, 1951.

124   Holloway, *Stalin and the Bomb*, pp. 198, 219.

125   Ibid., pp. 219–220; Podvig (ed.), *Russia's Strategic Nuclear Forces*, p. 485.

126   Athelstan Spilhaus, Research and Development Board, Memorandum for Chief, AFOAT-1, Subject: Review of Dogface Data, October 3, 1951. Apparently the code name for Joe-2 was Dogface; "Attachment A," to Joint Panel on Technical Objective IO-7, Memorandum to the Chairman, RDB Committee on Atomic Energy/Chairman, RDB Committee on Geophysics and Geography, Subject: Review of DOD Program for Long Range Detection of Atomic Operations, July 1, 1951. The four atomic tests that the United States conducted, collectively designated Greenhouse, at Eniwetok atoll between April 8 and May 25, 1951, resulted in "increased optimism" with respect to the ability of acoustic systems to detect and fix the location of atomic explosions at considerable distances. The sound from the first three explosions, whose yields ranged from 47 to 225 kilotons, was detected as far away as 2,400 miles. Usable seismic signals were also recorded during the test. See Science Applications International Corporation, *Fifty Year Commemorative History of Long Range Detection*, pp. 33–34; Charles P. Boner, Memorandum for Chairman, RDB Committee on Atomic Energy/Chairman, RDB Committee on Geophysics and Geography, Subject: Review of DoD Program for Long Range Detection of Atomic Operations. A test of aerial sampling, designated Green Run, was conducted in December 1949 and relied on releases from the Hanford facility. See General Accounting Office (GAO), *Examples of Post World War II Radiation Releases at U.S. Nuclear Sites* (Washington, D.C.: GAO, 1993).

127   Spilhaus, Subject: Review of Dogface Data.

128   Podvig (ed.), *Russia's Strategic Nuclear Forces*, p. 99; Bukharin, Cochran, and Norris, *New Perspectives on Russia's Ten Secret Cities*, pp. 22–27.

129   Podvig (ed.), *Russia's Strategic Nuclear Forces*, pp. 100, 106–107; Bukharin, Cochran, and Norris, *New Perspectives on Russia's Ten Secret Cities*, p. 30.

130   Riste, *The Norwegian Intelligence Service*, pp. 193–194.

131   Welch, "AFTAC Celebrates 50 Years of Long Range Detection," p. 12; AFOIN-1X, Memorandum for the Record, January 14, 1953, RG 341, Entry 214, File 4-6A to 4-191, NARA.

132 Joint Message Form, from: HQ USAF AFOIN to: USAIRA Tehran, Iran, Subject: B/65, July 30, 1952, RG 341, Entry 214, File No. 2-24400 to 2-24499, NARA; Memorandum for: Deputy Chief of Staff, Operations, Subject: (Top Secret), AFOAT-1 Operations in Iran, August 1, 1952, RG 341, Entry 214, File No. 2-24400 to 2-24499, NARA.

133 Maj. Gen. John A. Samford, "Commendation of Brigadier General D. J. Keirn," September 22, 1952, RG 341, Entry 214, File 2-35202, NARA; "Major General Donald J. Keirn," at www.af.mil/bios, accessed December 2, 2003.

134 Harry S. Truman, Memorandum for the Secretary of State and Secretary of Defense, Subject: Communications Intelligence Activities, October 24, 1952; Center for Cryptologic History, *The Origins of NSA* (Ft. Meade, Md.: NSA, n.d.), p. 4; National Security Council Intelligence Directive (NSCID) 9, Communications Intelligence, December 29, 1952.

135 Hans A. Bethe, "Comments on the History of the H-Bomb," *Los Alamos Science*, Fall 1982, pp. 43–53; "The Hydrogen Bomb: The Secret," and "The Hydrogen Bomb: Schematic," and " www.atomicarchive.com, accessed June 9, 2005; Herken, *Brotherhood of the Bomb*, pp. 217–218, 222.

136 Herken, *Brotherhood of the Bomb*, p. 236; Holloway, *Stalin and the Bomb*, pp. 302–303. For Ulam's highly sanitized account, see S. M. Ulam, *Adventures of a Mathematician* (New York: Scribner's, 1976), pp. 209–224.

137 Herken, *Brotherhood of the Bomb*, p. 257; Lewis L. Strauss, "A Chronology of the Thermonuclear Weapon Program to November 1952," August 14, 1953, Lewis L. Strauss Papers, Box 106, HHPL.

138 German A. Goncharov, "Beginnings of the Soviet H-Bomb Program," *Physics Today*, 49, 11 (November 1996), pp. 50–55 at p. 50; Holloway, *Stalin and the Bomb*, pp. 50, 448.

139 Goncharov, "Beginnings of the Soviet H-Bomb Program," p. 50.

140 Ibid., pp. 51–52.

141 Ibid., pp. 51–53; Holloway, *Stalin and the Bomb*, pp. 297, 451; Kragh, *Quantum Generations*, p. 436. Cerenkov electromagnetic radiation, usually a bluish light, is emitted by a beam of high-energy particles passing through a transparent medium at a speed greater than the speed of light in that medium. The effect consists of the radiation causing a shock wave in the electromagnetic medium. See http://teachers.web.cern.ch.

142 Holloway, *Stalin and the Bomb*, p. 451; Goncharov, "Beginnings of the Soviet H-Bomb Program," p. 54; Rhodes, *Dark Sun*, pp. 305–306.

143 German A. Goncharov, "The Race Accelerates," *Physics Today*, 49, 11 (November 1996), pp. 56–61 at p. 56; Goncharov, "On the History of the Creation of the Soviet Hydrogen Bomb," *Physics-Upsekhi*, 40, 8 (August 1997), pp. 859–867 at p. 862.

144 Holloway, *Stalin and the Bomb*, pp. 299, 305, 449. Tritium had an additional drawback. Its production required sacrificing the production of much larger quantities of plutonium that could be used in fission bombs.

145 Ibid., p. 306; Goncharov, "The Race Accelerates," p. 57; Central Intelligence Agency, "The Purge of L.P. Beria," July 10, 1953, www.foia.cia.gov.

146   Goncharov, "The Race Accelerates," p. 57; Andrei Sakharov, *Memoirs* (New York: Knopf, 1990), pp. 173–174.

147   Sakharov, *Memoirs*, p. 174.

148   Thomas K. Finletter, Memorandum for the Secretary of Defense, Subject: Action Necessary to Achieve an H-Bomb Capability, March 22, 1952; Extracts from Memo re SSG No. 215, by Chief, Military Capabilities Branch, to Chief, Targets Division, October 3, 1952; Directorate of Intelligence, USAF, Special Air Intelligence Estimate, Subject: An Analysis of Malenkov's H Bomb Statement, August 11, 1953—all in Herken *BoB* Documents, Box 7, Folder: USAF HQ documents, National Security Archive; Robert D. Little, Joint Atomic Energy Intelligence Committee, CIA/SI 13-52, National Scientific Intelligence Estimate, *Status of the Soviet Atomic Energy Program*, January 8, 1953; *A History of the Air Force Atomic Energy Program, 1943–1953, Volume II, Part II* (Washington, D.C.: Air Force Historical Division, n.d.), p. 253.

149   Lewis L. Strauss, Memorandum for the Files of Lewis Strauss, August 19, 1953, Strauss Papers, Box 68, HHPL. The NRL Rainbarrel project continued through this test. See Friedman, Lockhart, and Blifford, "Detecting the Soviet Bomb," p. 41.

150   Strauss, Memorandum for the Files of Lewis Strauss.

151   Lilse A. Rose and Neil H. Peterson, *Foreign Relations of the United States, National Security Affairs, Volume II, Part 2* (Washington, D.C.: U.S. Government Printing Office, 1984), p. 1186 n. 1.

152   Hans Bethe, *Analysis of Joe-4*, September 11, 1953, p. 1; Science Applications International Corporation, *Fifty Year Commemorative History of Long Range Detection*, p. 29; John A. McCone, Memorandum for: Military Representative of the President, Subject: Distribution of the Report of the Foreign Weapons Evaluation (Bethe) Panel (Meeting held 16–17 December 1961), n.d., CREST, NARA; Jeremy Bernstein, *Hans Bethe: Prophet of Energy* (New York: Basic Books, 1980), p. 4.

153   Bethe, *Analysis of Joe-4*, pp. 4–5.

154   Ibid., pp. 5–7; Zaloga, *The Kremlin's Nuclear Sword*, pp. 33–34, 263 n. 19; Bethe, "Comments on the History of the H-Bomb," p. 53; Interview with Richard Garwin, July 24, 2004. Bethe's assertion has been questioned by key Soviet scientists—see Khariton and Smirnov, "Khariton Version," as well as Goncharov, "Beginnings of the Soviet H-Bomb Program." The main cause of the dispute seems to be a difference of standards rather than an argument over the facts. See Holloway, *Stalin and the Bomb*, p. 308.

CHAPTER 3: THE VIEW FROM ABOVE

1   Pavel Podvig (ed.), *Russian Strategic Nuclear Forces* (Cambridge: MIT Press, 2001), p. 485; Steven Zaloga, *The Kremlin's Nuclear Sword: The Rise and Fall of Russia's Strategic Nuclear Forces, 1945–2000* (Washington, D.C.: Smithsonian Institution Press, 2002), p. 29.

2   Jay Miller, *Lockheed U-2* (Austin, Tex.: Aerofax, 1983), p. 16; Harry Kinney and Bob Trimble, "Flying the Stratosphere," *Air Classics*, 9, 10 (October 1973), pp. 26ff.

3   Central Intelligence Agency, NIE 11-3A-54, *Summary: The Soviet Atomic Energy Program to Mid-1957*, February 16, 1954, pp. 1–2.

4   Ibid., pp. 1–3.

5   Ibid., p. 3.

6   Oleg Bukharin, Thomas B. Cochran, and Robert S. Norris, *New Perspectives on Russia's Ten Secret Cities* (Washington, D.C.: Natural Resources Defense Council, 1999), p. 34; Podvig (ed.), *Russian Strategic Nuclear Forces*, pp. 466–467; Thomas B. Cochran, Robert S. Norris, and Oleg A. Bukharin, *Making the Russian Bomb: From Stalin to Yeltsin* (Boulder, Colo.: Westview, 1995), p. 47. Zaloga gives the date of the decree as July 31, and the official title as 6th State Central Proving Ground. See Zaloga, *The Kremlin's Nuclear Sword*, pp. 70, 268 n. 20.

7   Podvig (ed.), *Russian Strategic Nuclear Forces*, pp. 441–442.

8   Sherman Kent, Assistant Director, National Estimates, Memorandum for: The Director of Central Intelligence, Subject: A Broader Approach to Annual NIE on the Soviet Nuclear Program, August 1, 1955, RG 263, Box 185, Folder 9, NARA.

9   F. A. Valente, Memorandum for: Mr. Gerard C. Smith, Dr. A. K. Brewer, Col. Geo. E. McCord, Subject: Section 73 (Atomic Energy), NIS 26 (USSR), March 21, 1955 w/att: Central Intelligence Agency, *Chapter VII-NIS 26, Section 73: Atomic Energy*, n.d., www.foai.ucia.gov.

10   Central Intelligence Agency, *Chapter VII-NIS 26, Section 73*, pp. B-1–B-8, F-1–F-8.

11   Ibid., pp. A-2–A-4, E-9, E-15; Richard Rhodes, *Dark Sun: The Making of the Hydrogen Bomb* (New York: Simon & Schuster, 1995), p. 418.

12   Central Intelligence Agency, *Chapter VII-NIS 26, Section 73*, p. K-1.

13   Henry S. Lowenhaupt, "On the Soviet Nuclear Scent," *Studies in Intelligence*, 11, 4 (Fall 1967), pp. 13–29 at pp. 18–19, 27–28.

14   Ibid., pp. 27–28.

15   Ibid., pp. 27–29; Cochran, Norris, and Bukharin, *Making the Russian Bomb*, p. 183.

16   Podvig (ed.), *Russian Strategic Nuclear Forces*, pp. 441–442, 466, 486–487.

17   Ibid., pp. 95–96, 104; Central Intelligence Agency, *Chapter VII-NIS 26, Section 73*, p. E-16; Bukharin, Cochran, and Norris, *New Perspectives on Russia's Ten Secret Cities*, pp. 13, 25; David Holloway, *Stalin and the Bomb: The Soviet Union and Atomic Energy, 1939–1956* (New Haven: Yale University Press, 1995), p. 322.

18   Andrei Sakharov, *Memoirs* (New York: Knopf, 1990), pp. 182–190.

19   German A. Goncharov, "The Race Accelerates," *Physics Today*, 49, 11 (November 1996), pp. 56–61 at p. 58; G. A. Goncharov, "American and Soviet H-Bomb Development Programmes: Historical Background," *Physics-Uspekhi*, 39, 10 (October 1996), pp. 1033–1044 at p. 1041. On the origins of Soviet H-bomb ideas and the possible role of espionage, also see G. A. Goncharov, "On the History of Creation of the Soviet Hydrogen Bomb," *Physics-Upsekhi*, 40, 8 (August 1997), pp. 859–867, and V. E. Adamski and Yu N. Smirnov, "Once Again on the Creation of the Soviet Hydrogen Bomb," *Physics-Upsekhi*, 40, 8 (August 1997), pp. 855–858.

20   Goncharov, "The Race Accelerates," pp. 59, 61.

21   Sakharov, *Memoirs*, pp. 190–191.

22   Ibid., pp. 191–192.

23   R. Gordon Arneson, Memorandum for Col. Jack A. Gibbs, Deputy Chief, AFOAT-1, Office for Atomic Energy, DCS/O, March 26, 1954.

24   Gerard C. Smith to Colonel Jack A. Gibbs, Deputy Chief, AFOAT-1, Office for Atomic Energy, DCS/O, n.d.; P. J. Farley, Memorandum for File, Subject: Requirement for New Seismic Stations, December 15, 1954; Gerard C. Smith, Special Assistant to the Secretary to L. Corrin Strong, June 3, 1955; AFOAT-1, *History of the Atomic Energy Detection System, 1955* (Washington, D.C.: AFOAT-1, n.d.), p. 13.

25   Gerard C. Smith, Special Assistant to the Secretary, to L. Corrin Strong, June 3, 1955; Olav Riste, *The Norwegian Intelligence Service, 1945–1970* (London: Frank Cass, 1999), pp. 195–196.

26   Desmond Ball, *A Suitable Piece of Real Estate: American Installations in Australia* (Sydney: Hale and Iremonger, 1980), pp. 83–84, 87; Mary Welch, "AFTAC Celebrates 50 Years of Long Range Detection," *The Monitor*, October 1997, pp. 8–32 at pp. 12–13. The personnel at each site were given a team designation and assigned a team number: Pole Mountain (Team 110), Douglas (Team 141), Encampment (Team 142), Larson AFB (Team 155), Thule (Team 220), Ankara (Team 301), Camp King (Team 313A). The Teams later became Detachments. The stations themselves were designated by code names. Code names assigned to the Ankara, Thule, and Clark Air Force Base stations were Slip Stream, Polka Dot, and Fish Hawk, respectively. For Team numbers, see Welch, "AFTAC Celebrates 50 Years of Long Range Detection," pp. 12–13. For code names, see AFOAT-1, *History of the Atomic Energy Detection System, 1955*, pp. 16–17, 19.

27   AFOAT-1, *History of the Atomic Energy Detection System, 1955*, pp. 13, 16, 58–59; "Russian Nuclear Explosions," n.d. but circa August 4, 1955, DEFE 13/414, UKNA.

28   Science Applications International Corporation, *Fifty Year Commemorative History of Long Range Detection: The Creation, Development, and Operation of the United States Atomic Energy Detection System* (Satellite Beach, Fla.: SAIC, 1997), p. 61; AFOAT-1, *History of the Atomic Energy Detection System, 1955*, pp. 22–25.

29   AFOAT-1, *History of the Atomic Energy Detection System, 1955*, p. 5; "Russian Nuclear Explosions"; Podvig (ed.), *Russian Strategic Nuclear Forces*, p. 486.

30   AFOAT-1, *History of the Atomic Energy Detection System, 1955*, pp. 6–7; Selwyn Lloyd to Prime Minister, September 23, 1955, DEFE 13/414, UKNA. The British preliminary estimate of the yield was 10 to 15 kilotons.

31   AFOAT-1, *History of the Atomic Energy Detection System, 1955*, pp. 7–8; Selwyn Lloyd to Prime Minister, November 7, 1955, DEFE 13/414, UKNA.

32   AFOAT-1, *History of the Atomic Energy Detection System, 1955*, pp. 8–9.

33   Ibid., pp. 25–26, 28. The AFOAT-1 history mentions the code name—Oilskin—for a November test that was a B-36 target, but does not give the date or Joe number.

34   Central Intelligence Agency, SE 36/1, *Soviet Capabilities for Attack on the US Through Mid-1955*, August 3, 1953, p. 2, in National Security Archive, *The Soviet Estimate: US Analysis of the Soviet Union, 1947–1991* (Alexandria, Va.: Chadwick-Healey, 1995), Document 00149.

35   Sir Frederick Brundrett to Minister, January 17, 1955, DEFE 13/60, UKNA.

36   Ibid. There was also tension during the same period over what the British felt were premature U.S. announcements or leaks concerning Soviet tests. In an October 1954 memo to the prime minister, Harold Macmillan wrote that the "recent statement by the Atomic Energy Commission on the Russian atomic explosions was made against our wishes," explaining that "we may be asked whether these explosions were detected by us as well as by the Americans. To answer such questions must necessarily help the Russians to assess our capabilities of detection." In August 1955 the prime minister received another memo noting recent Soviet nuclear detonations and telling him that while U.S. and British atomic intelligence authorities would prefer no publicity given the uncertainties involved in the data, "we have . . . learnt by past experience that there may be a danger of a leak on the other side of the Atlantic." See Harold Macmillan to Prime Minister, October 28, 1954, DEFE 13/60, UKNA; Selwyn Lloyd to Prime Minister, August 4, 1955, DEFE 13/414, UKNA.

37   In January 1961 Kenneth Strong, the director of the British Joint Intelligence Bureau (JIB), which maintained the small Technical Research Unit to conduct atomic intelligence analysis, sent a memo to his boss, the minister of defense. He noted that "our exchanges with our opposite numbers in the U.S. are now so good that for the first time for some years British and American estimates of the amounts of Soviet produced plutonium and U-235 are nearly identical as it would be reasonable to expect. . . . For some years past the CIA estimate has been considerably higher than the British one." See K. W. D. Strong, JIB, "The Soviet Atomic Energy Programme: Note for Minister of Defence," January 25, 1961, DEFE 13/342, UKNA.

38   Podvig (ed.), *Russian Strategic Nuclear Forces*, pp. 487–488; Gerard C. Smith, Special Assistant to the Secretary, to Hon. Horace A. Hildreth, American Ambassador, Karchi, Pakistan, February 14, 1956; Science Applications International Corporation, *Fifty Year Commemorative History of Long Range Detection*, p. 119; Memorandum for the File, Subject: AFOAT-Iran, March 22, 1956; Philip J. Farley, Memorandum for File: AFOAT-Iran, June 27, 1956; Philip J. Farley, Acting Special Assistant to the Secretary to G. Hayden Raynor, Counselor of Embassy, Oslo, September 21, 1956; Riste, *The Norwegian Intelligence Service, 1945–1970*, p. 196.

39   Chris Pocock, *Dragon Lady: The History of the U-2 Spyplane* (Shrewsbury, England: Airlife, 1989), p. 27; Gregory W. Pedlow and Donald E. Welzenbach, *The Central Intelligence Agency and Overhead Reconnaissance: The U-2 and OXCART Programs, 1954–1974* (Washington, D.C.: CIA, 1992), pp. 104–105.

40   Jeffrey T. Richelson, *The Wizards of Langley: Inside the CIA's Directorate of Science and Technology* (Boulder, Colo.: Westview, 2001), pp. 12–13.

41   Pedlow and Welzenbach, *The Central Intelligence Agency and Overhead Reconnaissance*, pp. 105, 109; Pocock, *Dragon Lady*, pp. 27–28; Chris Pocock, *The U-2 Spyplane: Toward the Unknown* (Atglen, Pa.: Schiffer, 2000), p. 51.

42   Jay Miller, *Lockheed U-2* (Austin, Tex.: Aerofax, 1983), pp. 27, 30; Pedlow and Welzenbach, *The Central Intelligence Agency and Overhead Reconnaissance*, pp. 135, 139.

43   Pedlow and Welzenbach, *The Central Intelligence Agency and Overhead Reconnaissance*, pp. 135, 139, 143; Henry S. Lowenhaupt, "Mission to Birch Woods," *Studies in Intelligence*, 12, 4 (Fall 1968), pp. 1–12 at p. 3.

44   Lowenhaupt, "Mission to Birch Woods," pp. 3–5.

45   Ibid., pp. 5–6; Donald E. Welzenbach, "Observation Balloons and Reconnaissance Satellites," *Studies in Intelligence*, 30, 1 (Spring 1986), pp. 21–28. On the Genetrix program, see Jeffrey T. Richelson, *American Espionage and the Soviet Target* (New York: Morrow, 1987), pp. 129–139.

46   Lowenhaupt, "Mission to Birch Woods," pp. 4, 9.

47   Ibid., pp. 6–7.

48   Ibid., p. 7.

49   Ibid., pp. 7–8.

50   Ibid., p. 8.

51   Ibid., pp. 8–9.

52   Ibid., p. 9; Pocock, *The U-2 Spyplane*, p. 105; Pedlow and Welzenbach, *The Central Intelligence Agency and Overhead Reconnaissance*, p. 138.

53   Pocock, *The U-2 Spyplane*, p. 105; Pedlow and Welzenbach, *The Central Intelligence Agency and Overhead Reconnaissance*, pp. 138–139; Lowenhaupt, "Mission to Birch Woods," p. 9; Podvig (ed.), *Russian Strategic Nuclear Forces*, pp. 488–490.

54   Lowenhaupt, "Mission to Birch Woods," p. 10; Henry S. Lowenhaupt, "Ravelling Russia's Reactors," *Studies in Intelligence*, 16, 4 (Fall 1972), pp. 65–79 at p. 65; James Q. Reber, Memorandum for: Project Director, Subject: Presidential Briefings on TALENT Materials, October 9, 1957, CREST, NARA.

55   Lowenhaupt, "Mission to Birch Woods," p. 10.

56   Lowenhaupt, "Ravelling Russia's Reactors," pp. 65–79.

57   Podvig (ed.), *Russian Strategic Nuclear Forces*, pp. 488–491.

58   Pocock, *The U-2 Spyplane*, pp. 116, 120. Polmar refers to the U-2A-1S as WU-2As. See Norman Polmar, *Spyplane: The U-2 History Declassified* (Osceolo, Wis.: Motor Books International, 2001), p. 171.

59   Pocock, *The U-2 Spyplane*, pp. 120–121.

60   Riste, *The Norwegian Intelligence Service, 1945–1970*, pp. 196–198.

61   "Materials Relating to the USSR's Unilateral Suspension of Nuclear Weapons Tests," pp. 1–3, Papers of Lewis L. Strauss, Box 106, HHPL.

62   Henry S. Lowenhaupt, "Decryption of a Picture," *Studies in Intelligence*, 1, 3 (Summer 1957), pp. 41–53 at p. 41.

63   Ibid., pp. 41–53.

64   Ibid., pp. 41, 52.

65   Henry S. Lowenhaupt, "Somewhere in Siberia," *Studies in Intelligence*, 15, 1 (Winter 1971), pp. 35–51 at p. 35; Murrey Marder, "Reds Avow No Secrecy in A-Talks," *Washington Post and Times Herald*, September 2, 1958, pp. A1, A14; Murrey Marder, "Cooperation on Fusion Power Urged by U.S., Soviet Scientists at Geneva," *Washington Post and Times-Herald*, September 3, 1958, pp. A1, A7.

66   Lowenhaupt, "Somewhere in Siberia," p. 35.

67   Ibid.; Darrell Garwood, "Reds Built Big Nuclear Power Plant in Siberia," *Washington Post and Times Herald*, September 9, 1958, p. A6.

68   Lowenhaupt, "Somewhere in Siberia," pp. 37–38.

69   Ibid., p. 38.

70   Ibid., pp. 39–40, 43–44.

71   Ibid., pp. 39, 41; Photographic Intelligence Center, CIA, Photographic Intelligence Brief B-39-58, October 31, 1958, CREST, NARA.

72   Lowenhaupt, "Somewhere in Siberia," pp. 42–43.

73   Ibid., pp. 35, 43.

74   Department of Energy, DOE-NV-209-REV 15, *United States Nuclear Tests, July 1945 Through September 1992*, December 2000, pp. vii, 17, www.nv.doe.gov.

75   Pocock, *The U-2 Spyplane*, pp. 152–153; Pedlow and Welzenbach, *The Central Intelligence Agency and Overhead Reconnaissance*, pp. 162–163.

76   Pocock, *The U-2 Spyplane*, p. 153; Pedlow and Welzenbach, *The Central Intelligence Agency and Overhead Reconnaissance*, p. 163; National Foreign Assessment Center, CIA, *USSR: Nuclear Accident near Kyshtym in 1957–1958*, October 1981, p. 4.

77   Raymond Garthoff, *A Journey Through the Cold War: A Memoir of Containment and Coexistence* (Washington, D.C.: Brookings, 2001), pp. 2–3, 8, 39; "Raymond L. Garthoff," www.brookings.org/scholars/rgarthoff.htm, accessed January 5, 2004.

78   Garthoff, *A Journey Through the Cold War*, pp. 85–86; Raymond L. Garthoff, "Intelligence Aspects of Cold War Scientific Exchanges: US-USSR Atomic Energy Exchange Visits in 1959," *Intelligence and National Security*, 15, 1 (Spring 2000), pp. 1–13 at p. 2.

79   Garthoff, *A Journey Through the Cold War*, pp. 77, 90, 109; Garthoff, "Intelligence Aspects of Cold War Scientific Exchanges," p. 2.

80   Garthoff, *A Journey Through the Cold War*, pp. 91–92; Garthoff, "Intelligence Aspects of Cold War Scientific Exchanges," pp. 4–5.

81   Garthoff, *A Journey Through the Cold War*, pp. 93, 99; Garthoff, "Intelligence Aspects of Cold War Scientific Exchanges," p. 6.

82   Science Applications International Corporation, *Fifty Year Commemorative History of Long Range Detection*, p. 5.

83   Ibid., p. 12; United States Air Force Oral History Program, Interview #K239.0512-685 of Doyle Northrup, July 24, 1973, Patrick Air Force Base, Fla., pp. 30–31.

84   Glenn Seaborg, *Kennedy, Khrushchev, and the Test Ban* (Berkeley: University of California Press, 1983), pp. 14–15; Podvig (ed.), *Russian Strategic Nuclear Forces*, pp. 491–493; William D. Hall, "3-Power A-Test Talks Set Oct. 31; Senators Warn on China Loophole," *Washington Post and Times Herald*, September 12, 1958, p. A17.

85   Science Applications International Corporation, *Fifty Year Commemorative History of Long Range Detection*, pp. 61, 73–74; Riste, *The Norwegian Intelligence Service, 1945–1970*, p. 199.

86   Philip J. Farley, Special Assistant to the Secretary, to John J. Muccio, Ambassador to Iceland, March 4, 1959; H. O. Ekern, S/AE, Memorandum for the Files, Subject: Exploration of Additional Arrangements for AFOAT Sites, March 31, 1959; P. Rutter,

S/AE, Memorandum for the File, Subject: AFTAC Station Requirements in Thailand, Ceylon, and Ecuador, December 2, 1959.

87   P. Rutter, S/AE, Memorandum for the File, Subject: AFTAC Expansion Program, October 9, 1959 w/att.; Peter Rutter, S/AE, Subject: Air Force Requirements for Establishment of Backscatter Radar Station, October 9, 1959; Science Applications International Corporation, *Fifty Year Commemorative History of Long Range Detection*, p. 121. The nations and territories listed in the attachment to Rutter's October 9 memo included Australia, Pakistan, Libya, Canada, Philippines, Tahiti, South Africa, South Georgia, Liberia, Ecuador, Ceylon, Macquarie, Kerguelan Island, Hawaii, Fiji, Mascarene Island, Lower California, Puerto Rico, French West Africa, Argentina, New Zealand, Easter Island, Brazil, Uruguay, Thailand, Norway, Iceland, Chile, Pitcairn Island, Mariana Island, Azores, Ascension, Bouvet Island, Turkey, and Japan.

88   Richelson, *The Wizards of Langley*, pp. 24–25.

89   Robert McDonald (ed.), *CORONA: Between the Sun and the Earth, the First NRO Reconnaissance Eye in Space* (Bethesda, Md.: American Society for Photogrammetry and Remote Sensing, 1997), pp. 301–302, 305–306; Dino A. Brugioni, "The Kyshtym Connection," *Bulletin of the Atomic Scientists*, March 1990, p. 12; Jonathan McDowell, "Launch Listings," in Dwayne A. Day, John M. Lodgson, and Brian Latell, *Eye in the Sky: The Story of the CORONA Spy Satellites* (Washington, D.C.: Smithsonian Institution Press, 1998), p. 236.

90   Committee on Overhead Reconnaissance, "List of High Priority Targets," August 18, 1960; Letter from Dino Brugioni to author, January 18, 2004.

91   Central Intelligence Agency, Photographic Intelligence Center, *Atomic Energy Complex: Novosibirsk, USSR*, February 1961, CREST, NARA.

92   Central Intelligence Agency, National Photographic Interpretation Center, *Uranium Mining Intelligence and Mining Complex: Mayli-Say, USSR*, June 1961, p. 9, CREST, NARA; Central Intelligence Agency, National Foreign Assessment Center, *USSR: Nuclear Accident near Kyshtym in 1957-1958*, October 1981, p. 4.

93   Central Intelligence Agency, Report No. CS-K-3/465,141, Subject: Miscellaneous Information on Nuclear Installations in the USSR, February 16, 1961, in Zhores Medvedev, *Nuclear Disaster in the Urals* (New York: W. W. Norton, 1979), pp. 186–188; Central Intelligence Agency, National Foreign Assessment Center, *USSR: Nuclear Accident near Kyshtym in 1957–1958*, p. 4.

94   National Intelligence Estimates 11-2A-56 (September 5, 1956), 11-2-57 (May 7, 1957), 11-2A-58 (February 4, 1958), 11-2A-59 (August 18, 1959), and 11-2A-60 (June 21, 1960), all titled *The Soviet Atomic Energy Program*, are now available in the National Intelligence Council collection of declassified documents, available at its Web site: www.cia.gov/nic.

95   Director of Central Intelligence, NIE 11-2-61, *The Soviet Atomic Energy Program*, October 5, 1961, passim.

96   Ibid., pp. 2, 17, 18n; Cochran, Norris, and Bukharin, *Making the Russian Bomb*, p. 186.

97   Director of Central Intelligence, NIE 11-2-61 *The Soviet Atomic Energy Program*, p. 18; Cochran, Norris, and Bukharin, *Making the Russian Bomb*, p. 36.

98   Director of Central Intelligence, NIE 11-2-61, *The Soviet Atomic Energy Program*, p. 23; Podvig (ed.), *Russian Strategic Nuclear Forces*, p. 104; Private information.

99   Director of Central Intelligence, NIE 11-2-61, *The Soviet Atomic Energy Program*, p. 23. Any treatment of Novaya Zemlya has been redacted from the sanitized version.

100 "Is Russia Fooling U.S. on A-Bomb Tests?" *U.S. News & World Report*, December 19, 1960, pp. 72–76 at p. 72; Herbert Scoville Jr., Assistant Director, Scientific Intelligence, Memorandum for: Director of Central Intelligence, Subject: Comments on U.S. NEWS AND WORLD REPORT Interview with John McCone, December 20, 1960, CREST, NARA.

101 Director of Central Intelligence, SNIE 11-7-57, *Feasibility and Likelihood of Soviet Evasion of a Nuclear Test Moratorium*, December 10, 1957, p. 4, in National Security Archive, *The Soviet Estimate*, Document No. 00208.

102 Ibid., pp. 4–5. The issue of possible Soviet evasion was addressed in later estimates: Director of Central Intelligence, SNIE 11-9-59, *Probable Soviet Position on Nuclear Weapons Testing*, September 8, 1959, and Director of Central Intelligence, SNIE 11-9A-59, *Probable Soviet Position on Nuclear Weapons Testing*, September 8, 1959, both in National Security Archive, *The Soviet Estimate*, Documents 00232 and 00233, respectively.

103 Scoville, Memorandum for: Director of Central Intelligence, Subject: Comments on U.S. NEWS AND WORLD REPORT Interview with John McCone.

104 Director of Central Intelligence, NIE 11-9-61, *The Possibility of Soviet Nuclear Testing During the Moratorium*, April 25, 1961, pp. 1–3.

105 Ibid., p. 3.

106 Glenn T. Seaborg, *Kennedy, Khrushchev, and the Test Ban* (Berkeley: University of California Press, 1983), p. 77.

107 Herbert Scoville Jr., Chairman, JAEIC Statement, 1430 Hours, September 1, 1961; Podvig (ed.), *Russian Strategic Nuclear Forces*, p. 493.

108 Podvig (ed.), *Russian Strategic Nuclear Forces*, pp. 493–499; Herbert Scoville Jr., Chairman, JAEIC, "Statement, 1230 Hours, 4 November 1961," November 4, 1961.

109 Strobe Talbott (ed.), *Khrushchev Remembers* (Boston: Little, Brown, 1970), p. 71; Zaloga, *The Kremlin's Nuclear Sword*, pp. 71–72.

110 Sakharov, *Memoirs*, pp. 219–220.

111 Ibid., p. 221; Victor Adamsky and Yuri Smirnov, "Moscow's Biggest Bomb: The 50-Megaton Test of October 1961," *Cold War International History Project Bulletin*, 4 (Fall 1994), pp. 3, 19–21 at p. 3.

112 Jerry E. Knotts and Patrick O'Malley, *The Big Safari Story* (privately printed, n.d.), p. 7; Science Applications International Corporation, *Fifty Year Commemorative History of Long Range Detection*, p. 91.

113 William E. Burrows, *By Any Means Necessary: America's Secret Air War in the Cold War* (New York: Farrar, Straus & Giroux, 2001), p. 282.

114   Knotts and O'Malley, *The Big Safari Story*, p. 7; Seaborg, *Kennedy, Khrushchev, and the Test Ban*, p. 114; United States Air Force Oral History Program Interview #K239.0512-685 with Doyle Northrup, p. 40.

115   Talbot (ed.), *Khrushchev Remembers*, p. 71.

116   Knotts and O'Malley, *The Big Safari Story*, p. 7; John F. Kennedy to Robert McNamara, November 10, 1961, reproduced in Science Applications International Corporation, *Fifty Year Commemorative History of Long Range Detection*, p. 92.

117   Director of Central Intelligence, NIE 11-14-61, *The Soviet Strategic Military Posture, 1961–1967*, November 1961, in Gerald K. Haines and Robert E. Leggett, *CIA's Analysis of the Soviet Union, 1947–1991* (Washington, D.C.: CIA, 2001), pp. 230–238 at pp. 234–235.

118   Robert S. Norris, Andrew S. Burrows, and Richard W. Fieldhouse, *Nuclear Weapons Databook, Volume V: British, French, and Chinese Nuclear Weapons* (Boulder, Colo.: Westview, 1994), pp. 25, 184.

119   James Fetzer, "Clinging to Containment: China Policy," in Thomas G. Patterson (ed.), *Kennedy's Quest for Victory: American Foreign Policy, 1961–63* (New York: Oxford University Press, 1989), pp. 178–197 at p. 182.

CHAPTER 4: MAO'S EXPLOSIVE THOUGHTS

1   John Wilson Lewis and Xue Litai, *China Builds the Bomb* (Stanford: Stanford University Press, 1988), pp. 37–38, 44; Robert S. Norris, Andrew Burrows, and Richard Fieldhouse, *Nuclear Weapons Databook, Volume V: British, French, and Chinese Nuclear Weapons* (Boulder, Colo.: Westview, 1994), p. 328.

2   Lewis and Xue, *China Builds the Bomb*, p. 38; Patrick Tyler, *A Great Wall: Six Presidents and China—An Investigative History* (New York: Public Affairs, 1999), pp. 83–84.

3   Lewis and Xue, *China Builds the Bomb*, pp. 11–39; Gordon H. Chang, *Friends and Enemies: The United States, China, and the Soviet Union, 1948–1972* (Stanford: Stanford University Press, 1990), pp. 16–42; Xiaobing Li, "PLA Attacks and Amphibious Operations During the Taiwan Strait Crises of 1954–55 and 1958," in Mark A. Ryan, David M. Finkelstein, and Michael A. McDevitt, *Chinese Warfighting: The PLA Experience Since 1949* (Armonk, N.Y.; M. E. Sharpe, 2003), pp. 143–172.

4   Lewis and Xue, *China Builds the Bomb*, pp. 46–47.

5   Ibid., pp. 48–49, 54–59.

6   Ibid., pp. 90, 140–141; Norris, Burrows, and Fieldhouse, *Nuclear Weapons Databook, Volume V*, pp. 338, 340; "Selections from CHINA TODAY: National Defense S&T Undertakings," *Joint Publications Research Service*, JPRS-CST-94-009, May 23, 1994, p. 13.

7   Lewis and Xue, *China Builds the Bomb*, pp. 76–81, 86.

8   Ibid., pp. 85, 95.

9   Ibid., pp. 90–92.

10   Ibid., p. 97; Norris, Burrows, and Fieldhouse, *Nuclear Weapons Databook, Volume V*, pp. 338, 345.

11   Lewis and Xue, *China Builds the Bomb*, pp. 115–116.

12   Ibid., p. 111; Norris, Burrows, and Fieldhouse, *Nuclear Weapons Databook, Volume V*, p. 339; "Selections from CHINA TODAY," p. 16.

13   Lewis and Xue, *China Builds the Bomb*, p. 111.

14   Ibid., p. 175.

15   Ibid., pp. 175–176.

16   Ibid., p. 176.

17   Ibid.; "Selections from CHINA TODAY," p. 23.

18   Lewis and Xue, *China Builds the Bomb*, pp. 176–177.

19   Ibid., p. 177; "Selections from CHINA TODAY," p. 24.

20   Lewis and Xue, *China Builds the Bomb*, pp. 39, 41, 41n.

21   Ibid., pp. 60–72; Director of Central Intelligence, NIE 100-3-60, *Sino-Soviet Relations*, August 9, 1960, in National Intelligence Council, *Tracking the Dragon: National Intelligence Estimates on China During the Era of Mao, 1948–1976* (Washington, D.C.: U.S. Government Printing Office, 2004), pp. 218–247 at 222, 225; Central Intelligence Agency, *China: Plutonium Production Reactor Problems*, January 1988, p. 1; Odd Arne Westad, *Brothers in Arms: The Rise and Fall of the Sino-Soviet Alliance, 1945–63* (Stanford: Stanford University Press, 1998), pp. 157–159, 206–207; Jin Zhitao, Wang Shibo, Xu Yunjian, sun Zongyong, Tian Hongyao, and Lue Jie, "The 'Two Bombs' Star That Will Never Fall—The Republic's Father of 'Two Bombs and One Satellite,' Remembering Guo Yonghuai," *Beijing Renmin Ribao*, December 27, 2000, pp. 11*ff* (translation by Foreign Broadcast Information Service, FBIS-CHI-2000-1227); Director of Central Intelligence, NIE 11-12-66, *The Outlook for Sino-Soviet Relations*, December 1, 1966, p. 3. Also see Victor Gobarev, "Soviet Policy Toward China: Developing Nuclear Weapons, 1949–1969," *Journal of Slavic Military Studies*, 12, 4 (December 1999), pp. 17–53.

22   Norris, Burrows, and Fieldhouse, *Nuclear Weapons Databook, Volume V*, pp. 328–329; Lewis and Xue, *China Builds the Bomb*, pp. 44, 47, 148; "Selections from CHINA TODAY," p. 13.

23   Jin et al., "The 'Two Bombs' Star That Will Never Fall"; Norris, Burrows, and Fieldhouse, *Nuclear Weapons Databook, Volume V*, p. 328.

24   Norris, Burrows, and Fieldhouse, *Nuclear Weapons Databook, Volume V*, p. 329; Lewis and Xue, *China Builds the Bomb*, pp. 44, 99.

25   Interview with Karl Weber, Oakton, Va., May 5, 1999. On the programs to use modified P-2Vs for reconnaissance of China (designated ST/POLLY and then ST/SPIN), see Jeffrey T. Richelson, *The Wizards of Langley: Inside the CIA's Directorate of Science and Technology* (Boulder, Colo.: Westview, 2001), pp. 20, 96–97.

26   Donald P. Steury, "Introduction," in Donald P. Steury, *Sherman Kent and the Board of National Estimates: Collected Essays* (Washington, D.C.: Central Intelligence Agency, 1994), pp. ix–xxv at pp. ix–x.

27   Sherman Kent, AD/NE, Memorandum for the Director, Subject: Chinese Communist Capabilities for Developing an Effective Atomic Weapons Program and Weapons Delivery Program, June 24, 1955, pp. 2–3.

28   Geography Division, Office of Research and Reports, Central Intelligence Agency, Project Initiation Memorandum, October 3, 1960, CREST, NARA.

29   Director of Central Intelligence, NIE 13-60, *Communist China*, December 6, 1960, p. 13; Director of Central Intelligence, NIE 13-2-60, *The Chinese Communist Atomic Energy Program*, December 13, 1960. In an interview published in *U.S. News & World Report* on December 19, AEC chairman John McCone stated that "we have no evidence on China's weapons development program," a comment that OSI chief Herbert Scoville characterized as being an "underestimate [of] intelligence knowledge on this subject." See "Interview with John A. McCone, Chairman, Atomic Energy Commission: Is Russia Fooling U.S. on A-Bomb Tests?" *U.S. News & World Report*, December 19, 1960, pp. 72–76 at p. 75; Herbert Scoville Jr., Memorandum for: Director of Central Intelligence, Subject: Comments on U.S. NEWS AND WORLD REPORT Interview with John A. McCone, December 20, 1960, CREST, NARA.

30   Director of Central Intelligence, NIE 13-2-60, *The Chinese Communist Atomic Energy Program*, pp. 1–2; John M. Steeves, Bureau of Far Eastern Affairs to Roger Hilsman, Director, INR, "National Intelligence Estimate on Implications of Chinese Communist Nuclear Capability," April 12, 1961; Robert A. McDonald, "CORONA: Success for Space Reconnaissance, A Look into the Cold War and a Revolution for Intelligence," *Photogrammetric Engineering and Remote Sensing*, 60, 6 (June 1995), pp. 689–720 at p. 700.

31   Director of Central Intelligence, NIE 13-2-60, *The Chinese Communist Atomic Energy Program*, pp. 2–3. As was often the case, the air force's assistant chief of staff for intelligence was more pessimistic, writing in a footnote (p. 3n) that China would "probably detonate its first nuclear device in 1962, and possibly as early as late 1961."

32   Memorandum from the Joint Chiefs of Staff, "A Strategic Analysis of the Impact of the Acquisition by Communist China of a Nuclear Capability," June 26, 1961, in Edward C. Keefer, David W. Mabon, and Harriet Dashiell Schwar (eds.), *Foreign Relations of the United States, 1961–63, Volume XXII, Northeast Asia* (Washington, D.C.: U.S. Government Printing Office, 1996), pp. 84–85; George McGhee to Secretary of State Dean Rusk, "Anticipatory Action Pending Chinese Demonstration of a Nuclear Capability," September 13, 1961, pp. 1–2.

33   McGhee to Rusk, "Anticipatory Action Pending Chinese Demonstration of a Nuclear Capability," pp. 2–3.

34   William Burr and Jeffrey T. Richelson, "Whether to 'Strangle the Baby in the Cradle': The United States and the Chinese Nuclear Program, 1960–1964," *International Security*, 25, 3 (Winter 2000/01), pp. 54–99 at p. 62.

35   Chang, *Friends and Enemies*, p. 232; "Daily Brief," *Central Intelligence Bulletin*, October 14, 1961, p. 1, CREST, NARA.

36   Chief, CIA/PID (NPIC), Memorandum for: Director, NPIC, Subject: Information Concerning the PI Effort on the Chinese Atomic Energy Program, March 28, 1963, Attachment B, CREST, NARA; McDonald, "CORONA," pp. 689–720 at p. 700.

37   Chris Pocock, *Dragon Lady: The History of the U-2 Spyplane* (Shrewsbury, England: Airlife, 1989), pp. 90–93.

38   Director of Central Intelligence, NIE 13-2-62, *Chinese Communist Advanced Weapons Capabilities*, April 25, 1962, p. 12.

39   Ibid., pp. 3, 11.

40   R. L. Blachy, L. Goure, S. T. Hosmer, A. L. Hsieh, B. F. Jaeger, P. F. Langer, and M. G. Weiner, *Implications of a Communist Chinese Nuclear Capability: A Briefing* (Santa Monica, Calif.: RAND Corporation, August 1962), pp. v, 1–2.

41   Dean Rusk, Memorandum for: M—Mr. McGhee, "Program to Influence World Opinion with Respect to a Chinese Communist Nuclear Detonation," September 20, 1962 w/att: Program to Influence World Opinion with Respect to a Chinese Communist Nuclear Detonation, CREST, NARA; George C. McGhee, Memorandum for the Honorable John A. McCone, Central Intelligence Agency, Subject: Program to Influence World Opinion with Respect to a Chinese Communist Nuclear Detonation, September 25, 1962, CREST, NARA.

42   Interview with Robert Johnson, Washington, D.C., May 9, 2003; Burr and Richelson, "Whether to 'Strangle the Baby in the Cradle,'" p. 63.

43   Johnson interview; Burr and Richelson, "Whether to 'Strangle the Baby in the Cradle,'" p. 63.

44   Lewis and Xue, *China Builds the Bomb*, p. 103, 131–132, 134; Norris, Burrows, and Fieldhouse, *Nuclear Weapons Databook, Volume V*, p. 332.

45   "Selections from CHINA TODAY," p. 16; Lewis and Xue, *China Builds the Bomb*, pp. 54, 159.

46   Lewis and Xue, *China Builds the Bomb*, p. 141.

47   Ibid., pp. 97, 99, 103; Norris, Burrows, and Fieldhouse, *Nuclear Weapons Databook, Volume V*, p. 333. In late 1963, OSI completed a study on the institute. See Office of Scientific Intelligence, Central Intelligence Agency, *The Communist Chinese Institute of Atomic Energy*, December 16, 1963.

48   "Editorial Note," in Keefer, Mabon, and Schwar (eds.), *Foreign Relations of the United States, 1961–63, Volume XXII*, p. 339.

49   Arms Control and Disarmament Agency, "Summary and Appraisal of Latest Evidence on Chinese Communist Advanced Weapons Capabilities," July 10, 1963, p. 1; Jonathan McDowell, "Launch Listings," in Dwayne A. Day, John M. Logsdon, and Brian Latell (eds.), *Eye in the Sky: The Story of the CORONA Spy Satellites* (Washington, D.C.: Smithsonian Institution Press, 1998), p. 238; Chief, CIA/PID (NPIC), Memorandum for: Director, NPIC, Subject: Information Concerning the PI Effort on the Chinese Atomic Energy Program, Attachments B, C; Memorandum, "U-2 Overflights of Cuba, 29 August through 14 October 1962," February 27, 1963, in Mary S. McAuliffe (ed.), *CIA Documents on the Cuban Missile Crisis, 1962* (Washington, D.C.: Central Intelligence Agency, 1992), pp. 127–137 at pp. 127–128. According to the above-cited memo for the director of the NPIC, at the end of March 1963 approximately 35 percent of China had been covered by aerial photography, while 85 to 90 percent had been covered by Corona launches since August 1960 (although 40 percent of that coverage had been obscured by scattered to heavy clouds).

50   National Imagery and Mapping Agency, *America's Eyes: What We Were Seeing*, Sep-

tember 2002, pp. 2–3; Interview with Dino Brugioni, January 23, 2003; Jeffrey T. Richelson, *America's Secret Eyes in Space: The U.S. Keyhole Spy Satellite Program* (New York: Harper & Row, 1990), p. 77.

51   Director of Central Intelligence, SNIE 13-2-63, *Communist China's Advanced Weapons Program,* July 24, 1963, p. 4.

52   Ibid.; Lewis and Xue, *China Builds the Bomb,* pp. 134–135.

53   Arms Control and Disarmament Agency, "Summary and Appraisal of Latest Evidence on Chinese Communist Advanced Weapons Capabilities," Annex 3.

54   Director of Central Intelligence, SNIE 13-2-63, *Communist China's Advanced Weapons Program,* p. 5.

55   Ibid.

56   Ibid., pp. 5–6.

57   Arms Control and Disarmament Agency, "Summary and Appraisal of Latest Evidence on Chinese Communist Advanced Weapons Capabilities," Annex 3.

58   Director of Central Intelligence, SNIE 13-2-63, *Communist China's Advanced Weapons Program,* p. 1; Burr and Richelson, "Whether to "Strangle the Baby in the Cradle,'" p. 65. See Willis C. Armstrong, William Leonhart, William J. McCaffrey, and Herbert C. Rothenberg, "The Hazards of Single-Outcome Forecasting," in H. Bradford Westerfield (ed.), *Inside the CIA's Private World* (New Haven: Yale University Press, 1995), pp. 238–254, for a discussion of the estimate's errors and their cause.

59   Director of Central Intelligence, SNIE 13-2-63, *Communist China's Advanced Weapons Program,* p. 10.

60   Burr and Richelson, "Whether to 'Strangle the Baby in the Cradle,'" p. 76; Johnson interview.

61   "Editorial Note," in Keefer, Mabon, and Schwar (eds.), *Foreign Relations of the United States, 1961–63, Volume XXII,* p. 339.

62   Burr and Richelson, "Whether to 'Strangle the Baby in the Cradle,'" pp. 67–71; Telegram to Moscow Embassy, July 15, 1963, and Moscow Embassy telegram to State Department, July 27, 1963, both in David W. Mabon and David S. Patterson (eds.), *Foreign Relations of the United States, 1961–63, Volume VII, Arms Control and Disarmament* (Washington, D.C.: U.S. Government Printing Office, 1996), pp. 801, 860. About a week before his departure, Sherman Kent, still the head of the Office of National Estimates, had sent him a short memo noting that "the Soviets must realize that when the Chinese have such a [nuclear] capability, it might be directed westward against the USSR as well as eastward against the US." Sherman Kent, Memorandum for: Averell Harriman, Subject: What the Soviets Must Be Thinking as They Perceive the Chinese Communists Working Towards an Initial Advanced Weapons Capability—Nuclear Weapons and Missiles, July 8, 1963, in Mabon and Patterson (eds.), *Foreign Relations of the United States, 1961–63, Volume VII,* pp. 771–772.

63   U.S. Embassy, Moscow, telegram to State Department, July 27, 1963, in Mabon and Patterson (eds.), *Foreign Relations of the United States, Volume VII,* p. 860; Kendrick Oliver, *Kennedy, Macmillan, and the Nuclear Test Ban Debate* (New York: St. Mar-

tin's, 1998), pp. 205–206; Vladislav Zubok, "Look What Chaos in the Beautiful Socialist Camp: Deng Xiaoping and the Russians, 1956–1963," *Bulletin of the Cold War International History Project*, 10 (Winter 1997/98), pp. 152–162; Tyler, *A Great Wall*, p. 58.

64   "The President's News Conference of August 1, 1963," *Public Papers of the Presidents of the United States: John F. Kennedy, 1963* (Washington, D.C.: U.S. Government Printing Office, 1964), p. 616; Harriet Dashiell Schwar (ed.), *Foreign Relations of the United States, 1964–68, Volume XXX, China* (Washington, D.C.: U.S. Government Printing Office, 1998), p. 24 n. 7.

65   William E. Colby, Memorandum for McGeorge Bundy, "Meeting of General Chiang Ching-kuo with the President, September 10, 1963," September 19, 1963, pp. 3, 11.

66   Burr and Richelson, "Whether to 'Strangle the Baby in the Cradle,'" pp. 72–73.

67   Ibid., p. 73.

68   Benjamin Read to McGeorge Bundy, "The President's Meeting with Chinese Minister of Defense Chiang Ching-kuo on September 23 at 11:30 A.M.," September 18, 1965, w/att: Background Paper, "U.S.-GRC Consultations Concerning Possible Action Against the Mainland," and Memorandum for the Record: "Understandings Reached During Chiang-Ching Kuo's Visit."

69   George Rathjens, ACDA, *Destruction of Chinese Nuclear Weapons Capabilities*, December 14, 1964; Walt Rostow, Memorandum for the President, "The Implications of a Chinese Communist Nuclear Capability," April 17, 1964; Maxwell Taylor, Chairman JCS, Memorandum for: Gen. LeMay, Gen. Wheeler, Adm. McDonald, and Gen. Shoup, "Chinese Nuclear Development," November 18, 1963; Burr and Richelson, "Whether to 'Strangle the Baby in the Cradle,'" pp. 74–75; Interview with Albert Wheelon, Washington, D.C., April 9, 1997.

70   Schwar (ed.), *Foreign Relations of the United States, 1964–68 Volume XXX*, p. 24 n. 7; Robert Johnson to Walt Rostow, "Direct Action Against Chicom Nuclear Facilities," February 12, 1964, cited in Burr and Richelson, "Whether to 'Strangle the Baby in the Cradle,'" p. 74.

71   Burr and Richelson, "Whether to 'Strangle the Baby in the Cradle,'" p. 75.

72   Lewis and Xue, *China Builds the Bomb*, p. 136.

73   Ibid., pp. 166–168; Norris, Burrows, and Fieldhouse, *Nuclear Weapons Databook, Volume V*, p. 333.

74   "Selections from CHINA TODAY," p. 17; Norris, Burrows, and Fieldhouse, *Nuclear Weapons Databook, Volume V*, p. 333; Lewis and Xue, *China Builds the Bomb*, p. 168.

75   "Selections from CHINA TODAY," p. 17; Lewis and Xue, *China Builds the Bomb*, p. 169.

76   Lewis and Xue, *China Builds the Bomb*, pp. 126n, 169, 184; Defense Intelligence Agency, Biographic Sketch: Zhang Aiping, July 1979.

77   "Selections from CHINA TODAY," p. 17.

78   Lewis and Xue, *China Builds the Bomb*, pp. 183–184. The "596" designation was derived from the year and month that Soviet assistance ceased. See Norris, Burrows, and Fieldhouse, *Nuclear Weapons Databook, Volume V*, p. 337.

79 Burr and Richelson, "Whether to 'Strangle the Baby in the Cradle,'" pp. 83–84; Central Intelligence Agency, *Central Intelligence Bulletin*, March 18, 1964, p. 4, CREST, NARA.

80 National Photographic Interpretation Center, *Mission GRC 176, September 25, 1963*, October 1963, pp. 13–14, 17.

81 Pocock, *Dragon Lady*, p. 98; M. S. Kohli and Kenneth Conboy, *Spies in the Himalayas: Secret Missions and Perilous Climbs* (Lawrence: University Press of Kansas, 2003), pp. 23–25; Interview with Richard Bissell, Farmington, Conn., March 16, 1984; Wheelon interview.

82 Day, Logsdon, and Latell (eds.), *Eye in the Sky*, p. 233; McDowell, "Launch Listings," in Day, Logsdon, and Latell (eds.), *Eye in the Sky*, p. 238; McDonald, "CORONA," p. 716; [James Q. Reber], Chairman, Committee on Overhead Reconnaissance, Memorandum for: Director of Central Intelligence, Subject: Additional KH-4 Coverage of China, April 17, 1964, CREST, NARA.

83 Day, Logsdon, and Latell (eds.), *Eye in the Sky*, p. 233; McDowell, "Launch Listings," p. 238; McDonald, "CORONA," p. 716; Richelson, *America's Secret Eyes in Space*, p. 357; National Imagery and Mapping Agency, *America's Eyes*, pp. 2–3; Dwayne A. Day, "A Failed Phoenix: The KH-6 LANYARD Reconnaissance Satellite," *Spaceflight*, 39, 5 (May 1997), pp. 170–174 at p. 173.

84 National Photographic Interpretation Center, NPIC/R-740/64, *Probable Atomic Energy Complex Under Construction near Chih-Chin-Hsia, China*, August 1964, p. 7, CREST, NARA. National Photographic Interpretation Center, NPIC/R-155/64, *Oak—Part I, Mission 1004-2, 19-22 February 1964*, February 1964, p. 17, CREST, NARA.

85 John McCone, Memorandum for the Record, July 24, 1964, in Schwar (ed.), *Foreign Relations of the United States, 1964–68, Volume XXX*, p. 70; Central Intelligence Agency, "Communist Chinese Nuclear Weapons Capabilities," July 22, 1964.

86 National Photographic Interpretation Center, NPIC/R-740/64, *Probable Atomic Energy Complex Under Construction near Chin-Chin-Hsia, China*, pp. 1, 7. The previous report on the complex was National Photographic Interpretation Center, R-335/63, *Suspect Atomic Energy Complex Under Construction near Yu-men, China*, December 1963. A subsequent report was National Photographic Interpretation Center, NPIC/R-860/64, *Probable Atomic Energy Complex Under Construction near Chih-Chin-Hsia, China*, October 1964, CREST, NARA.

87 National Photographic Interpretation Center, NPIC/R-740/64, *Probable Atomic Energy Complex Under Construction near Chin-Chin-Hsia, China*, pp. 1–5.

88 McDowell, "Launch Listings," p. 238.

89 Frederic C. E. Oder, James C. Fitzpatrick, and Paul Worthman, *The CORONA Story* (Washington, D.C.: National Reconnaissance Office, 1997), p. 155; Director of Central Intelligence, SNIE 13-4-64, *The Chances of an Imminent Communist Chinese Nuclear Explosion*, August 26, 1964, in Kevin Ruffner (ed.), *CORONA: America's First Satellite Program* (Washington, D.C.: Central Intelligence Agency, 1995), pp. 239–244 at p. 239.

90   Director of Central Intelligence, SNIE 13-4-64, "The Chances of an Imminent Communist Chinese Nuclear Explosion," p. 239.
91   Ibid., p. 241.
92   Ibid., pp. 241–242.
93   Ibid., pp. 242–243; Burr and Richelson, "Whether to 'Strangle the Baby in the Cradle'," p. 85. In April 1964 the American consul in Hong Kong told a Japanese diplomat who inquired whether the United States had any evidence about such a connection, that the United States doubted France would assist China in that way. See Am Consul Hong Kong to Department of State, A-857, Subject: French Unwillingness to Supply Heavy Water to Communist China, April 10, 1964. The issue was of enough concern three years later that the *chef du cabinet* in the Ministry of Science, Space, and Atomic Affairs found it necessary to assure U.S. diplomats that there was "zero cooperation between the French and Chicoms on nuclear matters, military or nonmilitary." See Burr and Richelson, "Whether to 'Strangle the Baby in the Cradle,'" p. 85 n. 88. SNIE 13-4-64 contained a paragraph on the issue, but seven of the eight lines are blacked out in the released version.
94   Director of Central Intelligence, SNIE 13-4-64, "The Chances of an Imminent Communist Chinese Nuclear Explosion," pp. 243–244.
95   Wheelon interview; Telephone conversation with Albert Wheelon, September 16, 1999.
96   Burr and Richelson, "Whether to 'Strangle the Baby in the Cradle,'" p. 86.
97   Ibid.
98   Ibid., p. 87; John A. McCone, Memorandum for the Record, Subject: Memorandum of Discussion at Luncheon—September 15th, Secretary Rusk's Dining Room, September 15, 1964, in Schwar (ed.), *Foreign Relations of the United States, 1964–1968, Volume XXX*, pp. 95–96; McGeorge Bundy, Memorandum for the Record, September 15, 1964.
99   Burr and Richelson, "Whether to 'Strangle the Baby in the Cradle,'" p. 87; McCone, Memorandum for the Record, Subject: Memorandum of Discussion at Luncheon, September 15, 1964; Bundy, Memorandum for the Record, September 15, 1964. See also the discussion by Chang, *Friends and Enemies*, p. 250; John Lewis Gaddis, *Strategies of Containment: A Critical Appraisal of Postwar American National Security Policy* (New York: Oxford University Press, 1982), pp. 210–211.
100 McCone, Memorandum for the Record, September 17, 1964.
101 Interview with Thomas L. Hughes, Washington, D.C., September 8, 2004. In an October 5 memo, McCone recounts a meeting that day with Johnson, Rusk, McNamara, and McGeorge Bundy. According to the memo, McCone presented KH-4 imagery and stated that U-2 photography would provide more precise information on the last stages of construction at Lop Nur, which might aid in estimating the timing of the test. However, McCone records that he told them that unless the president and Rusk believed information concerning the time of detonation was important, he could not recommend the mission on the grounds that it was a deep penetration that pushed the U-2 to its limit and would cover no other important targets. Rusk stated

his opposition, according to McCone, on the grounds that the information was not of significant importance and the mission would involve overflying Burma and India. A CIA telegram to Taipei stated that the primary reasons were the election, satellite-obtained data, and Rusk's September 29 statement about an upcoming Chinese test. See John McCone, Memorandum for the Record, Subject: Discussion with the President, Secretary Rusk, Secretary McNamara and Mr. McGeorge Bundy—Monday, 5 October 4:45 p.m. October 5, 1964, in Schwar (ed.), *Foreign Relations of the United States, 1964–68, Volume XXX*, p. 106 (including no. 2).

102   Burr and Richelson, "Whether to 'Strangle the Baby in the Cradle,'" p. 87.

103   Memcon, September 25, 1964, in Schwar (ed.), *Foreign Relations of the United States, 1964–68, Volume XXX*, pp. 104–105.

104   David E. Kaiser, *American Tragedy: Kennedy, Johnson, and the Origins of the Vietnam War* (Cambridge: Harvard University Press, 2000), p. 254; Lyle L. Goldstein, "When China Was a 'Rogue State': The Impact of China's Nuclear Weapons Program on US-China Relations During the 1960s," *Journal of Contemporary China*, 12, 37 (November 2003), pp. 739–764 at p. 752. For Johnson's emphasis on avoiding conflict with China over Vietnam, see Larry Berman, *Planning a Tragedy: The Americanization of the Vietnam War* (New York: W. W. Norton, 1982), pp. 125, 142–143.

105   Assistant Director for Scientific Intelligence Donald Chamberlain to Deputy DCI Marshall Carter, "Estimated Imminence of a Chinese Nuclear Test," October 15, 1964, in Schwar (ed.), *Foreign Relations of the United States, 1964–68, Volume XXX*, pp. 107–08. For the Malian delegation and reports of an October 1 test, see "The Secretary's Staff Meeting," October 28 and November 27, 1964. A Malian delegation visited China on June 19–July 4 and met with Mao and Zhou, among other senior officials. A Gambit launch of August 14 resulted in a good KH-7 image of Lop Nur being obtained on August 16 and returned to earth on August 23—too late to use in the August 1964 special estimate. A KH-4A launched on September 14 returned the first of its two film buckets on September 19, possibly permitting its exploitation and the dissemination of results by September 25. See McDowell, "Launched Listings," p. 238; Richelson, *American's Secret Eyes in Space*, p. 357.

106   Burr and Richelson, "Whether to "Strangle the Baby in the Cradle,'" pp. 89–90.

107   Committee on Overhead Reconnaissance, Subject: Photographic Coverage Contemplated During the Next Six Months of Significant ChiCom Targets, October 2, 1964.

108   McDowell "Launch Listings," p. 240; Richelson, *America's Secret Eyes in Space*, p. 357; Assistant Director for Scientific Intelligence Donald Chamberlain to Deputy DCI Marshall Carter, "Estimated Imminence of a Chinese Nuclear Test," in Schwar (ed.), *Foreign Relations of the United States, 1964–68, Volume XXX*, pp. 107–108; John A. McCone, Memorandum for the Record, October 17, 1964, in Schwar (ed.), *Foreign Relations of the United States, 1964–68, Volume XXX*, pp. 110–111; "Classification of Intelligence Information," attachment to: Howard J. Osborn, Memorandum for: Legislative Counsel, Subject: Proposal DCI Statement Before the Special Subcommittee on Intelligence of the Armed Services Committee, House of Representatives (Nedzi Committee), March 21, 1972, CREST, NARA. Gambit satellites

photographed Baotou on March 12 and April 25, 1964, while Jiuquan was covered on April 27 and September 26. Lanzhou apparently was not covered in 1964.

109   Chamberlain to Carter, "Estimated Imminence of a Chinese Nuclear Test," pp. 107–108.

110   "Selections from CHINA TODAY," p. 29; Lewis and Xue, *China Builds the Bomb*, pp. 185–186.

111   "Selections from CHINA TODAY," p. 29; Lewis and Xue, *China Builds the Bomb*, p. 187; Norris, Burrows, and Fieldhouse, *Nuclear Weapons Databook, Volume V*, p. 328.

112   "Selections from CHINA TODAY," p. 29; Lewis and Xue, *China Builds the Bomb*, p. 187; "Nuclear Pursuits," *Bulletin of the Atomic Scientists*, May 1991, p. 49.

113   Lewis and Xue, *China Builds the Bomb*, pp. 187–188.

114   Ibid., pp. 188–189; "Selections from CHINA TODAY," p. 30; "Statement by China on Its A-Explosion," *Washington Post*, October 17, 1964, p. A10; "Red China Sets Off Atomic Explosion; Soviet Paper Condemns Khrushchev," *Washington Post*, October 17, 1964, p. 1; "China Tests Atomic Bomb, Asks Summit Talk on Ban; Johnson Minimizes Peril," *New York Times*, October 17, 1964, p. 1. The October 17 *Times* also carried a story by science writer Walter Sullivan that indicated the plutonium assumption was widespread outside of the CIA—"Use of Plutonium Hints at Handicap" (p. 11). Sullivan's story also demonstrated that the Tackle operation, although not its code name, was no secret. He wrote, "Specialists here are uncertain of the exact location of the test site, although it is almost certainly known to those with access to photographs taken by U-2 aircraft flown over China by Chinese Nationalist pilots from Taiwan."

115   Air Force Technical Applications Center, *History of the Air Force Technical Applications Center, 1 July–31 December 1964*, n.d., pp. 9, 11, 15; "Selections from CHINA TODAY," p. 30.

116   "Johnson's Statement on Chinese A-Blast," *Washington Post*, October 17, 1964, p. A10; State Department Executive Secretary Benjamin Read to National Security Assistant McGeorge Bundy, "Standby Statement for Chinese Communist Nuclear Test," September 30, 1964; Burr and Richelson, "Whether to 'Strangle the Baby in the Cradle,' " p. 92; Lyndon Baines Johnson, *The Vantage Point: Perspectives of the Presidency, 1963–1969* (New York: Holt, Rinehart and Winston, 1971), p. 469.

117   Department of State/Department of Defense, Message, Subject: Project CLEAR SKY, October 16, 1964.

118   Air Force Technical Applications Center, *History of the Air Force Technical Applications Center, 1 July–31 December 1964*, p. 25.

119   Ibid.; Glenn T. Seaborg with Benjamin S. Loeb, *Stemming the Tide: Arms Control in the Johnson Years* (Lexington, Mass.: Lexington Books, 1987), p. 116.

120   McCone, Memorandum for the Record, October 17, 1964, p. 110.

121   Ibid., p. 111.

122   V. Gupta and D. Rich, "Locating the Detonation Point of China's First Nuclear Explosive Test on 16 October 1964," *International Journal of Remote Sensing*, 17, 10

(1996), pp. 1969–1974; Burr and Richelson, "Whether to 'Strangle the Baby in the Cradle,'" p. 91; See also Seaborg with Loeb, *Stemming the Tide*, p. 116.

123   *Journals of Glenn Seaborg*, Vols. 7–9 (Berkeley, Calif.: Lawrence Berkeley, Laboratory, 1989), pp. 254–261; Seaborg with Loeb, *Stemming the Tide*, pp. 116–117.

124   Rathjens, *Destruction of Chinese Nuclear Weapons Capabilities*, December 14, 1964, pp. 5–7.

125   Pocock, *Dragon Lady*, pp. 100–101; R. E. Lawrence and Harry W. Woo, "Infrared Imagery in Overhead Reconnaissance," *Studies in Intelligence*, 11, 3 (Summer 1967), pp. 17–40 at p. 23; Central Intelligence Agency, *U-2 Reconnaissance Mission C025C, Flown 8 January 1965*, 1965, pp. 1–2.

126   Director of Central Intelligence, NIE 13-2-65, *Communist China's Advanced Weapons Program*, January 27, 1965, pp. 1–2, 6–7.

127   Central Intelligence Agency, "The Second Chinese Nuclear Test," *Weekly Review*, May 21, 1965, pp. 7, 9.

128   From: [deleted], Memorandum for: Deputy Director for Intelligence, Subject: Photo-Satellite Reconnaissance 1965, October 5, 1965, CREST, NARA.

129   Central Intelligence Agency, *Chronology of Reactor Construction, Chin-Chin-Hsia Atomic Energy Complex*, September 1965, p. 1, CREST, NARA. The twenty-two missions figure is from a date that has been deleted from the declassified version of the document. Given that five Gambit/KH-7 missions were flown prior to the report's being prepared, three of which were undertaken after the October 16, 1964, detonation, the twenty-two missions probably refer to those between that event and the time the report was prepared.

130   Science Applications International Corporation, *Fifty Year Commemorative History of Long Range Detection* (Satellite Beach, Fla.: SAIC, 1997), p. 119.

131   Ibid., pp. 63–64. Other detection techniques that were in use in 1965 included atmospheric fluorescence (pp. 137–138), which recorded nuclear explosion–induced fluorescence in the upper atmosphere; magnetic (p. 95), which relied on recording fluctuations in the earth's magnetic field caused by high-altitude nuclear detonations; vertical incidence (pp. 133–134), which detected nuclear explosions at high altitudes by measuring the disturbances in the ionosphere within a sixty-degree cone over the detection facility; and surface-based resonance scatter (p. 89), which relied on optical filtering equipment to detect certain atoms and ions of debris that would be trapped in the atmosphere as the result of a high-altitude nuclear explosion.

132   E-mail, Matthew Aid to author, December 17, 2003.

133   Ibid.; U.S. Army Security Agency, *Annual Historical Summary: United States Army Security Agency, Fiscal Year 1966* (Arlington, Va.: ASA, n.d.), pp. 96–97, 106–107, 117, 154–155, 158, 163, 166; U.S. Army Security Agency, *Annual Historical Summary: United States Army Security Agency, Fiscal Year 1967* (Arlington, Va.: ASA, 1971), p. 179. In July 1965 the Red Wind program was redesignated Blue Zephyr, and then terminated as an operational intelligence effort. Only Dawn Star sites were designated as Signal Research Units (SRUs), while only Red Wind sites were designated Signals Operations Units (SOUs).

134   Science Applications International Corporation, *Fifty Year Commemorative History of Long Range Detection*, p. 123; John R. London III, "Vela—A Space System Success Story." Paper presented at the 42nd Congress of the International Astronautical Federation, October 5–11, 1991, Montreal, Canada; Charles C. Bates, Advanced Research Projects Agency, Address before the Annual Conference of the Division of Earth Sciences, National Research Council, Subject: The Goals of Project VELA, April 29, 1961, Papers of Lee DuBridge, Box 175, Folder 175.1, California Institute of Technology Archives.

135   Science Applications International Corporation, *Fifty Year Commemorative History of Long Range Detection*, pp. 123–124; London, "Vela," pp. 2, 7; Sidney Singer, "The Vela Satellite Program for Detection of High-Altitude Nuclear Detonations," *Proceedings of the IEEE*, 53, 12 (December 1965), pp. 1935–1948 at p. 1935.

136   William F. Raborn and Glenn Seaborg (signators), Memorandum of Understanding Between the Atomic Energy Commission and the Central Intelligence Agency Concerning Work to Be Performed at the Lawrence Radiation Laboratory, August 3, 1965; Ann Parker, "Knowing the Enemy, Anticipating the Threat," *Science and Technology Review*, July/August 2002, pp. 24–31 at p. 25.

137   Albert D. Wheelon, DDS&T, Memorandum for: Director of Central Intelligence, Subject: Formation of a Nuclear Intelligence Panel, October 29, 1965, CREST, NARA; Memorandum for: Mr. Duckett, Subject: Scientific Advisory Panels, October 11, 1966, CREST, NARA.

138   Norris, Burrows, and Fieldhouse, *Nuclear Weapons Databook, Volume V*, p. 333; Office of Scientific Intelligence, Central Intelligence Agency, *Weekly Surveyor*, May 23, 1966.

139   Norris, Burrows, and Fieldhouse, *Nuclear Weapons Databook, Volume V*, p. 333; Lewis and Xue, *China Builds the Bomb*, p. 202; Central Intelligence Agency, "Chinese Demonstrate Nuclear Weapons Delivery Capability," *Weekly Summary*, November 4, 1966, pp. 5–6.

140   Director of Central Intelligence, SNIE 13-8-66, *Communist China's Advanced Weapons Program*, November 3, 1966, pp. 1–2. The earlier 1966 estimate was Director of Central Intelligence, *Communist China's Advanced Weapons Program*, July 1, 1966. That estimate continued to wrestle with the issue of where the U-235 for China's nuclear tests came from. It noted that "in theory" the Lanzhou facility "could by itself produce uranium of sufficient enrichment, make a nuclear device. But because it appears too small to hold a complete gaseous diffusion cascade using normal size stages it would have been necessary for the Chinese to crowd in a large number of small stages. It is highly unlikely that the Chinese had the technical capability to do this during the years that [Lanzhou] was being built." It still suggested that the final stage of enrichment might have been handled by electromagnetic separation at an undetected facility. A year later in the 1967 estimate (NIE 13-8-67, *Communist China's Strategic Weapons Program*, August 3, 1967), the estimators would write (on p. 4) that "we are now less confident of our estimate that the Chinese are using the electromagnetic process to 'top off' the U-235 production that has been partially enriched in the gaseous diffusion cascade at [Lanzhou]." The 1966 estimate did correctly note that China's primary production center was under construction near Yumen (Jiuquan), probably consisting of a large plutonium production reactor, a plutonium separation plant, and a third facility believed to contain a small experimental reactor and possibly a pilot chemical separation plant (pp. 6–7).

141 Lewis and Xue, *China Builds the Bomb*, p. 196.

142 Ibid., pp. 199–201.

143 Ibid., pp. 200–201; Norris, Burrows, and Fieldhouse, *Nuclear Weapons Databook, Volume V*, p. 333; Central Intelligence Agency, "Chinese Explode Fifth Nuclear Device," *Weekly Summary*, January 6, 1967, p. 7.

144 Lewis and Xue, *China Builds the Bomb*, pp. 205–206.

145 Ibid., p. 206; Norris, Burrows, and Fieldhouse, *Nuclear Weapons Databook, Volume V*, p. 334; Central Intelligence Agency, "Chinese Communists Test Thermonuclear Weapon," *Weekly Summary*, June 23, 1967, p. 8; Director of Central Intelligence, NIE 13-8-67, *Communist China's Strategic Weapons Program*, p. 1.

146 Hsichun Mike Hua, "The Black Cat Squadron," *Air Power History*, Spring 2002, pp. 4–19 at p. 16; Chris Pocock, *50 Years of the U-2: The Complete Illustrated History of the "Dragon Lady"* (Atglen, Pa.: Schiffer, 2005), p. 246. Interview with former CIA official.

147 Hua, "The Black Cat Squadron," p. 16; Interview with former CIA official. Use of the Tabasco sensor may have been the result of a major effort to generate a requirement for its use. The purpose of January 1967 meeting involving OSI and JAEIC chairman Donald Chamberlain, the chairman of COMOR, and representatives of the Office of Research and Development, which developed Tabasco along with Sandia Laboratories, was to "determine what actions are required to generate a requirement, to which OSA can respond, for the Project [deleted] operational mission." The memo reporting on the purpose of the meeting also included a "short description of the [7 characters deleted] equipment and its function." See Memorandum for the Record, IDEA-0047-67, Subject: Project [deleted], January 27, 1967, CREST, NARA. The IDEA indicates Idealist, the current, at the time, code name for CIA U-2 operations.

148 Richelson, *America's Secret Eyes in Space*, pp. 358–359; Norris, Burrows, and Fieldhouse, *Nuclear Weapons Databook, Volume V*, p. 334; E-mail, Tim Brown to author, February 3, 2004; Pocock, *50 Years of the U-2*, p. 251.

149 McDowell, "Launch Listings," p. 242; Day, Logdson, and Latell (eds.), *Eye in the Sky*, pp. 231–233.

150 London, "Vela," p. 7. Scientific Applications International Corporation, *Fifty Year Commemorative History of Long Range Detection*, p. 125.

151 Norris, Burrows, and Fieldhouse, *Nuclear Weapons Databook, Volume V*, p. 334.

152 George C. Denney Jr. to the Secretary, Subject: Chinese Nuclear Test May Have Been a Failure, December 29, 1967. Denney also noted that China had not announced the test, contrary to its usual practice. In addition, he pointed out that there were other reasons to believe that any test would have been planned to produce a large yield—the desire for "a spectacle to end another year of cultural revolution

activity, a desire to steal some of the USSR's 50th anniversary thunder, and to pay homage to Mao two days before his birthday." In April 1968 a memorandum to holders of NIE 13-8-67 also proclaimed that "Peking's official silence concerning the test," as well as other factors, "point toward failure." See Director of Central Intelligence Memorandum to Holders, National Intelligence Estimate 13-8-67, *Communist China's Strategic Weapons Program*, April 4, 1968, p. 4.

153   Pocock, *Dragon Lady*, p. 120; Norman Polmar, *Spyplane: The U-2 History Declassified* (Osceola, Wis.: MBI Publishing, 2001), p. 206.

154   Lewis and Xue, *China Builds the Bomb*, p. 103.

155   Norris, Burrows, and Fieldhouse, *Nuclear Weapons Databook, Volume V*, p. 350; Barry Naughton, "The Third Front: Defense Industrialization in the Chinese Frontier," *China Quarterly*, 115 (September 1988), pp. 351–386.

CHAPTER 5: AN ELATED GENERAL, A SMILING BUDDHA

1   Leslie R. Groves, *Now It Can Be Told: The Story of the Manhattan Project* (New York: Da Capo, 1983), pp. 33–34; Bertrand Goldschmidt, *Atomic Rivals* (New Brunswick, N.J.: Rutgers University Press, 1990), p. 296.

2   Maurice Goldsmith, *Frédéric Joliot-Curie: A Biography* (London: Lawrence and Wishart, 1976), pp. 75–79, 84–85.

3   Ibid., pp. 84–88; Margaret Gowing, *Britain and Atomic Energy, 1939–1945* (New York: St. Martin's, 1964), pp. 49–50; Goldschmidt, *Atomic Rivals*, pp. 76–80.

4   Gowing, *Britain and Atomic Energy, 1939–1945*, p. 49; Goldschmidt, *Atomic Rivals*, pp. 57–59, 287; Goldsmith, *Frédéric Joliot-Curie*, pp. 92, 99; Robert S. Norris, Andrew Burrows, and Richard Fieldhouse, *Nuclear Weapons Databook, Volume V: British, French, and Chinese Nuclear Weapons* (Boulder, Colo.: Westview, 1994), p. 182.

5   Goldschmidt, *Atomic Rivals*, p. 296.

6   Roger Faligot and Pascal Krop, *La Piscine: The French Secret Service Since 1944* (New York: Basil Blackwell, 1989), pp. 32–33.

7   Goldschmidt, *Atomic Rivals*, pp. 214–217, 242, 288; Goldsmith, *Frédéric Joliot-Curie*, p. 137; Robert S. Norris, *Racing for the Bomb: General Leslie R. Groves, the Manhattan Project's Indispensable Man* (South Royalton, Vt.: Steerforth Press, 2002), pp. 332–333.

8   Goldsmith, *Frédéric Joliot-Curie*, p. 140; Norris, Burrows, and Fieldhouse, *Nuclear Weapons Databook, Volume V*, p. 182; Lawrence Scheinman, *Atomic Energy Policy in France Under the Fourth Republic* (Princeton: Princeton University Press, 1965), pp. 7, 11, 18; Richard Rhodes, *The Making of the Atomic Bomb* (New York: Simon & Schuster, 1986), p. 321.

9   Goldschmidt, *Atomic Rivals*, p. 295.

10   Ibid., pp. 325, 328; Norris, Burrows, and Fieldhouse, *Nuclear Weapons Databook, Volume V*, p. 182.

11   Goldschmidt, *Atomic Rivals*, p. 294; Goldsmith, *Frédéric Joliot-Curie*, p. 149.

12   Norris, Burrows, and Fieldhouse, *Nuclear Weapons Databook, Volume V*, p. 183.

13   Goldschmidt, *Atomic Rivals*, p. 335.

14   Norris, Burrows, and Fieldhouse, *Nuclear Weapons Databook, Volume V*, p. 183; Scheinman, *Atomic Energy Policy in France Under the Fourth Republic*, p. 41.

15   Norris, Burrows, and Fieldhouse, *Nuclear Weapons Databook, Volume V*, p. 183; John Prados, *Operation Vulture* (New York: Ibooks, 2002), pp. 200–228.

16   Norris, Burrows, and Fieldhouse, *Nuclear Weapons Databook, Volume V*, p. 183; Scheinman, *Atomic Energy Policy in France Under the Fourth Republic*, p. 43.

17   Norris, Burrows, and Fieldhouse, *Nuclear Weapons Databook, Volume V*, pp. 183–184; Scheinman, *Atomic Energy Policy in France Under the Fourth Republic*, pp. 116, 171; Wynfred Joshua, *New Perspectives in U.S.-French Nuclear Relations* (Stanford: Stanford Research Institute, 1972), p. 10; Ambassade de France, White Paper, "France's First Atomic Explosion," February 1960, p. 9; George A. Kelly, "The Political Background of the French A-Bomb," *Orbis*, IV, 3 (Fall 1960), pp. 284–306 at p. 297.

18   Ambassade de France, White Paper, "France's First Atomic Explosion," p. 16; Norris, Burrows, and Fieldhouse, *Nuclear Weapons Databook, Volume V*, p. 184; Scheinman, *Atomic Energy Policy in France Under the Fourth Republic*, pp. 173, 182.

19   Jean-Marc Regnault, "France's Search for Nuclear Test Sites, 1957–1963," *Journal of Military History*, 67, 4 (July 2003), pp. 1223–1248 at p. 1224–1226; Ambassade de France, White Paper, "France's First Atomic Explosion," p. 29.

20   Ambassade de France, White Paper, "France's First Atomic Explosion," p. 12; Regnault, "France's Search for Nuclear Test Sites, 1957–1963," p. 1227; Douglas Porch, *The French Secret Services: A History of French Intelligence from the Dreyfus Affairs to the Gulf War* (New York: Farrar, Straus & Giroux, 1995), p. 396.

21   Ambassade de France, White Paper, "France's First Atomic Explosion," p. 13; Ambassade de France, Release No. 886, "France's First Atomic Explosion," February 13, 1960, p. 3.

22   Regnault, "France's Search for Nuclear Test Sites, 1957–1963," pp. 1227–1228.

23   Ambassade de France, Release No. 886, "France's First Atomic Explosion," pp. 1, 4; Norris, Burrows, and Fieldhouse, *Nuclear Weapons Databook, Volume V*, p. 205; W. Granger Blair, "DeGaulle Claims World Atom Role as Test Succeeds," *New York Times*, February 14, 1960, pp. 1, 2; "Firing Is Climax of 8-Year Effort," *New York Times*, February 14, 1960, p. 3; E. W. Kenworthy, "U.S. and Soviet Regret French Atomic Explosion," *New York Times*, February 14, 1960, pp. 1, 3; "France Set to Try Real Bomb Now," *Washington Post and Times Herald*, February 14, 1960, pp. A1, A7; "Ghana to Freeze Assets of French," *New York Times*, February 14, 1960, pp. 1, 4.

24   Norris, Burrows, and Fieldhouse, *Nuclear Weapons Databook, Volume V*, pp. 205, 405; Porch, *The French Secret Services*, pp. 396–403.

25   Norris, *Racing for the Bomb*, p. 641 n. 62.

26   Lt. Col. S. M. Skinner to Col. W. R. Shuler, Subject: Atomic Experiments in France, February 18, 1946, RG 226, Entry 210, Box 431, Folder 2, NARA.

27   Col. W. R. Shuler, Corps of Engineers and D. C. G. Gattiker, Memorandum for the Period of 17 January 1946 to 28 February 1946, February 28, 1946, RG 77, Entry 22, Box 168, Folder: 202.3-1 (Combined Intelligence Reports), NARA.

28   Maj. Paul O. Languth to Lt. Col. Richard H. Free, Subject: Atomic Energy Research in France, August 29, 1946, RG 77, Entry 22, Box 173, NARA.

29   H. S. Lowenhaupt, Memo to File, Subject: France's Atomic Energy Development, as Extracted from Joliot-Curie's Speech to the Committee on Atomic Energy, 19 March 1946, November 14, 1946, RG 77, Entry 22, Box 173, NARA.

30   Division of Biographic Information to Special Assistant, Intelligence, Biographic Bulletin No. 25, "Francis Perrin, French High Commissioner of Atomic Energy," April 24, 1951.

31   Garrison B. Coverdale, Office of the Assistant Chief of Staff, G-2, Intelligence, Memorandum for: Director of Central Intelligence, Special Assistant for Atomic Energy, Department of State, Subject: French AEC Personnel Changes and Appointments, December 23, 1952 w/att: French AEC Personnel Changes and Appointments.

32   Central Intelligence Agency, "French Position on Disarmament May Be Shifting," *Central Intelligence Bulletin*, May 29, 1957, CREST, NARA.

33   Director of Central Intelligence, NIE 100-6-57, *Nuclear Weapons Production in Fourth Countries: Likelihood and Consequences*, June 18, 1957, pp. 3, 5.

34   Director of Central Intelligence, *Annex to National Intelligence Estimate No. 100-2-58, Development of Nuclear Capabilities by Fourth Countries: Likelihood and Consequences*, July 1, 1958, p. 1; Director of Central Intelligence, NIE 100-2-58, *Development of Nuclear Capabilities by Fourth Countries: Likelihood and Consequences*, July 1, 1958, p. 4.

35   Central Intelligence Agency, "French Nuclear Weapons Program," *Current Intelligence Weekly Summary*, September 18, 1958, page number unknown.

36   Charles de Gaulle, *Memoirs of Hope: Renewal and Endeavor* (New York: Simon & Schuster, 1971), pp. 210, 213; Central Intelligence Agency, *The French Nuclear Weapons Program*, November 13, 1959, p. 1; Interview with a former CIA official.

37   Central Intelligence Agency, *The French Nuclear Weapons Program*, p. 3.

38   Ibid., pp. 1, 3, 6.

39   Ibid., pp. 4, 6.

40   Ibid., p. 6.

41   Ibid.

42   Ibid., p. 7.

43   Ibid., pp. 6–7.

44   Central Intelligence Agency, "The French Nuclear Energy Program," *Current Intelligence Weekly Summary*, January 28, 1960.

45   Central Intelligence Agency, "French Nuclear Test Plans," *Current Intelligence Weekly Summary*, February 25, 1960.

46   Regnault, "France's Search for Nuclear Test Sites, 1957–1963," p. 1232; Norris, Burrows, and Fieldhouse, *Nuclear Weapons Databook, Volume V*, pp. 205, 406.

47   Regnault, "France's Search for Nuclear Test Sites, 1957–1963," pp. 1235, 1242.

48   Ibid., pp. 1233, 1239, 1242–1243; Norris, Burrows, and Fieldhouse, *Nuclear Weapons Databook, Volume V*, pp. 205–206. The local traditional name for the

island Moruroa, which in the Maohi language of Polynesia means "Place of the Great Secret." The French military changed the name to Mururoa in the 1960s.

49   Regnault, "France's Search for Nuclear Test Sites, 1957–1963," p. 1244; Norris, Burrows, and Fieldhouse, *Nuclear Weapons Databook, Volume V*, p. 206; International Atomic Energy Agency, *Study of the Radiological Situation at the Atolls of Mururoa and Fangataufa* (Vienna, Austria: IAEA, 1998), Attachment 1, p. 1.

50   Norris, Burrows, and Fieldhouse, *Nuclear Weapons Databook, Volume V*, p. 206.

51   Ibid., p. 407; Tillman Durdin, "'Tactical' French A-Bomb Exploded at Pacific Atoll: Test Series Begins," *New York Times*, July 3, 1966, pp. 1, 13.

52   Norris, Burrows, and Fieldhouse, *Nuclear Weapons Databook, Volume V*, p. 407.

53   Pierre Billaud, "The Incredible Story of the French H-bomb: A Chaotic Process and a Scandalous Historical Falsification," p. 2, http://perso.club-internet.fr/pbillaud/hla.html, accessed February 9, 2004; Jean Lacoutre, *De Gaulle: The Ruler, 1945–1970* (New York: W. W. Norton, 1992), p. 419.

54   Norris, Burrows, and Fieldhouse, *Nuclear Weapons Databook, Volume V*, pp. 206, 407.

55   Billaud, "The Incredible Story of the French H-bomb," pp. 3–4.

56   Ibid., p. 5; "Did UK Scientist Give France Vital Clues About H-bomb?" *Nature*, December 5, 1996, p. 392; Norris, Burrows, and Fieldhouse, *Nuclear Weapons Databook, Volume V*, p. 33.

57   Norris, Burrows, and Fieldhouse, *Nuclear Weapons Databook, Volume V*, pp. 206, 408; John L. Hess, "France Explodes Her First H-Bomb in South Pacific," *New York Times*, August 25, 1968, pp. 1, 5.

58   Norris, Burrows, and Fieldhouse, *Nuclear Weapons Databook, Volume V*, pp. 206, 407–408; "Debré, Michel," www.britannica.com, accessed December 17, 2004.

59   Norris, Burrows, and Fieldhouse, *Nuclear Weapons Databook, Volume V*, p. 409.

60   Richard St. F. Post to William Witman II, "Coverage of French Underground Tests," August 4, 1961, RG 59, Records of Special Assistant to Secretary for Atomic Energy and Outer Space, Subject and Country Files, 1950–1962, Box 5, Folder: 1961-France-Testing, NARA; Letter, Howard Furnas to General Rodenhauser, August 15, 1961, RG 59, Records of Special Assistant to Secretary for Atomic Energy and Outer Space, Subject and Country Files, 1950-1962, Box 5, Folder: 1961-France-Testing, NARA.

61   Post to Witman, "Coverage of French Underground Tests."

62   Ibid.

63   Letter, Furnas to Rodenhauser.

64   Central Intelligence Agency, "France May Reassess Nuclear Force," *Current Intelligence Weekly Summary*, April 12, 1963, p. 16; McGeorge Bundy, National Security Action Memorandum No. 241, Subject: Report on French Gaseous Diffusion Plant, May 7, 1963, w/att: "France"; Central Intelligence Agency, *Central Intelligence Bulletin*, July 25, 1963, p. 8.

65   Central Intelligence Agency, *The French Nuclear Strike Force Program*, May 31, 1963, p. 1, www.cia.foia.gov; Glenn. T. Seaborg, "Forward," to Goldschmidt, *Atomic Rivals*, p. xi.

66   Director of Central Intelligence, SNIE 22-2-63, *The French Nuclear Weapons Program*, July 24, 1963, pp. i, 4-5.

67   Central Intelligence Agency, *The French Nuclear Weapon Program*, March 27, 1964.

68   E-mail, Tim Brown to author, March 7, 2004; Interview.

69   Interview with Brig. Gen. Jack Ledford, Arlington, Va., October 7, 1999; Gregory W. Pedlow and Donald E. Welzenbach, *The Central Intelligence Agency and Overhead Reconnaissance: The U-2 and OXCART Programs, 1954–1974* (Washington, D.C.: CIA, 1992), pp. 247–248; James A. Cunningham Jr., Memorandum for: Deputy Director of Central Intelligence, Subject: Proposed Operation of U-2 Aircraft from Aircraft Carrier, July 23, 1963, CREST, NARA; James A. Cunningham Jr., Memorandum for: Deputy for Field Activities, Office of Special Activities, Subject: Carrier Training Exercise with USS Kitty Hawk (Unclassified Codename WHALE TALE), July 23, 1963, CREST, NARA.

70   Chris Pocock, *Dragon Lady: The History of the U-2 Spyplane* (Shrewsbury, England: Airlife, 1989), pp. 107–109; Interview with a former CIA official; Central Intelligence Agency, *The French Pacific Nuclear Test Center*, August 6, 1965; Central Intelligence Agency, *U-2 Aircraft Carrier Operation: Project "WHALE TALE,"* December 1969, CREST, NARA; Chris Pocock, *50 Years of the U-2: The Complete Illustrated History of the "Dragon Lady"* (Atglen, Pa.: Schiffer, 2005), p. 204.

71   National Imagery and Mapping Agency, *America's Eyes: What We Were Seeing* (Reston, Va.: NIMA, 2002), p. 3; Jeffrey T. Richelson, *America's Secret Eyes in Space: The U.S. Keyhole Spy Satellite Program* (New York: Harper & Row, 1990), pp. 359–360. The numbers and dates for KH-4A, KH-4B, and KH-7 missions are based on examination of the U.S. Geological Survey Earth Explorer data base as well as viewing of some of the imagery.

72   Interview with Dino Brugioni, January 23, 2003.

73   Richelson, *America's Secret Eyes in Space*, pp. 105–121; Jeffrey T. Richelson, *The Wizards of Langley: Inside the CIA's Directorate of Science and Technology* (Boulder, Colo.: Westview, 2001), p. 158.

74   U.S. Army Security Agency (ASA), *Historical Summary of United States Army Security Agency and Subordinate Units, Fiscal Years 1968–1970* (Arlington, Va.: ASA, 1972), p. 135; E-mail, Matthew Aid to author, February 18, 2004.

75   Strategic Air Command, *SAC Reconnaissance History, January 1968–June 1971* (Offutt Air Force Base, Neb.: SAC, 1973), p. 93; Strategic Air Command, Operations Order 60-71-05, *Burning Light*, May 1, 1971; Strategic Air Command, *SAC Reconnaissance History, FY 74* (Offutt Air Force Base, Neb.: SAC, 1975), p. 73.

76   Strategic Air Command, *SAC Reconnaissance History, January 1968–June 1971*, p. 93; Nicky Hager, *Secret Power: New Zealand's Role in the International Spy Network* (Nelson, New Zealand: Craig Potton, 1996), pp. 63, 102.

77   U.S. Pacific Command, *CINCPAC Command History, 1970, Volume I*, Camp H.M. Smith, Hawaii: PACOM, n.d.), pp. 142–143; U.S. Pacific Command, *CINCPAC Command History 1973, Volume I* (Camp H. M. Smith, Hawaii: PACOM, n.d.), p. 246; "T-AGM-8 Wheeling," www.navsource.org/archives, accessed February 23, 2004.

78   Strategic Air Command, *History of SAC Reconnaissance Operations, FY 72* (Offutt Air Force Base, Neb.: SAC, 1974), p. 59; U.S. Pacific Command, *CINCPAC Command History 1973, Volume I*, pp. 246–248; Strategic Air Command, *History of SAC Reconnaissance Operations, FY 74*, pp. 73–75; Stewart Firth, *Nuclear Playground: Fight for an Independent and Nuclear Free Pacific* (Honolulu: University of Hawaii Press, 1987), p. 99.

79   U.S. Pacific Command, *CINCPAC Command History 1973, Volume I*, pp. 247–248; Durdin, "'Tactical' French A-Bomb Exploded at Pacific Atoll."

80   U.S. Pacific Command, *CINCPAC Command History 1973, Volume I*, p. 246; Strategic Air Command, *History of SAC Reconnaissance Operations, FY 74*, pp. 73, 75.

81   Strategic Air Command, *History of SAC Reconnaissance Operations, FY 74*, p. 77.

82   Science Applications International Corporation, *Fifty Year Commemorative History of Long Range Detection: The Creation, Development, and Operation of the United States Atomic Energy Detection System* (Satellite Beach, Fla.: SAIC, 1997), pp. 113–115; Jeffrey T. Richelson, *The U.S. Intelligence Community*, 4th ed. (Boulder, Colo.: Westview, 1999), pp. 231–235.

83   Jeffrey T. Richelson, *America's Space Sentinels: DSP Satellites and National Security* (Lawrence: University Press of Kansas, 1999), pp. 66–69.

84   Ibid., p. 65.

85   Science Applications International Corporation, *Fifty Year Commemorative History of Long Range Detection*, pp. 124–125; Ellis Lapin, "Surveillance by Satellite," *Journal of Defense Research*, 8, 2 (Summer 1976), pp. 169–186. The satellites also carried another set of nuclear detection sensors, designed to focus on explosions above 1,240 miles: an omnidirectional X-ray spectrometer, a neutron detector (which would measure the neutron flux from a detonation), and a gamma ray detector (which would detect the gamma radiation associated with the detonation).

86   Richelson, *America's Space Sentinels*, pp. 68–69; Barkley G. Sprague, *Evolution of the Missile Defense Alarm System (MIDAS), 1955–1982* (Maxwell Air Force Base, Ala.: Air Command and Staff College, 1985), pp. 29–30.

87   George Perkovich, *India's Nuclear Bomb: The Impact on Global Proliferation* (Berkeley: University of California Press, 1999), p. 1; "Location of Rajasthan in India," www.rajasthan.gov.in/location.SHTM, accessed February 28, 2004.

88   Perkovich, *India's Nuclear Bomb*, p. 1.

89   Ibid., p. 16; Raj Chengappa, *Weapons of Peace: The Secret Story of India's Quest to Be a Nuclear Power* (New Delhi: Harper Collins Publishers India, 2000), p. 74; Robert P. Crease and Charles C. Mann, *The Second Creation: Makers of the Revolution in Twentieth-Century Physics* (New Brunswick, N.J.: Rutgers University Press, 1996), p. 407; Helge Kragh, *Quantum Generations: A History of Physics in the Twentieth Century* (Princeton: Princeton University Press, 1999), pp. 196, 202, 292.

90   Perkovich, *India's Nuclear Bomb*, p. 16; Chengappa, *Weapons of Peace*, pp. 77–78; George Greenstein, "A Gentleman of the Old School: Homi Bhabha and the Development of Science in India," *American Scholar*, Summer 1992, pp. 409–419 at pp. 411–412.

91   Perkovich, *India's Nuclear Bomb*, pp. 17–18; Chengappa, *Weapons of Peace*, p. 71.

92   Perkovich, *India's Nuclear Bomb*, p. 20; Rajesh Kochhar, "S. S. Bhatnagar: Life and Times," *Resonance*, April 2002, pp. 82–89 at p. 82; E. S. Raja Gopal, "K. S. Krishnan–An Outstanding Scientist, 1898–1961," *Resonance*, December 2002, pp. 2–4.

93   Perkovich, *India's Nuclear Bomb*, pp. 21–22; "Department of Atomic Energy: Milestones," www.barc.enet.in, accessed February 28, 2004.

94   Perkovich, *India's Nuclear Bomb*, p. 26.

95   Ibid., pp. 17, 27–28, 33; Steve Weissman and Herbert Krosney, *The Islamic Bomb: The Nuclear Threat to Israel and the Middle East* (New York: Times Books, 1981), p. 130.

96   Perkovich, *India's Nuclear Bomb*, pp. 34–35; Weissman and Krosney, *The Islamic Bomb*, p. 131.

97   Perkovich, *India's Nuclear Bomb*, pp. 35, 37, 52, 56.

98   Ibid., pp. 60–61, 63–64.

99   Ibid., pp. 64–65, 67; Chengappa, *Weapons of Peace*, pp. 93–94.

100 Perkovich, *India's Nuclear Bomb*, pp. 74, 81–82.

101 Ibid., pp. 83–84.

102 Ibid., pp. 90–95, 113; Chengappa, *Weapons of Peace*, pp. 97–98; "Mont Blanc," http://lynx.uio.no/mbl/html, accessed February 28, 2004; "Plane Crashes," www.montblanc.to/uk/glacier/texte4.html, accessed February 29, 2004.

103 Perkovich, *India's Nuclear Bomb*, pp. 112–114; Raja Ramanna, *Years of Pilgrimage: An Autobiography* (New Delhi: Praguin Books, 1991), p. 75.

104 Perkovich, *India's Nuclear Bomb*, pp. 125–126; Chengappa, *Weapons of Peace*, p. 111.

105 Perkovich, *India's Nuclear Bomb*, pp. 140–141; Chengappa, *Weapons of Peace*, p. 118; "Department of Atomic Energy: Milestones."

106 Perkovich, *India's Nuclear Bomb*, p. 141; "India's First Bomb, 1967–1974," www.nuclearweaponarchive.org., accessed February 28, 2004.

107 Perkovich, *India's Nuclear Bomb*, pp. 141–142.

108 Ibid., p. 149; Chengappa, *Weapons of Peace*, pp. 121–122, 180.

109 Perkovich, *India's Nuclear Bomb*, p. 171; "India's First Bomb, 1967–1974"; Chengappa, *Weapons of Peace*, pp. 117, 154; Ramanna, *Years of Pilgrimage*, p. 76. Chengappa reports (p. 117) that Ramanna recalls Gandhi not saying yes or no, which "for us meant an approval."

110 Perkovich, *India's Nuclear Bomb*, pp. 172–173; "Smiling Buddha: 1974," pp. 1–3, http://nuclearweaponarchive.org/India/IndiaSmiling.html, accessed February 27, 2004.

111 Perkovich, *India's Nuclear Bomb*, p. 172; Chengappa, *Weapons of Peace*, pp. 185, 187.

112 Chengappa, *Weapons of Peace*, pp. 188–191.

113 Ibid., pp. 194–195; "Smiling Buddha: 1974, p. 4."

114 Chengappa, *Weapons of Peace*, pp. 196–197.

115 Central Intelligence Agency, *Indian Nuclear Energy Program*, March 18, 1958, p. 7.

116 Department of State Instruction, CA-11378, Subject: Indian Capability and Likelihood to Produce Atomic Energy, June 29, 1961, in National Security Archive Elec-

tronic Briefing Book No. 6: *India and Pakistan—On the Threshold*, Document 1, www.nsarchive.org.

117   Department of State Instruction, CA-11378, Subject: Indian Capability and Likelihood to Produce Atomic Energy, June 29, 1961; Director of Central Intelligence, NIE 4-3-61, *Nuclear Weapons and Delivery Capabilities of Free World Countries Other Than the US and UK*, September 21, 1961, pp. 2, 9.

118   Director of Central Intelligence, NIE 4-63, *Likelihood and Consequence of a Proliferation of Nuclear Weapons Systems*, June 28, 1963, p. 2.

119   Amconsul Bombay to Department of State, Subject: Inauguration of Indian Plutonium Separation Plant, April 29, 1964, w/att: Department of Atomic Energy, "Plutonium Plant at Trombay," n.d.

120   Director of Central Intelligence, NIE 4-2-64, *Prospects for a Proliferation of Nuclear Weapons over the Next Decade*, October 21, 1964, in David S. Patterson (ed.), *Foreign Relations of the United States, 1964–1968, Volume X, National Security Policy* (Washington, D.C.: U.S. Government Printing Office, 2002), pp. 168–170.

121   Central Intelligence Agency, Intelligence Information Cable, TDCS DB-315/01148-64, "Indian Government Policy on Development of Nuclear Weapons," October 22, 1964.

122   Amembassy, New Delhi to Sec State, Cable No. 1323, Washington, D.C., October 29, 1964.

123   Office of Scientific Intelligence, Central Intelligence Agency, *Indian Nuclear Energy Program*, November 6, 1964, pp. 1–5.

124   H. S. Rowen, "The Indian Nuclear Problem," December 24, 1964, in National Security Archive, *Nuclear Non-Proliferation Policy, 1945–1990* (Alexandria, Va.: Chadwyck-Healey, 1991), Document No. 01086, pp. 1, 5.

125   Dwayne A. Day, John M. Logsdon, and Brian Latell (eds.), *Eye in the Sky: The Story of the Corona Spy Satellites* (Washington, D.C.: Smithsonian Institution Press, 1998), p. 240; "Bhabha Atomic Research Centre, Trombay," www.globalsecurity.org, accessed February 28, 2004; Richelson, *America's Secret Eyes in Space*, p. 358.

126   Director of Central Intelligence, SNIE 31-1-65, *India's Nuclear Weapons Policy*, October 21, 1965, pp. 2–3. Much of the information in the SNIE was conveyed in a separate OSI memo on October 18 to a National Security Council staff member in response to Johnson's verbal request. See Donald F. Chamberlain, Director of Scientific Intelligence, Memorandum for: Charles E. Johnson, Subject: Indian Nuclear Weapons Capability, October 18, 1965.

127   Director of Central Intelligence, SNIE 31-1-65, *India's Nuclear Weapons Policy*, p. 2.

128   Ibid.

129   Ibid., p. 6.

130   Department of State to Amembassy, New Delhi, Subject: Possible Indian Nuclear Weapons Development, March 29, 1966, in *India and Pakistan—On the Nuclear Threshold*, National Security Archive Electronic Briefing Book No. 6, Document 8.

131   W. W. Rostow, National Security Action Memorandum 351, Subject: Indian Nuclear Weapons Problem, June 9, 1966.

132 Secretary of State, *Report to the President in Response to NSAM No. 351: The Indian Nuclear Weapons Problem*, July 25, 1966, pp. 5–6.

133 Ibid., pp. 17, 21; W. W. Rostow, National Security Action Memorandum No. 355, Subject: The Indian Nuclear Weapons Problem, further to NSAM 351, August 1, 1966.

134 "Bhabha Atomic Research Centre, Trombay," www.globalsecurity.org, accessed February 28, 2004; K. Srimivasan, "Nuclear Material Control in a Reprocessing Plant," n.d., p. 7; Brown e-mail.

135 Amembassy, New Delhi to Department of State, Subject: Uranium Exploration, Development and Exploitation in India, May 9, 1968, p. 1.

136 Amconsul Madras to Department of State, Subject: Atomic Power Project at Kalpakkam, Tamil Nadu, April 21, 1969; Amconsul Madras to Department of State, Subject: The Madras Atomic Power Project, July 12, 1971; Amembassy New Delhi to Department of State, Subject: India's Second Atomic Power Station, August 19, 1972; Perkovich, *India's Nuclear Bomb*, p. 249.

137 National Security Agency, "Capital Projects Planned in India," August 31, 1972.

138 Interview with Leonard Spector, Washington, D.C., March 5, 2003; Interview with Myron Kratzer, September 2, 2003.

139 Henry A. Kissinger, National Security Study Memorandum 156, Indian Nuclear Development, May 18, 1972; NSC Interdepartmental Group for the Near East and South Asia, *National Security Study Memorandum 156: Indian Nuclear Developments*, September 1, 1972, p. 1.

140 Chengappa, *Weapons of Peace*, pp. 197–198.

141 Ibid., pp. 3, 198–199. According to Chengappa (p. 3) there is substantial dispute about who said what and when.

142 Chengappa, *Weapons of Peace*, pp. 201, 203–204.

143 Bernard Weinraub, "India Becomes 6th Nation to Set Off Nuclear Device," *New York Times*, May 19, 1974, pp. 1, 18; Lewis M. Simons, "India Explodes A-Device, Cites 'Peaceful Use'," *Washington Post*, May 19, 1974, pp. A1, A12.

144 Chengappa, *Weapons of Peace*, p. 56; Central Intelligence Agency, "The 18 May 1974 Indian Nuclear Test," September 1974, p. 21.

145 Chengappa, *Weapons of Peace*, p. 126; Perkovich, *India's Nuclear Bomb*, pp. 173–175; Ramanna, *Years of Pilgrimage*, p. 92.

146 Central Intelligence Agency, "India: [Deleted]," *Central Intelligence Bulletin*, May 20, 1974, pp. 1–3.

147 Milo D. Nordyke, Lawrence Livermore Natural Library, Subject: The Indian Explosion, May 29, 1974; Memorandum, Milo D. Nordyke to Roger E. Batzel, Subject: More on the Indian Explosion, October 1, 1974.

148 Bureau of Intelligence and Research, "India: Uncertainty over Nuclear Policy," June 13, 1974, in *India and Pakistan—On the Threshold*, Document 19.

149 Daniel O. Graham, Memorandum, Subject: Forthcoming Community Post-Mortem Report Concerning the Indian Nuclear Detonation, May 24, 1974.

150   Intelligence Community Staff, *Post-Mortem Report: An Examination of the Intelligence Community's Performance Before the Indian Nuclear Test of May 1974*, July 1974, p. i.

151   Ibid.; Daniel O. Graham, Memorandum for: Director of Central Intelligence, Subject: Indian Post-Mortem Report, July 18, 1974.

152   Chief PRD/IC, Memorandum for: [deleted] Subject: IC Responses to Post-Mortem Recommendations, January 15, 1975, w/att: Analysis of Community Responses to Recommendations in ICS Post-Mortems, CREST, NARA.

CHAPTER 6: "PARIAHS"

1   For one treatment of the subject, see Benjamin Beit-Hallahmi, *The Israeli Connection: Who Israel Arms and Why* (New York: Pantheon, 1987), pp. 208–224.

2   Avner Cohen, *Israel and the Bomb* (New York: Columbia University Press, 1998), pp. 10, 15; Michael Bar-Zohar, *The Armed Prophet: A Biography of Ben Gurion* (London: Arthur Barker, 1967), p. 1.

3   Cohen, *Israel and the Bomb*, p. 15.

4   Ibid., pp. 21, 30–31; Peter Pry, *Israel's Nuclear Arsenal* (Boulder, Colo.: Westview, 1984), p. 5.

5   Cohen, *Israel and the Bomb*, pp. 32–33.

6   Ibid., p. 33.

7   Ibid., pp. 41–42.

8   Ibid., p. 43.

9   James Adams, *The Unnatural Alliance* (London: Quartet, 1984), p. 146; Shimon Peres, *Battling for Peace: A Memoir* (New York: Random House, 1995), p. 116.

10   Cohen, *Israel and the Bomb*, p. 53; Shimon Peres, *David's Sling* (London: Weidenfeld and Nicolson, 1970), pp. 31–65; Peres, *Battling for Peace*, p. 105.

11   Cohen, *Israel and the Bomb*, p. 53.

12   Ibid., pp. 54–55; Bertrand Goldschmidt, *The Atomic Complex: A Worldwide Political History of Nuclear Energy* (La Grange Park, Ill.: American Nuclear Society, 1982), p. 185; Bar-Zohar, *The Armed Prophet*, p. 251.

13   Cohen, *Israel and the Bomb*, p. 58.

14   Ibid., p. 59.

15   Ibid., p. 62; Leonard Spector with Jacqueline R. Smith, *Nuclear Ambitions: The Spread of Nuclear Weapons, 1989–1990* (Boulder, Colo.: Westview, 1990), p. 153. According to Spector (p. 153), Norway would conduct only one inspection.

16   Cohen, *Israel and the Bomb*, p. 68; Peres, *Battling for Peace*, p. 118.

17   "Israel's Negev Desert," www.negev.org, accessed March 8, 2004; "Dimona, Negev Nuclear Research Center," www.globalsecurity.org, accessed March 8, 2004; Peres, *Battling for Peace*, p. 119.

18   Cohen, *Israel and the Bomb*, p. 73.

19   Ibid., pp. 73–74; Adams, *The Unnatural Alliance*, p. 147; Goldschmidt, *The Atomic*

Complex, p. 186; Peres, *Battling for Peace*, pp. 122–124; Charles de Gaulle, *Memoirs of Hope: Renewal and Endeavor* (New York: Simon & Schuster, 1971), p. 266.

20   Cohen, *Israel and the Bomb*, p. 75; Adams, *The Unnatural Alliance*, p. 148; Yossi Melman and Dan Raviv, *The Imperfect Spies: The History of Israeli Intelligence* (London: Sidgwick & Jackson, 1990), p. 103.

21   Cohen, *Israel and the Bomb*, p. 75; Adams, *The Unnatural Alliance*, p. 148.

22   Spector with Smith, *Nuclear Ambitions*, pp. 172–173; "Atoms for Israel," *Architectural Forum*, April 1961, pp. 121–122.

23   George Johnson, *Strange Beauty: Murray Gell-Mann and the Revolution in Twentieth Century Physics* (New York: Knopf, 1999), pp. 199–201, 208, 386 no. 20; Robert P. Crease and Charles C. Mann, *The Second Creation: Makers of the Revolution in Twentieth-Century Physics* (New Brunswick, N.J.: Rutgers University Press, 1996), pp. 269–272; Cohen, *Israel and the Bomb*, p. 437; Condensed Vita, Professor Yuval Ne'eman, Chairman of the Techniya Party in Israel, n.d.

24   Cohen, *Israel and the Bomb*, pp. 229, 442; William E. Burrows and Robert Windrem, *Critical Mass: The Dangerous Race for Superweapons in a Fragmenting World* (New York: Simon & Schuster, 1994), p. 301; "Soreq," www.globalsecurity.org, accessed March 9, 2004; "The Beginning: Dr. Chaim Weizmann," http://80.70.129.78, accessed March 9, 2004.

25   Quoted in Cohen, *Israel and the Bomb*, p. 232.

26   Burrows and Windrem, *Critical Mass*, p. 302; Cohen, "The Last Nuclear Moment," *New York Times*, October 6, 2003, p. A17.

27   Melman and Raviv, *The Imperfect Spies*, pp. 107–108; Adams, *The Unnatural Alliance*, pp. 158–161.

28   Hannes Steyn, Richardt van der Walt, and Jan van Loggerenberg, *Armament and Disarmament: South Africa's Nuclear Weapons Experience* (Pretoria: Network Publishers, 2003), p. 31.

29   Steyn, van der Walt, and van Loggerenberg, *Armament and Disarmament*, pp. 31–32; Waldo Stumpf, "South Africa's Nuclear Weapons Program: From Deterrence to Dismantlement," *Arms Control Today*, December 1995/January 1996, pp. 3–8 at p. 3; David Albright, "South Africa and the Affordable Bomb," *Bulletin of the Atomic Scientists*, July/August 1994, pp. 39–40.

30   Leonard Spector, *Nuclear Proliferation Today: The Spread of Nuclear Weapons 1984* (Cambridge, Mass.: Ballinger, 1984), pp. 282–283.

31   Albright, "South Africa and the Affordable Bomb," pp. 40–41.

32   Ibid., p. 40; Steyn, van der Walt, and van Loggerenberg, *Armament and Disarmament*, p. 35; Mitchell Reiss, *Bridled Ambition: Why Nations Constrain Their Nuclear Capabilities* (Washington, D.C.: Woodrow Wilson Center, 1995), pp. 7–8; Stumpf, "South Africa's Nuclear Weapons Program," p. 3; Barbara Rogers and Zdenek Cervenka, *The Nuclear Axis: The Secret Collaboration Between West Germany and South Africa* (New York: Times Books, 1978), p. 43; Roy E. Horton III, *Out of (South) Africa: Pretoria's Nuclear Weapons Experience* (USAF Academy, Colo.: USAF Institute for National Security Studies, 1999), p. 42 n. 11; Kenneth L. Adelman and

Albion W. Knight, "Can South Africa Go Nuclear?" *Orbis*, 23, 3 (Fall 1979), pp. 633–647 at p. 637.

33   Reiss, *Bridled Ambition*, p. 8; Albright, "South Africa and the Affordable Bomb," p. 41; Stumpf, "South Africa's Nuclear Weapons Program," p. 4.

34   Albright, "South Africa and the Affordable Bomb," p. 41; Darryl Howlett and John Simpson, "Nuclearisation and Denuclearisation in South Africa," *Survival*, 35, 3 (Autumn 1993), pp. 154–173 at p. 154.

35   Stumpf, "South Africa's Nuclear Weapons Program," pp. 3–4; Howlett and Simpson, "Nuclearisation and Denuclearisation in South Africa," p. 155.

36   Steyn, van der Walt, and van Loggerenberg, *Armament and Disarmament*, p. 41; Stumpf, "South Africa's Nuclear Weapons Program," p. 4.

37   David Albright and Corey Gay, "Taiwan: Nuclear Nightmare Averted," *Bulletin of the Atomic Scientists*, January/February 1998, pp. 54–60 at p. 55; Amembassy Taipei to Sec State Wash DC, October 23, 1964; Amembassy Taipei to Sec State Wash DC, Subject: Effect of CCNE on GRC and Implications for US Policy, October 29, 1964.

38   Albright and Gay, "Taiwan," p. 55.

39   Ibid., p. 56; "The Ramon Magsaysay Award for Government Service, Biography: Ta-You Wu," pp. 3–4, 9, www.rmaf.org, accessed March 13, 2004; "Ta-You Wu Lecture," www.physics.lsa.umich.edu, accessed March 13, 2004.

40   Albright and Gay, "Taiwan," p. 56; Dr. Ta-you Wu, "A Historical Document—A Footnote to the History of Our Country's 'Nuclear Energy' Policies," pp. 2–3, 5, www.isis-online.org, accessed March 13, 2004.

41   Albright and Gay, "Taiwan," p. 56; Ta-you Wu, "A Historical Document," pp. 3, 5.

42   Albright and Gay, "Taiwan," p. 56; Ta-you Wu, "A Historical Document," p. 5.

43   Albright and Gay, "Taiwan," pp. 56–57.

44   Ibid., p. 57.

45   Office of Scientific Intelligence, Central Intelligence Agency, *Nuclear Activities of Foreign Nations, Volume IV, Asia and Africa*, September 30, 1956, pp. 1–6. In January 1956 Israel was added to the Third Category Priority List, which contained the least important intelligence targets, but not apparently out of a specific concern with its nuclear activities.

46   Cohen, *Israel and the Bomb*, p. 81; Director of Central Intelligence, NIE 100-6-57, *Nuclear Weapons Production in Fourth Countries: Likelihood and Consequences*, June 18, 1957, p. 4.

47   Director of Central Intelligence, *Post-Mortem of SNIE 100-8-60: Implications of the Acquisition by Israel of a Nuclear Weapons Capability*, January 31, 1961, p. 9; Cohen, *Israel and the Bomb*, pp. 82, 84.

48   Director of Central Intelligence, *Post-Mortem of SNIE 100-8-60*, pp. 10–11.

49   Ibid., p. 11.

50   Ibid., p. 2.

51   Dino Brugioni, *Eyeball to Eyeball: The Inside Story of the Cuban Missile Crisis* (New York: Random House, 1993), p. 33.

52   Seymour Hersh, *The Samson Option: Israel's Nuclear Arsenal and American Foreign*

Policy (New York: Random House, 1991), p. 52; Peres, *Battling for Peace*, pp. 119–120.

53   Hersh, *The Samson Option*, p. 52.

54   Ibid., pp. 52, 56.

55   Ibid., pp. 52–53.

56   Hersh, *The Samson Option*, pp. 53–54; Cohen, *Israel and the Bomb*, p. 83; Interview with Dino Brugioni, February 21, 2003.

57   Director of Central Intelligence, *Post-Mortem on SNIE 100-8-60*, pp. 4–5, 9.

58   Ibid., pp. 8, 11–12.

59   Cohen, *Israel and the Bomb*, p. 85.

60   Director of Central Intelligence, *Post-Mortem on SNIE 100-8-60*, pp. 12–13.

61   Hersh, *The Sampson Option*, p. 57; Director of Central Intelligence, *Post-Mortem on SNIE 100-8-60*, p. 13; Amembassy Paris to Sec State, Washington, D.C., Telegram No. G-766, November 22, 1960, in Avner Cohen (ed.), *Israel and the Bomb*, National Security Archive Electronic Briefing Book, Dimona Revealed Section, Document 2, www.narchive.org.

62   Paris to Secretary of State, Telegram No. 2162, November 26, 1960, in Cohen (ed.), *Israel and the Bomb*, National Security Archive Electronic Briefing Book, Dimona Revealed Section, Document 3; "History 205, History of Modern Science, Lecture 8: Energy & Nuclear Power," pp. 3, 5, www.umich.edu, accessed March 18, 2004; Department of State, Memorandum of Conversation, Subject: Israeli Atomic Energy Program, December 1, 1960, in Cohen (ed.), *Israel and the Bomb*, National Security Archive Electronic Briefing Book, Dimona Revealed Section, Document 4; Director of Central Intelligence, *Post-Mortem on SNIE 100-8-60*, p. 15.

63   Department of State, Memorandum of Conversation, Subject: Israeli Atomic Energy Program.

64   Cohen, *Israel and the Bomb*, p. 87.

65   Director of Central Intelligence, *Post-Mortem on SNIE 100-8-60*, pp. 1, 8; Cohen, *Israel and the Bomb*, pp. 87–88; National Security Council, "National Intelligence Estimates," May 25, 1962. While the postmortem has been declassified, the SNIE has not.

66   Marion W. Boggs, "Memorandum of Discussion at 470th Meeting of the National Security Council, December 8, 1960," in Suzanne E. Coffman and Charles S. Sampson (eds.), *Foreign Relations of the United States, 1958–1960, Volume XIII, Arab-Israeli Dispute; United Arab Republic; North Africa* (Washington, D.C.: U.S. Government Printing Office, 1992), pp. 391–392.

67   "Telegram from the Department of State to the Embassy in Israel," and Memorandum of a Conversation, Department of State, Washington, D.C., December 20, 1960, Subject: Israeli Atomic Energy Program, December 27, 1960, both in Coffman and Sampson (eds.), *Foreign Relations of the United States, 1958–1960, Volume XIII*, pp. 393–394, 396–398; John W. Finney, "U.S. Misled at First on Israeli Reactor," *New York Times*, December 12, 1960, pp. 1, 15.

68   Cohen, *Israel and the Bomb*, p. 90; Finney, "U.S. Misled at First on Israeli Reactor";

Dana Adams Schmidt, "Israel Assures U.S. on Reactor," *New York Times*, December 22, 1960, p. 5. A summary of the discussion at the December 19 meeting with the president is contained in Memorandum of Conference with the President—December 19, 1960, January 12, 1961, in Cohen (ed.), *Israel and the Bomb, National Security Archive* Electronic Briefing Book, Dimona Revealed Section, Document 7.

69   Cohen, *Israel and the Bomb*, p. 92–94; Tel Aviv to Secretary of State, Telegram 577, December 24, 1960, in Cohen (ed.), *Israel and the Bomb*, National Security Archive Electronic Briefing Book, Dimona Revealed Section, Document 8; "Telegram from the Department of State to the Embassy in Israel," in Coffman and Sampson (eds.), *Foreign Relations of the United States, 1958–1960, Volume XIII*, pp. 399–400; Alvin Shuster, "Israel Satisfies U.S. on Use of Reactor," *New York Times*, December 23, 1960, pp. 1, 6.

70   Cohen, *Israel and the Bomb*, pp. 94–95.

71   Richard Reeves, *President Kennedy: Profile of Power* (New York: Simon & Schuster, 1993), pp. 32–33. On the U.S.-Israeli confrontation over Dimona, also see Warren Bass, *Support Any Friend: Kennedy's Middle East and the Making of the U.S.-Israel Alliance* (New York: Oxford University Press, 2003), pp. 186–238.

72   Cohen, *Israel and the Bomb*, pp. 101–102.

73   Ibid., p. 102.

74   Director of Central Intelligence, *Post-Mortem on SNIE 100-8-60*, pp. 1–2.

75   Ibid., pp. 2–3; Central Intelligence Agency, Information Report No. OO-B-3,174,835, Subject: Nuclear Engineering Training/Large Nuclear and Electric Power Plant near Beerhseba/French Nuclear Assistance to Israel/Israeli Attitudes Towards the Announcement of Its Large-Scale Nuclear Effort/Opportunity for US Participation in Nuclear Powered Water Conversion, February 9, 1961, in Cohen (ed.), *Israel and the Bomb*, National Security Archive Electronic Briefing Book, Dimona Revealed Section, Document 5.

76   "France-Israeli Nuclear Collaboration," *Central Intelligence Bulletin*, April 27, 1961, pp. 5–6, NSF Country File, Box 119A, Folder: Israel, Subjects: Ben Gurion Visit, 5/20/61-6/2/61, JFKL.

77   Cohen, *Israel and the Bomb*, pp. 102–104.

78   U. M. Staebler and J. W. Croach Jr., "Notes on Visit to Israel," May 23, 1961, p. 1; Biographical Sketch Information: Jesse William Croach Jr., n.d., and Biographical Sketch Information: Ulysses Merriam Staebler, n.d., in Cohen (ed.), *Israel and the Bomb*, National Security Archive Electronic Briefing Book, First Look Section, Documents 12 and 13.

79   Staebler and Croach, "Notes on Visit to Israel," p. 1.

80   Ibid., pp. 11–15.

81   Lucius Battle, Memorandum for Mr. McGeorge Bundy, The White House, Subject: U.S. Scientists' Visits to Israel's Dimona Reactor," May 26, 1961, in Cohen (ed.), *Israel and the Bomb*, National Security Archive Electronic Briefing Book, First Look Section, Document 14.

82   Cohen, *Israel and the Bomb*, pp. 110–111; Merriman Smith, "Kennedy on Peace

Mission: Boards Jet After Talk in New York," *Washington Post and Times Herald*, May 31, 1961, pp. A1, A6; Irving Spiegel, "Kennedy and Ben-Gurion Hold 'Fruitful' Talk Here," *New York Times*, May 31, 1961, pp. 1, 6.

83   Director of Central Intelligence, NIE 4-3-61, *Nuclear Weapons and Delivery Capabilities of Free World Countries Other Than the US and UK*, September 21, 1961, pp. 2, 7.

84   Cohen, *Israel and the Bomb*, pp. 111–112; Bass, *Support Any Friend*, p. 206; Dean Rusk, CA-4726, Circular Airgram from the Department of State to Certain Posts, Subject: Israel's Dimona Reactor, October 31, 1962; Hersh, *The Samson Option*, pp. 107, 196.

85   Cohen, *Israel and the Bomb*, pp. 112, 116.

86   Sherman Kent, Office of National Estimates, Memorandum for the Director. Subject: Consequences of Israeli Acquisition of Nuclear Capability, March 6, 1963.

87   McGeorge Bundy, NSAM 231, *Middle Eastern Nuclear Capabilities*, March 26, 1963.

88   E-mail, Tim Brown to author, March 16, 2004.

89   Hersh, *The Samson Option*, p. 164.

90   Cohen, *Israel and the Bomb*, pp. 118–119.

91   Ibid., pp. 128–131.

92   Ibid., p. 133; Bass, *Support Any Friend*, p. 218.

93   Cohen, *Israel and the Bomb*, pp. 134–135, 154–155; Bass, *Support Any Friend*, pp. 220–222; John F. Kennedy, Letter to Levi Eshkol, July 5, 1963, in Cohen (ed.), *Israel and the Bomb*, National Security Archive Electronic Briefing Book, Exchange Section, Document 1.

94   Cohen, *Israel and the Bomb*, pp. 177–179.

95   Ibid., pp. 179–180; "Summary of Findings of Dimona Inspection Team," in Harriet Dashiell Schwar (ed.), *Foreign Relations of the United States, 1964–68, Volume XXVIII, Arab-Israeli Dispute* (Washington, D.C.: U.S. Government Printing Office, 2000), pp. 30–31.

96   "Summary of Findings of Dimona Inspection Team," p. 31 n. 7.

97   E-mail, Tim Brown to author, March 16, 2004. All KH-7 imagery has been declassified, except that of Israel. As a result the identification of KH-7 missions that might have photographed Dimona is based on inference.

98   Cohen, *Israel and the Bomb*, pp. 180–183.

99   Ibid., p. 183.

100 Memorandum from the Director of the Office of Near Eastern Affairs (Davies) to the Assistant Secretary of State for Near Eastern and South Asian Affairs (Talbot), Subject: Observations of H. Earle Russell During His Recent Trip to Israel Based on Conversations with Embassy Officers, March 5, 1965, in Schwar (ed.), *Foreign Relations of the United States, 1964–68, Volume XXVIII*, pp. 382–384; Hersh, *The Samson Option*, p. 164.

101 William N. Dale, Charge d'Affairs a.i., to Department of State, Subject: Current Status of Dimona Reactor, April 9, 1965, p. 2.

102 Dale to Department of State, Subject: Current Status of Dimona Reactor, pp. 2–6.

103   Nicholas Katzenbach, Under Secretary of State, to President Lyndon Johnson, Subject: The Arab-Israeli Arms Race and Status of U.S. Arms Control Efforts, May 1, 1967, in Schwar (ed.), *Foreign Relations of the United States, 1964–68, Volume XXVIII*, pp. 814–817.

104   "Taiwan Nuclear Research Facility—overview," www.fas.org, accessed September 16, 2002; Jonathan McDowell, "Launch Listings," in Dwayne A. Day, John M. Logsdon, and Brian Latell (eds.), *Eye in the Sky: The Story of the Corona Spy Satellites* (Washington, D.C.: Smithsonian Institution Press, 1998), p. 240; Amembassy Tel Aviv to Department of State, Subject: Nationalist Chinese Atomic Experts Visit Israel, March 19, 1966, and Amembassy Tel Aviv to Department of State, Subject: More on Nationalist Chinese Atomic Experts Visit to Israel, March 24, 1966—both in William Burr (ed.), *New Archival Evidence on Taiwanese "Nuclear Intentions,"* 1966–1976, National Security Archive Electronic Briefing Book No. 19, October 13, 1999, www.nsarchive.org.

105   Amembassy Bonn to Sec State, Subject: German Nuclear Reactor for Taiwan, March 26, 1966, and Amembassy Taipei to Department of State, Subject: GRC Request to IAEA Team for Advice on Location of Reactor for Possible Use by Military Research Institute, April 8, 1966, both in Burr (ed.), *New Archival Evidence on Taiwanese "Nuclear Intentions,"* 1966–1976.

106   Amembassy Taipei to Department of State, Subject: Indications GRC Continue to Pursue Atomic Weaponry, June 20, 1966, in Burr (ed.), *New Archival Evidence on Taiwanese "Nuclear Intentions,"* 1966–1976.

107   McDowell, "Launch Listings," pp. 242, 244; Amembassy Taipei to Department of State, Subject: GRC Plans for Purchase of 50 Megawatt Water Nuclear Power Plant, February 21, 1967, and Amembassy Bonn to Sec State Washington DC, Subject: GRC Plans to Purchase 50 Megawatt Heavy Water Nuclear Power Plant, March 15, 1967, both in Burr (ed.), *New Archival Evidence on Taiwanese "Nuclear Intentions,"* 1966–1976.

108   Brown e-mail; McDowell, "Launch Listings," pp. 242, 244; Jeffrey T. Richelson, *America's Secret Eyes in Space: The U.S. Keyhole Spy Satellite Program* (New York: Harper & Row, 1990), pp. 359–360.

109   Cohen, *Israel and the Bomb*, pp. 186, 331–332.

110   Brown e-mail.

111   Hedrick Smith, "U.S. Assumes the Israelis Have A-Bomb or Its Parts," *New York Times*, July 18, 1970, pp. 1, 8.

112   Smith, "U.S. Assumes the Israelis Have A-Bomb or Its Parts." In 1978 Carl Duckett, who served as the CIA's deputy director of science and technology from 1966 until 1976, claimed that in 1968 the CIA produced a national estimate concluding that Israel did have nuclear weapons, and was told by director of central intelligence Richard Helms not to publish it, and then President Johnson informed Helms not to inform secretary of state Dean Rusk or secretary of defense Robert McNamara. A search for such an estimate during preparation of an official history of U.S. foreign relations proved unsuccessful. See Nuclear Regulatory Commission, *Inquiry into*

Testimony of the Executive Director for Operations, Volume III, Interview, February 1978, p. 178; David S. Patterson (ed.), *Foreign Relations of the United States, 1964–68, Volume XX, Arab-Israeli Dispute 1967–1968* (Washington, D.C.: U.S. Government Printing Office, 2001), pp. 257–258. It is possible that Duckett was actually referring to an OSI study. It is difficult to understand how a national estimate would be produced without individuals in the State and Defense Departments being aware of its existence.

113 DS&T/CIA, "South Africa Seeks Uranium Hexafluoride Technology," *Weekly Surveyor,* May 4, 1970, pp. 1–2; DS&T/CIA, "South Africans Release Further Information on Their Isotope Separation Process," *Weekly Surveyor,* October 12, 1970, p. 1.

114 OSI/CIA, *Atomic Energy Activities in the Republic of South Africa,* March 1971, p. 1.

115 Ibid., pp. 2–8.

116 DS&T/CIA, "South Africans to Fund Preparatory Work for Full Scale Uranium Enrichment Plant," *Weekly Surveyor,* June 11, 1973, pp. 1–2; DS&T/CIA, "South African Uranium Isotope Enrichment Process Probably Aerodynamic," *Weekly Surveyor,* February 11, 1974, p. 1; DS&T/CIA, "South Africa to Stockpile Large Quantities of Uranium," *Weekly Surveyor,* February 11, 1974, pp. 2–3; Amconsul Johannesburg to Department of State, Subject: Uranium Enrichment in South Africa, July 22, 1974.

117 OSI-OWI/CIA, "South Africa Not Currently in Position to Produce Nuclear Weapons," *Weekly Surveyor,* July 22, 1974, p. 1.

118 EA/ROC, Leo J. Moser to EA—Mr. Green, Department of State, Subject: Nuclear Materials Reprocessing Plan for ROC—Information Memorandum, December 14, 1972, in Burr (ed.), *New Archival Evidence on Taiwanese "Nuclear Intentions," 1966–1976.*

119 State Department to Amembassies Bonn, Brussels, Taipei, Subject: Proposed Reprocessing Plant for Republic of China, January 4, 1973, in Burr (ed.), *New Archival Evidence on Taiwanese "Nuclear Intentions," 1966–1976.*

120 State Department to Embassies in Bonn, Brussels, and Taipei, Subject: Proposed Reprocessing Plant for Republic of China, January 20, 1973, in Burr (ed.), *New Archival Evidence on Taiwanese "Nuclear Intentions," 1966–1976.*

121 Amembassy Taipei to Sec State Wash DC, Subject: Proposed Reprocessing Plant, January 31, 1973, and Amembassy Taipei to Sec State Wash DC, Subject: ROC Decides Against Purchase of Nuclear Reprocessing Plant, February 8, 1973, both in Burr (ed.), *New Archival Evidence on Taiwanese "Nuclear Intentions," 1966–1976.*

122 Department of State, Memorandum of Conversation, Subject: Nuclear Programs in Republic of China, February 9, 1973, in Burr (ed.), *New Archival Evidence on Taiwanese "Nuclear Intentions," 1966–1976.* The memorandum also notes that the British representatives indicated the United States might already have seen the British reports.

123 Amembassy Taipei to Sec State Wash DC, Subject: Chung Shan Nuclear Research

Institute, February 24, 1973, in Burr (ed.), *New Archival Evidence on Taiwanese "Nuclear Intentions," 1966–1976.*

124   Ibid.

125   Department of State, Memorandum of Conversation, Subject: ROC Nuclear Intentions, April 5, 1973, w/att: INR, Nuclear Weapon Intentions of the Republic of China, March 30, 1973, in Burr (ed.), *New Archival Evidence on Taiwanese "Nuclear Intentions," 1966–1976.*

126   INR, Nuclear Weapon Intentions of the Republic of China.

127   Memorandum of Conversation, Subject: Reported ROC Nuclear Weapons Development Program, April 7, 1973, in Burr (ed.), *New Archival Evidence on Taiwanese "Nuclear Intentions," 1966–1976.*

128   Ibid.; Fm Sec State Wash DC to Amembassy Taipei, Subject: ROC Nuclear Intentions, April 17, 1973, in Burr (ed.), *New Archival Evidence on Taiwanese "Nuclear Intentions," 1966–1976.*

129   Sec State Wash DC to Amembassy Taipei, Subj: Atomic Energy Study Team Visit to Taiwan, October 1, 1973; Letter, William H. Gleysteen Jr., Deputy Chief of Mission to Thomas Bleha, Deputy Director, Republic of China Affairs, Department of State, November 23, 1973; Amembassy Taipei to Sec State Wash DC, Subject: FORMIN Reaffirms ROC Decision to Refrain from Acquiring Nuclear Reprocessing Plant, November 23, 1973.

130   James G. Poor, Atomic Energy Commission, to Chairman Ray, Commissioner Kriegsman, Commissioner Anders, "Prospect for Further Proliferation of Nuclear Weapons," October 2, 1974; Director of Central Intelligence, Memorandum, "Prospect for Further Proliferation of Nuclear Weapons," September 4, 1974, p. 1.

131   Director of Central Intelligence, Memorandum, "Prospect for Further Proliferation of Nuclear Weapons," pp. 2–3.

132   Ibid, p. 3.

133   Ibid.

134   "Taipei Denies Work on Atomic Weapons," *New York Times*, July 8, 1975, p. 8.

135   From CS To: C, SADF, "The Jericho Weapon System," March 31, 1975, p. 1.

136   Ibid, pp. 1–2.

137   William Beecher, "Israel Seen Holding 10 Nuclear Weapons," *Washington Post*, July 31, 1975, p. A34.

138   DS&T/CIA, "Further Evidence That the South African Uranium Enrichment Process Is Probably Similar to the Becker Nozzle Principle," *Weekly Surveyor*, March 24, 1975, p. 9.

139   DS&T/CIA, "South African Uranium Enrichment Plant in Operation," *Weekly Surveyor*, April 21, 1975, pp. 1–2.

140   DS&T/CIA, "Some Aspects of South African Uranium Enrichment Process Revealed," *Weekly Surveyor*, May 5, 1975, pp. 1–2.

141   Hersh, *The Samson Option*, p. 239; Arthur Kranish, "CIA: Israel Has 10-20 A-Weapons," *Washington Post*, March 15, 1976, p. A2; David Binder, "C.I.A. Says Israel

Has 10-20 A-Bombs," *New York Times*, March 16, 1976, pp. 1, 5. The author of the *Post* article did not name Duckett as the source of the revelation but there were plenty of witnesses. Not long afterward, Duckett, who had an alcohol problem, which may have contributed to his indiscretion, retired from the agency. See Jeffrey T. Richelson, *The Wizards of Langley: Inside the CIA's Directorate of Science and Technology* (Boulder, Colo.: Westview, 2001), pp. 192–193.

142 DS&T/CIA, "South African Discusses Delay in Uranium Enrichment Operations," *Weekly Surveyor*, June 28, 1976, p. 1; DS&T/CIA, "South Africa Reportedly Is Developing a Nuclear Fuel Reprocessing Capability," *Weekly Surveyor*, July 19, 1976, pp. 3–4.

143 DS&T/CIA, "South Africa Again Rumored to Be Working on Nuclear Weapons," *Weekly Surveyor*, September 13, 1976, pp. 1–2.

144 DS&T/CIA, "South Africa Probably Will Greatly Improve Its Uranium Enrichment Technology by Using Axial Compressors," *Weekly Surveyor*, September 27, 1976, pp. 1–2; DS&T/CIA, "South African Pilot Plant May Enrich Uranium to More Than 20% U-235," *Weekly Surveyor*, November 29, 1976, pp. 1–2.

145 National Security Decision Memorandum 248, Subject: Changes in U.S. Force Levels on Taiwan, March 14, 1974; Jack Anderson, "Secret Report Sees Taiwan near A-Bomb," *Washington Post*, January 25, 1982, p. C14.

146 Albright and Gay, "Taiwan," p. 58; Eduard Schumacher, "Taiwan Seen Reprocessing Nuclear Fuel," *Washington Post*, August 29, 1976, pp. A1, A8.

147 Albright and Gay, "Taiwan," p. 58.

148 Ibid.

149 Ibid.

150 Ibid.

151 Ibid.; David Binder, "U.S. Finds Taiwan Develops A-Fuel," *New York Times*, August 30, 1976, pp. 1, 4; Schumacher, "Taiwan Seen Reprocessing Nuclear Fuel." According to Albright and Gay, U.S. officials later denied having evidence that reprocessing had occurred.

152 Bob Woodward, *Veil: The Secret Wars of the CIA, 1981–1987* (New York: Simon & Schuster, 1987), p. 170.

153 Director of Central Intelligence, Interagency Intelligence Memorandum, *Prospects for Arms Production and Development in Republic of China*, May 1976, pp. 8–9.

154 Binder, "U.S. Finds Taiwan Develops A-Fuel"; Fox Butterfield, "Taiwan Denying Atomic Operation," *New York Times*, September 5, 1976, p. 5; Schumacher, "Taiwan Seen Reprocessing Nuclear Fuel."

155 Amembassy Taipei to Sec State Wash DC, Subject: ROC's Nuclear Intentions: Conversation with Premier Chiang Ching-kuo, September 15, 1976; Albright and Gay, "Taiwan," p. 58; Leonard Spector, *The Undeclared Bomb* (Cambridge, Mass.: Ballinger, 1988), p. 76; Leonard Unger, Department of State, Memorandum of Conversation, Subject: ROC Nuclear Intentions, November 18, 1976, in Burr (ed.), *New Archival Evidence on Taiwanese "Nuclear Intentions," 1966–1976*.

156 Unger, Department of State, Memorandum of Conversation, Subject: ROC Nuclear Intentions.

157   Albright and Gay, "Taiwan," p. 58.

158   Ibid., pp. 58–59.

159   Ibid., p. 59.

160   Ibid.

161   Stumpf, "South Africa's Nuclear Weapons Program," p. 5; Steyn, van der Walt, and Loggerenberg, *Armament and Disarmament*, p. 40.

162   Steyn, van der Walt, and Loggerenberg, *Armament and Disarmament*, p. 41; Howlett and Simpson, "Nuclearisaton and Denuclearisation in South Africa," p. 157.

163   Steyn, van der Walt, and Loggerenberg, *Armament and Disarmament*, p. 41.

164   Adams, *The Unnatural Alliance*, p. 183.

165   Robin Wright, "Vorster Urges Americans to Oppose Carter's Pressure on South Africa," *Washington Post*, August 7, 1977, p. A18.

166   Sec State Wash DC to Amembassy Tel Aviv, Subject: Israeli-South African Nuclear Cooperation Nuclear Cooperation, August 17, 1977; Graham Hovey, "South Africa Tells U.S. It Doesn't Plan Any Nuclear Testing," *New York Times*, August 24, 1977, pp. A1, A9; Murrey Marder and Don Oberdorfer, "How West, Soviet Acted to Defuse S. African A-Test," *Washington Post*, August 28, 1977, pp. A1, A16–A17.

167   Adams, *The Unnatural Alliance*, p. 182.

168   David Binder, "U.S. Asserts It Headed Off A-Test by Pretoria After Warning," *New York Times*, August 28, 1977, pp. 1, 6; Marder and Oberdorfer, "How West, Soviet Acted to Defuse S. African A-Test."

169   Steyn, van der Walt, and Loggerenberg, *Armament and Disarmament*, p. 41.

170   Richelson, *America's Secret Eyes in Space*, pp. 360–362.

171   Marder and Oberdorfer, "How West, Soviet Acted to Defuse S. African A-Test"; Hersh, *The Samson Option*, p. 267; Binder, "U.S. Asserts It Headed Off A-Test."

172   Marder and Oberdorfer, "How West, Soviet Acted to Defuse S. African A-Test."

173   William Parmenter, National Intelligence Officer for Africa, Memorandum for: The National Foreign Intelligence Board, Subject: Interagency Assessment: South Africa: Policy Considerations Regarding a Nuclear Test, August 18, 1977; William Parmenter, NIO for Africa, Memorandum for: Representatives of the National Foreign Intelligence Board, Subject: Oral Contributions Meeting on Political Aspects of South Africa's Consideration of a Nuclear Device Test, August 12, 1977, CREST, NARA; [deleted] Chief, Clearance Division, Memorandum for: Chief Receptionist, Subject: South Africa, August 15, 1977, CREST, NARA.

174   Parmenter, Memorandum for: The National Foreign Intelligence Board, Subject: Interagency Assessment: South Africa: Policy Considerations Regarding a Nuclear Test, w/att: Director of Central Intelligence, *Interagency Assessment: South Africa: Policy Considerations Regarding a Nuclear Test*, August 18, 1977, passim. The quote is from p. iii.

175   Director of Central Intelligence, *Interagency Assessment: South Africa: Policy Considerations Regarding a Nuclear Test*, pp. i, 2.

176   Ibid., p. i.

177   Steyn, van der Walt, and Loggerenberg, *Armament and Disarmament*, pp. 41–42;

Marder and Oberdorfer, "How West, Soviet Acted to Defuse S. African A-Test"; Fm. Amembassy Pretoria to Sec State Wash DC, Subject: Soviet Demarche on Nuclear Weapons Development by SAG, August 10, 1977, in Kenneth Mokoena (ed.), *South Africa and the United States: The Declassified History* (New York: New Press, 1993), p. 124.

178   Spector, *Nuclear Proliferation Today*, p. 292; Marder and Oberdorfer, "How West, Soviet Acted to Defuse S. African A-Test"; "Around the World," *Washington Post*, June 1, 1976, p. A10.

179   Hovey, "South Africa Tells U.S. It Doesn't Plan Any Nuclear Testing"; Murrey Marder, "Carter Says South Africa Has Pledged It Will Not Develop Nuclear Explosives," *Washington Post*, August 24, 1977, pp. A1, A3.

180   Director of Central Intelligence, *Interagency Assessment: South Africa: Policy Considerations Regarding a Nuclear Test*, p. ii.

CHAPTER 7: THE DOUBLE FLASH

1   "U.S. Disagrees with Vorster on A-Weapons," *Washington Post*, October 25, 1977, p. A16; Caryle Murphy, "Two Flashes near South Africa: Just What Happened That Night? (Johannesburg)," *Washington Post*, October 27, 1979, pp. A1, A20.

2   William E. Burrows and Robert Windrem, *Critical Mass: The Dangerous Race for Superweapons in a Fragmenting World* (New York: Simon & Schuster, 1994), pp. 451–452; Supreme Court of South Africa (Provincial Division Cape of Good Hope), *In the Matter of The State versus Johann Philip Derk Blaauw—Judgment*, September 9, 1988, pp. 21–24.

3   Mitchell Reiss, *Bridled Ambition: Why Countries Constrain Their Nuclear Capabilities* (Washington, D.C.: Woodrow Wilson Center, 1995), p. 9; Waldo Stumpf, "South Africa's Nuclear Weapons Program: From Deterrence to Dismantlement," *Arms Control Today*, January 1995/December 1996, pp. 3–8 at p. 5. The southern Africa portion of a Pentagon wargame, Alpha-80, developed in 1979, involved a scenario in which South Africa was willing to use nuclear weapons, if necessary, to defend its interests.

4   Hannes Steyn, Richardt van der Walt, and Jan van Loggerenberg, *Armament and Disarmament: South Africa's Nuclear Weapons Experience* (Pretoria: Network Publishers, 2003), p. 43; Reiss, *Bridled Ambition*, p. 9.

5   Stumpf, "South Africa's Nuclear Weapons Program," pp. 4–5.

6   Murphy, "Two Flashes near South Africa."

7   Central Intelligence Agency, Memorandum for: [Deleted], Subject: OER Contribution to the Draft of IIM: *South Africa's Nuclear Options and Decision-Making Structures*, February 6, 1978, p. 3; "South Africa: Uranium Enrichment Capability," *Scientific Intelligence Weekly Review*, December 18, 1978; "South Africa: Evidence of Compressor Failures at the Valindaba Uranium Enrichment Plant," *Scientific Intelligence Weekly Review*, January 8, 1979; "South Africa: Military Personnel at the Pelindaba Nuclear Research Center," *Scientific Intelligence Weekly Review*, April 30, 1979, p. 5.

8   Desmond Ball, "The U.S. Vela Nuclear Detection Satellite System and the Australian Connection," *Pacific Defence Reporter*, March 1982, pp. 15–19 at pp. 15–16; John R. London III, "Vela—A Space System Success Story," paper presented at 42nd Congress of the International Astronautical Federation, Montreal, Canada, October 5–11, 1991, p. 10; Thomas O'Toole, "Only 3 Vela Satellites Now Scout for Nuclear Blasts in Atmosphere," *Washington Post*, November 3, 1979, p. A9; B. N. Turman, "Detection of Lightning Superbolts," *Journal of Geophysical Research*, 82, 18 (June 20, 1977), pp. 2566–2568; Dennis Overbye, *Lonely Hearts of the Cosmos: The Story of the Scientific Quest for the Secret of the Universe* (New York: Harper Collins, 1991), pp. 103–104, 428; Kip Thorne, *Black Holes and Time Warps: Einstein's Outrageous Legacy* (New York: W. W. Norton, 1994), pp. 314–321. In contrast to the numbers assigned to satellites operated by the NRO, where the four-digit number indicates the program and the mission number, the "6911" is Vela's interrange operations number (IRON). Thus, whereas "5505" referred to the fifth mission of the KH-11 imaging satellite, the "69" represents the year of the Vela launch, with the last two digits distinguishing that satellite from others launched from the two military test ranges (at Cape Canaveral, Florida, and Vandenberg Air Force Base, California). The Vela launched in tandem with 6911 was designated 6909. The final two, launched in 1970, were designated Vela 7033 and 7044.

9   Interview with Spurgeon Keeny, Washington, D.C., February 6, 2003.

10   Turman, "Detection of Lightning Superbolts"; Don Oberdorfer and Thomas O'Toole, "Two Flashes near South Africa: Just What Happened That Night? (Washington)," *Washington Post*, October 27, 1980, p. A11; Gary H. Mauth, *Alert 747* (Albuquerque, N.M.: Sandia Laboratories, May 1, 1980), p. 2.

11   Eliot Marshall, "Flash Not Missed by Vela Still Veiled in Mist," *Science*, November 30, 1979, pp. 1051–1052; Mauth, *Alert 747*, p. 2.

12   Stephen Green, *Living by the Sword: America and Israel in the Middle East 1968–87* (Brattleboro, Vt.: Amana Books, 1988), p. 112.

13   Seymour Hersh, *The Samson Option: Israel's Nuclear Arsenal and American Foreign Policy* (New York: Random House, 1991), pp. 272–273; Keeny interview.

14   Jeffrey T. Richelson, *America's Space Sentinels: DSP Satellites and National Security* (Lawrence: University Press of Kansas, 1999), pp. 70, 79–80.

15   Ibid., pp. 73–74.

16   *History of the Directorate of Space, DCS/Research and Development, Headquarters, United States Air Force, 1 July 1974–31 December 1974*, p. 37.

17   Sylvia E. D. Ferry, *The Defense Meteorological Satellite System Sensors: An Historical Overview* (Los Angeles Air Force Base, Calif.: DMSS Program Office, 1989), pp. 1, 6–7, 9, 10, 13.

18   Science Applications International Corporation, *Fifty Year Commemorative History of Long Range Detection: The Creation, Development, and Operation of the United States Atomic Energy Detection System* (Satellite Beach, Fla.: SAIC, 1997), pp. 97–100.

19   Gerald E. Wright, *History of the Air Force Technical Applications Center, Patrick Air*

Force Base, Florida, 1 January 1979–31 December 1980, Volume I, Narrative (Patrick Air Force Base, Fla.: Air Force Technical Applications Center, 1982), pp. 25–26; Holsey G. Handyside, Deputy Assistant Secretary International Nuclear and Technical Programs, Department of Energy, Memorandum for Leslie H. Brown, Department of State, Subject: Responses to Congressional Questions on Nuclear Explosives, March 7, 1980, p. 16; Office of Science and Technology Policy, *Ad Hoc Panel Report on the September 22 Event*, May 23, 1980, p. 6; Martin Bailey, "South Africa's Island Bombshell," *London Sunday Observer*, December 28, 1986; Private information.

20 Thomas O'Toole, "Fallout Studied to Confirm Blast near S. Africa," *Washington Post*, November 14, 1979, pp. A1, A18.

21 Ibid.

22 "Scientists Back at Square One on Evidence of A-Bomb Test," *Washington Post*, November 27, 1979, p. A19; Marshall, "Flash Not Missed by Vela Still Veiled in Mist"; Eliot Marshall, "Scientists Fail to Solve Vela Mystery," *Science*, February 1, 1980, pp. 504–505; "Data Suggesting Bomb Test in Southern Region Revised," *New York Times*, November 27, 1979, p. A5.

23 "The Arecibo Observatory," www.naic.edu/about/ao/description.htm, accessed May 3, 2004; N. C. Gerson, "SIGINT in Space," *Studies in Intelligence*, 28, 2 (Summer 1984), pp. 41–48; Frank Drake and Dava Sobel, *Is Anyone Out There?: The Scientific Search for Extraterrestrial Intelligence* (New York: Delta, 1994), p. 73.

24 Marshall, "Scientists Fail to Solve Vela Mystery."

25 Christine Dodson, Memorandum, Subject: South Atlantic Nuclear Event, October 22, 1979; Untitled discussion paper, attachment to Dodson, Memorandum, Subject: South Atlantic Nuclear Event.

26 Untitled attachment to Dodson, Memorandum, Subject: South Atlantic Nuclear Event, p. 1.

27 Ibid., pp. 1–2; James Adams, *The Unnatural Alliance* (New York: Quartet, 1984), p. 188.

28 Untitled attachment to Dodson, Memorandum, Subject: South Atlantic Nuclear Event, p. 2.

29 Ibid., p. 4.

30 Ibid., pp. 4–5.

31 Murphy, "Two Flashes near South Africa"; Aleksandr Fursenko and Timoth Naftali, *"One Hell of a Gamble": Khrushchev, Castro, and Kennedy, 1958–1964* (New York: W. W. Norton, 1997), pp. 264–265ff; Bernard Gwertzman, "U.S. Monitors Signs of Atom Explosion near South Africa," *New York Times*, October 26, 1979, pp. A1, A27; Green, *Living by the Sword*, pp. 116–117; Sec State Wash DC to All Diplomatic Posts Worldwide, Subject: Suspected Nuclear Explosion—Secretary Vance Press Conference of October 26 in Gainesville, Florida, November 1, 1979, in National Security Archive, *South Africa: The Making of U.S. Policy, 1962–1989* (Alexandria, Va.: Chadwyck-Healey, 1991), Document No. 00979.

32 "A Top South African Denies Knowledge of Nuclear Explosion," *New York Times*,

October 26, 1979, p. A22; Murphy, "Two Flashes near South Africa"; Embassy Praetoria to Sec State Wash DC, Subject: South Africa: Suspected Nuclear Event, October 26, 1979, in National Security Archive, *South Africa*, Document No. 00969.

33   John F. Burns, "Pretoria Suggests Cause of 'Explosion'," *New York Times*, October 28,
1979, p. 14; "Soviet-Ship Theory Rejected," *New York Times*, October 28, 1979, p.
14; Amembassy, Praetoria to Sec State Wash DC, Subject: Suspected Nuclear Event:
South African Press Speculation," October 28, 1979, in National Security Archive,
South Africa, Document No. 00971; Thomas B. Cochran, William M. Arkin, Robert
S. Norris, and Jeffrey I. Sands, *Nuclear Weapons Databook, Volume V: Soviet Nuclear
Weapons* (New York: Harper & Row, 1989), pp. 171–172, 285.

34   Untitled attachment to Dodson, Memorandum, Subject: South Atlantic Nuclear
Event, p. 4; David Albright and Corey Gay, "A Flash from the Past," *Bulletin of the
Atomic Scientists*, November/December 1997, pp. 15–17.

35   Director of Central Intelligence, Interagency Intelligence Memorandum, *The 22
September 1979 Event*, December 1979, p. 1.

36   Ibid., pp. 1, 5.

37   Ibid., p. 5.

38   Ibid.

39   Ibid., pp. 5–6.

40   Ibid., pp. 6–7.

41   Ibid., p. 8.

42   Ibid., pp. 7–8.

43   Ibid., p. 11.

44   Ibid., p. 9.

45   Ibid.

46   Ibid., p. 10.

47   Arnold Kramish, "Nuclear Flashes in the Night," *Washington Quarterly*, 3, 3 (Summer 1980), pp. 3–11.

48   Ibid., pp. 4–7.

49   S. T. Cohen, "La Bombe," *New Republic*, January 17, 1981, pp. 13–14.

50   Ibid., pp. 13–14.

51   Ibid., p. 14.

52   "Richard L. Garwin," in Robert A. McDonald (ed.), *Beyond Expectations—Building
an American National Reconnaissance Capability: Recollections of the Pioneers and
Founders of National Reconnaissance* (Bethesda, Md.: American Society for Photogrammetry and Remote Sensing, 2003), pp. 17–24 at p. 22; *The R.V. Jones Intelligence Award Ceremony honoring Dr. Richard L. Garwin, March 13, 1996*
(Washington, D.C.: Central Intelligence Agency, 1996), unpaginated; Interview
with Richard Garwin, July 24, 2004.

53   "Richard L. Garwin," p. 22; Garwin interview.

54   Marshall, "Scientists Fail to Solve the Vela Mystery"; Sec State Wash DC, Subject:
Press Panel Review of South Atlantic Event, February 7, 1980, in Kenneth Mokoena
(ed.), *South Africa and the United States: The Declassified History* (New York: New

Press, 1993), pp. 134–139 at p. 135; Green, *Living by the Sword*, p. 114; Interview with Jack Ruina, July 19, 2004.

55   Office of Science and Technology Policy, *Ad Hoc Panel Report on the September 22 Event*, May 23, 1980, p. 1; Sec State Wash DC, Subject: Press Panel Review of South Atlantic Event, in Mokoena (ed.), *South Africa and the United States*, pp. 135–136; Green, *Living by the Sword*, p. 115.

56   Guy E. Barasch, *Light Flash Produced by an Atmospheric Nuclear Explosion* (Los Alamos, N.M.: Los Alamos Scientific Laboratory, 1979), pp. 1–3; Office of Science and Technology Policy, *Ad Hoc Panel on the September 22 Event*, p. 3; Turman, "Detection of Lightning Superbolts"; Walter Sullivan, "South Africa 'Blast' May Have Been Bolt," *New York Times*, November 1, 1979, p. D22.

57   D. S. Sappenfield, D. H. Sowle, and T. H. McCartor, *Possible Origins of Event 747 Optical Data* (Santa Barbara, Calif.: Mission Research Corporation, 1979), pp. 3–4.

58   Ibid., p. 5.

59   Ibid., pp. 5–6.

60   George N. Oetzel and Steven C. Johnson, *Vela Meteoroid Evaluation* (Menlo Park, Calif.: SRI International, 1980), pp. 1, 42–44. On the Pioneer space probe, see William Burrows, *Exploring Space: Voyages in the Solar System and Beyond* (New York: Random House, 1990), pp. 255–283.

61   Henry G. Horak, *Vela Event Alert 747* (Los Alamos, N.M.: Los Alamos Scientific Laboratory, 1980), pp. 2–3; N. Wyman Storer, *A Brief History of Astronomy at KU to 1968*, http://kuphsx2.phsx.ukans.edu/~dept/Astronomy/storer.html, accessed April 21, 2004.

62   Horak, *Vela Event Alert 747*, pp. 2, 10, 17.

63   Mauth, *Alert 747*, pp. 2, 54.

64   Ibid., pp. 18, 67.

65   Luis W. Alvarez, *Alvarez: Adventures of a Physicist* (New York: Basic Books, 1987), pp. 249–250; Office of Science and Technology Policy, *Ad Hoc Panel Report on the September 22 Event*, p. 1; Ruina interview.

66   Office of Science and Technology Policy, *Ad Hoc Panel Report on the September 22 Event*, p. 1.

67   Ibid., pp. 9, 15–16.

68   Ibid., pp. 16–17.

69   Ibid., p. 17; David Albright and Corey Gay, "A Flash from the Past," *Bulletin of the Atomic Scientists*, November/December 1997, pp. 15–17.

70   Office of Science and Technology Policy, *Ad Hoc Panel Report on the September 22 Event*, p. 17; Marshall, "Scientists Fail to Solve Vela Mystery"; Albright and Gay, "A Flash from the Past."

71   Marshall, "Scientists Fail to Solve Vela Mystery."

72   Office of Science and Technology Policy, *Ad Hoc Panel Report on the September 22 Event*, p. 9.

73   Ibid.

74   Ibid.

75   Ibid., pp. 9–10, 14; Adams, *The Unnatural Alliance*, pp. 190–191.

76   Office of Science and Technology Policy, *Ad Hoc Panel Report on the September 22 Event*, p. 10.

77   Ibid.

78   Ibid., p. 14.

79   Ibid., p. 15.

80   Alvarez, *Alvarez*, p. 249.

81   Office of Science and Technology Policy, *Ad Hoc Panel Report on the September 22 Event*, p. 2; "Debate Continues on the Bomb That Wasn't," *Science*, August 1, 1980, pp. 572–573.

82   Thomas O'Toole and Milton Benjamin, "Officials Hotly Debate Whether African Event Was Atom Blast," *Washington Post*, January 17, 1980, p. A11; Eliot Marshall, "Navy Lab Concludes Vela Saw a Bomb," *Science*, August 29, 1980, pp. 996–997.

83   Green, *Living by the Sword*, p. 125; Dr. John E. Mansfield and Lt. Col. Houston T. Hawkins, *The South Atlantic Mystery Flash: Nuclear or Not?* (Washington, D.C.: Defense Intelligence Agency, June 26, 1980), p. 19; Garwin interview.

84   Mansfield and Hawkins, *The South Atlantic Mystery Flash*, p. 10.

85   Ibid., pp. 23–27.

86   Richard Burt, "Panel Doubts Flash Sighted Off Africa Was Atomic," *New York Times*, July 15, 1980, p. A9; "DIA Concludes Mystery Flash Probable A-Test," *Washington Post*, July 15, 1980, p. A7; Green, *Living by the Sword*, p. 125; Garwin interview.

87   "Debate Continues on the Bomb That Wasn't."

88   Alan Berman, Director of Research, NRL, To: John Marcum, Senior Adviser for Technology and Arms Control, Executive Office of the President, Subj: Analysis of Marion Island Ionosonde Records, July 24, 1984; John M. Marcum, Office of Science and Technology Policy to Dr. Alan Berman, Director of Research, Naval Research Laboratory, January 31, 1980, in National Security Archive, *South Africa*, Document No. 00999; Interview with Alan Berman, Alexandria, Va., March 27, 2003.

89   Marcum to Alan Berman, January 31, 1980, in National Security Archive, *South Africa*, Document No. 00999; Frank J. Kelly, Memorandum for File, Subject: Project SEARCH Phone conservation with R.A. Helliwell of Stanford University, 1700–1720 EST 2/15/80, n.d., in National Security Archive, *South Africa*, Document No. 01019.

90   Alan Berman, Subject: Contact with Foreign National with Respect to OSTP Study, February 14, 1980, National Security Archive, *South Africa*, Document No. 01018; D. H. Sinnott, *The Development of Over-the-Horizon Radar in Australia* (Melbourne: Defence Science and Technology Organization, 1988), ch. 9–10.

91   Kelly, Memorandum for File, Subject; Project SEARCH Phone conversation with R. A. Helliwell of Stanford University; F. J. Kelly, Memo for File, Subject: Project SEARCH: Conversation with Dr. Nelson Spenser, Goddard Space Flight Center, (334-5001) on 25 February 1980; F. J. Kelly, Memo for File, Project SEARCH: Conversation with [deleted], February 26, 1980, n.d.

92 Alan Berman, Subject: Study of Events of 22 September 1979 for Office of Science and Technology, February 1, 1980, in National Security Archive, *South Africa*, Document 01002; John Goodman, Memo for File, Subject: Data from LANDSAT, TIROS, NIMBUS, 27 February 1980, n.d.; Alan Berman, Subject: TELCON with [deleted], 27 February 1980.

93 J. Goodman to A. Berman, Subject: Project Report on Project SEARCH, 27 February 1980, n.d.

94 John Goodman, Memo for File, Subject: FGGE Data, March 3, 1980; J. Goodman, Memo for File, Subject: Data Still Not Received and Outline of Processing Tasks, March 5, 1980.

95 J. Goodman, Memo for File, Subject: DMSP Data from the SSIP Sensor, March 5, 1980; J. Goodman, Memo for File, Subject: Data Still Not Received and Outline of Processing Tasks; National Security Archive, *U.S. Military Uses of Space, 1945–1991—Guide and Index* (Alexandria, Va.: Chadwyck-Healey, 1991), p. 170.

96 NRL, Project Status Report, March 21, 1980; Donald W. Strasburg, Environmental Sciences Division, NRL, Subject: Radiation and Biota of the Prince Edward Islands, April 21, 1980, in National Security Archive, *South Africa*, Document No. 01051.

97 Lothar H. Ruhnke, NRL, Subject: Preliminary Results and Recommendations on Project Search, June 9, 1980.

98 Ibid.

99 Ibid; Berman interview.

100 Marshall, "Navy Lab Concludes Vela Saw a Bomb"; Adams, *The Unnatural Alliance*, pp. 193–194.

101 Berman interview; Marshall, "Navy Lab Concludes Vela Saw a Bomb."

102 Berman interview. Apparently, some lab scientists believed the event originated from Antarctica. See Marshall, "Navy Lab Concludes Vela Saw a Bomb."

103 Berman interview.

104 Ibid.

105 Berman to Marcum, Subj: Analysis of Marion Island Ionosonde Records.

106 Letter, Alan Berman, Director of Research, NRL, to Mr. John Marcum, Office of Science and Technology Policy, Re: Evidence of the Possible Detection of Fission Products Related to VELA Event of 22 September 1979, November 3, 1980, in National Security Archive, *South Africa*, Document No. 01104.

107 Marshall, "Navy Lab Concludes Vela Saw a Bomb," p. 997; Alan Berman, Director of Research, NRL, Report of Conversation Between Alan Berman and John Fialka of the Washington Star, August 7, 1980.

108 Marshall, "Navy Lab Concludes Vela Saw a Bomb."

109 D. S. Sappenfield, D. H. Sowle, and T. H. McCartor, *Possible Origins of Event 747 Optical Data* (Santa Barbara, Calif.: Mission Research Corporation, 1980), pp. 2–3, 67.

110 E. W. Jones Jr., D. N. Maker, and W. C. Feldman, *Evaluation of Some Geophysical Events on 22 September 1979* (Los Alamos, N.M.: Los Alamos Scientific Laboratory, 1981), p. 1.

111   Ibid., pp. 16–17.

112   C. J. Rice, *Search for Correlative Data* (El Segundo, Calif.: Aerospace Corporation, 1982), pp. 5, 20.

113   E. M. Jones, R. W. Whitaker, H. G. Hersh, and J. W. Kodis, *Low-Yield Nuclear Explosion Calculations: The 9/22/79 VELA Signal* (Los Alamos, N.M.: Los Alamos National Laboratory, 1982), pp. 3, 6.

114   Adams, *The Unnatural Alliance*, p. 195; "Israel Reported Behind A-Blast off S. Africa," *Washington Post*, February 21, 1980, p. A6; "Israel Denies a Report It Tested Atom Bomb in the South Atlantic," *New York Times*, February 23, 1980, p. 5; Eliot Marshall, "White House Brushes Off Report of Israeli A-Blast," *Science*, March 14, 1980, p. 1185.

115   Benjamin Beit-Hallami, *The Israeli Connection: Who Israel Arms and Why* (New York: Pantheon, 1987), p. 134.

116   Hersh, *The Samson Option*, pp. 271–272; Albright and Gay, "A Flash from the Past"; Interview with Leonard Weiss, Silver Springs, Md., March 19, 2003.

117   Kathy DeLucas, "Blast from the Past: Lab Scientists Received Vindication," *LASL Daily News Bulletin*, July 11, 1997; William B. Scott, "Admission of 1979 Nuclear Test Finally Validates Vela Data," *Aviation Week & Space Technology*, July 21, 1997, p. 33; Albright and Gay, "A Flash from the Past."

118   William B. Scott, "Admission of 1979 Nuclear Test Finally Validates Vela Data"; Albright and Gay, "A Flash from the Past."

119   Interview with Stansfield Turner, April 17, 2003; Interview with Leonard Spector, Washington, D.C., March 5, 2003.

120   Weiss interview.

121   Ibid.

122   Alvarez, *Alvarez*, p. 249; Garwin interview; Ruina interview.

123   Reiss, *Bridled Ambition*, p. 11.

124   Keeny interview; Ruina interview.

CHAPTER 8: ROGUES

1   Thomas W. Lippman, "Qaddafi Seen as Libya's Sole Power Source," *Washington Post*, June 9, 1976, p. A16.

2   Joseph S. Bermudez Jr., *North Korean Special Forces* (Annapolis, Md.: Naval Institute Press, 1998), pp. 18–19, 64–89; William C. Triplett II, *Rogue State: How Nuclear North Korea Threatens America* (Washington, D.C.: Regnery, 2004), pp. 18, 22, 64, 84, 90; James Bamford, *The Puzzle Palace: A Report on NSA, America's Most Secret Agency* (Boston: Houghton Mifflin, 1982), pp. 184–185; Mitchell B. Lerner, *The Pueblo Incident: A Spy Ship and the Failure of American Foreign Policy* (Lawrence: University Press of Kansas, 2002).

3   John K. Cooley, *Libyan Sandstorm* (New York: Holt, Reinhart and Winston, 1982), pp. 1, 7, 129–186; David C. Martin and John Walcott, *Best Laid Plans: The Inside Story of America's War Against Terrorism* (New York: Harper & Row, 1988), pp.

73–74, 266–268; Central Intelligence Agency, *Libya: Supplying Terrorist Weapons*, December 3, 1984; Brian L. Davis, *Qaddafi, Terrorism, and the Origins of the U.S. Attack on Libya* (Westport, Conn.: Praeger, 1990), pp. 2–22.

4   Andrew Cockburn and Patrick Cockburn, *Out of the Ashes: The Resurrection of Saddam Hussein* (New York: HarperCollins, 1999), pp. 66–71, 75–77; Samir al-Khalil, *Republic of Fear: The Politics of Modern Iraq* (Berkeley: University of California Press, 1989), pp. 3–45.

5   Dennis Kux, *The United States and Pakistan, 1947–2000: Disenchanted Allies* (Baltimore: Johns Hopkins University Press, 2001), pp. 233–234, 293; William E. Burrows and Robert Windrem, *Critical Mass: The Dangerous Race for Superweapons in a Fragmenting World* (New York: Simon & Schuster, 1994), pp. 60–61.

6   Steve Weissman and Herbert Krosney, *The Islamic Bomb: The Nuclear Threat to Israel and the Middle East* (New York: Times Books, 1981), p. 89; Imad Khadduri, *Iraq's Nuclear Mirage: Memoirs and Delusions* (Toronto: Springhead, 2003), p. 41; Central Intelligence Agency, *The Iraqi Nuclear Program: Progress Despite Setbacks*, June 1983, p. 1.

7   Weissman and Krosney, *The Islamic Bomb*, pp. 93–94; Central Intelligence Agency, *Iraq's National Security Goals*, December 1988, p. 2.

8   Weissman and Krosney, *The Islamic Bomb*, pp. 99–100.

9   Khidhir Hamza with Jeff Stein, *Saddam's Bombmaker: The Terrifying Inside Story of the Iraqi Nuclear and Biological Weapons Agenda* (New York: Scribner, 2000), pp. 20–21; Joby Warrick, "Scientists Hold Key to Iraqi Arms Search," *Washington Post*, December 15, 2002, pp. A1, A39.

10   Burrows and Windrem, *Critical Mass*, pp. 35–37; Khadduri, *Iraq's Nuclear Mirage*, p. 45.

11   Burrows and Windrem, *Critical Mass*, pp. 36–38.

12   Ibid., p. 38; Warrick, "Scientists Hold Key to Iraqi Arms Search"; Khadduri, *Iraq's Nuclear Mirage*, p. 80.

13   Khadduri, *Iraq's Nuclear Mirage*, pp. 36, 42, 47, 54, 57–62, 69–70, 98–115.

14   Ibid., pp. 67–68; Weissman and Krosney, *The Islamic Bomb*, p. 239; Shlomo Nakdimon, *First Strike: The Exclusive Story of How Israel Foiled Iraq's Attempt to Get the Bomb* (New York: Summit, 1987), p. 120.

15   Weissman and Krosney, *The Islamic Bomb*, p. 89; Central Intelligence Agency, *Iraq's Nuclear Program*, p. 2; J. P. Smith, "Iraq's Nuclear Arms Option," *Washington Post*, August 8, 1978, p. 14.

16   Peter Scott Ford, *Israel's Attack on Osiraq: A Model for Future Preventive Strikes?* (Monterey, Calif.: Naval Postgraduate School, 2004), pp. 14, 17–18.

17   Ian Black and Benny Morris, *Israel's Secret Wars: A History of Israel's Intelligence Services* (New York: Grove Weidenfeld, 1991), pp. 333–334; Nakdimon, *First Strike*, p. 101.

18   Black and Morris, *Israel's Secret Wars*, p. 334; Weissman and Krosney, *The Islamic Bomb*, pp. 239–241.

19   Black and Morris, *Israel's Secret Wars*, pp. 334–335; Rodger W. Claire, *Raid on the*

Sun: Inside Israel's Secret Campaign That Denied Saddam the Bomb (New York: Broadway, 2004), pp. xvii.

20   Black and Morris, *Israel's Secret Wars*, p. 334; Claire, *Raid on the Sun*, pp. 172–199; Wolf Blitzer, *Territory of Lies, the Exclusive Story of Jonathan Jay Pollard: The American Who Spied on His Country for Israel and How He Was Betrayed* (New York: Harper & Row, 1989), passim; Tom Cooper and Farzad Bishop, "Target: Saddam's Reactor," *Air Enthusiast*, March/April 2004, pp. 2–12.

21   Khadduri, *Iraq's Nuclear Mirage*, p. 81; Hamza, *Saddam's Bombmaker*, p. 128.

22   "Statement by the Government of Israel on the Bombing of the Iraqi Nuclear Facility," June 8, 1981, www.us-israel.org/source/History/BombingJune81.hmtl

23   David A. Kay, "Denial and Deception Practices of WMD Proliferators: Iraq and Beyond," *Washington Quarterly*, 18, 1 (Winter 1995), pp. 85–105 at p. 87.

24   Khadduri, *Iraq's Nuclear Mirage*, pp. 82–84.

25   Burrows and Windrem, *Critical Mass*, p. 42; Jay C. Davis and David A. Kay, "Iraq's Secret Nuclear Weapons Program," *Physics Today*, July 1992, pp. 21–27 at p. 22.

26   Khadduri, *Iraq's Nuclear Mirage*, pp. 90–91, 93, 96, 109.

27   David Albright, *Iraq's Programs to Make Highly Enriched Uranium and Plutonium for Nuclear Weapons Prior to the Gulf War*, October 2002, pp. 4–5, 12, www.isis-online.org.

28   Ibid., pp. 5–6; Mahdi Obdei and Kurt Pitzer, *The Bomb in My Garden: The Secrets of Saddam's Nuclear Mastermind* (New York: Wiley, 2004), p. 54.

29   Burrows and Windrem, *Critical Mass*, p. 50.

30   David Albright, Corey Gay, and Khidhir Hamza, *Development of the Al-Tuwaitha Site: What if the Public or the IAEA Had Overhead Imagery?*, April 26, 1999, pp. 3–5, www.isis-online.org; Jeffrey Smith and Glenn Frankel, "Saddam's Nuclear Weapons Dream: A Lingering Nightmare," *Washington Post*, October 13, 1991, pp. A1, A44–A45; U.S. Congress, House Committee on Foreign Affairs, *Iraq's Nuclear Weapons Capability and IAEA Inspections in Iraq* (Washington, D.C.: U.S. Government Printing Office, 1993), p. 155.

31   Cooley, *Libyan Sandstorm*, p. 229; Leonard Spector, *Nuclear Proliferation Today* (Boston: Ballinger, 1984), p. 155.

32   Spector, *Nuclear Proliferation Today*, p. 150.

33   Ibid.; Cooley, *Libyan Sandstorm*, p. 230; Weissman and Krosney, *The Islamic Bomb*, p. 56; "Writer Reports Libya A-Bomb Bid," *Washington Post*, April 16, 1979, p. A9.

34   Joseph V. R. Micallef, "A Nuclear Bomb for Libya?" *Bulletin of the Atomic Scientists*, August/September 1981, pp. 14–15.

35   Spector, *Nuclear Proliferation Today*, p. 151.

36   Ibid., p. 152; Cooley, *Libyan Sandstorm*, pp. 230–231; Micallef, "A Nuclear Bomb for Libya?"

37   Spector, *Nuclear Proliferation Today*, pp. 152–153; Richard L. Homan, "Libya to Get Soviet-Built Nuclear Plant," *Washington Post*, June 3, 1975, pp. A1, A13; "Writer Reports Libya A-Bomb Bid."

38   Spector, *Nuclear Proliferation Today*, p. 154.

39   Ibid., p. 153.

40   Ibid., pp. 152–153; Cooley, *Libyan Sandstorm*, p. 233; Leonard Spector, *Going Nuclear* (Boston: Ballinger, 1987), p. 148.

41   Leonard S. Spector with Jacqueline R. Smith, *Nuclear Ambitions* (Boulder, Colo.: Westview, 1990), p. 177.

42   Spector with Smith, *Nuclear Ambitions*, p. 177.

43   Matin Zuberi, "The Road to Chagai," in K. K. Nayyar (ed.), *Pakistan at the Crossroads* (New Delhi: Rupa, 2003), pp. 203, 207–208.

44   Kux, *The United States and Pakistan, 1947–2000*, p. 205; Weissman and Krosney, *The Islamic Bomb*, pp. 40, 48; Ashok Kapur, *Pakistan's Nuclear Development* (London: Croon, Helm, 1987), pp. 87 n. 1, 107.

45   Weissman and Krosney, *The Islamic Bomb*, pp. 45–46; Leonard S. Spector, *The Undeclared Bomb* (Cambridge: Ballinger, 1988), pp. 120–121; Zuberi, "The Road to Chagai," pp. 215–216.

46   Kux, *The United States and Pakistan, 1947–2000*, p. 212; Spector, *Nuclear Proliferation Today*, pp. 71, 74, 108; Zuberi, "The Road to Chagai," pp. 217–220.

47   Zuberi, "The Road to Chagai," p. 238.

48   Spector, *The Undeclared Bomb*, p. 121; Burrows and Windrem, *Critical Mass*, p. 364; Weissman and Krosney, *The Islamic Bomb*, pp. 170–171; Kapur, *Pakistan's Nuclear Development*, p. 196; Kux, *The United States and Pakistan, 1947–2000*, p. 236.

49   Spector, *Nuclear Ambitions*, pp. 102, 115; Kapur, *Pakistan's Nuclear Development*, pp. 196–197.

50   Weissman and Krosney, *The Islamic Bomb*, p. 175; Spector, *The Undeclared Bomb*, p. 122; Zuberi, "The Road to Chagai," pp. 226–227.

51   Weissman and Krosney, *The Islamic Bomb*, p. 176; Burrows and Windrem, *Critical Mass*, p. 362.

52   Weissman and Krosney, *The Islamic Bomb*, pp. 177–179; Burrows and Windrem, *Critical Mass*, pp. 362–363.

53   Zuberi, "The Road to Chagai," p. 227; Weissman and Krosney, *The Islamic Bomb*, p. 180.

54   Weissman and Krosney, *The Islamic Bomb*, p. 180.

55   Spector, *The Undeclared Bomb*, pp. 122–123.

56   Ibid., p. 123.

57   Ibid., pp. 122–123; Burrows and Windrem, *Critical Mass*, p. 349; Weissman and Krosney, *The Islamic Bomb*, p. 182; Kapur, *Pakistan's Nuclear Development*, p. 160.

58   Spector, *The Undeclared Bomb*, pp. 124, 141; Weissman and Krosney, *The Islamic Bomb*, p. 182; Spector, *Nuclear Proliferation Today*, p. 108.

59   Spector, *The Undeclared Bomb*, pp. 124–125, 149; Leonard Weiss, "Pakistan: It's Déjà Vu All Over Again," *Bulletin of the Atomic Scientists*, May/June 2004, pp. 52–59 at p. 54.

60   Spector, *The Undeclared Bomb*, pp. 126, 129, 134; Andrew Koch and Jennifer Topping, "Pakistan's Nuclear Weapons Program: A Status Report," *Nonproliferation Review*, 4, 3 (Spring/Summer 1997), pp. 109–113.

61   Kapur, *Pakistan's Nuclear Development*, p. 210; "Wah Cantonment," www.global security.org, accessed May 29, 2004.

62   Spector, *Nuclear Ambitions*, p. 121; Don Oberdorfer, *The Two Koreas: A Contemporary History* (Reading, Mass.: Addison-Wesley, 1997), p. 252.

63   Burrows and Windrem, *Critical Mass*, p. 426; Oberdorfer, *The Two Koreas*, p. 252.

64   Oberdorfer, *The Two Koreas*, p. 253.

65   Ibid.; "A Physicist Defector's Account of North Korea's Nuke Labs, Comments by Lee Wha Rang," www.kimsoft.com/2002/nk-nuke4.htm, accessed July 2, 2004.

66   Burrows and Windrem, *Critical Mass*, pp. 426–427; Spector, *Nuclear Ambitions*, p. 123; David Albright, "North Korean Plutonium Production," *Science & Global Security*, 5, 1 (1994), pp. 63–87 at p. 72.

67   Jeffrey T. Richelson, *America's Secret Eyes in Space: The U.S. Keyhole Spy Satellite Program* (New York: Harper & Row, 1990), pp. 360, 362.

68   Director of Central Intelligence, Interagency Intelligence Assessment, *Implications of Israeli Attack on Iraq*, July 1, 1981, p. 3.

69   Central Intelligence Agency, *The Iraqi Nuclear Program*, p. iii.

70   Ibid., pp. iv, 12, 14.

71   Ibid., p. 11.

72   Ibid., pp. 12–13.

73   Ibid., p. 13.

74   Ibid.

75   Ibid., p. 6.

76   Ibid.

77   Ibid., pp. 12, 14.

78   Nuclear Control Institute, "Declassified U.S. Intelligence Report Reveals Chinese Nuclear Assistance to Iraq," July 1, 1991; U.S. Army Operational Group, [deleted] Nuclear Power Plant Development Plans, May 12, 1986.

79   Central Intelligence Agency, *Iraq's National Security Goals*, p. 2.

80   Central Intelligence Agency, *Qadhafi's Nuclear Weapons Aims*, May 1975, p. 1.

81   Central Intelligence Agency, *The Libyan Nuclear Program: A Technical Perspective*, February 1985, pp. 2–6, 17–21.

82   Ibid., pp. 8–14.

83   Ibid., p. iii.

84   National Intelligence Council, *The Dynamics of Nuclear Proliferation: Balance of Incentives and Constraints*, September 1985, p. 16.

85   Director of Central Intelligence, Memorandum: *Prospects for Further Proliferation of Nuclear Weapons*, September 4, 1974, pp. 3–4.

86   Central Intelligence Agency, "Pakistan Negotiating with Niger for Uranium," *Weekly Surveyor*, January 17, 1977, p. 7.

87   Central Intelligence Agency, "Pakistan-China: Nuclear Cooperation," *Weekly Surveyor*, June 6, 1977, pp. 2–3.

88   Untitled paper, April 26, 1978, CIA Electronic Reading Room, pp. 1, 3, www.cia.gov.

89   Ibid., pp. 12, 13.

90   Ibid., pp. 19, 21–22.

91   Ibid., p. 23.

92   Ibid., pp. 25–27.

93   Interview with Robert L. Gallucci, Washington, D.C., June 22, 2004.

94   Ibid.

95   Kux, *The United States and Pakistan, 1947–2000*, p. 236.

96   Gallucci interview.

97   Department of State, General Advisory Committee on Arms Control and Disarmament, *Friday Morning Session, September 14, 1979, 8:30 A.M.–12.32 P.M.*, 1979, pp. 309, 311–312, 316.

98   Richard Burt, "U.S. Aides Say Pakistan Is Reported to Be Building an A-Bomb Site," *New York Times*, August 17, 1979, p. A6.

99   Milton R. Benjamin, "Pakistan Building Secret Nuclear Plant," *Washington Post*, September 23, 1980, pp. A1, A12.

100 Ibid.

101 Steven Coll, *Ghost Wars: The Secret History of the CIA, Afghanistan, and Bin Laden, from the Soviet Invasion to September 10, 2001* (New York: Penguin Press, 2004), pp. 57, 69.

102 Burrows and Windrem, *Critical Mass*, pp. 70–71; Hedrick Smith, "A Bomb Ticks in Pakistan," *New York Times Magazine*, March 6, 1988, pp. 38*ff* at p. 104; Weiss, "Pakistan," p. 56; Zuberi, "The Road to Chagai," p. 232.

103 Kux, *The United States and Pakistan, 1947–2000*, p. 279.

104 National Intelligence Council, *The Dynamics of Nuclear Proliferation*, p. 8.

105 Bob Woodward, "Pakistan Reported near Atom Arms Production," *Washington Post*, November 4, 1986, pp. A1, A16; Smith, "A Bomb Ticks in Pakistan."

106 Woodward, "Pakistan Reported near Atom Arms Production."

107 Ibid.; Jack Anderson and Dale Van Atta, "Nuclear Exports to China?" *Washington Post*, November 3, 1985, p. C7; Patrick E. Tyler and Joanne Omang, "China-Iran Nuclear Link Is Reported," *Washington Post*, October 23, 1985, pp. A1, A19; Joanne Omang, "Nuclear Pact with China Wins Senate Approval," November 22, 1985, p. A3; Patrick E. Tyler, "A Few Spoken Words Sealed China Atom Pact," *Washington Post*, January 12, 1986, pp. A1, A20–21; Zuberi, "The Road to Chagai," p. 233.

108 Kux, *The United States and Pakistan, 1947–2000*, pp. 284–285.

109 Ibid., p. 285; Smith, "A Bomb Ticks in Pakistan."

110 Kux, *The United States and Pakistan, 1947–2000*, p. 299.

111 Ibid., pp. 299–300. Beg would later claim that Pakistan could afford to suspend production because the country already had produced enough fissile material for deterrent purposes.

112 U.S. Congress, Senate Committee on Governmental Affairs, *Nuclear and Missile Proliferation* (Washington, D.C.: U.S. Government Printing Office, 1989), p. 23; Burrows and Windrem, *Critical Mass*, pp. 80–81; Stephen Engelberg, "U.S. Sees Pakistan Seeking an A-Bomb," *New York Times*, June 11, 1989, p. 5.

113   Burrows and Windrem, *Critical Mass*, p. 81; Michael R. Gordon, "Nuclear Course Set by Pakistan Worrying U.S.," *New York Times*, October 12, 1989, pp. A1, A9.

114   "KEY JUDGMENTS: Pakistan—Progress Toward Advanced Weapons," *Science and Weapons Review*, October 13, 1989, pp. 8–9.

115   Kux, *The United States and Pakistan, 1947–2000*, pp. 306–307.

116   Ibid., pp. 307–308; Matin Zuberi points to a claim by Pakistani general K. M. Arif (K. M. Arif, *Working with Zia: Pakistan's Power Politics, 1977–1988* [Karachi: Oxford University Press, 1995], p. 341) that during a 1981 visit to Washington with foreign minister Agha Shahi, the two had meetings with President Reagan, Vice President Bush, and Secretary of State Alexander Haig, and Haig told them Pakistan's nuclear program would not become the linchpin of the new relationship. Zuberi believes that subsequent warnings by U.S. spokesmen were for the sake of the record. E-mail, Matin Zuberi to the author, October 18, 2004.

117   Joel S. Wit, Daniel B. Poneman, and Robert L. Gallucci, *Going Critical: The First North Korean Nuclear Crisis* (Washington, D.C.: Brookings, 2004), p. 1; E-mail, Tim Brown to the author, October 4, 2004.

118   Central Intelligence Agency, "NORTH KOREA: Nuclear Reactor," July 9, 1982; Wit, Poneman, and Gallucci, *Going Critical*, p. 1.

119   Ibid.

120   Central Intelligence Agency, *East Asia Brief* [deleted] for 20 April 1984, April 20, 1984.

121   Department of State, Briefing Paper, ca. January 5, 1985, in Robert Wampler (ed.), *North Korea and Nuclear Weapons: The Declassified U.S. Record*, National Security Archive Electronic Briefing Book No. 87, April 25, 2003, Document 5, www.nsarchive.org.

122   Central Intelligence Agency, *North Korea: Potential for Nuclear Weapons Development*, September 1986, p. 1.

123   Ibid., p. vi.

124   Central Intelligence Agency, *North Korea's Nuclear Efforts*, April 28, 1987, pp. 2–3.

125   Central Intelligence Agency, *North Korea's Expanding Nuclear Efforts*, May 3, 1988, pp. 2–4.

126   Stephen J. Hedges and Peter Cary, "Saddam's Secret Bomb," *U.S. News & World Report*, November 25, 1991, pp. 34–42 at p. 37; Peter D. Zimmerman, *Iraq's Nuclear Achievements: Components, Sources, and Stature* (Washington, D.C.: Congressional Research Service, February 18, 1993), p. 8.

127   Burrows and Windrem, *Critical Mass*, p. 44; Zimmerman, *Iraq's Nuclear Achievements*, p. 9; Hedges and Cary, "Saddam's Secret Bomb," p. 38.

128   House Committee on Foreign Affairs, *Iraq's Nuclear Weapons Capability and IAEA Inspections in Iraq* (Washington, D.C.: U.S. Government Printing Office, 1993), p. 155; Zimmerman, *Iraq's Nuclear Achievements*, pp. 9–10.

129   Burrows and Windrem, *Critical Mass*, p. 45; Zimmerman, *Iraq's Nuclear Achievements*, p. 10.

130   Burrows and Windrem, *Critical Mass*, pp. 45–46; House Committee on Foreign

Affairs, *Iraq's Nuclear Weapons Capability and IAEA Inspections in Iraq*, p. 155; Zimmerman, *Iraq's Nuclear Achievements*, p. 11; Tim Ripley, "Iraq's Nuclear Weapons Programme," *Jane's Intelligence Review*, December 1992, pp. 554–558; Hedges and Cary, "Saddam's Secret Bomb," p. 37.

131   Zimmerman, *Iraq's Nuclear Achievements*, pp. 1, 17–18.

132   Hedges and Cary, "Saddam's Secret Bomb," pp. 35–36.

133   Zimmerman, *Iraq's Nuclear Achievements*, pp. 38–40; Hedges and Cary, "Saddam's Secret Bomb," p. 38.

134   Burrows and Windrem, *Critical Mass*, p. 43.

135   Ibid., p. 44.

136   Joseph S. Bermudez Jr., "North Korea's Nuclear Programme," *Jane's Intelligence Review*, September 1991, pp. 404–411 at pp. 405, 408.

137   Ibid., pp. 406–409.

138   "Questions for Mr. Emel," in U.S. Congress, House Committee on Energy and Commerce, *Nuclear Nonproliferation: Failed Efforts to Curtail Iraq's Nuclear Weapons Program* (Washington, D.C.: U.S. Government Printing Office, 1991), pp. 686–690 at p. 686.

139   Rick Atkinson, *Crusade: The Untold Story of the Persian Gulf War* (Boston: Houghton Mifflin, 1993), p. 28; Bob Woodward, "CIA Aiding Iraq in Gulf War," *Washington Post*, December 15, 1986, pp. A1, A28.

140   John A. Gentry, *Lost Promise: How CIA Analysis Misserves the Nation—An Intelligence Assessment* (Lanham, Md.: University Press of America, 1993), p. 315; John A. Gentry, "A Framework for Reform of the U.S. Intelligence Community," unpublished paper, June 1995, p. 28.

141   Gentry, "A Framework for Reform of the U.S. Intelligence Community," pp. 28–29.

142   "Questions for Mr. Emel," and "Testimony of Roger K. Heuser," in U.S. Congress, House Committee on Energy and Commerce, *Nuclear Nonproliferation: Failed Efforts to Curtail Iraq's Nuclear Weapons Program*, pp. 686 and 32, respectively.

143   "Questions for Mr. Emel," p. 687.

144   U.S. Congress, House Committee on Energy and Commerce, *Nuclear Nonproliferation*, pp. 67, 708.

145   Patrick E. Tyler, "Specialists See Iraq Unlikely to Build A-Bomb in Near Future," *Washington Post*, November 8, 1990, p. A62; Bill Gertz, "Saddam Close to Nuclear Weapon," *Washington Times*, November 28, 1990, pp. A1, A6; Michael Wines, "Hard Data Lacking on Iraqi Nuclear Threat," *New York Times*, November 30, 1990, p. A12.

146   Malcolm W. Browne, "Unless Stopped Iraq Could Have A-Arms in 10 Years," *New York Times*, November 18, 1990, pp. 1, 14.

147   Browne, "Unless Stopped Iraq Could Have A-Arms in 10 Years"; Gertz, "Saddam Close to Nuclear Weapon."

148   Wines, "Hard Data Lacking on Iraqi Nuclear Threat"; Gertz, "Saddam Close to Nuclear Weapon."

149   Wines, "Hard Data Lacking on Iraqi Nuclear Threat."

150   Ibid.

151 Ibid.

152 Tyler, "Specialists See Iraq Unlikely to Build A-Bomb in Near Future."

153 Ibid.

154 U.S. Congress, House Committee on Energy and Commerce, *Nuclear Nonproliferation*, p. 2.

155 Wines, "Hard Data Lacking on Iraqi Nuclear Threat."

156 U.S. News & World Report, *Triumph Without Victory: The Unreported History of the Persian Gulf War* (New York: Random House, 1992), pp. 294, 394–395, 399.

157 Ibid., pp. 432–434.

158 Robin Bulman, "Koreas Sign Declaration Banning Nuclear Arms," *Washington Post*, January 1, 1992, p. A24.

159 Central Intelligence Agency, Special Analysis, *NORTH KOREA: Nuclear Program of Proliferation Concern*, March 22, 1989, p. 1.

160 Ibid., pp. 2, 4.

161 Don Oberdorfer, "North Koreans Pursue Nuclear Arms," *Washington Post*, July 29, 1989, p. A9; John J. Fialka, "North Korea May Be Developing Ability to Build Nuclear Weapons," *Wall Street Journal*, July 19, 1989, p. A16; Michael R. Gordon, "U.S. Concern Rises over North Korea Atom Plant," *New York Times*, October 25, 1989, p. A9.

162 Gordon, "U.S. Concern Rises over North Korea Atom Plant."

163 David E. Sanger, "Furor in Seoul over North's Atom Plant," *New York Times*, April 16, 1991, p. A3; "A Knock on the Nuclear Door?" *Newsweek*, April 29, 1991, pp. 38–40.

164 Andrew Mack, "North Korea and the Bomb," *Foreign Policy*, 83 (Summer 1991), pp. 87–104 at pp. 89–90; Department of State, Talking Points Paper for Under Secretary of State Bartholomew's Trip, ca. 30 May 1991, Subject: North Korean Nuclear Program (for China), in Wampler (ed.), *North Korea and Nuclear Weapons*, Document 15.

165 David E. Sanger, "Data Raise Fears of Nuclear Moves by North Koreans," *New York Times*, November 10, 1991, pp. 1, 10.

166 Ibid.

167 Robin Bulman, "Koreas Sign Declaration Banning Nuclear Arms," *Washington Post*, January 1, 1992, p. A24; Oderdorfer, *The Two Koreas*, p. 264.

CHAPTER 9: "PARIAHS" REVISITED

1 Seymour Hersh, *The Samson Option: Israel's Nuclear Arsenal and American Foreign Policy* (New York: Random House, 1991), p. 201; Frank Barnaby, *The Invisible Bomb: The Nuclear Arms Race in the Middle East* (London: I. B. Tauris, 1989), pp. 40–41.

2 Hersh, *The Samson Option*, pp. 198–199, 282.

3 David Hoffman, "Israel Army Major Was a Spy," *Washington Post*, June 3, 1993, p. A18; Wolf Blitzer, "U.S. Changed Rules of the Spy Game," *Jerusalem Post International Edition*, March 28, 1987, pp. A1, A20; Wolf Blitzer, *Territory of Lies: The Exclusive Story of Jonathan Jay Pollard: The American Who Spied on His Country for Israel and How He Was Betrayed* (New York: Harper & Row, 1989).

4   Louis Toscano, *Triple Cross: Israel, the Atomic Bomb and the Man Who Spilled the Secrets* (New York: Birch Lane Press, 1990), pp. 9, 11–12.

5   Ibid., p. 18; Yossi Melman and Dan Raviv, *The Imperfect Spies: The History of Israeli Intelligence* (London: Sidgwick & Jackson, 1989), p. 382.

6   Toscano, *Triple Cross*, pp. 19–20; Melman and Raviv, *The Imperfect Spies*, p. 383.

7   Toscano, *Triple Cross*, pp. 21, 23.

8   Ibid., pp. 23, 26, 51.

9   Ibid., p. 39.

10   Central Intelligence Agency, *Foreign Intelligence and Security Services: Israel* (Washington, D.C.: CIA, 1977), p. 25; Toscano, *Triple Cross*, pp. 39–41.

11   Toscano, *Triple Cross*, pp. 46–47.

12   Ibid., pp. 41, 54; Andrew Cockburn and Leslie Cockburn, *Dangerous Liaison: The Inside Story of the U.S.-Israeli Covert Relationship* (New York: HarperCollins, 1991), p. 95.

13   Toscano, *Triple Cross*, pp. 63–64; Melman and Raviv, *The Imperfect Spies*, pp. 385–386; "Peter Hounam," www.visionpaperbacks.co.uk, accessed July 22, 2004; Peter Hounam, *The Woman from Mossad: The Story of Mordecai Vanunu and the Israel's Nuclear Program* (London: Vision, 1999), p. 18.

14   C. F. Barnaby, "Expert Opinion of Charles Frank Barnaby in the Matter of Mordecai Vanunu," June 14, 2004, p. 2.

15   Ian Black and Benny Morris, *Israel's Secret Wars: A History of Israeli's Intelligence Services* (New York: Grove, Weidenfeld, 1991), p. 438; Toscano, *Triple Cross*, pp. 49, 51; "Inside Dimona, Israel's Nuclear Bomb Factory," *London Sunday Times*, October 5, 1986.

16   Toscano, *Triple Cross*, pp. 51–52; Cockburn and Cockburn, *Dangerous Liaison*, p. 95.

17   "Inside Dimona, Israel's Nuclear Bomb Factory."

18   Ibid.

19   Ibid.

20   Ibid.

21   Hersh, *The Samson Option*, p. 198.

22   Black and Morris, *Israel's Secret Wars*, p. 438; Melman and Raviv, *The Imperfect Spies*, pp. 386–387; Cockburn and Cockburn, *Dangerous Liaison*, p. 96; Hounam, *The Woman from Mossad*, pp. 78–79.

23   Hersh, *The Samson Option*, pp. 198–200.

24   Ibid., pp. 198–199.

25   Ibid., p. 199.

26   Ibid., p. 200.

27   Tim Weiner, "How a Spy Left Taiwan in the Cold," *New York Times*, December 20, 1997, p. A7.

28   Ibid.; "The Man Who Put an End to Taiwan's Dream of Becoming a Nuclear Power," October 14, 1999, www.taipeitimes.com; "About Us," n.d., www.ccit.edu.tw, accessed July 10, 2004.

29   Weiner, "How a Spy Left Taiwan in the Cold"; Leonard S. Spector, *The Undeclared Bomb* (Cambridge, Mass.: Ballinger, 1988), pp. 75, 77; David Albright and Corey Gay, "Taiwan: Nuclear Nightmare Averted," *Bulletin of the Atomic Scientists* (January/February 1998), pp. 54–60 at p. 59; R. Jeffrey Smith and Don Oberdorfer, "Taiwan to Close Nuclear Reactor," *Washington Post*, March 24, 1988, p. A32.

30   Weiner, "How a Spy Left Taiwan in the Cold."

31   Stephen Engleberg and Michael R. Gordon, "Taipei Halts Work on Secret Plant to Make Nuclear Bomb Ingredient," *New York Times*, March 23, 1988, pp. A1, A15; Albright and Gay, "Taiwan," p. 59; Smith and Oberdorfer, "Taiwan to Close Nuclear Reactor."

32   Weiner, "How a Spy Left Taiwan in the Cold."

33   Mitchel Reiss, *Bridled Ambition: Why Countries Constrain Their Nuclear Capabilities* (Washington, D.C.: Woodrow Wilson Center, 1995), p. 7.

34   INR/SPA –[deleted], To: [assorted State Department officials], Subject: February 1993 Visit to South Africa by US Nuclear Weapon Scientists, May 28, 1993; "Decision Brief," October 14, 1997, www.security-policy.org; "Houston Terry Hawkins," www.lanl.gov, accessed July 23, 2004.

35   INR/SPA –[deleted], To: [assorted State Department officials], Subject: February 1993 Visit to South Africa by US Nuclear Weapon Scientists; Private information. In 2004, Stumpf was unable to recall any pleas by the visitors for greater openness. Interview with Waldo Stumpf, September 13, 2004.

36   Ibid.; "De Klerk Discloses Nuclear Capability to Parliament," *FBIS-AFR-93-056*, March 25, 1993, p. 5.; "F. W. De Klerk," http://www.encyclopedia.thefreedictionary.com, accessed July 12, 2004; F. W. de Klerk, *The Last Trek—A New Beginning* (New York: St. Martin's, 1999), pp. 130–148.

37   De Klerk, *The Last Trek*, p. 272.

38   "De Klerk Discloses Nuclear Capability to Parliament," pp. 5–9.

39   De Klerk, *The Last Trek*, p. 273.

40   "De Klerk Discloses Nuclear Capability to Parliament," p. 6; David B. Ottaway, "South Africa Said to Abandon Pursuit of Nuclear Weapons," *Washington Post*, October 18, 1991, pp. A23, A26.

41   Joseph Cirincione with Jon B. Wolfsthal and Miriam Rajkumar, *Deadly Arsenals: Tracking Weapons of Mass Destruction* (Washingon, D.C.: Carnegie Endowment for International Peace, 2002), p. 365; R. Jeffrey Smith, "South Africa's 16-Year Secret: The Nuclear Bomb," *Washington Post*, May 12, 1993, pp. A1, A26; Waldo Stumpf, "Birth and Death of the South African Nuclear Weapons Program," p. 2, presentation given at Conference on "50 Years After Hiroshima," Castiglioncello, Italy, 28 September to 2 October 1995, www.fas.org.

42   David Albright, "A Curious Conversion," *Bulletin of the Atomic Scientists*, June 1993, pp. 8–11; Frank V. Pabian, "South Africa's Nuclear Weapon Program: Lessons for U.S. Nonproliferation Policy," *Nonproliferation Review*, 3, 1 (Fall 1995), pp. 1–19 at p. 6; Adolf von Baeckmann, Gary Dillon, and Demetrius Perricos, "Nuclear Verification in South Africa," p. 4, www.iaea.org, accessed July 21, 2004.

43   Reiss, *Bridled Ambition*, p. 11; David Albright, "South Africa's Nuclear Weapons Program," March 14, 2001, web.mit.edu/ssp/spring01/Albright.htm; Albright, "A Curious Conversion"; Waldo Stumpf, "South Africa's Nuclear Weapons Program: From Deterrence to Dismantlement," *Arms Control Today*, December 1995/January 1996, pp. 3–8 at p. 5.

44   Reiss, *Bridled Ambition*, pp. 11–12; Stumpf, "Birth and Death of the South African Nuclear Weapons Programme," p. 6; von Baeckman, Dillon, and Pellicos, "Nuclear Verification in South Africa," pp. 4–5.

45   Reiss, *Bridled Ambition*, p. 12.

46   Ibid., p. 13.

47   Ibid., p. 14; Peter Liberman, "The Rise and Fall of the South African Bomb," *International Security*, 26, 2 (Fall 2001), pp. 45–86 at p. 60.

48   Reiss, *Bridled Ambition*, p. 14; Pabian, "South Africa's Nuclear Weapons Program," p. 9.

49   Stumpf, "Birth and Death of the South African Nuclear Weapons Programme," p. 7.

50   Reiss, *Bridled Ambition*, p. 18; Darryl Howlett and John Simpson, "Nuclearisation and Denuclearisation in South Africa," *Survival*, 35, 3 (Autumn 1993), pp. 154–173 at p. 162; Smith, "South Africa's 16-Year Secret"; de Klerk, *The Last Trek*, p. 274.

51   Reiss, *Bridled Ambition*, p. 18; Smith, "South Africa's 16-Year Secret."

52   "De Klerk Discloses Nuclear Capability to Parliament," p. 6.

53   Hannes Steyn, Richard van der Walt, and Jan van Loggerenberg, *Armament and Disarmament: South Africa's Nuclear Weapons Experience* (Pretoria: Network Publishers, 2003), p. 85; Smith, "South Africa's 16-Year Secret"; David Albright, "South Africa's Secret Nuclear Weapons Program," p. 7, May 1994, www.isis-online.org; Pabian, "South Africa's Nuclear Weapon Program," p. 6; de Klerk, *The Last Trek*, p. 273.

54   Smith, "South Africa's 16-Year Secret"; David Albright, "South Africa and the Affordable Bomb," *Bulletin of the Atomic Scientists*, July/August 1994, pp. 37–47 at p. 43.

55   "Strategic Value of Simonstown Naval Base May Decrease," *DIA Weekly Intelligence Summary*, July 23, 1982, pp. 23–25.

56   Pabian, "South Africa's Nuclear Weapon Program," p. 12.

57   Central Intelligence Agency, *New Information on South Africa's Nuclear Program and South African-Israeli Nuclear and Military Cooperation*, March 30, 1983, pp. 1–2.

58   Ibid., p. 2.

59   Ibid., pp. 2–3.

60   Director of Central Intelligence, NIE 73/5-84, *Trends in South Africa's Nuclear Security Policies and Programs*, October 5, 1984, p. 1.

61   Ibid., p. 2.

62   Letter, Randall M. Fort, Deputy Assistant Secretary Intelligence and Research, State Department to [deleted], September 18, 1991.

63   Letter, Fort to [deleted].

64   Howlett and Simpson, "Nuclearisation and Denuclearisation in South Africa," p.

166; R. Jeffrey Smith, "S. Africa's Nuclear File to Be Age Tested," *Washington Post*, May 13, 1993, p. A24; von Baeckmann, Dillon, and Perricos, "Nuclear Verification in South Africa," pp. 1–3.

65   Howlett and Simpson, "Nuclearisation and Denuclearisation in South Africa," p. 166.

66   Ibid., pp. 166–167; R. Jeffrey Smith, "Pretoria's Candor on Nuclear Program Questioned," *Washington Post*, March 18, 1993, p. A30.

67   Steve Coll and Paul Taylor, "Tracking S. Africa's Elusive A-Program," *Washington Post*, March 18, 1993, pp. A1, A32.

68   Howlett and Simpson, "Nuclearisation and Denuclearisation in South Africa," p. 167.

69   Stumpf interview.

70   From INR/SPA, To: INR/SPA Files, Subject: South Africa's Options to Conceal Highly Enriched Uranium, March 3, 1992.

71   INR/SPA – [deleted] To: DCI/NPC – [deleted], Subject: PAWG Draft Paper on South African Nuclear Inventory, August 26, 1992.

72   Commission to Assess the Organization of the Federal Government to Combat the Proliferation of Weapons of Mass Destruction, *Combating Proliferation of Weapons of Mass Destruction*, July 14, 1999, p. 73; "Dr. Gordon Oehler, Senior Fellow and member of Board of Regents," www.potomacinstitute.org, accessed July 25, 2004.

73   INR/SPA – [deleted] To: DCI/NPC – [deleted], Subject: PAWG Draft Paper on South African Nuclear Inventory.

74   Ibid.

75   From INR/SPA – [deleted] To: DCI/NPC – [deleted], Subject: INR Comments on PAWG Draft, August 28, 1992.

76   From INR/SPA – [deleted] To: DCI/NPC – [deleted], Subject: INR Footnote to NPC Paper on South Africa, September 18, 1992.

77   From INR/SPA – Gary D. Dietrich To: INR – Douglas P. Mulholland, Subject: [Deleted], December 7, 1992; U.S. Department of State, *Telephone Directory Fall 1992* (Washington, D.C.: U.S. Government Printing Office, 1992), pp. State-12, State-13.

78   INR, "Underground Nuclear Facilities," December 9, 1992.

79   Smith, "Pretoria's Candor on Nuclear Program Questioned"; Smith, "S. Africa's Nuclear File to Be Age Tested."

80   Smith, "Pretoria's Candor on Nuclear Program Questioned."

81   Ibid.

82   Ibid.

83   Ibid.; Smith, "S. Africa's Nuclear File to Be Age Tested."

84   Smith, "Pretoria's Candor on Nuclear Program Questioned."

85   Ibid.; "De Klerk Discloses Nuclear Capability to Parliament."

86   Von Baeckmann, Dillon, and Pellicos, "Nuclear Verification in South Africa," pp. 3–4; Nita Lelyveld, "S. Africa Provides Cautionary Tale," March 13, 2003, www.latimes.com.

87   Von Baeckmann, Dillon, and Pellicos, "Nuclear Verification in South Africa," p. 5.

88   Smith, "S. Africa's Nuclear File to Be Age Tested."

89   Ibid.

90   Ibid.

91   International Atomic Energy Agency, *The Agency's Verification Activities in South Africa* (att to: Director-General, IAEA, *The Denuclearization of Africa: Report by the Director General*, September 9, 1993), Annex 2.

92   International Atomic Energy Agency, *The Agency's Verification Activities in South Africa*, pp. 2–3.

93   Reiss, *Bridled Ambition*, p. 25.

94   INR, *South Africa: Nuclear Case Closed?*, December 19, 1993.

95   Ibid.

96   Ibid.

97   Ibid.

98   Ibid.

99   Ibid.

CHAPTER 10: BIG BANGS

1   "The Nuclear Testing Tally," May 1998, www.armscontrol.org; Robert S. Norris, Andrew S. Burrows, and Richard W. Fieldhouse, *Nuclear Weapons Databook, Volume V, British, French, and Chinese Nuclear Weapons* (Boulder, Colo.: Westview, 1994), pp. 230, 255, 257, 287–288, 303–305, 314–315, 413–415.

2   Jeffrey T. Richelson, *A Century of Spies: Intelligence in the Twentieth Century* (New York: Oxford University Press, 1995), pp. 404–407.

3   "The Nuclear Testing Tally"; Norris, Burrows, and Fieldhouse, *Nuclear Weapons Databook, Volume V*, pp. 248, 259, 416; Robert S. Norris, "French and Chinese Nuclear Weapons Testing," *Security Dialogue*, 27, 1 (March 1996), pp. 39–54 at p. 46.

4   "Nuclear Testing Tally"; Norris, Burrows, and Fieldhouse, *Nuclear Weapons Databook, Volume V*, p. 260; Kenneth R. Timmerman, *The French Betrayal of America* (New York: Crown, 2004), p. 194; R. L. Garwin, R. E. Kidder, and C. E. Paine, *A Report on Discussions Regarding The Need for Nuclear Test Explosions To Maintain French Nuclear Weapons Under a Comprehensive Test Ban: Paris, France November 2–7, 1994* (Washington, D.C.: Federation of American Scientists and Natural Resources Defense Council, 1995), Executive Summary, p. 1.

5   William Drozdiak and R. Jeffrey Smith, "French Nuclear Program Closely Tied to U.S.," *Washington Post*, September 19, 1995, pp. A1, A9; Philip Shenon, "France, Despite Wide Protests, Explodes a Nuclear Device," *New York Times*, September 6, 1995, p. A3; William Drozdiak, "France Sets Off Nuclear Blast Despite Worldwide Protests," *Washington Post*, September 6, 1995, pp. A23, A27; William Drozdiak, "France Rebuffs Critics, Readies More A-Tests," *Washington Post*, September 7, 1995, p. A33.

6   Drozdiak, "France Sets Off Nuclear Blast Despite Worldwide Protests"; Shenon, "France, Despite Wide Protests, Explodes a Nuclear Device"; Drozdiak, "France Rebuffs Critics, Readies More A-Tests"; Amembassy Wellington to Sec State Wash DC, Subject: Lange Blast France's Testing, November 6, 1984.

7   "The Nuclear Testing Tally"; "France Takes More Heat over New Test," *Washington Times*, December 29, 1995, p. A13; Tariq Rauf, "French Nuclear Testing: A Fool's Errand," *Nonproliferation Review*, 3, 1 (Fall 1995), pp. 49–57 at p. 49; Shenon, "France, Despite Wide Protests, Explodes a Nuclear Device." Some believed that the tests were driven more by the desire to exercise diplomatic muscle than the need to collect useful data. See Martin Sieff, "French Nuclear Test Draws Only 'Regrets' from World Powers," *Washington Times*, October 3, 1995, p. A11.

8   John Cork and Bruce Scivally, *James Bond: The Legacy* (New York: Harry N. Abrams, 2002), p. 257.

9   Nicky Hager, *Secret Power: New Zealand's Role in the International Spy Network* (Nelson, New Zealand: Craig Potton, 1996), pp. 103–104, 156, 269.

10   Jeffrey T. Richelson, *The Wizards of Langley: Inside the CIA's Directorate of Science and Technology* (Boulder, Colo.: Westview, 2001), p. 276.

11   Science Applications International Corporation, *Fifty Year Commemorative History of Long Range Detection: The Creation, Development, and Operation of the United States Atomic Energy Detection System* (Satellite Beach, Fla.: SAIC, 1997), pp. 77–80. The other stations were established in Botswana (beginning in May 1993), Brazil (August 1993), Bolivia (August 1993), Antarctica (December 1993), Paraguay (July 1994), Central Africa Republic (September 1994), and Ivory Coast (September 1994). The network was originally designated the Global Telemetered Seismic Network. Subsequently it became the Auxiliary Seismic Network and the AFTAC Southern Network.

12   U.S. Congress, House Committee on Appropriations, *Department of Defense Appropriations for 1994, Part I* (Washington, D.C.: U.S. Government Printing Office, 1993), p. 48; Jeffrey T. Richelson, *The U.S. Intelligence Community*, 4th ed. (Boulder, Colo.: Westview, 1999), p. 234.

13   Letter, Kathryn I. Dyer, Information and Privacy Coordinator, CIA, to author, July 30, 2002.

14   "The Nuclear Testing Tally"; Central Intelligence Agency, "China Seeking Foreign Assistance to Address Concerns About Nuclear Stockpile Under CTBT," *Proliferation Digest*, March 29, 1996, pp. 17–18.

15   See chapter 8, pp. 342–344.

16   Norris, Burrows, and Fieldhouse, *Nuclear Weapons Databook, Volume V*, pp. 420–421; Office of the Historian, Strategic Air Command, *History of SAC Reconnaissance Operations, July 1975–December 1976* (Offutt Air Force Base, Neb.: SAC, 1978), pp. 149–150.

17   Jeffrey T. Richelson, *America's Secret Eyes in Space: The U.S. Keyhole Spy Satellite Program* (New York: Harper & Row, 1990), pp. 360–361; Office of the Historian, Strategic Air Command, *History of SAC Reconnaissance Operations, July 1975–December 1976*, p. 150.

18   Office of the Historian, Strategic Air Command, *History of SAC Reconnaissance Operations, July 1975–December 1976*, pp. 150–151; Jonathan Medalia, *Chinese Nuclear Testing and Warhead Development* (Washington, D.C.: Congressional Research Service, 1997), p. 18.

19   Norris, Burrows, and Fieldhouse, *Nuclear Weapons Databook, Volume V*, p. 421.

20   Vipin Gupta, "Assessment of the Chinese Nuclear Test Site near Lop Nor," *Jane's Intelligence Review*, August 1993, pp. 378–381; "Lop Nur Nuclear Weapons Test Base," June 1998, www.nti.org/db./china/lopnur.htm.

21   John R. Matzko, "Geology of the Chinese Nuclear Test Site near Lop Nor, Xinjiang Uygur Autonomous Region, China," *Engineering Geology*, 36 (1994), pp. 173–181; Gupta, "Assessment of the Chinese Nuclear Test Site near Lop Nor."

22   Lawrence Livermore National Laboratory, "Counterintelligence Briefing," n.d.; Lawrence Livermore National Laboratory, *Welcome: The People's Republic of China Science and Technology Delegation, February 18–19, 1994*, n.d., n.p.

23   Dan Stober and Ian Hoffman, *A Convenient Spy: WEN HO LEE and the Politics of Nuclear Espionage* (New York: Simon & Schuster, 2001), p. 47.

24   Ibid., pp. 47–48.

25   Ibid., pp. 49–50.

26   Ibid., pp. 50–52.

27   Ibid., pp. 52–53; Defense Intelligence Agency, "Biographic Sketch: ZHANG Aiping," July 1979.

28   Stober and Hoffman, *A Convenient Spy*, pp. 54–55.

29   Ibid., pp. 57–58.

30   Dan Stillman, "Inside China's Nuclear Weapons Program," October 10, 2001, http://web.mit.edu/ssp/fall01/stillman.htm; Steve Coll, "The Man Inside China's Bomb Labs," *Washington Post*, May 16, 2001, pp. A1, A14; Stober and Hoffman, *A Convenient Spy*, pp. 86, 88–89.

31   Coll, "The Man Inside China's Bomb Labs"; Stillman, "Inside China's Nuclear Weapons Program."

32   Stillman, "Inside China's Nuclear Weapons Program."

33   Tom Harper, LLNL to Bert Weinstein, LLNL, Subject: Chinese Personnel, August 4, 1993; Coll, "The Man Inside China's Nuclear Weapons Program."

34   Coll, "The Man Inside China's Nuclear Weapons Program"; Stillman, "Inside China's Nuclear Weapons Program"; Stober and Hoffman, *A Convenient Spy*, p. 91.

35   See Coll, "The Man Inside China's Nuclear Weapons Program"; Walter Pincus, "Experts Cite U.S. Intelligence Gains from China Programs," *Washington Post*, October 31, 1999, p. A2; Stober and Hoffman, *A Convenient Spy*, p. 67.

36   Office of Scientific and Weapons Research, CIA, "China: New Nuclear Test," *Science and Weapons Review*, July 31, 1990, p. 1.

37   Office of Scientific and Weapons Research, CIA, "[deleted] Nuclear Tests in 1992," *Science and Weapons Review*, January 23, 1992, p. 6; Sheryl WuDunn, "Disappearance of Atomic Official Stirs Beijing," *New York Times*, January 26, 1992, p. 4.

38   Medalia, *Chinese Nuclear Testing and Warhead Development*, p. 18; Director of

Central Intelligence, "CHINA: Underground Nuclear Test," *National Intelligence Daily*, May 22, 1992, p. 6; Bill Gertz, "Nuclear Blast Was Test for New Chinese ICBM," *Washington Times*, May 23, 1992, p. A3.

39   Bill Gertz, "Chines Nuke Test Releases Gas Cloud," *Washington Times*, June 11, 1992, p. A5.

40   Office of Scientific and Weapons Research, CIA, "CHINA: The 21 May Nuclear Test—A Multiple-Device Experiment?," *Science and Weapons Review*, August 6, 1992, www.foia.cia.gov.

41   Medalia, *Chinese Nuclear Testing and Warhead Development*, p. 18. The specific yields given in open sources for each test, as compiled by the CIA were: September 25, 1992 (15 kt), October 5, 1993 (20–40 kt), June 10, 1994 (10–40 kt), October 7, 1994 (40–150 kt), May 15, 1995 (40–150 kt), August 17, 1995 (20–80 kt), June 8, 1996 (20–80 kt), and July 29, 1966 (1–5 kt). On Chinese tests during this period, see also Norris, Burrows, and Fieldhouse, *Nuclear Weapons Databook, Volume V*, p. 421; "China Stages Nuclear Test, Incurs Global Criticism," *Washington Post*, August 8, 1995, p. A29; Steven Mufson, "China Conducts Nuclear Test While Negotiating Ban," *Washington Post*, June 9, 1996, p. A22.

42   R. Jeffrey Smith, "China Planning a Nuclear Test, U.S. Aides Say," *Washington Post*, September 17, 1993, pp. A1, A31; "China Set for New Nuke Test," *Washington Times*, May 22, 1996, p. A7; Central Intelligence Agency, "China Plans Ambitious Nuclear Test Schedule for 1996," *Proliferation Digest*, May 31, 1996, p. 21.

43   Director of Central Intelligence, "China: Accelerated Nuclear Testing Schedule," *National Intelligence Daily*, February 19, 1993, p. 8; Central Intelligence Agency, "China's Nuclear Test Program Facing Delays," *Proliferation Digest*, October 30, 1994, p. 10.

44   Director of Central Intelligence, "China: Nuclear Test [deleted]," *National Intelligence Daily*, August 29, 1994, p. 10; Director of Central Intelligence, "China Future of Nuclear Testing at Lop Nur," *National Intelligence Daily*, September 10, 1994, p. 10; Central Intelligence Agency, "China's Nuclear Test Program Facing Delays," *Proliferation Digest*, October 30, 1994, p. 10; Director of Central Intelligence, "China: Nuclear Test [deleted]," *National Intelligence Daily*, March 18, 1995, p. 7; Central Intelligence Agency, "China Accelerating Preparations for Next Nuclear Test," *Proliferation Digest*, March 31, 1995, p. 17; Director of Central Intelligence, "China: Nuclear Testing Progressing," *National Intelligence Daily*, April 22, 1996, p. 8. Other *NID or Proliferation Digest* articles that informed readers of tests or future test plans include Director of Central Intelligence, "China: Ambitious Nuclear Test Program," *National Intelligence Daily*, May 24, 1994, p. 12; Director of Central Intelligence, "China: Nuclear Test [deleted]," *National Intelligence Daily*, August 16, 1994, p. 10; Director of Central Intelligence, "40th Nuclear Warhead Test at Lop Nur," *National Intelligence Daily*, October 8, 1994, p. 7; Director of Central Intelligence, "China: Underground Nuclear Test Scheduled," *National Intelligence Daily*, January 18, 1995, p. 6; Director of Central Intelligence, "China: Nuclear Test [deleted]," *National Intelligence Daily*, March 7, 1995, p. 11; Director of Central

Intelligence, "China: Nuclear Test [deleted]," *National Intelligence Daily*, May 26, 1995, p. 6; Director of Central Intelligence, "China: [deleted] Nuclear Test at Lop Nur," *National Intelligence Daily*, June 21, 1995, p. 9; Director of Central Intelligence, "China: More Activity at Lop Nur," *National Intelligence Daily*, July 29, 1995, p. 6; Directorate of Intelligence, CIA, "China's Requirements for Continued Nuclear Testing," *Proliferation Digest*, July 31, 1995, p. 33; Director of Central Intelligence, "China: Nuclear Test Occurs," *National Intelligence Digest*, August 17, 1995, p. 8; Directorate of Intelligence, "China Plans Ambitious Nuclear Test Schedule for 1996," *Proliferation Digest*, May 31, 1996, p. 21; Director of Central Intelligence, "China: Simultaneous Nuclear Tests Conducted," *National Intelligence Daily*, June 8, 1996, p. 5; Director of Central Intelligence, "China: Nuclear Test Conducted at Lop Nur," *National Intelligence Daily*, July 29, 1996, p. 8; Director of Central Intelligence, "China: Nuclear Testing Contingencies," *National Intelligence Daily*, July 30, 1996, p. 10.

45   Central Intelligence Agency and Defense Intelligence Agency, *Chinese Nuclear Testing: Racing a Comprehensive Test Ban*, September 30, 1994, p. 5; Directorate of Intelligence, Central Intelligence Agency, "Chinese Nuclear Event in September," *Proliferation Digest*, November 30, 1995, pp. 13–14.

46   Senators Fred Thompson and Joseph Lieberman, *Department of Energy, FBI, and Department of Justice Handling of the Espionage Investigation into the Compromise of Design Information on the W-88 Warhead* (Washington, D.C.: Senate Committee on Governmental Affairs, 1999).

47   Bill Gertz, "China Continues Nuclear Testing: U.S. May Respond," *Washington Times*, October 24, 1992, p. A3.

48   Stober and Hoffman, *A Convenient Spy*, pp. 103–104; "Watkins Reorganizes DOE's Intelligence Work," *Washington Post*, April 18, 1990, p. A25.

49   Stober and Hoffman, *A Convenient Spy*, pp. 105–106; Notra Trulock, *Code Name KINDRED SPIRIT: Inside the Chinese Nuclear Espionage Scandal* (San Francisco: Encounter, 2003), pp. 16–25, 31, 34.

50   Stober and Hoffman, *A Convenient Spy*, pp. 43, 104; United States Navy Fact File, "*Trident Fleet Ballistic Missile*," www.chino.navy.mil, accessed August 18, 2004.

51   Stober and Hoffman, *A Convenient Spy*, pp. 107–108.

52   Ibid., p. 108; Matthew Purdy, "The Making of a Suspect: The Case of Wen Ho Lee," *New York Times*, February 4, 2001, pp. 1, 20–21.

53   Stober and Hoffman, *A Convenient Spy*, p. 108.

54   Ibid., pp. 108–109.

55   Ibid., pp. 109–110; William J. Broad, "Spies vs. Sweat: The Debate over China's Nuclear Advance," *New York Times*, September 7, 1999, pp. A1, A14–A15.

56   Stober and Hoffman, *A Convenient Spy*, p. 110; Trulock, *Code Name KINDRED SPIRIT*, p. 72.

57   Stober and Hoffman, *A Convenient Spy*, pp. 111–112; Trulock, *Code Name KINDRED SPIRIT*, pp. 72–73.

58   Defense Intelligence Agency, DEB-49-84, "Nuclear Weapons Systems in China,"

April 24, 1984, p. 2.

59   Stober and Hoffman, *A Convenient Spy*, p. 112–114; Trulock, *Code Name KINDRED SPIRIT*, p. 77.

60   Stober and Hoffman, *A Convenient Spy*, p. 115.

61   Ibid., p. 115; David Wise, "Inside the Chinese Spy Mystery," *GQ*, November 1999, pp. 285*ff*.

62   Stober and Hoffman, *A Convenient Spy*, p. 115; Broad, "Spies vs. Sweat."

63   Stober and Hoffman, *A Convenient Spy*, p. 116.

64   Ibid.

65   U.S. Congress, House of Representatives, *Report of the Select Committee on U.S. National Security and Military/Commercial Concerns with the People's Republic of China, Volume I* (Washington, D.C.: U.S. Government Printing Office, 1999), p. 68; James G. Prather, Memorandum to Jack Kemp, Subject: US National Security Impact Analysis: Release of "Redacted" Cox Committee Report, July 8, 1999; M. M. May (ed.), *The Cox Committee Report: An Assessment* (Stanford, Calif.: December 1999); Purdy, "The Making of a Suspect"; Vernon Loeb and Walter Pincus, "Guilty Plea, Release Leave Unresolved Questions in Lee Case," *Washington Post*, September 17, 2000, p. A12; Michael Isikoff, "Into the Sunshine," *Newsweek*, September 25, 2000, pp. 38–40.

66   Central Intelligence Agency, "DCI Tenet Announces Independent Panel," March 15, 1999; "NIC Personnel," www.cia.gov/nic/NIC_personnel.html, accessed August 18, 2004.

67   Central Intelligence Agency, "DCI Statement on Damage Assessment," April 21, 1999; Central Intelligence Agency, "Key Findings: The Intelligence Community Damage Assessment on the Implications of China's Acquisition of US Nuclear Weapons Information on the Development of Future Chinese Weapons," April 21, 1999.

68   Arms Control and Disarmament Agency, *Arms Control and Disarmament Agreements* (Washington, D.C.: U.S. Government Printing Office, 1982), pp. 167–170; Ronald Reagan, National Security Decision Directive 121, *Soviet Noncompliance with Arms Control Agreements*, January 14, 1984.

69   Lynn R. Sykes and Steven Ruggi, "Soviet Nuclear Testing," in Thomas B. Cochran, William M. Arkin, Robert S. Norris, and Jeffrey I. Sands, *Soviet Nuclear Weapons, Volume IV* (New York: Harper & Row, 1989), pp. 332–382 at p. 373; William Leith and David W. Simpson, "Monitoring Underground Nuclear Tests," in Michael Krepon, Peter D. Zimmerman, Leonard S. Spector, and Mary Umberger (eds.), *Commercial Observation Satellites and International Security* (New York: St. Martin's, 1990), pp. 115–124 at p. 117.

70   R. Jeffrey Smith, "Administration at Odds over Soviet Cheating," *Science*, May 10, 1985, pp. 695–696; Reagan, National Security Decision Directive 121, *Soviet Noncompliance with Arms Control Agreements*, p. 3.

71   Smith, "Administration at Odds over Soviet Cheating"; Ronald Reagan, National Security Decision Directive 161, *Soviet Noncompliance with Arms Control Agree-*

ments, February 6, 1985, pp. 2–3; Ronald Reagan, National Security Decision Directive 202, *Soviet Noncompliance with Arms Control Agreements,* December 20, 1985, p. 2.

72   The existence of such a source is indicated by a secret Defense Intelligence Agency report dated June 8, 1981, and titled *HUMINT from Degelen Mountain.* In March 1986 it was reported that satellite reconnaissance (i.e., KH-11) photographs showed that the Soviet Union had been digging holes and tunnels in which nuclear explosives could be placed and had moved monitoring equipment into a test area, indicating that the country might be planning to end the self-imposed moratorium on testing Mikhail Gorbachev had declared on July 30, 1985. Analysts were less than certain that a test was imminent, some suggesting that it might be a hedge against U.S. refusal to refrain from further testing. Soviet testing would not resume until February 26, 1987. See Michael R. Gordon, "Soviet Reported Acting Begin New Atom Tests," *New York Times,* March 18, 1986, pp. A1, A4; Sykes and Ruggi, "Soviet Nuclear Testing," p. 371.

73   Smith, "Administration at Odds over Soviet Cheating"; Michael R. Gordon, "CIA Changes Way It Measures Soviet Atom Tests," *New York Times,* April 2, 1986, pp. A1, A10.

74   Arms Control and Disarmament Agency, *Arms Control and Disarmament Agreements,* pp. 169–170; Richard A. Scribner, Theodore J. Ralston, and William D. Metz, *The Verification Challenge: Problems and Promise of Strategic Nuclear Arms Control Verification* (Boston: Birkhauser, 1985), pp. 80–81; Frode Ringdal, Peter D. Marshall, and Ralph W. Alewine, "Seismic Yield Determination of Soviet Underground Nuclear Explosions at the Shagan River Test Site," *Geophysical Journal International,* 109 (1992), pp. 65–77 at pp. 66–67.

75   Smith, "Administration at Odds over Soviet Cheating"; Jack F. Evernden and Gerald E. Marsh, "Yields of US and Soviet Nuclear Tests," *Physics Today,* August 1987, pp. 37–44.

76   Gordon, "CIA Changes Way It Measures Soviet Atom Tests." The DARPA Seismic Review Panel report was to be issued during the first quarter of 1986, according to Science Applications International Corporation, *Research and Development Studies at the Center for Seismic Studies* (Springfield, Va.: National Technical Information Service, April 28, 1986), p. 71. That report was apparently completed in late August under ARPA Order-5308: Jeffrey W. Given and George R. Mellman, *M(b)-Yield Relations for the Soviet Test Site at Shagan River Inferred from Comparison of Long-Period Measurement of Explosions Source Strength at NTS and Shagan River, Part 2* (Kirkland, Wash.: Sierra Geophysics, August 31, 1986).

77   Gordon, "CIA Changes Way It Measures Soviet Atom Tests."

78   Ibid.; Ronald Reagan, National Security Decision Directive 260, *Soviet Noncompliance with Arms Control Agreements,* February 17, 1987, p. 8.

79   R. Jeffrey Smith, "Soviets to Close Major Site of Underground Atomic Tests," *Washington Post,* March 10, 1990, pp. A1, A19; Bill Gertz, "U.S. Officials Suspect Russia Staged Nuclear Test This Year," *Washington Times,* March 7, 1986, p. A3.

80   Gertz, "U.S. Officials Suspect Russia Staged Nuclear Test This Year."

81   Ibid.

82   Ibid.; Bill Gertz, "Perry Cites Evidence of Russian Nuke Test," *Washington Times*, March 8, 1996, p. A8; R. Jeffrey Smith, "U.S. Asks for Assurance on Test Ban After Activity Detected at Russian Site," *Washington Post*, August 29, 1997, p. A34.

83   Smith, "U.S. Asks for Assurance on Test Ban After Activity Detected at Russian Site"; R. Jeffrey Smith, "U.S. Officials Acted Hastily in Nuclear Test Accusation," *Washington Post*, October 20, 1997, pp. A1, A6–A7; Bill Gertz, "Russia Suspected of Nuclear Testing," *Washington Times*, August 28, 1997, pp. A1, A10; Stephen Lee Myers, "U.S. Suspects Russia Set Off Nuclear Test," *New York Times*, August 29, 1997, p. A7; Lynn R. Sykes, Sergey Yunga, and Tatianna Rautian, *Intraplate Earthquakes and State of Stress in the Former Soviet Union* (New York: Columbia University Press, 1998), p. 1.

84   Smith, "U.S. Officials Acted Hastily in Nuclear Test Accusation."

85   Ibid.; Smith, "U.S. Asks for Assurance on Test Ban After Activity Detected at Russian Site"; Gertz, "Russia Suspected of Nuclear Testing."

86   Smith, "U.S. Officials Acted Hastily in Nuclear Test Accusation."

87   Ibid.

88   Ibid.; Gertz, "Russia Suspected of Nuclear Testing."

89   Smith, "U.S. Officials Acted Hastily in Nuclear Test Accusation"; Gertz, "Russia Suspected of Nuclear Testing"; Smith, "U.S. Asks for Assurance on Test Ban After Activity Detected at Russian Site."

90   Interview with Notra Trulock, Washington, D.C., March 28, 2003; Interview with Spurgeon Keeny, Washington, D.C., February 6, 2003; William J. Broad, "India Blasts Cited by Treaty Critics May Have Failed," *New York Times*, October 10, 1999, p. 8. In 1995, according to Broad, Turnbull briefed industry executives on how a nation might employ large mines or caves for small clandestine blasts, expecting that the surrounding air would soften the bomb's shock waves, reducing them to an undetectable level. Such a "decoupling" technique had been suggested decades earlier, as had the possibility of testing in the vicinity of the far side of the moon.

91   Smith, "U.S. Officials Acted Hastily in Nuclear Test Accusation"; Gertz, "Russia Suspected of Nuclear Testing"; Myers, "U.S. Suspects Russia Set Off Nuclear Test."

92   Smith, "U.S. Officials Acted Hastily in Nuclear Test Accusation." According to Smith, the British government view was echoed by the Norwegian and French governments, as well as independent scientific experts.

93   Smith, "U.S. Officials Acted Hastily in Nuclear Test Accusation." One theory that had been considered, but largely dismissed, involved one of the submarine reactors reaching critical and exploding.

94   Bill Gertz, "CIA Panel Gives Split View on Arctic Seismic Rumbling," *Washington Times*, November 4, 1997, p. A6; Smith, "U.S. Officials Acted Hastily in Nuclear Test Accusation"; "Roger L. Hagengruber," http://t8web.lanl.gov, accessed August 9, 2004; Richard Kerr, Roger Hagengruber, Eugene Herrin, and Sidney Drell, "Review of Activity and Events Related to Russian Nuclear Test Site on Novaya Zemlya," October 24, 1997.

95   Smith, "U.S. Officials Acted Hastily in Nuclear Test Accusation."

96   Kerr, Hagengruber, Herrin, and Drell, "Review of Activity and Events Related to Russian Nuclear Test Site on Novaya Zemlya."

97   Ibid.

98   George J. Tenet, Memorandum for: [Deleted], Subject: [Deleted] Results of Special Panel Meeting on Novaya Zemlya Test Site," October 28, 1997; Smith, "U.S. Officials Acted Hastily in Nuclear Test Association"; R. Jeffrey Smith, "U.S. Formally Drops Claim of Possible Nuclear Blast," *Washington Post*, November 4, 1997, p. A2; Myers, "U.S. Suspects Russia Set Off Nuclear Test."

99   Smith, "U.S. Officials Acted Hastily in Nuclear Test Accusation." Several "decision briefs" published by the Center for Security Policy challenge the view that the seismic events were not the result of Russian nuclear tests in violation of the comprehensive test ban treaty. See "Wake-Up Call from Novaya Zemlya: Zero-Yield Nuclear Test Ban Is Unverifiable, Russians Will Cheat, U.S. Will Suffer" (No. 97-D 119), "Nuclear Spin-Control: Clinton See-No-Evil Response to Apparent Russian Test Offers Bitter Foretaste of C.T.B." (No. 97-D 156), and "Sorry, Calling the Russian Seismic Event an 'Unresolved Mystery' *Reinforces*, Rather Than Eliminates C.T.B. Criticisms" (No. 97-D 166), all available at www.centerforsecuritypolicy.org.

100   Bill Gertz, "Russia Preparing Blast in Arctic, Satellite Shows," *Washington Times*, September 24, 1998, pp. A1, A6; "Pentagon Says It's Unsure if Russians Are Planning Arctic Nuclear Explosion," *Washington Times*, September 25, 1998, p. A13.

101   "Russia Confirms It Held 5 Nuclear Tests in Arctic," *Washington Times*, December 25, 1998, p. A12.

CHAPTER 11: POKHRAN SURPRISE

1   Private information.

2   Raj Chengappa, *Weapons of Peace: The Secret Story of India's Quest to Be a Nuclear Power* (New Delhi: Harper Collins India, 2000), pp. 219–221.

3   Ibid., p. 221.

4   Ibid., pp. 246–247.

5   Ibid., p. 247.

6   Ibid., pp. 256–257. The activity at the test site was also noted by the Indian press. The May 9–15 edition of *Sunday Magazine* carried an article by Shubhabrata Bhattacharya titled "Another Nuclear Blast at Pokhran?" (pp. 12–15), which noted that "for the past one year, army units posted in the vicinity of Pokhran have been engaged in activities similar to the ones carried out before the 1974 blast." It went on to report that villagers at Loharki claimed that the Indian army had cordoned off an area between the 1974 test site of Malka and Khelotai and that another detonation appeared to be scheduled. The report was probably picked up by the CIA's Foreign Broadcast Information Service, although it is not clear how much intelligence it would have added to what was collected by more clandestine means. See Vipin Gupta and Frank Pabian, "Investigating the Allegations of Indian Nuclear Test

Preparations in the Rajasthan Desert," *Science & Global Security*, 6 (1996), pp. 101–189 at pp. 110–111.

7   Chengappa, *Weapons of Peace*, p. 257. Perkovich dates the initial approval of the test as sometime in late 1982 or early 1983. See George Perkovich, *India's Nuclear Bomb: The Impact on Global Proliferation* (Berkeley: University of California Press, 1999), pp. 242–243.

8   Central Intelligence Agency, *India's Nuclear Program—Energy and Weapons*, July 1982, p. 3; National Security Agency, *India's Heavy Water Shortages*, October 1982.

9   "India Reportedly Gets Illegal Heavy Water," *Washington Times*, November 2, 1988, p. A9; Gary Milhollin, "Dateline New Delhi: India's Nuclear Cover-Up," *Foreign Policy*, 64 (Fall 1996), pp. 161–175; David B. Ottaway, "Signs Found India Building an H-Bomb," *Washington Post*, May 19, 1989, pp. A29–A30.

10   Richard M. Weintraub, "India and Pakistan Hold Maneuvers at Sensitive Frontier," *Washington Post*, January 25, 1987, p. A24; Central Intelligence Agency, *India: BJP Flexing Military Muscle with Large Exercises*, October 30, 1998, p. 8.

11   Seymour Hersh, "On the Nuclear Edge," *New Yorker*, March 29, 1993, pp. 56–73; Dennis Kux, *The United States and Pakistan, 1947–2000: Disenchanted Allies* (Washington, D.C.: Woodrow Wilson Center, 2001), p. 306; Mark Urban, *UK Eyes Alpha: The Inside Story of British Intelligence* (London: Faber and Faber, 1996), p. 148; Perkovich, *India's Nuclear Bomb*, pp. 306–313; Devin T. Hagerty, "Nuclear Deterrence in South Asia," *International Security*, 20, 3 (Winter 1995/1996), pp. 79–114.

12   David Albright, "India and Pakistan's Nuclear Arms Race: Out of the Closet but Not in the Street," *Arms Control Today*, June 1993, pp. 12–16; David Albright and Mark Hibbs, "India's Silent Bomb," *Bulletin of the Atomic Scientists*, September 1992, pp. 27–31; Office of the Secretary of Defense, *Proliferation: Threat and Response* (Washington, D.C.: U.S. Government Printing Office, 1996), pp. 38–41; Bill Gertz, *Betrayal: How the Clinton Administration Undermined American Security* (Washington, D.C.: Regnery, 1999), pp. 158–165.

13   Chengappa, *Weapons of Peace*, p. 391; Perkovich, *India's Nuclear Bomb*, pp. 333, 364–365; A. P. J. Kalam with Arun Tawari, *Wings of Fire: An Autobiography* (Hyderabad, India: Universities Press [India], 1999).

14   Chengappa, *Weapons of Peace*, pp. 391–392.

15   Ibid., p. 394.

16   George Wilson, "N-PIC Technicians Ferret Out Secrets Behind Closed Windows," *Los Angeles Times*, January 12, 1975, p. 25; Curtis Peebles, "Satellite Photographic Interpretation," *Spaceflight*, October 1982, pp. 161–163; Jeffrey T. Richelson, *The Wizards of Langley: Inside the CIA's Directorate of Science and Technology* (Boulder, Colo.: Westview, 2001), p. 229.

17   Richelson, *The Wizards of Langley*, pp. 247–249.

18   Strobe Talbott, *Engaging India: Diplomacy, Democracy, and the Bomb* (Washington, D.C.: Brookings, 2004), p. 37.

19   Sec State Wash DC, Subject: INTSUM: India: Nuclear Test Unlikely, January 24, 1996; Tim Weiner, "U.S. Suspects India Prepares for Nuclear Test," *New York Times*,

December 15, 1995, p. A6; R. Jeffrey Smith, "Possible Nuclear Arms Test by India Concerns U.S.," *Washington Post*, December 16, 1995, p. A17; John F. Burns, "India Denies Atom-Test Plan but Then Turns Ambiguous," *New York Times*, December 16, 1995, p. 4.

20   Weiner, "U.S. Suspects India Prepares for Nuclear Test"; Sec State Wash DC, Subject: INTSUM: INDO/US: Rocky Road Ahead, December 13, 1995.

21   James Risen and Tim Weiner, "U.S. May Have Helped India Hide Its Nuclear Activity," *New York Times*, May 25, 1998, p. A3; Perkovich, *India's Nuclear Bomb*, pp. 368, 370; Evan Thomas, John Barry, and Melinda Liu, "Ground Zero," *Newsweek*, May 25, 1998, pp. 28–32A; Talbott, *Engaging India*, p. 37. For a discussion of the factors in Rao's decision not to go ahead with the test, see Perkovich, p. 370.

22   Weiner, "U.S. Suspects India Prepares for Nuclear Test"; Private information; Gupta and Fabian, "Investigating the Allegations of Indian Nuclear Test Preparations in the Rajasthan Desert," pp. 113–114, 167–171.

23   Perkovich, *India's Nuclear Bomb*, p. 374.

24   Ibid., pp. 373–374; Chengappa, *Weapons of Peace*, p. 37.

25   Perkovich, *India's Nuclear Bomb*, p. 374. Perkovich bases his assertion about a bomb having been placed in a shaft on interviews with unidentified U.S. and Indian officials (p. 565 n. 128). Chengappa claims that according to the bomb team, the devices were never transported to Pokhran during the period in question. See Chengappa, *Weapons of Peace*, p. 395.

26   Perkovich, *India's Nuclear Bomb*, pp. 374–375, 407, 409.

27   Central Intelligence Agency, *India: BJP Flexing Muscles, but How Far Will It Go?*, May 29, 1998, p. 13; Stephen F. Burgess, *India's Emerging Security Strategy, Missile Defense, and Arms Control* (USAF Academy, Colo.: Institute for National Security Studies, 2004), p. 18.

28   Manoj Joshi, "Nuclear Shock Wave," *India Today International*, May 25, 1998, pp. 12–20 at pp. 12–14; Raj Chengappa, "The Bomb Makers," *India Today International*, June 22, 1998, pp. 26–32 at p. 31; Chengappa, *Weapons of Peace*, pp. 50–51, 414; Perkovich, *India's Nuclear Bomb*, p. 408. Perkovich (p. 412) suggests that initial authorization for the weaponeers to proceed may have come shortly after the March 28 vote of confidence.

29   Chengappa, "The Bomb Makers," p. 31; Chengappa, *Weapons of Peace*, pp. 20, 418, 420–421.

30   Joshi, "Nuclear Shock Wave," p. 13; Chengappa, *Weapons of Peace*, p. 427.

31   Chengappa, "The Bomb Makers," p. 26; Chengappa, *Weapons of Peace*, pp. 6, 20.

32   Joshi, "Nuclear Shock Wave," p. 12; Chengappa, *Weapons of Peace*, pp. 4–5.

33   Robert Windrem, "India Nuke Timeline," e-mail to author, July 17, 2000; "Indian Government Statement on Nuclear Tests," May 11, 1998, www.atomicarchive.com; "Indian Government Statement on Nuclear Tests," May 13, 1998, www.atomic archive.com

34   Walter Pincus, "2 New Tests Again Catch U.S. Intelligence off Guard," *Washington Post*, May 14, 1998, p. A28.

35   INR, *Secretary's Morning Summary for 5/13/98*, May 13, 1998; State RCI to White House, May 14, 1998.

36   Walter Pincus, "CIA Detects Preparations for Blast in Pakistan," *Washington Post*, May 15, 1998, p. A33; Private information.

37   Interview with former senior intelligence official.

38   INR, *Secretary's Morning Summary for 5/19/98*, May 19, 1998; INR, *Secretary's Morning Summary for 5/27/98*, May 27, 1998; Bill Gertz, "Pakistan Close to Nuclear Test Blast," *Washington Times*, May 27, 1998, pp. A1, A9; John F. Burns, "Pakistan, Answering India, Carries Out Nuclear Tests, Clinton's Appeal Rejected," *New York Times*, May 29, 1998, pp. A1, A8.

39   Talbott, *Engaging India*, p. 70.

40   "Pakistani Government Statement on Nuclear Tests," May 29, 1998, www.atomic archive.com; Burns, "Pakistan, Answering India, Carries Out Nuclear Tests"; John Ward Anderson and Kamran Khan, "Pakistan Again Explodes Bomb," *Washington Post*, May 31, 1998, pp. A1, A23; INR, *Secretary's Morning Summary for 5/31/98*, May 31, 1998.

41   "Press Conference," May 17, 1998, www.fas.org/news/india/1998/05/980500-conf.htm; Perkovich, *India's Nuclear Bomb*, p. 425.

42   John F. Burns, "India Detonated a Hydrogen Bomb, Experts Confirm," *New York Times*, May 18, 1998, pp. A1, A8.

43   Perkovich, *India's Nuclear Bomb*, p. 425.

44   "Press Conference."

45   Talbott, *Engaging India*, p. 71.

46   Terry C. Wallace, "The May 1998 India and Pakistan Nuclear Tests," *Seismological Research Letters*, 69, 5 (September/October 1998), pp. 386–391 at p. 389.

47   William B. Scott, "Upkeep of Nuclear Intelligence Infrastructure Questioned," *Aviation Week & Space Technology*, February 21, 2000, p. 122; "USAF Aircraft Monitors Fallout Nuclear Tests," *Jane's Defence Weekly*, May 20, 1998, p. 5; Air Combat Command, *Air Combat Command History, 1999* (Langley Air Force Base, Va.: ACC, n.d.), p. 177. The Air Staff, "due to insufficient funding," terminated the WC-135B air-sampling mission on October 1, 1993, with three of the WC-135B aircraft becoming OC-135B Open Skies (arms control verification) aircraft. Another aircraft assigned to Open Skies retained the capability to conduct air-sampling missions, and was apparently targeted on Chinese tests in 1994. See Lt. Col. Joseph E. Spivey and Lance L. Smith, Memorandum to COMACC, Subject: Air Sampling Capability, May 26, 1994; Lt. Col. James P. Brennan Jr. and Maj. Gen. Lee A. Downer, Memorandum to COMACC, Subject: Air Sampling Collection, October 21, 1994.

48   Curtis Suplee, "Yield Key to Mystery of Blasts," *Washington Post*, May 14, 1998, p. A28; Peter D. Zimmerman, "India's Testing: Something Doesn't Fit," *Los Angeles Times*, May 22, 1998, p. B9.

49   Zimmerman, "India's Testing"; William R. Walter, Arthur J. Rodgers, Kevin Mayeda, Stephen C. Myers, Michael Pasyanos, and Marvin Denny, *Preliminary Regional Seis-*

mic Analysis of Nuclear Explosions and Earthquakes in Southwest Asia, UCRL-JC-130745, n.d.; Wallace, "The May 1998 India and Pakistan Nuclear Tests," p. 386.

50   Suplee, "Yield Key to Mystery of Blasts"; Zimmerman, "India's Testing"; Burns, "India Detonated a Hydrogen Bomb, Experts Say"; Perkovich, *India's Nuclear Bomb*, p. 427. In later interviews Chidambaram revised his statement, claiming that the primary was a boosted-fission device (Perkovich, p. 427).

51   William J. Broad, "Experts Greet India's H-Bomb with Suspicion," *New York Times*, May 19, 1998, pp. C1, C5; Eliot Marshall, "Did Test Ban Watchdog Fail to Bark," *Science*, June 26, 1998, pp. 2038–2040.

52   Broad, "Experts Greet India's H-Bomb with Suspicion."

53   Jack F. Evernden, "Estimation of Yields of Underground Explosions with Emphasis on Recent Indian and Pakistani Explosions," *Physics and Society*, 27, 4 (October 1998), pp. 10–11; Wallace, "The May 1998 India and Pakistan Nuclear Tests"; S. K. Sikka, Falguni Roy, G. J. Nair, V. G. Kolvankar, and Anil Kakodkar, "Update on Yield of May 11–13, 1998 Nuclear Detonations at Pokhran," *BARC Newsletter*, 178 (November 1998); S.K. Sikka, G.J. Nair, Falguni Roy, Anil Kakodkar and R. Chidambaram, "The Recent Indian Nuclear Tests," A Seismic Overview," *Current Science*, 79, 9 (November 10, 2000), pp. 1359–1366 at p. 486; Pallava Bagla, "Size of Indian Blasts Still Disputed," *Science*, September 25, 1998, p. 1939; Carey Sublette, "What Are the Real Yields of India's Test?" November 8, 2001, http://nuclear weaponarchive.org.

      Evernden, relying on the magnitude of surface rather than body waves, concluded that the Indian estimates were largely correct. Sikka and colleagues argued in the November 1998 *BARC Newsletter* that Wallace's assumption that the geology of the Pokhran test site is similar to that of the Soviet Shagan River site is wrong and produced faulty conclusions. In the November 2000 *Current Science* article Sikka and coauthors claimed that the yield of the May 11, 1998, tests had been underestimated due to the "use of data from simultaneous spatially separated explosions without incorporating necessary corrections for source geometry and to the ad hoc assumptions used in the estimation of the yield from body waves."

      According to Perkovich, in private Chidambaram asserted that "the Americans" and other outsiders did not understand the characteristics of the geological formations at the test site and therefore had little basis for their evaluation of the seismic data. He also said that multiple accelerometers had been placed around each test shaft and produced reliable seismic data. At the same time, Perkovich reports that a September 1998 paper in the Indian journal *Current Science* defending the estimates was based on the assumption that the official Indian claim of a 13-kiloton yield for the 1974 blast was accurate. Based on that assumption the authors could compare the seismic signal from the 1998 tests to the 1974 test and estimate the yield. However, two former nuclear establishment leaders had acknowledged that the actual 1974 yield had been 8 kilotons. See Perkovich, *India's Nuclear Bomb*, pp. 426–427.

54   Mark Hibbs, "India May Test Again Because H-Bomb Failed, U.S. Believes," *Nucleonics Week*, November 26, 1998.

55   William J. Broad, "Explosion Is Detected by U.S. Scientists," *New York Times*, May 29, 1998, p. A10.

56   R. Jeffrey Smith, "Analysts Skeptical of Pakistan's Claims," *Washington Post*, May 29, 1998, p. A33; Perkovich, *India's Nuclear Bomb*, p. 433.

57   William J. Broad, "Experts Say Pakistan Test Was Either Small or Failure," *New York Times*, May 31, 1998, p. 8; INR, *Secretary's Morning Summary for 5/31/98*, May 31, 1998.

58   Broad, "Experts Say Pakistan Test Was Either Small or Failure"; Dana Priest, "U.S. Labs at Odds on Whether Pakistani Blast Used Plutonium," *Washington Post*, January 17, 1999, p. A2.

59   Mark Hibbs, "U.S. Now Believes Pakistan to Use Khushab Plutonium in Bomb Program," July 16, 1988, www.nyu.edu/globalbeat/nucwatch.

60   Priest, "U.S. Labs at Odds on Whether Pakistani Blast Used Plutonium"; Notra Trulock, *Code Name* KINDRED SPIRIT: *Inside the Chinese Nuclear Espionage Scandal* (San Francisco: Encounter, 2003), p. 26; Interview with David Kay, Arlington, Va., April 28, 2003. Kay also noted that while the rivalry did have value in producing different viewpoints, it also eased foreign denial and deception because policymakers could shop for intelligence. Kay found himself depressed by the lack of discipline—that no one was forcing different groups to focus on their differences. The British, who had knowledge of the disputes, would make "biting references" to the differences, according to Kay. There was "no adult leadership," he said.

61   Priest, "U.S. Labs at Odds on Whether Pakistani Blast Used Plutonium."

62   Sec State Wash DC, Subject: INR Viewpoint: Eurasian Foreign Policy Update, May 21, 1998.

63   R. Jeffrey Smith, "CIA Missed Signs of India's Tests, U.S. Officials Say," *Washington Post*, May 13, 1998, p. A1; Weiner, "U.S. May Have Helped India Hide Its Nuclear Activity"; Robin Wright, "U.S. Intelligence Failed to Warn of India's Atom Tests," *Los Angeles Times*, May 13, 1998, pp. A1, A4; Tim Weiner, "U.S. Blundered on Intelligence, Officials Admit," *New York Times*, May 13, 1998, pp. A1, A12; Interview with former senior intelligence official.

64   "Statement of R. James Woolsey," in U.S. Congress, Senate Committee on Foreign Relations, *Crisis in South Asia: India's Nuclear Tests; Pakistan's Nuclear Tests; India and Pakistan: What Next?* (Washington, D.C.: U.S. Government Printing Office, 1998), p. 32.

65   Jeffrey T. Richelson, *The U.S. Intelligence Community*, 4th ed. (Boulder, Colo.: Westview, 1999), pp. 40, 42–47.

66   Risen and Weiner, "U.S. May Have Helped India Hide Its Nuclear Activity"; Thomas, Barry, and Liu, "Ground Zero," p. 29; Smith, "CIA Missed Signs of India's Tests, U.S. Officials Say."

67   Risen and Weiner, "U.S. May Have Helped India Hide Its Nuclear Activity"; "Indian Experts Ready to Make Nuclear Bombs," *Washington Times*, March 7, 1998, p. A7; Weiner, "U.S. Blundered on Intelligence, Officials Admit"; Interview with Leonard Weiss, Silver Spring, Md., March 19, 2003.

68   Talbott, *Engaging India*, p. 50.

69   Risen and Weiner, "U.S. May Have Helped India Hide Its Nuclear Activity"; Talbott, *Engaging India*, p. 50.

70   Richard A. Best, *U.S. Intelligence and India's Nuclear Tests: Lessons Learned* (Washington, D.C.: Congressional Research Service, August 11, 1998), p. 2; Risen and Weiner, "U.S. May Have Helped India Hide Its Nuclear Activity."

71   Best, *U.S. Intelligence and India's Nuclear Tests*, p. 2; Risen and Weiner, "U.S. May Have Helped India Hide Its Nuclear Activity"; Smith, "CIA Missed Signs of India's Tests, U.S. Officials Say" John Diamond, "India Able to Evade Satellites," Associated Press, May 17, 1998; Chengappa, *Weapons of Peace*, pp. 404, 426.

72   Chengappa, *Weapons of Peace*, p. 426.

73   Ibid., pp. 426–427.

74   Risen and Weiner, "U.S. May Have Helped India Hide Its Nuclear Activity"; The Commission on the Intelligence Capabilities of the United States Regarding Weapons of Mass Destruction, *Report to the President & the United States*, (Washington, DC: U.S. Government Printing Office 2005), p. 355.

75   Risen and Weiner, "U.S. May Have Helped India Hide Its Nuclear Activity"; Patrick Radden Keefe, *Chatter: Dispatches from the Secret World of Global Eavesdropping* (New York: Random House, 2005), p. 214; Thomas, Barry, and Liu, "Ground Zero." According to Thomas, Barry, and Liu, India may have been able to penetrate the CIA. They report that in 1996 a naturalized Indian employee was fired for mishandling classified documents and possible espionage. One source told them that the fired employee "got everything there was on India, and there was a real fear that he went to the Indians with it" (p. 30).

76   Risen and Weiner, "U.S. May Have Helped India Hide Its Nuclear Activity"; Seymour Hersh, "The Intelligence Gap," *New Yorker*, December 6, 1999, pp. 58–77 at p. 58.

77   "Jeremiah News Conference," June 2, 1998, p. 1, www.cia.gov.

78   Ibid.

79   Ibid., p. 2; CIA, "Recommendations of the Jeremiah Report (Unclassified)," n.d..

80   "Jeremiah News Conference," p. 2; CIA, "Recommendations of the Jeremiah Report."

81   "Jeremiah News Conference," pp. 4, 8.

82   "Press Statement by the Director of Central Intelligence, George J. Tenet, on the Release of the Jeremiah Report," June 2, 1998.

CHAPTER 12: INSPECTORS AND SPIES

1   Gen. Sir Peter de la Billiere, *Storm Command: A Personal Account of the Gulf War* (New York: HarperCollins, 1993), pp. 314–315; Rick Atkinson, *Crusade: The Untold Story of the Persian Gulf War* (Boston: Houghton Mifflin, 1993), pp. 5–6, 8; Gen. H. Norman Schwarzkopf, *It Doesn't Take a Hero* (New York: Ballantine, 1993), p. 559.

2   Schwarzkopf, *It Doesn't Take a Hero*, pp. 555.

3   United Nations, *The United Nations and the Iraq-Kuwait Conflict, 1990–1996* (New

York: United Nations, 1996), pp. 193–198 at p. 195; U.S. News & World Report, *Triumph Without Victory: The Unreported History of the Persian Gulf War* (New York: Times Books, 1992), pp. 432–433, 437.

4   United Nations, *The United Nations and the Iraq-Kuwait Conflict, 1990–1996*, p. 196.

5   Ibid.

6   Tim Trevan, *Saddam's Secrets: The Hunt for Iraq's Hidden Weapons* (London: HarperCollins, 1999), pp. 46–49.

7   Interview with David Kay, Arlington, Va., April 28, 2003; David A. Kay, "Denial and Deception Practices of WMD Proliferators: Iraq and Beyond," *Washington Quarterly*, 18, 1 (Winter 1995), pp. 85–105 at p. 94; Trevan, *Saddam's Secrets*, p. 49. A variety of other reasons for the inspectors' failure to recognize what was going on at Tuwaitha are discussed in Kay's article, pp. 95–98.

8   Trevan, *Saddam's Secrets*, pp. 60–61.

9   "National Monitoring Directorate," www.globalsecurity.org/wmd/world/iraq/nmd.htm, accessed September 8, 2004; Ibrahim al-Marsahi, "How Iraq Conceals and Obtains Its Weapons of Mass Destruction," *Middle East Review of International Affairs*, 7, 1 (March 2003), pp. 51–65 at pp. 52, 55–56; Ibrahim al-Marashi, "Iraq's Security and Intelligence Network: A Guide and Analysis," *Middle East Review of International Affairs*, 6, 3 (September 2002), pp. 1–13.

10   Trevan, *Saddam's Secrets*, p. 396; Kay, "Denial and Deception Practices of WMD Proliferators," pp. 86, 89.

11   Kay interview; Interview with Robert Gallucci, Washington, D.C., June 22, 2004.

12   George J. Church, "How to Hide an A-Bomb," *Time*, July 8, 1991, p. 40; International Atomic Energy Agency, *Ongoing Monitoring and Verification in Iraq*, February 1996, slide 14; D. L. Dononhue and R. Zeisler, "Behind the Scenes: Scientific Analysis of Samples from Nuclear Inspections in Iraq," *IAEA Bulletin*, 34, 1 (1992), pp. 25–32.

13   Trevan, *Saddam's Secrets*, pp. 62–63, 396; United Nations, *The United Nations and the Iraq-Kuwait Conflict, 1990–1996*, p. 354; Stephen J. Hedges and Peter Cary, "Saddam's Secret Bomb," *U.S. News & World Report*, November 25, 1991, pp. 34–42 at p. 36; Kay, "Denial and Deception Practices of WMD Proliferators," p. 98.

14   Hedges and Cary, "Saddam's Secret Bomb," p. 36; David Albright, "Masters of Deception," *Bulletin of the Atomic Scientists*, May/June 1998, pp. 44–50 at p. 46.

15   Trevan, *Saddam's Secrets*, p. 63.

16   Ibid., p. 65; "David Kay, Senior Research Fellow," www.potomacinstitute.org, accessed September 9, 2004; Hedges and Cary, "Saddam's Secret Bomb," p. 37; Douglas Jehl, "For Leader of Arms Hunt, Report Is a Test of Faith," *New York Times*, October 3, 2003, p. A12; Mahdi Obeidi and Kurt Pitzer, *The Bomb in My Garden: The Secrets of Saddam's Nuclear Mastermind* (New York: Wiley, 2004), p. 145; Leslie Thorne, "IAEA Nuclear Inspections in Iraq," *IAEA Bulletin*, 34, 1 (1992), pp. 16–24 at p. 20.

17   Trevan, *Saddam's Secrets*, pp. 67–68, 72, 98; Kay interview.

18   Hedges and Cary, "Saddam's Secret Bomb," pp. 36–37; Church, "How to Hide an

A-Bomb"; Paul Lewis, "U.S. Shows Photos to Argue Iraq Hides Nuclear Material," *New York Times*, June 27, 1991, p. A12.

19   Church, "How to Hide an A-Bomb"; Lewis, "U.S. Shows Photos to Argue Iraq Hides Nuclear Material"; Hedges and Cary, "Saddam's Secret Bomb," p. 37; "Iraq's Shell Game," *Newsweek*, July 8, 1991, pp. 16–17.

20   Lewis, "U.S. Shows Photos to Argue Iraq Hides Nuclear Material."

21   Trevan, *Saddam's Secrets*, p. 65; Church, "How to Hide an A-Bomb."

22   Trevan, *Saddam's Secrets*, pp. 66–67; Robert Gallucci, "Reflections on Establishing and Implementing the Post Gulf-War Inspections of Iraq's Weapons of Mass Destruction Programs," address to the Institute of Science and International Security Conference on "Understanding the Lessons of Nuclear Monitoring in Iraq: A Ten Year Review," June 14–15, 2001, p. 8, at www.isis-online.org.

23   Trevan, *Saddam's Secrets*, p. 66.

24   Ibid., pp. 66–67.

25   Ibid., pp. 67–68.

26   S/22788, Note by the Secretary General, July 15, 1991 w/enclosure: International Atomic Energy Agency, *Consolidated Report on the First Two IAEA Inspections under Security Council Resolution 687 (1991) of Iraqi Nuclear Capabilities*, July 11, 1991, pp. 5–7, 11–13.

27   Trevan, *Saddam's Secrets*, pp. 68–78.

28   Hedges and Cary, "Saddam's Secret Bomb," p. 38.

29   Ibid.

30   Trevan, *Saddam's Secrets*, p. 79.

31   United Nations, *The United Nations and the Iraq-Kuwait Conflict, 1990–1996*, p. 354; Trevan, *Saddam's Secrets*, p. 79.

32   Trevan, *Saddam's Secrets*, p. 81.

33   Ibid., pp. 79, 81.

34   Ibid., pp. 81–82.

35   Ibid., p. 82.

36   S/22986, Note by the Secretary General, August 28, 1991 w/enclosure: International Atomic Energy Agency, *Report on the Fourth IAEA On-Site Inspection in Iraq Under Security Council Resolution 687 (1991), 27 July–10 August 1991*, pp. 4, 10–12, 14; Kay, "Denial and Deception Practices of WMD Proliferators," p. 98.

37   S/22986, Note by the Secretary General, August 28, 1991 w/enclosure: International Atomic Energy Agency, *Report on the Fourth IAEA On-Site Inspection in Iraq Under Security Council Resolution 687 (1991), 27 July–10 August 1991*, p. 13.

38   Ibid., p. 14.

39   Trevan, *Saddam's Secrets*, p. 85; U.S. News & World Report, *Triumph Without Victory*, pp. 445–448.

40   Trevan, *Saddam's Secrets*, pp. 87–89; International Atomic Energy Agency, *Ongoing Monitoring and Verification of Iraq*, slides 7, 9.

41   Trevan, *Saddam's Secrets*, p. 89.

42   Ibid., pp. 101–102.

43   Ibid., p. 103; "Saddam's Nuclear Secrets," *Newsweek*, October 7, 1991, pp. 28–35 at p. 28.

44   Trevan, *Saddam's Secrets*, p. 103. Gallucci recalls there being two separate sets of radios, with one being secure against Iraqi eavesdropping, and that a "we found it" message was transmitted via the secure radio system. Gallucci, "Reflections on Establishing and Implementing the Post Gulf-War Inspections of Iraq's Weapons of Mass Destruction Programs," p. 10.

45   Trevan, *Saddam's Secrets*, p. 104.

46   Ibid.

47   Ibid., p. 105.

48   "Saddam's Nuclear Secrets," p. 28; Trevan, *Saddam's Secrets*, pp. 108–109; "Report: U.S. Placed Spies on U.N. teams," January 8, 1999, www.msnbc.com.

49   Trevan, *Saddam's Secrets*, pp. 108–109.

50   Ibid., p. 109.

51   S/23122, Note by the Secretary General, October 8, 1991 w/enclosure: International Atomic Energy Agency, *First Report on the Sixth IAEA On-Site Inspection in Iraq under Security Council Resolution 687 (1991), 22–30 September 1991*, October 8, 1991, pp. 3, 10–27.

52   International Atomic Energy Agency, *First Report on the Sixth IAEA On-Site Inspection in Iraq Under Security Council Resolution 687 (1991), 22–30 September 1991*, pp. 4, 6; Trevan, *Saddam's Secrets*, p. 110; Anthony Fainberg, *Strengthening IAEA Safeguards: Lessons from Iraq* (Stanford: Center for International Security and Arms Control, Stanford University, 1993), p. 17.

53   Trevan, *Saddam's Secrets*, pp. 400, 403–405.

54   Paul Lewis, "U.N. Aides Discover Arms Concealed by Iraq," *New York Times*, October 8, 1991, pp. A1, A9.

55   William E. Burrows and Robert Windrem, *Critical Mass: The Dangerous Race for Superweapons in a Fragmenting World* (New York: Simon & Schuster, 1994), p. 54.

56   Ibid.; Bill Gertz, "Saddam Close to Nuclear Weapon," *Washington Times*, June 11, 1991, pp. A1, A9; Paul Lewis, "U.N. Aides Say Iraq May Be Concealing Nuclear Material," *New York Times*, June 15, 1991, pp. 1, 4; "Iraq's Shell Game," *Newsweek*, July 8, 1991, pp. 16–17; R. Jeffrey Smith, "Iraq's Secret A-Arms Effort: Grim Lesson to the World," *Washington Post*, August 11, 1991, pp. C1, C4.

57   Burrows and Windrem, *Critical Mass*, p. 55; "Iraq's Shell Game."

58   Michael Wines, "U.S. Is Building Up a Picture of Vast Iraqi Atom Program," *New York Times*, September 27, 1991, p. A8.

59   Ibid.; "Written statements submitted by the International Atomic Energy Agency (IAEA) at the hearings jointly held by three subcommittees of the Committee of Foreign Affairs of the 103rd Congress of the United States—Washington 29 June 1993," in U.S. Congress, House Committee on Foreign Affairs, *Iraq's Nuclear Weapons Capability and IAEA Inspections in Iraq* (Washington, D.C.: U.S. Government Printing Office, 1993), pp. 146–147.

60   Wines, "U.S. Is Building Up a Picture of Vast Iraqi Atom Program."

61   "Written statements submitted by the International Atomic Energy Agency (IAEA) at the hearings jointly held by three subcommittees of the Committee of Foreign Affairs of the 103rd Congress of the United States—Washington 29 June 1993," p. 155; Obeidi and Pitzer, *The Bomb in My Garden*, pp. 147–149; Albright, "Masters of Deception," p. 48.

62   Eric Schmitt, "U.S. Says It Missed 2 A-Plants in Iraq," *New York Times*, October 11, 1991, p. A6; R. Jeffrey Smith and Glenn Frankel, "Saddam's Nuclear-Weapons Dream: A Lingering Nightmare," *Washington Post*, October 13, 1991, pp. A1, A44–A45; Paul Lewis, "U.N. Aides Discover Arms Center Concealed by Iraq," *New York Times*, October 8, 1991, pp. A1, A9.

63   Wines, "U.S. Is Building Up a Picture of Vast Iraqi Atom Program"; Elaine Sciolino, "Iraq's Nuclear Program Shows the Holes in U.S. Intelligence," *New York Times*, October 20, 1991, p. E5; Paul Lewis, "U.N. Experts Now Say Baghdad Was Far from Making an A-Bomb Before Gulf War," *New York Times*, May 20, 1992, p. A6.

64   Paul Lewis, "U.N. Officials Seek Mastermind in Charge of Iraq's Nuclear Effort," *New York Times*, October 1, 1991, pp. A11; S/23122, Note by the Secretary-General, October 8, 1991, w/att: *First Report on the Sixth IAEA On-Site Inspection in Iraq Under Security Council Resolution 687 (1991), 22–30 September 1991*, p. 6.

65   S/23644, Note by the Secretary General, February 26, 1992, w/att: *Report of the Tenth IAEA On-Site Inspection in Iraq Under Security Council Resolution 687 (1991), 5–13 February 1992*, p. 3; Fainberg, *Strengthening IAEA Safeguards*, p. 17; "Written statements submitted by the International Atomic Energy Agency (IAEA) at the hearings jointly held by three subcommittees of the Committee of Foreign Affairs of the 103rd Congress of the United States—Washington 29 June 1993," pp. 157–158.

66   Sciolino, "Iraq's Nuclear Program Shows the Holes in U.S. Intelligence."

67   Kenneth Timmerman, *Iraq Rebuilds Its Military Industries*, June 29, 1993, in U.S. Congress, House Committee on Foreign Affairs, *Iraq's Nuclear Weapons Capability and IAEA Inspections in Iraq*, p. 89.

68   U.S. Congress, House Committee on Foreign Affairs, *Iraq's Nuclear Weapons Capability and IAEA Inspections in Iraq*, p. 47; Gertz, "Saddam Close to Nuclear Weapon."

69   U.S. Congress, House Committee on Foreign Affairs, *Iraq's Nuclear Weapons Capability and IAEA Inspections in Iraq*, p. 47; "Written statements submitted by the International Atomic Energy Agency (IAEA) at the hearings jointly held by three subcommittees of the Committee of Foreign Affairs of the 103rd Congress of the United States—Washington 29 June 1993," pp. 155–158.

70   "Written statements submitted by the International Atomic Energy Agency (IAEA) at the hearings jointly held by three subcommittees of the Committee of Foreign Affairs of the 103rd Congress of the United States—Washington 29 June 1993," p. 158.

71   Obeidi and Pitzer, *The Bomb in My Garden*, p. 6.

72   Ibid., pp. 6–7.

73   U.S. Congress, Senate Committee on Governmental Affairs, *Proliferation Threats of the 1990s* (Washington, D.C.: U.S. Government Printing Office, 1993), p. 161.

74   U.S. Arms Control and Disarmament Agency, *Adherence to and Compliance with Arms Control Agreements*, June 24, 1994, p. 15.

75   S/1995/287, Note by the Secretary General, April 11, 1995 w/enclosure, *Seventh Report of the Director General of the International Atomic Energy Agency on the Implementation of the Agency's Plan for Future Ongoing Monitoring and Verification of Iraq's Compliance with Paragraph 12 of Resolution 687* (1991), p. 3.

76   Andrew Cockburn and Patrick Cockburn, *Out of the Ashes: The Resurrection of Saddam Hussein* (New York: HarperCollins, 1999), pp. 191–192.

77   Ibid., p. 193; Trevan, *Saddam's Secrets*, pp. 34–35, 410.

78   "General Hussein Kamal UNSCOM/IAEA Briefing," p. 1, www.globalsecurity.org, accessed September 26, 2004.

79   Ibid., p. 1.

80   Ibid., p. 2; Obeidi and Pitzer, *The Bomb in My Garden*, p. 166.

81   "General Hussein Kamal UNSCOM/IAEA Briefing," p. 3.

82   Ibid., pp. 3–4.

83   Ibid., p. 3.

84   Ibid., p. 3; Trevan, *Saddam's Secrets*, p. 410; Obeidi and Pitzer, *The Bomb in My Garden*, pp. 168–169.

85   Trevan, *Saddam's Secrets*, pp. 372–373, 410–416.

86   S/1999/27, Letter dated 8 February 1999 from the Secretary General addressed to the President of the Security Council, February 9, 1999, w/enclosure: *Report of the Director General of the International Atomic Energy Agency in Connection with the Panel on Disarmament and Current and Future monitoring and Verification Issues (S/1999/100)*, pp. 14–15.

CHAPTER 13: FLAWED INTELLIGENCE

1   Tim McCarthy, "Progress on the Nuclear Highway," *Washington Times*, February 12, 2001, p. A15; Judith Miller, "Iraqi Tells of Renovations at Sites for Chemical and Nuclear Arms," *New York Times*, December 20, 2001, pp. A1, A4; Peter Beaumont and Ed Vullianey, "Spooks Dig for Secrets of Saddam," *Observer*, September 15, 2002.

2   David Rose, "Iraq's Arsenal of Terror," *Vanity Fair*, May 2002, pp. 120–131 at pp. 124, 130–131; U.S. Congress, Senate Select Committee on Intelligence, *Report on the U.S. Intelligence Community's Prewar Intelligence Assessments in Iraq* (Washington, D.C.: SSCI, 2004), p. 332; Joby Warrick, "In Assessing Iraq's Arsenal the Reality Is Uncertainty," *Washington Post*, July 31, 2002, pp. A1, A14.

3   U.S. Congress, Senate Select Committee on Intelligence, *Report on the U.S. Intelligence Community's Prewar Intelligence Assessments in Iraq*, p. 25.

4   Ibid., p. 36; Seymour Hersh, "The Stovepipe," *New Yorker*, October 27, 2003, pp. 77–87 at p. 79; Central Intelligence Agency, "Niger," in *The World Factbook*, www.cia.gov, accessed September 30, 2004.

5   U.S. Congress, Senate Select Committee on Intelligence, *Report on the U.S. Intelli-*

gence Community's Prewar Intelligence Assessments in Iraq, p. 36; Hersh, "The Stovepipe," p. 79; "Niger Scrutinized for Low Atomic Security," September 21, 2003, www.abcnews.com.

6   U.S. Congress, Senate Select Committee on Intelligence, *Report on the U.S. Intelligence Community's Prewar Intelligence Assessments in Iraq*, pp. 37–38; The Commission on the Intelligence Capabilities of the United States Regarding Weapons of Mass Destruction, *Report to the President of the United States* (Washington, D.C.: U.S. Government Printing Office, 2005), pp. 78, 213–214 n. 214.

7   Ibid., p. 38; Vernon Loeb, "CIA Is Stepping Up Attempts to Monitor Spread of Weapons," *Washington Post*, March 12, 2001, p. A15.

8   U.S. Congress, Senate Select Committee on Intelligence, *Report on the U.S. Intelligence Community's Prewar Intelligence Assessments in Iraq*, p. 39; Michael Duffy, "Leaking with a Vengeance," *Time*, October 13, 2003, pp. 28–37 at p. 30; Hersh, "The Stovepipe," p. 80; Richard Leiby and Walter Pincus, "Retired Envoy: Nuclear Report Ignored," *Washington Post*, July 6, 2003, p. A13.

9   U.S. Congress, Senate Select Committee on Intelligence, *Report on the U.S. Intelligence Community's Prewar Intelligence Assessments in Iraq*, pp. 40–41.

10   Ibid., p. 41.

11   Leiby and Pincus, "Retired Envoy"; U.S. Congress, Senate Select Committee on Intelligence, *Report on the U.S. Intelligence Community's Prewar Intelligence Assessments in Iraq*, p. 41; Joseph C. Wilson 4th, "What I Didn't Find in Africa," *New York Times*, July 6, 2003, Section 4, p. 9. In his article Wilson claims to have met with current Niger officials, although the Senate Select Committee on Intelligence report states that he agreed not to hold discussions with such individuals. The accuracy of Wilson's claims has been challenged in several areas. See Susan Schmidt, "Plame's Input Is Cited on Niger Mission," *Washington Post*, July 10, 2004, p. A9; Richard W. Stevenson and David Johnston, "New Reports Reopen Debate over Whether Iraq Sought Uranium in Niger," *New York Times*, July 18, 2004, p. 10; Mark Steyn, "A Review of the Politics of Lies," *Washington Times*, July 19, 2004, p. A17.

12   U.S. Congress, Senate Select Committee on Intelligence, *Report on the U.S. Intelligence Community's Prewar Intelligence Assessments in Iraq*, pp. 43–44; Walter Pincus, and Mike Allen, "Probe Focuses on Month Before Leak to Reporters," *Washington Post*, October 12, 2003, pp. A1, A18.

13   U.S. Congress, Senate Select Committee on Intelligence, *Report on the U.S. Intelligence Community's Prewar Intelligence Assessments in Iraq*, p. 43; Susan Schmidt, "Book Names Iraqi in Alleged '99 Bid to Buy Uranium," *Washington Post*, April 30, 2004, p. A16; Central Intelligence Agency, "Statement by George J. Tenet, Director of Central Intelligence," July 11, 2003, www.cia.gov.

14   U.S. Congress, Senate Select Committee on Intelligence, *Report on the U.S. Intelligence Community's Prewar Intelligence Assessments in Iraq*, p. 47. The year that the deliveries would begin has been deleted from the unclassified version of the Senate report.

15   U.S. Congress, Senate Select Committee on Intelligence, *Report on the U.S. Intelligence Community's Prewar Intelligence Assessments in Iraq*, pp. 52, 54; National Intelligence Council, *Iraq's Continuing Program for Weapons of Mass Destruction*, October 1, 2002, page numbers not available.

16   U.S. Congress, Senate Select Committee on Intelligence, *Report on the U.S. Intelligence Community's Prewar Intelligence Assessments in Iraq*, p. 88.

17   Ibid., p. 90; David Albright, *Iraq's Aluminum Tubes: Separating Fact from Fiction*, Washington, D.C.: Institute for Science and International Security, December 5, 2003), pp. 1–8; Australian Broadcasting Company, "Spinning the Tubes," transcript of *Four Corners* broadcast of October 27, 2003, pp. 1–2, www.abc.net.au; David Barstow, William J. Broad, and Jeff Gerth, "How White House Embraced Suspect Iraq Arms Intelligence," *New York Times*, October 3, 2004, pp. 1, 16–18.

18   U.S. Congress, Senate Select Committee on Intelligence, *Report on the U.S. Intelligence Community's Prewar Intelligence Assessments in Iraq*, p. 97; Australian Broadcasting Company, "Spinning the Tubes," p. 2.

19   U.S. Congress, Senate Select Committee on Intelligence, *Report on the U.S. Intelligence Community's Prewar Intelligence Assessments in Iraq*, pp. 121–122.

20   Ibid., p. 122.

21   Ibid., pp. 122–124.

22   Ibid., pp. 84–85.

23   Ibid., p. 88; Central Intelligence Agency, *A Consumer's Guide to Intelligence* (Washington, D.C.: CIA, 1998), p. 23; Walter Pincus, "PDB, the Only News Not Fit for Anyone Else to Read," *Washington Post*, August 27, 1994, p. A7.

24   Barstow, Broad, and Gerth, "How White House Embraced Suspect Iraq Arms Intelligence."

25   U.S. Congress, Senate Select Committee on Intelligence, *Report on the U.S. Intelligence Community's Prewar Intelligence Assessments in Iraq*, pp. 88–89.

26   Ibid., p. 89.

27   Dafna Linzer and Barton Gellman, "CIA Skewed Iraq Reporting, Senate Says," *Washington Post*, July 11, 2004, p. A19.

28   Interview with Greg Thielmann, Arlington, Va., October 20, 2004.

29   U.S. Congress, Senate Select Committee on Intelligence, *Report on the U.S. Intelligence Community's Prewar Intelligence Assessments in Iraq*, p. 90.

30   Ibid., p. 93.

31   The Commission on the Intelligence Capabilities of the United States Regarding Weapons of Mass Destruction, *Report to the President of the United States*, pp. 55, 67. The two analysts responsible for NGIC's position received performance awards in 2002 and the two following years. See Walter Pincus, "Analysts Behind Iraq Intelligence Were Rewarded," *Washington Post*, May 28, 2005, pp. A1, A16.

32   U.S. Congress, Senate Select Committee on Intelligence, *Report on the U.S. Intelligence Community's Prewar Intelligence Assessments in Iraq*, p. 70; Linzer and Gellman, "CIA Skewed Iraq Reporting, Senate Says."

33   U.S. Congress, Senate Select Committee on Intelligence, *Report on the U.S. Intelligence Community's Prewar Intelligence Assessments in Iraq*, pp. 91, 93.

34   Ibid., p. 91.

35   U.S. Congress, Senate Select Committee on Intelligence, *Report on the U.S. Intelligence Community's Prewar Intelligence Assessments in Iraq*, p. 92; The Commission of the Intelligence Capabilities of the United States Regarding Weapons of Mass Destruction, *Report to the President of the United States*, p. 69.

36   Ibid., p. 92.

37   Barstow, Broad, and Gerth, "How White House Embraced Suspect Iraq Arms Intelligence"; Thielmann interview.

38   U.S. Congress, Senate Select Committee on Intelligence, *Report on the U.S. Intelligence Community's Prewar Intelligence Assessments in Iraq*, pp. 36–37.

39   Ibid., p. 42.

40   Ibid., p. 48.

41   "President Bush's State of the Union Address to Congress and the Nation," *New York Times*, January 30, 2002, p. A22; "In Cheney's Words: The Administration Case for Removing Saddam Hussein," *New York Times*, August 27, 2002, p. A8; Jim Garmone, "Rumsfeld Discusses Iraq Inspections, WMD Capabilities," September 3, 2002, www.defenselink.mil.

42   White House, *A Decade of Deception and Defiance: Saddam Hussein's Defiance of the United Nations*, September 12, 2002, pp. 9–10.

43   U.S. Congress, Senate Select Committee on Intelligence, *Report on the U.S. Intelligence Community's Prewar Intelligence Assessments in Iraq*, p. 12; Eric Schmitt and Alison Mitchell, "U.S. Lacks Up-to-Date Review of Iraqi Arms," *New York Times*, September 11, 2002, p. A23; "CIA Accused of Obstructing Panel," *Washington Post*, October 4, 2002, p. A16.

44   U.S. Congress, Senate Select Committee on Intelligence, *Report on the U.S. Intelligence Community's Prewar Intelligence Assessments in Iraq*, pp. 12–13; National Intelligence Council, "NIC Personnel," www.cia.gov/nic/NIC_personnel.html, accessed October 1, 2004.

45   U.S. Congress, Senate Select Committee on Intelligence, *Report on the U.S. Intelligence Community's Prewar Intelligence Assessments in Iraq*, p. 95.

46   Ibid., pp. 13, 95; Barton Gellman and Walter Pincus, "Depiction of Threat Outgrew Supporting Evidence," *Washington Post*, August 10, 2003, pp. A1, A9; The Commission on the Intelligence Capabilities of the United States Regarding Weapons of Mass Destruction, *Report to the President of the United States*, pp. 70, 209 n. 154.

47   Barstow, Broad, and Gerth, "Skewed Intelligence in March to War in Iraq"; U.S. Congress, Senate Select Committee on Intelligence, *Report on the U.S. Intelligence Community's Prewar Intelligence Assessments in Iraq*, p. 95; Paul Sperry, "Energy Rep at Iraq Meeting Lacked Intelligence Savy," August 6, 2003, www.worldnetdaily.com; Paul Sperry, "$20,000 Bonus to Official Who Agreed on Nuke Claim," August 12, 2003, www.worldnetdaily.com; Kevin Drum, "Saddam's Nukes," *Washington Monthly*, August 13, 2003, www.washingtonmonthly.com.

48   U.S. Congress, Senate Select Committee on Intelligence, *Report on the U.S. Intelligence Community's Prewar Intelligence Assessments in Iraq*, p. 54; Bob Woodward, *Plan of Attack* (New York: Simon & Schuster, 2004), pp. 197, 199; National Intelligence Council, *Iraq's Continuing Programs for Weapons of Mass Destruction*, p. 1.

49   National Intelligence Council, *Iraq's Continuing Programs for Weapons of Mass Destruction*, pp. 1, 2; U.S. Congress, Senate Select Committee on Intelligence, *Report on the U.S. Intelligence Community's Prewar Intelligence Assessments in Iraq*, pp. 85–86.

50   National Intelligence Council, *Iraq's Continuing Programs for Weapons of Mass Destruction*, p. 2; "Tuwaitha Nuclear Center," www.globalsecurity.org, accessed September 10, 2002; David Albright and Corey Hinderstein, "Is the Activity at Al Qaim Related to Nuclear Efforts?" September 10, 2002, www.isis-online.org.

51   National Intelligence Council, *Iraq's Continuing Programs for Weapons of Mass Destruction*, Key Judgments Section, pp. 4–5.

52   Ibid., Key Judgments Section, p. 5.

53   Ibid.

54   U.S. Congress, Senate Select Committee on Intelligence, *Report on the U.S. Intelligence Community's Prewar Intelligence Assessments in Iraq*, pp. 95–96.

55   Ibid., pp. 52–53; National Intelligence Council, *Iraq's Continuing Programs for Weapons of Mass Destruction*, Key Judgments Section; Central Intelligence Agency, "Statement by George J. Tenet, Director of Central Intelligence," July 11, 2003, www.cia.gov.

56   U.S. Congress, Senate Select Committee on Intelligence, *Report on the U.S. Intelligence Community's Prewar Intelligence Assessments in Iraq*, p. 52; National Intelligence Council, *Iraq's Continuing Programs for Weapons of Mass Destruction*, page numbers not available.

57   National Intelligence Council, *Iraq's Continuing Programs for Weapons of Mass Destruction*, page numbers not available.

58   Ibid., Annex A.

59   Lord Butler, *Review of Intelligence on Weapons of Mass Destruction* (London: The Stationery Office, 2004), pp. 67–68. The report was produced by a committee of Privy Counsellors, chaired by Butler.

60   Joint Intelligence Committee, *Iraq's Weapons of Mass Destruction: The Assessment of the British Government*, September 2002, pp. 17, 25.

61   Ibid., p. 26.

62   Ibid., p. 27.

63   Parliamentary Joint Committee on ASIO, ASIS and DSD, *Intelligence on Iraq's Weapons of Mass Destruction* (Canberra: The Parliament of the Commonwealth of Australia, December 2003), pp. 30–31.

64   Ibid., pp. 38, 41.

65   Central Intelligence Agency, *Iraq's Weapons of Mass Destruction*, October 2002, p. 1.

66   Ibid., p. 6.

67   The White House, "President Bush Outlines Iraqi Threat," October 7, 2002, www.whitehouse.gov.

68   Ibid.

69   Ibid.

70   David E. Sanger, "Bush Sees 'Urgent Duty' to Pre-empt Attack by Iraq," *New York Times*, October 8, 2002, pp. A1, A13; "Declassified Intelligence Photos of Iraqi Nuclear Weapons-Related Facilities/Al Furat," October 9, 2002, http://brownback.senate.gov; "Ready for Business?" www.msnbc.com, accessed October 8, 2002.

71   Dana Priest, "Uranium Claim Was Known for Months to Be Weak," *Washington Post*, July 20, 2003, p. A22; U.S. Congress, Senate Select Committee on Intelligence, *Report on the U.S. Intelligence Community's Prewar Intelligence Assessments in Iraq*, p. 57; (Alleged) Letter from President of Niger to Saddam Hussein, July 27, 2000; (Alleged Cable), Minister of Foreign Affairs to Ambassador of Niger, Rome, Subject: Protocol of Agreement Between the Government of Niger and the Government of Iraq Related to the Supplying of Uranium, October 10, 2000; "Italian Ex-Spy Discusses Own Role in Iraq-Niger Uranium Traffic Hoax," *Il Giornale*, September 21, 2004, p. 4.

72   U.S. Congress, Senate Select Committee on Intelligence, *Report on the U.S. Intelligence Community's Prewar Intelligence Assessments in Iraq*, p. 58.

73   Ibid., p. 62.

74   Ibid., pp. 67–68.

75   Ibid., p. 69; Seymour Hersh, "Who Lied to Whom?" *New Yorker*, March 31, 2003, pp. 41–43.

76   U.S. Congress, Senate Select Committee on Intelligence, *Report on the U.S. Intelligence Community's Prewar Intelligence Assessments in Iraq*, pp. 59–60.

77   Ibid., p. 68; Jeffrey T. Richelson, "Task Force 157: The U.S. Navy's Secret Intelligence Service," *Intelligence and National Security*, April 1996, pp. 105–145.

78   U.S. Congress, Senate Select Committee on Intelligence, *Report on the U.S. Intelligence Community's Prewar Intelligence Assessments in Iraq*, pp. 69–70.

79   Ibid., p. 71.

80   Kenneth Katzman, *Iraq: Weapons Programs, U.N. Requirements, and U.S. Policy* (Washington, D.C.: Congressional Research Service, June 30, 2003), p. 3.

81   Romesh Rathnesar and Andrew Purvis, "To Catch a Cheat," *Time*, November 25, 2002, pp. 36–39; John F. Burns, "Pattern of Iraqi Cooperation Shifts as Plant Is Searched," *New York Times*, December 1, 2002, p. 20; Rajiv Chandrasekaran, "U.N. Team Searches 'Sensitive' Site in Iraq," *Washington Post*, December 1, 2002, pp. A26, A28.

82   David Watsell, "Iraqi Regime Hiding Scientists," *Washington Times*, December 11, 2002, p. A12.

83   Katzman, *Iraqi*, p. 3; U.S. Congress, Senate Select Committee on Intelligence, *Report on the U.S. Intelligence Community's Prewar Intelligence Assessments in Iraq*, p. 60.

84   Linzer and Gellman, "CIA Skewed Iraq Reporting, Senate Says"; Douglas Jehl, "CIA Admits It Didn't Give Weapon Data to the U.N.," *New York Times*, February 21, 2004, p. A7.

85   U.S. Congress, Senate Select Committee on Intelligence, *Report on the U.S. Intelli-

gence Community's Prewar Intelligence Assessments in Iraq, pp. 62–63. The paper's title is *Request for Evidence of Iraq's Nuclear Program Other Than the Aluminum Tube Procurement Effort*.

86   Katzman, *Iraq*, p. 3; "Nuclear Evidence Discovered in Iraq," *Washington Times*, January 19, 2003, pp. A1, A17; Mohamed ElBaradei, Statement to the United Nations Security Council, "The Status of Nuclear Inspections in Iraq," January 27, 2003, w/att: IAEA *Update Report for the Security Council Pursuant to Resoolution 1441* (2002), January 27, 2003, pp. 1, 4, at www.iaea.org.

87   Secretary Colin L. Powell, *Remarks to the United Nations Security Council*, February 5, 2003, pp. 2, 14, www.state.gov.

88   Ibid., p. 14.

89   Mohamed ElBaradei, *The Status of Nuclear Inspections in Iraq: 14 February 2003 Update*, February 14, 2003, p. 1, www.iaea.org.

90   Ibid., p. 2; Gellman and Pincus, "Depiction of Threat Outgrew Supporting Evidence."

91   Mohamed ElBaradei, *The Status of Nuclear Inspections in Iraq: An Update*, March 7, 2003, pp. 2–3.

92   Katzman, *Iraq*, pp. 3–4.

93   Stephen A. Cambone (Presenter), "Briefing on Iraq Survey Group," May 30, 2003, p. 9, www.defenselink.mil.

94   Ibid., pp. 1–2, 9; Kenneth Gerhart, "The Changing Face of the ISG's Home Base," *Communique*, July–August 2003, pp. 5–7.

95   Gerhart, "The Changing Face of the ISG's Home Base"; Australian Broadcasting Corporation, *Four Corners*, pp. 3–4.

96   Cambone (Presenter), "Briefing on Iraq Survey Group," pp. 2–3; Charles A. Duelfer, *Comprehensive Report of the Special Advisor to the DCI on Iraq's WMD, Volume I* September 30, 2004, pp. 1–2; Gerhart, "Changing Face of ISG's Home Base."

97   Central Intelligence Agency, "DCI Tenet Announces Appointment of David Kay as Special Advisor," June 11, 2003, www.cia.gov; Douglas Jehl, "For Leader of Arms Hunt, Report Is a Test of Faith," *New York Times*, October 3, 2003, p. A12; Central Intelligence Agency, "Statement by Dr. David Kay, Special Advisor to the Director of Central Intelligence," November 2, 2003, www.cia.gov; Hans Blix, *Disarming Iraq* (New York: Pantheon, 2004), p. 25.

98   Central Intelligence Agency, "DCI Tenet Announces Appointment of David Kay as Special Advisor"; James Risen, "U.S. Asks Ex-U.N. Inspector to Advise on Arms Search," *New York Times*, June 12, 2003, p. A14; Blix, *Disarming Iraq*, p. 25.

99   Mahdi Obeidi and Kurt Pitzer, *The Bomb in My Garden: The Secret of Saddam's Nuclear Mastermind* (New York: Wiley, 2004), p. 204; Joby Warrick, "Iraqi Scientist Turns over Nuclear Plans, Parts," *New York Times*, June 26, 2003, p. A14; Bill Gertz, "CIA Finds Papers, Parts in Iraq for Enriching Uranium," *Washington Times*, June 26, 2003, p. A3; "CIA Statement on Recently Acquired Iraqi Centrifuge Equipment," June 26, 2003, www.cia.gov; David E. Sanger, "Iraqi Says Hussein Planned to Revive the Nuclear Program Dismantled," *New York Times*, June 27, 2003, p. A10;

Barton Gellman, "Search in Iraq Fails to Find Nuclear Threat," *Washington Post*, October 26, 2003, pp. A1, A28.

100   Walter Pincus and Kevin Sullivan, "Scientists Still Deny Iraqi Arms Programs," *Washington Post*, July 31, 2003, pp. A1, A16; Rowan Scarborough, "Iraqi Arms Scientists Killed Before They Talk," *Washington Times*, August 23, 2004, pp. A1, A8; Hersh, "The Stovepipe," p. 86.

101   Statement by David Kay on the Interim Progress Report on the Activities of the Iraq Survey Group (ISG) before the House Permanent Select Committee on Intelligence, the House Committee on Appropriations, Subcommittee on Defense, and the Senate Select Committee on Intelligence, October 2, 2003, p. 2.

102   Statement by David Kay, pp. 2–3; Dimitri Perricos, who had succeeded Blix as UNMOVIC chairman, found little new in Kay's report. See Walter Pincus, "U.N. Inspector: Little New in U.S. Probe for Iraq Arms," *Washington Post*, December 14, 2003, p. A27.

103   Statement by David Kay, pp. 3, 6–7.

104   Ibid., p. 7; Barton Gellman, "Iraq's Arsenal Was Only on Paper," *Washington Post*, January 7, 2004, pp. A1, A14–A15.

105   Statement by David Kay, p. 7.

106   Ibid.

107   Dana Priest and Walter Pincus, "Kay Plans to Leave Search for Iraqi Arms," *Washington Post*, December 18, 2003, p. A42; Richard W. Stevenson, "Head of Iraqi Arms Search May Be Ready to Step Down," *New York Times*, December 19, 2003, p. A12; James Risen, "Ex-Inspector Says C.I.A. Missed Arms Chaos," *New York Times*, January 26, 2004, pp. A1, A10.

108   Central Intelligence Agency, "DCI Announces Dulfer to Succeed Kay as Special Advisor," January 23, 2004, www.cia.gov.

109   Douglas Jehl, "Skeptic May Take over Iraq Arms Hunt," January 23, 2004, p. A6; "William Harlow, Charles Duelfer Conference Call," January 23, 2004, pp. 1–2.

110   Richard W. Stevenson, "Iraq Illicit Arms Gone Before War, Inspector States," *New York Times*, January 24, 2004, pp. A1, A7; Risen, "Ex-Inspector Says C.I.A. Missed Iraqi Arms Chaos."

111   Central Intelligence Agency, "Testimony to the US Congress by Mr. Charles Duelfer, Director of Central Intelligence Special Advisor for Strategy Regarding Iraqi Weapons of Mass Destruction (WMD) Programs," March 30, 2004, p. 5, www.cia.gov.

112   Ibid.

113   Ibid.

114   Charles A. Duelfer Jr., *Comprehensive Report of the Special Advisor to the DCI for Iraqi Weapons of Mass Destruction, Volume II*, Nuclear Chapter, September 30, 2004, pp. 1–2.

115   Ibid., pp. 1–2.

116   Central Intelligence Agency, "Testimony to the US Congress by Mr. Charles Duelfer, Director of Central Intelligence Special Advisor for Strategy Regarding Iraqi Weapons of Mass Destruction (WMD) Programs," p. 5.

117   Walter Pincus and Dana Milbank, "Kay Backs Outside Probe of Iraq Data," *Washington Post*, January 29, 2004, pp. A1, A18.

CHAPTER 14: TROUBLE WAITING TO HAPPEN

1   Daniel Benjamin and Steven Simon, *The Age of Sacred Terror* (New York: Random House, 2002), pp. 151, 223–225; Robert D'A. Henderson, *Brassey's International Intelligence Handbook* (Washington, D.C.: Brassey's, 2003), pp. 87–88; Héctor Tobar, "1994 Jewish Center Attack Under Review," November 9, 2004, www.latimes.com.

2   Rodney W. Jones, Mark G. McDonough with Toby F. Dalton and Gregory D. Koblentz, *Tracking Nuclear Proliferation: A Guide in Maps and Charts, 1998* (Washington, D.C.: Carnegie Endowment for International Peace, 1998), pp. 184–185; "Esfahan/Isfahan Nuclear Technology Center," www.globalsecurity.org, accessed October 24, 2004; Leonard Spector with Jacqueline R. Smith, *Nuclear Ambitions: The Spread of Nuclear Weapons 1989–1990* (Boulder, Colo.: Westview, 1990), pp. 203–204, Chen Zak, *Iran's Nuclear Policy and the JAFA: An Evaluation of Program 93 & 2* (Washington, D.C.: Washington Institute for Near East Policy 2002), p. 29.

3   "Esfahan/Isfahan Nuclear Technology Center."

4   Victor Gilinsky, "Iran's 'Legal' Paths to the Bomb," in Henry Sokoloski and Patrick Clawson (eds.), *Checking Iran's Nuclear Ambitions* (Carlisle, Pa.: U.S. Army War College Strategic Studies Institute, 2004), pp. 23–38 at pp. 28–29; Sammy Salama and Karen Ruster, "A Preemptive Attack on Iran's Nuclear Facilities: Possible Consequences," August 12, 2004, p. 2, http://cns.miis.edu/pubs/week/040812.htm; Maria Golovnina, "Russian Announces Completed Nuke Plant," *Washington Times*, October 15, 2004, p. A15. On U.S. attempts to dissuade Russia from following through on the Bushehr reactor deal, see Steven Greenhouse, "Russia and China Pressed Not to Sell A-Plants to Iran," *New York Times*, January 25, 1995, p. A6; Michael R. Gordon, "Russia Plans to Sell Reactors to Iran Despite U.S. Protests," *New York Times*, March 7, 1998, p. A3.

5   Salama and Ruster, "A Preemptive Attack on Iran's Nuclear Facilities," p. 3; "Arak," www.globalsecurity.org, accessed October 24, 2004; National Council of Resistance of Iran, U.S. Representative Office, "Information on Two Top Secret Nuclear Sites of the Iranian Regime (Natanz & Arak)," December 2002, p. 2, www.iranwatch.org; Douglas Frantz, "Iran Closes in on Ability to Build a Nuclear Bomb," August 4, 2003, www.latimes.com.

6   Salama and Ruster, "A Preemptive Attack on Iran's Nuclear Facilities," p. 3; "Natanz," www.globalsecurity.org, accessed October 24, 2004; Gilinsky, "Iran's 'Legal' Paths to the Bomb," p. 31; National Council of Resistance of Iran, U.S. Representative Office, "Information on Two Top Secret Nuclear Sites of the Iranian Regime (Natanz & Arak)," pp. 1–2; Glenn Kessler, "Front Firms Aided Iran Nuclear Bomb Effort," *Washington Post*, December 19, 2002, p. A26.

7   "Iran: Nuclear Facilities," www.globalsecurity.org, accessed October 24, 2004; Jones

and McDonough with Dalton and Koblentz, *Tracking Nuclear Proliferation*, pp. 184–185; Andrew Koch and Jeanette Wolf, "Iran's Nuclear Procurement Program: How Close to the Bomb?" *Nonproliferation Review*, 5, 1 (Fall 1997), pp. 123–135 at pp. 123–124.

8   Kessler, "Front Firms Aided Iran Nuclear Bomb Effort."

9   "Ardekan [Ardakan] Nuclear Fuel Site," www.globalsecurity.org, accessed October, 24, 2004; "Kolahdouz," www.globasecurity.org, accessed October 24, 2004; "Dark-hovin," www.globasecurity.org, accessed October 24, 2004.

10   Nazila Fathi, "Iran Says It Has Developed Ability to Fuel Plants but Won't Seek Weapons," *New York Times*, February 10, 2003, p. A12. For other Iranian claims of peaceful intent, see Elaine Sciolino, "Iran Says It Plans 10 Nuclear Plant but No Atom Arms," *New York Times*, May 14, 1995, pp. 1, 10.

11   R. Jeffrey Smith, "Officials Say Iran Is Seeking Nuclear Weapons Capability," *Washington Post*, October 30, 1991, pp. A1, A20; Elaine Sciolino, "Report Says Iran Seeks Atomic Arms," *New York Times*, October 31, 1991, p. A7; Koch and Wolf, "Iran's Nuclear Procurement Program," p. 125.

12   Steve Coll, "U.S. Halted Nuclear Bid by Iran," *Washington Post*, November 17, 1992, pp. A1, A30.

13   Ibid.; Elaine Sciolino, "China Will Build A-Plant for Iran," *New York Times*, September 11, 1992, p. A6.

14   Joint Atomic Energy Intelligence Committee, "Iran's Nuclear Program: Building a Weapons Capability," February 1, 1993.

15   "Iran: The Emerging Threat," 1993, pp. 14–15. This paper was prepared by a New York law firm. The claim that Iran had at least three nuclear warheads became the foundation for a novel by Larry Collins, *The Road to Armageddon* (Beverly Hills, Calif.: New Millennium Press, 2003)—see pp. v–viii.

16   Bill Gertz, "U.S. Defuses Effort by Iran to Get Nukes," *Washington Times*, November 24, 1994, pp. A1, A8; Al J. Venter, "Iran's Nuclear Ambition: Innocuous Illusion or Ominous Truth?" *Jane's International Defence Review*, September 1997, pp. 29–31.

17   Chris Hedges, "Iran May Be Able to Build an Atomic Bomb," *New York Times*, January 5, 1995, p. A10.

18   Steven Greenhouse, "U.S. Gives Russia Secret Data on Iran to Fight Atom Deal," *New York Times*, April 3, 1995, pp. A1, A9.

19   Ibid.

20   Elaine Sciolino, "Beijing Rebuffs U.S. on Halting Iran Atom Deal," *New York Times*, April 18, 1995, pp. A1, A18; Jack Anderson and Michael Binstein, "Iran's Nuclear Ambitions," *Washington Post*, December 10, 1992, p. C7.

21   Ann Devroy, "President Will Ban All Trade with Iran," *Washington Post*, May 1, 1995, pp. A1, A12; Martin Sieff, "Iran's Nuke Plan Spurred Embargo," *Washington Times*, May 2, 1995, pp. A1, A20; Russell Watson, Karen Breslau, and John Barry, "So Who Needs Allies?" *Newsweek*, May 15, 1995, p. 36.

22   Charles J. Hanley, "Iran's Nuclear Effort behind Schedule," *Washington Times*, May

5, 1997, p. A13; Margaret Shapiro, "Russia Firm on Reactor Sale to Iran," *Washington Post*, May 4, 1995, p. A17; Fred Hiatt, "Russia Denies Plan to Sell Gas Centrifuge to Iran," *Washington Post*, May 5, 1995, p. A29.

23   R. Jeffrey Smith, "Administration Concerned About Russia's Nuclear Cooperation with Iran," *Washington Post*, July 3, 1997, p. A7.

24   Barton Gellman and John Pomfret, "U.S. Action Stymied China Sale to Iran," *Washington Post*, March 13, 1998, pp. A1, A20; Bill Gertz, "Iran Gets China's Help on Nuclear Arms," *Washington Times*, April 17, 1996, pp. A1, A10; Robert J. Einhorn, "Testimony Before Senate Foreign Relations Committee, Washington, D.C., "October 5, 2000, p. 2, www.state.gov.

25   Gellman and Pomfret, "U.S. Action Stymied China Sale to Iran."

26   Ibid.

27   James Risen and Judith Miller, "C.I.A. Tells Clinton an Iranian A-Bomb Can't Be Ruled Out," *New York Times*, January 17, 2000, pp. A1, A8.

28   Ibid.

29   Walter Pincus, "Russia: Laser Deal with Iran Blocked," *Washington Post*, September 20, 2000, p. A25.

30   Statement by John A. Lauder, Director, DCI Nonproliferation Center, to the Senate Committee on Foreign Relations, "Russian Proliferation to Iran's Weapons of Mass Destruction and Missile Programs," October 5, 2000, pp. 1–2, at www.cia.gov.

31   Director of Central Intelligence, *Unclassified Report to Congress on the Acquisition of Technology Relating to Weapons of Mass Destruction and Advanced Conventional Munitions, 1 January Through 30 June 2003*, 2003, p. 2. The same judgment appeared in the subsequent report: Director of Central Intelligence, *Unclassified Report to Congress on the Acquisition of Technology Relating to Weapons of Mass Destruction and Advanced Conventional Munitions, 1 July Through 30 December 2003*, 2003, p. 2.

32   Ibid., p. 2; Frantz, "Iran Closes in on Ability to Build a Nuclear Bomb"; Seymour M. Hersh, "The Iran Game," *New Yorker*, December 3, 2001, pp. 42–50.

33   Director of Central Intelligence, *Unclassified Report to Congress on the Acquisition of Technology Relating to Weapons of Mass Destruction and Advanced Conventional Munitions, 1 January Through 30 June 2003*, pp. 2–3; "Detailed Assessment of Feasible Uranium Enrichment Plant at Natanz, Iran," February 20, 2003; David Albright and Corey Hinderstein, "The Iranian Gas Centrifuge Uranium Enrichment Plant at Natanz: Drawing from Commercial Satellite Images," March 14, 2003.

34   Director of Central Intelligence, *Unclassified Report to Congress on the Acquisition of Technology Relating to Weapons of Mass Destruction and Advanced Conventional Munitions, 1 January Through 20 June 2003*, pp. 2–3.

35   Director General, International Atomic Energy Agency, *Implementation of the NPT Safeguards Agreement in the Islamic Republic of Iran*, February 24, 2004, pp. 5, 8; Peter Slevin and Joby Warrick, "U.N. Finds Uranium Enrichment Tools in Iran," *Washington Post*, February 20, 2004, p. A15; Karl Vick, "Another Nuclear Program Found in Iran," *Washington Post*, February 24, 2004, pp. A1, A14; Joby Warrick, "Iranian Nuclear Plans Found," *Washington Post*, February 13, 2004, pp. A1, A23.

36   Louis Charbonneau, "Diplomats: Iran Amassing Atomic Enrichment Machines,"
      January 13, 2004, www.abcnews.com; "Iran Said to Renege on Nuclear Promises,"
      January 20, 2004, www.abcnews.com; Ali Akbar Dareini, "Iranians to Resume
      Enriching Uranium," *Washington Post*, March 11, 2004, p. A22; Joby Warrick, "Ira-
      nians Bar Further Nuclear Inspections," *Washington Post*, March 14, 2004, p. A19;
      Eli J. Lake, "U.S. Wants U.N. Atomic Energy Agency to Probe, Cite Iran," *Washing-
      ton Times*, May 2, 2003, p. A18.

37   Director General, International Atomic Energy Agency, *Implementation of the NPT
      Safeguards in the Islamic Republic of Iran*, June 1, 2003, pp. 5, 7; "Nuclear Inspectors
      Arrive in Iran," April 13, 2004, www.latimes.com; Peter Slevin, "Watchdog Blasts
      Iran on Nuclear Program," *Washington Post*, June 2, 2004, p. A21.

38   Louis Charbonneau, "Iran Keeps Tabs on Nuclear Officials," *Washington Times*,
      April 29, 2004, p. A17.

39   Greg Miller, "U.S. Lacks Reliable Data on Iran Arms," November 27, 2004,
      www.latimes.com.

40   Dafna Linzer, "Nuclear Disclosures of Iran Unverified," November 19, 2004,
      www.washingtonpost.com; Douglas Jehl and William J. Broad, "Doubts Persist on
      Iran Nuclear Arms Goals," *New York Times*, November 20, 2004, p. A8.

41   Dafna Linzer, "U.S. Uses Drones to Probe Iran for Arms," *Washington Post*, February
      13, 2005, pp. A1, A26; David Fulghum, "Hide and Seek," *Aviation Week & Space
      Technology*, February 28, 2005, pp. 24-25.

42   "ISIS Imagery Brief: Destruction at Iranian Site Raises New Questions About Iran's
      Nuclear Activities," June 17, 2004, www.isis-online.org; Karl Vick, "Demolitions
      Raise Concern of Nuclear Coverup in Iran," *Washington Post*, June 20, 2004, p. A14;
      National Council for Resistance in Iran, "Disclosing a Major Secret Nuclear Site
      Under the Ministry of Defense," November 17, 2004, p. 2, www.globalsecurity.org.

43   National Council for Resistance in Iran, "Disclosing a Major Secret Nuclear Site
      under the Ministry of Defense."

44   David Albright and Corey Hinderstein, "Parchin: Possible Nuclear Weapons-Related
      Site in Iran," September 15, 2004, www.isis-online.org

45   Ibid.

46   Ibid.

47   Dafna Linzer and Walter Pincus, "U.S. Reviewing Its Intelligence on Iran," *Washing-
      ton Post*, February 12, 2005, p. A12; Douglas Jehl and Eric Schmitt, "Data Is Lacking
      on Iran's Arms, U.S. Panel Says," *New York Times*, March 9, 2005, pp. A1, A8.

48   Foreign Broadcast Information Service, CIA, *Iran: News Agency Posts Photos of Arak
      Heavy Water Facility*, n.d. (but late October 2004 or after); Foreign Broadcast Infor-
      mation Service, CIA, *Iran: News Agency Post Photos of Isfahan UCF*, n.d. (but late
      November 2004 or after); Foreign Broadcast Information Service, CIA, *Tehran TV
      Shows Khatami Visiting Natanz Nuclear Facility*, March 30, 2005, www.fas.org, p. 1.

49   David E. Sanger, "Iran Agrees to Inspection of Military Base," *New York Times*, Jan-
      uary 6, 2005, p. A6; Richard Bernstein, "Nuclear Agency Says Iran Has Blocked
      Investigation," March 2, 2005, p. A5.

50   Elaine Sciolino and David E. Sanger, "Pressed, Iran Admits Its Discussed Acquiring
      Tools for Nuclear Arms," *New York Times*, February 28, 2005, pp. A1, A7; "Iran Con-
      firms Processing Tons of Uranium Ore," *New York Times*, May 10, 2005, p. A10;
      Richard Bernstein, "Iran Said to Admit Test on Path to Atom Arms," *New York Times*,
      June 16, 2005, p. A12.

51   Dafna Linzer, "Iran Is Judged 10 Years from Nuclear Bomb," *Washington Post*,
      August 2, 2005, pp. A1, A10; Gary Milhollin, "Don't Underestimate the Mullahs,"
      New York Times, August 23, 2005, p. A23; "Europe's Iran Moment," *Wall Street Jour-
      nal*, August 3, 2005, p. A10.

52   Larry A. Niksch, *North Korea's Nuclear Weapons Program* (Washington, D.C.: Con-
      gressional Research Service, June 9, 2003), p. 9; Steven R. Weisman, "North Korea
      Signs Accord on Atom-Plant Inspections," *New York Times*, January 31, 1992, p. A2.

53   Niksch, *North Korea's Nuclear Weapons Program*, p. 9; Steven R. Weisman, "North
      Korean Leader's Statement Renews Doubt on Nuclear Issue," *New York Times*, Feb-
      ruary 21, 1992, p. A9.

54   T. R. Reid, "North Korea Reveals Existence of Nuclear Reactor Unknown in West,"
      Washington Post, April 17, 1992, p. A7; Don Oberdorfer, "N. Korea Releases Exten-
      sive Data on Nuclear Effort," *Washington Post*, May 6, 1992, p. A11; David Albright
      and Mark Hibbs, "North Korea's Plutonium Puzzle," *Bulletin of the Atomic Scien-
      tists*, November 1992, pp. 36–40 at p. 38; Jones and McDonough with Dalton and
      Koblentz, *Tracking Nuclear Proliferation*, p. 158.

55   T. R. Reid, "N. Korean Plutonium Plant Cited," *Washington Post*, May 17, 1992, pp.
      A1, A30.

56   Reid, "N. Korean Plutonium Plant Cited"; Sheryl WuDunn, "North Korean Site Has
      A-Bomb Hints," *New York Times*, May 17, 1993, pp. 1, 14.

57   David Albright, "How Much Plutonium Does North Korea Have?" *Bulletin of the
      Atomic Scientists*, September/October 1994, pp. 46–53 at p. 47.

58   Ibid., p. 48; Niksch, *North Korea's Nuclear Weapons Program*, pp. 9–10; David E.
      Sanger, "In Reversal, North Korea Bars Nuclear Inspectors," *New York Times*, Febru-
      ary 9, 1993, p. A13; R. Jeffrey Smith, "N. Korea and the Bomb: High Tech Hide-and-
      Seek," *Washington Post*, April 27, 1993, pp. A1, A11.

59   Albright, "How Much Plutonium Does North Korea Have?" p. 48.

60   Ibid., pp. 48, 50.

61   Bill Gertz, "North Korea Digs Tunnels for Nuclear Arms," *Washington Times*, Febru-
      ary 21, 1992, p. A9; R. Jeffrey Smith, "N. Koreans Accused of Arms Ploy," *Washing-
      ton Post*, February 28, 1992, p. A29.

62   R. Jeffrey Smith, "U.S. to Dangle Reactor Prospect at N. Korea," *Washington Post*,
      July 7, 1994, pp. A1, A14.

63   Smith, "N. Korea and the Bomb."

64   Ibid.

65   Albright, "How Much Plutonium Does North Korea Have?" p. 48.

66   Ibid.; Smith, "N. Korea and the Bomb."

67   Smith, "N. Korea and the Bomb."

68   Ibid.

69   Joel S. Wit, Daniel B. Poneman, and Robert L. Gallucci, *Going Critical: The First North Korean Nuclear Crisis* (Washington, D.C.: Brookings Institution, 2004), p. 20.

70   Smith, "North Korea and the Bomb."

71   Barbara Starr, "Woolsey Tackles Proliferation as the Problem Gets Worse," *Jane's Defence Weekly*, November 13, 1993, p. 23.

72   Elaine Sciolino, "C.I.A. Chief Says North Koreans Plan to Make Secret Atom Arms," *New York Times*, February 26, 1992, pp. A1, A5; Don Oberdorfer, "Gates Remains Suspicious of N. Korea," *Washington Post*, January 13, 1993, p. A17.

73   Elaine Sciolino, "U.S. Agencies Split over North Korea," *New York Times*, March 10, 1992, pp. A1, A12.

74   Oberdorfer, "Gates Remains Suspicious of N. Korea."

75   Jim Mann, "N. Korea Intent on Becoming a Nuclear Power, Experts Say," *Los Angeles Times*, March 31, 1993, p. A14; Bill Gertz, "U.S. Intelligence: North Korea Could Have Nukes," *Washington Times*, December 2, 1993, p. A3; Wit, Poneman, and Gallucci, *Going Critical*, p. 6.

76   R. Jeffrey Smith, "U.S. Analysts Are Pessimistic on Korean Nuclear Inspection," *Washington Post*, December 3, 1993, pp. A1, A35.

77   Ibid.

78   Stephen Engelberg with Michael R. Gordon, "Intelligence Study Says North Korea Has Nuclear Bomb," *New York Times*, December 26, 1993, pp. 1, 8.

79   Ibid.

80   Ibid.

81   Ibid.

82   Wit, Poneman, and Gallucci, *Going Critical*, p. xvi.

83   Niksch, *North Korea's Nuclear Weapons Program*, p. 10.

84   J. F. O. McAllister, "Frightening Face-Off," *Time*, December 13, 1993, p. 53; Bruce W. Nelan, "Down the Risky Path," *Time*, June 13, 1994, pp. 24–28 at p. 25; Jill Smolowe, "What If . . . ," *Time*, June 13, 1994, pp. 32–34; David E. Sanger, "U.S. to Withdraw from Arms Accord with North Korea," *New York Times*, October 20, 2002, pp. A1, A10.

85   Niksch, *North Korea's Nuclear Weapons Program*, pp. 10, 13; James A. Kelly, Statement to the Senate Foreign Relations Committee, "Dealing with North Korea's Nuclear Program," July 15, 2004, p. 2, www.state.gov. The detailed, inside account of the negotiations is Wit, Poneman, and Gallucci, *Going Critical*.

86   Niksch, *North Korea's Nuclear Weapons Program*, p. 11.

87   Wit, Poneman, and Gallucci, *Going Critical*, p. 250.

88   Don Oberdorfer, *The Two Koreas: A Contemporary History* (Boston: Addison-Wesley, 1997), pp. 339, 345.

89   Ibid., pp. 346–347; Wit, Poneman, and Gallucci, *Going Critical*, pp. 5–6.

90   Oberdorfer, *The Two Koreas*, p. 346.

91   Ibid., pp. 366, 368.

92   James Risen, "Russia Helped U.S. on Nuclear Spying Inside North Korea," *New York Times,* January 20, 2003, pp. A1, A11.

93   Risen, "Russia Helped U.S. on Nuclear Spying Inside North Korea." The day after the article reporting the operation appeared, Boris Labusov, a spokesman for the SVR categorically denied the report, stating that "we must assume that some forces in the United States fabricated this story . . . at a moment when Russia is making intense efforts to defuse the tension around North Korea's nuclear program." He went on to claim that "we are cooperating with foreign intelligence services not against [particular] countries, but against [dangerous] developments"—apparently developments that do not emanate from specific countries. See "Russian Intelligence Denies Helping CIA Monitor North Korea," *RFE/RL Newsline,* January 22, 2003, www.rferl.org.

94   Oberdorfer, *The Two Koreas,* pp. 400–403.

95   Ibid., p. 401; Bill Gertz, "Hwang Says N. Korea Has Atomic Weapons," *Washington Times,* June 5, 1997, p. A12.

96   Gertz, "Hwang Says N. Korea Has Atomic Weapons."

97   David E. Sanger, "North Korea Site an A-Bomb Plant, U.S. Agencies Say," *New York Times,* August 17, 1998; Dana Priest, "Activity Suggests N. Koreans Building Secret Nuclear Site," *Washington Post,* August 18, 1998, pp. A1, A12; Center for Nonproliferation Studies, Monterey Institute of International Studies, "Uncovering the Truth About North Korea's Alleged Underground Nuclear Facility: The Kumchang-ri Controversy," http://cns.miss.edu, accessed October 24, 2002.

98   Sanger, "North Korea Site an A-Bomb Plant, U.S. Agencies Say." Why hard-line North Korean Communist military officials are described as "right wing" might be hard to fathom, unless one considers that the description appeared in the *New York Times.*

99   Bill Gertz, "U.S. Suspects N. Korea Building Nuclear Reactor," *Washington Times,* January 27, 1997, p. A4.

100 Philip Shenon, "Suspected North Korean Atom Site Is Empty, U.S. Finds," *New York Times,* May 28, 1999, p. A3.

101 Steven Mufson, "N. Korean Site Passes a Test," *Washington Post,* May 29, 1999, p. A24; Shenon, "Suspected North Korean Atom Site Is Empty, U.S. Finds"; U.S. Department of State, Office of the Spokesman, Statement by James P. Rubin, Spokesman, "Report on the U.S. Visit to the Site at Kumchang-ni, Democratic People's Republic of Korea," June 25, 1999; Bill Gertz, "North Korean Site Yields Only a System of Empty Tunnels," *Washington Times,* May 28, 1999, pp. A1, A15; Center for Nonproliferation Studies, Monterey Institute of International Studies, "Uncovering the Truth About North Korea's Alleged Underground Nuclear Facility: The Kumchang-ri Controversy," pp. 3–5.

102 U.S. Department of State, Office of the Spokesman, Statement by James P. Rubin, Spokesman, "Report on the U.S. Visit to the Site at Kumchang-ni, Democratic People's Republic of Korea"; Holly Higgins, "The Foundation Is Shaken," in David Albright and Kevin O'Neill (eds.), *Solving the North Korean Nuclear Puzzle* (Wash-

ington, D.C.: Institute for Science and International Security, 2000), pp. 167–186 at p. 174.

103   John E. McLaughlin, "North Korea: Engagement or Confrontation," April 17, 2001, Remarks to Texas A&M Conference, *North Korea: Engagement or Confrontation*; "SSCI Questions for the Record: Regarding 11 February 2003 DCI Worldwide Threat Briefing," att to: Letter, Stanley M. Moskowitz, Director of Congressional Affairs, to Pat Roberts, Chairman, SSCI, August 18, 2003.

104   Gertz, ""North Korean Site Yields Only a System of Empty Tunnels."

105   Ibid.; Bill Gertz, "Pyongyang Working to Make Fuel for Nukes," *Washington Times*, March 11, 1999, pp. A1, A14.

106   Joby Warrick, "U.S. Followed the Aluminum," *Washington Post*, October 18, 2002, pp. A1, A24; Untitled, unclassified CIA assessment provided to Congress, November 2002; Jim Hoagland, "Nuclear Deceit," *Washington Post*, November 10, 2002, p. B7; David E. Sanger, "In North Korea and Pakistan, Deep Roots of Nuclear Barter," *New York Times*, November 24, 2002, pp. 1, 16; Central Intelligence Agency, *Unclassified Report to Congress on the Acquisition of Technology Relating to Weapons of Mass Destruction and Advanced Conventional Munitions, 1 July Through 31 December 2001*, January 7, 2003, pp. 5–6.

107   Walter Pincus, "N. Korea's Plans Were No Secret," *Washington Post*, February 1, 2003, pp. A1, A20; Seymour Hersh, "The Cold Test," *New Yorker*, January 27, 2003, pp. 42–47 at p. 42. According to one account, information from a defector was a significant factor in reaching that conclusion. See John Diamond, "N. Korea Keeps U.S. Intelligence Guessing," *USA Today*, March 11, 2003, pp. 1A, 5A.

108   Sanger, "In North Korea and Pakistan, Deep Roots of Nuclear Barter"; Niksch, *North Korea's Nuclear Weapons Program*, p. 1; Peter Slevin and Karen DeYoung, "N. Korea Admits Having Secret Nuclear Arms," *Washington Post*, October 17, 2002, pp. A1, A17.

109   Niksch, *North Korea's Nuclear Weapons Program*, pp. 2, 4; Richard W. Stevenson, "North Korea Begins to Reopen Plant for Processing Plutonium," *New York Times*, December 24, 2002, pp. A1, A8; Peter S. Goodman, "N. Korea Moves to Activate Complex," *Washington Post*, December 27, 2002, pp. A1, A17; James Brooke, "North Korea Says It Plans to Expel Nuclear Monitors," *New York Times*, December 28, 2002, pp. A1, A10; Sanger, "U.S. to Withdraw from Arms Accord with North Korea."

110   Bill Gertz, "N. Korea Seeks Aid from China on Nukes," *Washington Times*, December 9, 2002; Bill Gertz, "China Ships North Korea Ingredient for Nuclear Arms," *Washington Times*, December 17, 2002, p. A3.

111   Niksch, *North Korea's Nuclear Weapons Program*, pp. 2, 4; Seth Mydans, "North Korea Says It Is Withdrawing from Arms Treaty," *New York Times*, January 10, 2003, pp. A1, A11.

112   David S. Cloud and Jeanne Cummings, "Photos May Fan Korea Nuclear Tensions," *Wall Street Journal*, January 31, 2003, p. A3; David E. Sanger and Eric Schmitt, "Satellites Said to See Activity at North Korean Nuclear Site," *New York Times*, January 31, 2003, pp. A1, A10.

113   Sanger and Schmitt, "Satellites Said to See Activity at North Korean Nuclear Site"; Sonni Efron, "N. Korea May Be Intent on Sparking Crisis," February 2, 2003, www.latimes.com.

114   David E. Sanger, "U.S. Sees Quick Start of North Korea Nuclear Site," *New York Times*, March 1, 2003, pp. A1, A9; John Diamond, "N. Korea Keeps U.S. Intelligence Guessing," *USA Today*, March 11, 2003, pp. 1A, 5A; Glenn Kessler and Walter Pincus, "N. Korea Stymied on Plutonium Work," *Washington Post*, March 20, 2003, p. A24. One senior U.S. official said that through back-channel communications with U.S. officials the North Koreans have sent signals that they would not produce material for weapons and were prepared to "wait and wait" for the United States to come to the negotiating table. See Glenn Kessler, "N. Korea Standoff Sent to U.N. Council," *Washington Post*, February 13, 2003, pp. A1, A27.

115   Niksch, *North Korea's Nuclear Weapons Program*, p. 2; Glenn Kessler and Doug Struck, "N. Korean Statements Jeopardize New Talks," *Washington Post*, April 19, 2003, pp. A1, A10; Glenn Kessler, "N. Korea Says It Has Nuclear Arms," *Washington Post*, April 25, 2003, pp. A1, A18; Steven R. Weisman, "North Korea Said to Offer Small Nuclear Steps, at a Price," *New York Times*, April 29, 2003, p. A13; David E. Sanger, "North Korea Says It Now Possesses Nuclear Arsenal," *New York Times*, April 25, 2003, pp. A1, A18.

116   David E. Sanger and Howard W. French, "North Korea Prompts U.S. to Investigate Nuclear Boast," *New York Times*, May 1, 2003, p. A18; Sanger, "North Korea Says It Now Possesses Nuclear Arsenal."

117   Sanger and French, "North Korea Prompts U.S. to Investigate Nuclear Boast."

118   David E. Sanger, "U.S. Suspects North Korea Moved Ahead on Weapons," *New York Times*, May 8, 2003, p. A16; Daniel Cooley, "U.S. Satellite Photos Hint of Nuke Activity," *Washington Times*, May 9, 2003, p. A15.

119   David E. Sanger, "C.I.A. Said to Find Nuclear Advances by North Koreans," *New York Times*, July 1, 2003, pp. A1, A8.

120   Ibid.; Thom Shanker and David E. Sanger, "North Korea Hides New Nuclear Site, Evidence Suggests," *New York Times*, July 20, 2003, pp. 1, 6; Bill Gertz, "2nd N. Korean Nuclear Site Not Likely," *Washington Times*, July 22, 2003, p. A8.

121   Douglas Jehl, "Shutdown of Nuclear Complex Deepens North Korea Mystery," *New York Times*, September 13, 2003, p. A6; James Brooke, "Korea Claim Leaves U.S. Concerned, but Skeptical," *New York Times*, October 3, 2003, p. A6.

122   Glenn Kessler, "N. Korea Still Denies Enriching Uranium," *Washington Post*, January 13, 2004, p. 12; Glenn Kessler and Phillip P. Pan, "N. Korea Repeats Uranium Denial," *Washington Post*, February 26, 2004, p. A14; U.S. Congress, Senate Committee on Foreign Relations, *North Korea: Status Report on Nuclear Program, Humanitarian Issues, and Economic Reforms* (Washington, D.C.: U.S. Government Printing Office, 2004), p. vii.

123   U.S. Congress, Senate Committee on Foreign Relations, *North Korea*, pp. v, 16–17; Siegfried S. Hecker, "The Nuclear Crisis in North Korea," *Bridge*, Summer 2004, pp. 17–23 at p. 18.

124   U.S. Congress, Senate Committee on Foreign Relations, *North Korea*, p. 23; Hecker, "The Nuclear Crisis in North Korea," p. 22.

125   Hecker, "The Nuclear Crisis in North Korea," pp. 21–22.

126   Glenn Kessler, "N. Korea Nuclear Estimate to Rise," *Washington Post*, April 28, 2004, pp. A1, A16.

127   Ibid.

128   Serge Schemann, "U.N. Agency Demands North Korea End Atomic Program," *New York Times*, November 30, 2002, p. A10; Peter Selvin, "N. Korea Rejects Call for Inspections," *Washington Post*, December 5, 2002, p. A18; Glenn Kessler, "Powell Stresses 'Urgency' of Talks with North Korea," *Washington Post*, October 25, 2004, p. A12; Nicholas Kralev, "U.S. Urged to Be 'Flexible' Toward N. Korea," *Washington Times*, October 26, 2004, p. A13; Steven R. Weisman, "Powell Presses for Nuclear Talks with North Korea," *New York Times*, November 19, 2004, p. A10; James G. Lakely, "North Korea's Nukes at Top of U.S. Agenda," *Washington Times*, November 19, 2004, p. A4.

129   James Brooke and David E. Sanger, "North Koreans Say They Hold Nuclear Arms," *New York Times*, February 11, 2005, pp. A1, A8; David E. Sanger, "Steps at Reactor in North Korea Worry the U.S.," *New York Times*, April 18, 2005, pp. A1, A4.

130   Sanger, "North Koreans Say They Hold Nuclear Arms"; Barbara Slavin, "N. Korean Arsenal May Be Growing," USAToday.com, April 19, 2005.

131   James Brooke, "North Koreans Claim to Extract Fuel for Bombs," *New York Times*, May 12, 2005, pp. A1, A19.

132   Glenn Kessler, "Signs Stir Concern North Korea Might Test Nuclear Bomb," *Washington Post*, April 23, 2005, p. A13.

133   David E. Sanger and William J. Broad, "U.S. Cites Signs of Korean Steps to Nuclear Test," *New York Times*, May 6, 2005, pp. A1, A6.

134   Ibid.; Office of the Secretary of Defense, *Proliferation: Threat and Response*, p. 7, January 2001, www.defenselink.mil.

135   David E. Sanger, "U.S. in Warning to North Korea on Nuclear Test," *New York Times*, May 16, 2005, pp. A1, A9.

136   David E. Sanger, "What Are Koreans Up To?, U.S. Agencies Can't Agree," *New York Times*, May 12, 2005, p. A10; Joseph Kahn and David E. Sanger, "China Rules Out Using Sanctions on North Korea," *New York Times*, May 11, 2005, pp. A1, A6.

137   Joseph Kahn and David E. Sanger, "U.S.-Korean Deal on Arms Leaves Key Points Open," *New York Times*, September 20, 2005, pp. A1, A6; Jae-Soon Chang, "North Korea Hedges on Nuclear Deal," *Washington Times*, September 20, 2005, pp. A1, A13.

138   Bob Woodward, *Plan of Attack* (New York: Simon & Schuster, 2004), pp. 249–250; Thomas Powers, "The Vanishing Case for War," *New York Review of Books*, December 4, 2003, www.nybooks.com; Thomas Powers, "How Bush Got It Wrong," *New York Review of Books*, September 23, 2004, www.nybooks.com; John Prados, "Hiding Behind Secrecy," January 18, 2005, www.tompaine.com.

139   Kenneth M. Pollack, "Spies, Lies, and Weapons: What Went Wrong," *Atlantic*, January/February 2004, pp. 78–92 at p. 82.

140   Joseph Kahn, "China Questions U.S. Data on North Korea," *New York Times*, March 7, 2005, p. A5.

141   William J. Broad, David E. Sanger, and Raymond Bonner, "A Tale of Nuclear Proliferation: How Pakistani Built His Network," *New York Times*, December 12, 2004, pp. A1, A18; David E. Sanger and Judith Miller, "Libya to Give Up Arms Programs, Bush Announces," *New York Times*, December 20, 2003, pp. A1, A8; Patrick E. Tyler and James Risen, "Secret Diplomacy Won Libyan Pledge on Arms," *New York Times*, December 21, 2003, pp. A1, A21; Robin Wright, "Ship Incident May Have Swayed Libya," *Washington Post*, January 1, 2004, p. A18; Douglas Frontz, "A High-Risk Nuclear Stakeout," February 22, 2005, www.latimes.com; David Albright and Corey Henderson, "Unraveling the A Q Khan and Future Proliferation Networks," *Washington Quarterly*, 28, 2 (Spring 2005), pp. 111–20.

142   Joby Warrick, "Nuclear Program in Iran Tied to Pakistan," *Washington Post*, December 21, 2003, pp. A1, A36; William J. Broad, David Rohde, and David E. Sanger, "Inquiry Suggests Pakistanis Sold Nuclear Secrets," *New York Times*, December 22, 2003, pp. A1, A10; David E. Sanger and William J. Broad, "From Rogue Nuclear Programs Web of Trails Leads to Pakistan," *New York Times*, January 4, 2004, pp. 1, 8.

143   Joel Wit, "Clinton and North Korea: Past, Present, and Future," in Albright and O'Neill (eds.), *Solving the North Korean Nuclear Puzzle*, p. 205; Diamond, "N. Korea Keeps U.S. Intelligence Guessing."

144   For example, in early November 2004, China announced that it would oppose efforts aimed at referring the issue of Iran's nuclear program to the UN Security Council. China also has acted as if the United States and North Korea are equally to blame for the Korean nuclear crisis. See Nazila Fathi, "China Bolsters Iran in Dispute over Nuclear Program," *New York Times*, November 7, 2004, p. 8; Dan Blumenthal, "Unhelpful China," *Washington Post*, December 6, 2004, p. A21.

145   "Iran-EU Agreement on Nuclear Programs," November 14, 2004, www.global security.org; Elaine Sciolino, "Iran Gives Pledge on Uranium but Europeans Are Cautious," *New York Times*, November 15, 2004, p. A8; Dafna Linzer, "Diplomats Say Tehran Sends Wrong Signal," *Washington Post*, November 20, 2004, p. A8; Elaine Sciolino, "Iran Refuses to Terminate Nuclear Plans," *New York Times*, November 26, 2004, pp. A1, A14; Nazila Fathi, "Iran Says It Will Suspend but Will Not End Its Uranium Program," *New York Times*, December 1, 2004, p. A3; Elaine Sciolino, "Day Aer Nuclear Deal, Iran Is Cleared to Start W.T.O. Process," May 26, 2005, www.nytimes.co; Elaine Sciolino, "Europe Gets Iran to Extend Freeze in Nuclear Work," *New York Times*, May 1, 2005, pp. A1, A12.

146   Nazila Fathi, "Iran Says It Will Resume Uranium Enrichment, Jeopardizing Nuclear Talks with Europe," *New York Times*, August 1, 2005, p. A8; Dafna Linzer, "Europeans Warn Iran That Nuclear Work Would End Negotiations," *Washington Times*, August 3, 2005, p. A13; Steven R. Weisman, "Offer by Europe Would Give Iran Nuclear Future," August 5, 2005, pp. A1, A10; Nazila Fathi, "Atomic Activity Resumes in Iran Amid Warnings," *New York Times*, August 9, 2005, pp. A1, A18; "Bush Gives Stern Warning," *Washington Post*, August 14, 2005, p. A15; Dafna

Linzer, "U.S. Deploys Slide Show to Press Case Against Iran," *Washington Post*, September 14, 2005, p. A7; Mark Landler, "Nuclear Agency Votes to Report Iran to U.N. Security Council for Treaty Violations," *New York Times*, September 25, 2005, p. 6; John Ward Anderson, "U.N. Body Cites Iran on Nuclear Program," *Washington Post*, September 25, 2005, p. 6; "U.S. Praises Vote to Report Iran," *New York Times*, September 25, 2005, p. 6; Joel Brinkley, "Half a Step Forward to Rein In Iran," *New York Times*, September 27, 2005, p. A6; Steven R. Weisman, "U.S. and Europe Put Off Referral of Iran Case to Security Council," *New York Times*, November 23, 2005, p. A5.

147   William J. Broad and Elaine Sciolino, "Iran Retains Plutonium Plan in Nuclear Deal," *New York Times*, November 25, 2004, pp. A1, A16; "Appeasing Iran," *Wall Street Journal*, November 12, 2004, p. A12; "Moment of Truth on Iran," *Wall Street Journal*, November 22, 2004, p. A14.

EPILOGUE

1   Office of the Director of National Intelligence, "History of the Office of the Director of National Intelligence," www.dni.gov, accessed November 8, 2006.

2   Ibid.

3   Office of the Director of National Intelligence, ODNI News Release No. 2-06, "ODNI Announces Mission Managers and Senior Leadership Position," January 11, 2006, www .dni.gov.

4   John D. Negroponte, Director of National Intelligence, *Annual Threat Assessment of the Director of National Intelligence for the Senate Select Committee on Intelligence*, February 2, 2006, p. 13.

5   David E. Sanger, "U.S. Said to Weigh a New Approach on North Korea," *New York Times*, May 18, 2006, pp. A1, A10.

6   Negroponte, *Annual Threat Assessment of the Director of National Intelligence for the Senate Select Committee on Intelligence*, pp. 11–13.

7   William J. Broad and David E. Sanger, "Relying on Computer, U.S. Seeks to Prove Iran's Nuclear Aims," *New York Times*, November 13, 2005, pp. 1, 2.

8   Dafna Linzer, "Strong Leads and Dead Ends in Nuclear Case Against Iran," February 8, 2006, www.washingtonpost.com.

9   Ibid.

10   Broad and Sanger, "Relying on Computer, U.S. Seeks to Prove Iran's Nuclear Aims."

11   Alissa J. Rubin, "Iran Still Not Opening Up to the IAEA," *Los Angeles Times*, November 19, 2005, p. A3; Nazila Fathi, "Iran Parliament Votes to Close Atomic Sites to U.N. Monitors," *New York Times*, November 21, 2005, p. A10; Mohamed ElBaradei, Director General, IAEA, "Implementation of the NPT Safeguards Agreement in the Islamic Republic of Iran," November 18, 2005, p. 5.

12   ElBaradei, "Implementation of the NPT Safeguards Agreement in the Islamic Republic of Iran," November 18, 2005, p. 4.

13   Deputy Director General for Safeguards, IAEA, "Developments in the Implementation

of the NPT Safeguards Agreement in the Islamic Republic of Iran and Agency Verification of Iran's Suspension of Enrichment-Related, and Reprocessing Activities," January 31, 2006, pp. 2–3.

14   Alissa J. Rubin, "Rejecting Cooperation, Iran Asks IAEA to Remove Seals, Cameras," *Los Angeles Times*, February 7, 2006, p. A4; Mohamed ElBaradei, Director General, IAEA, "Implementation of the NPT Safeguards Agreement in the Islamic Republic of Iran," February 27, 2006, p. 9; Alissa J. Rubin, "Case Against Iran Differs from Iraq," *Los Angeles Times*, February 27, 2006, p. A4; Alissa J. Rubin, "Iran Report Raises More Suspicions," *Los Angeles Times*, February 28, 2006, p. A3.

15   Board of Governors, IAEA, "Implementation of the NPT Safeguards Agreement in the Islamic Republic of Iran—Resolution Adopted on 4 February 2006," February 4, 2006, p.2; ElBaradei, "Implementation of the NPT Safeguards Agreement in the Islamic Republic of Iran," February 27, 2006, pp. 6–8.

16   Paul Brannan and David Albright, Institute for Science and International Security, "ISIS Imagery Brief: New Activities at the Esafhan and Natanz Nuclear Sites in Iran," April 14, 2006.

17   William J. Broad, Nazila Fathi, and Joel Brinkley, "Analysts Say a Nuclear Iran Is Years Away," *New York Times*, April 13, 2006, pp. A1, A8; John Diamond, "U.S. Intelligence Agencies Say Iran Is Years Away from Building Nukes," April 14, 2006, www.usatoday .com. For an analysis of the key issues, written at this time, see David Albright and Corey Hinderstein, Institute for Science and International Security, "The Clock Is Ticking, But How Fast?" March 27, 2006; "National Counterproliferation Center," www.dni.gov, accessed November 19, 2006.

18   "Nuclear Inspectors Pay Visit to Iran," *Los Angeles Times*, April 9, 2006, p. A30; Mohamad ElBaradei, Director General, IAEA, "Implementation of the NPT Safeguards Agreement in the Islamic Republic of Iran," April 28, 2006, pp. 6–7; Elaine Sciolino, "U.N. Agency Says Iran Falls Short on Nuclear Data," *New York Times*, April 29, 2006, pp. A1, A6; William J. Broad, "U.N. Finds New Uranium Traces in Iran," *New York Times*, May 12, 2006, p. A8.

19   ElBaradei, "Implementation of the NPT Safeguards Agreement in the Islamic Republic of Iran," April 28, 2006, pp. 5–6; William J. Broad and Elaine Sciolino, "Iran's Secrecy Widens Gap in Nuclear Intelligence," *New York Times*, May 19, 2006, pp. A1, A14.

20   Broad and Sciolino, "Iran's Secrecy Widens Gap in Nuclear Intelligence"; The Commission on the Intelligence Capabilities of the United States Regarding Weapons of Mass Destruction, *Report to the President of the United States* (Washington, D.C.: U.S. Government Printing Office, 2005), p. 366; Department of Defense, News Transcript, "Radio Interview with Secretary Rumsfeld on the Laura Ingraham Show," April 18, 2006, www.defenselink.mil/transcripts.

21   U.S. Congress, House Permanent Select Committee on Intelligence, *Recognizing Iran as a Strategic Threat: An Intelligence Challenge for the United States*, August 23, 2006, pp. 5, 16.

22   Ibid., pp. 24–25.

23   Alissa J. Rubin, "Iran Declares Another Nuclear Advance," *Los Angeles Times*, August 27, 2006, p. A5.

24   Mohamad ElBaradei, Director General, IAEA, "Implementation of the NPT Safeguards Agreement in the Islamic Republic of Iran," August 31, 2006, p. 5; Dafna Linzer, "Iran Enriching More Uranium," August 30, 2006, www.washingtonpost.com; Elaine Sciolino, "Highly Enriched Uranium Is Found at an Iranian Plant," *New York Times*, September 1, 2006, p. A10.

25   Office of the Director of National Intelligence, "Interview of Ambassador John D. Negroponte, Director of National Intelligence, with Mr. Gary Thomas of Voice of America," October 3, 2006, p. 1, www.dni.gov.

26   David E. Sanger, "U.S. and Europe to Give Iranians New Atom Offer," *New York Times*, November 10, 2005, pp. A1, A10; Steven R. Weisman, "U.S. and Europe Put Off Referral of Iran Case to Security Council," *New York Times*, November 23, 2005, p. A5.

27   Elaine Sciolino, "Iran's Nuclear Team Fails to Keep a Date with the U.N.," *New York Times*, January 6, 2006, p. A3; John Daniszewski and Alissa J. Rubin, "Iran Breaks Atomic Seals amid West's Ire," *Los Angeles Times*, January 11, 2006, pp. A1, A6; Nazila Fathi, "U.N. Scrutiny Won't Make Iran Quit Nuclear Effort, President Says," *New York Times*, January 15, 2006, p. 10; Nazila Fathi, "Iran Rejects Russian Offer to Defuse Nuclear Dispute," *New York Times*, March 13, 2006, p. A11.

28   Warren Hoge, "U.N. Council Urges Iran to Halt Atom Activity," *New York Times*, March 30, 2006, p. A6; Glenn Kessler, "Iran Warned, but Russia, China Dissent on Action," March 31, 2006, www.washingtonpost.com; Steven R. Weisman, "Help with Reactor Included in European Offer to Iran," *New York Times*, May 17, 2006, p. A6; Colum Lynch, "Incentives Offered to Iran Detailed at Security Council," July 14, 2006, www.washingtonpost.com.

29   Karl Vick, "Iran Derides Incentive Bid to Resolve Nuclear Dispute," May 18, 2006, www.washingtonpost.com; Karl Vick and Dafna Linzer, "Proposal Would Let Iran Enrich Uranium," June 7, 2006, www.washingtonpost.com.

30   Islamic Republic of Iran, Islamic Republic of Iran's Response to the Package Presented on June 6, 2006, n.d.; Nazila Fathi, "Iran Says Answer on Atom Deal Will Take More Than a Month," *New York Times*, June 22, 2006, p. A14.

31   Nazila Fathi, "Iran Offers a Pledge and a Warning," *New York Times*, July 21, 2004, p. A4; Michael Slackman, "Iran Says It Will Ignore U.N. Deadline on Uranium Program," *New York Times*, August 7, 2006, p. A3; George Jahn, "Iran Denies Inspectors Access to Site," Associated Press, August 21, 2006, www.comcast.net.

32   Michael Slackman, "Iran Remains Steadfast in Pursuing Nuclear Plans as U.N. Deadline Arrives," *New York Times*, September 1, 2006, p. A10; Steven Lee Myers, "Russia Hints It Won't Back Any Penalties Against Iran," *New York Times*, September 2, 2006, p. A7; Maggie Farley, "France Now Opposes Iran Punishments," *Los Angeles Times*, September 19, 2006, p. A9.

33   Glenn Kessler, "Early October New Deadline for Iran," September 21, 2006, www.washingtonpost.com; "Iran Leader Rejects Even Brief Halt in Its Uranium Enrichment Efforts," *New York Times*, October 1, 2006, p. 10; Colum Lynch, "U.S., European Allies

at Odds on Terms of Iran Resolution," October 26, 2006, www.washingtonpost.com.

34   Kim Murphy, "Iran Warns U.N. on Sanctions," *Los Angeles Times*, November 11, 2006, p. A6; Nazila Fathi, "Iran Criticizes Security Council over Threat of Sanctions," *New York Times*, November 13, 2006, p. A12; Alk Akbar Dareini, "Iran Says Nuke Program Is Near Complete," Associated Press, November 14, 2006, www.comcast.net; George Jahn, "Plutonium Found in Iran Waste Facility," Associated Press, November 14, 2006, www.comcast.net; Alissa J. Rubin, "Iran's Nuclear Work Grows," *Los Angeles Times*, November 15, 2006, p. A4; William J. Broad and Nazila Fathi, "Iran's Leader Cites Progress on Nuclear Plans," *New York Times*, November 15, 2006, p. A8; Mohamad ElBaradei, Director General, IAEA, *Implementation of the NPT Safeguards Agree-ment in the Islamic Republic of Iran*, November 14, 2006, p. 3; Nazila Fathi, "Iran Says It Will Build Heavy-Water Reactor Without Agency's Help," *New York Times*, November 24, 2006, p. A8.

35   Maggie Farley, "U.N. Slaps Iran with Sanctions," *Los Angeles Times*, December 24, 2006, pp. A1, A14; Elissa Goodman, "Security Council Approves Sanctions Against Iran over Nuclear Program," *New York Times*, December 24, 2006, p. 8.

36   Nazila Fathi, "Iran Is Defiant, Vowing to U.N. It Will Continue Nuclear Efforts," *New York Times*, December 25, 2006, p. A10; Nazila Fathi, "Iran to 'Revise' Any Relations with Monitors in Nuclear Area," *New York Times*, December 26, 2006, p. A3.

37   Gordon Fairclough, "North Korea Faces Test on Its Pledge to Disarm," *Wall Street Journal*, November 8, 2005, p. A15; Warren Hoge, "U.N. Sets Aug. 31 Deadline for Iran to End Uranium Work," *New York Times*, August 1, 2006, p. A3.

38   Glenn Kessler, "North Rushes to Finish Reactor," November 9, 2005, www.washington post.com.

39   Ibid.

40   Jim Yardley, "Six-Nation Talks on North Korea Resume in China," *New York Times*, November 10, 2005, p. A10; Philip P. Pan, "New Round Opens in North Korea Talks," November 9, 2005, www.washingtonpost.com; Joseph Kahn, "North Korea and U.S. Spar, Causing Talks to Stall," *New York Times*, November 12, 2005, p. A5; Mark Magnier, "U.S., N. Korea Stick to Their Positions in Nuclear Talks," *Los Angeles Times*, November 12, 2005, p. A3; Larry A. Niksch, *North Korea's Nuclear Weapons Program*, Congressional Research Service, February 21, 2006, p. 1. On North Korean counterfeiting, see Ralph F. Perl and Dick N. Nanto, Congressional Research Service, *North Korean Counterfeiting of U.S. Currency*, March 22, 2006.

41   "North Korea Sees No Return to Talks," *Los Angeles Times*, April 10, 2006, p. A17; Norimitsu Onishi, "Key Diplomats Together Again, but Not Meeting on North Korea," *New York Times*, April 11, 2006, p. A8; Anthony Faiola, "Tokyo Trip Could Aid Talks on N. Korea," April 5, 2006, www.washingtonpost.com.

42   Sanger, "U.S. Said to Weigh a New Approach on North Korea"; Peter Baker, "U.S. and S. Korea to Push to Restart Nuclear Talks," September 15, 2006, www .washingtonpost.com.

43   Bob Woodward, *Bush at War* (New York: Simon & Schuster, 2002), p. 340; Norimitsu Onishi and David E. Sanger, "6 Missiles Fired by North Korea; Tests Protested," *New*

York Times, July 5, 2006, pp. A1, A8; Kongdan Oh and Ralph C. Hassig, "North Korea's Nuclear Politics," *Current History*, September 2004, pp. 273–279. On Kim's regime, see Jasper Becker, *Rogue Regime: Kim Jong Il and the Looming Threat of North Korea* (New York: Oxford University Press, 2006).

44   Bo-Mi Lim, "North Korea Says It Will Stage Nuke Test," Associated Press, October 3, 2006, www.comcast.net; Bruce Wallace and Julian E. Barnes, "N. Korea Plans a Nuclear Test," *Los Angeles Times*, October 4, 2006, pp. A1, A6; David E. Sanger, "North Koreans Say They Plan a Nuclear Test," *New York Times*, October 4, 2006, pp. A1, A6.

45   Dafna Linzer, "Pyongyang Warned on Weapon Testing," October 5, 2006, www.washingtonpost.com; David E. Sanger and Jim Yardley, "U.S. Sternly Warns North Korea Not to Conduct a Nuclear Test," *New York Times*, October 5, 2006, p. A8; Warren Hoge, "U.N. Council Presses North Korea to Drop Plans for Nuclear Test," *New York Times*, October 7, 2006, p. A3.

46   William B. Scott and David A. Fulghum, "Nuclear Poker," *Aviation Week & Space Technology*, October 9, 2006, pp. 30–31.

47   Sanger, "North Koreans Say They Plan a Nuclear Test"; "U.S. Agencies Looking into N. Korea Test," Associated Press, October 8, 2006, www.nytimes.com.

48   Wallace and Barnes, "N. Korea Plans a Nuclear Test"; Scott and Fulghum, "Nuclear Poker."

49   David E. Sanger, "N. Korea Reports 1st Nuclear Arms Test," October 9, 2006, www.nytimes.com; Burt Herman, "South Korea Quake Center Watches North," August 30, 2006, www.washingtontimes.com; Anthony Faiola, Glenn Kessler, and Dafna Linzer, "N. Korea Claims Nuclear Test," October 9, 2006, www.washingtonpost.com.

50   Faiola, "N. Korea Claims Nuclear Test"; White House, "President Bush's Statement on North Korea Nuclear Test," October 9, 2006, www.whitehouse.gov.

51   Faiola, "N. Korea Claims Nuclear Test."

52   Ibid.; William J. Broad and Mark Mazzetti, "Small Blast May Be Only a Partial Success, Experts Say," *New York Times*, October 10, 2006, p. A8.

53   David Stout and John O'Neil, "Analysts Say Blast Was Small for a Nuclear Weapon," October 9, 2006, www.nytimes.com.

54   Greg Miller and Karen Kaplan, "Even if a Device Was Flawed, Test Crossed a Threshold," *Los Angeles Times*, October 10, 2006, pp. A1, A8; Dafna Linzer, "Low Yield of Blast Surprises Analysts," October 10, 2006, www.washingtonpost.com; David E. Sanger and William J. Broad, "Small Blast or 'Big Deal'? U.S. Experts Look for Clues," *New York Times*, October 11, 2006, p. A10. For additional analyses, see Richard L. Garwin and Frank N. von Hippel, "A Technical Analysis: Deconstructing North Korea's October 9 Nuclear Test," *Arms Control Today*, November 2006, pp. 14–16; Graham P. Collins, "Kim's Big Fizzle," *Scientific American*, January 2007, pp. 18–20.

55   Broad and Mazzetti, "Small Blast May Be Only a Partial Success, Experts Say."

56   Ibid.; Dafna Linzer and Thomas E. Ricks, "U.S. Waits for Firm Information on Nature and Success of Device," October 11, 2006, www.washingtonpost.com.

57   Linzer and Ricks, "U.S. Waits for Firm Information on Nature and Success of Device"; Robert Block, "U.S. Seeks Data on North Korea's Nuclear Test Claim," *Wall Street Jour-*

nal, October 11, 2006, p. A4; "N. Korea Air Sample Has No Radioactivity," Associated Press, October 13, 2006, www.nytimes.com.

58   "N. Korea Air Sample Has No Radioactivity"; "U.S. Has Yet to Draw Conclusion about Blast, Official Says," Associated Press, October 13, 2006, www.nytimes.com.

59   "U.S. Has Yet to Draw Conclusion about Blast, Official Says"; Bill Gertz and Betsy Pisik, "U.S. Finding Indicates Nuclear Test," October 14, 2006, www.washingtontimes.com; Bill Gertz, "Korean Test Seen as Only Partial Blast," October 13, 2006, www.washing tontimes.com; Dafna Linzer and Walter Pincus, "U.S. Detects Signs of Radiation Consistent with Test," October 14, 2006, www.washingtonpost.com; Mark Mazzetti, "Preliminary Samples Hint at North Korean Nuclear Test," *New York Times*, October 14, 2006, p. A7. For a technical analysis based on public data, see Richard L. Garwin and Frank N. von Hippel, "A Technical Analysis of North Korea's Oct. 9 Nuclear Test," *Arms Control Today*, November 2006, pp. 14–16.

60   United Nations Security Council, Resolution 1718 (2006), October 14, 2006; Warren Hoge, "U.S. Hits Obstacle in Getting a Vote on North Korea," *New York Times*, October 14, 2006, pp. A1, A7; Warren Hoge, "Security Council Supports Sanctions on North Korea," *New York Times*, October 15, 2006, pp. 1, 10; Emma Chanlett-Avery and Sharon Squassoni, Congressional Research Service, *North Korea's Nuclear Test: Motivations, Implications, and U.S. Options*, October 24, 2006, p. 3.

61   Office of the Director of National Intelligence, ODNI News Release No. 19-06, "Statement by the Office of the Director of National Intelligence on the North Korea Nuclear Test," October 16, 2006.

62   Glenn Kessler and Dafna Linzer, "Rice Trip to Push Full Sanctions for N. Korea," October 17, 2006, www.washingtonpost.com; Thom Shanker and David E. Sanger, "North Korean Fuel Said to Be Plutonium," *New York Times*, October 17, 2006, p. A9.

63   Shanker and Sanger, "North Korean Fuel Said to Be Plutonium."

64   Bo-Mi Lim, "N. Korea Apparently Preparing Nuke Test," Associated Press, October 17, 2006, www.comcast.net.

65   Joseph Kahn and Helene Cooper, "North Korea Will Resume Nuclear Talks," *New York Times*, November 1, 2006, pp. A1, A14; "North Korea Will Resume Nuclear Talks," *Wall Street Journal*, November 1, 2006, p. A6; Josh Meyer, "Squeeze on North Korea's Money Supply Yields Results," *Los Angeles Times*, November 2, 2006, pp. A1, A8.

66   "Iran Should Give Sanctions 'Serious Response,' China Says," *New York Times*, January 6, 2007, p. A6; Steven R. Weisman, "Europe Resists U.S. on Curbing Ties with Iran," *New York Times*, January 30, 2007, pp. A1, A6.

67   Nazila Fathi, "Iran Bars Inspectors; Dissident Cleric Condemns President's Stance," *New York Times*, January 23, 2007, p. A7; Mark Lander and David E. Sanger, "Chief U.N. Nuclear Monitor Cites Iran Enrichment Plan," *New York Times*, January 27, 2007, p. A7; "Iran Said to Have Set Up Centrifuges," *Los Angeles Times*, February 6, 2007, p. A4; Nasser Karimi, "No 'Brakes' on Iran Nuclear Effort," February 26, 2007, www.wash ingtonpost.com.

68   Dafna Linzer, "Iran Asserts Expansion of Nuclear Operations," April 10, 2007, www

.washington.com; Nazila Fathi, "Iran Says It Can Enrich Uranium on an Industrial Scale," *New York Times*, April 10, 2007, p. A3.

69   William J. Broad, "World Atomic Agency Suspends 22 Programs of Aid to Iran," *New York Times*, February 10, 2007, p. A8; Board of Governors, IAEA, GOV/2007/7, *Cooperation Between the Islamic Republic of Iran and the Agency in the Light of United Nations Security Council Resolution 1737 (2006)*, February 8, 2007; Steven R. Weisman, "European Officials Agree to Widen Economic Sanctions Against Iran over Nuclear Program," *New York Times*, February 13, 2007, p. A10; Thom Shanker, "Security Council Adds Sanctions to Press Iran," *New York Times*, March 25, 2007, pp. 1, 4.

70   Andrew E. Kramer, "Russia Will Slow Work on Iran's Nuclear Plant," *New York Times*, February 20, 2007, p. A8; Elaine Sciolino, "Russia Gives Iran an Ultimatum on Enrichment," *New York Times*, March 20, 2007, pp. A1, A7; see also William R. Hawkins, "Iran Calls the UN's Bluff," April 11, 2007, www.frontpagemag.com.

71   Nazila Fathi, "Iran Has Guests in to See, but Not Inspect, Nuclear Site," *New York Times*, February 4, 2007, p. 4; Kim Murphy, "Iran Gives Visitors Inside Look at Nuclear Facility," *Los Angeles Times*, February 4, 2007, p. A3; David E. Sanger and William J. Broad, "Iran Expanding Nuclear Effort, Agency Reports," *New York Times*, February 23, 2007, pp. A1, A8; Bob Drogin, "Iran's Nuclear Effort in High Gear, U.N. Says," *Los Angeles Times*, February 23, 2007, pp. A1, A6–A7; Board of Governors, IAEA, GOV/2007/8, *Implementation of the NPT Safeguards Agreement and Relevant Provisions of Security Council Resolution 1737 (2006) in the Islamic Republic of Iran*, February 22, 2007.

72   Board of Governors, IAEA, GOV/2007/8, *Implementation of the NPT Safeguards Agreement and Relevant Provisions of Security Council Resolution 1737 (2006) in the Islamic Republic of Iran*, p. 3; Bob Drogin and Kim Murphy, "U.N. Calls U.S. Data on Iran's Nuclear Aims Unreliable," *Los Angeles Times*, February 25, 2007, pp. A1, A9.

73   "ElBaradei Disputes Tehran's Claim of 3,000 Centrifuges" *Los Angeles Times*, April 13, 2007, p. A4.

74   Olli Heinonen, Deputy Director General, IAEA, to H. E. Ali Asghar, April 18, 2007; David E. Sanger, "Atomic Agency Confirms Advances by Iran's Nuclear Program," *New York Times*, April 19, 2007, p. A10; Dafna Linzer, "Booster in Iran's Capacity to Enrich Uranium Noted," April 19, 2007, www.washingtonpost.com.

75   David E. Sanger, "Inspectors Cite Big Gain by Iran on Nuclear Fuel," *New York Times*, May 15, 2007, pp. A1, A2; Bob Drogin, "U.S. Cautious over New Iran Nuclear Report," *Los Angeles Times*, May 16, 2007, p. A4.

76   Joseph Kahn, "Talks End on North Korea's Nuclear Weapons," *New York Times*, December 23, 2006, p. A7; Jim Yardley, "Private Talks Held in Berlin Spurred Sides to Reach Deal," *New York Times*, February 14, 2007, p. A10; Jim Yardley and David E. Sanger, "Deal to Shut Down Major North Korean Nuclear Facilities Appears Closer," *New York Times*, February 10, 2007, p. A6; Jim Yardley and David E. Sanger, "Nuclear Talks on North Korea Hit a Roadblock," *New York Times*, February 12, 2007, pp. A1, A11; "Nuclear Bargaining," February 14, 2007, www.washingtonpost.com.

77   Yardley and Sanger, "Deal to Shut Down Major North Korean Facilities Appears

Closer"; "Nuclear Bargaining"; Yardley and Sanger, "Nuclear Talks on North Korea Hit a Roadblock," pp. A1, A11; Jim Yardley and David E. Sanger, "In Shift, Accord on North Korea Seems to Be Set," *New York Times*, February 13, 2007, pp. A1, A11; Bob Drogin, "U.N. Nuclear Monitor Is Invited to North Korea," *Los Angeles Times*, February 24, 2007, pp. A1, A5; Helene Cooper and Jim Yardley, "Pact with North Korea Draws Fire from a Wide Range of Critics in the U.S.," *New York Times*, February 14, 2007, p. A10.

78   Bill Gertz, "Bolton Hits Agreement as a 'Bad Signal' to Iran," February 14, 2007, www.washingtontimes.com; David E. Sanger, "Sensing Shift in Bush Policy, Another Hawk Joins Exodus," *New York Times*, March 23, 2007, pp. A1, A8; Maureen Fan, "Six-Party Talks Break Down as N. Korea Balks on Funds," March 23, 2007, www.washingtonpost.com; David E. Sanger, "Money Shift Could Clear Way to Shut North Korea Reactor," *New York Times*, April 7, 2007, p. A5; Maura Reynolds, "Bush and Abe Warn North Korea to Fulfill Pact," *Los Angeles Times*, April 28, 2007, p. A3.

79   Bill Gertz and Rowan Scarborough, "Inside the Ring." April 27, 2007, www.washingtontimes.com; "Kim Jong Il's Word," *Wall Street Journal*, March 5, 2007, p. A16.

80   See pp. 376–380, 397.

81   David E. Sanger and William J. Broad, "U.S. Concedes Uncertainty on Korean Uranium Effort," *New York Times*, March 1, 2007, pp. A1, A10; "Creative Interpretation," *Newsweek*, March 12, 2007, p. 11.

82   Sanger and Broad, "U.S. Concedes Uncertainty on Korea Uranium Effort"; Office of the Director of National Intelligence, ODNI News Release No. 04-07, "Statement by Ambassador Joseph De Trani, North Korean Mission Manager," March 4, 2007.

83   Glenn Kessler, "New Doubts on Nuclear Efforts by North Korea," March 1, 2007, www.washingtonpost.com; John R. Bolton, "North Korea Climbdown," *Wall Street Journal*, March 5, 2007, p. A17.

84   For an argument to make more of the intelligence concerning the Iranian nuclear program public, see Micah Zenko, "Share the Evidence on Iran," August 29, 2006, www.washingtonpost.com.

85   Steve Coll, "Nuke Rebuke," October 23, 2006, www.newyorker.com; Donald Gregg and Don Oberdorfer, "Wrong Path on North Korea," September 6, 2006, www.washingtonpost.com. Coll's article is an excellent example of ideological venting in the place of reasoned analysis. At one point Coll refers to the Nuclear Non-Proliferation Treaty regime as being "burdened by Israel's defiance"—ignoring the evidence that Israel had acquired a nuclear capability (in 1966) before the treaty was signed. He also condemns India's Hindu nationalist leaders for "shattering" the non-proliferation momentum when they tested in 1998. The concept that India and Israel, as free democratic societies that never signed the NPT, might have a right to choose what weapons they require for their defense does not seem to be one that has occurred to Coll. Indeed, Coll also charges that "the global system that encourages states to acquire nuclear weapons is complex and difficult to manipulate. So is the system that girded the colonial slave trade. Both are immoral." But the slave trade was a gross violation of individual rights, whereas the system that "encourages" states to acquire nuclear weapons is national sovereignty

and reality—neither of which is likely to, or should, change. Coll also asserts that "arduous diplomacy" by the Clinton administration was instrumental in South Africa, Brazil, and Argentina giving up nuclear weapons. But only South Africa actually built such weapons, and made the decision to give them up for its own reasons, long before Bill Clinton assumed the presidency. Finally, Coll blames President Bush's "axis of evil" speech for stoking the paranoia of the regimes in Pyongyang and Tehran—as if the leaders of those regimes did not already qualify as world-class paranoids. There is no evidence to support Gregg and Oberdorfer's claim that negotiation is the only possible path to success. And it will take some time to prove that the current agreement will be fully implemented. Based on past experience it would hardly be shocking if it were not.

86   Michael Rubin, "The U.S. vs. Iran," *Wall Street Journal,* September 20, 2006, p. A26; Dr. Chen Kane, "Nuclear Decision-Making in Iran: A Rare Glimpse," *Middle East Brief,* May 2006.

87   Norimitsu Onishi, "South Korea Won't Intercept Cargo Ships from the North," *New York Times,* November 14, 2006, p. A8; "The Arms-Control Illusion," *Wall Street Journal,* October 14–15, 2006, p. A6; "Kremlin Rules," *Wall Street Journal,* October 7–8, 2006, p. A6; "Iran Stalls," August 24, 2006, www.washingtonpost.com; Evan Ramstad, "South Korea Imposes Package of Mild Penalties on the North," *Wall Street Journal,* November 14, 2006, p. A6.

INDEX

Page numbers in *italics* refer to illustrations. Page numbers after 574 refer to endnotes.